W9-DFR-369

Critical Values of the *t* Distribution

Degrees of Freedom	$t_{.100}$	$t_{.050}$	$t_{.025}$	$t_{.010}$	$t_{.005}$
1	3.078	6.314	12.706	31.821	63.657
2	1.886	2.920	4.303	6.965	9.925
3	1.638	2.353	3.182	4.541	5.841
4	1.533	2.132	2.776	3.747	4.604
5	1.476	2.015	2.571	3.365	4.032
6	1.440	1.943	2.447	3.143	3.707
7	1.415	1.895	2.365	2.998	3.499
8	1.397	1.860	2.306	2.896	3.355
9	1.383	1.833	2.262	2.821	3.250
10	1.372	1.812	2.228	2.764	3.169
11	1.363	1.796	2.201	2.718	3.106
12	1.356	1.782	2.179	2.681	3.055
13	1.350	1.771	2.160	2.650	3.012
14	1.345	1.761	2.145	2.624	2.977
15	1.341	1.753	2.131	2.602	2.947
16	1.337	1.746	2.120	2.583	2.921
17	1.333	1.740	2.110	2.567	2.898
18	1.330	1.734	2.101	2.552	2.878
19	1.328	1.729	2.093	2.539	2.861
20	1.325	1.725	2.086	2.528	2.845
21	1.323	1.721	2.080	2.518	2.831
22	1.321	1.717	2.074	2.508	2.819
23	1.319	1.714	2.069	2.500	2.807
24	1.318	1.711	2.064	2.492	2.797
25	1.316	1.708	2.060	2.485	2.787
26	1.315	1.706	2.056	2.479	2.779
27	1.314	1.703	2.052	2.473	2.771
28	1.313	1.701	2.048	2.467	2.763
29	1.311	1.699	2.045	2.462	2.756
30	1.310	1.697	2.042	2.457	2.750
40	1.303	1.684	2.021	2.423	2.704
60	1.296	1.671	2.000	2.390	2.660
120	1.289	1.658	1.980	2.358	2.617
∞	1.282	1.645	1.960	2.326	2.576
C.I.	80%	90%	95%	98%	99%

Critical Points of *Z* for Selected Levels of Significance

Level of Significance α:

	0.05	0.01
One-Tailed Test	+ or 1.645 −	+ or 2.326 −
Two-Tailed Test	+ and 1.96 −	+ and 2.576 −

Note: + or − means we use the positive value in the table for a right-hand-tailed test and the negative value for a left-hand-tailed test. In a two tailed test, we use both the positive and the negative values.

Source: M. Merrington, "Table of Percentage Points of the *t*-Distribution," *Biometrika* 32 (1941), p. 300. Reproduced by permission of the *Biometrika* Trustees.

Complete
Business
Statistics

The McGraw-Hill/Irwin Series
Operations and Decision Sciences

BUSINESS STATISTICS

Aczel and Sounderpandian, *Complete Business Statistics,* Seventh Edition

ALEKS Corporation, *ALEKS for Business Statistics,* First Edition

Alwan, *Statistical Process Analysis,* First Edition

Bowerman, O'Connell, and Murphree, *Business Statistics in Practice,* Fifth Edition

Bowerman, O'Connell, Orris, and Porter, *Essentials of Business Statistics,* Second Edition

Bryant and Smith, *Practical Data Analysis: Case Studies in Business Statistics,* Volumes I, II, and III*

Cooper and Schindler, *Business Research Methods,* Tenth Edition

Doane, *LearningStats CD Rom,* First Edition, 1.2

Doane, Mathieson, and Tracy, *Visual Statistics,* Second Edition, 2.0

Doane and Seward, *Applied Statistics in Business and Economics,* Second Edition

Doane and Seward, *Essential Statistics in Business and Economics,* First Edition

Gitlow, Oppenheim, Oppenheim, and Levine, *Quality Management,* Third Edition

Kutner, Nachtsheim, and Neter, *Applied Linear Regression Models,* Fourth Edition

Kutner, Nachtsheim, Neter, and Li, *Applied Linear Statistical Models,* Fifth Edition

Lind, Marchal, and Wathen, *Basic Statistics for Business and Economics,* Sixth Edition

Lind, Marchal, and Wathen, *Statistical Techniques in Business and Economics,* Thirteenth Edition

Merchant, Goffinet, and Koehler, *Basic Statistics Using Excel for Office XP,* Fourth Edition

Olson and Shi, *Introduction to Business Data Mining,* First Edition

Orris, *Basic Statistics Using Excel and MegaStat,* First Edition

Siegel, *Practical Business Statistics,* Fifth Edition

Wilson, Keating, and John Galt Solutions, Inc., *Business Forecasting,* Fifth Edition

Zagorsky, *Business Information,* First Edition

QUANTITATIVE METHODS AND MANAGEMENT SCIENCE

Hillier and Hillier, *Introduction to Management Science,* Third Edition

Kros, *Spreadsheet Modeling for Business Decisions,* First Edition

Stevenson and Ozgur, *Introduction to Management Science with Spreadsheets,* First Edition

*Available only through McGraw-Hill's PRIMIS Online Assets Library.

Complete Business Statistics

SEVENTH EDITION

Amir D. Aczel
Boston University
University of New Hampshire

Jayavel Sounderpandian
University of Wisconsin–Parkside

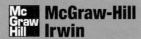

McGraw-Hill
Irwin

Boston   Burr Ridge, IL   Dubuque, IA   New York   San Francisco   St. Louis
Bangkok   Bogotá   Caracas   Kuala Lumpur   Lisbon   London   Madrid   Mexico City
Milan   Montreal   New Delhi   Santiago   Seoul   Singapore   Sydney   Taipei   Toronto

The McGraw-Hill Companies

**McGraw-Hill
Irwin**

COMPLETE BUSINESS STATISTICS

Published by McGraw-Hill/Irwin, a business unit of The McGraw-Hill Companies, Inc., 1221
Avenue of the Americas, New York, NY, 10020. Copyright © 2009, 2006, 2002, 1999, 1996, 1993, 1989
by The McGraw-Hill Companies, Inc. All rights reserved. No part of this publication may be reproduced
or distributed in any form or by any means, or stored in a database or retrieval system, without the prior
written consent of The McGraw-Hill Companies, Inc., including, but not limited to, in any network or
other electronic storage or transmission, or broadcast for distance learning.

Some ancillaries, including electronic and print components, may not be available to customers outside
the United States.

This book is printed on acid-free paper.

1 2 3 4 5 6 7 8 9 0 VNH/VNH 0 9 8

ISBN   978-0-07-337360-7
MHID   0-07-337360-5

Editorial director: *Stewart Mattson*
Executive editor: *Scott Isenberg*
Senior developmental editor: *Wanda J. Zeman*
Senior marketing manager: *Sankha Basu*
Project manager: *Bruce Gin*
Lead production supervisor: *Carol A. Bielski*
Lead designer: *Matthew Baldwin*
Senior media project manager: *Matthew Perry*
Cover design: *Kay Lieberher*
Interior design: *Kay Lieberher*
Cover images: © *Veer,* © *Jim Zook/Images.com,* © *Fotosearch*
Typeface: *10/12 Baskerville BE*
Compositor: *ICC Macmillan Inc.*
Printer: *Von Hoffmann Corporation*

Library of Congress Cataloging-in-Publication Data

Aczel, Amir D.
        Complete business statistics / Amir D. Aczel, Jayavel Sounderpandian. – 7th ed.
            p. cm. – (The McGraw-Hill/Irwin series Operations and decision sciences)
        Includes index.
        ISBN-13: 978-0-07-337360-7 (alk. paper)
        ISBN-10: 0-07-337360-5 (alk. paper)
        1. Commercial statistics.   2. Statistics.   I. Sounderpandian, Jayavel.   II. Title.
    HF1017.A26 2009
        519.5–dc22

                                                                                    2007043509

www.mhhe.com

To the memories of my father, Captain E. L. Aczel, and my mother, Miriam Aczel

Amir D. Aczel

Amir D. Aczel is with the Center for Philosophy and History of Science at Boston University and with the University of New Hampshire, and is an occasional business commentator on CNN. He earned his B.A. in mathematics and M.S. in operations research from the University of California–Berkeley, and he was awarded his Ph.D. in statistics from the University of Oregon. Prior to assuming his current position, Aczel lived and taught in California, Alaska, Europe, the Middle East, and the Far East.

Aczel is the author of 14 books on mathematics, business, and statistics. His best known book, *Fermat's Last Theorem,* discusses the quest to prove a heretofore unprovable mathematical theorem. The recently published *Chance* is a popular description of the theory of probability.

Aczel's wide-ranging interests, which are evident in *Complete Business Statistics,* reflect the international scope of the author's experience, the authority of his educational background, and the practical bent he has displayed in his other writing. Aczel lives with his wife and daughter in the greater Boston area.

Jayavel Sounderpandian, now deceased, was a professor of quantitative methods at the University of Wisconsin–Parkside, where he taught business statistics and operations management for 24 years. He earned his doctoral and master's degrees in business from Kent State University and received his bachelor's degree in mechanical engineering from the Indian Institute of Technology, Madras. Before turning to academia, Sounderpandian worked as an engineer for seven years at an aircraft manufacturing company in India.

Besides this textbook, Sounderpandian wrote four supplemental textbooks that focus on the use of spreadsheets in business statistics, market research, and operations management. He was devoted to the use of spreadsheet templates in the classroom, and applied that expertise in designing the more than 100 templates in this textbook. Sounderpandian's research interests were in decision and risk analysis, and he published widely in leading journals such as *Operations Research, Abacus, Journal of Risk and Uncertainty, International Journal of Production Economics,* and *Interfaces.*

Professor Sounderpandian's interest in composing and solving mathematical puzzles informed many of the case studies in this textbook. He and his wife resided in Racine, Wisconsin, where they raised three daughters.

Regrettably, Professor Jayavel Sounderpandian passed away before the revision of the text commenced. He had been a consistent champion of the book, first as a loyal user and later as a productive co-author. His many contributions and contagious enthusiasm will be sorely missed. In the seventh edition of *Complete Business Statistics,* we focus on many improvements in the text, driven largely by recommendations from dedicated users and others who teach business statistics. In their reviews, these professors suggested ways to improve the book by maintaining the Excel feature while incorporating MINITAB, as well as by adding new content and pedagogy, and by updating the source material. Additionally, there is increased emphasis on good applications of statistics, and a wealth of excellent real-world problems has been incorporated in this edition. The book continues to attempt to instill a deep understanding of statistical methods and concepts with its readers.

The seventh edition, like its predecessors, retains its global emphasis, maintaining its position of being at the vanguard of international issues in business. The economies of countries around the world are becoming increasingly intertwined. Events in Asia and the Middle East have direct impact on Wall Street, and the Russian economy's move toward capitalism has immediate effects on Europe as well as on the United States. The publishing industry, in which large international conglomerates have acquired entire companies; the financial industry, in which stocks are now traded around the clock at markets all over the world; and the retail industry, which now offers consumer products that have been manufactured at a multitude of different locations throughout the world—all testify to the ubiquitous globalization of the world economy. A large proportion of the problems and examples in this new edition are concerned with international issues. We hope that instructors welcome this approach as it increasingly reflects that context of almost all business issues.

A number of people have contributed greatly to the development of this seventh edition and we are grateful to all of them. Major reviewers of the text are:

C. Lanier Benkard, Stanford University
Robert Fountain, Portland State University
Lewis A. Litteral, University of Richmond
Tom Page, Michigan State University
Richard Paulson, St. Cloud State University
Simchas Pollack, St. John's University
Patrick A. Thompson, University of Florida
Cindy van Es, Cornell University

We would like to thank them, as well as the authors of the supplements that have been developed to accompany the text. Lou Patille, Keller Graduate School of Management, updated the Instructor's Manual and the Student Problem Solving Guide. Alan Cannon, University of Texas–Arlington, updated the Test Bank, and Lloyd Jaisingh, Morehead State University, created data files and updated the PowerPoint Presentation Software. P. Sundararaghavan, University of Toledo, provided an accuracy check of the page proofs. Also, a special thanks to David Doane, Ronald Tracy, and Kieran Mathieson, all of Oakland University, who permitted us to include their statistical package, *Visual Statistics,* on the CD-ROM that accompanies this text.

We are indebted to the dedicated personnel at McGraw-Hill/Irwin. We are thankful to Scott Isenberg, executive editor, for his strategic guidance in updating this text to its seventh edition. We appreciate the many contributions of Wanda Zeman, senior developmental editor, who managed the project well, kept the schedule on time and the cost within budget. We are thankful to the production team at McGraw-Hill/Irwin for the high-quality editing, typesetting, and printing. Special thanks are due to Saeideh Fallah Fini for her excellent work on computer applications.

Amir D. Aczel
Boston University

CONTENTS IN BRIEF

Chapter 1   Introduction and Descriptive Statistics   2

Chapter 2   Probability   50

Chapter 3   Random Variables   90

Chapter 4   The Normal Distribution   146

Chapter 5   Sampling and Sampling Distributions   180

Chapter 6   Confidence Intervals   218

Chapter 7   Hypothesis Testing   256

Chapter 8   The Comparison of Two Populations   302

Chapter 9   Analysis of Variance   348

Chapter 10 Simple Linear Regression and Correlation   408

Chapter 11 Multiple Regression   468

Chapter 12 Time Series, Forecasting, and Index Numbers   560

Chapter 13 Quality Control and Improvement   594

Chapter 14 Nonparametric Methods and Chi-Square Tests   620

Chapter 15 Bayesian Statistics and Decision Analysis   686

Appendix A References   740

Appendix B Answers to Most Odd-Numbered Problems   743

Appendix C Statistical Tables   755

ON the CD

Chapter 16 Sampling Methods

Chapter 17 Multivariate Analysis

            Working with Templates
            Introduction to Excel Basics

            Index   793

CONTENTS

Chapter 1   Introduction and Descriptive Statistics   2

1-1   Using Statistics   3
   Samples and Populations   5
   Data and Data Collection   5
1-2   Percentiles and Quartiles   8
1-3   Measures of Central Tendency   10
1-4   Measures of Variability   14
1-5   Grouped Data and the Histogram   20
1-6   Skewness and Kurtosis   22
1-7   Relations between the Mean and the Standard
         Deviation   24
   Chebyshev's Theorem   24
   The Empirical Rule   24
1-8   Methods of Displaying Data   25
   Pie Charts   25
   Bar Charts   25
   Frequency Polygons and Ogives   25
   A Caution about Graphs   27
   Time Plots   28
1-9   Exploratory Data Analysis   29
   Stem-and-Leaf Displays   30
   Box Plots   31
1-10 Using the Computer   35
   Using Excel for Descriptive Statistics and Plots   35
   Using MINITAB for Descriptive Statistics and Plots   39
1-11 Summary and Review of Terms   41
Case 1: NASDAQ Volatility   48

Chapter 2   Probability   50

2-1   Using Statistics   51
2-2   Basic Definitions: Events, Sample Space,
         and Probabilities   53
2-3   Basic Rules for Probability   57
   The Range of Values   57
   The Rule of Complements   58
   Mutually Exclusive Events   59
2-4   Conditional Probability   61
2-5   Independence of Events   66
   Product Rules for Independent Events   67
2-6   Combinatorial Concepts   70

2–7   The Law of Total Probability and Bayes' Theorem   73
   The Law of Total Probability   73
   Bayes' Theorem   75
2–8   The Joint Probability Table   79
2–9   Using the Computer   80
   Excel Templates and Formulas   80
   Using MINITAB   81
2–10 Summary and Review of Terms   84
Case 2: Job Applications   89

Chapter 3   Random Variables   90

3–1   Using Statistics   91
   Discrete and Continuous Random Variables   95
   Cumulative Distribution Function   96
3–2   Expected Values of Discrete Random Variables   102
   The Expected Value of a Function of a Random Variable   103
   Variance and Standard Deviation of a Random Variable   104
   Variance of a Linear Function of a Random Variable   106
3–3   Sum and Linear Composites of Random Variables   107
   Chebyshev's Theorem   108
   The Templates for Random Variables   109
3–4   Bernoulli Random Variable   112
3–5   The Binomial Random Variable   113
   Conditions for a Binomial Random Variable   113
   Binomial Distribution Formulas   114
   The Template   115
   Problem Solving with the Template   116
3–6   Negative Binomial Distribution   118
   Negative Binomial Distribution Formulas   118
   Problem Solving with the Template   119
3–7   The Geometric Distribution   120
   Geometric Distribution Formulas   120
   Problem Solving with the Template   121
3–8   The Hypergeometric Distribution   121
   Hypergeometric Distribution Formulas   122
   Problem Solving with the Template   123
3–9   The Poisson Distribution   124
   Problem Solving with the Template   125
3–10 Continuous Random Variables   126
3–11 The Uniform Distribution   129
   Problem Solving with the Template   130
3–12 The Exponential Distribution   130
   A Remarkable Property   131
   The Template   131
   Value at Risk   132

3–13 Using the Computer   133
  Using Excel Formulas for Some Standard Distributions   *133*
  Using MINITAB for Some Standard Distributions   *134*
3–14 Summary and Review of Terms   135
Case 3: Concepts Testing   145

Chapter 4   The Normal Distribution   146

4–1 Using Statistics   147
4–2 Properties of the Normal Distribution   148
4–3 The Standard Normal Distribution   151
  *Finding Probabilities of the Standard Normal
    Distribution*   *151*
  Finding Values of Z Given a Probability   *153*
4–4 The Transformation of Normal Random
      Variables   156
  Using the Normal Transformation   *157*
4–5 The Inverse Transformation   162
4–6 The Template   166
  Problem Solving with the Template   *167*
4–7 Normal Approximation of Binomial Distributions   169
4–8 Using the Computer   171
  Using Excel Functions for a Normal Distribution   *171*
  Using MINITAB for a Normal Distribution   *172*
4–9 Summary and Review of Terms   172
Case 4: Acceptable Pins   177
Case 5: Multicurrency Decision   177

Chapter 5   Sampling and Sampling Distributions   180

5–1 Using Statistics   181
5–2 Sample Statistics as Estimators of Population
      Parameters   183
  Obtaining a Random Sample   *186*
  Other Sampling Methods   *187*
  Nonresponse   *188*
5–3 Sampling Distributions   190
  The Central Limit Theorem   *194*
  The History of the Central Limit Theorem   *198*
  *The Standardized Sampling Distribution of the
    Sample Mean When σ Is Not Known*   *198*
  The Sampling Distribution of the Sample Proportion $\hat{P}$ *198*
5–4 Estimators and Their Properties   201
  *Applying the Concepts of Unbiasedness, Efficiency,
    Consistency, and Sufficiency*   *203*
5–5 Degrees of Freedom   205

5–6   Using the Computer   209
Using Excel for Generating Sampling Distributions   209
Using MINITAB for Generating Sampling Distributions   212
5–7   Summary and Review of Terms   213
Case 6: Acceptance Sampling of Pins   216

Chapter 6   Confidence Intervals   218

6–1   Using Statistics   219
6–2   Confidence Interval for the Population Mean
      When the Population Standard Deviation
      Is Known   220
The Template   225
6–3   Confidence Intervals for μ When σ Is Unknown—
      The t Distribution   228
The t Distribution   228
6–4   Large-Sample Confidence Intervals for
      the Population Proportion p 235
The Template   237
6–5   Confidence Intervals for the Population
      Variance   239
The Template   242
6–6   Sample-Size Determination   243
6–7   The Templates   245
Optimizing Population Mean Estimates   245
Determining the Optimal Half-Width   245
Using the Solver   247
Optimizing Population Proportion Estimates   247
6–8   Using the Computer   248
*Using Excel Built-In Functions for Confidence Interval
  Estimation   248*
Using MINITAB for Confidence Interval Estimation   249
6–9   Summary and Review of Terms   250
Case 7: Presidential Polling   254
Case 8: Privacy Problem   255

Chapter 7   Hypothesis Testing   256

7–1   Using Statistics   257
The Null Hypothesis   257
7–2   The Concepts of Hypothesis Testing   260
Evidence Gathering   260
Type I and Type II Errors   260
The p-Value   261
The Significance Level   262
*Optimal α and the Compromise between Type I
  and Type II Errors   263*
β and Power   264
Sample Size   264

7–3   Computing the *p*-Value   265

The Test Statistic   266

p-Value Calculations   266

One-Tailed and Two-Tailed Tests   267

Computing β   269

7–4   The Hypothesis Test   272

Testing Population Means   272

A Note on t *Tables and* p*-Values   273*

The Templates   274

Testing Population Proportions   276

Testing Population Variances   278

7–5   Pretest Decisions   289

Testing Population Means   289

Manual Calculation of Required Sample Size   290

Testing Population Proportions   294

Manual Calculation of Sample Size   295

7–6   Using the Computer   298

Using Excel for One-Sample Hypothesis Testing   298

Using MINITAB for One-Sample Hypothesis Testing   299

7–7   Summary and Review of Terms   300

Case 9: Tiresome Tires I   301

Chapter 8   The Comparison of Two Populations   302

8–1   Using Statistics   303

8–2   Paired-Observation Comparisons   304

The Template   306

Confidence Intervals   307

The Template   308

8–3   A Test for the Difference between Two Population Means Using Independent Random Samples   310

The Templates   314

Confidence Intervals   316

The Templates   318

Confidence Intervals   321

8–4   A Large-Sample Test for the Difference between Two Population Proportions   324

Confidence Intervals   327

The Template   328

8–5   The *F* Distribution and a Test for Equality of Two Population Variances   330

A Statistical Test for Equality of Two Population Variances   333

The Templates   336

8–6   Using the Computer   338

Using Excel for Comparison of Two Populations   338

Using MINITAB for Comparison of Two Samples   340

8–7   Summary and Review of Terms   341

Case 10: Tiresome Tires II   346

Chapter 9   Analysis of Variance   348

9–1   Using Statistics   349
9–2   The Hypothesis Test of Analysis of Variance   350
      The Test Statistic   351
9–3   The Theory and the Computations of ANOVA   355
      The Sum-of-Squares Principle   358
      The Degrees of Freedom   361
      The Mean Squares   362
      *The Expected Values of the Statistics MSTR and MSE
        under the Null Hypothesis   362*
      The F Statistic   363
9–4   The ANOVA Table and Examples   364
9–5   Further Analysis   371
      The Tukey Pairwise-Comparisons Test   373
      Conducting the Tests   375
      *The Case of Unequal Sample Sizes, and
        Alternative Procedures   376*
      The Template   376
9–6   Models, Factors, and Designs   378
      One-Factor versus Multifactor Models   378
      Fixed-Effects versus Random-Effects Models   379
      Experimental Design   379
9–7   Two-Way Analysis of Variance   380
      The Two-Way ANOVA Model   381
      The Hypothesis Tests in Two-Way ANOVA   382
      *Sums of Squares, Degrees of Freedom, and
        Mean Squares   383*
      The F Ratios and the Two-Way ANOVA Table   384
      The Template   388
      The Overall Significance Level   388
      The Tukey Method for Two-Way Analysis   388
      Extension of ANOVA to Three Factors   389
      Two-Way ANOVA with One Observation per Cell   389
9–8   Blocking Designs   393
      Randomized Complete Block Design   393
      The Template   396
9–9   Using the Computer   398
      Using Excel for Analysis of Variance   398
      Using MINITAB for Analysis of Variance   400
9–10 Summary and Review of Terms   403
      Case 11: Rating Wines   406
      Case 12: Checking Out Checkout   406

Chapter 10   Simple Linear Regression and Correlation   408

10–1 Using Statistics   409
      Model Building   410
10–2 The Simple Linear Regression Model   411

10–3 Estimation: The Method of Least Squares 414

The Template 421

10–4 Error Variance and the Standard Errors
of Regression Estimators 424

Confidence Intervals for the Regression Parameters 426

10–5 Correlation 429

10–6 Hypothesis Tests about the Regression Relationship 434

Other Tests 437

10–7 How Good Is the Regression? 438

10–8 Analysis-of-Variance Table and an *F* Test of the
Regression Model 443

10–9 Residual Analysis and Checking for
Model Inadequacies 445

A Check for the Equality of Variance of the Errors 445

Testing for Missing Variables 446

Detecting a Curvilinear Relationship between Y and X 447

The Normal Probability Plot 448

10–10 Use of the Regression Model for Prediction 454

Point Predictions 454

Prediction Intervals 455

*A Confidence Interval for the Average Y, Given a
Particular Value of X 457*

10–11 Using the Computer 458

The Excel Solver Method for Regression 458

The Excel LINEST Function 461

Using MINITAB for Simple Linear Regression Analysis 463

10–12 Summary and Review of Terms 464

Case 13: Firm Leverage and Shareholder Rights 466

Case 14: Risk and Return 467

Chapter 11   Multiple Regression   468

11–1 Using Statistics 469

11–2 The *k*-Variable Multiple Regression Model 469

The Estimated Regression Relationship 472

11–3 The *F* Test of a Multiple Regression Model 473

11–4 How Good Is the Regression? 477

11–5 Tests of the Significance of Individual
Regression Parameters 482

11–6 Testing the Validity of the Regression Model 494

Residual Plots 494

Standardized Residuals 494

The Normal Probability Plot 496

Outliers and Influential Observations 496

Lack of Fit and Other Problems 498

11–7 Using the Multiple Regression Model for Prediction 500

The Template 502

Setting Recalculation to "Manual" on the Template 502

11–8 Qualitative Independent Variables   503
   Interactions between Qualitative and Quantitative Variables   510
11–9 Polynomial Regression   513
   Other Variables and Cross-Product Terms   517
11–10 Nonlinear Models and Transformations   521
   Variance-Stabilizing Transformations   527
   Regression with Dependent Indicator Variable   528
11–11 Multicollinearity   531
   Causes of Multicollinearity   532
   Detecting the Existence of Multicollinearity   533
   Solutions to the Multicollinearity Problem   537
11–12 Residual Autocorrelation and the Durbin-Watson Test   539
11–13 Partial *F* Tests and Variable Selection Methods   542
   Partial F *Tests   542*
   Variable Selection Methods   545
11–14 Using the Computer   548
   Multiple Regression Using the Solver   548
   LINEST Function for Multiple Regression   550
   Using MINITAB for Multiple Regression   551
11–15 Summary and Review of Terms   554
   Case 15: Return on Capital for Four Different Sectors   556

Chapter 12   Time Series, Forecasting, and Index Numbers   560
12–1 Using Statistics   561
12–2 Trend Analysis   561
12–3 Seasonality and Cyclical Behavior   566
12–4 The Ratio-to-Moving-Average Method   569
   The Template   574
   The Cyclical Component of the Series   574
   Forecasting a Multiplicative Series   576
12–5 Exponential Smoothing Methods   577
   The Template   581
12–6 Index Numbers   582
   The Consumer Price Index   585
   The Template   587
12–7 Using the Computer   588
   Using Microsoft Excel in Forecasting and Time Series   588
   Using MINITAB in Forecasting and Time Series   589
12–8 Summary and Review of Terms   591
   Case 16: Auto Parts Sales Forecast   592

Chapter 13   Quality Control and Improvement   594
13–1 Using Statistics   595
13–2 W. Edwards Deming Instructs   596

13–3 Statistics and Quality   596
   Deming's 14 Points   *597*
   Process Capability   *598*
   Control Charts   *598*
   Pareto Diagrams   *601*
   Six Sigma   *602*
   Acceptance Sampling   *602*
   Analysis of Variance and Experimental Design   *602*
   Taguchi Methods   *602*
   The Template   *603*
13–4 The $\bar{x}$ Chart   604
   The Template   *606*
13–5 The R Chart and the s Chart   608
   The R Chart   *608*
   The s Chart   *608*
13–6 The p Chart   611
   The Template   *612*
13–7 The c Chart   614
   The Template   *614*
13–8 The x Chart   615
13–9 Using the Computer   616
   Using MINITAB for Quality Control   *616*
13–10 Summary and Review of Terms   617
Case 17: Quality Control and Improvement
   at Nashua Corporation   618

Chapter 14   Nonparametric Methods and Chi-Square Tests   620
14–1 Using Statistics   621
14–2 The Sign Test   621
14–3 The Runs Test—A Test for Randomness   626
   Large-Sample Properties   *628*
   The Template   *629*
   The Wald-Wolfowitz Test   *630*
14–4 The Mann-Whitney U Test   633
   The Computational Procedure   *634*
14–5 The Wilcoxon Signed-Rank Test   639
   The Paired-Observations Two-Sample Test   *639*
   Large-Sample Version of the Test   *640*
   A Test for the Mean or Median of a Single
   Population   *642*
   The Template   *643*
14–6 The Kruskal-Wallis Test—A Nonparametric
   Alternative to One-Way ANOVA   645
   The Template   *648*
   Further Analysis   *650*
14–7 The Friedman Test for a Randomized Block Design   653
   The Template   *655*

14–8 The Spearman Rank Correlation Coefficient 657
  The Template 659
14–9 A Chi-Square Test for Goodness of Fit 661
  A Goodness-of-Fit Test for the Multinomial Distribution 663
  The Template 664
  Unequal Probabilities 664
  The Template 668
14–10 Contingency Table Analysis—A Chi-Square Test
       for Independence 669
  The Template 672
14–11 A Chi-Square Test for Equality of Proportions 675
  The Median Test 677
14–12 Using the Computer 680
  Using MINITAB for Nonparametric Tests 680
14–13 Summary and Review of Terms 682
Case 18: The Nine Nations of North America 684

Chapter 15   Bayesian Statistics and Decision Analysis   686

15–1 Using Statistics 687
15–2 Bayes' Theorem and Discrete Probability
      Models 688
  The Template 692
15–3 Bayes' Theorem and Continuous
      Probability Distributions 695
  The Normal Probability Model 696
  Credible Sets 698
  The Template 699
15–4 The Evaluation of Subjective Probabilities 701
  Assessing a Normal Prior Distribution 701
15–5 Decision Analysis: An Overview 702
  Actions 703
  Chance Occurrences 703
  Probabilities 704
  Final Outcomes 704
  Additional Information 704
  Decision 704
15–6 Decision Trees 705
  The Payoff Table 706
15–7 Handling Additional Information Using
      Bayes' Theorem 714
  Determining the Payoffs 716
  Determining the Probabilities 716
15–8 Utility 725
  A Method of Assessing Utility 727
15–9 The Value of Information 728

15–10 Using the Computer   731
    The Template   731
15–11 Summary and Review of Terms   733
Case 19: Pizzas 'R' Us   735
Case 20: New Drug Development   736

Appendix A   References   740

Appendix B   Answers to Most Odd-Numbered Problems   743

Appendix C   Statistical Tables   755

On the CD

Chapter 16   Sampling Methods
    16–1 Using Statistics
    16–2 Nonprobability Sampling and Bias
    16–3 Stratified Random Sampling
       Practical Applications
       Confidence Intervals
       The Template
       Stratified Sampling for the Population Proportion
       The Template
       What Do We Do When the Population Strata
         Weights Are Unknown?
       How Many Strata Should We Use?
       Postsampling Stratification
       Optimum Allocation
       The Template
    16–4 Cluster Sampling
       The Relation with Stratified Sampling
       Single-Stage Cluster Sampling for the Population Mean
       Single-Stage Cluster Sampling for the Population
         Proportion
       The Templates
       Two-Stage Cluster Sampling
    16–5 Systematic Sampling
       The Advantages of Systematic Sampling
       Estimation of the Population Mean in Systematic
         Sampling
       The Template
    16–6 Nonresponse
    16–7 Summary and Review of Terms
    Case 21: The Boston Redevelopment Authority

Chapter 17   Multivariate Analysis
   17–1 Using Statistics
   17–2 The Multivariate Normal Distribution
   17–3 Discriminant Analysis
      Developing a Discriminant Function
      Evaluating the Performance of the Model
      Discriminant Analysis with More Than Two Groups
   17–4 Principal Components and Factor Analysis
      Principal Components
      The Extraction of the Components
      Factor Analysis
      The Extraction of Factors
      The Rotation of Factors
   17–5 Using the Computer
      Using MINITAB for Discriminant and Principal
         Component Analysis
   17–6 Summary and Review of Terms
   Case 22: Predicting Company Failure

   Working with Templates
   The Idea of Templates
      The Dangers of Templates and How to Avoid Them
      Conventions Employed in the Templates
   Working with Templates
      Protecting and Unprotecting a Sheet
      Entering Data into the Templates
   The Autocalculate Command
   The Data|Table Command
   The Goal Seek Command
   The Solver Macro
      Solver Installation
   Some Formatting Tips
   Saving the Templates

   Introduction to Excel Basics
   Excel Formulas
      Copying Formulas
   Excel Functions
   The Need for Templates
      Creating the Template
      Limitations of the Template
      Exercise

   Index   793

Complete
Business
Statistics

1

INTRODUCTION AND DESCRIPTIVE STATISTICS

1-1   Using Statistics   3
1-2   Percentiles and Quartiles   8
1-3   Measures of Central Tendency   10
1-4   Measures of Variability   14
1-5   Grouped Data and the Histogram   20
1-6   Skewness and Kurtosis   22
1-7   Relations between the Mean and the Standard Deviation   24
1-8   Methods of Displaying Data   25
1-9   Exploratory Data Analysis   29
1-10   Using the Computer   35
1-11   Summary and Review of Terms   41
Case 1   NASDAQ Volatility   48

LEARNING OBJECTIVES

After studying this chapter, you should be able to:

- Distinguish between qualitative and quantitative data.
- Describe nominal, ordinal, interval, and ratio scales of measurement.
- Describe the difference between a population and a sample.
- Calculate and interpret percentiles and quartiles.
- Explain measures of central tendency and how to compute them.
- Create different types of charts that describe data sets.
- Use Excel templates to compute various measures and create charts.

It is better to be roughly right than precisely wrong.
–John Maynard Keynes

You all have probably heard the story about Malcolm Forbes, who once got lost floating for miles in one of his famous balloons and finally landed in the middle of a cornfield. He spotted a man coming toward him and asked, "Sir, can you tell me where I am?" The man said, "Certainly, you are in a basket in a field of corn." Forbes said, "You must be a statistician." The man said, "That's amazing, how did you know that?" "Easy," said Forbes, "your information is concise, precise, and absolutely useless!"[1]

The purpose of this book is to convince you that information resulting from a good statistical analysis is always concise, often precise, and never useless! The spirit of statistics is, in fact, very well captured by the quotation above from Keynes. This book should teach you how to be at least roughly right a high percentage of the time. Statistics is a science that helps us make better decisions in business and economics as well as in other fields. Statistics teach us how to summarize data, analyze them, and draw meaningful inferences that then lead to improved decisions. These better decisions we make help us improve the running of a department, a company, or the entire economy.

The word *statistics* is derived from the Italian word *stato,* which means "state," and *statista* refers to a person involved with the affairs of state. Therefore, *statistics* originally meant the collection of facts useful to the *statista.* Statistics in this sense was used in 16th-century Italy and then spread to France, Holland, and Germany. We note, however, that surveys of people and property actually began in ancient times.[2] Today, statistics is not restricted to information about the state but extends to almost every realm of human endeavor. Neither do we restrict ourselves to merely collecting numerical information, called *data.* Our data are summarized, displayed in meaningful ways, and analyzed. Statistical analysis often involves an attempt to generalize from the data. Statistics is a science–the science of information. Information may be *qualitative* or *quantitative.* To illustrate the difference between these two types of information, let's consider an example.

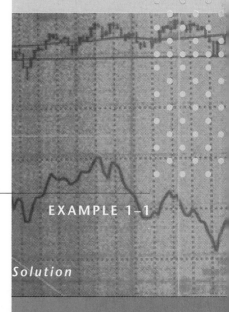

EXAMPLE 1–1

Realtors who help sell condominiums in the Boston area provide prospective buyers with the information given in Table 1–1. Which of the variables in the table are quantitative and which are qualitative?

Solution

The asking price is a *quantitative* variable: it conveys a quantity–the asking price in dollars. The number of rooms is also a quantitative variable. The direction the apartment faces is a *qualitative* variable since it conveys a quality (east, west, north, south). Whether a condominium has a washer and dryer in the unit (yes or no) and whether there is a doorman are also qualitative variables.

---

[1]From an address by R. Gnanadesikan to the American Statistical Association, reprinted in *American Statistician* 44, no. 2 (May 1990), p. 122.

[2]See Anders Hald, *A History of Probability and Statistics and Their Applications before 1750* (New York: Wiley, 1990), pp. 81–82.

TABLE 1–1   Boston Condominium Data

Asking Price	Number of Bedrooms	Number of Bathrooms	Direction Facing	Washer/Dryer?	Doorman?
$709,000	2	1	E	Y	Y
812,500	2	2	N	N	Y
980,000	3	3	N	Y	Y
830,000	1	2	W	N	N
850,900	2	2	W	Y	N

Source: Boston.condocompany.com, March 2007.

A **quantitative variable** can be described by a number for which arithmetic operations such as averaging make sense. A **qualitative** (or **categorical**) **variable** simply records a quality. If a number is used for distinguishing members of different categories of a qualitative variable, the number assignment is arbitrary.

The field of statistics deals with **measurements**–some quantitative and others qualitative. The measurements are the actual numerical values of a variable. (Qualitative variables could be described by numbers, although such a description might be arbitrary; for example, $N = 1$, $E = 2$, $S = 3$, $W = 4$, $Y = 1$, $N = 0$.)

The four generally used **scales of measurement** are listed here from weakest to strongest.

Nominal Scale.   In the **nominal scale** of measurement, numbers are used simply as labels for groups or classes. If our data set consists of blue, green, and red items, we may designate blue as 1, green as 2, and red as 3. In this case, the numbers 1, 2, and 3 stand only for the category to which a data point belongs. "Nominal" stands for "name" of category. The nominal scale of measurement is used for qualitative rather than quantitative data: blue, green, red; male, female; professional classification; geographic classification; and so on.

Ordinal Scale.   In the **ordinal scale** of measurement, data elements may be ordered according to their relative size or quality. Four products ranked by a consumer may be ranked as 1, 2, 3, and 4, where 4 is the best and 1 is the worst. In this scale of measurement we do not know how much better one product is than others, only that it is better.

Interval Scale.   In the **interval scale** of measurement the value of zero is assigned arbitrarily and therefore we cannot take ratios of two measurements. But *we can take ratios of intervals.* A good example is how we measure time of day, which is in an interval scale. We cannot say 10:00 A.M. is twice as long as 5:00 A.M. But we can say that the interval between 0:00 A.M. (midnight) and 10:00 A.M., which is a duration of 10 hours, is twice as long as the interval between 0:00 A.M. and 5:00 A.M., which is a duration of 5 hours. This is because 0:00 A.M. does not mean absence of any time. Another example is temperature. When we say 0°F, we do not mean zero heat. A temperature of 100°F is not twice as hot as 50°F.

Ratio Scale.   If two measurements are in **ratio scale,** then we can take ratios of those measurements. The zero in this scale is an absolute zero. Money, for example, is measured in a ratio scale. A sum of $100 is twice as large as $50. A sum of $0 means absence of any money and is thus an absolute zero. We have already seen that measurement of duration (but not time of day) is in a ratio scale. In general, the interval between two interval scale measurements will be in ratio scale. Other examples of the ratio scale are measurements of weight, volume, area, or length.

Samples and Populations

In statistics we make a distinction between two concepts: a population and a sample.

> The **population** consists of the set of all measurements in which the investigator is interested. The population is also called the **universe**.
>
> A **sample** is a subset of measurements selected from the population. Sampling from the population is often done randomly, such that every possible sample of *n* elements will have an equal chance of being selected. A sample selected in this way is called a **simple random sample**, or just a **random sample**. A random sample allows chance to determine its elements.

For example, Farmer Jane owns 1,264 sheep. These sheep constitute her entire *population* of sheep. If 15 sheep are selected to be sheared, then these 15 represent a *sample* from Jane's population of sheep. Further, if the 15 sheep were selected at *random* from Jane's population of 1,264 sheep, then they would constitute a *random sample* of sheep.

The definitions of *sample* and *population* are relative to what we want to consider. If Jane's sheep are all we care about, then they constitute a population. If, however, we are interested in all the sheep in the county, then all Jane's 1,264 sheep are a sample of that larger population (although this sample would not be random).

The distinction between a sample and a population is very important in statistics.

Data and Data Collection

A set of measurements obtained on some variable is called a **data set.** For example, heart rate measurements for 10 patients may constitute a data set. The variable we're interested in is heart rate, and the scale of measurement here is a ratio scale. (A heart that beats 80 times per minute is twice as fast as a heart that beats 40 times per minute.) Our actual observations of the patients' heart rates, the data set, might be 60, 70, 64, 55, 70, 80, 70, 74, 51, 80.

Data are collected by various methods. Sometimes our data set consists of the entire population we're interested in. If we have the actual point spread for five football games, and if we are interested only in these five games, then our data set of five measurements is the entire population of interest. (In this case, our data are on a ratio scale. Why? Suppose the data set for the five games told only whether the home or visiting team won. What would be our measurement scale in this case?)

In other situations data may constitute a sample from some population. If the data are to be used to draw some conclusions about the larger population they were drawn from, then we must collect the data with great care. A conclusion drawn about a population based on the information in a sample from the population is called a **statistical inference.** Statistical inference is an important topic of this book. To ensure the accuracy of statistical inference, data must be drawn randomly from the population of interest, and we must make sure that every segment of the population is adequately and proportionally represented in the sample.

Statistical inference may be based on data collected in surveys or experiments, which must be carefully constructed. For example, when we want to obtain information from people, we may use a mailed questionnaire or a telephone interview as a convenient instrument. In such surveys, however, we want to minimize any **nonresponse bias.** This is the biasing of the results that occurs when we disregard the fact that some people will simply not respond to the survey. The bias distorts the findings, because the people who do not respond may belong more to one segment of the population than to another. In social research some questions may be sensitive—for example, "Have you ever been arrested?" This may easily result in a nonresponse bias, because people who have indeed been arrested may be less likely to answer the question (unless they can be perfectly certain of remaining anonymous). Surveys conducted by popular magazines often suffer from nonresponse bias, especially when their questions are provocative. What makes good magazine reading often makes bad statistics. An article in the *New York Times* reported on a survey about Jewish life in America. The survey was conducted by calling people at home on a Saturday–thus strongly biasing the results since Orthodox Jews do not answer the phone on Saturday.[3]

Suppose we want to measure the speed performance or gas mileage of an automobile. Here the data will come from experimentation. In this case we want to make sure that a variety of road conditions, weather conditions, and other factors are represented. Pharmaceutical testing is also an example where data may come from experimentation. Drugs are usually tested against a placebo as well as against no treatment at all. When an experiment is designed to test the effectiveness of a sleeping pill, the variable of interest may be the time, in minutes, that elapses between taking the pill and falling asleep.

In experiments, as in surveys, it is important to **randomize** if inferences are indeed to be drawn. People should be randomly chosen as subjects for the experiment if an inference is to be drawn to the entire population. Randomization should also be used in assigning people to the three groups: pill, no pill, or placebo. Such a design will minimize potential biasing of the results.

In other situations data may come from published sources, such as statistical abstracts of various kinds or government publications. The published unemployment rate over a number of months is one example. Here, data are "given" to us without our having any control over how they are obtained. Again, caution must be exercised. The unemployment rate over a given period is not a random sample of any *future* unemployment rates, and making statistical inferences in such cases may be complex and difficult. If, however, we are interested only in the period we have data for, then our data do constitute an entire population, which may be described. In any case, however, we must also be careful to note any missing data or incomplete observations.

In this chapter, we will concentrate on the processing, summarization, and display of data—the first step in statistical analysis. In the next chapter, we will explore the theory of probability, the connection between the random sample and the population. Later chapters build on the concepts of probability and develop a system that allows us to draw a logical, consistent inference from our sample to the underlying population.

Why worry about inference and about a population? Why not just look at our data and interpret them? Mere inspection of the data will suffice when interest centers on the particular observations you have. If, however, you want to draw meaningful conclusions with implications extending beyond your limited data, statistical inference is the way to do it.

In marketing research, we are often interested in the relationship between advertising and sales. A data set of randomly chosen sales and advertising figures for a given firm may be of some interest in itself, but the information in it is much more useful if it leads to implications about the underlying process—the relationship between the firm's level of advertising and the resulting level of sales. An understanding of the true relationship between advertising and sales—the relationship in the population of advertising and sales possibilities for the firm—would allow us to predict sales for any level of advertising and thus to set advertising at a level that maximizes profits.

A pharmaceutical manufacturer interested in marketing a new drug may be required by the Food and Drug Administration to prove that the drug does not cause serious side effects. The results of tests of the drug on a random sample of people may then be used in a statistical inference about the entire population of people who may use the drug if it is introduced.

[3]Laurie Goodstein, "Survey Finds Slight Rise in Jews Intermarrying," *The New York Times,* September 11, 2003, p. A13.

A bank may be interested in assessing the popularity of a particular model of automatic teller machines. The machines may be tried on a randomly chosen group of bank customers. The conclusions of the study could then be generalized by statistical inference to the entire population of the bank's customers.

A quality control engineer at a plant making disk drives for computers needs to make sure that no more than 3% of the drives produced are defective. The engineer may routinely collect random samples of drives and check their quality. Based on the random samples, the engineer may then draw a conclusion about the proportion of defective items in the entire population of drives.

These are just a few examples illustrating the use of statistical inference in business situations. In the rest of this chapter, we will introduce the descriptive statistics needed to carry out basic statistical analyses. The following chapters will develop the elements of inference from samples to populations.

PROBLEMS

1-1. A survey by an electric company contains questions on the following:

1. Age of household head.
2. Sex of household head.
3. Number of people in household.
4. Use of electric heating (yes or no).
5. Number of large appliances used daily.
6. Thermostat setting in winter.
7. Average number of hours heating is on.
8. Average number of heating days.
9. Household income.
10. Average monthly electric bill.
11. Ranking of this electric company as compared with two previous electricity suppliers.

Describe the variables implicit in these 11 items as quantitative or qualitative, and describe the scales of measurement.

1-2. Discuss the various data collection methods described in this section.

1-3. Discuss and compare the various scales of measurement.

1-4. Describe each of the following variables as qualitative or quantitative.

The Richest People on Earth 2007

Name	Wealth ($ billion)	Age	Industry	Country of Citizenship
William Gates III	56	51	Technology	U.S.A.
Warren Buffett	52	76	Investment	U.S.A.
Carlos Slim Helú	49	67	Telecom	Mexico
Ingvar Kamprad	33	80	Retail	Sweden
Bernard Arnault	26	58	Luxury goods	France

Source: *Forbes*, March 26, 2007 (the "billionaires" issue), pp. 104–156.

1-5. Five ice cream flavors are rank-ordered by preference. What is the scale of measurement?

1-6. What is the difference between a qualitative and a quantitative variable?

1-7. A town has 15 neighborhoods. If you interviewed everyone living in one particular neighborhood, would you be interviewing a population or a sample from the town?

Would this be a random sample? If you had a list of everyone living in the town, called a **frame,** and you randomly selected 100 people from all the neighborhoods, would this be a random sample?

1–8.   What is the difference between a sample and a population?

1–9.   What is a random sample?

1–10.   For each tourist entering the United States, the U.S. Immigration and Naturalization Service computer is fed the tourist's nationality and length of intended stay. Characterize each variable as quantitative or qualitative.

1–11.   What is the scale of measurement for the color of a karate belt?

1–12.   An individual federal tax return form asks, among other things, for the following information: income (in dollars and cents), number of dependents, whether filing singly or jointly with a spouse, whether or not deductions are itemized, amount paid in local taxes. Describe the scale of measurement of each variable, and state whether the variable is qualitative or quantitative.

1–2 Percentiles and Quartiles

Given a set of numerical observations, we may order them according to magnitude. Once we have done this, it is possible to define the boundaries of the set. Any student who has taken a nationally administered test, such as the Scholastic Aptitude Test (SAT), is familiar with *percentiles*. Your score on such a test is compared with the scores of all people who took the test at the same time, and your position within this group is defined in terms of a percentile. If you are in the 90th percentile, 90% of the people who took the test received a score lower than yours. We define a percentile as follows.

> The Pth **percentile** of a group of numbers is that value below which lie $P\%$ (P percent) of the numbers in the group. The position of the Pth percentile is given by $(n + 1)P/100$, where n is the number of data points.

Let's look at an example.

EXAMPLE 1–2

The magazine *Forbes* publishes annually a list of the world's wealthiest individuals. For 2007, the net worth of the 20 richest individuals, in billions of dollars, in no particular order, is as follows:[4]

> 33, 26, 24, 21, 19, 20, 18, 18, 52, 56, 27, 22, 18, 49, 22, 20, 23, 32, 20, 18

Find the 50th and 80th percentiles of this set of the world's top 20 net worths.

Solution   First, let's order the data from smallest to largest:

> 18, 18, 18, 18, 19, 20, 20, 20, 21, 22, 22, 23, 24, 26, 27, 32, 33, 49, 52, 56

To find the 50th percentile, we need to determine the data point in position $(n + 1)P/100 = (20 + 1)(50/100) = (21)(0.5) = 10.5$. Thus, we need the data point in position 10.5. Counting the observations from smallest to largest, we find that the 10th observation is 22, and the 11th is 22. Therefore, the observation that would lie in position 10.5 (halfway between the 10th and 11th observations) is 22. Thus, the 50th percentile is 22.

Similarly, we find the 80th percentile of the data set as the observation lying in position $(n + 1)P/100 = (21)(80/100) = 16.8$. The 16th observation is 32, and the 17th is 33; therefore, the 80th percentile is a point lying 0.8 of the way from 32 to 33, that is, 32.8.

---

[4]*Forbes,* March 26, 2007 (the "billionaires" issue), pp. 104–186.

Certain percentiles have greater importance than others because they break down the **distribution** of the data (the way the data points are distributed along the number line) into four groups. These are the quartiles. **Quartiles** are the percentage points that break down the data set into quarters—first quarter, second quarter, third quarter, and fourth quarter.

The **first quartile** is the 25th percentile. It is that point below which lie one-fourth of the data.

Similarly, the second quartile is the 50th percentile, as we computed in Example 1–2. This is a most important point and has a special name—the *median.*

The **median** is the point below which lie half the data. It is the 50th percentile.

We define the third quartile correspondingly:

The **third quartile** is the 75th percentile point. It is that point below which lie 75 percent of the data.

The 25th percentile is often called the **lower quartile;** the 50th percentile point, the median, is called the **middle quartile;** and the 75th percentile is called the **upper quartile.**

Find the lower, middle, and upper quartiles of the billionaires data set in Example 1–2.   **EXAMPLE 1–3**

Based on the procedure we used in computing the 80th percentile, we find that *Solution* the lower quartile is the observation in position $(21)(0.25) = 5.25$, which is 19.25. The middle quartile was already computed (it is the 50th percentile, the median, which is 22). The upper quartile is the observation in position $(21)(75/100) = 15.75$, which is 30.75.

We define the **interquartile range** as the difference between the first and third quartiles.

The interquartile range is a measure of the spread of the data. In Example 1–2, the interquartile range is equal to Third quartile − First quartile = 30.75 − 19.25 = 11.5.

PROBLEMS

1–13. The following data are numbers of passengers on flights of Delta Air Lines between San Francisco and Seattle over 33 days in April and early May.

128, 121, 134, 136, 136, 118, 123, 109, 120, 116, 125, 128, 121, 129, 130, 131, 127, 119, 114, 134, 110, 136, 134, 125, 128, 123, 128, 133, 132, 136, 134, 129, 132

Find the lower, middle, and upper quartiles of this data set. Also find the 10th, 15th, and 65th percentiles. What is the interquartile range?

1–14. The following data are annualized returns on a group of 15 stocks.

12.5, 13, 14.8, 11, 16.7, 9, 8.3, −1.2, 3.9, 15.5, 16.2, 18, 11.6, 10, 9.5

Find the median, the first and third quartiles, and the 55th and 85th percentiles for these data.

1–15. The following data are the total 1-year return, in percent, for 10 midcap mutual funds:[5]

$0.7, 0.8, 0.1, -0.7, -0.7, 1.6, 0.2, -0.5, -0.4, -1.3$

Find the median and the 20th, 30th, 60th, and 90th percentiles.

1–16. Following are the numbers of daily bids received by the government of a developing country from firms interested in winning a contract for the construction of a new port facility.

$2, 3, 2, 4, 3, 5, 1, 1, 6, 4, 7, 2, 5, 1, 6$

Find the quartiles and the interquartile range. Also find the 60th percentile.

1–17. Find the median, the interquartile range, and the 45th percentile of the following data.

$23, 26, 29, 30, 32, 34, 37, 45, 57, 80, 102, 147, 210, 355, 782, 1{,}209$

1–3   Measures of Central Tendency

CHAPTER 1

Percentiles, and in particular quartiles, are measures of the relative positions of points within a data set or a population (when our data set constitutes the entire population). The median is a special point, since it lies in the center of the data in the sense that half the data lie below it and half above it. The median is thus a measure of the *location* or *centrality* of the observations.

In addition to the median, two other measures of central tendency are commonly used. One is the *mode* (or modes—there may be several of them), and the other is the *arithmetic mean,* or just the *mean.* We define the mode as follows.

> The **mode** of the data set is the value that occurs most frequently.

Let us look at the frequencies of occurrence of the data values in Example 1–2, shown in Table 1–2. We see that the value 18 occurs most frequently. Four data points have this value—more points than for any other value in the data set. Therefore, the mode is equal to 18.

The most commonly used measure of central tendency of a set of observations is the mean of the observations.

> The **mean** of a set of observations is their **average.** It is equal to the sum of all observations divided by the number of observations in the set.

Let us denote the observations by $x_1, x_2, \ldots x_n$. That is, the first observation is denoted by x_1, the second by x_2, and so on to the nth observation, x_n. (In Example 1–2, $x_1 = 33$, $x_2 = 26, \ldots$, and $x_n = x_{20} = 18$.) The sample mean is denoted by $\bar{x}$

> Mean of a sample:
>
> $$\bar{x} = \frac{\sum\limits_{i=1}^{n} x_i}{n} = \frac{x_1 + x_2 + \cdots + x_n}{n} \qquad (1\text{–}1)$$

where Σ is summation notation. The summation extends over all data points.

TABLE 1–2   Frequencies of Occurrence of Data Values in Example 1–2

Value	Frequency
18	4
19	1
20	3
21	1
22	2
23	1
24	1
26	1
27	1
32	1
33	1
49	1
52	1
56	1

---

[5]"The Money 70," *Money,* March 2007, p. 63.

When our observation set constitutes an entire population, instead of denoting the mean by $\bar{x}$ we use the symbol μ (the Greek letter mu). For a population, we use N as the number of elements instead of n. The population mean is defined as follows.

Mean of a population:

$$\mu = \frac{\sum_{i=1}^{N} x_i}{N} \qquad (1\text{–}2)$$

The mean of the observations in Example 1–2 is found as

$$\begin{aligned}
\bar{x} &= (x_1 + x_2 + \cdots + x_{20})/20 = (33 + 26 + 24 + 21 + 19 \\
&\quad + 20 + 18 + 18 + 52 + 56 + 27 + 22 + 18 + 49 + 22 \\
&\quad + 20 + 23 + 32 + 20 + 18)/20 \\
&= 538/20 = 26.9
\end{aligned}$$

The mean of the observations of Example 1–2, their average, is 26.9.

Figure 1–1 shows the data of Example 1–2 drawn on the number line along with the mean, median, and mode of the observations. If you think of the data points as little balls of equal weight located at the appropriate places on the number line, the mean is that point where all the weights balance. It is the *fulcrum* of the point-weights, as shown in Figure 1–1.

What characterizes the three measures of centrality, and what are the relative merits of each? The mean summarizes all the information in the data. It is the average of all the observations. The mean is a single point that can be viewed as the point where all the mass–the weight–of the observations is concentrated. It is the center of mass of the data. If all the observations in our data set were the same size, then (assuming the total is the same) each would be equal to the mean.

The median, on the other hand, is an observation (or a point between two observations) in the center of the data set. One-half of the data lie above this observation, and one-half of the data lie below it. When we compute the median, we do not consider the exact location of each data point on the number line; we only consider whether it falls in the half lying above the median or in the half lying below the median.

What does this mean? If you look at the picture of the data set of Example 1–2, Figure 1–1, you will note that the observation $x_{10} = 56$ lies to the far right. If we shift this particular observation (or any other observation to the right of 22) to the right, say, move it from 56 to 100, what will happen to the median? The answer is: absolutely *nothing* (prove this to yourself by calculating the new median). The exact location of any data point is not considered in the computation of the median, only

FIGURE 1–1   Mean, Median, and Mode for Example 1–2

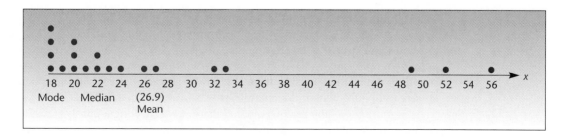

its relative standing with respect to the central observation. *The median is resistant to extreme observations.*

The mean, on the other hand, is sensitive to extreme observations. Let us see what happens to the mean if we change x_{10} from 56 to 100. The new mean is

$$\bar{x} = (33 + 26 + 24 + 21 + 19 + 20 + 18 + 18 + 52 + 100 + 27 \\ + 22 + 18 + 49 + 22 + 20 + 23 + 32 + 20 + 18)/20 \\ = 29.1$$

We see that the mean has shifted 2.2 units to the right to accommodate the change in the single data point x_{10}.

The mean, however, does have strong advantages as a measure of central tendency. *The mean is based on information contained in all the observations in the data set,* rather than being an observation lying "in the middle" of the set. The mean also has some desirable mathematical properties that make it useful in many contexts of statistical inference. In cases where we want to guard against the influence of a few outlying observations (called *outliers*), however, we may prefer to use the median.

EXAMPLE 1–4

To continue with the condominium prices from Example 1–1, a larger sample of asking prices for two-bedroom units in Boston (numbers in thousand dollars, rounded to the nearest thousand) is

789, 813, 980, 880, 650, 700, 2,990, 850, 690

What are the mean and the median? Interpret their meaning in this case.

Solution

Arranging the data from smallest to largest, we get

650, 690, 700, 789, 813, 850, 880, 980, 2,990

There are nine observations, so the median is the value in the middle, that is, in the fifth position. That value is 813 thousand dollars.

To compute the mean, we add all data values and divide by 9, giving 1,038 thousand dollars—that is, \$1,038,000. Now notice some interesting facts. The value 2,990 is clearly an *outlier*. It lies far to the right, away from the rest of the data bunched together in the 650–980 range.

In this case, the median is a very descriptive measure of this data set: it tells us where our data (with the exception of the outlier) are located. The mean, on the other hand, pays so much attention to the large observation 2,990 that it locates itself at 1,038, a value larger than our largest observation, except for the outlier. If our outlier had been more like the rest of the data, say, 820 instead of 2,990, the mean would have been 796.9. Notice that the median does not change and is still 813. This is so because 820 is on the same side of the median as 2,990.

Sometimes an outlier is due to an error in recording the data. In such a case it should be removed. Other times it is "out in left field" (actually, right field in this case) for good reason.

As it turned out, the condominium with asking price of \$2,990,000 was quite different from the rest of the two-bedroom units of roughly equal square footage and location. This unit was located in a prestigious part of town (away from the other units, geographically as well). It had a large whirlpool bath adjoining the master bedroom; its floors were marble from the Greek island of Paros; all light fixtures and faucets were gold-plated; the chandelier was Murano crystal. "This is not your average condominium," the realtor said, inadvertently reflecting a purely statistical fact in addition to the intended meaning of the expression.

FIGURE 1–2 **A Symmetrically Distributed Data Set**

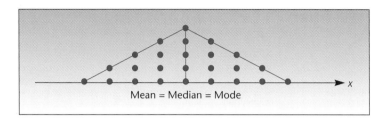

Mean = Median = Mode

The mode tells us our data set's most frequently occurring value. There may be several modes. In Example 1–2, our data set actually possesses three modes: 18, 20, and 22. Of the three measures of central tendency, we are most interested in the mean.

If a data set or population is *symmetric* (i.e., if one side of the distribution of the observations is a mirror image of the other) and if the distribution of the observations has only one mode, then the mode, the median, and the mean are all equal. Such a situation is demonstrated in Figure 1–2. Generally, when the data distribution is not symmetric, then the mean, median, and mode will not all be equal. The relative positions of the three measures of centrality in such situations will be discussed in section 1–6.

In the next section, we discuss measures of variability of a data set or population.

PROBLEMS

1–18. Discuss the differences among the three measures of centrality.

1–19. Find the mean, median, and mode(s) of the observations in problem 1–13.

1–20. Do the same as problem 1–19, using the data of problem 1–14.

1–21. Do the same as problem 1–19, using the data of problem 1–15.

1–22. Do the same as problem 1–19, using the data of problem 1–16.

1–23. Do the same as problem 1–19, using the observation set in problem 1–17.

1–24. Do the same as problem 1–19 for the data in Example 1–1.

1–25. Find the mean, mode, and median for the data set 7, 8, 8, 12, 12, 12, 14, 15, 20, 47, 52, 54.

1–26. For the following stock price one-year percentage changes, plot the data and identify any outliers. Find the mean and median.[6]

Intel	−6.9%
AT&T	46.5
General Electric	12.1
ExxonMobil	20.7
Microsoft	16.9
Pfizer	17.2
Citigroup	16.5

[6]"Stocks," *Money*, March 2007, p. 128.

1–27.   The following data are the median returns on investment, in percent, for 10 industries.[7]

Consumer staples	24.3%
Energy	23.3
Health care	22.1
Financials	21.0
Industrials	19.2
Consumer discretionary	19.0
Materials	18.1
Information technology	15.1
Telecommunication services	11.0
Utilities	10.4

Find the median of these medians and their mean.

1–4   Measures of Variability

CHAPTER 1

Consider the following two data sets.

Set I: 1, 2, 3, 4, 5, 6, 6, 7, 8, 9, 10, 11
Set II: 4, 5, 5, 5, 6, 6, 6, 6, 7, 7, 7, 8

Compute the mean, median, and mode of each of the two data sets. As you see from your results, the two data sets have the same mean, the same median, and the same mode, all equal to 6. The two data sets also happen to have the same number of observations, $n = 12$. But the two data sets are different. What is the main difference between them?

Figure 1–3 shows data sets I and II. The two data sets have the same central tendency (as measured by any of the three measures of centrality), but they have a different *variability*. In particular, we see that data set I is more variable than data set II. The values in set I are more spread out: they lie farther away from their mean than do those of set II.

There are several measures of **variability**, or **dispersion.** We have already discussed one such measure—the interquartile range. (Recall that the interquartile range

FIGURE 1–3   Comparison of Data Sets I and II

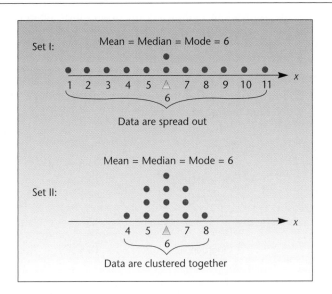

---

[7]"Sector Snapshot," *BusinessWeek,* March 26, 2007, p. 62.

is defined as the difference between the upper quartile and the lower quartile.) The interquartile range for data set I is 5.5, and the interquartile range of data set II is 2 (show this). The interquartile range is one measure of the dispersion or variability of a set of observations. Another such measure is the *range*.

> The **range** of a set of observations is the difference between the largest observation and the smallest observation.

The range of the observations in Example 1–2 is Largest number − Smallest number = 56 − 18 = 38. The range of the data in set I is 11 − 1 = 10, and the range of the data in set II is 8 − 4 = 4. We see that, conforming with what we expect from looking at the two data sets, the range of set I is greater than the range of set II. Set I is more variable.

The range and the interquartile range are measures of the dispersion of a set of observations, the interquartile range being more resistant to extreme observations. There are also two other, more commonly used measures of dispersion. These are the *variance* and the square root of the variance—the *standard deviation*.

The variance and the standard deviation are more useful than the range and the interquartile range because, like the mean, they use the information contained in all the observations in the data set or population. (The range contains information only on the distance between the largest and smallest observations, and the interquartile range contains information only about the difference between upper and lower quartiles.) We define the variance as follows.

> The **variance** of a set of observations is the average squared deviation of the data points from their mean.

When our data constitute a sample, the variance is denoted by s^2, and the averaging is done by dividing the sum of the squared deviations from the mean by $n − 1$. (The reason for this will become clear in Chapter 5.) When our observations constitute an entire population, the variance is denoted by σ^2, and the averaging is done by dividing by N. (And σ is the Greek letter sigma; we call the variance *sigma squared*. The capital sigma is known to you as the symbol we use for summation, Σ.)

> Sample variance:
> $$s^2 = \frac{\sum_{i=1}^{n}(x_i - \bar{x})^2}{n - 1}$$
> (1–3)

Recall that $\bar{x}$ is the sample mean, the average of all the observations in the sample. Thus, the numerator in equation 1–3 is equal to the sum of the squared differences of the data points x_i (where $i = 1, 2, \ldots, n$) from their mean $\bar{x}$. When we divide the numerator by the denominator $n − 1$, we get a kind of average of the items summed in the numerator. This average is based on the assumption that there are only $n − 1$ data points. (Note, however, that the summation in the numerator extends over all n data points, not just $n − 1$ of them.) This will be explained in section 5–5.

When we have an entire population at hand, we denote the total number of observations in the population by N. We define the population variance as follows.

> Population variance:
> $$\sigma^2 = \frac{\sum_{i=1}^{N}(x_i - \mu)^2}{N}$$
> (1–4)
>
> where μ is the population mean.

Unless noted otherwise, we will assume that all our data sets are samples and do not constitute entire populations; thus, we will use equation 1–3 for the variance, and not equation 1–4. We now define the standard deviation.

> The **standard deviation** of a set of observations is the (positive) square root of the variance of the set.

The standard deviation of a sample is the square root of the sample variance, and the standard deviation of a population is the square root of the variance of the population.[8]

Sample standard deviation:

$$s = \sqrt{s^2} = \sqrt{\frac{\sum_{i=1}^{n}(x_i - \bar{x})^2}{n - 1}} \qquad (1\text{–}5)$$

Population standard deviation:

$$\sigma = \sqrt{\sigma^2} = \sqrt{\frac{\sum_{i=1}^{n}(x_i - \mu)^2}{n - 1}} \qquad (1\text{–}6)$$

Why would we use the standard deviation when we already have its square, the variance? The standard deviation is a more meaningful measure. The variance is the average squared deviation from the mean. It is squared because if we just compute the deviations from the mean and then averaged them, we get zero (prove this with any of the data sets). Therefore, when seeking a measure of the variation in a set of observations, we square the deviations from the mean; this removes the negative signs, and thus the measure is not equal to zero. The measure we obtain—the variance—is still a *squared* quantity; it is an average of squared numbers. By taking its square root, we "unsquare" the units and get a quantity denoted in the original units of the problem (e.g., dollars instead of dollars squared, which would have little meaning in most applications). The variance tends to be large because it is in squared units. Statisticians like to work with the variance because its mathematical properties simplify computations. People applying statistics prefer to work with the standard deviation because it is more easily interpreted.

Let us find the variance and the standard deviation of the data in Example 1–2. We carry out hand computations of the variance by use of a table for convenience. After doing the computation using equation 1–3, we will show a shortcut that will help in the calculation. Table 1–3 shows how the mean $\bar{x}$ is subtracted from each of the values and the results are squared and added. At the bottom of the last column we find the sum of all squared deviations from the mean. Finally, the sum is divided by $n - 1$, giving s^2, the sample variance. Taking the square root gives us s, the sample standard deviation.

---

[8]A note about calculators: If your calculator is designed to compute means and standard deviations, find the key for the standard deviation. Typically, there will be two such keys. Consult your owner's handbook to be sure you are using the key that will produce the correct computation for a sample (division by $n - 1$) versus a population (division by N).

TABLE 1–3 Calculations Leading to the Sample Variance in Example 1–2

x	$x - \bar{x}$	$(x - \bar{x})^2$
18	$18 - 26.9 = -8.9$	79.21
18	$18 - 26.9 = -8.9$	79.21
18	$18 - 26.9 = -8.9$	79.21
18	$18 - 26.9 = -8.9$	79.21
19	$19 - 26.9 = -7.9$	62.41
20	$20 - 26.9 = -6.9$	47.61
20	$20 - 26.9 = -6.9$	47.61
20	$20 - 26.9 = -6.9$	47.61
21	$21 - 26.9 = -5.9$	34.81
22	$22 - 26.9 = -4.9$	24.01
22	$22 - 26.9 = -4.9$	24.01
23	$23 - 26.9 = -3.9$	15.21
24	$24 - 26.9 = -2.9$	8.41
26	$26 - 26.9 = -0.9$	0.81
27	$27 - 26.9 = 0.1$	0.01
32	$32 - 26.9 = 5.1$	26.01
33	$33 - 26.9 = 6.1$	37.21
49	$49 - 26.9 = 22.1$	488.41
52	$52 - 26.9 = 25.1$	630.01
56	$56 - 26.9 = 29.1$	846.81
	0	2,657.8

By equation 1–3, the variance of the sample is equal to the sum of the third column in the table, 2,657.8, divided by $n - 1$: $s^2 = 2,657.8/19 = 139.88421$. The standard deviation is the square root of the variance: $s = \sqrt{139.88421} = 11.827266$, or, using two-decimal accuracy,[9] $s = 11.83$.

If you have a calculator with statistical capabilities, you may avoid having to use a table such as Table 1–3. If you need to compute by hand, there is a shortcut formula for computing the variance and the standard deviation.

Shortcut formula for the sample variance:

$$s^2 = \frac{\sum_{i=1}^{n} x_i^2 - \left(\sum_{i=1}^{n} x_i\right)^2 \Big/ n}{n - 1} \qquad (1\text{–}7)$$

Again, the standard deviation is just the square root of the quantity in equation 1–7. We will now demonstrate the use of this computationally simpler formula with the data of Example 1–2. We will then use this simpler formula and compute the variance and the standard deviation of the two data sets we are comparing: set I and set II.

As before, a table will be useful in carrying out the computations. The table for finding the variance using equation 1–7 will have a column for the data points x and

---

[9]In quantitative fields such as statistics, decimal accuracy is always a problem. How many digits after the decimal point should we carry? This question has no easy answer; everything depends on the required level of accuracy. As a rule, we will use only two decimals, since this suffices in most applications in this book. In some procedures, such as regression analysis, more digits need to be used in computations (these computations, however, are usually done by computer).

TABLE 1–4 Shortcut Computations for the Variance in Example 1–2

x	x^2
18	324
18	324
18	324
18	324
19	361
20	400
20	400
20	400
21	441
22	484
22	484
23	529
24	576
26	676
27	729
32	1,024
33	1,089
49	2,401
52	2,704
56	3,136
538	17,130

a column for the squared data points x^2. Table 1–4 shows the computations for the variance of the data in Example 1–2.

Using equation 1–7, we find

$$s^2 = \frac{\sum_{i=1}^{n} x_i^2 - \left(\sum_{i=1}^{n} x_i\right)^2 \big/ n}{n - 1} = \frac{17{,}130 - (538)^2/20}{19} = \frac{17{,}130 - 289{,}444/20}{19}$$
$$= 139.88421$$

The standard deviation is obtained as before: $s = \sqrt{139.88421} = 11.83$. Using the same procedure demonstrated with Table 1–4, we find the following quantities leading to the variance and the standard deviation of set I and of set II. Both are assumed to be samples, not populations.

Set I: $\Sigma x = 72$, $\Sigma x^2 = 542$, $s^2 = 10$, and $s = \sqrt{10} = 3.16$
Set II: $\Sigma x = 72$, $\Sigma x^2 = 446$, $s^2 = 1.27$, and $s = \sqrt{1.27} = 1.13$

As expected, we see that the variance and the standard deviation of set II are smaller than those of set I. While each has a mean of 6, set I is more variable. That is, the values in set I vary more about their mean than do those of set II, which are clustered more closely together.

The sample standard deviation and the sample mean are very important statistics used in inference about populations.

EXAMPLE 1–5

In financial analysis, the standard deviation is often used as a measure of *volatility* and of the *risk* associated with financial variables. The data below are exchange rate values of the British pound, given as the value of one U.S. dollar's worth in pounds. The first column of 10 numbers is for a period in the beginning of 1995, and the second column of 10 numbers is for a similar period in the beginning of 2007.[10] During which period, of these two precise sets of 10 days each, was the value of the pound more volatile?

1995	2007
0.6332	0.5087
0.6254	0.5077
0.6286	0.5100
0.6359	0.5143
0.6336	0.5149
0.6427	0.5177
0.6209	0.5164
0.6214	0.5180
0.6204	0.5096
0.6325	0.5182

Solution We are looking at two *populations* of 10 specific days at the start of each year (rather than a random sample of days), so we will use the formula for the population standard deviation. For the 1995 period we get $\sigma = 0.007033$. For the 2007 period we get $\sigma = 0.003938$. We conclude that during the 1995 ten-day period the British pound was

[10]From data reported in "Business Day," *The New York Times*, in March 2007, and from Web information.

more volatile than in the same period in 2007. Notice that if these had been random samples of days, we would have used the sample standard deviation. In such cases we might have been interested in statistical inference to some population.

EXAMPLE 1–6

The data for second quarter earnings per share (EPS) for major banks in the Northeast are tabulated below. Compute the mean, the variance, and the standard deviation of the data.

Name	EPS
Bank of New York	$2.53
Bank of America	4.38
Banker's Trust/New York	7.53
Chase Manhattan	7.53
Citicorp	7.96
Brookline	4.35
MBNA	1.50
Mellon	2.75
Morgan JP	7.25
PNC Bank	3.11
Republic	7.44
State Street	2.04
Summit	3.25

Solution

$$\sum x = \$61.62; \qquad \bar{x} = \$4.74; \qquad \sum x^2 = 363.40;$$

$$s^2 = 5.94; \qquad s = \$2.44.$$

Figure 1–4 shows how Excel commands can be used for obtaining a group of the most useful and common descriptive statistics using the data of Example 1–2. In section 1–10, we will see how a complete set of descriptive statistics can be obtained from a spreadsheet template.

FIGURE 1–4 Using Excel for Example 1–2

	A	B	C	D	E	F	G	H
1								
2		Wealth ($billion)						
3		33						
4		26						
5		24		Descriptive Statistics	Excel Command	Result		
6		21						
7		19						
8		20		Mean	=AVERAGE(A3:A22)	26.9		
9		18		Median	=MEDIAN(A3:A22)	22		
10		18		Mode	=MODE(A3:A22)	18		
11		52		Standard Deviation	=STDEV(A3:A22)	11.8272656		
12		56		Standard Error	=F11/SQRT(20)	2.64465698		
13		27		Kurtosis	=KURT(A3:A22)	1.60368514		
14		22		Skewness	=SKEW(A3:A22)	1.65371559		
15		18		Range	=MAX(A3:A22)-MIN(A3:A22)	38		
16		49		Minimum	=MIN(A3:A22)	18		
17		22		Maximum	=MAX(A3:A22)	56		
18		20		Sum	=SUM(A3:A22)	538		
19		23		Count	=COUNT(A3:A22)	20		
20		32						
21		20						
22		18						
23								

1–28. Explain why we need measures of variability and what information these measures convey.

1–29. What is the most important measure of variability and why?

1–30. What is the computational difference between the variance of a sample and the variance of a population?

1–31. Find the range, the variance, and the standard deviation of the data set in problem 1–13 (assumed to be a sample).

1–32. Do the same as problem 1–31, using the data in problem 1–14.

1–33. Do the same as problem 1–31, using the data in problem 1–15.

1–34. Do the same as problem 1–31, using the data in problem 1–16.

1–35. Do the same as problem 1–31, using the data in problem 1–17.

1–5   Grouped Data and the Histogram

Data are often grouped. This happened naturally in Example 1–2, where we had a group of four points with a value of 18, a group of three points with a value of 20, and a group of two points with a value of 22. In other cases, especially when we have a large data set, the collector of the data may break the data into groups even if the points in each group are not equal in value. The data collector may set some (often arbitrary) group boundaries for ease of recording the data. When the salaries of 5,000 executives are considered, for example, the data may be reported in the form: 1,548 executives in the salary range $60,000 to $65,000; 2,365 executives in the salary range $65,001 to $70,000; and so on. In this case, the data collector or analyst has processed all the salaries and put them into groups with defined boundaries. In such cases, there is a loss of information. We are unable to find the mean, variance, and other measures because we do not know the actual values. (Certain formulas, however, allow us to find the approximate mean, variance, and standard deviation. The formulas assume that all data points in a group are placed in the midpoint of the interval.) In this example, we assume that all 1,548 executives in the $60,000–$65,000 *class* make exactly ($60,000 + $65,000)/2 = $62,500; we estimate similarly for executives in the other groups.

> We define a group of data values within specified group boundaries as a **class.**

When data are grouped into classes, we may also plot a frequency distribution of the data. Such a frequency plot is called a *histogram.*

> A **histogram** is a chart made of bars of different heights. The height of each bar represents the **frequency** of values in the class represented by the bar. Adjacent bars share sides.

We demonstrate the use of histograms in the following example. Note that a histogram is used only for measured, or ordinal, data.

EXAMPLE 1–7   Management of an appliance store recorded the amounts spent at the store by the 184 customers who came in during the last day of the big sale. The data, amounts spent, were grouped into categories as follows: $0 to less than $100, $100 to less than $200, and so on up to $600, a bound higher than the amount spent by any single buyer. The classes and the frequency of each class are shown in Table 1–5. The frequencies, denoted by $f(x)$, are shown in a histogram in Figure 1–5.

TABLE 1–5   Classes and Frequencies for Example 1–7

x Spending Class ($)	f(x) Frequency (Number of Customers)
0 to less than 100	30
100 to less than 200	38
200 to less than 300	50
300 to less than 400	31
400 to less than 500	22
500 to less than 600	13
	184

FIGURE 1–5   A Histogram of the Data in Example 1–7

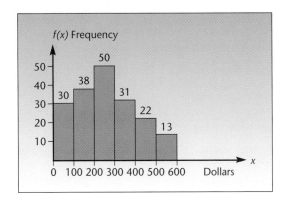

TABLE 1–6   Relative Frequencies for Example 1–7

x Class ($)	f(x) Relative Frequency
0 to less than 100	0.163
100 to less than 200	0.207
200 to less than 300	0.272
300 to less than 400	0.168
400 to less than 500	0.120
500 to less than 600	0.070
	1.000

As you can see from Figure 1–5, a histogram is just a convenient way of plotting the frequencies of grouped data. Here the frequencies are *absolute frequencies* or **counts** of data points. It is also possible to plot *relative frequencies*.

The **relative frequency** of a class is the count of data points in the class divided by the total number of data points.

Solution

The relative frequency in the first class, $0 to less than $100, is equal to count/total = $30/184 = 0.163$. We can similarly compute the relative frequencies for the other classes. The advantage of relative frequencies is that they are standardized: They add to 1.00. The relative frequency in each class represents the proportion of the total sample in the class. Table 1–6 gives the relative frequencies of the classes.

Figure 1–6 is a histogram of the relative frequencies of the data in this example. Note that the shape of the histogram of the relative frequencies is the same as that of

FIGURE 1–6   A Histogram of the Relative Frequencies in Example 1–7

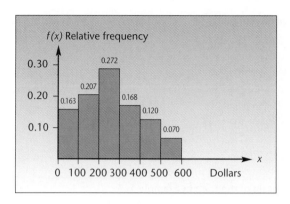

the absolute frequencies, the counts. The shape of the histogram does not change; only the labeling of the $f(x)$ axis is different.

Relative frequencies—proportions that add to 1.00—may be viewed as probabilities, as we will see in the next chapter. Hence, such frequencies are very useful in statistics, and so are their histograms.

CHAPTER 1
CHAPTER 3

1–6   Skewness and Kurtosis

In addition to measures of location, such as the mean or median, and measures of variation, such as the variance or standard deviation, two more attributes of a frequency distribution of a data set may be of interest to us. These are *skewness* and *kurtosis*.

Skewness is a measure of the degree of asymmetry of a frequency distribution.

When the distribution stretches to the right more than it does to the left, we say that the distribution is *right skewed*. Similarly, a *left-skewed* distribution is one that stretches asymmetrically to the left. Four graphs are shown in Figure 1–7: a symmetric distribution, a right-skewed distribution, a left-skewed distribution, and a symmetrical distribution with two modes.

Recall that a symmetric distribution with a single mode has mode = mean = median. Generally, for a right-skewed distribution, the mean is to the right of the median, which in turn lies to the right of the mode (assuming a single mode). The opposite is true for left-skewed distributions.

Skewness is calculated[11] and reported as a number that may be positive, negative, or zero. *Zero skewness* implies a symmetric distribution. A *positive skewness* implies a right-skewed distribution, and a *negative skewness* implies a left-skewed distribution.

Two distributions that have the same mean, variance, and skewness could still be significantly different in their shape. We may then look at their kurtosis.

Kurtosis is a measure of the peakedness of a distribution.

The larger the kurtosis, the more peaked will be the distribution. The kurtosis is calculated[12] and reported either as an absolute or a relative value. *Absolute kurtosis* is

---

[11]The formula used for calculating the skewness of a population is $\sum_{i=1}^{N}\left[\dfrac{x_i - \mu}{\sigma}\right]^3 \Big/ N.$

[12]The formula used for calculating the absolute kurtosis of a population is $\sum_{i=1}^{N}\left[\dfrac{x_i - \mu}{\sigma}\right]^4 \Big/ N.$

FIGURE 1–7   Skewness of Distributions

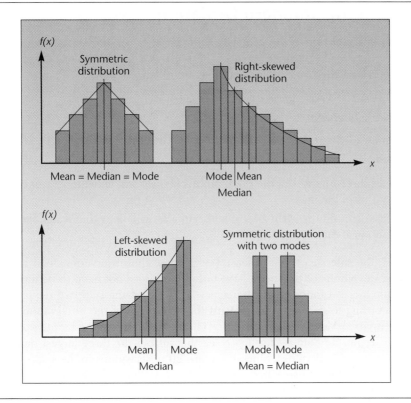

FIGURE 1–8   Kurtosis of Distributions

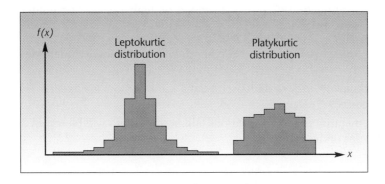

always a positive number. The absolute kurtosis of a *normal distribution,* a famous distribution about which we will learn in Chapter 4, is 3. This value of 3 is taken as the datum to calculate the *relative kurtosis.* The two are related by the equation

$$\text{Relative kurtosis} = \text{Absolute kurtosis} - 3$$

The relative kurtosis can be negative. We will always work with relative kurtosis. As a result, in this book, "kurtosis" means "relative kurtosis."

A negative kurtosis implies a flatter distribution than the normal distribution, and it is called *platykurtic.* A positive kurtosis implies a more peaked distribution than the normal distribution, and it is called *leptokurtic.* Figure 1–8 shows these examples.

1–7   Relations between the Mean and the Standard Deviation

The mean is a measure of the centrality of a set of observations, and the standard deviation is a measure of their spread. There are two general rules that establish a relation between these measures and the set of observations. The first is called Chebyshev's theorem, and the second is the empirical rule.

Chebyshev's Theorem

A mathematical theorem called **Chebyshev's theorem** establishes the following rules:

1. At least three-quarters of the observations in a set will lie within 2 standard deviations of the mean.
2. At least eight-ninths of the observations in a set will lie within 3 standard deviations of the mean.

In general, the rule states that at least $1 - 1/k^2$ of the observations will lie within k standard deviations of the mean. (We note that k does not have to be an integer.) In Example 1–2 we found that the mean was 26.9 and the standard deviation was 11.83. According to rule 1 above, at least three-quarters of the observations should fall in the interval Mean $\pm 2s = 26.9 \pm 2(11.83)$, which is defined by the points 3.24 and 50.56. From the data set itself, we see that all but the three largest data points lie within this range of values. Since there are 20 observations in the set, seventeen-twentieths are within the specified range, so the rule that at least three-quarters will be within the range is satisfied.

The Empirical Rule

If the distribution of the data is mound-shaped—that is, if the histogram of the data is more or less symmetric with a single mode or high point—then tighter rules will apply. This is the **empirical rule:**

1. Approximately 68% of the observations will be within 1 standard deviation of the mean.
2. Approximately 95% of the observations will be within 2 standard deviations of the mean.
3. A vast majority of the observations (all, or almost all) will be within 3 standard deviations of the mean.

Note that Chebyshev's theorem states *at least* what percentage will lie within k standard deviations in any distribution, whereas the empirical rule states *approximately* what percentage will lie within k standard deviations in a *mound-shaped* distribution.

For the data set in Example 1–2, the distribution of the data set is not symmetric, and the empirical rule holds only approximately.

PROBLEMS

1–36. Check the applicability of Chebyshev's theorem and the empirical rule for the data set in problem 1–13.

1–37. Check the applicability of Chebyshev's theorem and the empirical rule for the data set in problem 1–14.

1–38. Check the applicability of Chebyshev's theorem and the empirical rule for the data set in problem 1–15.

1–39. Check the applicability of Chebyshev's theorem and the empirical rule for the data set in problem 1–16.

1–40. Check the applicability of Chebyshev's theorem and the empirical rule for the data set in problem 1–17.

1–8 Methods of Displaying Data

In section 1–5, we saw how a histogram is used to display frequencies of occurrence of values in a data set. In this section, we will see a few other ways of displaying data, some of which are descriptive only. We will introduce frequency polygons, cumulative frequency plots (called *ogives*), pie charts, and bar charts. We will also see examples of how descriptive graphs can sometimes be misleading. We will start with pie charts.

Pie Charts

A **pie chart** is a simple descriptive display of data that sum to a given total. A pie chart is probably the most illustrative way of displaying quantities as percentages of a given total. The total area of the pie represents 100% of the quantity of interest (the sum of the variable values in all categories), and the size of each slice is the percentage of the total represented by the category the slice denotes. Pie charts are used to present frequencies for categorical data. The scale of measurement may be nominal or ordinal. Figure 1–9 is a pie chart of the percentages of all kinds of investments in a typical family's portfolio.

Bar Charts

Bar charts (which use horizontal or vertical rectangles) are often used to display categorical data where there is no emphasis on the percentage of a total represented by each category. The scale of measurement is nominal or ordinal.

Charts using horizontal bars and those using vertical bars are essentially the same. In some cases, one may be more convenient than the other for the purpose at hand. For example, if we want to write the name of each category inside the rectangle that represents that category, then a horizontal bar chart may be more convenient. If we want to stress the height of the different columns as measures of the quantity of interest, we use a vertical bar chart. Figure 1–10 is an example of how a bar chart can be used effectively to display and interpret information.

Frequency Polygons and Ogives

A **frequency polygon** is similar to a histogram except that there are no rectangles, only a point in the midpoint of each interval at a height proportional to the frequency

FIGURE 1–9 Investments Portfolio Composition

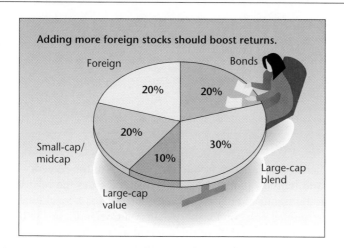

Source: Carolyn Bigda, "The Fast Track to Kicking Back," *Money*, March 2007, p. 60.

FIGURE 1–10   The Web Takes Off

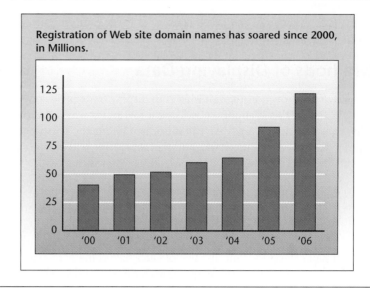

Registration of Web site domain names has soared since 2000, in Millions.

Source: S. Hammand and M. Tucker, "How Secure Is Your Domain," *BusinessWeek*, March 26, 2007, p. 118.

TABLE 1–7   Pizza Sales

Sales ($000)	Relative Frequency
6–14	0.20
15–22	0.30
23–30	0.25
31–38	0.15
39–46	0.07
47–54	0.03

FIGURE 1–11   Relative-Frequency Polygon for Pizza Sales

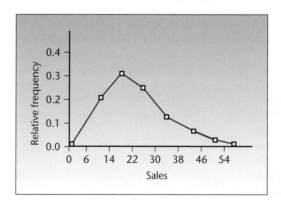

or relative frequency (in a relative-frequency polygon) of the category of the interval. The rightmost and leftmost points are zero. Table 1–7 gives the relative frequency of sales volume, in thousands of dollars per week, for pizza at a local establishment.

A relative-frequency polygon for these data is shown in Figure 1–11. Note that the frequency is located in the middle of the interval as a point with height equal to the relative frequency of the interval. Note also that the point zero is added at the left

FIGURE 1–12   Excel-Produced Graph of the Data in Example 1–2

	A	B	C	D	E	F	G	H	I	J	K
1											
2		**Wealth ($billion)**									
3		33									
4		26									
5		24									
6		21									
7		19									
8		20									
9		18									
10		18									
11		52									
12		56									
13		27									
14		22									
15		18									
16		49									
17		22									
18		20									
19		23									
20		32									
21		20									
22		18									
23											

Frequency of occurrence of data values (bar chart with x-axis values: 18 19 20 21 22 23 24 26 27 32 33 49 52 56)

FIGURE 1–13   Ogive of Pizza Sales

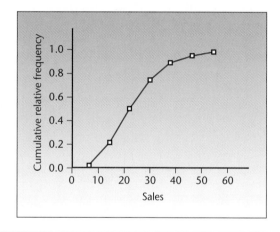

boundary and the right boundary of the data set: The polygon starts at zero and ends at zero relative frequency.

Figure 1–12 shows the worth of the 20 richest individuals from Example 1–2 displayed as a column chart. This is done using Excel's Chart Wizard.

An **ogive** is a cumulative-frequency (or cumulative relative-frequency) graph. An ogive starts at 0 and goes to 1.00 (for a relative-frequency ogive) or to the maximum cumulative frequency. The point with height corresponding to the cumulative frequency is located at the right endpoint of each interval. An ogive for the data in Table 1–7 is shown in Figure 1–13. While the ogive shown is for the cumulative *relative* frequency, an ogive can also be used for the cumulative absolute frequency.

A Caution about Graphs

A picture is indeed worth a thousand words, but pictures can sometimes be deceiving. Often, this is where "lying with statistics" comes in: presenting data graphically on a stretched or compressed scale of numbers with the aim of making the data show whatever you want them to show. This is one important argument against a

FIGURE 1–14   German Wage Increases (%)

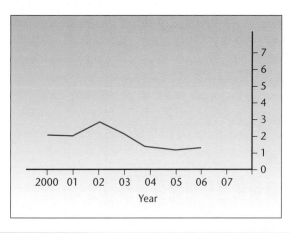 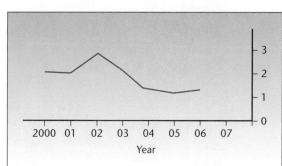

Source: "Economic Focus," *The Economist*, March 3, 2007, p. 82. Reprinted by permission.

FIGURE 1–15   The S&P 500, One Year, to March 2007

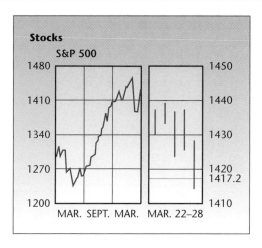

Source: Adapted from "Economic Focus," *The Economist*, March 3, 2007, p. 82.

merely descriptive approach to data analysis and an argument for statistical *inference*. Statistical tests tend to be more objective than our eyes and are less prone to deception as long as our assumptions (random sampling and other assumptions) hold. As we will see, statistical inference gives us tools that allow us to objectively evaluate what we see in the data.

Pictures are sometimes deceptive even though there is no intention to deceive. When someone shows you a graph of a set of numbers, there may really be no particular scale of numbers that is "right" for the data.

The graph on the left in Figure 1–14 is reprinted from *The Economist*. Notice that there is *no scale* that is the "right" one for this graph. Compare this graph with the one on the right side, which has a different scale.

Time Plots

Often we want to graph changes in a variable over time. An example is given in Figure 1–15.

1–41. The following data are estimated worldwide appliance sales (in millions of dollars). Use the data to construct a pie chart for the worldwide appliance sales of the listed manufacturers.

Electrolux	$5,100
General Electric	4,350
Matsushita Electric	4,180
Whirlpool	3,950
Bosch-Siemens	2,200
Philips	2,000
Maytag	1,580

1–42. Draw a bar graph for the data on the first five stocks in problem 1–14. Is any one of the three kinds of plot more appropriate than the others for these data? If so, why?

1–43. Draw a bar graph for the endowments (stated in billions of dollars) of each of the universities specified in the following list.

Harvard	$3.4
Texas	2.5
Princeton	1.9
Yale	1.7
Stanford	1.4
Columbia	1.3
Texas A&M	1.1

1–44. The following are the top 10 private equity deals of all time, in billions of dollars.[13]

38.9, 32.7, 31.1, 27.4, 25.7, 21.6, 17.6, 17.4, 15.0, 13.9

Find the mean, median, and standard deviation. Draw a bar graph.

1–45. The following data are credit default swap values:[14] 6, 10, 12, 13, 18, 21 (in trillions of dollars). Draw a pie chart of these amounts. Find the mean and median.

1–46. The following are the amounts from the sales slips of a department store (in dollars): 3.45, 4.52, 5.41, 6.00, 5.97, 7.18, 1.12, 5.39, 7.03, 10.25, 11.45, 13.21, 12.00, 14.05, 2.99, 3.28, 17.10, 19.28, 21.09, 12.11, 5.88, 4.65, 3.99, 10.10, 23.00, 15.16, 20.16. Draw a frequency polygon for these data (start by defining intervals of the data and counting the data points in each interval). Also draw an ogive and a column graph.

1–9   Exploratory Data Analysis

Exploratory data analysis (EDA) is the name given to a large body of statistical and graphical techniques. These techniques provide ways of looking at data to determine relationships and trends, identify outliers and influential observations, and quickly describe or summarize data sets. Pioneering methods in this field, as well as the name *exploratory data analysis,* derive from the work of John W. Tukey [John W. Tukey, *Exploratory Data Analysis* (Reading, Massachusetts: Addison-Wesley, 1977)].

---

[13]R. Kirkland, "Private Money," *Fortune,* March 5, 2007, p. 58.

[14]John Ferry, "Gimme Shelter," *Worth,* April 2007, p. 89.

Stem-and-Leaf Displays

A **stem-and-leaf display** is a quick way of looking at a data set. It contains some of the features of a histogram but avoids the loss of information in a histogram that results from aggregating the data into intervals. The stem-and-leaf display is based on the tallying principle: | || ||| |||| ||||; but it also uses the decimal base of our number system. In a stem-and-leaf display, the *stem* is the number without its rightmost digit (the *leaf*). The stem is written to the left of a vertical line separating the stem from the leaf. For example, suppose we have the numbers 105, 106, 107, 107, 109. We display them as

10 | 56779

With a more complete data set with different stem values, the last digit of each number is displayed at the appropriate place to the right of its stem digit(s). Stem-and-leaf displays help us identify, at a glance, numbers in our data set that have high frequency. Let's look at an example.

EXAMPLE 1–8

Virtual reality is the name given to a system of simulating real situations on a computer in a way that gives people the feeling that what they see on the computer screen is a real situation. Flight simulators were the forerunners of virtual reality programs. A particular virtual reality program has been designed to give production engineers experience in real processes. Engineers are supposed to complete certain tasks as responses to what they see on the screen. The following data are the time, in seconds, it took a group of 42 engineers to perform a given task:

11, 12, 12, 13, 15, 15, 15, 16, 17, 20, 21, 21, 21, 22, 22, 22, 23, 24, 26, 27, 27, 27, 28, 29, 29, 30, 31, 32, 34, 35, 37, 41, 41, 42, 45, 47, 50, 52, 53, 56, 60, 62

Use a stem-and-leaf display to analyze these data.

Solution   The data are already arranged in increasing order. We see that the data are in the 10s, 20s, 30s, 40s, 50s, and 60s. We will use the first digit as the stem and the second digit of each number as the leaf. The stem-and-leaf display of our data is shown in Figure 1–16.

As you can see, the stem-and-leaf display is a very quick way of arranging the data in a kind of a histogram (turned sideways) that allows us to see what the data look like. Here, we note that the data do not seem to be symmetrically distributed; rather, they are skewed to the right.

FIGURE 1–16 Stem-and-Leaf Display of the Task Performance Times of Example 1–8

1	122355567
2	0111222346777899
3	012457
4	11257
5	0236
6	02

We may feel that this display does not convey very much information because there are too many values with first digit 2. To solve this problem, we may split the groups into two subgroups. We will denote the stem part as 1* for the possible numbers 10, 11, 12, 13, 14 and as 1. for the possible numbers 15, 16, 17, 18, 19. Similarly, the stem 2* will be used for the possible numbers 20, 21, 22, 23, and 24; stem 2. will be used for the numbers 25, 26, 27, 28, and 29; and so on for the other numbers. Our stem-and-leaf diagram for the data of Example 1–8 using this convention is shown in Figure 1–17. As you can see from the figure, we now have a more spread-out histogram of the data. The data still seem skewed to the right.

If desired, a further refinement of the display is possible by using the symbol * for a stem followed by the leaf values 0 and 1; the symbol t for leaf values 2 and 3; the symbol f for leaf values 4 and 5; s for 6 and 7; and . for 8 and 9. Also, the class containing the median observation is often denoted with its stem value in parentheses.

We demonstrate this version of the display for the data of Example 1–8 in Figure 1–18. Note that the median is 27 (why?).

Note that for the data set of this example, the refinement offered in Figure 1–18 may be too much: We may have lost the general picture of the data. In cases where there are many observations with the same value (for example, 22, 22, 22, 22, 22, 22, 22, . . .), the use of a more stretched-out display may be needed in order to get a good picture of the way our data are clustered.

Box Plots

A *box plot* (also called a *box-and-whisker plot*) is another way of looking at a data set in an effort to determine its central tendency, spread, skewness, and the existence of outliers.

A **box plot** is a set of five summary measures of the distribution of the data:

1. The median of the data
2. The lower quartile
3. The upper quartile
4. The smallest observation
5. The largest observation

These statements require two qualifications. First, we will assume that the *hinges* of the box plot are essentially the quartiles of the data set. (We will define hinges shortly.) The median is a line inside the box.

FIGURE 1–17 Refined Stem-and-Leaf Display for Data of Example 1–8

1*	1223
1.	55567
2*	011122234
2.	6777899
3*	0124
3.	57
4*	112
4.	57
5*	023
5.	6
6*	02

CHAPTER 1

FIGURE 1–18 Further Refined Stem-and-Leaf Display of Data of Example 1–8

	1*	1
	t	223
	f	555
	s	67
	.	
	2*	0111
	t	2223
	f	4
(Median in this class)	(s)	6777
	.	899
	3*	01
	t	2
	f	45
	s	7
	.	
	4*	11
	t	2
	f	5
	s	7
	.	
	5*	0
	t	23
	f	
	s	6
	.	
	6*	0
	t	2

Second, the **whiskers** of the box plot are made by extending a line from the upper quartile to the largest observation and from the lower quartile to the smallest observation, only if the largest and smallest observations are within a distance of 1.5 times the interquartile range from the appropriate hinge (quartile). If one or more observations are farther away than that distance, they are marked as suspected outliers. If these observations are at a distance of over 3 times the interquartile range from the appropriate hinge, they are marked as outliers. The whisker then extends to the largest or smallest observation that is at a distance less than or equal to 1.5 times the interquartile range from the hinge.

Let us make these definitions clearer by using a picture. Figure 1–19 shows the parts of a box plot and how they are defined. The median is marked as a vertical line across the box. The **hinges** of the box are the upper and lower quartiles (the rightmost and leftmost sides of the box). The interquartile range (IQR) is the distance from the upper quartile to the lower quartile (the length of the box from hinge to hinge): IQR = $Q_U - Q_L$. We define the **inner fence** as a point at a distance of 1.5(IQR) above the upper quartile; similarly, the lower inner fence is $Q_L - 1.5(\text{IQR})$. The **outer fences** are defined similarly but are at a distance of 3(IQR) above or below the appropriate hinge. Figure 1–20 shows the fences (these are not shown on the actual box plot; they are only guidelines for defining the whiskers, suspected outliers, and outliers) and demonstrates how we mark outliers.

FIGURE 1–19   The Box Plot

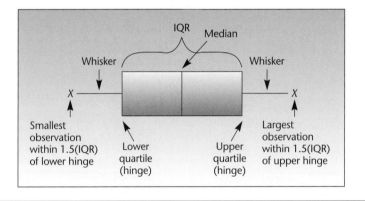

FIGURE 1–20   The Elements of a Box Plot

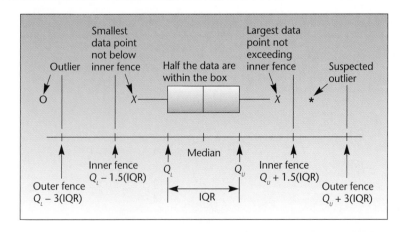

Box plots are very useful for the following purposes.

1. To identify the location of a data set based on the median.
2. To identify the spread of the data based on the length of the box, hinge to hinge (the interquartile range), and the length of the whiskers (the range of the data without extreme observations: outliers or suspected outliers).
3. To identify possible skewness of the distribution of the data set. If the portion of the box to the right of the median is longer than the portion to the left of the median, and/or the right whisker is longer than the left whisker, the data are right-skewed. Similarly, a longer left side of the box and/or left whisker implies a left-skewed data set. If the box and whiskers are symmetric, the data are symmetrically distributed with no skewness.
4. To identify suspected outliers (observations beyond the inner fences but within the outer fences) and outliers (points beyond the outer fences).
5. To compare two or more data sets. By drawing a box plot for each data set and displaying the box plots on the same scale, we can compare several data sets.

A special form of a box plot may even be used for conducting a test of the equality of two population medians. The various uses of a box plot are demonstrated in Figure 1–21.

Let us now construct a box plot for the data of Example 1–8. For this data set, the median is 27, and we find that the lower quartile is 20.75 and the upper quartile is 41. The interquartile range is IQR = 41 − 20.75 = 20.25. One and one-half times this distance is 30.38; hence, the inner fences are −9.63 and 71.38. Since no observation lies beyond either point, there are no suspected outliers and no outliers, so the whiskers extend to the extreme values in the data: 11 on the left side and 62 on the right side.

As you can see from the figure, there are no outliers or suspected outliers in this data set. The data set is skewed to the right. This confirms our observation of the skewness from consideration of the stem-and-leaf diagrams of the same data set, in Figures 1–16 to 1–18.

FIGURE 1–21   Box Plots and Their Uses

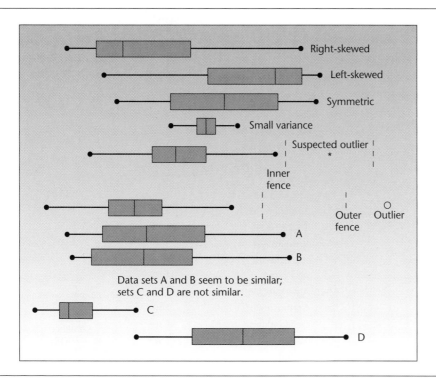

1–47. The following data are monthly steel production figures, in millions of tons.

7.0, 6.9, 8.2, 7.8, 7.7, 7.3, 6.8, 6.7, 8.2, 8.4, 7.0, 6.7, 7.5, 7.2, 7.9, 7.6, 6.7, 6.6, 6.3, 5.6, 7.8, 5.5, 6.2, 5.8, 5.8, 6.1, 6.0, 7.3, 7.3, 7.5, 7.2, 7.2, 7.4, 7.6

Draw a stem-and-leaf display of these data.

1–48. Draw a box plot for the data in problem 1–47. Are there any outliers? Is the distribution of the data symmetric or skewed? If it is skewed, to what side?

1–49. What are the uses of a stem-and-leaf display? What are the uses of a box plot?

1–50. Worker participation in management is a new concept that involves employees in corporate decision making. The following data are the percentages of employees involved in worker participation programs in a sample of firms. Draw a stem-and-leaf display of the data.

5, 32, 33, 35, 42, 43, 42, 45, 46, 44, 47, 48, 48, 48, 49, 49, 50, 37, 38, 34, 51, 52, 52, 47, 53, 55, 56, 57, 58, 63, 78

1–51. Draw a box plot of the data in problem 1–50, and draw conclusions about the data set based on the box plot.

1–52. Consider the two box plots in Figure 1–24 (on page 38), and draw conclusions about the data sets.

1–53. Refer to the following data on distances between seats in business class for various airlines. Find μ, σ, σ^2, draw a box plot, and find the mode and any outliers.

Characteristics of Business-Class Carriers

	Distance between Rows (in cm)
Europe	
Air France	122
Alitalia	140
British Airways	127
Iberia	107
KLM/Northwest	120
Lufthansa	101
Sabena	122
SAS	132
SwissAir	120
Asia	
All Nippon Airw	127
Cathay Pacific	127
JAL	127
Korean Air	127
Malaysia Air	116
Singapore Airl	120
Thai Airways	128
Vietnam Airl	140
North America	
Air Canada	140
American Airl	127
Continental	140
Delta Airlines	130
TWA	157
United	124

1–54.   The following data are the daily price quotations for a certain stock over a period of 45 days. Construct a stem-and-leaf display for these data. What can you conclude about the distribution of daily stock prices over the period under study?

10, 11, 10, 11, 11, 12, 12, 13, 14, 16, 15, 11, 18, 19, 20, 15, 14, 14, 22, 25, 27, 23, 22, 26, 27, 29, 28, 31, 32, 30, 32, 34, 33, 38, 41, 40, 42, 53, 52, 47, 37, 23, 11, 32, 23

1–55.   Discuss ways of dealing with outliers—their detection and what to do about them once they are detected. Can you always discard an outlier? Why or why not?

1–56.   Define the inner fences and the outer fences of a box plot; also define the whiskers and the hinges. What portion of the data is represented by the box? By the whiskers?

1–57.   The following data are the number of ounces of silver per ton of ore for two mines.

Mine A: 34, 32, 35, 37, 41, 42, 43, 45, 46, 45, 48, 49, 51, 52, 53, 60, 73, 76, 85
Mine B: 23, 24, 28, 29, 32, 34, 35, 37, 38, 40, 43, 44, 47, 48, 49, 50, 51, 52, 59

Construct a stem-and-leaf display for each data set and a box plot for each data set. Compare the two displays and the two box plots. Draw conclusions about the data.

1–58.   Can you compare two *populations* by looking at box plots or stem-and-leaf displays of random samples from the two populations? Explain.

1–59.   The following data are daily percentage changes in stock prices for 20 stocks called "The Favorites."[15]

−0.1, 0.5, 0.6, 0.7, 1.4, 0.7, 1.3, 0.3, 1.6, 0.6, −3.5, 0.6, 1.1, 1.3, −0.1, 2.5, −0.3, 0.3, 0.2, 0.4

Draw a box plot of these data.

1–60.   Consult the following data on a sports car 0 to 60 times, in seconds.[16]

4.9, 4.6, 4.2, 5.1, 5.2, 5.1, 4.8, 4.7, 4.9, 5.3

Find the mean and the median. Compare the two. Also construct a box plot. Interpret your findings.

1–10   Using the Computer

Using Excel for Descriptive Statistics and Plots

If you need to develop any statistical or engineering analyses, you can use the **Excel Analysis Toolpack.** One of the applicable features available in the Analysis Toolpack is Descriptive Statistics. To access this tool, click Data Analysis in the Analysis Group on the Data tab. Then choose Descriptive Statistics. You can define the range of input and output in this window. Don't forget to select the Summary Statistics check box. Then press OK. A table containing the descriptive statistics of your data set will be created in the place that you have specified for output range.

If the Data Analysis command is not available in the Data tab, you need to load the Analysis Toolpack add-in program. For this purpose follow the next steps:

- Click the Microsoft Office button, and then click Excel Options.
- Click Add-ins, and then in the Manage box, select Excel Add-ins.
- Click Go.
- In the Add-ins Available box, select the Analysis Toolpack check box, and then click OK.

---

[15]Data reported in "Business Day," *The New York Times*, Thursday, March 15, 2007, p. C11.

[16]"Sports Stars," *BusinessWeek*, March 5, 2007, p. 140.

FIGURE 1–22   Template for Calculating Basic Statistics
[Basic Statistics.xls]

	A	B	C	D	E	F	G	H	I	J	K
1		**Basic Statistics from Raw Data**				Sales Data					
2											**Data Entry**
3		Measures of Central tendency								1	33
4										2	26
5		Mean	26.9		Median	22	Mode	18		3	24
6										4	21
7		Measures of Dispersion								5	19
8				If the data is of a						6	20
9				Sample	Population					7	18
10			Variance	139.884211	132.89	Range	38			8	18
11			St. Dev.	11.8272656	11.5277925	IQR	8.5			9	52
12										10	56
13		Skewness and Kurtosis								11	27
14				If the data is of a						12	22
15				Sample	Population					13	18
16			Skewness	1.65371559	1.52700876					14	49
17			(Relative) Kurtosis	1.60368514	0.94417958					15	22
18										16	20
19		Percentile and Percentile Rank Calculations								17	23
20				x-th			Percentile			18	32
21			x	Percentile		y	rank of y			19	20
22			50	22		22.0	47			20	18
23			80	32.2		32.2	80				
24			90	49.3		49.3	90				
25											
26		Quartiles									
27			1st Quartile	19.75							
28			Median	22		IQR	8.5				
29			3rd Quartile	28.25							
30											
31		Other Statistics									
32			Sum	538							
33			Size	22							
34			Maximum	56							
35			Minimum	18							

In addition to the useful features of the Excel Analysis Toolpak and the direct use of Excel commands as shown in Figure 1–4, we also will discuss the use of Excel templates that we have developed for computations and charts covered in the chapter. General instructions about using templates appear on the Student CD.

Figure 1–22 shows the template that can be used for calculating basic statistics of a data set. As soon as the data are entered in the shaded area in column K, all the statistics are automatically calculated and displayed. All the statistics have been explained in this chapter, but some aspects of this template will be discussed next.

PERCENTILE AND PERCENTILE RANK COMPUTATION

The percentile and percentile rank computations are done slightly differently in Excel. Do not be alarmed if your manual calculation differs (slightly) from the result you see in the template. These discrepancies in percentile and percentile rank computations occur because of approximation and rounding off. In Figure 1–22, notice that the 50th percentile is 22, but the percentile rank of 22 is 47. Such discrepancies will get smaller as the size of the data set increases. For large data sets, the discrepancy will be negligible or absent.

HISTOGRAMS

A histogram can be drawn either from raw data or from grouped data, so the workbook contains one sheet for each case. Figure 1–23 shows the template that used raw data. After entering the data in the shaded area in column Q, select appropriate values for the start, interval width, and end values for the histogram in

FIGURE 1–23   **Template for Histograms and Related Charts**
[Histogram.xls; Sheet: from Raw Data]

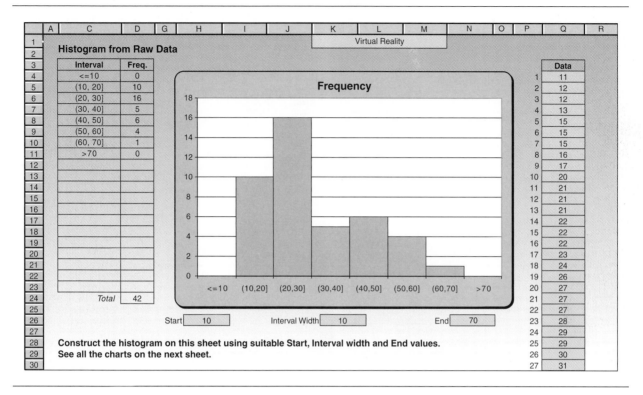

cells H26, K26, and N26 respectively. When selecting the start and end values, make sure that the first bar and the last bar of the chart have zero frequencies. This will ensure that no value in the data has been omitted. The interval width should be selected to make the histogram a good representation of the distribution of the data.

After constructing the histogram on this sheet, go to the next sheet, named "Charts," to see all the related charts: Relative Frequency, Frequency Polygon, Relative Frequency Polygon, and Ogive.

At times, you may have grouped data rather than raw data to start with. In this case, go to the grouped data sheet and enter the data in the shaded area on the right. This sheet contains a total of five charts. If any of these is not needed, unprotect the sheet and delete it before printing. Another useful template provided in the CD is Frequency Polygon.xls, which is used to compare two distributions.

An advantage of frequency polygons is that unlike histograms, we can superpose two or more polygons to compare the distributions.

PIE CHARTS

Pie chart.xls is one of the templates in the CD for creating pie charts. Note that the data entered in this template for creating a pie chart need not be percentages, and even if they are percentages, they need not add up to 100%, since the spreadsheet recalculates the proportions.

If you wish to modify the format of the chart, for example, by changing the colors of the slices or the location of legends, unprotect the sheet and use the Chart Wizard.

To use the Chart Wizard, click on the icon that looks like this: 📊 . Protect the sheet after you are done.

FIGURE 1–24   Box Plot Template to Compare Two Data Sets
              [Box Plot 2.xls]

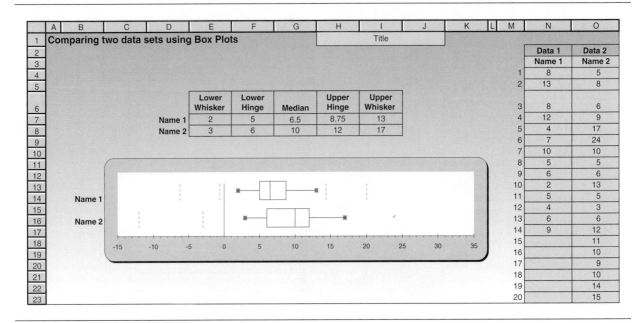

BAR CHARTS

Bar chart.xls is the template that can be used to draw bar charts. Many refinements are possible on the bar charts, such as making it a 3-D chart. You can unprotect the sheet and use the Chart Wizard to make the refinements.

BOX PLOTS

Box plot.xls is the template that can be used to create box plots. Box plot2.xls is the template that draws two box plots of two different data sets. Thus it can be used to compare two data sets. Figure 1–24 shows the comparison between two data sets using this template. Cells N3 and O3 are used to enter the name for each data set. The comparison shows that the second data set is more varied and contains relatively larger numbers than the first set.

TIME PLOTS

Time plot.xls is the template that can be used to create time plots.

To compare two data sets, use the template timeplot2.xls. Comparing sales in years 2006 and 2007, Figure 1–25 shows that Year 2007 sales were consistently below those of Year 2006, except in April. Moreover, the Year 2007 sales show less variance than those of Year 2006. Reasons for both facts may be worth investigating.

SCATTER PLOTS

Scatter plots are used to identify and report any underlying relationships among pairs of data sets. For example, if we have the data on annual sales of a product and on the annual advertising budgets for that product during the same period, then we can plot them on the same graph to see if a pattern emerges that brings out a relationship between the data sets. We might expect that whenever the advertising budget was high, the sales would also be high. This can be verified on a scatter plot.

The plot consists of a scatter of points, each point representing an observation. For instance, if the advertising budget in one year was x and the sales in the same year was y, then a point is marked on the plot at coordinates (x, y). Scatter plot.xls is the template that can be used to create a scatter plot.

FIGURE 1–25   **Time Plot Comparison**
[Time Plot 2.xls]

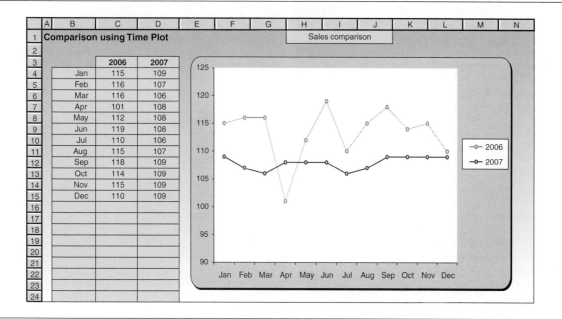

Sometimes we have several data sets, and we may want to know if a relation exists between any two of them. Plotting every pair of them can be tedious, so it would be faster and easier if a bunch of scatter plots are produced together. The template Scatter plot.xls has another sheet named "5 Variables" which accommodates data on five variables and produces a scatter plot for every pair of variables. A glance at the scatter plots can quickly reveal an apparent correlation between any pair.

Using MINITAB for Descriptive Statistics and Plots

MINITAB can use data from different sources: previously saved MINITAB worksheet files, text files, and Microsoft Excel files. To place data in MINITAB, we can:

- Type directly into MINITAB.
- Copy and paste from other applications.
- Open from a variety of file types, including Excel or text files.

In this section we demonstrate the use of MINITAB in producing descriptive statistics and corresponding plots with the data of Example 1–2. If you are using a keyboard to type the data into the worksheet, begin in the row above the horizontal line containing the numbered row. This row is used to provide a label for each variable. In the first column (labeled C1) enter the label of your variable (wealth) and press Enter. By moving the cursor to the cell in the next row, you can start entering data in the first column.

To open data from a file, choose File ▶ Open Worksheet. This will provide you with the open worksheet dialog box. Many different files, including Minitab worksheet files (.MTW), Microsoft Excel (.XLS), data (.DAT), and text (.TXT), can be opened from this dialog box. Make sure that the proper file type appears in the List of Files of Type Box. You can also use the Session window and type the command to set the data into the columns.

For obtaining descriptive statistics, you can type the appropriate command in the Session window or use the menu. Figure 1–26 shows the command, data, and output for Example 1–2.

FIGURE 1–26   Using MINITAB to Describe Data

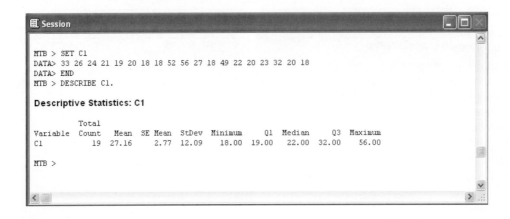

FIGURE 1–27   MINITAB Output

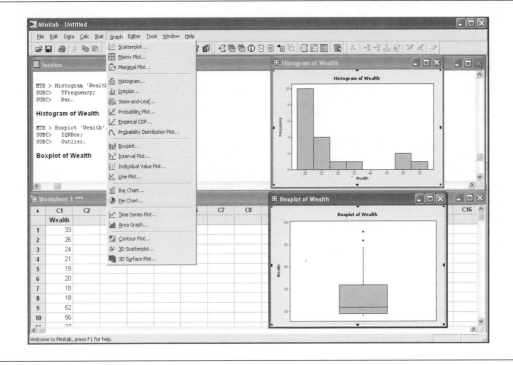

To obtain descriptive statistics using the menu, choose Stat ▶ Basic Statistics ▶ Display Descriptive Statistics. In the Descriptive Statistics dialog box choose C1 in the Variable List box and then press zero. The result will be shown in the Session window. Some users find menu commands quicker to use than session commands.

As was mentioned earlier in the chapter, we can use graphs to explore data and assess relationships among the variables. You can access MINITAB's graph from the Graph and Stat menus. Using the Graph menu enables you to obtain a large variety of graphs. Figure 1–27 shows the histogram and box plot obtained using the Graph menu.

Finally, note that MINITAB does not display the command prompt by default. To enter commands directly into the Session window, you must enable this prompt by choosing Editor ▶ Enable Commands. A check appears next to the menu item.

When you execute a command from a menu and session commands are enabled, the corresponding session command appears in the Session window along with the text output. This technique provides a convenient way to learn session commands.

1–11 Summary and Review of Terms

In this chapter we introduced many terms and concepts. We defined a **population** as the set of all measurements in which we are interested. We defined a **sample** as a smaller group of measurements chosen from the larger population (the concept of random sampling will be discussed in detail in Chapter 4). We defined the process of using the sample for drawing conclusions about the population as **statistical inference.**

We discussed **descriptive statistics** as quantities computed from our data. We also defined the following statistics: **percentile,** a point below which lie a specified percentage of the data, and **quartile,** a percentile point in multiples of 25. The first quartile, the 25th percentile point, is also called the **lower quartile.** The 50th percentile point is the second quartile, also called the middle quartile, or the **median.** The 75th percentile is the **third quartile,** or the upper quartile. We defined the **interquartile range** as the difference between the upper and lower quartiles. We said that the median is a measure of central tendency, and we defined two other measures of central tendency: the **mode,** which is a *most frequent* value, and the **mean.** We called the mean the most important measure of central tendency, or location, of the data set. We said that the mean is the average of all the data points and is the point where the entire distribution of data points balances.

We defined measures of variability: the **range,** the **variance,** and the **standard deviation.** We defined the range as the difference between the largest and smallest data points. The variance was defined as the average squared deviation of the data points from their mean. For a sample (rather than a population), we saw that this averaging is done by dividing the sum of the squared deviations from the mean by $n - 1$ instead of by n. We defined the standard deviation as the square root of the variance.

We discussed grouped data and **frequencies** of occurrence of data points in **classes** defined by intervals of numbers. We defined **relative frequencies** as the absolute frequencies, or counts, divided by the total number of data points. We saw how to construct a **histogram** of a data set: a graph of the frequencies of the data. We mentioned **skewness,** a measure of the asymmetry of the histogram of the data set. We also mentioned **kurtosis,** a measure of the flatness of the distribution. We introduced **Chebyshev's theorem** and the **empirical rule** as ways of determining the proportions of data lying within several standard deviations of the mean.

We defined four scales of measurement of data: **nominal**—name only; **ordinal**—data that can be ordered as greater than or less than; **interval**—with meaningful distances as intervals of numbers; and **ratio**—a scale where ratios of distances are also meaningful.

The next topic we discussed was graphical techniques. These extended the idea of a histogram. We saw how a **frequency polygon** may be used instead of a histogram. We also saw how to construct an **ogive:** a cumulative frequency graph of a data set. We also talked about **bar charts** and **pie charts,** which are types of charts for displaying data, both categorical and numerical.

Then we discussed **exploratory data analysis,** a statistical area devoted to analyzing data using graphical techniques and other techniques that do not make restrictive assumptions about the structure of the data. Here we encountered two useful techniques for plotting data in a way that sheds light on their structure: **stem-and-leaf displays** and **box plots.** We saw that a stem-and-leaf display, which can be drawn quickly, is a type of histogram that makes use of the decimal structure of our number system. We saw how a box plot is made out of five quantities: the median, the two **hinges,** and the two **whiskers.** And we saw how the whiskers, as well as outliers and suspected outliers, are determined by the **inner fences** and **outer fences;** the first lies at a distance of 1.5 times the interquartile range from the hinges, and the second is found at 3 times the interquartile range from the hinges.

Finally, was saw the use of **templates** to compute population parameters and sample statistics, create histograms and frequency polygons, create bar charts and pie charts, draw box plots, and produce scatter plots.

1–61. Open the workbook named Problem 1–61.xls. Study the statistics that have been calculated in the worksheet. Of special interest to this exercise are the two cells marked Mult and Add. If you enter 2 under Mult, all the data points will be multiplied by 2, as seen in the modified data column. Entering 1 under Mult leaves the data unchanged, since multiplying a number by 1 does not affect it. Similarly, entering 5 under Add will add 5 to all the data points. Entering 0 under Add will leave the data unchanged.

1. Set Mult = 1 and Add = 5, which corresponds to adding 5 to all data points. Observe how the statistics have changed in the modified statistics column. Keeping Mult = 1 and changing Add to different values, observe how the statistics change. Then make a formal statement such as "If we add x to all the data points, then the average would increase by x," for each of the statistics, starting with average.

2. Add an explanation for each statement made in part 1 above. For the average, this will be "If we add x to all the data points, then the sum of all the numbers will increase by $x*n$ where n is the number of data points. The sum is divided by n to get the average. So the average will increase by x."

3. Repeat part 1 for multiplying all the data points by some number. This would require setting Mult equal to desired values and Add = 0.

4. Repeat part 1 for multiplying and adding at once. This would require setting both Mult and Add to desired values.

1–62. *Fortune* published a list of the 10 largest "green companies"–those that follow environmental policies. Their annual revenues, in $ billions, are given below.[17]

Company	Revenue $ Billion
Honda	$84.2
Continental Airlines	13.1
Suncor	13.6
Tesco	71.0
Alcan	23.6
PG&E	12.5
S.C. Johnson	7.0
Goldman Sachs	69.4
Swiss RE	24.0
Hewlett-Packard	91.7

Find the mean, variance, and standard deviation of the annual revenues.

1–63. The following data are the number of tons shipped weekly across the Pacific by a shipping company.

398, 412, 560, 476, 544, 690, 587, 600, 613, 457, 504, 477, 530, 641, 359, 566, 452, 633, 474, 499, 580, 606, 344, 455, 505, 396, 347, 441, 390, 632, 400, 582

Assume these data represent an entire population. Find the population mean and the population standard deviation.

1–64. Group the data in problem 1–63 into classes, and draw a histogram of the frequency distribution.

---

[17]"Green Is Good: Ten Green Giants," *Fortune*, April 2, 2007, pp. 44–50.

1–65. Find the 90th percentile, the quartiles, and the range of the data in problem 1–63.

1–66. The following data are numbers of color television sets manufactured per day at a given plant: 15, 16, 18, 19, 14, 12, 22, 23, 25, 20, 32, 17, 34, 25, 40, 41. Draw a frequency polygon and an ogive for these data.

1–67. Construct a stem-and-leaf display for the data in problem 1–66.

1–68. Construct a box plot for the data in problem 1–66. What can you say about the data?

1–69. The following data are the number of cars passing a point on a highway per minute: 10, 12, 11, 19, 22, 21, 23, 22, 24, 25, 23, 21, 28, 26, 27, 27, 29, 26, 22, 28, 30, 32, 25, 37, 34, 35, 62. Construct a stem-and-leaf display of these data. What does the display tell you about the data?

1–70. For the data problem 1–69, construct a box plot. What does the box plot tell you about these data?

1–71. An article by Julia Moskin in the *New York Times* reports on the use of cheap wine in cooking.[18] Assume that the following results are taste-test ratings, from 1 to 10, for food cooked in cheap wine.

7, 7, 5, 6, 9, 10, 10, 10, 10, 7, 3, 8, 10, 10, 9

Find the mean, median, and modes of these data. Based on these data alone, do you think cheap wine works?

1–72. The following are a sample of Motorola's stock prices in March 2007.[19]

20, 20.5, 19.8, 19.9, 20.1, 20.2, 20.7, 20.6, 20.8, 20.2, 20.6, 20.2

Find the mean and the variance, plot the data, determine outliers, and construct a box plot.

1–73. Consult the corporate data shown below. Plot data; find μ, σ, σ^2; and identify outliers.

Morgan Stanley	91.36%
Merrill Lynch	40.26
Travelers	39.42
Warner-Lambert	35.00
Microsoft	32.95
J.P. Morgan & Co.	29.62
Lehman Brothers	28.25
US Airways	26.71
Sun Microsystems	25.99
Marriott	25.81
Bankers Trust	25.53
General Mills	25.41
MCI	24.39
AlliedSignal	24.23
ITT Industries	24.14

1–74. The following are quoted interest rates (%) on Italian bonds.

2.95, 4.25, 3.55, 1.90, 2.05, 1.78, 2.90, 1.85, 3.45, 1.75, 3.50, 1.69, 2.85, 4.10, 3.80, 3.85, 2.85, 8.70, 1.80, 2.87, 3.95, 3.50, 2.90, 3.45, 3.40, 3.55, 4.25, 1.85, 2.95

Plot the data; find μ, σ, and σ^2; and identify outliers (one is private, the rest are banks and government).

---

[18] Julia Moskin, "It Boils Down to This: Cheap Wine Works Fine," *The New York Times,* March 21, 2007, p. D1.

[19] Adapted from a chart in R. Farzad, "Activist Investors Not Welcome," *BusinessWeek,* April 9, 2007, p. 36.

1–75. Refer to the box plot below to answer the questions.

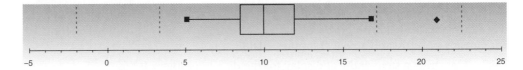

1. What is the interquartile range for this data set?
2. What can you say about the skewness of this data set?
3. For this data set, the value of 9.5 is more likely to be (choose one)

   a. The first quartile rather than the median.

   b. The median rather than the first quartile.

   c. The mean rather than the mode.

   d. The mode rather than the mean.

4. If a data point that was originally 13 is changed to 14, how would the box plot be affected?

1–76. The following table shows changes in bad loans and in provisions for bad loans, from 2005 to 2006, for 19 lending institutions.[20] Verify the reported averages, and find the medians. Which measure is more meaningful, in your opinion? Also find the standard deviation and identify outliers for change in bad loans and change in provision for bad loans.

	Menacing Loans	
Bank/Assets $ Billions	Change in Bad Loans* 12/06 vs. 12/05	Change in Provisions for Bad Loans
Bank of America ($1,459.0)	16.8%	12.1%
Wachovia (707.1)	91.7	23.3
Wells Fargo (481.9)	24.5	−2.8
Suntrust Banks (182.2)	123.5	4.4
Bank of New York (103.4)	42.3	−12.0
Fifth Third Bancorp (100.7)	19.7	3.6
Northern Trust (60.7)	15.2	12.0
Comerica (58.0)	55.1	−4.5
M&T Bank (57.0)	44.9	1.9
Marshall & Isley (56.2)	96.5	15.6
Commerce Bancorp ($45.3)	45.5	13.8
TD Banknorth (40.2)	116.9	25.4
First Horizon National (37.9)	79.2	14.0
Huntington Bancshares (35.3)	22.9	1.4
Compass Bancshares (34.2)	17.3	8.9
Synovus Financial (31.9)	17.6	8.6
Associated Banc-Corp (21.0)	43.4	0.0
Mercantile Bankshares (17.72)	37.2	−8.7
W Holding (17.2)	159.1	37.3
Average** (149.30)	11.00	4.1

*Nonperforming loans.
**At 56 banks with more than $10 billion in assets.
Data: SNL financial.

---

[20]Mara der Hovanesian, "Lender Woes Go beyond Subprime," *BusinessWeek*, March 12, 2007, p. 38. Reprinted by permission.

1-77. Repeat problem 1-76 for the bank assets data, shown in parentheses in the table at the bottom of the previous page.

1-78. A country's percentage approval of its citizens in European Union membership is given below.[21]

Ireland	78%	Luxembourg	75%	Netherlands	70%
Belgium	68	Spain	62	Denmark	60
Germany	58	Greece	57	Italy	52
France	52	Portugal	48	Sweden	48
Finland	40	Austria	39	Britain	37

Find the mean, median, and standard deviation for the percentage approval. Compare the mean and median to the entire EU approval percentage, 53%.

1-79. The following display is adapted from an article in *Fortune*.[22]

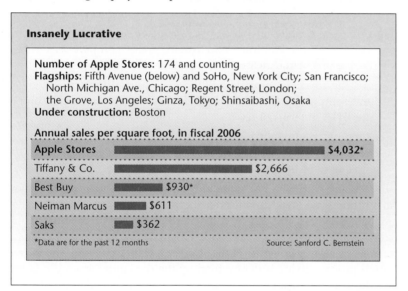

Interpret the chart, and find the mean and standard deviation of the data, viewed as a population.

1-80. The future Euroyen is the price of the Japanese yen as traded in the European futures market. The following are 30-day Euroyen prices on an index from 0 to 100%: 99.24, 99.37, 98.33, 98.91, 98.51, 99.38, 99.71, 99.21, 98.63, 99.10. Find μ, σ, σ^2, and the median.

1-81. The daily expenditure on food by a traveler, in dollars in summer 2006, was as follows: 17.5, 17.6, 18.3, 17.9, 17.4, 16.9, 17.1, 17.1, 18.0, 17.2, 18.3, 17.8, 17.1, 18.3, 17.5, 17.4. Find the mean, standard deviation, and variance.

1-82. For the following data on financial institutions' net income, find the mean and the standard deviation.[23]

Goldman Sachs	$ 9.5 billion
Lehman Brothers	4.0 billion
Moody's	$753 million
T. Rowe Price	$530 million
PNC Financial	$ 2.6 billion

[21]"Four D's for Europe: Dealing with the Dreaded Democratic Deficit," *The Economist*, March 17, 2007, p. 16.

[22]Jerry Useem, "Simply Irresistible: Why Apple Is the Best Retailer in America," *Fortune*, March 19, 2007, p. 108.

[23]"The Rankings," *BusinessWeek*, March 26, 2007, pp. 74–90.

1–83. The following are the percentage profitability data (%) for the top 12 American corporations.[24]

39, 33, 63, 41, 46, 32, 27, 13, 55, 35, 32, 30

Find the mean, median, and standard deviation of the percentages.

1–84. Find the daily stock price of Wal-Mart for the last three months. (A good source for the data is http://moneycentral.msn.com. You can ask for the three-month chart and export the data to a spreadsheet.)

1. Calculate the mean and the standard deviation of the stock prices.
2. Get the corresponding data for Kmart and calculate the mean and the standard deviation.
3. The coefficient of variation (CV) is defined as the ratio of the standard deviation over the mean. Calculate the CV of Wal-Mart and Kmart stock prices.
4. If the CV of the daily stock prices is taken as an indicator of risk of the stock, how do Wal-Mart and Kmart stocks compare in terms of risk? (There are better measures of risk, but we will use CV in this exercise.)
5. Get the corresponding data of the Dow Jones Industrial Average (DJIA) and compute its CV. How do Wal-Mart and Kmart stocks compare with the DJIA in terms of risk?
6. Suppose you bought 100 shares of Wal-Mart stock three months ago and held it. What are the mean and the standard deviation of the daily market price of your holding for the three months?

1–85. To calculate variance and standard deviation, we take the deviations from the mean. At times, we need to consider the deviations from a target value rather than the mean. Consider the case of a machine that bottles cola into 2-liter (2,000-cm^3) bottles. The target is thus 2,000 cm^3. The machine, however, may be bottling 2,004 cm^3 on average into every bottle. Call this 2,004 cm^3 the *process mean*. The damage from process errors is determined by the deviations from the target rather than from the process mean. The variance, though, is calculated with deviations from the process mean, and therefore is not a measure of the damage. Suppose we want to calculate a new variance using deviations from the target value. Let "SSD(Target)" denote the sum of the squared deviations from the target. [For example, SSD(2,000) denotes the sum of squared deviations when the deviations are taken from 2,000.] Dividing the SSD by the number of data points gives the Average SSD(Target).

The following spreadsheet is set up to calculate the deviations from the target, SSD(Target), and the Average SSD(Target). Column B contains the data, showing a process mean of 2,004. (Strictly speaking, this would be sample data. But to simplify matters, let us assume that this is population data.) Note that the population variance (VARP) is 3.5 and the Average SSD(2,000) is 19.5.

In the range G5:H13, a table has been created to see the effect of changing the target on Average SSD(Target). The offset refers to the difference between the target and the process mean.

1. Study the table and find an equation that relates the Average SSD to VARP and the Offset. [Hint: Note that while calculating SSD, the deviations are squared, so think in squares.]
2. Using the equation you found in part 1, prove that the Average SSD(Target) is minimized when the target equals the process mean.

---

[24]From "Inside the Rankings," *BusinessWeek*, March 26, 2007, p. 92.

Working with Deviations from a Target
[Problem 1–85.xls]

Deviations from a Target

Target: 2000

Data	Deviation from Target	Squared Deviation		Offset	Target	Average SSd
2003	3	9				
2002	2	4		-4	2000	19.5
2005	5	25		-3	2001	12.5
2004	4	16		-2	2002	7.5
2006	6	36		-1	2003	4.5
2001	1	1		0	2004	3.5 <- VARP
2004	4	16		1	2005	4.5
2007	7	49		2	2006	7.5
				3	2007	12.5
Mean 2004	**SSd**	156		4	2008	19.5
VARP 3.5	**Avg. SSd**	19.5				

1–86. The Consumer Price Index (CPI) is an important indicator of the general level of prices of essential commodities. It is widely used in making cost of living adjustments to salaries, for example.

1. Log on to the Consumer Price Index (CPI) home page of the Bureau of Labor Statistics Web site (stats.bls.gov/cpihome.htm). Get a table of the last 48 months' CPI for U.S. urban consumers with 1982–1984 as the base. Make a time plot of the data. Discuss any seasonal pattern you see in the data.

2. Go to the Average Price Data area and get a table of the last 48 months' average price of unleaded regular gasoline. Make a comparison time plot of the CPI data in part 1 and the gasoline price data. Comment on the gasoline prices.

1–87. Log on to the Center for Disease Control Web site and go to the HIV statistics page (www.cdc.gov/hiv/stats.htm).

1. Download the data on the cumulative number of AIDS cases reported in the United States and its age-range breakdown. Draw a pie chart of the data.

2. Download the race/ethnicity breakdown of the data. Draw a pie chart of the data.

1–88. Search the Web for major league baseball (MLB) players' salaries. ESPN and *USA Today* are good sources.

1. Get the Chicago Cubs players' salaries for the current year. Draw a box plot of the data. (Enter the data in thousands of dollars to make the numbers smaller.) Are there any outliers?

2. Get the Chicago White Sox players' salaries for the current year. Make a comparison box plot of the two data. Describe your comparison based on the plot.

1-89. The following data are bank yields (in percent) for 6-month CDs.[25]

3.56, 5.44, 5.37, 5.28, 5.19, 5.35, 5.48, 5.27, 5.39

Find the mean and standard deviation.

---

[25]"Wave and You've Paid," *Money*, March 2007, p. 40.

CASE 1   NASDAQ Volatility

The NASDAQ Combined Composite Index is a measure of the aggregate value of technological stocks. During the year 2007, the index moved up and down considerably, indicating the rapid changes in e-business that took place in that year and the high uncertainty in the profitability of technology-oriented companies. Historical data of the index are available at many Web sites, including **Finance.Yahoo.com.**

1. Download the monthly data of the index for the calendar year 2007 and make a time plot of the data. Comment on the volatility of the index, looking at the plot. Report the standard deviation of the data.

2. Download the monthly data of the index for the calendar year 2006 and compare the data for 2006 and 2007 on a single plot. Which year has been more volatile? Calculate the standard deviations of the two sets of data. Do they confirm your answer about the relative volatility of the two years?

3. Download the monthly data of the S&P 500 index for the year 2007. Compare this index with the NASDAQ index for the same year on a single plot. Which index has been more volatile? Calculate and report the standard deviations of the two sets of data.

4. Download the monthly data of the Dow Jones Industrial Average for the year 2007. Compare this index with the NASDAQ index for the same year on a single plot. Which index has been more volatile? Calculate and report the standard deviations of the two sets of data.

5. Repeat part 1 with the monthly data for the latest 12 full months.

2

PROBABILITY

2–1   Using Statistics   51
2–2   Basic Definitions: Events, Sample Space, and Probabilities   53
2–3   Basic Rules for Probability   57
2–4   Conditional Probability   61
2–5   Independence of Events   66
2–6   Combinatorial Concepts   70
2–7   The Law of Total Probability and Bayes' Theorem   73
2–8   The Joint Probability Table   79
2–9   Using the Computer   80
2–10 Summary and Review of Terms   84
Case 2   Job Applications   89

LEARNING OBJECTIVES

After studying this chapter, you should be able to:

- Define probability, sample space, and event.
- Distinguish between subjective and objective probability.
- Describe the complement of an event and the intersection and union of two events.
- Compute probabilities of various types of events.
- Explain the concept of conditional probability and how to compute it.
- Describe permutation and combination and their use in certain probability computations.
- Explain Bayes' theorem and its application.

A Missed Pickup Is a Missed Opportunity

A bizarre sequence of events took place on the University of California campus at Berkeley on October 20, 2003. An employee of the university took a package containing 30 applications by graduate students at the university for the prestigious Fulbright Fellowship, administered by the U.S. Department of Education, and dropped them at the Federal Express pickup box on campus. October 20 was the deadline the Department of Education had set for posting by each university of all its applications for awards on behalf of its students.

But just that day, something that had never happened before took place. Because of a "computer glitch," as Federal Express later described it, there was no pickup by the company from its box on Sproul Plaza on the U.C. campus. When the problem became apparent to the university, an employee sent an e-mail message late that night to the Department of Education in Washington, apologizing for the mishap, which was not the University's fault, and requesting an extension of time for its students. The Department of Education refused.

There ensued a long sequence of telephone calls, and the Chancellor of the University, Robert M. Berdahl, flew to Washington to beg the authorities to allow his students to be considered. The Department of Education refused. At one point, one of the attorneys for the Department told the University that had the e-mail message not been sent, everything would have been fine since FedEx would have shown the date of posting as October 20. But since the e-mail message had been sent, the fate of the applications was sealed. Usually, 15 out of 30 applications from U.C. Berkeley result in awards. But because of this unfortunate sequence of events, no Berkeley graduate students were to receive a Fulbright Fellowship in 2004.

Dean E. Murphy, "Missed Pickup Means a Missed Opportunity for 30 Seeking a Fellowship," *The New York Times,* February 5, 2004, p. A14.

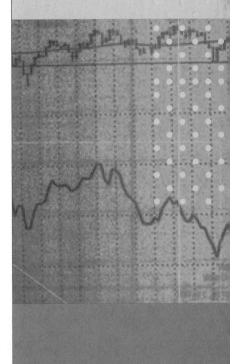

This story demonstrates how probabilities affect everything in our lives. A priori, there was an extremely small chance that a pickup would be missed: According to FedEx this simply doesn't happen. The university had relied on the virtually sure probability of a pickup, and thus posted the applications on the last possible day. Moreover, the chance that an employee of the university would find out that the pickup was missed on that same day and e-mail the Department of Education was very small. Yet the sequence of rare events took place, with disastrous results for the graduate students who had worked hard to apply for these important awards.

A **probability** is a quantitative measure of uncertainty—a number that conveys the strength of our belief in the occurrence of an uncertain event. Since life is full of uncertainty, people have always been interested in evaluating probabilities. The statistician I. J. Good suggests that "the theory of probability is much older than the human species," since the assessment of uncertainty incorporates the idea of learning from experience, which most creatures do.[1]

[1] I. J. Good, "Kinds of Probability," *Science,* no. 129 (February 20, 1959), pp. 443–47.

The theory of probability as we know it today was largely developed by European mathematicians such as Galileo Galilei (1564–1642), Blaise Pascal (1623–1662), Pierre de Fermat (1601–1665), Abraham de Moivre (1667–1754), and others.

As in India, the development of probability theory in Europe is often associated with gamblers, who pursued their interests in the famous European casinos, such as the one at Monte Carlo. Many books on probability and statistics tell the story of the Chevalier de Mère, a French gambler who enlisted the help of Pascal in an effort to obtain the probabilities of winning at certain games of chance, leading to much of the European development of probability.

Today, the theory of probability is an indispensable tool in the analysis of situations involving uncertainty. It forms the basis for inferential statistics as well as for other fields that require quantitative assessments of chance occurrences, such as quality control, management decision analysis, and areas in physics, biology, engineering, and economics.

While most analyses using the theory of probability have nothing to do with games of chance, gambling models provide the clearest examples of probability and its assessment. The reason is that games of chance usually involve dice, cards, or roulette wheels—mechanical devices. If we assume there is no cheating, these mechanical devices tend to produce sets of outcomes that are *equally likely,* and this allows us to compute probabilities of winning at these games.

Suppose that a single die is rolled and that you win a dollar if the number 1 or 2 appears. What are your chances of winning a dollar? Since there are six equally likely numbers (assuming the die is fair) and you win as a result of either of two numbers appearing, the probability that you win is 2/6, or 1/3.

As another example, consider the following situation. An analyst follows the price movements of IBM stock for a time and wants to assess the probability that the stock will go up in price in the next week. This is a different type of situation. The analyst does not have the luxury of a known set of equally likely outcomes, where "IBM stock goes up next week" is one of a given number of these equally likely possibilities. Therefore, the analyst's assessment of the probability of the event will be a *subjective* one. The analyst will base her or his assessment of this probability on knowledge of the situation, guesses, or intuition. Different people may assign different probabilities to this event depending on their experience and knowledge, hence the name *subjective* probability.

Objective probability is probability based on symmetry of games of chance or similar situations. It is also called *classical probability.* This probability is based on the idea that certain occurrences are equally likely (the term *equally likely* is intuitively clear and will be used as a starting point for our definitions): The numbers 1, 2, 3, 4, 5, and 6 on a fair die are each equally likely to occur. Another type of objective probability is long-term *relative-frequency* probability. If, in the long run, 20 out of 1,000 consumers given a taste test for a new soup like the taste, then we say that the probability that a given consumer will like the soup is 20/1,000 = 0.02. If the probability that a head will appear on any one toss of a coin is 1/2, then if the coin is tossed a large number of times, the proportion of heads will approach 1/2. Like the probability in games of chance and other symmetric situations, relative-frequency probability is objective in the sense that no personal judgment is involved.

Subjective probability, on the other hand, involves personal judgment, information, intuition, and other subjective evaluation criteria. The area of subjective probability—which is relatively new, having been first developed in the 1930s—is somewhat controversial.[2] A physician assessing the probability of a patient's recovery and an expert assessing the probability of success of a merger offer are both making a personal judgment based on what they know and feel about the situation. Subjective

---

[2]The earliest published works on subjective probability are Frank Ramsey's *The Foundation of Mathematics and Other Logical Essays* (London: Kegan Paul, 1931) and the Italian statistician Bruno de Finetti's "La Prévision: Ses Lois Logiques, Ses Sources Subjectives," *Annales de L'Institut Henri Poincaré* 7, no. 1 (1937).

probability is also called *personal probability*. One person's subjective probability may very well be different from another person's subjective probability of the same event.

Whatever the kind of probability involved, the same set of mathematical rules holds for manipulating and analyzing probability. We now give the general rules for probability as well as formal definitions. Some of our definitions will involve counting the number of ways in which some event may occur. The counting idea is implementable only in the case of objective probability, although conceptually this idea may apply to subjective probability as well, if we can imagine a kind of lottery with a known probability of occurrence for the event of interest.

2–2 Basic Definitions: Events, Sample Space, and Probabilities

To understand probability, some familiarity with sets and with operations involving sets is useful.

A **set** is a collection of elements.

The elements of a set may be people, horses, desks, cars, files in a cabinet, or even numbers. We may define our set as the collection of all horses in a given pasture, all people in a room, all cars in a given parking lot at a given time, all the numbers between 0 and 1, or all integers. The number of elements in a set may be infinite, as in the last two examples.

A set may also have no elements.

The **empty set** is the set containing *no elements*. It is denoted by ∅.

We now define the universal set.

The **universal set** is the set containing *everything* in a given context. We denote the universal set by S.

Given a set A, we may define its *complement*.

The **complement** of set A is the set containing all the elements in the universal set S that are *not* members of set A. We denote the complement of A by $\overline{A}$. The set $\overline{A}$ is often called "not A."

A **Venn diagram** is a schematic drawing of sets that demonstrates the relationships between different sets. In a Venn diagram, sets are shown as circles, or other closed figures, within a rectangle corresponding to the universal set, S. Figure 2–1 is a Venn diagram demonstrating the relationship between a set A and its complement $\overline{A}$.

As an example of a set and its complement, consider the following. Let the universal set S be the set of all students at a given university. Define A as the set of all students who own a car (at least one car). The complement of A, or $\overline{A}$, is thus the set of all students at the university who do *not* own a car.

Sets may be related in a number of ways. Consider two sets A and B within the context of the same universal set S. (We say that A and B are *subsets* of the universal set S.) If A and B have some elements in common, we say they *intersect*.

The **intersection** of A and B, denoted A ∩ B, is the set containing all elements that are members of *both* A and B.

When we want to consider all the elements of two sets A and B, we look at their *union*.

The **union** of A and B, denoted A ∪ B, is the set containing all elements that are members of *either* A *or* B or *both*.

FIGURE 2–1   A Set A and Its Complement Ā

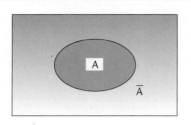

FIGURE 2–2   Sets A and B and Their Intersection

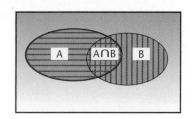

FIGURE 2–3   The Union of A and B

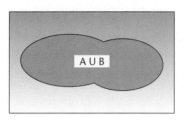

FIGURE 2–4   Two Disjoint Sets

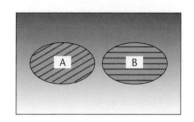

As you can see from these definitions, the union of two sets contains the intersection of the two sets. Figure 2–2 is a Venn diagram showing two sets A and B and their intersection A ∩ B. Figure 2–3 is a Venn diagram showing the union of the same sets.

As an example of the union and intersection of sets, consider again the set of all students at a university who own a car. This is set A. Now define set B as the set of all students at the university who own a bicycle. The universal set S is, as before, the set of all students at the university. And A ∩ B is the intersection of A and B—it is the set of all students at the university who own *both* a car and a bicycle. And A ∪ B is the union of A and B—it is the set of all students at the university who own either a car or a bicycle or both.

Two sets may have no intersection: They may be **disjoint.** In such a case, we say that the intersection of the two sets is the empty set ∅. In symbols, when A and B are disjoint, A ∩ B = ∅. As an example of two disjoint sets, consider the set of all students enrolled in a business program at a particular university and all the students at the university who are enrolled in an art program. (Assume no student is enrolled in both programs.) A Venn diagram of two disjoint sets is shown in Figure 2–4.

In probability theory we make use of the idea of a set and of operations involving sets. We will now provide some basic definitions of terms relevant to the computation of probability. These are an *experiment,* a *sample space,* and an *event.*

> An **experiment** is a process that leads to one of several possible **outcomes.**
> An **outcome** of an experiment is some observation or measurement.

Drawing a card out of a deck of 52 cards is an experiment. One outcome of the experiment may be that the queen of diamonds is drawn.

A single outcome of an experiment is called a *basic outcome* or an *elementary event.* Any particular card drawn from a deck is a basic outcome.

> The **sample space** is the universal set S pertinent to a given experiment.
> The sample space is the set of all possible outcomes of an experiment.

FIGURE 2–5   Sample Space for Drawing a Card

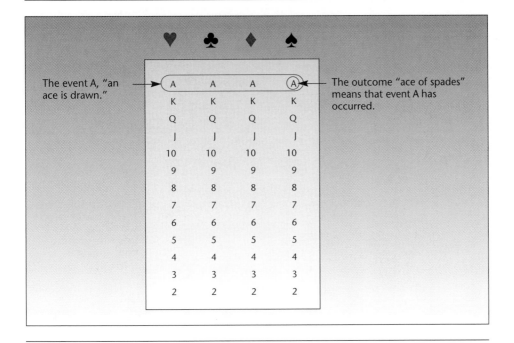

The event A, "an ace is drawn." → [the four aces row] ← The outcome "ace of spades" means that event A has occurred.

The sample space for the experiment of drawing a card out of a deck is the set of all cards in the deck. The sample space for an experiment of reading the temperature is the set of all numbers in the range of temperatures.

> An **event** is a subset of a sample space. It is a set of basic outcomes. We say that the event *occurs* if the experiment gives rise to a basic outcome belonging to the event.

For example, the event "an ace is drawn out of a deck of cards" is the set of the four aces within the sample space consisting of all 52 cards. This event occurs whenever one of the four aces (the basic outcomes) is drawn.

The sample space for the experiment of drawing a card out of a deck of 52 cards is shown in Figure 2–5. The figure also shows event A, the event that an ace is drawn.

In this context, for a given experiment we have a sample space with equally likely basic outcomes. When a card is drawn out of a well-shuffled deck, every one of the cards (the basic outcomes) is as likely to occur as any other. In such situations, it seems reasonable to define the probability of an event as the *relative size* of the event with respect to the size of the sample space. Since a deck has 4 aces and 52 cards, the size of A is 4 and the size of the sample space is 52. Therefore, the probability of A is equal to 4/52.

The rule we use in computing probabilities, assuming equal likelihood of all basic outcomes, is as follows:

Probability of event A:

$$P(A) = \frac{n(A)}{n(S)} \tag{2-1}$$

where

$n(A)$ = the number of elements in the set of the event A
$n(S)$ = the number of elements in the sample space S

FIGURE 2–6   The Events A and ♥ and Their Union and Intersection

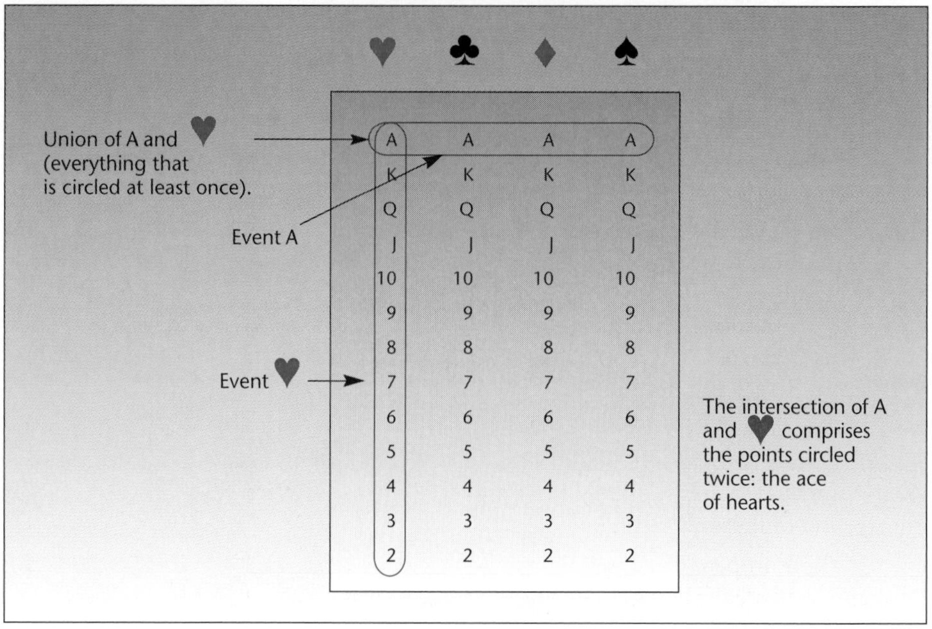

The probability of drawing an ace is $P(\text{A}) = n(\text{A})/n(\text{S}) = 4/52$.

EXAMPLE 2–1

Roulette is a popular casino game. As the game is played in Las Vegas or Atlantic City, the roulette wheel has 36 numbers, 1 through 36, and the number 0 as well as the number 00 (double zero). What is the probability of winning on a single number that you bet?

Solution

The sample space S in this example consists of 38 numbers (0, 00, 1, 2, 3,..., 36), each of which is equally likely to come up. Using our counting rule P (any one given number) $= 1/38$.

Let's now demonstrate the meaning of union and intersection with the example of drawing a card from a deck. Let A be the event that an ace is drawn and ♥ the event that a heart is drawn. The sample space is shown in Figure 2–6. Note that the event A ∩ ♥ is the event that the card drawn is both an ace and a heart (i.e., the ace of hearts). The event A ∪ ♥ is the event that the card drawn is either an ace or a heart or both.

PROBLEMS

2–1.   What are the two main types of probability?

2–2.   What is an event? What is the union of two events? What is the intersection of two events?

2–3.   Define a sample space.

2–4.   Define the probability of an event.

2–5. Let G be the event that a girl is born. Let F be the event that a baby over 5 pounds is born. Characterize the union and the intersection of the two events.

2–6. Consider the event that a player scores a point in a game against team A and the event that the same player scores a point in a game against team B. What is the union of the two events? What is the intersection of the two events?

2–7. A die is tossed twice and the two outcomes are noted. Draw the Venn diagram of the sample space and indicate the event "the second toss is greater than the first." Calculate the probability of the event.

2–8. Ford Motor Company advertises its cars on radio and on television. The company is interested in assessing the probability that a randomly chosen person is exposed to at least one of these two modes of advertising. If we define event R as the event that a randomly chosen person was exposed to a radio advertisement and event T as the event that the person was exposed to a television commercial, define R ∪ T and R ∩ T in this context.

2–9. A brokerage firm deals in stocks and bonds. An analyst for the firm is interested in assessing the probability that a person who inquires about the firm will eventually purchase stock (event S) or bonds (event B). Define the union and the intersection of these two events.

2–10. The European version of roulette is different from the U.S. version in that the European roulette wheel doesn't have 00. How does this change the probability of winning when you bet on a single number? European casinos charge a small admission fee, which is not the case in U.S. casinos. Does this make sense to you, based on your answer to the earlier question?

2–3 Basic Rules for Probability

We have explored probability on a somewhat intuitive level and have seen rules that help us evaluate probabilities in special cases when we have a known sample space with equally likely basic outcomes. We will now look at some general probability rules that hold regardless of the particular situation or kind of probability (objective or subjective). First, let us give a general definition of probability.

> Probability is a measure of uncertainty. The **probability** of event A is a numerical measure of the likelihood of the event's occurring.

The Range of Values

Probability obeys certain rules. The first rule sets the range of values that the probability measure may take.

For any event A, the probability $P(A)$ satisfies

$$0 \le P(A) \le 1 \qquad\qquad (2\text{–}2)$$

When an event cannot occur, its probability is zero. The probability of the empty set is zero: $P(\varnothing) = 0$. In a deck where half the cards are red and half are black, the probability of drawing a green card is zero because the set corresponding to that event is the empty set: There are no green cards.

Events that are certain to occur have probability 1.00. The probability of the entire sample space S is equal to 1.00: $P(S) = 1.00$. If we draw a card out of a deck, 1 of the 52 cards in the deck will certainly be drawn, and so the probability of the sample space, the set of all 52 cards, is equal to 1.00.

FIGURE 2–7   Interpretation of a Probability

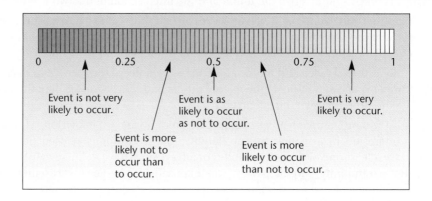

Within the range of values 0 to 1, the greater the probability, the more confidence we have in the occurrence of the event in question. A probability of 0.95 implies a very high confidence in the occurrence of the event. A probability of 0.80 implies a high confidence. When the probability is 0.5, the event is as likely to occur as it is not to occur. When the probability is 0.2, the event is not very likely to occur. When we assign a probability of 0.05, we believe the event is unlikely to occur, and so on. Figure 2–7 is an informal aid in interpreting probability.

Note that probability is a measure that goes from 0 to 1. In everyday conversation we often describe probability in less formal terms. For example, people sometimes talk about **odds.** If the odds are 1 to 1, the probability is 1/2; if the odds are 1 to 2, the probability is 1/3; and so on. Also, people sometimes say, "The probability is 80 percent." Mathematically, this probability is 0.80.

The Rule of Complements

Our second rule for probability defines the probability of the complement of an event in terms of the probability of the original event. Recall that the complement of set A is denoted by $\overline{A}$.

Probability of the complement:

$$P(\overline{A}) = 1 - P(A) \qquad (2\text{–}3)$$

As a simple example, if the probability of rain tomorrow is 0.3, then the probability of no rain tomorrow must be $1 - 0.3 = 0.7$. If the probability of drawing an ace is 4/52, then the probability of the drawn card's not being an ace is $1 - 4/52 = 48/52$.

The Rule of Unions.   We now state a very important rule, the **rule of unions.** The rule of unions allows us to write the probability of the union of two events in terms of the probabilities of the two events and the probability of their intersection:[3]

The rule of unions:

$$P(A \cup B) = P(A) + P(B) - P(A \cap B) \qquad (2\text{–}4)$$

---

[3]The rule can be extended to more than two events. In the case of three events, we have $P(A \cup B \cup C) = P(A) + P(B) + P(C) - P(A \cap B) - P(A \cap C) - P(B \cap C) + P(A \cap B \cap C)$. With more events, this becomes even more complicated.

[The probability of the intersection of two events $P(A \cap B)$ is called their **joint probability**.] The meaning of this rule is very simple and intuitive: When we add the probabilities of A and B, we are measuring, or counting, the probability of their inter-section *twice*—once when measuring the relative size of A within the sample space and once when doing this with B. Since the relative size, or probability, of the intersection of the two sets is counted twice, we subtract it once so that we are left with the true proba-bility of the union of the two events (refer to Figure 2–6). Note that instead of finding the probability of $A \cup B$ by direct counting, we can use the rule of unions: We know that the probability of an ace is 4/52, the probability of a heart is 13/52, and the probability of their intersection—the drawn card being the ace of hearts—is 1/52. Thus, $P(A \cup \heartsuit) = 4/52 + 13/52 - 1/52 = 16/52$, which is exactly what we find from direct counting.

The rule of unions is especially useful when we do not have the sample space for the union of events but do have the separate probabilities. For example, suppose your chance of being offered a certain job is 0.4, your probability of getting another job is 0.5, and your probability of being offered both jobs (i.e., the intersection) is 0.3. By the rule of unions, your probability of being offered at least one of the two jobs (their union) is $0.4 + 0.5 - 0.3 = 0.6$.

Mutually Exclusive Events

When the sets corresponding to two events are disjoint (i.e., have no intersection), the two events are called **mutually exclusive** (see Figure 2–4). For mutually exclusive events, the probability of the intersection of the events is zero. This is so because the intersection of the events is the empty set, and we know that the probability of the empty set $\varnothing$ is zero.

> For mutually exclusive events A and B:
> $$P(A \cap B) = 0 \qquad\qquad (2\text{–}5)$$

This fact gives us a special rule for unions of mutually exclusive events. Since the probability of the intersection of the two events is zero, there is no need to subtract $P(A \cap B)$ when the probability of the union of the two events is computed. Therefore,

> For mutually exclusive events A and B:
> $$P(A \cup B) = P(A) + P(B) \qquad\qquad (2\text{–}6)$$

This is not really a new rule since we can always use the rule of unions for the union of two events: If the events happen to be mutually exclusive, we subtract zero as the probability of the intersection.

To continue our cards example, what is the probability of drawing either a heart or a club? We have $P(\heartsuit \cup \clubsuit) = P(\heartsuit) + P(\clubsuit) = 13/52 + 13/52 = 26/52 = 1/2$. We need not subtract the probability of an intersection, since no card is both a club and a heart.

PROBLEMS

2-11. According to an article in *Fortune,* institutional investors recently changed the proportions of their portfolios toward public sector funds.[4] The article implies that 8% of investors studied invest in public sector funds and 6% in corporate funds. Assume that 2% invest in both kinds. If an investor is chosen at random, what is the probability that this investor has either public or corporate funds?

---

[4]"Fueling the Fire," *Fortune,* March 5, 2007, p. 60.

2–12. According to *The New York Times,* 5 million BlackBerry users found their devices nonfunctional on April 18, 2007.[5] If there were 18 million users of handheld data devices of this kind on that day, what is the probability that a randomly chosen user could not use a device?

2–13. In problem 2–12, assume that 3 million out of 18 million users could not use their devices as cellphones, and that 1 million could not use their devices as a cellphone and for data device. What is the probability that a randomly chosen device could not be used either for data or for voice communication?

2–14. According to a report on CNN Business News in April 1995, the probability of being murdered (in the United States) in 1 year is 9 in 100,000. How might such a probability have been obtained?

2–15. Assign a reasonable numerical probability to the statement "Rain is very likely tonight."

2–16. How likely is an event that has a 0.65 probability? Describe the probability in words.

2–17. If a team has an 80% chance of winning a game, describe its chances in words.

2–18. ShopperTrak is a hidden electric eye designed to count the number of shoppers entering a store. When two shoppers enter a store together, one walking in front of the other, the following probabilities apply: There is a 0.98 probability that the first shopper will be detected, a 0.94 probability that the second shopper will be detected, and a 0.93 probability that both of them will be detected by the device. What is the probability that the device will detect at least one of two shoppers entering together?

2–19. A machine produces components for use in cellular phones. At any given time, the machine may be in one, and only one, of three states: operational, out of control, or down. From experience with this machine, a quality control engineer knows that the probability that the machine is out of control at any moment is 0.02, and the probability that it is down is 0.015.

  a. What is the relationship between the two events "machine is out of control" and "machine is down"?

  b. When the machine is either out of control or down, a repair person must be called. What is the probability that a repair person must be called right now?

  c. Unless the machine is down, it can be used to produce a single item. What is the probability that the machine can be used to produce a single component right now? What is the relationship between this event and the event "machine is down"?

2–20. Following are age and sex data for 20 midlevel managers at a service company: 34 F, 49 M, 27 M, 63 F, 33 F, 29 F, 45 M, 46 M, 30 F, 39 M, 42 M, 30 F, 48 M, 35 F, 32 F, 37 F, 48 F, 50 M, 48 F, 61 F. A manager must be chosen at random to serve on a companywide committee that deals with personnel problems. What is the probability that the chosen manager will be either a woman or over 50 years old or both? Solve both directly from the data and by using the law of unions. What is the probability that the chosen manager will be under 30?

2–21. Suppose that 25% of the population in a given area is exposed to a television commercial for Ford automobiles, and 34% is exposed to Ford's radio advertisements. Also, it is known that 10% of the population is exposed to both means of advertising. If a person is randomly chosen out of the entire population in this area, what is the probability that he or she was exposed to at least one of the two modes of advertising?

2–22. Suppose it is known that 85% of the people who inquire about investment opportunities at a brokerage house end up purchasing stock, and 33% end up purchasing bonds. It is also known that 28% of the inquirers end up getting a portfolio

[5]Brad Stone, "Bereft of BlackBerrys, the Untethered Make Do," *The New York Times,* April 19, 2007, p. C1.

with both stocks and bonds. If a person is just making an inquiry, what is the probability that she or he will get stock or bonds or both (i.e., open any portfolio)?

2–23. A firm has 550 employees; 380 of them have had at least some college education, and 412 of the employees underwent a vocational training program. Furthermore, 357 employees both are college-educated and have had the vocational training. If an employee is chosen at random, what is the probability that he or she is college-educated or has had the training or both?

2–24. In problem 2–12, what is the probability that a randomly chosen user could use his or her device?

2–25. As part of a student project for the 1994 Science Fair in Orange, Massachusetts, 28 horses were made to listen to Mozart and heavy-metal music. The results were as follows: 11 of the 28 horses exhibited some head movements when Mozart was played; 8 exhibited some head movements when the heavy metal was played; and 5 moved their heads when both were played. If a horse is chosen at random, what is the probability the horse exhibited head movements to Mozart or to heavy metal or to both?

2–4 Conditional Probability

As a measure of uncertainty, probability depends on information. Thus, the probability you would give the event "Xerox stock price will go up tomorrow" depends on what you know about the company and its performance; the probability is *conditional* upon your information set. If you know much about the company, you may assign a different probability to the event than if you know little about the company. We may define the probability of event A *conditional* upon the occurrence of event B. In this example, event A may be the event that the stock will go up tomorrow, and event B may be a favorable quarterly report.

The **conditional probability** of event A given the occurrence of event B is

$$P(A|B) = \frac{P(A \cap B)}{P(B)} \tag{2-7}$$

assuming $P(B) \neq 0$.

The vertical line in $P(A \mid B)$ is read *given,* or *conditional upon.* The probability of event A given the occurrence of event B is defined as the probability of the intersection of A and B, divided by the probability of event B.

As part of a drive to modernize the economy, the government of an eastern European country is pushing for starting 100 new projects in computer development and telecommunications. Two U.S. giants, IBM and AT&T, have signed contracts

EXAMPLE 2–2

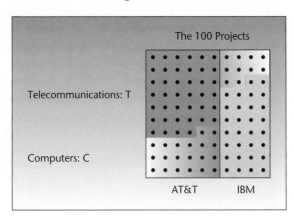

The 100 Projects

Telecommunications: T

Computers: C

AT&T   IBM

for these projects: 40 projects for IBM and 60 for AT&T. Of the IBM projects, 30 are in the computer area and 10 are in telecommunications; of the AT&T projects, 40 are in telecommunications and 20 are in computer areas. Given that a randomly chosen project is in telecommunications, what is the probability that it is undertaken by IBM?

Solution

$$P(\text{IBM}|\text{T}) = \frac{P(\text{IBM} \cap \text{T})}{P(\text{T})} = \frac{10/100}{50/100} = 0.2$$

But we see this directly from the fact that there are 50 telecommunications projects and 10 of them are by IBM. This confirms the definition of conditional probability in an intuitive sense.

When two events and their complements are of interest, it may be convenient to arrange the information in a **contingency table**. In Example 2–2 the table would be set up as follows:

	AT&T	IBM	Total
Telecommunications	40	10	50
Computers	20	30	50
Total	60	40	100

Contingency tables help us visualize information and solve problems. The definition of conditional probability (equation 2–7) takes two other useful forms.

> Variation of the conditional probability formula:
>
> $$P(A \cap B) = P(A \mid B)P(B)$$
>
> and
>
> $$P(A \cap B) = P(B \mid A)P(A) \qquad (2\text{–}8)$$

These are illustrated in Example 2–3.

EXAMPLE 2–3

A consulting firm is bidding for two jobs, one with each of two large multinational corporations. The company executives estimate that the probability of obtaining the consulting job with firm A, event A, is 0.45. The executives also feel that if the company should get the job with firm A, then there is a 0.90 probability that firm B will also give the company the consulting job. What are the company's chances of getting *both* jobs?

Solution

We are given $P(A) = 0.45$. We also know that $P(B \mid A) = 0.90$, and we are looking for $P(A \cap B)$, which is the probability that both A and B will occur. From the equation we have $P(A \cap B) = P(B \mid A)P(A) = 0.90 \times 0.45 = 0.405$.

EXAMPLE 2–4

Twenty-one percent of the executives in a large advertising firm are at the top salary level. It is further known that 40% of all the executives at the firm are women. Also, 6.4% of all executives are women *and* are at the top salary level. Recently, a question arose among executives at the firm as to whether there is any evidence of salary inequity. Assuming that some statistical considerations (explained in later chapters) are met, do the percentages reported above provide any evidence of salary inequity?

Solution

To solve this problem, we pose it in terms of probabilities and ask whether the probability that a randomly chosen executive will be at the top salary level is approximately equal to the probability that the executive will be at the top salary level given the executive is a woman. To answer, we need to compute the probability that the executive will be at the top level given the executive is a woman. Defining T as the event of a top salary and W as the event that an executive is a woman, we get

$$P(T|W) = \frac{P(T \cap W)}{P(W)} = \frac{0.064}{0.40} = 0.16$$

Since 0.16 is smaller than 0.21, we may conclude (subject to statistical considerations) that salary inequity does exist at the firm, because an executive is less likely to make a top salary if she is a woman.

Example 2–4 may incline us to think about the relations among different events. Are different events related, or are they independent of each other? In this example, we concluded that the two events, being a woman and being at the top salary level, are related in the sense that the event W made event T less likely. Section 2–5 quantifies the relations among events and defines the concept of independence.

PROBLEMS

2–26. SBC Warburg, Deutsche Morgan Grenfell, and UBS are foreign. Given that a security is foreign-underwritten, find the probability that it is by SBC Warburg (see the accompanying table).[6]

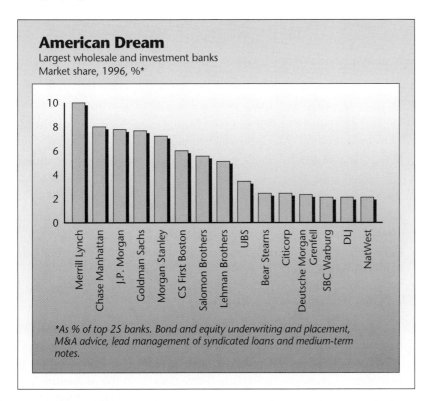

American Dream
Largest wholesale and investment banks
Market share, 1996, %*

As % of top 25 banks. Bond and equity underwriting and placement, M&A advice, lead management of syndicated loans and medium-term notes.

---

[6]From "Out of Their League?" *The Economist,* June 21, 1997, pp. 71–72. © 1997 The Economist Newspaper Group, Inc. Reprinted with permission. Further reproduction prohibited. www.economist.com.

2–27. If a large competitor will buy a small firm, the firm's stock will rise with probability 0.85. The purchase of the company has a 0.40 probability. What is the probability that the purchase will take place and the firm's stock will rise?

2–28. A financial analyst believes that if interest rates decrease in a given period, then the probability that the stock market will go up is 0.80. The analyst further believes that interest rates have a 0.40 chance of decreasing during the period in question. Given the above information, what is the probability that the market will go up and interest rates will go down during the period in question?

2–29. A bank loan officer knows that 12% of the bank's mortgage holders lose their jobs and default on the loan in the course of 5 years. She also knows that 20% of the bank's mortgage holders lose their jobs during this period. Given that one of her mortgage holders just lost his job, what is the probability that he will now default on the loan?

2–30. An express delivery service promises overnight delivery of all packages checked in before 5 P.M. The delivery service is not perfect, however, and sometimes delays do occur. Management knows that if delays occur in the evening flight to a major city from which distribution is made, then a package will not arrive on time with probability 0.25. It is also known that 10% of the evening flights to the major city are delayed. What percentage of the packages arrive late? (Assume that all packages are sent out on the evening flight to the major city and that all packages arrive on time if the evening flight is not delayed.)

2–31. The following table gives numbers of claims at a large insurance company by kind and by geographic region.

	East	South	Midwest	West
Hospitalization	75	128	29	52
Physician's visit	233	514	104	251
Outpatient treatment	100	326	65	99

Compute column totals and row totals. What do they mean?

    a. If a bill is chosen at random, what is the probability that it is from the Midwest?

    b. What is the probability that a randomly chosen bill is from the East?

    c. What is the probability that a randomly chosen bill is either from the Midwest or from the South? What is the relation between these two events?

    d. What is the probability that a randomly chosen bill is for hospitalization?

    e. Given that a bill is for hospitalization, what is the probability that it is from the South?

    f. Given that a bill is from the East, what is the probability that it is for a physician's visit?

    g. Given that a bill is for outpatient treatment, what is the probability that it is from the West?

    h. What is the probability that a randomly chosen bill is either from the East or for outpatient treatment (or both)?

    i. What is the probability that a randomly selected bill is either for hospitalization or from the South (or both)?

2–32. One of the greatest problems in marketing research and other survey fields is the problem of nonresponse to surveys. In home interviews the problem arises when the respondent is not home at the time of the visit or, sometimes, simply refuses to answer questions. A market researcher believes that a respondent will answer all questions with probability 0.94 if found at home. He further believes that the probability that a given person will be found at home is 0.65. Given this information, what percentage of the interviews will be successfully completed?

2–33. An investment analyst collects data on stocks and notes whether or not dividends were paid and whether or not the stocks increased in price over a given period. Data are presented in the following table.

	Price Increase	No Price Increase	Total
Dividends paid	34	78	112
No dividends paid	85	49	134
Total	119	127	246

    a. If a stock is selected at random out of the analyst's list of 246 stocks, what is the probability that it increased in price?

    b. If a stock is selected at random, what is the probability that it paid dividends?

    c. If a stock is randomly selected, what is the probability that it both increased in price and paid dividends?

    d. What is the probability that a randomly selected stock neither paid dividends nor increased in price?

    e. Given that a stock increased in price, what is the probability that it also paid dividends?

    f. If a stock is known not to have paid dividends, what is the probability that it increased in price?

    g. What is the probability that a randomly selected stock was worth holding during the period in question; that is, what is the probability that it increased in price or paid dividends or did both?

2–34. The following table lists the number of firms where the top executive officer made over \$1 million per year. The table also lists firms according to whether shareholder return was positive during the period in question.

	Top Executive Made More than \$1 Million	Top Executive Made Less than \$1 Million	Total
Shareholders made money	1	6	7
Shareholders lost money	2	1	3
Total	3	7	10

    a. If a firm is randomly chosen from the list of 10 firms studied, what is the probability that its top executive made over \$1 million per year?

    b. If a firm is randomly chosen from the list, what is the probability that its shareholders lost money during the period studied?

    c. Given that one of the firms in this group had negative shareholder return, what is the probability that its top executive made over \$1 million?

    d. Given that a firm's top executive made over \$1 million, what is the probability that the firm's shareholder return was positive?

2–35. According to *Fortune,* 90% of endangered species depend on forests for the habitat they provide.[7] If 30% of endangered species are in critical danger and depend on forests for their habitat, what is the probability that an endangered species that depends on forests is in critical danger?

---

[7]"Environmental Steward," *Fortune,* March 5, 2007, p. 54.

2–5   Independence of Events

In Example 2–4 we concluded that the probability that an executive made a top salary was lower when the executive was a woman, and we concluded that the two events T and W were *not* independent. We now give a formal definition of statistical independence of events.

Two events A and B are said to be *independent* of each other if and only if the following three conditions hold:

Conditions for the **independence of two events** A and B:

$$P(A \mid B) = P(A)$$
$$P(B \mid A) = P(B) \tag{2–9}$$

and, most useful:

$$P(A \cap B) = P(A)P(B) \tag{2–10}$$

The first two equations have a clear, intuitive appeal. The top equation says that when A and B are independent of each other, then the probability of A stays the same even when we know that B has occurred—it is a simple way of saying that knowledge of B tells us nothing about A when the two events are independent. Similarly, when A and B are independent, then knowledge that A has occurred gives us absolutely no information about B and its likelihood of occurring.

The third equation, however, is the most useful in applications. It tells us that when A and B are independent (and only when they are independent), we can obtain the probability of the joint occurrence of A and B (i.e., the probability of their intersection) simply by multiplying the two separate probabilities. This rule is thus called the **product rule** for independent events. (The rule is easily derived from the first rule, using the definition of conditional probability.)

As an example of independent events, consider the following: Suppose I roll a single die. What is the probability that the number 6 will turn up? The answer is 1/6. Now suppose that I told you that I just tossed a coin and it turned up heads. What is now the probability that the die will show the number 6? The answer is unchanged, 1/6, because events of the die and the coin are independent of each other. We see that $P(6 \mid H) = P(6)$, which is the first rule above.

In Example 2–2, we found that the probability that a project belongs to IBM given that it is in telecommunications is 0.2. We also knew that the probability that a project belongs to IBM was 0.4. Since these two numbers are not equal, the two events IBM and telecommunications are not independent.

When two events are not independent, neither are their complements. Therefore, AT&T and computers are not independent events (and neither are the other two possibilities).

EXAMPLE 2–5

The probability that a consumer will be exposed to an advertisement for a certain product by seeing a commercial on television is 0.04. The probability that the consumer will be exposed to the product by seeing an advertisement on a billboard is 0.06. The two events, being exposed to the commercial and being exposed to the billboard ad, are assumed to be independent. (*a*) What is the probability that the consumer will be exposed to both advertisements? (*b*) What is the probability that he or she will be exposed to at least one of the ads?

Solution

(*a*) Since the two events are independent, the probability of the intersection of the two (i.e., being exposed to *both* ads) is $P(A \cap B) = P(A)P(B) = 0.04 \times 0.06 = 0.0024$. (*b*) We note that being exposed to at least one of the advertisements is, by definition, the union of the two events, and so the rule for union applies. The probability of the intersection was computed above, and we have $P(A \cup B) = P(A) + P(B) - P(A \cap B) = 0.04 + 0.06 - 0.0024 = 0.0976$. The computation of such probabilities is important in advertising research. Probabilities are meaningful also as proportions of the population exposed to different modes of advertising, and are thus important in the evaluation of advertising efforts.

Product Rules for Independent Events

The rules for the union and the intersection of two independent events extend nicely to sequences of more than two events. These rules are very useful in **random sampling.**

Much of statistics involves random sampling from some population. When we sample randomly from a large population, or when we sample randomly with replacement from a population of any size, the elements are independent of one another. For example, suppose that we have an urn containing 10 balls, 3 of them red and the rest blue. We randomly sample one ball, note that it is red, and return it to the urn (this is sampling *with* replacement). What is the probability that a second ball we choose at random will be red? The answer is still 3/10 because the second drawing does not "remember" that the first ball was red. Sampling with replacement in this way ensures independence of the elements. The same holds for random sampling without replacement (i.e., without returning each element to the population before the next draw) *if* the population is relatively large in comparison with the size of the sample. Unless otherwise specified, we will assume random sampling from a large population.

Random sampling from a large population implies independence.

Intersection Rule

The probability of the intersection of several independent events is just the product of the separate probabilities.

The rate of defects in corks of wine bottles is very high, 75%. Assuming independence, if four bottles are opened, what is the probability that all four corks are defective? Using this rule: *P* (all 4 are defective) = *P* (first cork is defective) × *P* (second cork is defective) × *P* (third cork is defective) × *P* (fourth cork is defective) = 0.75 × 0.75 × 0.75 × 0.75 = 0.316.

If these four bottles were randomly selected, then we would not have to specify independence—a random sample always implies independence.

Union Rule

The probability of the union of several independent events—$A_1, A_2, ..., A_n$—is given by the following equation:

$$P(A_1 \cup A_2 \cup \cdots \cup A_n) = 1 - P(\bar{A}_1) P(\bar{A}_2) \cdots P(\bar{A}_n) \qquad (2\text{–}11)$$

The union of several events is the event that at least one of the events happens. In the example of the wine corks, suppose we want to find the probability that at least one of the four corks is defective. We compute this probability as follows: *P* (at least one is defective) = $1 - P$ (none are defective) = $1 - 0.25 \times 0.25 \times 0.25 \times 0.25 = 0.99609$.

EXAMPLE 2-6   Read the accompanying article. Three women (assumed a random sample) in a developing country are pregnant. What is the probability that at least one will die?

Poor Nations' Mothers at Serious Health Risk

In the industrialized world, a woman's odds of dying from problems related to pregnancy are 1 in 1,687. But in the developing world the figure is 1 in 51. The World Bank also says that each year 7 million newborns die within a week of birth because of maternal health problems. The bank and the United Nations are in the midst of an initiative to cut maternal illnesses and deaths.

Edward Epstein, "Poor Nations' Mothers at Serious Health Risk," World Insider, *San Francisco Chronicle*, August 10, 1993, p. A9. © 1993 San Francisco Chronicle. Reprinted by permission.

Solution

$$P(\text{at least 1 will die}) = 1 - P(\text{all 3 will survive}) = 1 - (50/51)^3 = 0.0577$$

EXAMPLE 2-7   A marketing research firm is interested in interviewing a consumer who fits certain qualifications, for example, use of a certain product. The firm knows that 10% of the public in a certain area use the product and would thus qualify to be interviewed. The company selects a random sample of 10 people from the population as a whole. What is the probability that at least 1 of these 10 people qualifies to be interviewed?

Solution   First, we note that if a sample is drawn at random, then the event that any one of the items in the sample fits the qualifications is independent of the other items in the sample. This is an important property in statistics. Let Q_i, where $i = 1, 2, \ldots, 10$, be the event that person i qualifies. Then the probability that at least 1 of the 10 people will qualify is the probability of the union of the 10 events Q_i ($i = 1, \ldots, 10$). We are thus looking for $P(Q_1 \cup Q_2 \cup \cdots \cup Q_{10})$.

Now, since 10% of the people qualify, the probability that person i does not qualify, or $P(\overline{Q}_i)$, is equal to 0.90 for each $i = 1, \ldots, 10$. Therefore, the required probability is equal to $1 - (0.9)(0.9) \cdots (0.9)$ (10 times), or $1 - (0.9)^{10}$. This is equal to 0.6513.

Be sure that you understand the difference between *independent* events and *mutually exclusive* events. Although these two concepts are very different, they often cause some confusion when introduced. When two events are mutually exclusive, they are *not* independent. In fact, they are dependent events in the sense that if one happens, the other one cannot happen. The probability of the intersection of two mutually exclusive events is equal to zero. The probability of the intersection of two independent events is *not* zero; it is equal to the product of the probabilities of the separate events.

2–36. According to *USA Today,* 65% of Americans are overweight or obese.[8] If five Americans are chosen at random, what is the probability that at least one of them is overweight or obese?

2–37. The chancellor of a state university is applying for a new position. At a certain point in his application process, he is being considered by seven universities. At three of the seven he is a finalist, which means that (at each of the three universities) he is in the final group of three applicants, one of which will be chosen for the position. At two of the seven universities he is a semifinalist, that is, one of six candidates (in each of the two universities). In two universities he is at an early stage of his application and believes there is a pool of about 20 candidates for each of the two positions. Assuming that there is no exchange of information, or influence, across universities as to their hiring decisions, and that the chancellor is as likely to be chosen as any other applicant, what is the chancellor's probability of getting at least one job offer?

2–38. A package of documents needs to be sent to a given destination, and delivery within one day is important. To maximize the chances of on-time delivery, three copies of the documents are sent via three different delivery services. Service A is known to have a 90% on-time delivery record, service B has an 88% on-time delivery record, and service C has a 91% on-time delivery record. What is the probability that at least one copy of the documents will arrive at its destination on time?

2–39. The projected probability of increase in online holiday sales from 2004 to 2005 is 95% in the United States, 90% in Australia, and 85% in Japan. Assume these probabilities are independent. What is the probability that holiday sales will increase in all three countries from 2004 to 2005?

2–40. An electronic device is made up of two components A and B such that the device would work satisfactorily as long as at least one of the components works. The probability of failure of component A is 0.02 and that of B is 0.1 in some fixed period of time. If the components work independently, find the probability that the device will work satisfactorily during the period.

2–41. A recent survey conducted by Towers Perrin and published in the *Financial Times* showed that among 460 organizations in 13 European countries, 93% have bonus plans, 55% have cafeteria-style benefits, and 70% employ home-based workers. If the types of benefits are independent, what is the probability that an organization selected at random will have at least one of the three types of benefits?

2–42. Credit derivatives are a new kind of investment instrument: they protect investors from risk.[9] If such an investment offered by ABN Amro has a 90% chance of making money, another by AXA has a 75% chance of success, and one by the ING Group has a 60% chance of being profitable, and the three are independent of each other, what is the chance that at least one investment will make money?

2–43. In problem 2–42, suppose that American investment institutions enter this new market, and that their probabilities for successful instruments are:

Goldman Sachs	70%
Salomon Brothers	82%
Fidelity	80%
Smith Barney	90%

What is the probability that at least one of these four instruments is successful? Assume independence.

---

[8]Nancy Hellmich, "A Nation of Obesity," *USA Today,* October 14, 2003, p. 7D.

[9] John Ferry, "Gimme Shelter," *Worth,* April 2007, pp. 88–90.

2–44. In problem 2–31, are the events "hospitalization" and "the claim being from the Midwest" independent of each other?

2–45. In problem 2–33, are "dividends paid" and "price increase" independent events?

2–46. In problem 2–34, are the events "top executive made more than $1 million" and "shareholders lost money" independent of each other? If this is true for all firms, how would you interpret your finding?

2–47. The accompanying table shows the incidence of malaria and two other similar illnesses. If a person lives in an area affected by all three diseases, what is the probability that he or she will develop at least one of the three illnesses? (Assume that contracting one disease is an event independent from contracting any other disease.)

	Cases	Number at Risk (Millions)
Malaria	110 million per year	2,100
Schistosomiasis	200 million	600
Sleeping sickness	25,000 per year	50

2–48. A device has three components and works as long as at least one of the components is functional. The reliabilities of the components are 0.96, 0.91, and 0.80. What is the probability that the device will work when needed?

2–49. In 2003, there were 5,732 deaths from car accidents in France.[10] The population of France is 59,625,919. If I am going to live in France for five years, what is my probability of dying in a car crash?

2–50. The probabilities that three drivers will be able to drive home safely after drinking are 0.5, 0.25, and 0.2, respectively. If they set out to drive home after drinking at a party, what is the probability that at least one driver drives home safely?

2–51. When one is randomly sampling four items from a population, what is the probability that all four elements will come from the top quartile of the population distribution? What is the probability that at least one of the four elements will come from the bottom quartile of the distribution?

2–6 Combinatorial Concepts

In this section we briefly discuss a few combinatorial concepts and give some formulas useful in the analysis. The interested reader may find more on combinatorial rules and their applications in the classic book by W. Feller or in other books on probability.[11]

> If there are n events and event i can occur in N_i possible ways, then the number of ways in which the sequence of n events may occur is $N_1 N_2 \cdots N_n$.

Suppose that a bank has two branches, each branch has two departments, and each department has three employees. Then there are $(2)(2)(3)$ choices of employees, and the probability that a particular one will be randomly selected is $1/(2)(2)(3) = 1/12$.

We may view the choice as done sequentially: First a branch is randomly chosen, then a department within the branch, and then the employee within the department. This is demonstrated in the tree diagram in Figure 2–8.

> For any positive integer n, we define n **factorial** as

$$n(n - 1)(n - 2) \cdots 1$$

> We denote n factorial by $n!$. The number $n!$ is the number of ways in which n objects can be ordered. By definition, $0! = 1$.

[10]Elaine Sciolino, "Garçon! The Check, Please, and Wrap Up the Bordelais!," *The New York Times,* January 26, 2004, p. A4.

[11]William Feller, *An Introduction to Probability Theory and Its Applications,* vol. I, 3d ed. (New York: John Wiley & Sons, 1968).

FIGURE 2–8   Tree Diagram for Computing the Total Number of Employees by Multiplication

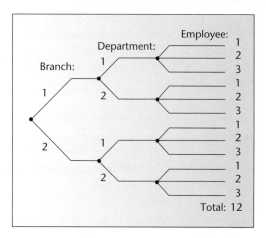

For example, 6! is the number of possible arrangements of six objects. We have 6! = (6)(5)(4)(3)(2)(1) = 720. Suppose that six applications arrive at a center on the same day, all written at different times. What is the probability that they will be read in the order in which they were written? Since there are 720 ways to order six applications, the probability of a particular order (the order in which the applications were written) is 1/720.

Permutations are the possible ordered selections of r objects out of a total of n objects. The number of permutations of n objects taken r at a time is denoted $n\mathbf{P}r$.

$$n\mathbf{P}r = \frac{n!}{(n - r)!} \qquad (2\text{--}12)$$

Suppose that 4 people are to be randomly chosen out of 10 people who agreed to be interviewed in a market survey. The four people are to be assigned to four interviewers. How many possibilities are there? The first interviewer has 10 choices, the second 9 choices, the third 8, and the fourth 7. Thus, there are $(10)(9)(8)(7) = 5,040$ selections. You can see that this is equal to $n(n - 1)(n - 2) \cdots (n - r + 1)$, which is equal to $n!/(n - r)!$. If choices are made randomly, the probability of any predetermined assignment of 4 people out of a group of 10 is 1/5,040.

Combinations are the possible selections of r items from a group of n items regardless of the order of selection. The number of combinations is denoted by $\binom{n}{r}$ and is read n choose r. An alternative notation is $n\mathbf{C}r$. We define the number of combinations of r out of n elements as

$$\binom{n}{r} = \frac{n!}{r!(n - r)!} \qquad (2\text{--}13)$$

This is the most important of the combinatorial rules given in this chapter and is the only one we will use extensively. This rule is basic to the formula of the binomial distribution presented in the next chapter and will find use also in other chapters.

Suppose that 3 out of the 10 members of the board of directors of a large corporation are to be randomly selected to serve on a particular task committee. How many possible selections are there? Using equation 2–13, we find that the number of combinations is $\binom{10}{3} = 10!/(3!7!) = 120$. If the committee is chosen in a truly random fashion, what is the probability that the three committee members chosen will be the three senior board members? This is 1 combination out of a total of 120, so the answer is $1/120 = 0.00833$.

EXAMPLE 2–8   A certain university held a meeting of administrators and faculty members to discuss some important issues of concern to both groups. Out of eight members, two were faculty, and both were missing from the meeting. If two members are absent, what is the probability that they should be the two faculty members?

Solution   By definition, there are $\binom{8}{2}$ ways of selecting two people out of a total of eight people, disregarding the order of selection. Only one of these ways corresponds to the pair's being the two faculty members. Hence, the probability is $1/\binom{8}{2} = 1/[8!/(2!6!)] = 1/28 = 0.0357$. This assumes randomness.

PROBLEMS

2–52. A company has four departments: manufacturing, distribution, marketing, and management. The number of people in each department is 55, 30, 21, and 13, respectively. Each department is expected to send one representative to a meeting with the company president. How many possible sets of representatives are there?

2–53. Nine sealed bids for oil drilling leases arrive at a regulatory agency in the morning mail. In how many different orders can the nine bids be opened?

2–54. Fifteen locations in a given area are believed likely to have oil. An oil company can only afford to drill at eight sites, sequentially chosen. How many possibilities are there, in order of selection?

2–55. A committee is evaluating six equally qualified candidates for a job. Only three of the six will be invited for an interview; among the chosen three, the order of invitation is of importance because the first candidate will have the best chance of being accepted, the second will be made an offer only if the committee rejects the first, and the third will be made an offer only if the committee should reject both the first and the second. How many possible ordered choices of three out of six candidates are there?

2–56. In the analysis of variance (discussed in Chapter 9) we compare several population means to see which is largest. After the primary analysis, pairwise comparisons are made. If we want to compare seven populations, each with all the others, how many pairs are there? (We are looking for the number of choices of seven items taken two at a time, regardless of order.)

2–57. In a shipment of 14 computer parts, 3 are faulty and the remaining 11 are in working order. Three elements are randomly chosen out of the shipment. What is the probability that all three faulty elements will be the ones chosen?

2–58. Megabucks is a lottery game played in Massachusetts with the following rules. A random drawing of 6 numbers out of all 36 numbers from 1 to 36 is made every Wednesday and every Saturday. The game costs $1 to play, and to win a person must have the correct six numbers drawn, regardless of their order. (The numbers are sequentially drawn from a bin and are arranged from smallest to largest. When a player buys a ticket prior to the drawing, the player must also arrange his or her chosen numbers in ascending order.) The jackpot depends on the number of players and is usually worth several million dollars. What is the probability of winning the jackpot?

2–59. In Megabucks, a player who correctly chooses five out of the six winning numbers gets $400. What is the probability of winning $400?

2–7 The Law of Total Probability and Bayes' Theorem

In this section we present two useful results of probability theory. The first one, **the law of total probability,** allows us at times to evaluate probabilities of events that are difficult to obtain alone, but become easy to calculate once we *condition* on the occurrence of a related event. First we assume that the related event occurs, and then we assume it does not occur. The resulting conditional probabilities help us compute the total probability of occurrence of the event of interest.

The second rule, the famous **Bayes' theorem,** is easily derived from the law of total probability and the definition of conditional probability. The rule, discovered in 1761 by the English clergyman Thomas Bayes, has had a profound impact on the development of statistics and is responsible for the emergence of a new philosophy of science. Bayes himself is said to have been unsure of his extraordinary result, which was presented to the Royal Society by a friend in 1763—after Bayes' death.

The Law of Total Probability

Consider two events A and B. Whatever may be the relation between the two events, we can *always* say that the probability of A is equal to the probability of the intersection of A and B, plus the probability of the intersection of A and the complement of B (event $\overline{B}$).

The law of total probability:

$$P(A) = P(A \cap B) + P(A \cap \overline{B}) \tag{2–14}$$

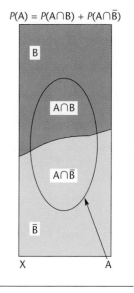

FIGURE 2–9
Partition of Set A into Its Intersections with the Two Sets B and $\overline{B}$, and the Implied Law of Total Probability

$P(A) = P(A \cap B) + P(A \cap \overline{B})$

The sets B and $\overline{B}$ form a **partition** of the sample space. A partition of a space is the division of the space into a set of events that are mutually exclusive (disjoint sets) and cover the whole space. Whatever event B may be, either B or $\overline{B}$ must occur, but not both. Figure 2–9 demonstrates this situation and the law of total probability.

The law of total probability may be extended to more complex situations, where the sample space X is partitioned into more than two events. Say we partition the space into a collection of n sets $B_1, B_2, \ldots, B_n$. The law of total probability in this situation is

$$P(A) = \sum_{i=1}^{n} P(A \cap B_i) \tag{2–15}$$

Figure 2–10 shows the partition of a sample space into the four events B_1, B_2, B_3, and B_4 and shows their intersections with set A.

We demonstrate the rule with a more specific example. Define A as the event that a picture card is drawn out of a deck of 52 cards (the picture cards are the aces, kings, queens, and jacks). Letting H, C, D, and S denote the events that the card drawn is a heart, club, diamond, or spade, respectively, we find that the probability of a picture

FIGURE 2–10   The Partition of Set A into Its Intersection with Four Partition Sets

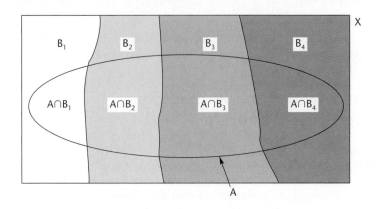

FIGURE 2–11   The Total Probability of Drawing a Picture Card as the Sum of the Probabilities of Drawing a Card in the Intersections of Picture and Suit

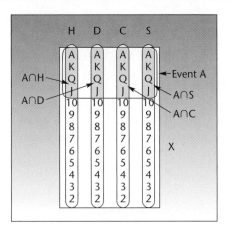

card is $P(A) = P(A \cap H) + P(A \cap C) + P(A \cap D) + P(A \cap S) = 4/52 + 4/52 + 4/52 + 4/52 = 16/52$, which is what we know the probability of a picture card to be just by counting 16 picture cards out of a total of 52 cards in the deck. This demonstrates equation 2–15. The situation is shown in Figure 2–11. As can be seen from the figure, the event A is the set addition of the intersections of A with each of the four sets H, D, C, and S. Note that in these examples we denote the sample space X.

The law of total probability can be extended by using the definition of conditional probability. Recall that $P(A \cap B) = P(A \mid B)P(B)$ (equation 2–8) and, similarly, $P(A \cap \overline{B}) = P(A \mid \overline{B})P(\overline{B})$. Substituting these relationships into equation 2–14 gives us another form of the law of total probability. This law and its extension to a partition consisting of more than two sets are given in equations 2–16 and 2–17. In equation 2–17, we have a set of conditioning events B_i that span the entire sample space, instead of just two events spanning it, B and $\overline{B}$.

The **law of total probability** using conditional probabilities:

Two-set case:

$$P(A) = P(A \mid B)P(B) + P(A \mid \overline{B})P(\overline{B}) \qquad (2–16)$$

More than two sets in the partition:

$$P(A) = \sum_{i=1}^{n} P(A|B_i)P(B_i) \qquad (2\text{--}17)$$

where there are n sets in the partition: B_i, $i = 1, \ldots, n$.

An analyst believes the stock market has a 0.75 probability of going up in the next year if the economy should do well, and a 0.30 probability of going up if the economy should not do well during the year. The analyst further believes there is a 0.80 probability that the economy will do well in the coming year. What is the probability that the stock market will go up next year (using the analyst's assessments)?

EXAMPLE 2–9

We define U as the event that the market will go up and W as the event the economy will do well. Using equation 2–16, we find $P(U) = P(U \mid W)P(W) + P(U \mid \overline{W})P(\overline{W}) = (0.75)(0.80) + (0.30)(0.20) = 0.66$.

Solution

Bayes' Theorem

We now develop the well-known Bayes' theorem. The theorem allows us to reverse the conditionality of events: we can obtain the probability of B given A from the probability of A given B (and other information).

By the definition of conditional probability, equation 2–7,

$$P(B|A) = \frac{P(A \cap B)}{P(A)} \qquad (2\text{--}18)$$

By another form of the same definition, equation 2–8,

$$P(A \cap B) = P(A \mid B)P(B) \qquad (2\text{--}19)$$

Substituting equation 2–19 into equation 2–18 gives

$$P(B|A) = \frac{P(A|B)P(B)}{P(A)} \qquad (2\text{--}20)$$

From the law of total probability using conditional probabilities, equation 2–16, we have

$$P(A) = P(A|B)P(B) + P(A|\overline{B})P(\overline{B})$$

Substituting this expression for $P(A)$ in the denominator of equation 2–20 gives us Bayes' theorem.

Bayes' Theorem

$$P(B|A) = \frac{P(A|B)P(B)}{P(A|B)P(B) + P(A|\overline{B})P(\overline{B})} \qquad (2\text{--}21)$$

As we see from the theorem, the probability of B given A is obtained from the probabilities of B and $\overline{B}$ and from the conditional probabilities of A given B and A given $\overline{B}$.

The probabilities $P(B)$ and $P(\overline{B})$ are called **prior probabilities** of the events B and $\overline{B}$; the probability $P(B|A)$ is called the **posterior probability** of B. Bayes' theorem may be written in terms of $\overline{B}$ and A, thus giving the posterior probability of $\overline{B}$, $P(\overline{B}|A)$. Bayes' theorem may be viewed as a means of transforming our prior probability of an event B into a posterior probability of the event B—posterior to the known occurrence of event A.

The use of prior probabilities in conjunction with other information—often obtained from experimentation—has been questioned. The controversy arises in more involved statistical situations where Bayes' theorem is used in mixing the objective information obtained from sampling with prior information that could be subjective. We will explore this topic in greater detail in Chapter 15. We now give some examples of the use of the |.

EXAMPLE 2–10

Consider a test for an illness. The test has a known reliability:

1. When administered to an ill person, the test will indicate so with probability 0.92.
2. When administered to a person who is not ill, the test will erroneously give a positive result with probability 0.04.

Suppose the illness is rare and is known to affect only 0.1% of the entire population. If a person is randomly selected from the entire population and is given the test and the result is positive, what is the posterior probability (posterior to the test result) that the person is ill?

Solution

Let Z denote the event that the test result is positive and I the event that the person tested is ill. The preceding information gives us the following probabilities of events:

$$P(I) = 0.001 \qquad P(\overline{I}) = 0.999 \qquad P(Z|I) = 0.92 \qquad P(Z|\overline{I}) = 0.04$$

We are looking for the probability that the person is ill given a positive test result; that is, we need $P(I|Z)$. Since we have the probability with the reversed conditionality, $P(Z|I)$, we know that Bayes' theorem is the rule to be used here. Applying the rule, equation 2–21, to the events Z, I, and $\overline{I}$, we get

$$P(I|Z) = \frac{P(Z|I)P(I)}{P(Z|I)P(I) + P(Z|\overline{I})P(\overline{I})} = \frac{(0.92)(0.001)}{(0.92)(0.001) + (0.04)(0.999)}$$

$$= 0.0225$$

This result may surprise you. A test with a relatively high reliability (92% correct diagnosis when a person is ill and 96% correct identification of people who are not ill) is administered to a person, the result is positive, and yet the probability that the person is actually ill is only 0.0225!

The reason for the low probability is that we have used two sources of information here: the reliability of the test and the very small probability (0.001) that a randomly selected person is ill. The two pieces of information were mixed by Bayes' theorem, and the posterior probability reflects the mixing of the high reliability of the test with the fact that the illness is rare. The result is perfectly correct as long as the information we have used is accurate. Indeed, subject to the accuracy of our information, if the test were administered to a large number of people selected randomly from the entire population, it would be found that about 2.25% of the people in the sample who test positive are indeed ill.

Problems with Bayes' theorem arise when we are not careful with the use of prior information. In this example, suppose the test is administered to people in a hospital. Since people in a hospital are more likely to be ill than people in the population as a whole, the overall population probability that a person is ill, 0.001, no longer applies. If we applied this low probability in the hospital, our results would not be correct. This caution extends to all situations where prior probabilities are used: We must always examine the appropriateness of the prior probabilities.

Bayes' theorem may be extended to a partition of more than two sets. This is done using equation 2–17, the law of total probability involving a partition of sets B_1, $B_2, \ldots, B_n$. The resulting extended form of Bayes' theorem is given in equation 2–22. The theorem gives the probability of one of the sets in partition B_1 given the occurrence of event A. A similar expression holds for any of the events B_i.

Extended Bayes' Theorem

$$P(B_1|A) = \frac{P(A|B_1)P(B_1)}{\sum\limits_{i=1}^{n} P(A|B_i)P(B_i)} \qquad (2\text{–}22)$$

We demonstrate the use of equation 2–22 with the following example. In the solution, we use a table format to facilitate computations. We also demonstrate the computations using a tree diagram.

An economist believes that during periods of high economic growth, the U.S. dollar appreciates with probability 0.70; in periods of moderate economic growth, the dollar appreciates with probability 0.40; and during periods of low economic growth, the dollar appreciates with probability 0.20. During any period of time, the probability of high economic growth is 0.30, the probability of moderate growth is 0.50, and the probability of low economic growth is 0.20. Suppose the dollar has been appreciating during the present period. What is the probability we are experiencing a period of high economic growth?

EXAMPLE 2–11

Figure 2–12 shows solution by template. Below is the manual solution.

Solution

Our partition consists of three events: high economic growth (event H), moderate economic growth (event M), and low economic growth (event L). The prior probabilities of the three states are $P(H) = 0.30$, $P(M) = 0.50$, and $P(L) = 0.20$. Let A denote

FIGURE 2–12   Bayesian Revision of Probabilities
[Bayes Revision.xls; Sheet: Empirical]

	A	B	C	D	E	F	G	H	I	J	K	L	M
1	Bayesian Revision based on Empirical Conditional Probabilities									Example 2-11			
2													
3			High	Moderate	Low								
4			s1	s2	s3	s4	s5	s6	s7	s8		Total	
5	Prior Probability		0.3	0.5	0.2							1	
6													
7		Conditional Probabilities											
8			s1	s2	s3	s4	s5	s6	s7	s8			
9	$ Appreciates	P(I1 | .)	0.7	0.4	0.2								
10	$ Depreciates	P(I2 | .)	0.3	0.6	0.8								
11		P(I3 | .)											
12		P(I4 | .)											
13		P(I5 | .)											
14		Total	1	1	1	0	0	0	0	0			
15													
16		Joint Probabilities											
17			s1	s2	s3	s4	s5	s6	s7	s8		Marginal	
18		I1	0.2100	0.2000	0.0400							0.4500	
19		I2	0.0900	0.3000	0.1600							0.5500	
20		I3											
21		I4											
22		I5											
23													
24		Posterior Probabilities											
25			s1	s2	s3	s4	s5	s6	s7	s8			
26		P(. | I1)	0.4667	0.4444	0.0889								
27		P(. | I2)	0.1636	0.5455	0.2909								
28		P(. | I3)											
29		P(. | I4)											
30		P(. | I5)											

the event that the dollar appreciates. We have the following conditional probabilities: $P(A \mid H) = 0.70$, $P(A \mid M) = 0.40$, and $P(A \mid L) = 0.20$. Applying equation 2–22 while using three sets $(n = 3)$, we get

$$
\begin{aligned}
P(H \mid A) &= \frac{P(A \mid H)P(H)}{P(A \mid H)P(H) + P(A \mid M)P(M) + P(A \mid L)P(L)} \\
&= \frac{(0.70)(0.30)}{(0.70)(0.30) + (0.40)(0.50) + (0.20)(0.20)} = 0.467
\end{aligned}
$$

We can obtain this answer, along with the posterior probabilities of the other two states, M and L, by using a table. In the first column of the table we write the prior probabilities of the three states H, M, and L. In the second column we write the three conditional probabilities $P(A \mid H)$, $P(A \mid M)$, and $P(A \mid L)$. In the third column we write the joint probabilities $P(A \cap H)$, $P(A \cap M)$, and $P(A \cap L)$. The joint probabilities are obtained by multiplying across in each of the three rows (these operations make use of equation 2–8). The sum of the entries in the third column is the total probability of event A (by equation 2–15). Finally, the posterior probabilities $P(H \mid A)$, $P(M \mid A)$, and $P(L \mid A)$ are obtained by dividing the appropriate joint probability by the total probability of A at the bottom of the third column. For example, $P(H \mid A)$ is obtained by dividing $P(H \cap A)$ by the probability $P(A)$. The operations and the results are given in Table 2–1 and demonstrated in Figure 2–13.

Note that both the prior probabilities and the posterior probabilities of the three states add to 1.00, as required for probabilities of all the possibilities in a

TABLE 2–1   Bayesian Revision of Probabilities for Example 2–11

Event	Prior Probability	Conditional Probability	Joint Probability	Posterior Probability
H	$P(H) = 0.30$	$P(A \mid H) = 0.70$	$P(A \cap H) = 0.21$	$P(H \mid A) = \dfrac{0.21}{0.45} = 0.467$
M	$P(M) = 0.50$	$P(A \mid M) = 0.40$	$P(A \cap M) = 0.20$	$P(M \mid A) = \dfrac{0.20}{0.45} = 0.444$
L	$P(L) = 0.20$	$P(A \mid L) = 0.20$	$P(A \cap L) = 0.04$	$P(L \mid A) = \dfrac{0.04}{0.45} = 0.089$
	Sum $= \overline{1.00}$		$P(A) = 0.45$	Sum $= \overline{1.000}$

FIGURE 2–13   Tree Diagram for Example 2–11

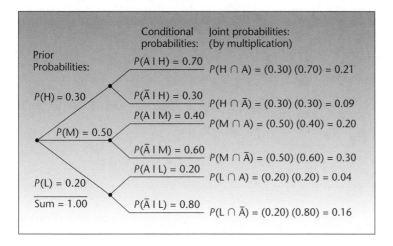

given situation. We conclude that, given that the dollar has been appreciating, the probability that our period is one of high economic growth is 0.467, the probability that it is one of moderate growth is 0.444, and the probability that our period is one of low economic growth is 0.089. The advantage of using a table is that we can obtain all posterior probabilities at once. If we use the formula directly, we need to apply it once for the posterior probability of each state.

2–8   The Joint Probability Table

A **joint probability table** is similar to a contingency table, except that it has probabilities in place of frequencies. For example, the case in Example 2–11 can be summarized with the joint probabilities shown in Table 2–2. The body of the table can be visualized as the sample space partitioned into row-events and column-events.

TABLE 2–2   Joint Probability Table

	High	Medium	Low	Total
$ Appreciates	0.21	0.2	0.04	0.45
$ Depreciates	0.09	0.3	0.16	0.55
Total	0.3	0.5	0.2	1

Every cell is a joint event of that row and column. Thus the joint probability of High and $ Appreciates is 0.21.

The row totals and column totals are known as **marginal probabilities.** For example, the marginal probability of the event "High" is 0.3. In Example 2–11, this was the prior probability of High. The marginal probability of the event "$ Appreciates" is 0.45. The computations shown in Table 2–1 yield the top row of values in the joint probability table. Knowing the column totals (which are the prior or marginal probabilities of High, Medium, and Low), we can quickly infer the second row of values.

The joint probability table is also a clear means to compute conditional probabilities. For example, the conditional probability that $ Appreciates when economic growth is High can be computed using the Bayes' formula:

$$P(\$ \text{ Appreciates} \,|\, \text{High}) \;=\; \frac{P(\$ \text{ Appreciates } and \text{ High})}{P(\text{High})}$$

Note that the numerator in the formula is a joint probability and the denominator is a marginal probability.

$$P(\$ \text{ Appreciates} \,|\, \text{High}) \;=\; \frac{0.21}{0.45} = 0.467$$

which is the posterior probability sought in Example 2–11.

If you use the template Bayesian Revision.xls to solve a problem, you will note that the template produces the joint probability table in the range C18:J22. It also computes all marginal and all conditional probabilities.

2–9   Using the Computer

Excel Templates and Formulas

Figure 2–14 shows the template which is used for calculating joint, marginal, and conditional probabilities starting from a contingency table. If the starting point is a joint probability table, rather than a contingency table, this template can still be used. Enter the joint probability table in place of the contingency table.

The user needs to know how to read off the conditional probabilities from this template. The conditional probability of 0.6667 in cell C23 is $P(\text{Telecom} \,|\, \text{AT\&T})$, which is the row label in cell B23 and the column label in cell C22 put together. Similarly, the conditional probability of 0.8000 in cell K14 is $P(\text{AT\&T} \,|\, \text{Telecom})$.

Figure 2–12 shows the template that can be used to solve conditional probability problems using Bayes' revision of probabilities. It was used to solve Example 2–11.

In addition to the template mentioned above, you can also directly use Excel functions for some of the calculations in this chapter. For example, functions COMBIN (number of items, number to choose) and PERMUT (number of items, number to choose) are used to provide us with the number of combinations and permutations of the number of items chosen some at a time. The function FACT (number) also returns the factorial of a number. The numeric arguments of all these functions should be nonnegative, and they will be truncated if they are not integers. Note that the entries in the range C10:E10 of probabilities of the dollar depreciating have been

FIGURE 2–14   Template for Calculating Probabilities from a Contingency Table
[Contingency Table.xls]

	A	B	C	D	E	F	G	H	I	J	K	L	M
1		Contingency Table and Conditional Probabilities								Title			
2													
3		Contingency Table											
4			AT&T	IBM				Total					
5		Telecom	40	10				50					
6		Comp	20	30				50					
7													
8													
9													
10		Total	60	40				100					
11													
12		Joint Probabilities								Row-Conditional Probabilities			
13			AT&T	IBM				Marginal			P(AT&T	P(IBM	
14		Telecom	0.4000	0.1000				0.5000		|Telecom)	0.8000	0.2000	
15		Comp	0.2000	0.3000				0.5000		|Comp)	0.4000	0.6000	
16													
17													
18													
19		Marginal	0.6000	0.4000				1.0000					
20													
21		Column-Conditional Probabilities											
22			|AT&T)	|IBM)								
23		P(Telecom	0.6667	0.2500									
24		P(comp	0.3333	0.7500									
25													
26													
27													
28													

entered for completeness. The questions in the example can be answered without those entries.

Using MINITAB

We can use **MINITAB** to find a large number of arithmetic operations such as factorial, combination, and permutation. The command `Let C1 = FACTORIAL(n)` calculates n factorial $(n!)$, the product of all the consecutive integers from 1 to n inclusive, and puts the result in the first cell of column C1. The value of n (**number of items**) must be greater than or equal to 0. You can enter a column or constant and missing values are not allowed. You can also use the menu by choosing Calc ▶ Calculator. In the list of functions choose FACTORIAL and then specify the number of items. You need also define the name of the variable that will store the result, for example, C1, then press OK.

The command `Let C1 = COMBINATIONS(n,k)` calculates the number of combinations of n items chosen k at a time. You can specify the **number of items** (n) and the **number to choose** (k) as columns or constants. The **number of items** must be greater than or equal to 1, and the **number to choose** must be greater than or equal to 0. Missing values are not allowed. The same as before, you can use menu Calc ▶ Calculator and choose COMBINATIONS in the list of functions. Then specify the number of items, the number to choose, and the name of the variable that will store the results. Then press OK.

The next command is `Let C1 = PERMUTATIONS(n,k)`, which calculates the number of permutations of n things taken k at a time. Specify the **number of items** (n) and the **number to choose** (k). The **number of items** must be greater than or equal to 1, and the **number to choose** must be greater than or equal to 0. Missing values are not allowed.

Figure 2–15 shows how we can use session commands and the menu to obtain permutations and combinations.

FIGURE 2–15   Using MINITAB for Permutation and Combination Problems

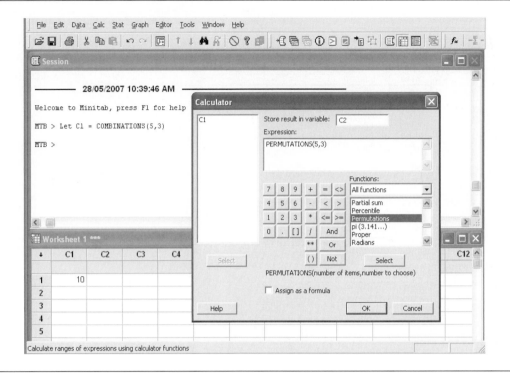

2–60.   In a takeover bid for a certain company, management of the raiding firm believes that the takeover has a 0.65 probability of success if a member of the board of the raided firm resigns, and a 0.30 chance of success if she does not resign. Management of the raiding firm further believes that the chances for a resignation of the member in question are 0.70. What is the probability of a successful takeover?

2–61.   A drug manufacturer believes there is a 0.95 chance that the Food and Drug Administration (FDA) will approve a new drug the company plans to distribute if the results of current testing show that the drug causes no side effects. The manufacturer further believes there is a 0.50 probability that the FDA will approve the drug if the test shows that the drug does cause side effects. A physician working for the drug manufacturer believes there is a 0.20 probability that tests will show that the drug causes side effects. What is the probability that the drug will be approved by the FDA?

2–62.   An import–export firm has a 0.45 chance of concluding a deal to export agricultural equipment to a developing nation if a major competitor does not bid for the contract, and a 0.25 probability of concluding the deal if the competitor does bid for it. It is estimated that the competitor will submit a bid for the contract with probability 0.40. What is the probability of getting the deal?

2–63.   A realtor is trying to sell a large piece of property. She believes there is a 0.90 probability that the property will be sold in the next 6 months if the local economy continues to improve throughout the period, and a 0.50 probability the property will be sold if the local economy does not continue its improvement during the period. A state economist consulted by the realtor believes there is a 0.70 chance the economy will continue its improvement during the next 6 months. What is the probability that the piece of property will be sold during the period?

2–64. Holland America Cruise Lines has three luxury cruise ships that sail to Alaska during the summer months. Since the business is very competitive, the ships must run full during the summer if the company is to turn a profit on this line. A tourism expert hired by Holland America believes there is a 0.92 chance the ships will sail full during the coming summer if the dollar does not appreciate against European currencies, and a 0.75 chance they will sail full if the dollar does appreciate in Europe (appreciation of the dollar in Europe draws U.S. tourists there, away from U.S. destinations). Economists believe the dollar has a 0.23 chance of appreciating against European currencies soon. What is the probability the ships will sail full?

2–65. Saflok is an electronic door lock system made in Troy, Michigan, and used in modern hotels and other establishments. To open a door, you must insert the electronic card into the lock slip. Then a green light indicates that you can turn the handle and enter; a yellow light indicates that the door is locked from inside, and you cannot enter. Suppose that 90% of the time when the card is inserted, the door should open because it is not locked from inside. When the door should open, a green light will appear with probability 0.98. When the door should not open, a green light may still appear (an electronic error) 5% of the time. Suppose that you just inserted the card and the light is green. What is the probability that the door will actually open?

2–66. A chemical plant has an emergency alarm system. When an emergency situation exists, the alarm sounds with probability 0.95. When an emergency situation does not exist, the alarm system sounds with probability 0.02. A real emergency situation is a rare event, with probability 0.004. Given that the alarm has just sounded, what is the probability that a real emergency situation exists?

2–67. When the economic situation is "high," a certain economic indicator rises with probability 0.6. When the economic situation is "medium," the economic indicator rises with probability 0.3. When the economic situation is "low," the indicator rises with probability 0.1. The economy is high 15% of the time, it is medium 70% of the time, and it is low 15% of the time. Given that the indicator has just gone up, what is the probability that the economic situation is high?

2–68. An oil explorer orders seismic tests to determine whether oil is likely to be found in a certain drilling area. The seismic tests have a known reliability: When oil does exist in the testing area, the test will indicate so 85% of the time; when oil does not exist in the test area, 10% of the time the test will erroneously indicate that it does exist. The explorer believes that the probability of existence of an oil deposit in the test area is 0.4. If a test is conducted and indicates the presence of oil, what is the probability that an oil deposit really exists?

2–69. Before marketing new products nationally, companies often test them on samples of potential customers. Such tests have a known reliability. For a particular product type, a test will indicate success of the product 75% of the time if the product is indeed successful and 15% of the time when the product is not successful. From past experience with similar products, a company knows that a new product has a 0.60 chance of success on the national market. If the test indicates that the product will be successful, what is the probability that it really will be successful?

2–70. A market research field worker needs to interview married couples about use of a certain product. The researcher arrives at a residential building with three apartments. From the names on the mailboxes downstairs, the interviewer infers that a married couple lives in one apartment, two men live in another, and two women live in the third apartment. The researcher goes upstairs and finds that there are no names or numbers on the three doors, so that it is impossible to tell in which of the three apartments the married couple lives. The researcher chooses a door at random and knocks. A woman answers the door. Having seen a woman at the door, what *now* is the probability of having reached the married couple? Make the (possibly unrealistic) assumptions that if the two men's apartment was reached, a woman cannot answer the door; if the two women's apartment was reached, then only a woman can answer; and that if the married couple was reached, then the probability of a woman at the door is 1/2. Also assume a 1/3 prior probability of reaching the married couple. Are you surprised by the numerical answer you obtained?

2–10   Summary and Review of Terms

In this chapter, we discussed the basic ideas of probability. We defined **probability** as a relative measure of our belief in the occurrence of an **event**. We defined a **sample space** as the set of all possible outcomes in a given situation and saw that an event is a set within the sample space. We set some rules for handling probabilities: the **rule of unions**, the definition of **conditional probability**, the **law of total probability**, and **Bayes' theorem**. We also defined **mutually exclusive events** and **independence of events**. We saw how certain computations are possible in the case of independent events, and we saw how we may test whether events are independent.

In the next chapter, we will extend the ideas of probability and discuss random variables and probability distributions. These will bring us closer to statistical inference, the main subject of this book.

PROBLEMS

2–71.   AT&T was running commercials in 1990 aimed at luring back customers who had switched to one of the other long-distance phone service providers. One such commercial shows a businessman trying to reach Phoenix and mistakenly getting Fiji, where a half-naked native on a beach responds incomprehensibly in Polynesian. When asked about this advertisement, AT&T admitted that the portrayed incident did not actually take place but added that this was an enactment of something that "could happen."[12] Suppose that one in 200 long-distance telephone calls is misdirected. What is the probability that at least one in five attempted telephone calls reaches the wrong number? (Assume independence of attempts.)

2–72.   Refer to the information in the previous problem. Given that your long-distance telephone call is misdirected, there is a 2% chance that you will reach a foreign country (such as Fiji). Suppose that I am now going to dial a single long-distance number. What is the probability that I will erroneously reach a foreign country?

2–73.   The probability that a builder of airport terminals will win a contract for construction of terminals in country A is 0.40, and the probability that it will win a contract in country B is 0.30. The company has a 0.10 chance of winning the contracts in both countries. What is the probability that the company will win at least one of these two prospective contracts?

2–74.   According to *BusinessWeek*, 50% of top managers leave their jobs within 5 years.[13] If 25 top managers are followed over 5 years after they assume their positions, what is the probability that none will have left their jobs? All of them will have

---

[12]While this may seem virtually impossible due to the different dialing procedure for foreign countries, AT&T argues that erroneously dialing the prefix 679 instead of 617, for example, would get you Fiji instead of Massachusetts.

[13]Roger O. Crockett, "At the Head of the Headhunting Pack," *BusinessWeek*, April 9, 2007, p. 80.

left their jobs? At least one will have left the position? What implicit assumption are you making and how do you justify it?

2–75. The probability that a consumer entering a retail outlet for microcomputers and software packages will buy a computer of a certain type is 0.15. The probability that the consumer will buy a particular software package is 0.10. There is a 0.05 probability that the consumer will buy both the computer and the software package. What is the probability that the consumer will buy the computer or the software package or both?

2–76. The probability that a graduating senior will pass the certified public accountant (CPA) examination is 0.60. The probability that the graduating senior will both pass the CPA examination and get a job offer is 0.40. Suppose that the student just found out that she passed the CPA examination. What is the probability that she will be offered a job?

2–77. Two stocks A and B are known to be related in that both are in the same industry. The probability that stock A will go up in price tomorrow is 0.20, and the probability that both stocks A and B will go up tomorrow is 0.12. Suppose that tomorrow you find that stock A did go up in price. What is the probability that stock B went up as well?

2–78. The probability that production will increase if interest rates decline more than 0.5 percentage point for a given period is 0.72. The probability that interest rates will decline by more than 0.5 percentage point in the period in question is 0.25. What is the probability that, for the period in question, both the interest rate will decline and production will increase?

2–79. A large foreign automaker is interested in identifying its target market in the United States. The automaker conducts a survey of potential buyers of its high-performance sports car and finds that 35% of the potential buyers consider engineering quality among the car's most desirable features and that 50% of the people surveyed consider sporty design to be among the car's most desirable features. Out of the people surveyed, 25% consider both engineering quality and sporty design to be among the car's most desirable features. Based on this information, do you believe that potential buyers' perceptions of the two features are independent? Explain.

2–80. Consider the situation in problem 2–79. Three consumers are chosen randomly from among a group of potential buyers of the high-performance automobile. What is the probability that all three of them consider engineering quality to be among the most important features of the car? What is the probability that at least one of them considers this quality to be among the most important ones? How do you justify your computations?

2–81. A financial service company advertises its services in magazines, runs billboard ads on major highways, and advertises its services on the radio. The company estimates that there is a 0.10 probability that a given individual will see the billboard ad during the week, a 0.15 chance that he or she will see the ad in a magazine, and a 0.20 chance that she or he will hear the advertisement on the radio during the week. What is the probability that a randomly chosen member of the population in the area will be exposed to at least one method of advertising during a given week? (Assume independence.)

2–82. An accounting firm carries an advertisement in *The Wall Street Journal*. The firm estimates that 60% of the people in the potential market read *The Wall Street Journal;* research further shows that 85% of the people who read the *Journal* remember seeing the advertisement when questioned about it afterward. What percentage of the people in the firm's potential market see and remember the advertisement?

2–83. A quality control engineer knows that 10% of the microprocessor chips produced by a machine are defective. Out of a large shipment, five chips are chosen at random. What is the probability that none of them is defective? What is the probability that at least one is defective? Explain.

2–84. A fashion designer has been working with the colors green, black, and red in preparing for the coming season's fashions. The designer estimates that there is a 0.3 chance that the color green will be "in" during the coming season, a 0.2 chance that black will be among the season's colors, and a 0.15 chance that red will be popular. Assuming that colors are chosen independently of each other for inclusion in new fashions, what is the probability that the designer will be successful with at least one of her colors?

2–85. A company president always invites one of her three vice presidents to attend business meetings and claims that her choice of the accompanying vice president is random. One of the three has not been invited even once in five meetings. What is the probability of such an occurrence if the choice is indeed random? What conclusion would you reach based on your answer?

2–86. A multinational corporation is considering starting a subsidiary in an Asian country. Management realizes that the success of the new subsidiary depends, in part, on the ensuing political climate in the target country. Management estimates that the probability of success (in terms of resulting revenues of the subsidiary during its first year of operation) is 0.55 if the prevailing political situation is favorable, 0.30 if the political situation is neutral, and 0.10 if the political situation during the year is unfavorable. Management further believes that the probabilities of favorable, neutral, and unfavorable political situations are 0.6, 0.2, and 0.2, respectively. What is the success probability of the new subsidiary?

2–87. The probability that a shipping company will obtain authorization to include a certain port of call in its shipping route is dependent on whether certain legislation is passed. The company believes there is a 0.5 chance that both the relevant legislation will pass and it will get the required authorization to visit the port. The company further estimates that the probability that the legislation will pass is 0.75. If the company should find that the relevant legislation just passed, what is the probability that authorization to visit the port will be granted?

2–88. The probability that a bank customer will default on a loan is 0.04 if the economy is high and 0.13 if the economy is not high. Suppose the probability that the economy will be high is 0.65. What is the probability that the person will default on the loan?

2–89. Researchers at Kurume University in Japan surveyed 225 workers aged 41 to 60 years and found that 30% of them were skilled workers and 70% were unskilled. At the time of survey, 15% of skilled workers and 30% of unskilled workers were on an assembly line. A worker is selected at random from the age group 41 to 60.

>   *a.* What is the probability that the worker is on an assembly line?
>
>   *b.* Given that the worker is on an assembly line, what is the probability that the worker is unskilled?

2–90. SwissAir maintains a mailing list of people who have taken trips to Europe in the last three years. The airline knows that 8% of the people on the mailing list will make arrangements to fly SwissAir during the period following their being mailed a brochure. In an experimental mailing, 20 people are mailed a brochure. What is the probability that at least one of them will book a flight with SwissAir during the coming season?

2–91. A company's internal accounting standards are set to ensure that no more than 5% of the accounts are in error. From time to time, the company collects a random sample of accounts and checks to see how many are in error. If the error rate is indeed 5% and 10 accounts are chosen at random, what is the probability that none will be in error?

2–92. At a certain university, 30% of the students who take basic statistics are first-year students, 35% are sophomores, 20% are juniors, and 15% are seniors. From records of the statistics department it is found that out of the first-year students who take the basic statistics course 20% get As; out of the sophomores who take the course 30% get As; out of the juniors 35% get As; and out of the seniors who take the course 40% get As. Given that a student got an A in basic statistics, what is the probability that she or he is a senior?

2–93. The probability that a new product will be successful if a competitor does not come up with a similar product is 0.67. The probability that the new product will be successful in the presence of a competitor's new product is 0.42. The probability that the competing firm will come out with a new product during the period in question is 0.35. What is the probability that the product will be a success?

2–94. In 2007, Starbucks inaugurated its Dulce de Leche Latte.[14] If 8% of all customers who walk in order the new drink, what is the probability that out of 13 people, at least 1 will order a Dulce de Leche Latte? What assumption are you making?

2–95. Blackjack is a popular casino game in which the objective is to reach a card count greater than the dealer's without exceeding 21. One version of the game is referred to as the "hole card" version. Here, the dealer starts by drawing a card for himself or herself and putting it aside, face down, without the player's seeing what it is. This is the dealer's *hole card* (and the origin of the expression "an ace in the hole"). At the end of the game, the dealer has the option of turning this additional card face up if it may help him or her win the game. The no-hole-card version of the game is exactly the same, except that at the end of the game the dealer has the option of drawing the additional card from the deck for the same purpose (assume that the deck is shuffled prior to this draw). Conceptually, what is the difference between the two versions of the game? Is there any practical difference between the two versions as far as a player is concerned?

2–96. For the United States, automobile fatality statistics for the most recent year of available data are 40,676 deaths from car crashes, out of a total population of 280 million people. Compare the car fatality probability for one year in the United States and in France. What is the probability of dying from a car crash in the United States in the next 20 years?

2–97. Recall from Chapter 1 that the median is that number such that one-half the observations lie above it and one-half the observations lie below it. If a random sample of two items is to be drawn from some population, what is the probability that the population median will lie between these two data points?

2–98. Extend your result from the previous problem to a general case as follows. A random sample of n elements is to be drawn from some population and arranged according to their value, from smallest to largest. What is the probability that the population median will lie somewhere between the smallest and the largest values of the drawn data?

2–99. A research journal states: "Rejection rate for submitted manuscripts: 86%." A prospective author believes that the editor's statement reflects the probability of acceptance of any author's *first* submission to the journal. The author further believes that for any subsequent submission, an author's acceptance probability is 10% lower than the probability he or she had for acceptance of the preceding submission. Thus,

---

[14]Burt Helm, "Saving Starbucks' Soul," *BusinessWeek*, April 9, 2007, p. 56.

the author believes that the probability of acceptance of a first submission to the journal is $1 - 0.86 = 0.14$, the probability of acceptance of the second submission is 10% lower, that is, $(0.14)(0.90) = 0.126$, and so on for the third submission, fourth submission, etc. Suppose the author plans to continue submitting papers to the journal indefinitely until one is accepted. What is the probability that at least one paper will eventually be accepted by the journal?[15]

2–100. (*The Von Neumann device*) Suppose that one of two people is to be randomly chosen, with equal probability, to attend an important meeting. One of them claims that using a coin to make the choice is not fair because the probability that it will land on a head or a tail is not exactly 0.50. How can the coin still be used for making the choice? (*Hint:* Toss the coin *twice,* basing your decision on two possible outcomes.) Explain your answer.

2–101. At the same time as new hires were taking place, many retailers were cutting back. Out of 1,000 Kwik Save stores in Britain, 107 were to be closed. Out of 424 Somerfield stores, 424 were to be closed. Given that a store is closing, what is the probability that it is a Kwik Save? What is the probability that a randomly chosen store is either closing or Kwik Save? Find the probability that a randomly selected store is not closing given that it is a Somerfield.

2–102. Major hirings in retail in Britain are as follows: 9,000 at Safeway; 5,000 at Boots; 3,400 at Debenhams; and 1,700 at Marks and Spencer. What is the probability that a randomly selected new hire from these was hired by Marks and Spencer?

2–103. The House Ways and Means Committee is considering lowering airline taxes. The committee has 38 members and needs a simple majority to pass the new legislation. If the probability that each member votes yes is 0.25, find the probability that the legislation will pass. (Assume independence.)

Given that taxes are reduced, the probability that Northwest Airlines will compete successfully is 0.7. If the resolution does not pass, Northwest cannot compete successfully. Find the probability that Northwest can compete successfully.

2–104. Hong Kong's Mai Po marsh is an important migratory stopover for more than 100,000 birds per year from Siberia to Australia. Many of the bird species that stop in the marsh are endangered, and there are no other suitable wetlands to replace Mai Po. Currently the Chinese government is considering building a large housing project at the marsh's boundary, which could adversely affect the birds. Environmentalists estimate that if the project goes through, there will be a 60% chance that the black-faced spoonbill (current world population = 450) will not survive. It is estimated that there is a 70% chance the Chinese government will go ahead with the building project. What is the probability of the species' survival (assuming no danger if the project doesn't go through)?

2–105. Three machines A, B, and C are used to produce the same part, and their outputs are collected in a single bin. Machine A produced 26% of the parts in the bin, machine B 38%, and machine C the rest. Of the parts produced by machine A, 8% are defective. Similarly, 5% of the parts from B and 4% from C are defective. A part is picked at random from the bin.

a. If the part is defective, what is the probability it was produced by machine A?

b. If the part is good, what is the probability it was produced by machine B?

[15]Since its appearance in the first edition of the book, this interesting problem has been generalized. See N. H. Josephy and A. D. Aczel, "A Note on a Journal Selection Problem," *ZOR-Methods and Models of Operations Research* 34 (1990), pp. 469–76.

CASE 2 Job Applications

A business graduate wants to get a job in any one of the top 10 accounting firms. Applying to any of these companies requires a lot of effort and paperwork and is therefore costly. She estimates the cost of applying to each of the 10 companies and the probability of getting a job offer there. These data are tabulated below. The tabulation is in the decreasing order of cost.

1. If the graduate applies to all 10 companies, what is the probability that she will get at least one offer?

2. If she can apply to only one company, based on cost and success probability criteria alone, should she apply to company 5? Why or why not?

3. If she applies to companies 2, 5, 8, and 9, what is the total cost? What is the probability that she will get at least one offer?

4. If she wants to be at least 75% confident of getting at least one offer, to which companies should she apply to minimize the total cost? (*This is a trial-and-error problem.*)

5. If she is willing to spend $1,500, to which companies should she apply to maximize her chances of getting at least one job? (*This is a trial-and-error problem.*)

Company	1	2	3	4	5	6	7	8	9	10
Cost	$870	$600	$540	$500	$400	$320	$300	$230	$200	$170
Probability	0.38	0.35	0.28	0.20	0.18	0.18	0.17	0.14	0.14	0.08

RANDOM VARIABLES

3–1   Using Statistics   91

3–2   Expected Values of Discrete Random Variables   102

3–3   Sum and Linear Composites of Random Variables   107

3–4   Bernoulli Random Variable   112

3–5   The Binomial Random Variable   113

3–6   Negative Binomial Distribution   118

3–7   The Geometric Distribution   120

3–8   The Hypergeometric Distribution   121

3–9   The Poisson Distribution   124

3–10 The Continuous Random Variables   126

3–11 The Uniform Distribution   129

3–12 The Exponential Distribution   130

3–13 Using the Computer   133

3–14 Summary and Review of Terms   135

Case 3   Concepts Testing   145

LEARNING OBJECTIVES

After studying this chapter, you should be able to:

- Distinguish between discrete and continuous random variables.
- Explain how a random variable is characterized by its probability distribution.
- Compute statistics about a random variable.
- Compute statistics about a function of a random variable.
- Compute statistics about the sum of a linear composite of random variables.
- Identify which type of distribution a given random variable is most likely to follow.
- Solve problems involving standard distributions manually using formulas.
- Solve business problems involving standard distributions using spreadsheet templates.

Recent work in genetics makes assumptions about the distribution of babies of the two sexes. One such analysis concentrated on the probabilities of the number of babies of each sex in a given number of births. Consider the sample space made up of the 16 equally likely points:

BBBB	BBBG	BGGB	GBGG
GBBB	GGBB	BGBG	GGBG
BGBB	GBGB	BBGG	GGGB
BBGB	GBBG	BGGG	GGGG

All these 16 points are equally likely because when four children are born, the sex of each child is assumed to be independent of those of the other three. Hence the probability of each quadruple (e.g., GBBG) is equal to the product of the probabilities of the four separate, single outcomes—G, B, B, and G—and is thus equal to $(1/2)(1/2)(1/2)(1/2) = 1/16$.

Now, let's look at the variable "the number of girls out of four births." This number *varies* among points in the sample space, and it is *random*—given to chance. That's why we call such a number a **random variable.**

A **random variable** is an uncertain quantity whose value depends on chance.

A random variable has a probability law—a rule that assigns probabilities to the different values of the random variable. The probability law, the probability assignment, is called the **probability distribution** of the random variable. We usually denote the random variable by a capital letter, often X. The probability distribution will then be denoted by $P(X)$.

Look again at the sample space for the sexes of four babies, and remember that our variable is the number of girls out of four births. The first point in the sample space is BBBB; because the number of girls is zero here, $X = 0$. The next four points in the sample space all have one girl (and three boys). Hence, each one leads to the value $X = 1$. Similarly, the next six points in the sample space all lead to $X = 2$; the next four points to $X = 3$; and, finally, the last point in our sample space gives $X = 4$. The correspondence of points in the sample space with values of the random variable is as follows:

Sample Space	Random Variable
BBBB }	$X = 0$
GBBB	
BGBB	
BBGB	$X = 1$
BBBG	
GGBB	
GBGB	
GBBG	
BGGB	$X = 2$
BGBG	
BBGG	
BGGG	
GBGG	
GGBG	$X = 3$
GGGB	
GGGG}	$X = 4$

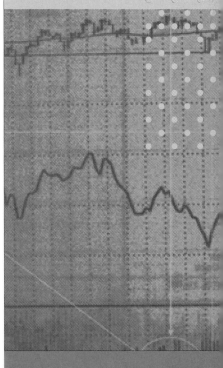

This correspondence, when a sample space clearly exists, allows us to define a random variable as follows:

A **random variable** is a function of the sample space.

What is this function? The correspondence between points in the sample space and values of the random variable allows us to determine the probability distribution of X as follows: Notice that 1 of the 16 equally likely points of the sample space leads to $X = 0$. Hence, the probability that $X = 0$ is $1/16$. Because 4 of the 16 equally likely points lead to a value $X = 1$, the probability that $X = 1$ is $4/16$, and so forth. Thus, looking at the sample space and counting the number of points leading to each value of X, we find the following probabilities:

$$P(X = 0) = 1/16 = 0.0625$$
$$P(X = 1) = 4/16 = 0.2500$$
$$P(X = 2) = 6/16 = 0.3750$$
$$P(X = 3) = 4/16 = 0.2500$$
$$P(X = 4) = 1/16 = 0.0625$$

The probability statements above constitute the probability distribution of the random variable X = the number of girls in four births. Notice how this probability law was obtained simply by associating values of X with sets in the sample space. (For example, the set GBBB, BGBB, BBGB, BBBG leads to $X = 1$.) Writing the probability distribution of X in a table format is useful, but first let's make a small, simplifying notational distinction so that we do not have to write complete probability statements such as $P(X = 1)$.

As stated earlier, we use a capital letter, such as X, to denote the random variable. But we use a lowercase letter to denote a particular value that the random variable can take. For example, $x = 3$ means that some particular set of four births resulted in three girls. Think of X as random and x as known. Before a coin is tossed, the number of heads (in one toss) is an unknown, X. Once the coin lands, we have $x = 0$ or $x = 1$.

Now let's return to the number of girls in four births. We can write the probability distribution of this random variable in a table format, as shown in Table 3–1.

Note an important fact: The sum of the probabilities of all the values of the random variable X must be 1.00. A picture of the probability distribution of the random variable X is given in Figure 3–1. Such a picture is a **probability bar chart** for the random variable.

Marilyn is interested in the number of girls (or boys) in any fixed number of births, not necessarily four. Thus her discussion extends beyond this case. In fact, the

TABLE 3–1   **Probability Distribution of the Number of Girls in Four Births**

Number of Girls x	Probability $P(x)$
0	1/16
1	4/16
2	6/16
3	4/16
4	1/16
	16/16 = 1.00

FIGURE 3–1   Probability Bar Chart

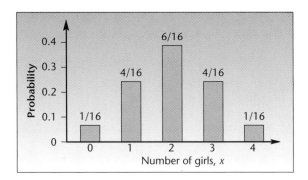

random variable she describes, which in general counts the number of "successes" (here, a girl is a success) in a fixed number *n* of trials, is called a *binomial random variable*. We will study this particular important random variable in section 3–3.

Figure 3–2 shows the sample space for the experiment of rolling two dice. As can be seen from the sample space, the probability of every pair of outcomes is 1/36. This can be seen from the fact that, by the independence of the two dice, for example, P(6 on red die $\cap$ 5 on green die) $= P$(6 on red die) $\times P$(5 on green die) $= (1/6)(1/6) =$ 1/36, and that this holds for all 36 pairs of outcomes. Let $X =$ the sum of the dots on the two dice. What is the distribution of *x*?

EXAMPLE 3–1

Figure 3–3 shows the correspondence between sets in our sample space and the values of X. The probability distribution of X is given in Table 3–2. The probability distribution allows us to answer various questions about the random variable of interest. Draw a picture of this probability distribution. Such a graph need not be a histogram, used earlier, but can also be a bar graph or column chart of the probabilities of the different values of the random variable. Note from the graph you produced that the distribution of the random variable "the sum of two dice" is symmetric. The central value is $x = 7$, which has the highest probability, $P(7) = 6/36 = 1/6$. This is the *mode,*

Solution

FIGURE 3–2   Sample Space for Two Dice

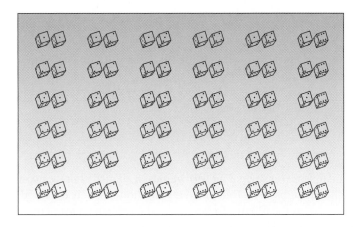

FIGURE 3–3   Correspondence between Sets and Values of X

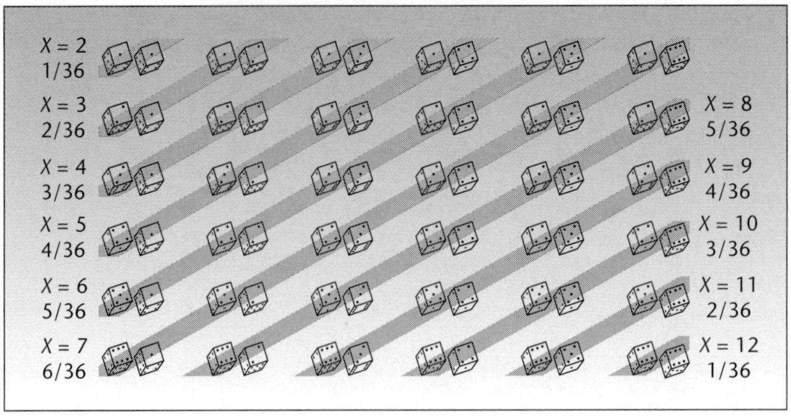

TABLE 3–2   Probability Distribution of the Sum of Two Dice

x	P(x)
2	1/36
3	2/36
4	3/36
5	4/36
6	5/36
7	6/36
8	5/36
9	4/36
10	3/36
11	2/36
12	1/36
	36/36 = 1.00

the most likely value. Thus, if you were to bet on one sum of two dice, the best bet is that the sum will be 7.

We can answer other probability questions, such as: What is the probability that the sum will be at most 5? This is $P(X \leq 5)$. Notice that to answer this question, we require the sum of all the probabilities of the values that are less than or equal to 5:

$$P(2) + P(3) + P(4) + P(5) = 1/36 + 2/36 + 3/36 + 4/36 = 10/36$$

Similarly, we may want to know the probability that the sum is greater than 9. This is calculated as follows:

$$P(X > 9) = P(10) + P(11) + P(12) = 3/36 + 2/36 + 1/36 = 6/36 = 1/6$$

Most often, unless we are dealing with games of chance, there is no evident sample space. In such situations the probability distribution is often obtained from lists or other data that give us the relative frequency in the recorded past of the various values of the random variable. This is demonstrated in Example 3–2.

800, 900, and Now: the 500 Telephone Numbers

EXAMPLE 3–2

The new code 500 is for busy, affluent people who travel a lot: It can work with a cellular phone, your home phone, office phone, second-home phone, up to five additional phones besides your regular one. The computer technology behind this service is astounding—the new phone service can find you wherever you may be on the planet at a given moment (assuming one of the phones you specify is cellular and you keep it with you when you are not near one of your stationary telephones). What the computer does is to first ring you up at the telephone number you specify as your primary one (your office phone, for example). If there is no answer, the computer switches to search for you at your second-specified phone number (say, home); if you do not answer there, it will switch to your third phone (maybe the phone at a close companion's home, or your car phone, or a portable cellular phone); and so on up to five allowable switches. The switches are the expensive part of this service (besides arrangements to have your cellular phone reachable overseas), and the service provider wants to get information on these switches. From data available on an experimental run of the 500 program, the following probability distribution is constructed for the number of dialing switches that are necessary before a person is reached. When $X = 0$, the person was reached on her or his primary phone (no switching was necessary); when $X = 1$, a dialing switch was necessary, and the person was found at the secondary phone; and so on up to five switches. Table 3–3 gives the probability distribution for this random variable.

A plot of the probability distribution of this random variable is given in Figure 3–4. When more than two switches occur on a given call, extra costs are incurred. What is the probability that for a given call there would be extra costs?

TABLE 3–3
The Probability Distribution
of the Number of Switches

x	P(x)
0	0.1
1	0.2
2	0.3
3	0.2
4	0.1
5	0.1
	1.00

Solution

$$P(X > 2) = P(3) + P(4) + P(5) = 0.2 + 0.1 + 0.1 = 0.4$$

What is the probability that at least one switch will occur on a given call? $1 - P(0) = 0.9$, a high probability.

Discrete and Continuous Random Variables

Refer to Example 3–2. Notice that when switches occur, the number X jumps by 1. It is impossible to have one-half a switch or 0.13278 of one. The same is true for the number of dots on two dice (you cannot see 2.3 dots or 5.87 dots) and, of course, the number of girls in four births.

> A **discrete random variable** can assume at most a countable number of values.

The values of a discrete random variable do not have to be positive whole numbers; they just have to "jump" from one possible value to the next without being able to have any value in between. For example, the amount of money you make on an investment may be $500, or it may be a loss: −$200. At any rate, it can be measured at best to the nearest *cent,* so this variable is discrete.

What are continuous random variables, then?

> A **continuous random variable** may take on any value in an interval of numbers (i.e., its possible values are uncountably infinite).

FIGURE 3–4
The Probability Distribution
of the Number of Switches

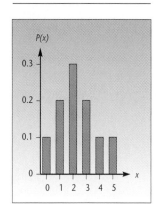

FIGURE 3–5   Discrete and Continuous Random Variables

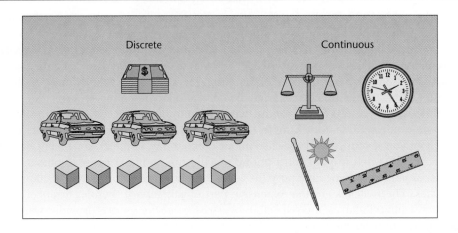

The values of continuous random variables can be measured (at least in theory) to any degree of accuracy. They move continuously from one possible value to another, without having to jump. For example, temperature is a continuous random variable, since it can be measured as $72.00340981136\ldots°$. Weight, height, and time are other examples of continuous random variables.

The difference between discrete and continuous random variables is illustrated in Figure 3–5. Is wind speed a discrete or a continuous random variable?

The probability distribution of a discrete random variable X must satisfy the following two conditions.

$$1.\ \ P(x) \geq 0 \text{ for all values } x \qquad\qquad (3\text{–}1)$$

$$2.\ \ \sum_{\text{all } x} P(x) = 1 \qquad\qquad (3\text{–}2)$$

These conditions must hold because the $P(x)$ values are probabilities. Equation 3–1 states that all probabilities must be greater than or equal to zero, as we know from Chapter 2. For the second rule, equation 3–2, note the following. For each value x, $P(x) = P(X = x)$ is the probability of the event that the random variable equals x. Since by definition *all x* means all the values the random variable X may take, and since X may take on only one value at a time, the occurrences of these values are mutually exclusive events, and one of them must take place. Therefore, the sum of all the probabilities $P(x)$ must be 1.00.

Cumulative Distribution Function

The probability distribution of a discrete random variable lists the probabilities of occurrence of different values of the random variable. We may be interested in *cumulative* probabilities of the random variable. That is, we may be interested in the probability that the value of the random variable is *at most* some value x. This is the sum of all the probabilities of the values i of X that are less than or equal to x.

TABLE 3–4   Cumulative Distribution Function of the Number of Switches (Example 3–2)

x	P(x)	F(x)
0	0.1	0.1
1	0.2	0.3
2	0.3	0.6
3	0.2	0.8
4	0.1	0.9
5	0.1	1.00
	1.00	

We define the *cumulative distribution function* (also called *cumulative probability function*) as follows.

> The **cumulative distribution function,** $F(x)$, of a discrete random variable X is
>
> $$F(x) = P(X \le x) = \sum_{\text{all } i \le x} P(i) \qquad (3\text{–}3)$$

Table 3–4 gives the cumulative distribution function of the random variable of Example 3–2. Note that each entry of $F(x)$ is equal to the sum of the corresponding values of $P(i)$ for all values i less than or equal to x. For example, $F(3) = P(X \le 3) = P(0) + P(1) + P(2) + P(3) = 0.1 + 0.2 + 0.3 + 0.2 = 0.8$. Of course, $F(5) = 1.00$ because $F(5)$ is the sum of the probabilities of all values that are less than or equal to 5, and 5 is the largest value of the random variable.

Figure 3–6 shows $F(x)$ for the number of switches on a given call. All cumulative distribution functions are nondecreasing and equal 1.00 at the largest possible value of the random variable.

Let us consider a few probabilities. The probability that the number of switches will be less than or equal to 3 is given by $F(3) = 0.8$. This is illustrated, using the probability distribution, in Figure 3–7.

FIGURE 3–6   Cumulative Distribution Function of Number of Switches

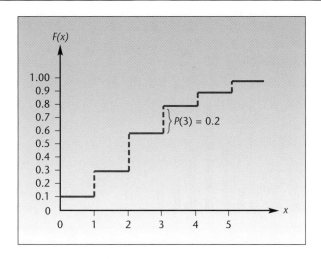

FIGURE 3–7　The Probability That at Most Three Switches Will Occur

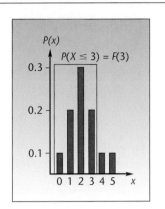

FIGURE 3–8　Probability That More than One Switch Will Occur

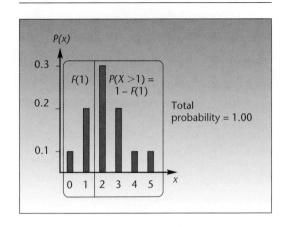

The probability that *more than* one switch will occur, $P(X > 1)$, is equal to $1 - F(1) = 1 - 0.3 = 0.7$. This is so because $F(1) = P(X \leq 1)$, and $P(X \leq 1) + P(X > 1) = 1$ (the two events are complements of each other). This is demonstrated in Figure 3–8.

The probability that anywhere from one to three switches will occur is $P(1 \leq X \leq 3)$. From Figure 3–9 we see that this is equal to $F(3) - F(0) = 0.8 - 0.1 = 0.7$. (This is the probability that the number of switches that occur will be less than or equal to 3 and greater than 0.) This, and other probability questions, could certainly be answered directly, without use of $F(x)$. We could just add the probabilities: $P(1) + P(2) + P(3) = 0.2 + 0.3 + 0.2 = 0.7$. The advantage of $F(x)$ is that probabilities may be computed by few operations [usually subtraction of two values of $F(x)$, as in this example], whereas use of $P(x)$ often requires lengthier computations.

If the probability distribution is available, use it directly. If, on the other hand, you have a cumulative distribution function for the random variable in question, you may use it as we have demonstrated. In either case, drawing a picture of the probability distribution is always helpful. You can look at the signs in the probability statement, such as $P(X \leq x)$ versus $P(X < x)$, to see which values to include and which ones to leave out of the probability computation.

FIGURE 3–9　Probability That Anywhere from One to Three Switches Will Occur

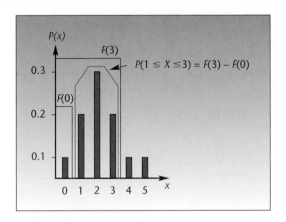

3–1. The number of telephone calls arriving at an exchange during any given minute between noon and 1:00 P.M. on a weekday is a random variable with the following probability distribution.

x	P(x)
0	0.3
1	0.2
2	0.2
3	0.1
4	0.1
5	0.1

   a. Verify that $P(x)$ is a probability distribution.

   b. Find the cumulative distribution function of the random variable.

   c. Use the cumulative distribution function to find the probability that between 12:34 and 12:35 P.M. more than two calls will arrive at the exchange.

3–2. According to an article in *Travel and Leisure,* every person in a small study of sleep during vacation was found to sleep longer than average during the first vacation night.[1] Suppose that the number of additional hours slept in the first night of a vacation, over the person's average number slept per night, is given by the following probability distribution:

x	P(x)
0	0.01
1	0.09
2	0.30
3	0.20
4	0.20
5	0.10
6	0.10

   a. Verify that $P(x)$ is a probability distribution.

   b. Find the cumulative distribution function.

   c. Find the probability that at most four additional hours are slept.

   d. Find the probability that at least two additional hours are slept per night.

3–3. The percentage of people (to the nearest 10) responding to an advertisement is a random variable with the following probability distribution:

x(%)	P(x)
0	0.10
10	0.20
20	0.35
30	0.20
40	0.10
50	0.05

   a. Show that $P(x)$ is a probability distribution.

   b. Find the cumulative distribution function.

   c. Find the probability that more than 20% will respond to the ad.

---

[1]Amy Farley, "Health and Fitness on the Road," *Travel and Leisure,* April 2007, p. 182.

3–4. An automobile dealership records the number of cars sold each day. The data are used in calculating the following probability distribution of daily sales:

x	P(x)
0	0.1
1	0.1
2	0.2
3	0.2
4	0.3
5	0.1

   a. Find the probability that the number of cars sold tomorrow will be between two and four (both inclusive).

   b. Find the cumulative distribution function of the number of cars sold per day.

   c. Show that $P(x)$ is a probability distribution.

3–5. Consider the roll of a pair of dice, and let X denote the sum of the two numbers appearing on the dice. Find the probability distribution of X, and find the cumulative distribution function. What is the most likely sum?

3–6. The number of intercity shipment orders arriving daily at a transportation company is a random variable X with the following probability distribution:

x	P(x)
0	0.1
1	0.2
2	0.4
3	0.1
4	0.1
5	0.1

   a. Verify that $P(x)$ is a probability distribution.

   b. Find the cumulative probability function of X.

   c. Use the cumulative probability function computed in (*b*) to find the probability that anywhere from one to four shipment orders will arrive on a given day.

   d. When more than three orders arrive on a given day, the company incurs additional costs due to the need to hire extra drivers and loaders. What is the probability that extra costs will be incurred on a given day?

   e. Assuming that the numbers of orders arriving on different days are independent of each other, what is the probability that no orders will be received over a period of five working days?

   f. Again assuming independence of orders on different days, what is the probability that extra costs will be incurred two days in a row?

3–7. An article in *The New York Times* reports that several hedge fund managers now make more than a *billion dollars a year.*[2] Suppose that the annual income of a hedge

---

[2]Jenny Anderson and Julie Creswell, "Make Less Than $240 Million? You're Off Top Hedge Fund List," *The New York Times,* April 24, 2007, p. A1.

fund manager in the top tier, in millions of dollars a year, is given by the following probability distribution:

x ($ millions)	P(x)
$1,700	0.2
1,500	0.2
1,200	0.3
1,000	0.1
800	0.1
600	0.05
400	0.05

a. Find the probability that the annual income of a hedge fund manager will be between $400 million and $1 billion (both inclusive).

b. Find the cumulative distribution function of X.

c. Use $F(x)$ computed in (b) to evaluate the probability that the annual income of a hedge fund manager will be less than or equal to $1 billion.

d. Find the probability that the annual income of a hedge fund manager will be greater than $600 million and less than or equal to $1.5 billion.

3–8. The number of defects in a machine-made product is a random variable X with the following probability distribution:

x	P(x)
0	0.1
1	0.2
2	0.3
3	0.3
4	0.1

a. Show that $P(x)$ is a probability distribution.

b. Find the probability $P(1 < X \le 3)$.

c. Find the probability $P(1 < X \le 4)$.

d. Find $F(x)$.

3–9. Returns on investments overseas, especially in Europe and the Pacific Rim, are expected to be higher than those of U.S. markets in the near term, and analysts are now recommending investments in international portfolios. An investment consultant believes that the probability distribution of returns (in percent per year) on one such portfolio is as follows:

x(%)	P(x)
9	0.05
10	0.15
11	0.30
12	0.20
13	0.15
14	0.10
15	0.05

a. Verify that $P(x)$ is a probability distribution.

b. What is the probability that returns will be at least 12%?

c. Find the cumulative distribution of returns.

3–10. The daily exchange rate of one dollar in euros during the first three months of 2007 can be inferred to have the following distribution.[3]

x	P(x)
0.73	0.05
0.74	0.10
0.75	0.25
0.76	0.40
0.77	0.15
0.78	0.05

a. Show that $P(x)$ is a probability distribution.

b. What is the probability that the exchange rate on a given day during this period will be at least 0.75?

c. What is the probability that the exchange rate on a given day during this period will be less than 0.77?

d. If daily exchange rates are independent of one another, what is the probability that for two days in a row the exchange rate will be above 0.75?

3–2　Expected Values of Discrete Random Variables

In Chapter 1, we discussed summary measures of data sets. The most important summary measures discussed were the mean and the variance (also the square root of the variance, the standard deviation). We saw that the mean is a measure of *centrality,* or *location,* of the data or population, and that the variance and the standard deviation measure the *variability,* or *spread,* of our observations.

The mean of a probability distribution of a random variable is a measure of the centrality of the probability distribution. It is a measure that considers both the values of the random variable and their probabilities. The mean is a *weighted average* of the possible values of the random variable—the weights being the probabilities.

The mean of the probability distribution of a random variable is called the *expected value* of the random variable (sometimes called the *expectation* of the random variable). The reason for this name is that the mean is the (probability-weighted) average value of the random variable, and therefore it is the value we "expect" to occur. We denote the mean by two notations: μ for *mean* (as in Chapter 1 for a population) and $E(X)$ for *expected value of X.* In situations where no ambiguity is possible, we will often use μ. In cases where we want to stress the fact that we are talking about the expected value of a particular random variable (here, X), we will use the notation $E(X)$. The expected value of a discrete random variable is defined as follows.

The **expected value** of a discrete random variable X is equal to the sum of all values of the random variable, each value multiplied by its probability.

$$\mu = E(X) = \sum_{\text{all } x} xP(x) \qquad (3\text{–}4)$$

Suppose a coin is tossed. If it lands heads, you win a dollar; but if it lands tails, you lose a dollar. What is the expected value of this game? Intuitively, you know you have an even chance of winning or losing the same amount, and so the average or expected

---

[3]Inferred from a chart of dollars in euros published in "Business Day," *The New York Times,* April 20, 2007, p. C10.

TABLE 3–5   Computing the Expected Number of Switches for Example 3–2

x	P(x)	xP(x)
0	0.1	0
1	0.2	0.2
2	0.3	0.6
3	0.2	0.6
4	0.1	0.4
5	0.1	0.5
	1.00	2.3 ← Mean, E(X)

value is zero. Your payoff from this game is a random variable, and we find its expected value from equation 3–4: $E(X) = (1)(1/2) + (-1)(1/2) = 0$. The definition of an expected value, or mean, of a random variable thus conforms with our intuition. Incidentally, games of chance with an expected value of zero are called *fair games*.

Let us now return to Example 3–2 and find the expected value of the random variable involved—the expected number of switches on a given call. For convenience, we compute the mean of a discrete random variable by using a table. In the first column of the table we write the values of the random variable. In the second column we write the probabilities of the different values, and in the third column we write the products $xP(x)$ for each value x. We then add the entries in the third column, giving us $E(X) = \Sigma xP(x)$, as required by equation 3–4. This is shown for Example 3–2 in Table 3–5.

As indicated in the table, $\mu = E(X) = 2.3$. We can say that, on the average, 2.3 switches occur per call. As this example shows, the mean does not have to be one of the values of the random variable. No calls have 2.3 switches, but 2.3 is the average number of switches. It is the *expected* number of switches per call, although here the exact expectation will not be realized on any call.

As the weighted average of the values of the random variable, with probabilities as weights, the mean is the *center of mass* of the probability distribution. This is demonstrated for Example 3–2 in Figure 3–10.

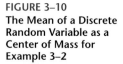

FIGURE 3–10
The Mean of a Discrete Random Variable as a Center of Mass for Example 3–2

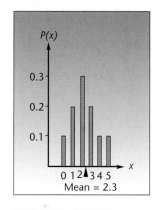

The Expected Value of a Function of a Random Variable

The expected value of a *function* of a random variable can be computed as follows. Let $h(X)$ be a function of the discrete random variable X.

The expected value of $h(X)$, a function of the discrete random variable X, is

$$E[h(X)] = \sum_{\text{all } x} h(x)P(x) \qquad (3\text{–}5)$$

The function $h(X)$ could be X^2, $3X^4$, $\log X$, or any function. As we will see shortly, equation 3–5 is most useful for computing the expected value of the special function $h(X) = X^2$. But let us first look at a simpler example, where $h(X)$ is a *linear* function of X. A linear function of X is a straight-line relation: $h(X) = a + bX$, where a and b are numbers.

Monthly sales of a certain product, recorded to the nearest thousand, are believed to follow the probability distribution given in Table 3–6. Suppose that the company has a fixed monthly production cost of $8,000 and that each item brings $2. Find the expected monthly profit from product sales.

EXAMPLE 3–3

TABLE 3–6   Probability Distribution of Monthly Product Sales for Example 3–3

Number of Items x	P(x)
5,000	0.2
6,000	0.3
7,000	0.2
8,000	0.2
9,000	0.1
	1.00

TABLE 3–7   Computing Expected Profit for Example 3–3

x	h(x)	P(x)	h(x)P(x)
5,000	2,000	0.2	400
6,000	4,000	0.3	1,200
7,000	6,000	0.2	1,200
8,000	8,000	0.2	1,600
9,000	10,000	0.1	1,000
			$E[h(X)] = 5,400$

Solution   The company's profit function from sales of the product is $h(X) = 2X - 8,000$. Equation 3–5 tells us that the expected value of $h(X)$ is the sum of the values of $h(X)$, each value multiplied by the probability of the particular value of X. We thus add two columns to Table 3–6: a column of values of $h(x)$ for all x and a column of the products $h(x)P(x)$. At the bottom of this column we find the required sum $E[h(X)] = \Sigma_{\text{all } x} h(x)P(x)$. This is done in Table 3–7. As shown in the table, expected monthly profit from sales of the product is $5,400.

In the case of a linear function of a random variable, as in Example 3–3, there is a possible simplification of our calculation of the mean of $h(X)$. The simplified formula of the expected value of a linear function of a random variable is as follows:

The expected value of a linear function of a random variable is

$$E(aX + b) = aE(X) + b \qquad (3–6)$$

where *a* and *b* are fixed numbers.

Equation 3–6 holds for *any* random variable, discrete or continuous. Once you know the expected value of X, the expected value of $aX + b$ is just $aE(X) + b$. In Example 3–3 we could have obtained the expected profit by finding the mean of X first, and then multiplying the mean of X by 2 and subtracting from this the fixed cost of $8,000. The mean of X is 6,700 (prove this), and the expected profit is therefore $E[h(X)] = E(2X - 8,000) = 2E(X) - 8,000 = 2(6,700) - 8,000 = \$5,400$, as we obtained using Table 3–7.

As mentioned earlier, the most important expected value of a function of X is the expected value of $h(X) = X^2$. This is because this expected value helps us compute the *variance* of the random variable X and, through the variance, the standard deviation.

Variance and Standard Deviation of a Random Variable

The variance of a random variable is the expected squared deviation of the random variable from its mean. The idea is similar to that of the variance of a data set or a population, defined in Chapter 1. Probabilities of the values of the random variable are used as weights in the computation of the expected squared deviation from the mean of a discrete random variable. The definition of the variance follows. As with a population, we denote the variance of a random variable by σ^2. Another notation for the variance of X is $V(X)$.

The **variance** of a discrete random variable X is given by

$$\sigma^2 = V(X) = E[(X - \mu)^2] = \sum_{\text{all } x}(x - \mu)^2 P(x) \qquad (3\text{--}7)$$

Using equation 3–7, we can compute the variance of a discrete random variable by subtracting the mean μ from each value x of the random variable, squaring the result, multiplying it by the probability $P(x)$, and finally adding the results for all x. Let us apply equation 3–7 and find the variance of the number of dialing switches in Example 3–2:

$$\sigma^2 = \Sigma(x - \mu)^2 P(x)$$
$$= (0 - 2.3)^2(0.1) + (1 - 2.3)^2(0.2) + (2 - 2.3)^2(0.3)$$
$$\quad + (3 - 2.3)^2(0.2) + (4 - 2.3)^2(0.1) + (5 - 2.3)^2(0.1)$$
$$= 2.01$$

The variance of a discrete random variable can be computed more easily. Equation 3–7 can be shown mathematically to be equivalent to the following computational form of the variance.

Computational formula for the variance of a random variable:
$$\sigma^2 = V(X) = E(X^2) - [E(X)]^2 \qquad (3\text{--}8)$$

Equation 3–8 has the same relation to equation 3–7 as equation 1–7 has to equation 1–3 for the variance of a set of points.

Equation 3–8 states that the variance of X is equal to the expected value of X^2 minus the squared mean of X. In computing the variance using this equation, we use the definition of the expected value of a function of a discrete random variable, equation 3–5, in the special case $h(X) = X^2$. We compute x^2 for each x, multiply it by $P(x)$, and add for all x. This gives us $E(X^2)$. To get the variance, we subtract from $E(X^2)$ the mean of X, squared.

We now compute the variance of the random variable in Example 3–2, using this method. This is done in Table 3–8. The first column in the table gives the values of X, the second column gives the probabilities of these values, the third column gives the products of the values and their probabilities, and the fourth column is the product of the third column and the first [because we get $x^2 P(x)$ by just multiplying each entry $xP(x)$ by x from column 1]. At the bottom of the third column we find the mean of X, and at the bottom of the fourth column we find the mean of X^2. Finally, we perform the subtraction $E(X^2) - [E(X)]^2$ to get the variance of X:

$$V(X) = E(X^2) - [E(X)]^2 = 7.3 - (2.3)^2 = 2.01$$

TABLE 3–8   Computations Leading to the Variance of the Number of Switches in Example 3–2
Using the Shortcut Formula (Equation 3–8)

x	$P(x)$	$xP(x)$	$x^2P(x)$
0	0.1	0	0
1	0.2	0.2	0.2
2	0.3	0.6	1.2
3	0.2	0.6	1.8
4	0.1	0.4	1.6
5	0.1	0.5	2.5
	1.00	2.3 ← Mean of X	7.3 ← Mean of X^2

This is the same value we found using the other formula for the variance, equation 3–7. Note that equation 3–8 holds for *all* random variables, discrete or otherwise. Once we obtain the expected value of X^2 and the expected value of X, we can compute the variance of the random variable using this equation.

For random variables, as for data sets or populations, the standard deviation is equal to the (positive) square root of the variance. We denote the standard deviation of a random variable X by σ or by $SD(X)$.

> The **standard deviation** of a random variable:
> $$\sigma = SD(X) = \sqrt{V(X)} \qquad (3\text{–}9)$$

In Example 3–2, the standard deviation is $\sigma = \sqrt{2.01} = 1.418$.

What are the variance and the standard deviation, and how do we interpret their meaning? By definition, the variance is the weighted average squared deviation of the values of the random variable from their mean. Thus, it is a measure of the *dispersion* of the possible values of the random variable about the mean. The variance gives us an idea of the variation or uncertainty associated with the random variable: The larger the variance, the farther away from the mean are possible values of the random variable. Since the variance is a squared quantity, it is often more useful to consider its square root—the standard deviation of the random variable. When two random variables are compared, the one with the larger variance (standard deviation) is the more variable one. The risk associated with an investment is often measured by the standard deviation of investment returns. When comparing two investments with the same average (*expected*) return, the investment with the higher standard deviation is considered riskier (although a higher standard deviation implies that returns are expected to be more variable—both below and above the mean).

Variance of a Linear Function of a Random Variable

There is a formula, analogous to equation 3–6, that gives the variance of a linear function of a random variable. For a linear function of X given by $aX + b$, we have the following:

> Variance of a linear function of a random variable is
> $$V(aX + b) = a^2V(X) = a^2\sigma^2 \qquad (3\text{–}10)$$
> where a and b are fixed numbers.

Using equation 3–10, we will find the variance of the profit in Example 3–3. The profit is given by $2X - 8,000$. We need to find the variance of X in this example. We find

$$E(X^2) = (5,000)^2(0.2) + (6,000)^2(0.3) + (7,000)^2(0.2) + (8,000)^2(0.2)$$
$$+ (9,000)^2(0.1)$$
$$= 46,500,000$$

The expected value of X is $E(X) = 6,700$. The variance of X is thus

$$V(X) = E(X^2) - [E(X)]^2 = 46,500,000 - (6,700)^2 = 1,610,000$$

Finally, we find the variance of the profit, using equation 3–10, as $2^2(1,610,000) = 6,440,000$. The standard deviation of the profit is $\sqrt{6,440,000} = 2,537.72$.

3–3 Sum and Linear Composites of Random Variables

Sometimes we are interested in the sum of several random variables. For instance, a business may make several investments, and each investment may have a random return. What finally matters to the business is the sum of all the returns. Sometimes what matters is a **linear composite** of several random variables. A linear composite of random variables $X_1, X_2, \ldots, X_k$ will be of the form

$$a_1 X_1 + a_2 X_2 + \cdots + a_k X_k$$

where $a_1, a_2, \ldots, a_k$ are constants. For instance, let $X_1, X_2, \ldots, X_k$ be the random quantities of k different items that you buy at a store, and let $a_1, a_2, \ldots, a_k$ be their respective prices. Then $a_1 X_1 + a_2 X_2 + \cdots + a_k X_k$ will be the random total amount you have to pay for the items. Note that the sum of the variables is a linear composite where all a's are 1. Also, $X_1 - X_2$ is a linear composite with $a_1 = 1$ and $a_2 = -1$.

We therefore need to know how to calculate the expected value and variance of the sum or linear composite of several random variables. The following results are useful in computing these statistics.

> The expected value of the sum of several random variables is the sum of the individual expected values. That is,
>
> $$E(X_1 + X_2 + \cdots + X_k) = E(X_1) + E(X_2) + \cdots + E(X_k)$$
>
> Similarly, the expected value of a linear composite is given by
>
> $$E(a_1 X_1 + a_2 X_2 + \cdots + a_k X_k) = a_1 E(X_1) + a_2 E(X_2) + \cdots + a_k E(X_k)$$

In the case of variance, we will look only at the case where $X_1, X_2, \ldots, X_k$ are **mutually independent,** because if they are not mutually independent, the computation involves covariances, which we will learn about in Chapter 10. Mutual independence means that any event $X_i = x$ and any other event $X_j = y$ are independent. We can now state the result.

> If $X_1, X_2, \ldots, X_k$ are mutually independent, then the variance of their sum is the sum of their individual variances. That is,
>
> $$V(X_1 + X_2 + \cdots + X_k) = V(X_1) + V(X_2) + \cdots + V(X_k)$$
>
> Similarly, the variance of a linear composite is given by
>
> $$V(a_1X_1 + a_2X_2 + \cdots + a_kX_k) = a_1^2 V(X_1) + a_2^2 V(X_2) + \cdots + a_k^2 V(X_k)$$

We will see the application of these results through an example.

EXAMPLE 3–4

A portfolio includes stocks in three industries: financial, energy, and consumer goods (in equal proportions). Assume that these three sectors are independent of each other and that the expected annual return (in dollars) and standard deviations are as follows: financial: 1,000 and 700; energy 1,200 and 1,100; and consumer goods 600 and 300 (respectively). What are the mean and standard deviation of annual dollar-value return on this portfolio?

Solution

The mean of the sum of the three random variables is the sum of the means $1,000 + 1,200 + 600 = \$2,800$. Since the three sectors are assumed independent, the variance is the sum of the three variances. It is equal to $700^2 + 1,100^2 + 300^2 = 1,790,000$. So the standard deviation is $\sqrt{1,790,000} = \$1,337.90$.

Chebyshev's Theorem

The standard deviation is useful in obtaining bounds on the possible values of the random variable with certain probability. The bounds are obtainable from a well-known theorem, *Chebyshev's theorem* (the name is sometimes spelled Tchebychev, Tchebysheff, or any of a number of variations). The theorem says that for any number k greater than 1.00, the probability that the value of a given random variable will be *within k standard deviations* of the mean is at least $1 - 1/k^2$. In Chapter 1, we listed some results for data sets that are derived from this theorem.

> **Chebyshev's Theorem**
>
> For a random variable X with mean μ and standard deviation σ, and for any number $k > 1$,
>
> $$P(|X - \mu| < k\sigma) \geq 1 - 1/k^2 \qquad (3\text{–}11)$$

Let us see how the theorem is applied by selecting values of k. While k does not have to be an integer, we will use integers. When $k = 2$, we have $1 - 1/k^2 = 0.75$: The theorem says that the value of the random variable will be within a distance of 2 standard deviations away from the mean with at least a 0.75 probability. Letting $k = 3$, we find that X will be within 3 standard deviations of its mean with at least a 0.89 probability. We can similarly apply the rule for other values of k. The rule holds for data sets and populations in a similar way. When applied to a sample of observations, the rule says that at least 75% of the observations lie within 2 standard deviations of the sample mean $\bar{x}$. It says that at least 89% of the observations lie within 3 standard deviations of the mean, and so on. Applying the theorem to the random variable of Example 3–2, which has mean 2.3 and standard deviation 1.418, we find that the probability that X will be anywhere from $2.3 - 2(1.418)$ to $2.3 + 2(1.418) = -0.536$ to 5.136 is at least 0.75. From the actual probability distribution in this example, Table 3–3, we know that the probability that X will be between 0 and 5 is 1.00.

Often, we will know the distribution of the random variable in question, in which case we will be able to use the distribution for obtaining actual probabilities rather than the bounds offered by Chebyshev's theorem. If the exact distribution of the random variable is not known, but we may assume an approximate distribution, the approximate probabilities may still be better than the general bounds offered by Chebyshev's theorem.

The Templates for Random Variables

The template shown in Figure 3–11 can be used to calculate the descriptive statistics of a random variable and also those of a function *h(x)* of that random variable. To calculate the statistics of $h(x)$, the Excel formula for the function must be entered in cell G12. For instance, if $h(x) = 5x^2 + 8$, enter the Excel formula `=5*x^2+8` in cell G12.

The template shown in Figure 3–12 can be used to compute the statistics about the sum of mutually independent random variables. While entering the variance of the individual X's, be careful that what you enter is the variance and not the standard deviation. At times, you know only the standard deviation and not the variance. In such cases, you can make the template calculate the variance from the standard deviation. For example, if the standard deviation is 1.23, enter the formula `=1.23^2`, which will compute and use the variance.

The template shown in Figure 3–13 can be used to compute the statistics about linear composites of mutually independent random variables. You will enter the coefficients (the a_i's) in column B.

FIGURE 3–11 Descriptive Statistics of a Random Variable *X* and *h*(*x*) [Random Variable.xls]

Statistics of a Random Variable — Title

x	P(*x*)	F(*x*)
0	0.1	0.1
1	0.2	0.3
2	0.3	0.6
3	0.2	0.8
4	0.1	0.9
5	0.1	1

Statistics of *X*	
Mean	2.3
Variance	2.01
Std. Devn.	1.41774
Skewness	0.30319
(Relative) Kurtosis	-0.63132

Definition of h(*x*)		*x*
h(*x*) =	8	0

Statistics of h(*x*)	
Mean	44.5
Variance	1400.25
Std. Devn.	37.4199
Skewness	1.24449
(Relative) Kurtosis	0.51413

FIGURE 3–12 Template for the Sum of Independent Variables

Sum of Independent Random Variables

	Mean	Variance	Std Devn.
X_1	18.72	5.2416	2.289454
X_2	4.9	3.185	1.784657
X_3	2.4	2.4	1.549193
X_4			
X_5			
X_6			
X_7			
X_8			
X_9			
X_{10}			
Sum	26.02	10.8266	3.29038
	Mean	Variance	Std Devn.

FIGURE 3–13   Template for Linear Composites of Independent Variables
                [Random Variables.xls, Sheet: Composite]

	A	B	C	D	E	F	G
1		Linear Composite of Independent Random Variables					
2							
3		Coef.		Mean	Variance	Std Devn.	
4		20	X_1	18.72	5.2416	2.289454	
5		10	X_2	4.9	3.185	1.784657	
6		30	X_3	2.4	2.4	1.549193	
7			X_4				
8			X_5				
9			X_6				
10			X_7				
11			X_8				
12			X_9				
13			X_{10}				
14							
15			Composite	495.4	4575.14	67.63978	
16				Mean	Variance	Std Devn.	

PROBLEMS

3–11. Find the expected value of the random variable in problem 3–1. Also find the variance of the random variable and its standard deviation.

3–12. Find the mean, variance, and standard deviation of the random variable in problem 3–2.

3–13. What is the expected percentage of people responding to an advertisement when the probability distribution is the one given in problem 3–3? What is the variance of the percentage of people who respond to the advertisement?

3–14. Find the mean, variance, and standard deviation of the number of cars sold per day, using the probability distribution in problem 3–4.

3–15. What is the expected number of dots appearing on two dice? (Use the probability distribution you computed in your answer to problem 3–5.)

3–16. Use the probability distribution in problem 3–6 to find the expected number of shipment orders per day. What is the probability that on a given day there will be more orders than the average?

3–17. Find the mean, variance, and standard deviation of the annual income of a hedge fund manager, using the probability distribution in problem 3–7.

3–18. According to Chebyshev's theorem, what is the minimum probability that a random variable will be within 4 standard deviations of its mean?

3–19. At least eight-ninths of a population lies within how many standard deviations of the population mean? Why?

3–20. The average annual return on a certain stock is 8.3%, and the variance of the returns on the stock is 2.3. Another stock has an average return of 8.4% per year and a variance of 6.4. Which stock is riskier? Why?

3–21. Returns on a certain business venture, to the nearest $1,000, are known to follow the probability distribution

x	$P(x)$
−2,000	0.1
−1,000	0.1
0	0.2
1,000	0.2
2,000	0.3
3,000	0.1

    a. What is the most likely monetary outcome of the business venture?

    b. Is the venture likely to be successful? Explain.

    c. What is the long-term average earning of business ventures of this kind? Explain.

    d. What is a good measure of the risk involved in a venture of this kind? Why? Compute this measure.

3–22. Management of an airline knows that 0.5% of the airline's passengers lose their luggage on domestic flights. Management also knows that the average value claimed for a lost piece of luggage on domestic flights is $600. The company is considering increasing fares by an appropriate amount to cover expected compensation to passengers who lose their luggage. By how much should the airline increase fares? Why? Explain, using the ideas of a random variable and its expectation.

3–23. Refer to problem 3–7. Suppose that hedge funds must withhold $300 million from the income of the manager and an additional 5% of the remaining income. Find the expected net income of a manager in this group. What property of expected values are you using?

3–24. Refer to problem 3–4. Suppose the car dealership's operation costs are well approximated by the square root of the number of cars sold, multiplied by $300. What is the expected daily cost of the operation? Explain.

3–25. In problem 3–2, suppose that a cost is imposed of an amount equal to the square of the number of additional hours of sleep. What is the expected cost? Explain.

3–26. All voters of Milwaukee County were asked a week before election day whether they would vote for a certain presidential candidate. Of these, 48% answered yes, 45% replied no, and the rest were undecided. If a yes answer is coded +1, a no answer is coded −1, and an undecided answer is coded 0, find the mean and the variance of the code.

3–27. Explain the meaning of the variance of a random variable. What are possible uses of the variance?

3–28. Why is the standard deviation of a random variable more meaningful than its variance for interpretation purposes?

3–29. Refer to problem 3–23. Find the variance and the standard deviation of hedge fund managers' income.

3–30. For problem 3–10, find the mean and the standard deviation of the dollar to euros exchange rate.

3–31. Lobsters vary in sizes. The bigger the size, the more valuable the lobster per pound (a 6-pound lobster is more valuable than two 3-pound ones). Lobster merchants will sell entire boatloads for a certain price. The boatload has a mixture of sizes. Suppose the distribution is as follows:

x(pound)	P(x)	v(x) ($)
½	0.1	2
¾	0.1	2.5
1	0.3	3.0
1¼	0.2	3.25
1½	0.2	3.40
1¾	0.05	3.60
2	0.05	5.00

What is a fair price for the shipload?

TABLE 3–9
Bernoulli Distribution

x	$P(x)$
1	p
0	$1 - p$

3–4 Bernoulli Random Variable

The first standard random variable we shall study is the *Bernoulli random variable*, named in honor of the mathematician Jakob Bernoulli (1654–1705). It is the building block for other random variables in this chapter. The distribution of a Bernoulli random variable X is given in Table 3–9. As seen in the table, x is 1 with probability p and 0 with probability $(1 - p)$. The case where $x = 1$ is called "success" and the case where $x = 0$ is called "failure."

Observe that

$$E(X) = 1 * p + 0 * (1 - p) = p$$
$$E(X^2) = 1^2 * p + 0^2 * (1 - p) = p$$
$$V(X) = E(X^2) - [E(X)]^2 = p - p^2 = p(1 - p)$$

Often the quantity $(1 - p)$, which is the probability of failure, is denoted by the symbol q, and thus $V(X) = pq$. If X is a Bernoulli random variable with probability of success p, then we write $X \sim \text{BER}(p)$, where the symbol "$\sim$" is read "is distributed as" and BER stands for Bernoulli. The characteristics of a Bernoulli random variable are summarized in the following box.

Bernoulli Distribution

If $X \sim \text{BER}(p)$, then

$$P(1) = p; \qquad P(0) = 1 - p$$
$$E[X] = p$$
$$V(X) = p(1 - p)$$

For example, if $p = 0.8$, then

$$E[X] = 0.8$$
$$V(X) = 0.8 * 0.2 = 0.16$$

Let us look at a practical instance of a Bernoulli random variable. Suppose an operator uses a lathe to produce pins, and the lathe is not perfect in that it does not always produce a good pin. Rather, it has a probability p of producing a good pin and $(1 - p)$ of producing a defective one.

Just after the operator produces one pin, let X denote the "number of good pins produced." Clearly, X is 1 if the pin is good and 0 if it is defective. Thus, X follows exactly the distribution in Table 3–9, and therefore $X \sim \text{BER}(p)$.

If the outcome of a trial can only be either a success or a failure, then the trial is a **Bernoulli trial**.

The number of successes X in one Bernoulli trial, which can be 1 or 0, is a **Bernoulli random variable**.

Another example is tossing a coin. If we take heads as 1 and tails as 0, then the outcome of a toss is a Bernoulli random variable.

A Bernoulli random variable is too simple to be of immediate practical use. But it forms the building block of the binomial random variable, which is quite useful in practice. The binomial random variable in turn is the basis for many other useful cases.

3–5 The Binomial Random Variable

In the real world we often make several trials, not just one, to achieve one or more successes. Since we now have a handle on Bernoulli-type trials, let us consider cases where there are n number of Bernoulli trials. A condition we need to impose on these trials is that the outcome of any trial be independent of the outcome of any other trial. Very often this independence condition is true. For example, when we toss a coin several times, the outcome of one toss is not affected by the outcome of any other toss.

Consider n number of *identically and independently distributed* Bernoulli random variables $X_1, X_2, \ldots, X_n$. Here, identically means that they all have the same p, and independently means that the value of one X does not in any way affect the value of another. For example, the value of X_2 does not affect the value of X_3 or X_5, and so on. Such a *sequence* of identically and independently distributed Bernoulli variables is called a **Bernoulli process.**

Suppose an operator produces n pins, one by one, on a lathe that has probability p of making a good pin at each trial. If this p remains constant throughout, then independence is guaranteed and the sequence of numbers (1 or 0) denoting the good and bad pins produced in each of the n trials is a Bernoulli process. For example, in the sequence of eight trials denoted by

$$0\ 0\ 1\ 0\ 1\ 1\ 0\ 0$$

the third, fifth, and sixth are good pins, or successes. The rest are failures.

In practice, we are usually interested in the total number of good pins rather than the sequence of 1's and 0's. In the example above, three out of eight are good. In the general case, let X denote the total number of good pins produced in n trials. We then have

$$X = X_1 + X_2 + \cdots + X_n$$

where all $X_i \sim \text{BER}(p)$ and are independent.

An X that counts the number of successes in many independent, identical Bernoulli trials is called a **binomial random variable.**

Conditions for a Binomial Random Variable

Note the conditions that need to be satisfied for a binomial random variable:

1. The trials must be Bernoulli trials in that the outcomes can only be either success or failure.
2. The outcomes of the trials must be independent.
3. The probability of success in each trial must be constant.

The first condition is easy to understand. Coming to the second condition, we already saw that the outcomes of coin tosses will be independent. As an example of dependent outcomes, consider the following experiment. We toss a fair coin and if it is heads we record the outcome as success, or 1, and if it is tails we record it as failure, or 0. For the second outcome, we do not toss the coin but we record the opposite of the previous outcome. For the third outcome, we toss the coin again and repeat the process of writing the opposite result for every other outcome. Thus in the sequence of all outcomes, every other outcome will be the opposite of the previous outcome. We stop after recording 20 outcomes. In this experiment, all outcomes are random and of Bernoulli type with success probability 0.5. But they are not independent in that every other outcome is the opposite of, and thus dependent on, the previous outcome. And for this reason, the number of successes in such an experiment will not be binomially distributed. (In fact, the number is not even random. Can you guess what that number will be?)

The third condition of constant probability of success is important and can be easily violated. Tossing two different coins with differing probabilities of success will violate the third condition (but not the other two). Another case that is relevant to the third condition, which we need to be aware of, is *sampling with and without replacement.* Consider an urn that contains 10 green marbles (successes) and 10 red marbles (failures). We pick a marble from the urn at random and record the outcome. The probability of success is $10/20 = 0.5$. For the second outcome, suppose *we replace the first* marble drawn and then pick one at random. In this case the probability of success remains at $10/20 = 0.5$, and the third condition is satisfied. But if *we do not replace the first* marble before picking the second, then the probability of the second outcome being a success is $9/19$ if the first was a success and $10/19$ if the first was a failure. Thus the probability of success does not remain constant (and is also dependent on the previous outcomes). Therefore, the third condition is violated (as is the second condition). This means that sampling with replacement will follow a binomial distribution, but sampling without replacement will not. Later we will see that sampling without replacement will follow a hypergeometric distribution.

Binomial Distribution Formulas

Consider the case where five trials are made, and in each trial the probability of success is 0.6. To get to the formula for calculating binomial probabilities, let us analyze the probability that the number of successes in the five trials is exactly three.

First, we note that there are $\binom{5}{3}$ ways of getting three successes out of five trials. Next we observe that each of these $\binom{5}{3}$ possibilities has $0.6^3 * 0.4^2$ probability of occurrence corresponding to 3 successes and 2 failures. Therefore,

CHAPTER 4

$$P(X = 3) = \binom{5}{3} * 0.6^3 * 0.4^2 = 0.3456$$

We can generalize this equation with n denoting the number of trials and p the probability of success:

$$P(X = x) = \binom{n}{x} p^x (1 - p)^{(n-x)} \qquad \text{for } x = 0, 1, 2, \ldots, n \qquad (3\text{–}12)$$

Equation 3–12 is the famous binomial probability formula.

To describe a binomial random variable we need two parameters, n and p. We write $X \sim B(n, p)$ to indicate that X is binomially distributed with n number of trials and p probability of success in each trial. The letter B in the expression stands for binomial.

With any random variable, we will be interested in its expected value and its variance. Let us consider the expected value of a binomial random variable X. We note that X is the sum of n number of Bernoulli random variables, each of which has an expected value of p. Hence the expected value of X must be np, that is, $E(X) = np$. Furthermore, the variance of each Bernoulli random variable is $p(1 - p)$, and they are all independent. Therefore variance of X is $np(1 - p)$, that is, $V(X) = np(1 - p)$. The formulas for the binomial distribution are summarized in the next box, which also presents sample calculations that use these formulas.

Binomial Distribution

If $X \sim B(n, p)$, then

$$P(X = x) = \binom{n}{x} p^x (1 - p)^{(n-x)} \qquad x = 0, 1, 2, \ldots, n$$

$$E(X) = np$$
$$V(X) = np(1 - p)$$

For example, if $n = 5$ and $p = 0.6$, then

$$P(X = 3) = 10 * 0.6^3 * 0.4^2 = 0.3456$$
$$E(X) = 5 * 0.6 = 3$$
$$V(X) = 5 * 0.6 * 0.4 = 1.2$$

The Template

The calculation of binomial probabilities, especially the cumulative probabilities, can be tedious. Hence we shall use a spreadsheet template. The template that can be used to calculate binomial probabilities is shown in Figure 3–14. When we enter the values for n and p, the template automatically tabulates the probability of "Exactly x," "At most x," and "At least x" number of successes. This tabulation can be used to solve many kinds of problems involving binomial probabilities, as explained in the next section. Besides the tabulation, a histogram is also created on the right. The histogram helps the user to visualize the shape of the distribution.

FIGURE 3–14   **Binomial Distribution Template [Binomial.xls]**

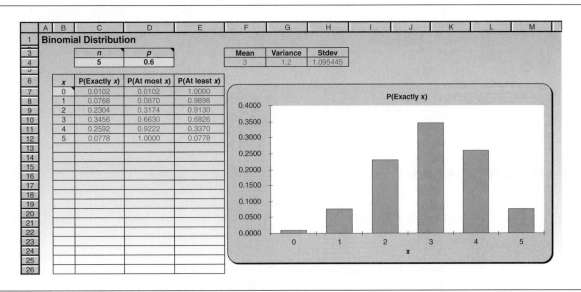

Problem Solving with the Template

Suppose an operator wants to produce *at least* two good pins. (In practice, one would want *at least* some number of *good* things, or *at most* some number of *bad* things. Rarely would one want *exactly* some number of good or bad things.) He produces the pins using a lathe that has 0.6 probability of making a good pin in each trial, and this probability stays constant throughout. Suppose he produces five pins. What is the probability that he would have made at least two good ones?

Let us see how we can answer the question using the template. After making sure that *n* is filled in as 5 and *p* as 0.6, the answer is read off as 0.9130 (in cell E9). That is, the operator can be 91.3% confident that he would have at least two good pins.

Let us go further with the problem. Suppose it is critical that the operator have at least two good pins, and therefore he wants to be at least 99% confident that he would have at least two good pins. (In this type of situation, the phrases "at least" and "at most" occur often. You should read carefully.) With five trials, we just found that he can be only 91.3% confident. To increase the confidence level, one thing he can do is increase the number of trials. How many more trials? Using the spreadsheet template, we can answer this question by progressively increasing the value of *n* and stopping when *P*(At least 2) in cell E9 just exceeds 99%. On doing this, we find that eight trials will do and seven will not. Hence the operator should make at least eight trials.

Increasing *n* is not the only way to increase confidence. We can increase *p*, if that is possible in practice. To see it, we pose another question.

Suppose the operator has enough time to produce only five pins, but he still wants to have at least 99% confidence of producing at least two good pins by improving the lathe and thus increasing *p*. How much should *p* be increased? To answer this, we can keep increasing *p* and stop when *P*(At least 2) just exceeds 99%. But this process could get tiresome if we need, say, four decimal place accuracy for *p*. This is where the Goal seek . . . command (see the Working with Templates file found on the student CD) in the spreadsheet comes in handy. The Goal seek command yields 0.7777. That is, *p* must be increased to at least 0.7777 in order to be 99% confident of getting at least two good pins in five trials.

We will complete this section by pointing out the use of the AutoCalculate command. We first note that the probability of at most *x* number of successes is the same as the cumulative probability $F(x)$. Certain types of probabilities are easily calculated using $F(x)$ values. For example, in our operator's problem, consider the probability that the number of successes will be between 1 and 3, both inclusive. We know that

$$P(1 \leq x \leq 3) = F(3) - F(0)$$

Looking at the template in Figure 3–14, we calculate this as $0.6630 - 0.0102 = 0.6528$. A quicker way is to use the AutoCalculate facility. When the range of cells containing $P(1)$ to $P(3)$ is selected, the sum of the probabilities appears in the AutoCalculate area as 0.6528.

PROBLEMS

3–32. Three of the 10 airplane tires at a hangar are faulty. Four tires are selected at random for a plane; let *F* be the number of faulty tires found. Is *F* a binomial random variable? Explain.

3–33. A salesperson finds that, in the long run, two out of three sales calls are successful. Twelve sales calls are to be made; let *X* be the number of concluded sales. Is *X* a binomial random variable? Explain.

3–34. A large shipment of computer chips is known to contain 10% defective chips. If 100 chips are randomly selected, what is the expected number of defective ones? What is the standard deviation of the number of defective chips? Use Chebyshev's theorem to give bounds such that there is at least a 0.75 chance that the number of defective chips will be within the two bounds.

3–35. A new treatment for baldness is known to be effective in 70% of the cases treated. Four bald members of the same family are treated; let X be the number of successfully treated members of the family. Is X a binomial random variable? Explain.

3–36. What are Bernoulli trials? What is the relationship between Bernoulli trials and the binomial random variable?

3–37. Look at the histogram of probabilities in the binomial distribution template [Binomial.xls] for the case $n = 5$ and $p = 0.6$.

  a. Is this distribution symmetric or skewed? Now, increase the value of n to 10, 15, 20, . . . Is the distribution becoming more symmetric or more skewed? Make a formal statement about what happens to the distribution's shape when n increases.

  b. With $n = 5$, change the p value to 0.1, 0.2, . . . Observe particularly the case of $p = 0.5$. Make a formal statement about how the skewness of the distribution changes with p.

3–38. A salesperson goes door-to-door in a residential area to demonstrate the use of a new household appliance to potential customers. At the end of a demonstration, the probability that the potential customer would place an order for the product is a constant 0.2107. To perform satisfactorily on the job, the salesperson needs at least four orders. Assume that each demonstration is a Bernoulli trial.

  a. If the salesperson makes 15 demonstrations, what is the probability that there would be exactly 4 orders?

  b. If the salesperson makes 16 demonstrations, what is the probability that there would be at most 4 orders?

  c. If the salesperson makes 17 demonstrations, what is the probability that there would be at least 4 orders?

  d. If the salesperson makes 18 demonstrations, what is the probability that there would be anywhere from 4 to 8 (both inclusive) orders?

  e. If the salesperson wants to be at least 90% confident of getting at least 4 orders, at least how many demonstrations should she make?

  f. The salesperson has time to make only 22 demonstrations, and she still wants to be at least 90% confident of getting at least 4 orders. She intends to gain this confidence by improving the quality of her demonstration and thereby improving the chances of getting an order at the end of a demonstration. At least to what value should this probability be increased in order to gain the desired confidence? Your answer should be accurate to four decimal places.

3–39. An MBA graduate is applying for nine jobs, and believes that she has in each of the nine cases a constant and independent 0.48 probability of getting an offer.

  a. What is the probability that she will have at least three offers?

  b. If she wants to be 95% confident of having at least three offers, how many more jobs should she apply for? (Assume each of these additional applications will also have the same probability of success.)

  c. If there are no more than the original nine jobs that she can apply for, what value of probability of success would give her 95% confidence of at least three offers?

3–40. A computer laboratory in a school has 33 computers. Each of the 33 computers has 90% reliability. Allowing for 10% of the computers to be down, an instructor specifies an enrollment ceiling of 30 for his class. Assume that a class of 30 students is taken into the lab.

> *a.* What is the probability that each of the 30 students will get a computer in working condition?
>
> *b.* The instructor is surprised to see the low value of the answer to (*a*) and decides to improve it to at least 95% by doing one of the following:
>
>> i. Decreasing the enrollment ceiling.
>>
>> ii. Increasing the number of computers in the lab.
>>
>> iii. Increasing the reliability of all the computers.

To help the instructor, find out what the increase or decrease should be for each of the three alternatives.

3–41. A commercial jet aircraft has four engines. For an aircraft in flight to land safely, at least two engines should be in working condition. Each engine has an independent reliability of $p = 92\%$.

> *a.* What is the probability that an aircraft in flight can land safely?
>
> *b.* If the probability of landing safely must be at least 99.5%, what is the minimum value for p? Repeat the question for probability of landing safely to be 99.9%.
>
> *c.* If the reliability cannot be improved beyond 92% but the number of engines in a plane can be increased, what is the minimum number of engines that would achieve at least 99.5% probability of landing safely? Repeat for 99.9% probability.
>
> *d.* One would certainly desire 99.9% probability of landing safely. Looking at the answers to (*b*) and (*c*), what would you say is a better approach to safety, increasing the number of engines or increasing the reliability of each engine?

3–6   Negative Binomial Distribution

Consider again the case of the operator who wants to produce two good pins using a lathe that has 0.6 probability of making one good pin in each trial. Under binomial distribution, we assumed that he produces five pins and calculated the probability of getting at least two good ones. In practice, though, if only two pins are needed, the operator would produce the pins one by one and stop when he gets two good ones. For instance, if the first two are good, then he would stop right there; if the first and the third are good, then he would stop with the third; and so on. Notice that in this scenario, the number of successes is held constant at 2, and the number of trials is random. The number of trials could be 2, 3, 4, ... (Contrast this with the binomial distribution where the number of trials is fixed and the number of successes is random.)

The number of trials made in this scenario is said to follow a **negative binomial distribution.** Let *s* denote the exact number of successes desired and *p* the probability of success in each trial. Let *X* denote the number of trials made until the desired number of successes is achieved. Then *X* will follow a negative binomial distribution and we shall write $X \sim NB(s, p)$ where NB denotes negative binomial.

Negative Binomial Distribution Formulas

What is the formula for $P(X = x)$ when $X \sim NB(s, p)$? We know that the very last trial must be a success; otherwise, we would have already had the desired number of successes with $x - 1$ trials, and we should have stopped right there. The last trial being a success, the first $x - 1$ trials should have had $s - 1$ successes. Thus the formula should be

$$P(X = x) = \binom{x - 1}{s - 1} p^s(1 - p)^{(x-s)}$$

The formula for the mean can be arrived at intuitively. For instance, if $p = 0.3$, and 3 successes are desired, then the expected number of trials to achieve 3 successes is 10. Thus the mean should have the formula $\mu = s/p$. The variance is given by the formula $\sigma^2 = s(1 - p)/p^2$.

Negative Binomial Distribution

If $X \sim NB(s, p)$, then

$$P(X = x) = \binom{x - 1}{s - 1} p^s(1 - p)^{(x-s)} \qquad x = s, s + 1, s + 2, \ldots$$

$$E(X) = s/p$$
$$V(X) = s(1 - p)/p^2$$

For example, if $s = 2$ and $p = 0.6$, then

$$P(X = 5) = \binom{4}{1} * 0.6^2 * 0.4^3 = 0.0922$$

$$E(X) = 2/0.6 = 3.3333$$
$$V(X) = 2 * 0.4/0.6^2 = 2.2222$$

Problem Solving with the Template

Figure 3–15 shows the negative binomial distribution template. When we enter the s and p values, the template updates the probability tabulation and draws a histogram on the right.

FIGURE 3–15   Negative Binomial Distribution Template
             [Negative Binomial.xls]

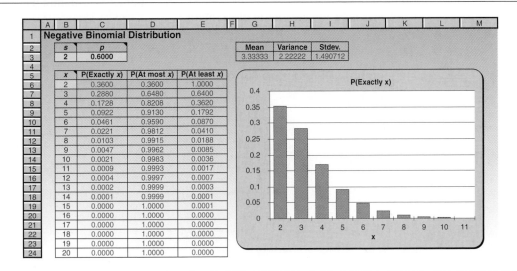

Let us return to the operator who wants to keep producing pins until he has two good ones. The probability of getting a good one at any trial is 0.6. What is the probability that he would produce exactly five? Looking at the template, we see that the answer is 0.0922, which agrees with the calculation in the preceding box. We can, in addition, see that the probability of producing at most five is 0.9130 and at least five is 0.1792.

Suppose the operator has enough time to produce only four pins. How confident can he be that he would have two good ones within the available time? Looking at the template, we see that the probability of needing at most four trials is 0.8208 and hence he can be about 82% confident.

If he wants to be at least 95% confident, at least how many trials should he be prepared for? Looking at the template in the "At most" column, we infer that he should be prepared for at least six trials, since five trials yield only 91.30% confidence and six trials yield 95.90%.

Suppose the operator has enough time to produce only four pins and still wants to be at least 95% confident of getting two good pins within the available time. Suppose, further, he wants to achieve this by increasing the value of p. What is the minimum p that would achieve this? Using the **Goal Seek** command, this can be answered as 0.7514. Specifically, you set cell D8 to 0.95 by changing cell C3.

3–7   The Geometric Distribution

In a negative binomial distribution, the number of desired successes s can be any number. But in some practical situations, the number of successes desired is just one. For instance, if you are attempting to pass a test or get some information, it is enough to have just one success. Let X be the (random) number of Bernoulli trials, each having p probability of success, required to achieve just one success. Then X follows a **geometric distribution,** and we shall write $X \sim G(p)$. Note that the geometric distribution is a special case of the negative binomial distribution where $s = 1$. The reason for the name "geometric distribution" is that the sequence of probabilities $P(X = 1)$, $P(X = 2)$, . . . , follows a *geometric progression.*

Geometric Distribution Formulas

Because the geometric distribution is a special case of the negative binomial distribution where $s = 1$, the formulas for the negative binomial distribution with s fixed as 1 can be used for the geometric distribution.

Geometric Distribution Formulas

If $X \sim G(p)$, then

$$P(X = x) = p(1 - p)^{(x-1)} \qquad x = 1, 2, \ldots$$
$$E(X) = 1/p$$
$$V(X) = (1 - p)/p^2$$

For example, if $p = 0.6$, then

$$P(X = 5) = 0.6 * 0.4^4 = 0.0154$$
$$E(X) = 1/0.6 = 1.6667$$
$$V(X) = 0.4/0.6^2 = 1.1111$$

FIGURE 3–16   Geometric Distribution Template
[Geometric.xls]

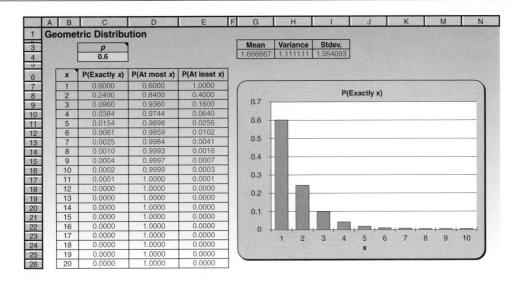

x	P(Exactly x)	P(At most x)	P(At least x)
1	0.6000	0.6000	1.0000
2	0.2400	0.8400	0.4000
3	0.0960	0.9360	0.1600
4	0.0384	0.9744	0.0640
5	0.0154	0.9898	0.0256
6	0.0061	0.9959	0.0102
7	0.0025	0.9984	0.0041
8	0.0010	0.9993	0.0016
9	0.0004	0.9997	0.0007
10	0.0002	0.9999	0.0003
11	0.0001	1.0000	0.0001
12	0.0000	1.0000	0.0000
13	0.0000	1.0000	0.0000
14	0.0000	1.0000	0.0000
15	0.0000	1.0000	0.0000
16	0.0000	1.0000	0.0000
17	0.0000	1.0000	0.0000
18	0.0000	1.0000	0.0000
19	0.0000	1.0000	0.0000
20	0.0000	1.0000	0.0000

Mean 1.666667 Variance 1.111111 Stdev. 1.054093

p = 0.6

Problem Solving with the Template

Consider the operator who produces pins one by one on a lathe that has 0.6 probability of producing a good pin at each trial. Suppose he wants only one good pin and stops as soon as he gets one. What is the probability that he would produce exactly five pins? The template that can be used to answer this and related questions is shown in Figure 3–16. On that template, we enter the value 0.6 for p. The answer can now be read off as 0.0154, which agrees with the example calculation in the preceding box. Further, we can read on the template that the probability of at most five is 0.9898 and at least five is 0.0256. Also note that the probability of exactly 1, 2, 3, . . . , trials follows the sequence 0.6, 0.24, 0.096, 0.0384, . . . , which is indeed a geometric progression with common ratio 0.4.

Now suppose the operator has time enough for at most two pins; how confident can he be of getting a good one within the available time? From the template, the answer is 0.8400, or 84%. What if he wants to be at least 95% confident? Again from the template, he must have enough time for four pins, because three would yield only 93.6% confidence and four yields 97.44%.

Suppose the operator wants to be 95% confident of getting a good pin by producing at most two pins. What value of p will achieve this? Using the Goal Seek command the answer is found to be 0.7761.

3–8   The Hypergeometric Distribution

Assume that a box contains 10 pins of which 6 are good and the rest defective. An operator picks 5 pins at random from the 10, and is interested in the number of good pins picked. Let X denote the number of good pins picked. We should first note that this is a case of sampling without replacement and therefore X is *not* a binomial random variable. The probability of success p, which is the probability of picking a good pin, is neither constant nor independent from trial to trial. The first pin picked has 0.6 probability of being good; the second has either 5/9 or 6/9 probability, depending on whether or not the first was good. Therefore, X does not follow a binomial distribution, but follows what is called a **hypergeometric distribution.** In general, when a pool of size N contains S successes and $(N - S)$ failures, and a random sample of size n is drawn from the pool, the number of successes X in the sample follows

CHAPTER 4

FIGURE 3–17   Schematic for Hypergeometric Distribution

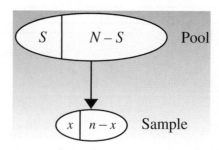

a hypergeometric distribution. We shall then write $X \sim \mathrm{HG}(n, S, N)$. The situation is depicted in Figure 3–17.

Hypergeometric Distribution Formulas

Let us derive the formula for $P(X = x)$ when X is hypergeometrically distributed. The x number of successes have to come from the S successes in the pool, which can happen in $\binom{S}{x}$ ways. The $(n - x)$ failures have to come from the $(N - S)$ failures in the pool, which can happen in $\binom{N-S}{n-x}$ ways. Together the x successes and $(n - x)$ failures can happen in $\binom{S}{x}\binom{N-S}{n-x}$ ways. Finally, there are $\binom{N}{n}$ ways of selecting a sample of size n. Putting them all together,

$$P(X = x) = \frac{\binom{S}{x}\binom{N - S}{n - x}}{\binom{N}{n}}$$

In this formula n cannot exceed N since the sample size cannot exceed the pool size. There is also a minimum possible value and a maximum possible value for x, depending on the values of n, S, and N. For instance, if $n = 9$, $S = 5$, and $N = 12$, you may verify that there would be at least two successes and at most five. In general, the minimum possible value for x is $\mathrm{Max}(0, n - N + S)$ and the maximum possible value is $\mathrm{Min}(n, S)$.

Hypergeometric Distribution Formulas

If $X \sim \mathrm{HG}(n, S, N)$, then

$$P(X = x) = \frac{\binom{S}{x}\binom{N - S}{n - x}}{\binom{N}{n}} \qquad \mathrm{Max}(0, n - N + S) \le x \le \mathrm{Min}(n, S)$$

$$E(X) = np \qquad \text{where } p = S/N$$

$$V(X) = np(1 - p)\left[\frac{N - n}{N - 1}\right]$$

For example, if $n = 5$, $S = 6$, and $N = 10$, then

$$P(X = 2) = \frac{\binom{6}{2}\binom{10-6}{5-2}}{\binom{10}{5}} = 0.2381$$

$$E(X) = 5 * (6/10) = 3.00$$
$$V(X) = 5 * 0.6 * (1 - 0.6) * (10 - 5)/(10 - 1) = 0.6667$$

The proportion of successes in the pool, which is the ratio S/N, is the probability of the first trial being a success. This ratio is denoted by the symbol p since it resembles the p used in the binomial distribution. The expected value and variance of X are expressed using p as

$$E(X) = np$$

$$V(X) = np(1 - p)\left[\frac{N - n}{N - 1}\right]$$

Notice that the formula for $E(X)$ is the same as for the binomial case. The formula for $V(X)$ is similar to but not the same as the binomial case. The difference is the additional factor in square brackets. This additional factor approaches 1 as N becomes larger and larger compared to n and may be dropped when N is, say, 100 times as large as n. We can then approximate the hypergeometric distribution as a binomial distribution.

Problem Solving with the Template

Figure 3–18 shows the template used for the hypergeometric distribution. Let us consider the case where a box contains 10 pins out of which 6 are good, and the operator picks 5 at random. What is the probability that exactly 2 good pins are picked? The answer is 0.2381 (cell C8). Additionally, the probabilities that at most two and at least two good ones are picked are, respectively, 0.2619 and 0.9762.

Suppose the operator needs at least three good pins. How confident can he be of getting at least three good pins? The answer is 0.7381 (cell E9). Suppose the operator wants to increase this confidence to 90% by adding some good pins to the pool. How many good pins should be added to the pool? This question, unfortunately, cannot be answered using the Goal Seek command for three reasons. First, the Goal Seek command works on a continuous scale, whereas S and N must be integers. Second, *when* n, S, *or* N *is changed the tabulation may shift and* P *(at least 3) may not be in cell E9!* Third, the Goal Seek command can change only one cell at a time. But in many problems, two cells (S and N) may have to change. Hence do not use the Goal Seek or the Solver on this template. Also, be careful to read the probabilities from the correct cells.

Let us solve this problem without using the Goal Seek command. If a good pin is added to the pool, what happens to S and N? They *both* increase by 1. Thus we should enter 7 for S and 11 for N. When we do, P(at least 3) = 0.8030, which is less than the desired 90% confidence. So we add one more good pin to the pool. Continuing in this fashion, we find that at least four good pins must be added to the pool.

Another way to increase P(at least 3) is to remove a bad pin from the pool. What happens to S and N when a bad pin is removed? S will remain the same and N will decrease by one. Suppose the operator wants to be 80% confident that at least three

FIGURE 3–18   The Template for the Hypergeometric Distribution
[Hypergeometric.xls]

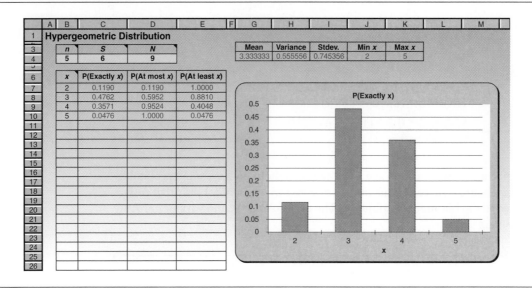

good pins will be selected. How many bad pins must be removed from the pool? Decreasing N one by one, we find that removing one bad pin is enough.

3–9   The Poisson Distribution

Imagine an automatic lathe that mass produces pins. On rare occasions, let us assume that the lathe produces a gem of a pin which is so perfect that it can be used for a very special purpose. To make the case specific, let us assume the lathe produces 20,000 pins and has 1/10,000 chance of producing a perfect one. Suppose we are interested in the number of perfect pins produced. We could try to calculate this number by using the binomial distribution with $n = 20,000$ and $p = 1/10,000$. But the calculation would be almost impossible because n is so large, p is so small, and the binomial formula calls for $n!$ and p^{n-x}, which are hard to calculate even on a computer. However, the expected number of perfect pins produced is $np = 20,000*(1/10,000) = 2$, which is neither too large nor too small. It turns out that as long as the expected value $\mu = np$ is neither too large nor too small, say, lies between 0.01 and 50, the binomial formula for $P(X = x)$ can be approximated as

$$P(X = x) = \frac{e^{-\mu}\mu^{x}}{x!} \qquad x = 0, 1, 2, \ldots$$

where e is the natural base of logarithms, equal to 2.71828. . . . This formula is known as the **Poisson formula,** and the distribution is called the **Poisson distribution.** In general, if we count the number of times a rare event occurs during a fixed interval, then that number would follow a Poisson distribution. We know the mean $\mu = np$.

Considering the variance of a Poisson distribution, we note that the binomial variance is $np(1 - p)$. But since p is very small, $(1 - p)$ is close to 1 and therefore can be omitted. Thus the variance of a Poisson random variable is np, which happens to be the same as its mean. The Poisson formula needs only μ, and not n or p.

We suddenly realize that we need not know n and p separately. All we need to know is their product, μ, which is the mean and the variance of the distribution. Just one number, μ, is enough to describe the whole distribution, and in this sense, the Poisson distribution is a simple one, even simpler than the binomial. If *X* follows a Poisson distribution, we shall write $X \sim P(\mu)$ where μ is the expected value of the distribution. The following box summarizes the Poisson distribution.

Poisson Distribution Formulas

If $X \sim P(\mu)$, then

$$P(X = x) = \frac{e^{-\mu}\mu^x}{x!} \qquad x = 0, 1, 2, \ldots$$

$$E(X) = np = \mu$$

$$V(X) = np = \mu$$

For example, if μ = 2, then

$$P(X = 3) = \frac{e^{-2}2^3}{3!} = 0.1804$$

$$E(X) = \mu = 2.00$$

$$V(X) = \mu = 2.00$$

The Poisson template is shown in Figure 3–19. The only input needed is the mean μ in cell C4. The starting value of *x* in cell B7 is usually zero, but it can be changed as desired.

Problem Solving with the Template

Let us return to the case of the automatic lathe that produces perfect pins on rare occasions. Assume that the lathe produces on the average two perfect pins a day, and an operator wants at least three perfect pins. What is the probability that it will produce at least three perfect pins on a given day? Looking at the template, we find the answer to be 0.3233. Suppose the operator waits for two days. In two days the lathe

**FIGURE 3–19 Poisson Distribution Template
[Poisson.xls]**

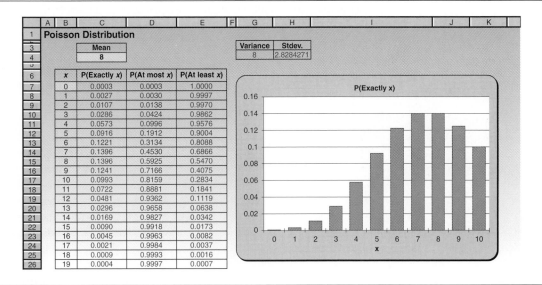

will produce on average four perfect pins. We should therefore change the mean in cell C4 to 4. What is the probability that the lathe will produce at least three perfect pins in two days? Using the template, we find the answer to be 0.7619. If the operator wants to be at least 95% confident of producing at least three perfect pins, how many days should he be prepared to wait? Again, using the template, we find that the operator should be prepared to wait at least four days.

A Poisson distribution also occurs in other types of situations leading to other forms of analysis. Consider an emergency call center. The number of distress calls received within a specific period, being a count of rare events, is usually Poisson-distributed. In this context, suppose the call center receives on average two calls per hour. In addition, suppose the crew at the center can handle up to three calls in an hour. What is the probability that the crew can handle all the calls received in a given hour? Since the crew can handle up to three calls, we look for the probability of at most three calls. From the template, the answer is 0.8571. If the crew wanted to be at least 95% confident of handling all the calls received during a given hour, how many calls should it be prepared to handle? Again, from the template, the answer is five, because the probability of at most four calls is less than 95% and of at most five calls is more than 95%.

3–10 Continuous Random Variables

Instead of depicting probability distributions by simple graphs, where the height of the line above each value represents the probability of that value of the random variable, let us use a histogram. We will associate the *area* of each rectangle of the histogram with the probability of the particular value represented. Let us look at a simple example. Let X be the time, measured in minutes, it takes to complete a given task. A histogram of the probability distribution of X is shown in Figure 3–20.

The probability of each value is the area of the rectangle over the value and is written on top of the rectangle. Since the rectangles all have the same base, the height of each rectangle is proportional to the probability. Note that the probabilities add to 1.00, as required. Now suppose that X can be measured more accurately. The distribution of X, with time now measured to the nearest half-minute, is shown in Figure 3–21.

Let us continue the process. Time is a continuous random variable; it can take on any value measured on an interval of numbers. We may, therefore, refine our measurement to the nearest quarter-minute, the nearest 5 seconds, or the nearest second, or we can use even more finely divided units. As we refine the measurement scale, the number of rectangles in the histogram increases and the width of each rectangle decreases. The probability of each value is still measured by the area of the rectangle above it, and the total area of all rectangles remains 1.00, as required of all probability distributions. As we keep refining our measurement scale, the discrete distribution of

FIGURE 3–20 **Histogram of the Probability Distribution of Time to Complete a Task, with Time Measured to the Nearest Minute**

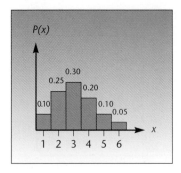

FIGURE 3–21 **Histogram of the Probability Distribution of Time to Complete a Task, with Time Measured to the Nearest Half-Minute**

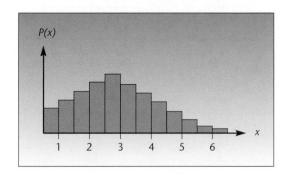

FIGURE 3–22   **Histograms of the Distribution of Time to Complete a Task as Measurement Is Refined to Smaller and Smaller Intervals of Time, and the Limiting Density Function** *f*(*x*)

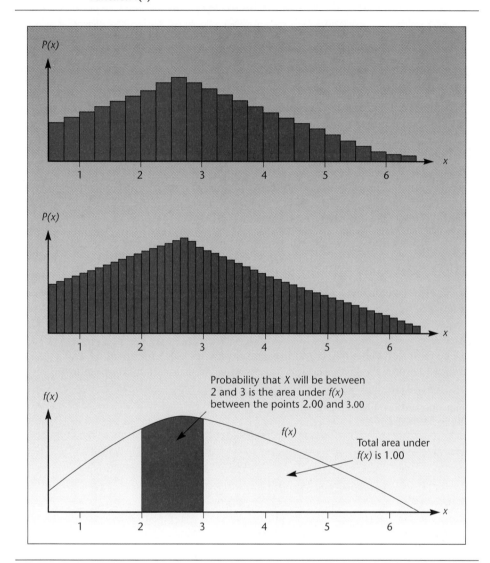

X tends to a continuous probability distribution. The steplike surface formed by the tops of the rectangles in the histogram tends to a smooth function. This function is denoted by $f(x)$ and is called the **probability density function** of the continuous random variable X. Probabilities are still measured as areas under the curve. The probability that the task will be completed in 2 to 3 minutes is the area under $f(x)$ between the points $x = 2$ and $x = 3$. Histograms of the probability distribution of X with our measurement scale refined further and further are shown in Figure 3–22. Also shown is the density function $f(x)$ of the limiting continuous random variable X. The density function is the limit of the histograms as the number of rectangles approaches infinity and the width of each rectangle approaches zero.

Now that we have developed an intuitive feel for continuous random variables, and for probabilities of intervals of values as areas under a density function, we make some formal definitions.

A **continuous random variable** is a random variable that can take on any value in an interval of numbers.

The probabilities associated with a continuous random variable X are determined by the **probability density function** of the random variable. The function, denoted $f(x)$, has the following properties.

1. $f(x) \geq 0$ for all x.
2. The probability that X will be between two numbers a and b is equal to the area under $f(x)$ between a and b.
3. The total area under the entire curve of $f(x)$ is equal to 1.00.

When the sample space is continuous, the probability of any single given value is zero. For a continuous random variable, therefore, the probability of occurrence of any given value is zero. We see this from property 2, noting that the area under a curve between a point and itself is the area of a line, which is zero. *For a continuous random variable, nonzero probabilities are associated only with intervals of numbers.*

We define the cumulative distribution function $F(x)$ for a continuous random variable similarly to the way we defined it for a discrete random variable: $F(x)$ is the probability that X is less than (or equal to) x.

The **cumulative distribution function** of a continuous random variable:[4]

$$F(x) = P(X \leq x) = \text{area under } f(x) \text{ between the } smallest \text{ possible value of } X \text{ (often } -\infty) \text{ and point } x$$

The cumulative distribution function $F(x)$ is a smooth, nondecreasing function that increases from 0 to 1.00. The connection between $f(x)$ and $F(x)$ is demonstrated in Figure 3–23.

The expected value of a continuous random variable X, denoted by $E(X)$, and its variance, denoted by $V(X)$, require the use of calculus for their computation.[5]

FIGURE 3–23   Probability Density Function and Cumulative Distribution Function of a Continuous Random Variable

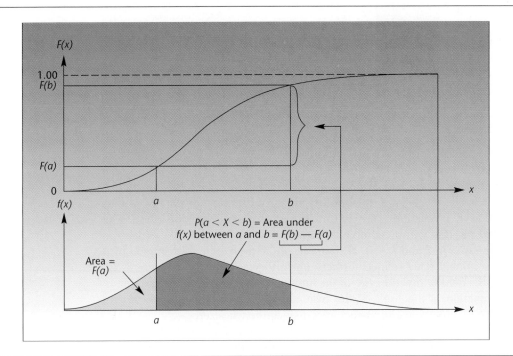

---

[4]If you are familiar with calculus, you know that the area under a curve of a function is given by the integral of the function. The probability that X will be between a and b is the definite integral of $f(x)$ between these two points: $P(a < X < b) = \int_a^b f(x)\, dx$. In calculus notation, we define the cumulative distribution function as $F(x) = \int_{-\infty}^x f(y)\, dy$.

[5]$E(X) = \int_{-\infty}^\infty x f(x)\, dx; \ V(X) = \int_{-\infty}^\infty [x - E(X)]^2 f(x)\, dx$.

3–11   The Uniform Distribution

The uniform distribution is the simplest of continuous distributions. The probability density function is

$$f(x) = 1/(b - a) \qquad a \leq x \leq b$$
$$= 0 \qquad \text{all other } x$$

where a is the minimum possible value and b is the maximum possible value of X. The graph of $f(x)$ is shown in Figure 3–24. Because the curve of $f(x)$ is a flat line, the area under it between any two points x_1 and x_2, where $a \leq x_1 < x_2 \leq b$, will be a rectangle with height $1/(b - a)$ and width $(x_2 - x_1)$. Thus $P(x_1 \leq X \leq x_2) = (x_2 - x_1)/(b - a)$. If X is uniformly distributed between a and b, we shall write $X \sim U(a, b)$.

The mean of the distribution is the midpoint between a and b, which is $(a + b)/2$. By using integration, it can be shown that the variance is $(b - a)^2/12$. Because the shape of a uniform distribution is always a rectangle, the skewness and kurtosis are the same for all uniform distributions. The skewness is zero. (Why?) Because the shape is flat, the (relative) kurtosis is negative, always equal to -1.2.

The formulas for uniform distribution are summarized in the following box. Because the probability calculation is simple, there is no special spreadsheet function for uniform distribution. The box contains some sample calculations.

Uniform Distribution Formulas

If $X \sim U(a, b)$, then

$$f(x) = 1/(b - a) \qquad\qquad a \leq x \leq b$$
$$= 0 \qquad\qquad\qquad \text{all other } x$$
$$P(x_1 \leq X \leq x_2) = (x_2 - x_1)/(b - a) \qquad a \leq x_1 < x_2 \leq b$$
$$E(X) = (a + b)/2$$
$$V(X) = (b - a)^2/12$$

For example, if $a = 10$ and $b = 20$, then

$$P(12 \leq X \leq 18) = (18 - 12)/(20 - 10) = 0.6$$
$$E(X) = (10 + 20)/2 = 15$$
$$V(X) = (20 - 10)^2/12 = 8.3333$$

A common instance of uniform distribution is waiting time for a facility that goes in cycles. Two good examples are a shuttle bus and an elevator, which move, roughly, in cycles with some cycle time. If a user comes to a stop at a random time and waits till the facility arrives, the waiting time will be uniformly distributed between a minimum of zero and a maximum equal to the cycle time. In other words, if a shuttle bus has a cycle time of 20 minutes, the waiting time would be uniformly distributed between 0 and 20 minutes.

FIGURE 3–24   The Uniform Distribution

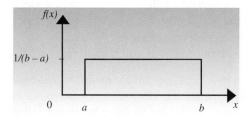

FIGURE 3–25   Template for the Uniform Distribution
[Uniform.xls]

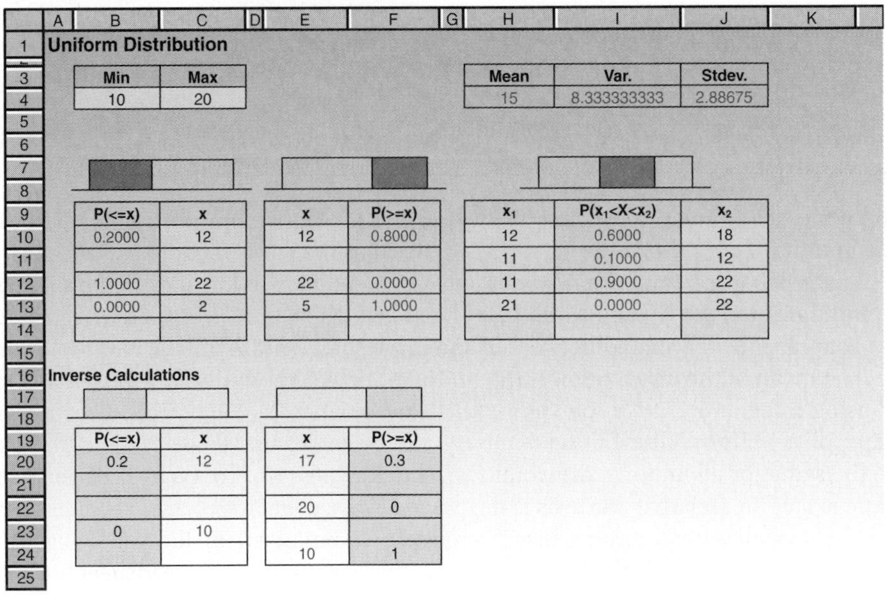

Problem Solving with the Template

Figure 3–25 shows the template for the uniform distributions. If $X \sim U(10, 20)$, what is $P(12 \leq X \leq 18)$? In the template, make sure the Min and Max are set to 10 and 20 in cells B4 and C4. Enter 12 and 18 in cells H10 and J10. The answer of 0.6 appears in cell I10.

What is the probability $P(X < 12)$? To answer this, enter 12 in cell C10. The answer 0.2 appears in cell B10. What is $P(X > 12)$? To answer this, enter 12 in cell E10. The answer 0.8 appears in F10.

Inverse calculations are possible in the bottom area of the template. Suppose you want to find x such that $P(X < x) = 0.2$. Enter 0.2 in cell B20. The answer, 12, appears in cell C20. To find x such that $P(X > x) = 0.3$, enter 0.3 in cell F20. The answer, 17, appears in cell E20.

As usual, you may also use facilities such as the Goal Seek command or the Solver tool in conjunction with this template.

3–12   The Exponential Distribution

Suppose an event occurs with an average frequency of λ occurrences per hour and this average frequency is constant in that the probability that the event will occur during any tiny duration t is λt. Suppose further we arrive at the scene at any given time and wait till the event occurs. The waiting time will then follow an **exponential distribution,** which is the continuous limit of the geometric distribution. Suppose our waiting time was x. For the event (or success) to occur at time x, every tiny duration t from time 0 to time x should be a failure and the interval x to $x + t$ must be a success. This is nothing but a geometric distribution. To get the continuous version, we take the limit of this process as t approaches zero.

The exponential distribution is fairly common in practice. Here are some examples.

1. The time between two successive breakdowns of a machine will be exponentially distributed. This information is relevant to maintenance engineers. The mean μ in this case is known as the **mean time between failures,** or **MTBF.**

2. The life of a product that fails by accident rather than by wear-and-tear follows an exponential distribution. Electronic components are good examples. This information is relevant to warranty policies.

3. The time gap between two successive arrivals to a waiting line, known as the **interarrival time,** will be exponentially distributed. This information is relevant to waiting line management.

When X is exponentially distributed with frequency λ, we shall write $X \sim E(\lambda)$. The probability density function $f(x)$ of the exponential distribution has the form

$$f(x) = \lambda e^{-\lambda x}$$

where λ is the frequency with which the event occurs. The frequency λ is expressed as so many times per unit time, such as 1.2 times per month. The mean of the distribution is $1/\lambda$ and the variance is $(1/\lambda)^2$. Just like the geometric distribution, the exponential distribution is positively skewed.

A Remarkable Property

The exponential distribution has a remarkable property. Suppose the time between two successive breakdowns of a machine is exponentially distributed with an MTBF of 100 hours, and we have just witnessed one breakdown. If we start a stopwatch as soon as it is repaired and put back into service so as to measure the time until the next failure, then that time will, of course, be exponentially distributed with a μ of 100 hours. What is remarkable is the following. Suppose we arrive at the scene at some random time and start the stopwatch (instead of starting it immediately after a breakdown); the time until next breakdown will still be exponentially distributed with the same μ of 100 hours. In other words, it is immaterial when the event occurred last and how much later we start the stopwatch. For this reason, an exponential process is known as a *memoryless process*. It does not depend on the past at all.

The Template

The template for this distribution is seen in Figure 3–26. The following box summarizes the formulas and provides example calculations.

Exponential Distribution Formulas

If $X \sim E(\lambda)$, then

$$f(x) = \lambda e^{-\lambda x} \qquad x \geq 0$$
$$P(X \leq x) = 1 - e^{-\lambda x} \qquad \text{for } x \geq 0$$
$$P(X \geq x) = e^{-\lambda x} \qquad \text{for } x \geq 0$$
$$P(x_1 \leq X \leq x_2) = e^{-\lambda x_1} - e^{-\lambda x_2} \qquad 0 \leq x_1 < x_2$$
$$E(X) = 1/\lambda$$
$$V(X) = 1/\lambda^2$$

For example, if $\lambda = 1.2$, then

$$P(X \geq 0.5) = e^{-1.2*0.5} = 0.5488$$
$$P(1 \leq X \leq 2) = e^{-1.2*1} - e^{-1.2*2} = 0.2105$$
$$E(X) = 1/1.2 = 0.8333$$
$$V(X) = 1/1.2^2 = 0.6944$$

To use the exponential distribution template seen in Figure 3–26, the value of λ must be entered in cell B4. At times, the mean μ rather than λ may be known, in which case its reciprocal $1/\mu$ is what should be entered as λ in cell B4. Note that λ is

FIGURE 3–26   Exponential Distribution Template
[Exponential.xls]

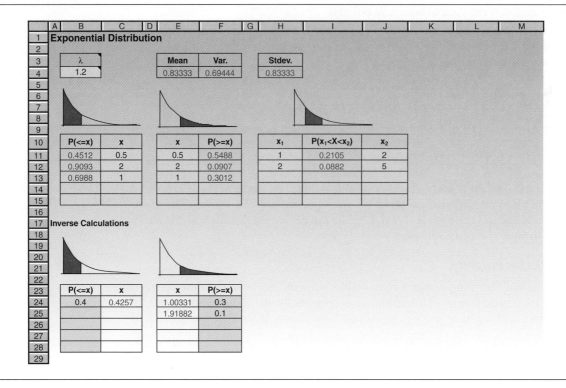

the average number of occurrences of a rare event in unit time and μ is the average time gap between two successive occurrences. The shaded cells are the input cells and the rest are protected. As usual, the Goal Seek command and the Solver tool can be used in conjunction with this template to solve problems.

EXAMPLE 3–5

A particular brand of handheld computers fails following an exponential distribution with a μ of 54.82 months. The company gives a warranty for 6 months.

    a. What percentage of the computers will fail within the warranty period?

    b. If the manufacturer wants only 8% of the computers to fail during the warranty period, what should be the average life?

Solution

    a. Enter the reciprocal of 54.82 = 0.0182 as λ in the template. (You may enter the formula "=1/54.82" in the cell. But then you will not be able to use the Goal Seek command to change this entry. The Goal Seek command requires that the changing cell contain a number rather than a formula.) The answer we are looking for is the area to the left of 6. Therefore, enter 6 in cell C11. The area to the left, 0.1037, appears in cell B11. Thus 10.37% of the computers will fail within the warranty period.

    b. Enter 0.08 in cell B25. Invoke the Goal Seek command to set cell C25 to the value of 6 by changing cell B4. The λ value in cell B4 reaches 0.0139, which corresponds to a μ value of 71.96 months, as seen in cell E4. Therefore, the average life of the computers must be 71.96 months.

Value at Risk

When a business venture involves chances of large losses, a measure of risk that many companies use is the **value at risk.** Suppose the profit from a venture has a negatively

FIGURE 3–27   Distribution of Profit Showing Value at Risk

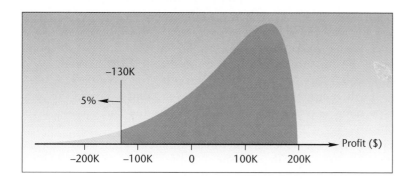

FIGURE 3–28   Distribution of Loss Showing Value at Risk

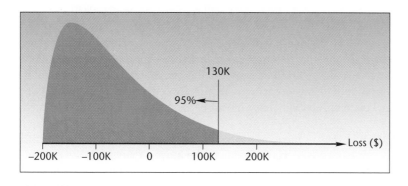

skewed distribution, shown in Figure 3–27. A negative profit signifies loss. The distribution shows that large losses are possible. A common definition of value at risk is the amount of loss at the 5th percentile of the distribution. In Figure 3–27, the 5th percentile is $–130,000, meaning a loss of $130,000. Thus the value at risk is $130,000.

If the profit is a discrete random variable, then the percentile used may be a convenient one closest to 5%.

If the distribution of loss rather than profit is plotted, then we will have the mirror image of Figure 3–27, which is shown in Figure 3–28. In this case, the value at risk is the 95th percentile.

Keep in mind that value at risk applies only to distributions of profit/loss where there exist small chances of large losses.

3–13   Using the Computer

Using Excel Formulas for Some Standard Distributions

Excel has built-in functions that you may use to calculate certain probabilities without using templates. These formulas are described in this section.

You can use **BINOMDIST** to obtain the individual term binomial distribution probability. In the formula BINOMDIST(x, n, p, cumulative), x is the number of successes in trials, n is the number of independent trials, p is the probability of success on each trial, and cumulative is a logical value that determines the form of the function. If cumulative is TRUE, then BINOMDIST returns the cumulative distribution function, which is the probability that there are at most x successes; if FALSE, it returns the probability mass function, which is the probability that there are x successes.

NEGBINOMDIST returns the negative binomial distribution. By using the formula NEGBINOMDIST(f, s, p) you can obtain the probability that there will be f failures before the sth success, when the constant probability of a success is p. As we can see, the conventions for negative binomial distributions are slightly different in Excel. We have used the symbol x in this chapter to denote the total number of trials until the sth success is achieved, but in the Excel formula we count the total number of failures before the sth success. For example, NEGBINOMDIST (3,2,0.5) will return the probability of three failures before the 2nd success, which is the same as probability of 5 trials before the 2nd success. It returns the value 0.0922.

No function is available for geometric distribution per se, but the negative binomial formula can be used with s=1. For example, the geometric probability of 5 trials when p=0.6 can be computed using the formula NEGBINOMDIST(4,1,0.6). It returns the value of 0.2381.

HYPGEOMDIST returns the hypergeometric distribution. Using the formula HYPGEOMDIST(x, n, s, N) you can obtain the probability of x success in a random sample of size n, when the population has s success and size N. For example, the formula HYPGEOMDIST(2,5,6,10) will return a value of 0.2381.

POISSON returns the Poisson distribution. In the formula POISSON(x, mean, cumulative), x is the number of events, *mean* is the expected numeric value and *cumulative* is a logical value that determines the form of the probability distribution returned. If cumulative is TRUE, POISSON returns the cumulative Poisson probability that the number of random events occurring will be between zero and x inclusive; if FALSE, it returns the Poisson probability mass function that the number of events occurring will be exactly x.

EXPONDIST returns the exponential distribution. In the formula EXPONDIST (x, lambda, cumulative), x is the value of the function, *lambda* is the parameter value, and *cumulative* is a logical value that indicates which form of the exponential function to provide. If cumulative is TRUE, EXPONDIST returns the cumulative distribution function; if FALSE, it returns the probability density function. For example, EXPONDIST (0.5, 1.2, TRUE) will return the cumulative exponential probability $P(X < x)$, which is 0.4512, while EXPONDIST(0.5, 1.2, FALSE) will return the exponential probability density function $f(x)$, which we do not need for any practical purpose.

No probability function is available for the uniform distribution but the probability formulas are simple enough to compute manually.

Using MINITAB for Some Standard Distributions

In this section we will demonstrate how we can use MINITAB to obtain the probability density function or cumulative distribution function of various random variables.

Start by choosing Calc ▶ Probability Distributions from the menu. This option will display commands that allow you to compute probability densities and cumulative probabilities for continuous and discrete distributions. For example when you select Calc ▶ Probability Distributions ▶ Binomial, the Binomial Distribution dialog box will appear. From the items available in the dialog box, you can choose to calculate probabilities or cumulative probabilities. You also need to specify the parameters of the binomial distribution, which are number of trials and event probability. In the input section the values for which you aim to obtain probability densities or cumulative probabilities are specified. These values can be a constant or a set of values that have been defined in a column. Then press OK to observe the obtained result in the Session window. Figure 3–29 shows how MINITAB has been used for obtaining probability distributions for a binomial distribution with parameters 4 and 0.6. The final result and corresponding session commands are presented in the session window.

FIGURE 3–29   Using MINITAB for Generating a Binomial Distribution

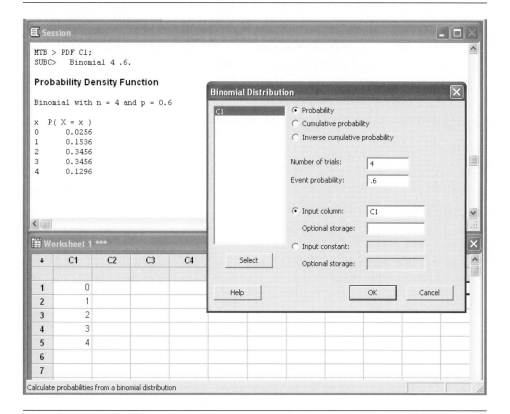

3–14   Summary and Review of Terms

In this chapter we described several important standard random variables, the associated formulas, and problem solving with spreadsheets. In order to use a spreadsheet template, you need to know *which* template to use, but first you need to know the kind of random variable at hand. This summary concentrates on this question.

A **discrete random variable** X will follow a **binomial distribution** if it is the number of successes in n independent **Bernoulli trials.** Make sure that the probability of success, p, remains constant in all trials. X will follow a **negative binomial distribution** if it is the number of Bernoulli trials made to achieve a desired number of successes. It will follow a **geometric distribution** when the desired number of successes is one. X will follow a **hypergeometric distribution** if it is the number of successes in a random sample drawn from a finite pool of successes and failures. X will follow a **Poisson distribution** if it is the number of occurrences of a rare event during a finite period.

Waiting time for an event that occurs periodically is **uniformly distributed.** Waiting time for a rare event is **exponentially distributed.**

3–42. An investment portfolio has equal proportions invested in five stocks. The expected returns and standard deviations (both in percent per year) are (8, 3), (5, 2), (12, 8), (7, 9), (14, 15). What are average return and standard deviation for this portfolio?

3–43. A graduating student keeps applying for jobs until she has three offers. The probability of getting an offer at any trial is 0.48.

  a. What is the expected number of applications? What is the variance?

  b. If she has enough time to complete only six applications, how confident can she be of getting three offers within the available time?

  c. If she wants to be at least 95% confident of getting three offers, how many applications should she prepare?

  d. Suppose she has time for at most six applications. For what minimum value of p can she still have 95% confidence of getting three offers within the available time?

3–44. A real estate agent has four houses to sell before the end of the month by contacting prospective customers one by one. Each customer has an independent 0.24 probability of buying a house on being contacted by the agent.

  a. If the agent has enough time to contact only 15 customers, how confident can she be of selling all four houses within the available time?

  b. If the agent wants to be at least 70% confident of selling all the houses within the available time, at least how many customers should she contact? (If necessary, extend the template downward to more rows.)

  c. What minimum value of p will yield 70% confidence of selling all four houses by contacting at most 15 customers?

  d. To answer (*c*) above more thoroughly, tabulate the confidence for p values ranging from 0.2 to 0.6 in steps of 0.05.

3–45. A graduating student keeps applying for jobs until she gets an offer. The probability of getting an offer at any trial is 0.35.

  a. What is the expected number of applications? What is the variance?

  b. If she has enough time to complete at most four applications, how confident can she be of getting an offer within the available time?

  c. If she wants to be at least 95% confident of getting an offer, how many applications should she prepare?

  d. Suppose she has time for at most four applications. For what minimum value of p can she have 95% confidence of getting an offer within the available time?

3–46. A shipment of pins contains 25 good ones and 2 defective ones. At the receiving department, an inspector picks three pins at random and tests them. If any defective pin is found among the three that are tested, the shipment would be rejected.

  a. What is the probability that the shipment would be accepted?

  b. To increase the probability of acceptance to at least 90%, it is decided to do one of the following:

  i. Add some good pins to the shipment.

  ii. Remove some defective pins in the shipment.

For each of the two options, find out exactly how many pins should be added or removed.

3–47. A committee of 7 members is to be formed by selecting members at random from a pool of 14 candidates consisting of 5 women and 9 men.

  a. What is the probability that there will be at least three women in the committee?

b. It is desired to increase the chance that there are at least three women in the committee to 80% by doing one of the following:

i. Adding more women to the pool.

ii. Removing some men from the pool.

For each of the two options, find out how many should be added or removed.

3–48. A mainframe computer in a university crashes on the average 0.71 time in a semester.

a. What is the probability that it will crash at least two times in a given semester?

b. What is the probability that it will not crash at all in a given semester?

c. The MIS administrator wants to increase the probability of no crash at all in a semester to at least 90%. What is the largest μ that will achieve this goal?

3–49. The number of rescue calls received by a rescue squad in a city follows a Poisson distribution with $\mu = 2.83$ per day. The squad can handle at most four calls a day.

a. What is the probability that the squad will be able to handle all the calls on a particular day?

b. The squad wants to have at least 95% confidence of being able to handle all the calls received in a day. At least how many calls a day should the squad be prepared for?

c. Assuming that the squad can handle at most four calls a day, what is the largest value of μ that would yield 95% confidence that the squad can handle all calls?

3–50. A student takes the campus shuttle bus to reach the classroom building. The shuttle bus arrives at his stop every 15 minutes but the actual arrival time at the stop is random. The student allows 10 minutes waiting time for the shuttle in his plan to make it in time to the class.

a. What is the expected waiting time? What is the variance?

b. What is the probability that the wait will be between four and six minutes?

c. What is the probability that the student will be in time for the class?

d. If he wants to be 95% confident of being on time for the class, how much time should he allow for waiting for the shuttle?

3–51. A hydraulic press breaks down at the rate of 0.1742 time per day.

a. What is the MTBF?

b. On a given day, what is the probability that it will break down?

c. If four days have passed without a breakdown, what is the probability that it will break down on the fifth day?

d. What is the probability that five consecutive days will pass without any breakdown?

3–52. Laptop computers produced by a company have an average life of 38.36 months. Assume that the life of a computer is exponentially distributed (which is a good assumption).

a. What is the probability that a computer will fail within 12 months?

b. If the company gives a warranty period of 12 months, what proportion of computers will fail during the warranty period?

c. Based on the answer to (*b*), would you say the company can afford to give a warranty period of 12 months?

d. If the company wants not more than 5% of the computers to fail during the warranty period, what should be the warranty period?

e. If the company wants to give a warranty period of three months and still wants not more than 5% of the computers to fail during the warranty period, what should be the minimum average life of the computers?

3–53. In most statistics textbooks, you will find cumulative binomial probability tables in the format shown below. These can be created using spreadsheets using the Binomial template and Data|Table commands.

$n = 5$		p								
		0.1	0.2	0.3	0.4	0.5	0.6	0.7	0.8	0.9
	0	0.5905	0.3277	0.1681	0.0778	0.0313	0.0102	0.0024	0.0003	0.0000
	1	0.9185	0.7373	0.5282	0.3370	0.1875	0.0870	0.0308	0.0067	0.0005
x	2	0.9914	0.9421	0.8369	0.6826	0.5000	0.3174	0.1631	0.0579	0.0086
	3	0.9995	0.9933	0.9692	0.9130	0.8125	0.6630	0.4718	0.2627	0.0815
	4	1.0000	0.9997	0.9976	0.9898	0.9688	0.9222	0.8319	0.6723	0.4095

a. Create the above table.

b. Create a similar table for $n = 7$.

3–54. Look at the shape of the binomial distribution for various combinations of n and p. Specifically, let $n = 5$ and try $p = 0.2$, 0.5, and 0.8. Repeat the same for other values of n. Can you say something about how the skewness of the distribution is affected by p and n?

3–55. Try various values of s and p on the negative binomial distribution template and answer this question: How is the skewness of the negative binomial distribution affected by s and p values?

3–56. An MBA graduate keeps interviewing for jobs, one by one, and will stop interviewing on receiving an offer. In each interview he has an independent probability 0.2166 of getting the job.

a. What is the expected number of interviews? What is the variance?

b. If there is enough time for only six interviews, how confident can he be of getting a job within the available time?

c. If he wants to be at least 95% confident of getting a job, how many interviews should he be prepared for?

d. Suppose there is enough time for at most six interviews. For what minimum value of p can he have 95% confidence of getting a job within the available time?

e. In order to answer (*d*) more thoroughly, tabulate the confidence level for p values ranging from 0.1 to 0.5 in steps of 0.05.

3–57. A shipment of thousands of pins contains some percentage of defectives. To decide whether to accept the shipment, the consumer follows a sampling plan where 80 items are chosen at random from the sample and tested. If the number of defectives in the sample is at most three, the shipment is accepted. (The number 3 is known as the *acceptance number* of the sampling plan.)

a. Assuming that the shipment includes 3% defectives, what is the probability that the shipment will be accepted? (*Hint:* Use the binomial distribution.)

b. Assuming that the shipment includes 6% defectives, what is the probability that the shipment will be accepted?

    c. Using the Data|Table command, tabulate the probability of acceptance for defective percentage ranging from 0% to 15% in steps of 1%.

    d. Plot a line graph of the table created in (*c*). (This graph is known as the *operating characteristic curve* of the sampling plan.)

3–58. A shipment of 100 pins contains some defectives. To decide whether to accept the shipment, the consumer follows a sampling plan where 15 items are chosen at random from the sample and tested. If the number of defectives in the sample is at most one, the shipment is accepted. (The number 1 is known as the *acceptance number* of the sampling plan.)

    a. Assuming that the shipment includes 5% defectives, what is the probability that the shipment will be accepted? (*Hint:* Use the hypergeometric distribution.)

    b. Assuming that the shipment includes 8% defectives, what is the probability that the shipment will be accepted?

    c. Using the Data|Table command, tabulate the probability of acceptance for defective percentage ranging from 0% to 15% in steps of 1%.

    d. Plot a line graph of the table created in part (*c*) above. (This graph is known as the *operating characteristic curve* of the sampling plan.)

3–59. A recent study published in the *Toronto Globe and Mail* reveals that 25% of mathematics degrees from Canadian universities and colleges are awarded to women. If five recent graduates from Canadian universities and colleges are selected at random, what is the probability that

    a. At least one would be a woman.

    b. None of them would be a woman.

3–60. An article published in *Access* magazine states that according to a survey conducted by the American Management Association, 78% of major U.S. companies electronically monitor their employees. If five such companies are selected at random, find the probability that

    a. At most one company monitors its employees electronically.

    b. All of them monitor their employees electronically.

3–61. An article published in *Business Week* says that according to a survey by a leading organization 45% of managers change jobs for intellectual challenge, 35% for pay, and 20% for long-term impact on career. If nine managers who recently changed jobs are randomly chosen, what is the probability that

    a. Three changed for intellectual challenges.

    b. Three changed for pay reasons.

    c. Three changed for long-term impact.

3–62. Estimates published by the World Health Organization state that one out of every three workers may be toiling away in workplaces that make them sick. If seven workers are selected at random, what is the probability that a majority of them are made sick by their workplace?

3–63. Based on the survey conducted by a municipal administration in the Netherlands, Monday appeared to be managements' preferred day for laying off workers. Of the total number of workers laid off in a given period, 30% were on Monday, 25% on Tuesday, 20% on Wednesday, 13% on Thursday, and 12% on Friday. If a random sample of 15 layoffs is taken, what is the probability that

    a. Five were laid off on Monday.

    b. Four were laid off on Tuesday.

    c. Three were laid off on Wednesday.

    d. Two were laid off on Thursday.

    e. One was laid off on Friday.

3–64. A recent survey published in *BusinessWeek* concludes that Gatorade commands an 83% share of the sports drink market versus 11% for Coca-Cola's PowerAde and 3% for Pepsi's All Sport. A market research firm wants to conduct a new taste test for which it needs Gatorade drinkers. Potential participants for the test are selected by random screening of drink users to find Gatorade drinkers. What is the probability that

    a. The first randomly selected drinker qualifies.

    b. Three soft drink users will have to be interviewed to find the first Gatorade drinker.

3–65. The time between customer arrivals at a bank has an exponential distribution with a mean time between arrivals of three minutes. If a customer just arrived, what is the probability that another customer will not arrive for at least two minutes?

3–66. Lightbulbs manufactured by a particular company have an exponentially distributed life with mean 100 hours.

    a. What is the probability that the lightbulb I am now putting in will last at least 65 hours?

    b. What is the standard deviation of the lifetime of a lightbulb?

3–67. The Bombay Company offers reproductions of classic 18th- and 19th-century English furniture pieces, which have become popular in recent years. The following table gives the probability distribution of the number of Raffles tables sold per day at a particular Bombay store.

Number of Tables	Probability
0	0.05
1	0.05
2	0.10
3	0.15
4	0.20
5	0.15
6	0.15
7	0.10
8	0.05

    a. Show that the probabilities above form a proper probability distribution.

    b. Find the cumulative distribution function of the number of Raffles tables sold daily.

    c. Using the cumulative distribution function, find the probability that the number of tables sold in a given day will be at least three and less than seven.

    d. Find the probability that at most five tables will be sold tomorrow.

    e. What is the expected number of tables sold per day?

    f. Find the variance and the standard deviation of the number of tables sold per day.

    g. Use Chebyshev's theorem to determine bounds of at least 0.75 probability on the number of tables sold daily. Compare with the actual probability for these bounds using the distribution itself.

3–68. According to an article in *USA Today,* 90% of Americans will suffer from high blood pressure as they age. Out of 20 randomly chosen people what is the probability that at most 3 will suffer from high blood pressure?

3-69. The number of orders for installation of a computer information system arriving at an agency per week is a random variable X with the following probability distribution:

x	$P(x)$
0	0.10
1	0.20
2	0.30
3	0.15
4	0.15
5	0.05
6	0.05

a. Prove that $P(X)$ is a probability distribution.

b. Find the cumulative distribution function of X.

c. Use the cumulative distribution function to find probabilities $P(2 < X \leq 5)$, $P(3 \leq X \leq 6)$, and $P(X > 4)$.

d. What is the probability that either four or five orders will arrive in a given week?

e. Assuming independence of weekly orders, what is the probability that three orders will arrive next week and the same number of orders the following week?

f. Find the mean and the standard deviation of the number of weekly orders.

3-70. Consider the situation in the previous problem, and assume that the distribution holds for all weeks throughout the year and that weekly orders are independent from week to week. Let Y denote the number of weeks in the year in which no orders are received (assume a year of 52 weeks).

a. What kind of random variable is Y? Explain.

b. What is the expected number of weeks with no orders?

3-71. An analyst kept track of the daily price quotation for a given stock. The frequency data led to the following probability distribution of daily stock price:

Price x in Dollars	$P(x)$
17	0.05
17.125	0.05
17.25	0.10
17.375	0.15
17.5	0.20
17.625	0.15
17.75	0.10
17.875	0.05
18	0.05
18.125	0.05
18.25	0.05

Assume that the stock price is independent from day to day.

a. If 100 shares are bought today at 17 1/4 and must be sold tomorrow, by prearranged order, what is the expected profit, disregarding transaction costs?

b. What is the standard deviation of the stock price? How useful is this information?

c. What are the limitations of the analysis in part (a)? Explain.

3-72. In problem 3-69, suppose that the company makes $1,200 on each order but has to pay a fixed weekly cost of $1,750. Find the expected weekly profit and the standard deviation of weekly profits.

3–73. Out of 140 million cellular telephone subscribers in the United States, 36 million use Verizon.[6]

    a. Ten wireless customers are chosen. Under what conditions is the number of Verizon customers a binomial random variable?

    b. Making the required assumptions above, find the probability that at least two are Verizon customers.

3–74. An advertisement claims that two out of five doctors recommend a certain pharmaceutical product. A random sample of 20 doctors is selected, and it is found that only 2 of them recommend the product.

    a. Assuming the advertising claim is true, what is the probability of the observed event?

    b. Assuming the claim is true, what is the probability of observing two or fewer successes?

    c. Given the sampling results, do you believe the advertisement? Explain.

    d. What is the expected number of successes in a sample of 20?

3–75. Five percent of the many cars produced at a plant are defective. Ten cars made at the plant are sent to a dealership. Let X be the number of defective cars in the shipment.

    a. Under what conditions can we assume that X is a binomial random variable?

    b. Making the required assumptions, write the probability distribution of X.

    c. What is the probability that two or more cars are defective?

    d. What is the expected number of defective cars?

3–76. Refer to the situation in the previous problem. Suppose that the cars at the plant are checked one by one, and let X be the number of cars checked until the first defective car is found. What type of probability distribution does X have?

3–77. Suppose that 5 of a total of 20 company accounts are in error. An auditor selects a random sample of 5 out of the 20 accounts. Let X be the number of accounts in the sample that are in error. Is X binomial? If not, what distribution does it have? Explain.

3–78. The time, in minutes, necessary to perform a certain task has the uniform [5, 9] distribution.

    a. Write the probability density function of this random variable.

    b. What is the probability that the task will be performed in less than 8 minutes? Explain.

    c. What is the expected time required to perform the task?

3–79. Suppose X has the following probability density function:

$$f(x) = \begin{cases} (1/8)(x - 3) & \text{for } 3 \le x \le 7 \\ 0 & \text{otherwise} \end{cases}$$

    a. Graph the density function.

    b. Show that $f(x)$ is a density function.

    c. What is the probability that X is greater than 5.00?

3–80. Recently, the head of the Federal Deposit Insurance Corporation (FDIC) revealed that the agency maintains a secret list of banks suspected of being in financial trouble. The FDIC chief further stated that of the nation's 14,000 banks, 1,600 were on the list at the time. Suppose that, in an effort to diversify your savings, you randomly choose six banks and split your savings among them. What is the probability that no more than three of your banks are on the FDIC's suspect list?

---

[6]Matt Richtel and Andrew Ross Sorkin, "AT&T Wireless for Sale as a Shakeout Starts," *The New York Times,* January 21, 2004, p. C1.

3–81. Corporate raider Asher Adelman, teaching a course at Columbia University's School of Business, made the following proposal to his students. He would pay $100,000 to any student who would give him the name of an undervalued company, which Adelman would then buy.[7] Suppose that Adelman has 15 students in his class and that 5% of all companies in this country are undervalued. Suppose also that due to liquidity problems, Adelman can give the award to at most three students. Finally, suppose each student chooses a single company at random without consulting others. What is the probability that Adelman would be able to make good on his promise?

3–82. An applicant for a faculty position at a certain university is told by the department chair that she has a 0.95 probability of being invited for an interview. Once invited for an interview, the applicant must make a presentation and win the votes of a majority (at least 8) of the department's 14 current members. From previous meetings with four of these members, the candidate believes that three of them would certainly vote for her while one would not. She also feels that any member she has not yet met has a 0.50 probability of voting for her. Department members are expected to vote independently and with no prior consultation. What are the candidate's chances of getting the position?

3–83. The ratings of viewership for the three major networks during prime time recently were as follows. Also shown is the proportion of viewers watching each program.

Program	Network	Rating	Proportion
20/20	ABC	13.8	0.44
CSI	CBS	10.4	0.33
Law and Order	NBC	7.5	0.23

 a. What is the mean rating given a program that evening?

 b. How many standard deviations above or below the mean is the rating for each one of the programs?

3–84. A major ski resort in the eastern United States closes in late May. Closing day varies from year to year depending on when the weather becomes too warm for making and preserving snow. The day in May and the number of years in which closing occurred that day are reported in the table:

Day	Number of Years
21	2
22	5
23	1
24	3
25	3
26	1
27	2
28	1

 a. Based only on this information, estimate the probability that you could ski at this resort after May 25 next year.

 b. What is the average closing day based on history?

3–85. Ten percent of the items produced at a plant are defective. A random sample of 20 items is selected. What is the probability that more than three items in the sample are defective? If items are selected randomly until the first defective item is encountered, how many items, on average, will have to be sampled before the first defective item is found?

---

[7]Columbia has since questioned this offer on ethical grounds, and the offer has been retracted.

3–86. Lee Iacocca volunteered to drive one of his Chryslers into a brick wall to demonstrate the effectiveness of airbags used in these cars. Airbags are known to activate at random when the car decelerates anywhere from 9 to 14 miles per hour per second (mph/s). The probability distribution for the deceleration speed at which bags activate is given below.

mph/s	Probability
9	0.12
10	0.23
11	0.34
12	0.21
13	0.06
14	0.04

    a. If the airbag activates at a deceleration of 12 mph/s or more, Iacocca would get hurt. What is the probability of his being hurt in this demonstration?

    b. What is the mean deceleration at airbag activation moment?

    c. What is the standard deviation of deceleration at airbag activation time?

3–87. In the previous problem, the time that it takes the airbag to completely fill up from the moment of activation has an exponential distribution with mean 1 second. What is the probability that the airbag will fill up in less than 1/2 second?

3–88. The time interval between two successive customers entering a store in a mall is exponentially distributed with a mean of 6.55 seconds.

    a. What is the probability that the time interval is more than 10 seconds?

    b. What is the probability that the time interval is between 10 and 20 seconds?

    c. On a particular day a security camera is installed. Using an entry sensor, the camera takes pictures of every customer entering the shop. It needs 0.75 second after a picture is taken to get ready for the next picture. What is the probability that the camera will miss an entering customer?

    d. How quick should the camera be if the store owner wants to photograph at least 95% of entering customers?

3–89. The Dutch consumer-electronics giant, Philips, is protected against takeovers by a unique corporate voting structure that gives power only to a few trusted shareholders. A decision of whether to sever Philips' links with the loss-producing German electronics firm Grundig had to be made. The decision required a simple majority of nine decision-making shareholders. If each is believed to have a 0.25 probability of voting yes on the issue, what is the probability that Grundig will be dumped?

3–90. According to a front-page article in *The Wall Street Journal,* 30% of all students in American universities miss classes due to drinking.[8] If 10 students are randomly chosen, what is the probability that at most 3 of them miss classes due to drinking?

3–91. According to an article in *USA Today,* 60% of 7- to 12-year-olds who use the Internet do their schoolwork on line.[9] If 8 kids within this age group who use the Internet are randomly chosen, what is the probability that 2 of them do their schoolwork on line? What is the probability that no more than 5 of them do their schoolwork on line?

[8]Bryan Gruley, "How One University Stumbled in Its Attack on Alcohol Abuse," *The Wall Street Journal,* October 14, 2003, p. 1A.

[9]Ruth Peters, "Internet: Boon or Bane for Kids?" *USA Today,* October 15, 2003, p. 19A.

3–92. The cafeteria in a building offers three different lunches. The demands for the three types of lunch on any given day are independent and Poisson distributed with means 4.85, 12.70, and 27.61. The cost of the three types are $12.00, $8.50, and $6.00, respectively. Find the expected value and variance of the total cost of lunches bought on a particular day.

3–93. The mean time between failures (MTBF) of a hydraulic press is to be estimated assuming that the time between failures (TBF) is exponentially distributed. A foreman observes that the chance that the TBF is more than 72 hours is 50%, and he quotes 72 hours as the MTBF.

    a. Is the foreman right? If not, what is the MTBF?

    b. If the MTBF is indeed 72 hours, 50% of the time the TBF will be more than how many hours?

    c. Why is the mean of an exponential distribution larger than its median?

3–94. An operator needs to produce 4 pins and 6 shafts using a lathe which has 72% chance of producing a defect-free pin at each trial and 65% chance of producing a defect-free shaft at each trial. The operator will first produce pins one by one until he has 4 defect-free pins and then produce shafts one by one until he has 6 defect-free shafts.

    a. What is the expected value and variance of the total number of trials that the operator will make?

    b. Suppose each trial for pins takes 12 minutes and each trial for shafts takes 25 minutes. What is the expected value and variance of the total time required?

CASE 3   Concepts Testing

Hedge funds are institutions that invest in a wide variety of instruments, from stocks and bonds to commodities and real estate. One of the reasons for the success of this industry is that it manages expected return and risk better than other financial institutions. Using the concepts and ideas described in this chapter, discuss how a hedge fund might maximize expected return and minimize risk by investing in various financial instruments. Include in your discussion the concepts of means and variances of linear composites of random variables and the concept of independence.

4

THE NORMAL DISTRIBUTION

4–1 Using Statistics 147

4–2 Properties of the Normal Distribution 148

4–3 The Standard Normal Distribution 151

4–4 The Transformation of Normal Random Variables 156

4–5 The Inverse Transformation 162

4–6 The Template 166

4–7 Normal Approximation of Binomial Distributions 169

4–8 Using the Computer 171

4–9 Summary and Review of Terms 172

Case 4 Acceptable Pins 177

Case 5 Multicurrency Decision 177

LEARNING OBJECTIVES

After studying this chapter, you should be able to:

- Identify when a random variable will be normally distributed.
- Use the properties of the normal distribution.
- Explain the significance of the standard normal distribution.
- Compute probabilities using normal distribution tables.
- Transform a normal distribution into a standard normal distribution.
- Convert a binomial distribution into an approximated normal distribution.
- Solve normal distribution problems using spreadsheet templates.

4–1 Using Statistics

The **normal distribution** is an important continuous distribution because a good number of random variables occurring in practice can be approximated to it. *If a random variable is affected by many independent causes, and the effect of each cause is not overwhelmingly large compared to other effects, then the random variable will closely follow a normal distribution.* The lengths of pins made by an automatic machine, the times taken by an assembly worker to complete the assigned task repeatedly, the weights of baseballs, the tensile strengths of a batch of bolts, and the volumes of soup in a particular brand of canned soup are good examples of normally distributed random variables. All of these are affected by several independent causes where the effect of each cause is small. For example, the length of a pin is affected by many independent causes such as vibrations, temperature, wear and tear on the machine, and raw material properties.

Additionally, in the next chapter, on sampling theory, we shall see that many of the sample statistics are normally distributed.

For a normal distribution with mean μ and standard deviation σ, the probability density function $f(x)$ is given by the complicated formula

$$f(x) = \frac{1}{\sqrt{2\pi}\sigma} e^{-\frac{1}{2}\left(\frac{x-\mu}{\sigma}\right)^2} \qquad -\infty < x < +\infty \qquad (4\text{–}1)$$

In equation 4–1, e is the natural base logarithm, equal to 2.71828 . . . By substituting desired values for μ and σ, we can get any desired density function. For example, a distribution with mean 100 and standard deviation 5 will have the density function

$$f(x) = \frac{1}{\sqrt{2\pi}5} e^{-\frac{1}{2}\left(\frac{x-100}{5}\right)^2} \qquad -\infty < x < +\infty \qquad (4\text{–}2)$$

This function is plotted in Figure 4–1. This is the famous bell-shaped normal curve.

Over the years, many mathematicians have worked on the mathematics behind the normal distribution and have made many independent discoveries. The discovery

FIGURE 4–1 A Normal Distribution with Mean 100 and Standard Deviation 5

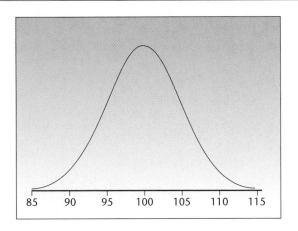

FIGURE 4–2   Three Normal Distributions

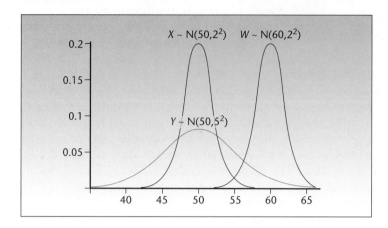

of equation 4–1 for the normal density function is attributed to Carl Friedrich Gauss (1777–1855), who did much work with the formula. In science books, this distribution is often called the *Gaussian distribution*. But the formula was first discovered by the French-born English mathematician Abraham De Moivre (1667–1754). Unfortunately for him, his discovery was not discovered until 1924.

As seen in Figure 4–1, the normal distribution is symmetric about its mean. It has a (relative) kurtosis of 0, which means it has average peakedness. The curve reaches its peak at the mean of 100, and therefore its mode is 100. Due to symmetry, its median is 100 too. In the figure the curve seems to touch the horizontal axis at 85 on the left and at 115 on the right; these points are 3 standard deviations away from the center on either side. Theoretically, the curve never touches the horizontal axis and extends to infinity on both sides.

If X is normally distributed with mean μ and variance σ^2, we write $X \sim N(\mu, \sigma^2)$. If the mean is 100 and the variance is 9, we write $X \sim N(100, 3^2)$. Note how the variance is written. By writing 9 as 3^2, we explicitly show that the standard deviation is 3. Figure 4–2 shows three normal distributions: $X \sim N(50, 2^2)$; $Y \sim N(50, 5^2)$; $W \sim N(60, 2^2)$. Note their shapes and positions.

4–2   Properties of the Normal Distribution

CHAPTER 5

There is a remarkable property possessed only by the normal distribution:

> If several *independent* random variables are normally distributed, then their sum will also be normally distributed. The mean of the sum will be the sum of all the individual means, and by virtue of the independence, the variance of the sum will be the sum of all the individual variances.

We can write this in algebraic form as

If $X_1, X_2, \ldots, X_n$ are independent random variables that are normally distributed, then their sum S will also be normally distributed with

$$E(S) = E(X_1) + E(X_2) + \cdots + E(X_n)$$

and

$$V(S) = V(X_1) + V(X_2) + \cdots + V(X_n)$$

Note that it is the *variances* that can be added as in the preceding box, and *not the standard deviations*. We will never have an occasion to add standard deviations.

We see intuitively that the sum of many normal random variables will also be normally distributed, because the sum is affected by many independent individual causes, namely, those causes that affect each of the original random variables.

Let us see the application of this result through a few examples.

EXAMPLE 4–1

Let X_1, X_2, and X_3 be independent random variables that are normally distributed with means and variances as follows:

	Mean	Variance
X_1	10	1
X_2	20	2
X_3	30	3

Find the distribution of the sum $S = X_1 + X_2 + X_3$. Report the mean, variance, and standard deviation of S.

Solution

The sum S will be normally distributed with mean $10 + 20 + 30 = 60$ and variance $1 + 2 + 3 = 6$. The standard deviation of $S = \sqrt{6} = 2.45$.

EXAMPLE 4–2

The weight of a module used in a spacecraft is to be closely controlled. Since the module uses a bolt-nut-washer assembly in numerous places, a study was conducted to find the distribution of the weights of these parts. It was found that the three weights, in grams, are normally distributed with the following means and variances:

	Mean	Variance
Bolt	312.8	2.67
Nut	53.2	0.85
Washer	17.5	0.21

Find the distribution of the weight of the assembly. Report the mean, variance, and standard deviation of the weight.

Solution

The weight of the assembly is the sum of the weights of the three component parts, which are three normal random variables. Furthermore, the individual weights are independent since the weight of any one component part does not influence the weight of the other two. Therefore, the weight of the assembly will be normally distributed.

The mean weight of the assembly will be the sum of the mean weights of the individual parts: $312.8 + 53.2 + 17.5 = 383.5$ grams.

The variance will be the sum of the individual variances: $2.67 + 0.85 + 0.21 = 3.73$ gram^2.

The standard deviation $= \sqrt{3.73} = 1.93$ grams.

Another interesting property of the normal distribution is that if X is normally distributed, then $aX + b$ will also be normally distributed with mean $aE(X) + b$ and variance $a^2 V(X)$. For example, if X is normally distributed with mean 10 and variance 3, then $4X + 5$ will be normally distributed with mean $4 * 10 + 5 = 45$ and variance $4^2 * 3 = 48$.

We can combine the above two properties and make the following statement:

If X_1, X_2, ..., X_n are independent random variables that are normally distributed, then the random variable Q defined as $Q = a_1X_1 + a_2X_2 + \cdots + a_nX_n + b$ will also be normally distributed with

$$E(Q) = a_1E(X_1) + a_2E(X_2) + \cdots + a_nE(X_n) + b$$

and

$$V(Q) = a_1^2V(X_1) + a_2^2V(X_2) + \cdots + a_n^2V(X_n)$$

The application of this result is illustrated in the following sample problems.

EXAMPLE 4–3

The four independent normal random variables X_1, X_2, X_3, and X_4 have the following means and variances:

	Mean	Variance
X_1	12	4
X_2	−5	2
X_3	8	5
X_4	10	1

Find the mean and variance of $Q = X_1 - 2X_2 + 3X_3 - 4X_4 + 5$. Find also the standard deviation of Q.

Solution

$$E(Q) = 12 - 2(-5) + 3(8) - 4(10) + 5 = 12 + 10 + 24 - 40 + 5 = 11$$
$$V(Q) = 4 + (-2)^2\,(2) + 3^2\,(5) + (-4)^2\,(1) = 4 + 8 + 45 + 16 = 73$$
$$\mathrm{SD}(Q) = \sqrt{73} = 8.544$$

EXAMPLE 4–4

A cost accountant needs to forecast the unit cost of a product for next year. He notes that each unit of the product requires 12 hours of labor and 5.8 pounds of raw material. In addition, each unit of the product is assigned an overhead cost of $184.50. He estimates that the cost of an hour of labor next year will be normally distributed with an expected value of $45.75 and a standard deviation of $1.80; the cost of the raw material will be normally distributed with an expected value of $62.35 and a standard deviation of $2.52. Find the distribution of the unit cost of the product. Report its expected value, variance, and standard deviation.

Solution

Let L be the cost of labor and M be the cost of the raw material. Denote the unit cost of the product by Q. Then $Q = 12L + 5.8M + 184.50$. Since the cost of labor L may not influence the cost of raw material M, we can assume that the two are independent. This makes the unit cost of the product Q a normal random variable. Then

$$E(Q) = 12 \times 45.75 + 5.8 \times 62.35 + 184.50 = \$1095.13$$
$$V(Q) = 12^2 \times 1.80^2 + 5.8^2 \times 2.52^2 = 680.19$$
$$\mathrm{SD}(Q) = \sqrt{680.19} = \$26.08$$

4–3   The Standard Normal Distribution

Since, as noted earlier, infinitely many normal random variables are possible, one is selected to serve as our *standard*. Probabilities associated with values of this standard normal random variable are tabulated. A special transformation then allows us to apply the tabulated probabilities to *any* normal random variable. The standard normal random variable has a special name, Z (rather than the general name X we use for other random variables).

> We define the **standard normal random variable Z** as the normal random variable with mean $\mu = 0$ and standard deviation $\sigma = 1$.

In the notation established in the previous section, we say

$$Z \sim N(0, 1^2) \qquad (4\text{–}3)$$

Since $1^2 = 1$, we may drop the superscript 2 as no confusion of the standard deviation and the variance is possible. A graph of the standard normal density function is given in Figure 4–3.

Finding Probabilities of the Standard Normal Distribution

Probabilities of intervals are areas under the density $f(z)$ over the intervals in question. From the range of values in equation 4–1, $-\infty < x < \infty$, we see that any normal random variable is defined over the entire real line. Thus, the intervals in which we will be interested are sometimes *semi-infinite* intervals, such as a to ∞ or $-\infty$ to b (where a and b are numbers). While such intervals have infinite length, the probabilities associated with them are finite; they are, in fact, no greater than 1.00, as required of all probabilities. The reason for this is that the area in either of the "tails" of the distribution (the two narrow ends of the distribution, extending toward $-\infty$ and $+\infty$) becomes very small very quickly as we move away from the center of the distribution.

Tabulated areas under the standard normal density are probabilities of intervals extending from the mean $\mu = 0$ to points z to its right. Table 2 in Appendix C gives areas under the standard normal curve between 0 and points $z > 0$. The total area under the normal curve is equal to 1.00, and since the curve is symmetric, the area from 0 to $-\infty$ is equal to 0.5. The *table area* associated with a point z is thus equal to the value of the cumulative distribution function $F(z)$ minus 0.5.

> We define the **table area** as
> $$TA = F(z) - 0.5 \qquad (4\text{–}4)$$

FIGURE 4–3   **The Standard Normal Density Function**

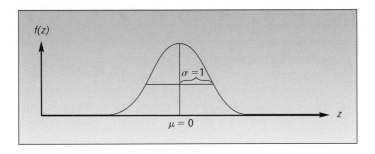

FIGURE 4–4   The Table Area TA for a Point **z** of the Standard Normal Distribution

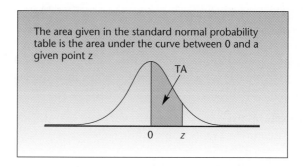

The area given in the standard normal probability table is the area under the curve between 0 and a given point z

TA

0   z

TABLE 4–1   Standard Normal Probabilities

z	.00	.01	.02	.03	.04	.05	.06	.07	.08	.09
0.0	.0000	.0040	.0080	.0120	.0160	.0199	.0239	.0279	.0319	.0359
0.1	.0398	.0438	.0478	.0517	.0557	.0596	.0636	.0675	.0714	.0753
0.2	.0793	.0832	.0871	.0910	.0948	.0987	.1026	.1064	.1103	.1141
0.3	.1179	.1217	.1255	.1293	.1331	.1368	.1406	.1443	.1480	.1517
0.4	.1554	.1591	.1628	.1664	.1700	.1736	.1772	.1808	.1844	.1879
0.5	.1915	.1950	.1985	.2019	.2054	.2088	.2123	.2157	.2190	.2224
0.6	.2257	.2291	.2324	.2357	.2389	.2422	.2454	.2486	.2517	.2549
0.7	.2580	.2611	.2642	.2673	.2704	.2734	.2764	.2794	.2823	.2852
0.8	.2881	.2910	.2939	.2967	.2995	.3023	.3051	.3078	.3106	.3133
0.9	.3159	.3186	.3212	.3238	.3264	.3289	.3315	.3340	.3365	.3389
1.0	.3413	.3438	.3461	.3485	.3508	.3531	.3554	.3577	.3599	.3621
1.1	.3643	.3665	.3686	.3708	.3729	.3749	.3770	.3790	.3810	.3830
1.2	.3849	.3869	.3888	.3907	.3925	.3944	.3962	.3980	.3997	.4015
1.3	.4032	.4049	.4066	.4082	.4099	.4115	.4131	.4147	.4162	.4177
1.4	.4192	.4207	.4222	.4236	.4251	.4265	.4279	.4292	.4306	.4319
1.5	.4332	.4345	.4357	.4370	.4382	.4394	.4406	.4418	.4429	.4441
1.6	.4452	.4463	.4474	.4484	.4495	.4505	.4515	.4525	.4535	.4545
1.7	.4554	.4564	.4573	.4582	.4591	.4599	.4608	.4616	.4625	.4633
1.8	.4641	.4649	.4656	.4664	.4671	.4678	.4686	.4693	.4699	.4706
1.9	.4713	.4719	.4726	.4732	.4738	.4744	.4750	.4756	.4761	.4767
2.0	.4772	.4778	.4783	.4788	.4793	.4798	.4803	.4808	.4812	.4817
2.1	.4821	.4826	.4830	.4834	.4838	.4842	.4846	.4850	.4854	.4857
2.2	.4861	.4864	.4868	.4871	.4875	.4878	.4881	.4884	.4887	.4890
2.3	.4893	.4896	.4898	.4901	.4904	.4906	.4909	.4911	.4913	.4916
2.4	.4918	.4920	.4922	.4925	.4927	.4929	.4931	.4932	.4934	.4936
2.5	.4938	.4940	.4941	.4943	.4945	.4946	.4948	.4949	.4951	.4952
2.6	.4953	.4955	.4956	.4957	.4959	.4960	.4961	.4962	.4963	.4964
2.7	.4965	.4966	.4967	.4968	.4969	.4970	.4971	.4972	.4973	.4974
2.8	.4974	.4975	.4976	.4977	.4977	.4978	.4979	.4979	.4980	.4981
2.9	.4981	.4982	.4982	.4983	.4984	.4984	.4985	.4985	.4986	.4986
3.0	.4987	.4987	.4987	.4988	.4988	.4989	.4989	.4989	.4990	.4990

The table area TA is shown in Figure 4–4. Part of Table 2 is reproduced here as Table 4–1. Let us see how the table is used in obtaining probabilities for the standard normal random variable. In the following examples, refer to Figure 4–4 and Table 4–1.

FIGURE 4–5   Finding the Probability That Z Is Less Than −2.47

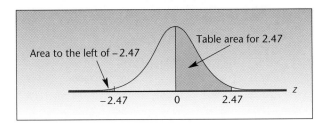

1. Let us find the probability that the value of the standard normal random variable will be between 0 and 1.56. That is, we want $P(0 < Z < 1.56)$. In Figure 4–4, substitute 1.56 for the point z on the graph. We are looking for the table area in the row labeled 1.5 and the column labeled 0.06. In the table, we find the probability 0.4406.

2. Let us find the probability that Z will be less than -2.47. Figure 4–5 shows the required area for the probability $P(Z < -2.47)$. By the symmetry of the normal curve, the area to the left of -2.47 is exactly equal to the area to the right of 2.47. We find

$$P(Z < -2.47) = P(Z > 2.47) = 0.5000 - 0.4932 = 0.0068$$

3. Find $P(1 < Z < 2)$. The required probability is the area under the curve between the two points 1 and 2. This area is shown in Figure 4–6. The table gives us the area under the curve between 0 and 1, and the area under the curve between 0 and 2. Areas are additive; therefore, $P(1 < Z < 2) = \text{TA}(\text{for } 2.00) - \text{TA}(\text{for } 1.00) = 0.4772 - 0.3413 = 0.1359$.

In cases where we need probabilities based on values with greater than second-decimal accuracy, we may use a linear interpolation between two probabilities obtained from the table. For example, $P(0 \le Z \le 1.645)$ is found as the midpoint between the two probabilities $P(0 \le Z \le 1.64)$ and $P(0 \le Z \le 1.65)$. This is found, using the table, as the midpoint of 0.4495 and 0.4505, which is 0.45. If even greater accuracy is required, we may use computer programs designed to produce standard normal probabilities.

Finding Values of Z Given a Probability

In many situations, instead of finding the probability that a standard normal random variable will be within a given interval, we may be interested in the reverse: finding an interval with a given probability. Consider the following examples.

FIGURE 4–6   Finding the Probability That Z Is between 1 and 2

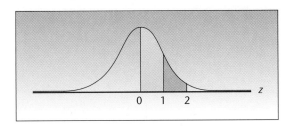

FIGURE 4–7   Using the Normal Table to Find a Value, Given a Probability

z	.00	.01	.02	.03	.04	.05	.06	.07	.08	.09
0.0	.0000	.0040	.0080	.0120	.0160	.0199	.0239	.0279	.0319	.0359
0.1	.0398	.0438	.0478	.0517	.0557	.0596	.0636	.0675	.0714	.0753
0.2	.0793	.0832	.0871	.0910	.0948	.0987	.1026	.1064	.1103	.1141
0.3	.1179	.1217	.1255	.1293	.1331	.1368	.1406	.1443	.1480	.1517
0.4	.1554	.1591	.1628	.1664	.1700	.1736	.1772	.1808	.1844	.1879
0.5	.1915	.1950	.1985	.2019	.2054	.2088	.2123	.2157	.2190	.2224
0.6	.2257	.2291	.2324	.2357	.2389	.2422	.2454	.2486	.2517	.2549
0.7	.2580	.2611	.2642	.2673	.2704	.2734	.2764	.2794	.2823	.2852
0.8	.2881	.2910	.2939	.2967	.2995	.3023	.3051	.3078	.3106	.3133
0.9	.3159	.3186	.3212	.3238	.3264	.3289	.3315	.3340	.3365	.3389
1.0	.3413	.3438	.3461	.3485	.3508	.3531	.3554	.3577	.3599	.3621
1.1	.3643	.3665	.3686	.3708	.3729	.3749	.3770	.3790	.3810	.3830
1.2	.3849	.3869	.3888	.3907	.3925	.3944	.3962	.3980	.3997	.4015
1.3	.4032	.4049	.4066	.4082	.4099	.4115	.4131	.4147	.4162	.4177
1.4	.4192	.4207	.4222	.4236	.4251	.4265	.4279	.4292	.4306	.4319
1.5	.4332	.4345	.4357	.4370	.4382	.4394	.4406	.4418	.4429	.4441

1. Find a value z of the standard normal random variable such that the probability that the random variable will have a value between 0 and z is 0.40. We look *inside* the table for the value closest to 0.40; we do this by searching through the values inside the table, noting that they increase from 0 to numbers close to 0.5000 as we go down ↓ the columns and across the rows. The closest value we find to 0.40 is the table area .3997. This value corresponds to 1.28 (row 1.2 and column .08). This is illustrated in Figure 4–7.

2. Find the value of the standard normal random variable that cuts off an area of 0.90 to its left. Here, we reason as follows: Since the area to the left of the given point z is greater than 0.50, z *must be on the right side of 0*. Furthermore, the area to the left of 0 all the way to $-\infty$ is equal to 0.5. Therefore, TA = $0.9 - 0.5 = 0.4$. We need to find the point z such that TA = 0.4. We know the answer from the preceding example: $z = 1.28$. This is shown in Figure 4–8.

3. Find a 0.99 probability interval, symmetric about 0, for the standard normal random variable. The required area between the two z values that are equidistant from 0 on either side is 0.99. Therefore, the area under the curve between 0 and the positive z value is TA = $0.99/2 = 0.495$. We now look in our normal probability table for the area closest to 0.495. The area 0.495 lies exactly between the two areas 0.4949 and 0.4951, corresponding to $z = 2.57$ and $z = 2.58$. Therefore, a simple linear interpolation between the two values gives us $z = 2.575$. This is correct to within the accuracy of the linear interpolation. The answer, therefore, is $z = \pm 2.575$. This is shown in Figure 4–9.

FIGURE 4–8   Finding z Such That $P(Z \le z) = 0.9$

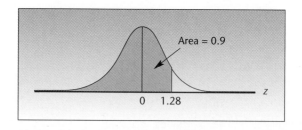

FIGURE 4–9   A Symmetric 0.99 Probability Interval about 0 for a
             Standard Normal Random Variable

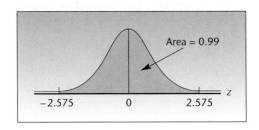

4–1. Find the following probabilities: $P(-1 < Z < 1)$, $P(-1.96 < Z < 1.96)$, $P(-2.33 < Z < 2.33)$.

4–2. What is the probability that a standard normal random variable will be between the values -2 and 1?

4–3. Find the probability that a standard normal random variable will have a value between -0.89 and -2.50.

4–4. Find the probability that a standard normal random variable will have a value greater than 3.02.

4–5. Find the probability that a standard normal random variable will be between 2 and 3.

4–6. Find the probability that a standard normal random variable will have a value less than or equal to -2.5.

4–7. Find the probability that a standard normal random variable will be greater in value than -2.33.

4–8. Find the probability that a standard normal random variable will have a value between -2 and 300.

4–9. Find the probability that a standard normal variable will have a value less than -10.

4–10. Find the probability that a standard normal random variable will be between -0.01 and 0.05.

4–11. A sensitive measuring device is calibrated so that errors in the measurements it provides are normally distributed with mean 0 and variance 1.00. Find the probability that a given error will be between -2 and 2.

4–12. Find two values defining tails of the normal distribution with an area of 0.05 each.

4–13. Is it likely that a standard normal random variable will have a value less than -4? Explain.

4–14. Find a value such that the probability that the standard normal random variable will be above it is 0.85.

4–15. Find a value of the standard normal random variable cutting off an area of 0.685 to its left.

4–16. Find a value of the standard normal random variable cutting off an area of 0.50 to its right. (Do you need the table for this probability? Explain.)

4–17. Find z such that $P(Z > z) = 0.12$.

4–18. Find two values, equidistant from 0 on either side, such that the probability that a standard normal random variable will be between them is 0.40.

4–19. Find two values of the standard normal random variable, z and $-z$, such that $P(-z < Z < z) = 0.95$.

4–20. Find two values of the standard normal random variable, z and $-z$, such that the two corresponding tail areas of the distribution (the area to the right of z and the area to the left of $-z$) add to 0.01.

4–21. The deviation of a magnetic needle from the magnetic pole in a certain area in northern Canada is a normally distributed random variable with mean 0 and standard deviation 1.00. What is the probability that the absolute value of the deviation from the north pole at a given moment will be more than 2.4?

4–4   The Transformation of Normal Random Variables

The importance of the standard normal distribution derives from the fact that any normal random variable may be transformed to the standard normal random variable. We want to transform X, where $X \sim N(\mu, \sigma^2)$, into the standard normal random variable $Z \sim N(0, 1^2)$. Look at Figure 4–10. Here we have a normal random variable X with mean $\mu = 50$ and standard deviation $\sigma = 10$. We want to transform this random variable to a normal random variable with $\mu = 0$ and $\sigma = 1$. How can we do this?

We move the distribution from its center of 50 to a center of 0. This is done by *subtracting* 50 from all the values of X. Thus, we shift the distribution 50 units back so that its new center is 0. The second thing we need to do is to make the width of the distribution, its standard deviation, equal to 1. This is done by squeezing the width down from 10 to 1. Because the total probability under the curve must remain 1.00, the distribution must grow upward to maintain the same area. This is shown in Figure 4–10. Mathematically, squeezing the curve to make the width 1 is equivalent to dividing the random variable by its standard deviation. The area under the curve adjusts so that the total remains the same. *All probabilities* (areas under the curve) *adjust accordingly.* The mathematical transformation from X to Z is thus achieved by first subtracting μ from X and then dividing the result by σ.

The transformation of X to Z:

$$Z = \frac{X - \mu}{\sigma}$$

                                                    (4–5)

FIGURE 4–10   **Transforming a Normal Random Variable with Mean 50 and Standard Deviation 10 into the Standard Normal Random Variable**

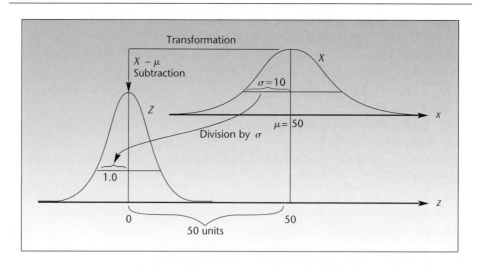

The transformation of equation 4–5 takes us from a random variable X with mean μ and standard deviation σ to the standard normal random variable. We also have an opposite, or *inverse,* transformation, which takes us from the standard normal random variable Z to the random variable X with mean μ and standard deviation σ. The inverse transformation is given by equation 4–6.

The inverse transformation of Z to X:

$$X = \mu + Z\sigma \qquad\qquad (4\text{–}6)$$

You can verify mathematically that equation 4–6 does the opposite of equation 4–5. Note that multiplying the random variable Z by the number σ increases the width of the curve from 1 to σ, thus making σ the new standard deviation. Adding μ makes μ the new mean of the random variable. The actions of multiplying and then adding are the opposite of subtracting and then dividing. We note that the two transformations, one an inverse of the other, transform a *normal* random variable into a *normal* random variable. If this transformation is carried out on a random variable that is not normal, the result will not be a normal random variable.

Using the Normal Transformation

Let us consider our random variable X with mean 50 and standard deviation 10, $X \sim N(50, 10^2)$. Suppose we want the probability that X is greater than 60. That is, we want to find $P(X > 60)$. We cannot evaluate this probability directly, but if we can transform X to Z, we will be able to find the probability in the Z table, Table 2 in Appendix C. Using equation 4–5, the required transformation is $Z = (X - \mu)/\sigma$. Let us carry out the transformation. In the probability statement $P(X > 60)$, we will substitute Z for X. If, however, we carry out the transformation on one side of the probability inequality, we must also do it on the other side. In other words, transforming X into Z requires us also to transform the value 60 into the appropriate value of the standard normal distribution. We transform the value 60 into the value $(60 - \mu)/\sigma$. The new probability statement is

$$
\begin{aligned}
P(X > 60) &= P\left(\frac{X - \mu}{\sigma} > \frac{60 - \mu}{\sigma}\right) = P\left(Z > \frac{60 - \mu}{\sigma}\right) \\
&= P\left(Z > \frac{60 - 50}{10}\right) = P(Z > 1)
\end{aligned}
$$

Why does the inequality still hold? We subtracted a number from each side of an inequality; this does not change the inequality. In the next step we divide both sides of the inequality by the standard deviation σ. The inequality does not change because we can divide both sides of an inequality by a positive number, and a standard deviation is always a positive number. (Recall that dividing by 0 is not permissible; and dividing, or multiplying, by a negative value would reverse the direction of the inequality.) From the transformation, we find that the probability that a normal random variable with mean 50 and standard deviation 10 will have a value greater than 60 is exactly the probability that the standard normal random variable Z will be greater than 1. The latter probability can be found using Table 2 in Appendix C. We find: $P(X > 60) = P(Z > 1) = 0.5000 - 0.3413 = 0.1587$. Let us now look at a few examples of the use of equation 4–5.

EXAMPLE 4–5

Suppose that the time it takes the electronic device in the car to respond to the signal from the toll plaza is normally distributed with mean 160 microseconds and standard deviation 30 microseconds. What is the probability that the device in the car will respond to a given signal within 100 to 180 microseconds?

Solution

Figure 4–11 shows the normal distribution for $X \sim N(160, 30^2)$ and the required area on the scale of the original problem and on the transformed z scale. We have the following (where the probability statement inequality has three sides and we carry out the transformation of equation 4–5 on all three sides):

$$
\begin{aligned}
P(100 < X < 180) &= P\left(\frac{100 - \mu}{\sigma} < \frac{X - \mu}{\sigma} < \frac{180 - \mu}{\sigma}\right) \\
&= P\left(\frac{100 - 160}{30} < Z < \frac{180 - 160}{30}\right) \\
&= P(-2 < Z < 0.6666) = 0.4772 + 0.2475 = 0.7247
\end{aligned}
$$

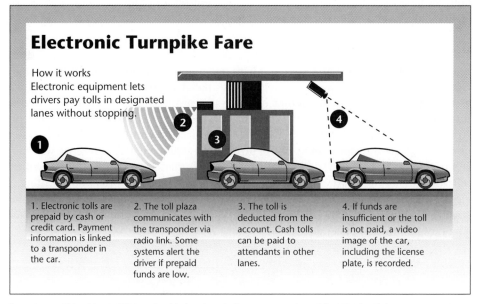

Electronic Turnpike Fare

How it works
Electronic equipment lets drivers pay tolls in designated lanes without stopping.

1. Electronic tolls are prepaid by cash or credit card. Payment information is linked to a transponder in the car.

2. The toll plaza communicates with the transponder via radio link. Some systems alert the driver if prepaid funds are low.

3. The toll is deducted from the account. Cash tolls can be paid to attendants in other lanes.

4. If funds are insufficient or the toll is not paid, a video image of the car, including the license plate, is recorded.

From *Boston Globe*, May 9, 1995, p. 1, with data from industry reports. Copyright 1995 by Globe Newspaper Co. (MA). Reproduced with permission via Copyright Clearance Center.

FIGURE 4–11   Probability Computation for Example 4–5

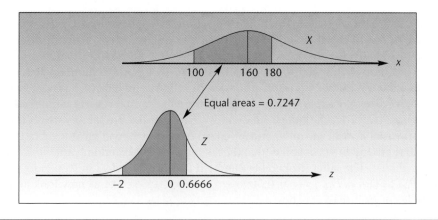

(Table area values were obtained by linear interpolation.) Thus, the chance that the device will respond within 100 to 180 microseconds is 0.7247.

EXAMPLE 4–6

The concentration of impurities in a semiconductor used in the production of microprocessors for computers is a normally distributed random variable with mean 127 parts per million and standard deviation 22. A semiconductor is acceptable only if its concentration of impurities is below 150 parts per million. What proportion of the semiconductors are acceptable for use?

Now $X \sim N(127, 22^2)$, and we need $P(X < 150)$. Using equation 4–5, we have

$$P(X < 150) = P\left(\frac{X - \mu}{\sigma} < \frac{150 - \mu}{\sigma}\right) = P\left(Z < \frac{150 - 127}{22}\right)$$
$$= P(Z < 1.045) = 0.5 + 0.3520 = 0.8520$$

(The TA of 0.3520 was obtained by interpolation.) Thus, 85.2% of the semiconductors are acceptable for use. This also means that the probability that a randomly chosen semiconductor will be acceptable for use is 0.8520. The solution of this example is illustrated in Figure 4–12.

FIGURE 4–12   Probability Computation for Example 4–6

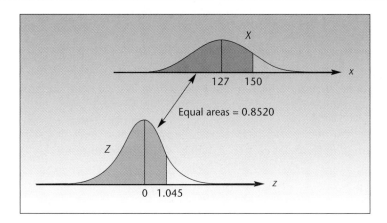

EXAMPLE 4–7

Fluctuations in the prices of precious metals such as gold have been empirically shown to be well approximated by a normal distribution when observed over short intervals of time. In May 1995, the daily price of gold (1 troy ounce) was believed to have a mean of $383 and a standard deviation of $12. A broker, working under these assumptions, wanted to find the probability that the price of gold the next day would be between $394 and $399 per troy ounce. In this eventuality, the broker had an order from a client to sell the gold in the client's portfolio. What is the probability that the client's gold will be sold the next day?

Figure 4–13 shows the setup for this problem and the transformation of X, where $X \sim N(383, 12^2)$, into the standard normal random variable Z. Also shown are the required areas under the X curve and the transformed Z curve. We have

FIGURE 4–13   Probability Computation for Example 4–7

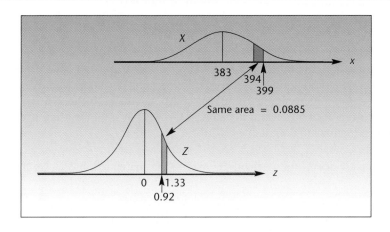

$$P(394 < X < 399) = P\left(\frac{394 - \mu}{\sigma} < \frac{X - \mu}{\sigma} < \frac{399 - \mu}{\sigma}\right)$$

$$= P\left(\frac{394 - 383}{12} < Z < \frac{399 - 383}{12}\right)$$

$$= P(0.9166 < Z < 1.3333) = 0.4088 - 0.3203 = 0.0885$$

(Both TA values were obtained by linear interpolation, although this is not necessary if less accuracy is acceptable.)

Let us summarize the transformation procedure used in computing probabilities of events associated with a normal random variable $X \sim N(\mu, \sigma^2)$.

Transformation formulas of X to Z, where a and b are numbers:

$$P(X < a) = P\left(Z < \frac{a - \mu}{\sigma}\right)$$

$$P(X > b) = P\left(Z > \frac{b - \mu}{\sigma}\right)$$

$$P(a < X < b) = P\left(\frac{a - \mu}{\sigma} < Z < \frac{b - \mu}{\sigma}\right)$$

PROBLEMS

4–22. For a normal random variable with mean 650 and standard deviation 40, find the probability that its value will be below 600.

4–23. Let X be a normally distributed random variable with mean 410 and standard deviation 2. Find the probability that X will be between 407 and 415.

4–24. If X is normally distributed with mean 500 and standard deviation 20, find the probability that X will be above 555.

4–25. For a normally distributed random variable with mean -44 and standard deviation 16, find the probability that the value of the random variable will be above 0.

4–26. A normal random variable has mean 0 and standard deviation 4. Find the probability that the random variable will be above 2.5.

4–27. Let X be a normally distributed random variable with mean $\mu = 16$ and standard deviation $\sigma = 3$. Find $P(11 < X < 20)$. Also find $P(17 < X < 19)$ and $P(X > 15)$.

4–28. The time it takes an international telephone operator to place an overseas phone call is normally distributed with mean 45 seconds and standard deviation 10 seconds.

   a. What is the probability that my call will go through in less than 1 minute?

   b. What is the probability that I will get through in less than 40 seconds?

   c. What is the probability that I will have to wait more than 70 seconds for my call to go through?

4–29. The number of votes cast in favor of a controversial proposition is believed to be approximately normally distributed with mean 8,000 and standard deviation 1,000. The proposition needs at least 9,322 votes in order to pass. What is the probability that the proposition will pass? (Assume numbers are on a continuous scale.)

4–30. Under the system of floating exchange rates, the rate of foreign money to the U.S. dollar is affected by many random factors, and this leads to the assumption of a normal distribution of small daily fluctuations. The rate of U.S. dollar per euro is believed in April 2007 to have a mean of 1.36 and a standard deviation of 0.03.[1] Find the following.

   a. The probability that tomorrow's rate will be above 1.42.

   b. The probability that tomorrow's rate will be below 1.35.

   c. The probability that tomorrow's exchange rate will be between 1.16 and 1.23.

4–31. *Wine Spectator* rates wines on a point scale of 0 to 100. It can be inferred from the many ratings in this magazine that the average rating is 87 and the standard deviation is 3 points. Wine ratings seem to follow a normal distribution. In the May 15, 2007, issue of the magazine, the burgudy Domaine des Perdrix received a rating of 89.[2] What is the probability that a randomly chosen wine will score this high or higher?

4–32. The weights of domestic, adult cats are normally distributed with a mean of 10.42 pounds and a standard deviation of 0.87 pounds. A cat food manufacturer sells three types of foods for underweight, normal, and overweight cats. The manufacturer considers the bottom 5% of the cats underweight and the top 10% overweight. Compute what weight range must be specified for each of the three categories.

4–33. Daily fluctuations of the French CAC-40 stock index from March to June 1997 seem to follow a normal distribution with mean of 2,600 and standard deviation of 50. Find the probability that the CAC-40 will be between 2,520 and 2,670 on a random day in the period of study.

4–34. According to global analyst Olivier Lemaigre, the average price-to-earnings ratio for companies in emerging markets is 12.5.[3] Assume a normal distribution and a standard deviation of 2.5. If a company in emerging markets is randomly selected, what is the probability that its price-per-earnings ratio is above 17.5, which, according to Lemaigre, is the average for companies in the developed world?

4–35. Based on the research of Ibbotson Associates, a Chicago investment firm, and Prof. Jeremy Siegel of the Wharton School of the University of Pennsylvania, the

---

[1]This information is inferred from data on foreign exchange rates in *The New York Times,* April 20, 2007, p. C10.

[2]"The Ratings," *Wine Spectator,* May 15, 2007, p. 156.

[3]Mitchell Martin, "Stock Focus: Ride the Rocket," *Forbes,* April 26, 2004, p. 138.

average return on large-company stocks since 1920 has been 10.5% per year and the standard deviation has been 4.75%. Assuming a normal distribution for stock returns (and that the trend will continue this year), what is the probability that a large-company stock you've just bought will make in 1 year at least 12%? Will lose money? Will make at least 5%?

4–36. A manufacturing company regularly consumes a special type of glue purchased from a foreign supplier. Because the supplier is foreign, the time gap between placing an order and receiving the shipment against that order is long and uncertain. This time gap is called "lead time." From past experience, the materials manager notes that the company's demand for glue during the uncertain lead time is normally distributed with a mean of 187.6 gallons and a standard deviation of 12.4 gallons. The company follows a policy of placing an order when the glue stock falls to a predetermined value called the "reorder point." Note that if the reorder point is x gallons and the demand during lead time exceeds x gallons, the glue would go "stock-out" and the production process would have to stop. Stock-out conditions are therefore serious.

    a. If the reorder point is kept at 187.6 gallons (equal to the mean demand during lead time) what is the probability that a stock-out condition would occur?

    b. If the reorder point is kept at 200 gallons, what is the probability that a stock-out condition would occur?

    c. If the company wants to be 95% confident that the stock-out condition will not occur, what should be the reorder point? The reorder point minus the mean demand during lead time is known as the "safety stock." What is the safety stock in this case?

    d. If the company wants to be 99% confident that the stock-out condition will not occur, what should be the reorder point? What is the safety stock in this case?

4–37. The daily price of orange juice 30-day futures is normally distributed. In March through April 2007, the mean was 145.5 cents per pound, and standard deviation = 25.0 cents per pound.[4] Assuming the price is independent from day to day, find $P(x < 100)$ on the next day.

4–5 The Inverse Transformation

Let us look more closely at the relationship between X, a normal random variable with mean μ and standard deviation σ, and the standard normal random variable. The fact that the standard normal random variable has mean 0 and standard deviation 1 has some important implications. When we say that Z is greater than 2, we are also saying that Z is more than 2 *standard deviations above its mean*. This is so because the mean of Z is 0 and the standard deviation is 1; hence, $Z > 2$ is the same event as $Z > [0 + 2(1)]$.

Now consider a normal random variable X with mean 50 and standard deviation 10. Saying that X is greater than 70 is exactly the same as saying that X is 2 standard deviations above its mean. This is so because 70 is 20 units above the mean of 50, and 20 units = 2(10) units, or 2 standard deviations of X. Thus, the event $X > 70$ is the same as the event $X > (2$ standard deviations above the mean). This event is identical to the event $Z > 2$. Indeed, this is what results when we carry out the transformation of equation 4–5:

$$P(X > 70) = P\left(\frac{X - \mu}{\sigma} > \frac{70 - \mu}{\sigma}\right) = P\left(Z > \frac{70 - 50}{10}\right) = P(Z > 2)$$

---

[4] "Futures," *The New York Times*, April 26, 2007, p. C9.

Normal random variables are related to one another by the fact that the probability that a normal random variable will be above (or below) its mean a certain number of standard deviations is exactly equal to the probability that any other normal random variable will be above (or below) its mean the same number of (its) standard deviations. In particular, this property holds for the standard normal random variable. The probability that a normal random variable will be greater than (or less than) z standard-deviation units above its mean is the same as the probability that the standard normal random variable will be greater than (less than) z. The change from a z *value* of the random variable Z to z *standard deviations* above the mean for a given normal random variable X should suggest to us the inverse transformation, equation 4–6:

$$x = \mu + z\sigma$$

That is, the value of the random variable X may be written in terms of the number z of standard deviations σ it is above or below the mean μ. Three examples are useful here. We know from the standard normal probability table that the probability that Z is greater than -1 and less than 1 is 0.6826 (show this). Similarly, we know that the probability that Z is greater than -2 and less than 2 is 0.9544. Also, the probability that Z is greater than -3 and less than 3 is 0.9974. These probabilities may be applied to *any* normal random variable as follows:[5]

1. The probability that a normal random variable will be within a distance of *1 standard deviation* from its mean (on either side) is 0.6826, or *approximately 0.68.*
2. The probability that a normal random variable will be within *2 standard deviations* of its mean is 0.9544, or *approximately 0.95.*
3. The probability that a normal random variable will be within *3 standard deviations* of its mean is 0.9974.

We use the inverse transformation, equation 4–6, when we want to get from a given probability to the value or values of a normal random variable X. We illustrate the procedure with a few examples.

PALCO Industries, Inc., is a leading manufacturer of cutting and welding products. One of the company's products is an acetylene gas cylinder used in welding. The amount of nitrogen gas in a cylinder is a normally distributed random variable with mean 124 units of volume and standard deviation 12. We want to find the amount of nitrogen x such that 10% of the cylinders contain more nitrogen than this amount.

EXAMPLE 4–8

We have $X \sim N(124, 12^2)$. We are looking for the value of the random variable X such that $P(X > x) = 0.10$. In order to find it, we look for the value of the standard normal random variable Z such that $P(Z > z) = 0.10$. Figure 4–14 illustrates how we find the value z and transform it to x. If the area to the right of z is equal to 0.10, the area between 0 and z (the table area) is equal to $0.5 - 0.10 = 0.40$. We look inside the table for the z value corresponding to TA $= 0.40$ and find $z = 1.28$ (actually, TA $= 0.3997$,

Solution

---

[5]This is the origin of the *empirical rule* (in Chapter 1) for mound-shaped data distributions. Mound-shaped data sets approximate the distribution of a normal random variable, and hence the proportions of observations within a given number of standard deviations away from the mean roughly equal those predicted by the normal distribution. Compare the empirical rule (section 1–7) with the numbers given here.

FIGURE 4-14   Solution of Example 4-8

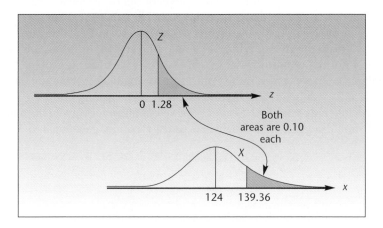

which is close enough to 0.4). We need to find the appropriate x value. Here we use equation 4-6:

$$x = \mu + z\sigma = 124 + (1.28)(12) = 139.36$$

Thus, 10% of the acetylene cylinders contain more than 139.36 units of nitrogen.

EXAMPLE 4-9

The amount of fuel consumed by the engines of a jetliner on a flight between two cities is a normally distributed random variable X with mean $\mu = 5.7$ tons and standard deviation $\sigma = 0.5$. Carrying too much fuel is inefficient as it slows the plane. If, however, too little fuel is loaded on the plane, an emergency landing may be necessary. The airline would like to determine the amount of fuel to load so that there will be a 0.99 probability that the plane will arrive at its destination.

Solution

We have $X \sim N(5.7, 0.5^2)$. First, we must find the value z such that $P(Z < z) = 0.99$. Following our methodology, we find that the required table area is TA $= 0.99 - 0.5 = 0.49$, and the corresponding z value is 2.33. Transforming the z value to an x value, we get $x = \mu + z\sigma = 5.7 + (2.33)(0.5) = 6.865$. Thus, the plane should be loaded with 6.865 tons of fuel to give a 0.99 probability that the fuel will last throughout the flight. The transformation is shown in Figure 4-15.

FIGURE 4-15   Solution of Example 4-9

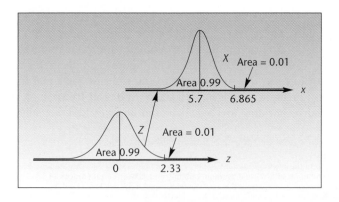

EXAMPLE 4–10

Weekly sales of Campbell's soup cans at a grocery store are believed to be approximately normally distributed with mean 2,450 and standard deviation 400. The store management wants to find two values, symmetrically on either side of the mean, such that there will be a 0.95 probability that sales of soup cans during the week will be between the two values. Such information is useful in determining levels of orders and stock.

Here $X \sim N(2,450, 400^2)$. From the section on the standard normal random variable, we know how to find two values of Z such that the area under the curve between them is 0.95 (or any other area). We find that $z = 1.96$ and $z = -1.96$ are the required values. We now need to use equation 4–6. Since there are *two* values, one the negative of the other, we may combine them in a single transformation:

$$x = \mu \pm z\sigma \qquad\qquad (4\text{–}7)$$

Applying this special formula we get $x = 2,450 \pm (1.96)(400) = 1,666$ and 3,234. Thus, management may be 95% sure that sales on any given week will be between 1,666 and 3,234 units.

The procedure of obtaining values of a normal random variable, given a probability, is summarized:

1. Draw a picture of the normal distribution in question and the standard normal distribution.
2. In the picture, shade in the area corresponding to the probability.
3. Use the table to find the z value (or values) that gives the required probability.
4. Use the transformation from Z to X to get the appropriate value (or values) of the original normal random variable.

PROBLEMS

4–38. If X is a normally distributed random variable with mean 120 and standard deviation 44, find a value x such that the probability that X will be less than x is 0.56.

4–39. For a normal random variable with mean 16.5 and standard deviation 0.8, find a point of the distribution such that there is a 0.85 probability that the value of the random variable will be above it.

4–40. For a normal random variable with mean 19,500 and standard deviation 400, find a point of the distribution such that the probability that the random variable will exceed this value is 0.02.

4–41. Find two values of the normal random variable with mean 88 and standard deviation 5 lying symmetrically on either side of the mean and covering an area of 0.98 between them.

4–42. For $X \sim N(32, 7^2)$, find two values x_1 and x_2, symmetrically lying on each side of the mean, with $P(x_1 < X < x_2) = 0.99$.

4–43. If X is a normally distributed random variable with mean -61 and standard deviation 22, find the value such that the probability that the random variable will be above it is 0.25.

4–44. If X is a normally distributed random variable with mean 97 and standard deviation 10, find x_2 such that $P(102 < X < x_2) = 0.05$.

4–45. Let X be a normally distributed random variable with mean 600 and variance 10,000. Find two values x_1 and x_2 such that $P(X > x_1) = 0.01$ and $P(X < x_2) = 0.05$.

4–46. Pierre operates a currency exchange office at Orly Airport in Paris. His office is open at night when the airport bank is closed, and he makes most of his business on returning U.S. tourists who need to change their remaining euros back to U.S. dollars. From experience, Pierre knows that the demand for dollars on any given night during high season is approximately normally distributed with mean $25,000 and standard deviation $5,000. If Pierre carries too much cash in dollars overnight, he pays a penalty: interest on the cash. On the other hand, if he runs short of cash during the night, he needs to send a person downtown to an all-night financial agency to get the required cash. This, too, is costly to him. Therefore, Pierre would like to carry overnight an amount of money such that the demand on 85% of the nights will not exceed this amount. Can you help Pierre find the required amount of dollars to carry?

4–47. The demand for high-grade gasoline at a service station is normally distributed with mean 27,009 gallons per day and standard deviation 4,530. Find two values that will give a symmetric 0.95 probability interval for the amount of high-grade gasoline demanded daily.

4–48. The percentage of protein in a certain brand of dog food is a normally distributed random variable with mean 11.2% and standard deviation 0.6%. The manufacturer would like to state on the package that the product has a protein content of at least x_1% and no more than x_2%. It wants the statement to be true for 99% of the packages sold. Determine the values x_1 and x_2.

4–49. Private consumption as a share of GDP is a random quantity that follows a roughly normal distribution. According to an article in *BusinessWeek*, for the United States that was about 71%.[6] Assuming that this value is the mean of a normal distribution, and that the standard deviation of the distribution is 3%, what is the value of private consumption as share of GDP such that you are 90% sure that the actual value falls below it?

4–50. The daily price of coffee is approximately normally distributed over a period of 15 days with a mean in April 2007 of $1.35 per pound (on the wholesale market) and standard deviation of $0.15. Find a price such that the probability in the next 15 days that the price will go below it will be 0.90.

4–51. The daily price in dollars per metric ton of cocoa in 2007 was normally distributed with $\mu = \$2,014$ per metric ton and $\sigma = \$2.00$. Find a price such that the probability that the actual price will be above it is 0.80.

4–6 The Template

This normal distribution template is shown in Figure 4–16. As usual, it can be used in conjunction with the Goal Seek command and the Solver tool to solve many types of problems.

To use the template, make sure that the correct values are entered for the mean and the standard deviation in cells B4 and C4. Cell B11 gives the area to the left of the value entered in cell C11. The five cells below C11 can be similarly used. Cell F11 gives the area to the right of the value entered in cell E11. Cell I11 contains the area between the values entered in cells H11 and J11. In the area marked "Inverse Calculations," you can input areas (probabilities) and get x values corresponding to those areas. For example, on entering 0.9 in cell B25, we get the x value of 102.56 in cell C25. This implies that the area to the left of 102.56 is 0.9. Similarly, cell F25 has been used to get the x value that has 0.9 area to its right.

---

[6]Dexter Roberts, "Slower to Spend," *BusinessWeek*, April 30, 2007, p. 34.

FIGURE 4–16   Normal Distribution Template
              [Normal Distribution.xls; Sheet: Normal]

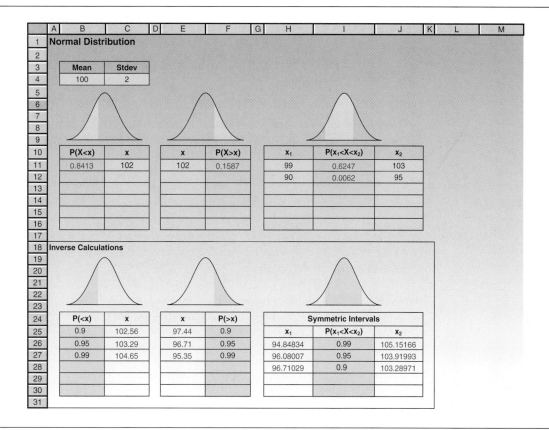

Sometimes we are interested in getting the *narrowest* interval that contains a desired amount of area. A little thought reveals that the narrowest interval has to be symmetric about the mean, because the distribution is symmetric and it peaks at the mean. In later chapters, we will study *confidence intervals,* many of which are also the narrowest intervals that contain a desired amount of area. Naturally, these confidence intervals are symmetric about the mean. For this reason, we have the "Symmetric Intervals" area in the template. Once the desired area is entered in cell I26, the limits of the symmetric interval that contains that much area appear in cells H26 and J26. In the example shown in the Figure 4–16, the symmetric interval (94.85, 105.15) contains the desired area of 0.99.

Problem Solving with the Template

Most questions about normal random variables can be answered using the template in Figure 4–16. We will see a few problem-solving strategies through examples.

Suppose $X \sim N(100, 2^2)$. Find x_2 such that $P(99 \leq X \leq x_2) = 60\%$.   **EXAMPLE 4–11**

Fill in cell B4 with the mean 100 and cell C4 with standard deviation 2. Fill in cell   *Solution*
H11 with 99. Then on the Data tab, in the Data Tools group, click **What If Analysis,**
and then click **Goal Seek.** In the dialog box, ask to set cell I11 to value 0.6 by changing cell J11. Click **OK** when the computer finds the answer. The required value of 102.66 for x_2 appears in cell J11.

EXAMPLE 4–12

Suppose $X \sim \text{N}(\mu, 0.5^2)$; $P(X > 16.5) = 0.20$. What is μ?

Solution

Enter the σ of 0.5 in cell C4. Since we do not know μ, enter a *guessed* value of 15 in cell B4. Then enter 16.5 in cell F11. Now invoke the **Goal Seek** command to set cell F11 to value 0.20 by changing cell B4. The computer finds the value of μ in cell B4 to be 16.08.

The **Goal Seek** command can be used if there is only one unknown. With more than one unknown, the Solver tool has to be used. We shall illustrate the use of the Solver in the next example.

EXAMPLE 4–13

Suppose $X \sim \text{N}(\mu, \sigma^2)$; $P(X > 28) = 0.80$; $P(X > 32) = 0.40$. What are μ and σ?

Solution

One way to solve this problem is to use the Solver to find μ and σ with the objective of making $P(X > 28) = 0.80$ subject to the constraint $P(X > 32) = 0.40$. The following detailed steps will do just that:

- Fill in cell B4 with 30 (which is a guessed value for μ).
- Fill in cell C4 with 2 (which is a guessed value for σ).
- Fill in cell E11 with 28.
- Fill in cell E12 with 32.
- Under the Analysis group on the Data tab select the Solver.
- In the **Set Cell** box enter F11.
- In the **To Value** box enter 0.80 [which sets up the objective of $P(X > 28) = 0.80$].
- In the **By Changing Cells** box enter B4:C4.
- Click on the **Constraints** box and the **Add** button.
- In the dialog box on the left-hand side enter F12.
- Select the = sign in the middle drop down box.
- Enter 0.40 in the right-hand-side box [which sets up the constraint of $P(X > 32) = 0.40$].
- Click the OK button.
- In the Solver dialog box that reappears, click the **Solve** button.
- In the dialog box that appears at the end, select the **Keep Solver Solution** option.

The Solver finds the correct values for the cells B4 and C4 as $\mu = 31.08$ and $\sigma = 3.67$.

EXAMPLE 4–14

A customer who has ordered 1-inch-diameter pins in bulk will buy only those pins with diameters in the interval 1 ± 0.003 inches. An automatic machine produces pins whose diameters are normally distributed with mean 1.002 inches and standard deviation 0.0011 inch.

1. What percentage of the pins made by the machine will be acceptable to the customer?
2. If the machine is adjusted so that the mean of the pins made by the machine is reset to 1.000 inch, what percentage of the pins will be acceptable to the customer?
3. Looking at the answer to parts 1 and 2, can we say that the machine must be reset?

1. Enter $\mu = 1.002$ and $\sigma = 0.0011$ into the template. From the template $P(0.997 < X < 1.003) = 0.8183$. Thus, 81.83% of the pins will be acceptable to the consumer. *Solution*

2. Change μ to 1.000 in the template. Now, $P(0.997 < X < 1.003) = 0.9936$. Thus, 99.36% of the pins will be acceptable to the consumer.

3. Resetting the machine has considerably increased the percentage of pins acceptable to the consumer. Therefore, resetting the machine is highly desirable.

4–7 Normal Approximation of Binomial Distributions

When the number of trials n in a binomial distribution is large ($>1{,}000$), the calculation of probabilities becomes difficult for the computer, because the calculation encounters some numbers that are too large and some that are too small to handle with needed accuracy. Fortunately, the binomial distribution approaches the normal distribution as n increases and therefore we can approximate it as a normal distribution. Note that the mean is np and the standard deviation is $\sqrt{np(1 - p)}$. The template is shown in Figure 4–17. When the values for n and p of the binomial distribution are entered in cells B4 and C4, the mean and the standard deviation of the corresponding normal distribution are calculated in cells E4 and F4. The rest of the template is similar to the normal distribution template we already saw.

Whenever a binomial distribution is approximated as a normal distribution, a **continuity correction** is required because a binomial is discrete and a normal is continuous. Thus, a column in the histogram of a binomial distribution for, say, $X = 10$, covers, in the continuous sense, the interval [9.5, 10.5]. Similarly, if we include the columns for $X = 10$, 11, and 12, then in the continuous case, the bars occupy the interval [9.5, 12.5], as seen in Figure 4–18. Therefore, when we calculate

FIGURE 4–17 The Template for Normal Approximation of Binomial Distribution [Normal Distribution.xls; Sheet: Normal Approximation]

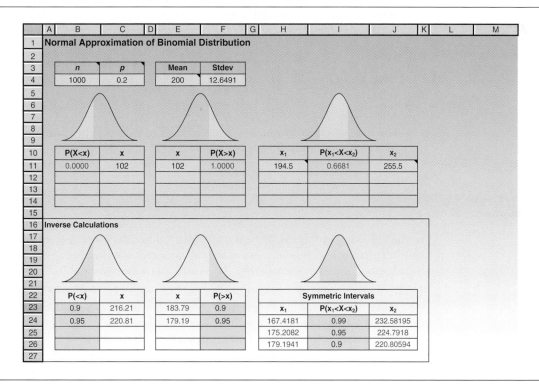

FIGURE 4–18   Continuity Correction

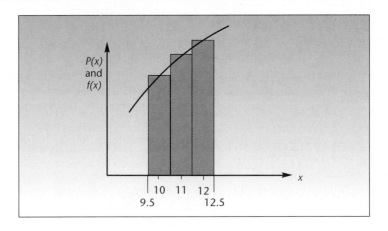

the binomial probability of an interval, say, $P(195 \leq X \leq 255)$, *we should subtract 0.5 from the left limit and add 0.5 to the right limit* to get the corresponding normal probability, namely, $P(194.5 < X < 255.5)$. Adding and subtracting 0.5 in this manner is known as the *continuity correction*. In Figure 4–17, this correction has been applied in cells H11 and J11. Cell I11 has the binomial probability of $P(195 \leq X \leq 255)$.

EXAMPLE 4–15

A total of 2,058 students take a difficult test. Each student has an independent 0.6205 probability of passing the test.

 a. What is the probability that between 1,250 and 1,300 students, both numbers inclusive, will pass the test?

 b. What is the probability that at least 1,300 students will pass the test?

 c. If the probability of at least 1,300 students passing the test has to be at least 0.5, what is the minimum value for the probability of each student passing the test?

Solution

 a. On the template for normal approximation, enter 2,058 for *n* and 0.6205 for *p*. Enter 1,249.5 in cell H11 and 1,300.5 in cell J11. The answer 0.7514 appears in cell I11.

 b. Enter 1,299.5 in cell E11. The answer 0.1533 appears in cell F11.

 c. Use the **Goal Seek** command to set cell F11 to value 0.5 by changing cell C4. The computer finds the answer as $p = 0.6314$.

PROBLEMS

In the following problems, use a normal distribution to compute the required probabilities. In each problem, also state the assumptions necessary for a binomial distribution, and indicate whether the assumptions are reasonable.

4–52.   The manager of a restaurant knows from experience that 70% of the people who make reservations for the evening show up for dinner. The manager decides one evening to overbook and accept 20 reservations when only 15 tables are available. What is the probability that more than 15 parties will show up?

4–53.   An advertising research study indicates that 40% of the viewers exposed to an advertisement try the product during the following four months. If 100 people are exposed to the ad, what is the probability that at least 20 of them will try the product in the following four months?

4–54. According to *The Economist,* 77.9% of Google stockholders have voting power.[7] If 2,000 stockholders are gathered in a meeting, what is the probability that at least 1,500 of them can vote?

4–55. Sixty percent of the managers who enroll in a special training program will successfully complete the program. If a large company sends 328 of its managers to enroll in the program, what is the probability that at least 200 of them will pass?

4–56. A large state university sends recruiters throughout the state to recruit graduating high school seniors to enroll in the university. University records show that 25% of the students who are interviewed by the recruiters actually enroll. If last spring the university recruiters interviewed 1,889 graduating seniors, what is the probability that at least 500 of them will enroll this fall?

4–57. According to *Fortune,* Missouri is within 500 miles of 44% of all U.S. manufacturing plants.[8] If a Missouri company needs parts manufactured in 122 different plants, what is the probability that at least half of them can be found within 500 miles of the state? (Assume independence of parts and of plants.)

4–58. According to *Money,* 59% of full-time workers believe that technology has lengthened their workday.[9] If 200 workers are randomly chosen, what is the probability that at least 120 of them believe that technology has lengthened their workday?

4–8   Using the Computer

Using Excel Functions for a Normal Distribution

In addition to the templates discussed in this chapter, you can use the built-in functions of Excel to evaluate probabilities for normal random variables.

The **NORMDIST** function returns the normal distribution for the specified mean and standard deviation. In the formula NORMDIST(x, mean, stdev, cumulative), *x* is the value for which you want the distribution, *mean* is the arithmetic mean of the distribution, *stdev* is the standard deviation of the distribution, and *cumulative* is a logical value that determines the form of the function. If cumulative is TRUE, NORMDIST returns the cumulative distribution function; if FALSE, it returns the probability density function. For example, NORMDIST(102,100,2,TRUE) will return the area to the left of 102 in a normal distribution with mean 100 and standard deviation 2. This value is 0.8413. NORMDIST(102,100,2,FALSE) will return the density function $f(x)$, which is not needed for most practical purposes.

NORMSDIST(z) returns the standard normal cumulative distribution function, which means the area to the left of z in a standard normal distribution. You can use this function in place of a table of standard normal curve areas. For example NORMSDIST(1) will return the value 0.8413.

NORMINV(probability, mean, stdev) returns the inverse of the normal cumulative distribution for the specified mean and standard deviation. For example NORMINV(0.8413, 100, 2) will return the value of *x* on the normal distribution with mean 100 and standard deviation 2 for which $P(X \le x) = 0.8413$. The value of *x* is 102.

The function NORMSINV(Probability) returns the inverse of the standard normal cumulative distribution. For example, the formula NORMSINV(0.8413) will return the value 1, for which $P(Z \le 1) = 0.8413$.

---

[7]"Our Company Right or Wrong," *The Economist,* March 17, 2007, p. 77.

[8]"Missouri," *Fortune,* March 19, 2007, p. 177.

[9]Jean Chatzky, "Confessions of an E-Mail Addict," *Money,* March 28, 2007, p. 28.

FIGURE 4–19   Using MINITAB for Generating Cumulative and Inverse Cumulative Distribution Functions of a Normal Distribution

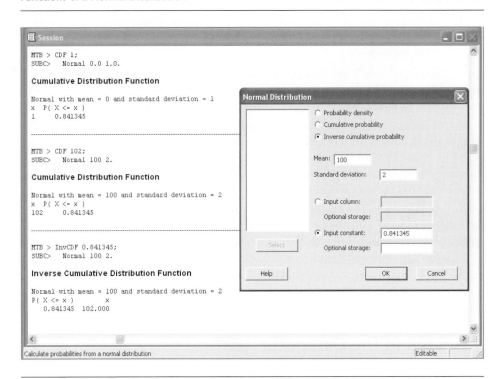

Using MINITAB for a Normal Distribution

As in the previous chapter, choose Calc ▶ Probability Distributions ▶ Normal from the menu. The Normal Distribution dialog box will appear. Using the items available in the dialog box, you can choose to calculate probabilities, cumulative probabilities, or inverse cumulative probabilities for a normal distribution. You also need to specify the mean and standard deviation of the normal distribution. In the input section the values for which you aim to obtain probability densities, cumulative probabilities, or inverse cumulative probabilities are specified. These values can be a constant or a set of values that have been defined in a column. Then press OK to observe the obtained result in the Session window. Figure 4–19 shows the Session commands for obtaining the cumulative distribution in a standard normal distribution as well as a normal distribution with mean 100 and standard deviation 2. It also shows the dialog box and Session commands for obtaining inverse cumulative probabilities for a normal distribution with mean 100 and standard deviation 2.

4–9   Summary and Review of Terms

In this chapter, we discussed the **normal probability distribution,** the most important probability distribution in statistics. We defined the **standard normal random variable** as the normal random variable with mean 0 and standard deviation 1. We saw how to use a table of probabilities for the standard normal random variable and how to transform a normal random variable with any mean and any standard deviation to the standard normal random variable by using the **normal transformation.**

We also saw how the standard normal random variable may, in turn, be transformed into any other normal random variable with a specified mean and standard deviation, and how this allows us to find values of a normal random variable that conform with some probability statement. We discussed a method of determining the mean and/or the standard deviation of a normal random variable from probability statements about the random variable. We saw how the normal distribution is used as a model in many real-world situations, both as the true distribution (a continuous one) and as an approximation to discrete distributions. In particular, we illustrated the use of the normal distribution as an approximation to the binomial distribution.

In the following chapters, we will make much use of the material presented here. Most statistical theory relies on the normal distribution and on distributions that are derived from it.

ADDITIONAL PROBLEMS

4–59. The time, in hours, that a copying machine may work without breaking down is a normally distributed random variable with mean 549 and standard deviation 68. Find the probability that the machine will work for at least 500 hours without breaking down.

4–60. The yield, in tons of ore per day, at a given coal mine is approximately normally distributed with mean 785 tons and standard deviation 60. Find the probability that at least 800 tons of ore will be mined on a given day. Find the proportion of working days in which anywhere from 750 to 850 tons is mined. Find the probability that on a given day, the yield will be below 665 tons.

4–61. Scores on a management aptitude examination are believed to be normally distributed with mean 650 (out of a total of 800 possible points) and standard deviation 50. What is the probability that a randomly chosen manager will achieve a score above 700? What is the probability that the score will be below 750?

4–62. The price of a share of Kraft stock is normally distributed with mean 33.30 and standard deviation 6.[10] What is the probability that on a randomly chosen day in the period for which our assumptions are made, the price of the stock will be more than $40 per share? Less than $30 per share?

4–63. The amount of oil pumped daily at Standard Oil's facilities in Prudhoe Bay is normally distributed with mean 800,000 barrels and standard deviation 10,000. In determining the amount of oil the company must report as its lower limit of daily production, the company wants to choose an amount such that for 80% of the days, at least the reported amount x is produced. Determine the value of the lower limit x.

4–64. An analyst believes that the price of an IBM stock is a normally distributed random variable with mean $105 and variance 24. The analyst would like to determine a value such that there is a 0.90 probability that the price of the stock will be greater than that value.[11] Find the required value.

4–65. Weekly rates of return (on an annualized basis) for certain securities over a given period are believed to be normally distributed with mean 8.00% and variance 0.25. Give two values x_1 and x_2 such that you are 95% sure that annualized weekly returns will be between the two values.

4–66. The impact of a television commercial, measured in terms of excess sales volume over a given period, is believed to be approximately normally distributed with mean 50,000 and variance 9,000,000. Find 0.99 probability bounds on the volume of excess sales that would result from a given airing of the commercial.

4–67. A travel agency believes that the number of people who sign up for tours to Hawaii during the Christmas–New Year's holiday season is an approximately normally distributed random variable with mean 2,348 and standard deviation 762. For reservation purposes, the agency's management wants to find the number of people

---

[10]Inferred from data in "Business Day," *The New York Times*, April 4, 2007, p. C11.

[11]Inferred from data in "Business Day," *The New York Times*, March 14, 2007, p. C10.

such that the probability is 0.85 that at least that many people will sign up. It also needs 0.80 probability bounds on the number of people who will sign up for the trip.

4–68.   A loans manager at a large bank believes that the percentage of her customers who default on their loans during each quarter is an approximately normally distributed random variable with mean 12.1% and standard deviation 2.5%. Give a lower bound x with 0.75 probability that the percentage of people defaulting on their loans is at least x. Also give an upper bound x' with 0.75 probability that the percentage of loan defaulters is below x'.

4–69.   The power generated by a solar electric generator is normally distributed with mean 15.6 kilowatts and standard deviation of 4.1 kilowatts. We may be 95% sure that the generator will deliver at least how many kilowatts?

4–70.   Short-term rates fluctuate daily. It may be assumed that the yield for 90-day Treasury bills in early 2007 was approximately normally distributed with mean 4.92% and standard deviation 0.3%.[12] Find a value such that 95% of the time during that period the yield of 90-day T-bills was below this value.

4–71.   In quality-control projects, engineers use charts where item values are plotted and compared with 3-standard-deviation bounds above and below the mean for the process. When items are found to fall outside the bounds, they are considered nonconforming, and the process is stopped when "too many" items are out of bounds. Assuming a normal distribution of item values, what percentage of values would you expect to be out of bounds when the process is in control? Accordingly, how would you define "too many"? What do you think is the rationale for this practice?

4–72.   Total annual textbook sales in a certain discipline are normally distributed. Forty-five percent of the time, sales are above 671,000 copies, and 10% of the time, sales are above 712,000 copies. Find the mean and the variance of annual sales.

4–73.   Typing speed on a new kind of keyboard for people at a certain stage in their training program is approximately normally distributed. The probability that the speed of a given trainee will be greater than 65 words per minute is 0.45. The probability that the speed will be more than 70 words per minute is 0.15. Find the mean and the standard deviation of typing speed.

4–74.   The number of people responding to a mailed information brochure on cruises of the Royal Viking Line through an agency in San Francisco is approximately normally distributed. The agency found that 10% of the time, over 1,000 people respond immediately after a mailing, and 50% of the time, at least 650 people respond right after the mailing. Find the mean and the standard deviation of the number of people who respond following a mailing.

4–75.   The Tourist Delivery Program was developed by several European automakers. In this program, a tourist from outside Europe—most are from the United States—may purchase an automobile in Europe and drive it in Europe for as long as six months, after which the manufacturer will ship the car to the tourist's home destination at no additional cost. In addition to the time limitations imposed, some countries impose mileage restrictions so that tourists will not misuse the privileges of the program. In setting the limitation, some countries use a normal distribution assumption. It is believed that the number of kilometers driven by a tourist in the program is normally distributed with mean 4,500 and standard deviation 1,800. If a country wants to set the mileage limit at a point such that 80% of the tourists in the program will want to drive fewer kilometers, what should the limit be?

4–76.   The number of newspapers demanded daily in a large metropolitan area is believed to be an approximately normally distributed random variable. If more newspapers are demanded than are printed, the paper suffers an opportunity loss,

---

[12]From "Business Day," *The New York Times*, March 14, 2007, p. C11.

in that it could have sold more papers, and a loss of public goodwill. On the other hand, if more papers are printed than will be demanded, the unsold papers are returned to the newspaper office at a loss. Suppose that management believes that guarding against the first type of error, unmet demand, is most important and would like to set the number of papers printed at a level such that 75% of the time, demand for newspapers will be lower than that point. How many papers should be printed daily if the average demand is 34,750 papers and the standard deviation of demand is 3,560?

4–77. The Federal Funds rate in spring 2007 was approximately normal with $\mu = 5.25\%$ and $\sigma = 0.05\%$. Find the probability that the rate on a given day will be less than 1.1%.[13]

4–78. Thirty-year fixed mortgage rates in April 2007 seemed normally distributed with mean 6.17%.[14] The standard deviation is believed to be 0.25%. Find a bound such that the probability that the actual rate obtained will be this number or below it is 90%.

4–79. A project consists of three phases to be completed one after the other. The duration of each phase, in days, is normally distributed as follows: Duration of Phase I ~ N(84, 3^2); Duration of Phase II ~ N(102, 4^2); Duration of Phase III ~ N(62, 2^2). The durations are independent.

  a. Find the distribution of the project duration. Report the mean and the standard deviation.

  b. If the project duration exceeds 250 days, a penalty will be assessed. What is the probability that the project will be completed within 250 days?

  c. If the project is completed within 240 days, a bonus will be earned. What is the probability that the project will be completed within 240 days?

4–80. The GMAT scores of students who are potential applicants to a university are normally distributed with a mean of 487 and a standard deviation of 98.

  a. What percentage of students will have scores exceeding 500?

  b. What percentage of students will have scores between 600 and 700?

  c. If the university wants only the top 75% of the students to be eligible to apply, what should be the minimum GMAT score specified for eligibility?

  d. Find the narrowest interval that will contain 75% of the students' scores.

  e. Find x such that the interval $[x, 2x]$ will contain 75% of the students' scores. (There are two answers. See if you can find them both.)

4–81. The profit (or loss) from an investment is normally distributed with a mean of $11,200 and a standard deviation of $8,250.

  a. What is the probability that there will be a loss rather than a profit?

  b. What is the probability that the profit will be between $10,000 and $20,000?

  c. Find x such that the probability that the profit will exceed x is 25%.

  d. If the loss exceeds $10,000 the company will have to borrow additional cash. What is the probability that the company will have to borrow additional cash?

  e. Calculate the value at risk.

4–82. The weight of connecting rods used in an automobile engine is to be closely controlled to minimize vibrations. The specification is that each rod must be 974 ± 1.2 grams. The half-width of the specified interval, namely, 1.2 grams, is known as the *tolerance*. The manufacturing process at a plant produces rods whose weights are

---

[13]www.federalreserve.gov

[14]"Figures of the Week," *BusinessWeek,* April 30, 2007, p. 95.

normally distributed with a mean μ of 973.8 grams and a standard deviation σ of 0.32 grams.

- a. What proportion of the rods produced by this process will be acceptable according to the specification?

- b. The *process capability index,* denoted by C_p, is given by the formula

$$C_p = \frac{\text{Tolerance}}{3 * \sigma}$$

  Calculate C_p for this process.

- c. Would you say a larger value or a smaller value of C_p is preferable?

- d. The mean of the process is 973.8 grams, which does not coincide with the target value of 974 grams. The difference between the two is the *offset,* defined as the difference and therefore always positive. Clearly, as the offset increases, the chances of a part going outside the specification limits increase. To take into account the effect of the offset, another index, denoted by C_{pk}, is defined as

$$C_{pk} = C_p - \frac{\text{Offset}}{3 * \sigma}$$

  Calculate C_{pk} for this process.

- e. Suppose the process is adjusted so that the offset is zero, and σ remains at 0.32 gram. Now, what proportion of the parts made by the process will fall within specification limits?

- f. A process has a C_p of 1.2 and a C_{pk} of 0.9. What proportion of the parts produced by the process will fall within specification limits? (*Hint:* One way to proceed is to assume that the target value is, say, 1,000, and $\sigma = 1$. Next, find the tolerance, the specification limits, and the offset. You should then be able to answer the question.)

4–83. A restaurant has three sources of revenue: eat-in orders, takeout orders, and the bar. The daily revenue from each source is normally distributed with mean and standard deviation shown in the table below.

	Mean	Standard Deviation
Eat in	$5,780	$142
Takeout	641	78
Bar	712	72

- a. Will the total revenue on a day be normally distributed?

- b. What are the mean and standard deviation of the total revenue on a particular day?

- c. What is the probability that the revenue will exceed $7,000 on a particular day?

CASE 4   Acceptable Pins

A company supplies pins in bulk to a customer. The company uses an automatic lathe to produce the pins. Due to many causes—vibration, temperature, wear and tear, and the like—the lengths of the pins made by the machine are normally distributed with a mean of 1.012 inches and a standard deviation of 0.018 inch. The customer will buy only those pins with lengths in the interval 1.00 ± 0.02 inch. In other words, the customer wants the length to be 1.00 inch but will accept up to 0.02 inch deviation on either side. This 0.02 inch is known as the *tolerance*.

1. What percentage of the pins will be acceptable to the consumer?

In order to improve percentage accepted, the production manager and the engineers discuss adjusting the population mean and standard deviation of the length of the pins.

2. If the lathe can be adjusted to have the mean of the lengths to any desired value, what should it be adjusted to? Why?

3. Suppose the mean cannot be adjusted, but the standard deviation can be reduced. What maximum value of the standard deviation would make 90% of the parts acceptable to the consumer? (Assume the mean to be 1.012.)

4. Repeat question 3, with 95% and 99% of the pins acceptable.

5. In practice, which one do you think is easier to adjust, the mean or the standard deviation? Why?

The production manager then considers the costs involved. The cost of resetting the machine to adjust the population mean involves the engineers' time and the cost of production time lost. The cost of reducing the population standard deviation involves, in addition to these costs, the cost of overhauling the machine and reengineering the process.

6. Assume it costs $150 x^2 to decrease the standard deviation by $(x/1000)$ inch. Find the cost of reducing the standard deviation to the values found in questions 3 and 4.

7. Now assume that the mean has been adjusted to the best value found in question 2 at a cost of $80. Calculate the reduction in standard deviation necessary to have 90%, 95%, and 99% of the parts acceptable. Calculate the respective costs, as in question 6.

8. Based on your answers to questions 6 and 7, what are your recommended mean and standard deviation?

CASE 5   Multicurrency Decision

A company sells precision grinding machines to four customers in four different countries. It has just signed a contract to sell, two months from now, a batch of these machines to each customer. The following table shows the number of machines (batch quantity) to be delivered to the four customers. The selling price of the machine is fixed in the local currency, and the company plans to convert the local currency at the exchange rate prevailing at the time of delivery. As usual, there is uncertainty in the exchange rates. The sales department estimates the exchange rate for each currency and its standard deviation, expected at the time of delivery, as shown in the table. Assume that the exchange rates are normally distributed and independent.

Customer	Batch Quantity	Selling Price	Exchange Rate Mean	Exchange Rate Standard Deviation
1	12	£ 57,810	$1.41/£	$0.041/£
2	8	¥ 8,640,540	$0.00904/¥	$0.00045/¥
3	5	€97,800	$0.824/€	$0.0342/€
4	2	R 4,015,000	$0.0211/R	$0.00083/R

1. Find the distribution of the uncertain revenue from the contract in U.S. dollars. Report the mean, the variance, and the standard deviation.

2. What is the probability that the revenue will exceed $2,250,000?

3. What is the probability that the revenue will be less than $2,150,000?

4. To remove the uncertainty in the revenue amount, the sales manager of the company looks for someone who would assume the risk. An international bank offers to pay a sure sum of $2,150,000 in return for the revenue in local currencies. What useful facts can you tell the sales manager about the offer, without involving any of your personal judgment?

5. What is your recommendation to the sales manager, based on your personal judgment?

6. If the sales manager is willing to accept the bank's offer, but the CEO of the company is not, who is more risk-averse?

7. Suppose the company accepts the bank's offer. Now consider the bank's risk, assuming that the bank will convert all currencies into U.S. dollars at the prevailing exchange rates. What is the probability that the bank will incur a loss?

8. The bank defines its value at risk as the loss that occurs at the 5th percentile of the uncertain revenue. What is the bank's value at risk?

9. What is the bank's expected profit?

10. Express the value at risk as a percentage of the expected profit. Based on this percentage, what is your evaluation of the risk faced by the bank?

11. Suppose the bank does not plan to convert all currencies into U.S. dollars, but plans to spend or save them as local currency or convert them into some other needed currency. Will this increase or decrease the risk faced by the bank?

12. Based on the answer to part 11, is the assumption (made in parts 7 to 10) that the bank will convert all currencies into U.S. dollars a good assumption?

5

SAMPLING AND SAMPLING DISTRIBUTIONS

5–1   Using Statistics   181
5–2   Sample Statistics as Estimators of Population Parameters   183
5–3   Sampling Distributions   190
5–4   Estimators and Their Properties   201
5–5   Degrees of Freedom   205
5–6   Using the Computer   209
5–7   Summary and Review of Terms   213
Case 6   Acceptance Sampling of Pins   216

LEARNING OBJECTIVES

After studying this chapter, you should be able to:

- Take random samples from populations.
- Distinguish between population parameters and sample statistics.
- Apply the central limit theorem.
- Derive sampling distributions of sample means and proportions.
- Explain why sample statistics are good estimators of population parameters.
- Judge one estimator as better than another based on desirable properties of estimators.
- Apply the concept of degrees of freedom.
- Identify special sampling methods.
- Compute sampling distributions and related results using templates.

Statistics is a science of *inference*. It is the science of generalization from a *part* (the randomly chosen sample) to the *whole* (the population).[1] Recall from Chapter 1 that the population is the entire collection of measurements in which we are interested, and the sample is a smaller set of measurements selected from the population. A random sample of *n* elements is a sample selected from the population in such a way that every set of *n* elements is as likely to be selected as any other set of *n* elements.[2] It is important that the sample be drawn randomly from the entire population under study. This increases the likelihood that our sample will be truly representative of the population of interest and minimizes the chance of errors. As we will see in this chapter, random sampling also allows us to compute the probabilities of sampling errors, thus providing us with knowledge of the degree of accuracy of our sampling results. The need to sample correctly is best illustrated by the well-known story of the *Literary Digest* (see page 182).

In 1936, the widely quoted *Literary Digest* embarked on the project of predicting the results of the presidential election to be held that year. The magazine boasted it would predict, to within a fraction of the percentage of the votes, the winner of the election—incumbent President Franklin Delano Roosevelt or the Republican governor of Kansas, Alfred M. Landon. The *Digest* tried to gather a sample of staggering proportion—10 million voters! One problem with the survey was that only a fraction of the people sampled, 2.3 million, actually provided the requested information. Should a link have existed between a person's inclination to answer the survey and his or her voting preference, the results of the survey would have been *biased:* slanted toward the voting preference of those who did answer. Whether such a link did exist in the case of the *Digest is not known.* (This problem, *nonresponse bias,* is discussed in Chapter 16.) A very serious problem with the *Digest*'s poll, and one known to have affected the results, is the following.

The sample of voters chosen by the *Literary Digest* was obtained from lists of telephone numbers, automobile registrations, and names of *Digest* readers. Remember that this was 1936—not as many people owned phones or cars as today, and those who did tended to be wealthier and more likely to vote Republican (and the same goes for readers of the *Digest*). The selection procedure for the sample of voters was thus biased (slanted toward one kind of voter) because the sample was not randomly chosen from the entire population of voters. Figure 5–1 demonstrates a correct sampling procedure versus the sampling procedure used by the *Literary Digest*.

As a result of the *Digest* error, the magazine does not exist today; it went bankrupt soon after the 1936 election. Some say that hindsight is useful and that today we know more statistics, making it easy for us to deride mistakes made more than 60 years ago. Interestingly enough, however, the ideas of sampling bias were understood in 1936. A few weeks *before* the election, a small article in *The New York Times* criticized the methodology of the *Digest* poll. Few paid it any attention.

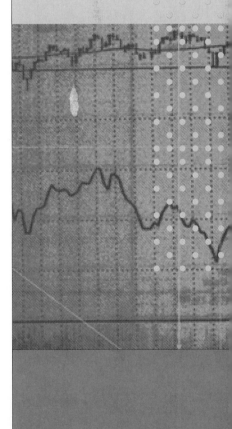

---

[1]Not all of statistics concerns inferences about populations. One branch of statistics, called *descriptive statistics,* deals with describing data sets—possibly with no interest in an underlying population. The descriptive statistics of Chapter 1, when *not* used for inference, fall in this category.

[2]This is the definition of *simple random sampling,* and we will assume throughout that all our samples are simple random samples. Other methods of sampling are discussed in Chapter 6.

Digest Poll Gives Landon 32 States
Landon Leads 4–3 in Last Digest Poll

**Final Tabulation Gives Him
370 Electoral Votes to 161 for
President Roosevelt**

Governor Landon will win the election by an electoral vote of 370 to 161, will carry thirty-two of the forty-eight States, and will lead President Roosevelt about four to three in their share of the popular vote, if the final figures in The Literary Digest poll, made public yesterday, are verified by the count of the ballots next Tuesday.

The New York Times, October 30, 1936. Copyright © 1936 by The New York Times Company. Reprinted by permission.

Roosevelt's Plurality Is 11,000,000
History's Largest Poll
46 States Won by President,
Maine and Vermont by Landon
Many Phases to Victory

**Democratic Landslide Looked Upon
as Striking Personal Triumph for
Roosevelt**

By Arthur Krock

As the count of ballots cast Tuesday in the 1936 Presidential election moved toward completion yesterday, these facts appeared:

Franklin Delano Roosevelt was re-elected President, and John N. Garner Vice President, by the largest popular and electoral majority since the United States became a continental nation—a margin of approximately 11,000,000 plurality of all votes cast, and 523 votes in the electoral college to 8 won by the Republican Presidential candidate, Governor Alfred M. Landon of Kansas. The latter carried only Maine and Vermont of the forty-eight States of the Union . . . .

The New York Times, November 5, 1936. Copyright © 1936 by The New York Times Company. Reprinted by permission.

Sampling is very useful in many situations besides political polling, including business and other areas where we need to obtain information about some population. Our information often leads to a *decision.* There are also situations, as demonstrated by the examples in the introduction to this book, where we are interested in a *process* rather than a single population. One such process is the relationship between advertising and sales. In these more involved situations, we still make the assumption of an underlying population—here, the population of *pairs* of possible advertising and sales values. Conclusions about the process are reached based on information in our data, which are assumed to constitute a random sample from the entire population. The ideas of a population and of a random sample drawn from the population are thus essential to all inferential statistics.

FIGURE 5–1   A Good Sampling Procedure and the One Used by the *Literary Digest*

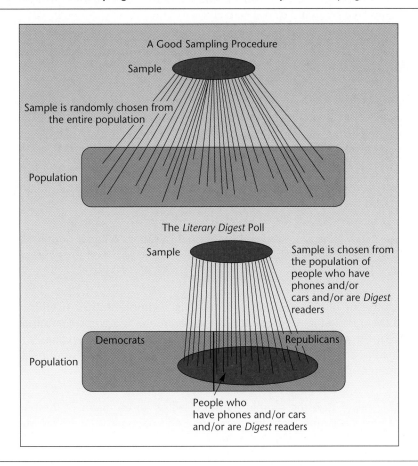

In statistical inference we are concerned with populations; the samples are of no interest to us in their own right. We wish to use our *known* random sample in the extraction of information about the *unknown* population from which it is drawn. The information we extract is in the form of summary statistics: a sample mean, a sample standard deviation, or other measures computed from the sample. A statistic such as the sample mean is considered an *estimator* of a population *parameter*—the population mean. In the next section, we discuss and define sample estimators and population parameters. Then we explore the relationship between statistics and parameters via the *sampling distribution*. Finally, we discuss desirable properties of statistical estimators.

5–2   Sample Statistics as Estimators of Population Parameters

A population may be a large, sometimes infinite, collection of elements. The population has a *frequency distribution*—the distribution of the frequencies of occurrence of its elements. The population distribution, when stated in relative frequencies, is also the probability distribution of the population. This is so because the relative frequency of a value in the population is also the probability of obtaining the particular value when an element is randomly drawn from the entire population. As with random variables, we may associate with a population its mean and its standard deviation.

In the case of populations, the mean and the standard deviation are called *parameters*. They are denoted by μ and σ, respectively.

> A numerical measure of a population is called a **population parameter,** or simply a **parameter.**

Recall that in Chapter 4 we referred to the mean and the standard deviation of a normal probability distribution as the distribution parameters. Here we view parameters as descriptive measures of populations. Inference drawn about a population parameter is based on sample statistics.

> A numerical measure of the sample is called a **sample statistic,** or simply a **statistic.**

Population parameters are estimated by sample statistics. When a sample statistic is used to estimate a population parameter, the statistic is called an *estimator* of the parameter.

> An **estimator** of a population parameter is a sample statistic used to estimate the parameter. An **estimate** of the parameter is a *particular* numerical value of the estimator obtained by sampling. When a single value is used as an estimate, the estimate is called a **point estimate** of the population parameter.

The sample mean $\overline{X}$ is the sample statistic used as an estimator of the population mean μ. Once we sample from the population and obtain a value of $\overline{X}$ (using equation 1–1), we will have obtained a *particular* sample mean; we will denote this particular value by $\overline{x}$. We may have, for example, $\overline{x} = 12.53$. This value is our estimate of μ. The estimate is a point estimate because it constitutes a single number. In this chapter, every estimate will be a point estimate—a single number that, we hope, lies close to the population parameter it estimates. Chapter 6 is entirely devoted to the concept of an *interval estimate*—an estimate constituting an interval of numbers rather than a single number. An interval estimate is an interval believed likely to contain the unknown population parameter. It conveys more information than just the point estimate on which it is based.

In addition to the sample mean, which estimates the population mean, other statistics are useful. The sample variance S^2 is used as an estimator of the population variance σ^2. A particular estimate obtained will be denoted by s^2. (This estimate is computed from the data using equation 1–3 or an equivalent formula.)

As demonstrated by the political polling example with which we opened this chapter, interest often centers not on a mean or standard deviation of a population, but rather on a population *proportion*. The population proportion parameter is also called a binomial proportion parameter.

> The **population proportion** p is equal to the number of elements in the population belonging to the category of interest, divided by the total number of elements in the population.

The population proportion of voters for Governor Landon in 1936, for example, was the number of people who intended to vote for the candidate, divided by the total number of voters. The estimator of the population proportion p is the *sample proportion* $\hat{P}$, defined as the number of *binomial successes* in the sample (i.e., the number of elements in the sample that belong to the category of interest), divided by the sample size n. A particular estimate of the population proportion p is the sample proportion $\hat{p}$.

The **sample proportion** is

$$\hat{p} = \frac{x}{n} \qquad\qquad (5\text{–}1)$$

where x is the number of elements in the sample found to belong to the category of interest and n is the sample size.

Suppose that we want to estimate the proportion of consumers in a certain area who are users of a certain product. The (unknown) population proportion is p. We estimate p by the statistic $\hat{P}$, the sample proportion. Suppose a random sample of 100 consumers in the area reveals that 26 are users of the product. Our point estimate of p is then $\hat{p} = x/n = 26/100 = 0.26$. As another example, let's look at a very important problem, whose seriousness became apparent in early 2007, when more than a dozen dogs and cats in the United States became sick, and some died, after being fed pet food contaminated with an unknown additive originating in China. The culprit was melamine, an artificial additive derived from coal, which Chinese manufacturers have been adding to animal feed, and it was the cause of the death of pets and has even caused problems with the safety of eating farm products.[3] The wider problem of just how this harmful additive ended up in animal feed consumed in the United States is clearly statistical in nature, and it could have been prevented by effective use of sampling. It turned out that in the whole of 2006, Food and Drug Administration (FDA) inspectors sampled only 20,662 shipments out of 8.9 million arriving at American ports.[4] While this sampling percentage is small (about 0.2%), in this chapter you will learn that correct scientific sampling methods do not require larger samples, and good information can be gleaned from random samples of this size when they truly represent the population of all shipments. Suppose that this had indeed been done, and that 853 of the sampled shipments contained melamine. What is the sample estimate of the proportion of all shipments to the United States tainted with melamine? Using equation 5–1, we see that the estimate is $853/20{,}662 = 0.0413$, or about 4.13%.

In summary, we have the following estimation relationships:

Estimator (Sample Statistic)		Population Parameter
$\bar{X}$	$\xrightarrow{\text{estimates}}$	μ
S^2	$\xrightarrow{\text{estimates}}$	σ^2
$\hat{P}$	$\xrightarrow{\text{estimates}}$	p

Let us consider sampling to estimate the population mean, and let us try to visualize how this is done. Consider a population with a certain frequency distribution. The frequency distribution of the values of the population is the probability distribution of the value of an element in the population, drawn at random. Figure 5–2 shows a frequency distribution of some population and the population mean μ. If we knew the exact frequency distribution of the population, we would be able to determine μ directly in the same way we determine the mean of a random variable when we know its probability distribution. In reality, the frequency distribution of a population is not known; neither is the mean of the population. We try to estimate the population mean by the sample mean, computed from a random sample. Figure 5–2 shows the values of a random sample obtained from the population and the resulting sample mean $\bar{x}$, computed from the data.

[3]Alexei Barrionuevo, "U.S. Says Some Chicken Feed Tainted," *The New York Times,* May 1, 2007, p. C6.

[4]Alexei Barrionuevo, "Food Imports Often Escape Scrutiny," *The New York Times,* May 1, 2007, p. C1.

FIGURE 5–2   A Population Distribution, a Random Sample from the Population, and Their
              Respective Means

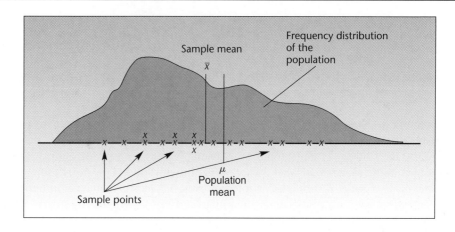

In this example, $\bar{x}$ happens to lie close to μ, the population parameter it estimates, although this does not always happen. The sample statistic $\bar{X}$ is a *random
variable* whose actual value depends on the particular random sample obtained. The
random variable $\bar{X}$ has a relatively high probability of being close to the population
mean it estimates, and it has decreasing probabilities of falling farther and farther
from the population mean. Similarly, the sample statistic S is a random variable with
a relatively high probability of being close to σ, the population parameter it estimates.
Also, when sampling for a population proportion p, the estimator $\hat{P}$ has a relatively
high probability of being close to p. How high a probability, and how close to the
parameter? The answer to this question is the main topic of this chapter, presented in
the next section. Before discussing this important topic, we will say a few things about
the mechanics of obtaining random samples.

Obtaining a Random Sample

CHAPTER 8

All along we have been referring to random samples. We have stressed the importance
of the fact that our sample should always be drawn randomly from the entire population about which we wish to draw an inference. How do we draw a random sample?

To obtain a random sample from the entire population, we need a list of all the elements in the population of interest. Such a list is called a *frame*. The frame allows us
to draw elements from the population by randomly generating the numbers of the
elements to be included in the sample. Suppose we need a simple random sample of
100 people from a population of 7,000. We make a list of all 7,000 people and assign
each person an identification number. This gives us a list of 7,000 numbers—our frame
for the experiment. Then we generate by computer or by other means a set of 100 random numbers in the range of values from 1 to 7,000. This procedure gives every set
of 100 people in the population an equal chance of being included in the sample.

As mentioned, a computer (or an advanced calculator) may be used for generating random numbers. We will demonstrate an alternative method of choosing random numbers—a random number table. Table 5–1 is a part of such a table. A random
number table is given in Appendix C as Table 14. To use the table, we start at any
point, pick a number from the table, and continue in the same row or the same column (it does not matter which), systematically picking out numbers with the number
of digits appropriate for our needs. If a number is outside our range of required numbers, we ignore it. We also ignore any number already obtained.

For example, suppose that we need a random sample of 10 data points from a population with a total of 600 elements. This means that we need 10 random drawings of

TABLE 5–1   Random Numbers

10480	15011	01536	02011	81647	91646	69179	14194
22368	46573	25595	85393	30995	89198	27982	53402
24130	48360	22527	97265	76393	64809	15179	24830
42167	93093	06243	61680	07856	16376	93440	53537
37570	39975	81837	16656	06121	91782	60468	81305
77921	06907	11008	42751	27756	53498	18602	70659

elements from our frame of 1 through 600. To do this, we note that the number 600 has three digits; therefore, we draw random numbers with three digits. Since our population has only 600 units, however, we ignore any number greater than 600 and take the next number, assuming it falls in our range. Let us decide arbitrarily to choose the first three digits in each set of five digits in Table 5–1; and we proceed by row, starting in the first row and moving to the second row, continuing until we have obtained our 10 required random numbers. We get the following random numbers: 104, 150, 15, 20, 816 (discard), 916 (discard), 691 (discard), 141, 223, 465, 255, 853 (discard), 309, 891 (discard), 279. Our random sample will, therefore, consist of the elements with serial numbers 104, 150, 15, 20, 141, 223, 465, 255, 309, and 279. A similar procedure would be used for obtaining the random sample of 100 people from the population of 7,000 mentioned earlier. Random number tables are included in books of statistical tables.

In many situations obtaining a frame of the elements in the population is impossible. In such situations we may still randomize some aspect of the experiment and thus obtain a random sample. For example, we may randomize the location and the time and date of the collection of our observations, as well as other factors involved. In estimating the average miles-per-gallon rating of an automobile, for example, we may randomly choose the dates and times of our trial runs as well as the particular automobiles used, the drivers, the roads used, and so on.

Other Sampling Methods

Sometimes a population may consist of distinct subpopulations, and including a certain number of samples from each subpopulation may be useful. For example, the students at a university may consist of 54% women and 46% men. We know that men and women may have very different opinions on the topic of a particular survey. Thus having proper representation of men and women in the random sample is desirable. If the total sample size is going to be 100, then a proper representation would mean 54 women and 46 men. Accordingly, the 54 women may be selected at random from a frame of only women students, and the 46 men may be selected similarly. Together they will make up a random sample of 100 with proper representation. This method of sampling is called **stratified sampling**.

> In a stratified sampling the population is partitioned into two or more subpopulations called **strata**, and from each stratum a desired number of samples are selected at random.

Each stratum must be distinct in that it differs from other strata in some aspect that is relevant to the sampling experiment. Otherwise, stratification would yield no benefit. Besides sex, another common distinction between strata is their individual variances. For example, suppose we are interested in estimating the average income of all the families in a city. Three strata are possible: high-income, medium-income, and low-income families. High-income families may have a large variance in their incomes, medium-income families a smaller variance, and low-income families the least variance.

Then, by properly representing the three strata in a stratified sampling process, we can achieve a greater accuracy in the estimate than by a regular sampling process.

Sometimes, we may have to deviate from the regular sampling process for practical reasons. For example, suppose we want to find the average opinion of all voters in the state of Michigan on a state legislation issue. Assume that the budget for the sampling experiment is limited. A normal random sampling process will choose voters all over the state. It would be too costly to visit and interview every selected voter. Instead, we could choose a certain number of counties at random and from within the chosen counties select voters at random. This way, the travel will be restricted to chosen counties only. This method of sampling is called **cluster sampling.** Each county in our example is a *cluster.* After choosing a cluster at random if we sample every item or person in that cluster, then the method would be **single-stage cluster sampling.** If we choose a cluster at random and select items or people at random within the chosen clusters, as mentioned in our example, then that is **two-stage cluster sampling.** **Multistage cluster sampling** is also possible. For example, we might choose counties at random, then choose townships at random within the chosen counties, and finally choose voters at random within the chosen townships.

At times, the frame we have for a sampling experiment may itself be in random order. In such cases we could do a **systematic sampling.** Suppose we have a list of 3,000 customers and the order of customers in the list is random. Assume that we need a random sample of 100 customers. We first note that $3,000/100 = 30$. We then pick a number between 1 and 30 at random–say, 18. We select the 18th customer in the list and from there on, we pick every 30th customer in the list. In other words, we pick the 18th, 48th, 78th, and so on. In general, if N is the population size and n is the sample size, let $N/n = k$ where k is a rounded integer. We pick a number at random between 1 and k–say, l. We then pick the kth, $(l + k)$th, $(l + 2k)$th, $\ldots$, items from the frame.

Systematic sampling may also be employed when a frame cannot be prepared. For example, a call center manager may want to select calls at random for monitoring purposes. Here a frame is impossible but the calls can reasonably be assumed to arrive in a random sequence, thus justifying a systematic selection of calls. Starting at a randomly selected time, one may choose every kth call where k depends on the call volume and the sample size desired.

Nonresponse

Nonresponse to sample surveys is one of the most serious problems that occur in practical applications of sampling methodology. The example of polling Jewish people, many of whom do not answer the phone on Saturday, mentioned in the *New York Times* article in 2003 (see Chapter 1), is a case in point. The problem is one of loss of information. For example, suppose that a survey questionnaire dealing with some issue is mailed to a randomly chosen sample of 500 people and that only 300 people respond to the survey. The question is: What can you say about the 200 people who did not respond? This is a very important question, and there is no immediate answer to it, precisely because the people did not respond; we know nothing about them. Suppose that the questionnaire asks for a yes or no answer to a particular public issue over which people have differing views, and we want to estimate the proportion of people who would respond yes. People may have such strong views about the issue that those who would respond no may refuse to respond altogether. In this case, the 200 nonrespondents to our survey will contain a higher proportion of "no" answers than the 300 responses we have. But, again, we would not know about this. The result will be a bias. How can we compensate for such a possible bias?

We may want to consider the population as made up of two *strata:* the respondents' stratum and the nonrespondents' stratum. In the original survey, we managed to sample only the respondents' stratum, and this caused the bias. What we need to do is to obtain a random sample from the nonrespondents' stratum. This is easier said than done. Still, there are ways we can at least reduce the bias and get some idea about the proportion of "yes" answers in the nonresponse stratum. This entails *callbacks:* returning to the nonrespondents and asking them again. In some mail questionnaires, it is common to send several requests for response, and these reduce the uncertainty. There may, however, be hard-core refusers who just do not want to answer the questionnaire. Such people are likely to have very distinct views about the issue in question, and if you leave them out, there will be a significant bias in your conclusions. In such a situation, gathering a small random sample of the hard-core refusers and offering them some monetary reward for their answers may be useful. In cases where people may find the question embarrassing or may worry about revealing their personal views, a random-response mechanism whereby the respondent randomly answers one of two questions–one the sensitive question, and the other an innocuous question of no relevance–may elicit answers. The interviewer does not know which question any particular respondent answered but does know the probability of answering the sensitive question. This still allows for computation of the aggregated response to the sensitive question while protecting any given respondent's privacy.

PROBLEMS

5–1. Discuss the concepts of a parameter, a sample statistic, an estimator, and an estimate. What are the relations among these entities?

5–2. An auditor selected a random sample of 12 accounts from all accounts receivable of a given firm. The amounts of the accounts, in dollars, are as follows: 87.50, 123.10, 45.30, 52.22, 213.00, 155.00, 39.00, 76.05, 49.80, 99.99, 132.00, 102.11. Compute an estimate of the mean amount of all accounts receivable. Give an estimate of the variance of all the amounts.

5–3. In problem 5–2, suppose the auditor wants to estimate the proportion of all the firm's accounts receivable with amounts over $100. Give a point estimate of this parameter.

5–4. An article in the *New York Times* describes an interesting business phenomenon. The owners of small businesses tend to pay themselves much smaller salaries than they would earn had they been working for someone else.[5] Suppose that a random sample of small business owners' monthly salaries, in dollars, are as follows: 1,000, 1,200, 1,700, 900, 2,100, 2,300, 830, 2,180, 1,300, 3,300, 7,150, 1,500. Compute point estimates of the mean and the standard deviation of the population monthly salaries of small business owners.

5–5. Starbucks regularly introduces new coffee drinks and attempts to evaluate how these drinks fare by estimating the price its franchises can charge for them and sell enough cups to justify marketing the drink.[6] Suppose the following random sample of prices a new drink sells for in New York (in dollars) is available: 4.50, 4.25, 4.10, 4.75, 4.80, 3.90, 4.20, 4.55, 4.65, 4.85, 3.85, 4.15, 4.85, 3.95, 4.30, 4.60, 4.00. Compute the sample estimators of the population mean and standard deviation.

5–6. A market research worker interviewed a random sample of 18 people about their use of a certain product. The results, in terms of Y or N (for Yes, a user of the product, or No, not a user of the product), are as follows: Y N N Y Y Y N Y N Y Y Y N Y N Y Y N. Estimate the population proportion of users of the product.

---

[5]Eva Tahmincioglu, "When the Boss Is Last in Line for a Paycheck," *The New York Times,* March 22, 2007, p. C5.

[6]Burt Helm, "Saving Starbucks' Soul," *BusinessWeek,* April 9, 2007, p. 56.

5–7. Use a random number table (you may use Table 5–1) to find identification numbers of elements to be used in a random sample of size $n = 25$ from a population of 950 elements.

5–8. Find five random numbers from 0 to 5,600.

5–9. Assume that you have a frame of 40 million voters (something the *Literary Digest* should have had for an unbiased polling). Randomly generate the numbers of five sampled voters.

5–10. Suppose you need to sample the concentration of a chemical in a production process that goes on continuously 24 hours per day, 7 days per week. You need to generate a random sample of six observations of the process over a period of one week. Use a computer, a calculator, or a random number table to generate the six observation times (to the nearest minute).

5–3   Sampling Distributions

CHAPTER 8

> The **sampling distribution** of a statistic is the probability distribution of all possible values the statistic may take when computed from random samples of the same size, drawn from a specified population.

Let us first look at the sample mean $\overline{X}$. The sample mean is a random variable. The possible values of this random variable depend on the possible values of the elements in the random sample from which $\overline{X}$ is to be computed. The random sample, in turn, depends on the distribution of the population from which it is drawn. As a random variable, $\overline{X}$ has a *probability distribution*. This probability distribution is the sampling distribution of $\overline{X}$.

> The **sampling distribution of $\overline{X}$** is the probability distribution of all possible values the random variable $\overline{X}$ may take when a sample of size *n* is taken from a specified population.

Let us derive the sampling distribution of $\overline{X}$ in the simple case of drawing a sample of size $n = 2$ items from a population uniformly distributed over the integers 1 through 8. That is, we have a large population consisting of equal proportions of the values 1 to 8. At each draw, there is a $1/8$ probability of obtaining any of the values 1 through 8 (alternatively, we may assume there are only eight elements, 1 through 8, and that the sampling is done with replacement). The sample space of the values of the two sample points drawn from this population is given in Table 5–2. This is an example. In real situations, sample sizes are much larger.

TABLE 5–2   Possible Values of Two Sample Points from a Uniform Population of the Integers 1 through 8

Second Sample Point	First Sample Point							
	1	2	3	4	5	6	7	8
1	1,1	2,1	3,1	4,1	5,1	6,1	7,1	8,1
2	1,2	2,2	3,2	4,2	5,2	6,2	7,2	8,2
3	1,3	2,3	3,3	4,3	5,3	6,3	7,3	8,3
4	1,4	2,4	3,4	4,4	5,4	6,4	7,4	8,4
5	1,5	2,5	3,5	4,5	5,5	6,5	7,5	8,5
6	1,6	2,6	3,6	4,6	5,6	6,6	7,6	8,6
7	1,7	2,7	3,7	4,7	5,7	6,7	7,7	8,7
8	1,8	2,8	3,8	4,8	5,8	6,8	7,8	8,8

TABLE 5–3 The Sampling Distribution of $\overline{X}$ for a Sample of Size 2 from a Uniformly Distributed Population of the Integers 1 to 8

Particular Value $\overline{x}$	Probability of $\overline{x}$	Particular Value $\overline{x}$	Probability of $\overline{x}$
1	1/64	5	7/64
1.5	2/64	5.5	6/64
2	3/64	6	5/64
2.5	4/64	6.5	4/64
3	5/64	7	3/64
3.5	6/64	7.5	2/64
4	7/64	8	1/64
4.5	8/64		1.00

Using the sample space from the table, we will now find all possible values of the sample mean $\overline{X}$ and their probabilities. We compute these probabilities, using the fact that all 64 sample pairs shown are equally likely. This is so because the population is uniformly distributed and because in random sampling each drawing is independent of the other; therefore, the probability of a given pair of sample points is the product $(1/8)(1/8) = 1/64$. From Table 5–2, we compute the sample mean associated with each of the 64 pairs of numbers and find the probability of occurrence of each value of the sample mean. The values and their probabilities are given in Table 5–3. The table thus gives us the sampling distribution of $\overline{X}$ in this particular sampling situation. Verify the values in Table 5–3 using the sample space given in Table 5–2. Figure 5–3 shows the uniform distribution of the population and the sampling distribution of $\overline{X}$, as listed in Table 5–3.

Let us find the mean and the standard deviation of the *population*. We can do this by treating the population as a random variable (the random variable being the value of a single item randomly drawn from the population; each of the values 1 through 8 has a 1/8 probability of being drawn). Using the appropriate equations from Chapter 3, we find $\mu = 4.5$ and $\sigma = 2.29$ (verify these results).

Now let us find the expected value and the standard deviation of the random variable $\overline{X}$. Using the sampling distribution listed in Table 5–3, we find $E(\overline{X}) = 4.5$ and $\sigma_{\overline{x}} = 1.62$ (verify these values by computation). Note that the expected value of $\overline{X}$ is equal to the mean of the population; each is equal to 4.5. The standard deviation of $\overline{X}$, denoted $\sigma_{\overline{x}}$, is equal to 1.62, and the population standard deviation σ is 2.29. But observe an interesting fact: $2.29/\sqrt{2} = 1.62$. The facts we have discovered in this example are not an accident—they hold in all cases. The expected value of the sample

FIGURE 5–3 The Population Distribution and the Sampling Distribution of the Sample Mean

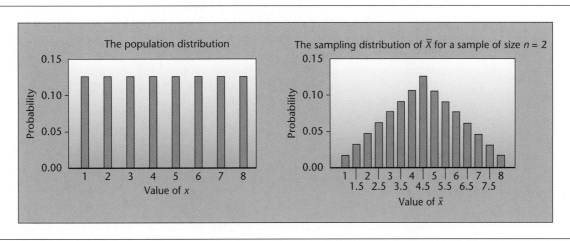

mean $\overline{X}$ is equal to the population mean μ and the standard deviation of $\overline{X}$ is equal to the population standard deviation divided by the square root of the sample size. Sometimes the estimated standard deviation of a statistic is called its *standard error*.

The expected value of the sample mean is[7]

$$E(\overline{X}) = \mu \tag{5-2}$$

The standard deviation of the sample mean is[8]

$$SD(\overline{X}) = \sigma_{\overline{x}} = \sigma/\sqrt{n} \tag{5-3}$$

We know the two parameters of the sampling distribution of $\overline{X}$: We know the mean of the distribution (the expected value of $\overline{X}$) and we know its standard deviation. What about the shape of the sampling distribution? If the population itself is *normally distributed*, the sampling distribution of $\overline{X}$ is also normal.

When sampling is done from a *normal distribution* with mean μ and standard deviation σ, the sample mean $\overline{X}$ has a **normal sampling distribution:**

$$\overline{X} \sim N(\mu, \sigma^2/n) \tag{5-4}$$

Thus, when we sample from a normally distributed population with mean μ and standard deviation σ, the sample mean has a normal distribution with the same *center*, μ, as the population but with *width* (standard deviation) that is $1/\sqrt{n}$ the size of the width of the population distribution. This is demonstrated in Figure 5–4, which shows a normal population distribution and the sampling distribution of $\overline{X}$ for different sample sizes.

The fact that the sampling distribution of $\overline{X}$ has mean μ is very important. It means that, *on the average,* the sample mean is equal to the population mean. The distribution of the statistic is *centered* on the parameter to be estimated, and this makes the statistic $\overline{X}$ a good estimator of μ. This fact will become clearer in the next section, where we discuss estimators and their properties. The fact that the standard deviation of $\overline{X}$ is $\sigma/\sqrt{n}$ means that as the sample size *increases,* the standard deviation of $\overline{X}$ *decreases,* making $\overline{X}$ more likely to be close to μ. This is another desirable property of a good estimator, to be discussed later. Finally, when the sampling distribution of $\overline{X}$ is normal, this allows us to compute probabilities that $\overline{X}$ will be within specified distances of μ. What happens in cases where the population itself is *not* normally distributed?

In Figure 5–3, we saw the sampling distribution of $\overline{X}$ when sampling is done from a uniformly distributed population and with a sample of size $n = 2$. Let us now see what happens as we increase the sample size. Figure 5–5 shows results of a simulation giving the sampling distribution of $\overline{X}$ when the sample size is $n = 5$, when the sample size is $n = 20$, and the *limiting* distribution of $\overline{X}$—the distribution of $\overline{X}$ as the sample size increases indefinitely. As can be seen from the figure, the limiting distribution of $\overline{X}$ is, again, the *normal distribution*.

---

[7]The proof of equation 5–2 relies on the fact that the expected value of the sum of several random variables is equal to the sum of their expected values. Also, from equation 3–6 we know that the expected value of aX, where a is a number, is equal to a times the expected value of X. We also know that the expected value of each element X drawn from the population is equal to μ, the population mean. Using these facts, we find the following: $E(\overline{X}) = E(\Sigma X/n) = (1/n)E(\Sigma X) = (1/n)n\mu = \mu$.

[8]The proof of equation 5–3 relies on the fact that, when several random variables are *independent* (as happens in random sampling), the variance of the sum of the random variables is equal to the sum of their variances. Also, from equation 3–10, we know that the variance of aX is equal to $a^2V(X)$. The variance of each X drawn from the population is equal to σ^2. Using these facts, we find $V(\overline{X}) = V(\Sigma X/n) = (1/n)^2(\Sigma\sigma^2) = (1/n)^2(n\sigma^2) = \sigma^2/n$. Hence, SD $(\overline{X}) = \sigma/\sqrt{n}$.

FIGURE 5–4   **A Normally Distributed Population and the Sampling Distribution of the Sample Mean for Different Sample Sizes**

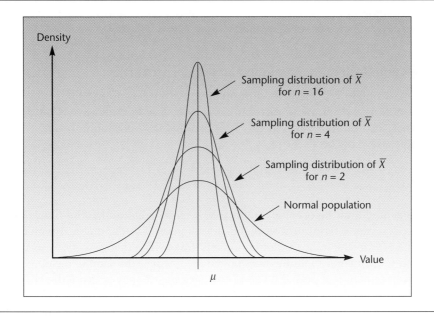

FIGURE 5–5   **The Sampling Distribution of $\overline{X}$ as the Sample Size Increases**

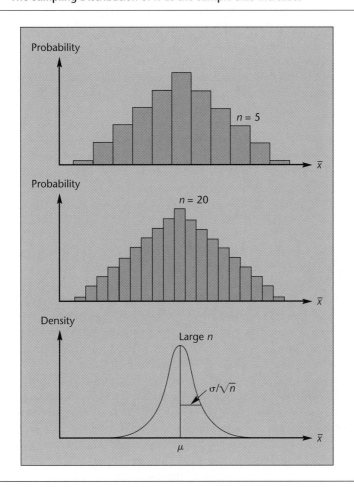

The Central Limit Theorem

The result we just stated—that the distribution of the sample mean $\overline{X}$ tends to the normal distribution as the sample size increases—is one of the most important results in statistics. It is known as the *central limit theorem.*

CHAPTER 7

The Central Limit Theorem (and additional properties)

When sampling is done from a population with mean μ and finite standard deviation σ, the sampling distribution of the sample mean $\overline{X}$ will tend to a normal distribution with mean μ and standard deviation $\sigma/\sqrt{n}$ as the sample size n becomes large.

$$\text{For "large enough" } n \qquad \overline{X} \sim N(\mu, \sigma^2/n) \qquad\qquad (5\text{–}5)$$

The central limit theorem is remarkable because it states that the distribution of the sample mean $\overline{X}$ tends to a normal distribution *regardless* of the distribution of the population from which the random sample is drawn. The theorem allows us to make probability statements about the possible range of values the sample mean may take. It allows us to compute probabilities of how far away $\overline{X}$ may be from the population mean it estimates. For example, using our rule of thumb for the normal distribution, we know that the probability that the distance between $\overline{X}$ and μ will be less than $\sigma/\sqrt{n}$ is approximately 0.68. This is so because, as you remember, the probability that the value of a normal random variable will be within 1 standard deviation of its mean is 0.6826; here our normal random variable has mean μ and standard deviation $\sigma/\sqrt{n}$. Other probability statements can be made as well; we will see their use shortly. When is a sample size n "large enough" that we may apply the theorem?

The central limit theorem says that, *in the limit,* as n goes to infinity $(n \to \infty)$, the distribution of $\overline{X}$ becomes a normal distribution (regardless of the distribution of the population). The *rate* at which the distribution approaches a normal distribution does depend, however, on the shape of the distribution of the parent population. If the population itself is normally distributed, the distribution of $\overline{X}$ is normal for *any* sample size n, as stated earlier. On the other hand, for population distributions that are very different from a normal distribution, a relatively large sample size is required to achieve a good normal approximation for the distribution of $\overline{X}$. Figure 5–6 shows several parent population distributions and the resulting sampling distributions of $\overline{X}$ for different sample sizes.

Since we often do not know the shape of the population distribution, some general rule of thumb telling us when a sample is large enough that we may apply the central limit theorem would be useful.

In general, a sample of 30 or more elements is considered **large enough** for the central limit theorem to take effect.

We emphasize that this is a *general,* and somewhat arbitrary, rule. A larger minimum sample size may be required for a good normal approximation when the population distribution is very different from a normal distribution. By the same token, a smaller minimum sample size may suffice for a good normal approximation when the population distribution is close to a normal distribution.

Throughout this book, we will make reference to *small* samples versus *large* samples. By a small sample, we generally mean a sample of fewer than 30 elements. A large sample will generally mean a sample of 30 or more elements. The results we will discuss as applicable for large samples will be more meaningful, however, the larger the sample size. (By the central limit theorem, the larger the sample size, the better the approximation offered by the normal distribution.) The "30 rule" should, therefore, be applied with caution. Let us now look at an example of the use of the central limit theorem.

FIGURE 5–6   **The Effects of the Central Limit Theorem: The Distribution of $\overline{X}$ for Different Populations and Different Sample Sizes**

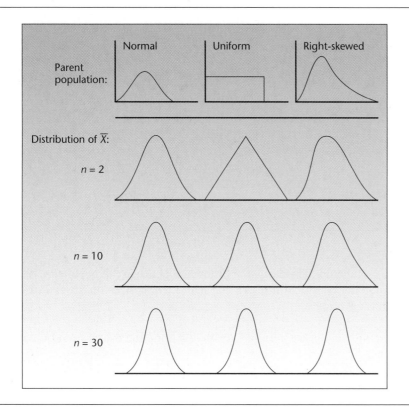

Mercury makes a 2.4-liter V-6 engine, the Laser XRi, used in speedboats. The company's engineers believe that the engine delivers an average power of 220 horsepower and that the standard deviation of power delivered is 15 horsepower. A potential buyer intends to sample 100 engines (each engine to be run a single time). What is the probability that the sample mean $\overline{X}$ will be less than 217 horsepower?

EXAMPLE 5–1

In solving problems such as this one, we use the techniques of Chapter 4. There we used μ as the mean of the normal random variable and σ as its standard deviation. Here our random variable $\overline{X}$ is normal (at least approximately so, by the central limit theorem because our sample size is large) and has mean μ. Note, however, that the standard deviation of our random variable $\overline{X}$ is $\sigma/\sqrt{n}$ and not just σ. We proceed as follows:

Solution

$$P(\overline{X} < 217) = P\left(Z < \frac{217 - \mu}{\sigma/\sqrt{n}} \right)$$

$$= P\left(Z < \frac{217 - 220}{15/\sqrt{100}} \right) = P(Z < -2) = 0.0228$$

Thus, if the population mean is indeed $\mu = 220$ horsepower and the standard deviation is $\sigma = 15$ horsepower, the probability that the potential buyer's tests will result in a sample mean less than 217 horsepower is rather small.

FIGURE 5–7 A (Nonnormal) Population Distribution and the Normal Sampling Distribution
of the Sample Mean When a Large Sample Is Used

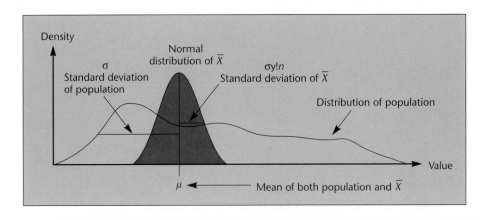

Figure 5–7 should help clarify the distinction between the population distribution and the sampling distribution of $\overline{X}$. The figure emphasizes the three aspects of the central limit theorem:

1. When the sample size is large enough, the sampling distribution of $\overline{X}$ is normal.
2. The expected value of $\overline{X}$ is μ.
3. The standard deviation of $\overline{X}$ is $\sigma/\sqrt{n}$.

The last statement is the key to the important fact that as the sample size increases, the variation of $\overline{X}$ about its mean μ decreases. Stated another way, as we buy *more information* (take a larger sample), our *uncertainty* (measured by the standard deviation) about the parameter being estimated *decreases*.

EXAMPLE 5–2

**Eastern-Based Financial Institutions
Second-Quarter EPS and Statistical Summary**

Corporation	EPS ($)	Summary	
Bank of New York	2.53	Sample size	13
Bank Boston	4.38	Mean EPS	4.7377
Banker's Trust NY	7.53	Median EPS	4.3500
Chase Manhattan	7.53	Standard deviation	2.4346
Citicorp	7.93		
Fleet	4.35		
MBNA	1.50		
Mellon	2.75		
JP Morgan	7.25		
PNC Bank	3.11		
Republic Bank	7.44		
State Street Bank	2.04		
Summit	3.25		

This example shows random samples from the data above. Here 100 random samples of five banks each are chosen with replacement. The mean for each sample is computed, and a frequency distribution is drawn. Note the shape of this distribution (Figure 5–8).

Data Set:
2.53
4.38
7.53
7.53
7.93
4.35
1.50
2.75
7.25
3.11
7.44
2.04
3.25

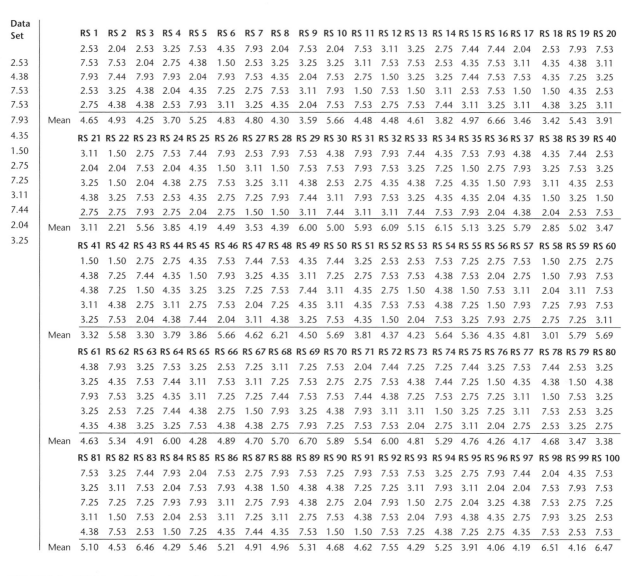

	RS 1	RS 2	RS 3	RS 4	RS 5	RS 6	RS 7	RS 8	RS 9	RS 10	RS 11	RS 12	RS 13	RS 14	RS 15	RS 16	RS 17	RS 18	RS 19	RS 20
	2.53	2.04	2.53	3.25	7.53	4.35	7.93	2.04	7.53	2.04	7.53	3.11	3.25	2.75	7.44	7.44	2.04	2.53	7.93	7.53
	7.53	7.53	2.04	2.75	4.38	1.50	2.53	3.25	3.25	3.25	3.11	7.53	7.53	2.53	4.35	7.53	3.11	4.35	4.38	3.11
	7.93	7.44	7.93	7.93	2.04	7.93	7.53	4.35	2.04	7.53	2.75	1.50	3.25	3.25	7.44	7.53	7.53	4.35	7.25	3.25
	2.53	3.25	4.38	2.04	4.35	7.25	2.75	7.53	3.11	7.93	1.50	7.53	1.50	3.11	2.53	7.53	1.50	1.50	4.35	2.53
	2.75	4.38	4.38	2.53	7.93	3.11	3.25	4.35	2.04	7.53	7.53	2.75	7.53	7.44	3.11	3.25	3.11	4.38	3.25	3.11
Mean	4.65	4.93	4.25	3.70	5.25	4.83	4.80	4.30	3.59	5.66	4.48	4.48	4.61	3.82	4.97	6.66	3.46	3.42	5.43	3.91

	RS 21	RS 22	RS 23	RS 24	RS 25	RS 26	RS 27	RS 28	RS 29	RS 30	RS 31	RS 32	RS 33	RS 34	RS 35	RS 36	RS 37	RS 38	RS 39	RS 40
	3.11	1.50	2.75	7.53	7.44	7.93	2.53	7.93	7.53	4.38	7.93	7.93	7.44	4.35	7.53	7.93	4.38	4.35	7.44	2.53
	2.04	2.04	7.53	2.04	4.35	1.50	3.11	1.50	7.53	7.53	7.93	7.53	3.25	7.25	1.50	2.75	7.93	3.25	7.53	3.25
	3.25	1.50	2.04	4.38	2.75	7.53	3.25	3.11	4.38	2.53	2.75	4.35	4.38	7.25	4.35	1.50	7.93	3.11	4.35	2.53
	4.38	3.25	7.53	2.53	4.35	2.75	7.25	7.93	7.44	3.11	7.93	7.53	3.25	4.35	4.35	2.04	4.35	1.50	3.25	1.50
	2.75	2.75	7.93	2.75	2.04	2.75	1.50	1.50	3.11	7.44	3.11	3.11	7.44	7.53	7.93	2.04	4.38	2.04	2.53	7.53
Mean	3.11	2.21	5.56	3.85	4.19	4.49	3.53	4.39	6.00	5.00	5.93	6.09	5.15	6.15	5.13	3.25	5.79	2.85	5.02	3.47

	RS 41	RS 42	RS 43	RS 44	RS 45	RS 46	RS 47	RS 48	RS 49	RS 50	RS 51	RS 52	RS 53	RS 54	RS 55	RS 56	RS 57	RS 58	RS 59	RS 60
	1.50	1.50	2.75	2.75	4.35	7.53	7.44	7.53	4.35	7.44	3.25	2.53	2.53	7.53	7.25	2.75	7.53	1.50	2.75	2.75
	4.38	7.25	7.44	4.35	1.50	7.93	3.25	4.35	3.11	7.25	2.75	7.53	7.53	4.38	7.53	2.04	2.75	1.50	7.93	7.53
	4.38	7.25	1.50	4.35	3.25	3.25	7.25	7.53	7.44	3.11	4.35	2.75	1.50	4.38	1.50	7.53	3.11	2.04	3.11	7.53
	3.11	4.38	2.75	3.11	2.75	7.53	2.04	7.25	4.35	3.11	4.35	7.53	7.53	4.38	7.25	1.50	7.93	7.25	7.93	7.53
	3.25	7.53	2.04	4.38	7.44	2.04	3.11	4.38	3.25	7.53	4.35	1.50	2.04	7.53	3.25	7.93	2.75	2.75	7.25	3.11
Mean	3.32	5.58	3.30	3.79	3.86	5.66	4.62	6.21	4.50	5.69	3.81	4.37	4.23	5.64	5.36	4.35	4.81	3.01	5.79	5.69

	RS 61	RS 62	RS 63	RS 64	RS 65	RS 66	RS 67	RS 68	RS 69	RS 70	RS 71	RS 72	RS 73	RS 74	RS 75	RS 76	RS 77	RS 78	RS 79	RS 80
	4.38	7.93	3.25	7.53	3.25	2.53	7.25	3.11	7.25	7.53	2.04	7.44	7.25	7.25	7.44	3.25	7.53	7.44	2.53	3.25
	3.25	4.35	7.53	7.44	3.11	7.53	3.11	7.25	7.53	2.75	2.75	7.53	4.38	7.44	7.25	1.50	4.35	4.38	1.50	4.38
	7.93	7.53	3.25	4.35	3.11	7.25	7.25	7.44	7.53	7.53	7.44	4.38	7.25	7.53	2.75	7.25	3.11	1.50	7.53	3.25
	3.25	2.53	7.25	7.44	4.38	2.75	1.50	7.93	3.25	4.38	7.93	3.11	3.11	1.50	3.25	7.25	3.11	7.53	2.53	3.25
	4.35	4.38	3.25	3.25	7.53	4.38	4.38	2.75	7.93	7.25	7.53	7.53	2.04	2.75	3.11	2.04	2.75	2.53	3.25	2.75
Mean	4.63	5.34	4.91	6.00	4.28	4.89	4.70	5.70	6.70	5.89	5.54	6.00	4.81	5.29	4.76	4.26	4.17	4.68	3.47	3.38

	RS 81	RS 82	RS 83	RS 84	RS 85	RS 86	RS 87	RS 88	RS 89	RS 90	RS 91	RS 92	RS 93	RS 94	RS 95	RS 96	RS 97	RS 98	RS 99	RS 100
	7.53	3.25	7.44	7.93	2.04	7.53	2.75	7.93	7.53	7.25	7.93	7.53	7.53	3.25	2.75	7.93	7.44	2.04	4.35	7.53
	3.25	3.11	7.53	2.04	7.53	7.93	4.38	1.50	4.38	4.38	7.25	7.25	3.11	7.93	3.11	2.04	2.04	7.53	7.93	7.53
	7.25	7.25	7.25	7.93	7.93	3.11	2.75	7.93	4.38	2.75	2.04	7.93	1.50	2.75	2.04	3.25	4.38	7.53	2.75	7.25
	3.11	1.50	7.53	2.04	2.53	3.11	7.25	3.11	2.75	7.53	4.38	7.53	2.04	7.93	4.38	4.35	2.75	7.93	3.25	2.53
	4.38	7.53	2.53	1.50	7.25	4.35	7.44	4.35	7.53	1.50	1.50	7.53	7.25	4.38	7.25	2.75	4.35	7.53	2.53	7.53
Mean	5.10	4.53	6.46	4.29	5.46	5.21	4.91	4.96	5.31	4.68	4.62	7.55	4.29	5.25	3.91	4.06	4.19	6.51	4.16	6.47

FIGURE 5–8 EPS Mean Distribution—Excel Output

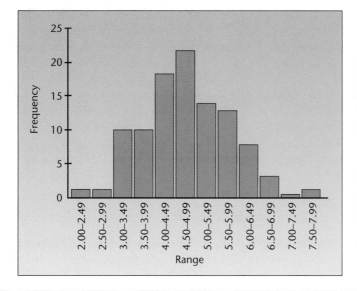

	A	B
1	Distribution	
2		
3	2.00−2.49	1
4	2.50−2.99	1
5	3.00−3.49	10
6	3.50−3.99	10
7	4.00−4.49	18
8	4.50−4.99	21
9	5.00−5.49	14
10	5.50−5.99	13
11	6.00−6.49	8
12	6.50−6.99	3
13	7.00−7.49	0
14	7.50−7.99	1

Figure 5–8 shows a graph of the means of the samples from the banks' data using Excel.

The History of the Central Limit Theorem

What we call the central limit theorem actually comprises several theorems developed over the years. The first such theorem was discussed at the beginning of Chapter 4 as the discovery of the normal curve by Abraham De Moivre in 1733. Recall that De Moivre discovered the normal distribution as the *limit* of the binomial distribution. The fact that the normal distribution appears as a limit of the binomial distribution as *n* increases is a form of the central limit theorem. Around the turn of the twentieth century, Liapunov gave a more general form of the central limit theorem, and in 1922 the final form we use in applied statistics was given by Lindeberg. The proof of the necessary condition of the theorem was given in 1935 by W. Feller [see W. Feller, *An Introduction to Probability Theory and Its Applications* (New York: Wiley, 1971), vol. 2]. A proof of the central limit theorem is beyond the scope of this book, but the interested reader is encouraged to read more about it in the given reference or in other books.

The Standardized Sampling Distribution of the Sample Mean When σ Is Not Known

To use the central limit theorem, we need to know the population standard deviation, σ. When σ is not known, we use its estimator, the sample standard deviation *S*, in its place. In such cases, the distribution of the standardized statistic

$$\frac{\overline{X} - \mu}{S/\sqrt{n}} \qquad (5\text{–}6)$$

(where *S* is used in place of the unknown σ) is no longer the standard normal distribution. *If the population itself is normally distributed, the statistic in equation 5–6 has a* t *distribution with* n − 1 *degrees of freedom.* The *t* distribution has wider tails than the standard normal distribution. Values and probabilities of *t* distributions with different degrees of freedom are given in Table 3 in Appendix C. The *t* distribution and its uses will be discussed in detail in Chapter 6. The idea of degrees of freedom is explained in section 5–5 of this chapter.

The Sampling Distribution of the Sample Proportion $\hat{P}$

The sampling distribution of the sample proportion $\hat{P}$ is based on the binomial distribution with parameters *n* and *p*, where *n* is the sample size and *p* is the population proportion. Recall that the binomial random variable *X* counts the number of successes in *n* trials. Since $\hat{P} = X/n$ and *n* is fixed (determined before the sampling), the distribution of the number of successes *X* leads to the distribution of $\hat{P}$.

As the sample size increases, the central limit theorem applies here as well. Figure 5–9 shows the effects of the central limit theorem for a binomial distribution with $p = 0.3$. The distribution is skewed to the right for small values of *n* but becomes more symmetric and approaches the normal distribution as *n* increases.

We now state the central limit theorem when sampling for the population proportion *p*.

> As the sample size *n* increases, the sampling distribution of $\hat{P}$ approaches a **normal distribution** with mean *p* and standard deviation $\sqrt{p(1 - p)/n}$.

(The estimated standard deviation of $\hat{P}$ is also called its *standard error*.) In order for us to use the normal approximation for the sampling distribution of $\hat{P}$, the sample size needs to be large. A commonly used rule of thumb says that the normal approximation to the distribution of $\hat{P}$ may be used only if *both np and n(1 − p) are greater than* 5. We demonstrate the use of the theorem with Example 5–3.

FIGURE 5–9 The Sampling Distribution of $\hat{P}$ When $p = 0.3$, as n Increases

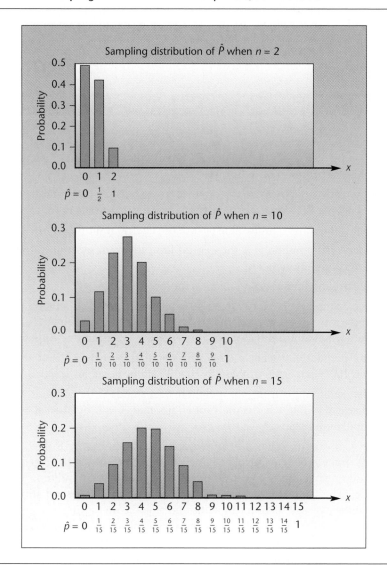

In recent years, convertible sport coupes have become very popular in Japan. Toyota is currently shipping Celicas to Los Angeles, where a customizer does a roof lift and ships them back to Japan. Suppose that 25% of all Japanese in a given income and lifestyle category are interested in buying Celica convertibles. A random sample of 100 Japanese consumers in the category of interest is to be selected. What is the probability that at least 20% of those in the sample will express an interest in a Celica convertible?

EXAMPLE 5–3

We need $P(\hat{P} \geq 0.20)$. Since $np = 100(0.25) = 25$ and $n(1 - p) = 100(0.75) = 75$, both numbers greater than 5, we may use the normal approximation to the distribution of $\hat{P}$. The mean of $\hat{P}$ is $p = 0.25$, and the standard deviation of $\hat{P}$ is $\sqrt{p(1 - p)/n} = 0.0433$. We have

Solution

$$P(\hat{P} \geq 0.20) = P\left(Z \geq \frac{0.20 - 0.25}{0.0433}\right) = P(Z \geq -1.15) = 0.8749$$

Sampling distributions are essential to statistics. In the following chapters, we will make much use of the distributions discussed in this section, as well as others that will be introduced as we go along. In the next section, we discuss properties of good estimators.

PROBLEMS

5–11. What is a sampling distribution, and what are the uses of sampling distributions?

5–12. A sample of size $n = 5$ is selected from a population. Under what conditions is the sampling distribution of $\overline{X}$ normal?

5–13. In problem 5–12, suppose the population mean is $\mu = 125$ and the population standard deviation is 20. What are the expected value and the standard deviation of $\overline{X}$?

5–14. What is the most significant aspect of the central limit theorem?

5–15. Under what conditions is the central limit theorem most useful in sampling to estimate the population mean?

5–16. What are the limitations of small samples?

5–17. When sampling is done from a population with population proportion $p = 0.1$, using a sample size $n = 2$, what is the sampling distribution of $\hat{P}$? Is it reasonable to use a normal approximation for this sampling distribution? Explain.

5–18. If the population mean is 1,247, the population variance is 10,000, and the sample size is 100, what is the probability that $\overline{X}$ will be less than 1,230?

5–19. When sampling is from a population with standard deviation $\sigma = 55$, using a sample of size $n = 150$, what is the probability that $\overline{X}$ will be at least 8 units away from the population mean μ?

5–20. The Colosseum, once the most popular monument in Rome, dates from about AD 70. Since then, earthquakes have caused considerable damage to the huge structure, and engineers are currently trying to make sure the building will survive future shocks. The Colosseum can be divided into several thousand small sections. Suppose that the average section can withstand a quake measuring 3.4 on the Richter scale with a standard deviation of 1.5. A random sample of 100 sections is selected and tested for the maximum earthquake force they can withstand. What is the probability that the average section in the sample can withstand an earthquake measuring at least 3.6 on the Richter scale?

5–21. According to *Money,* in the year prior to March 2007, the average return for firms of the S&P 500 was 13.1%.[9] Assume that the standard deviation of returns was 1.2%. If a random sample of 36 companies in the S&P 500 is selected, what is the probability that their average return for this period will be between 12% and 15%?

5–22. An economist wishes to estimate the average family income in a certain population. The population standard deviation is known to be $4,500, and the economist uses a random sample of size $n = 225$. What is the probability that the sample mean will fall within $800 of the population mean?

5–23. When sampling is done for the proportion of defective items in a large shipment, where the population proportion is 0.18 and the sample size is 200, what is the probability that the sample proportion will be at least 0.20?

5–24. A study of the investment industry claims that 58% of all mutual funds outperformed the stock market as a whole last year. An analyst wants to test this claim and obtains a random sample of 250 mutual funds. The analyst finds that only 123

---

[9]"Market Benchmarks," *Money,* March 2007, p. 128.

of the funds outperformed the market during the year. Determine the probability that another random sample would lead to a sample proportion as low as or lower than the one obtained by the analyst, assuming the proportion of all mutual funds that outperformed the market is indeed 0.58.

5–25. According to a recent article in *Worth*, the average price of a house on Marco Island, Florida, is $2.6 million.[10] Assume that the standard deviation of the prices is $400,000. A random sample of 75 houses is taken and the average price is computed. What is the probability that the sample mean exceeds $3 million?

5–26. It has been suggested that an investment portfolio selected randomly by throwing darts at the stock market page of *The Wall Street Journal* may be a sound (and certainly well-diversified) investment.[11] Suppose that you own such a portfolio of 16 stocks randomly selected from all stocks listed on the New York Stock Exchange (NYSE). On a certain day, you hear on the news that the average stock on the NYSE rose 1.5 points. Assuming that the standard deviation of stock price movements that day was 2 points and assuming stock price movements were normally distributed around their mean of 1.5, what is the probability that the average stock price of your portfolio increased?

5–27. An advertisement for Citicorp Insurance Services, Inc., claims "one person in seven will be hospitalized this year." Suppose you keep track of a random sample of 180 people over an entire year. Assuming Citicorp's advertisement is correct, what is the probability that fewer than 10% of the people in your sample will be found to have been hospitalized (at least once) during the year? Explain.

5–28. Shimano mountain bikes are displayed in chic clothing boutiques in Milan, Italy, and the average price for the bike in the city is $700. Suppose that the standard deviation of bike prices is $100. If a random sample of 60 boutiques is selected, what is the probability that the average price for a Shimano mountain bike in this sample will be between $680 and $720?

5–29. A quality-control analyst wants to estimate the proportion of imperfect jeans in a large warehouse. The analyst plans to select a random sample of 500 pairs of jeans and note the proportion of imperfect pairs. If the actual proportion in the entire warehouse is 0.35, what is the probability that the sample proportion will deviate from the population proportion by more than 0.05?

5–4 Estimators and Their Properties[12]

The sample statistics we discussed—$\bar{X}$, S, and $\hat{P}$—as well as other sample statistics to be introduced later, are used as estimators of population parameters. In this section, we discuss some important properties of good statistical estimators: *unbiasedness, efficiency, consistency,* and *sufficiency.*

> An estimator is said to be **unbiased** if its expected value is equal to the population parameter it estimates.

CHAPTER 8

Consider the sample mean $\bar{X}$. From equation 5–2, we know $E(\bar{X}) = \mu$. *The sample mean $\bar{X}$ is, therefore, an unbiased estimator of the population mean μ.* This means that if we sample repeatedly from the population and compute $\bar{X}$ for each of our samples, *in the long run,* the average value of $\bar{X}$ will be the parameter of interest μ. This is an important property of the estimator because it means that there is no systematic *bias* away from the parameter of interest.

---

[10]Elizabeth Harris, "Luxury Real Estate Investment," *Worth,* April 2007, p. 76.

[11]See the very readable book by Burton G. Malkiel, *A Random Walk Down Wall Street* (New York: W. W. Norton, 2003).

[12]An optional, but recommended, section.

FIGURE 5–10   The Sample Mean $\overline{X}$ as an Unbiased Estimator of the Population Mean μ

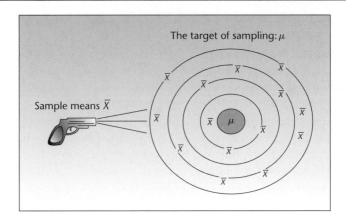

If we view the gathering of a random sample and the calculating of its mean as shooting at a target—the target being the population parameter, say, μ—then the fact that $\overline{X}$ is an unbiased estimator of μ means that the device producing the estimates is aiming at the *center* of the target (the parameter of interest), with no systematic deviation away from it.

> Any *systematic* deviation of the estimator away from the parameter of interest is called a **bias.**

The concept of unbiasedness is demonstrated for the sample mean $\overline{X}$ in Figure 5–10.

Figure 5–11 demonstrates the idea of a biased estimator of μ. The hypothetical estimator we denote by Y is centered on some point M that lies away from the parameter μ. The distance between the expected value of Y (the point M) and μ is the *bias*.

It should be noted that, in reality, we usually sample *once* and obtain our estimate. The multiple estimates shown in Figures 5–10 and 5–11 serve only as an illustration of the expected value of an estimator as the center of a large collection of the actual estimates that would be obtained in repeated sampling. (Note also that, in reality, the "target" at which we are "shooting" is one-dimensional—on a straight line rather than on a plane.)

FIGURE 5–11   An Example of a Biased Estimator of the Population Mean μ

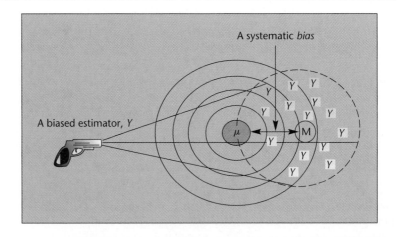

FIGURE 5–12   Two Unbiased Estimators of μ, Where the Estimator X Is Efficient Relative to the Estimator Z

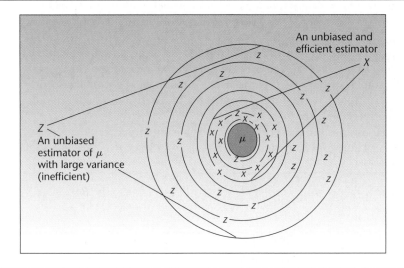

The next property of good estimators we discuss is *efficiency*.

An estimator is **efficient** if it has a relatively small variance (and standard deviation).

Efficiency is a relative property. We say that one estimator is efficient *relative* to another. This means that the estimator has a smaller variance (also a smaller standard deviation) than the other. Figure 5–12 shows two hypothetical unbiased estimators of the population mean μ. The two estimators, which we denote by $\overline{X}$ and Z, are unbiased: Their distributions are centered at μ. The estimator $\overline{X}$, however, is more efficient than the estimator Z because it has a smaller variance than that of Z. This is seen from the fact that repeated estimates produced by Z have a larger spread about their mean μ than repeated estimates produced by $\overline{X}$.

Another desirable property of estimators is *consistency*.

An estimator is said to be **consistent** if its probability of being close to the parameter it estimates increases as the sample size increases.

The sample mean $\overline{X}$ is a consistent estimator of μ. This is so because the standard deviation of $\overline{X}$ is $\sigma_{\overline{x}} = \sigma/\sqrt{n}$. As the sample size n increases, the standard deviation of $\overline{X}$ decreases and, hence, the probability that $\overline{X}$ will be close to its expected value μ increases.

We now define a fourth property of good estimators: *sufficiency*.

An estimator is said to be **sufficient** if it contains all the information in the data about the parameter it estimates.

Applying the Concepts of Unbiasedness, Efficiency, Consistency, and Sufficiency

We may evaluate possible estimators of population parameters based on whether they possess important properties of estimators and thus choose the best estimator to be used.

For a *normally distributed population*, for example, both the sample mean and the sample median are *unbiased* estimators of the population mean μ. The sample mean, however, is more *efficient* than the sample median. This is so because the variance of the sample median happens to be 1.57 times as large as the variance of the sample mean. In addition, the sample mean is a *sufficient* estimator because in computing it we use the *entire* data set. The sample median is not sufficient; it is found as the point in the middle of the data set, regardless of the exact magnitudes of all other data elements. The sample mean $\overline{X}$ is the *best* estimator of the population mean μ, because it is unbiased and has the smallest variance of all unbiased estimators of μ. The sample mean is also *consistent*. (Note that while the sample mean is best, the sample median is sometimes used because it is more resistant to extreme observations.)

The sample proportion $\hat{P}$ is the best estimator of the population proportion p. Since $E(\hat{P}) = p$, the estimator $\hat{P}$ is unbiased. It also has the smallest variance of all unbiased estimators of p.

What about the sample variance S^2? The sample variance, as defined in equation 1–3, is an unbiased estimator of the population variance σ^2. Recall equation 1–3:

$$S^2 = \frac{\Sigma(x_i - \overline{x})^2}{n - 1}$$

Dividing the sum of squared deviations in the equation by n rather than by $n - 1$ seems logical because we are seeking the *average* squared deviation from the sample mean. We have n deviations from the mean, so why not divide by n? It turns out that if we were to divide by n rather than by $n - 1$, our estimator of σ^2 would be biased. Although the bias becomes small as n increases, we will always use the statistic given in equation 1–3 as an estimator of σ^2. The reason for dividing by $n - 1$ rather than n will become clearer in the next section, when we discuss the concept of degrees of freedom.

Note that while S^2 is an unbiased estimator of the population variance σ^2, the sample standard deviation S (the square root of S^2) is *not* an unbiased estimator of the population standard deviation σ. Still, we will use S as our estimator of the population standard deviation, ignoring the small bias that results and relying on the fact that S^2 is the unbiased estimator of σ^2.

PROBLEMS

5–30. Suppose that you have two statistics A and B as possible estimators of the same population parameter. Estimator A is unbiased, but has a large variance. Estimator B has a small bias, but has only one-tenth the variance of estimator A. Which estimator is better? Explain.

5–31. Suppose that you have an estimator with a relatively large bias. The estimator is consistent and efficient, however. If you had a generous budget for your sampling survey, would you use this estimator? Explain.

5–32. Suppose that in a sampling survey to estimate the population variance, the biased estimator (with n instead of $n - 1$ in the denominator of equation 1–3) was used instead of the unbiased one. The sample size used was $n = 100$, and the estimate obtained was 1,287. Can you find the value of the unbiased estimate of the population variance?

5–33. What are the advantages of a sufficient statistic? Can you think of a possible disadvantage of sufficiency?

5–34. Suppose that you have two biased estimators of the same population parameter. Estimator A has a bias equal to $1/n$ (that is, the mean of the estimator is $1/n$ unit away from the parameter it estimates), where n is the sample size used. Estimator B has a bias equal to 0.01 (the mean of the estimator is 0.01 unit away from the parameter of interest). Under what conditions is estimator A better than B?

5–35. Why is consistency an important property?

5–5   Degrees of Freedom

Suppose you are asked to choose 10 numbers. You then have the freedom to choose 10 numbers as you please, and we say you have 10 **degrees of freedom**. But suppose a condition is imposed on the numbers. The condition is that the sum of all the numbers you choose must be 100. In this case, you cannot choose all 10 numbers as you please. After you have chosen the ninth number, let's say the sum of the nine numbers is 94. Your tenth number then has to be 6, and you have no choice. Thus you have only 9 degrees of freedom. In general, if you have to choose n numbers, and a condition on their total is imposed, you will have only $(n-1)$ degrees of freedom.

As another example, suppose that I wrote five checks last month, and the total amount of these checks is \$80. Now if I know that the first four checks were for \$30, \$20, \$15, and \$5, then I don't need to be told that the fifth check was for \$10. I can simply deduce this information by subtraction of the other four checks from \$80. My degrees of freedom are thus four, and not five.

In Chapter 1, we saw the formula for the sample variance

$$S^2 = \text{SSD}/(n-1)$$

where SSD is the sum of squared deviations from the sample mean. In particular, note that SSD is to be divided by $(n-1)$ rather than n. The reason concerns the degrees of freedom for the deviations. A more complex case of degrees of freedom occurs in the use of a technique called ANOVA, which is discussed in Chapter 9. In the following paragraphs, we shall see the details of these cases.

We first note that in the calculation of SSD, the deviations are taken from the sample mean $\bar{x}$ and not from the population mean μ. The reason is simple: While sampling, almost always, the population mean μ is not known. Not knowing the population mean, we take the deviations from the sample mean. But this introduces a downward bias in the deviations. To see the bias, refer to Figure 5–13, which shows the deviation of a sample point x from the sample mean and from the population mean.

It can be seen from Figure 5–13 that for sample points that fall to the right of the midpoint between μ and $\bar{x}$, the deviation from the sample mean will be smaller than the deviation from the population mean. Since the sample mean is where the sample points gravitate, a majority of the sample points are expected to fall to the right of the midpoint. Thus, overall, the deviations will have a downward bias.

To compensate for the downward bias, we use the concept of degrees of freedom. Let the population be a uniform distribution of the values $\{1, 2, \ldots, 10\}$. The mean of this population is 5.5. Suppose a random sample of size 10 is taken from this population. Assume that we are told to take the deviations from this population mean.

FIGURE 5–13   Deviations from the Population Mean and the Sample Mean

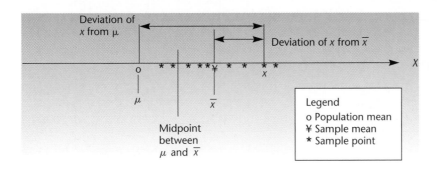

FIGURE 5–14   SSD and df

df = 10				
	Sample	Deviation from	Deviation	Deviation Squared
1	10	5.5	4.5	20.25
2	3	5.5	−2.5	6.25
3	2	5.5	−3.5	12.25
4	6	5.5	0.5	0.25
5	1	5.5	−4.5	20.25
6	9	5.5	3.5	12.25
7	6	5.5	0.5	0.25
8	4	5.5	−1.5	2.25
9	10	5.5	4.5	20.25
10	7	5.5	1.5	2.25
			SSD	96.5

In Figure 5–14, the Sample column shows the sampled values. The calculation of SSD is shown taking deviations from the population mean of 5.5. The SSD works out to 96.5. *Since we had no freedom in taking the deviations, all the 10 deviations are completely left to chance.* Hence we say that the deviations have 10 degrees of freedom.

Suppose we do not know the population mean and are told that we can take the deviation from any number we choose. The best number to choose then is the sample mean, which will minimize the SSD (see problem 1–85). Figure 5–15a shows the calculation of SSD where the deviations are taken from the sample mean of 5.8. Because of the downward bias, the SSD has decreased to 95.6. The SSD would decrease further if we were allowed to select two different numbers from which the deviations are taken. Suppose we are allowed to use one number for the first five data points and another for the next five. Our best choices are the average of the first five numbers, 4.4, and the average of next five numbers, 7.2. Only these choices will minimize the SSD. The minimized SSD works out to 76, as seen in Figure 5–15b.

We can carry this process further. If we were allowed 10 different numbers from which the deviations are taken, then we could reduce the SSD all the way to zero.

FIGURE 5–15   SSD and df (*continued*)

df = 10 − 1 = 9					df = 10 − 2 = 8				
	Sample	Deviation from	Deviation	Deviation Squared		Sample	Deviation from	Deviation	Deviation Squared
1	10	5.8	4.2	17.64		10	4.4	5.6	31.36
2	3	5.8	−2.8	7.84		3	4.4	−1.4	1.96
3	2	5.8	−3.8	14.44		2	4.4	−2.4	5.76
4	6	5.8	0.2	0.04		6	4.4	1.6	2.56
5	1	5.8	−4.8	23.04		1	4.4	−3.4	11.56
6	9	5.8	3.2	10.24		9	7.2	1.8	3.24
7	6	5.8	0.2	0.04		6	7.2	−1.2	1.44
8	4	5.8	−1.8	3.24		4	7.2	−3.2	10.24
9	10	5.8	4.2	17.64		10	7.2	2.8	7.84
10	7	5.8	1.2	1.44		7	7.2	−0.2	0.04
			SSD	95.6				SSD	76
		(a)					(b)		

FIGURE 5–16　SSD and df (*continued*)

df = 10 − 10 = 0				
	Sample	Deviation from	Deviation	Deviation Squared
1	10	10	0	0
2	3	3	0	0
3	2	2	0	0
4	6	6	0	0
5	1	1	0	0
6	9	9	0	0
7	6	6	0	0
8	4	4	0	0
9	10	10	0	0
10	7	7	0	0
			SSD	0

How? See Figure 5–16. We choose the 10 numbers equal to the 10 sample points (which in effect are 10 means). In the case of Figure 5–15*a*, we had one choice, and this takes away 1 degree of freedom from the deviations. The df of SSD is then declared as $10 - 1 = 9$. In Figure 5–15*b*, we had two choices and this took away 2 degrees of freedom from the deviations. Thus the df of SSD is $10 - 2 = 8$. In Figure 5–16, the df of SSD is $10 - 10 = 0$.

In every one of these cases, *dividing the SSD by only its corresponding df will yield an unbiased estimate of the population variance* σ^2. Hence the concept of the degrees of freedom is important. This also explains the denominator of $(n - 1)$ in the formula for sample variance S^2. For the case in Figure 5–15*a*, SSD/df $= 95.6/9 = 10.62$, and this is an unbiased estimate of the population variance.

We can now summarize how the number of degrees of freedom is determined. If we take a sample of size n and take the deviations from the (known) population mean, then the deviations, and therefore the SSD, will have df $= n$. But if we take the deviations from the sample mean, then the deviations, and therefore the SSD, will have df $= n - 1$. If we are allowed to take the deviations from $k (\leq n)$ different numbers that we choose, then the deviations, and therefore the SSD, will have df $= n - k$. While choosing each of the k numbers, we should choose the mean of the sample points to which that number applies. The case of $k > 1$ will be seen in Chapter 9, "Analysis of Variance."

A sample of size 10 is given below. We are to choose three different numbers from which the deviations are to be taken. The first number is to be used for the first five sample points; the second number is to be used for the next three sample points; and the third number is to be used for the last two sample points.

EXAMPLE 5–4

	Sample
1	93
2	97
3	60
4	72
5	96
6	83
7	59
8	66
9	88
10	53

1. What three numbers should we choose to minimize the SSD?
2. Calculate the SSD with the chosen numbers.
3. What is the df for the calculated SSD?
4. Calculate an unbiased estimate of the population variance.

Solution

1. We choose the means of the corresponding sample points: 83.6, 69.33, 70.5.
2. SSD = 2030.367. See the spreadsheet calculation below.
3. df = 10 − 3 = 7.
4. An unbiased estimate of the population variance is SSD/df = 2030.367/7 = 290.05.

	Sample	Mean	Deviation	Deviation Squared
1	93	83.6	9.4	88.36
2	97	83.6	13.4	179.56
3	60	83.6	−23.6	556.96
4	72	83.6	−11.6	134.56
5	96	83.6	12.4	153.76
6	83	69.33	13.6667	186.7778
7	59	69.33	−10.3333	106.7778
8	66	69.33	−3.33333	11.11111
9	88	70.5	17.5	306.25
10	53	70.5	−17.5	306.25
			SSD	2030.367
			SSD/df	290.0524

PROBLEMS

5–36. Three random samples of sizes, 30, 48, and 32, respectively, are collected, and the three sample means are computed. What is the total number of degrees of freedom for deviations from the means?

5–37. The data points in a sample of size 9 are 34, 51, 40, 38, 47, 50, 52, 44, 37.

a. If you can take the deviations of these data from any number you select, and you want to minimize the sum of the squared deviations (SSD), what number would you select? What is the minimized SSD? How many degrees of freedom are associated with this SSD? Calculate the mean squared deviation (MSD) by dividing the SSD by its degrees of freedom. (This MSD is an unbiased estimate of population variance.)

b. If you can take the deviations from three different numbers you select, and the first number is to be used with the first four data points to get the deviations, the second with the next three data points, and the third with the last two data points, what three numbers would you select? What is the minimized SSD? How many degrees of freedom are associated with this SSD? Calculate MSD.

c. If you can select nine different numbers to be used with each of the nine data points, what numbers would you select? What is the minimized SSD? How many degrees of freedom are associated with this SSD? Does MSD make sense in this case?

d. If you are told that the deviations are to be taken with respect to 50, what is the SSD? How many degrees of freedom are associated with this SSD? Calculate MSD.

5–38. Your bank sends you a summary statement, giving the average amount of all checks you wrote during the month. You have a record of the amounts of 17 out of the 19 checks you wrote during the month. Using this and the information provided by the bank, can you figure out the amounts of the two missing checks? Explain.

5–39. In problem 5–38, suppose you know the amounts of 18 of the 19 checks you wrote and the average of all the checks. Can you figure out the amount of the missing check? Explain.

5–40. You are allowed to take the deviations of the data points in a sample of size n, from k numbers you select, in order to calculate the sum of squared deviations (SSD). You select them to minimize SSD. How many degrees of freedom are associated with this SSD? As k increases, what happens to the degrees of freedom? What happens to SSD? What happens to MSD = SSD/df(SSD)?

5–6   Using the Computer

Using Excel for Generating Sampling Distributions

Figure 5–17 shows the template that can be used to calculate the sampling distribution of a sample mean. It is largely the same as the normal distribution template. The additional items are the population distribution entries at the top. To use the template, enter the population mean and standard deviation in cells B5 and C5. Enter the sample size in cell B8. In the drop-down box in cell I4, select Yes or No to answer the question "Is the population normally distributed?" The sample mean will follow

FIGURE 5–17   **The Template for Sampling Distribution of a Sample Mean**
[Sampling Distribution.xls; Sheet: X-bar]

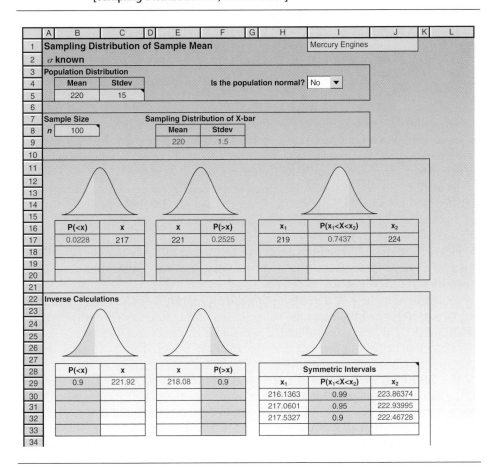

FIGURE 5–18   The Template for Sampling Distribution of a Sample Proportion
[Sampling Distribution.xls; Sheet: P-hat]

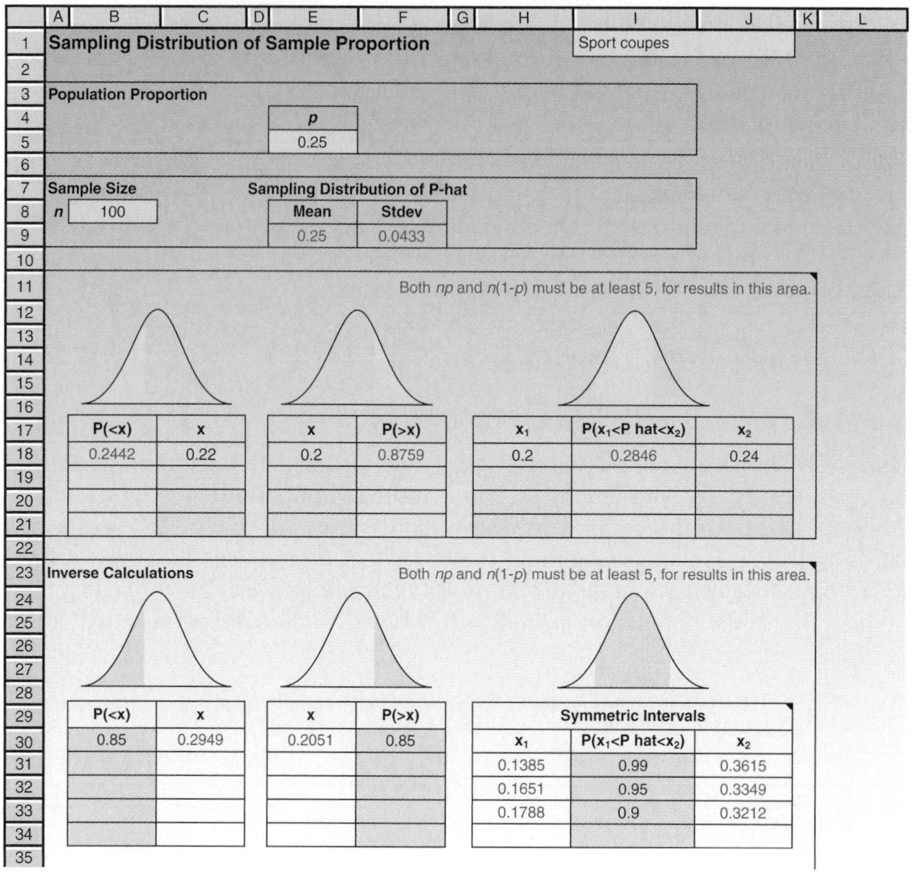

a normal distribution if either the population is normally distributed or the sample size is at least 30. Only in such cases should this template be used. In other cases, a warning message—"Warning: The sampling distribution cannot be approximated as normal. Results appear anyway"—will appear in cell A10.

To solve Example 5–1, enter the population mean 220 in cell B5 and the population standard deviation 15 in cell C5. Enter the sample size 100 in cell B8. To find the probability that the sample mean will be less than 217, enter 217 in cell C17. The answer 0.0228 appears in cell B17.

Figure 5–18 shows the template that can be used to calculate the sampling distribution of a sample proportion. To use the template, enter the population proportion in cell E5 and the sample size in cell B8.

To solve Example 5–3, enter the population proportion 0.25 in cell E5 and the sample size 100 in cell B8. Enter the value 0.2 in cell E17 to get the probability of the sample proportion being more than 0.2 in cell F17. The answer is 0.8749.

In addition to the templates discussed above, you can use Excel statistical tools to develop a variety of statistical analyses.

The **Sampling** analysis tool of Excel creates a sample from a population by treating the input range as a population. You can also create a sample that contains only the values from a particular part of a cycle if you believe that the input data is periodic. The Sampling analysis tool is accessible via Data Analysis in the Analysis group on the Data tab. If the Data Analysis command is not available, you need to load the Analysis ToolPack add-in program as described in Chapter 1.

FIGURE 5–19   Generating a Random Sample by Excel

	A	B	C	D	E	F	G	H	I	J	K
1											
2		**Initial Sample**		**Generated Sample**		Sampling					
3		3		2		Input				OK	
4		4		6		Input Range:		$B$3:$B$12		Cancel	
5		2		2		☑ Labels					
6		6		4		Sampling Method				Help	
7		3		4		○ Periodic					
8		7		4		Period:					
9		1		7		⦿ Random					
10		2		4		Number of Samples:		15			
11		8		3		Output options					
12		4		4		⦿ Output Range:		$D$3			
13				3		○ New Worksheet Ply:					
14				3		○ New Workbook					
15				6							
16				8							
17				6							

As an example, imagine you have a sample of size 10 from a population and you wish to generate another sample of size 15 from this population. You can start by choosing Sampling from Data Analysis. The Sampling dialog box will appear as shown in Figure 5–19. Specify the input range which represents your initial sample, cells B3 to B12. In the Sampling Method section you can indicate that you need a random sample of size 15. Determine the output range in the Output Options section. In Figure 5–19 the output has been placed in the column labeled Generated Sample starting from cell D3.

Another very useful tool of Excel is the **Random Number Generation** analysis tool, which fills a range with independent random numbers that are drawn from one of several distributions. Start by choosing the Random Number Generation analysis tool from Data Analysis in the Analysis group on the Data tab. Then the Random Number Generation dialog box will appear as shown in Figure 5–20. The number of

FIGURE 5–20   Generating Random Samples from Specific Distributions

	A	B	C	D	E	F	G	H	I	J	K
1						Random Number Generation					
2		**Sample 1**	**Sample 2**								
3		7.9323	6.3182		Number of Variables:		2		OK		
4		9.2926	8.3402		Number of Random Numbers:		10		Cancel		
5		9.0290	6.2854		Distribution:		Normal		Help		
6		8.5094	4.3010		Parameters						
7		7.6303	5.1313								
8		6.9048	8.0530		Mean =		7				
9		8.1731	6.8267		Standard deviation =		1.5				
10		7.3468	4.8941								
11		6.4296	7.0003								
12		5.3373	7.3525		Random Seed:						
13					Output options						
14					⦿ Output Range:		$B$3				
15					○ New Worksheet Ply:						
16					○ New Workbook						
17											
18											

variables and number of random numbers at each set are defined by the values 2 and 10, respectively. The type of distribution and its parameters are defined in the next section. Define the output range in the Output Options. The two sets of random numbers are labeled Sample 1 and Sample 2 in Figure 5–20.

Using MINITAB for Generating Sampling Distributions

In this section we will illustrate how to use the Random Number Generation tool of MINITAB for simulating sampling distributions. To develop a random sample from a specific distribution you have to start by choosing Calc ▶ Random Data from the menu. You will observe a list of all distributions. Let's start by generating a random sample of size 10 from a binomial distribution with parameters 10 and 0.6 for number of trials and event probability, respectively. After choosing Calc ▶ Random Data ▶ Binomial from the menu, the Binomial Distribution dialog box will appear as shown in Figure 5–21. You need to specify the size of your sample as the number of rows of data to generate. As can be seen, the number 10 has been entered in the corresponding edit box. Specify the name of the column that will store the generated random numbers. Define the parameters of the binomial distribution in the next section. Then press the OK button. The generated binomial random numbers as well as corresponding Session commands will appear as shown in Figure 5–21.

MINITAB also enables you to generate a sample with an arbitrary size from a specific sample space with or without replacement. You need to specify the members of your sample space in a column. Imagine we need to generate a sample of size 8 from a sample space that has been defined in the first column. Start by choosing Calc ▶ Random Data ▶ Sample Form Columns from the menu bar. You need to specify

FIGURE 5–21   Using MINITAB for Generating Sampling Distributions

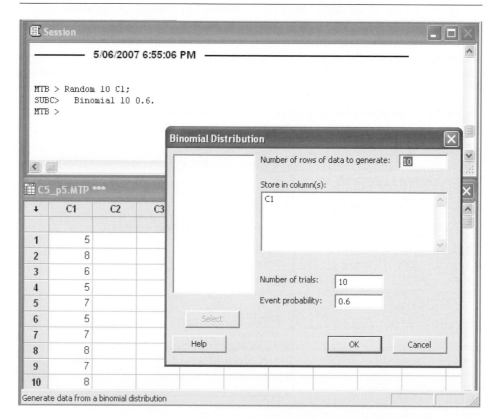

the size of your sample, the column that contains your sample space, and the column that will store the generated random numbers. You can also specify that the sampling occurs with or without replacement.

5–7 Summary and Review of Terms

In this chapter, we saw how samples are randomly selected from populations for the purpose of drawing inferences about **population parameters**. We saw how **sample statistics** computed from the data—the sample mean, the sample standard deviation, and the sample proportion—are used as **estimators** of population parameters. We presented the important idea of a **sampling distribution** of a statistic, the probability distribution of the values the statistic may take. We saw how the **central limit theorem** implies that the sampling distributions of the sample mean and the sample proportion approach normal distributions as the sample size increases. Sampling distributions of estimators will prove to be the key to the construction of confidence intervals in the following chapter, as well as the key to the ideas presented in later chapters. We also presented important properties we would like our estimators to possess: **unbiasedness, efficiency, consistency,** and **sufficiency.** Finally, we discussed the idea of **degrees of freedom.**

ADDITIONAL PROBLEMS

5–41. Suppose you are sampling from a population with mean $\mu = 1{,}065$ and standard deviation $\sigma = 500$. The sample size is $n = 100$. What are the expected value and the variance of the sample mean $\overline{X}$?

5–42. Suppose you are sampling from a population with population variance $\sigma^2 = 1{,}000{,}000$. You want the standard deviation of the sample mean to be at most 25. What is the minimum sample size you should use?

5–43. When sampling is from a population with mean 53 and standard deviation 10, using a sample of size 400, what are the expected value and the standard deviation of the sample mean?

5–44. When sampling is for a population proportion from a population with actual proportion $p = 0.5$, using a sample of size $n = 120$, what is the standard deviation of our estimator $\hat{P}$?

5–45. What are the expected value and the standard deviation of the sample proportion $\hat{P}$ if the true population proportion is 0.2 and the sample size is $n = 90$?

5–46. For a fixed sample size, what is the value of the true population proportion p that maximizes the variance of the sample proportion $\hat{P}$? (*Hint:* Try several values of p on a grid between 0 and 1.)

5–47. The average value of $1.00 in euros in early 2007 was 0.76.[13] If $\sigma = 0.02$ and $n = 30$, find $P(0.72 < \overline{X} < 0.82)$.

5–48. In problem 5–41, what is the probability that the sample mean will be at least 1,000? Do you need to use the central limit theorem to answer this question? Explain.

5–49. In problem 5–43, what is the probability that the sample mean will be between 52 and 54?

5–50. In problem 5–44, what is the probability that the sample proportion will be at least 0.45?

---

[13]From "Foreign Exchange," *The New York Times*, May 2, 2007, p. C16.

5–51. Searches at Switzerland's 406 commercial banks turned up only $3.3 million in accounts belonging to Zaire's deposed president, Mobutu Sese Seko. The Swiss banks had been asked to look a little harder after finding nothing at all the first time round.

    a. If President Mobutu's money was distributed in *all* 406 banks, how much was found, on average, per bank?

    b. If a random sample of 16 banks was first selected in a preliminary effort to estimate how much money was in all banks, then assuming that amounts were normally distributed with standard deviation of $2,000, what was the probability that the mean of this sample would have been less than $7,000?

5–52. The proportion of defective microcomputer disks of a certain kind is believed to be anywhere from 0.06 to 0.10. The manufacturer wants to draw a random sample and estimate the proportion of all defective disks. How large should the sample be to ensure that the standard deviation of the estimator is *at most* 0.03?

5–53. Explain why we need to draw random samples and how such samples are drawn. What are the properties of a (simple) random sample?

5–54. Explain the idea of a bias and its ramifications.

5–55. Is the sample median a biased estimator of the population mean? Why do we usually prefer the sample mean to the sample median as an estimator for the population mean? If we use the sample median, what must we assume about the population? Compare the two estimators.

5–56. Explain why the sample variance is defined as the sum of squared deviations from the sample mean, divided by $n - 1$ and not by n.

5–57. Residential real estate in New York rents for an average of $44 per square foot, for a certain segment of the market.[14] If the population standard deviation is $7, and a random sample of 50 properties is chosen, what is the probability that the sample average will be below $35?

5–58. In problem 5–57, give 0.95 probability bounds on the value of the sample mean that would be obtained. Also give 0.90 probability bounds on the value of the sample mean.

5–59. According to *Money,* the average U.S. government bond fund earned 3.9% over the 12 months ending in February 2007.[15] Assume a standard deviation of 0.5%. What is the probability that the average earning in a random sample of 25 bonds exceeded 3.0%?

5–60. You need to fill in a table of five rows and three columns with numbers. All the row totals and column totals are given to you, and the numbers you fill in must add to these given totals. How many degrees of freedom do you have?

5–61. Thirty-eight percent of all shoppers at a large department store are holders of the store's charge card. If a random sample of 100 shoppers is taken, what is the probability that at least 30 of them will be found to be holders of the card?

5–62. When sampling is from a normal population with an unknown variance, is the sampling distribution of the sample mean normal? Explain.

5–63. When sampling is from a normal population with a known variance, what is the smallest sample size required for applying a normal distribution for the sample mean?

5–64. Which of the following estimators are unbiased estimators of the appropriate population parameters: $\overline{X}$, $\hat{P}$, S^2, S? Explain.

---

[14]"Square Feet," *The New York Times,* May 2, 2007, p. C7.

[15]"Money Benchmarks," *Money,* March 2007, p. 130.

5–65. Suppose a new estimator for the population mean is discovered. The new estimator is unbiased and has variance equal to σ^2/n^2. Discuss the merits of the new estimator compared with the sample mean.

5–66. Three independent random samples are collected, and three sample means are computed. The total size of the combined sample is 124. How many degrees of freedom are associated with the deviations from the sample means in the combined data set? Explain.

5–67. Discuss, in relative terms, the sample size needed for an application of a normal distribution for the sample mean when sampling is from each of the following populations. (Assume the population standard deviation is known in each case.)

    a. A normal population

    b. A mound-shaped population, close to normal

    c. A discrete population consisting of the values 1,006, 47, and 0, with equal frequencies

    d. A slightly skewed population

    e. A highly skewed population

5–68. When sampling is from a normally distributed population, is there an advantage to taking a large sample? Explain.

5–69. Suppose that you are given a new sample statistic to serve as an estimator of some population parameter. You are unable to assume any theoretical results such as the central limit theorem. Discuss how you would empirically determine the sampling distribution of the new statistic.

5–70. Recently, the federal government claimed that the state of Alaska had overpaid 20% of the Medicare recipients in the state. The director of the Alaska Department of Health and Social Services planned to check this claim by selecting a random sample of 250 recipients of Medicare checks in the state and determining the number of overpaid cases in the sample. Assuming the federal government's claim is correct, what is the probability that less than 15% of the people in the sample will be found to have been overpaid?

5–71. A new kind of alkaline battery is believed to last an average of 25 hours of continuous use (in a given kind of flashlight). Assume that the population standard deviation is 2 hours. If a random sample of 100 batteries is selected and tested, is it likely that the average battery in the sample will last less than 24 hours of continuous use? Explain.

5–72. Häagen-Dazs ice cream produces a frozen yogurt aimed at health-conscious ice cream lovers. Before marketing the product in 2007, the company wanted to estimate the proportion of grocery stores currently selling Häagen-Dazs ice cream that would sell the new product. If 60% of the grocery stores would sell the product and a random sample of 200 stores is selected, what is the probability that the percentage in the sample will deviate from the population percentage by no more than 7 percentage points?

5–73. Japan's birthrate is believed to be 1.57 per woman. Assume that the population standard deviation is 0.4. If a random sample of 200 women is selected, what is the probability that the sample mean will fall between 1.52 and 1.62?

5–74. The Toyota Prius uses both gasoline and electric power. Toyota claims its mileage per gallon is 52. A random sample of 40 cars is taken and each sampled car is tested for its fuel efficiency. Assuming that 52 miles per gallon is the population mean and 2.4 miles per gallon is the population standard deviation, calculate the probability that the sample mean will be between 52 and 53.

5–75. A bank that employs many part-time tellers is concerned about the increasing number of errors made by the tellers. To estimate the proportion of errors made in a day, a random sample of 400 transactions on a particular day was checked. The proportion of the transactions with errors was computed. If the true proportion of transactions that had errors was 6% that day, what is the probability that the estimated proportion is less than 5%?

5–76. The daily number of visitors to a Web site follows a normal distribution with mean 15,830 and standard deviation 458. The average number of visitors on 10 randomly chosen days is computed. What is the probability that the estimated average exceeds 16,000?

5–77. According to *BusinessWeek,* profits in the energy sector have been rising, with one company averaging $3.42 monthly per share.[16] Assume this is an average from a population with standard deviation of $1.5. If a random sample of 30 months is selected, what is the probability that its average will exceed $4.00?

---

[16]Gene G. Marcial, "Tremendous Demand for Superior Energy Services," *BusinessWeek*, March 26, 2007, p. 132.

CASE 6   Acceptance Sampling of Pins

A company supplies pins in bulk to a customer. The company uses an automatic lathe to produce the pins. Factors such as vibration, temperature, and wear and tear affect the pins, so that the lengths of the pins made by the machine are normally distributed with a mean of 1.008 inches and a standard deviation of 0.045 inch. The company supplies the pins in large batches to a customer. The customer will take a random sample of 50 pins from the batch and compute the sample mean. If the sample mean is within the interval 1.000 inch ± 0.010 inch, then the customer will buy the whole batch.

1. What is the probability that a batch will be acceptable to the consumer? Is the probability large enough to be an acceptable level of performance?

To improve the probability of acceptance, the production manager and the engineers discuss adjusting the population mean and standard deviation of the lengths of the pins.

2. If the lathe can be adjusted to have the mean of the lengths at any desired value, what should it be adjusted to? Why?

3. Suppose the mean cannot be adjusted, but the standard deviation can be reduced. What maximum value of the standard deviation would make 90% of the parts acceptable to

the consumer? (Assume the mean continues to be 1.008 inches.)

4. Repeat part 3 with 95% and 99% of the pins acceptable.

5. In practice, which one do you think is easier to adjust, the mean or the standard deviation? Why?

The production manager then considers the costs involved. The cost of resetting the machine to adjust the population mean involves the engineers' time and the cost of production time lost. The cost of reducing the population standard deviation involves, in addition to these costs, the cost of overhauling the machine and reengineering the process.

6. Assume it costs $150x^2$ to decrease the standard deviation by $(x/1{,}000)$ inch. Find the cost of reducing the standard deviation to the values found in parts 3 and 4.

7. Now assume that the mean has been adjusted to the best value found in part 2 at a cost of $80. Calculate the reduction in standard deviation necessary to have 90%, 95%, and 99% of the parts acceptable. Calculate the respective costs, as in part 6.

8. Based on your answers to parts 6 and 7, what are your recommended mean and standard deviation to which the machine should be adjusted?

6

CONFIDENCE INTERVALS

6–1   Using Statistics   219

6–2   Confidence Interval for the Population Mean When the Population Standard Deviation Is Known   220

6–3   Confidence Intervals for μ When σ Is Unknown—The t Distribution   228

6–4   Large-Sample Confidence Intervals for the Population Proportion p 235

6–5   Confidence Intervals for the Population Variance   239

6–6   Sample-Size Determination   243

6–7   The Templates   245

6–8   Using the Computer   248

6–9   Summary and Review of Terms   250

Case 7   Presidential Polling   254

Case 8   Privacy Problem   255

LEARNING OBJECTIVES

After studying this chapter, you should be able to:

- Explain confidence intervals.
- Compute confidence intervals for population means.
- Compute confidence intervals for population proportions.
- Compute confidence intervals for population variances.
- Compute minimum sample sizes needed for an estimation.
- Compute confidence intervals for special types of sampling methods.
- Use templates for all confidence interval and sample-size computations.

6-1 Using Statistics

The alcoholic beverage industry, like many others, has to reinvent itself every few years: from beer to wine, to wine coolers, to cocktails. In 2007 it was clear that the gin-based martini was back as a reigning libation. But which gin was best for this cocktail? *The New York Times* arranged for experts to sample 80 martinis made with different kinds of gin, to determine the best. It also wanted to estimate the average number of stars that any given martini would get—its rating by an average drinker. This is an example of statistical inference, which we study in this chapter and the following ones. In actuality here, four people sampled a total of 80 martinis and determined that the best value was Plymouth English Gin, which received 3½ stars.[1]

In the following chapters we will learn how to compare several populations. In this chapter you will learn how to estimate a parameter of a single population and also provide a *confidence interval* for such a parameter. Thus, for example, you will be able to assess the average number of stars awarded a given gin by the average martini drinker.

In the last chapter, we saw how sample statistics are used as estimators of population parameters. We defined a point estimate of a parameter as a single value obtained from the estimator. We saw that an estimator, a sample statistic, is a random variable with a certain probability distribution—its sampling distribution. A given point estimate is a single realization of the random variable. The actual estimate may or may not be close to the parameter of interest. Therefore, if we only provide a point estimate of the parameter of interest, we are not giving any information about the *accuracy* of the estimation procedure. For example, saying that the sample mean is 550 is giving a point estimate of the population mean. This estimate does not tell us how close μ may be to its estimate, 550. Suppose, on the other hand, that we also said: "We are *99% confident* that μ is in the interval [449, 551]." This conveys much more information about the possible value of μ. Now compare this interval with another one: "We are *90% confident* that μ is in the interval [400, 700]." This interval conveys less information about the possible value of μ, both because it is wider and because the level of confidence is lower. (When based on the same information, however, an interval of lower confidence level is narrower.)

> A **confidence interval** is a *range of numbers* believed to include an unknown population parameter. Associated with the interval is a measure of the *confidence* we have that the interval does indeed contain the parameter of interest.

The sampling distribution of the statistic gives a *probability* associated with a range of values the statistic may take. After the sampling has taken place and a *particular estimate* has been obtained, this probability is transformed to a *level of confidence* for a range of values that may contain the unknown parameter.

In the next section, we will see how to construct confidence intervals for the population mean μ when the population standard deviation σ is known. Then we will alter this situation and see how a confidence interval for μ may be constructed without knowledge of σ. Other sections present confidence intervals in other situations.

---

[1]Eric Asimov, "No, Really, It Was Tough: 4 People, 80 Martinis," *The New York Times,* May 2, 2007, p. D1.

6–2   Confidence Interval for the Population Mean When the Population Standard Deviation Is Known

CHAPTER 9

The central limit theorem tells us that when we select a large random sample from any population with mean μ and standard deviation σ, the sample mean $\overline{X}$ is (at least approximately) normally distributed with mean μ and standard deviation $\sigma/\sqrt{n}$. If the population itself is normal, $\overline{X}$ is normally distributed for any sample size. Recall that the standard normal random variable Z has a 0.95 probability of being within the range of values -1.96 to 1.96 (you may check this using Table 2 in Appendix C). Transforming Z to the random variable $\overline{X}$ with mean μ and standard deviation $\sigma/\sqrt{n}$, we find that—*before the sampling*—there is a 0.95 probability that $\overline{X}$ will fall within the interval:

$$\mu \pm 1.96\frac{\sigma}{\sqrt{n}} \qquad (6\text{–}1)$$

Once we have obtained our random sample, we have a particular value $\overline{x}$. This particular $\overline{x}$ either lies within the range of values specified by equation 6–1 or does not lie within this range. Since we do not know the (fixed) value of the population parameter μ, we have no way of knowing whether $\overline{x}$ is indeed within the range given in equation 6–1. Since the random sampling has already taken place and a particular $\overline{x}$ has been computed, we no longer have a random variable and may no longer talk about probabilities. We do know, however, that since the presampling probability that $\overline{X}$ will fall in the interval in equation 6–1 is 0.95, about 95% of the values of $\overline{X}$ obtained in a large number of repeated samplings will fall within the interval. Since we have a single value $\overline{x}$ that was obtained by this process, we may say that we are *95% confident that $\overline{x}$ lies within the interval*. This idea is demonstrated in Figure 6–1.

Consider a particular $\overline{x}$, and note that the distance between $\overline{x}$ and μ is the same as the distance between μ and $\overline{x}$. Thus, $\overline{x}$ falls inside the interval $\mu \pm 1.96\sigma/\sqrt{n}$ *if and only if* μ happens to be inside the interval $\overline{x} \pm 1.96\sigma/\sqrt{n}$. In a large number of repeated trials, this would happen about 95% of the time. We therefore call the interval $\overline{x} \pm 1.96\sigma/\sqrt{n}$ a *95% confidence interval for the unknown population mean μ*. This is demonstrated in Figure 6–2.

Instead of measuring a distance of $1.96\sigma/\sqrt{n}$ on either side of μ (an impossible task since μ is unknown), we measure the same distance of $1.96\sigma/\sqrt{n}$ on either side of our *known* sample mean $\overline{x}$. Since, *before the sampling*, the random interval $\overline{X} \pm 1.96\sigma/\sqrt{n}$ had a 0.95 probability of capturing μ, *after the sampling* we may be 95% confident that our particular interval $\overline{x} \pm 1.96\sigma/\sqrt{n}$ indeed contains the population mean μ. We cannot say that there is a 0.95 *probability* that μ is inside the interval, because the interval $\overline{x} \pm 1.96\sigma/\sqrt{n}$ is not random, and neither is μ. The population mean μ is unknown to us but is a fixed quantity—not a random variable.[2] Either μ lies inside the confidence interval (in which case the probability of this event is 1.00), or it does not (in which case the probability of the event is 0). We do know, however,

---

[2]We are using what is called the *classical*, or *frequentist*, interpretation of confidence intervals. An alternative view, the Bayesian approach, will be discussed in Chapter 15. The Bayesian approach allows us to treat an unknown population parameter as a random variable. As such, the unknown population mean μ may be stated to have a 0.95 *probability* of being within an interval.

FIGURE 6–1   Probability Distribution of $\overline{X}$ and Some Resulting Values of the Statistic in Repeated Samplings

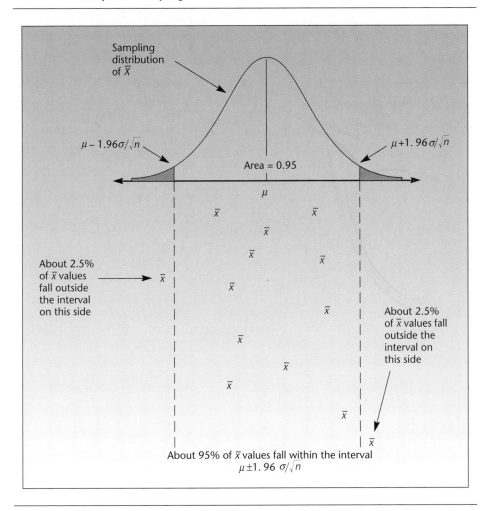

that 95% of all possible intervals constructed in this manner will contain μ. Therefore, we may say that we are *95% confident* that μ lies in the particular interval we have obtained.

A 95% confidence interval for μ when σ is known and sampling is done from a normal population, or a large sample is used, is

$$\overline{X} \pm 1.96\frac{\sigma}{\sqrt{n}} \qquad (6\text{–}2)$$

The quantity $1.96\sigma/\sqrt{n}$ is often called the *margin of error* or the *sampling error*. Its data-derived estimate (using s instead of the unknown σ) is commonly reported.

To compute a 95% confidence interval for μ, all we need to do is substitute the values of the required entities in equation 6–2. Suppose, for example, that we are sampling from a normal population, in which case the random variable $\overline{X}$ is normally distributed for any sample size. We use a sample of size $n = 25$, and we get a sample mean $\overline{x} = 122$. Suppose we also know that the population standard deviation is $\sigma = 20$.

FIGURE 6–2   Construction of a 95% Confidence Interval for the Population Mean μ

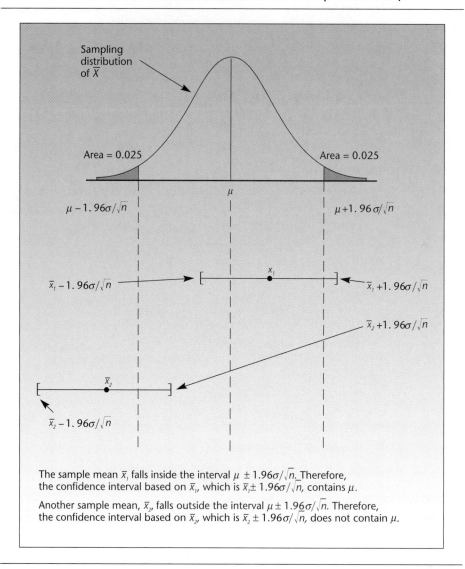

The sample mean $\bar{x}_1$ falls inside the interval $\mu \pm 1.96\sigma/\sqrt{n}$. Therefore, the confidence interval based on $\bar{x}_1$, which is $\bar{x}_1 \pm 1.96\sigma/\sqrt{n}$, contains μ.

Another sample mean, $\bar{x}_2$, falls outside the interval $\mu \pm 1.96\sigma/\sqrt{n}$. Therefore, the confidence interval based on $\bar{x}_2$, which is $\bar{x}_2 \pm 1.96\sigma/\sqrt{n}$, does not contain μ.

Let us compute a 95% confidence interval for the unknown population mean μ. Using equation 6–2, we get

$$\bar{x} \pm 1.96\,\frac{\sigma}{\sqrt{n}} \;=\; 122 \pm 1.96\,\frac{20}{\sqrt{25}} \;=\; 122 \pm 7.84 \;=\; [114.16, 129.84]$$

Thus, we may be 95% confident that the unknown population mean μ lies anywhere between the values 114.16 and 129.84.

In business and other applications, the 95% confidence interval is commonly used. There are, however, many other possible levels of confidence. You may choose any level of confidence you wish, find the appropriate z value from the standard normal table, and use it instead of 1.96 in equation 6–2 to get an interval of the chosen level of confidence. Using the standard normal table, we find, for example, that for a

90% confidence interval we use the z value 1.645, and for a 99% confidence interval we use $z = 2.58$ (or, using an accurate interpolation, 2.576). Let us formalize the procedure and make some definitions.

We define $z_{\alpha/2}$ as the z value that cuts off a right-tail area of $\alpha/2$ under the standard normal curve.

For example, 1.96 is $z_{\alpha/2}$ for $\alpha/2 = 0.025$ because $z = 1.96$ cuts off an area of 0.025 to its right. (We find from Table 2 that for $z = 1.96$, TA = 0.475; therefore, the right-tail area is $\alpha/2 = 0.025$.) Now consider the two points 1.96 and -1.96. Each of them cuts off a tail area of $\alpha/2 = 0.025$ in the respective direction of its tail. The area between the two values is therefore equal to $1 - \alpha = 1 - 2(0.025) = 0.95$. The area under the curve excluding the tails, $1 - \alpha$, is called the **confidence coefficient.** (And the combined area in both tails α is called the **error probability.** This probability will be important to us in the next chapter.) The confidence coefficient multiplied by 100, expressed as a percentage, is the **confidence level.**

A $(1 - \alpha)$ 100% confidence interval for μ when σ is known and sampling is done from a normal population, or with a large sample, is

$$\overline{X} \pm Z_{\alpha/2} \frac{\sigma}{\sqrt{n}} \qquad (6\text{–}3)$$

Thus, for a 95% confidence interval for μ we have

$$(1 - \alpha)100\% = 95\%$$
$$1 - \alpha = 0.95$$
$$\alpha = 0.05$$
$$\frac{\alpha}{2} = 0.025$$

From the normal table, we find $z_{\alpha/2} = 1.96$. This is the value we substitute for $z_{\alpha/2}$ in equation 6–3.

For example, suppose we want an 80% confidence interval for μ. We have $1 - \alpha = 0.80$ and $\alpha = 0.20$; therefore, $\alpha/2 = 0.10$. We now look in the standard normal table for the value of $z_{0.10}$, that is, the z value that cuts off an area of 0.10 to its right. We have TA $= 0.5 - 0.1 = 0.4$, and from the table we find $z_{0.10} = 1.28$. The confidence interval is therefore $\overline{x} \pm 1.28\sigma/\sqrt{n}$. This is demonstrated in Figure 6–3.

Let us compute an 80% confidence interval for μ using the information presented earlier. We have $n = 25$, and $\overline{x} = 122$. We also assume $\sigma = 20$. To compute an 80% confidence interval for the unknown population mean μ, we use equation 6–3 and get

$$\overline{x} \pm z_{\alpha/2} \frac{\sigma}{\sqrt{n}} = 122 \pm 1.28 \frac{20}{\sqrt{25}} = 122 \pm 5.12 = [116.88, 127.12]$$

FIGURE 6–3   Construction of an 80% Confidence Interval for μ

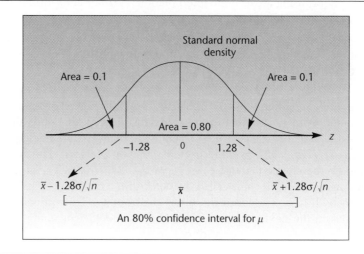

Comparing this interval with the 95% confidence interval for μ we computed earlier, we note that the present interval is *narrower*. This is an important property of confidence intervals.

> When sampling is from the same population, using a fixed sample size, *the higher the confidence level, the wider the interval.*

Intuitively, a wider interval has more of a presampling chance of "capturing" the unknown population parameter. If we want a 100% confidence interval for a parameter, the interval must be $[-\infty, \infty]$. The reason for this is that 100% confidence is derived from a presampling probability of 1.00 of capturing the parameter, and the only way to get such a probability using the standard normal distribution is by allowing Z to be anywhere from $-\infty$ to ∞. If we are willing to be more realistic (nothing is *certain*) and accept, say, a 99% confidence interval, our interval will be finite and based on $z = 2.58$. The width of our interval will then be $2(2.58\sigma/\sqrt{n})$. If we further reduce our confidence requirement to 95%, the width of our interval will be $2(1.96\sigma/\sqrt{n})$. Since both σ and n are fixed, the 95% interval must be narrower. The more confidence you require, the more you need to sacrifice in terms of a wider interval.

If you want both a narrow interval *and* a high degree of confidence, you need to acquire a large amount of information—take a large sample. This is so because the larger the sample size n, the narrower the interval. This makes sense in that if you buy more information, you will have less uncertainty.

> When sampling is from the same population, using a fixed confidence level, *the larger the sample size* n, *the narrower the confidence interval.*

Suppose that the 80% confidence interval developed earlier was based on a sample size $n = 2,500$, instead of $n = 25$. Assuming that $\bar{x}$ and σ are the same, the new confidence interval should be 10 times as narrow as the previous one (because $\sqrt{2,500} = 50$, which is 10 times as large as $\sqrt{25}$). Indeed, the new interval is

$$\bar{x} \pm z_{\alpha/2}\frac{\sigma}{\sqrt{n}} = 122 \pm 1.28\frac{20}{\sqrt{2,500}} = 122 \pm 0.512 = [121.49, 122.51]$$

This interval has width $2(0.512) = 1.024$, while the width of the interval based on a sample of size $n = 25$ is $2(5.12) = 10.24$. This demonstrates the value of information. The two confidence intervals are shown in Figure 6–4.

EXAMPLE 6–1

Comcast, the computer services company, is planning to invest heavily in online tele-vision service.[3] As part of the decision, the company wants to estimate the average number of online shows a family of four would watch per day. A random sample of $n = 100$ families is obtained, and in this sample the average number of shows viewed per day is 6.5 and the population standard deviation is known to be 3.2. Construct a 95% confidence interval for the average number of online television shows watched by the entire population of families of four.

We have

Solution

$$\bar{x} \pm z_{\alpha/2} \frac{\sigma}{\sqrt{n}} = 6.5 \pm 1.96 \frac{3.2}{\sqrt{100}} = 6.5 \pm 0.6272 = [5.8728, 7.1272]$$

Thus Comcast can be 95% confident that the average family of four within its popu-lation of subscribers will watch an average daily number of online television shows between about 5.87 and 7.13.

The Template

The workbook named Estimating Mean.xls contains sheets for computing confi-dence intervals for population means when

1. The sample statistics are known.
2. The sample data are known.

Figure 6–5 shows the first sheet. In this template, we enter the sample statistics in the top or bottom panel, depending on whether the population standard deviation σ is known or unknown.

Since the population standard deviation σ may not be known for certain, on the extreme right, not seen in the figure, there is a sensitivity analysis of the confidence interval with respect to σ. As can be seen in the plot below the panel, the half-width of the confidence interval is linearly related to σ.

Figure 6–6 shows the template to be used when the sample data are known. The data must be entered in column B. The sample size, the sample mean, and the sample standard deviation are automatically calculated and entered in cells F7, F8, F18, F19, and F20 as needed.

Note that in real-life situations we hardly ever know the population standard deviation. The following sections present more realistic applications.

FIGURE 6–4
Width of a Confidence Interval as a Function of Sample Size

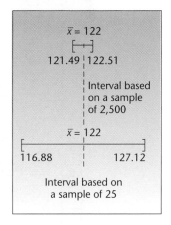

[3]Ronald Grover, "Comcast Joins the Party," *BusinessWeek,* May 7, 2007, p. 26.

**FIGURE 6–5   The Template for Estimating μ with Sample Statistics
[Estimating Mean.xls; Sheet: Sample Stats]**

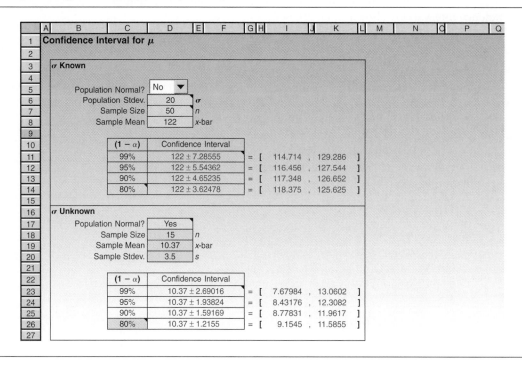

**FIGURE 6–6   The Template for Estimating μ with Sample Data
[Estimating Mean.xls; Sheet: Sample Data]**

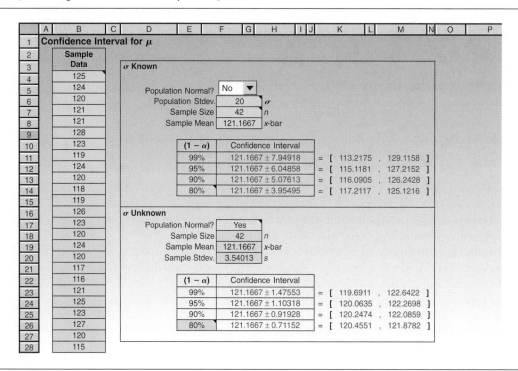

6–1. What is a confidence interval, and why is it useful? What is a confidence level?

6–2. Explain why in classical statistics describing a confidence interval in terms of probability makes no sense.

6–3. Explain how the postsampling confidence level is derived from a presampling probability.

6–4. Suppose that you computed a 95% confidence interval for a population mean. The user of the statistics claims your interval is too wide to have any meaning in the specific use for which it is intended. Discuss and compare two methods of solving this problem.

6–5. A real estate agent needs to estimate the average value of a residential property of a given size in a certain area. The real estate agent believes that the standard deviation of the property values is $\sigma = \$5,500.00$ and that property values are approximately normally distributed. A random sample of 16 units gives a sample mean of $89,673.12. Give a 95% confidence interval for the average value of all properties of this kind.

6–6. In problem 6–5, suppose that a 99% confidence interval is required. Compute the new interval, and compare it with the 95% confidence interval you computed in problem 6–5.

6–7. A car manufacturer wants to estimate the average miles-per-gallon highway rating for a new model. From experience with similar models, the manufacturer believes the miles-per-gallon standard deviation is 4.6. A random sample of 100 highway runs of the new model yields a sample mean of 32 miles per gallon. Give a 95% confidence interval for the population average miles-per-gallon highway rating.

6–8. In problem 6–7, do we need to assume that the population of miles-per-gallon values is normally distributed? Explain.

6–9. A wine importer needs to report the average percentage of alcohol in bottles of French wine. From experience with previous kinds of wine, the importer believes the population standard deviation is 1.2%. The importer randomly samples 60 bottles of the new wine and obtains a sample mean $\bar{x} = 9.3\%$. Give a 90% confidence interval for the average percentage of alcohol in all bottles of the new wine.

6–10. British Petroleum has recently been investing in oil fields in the former Soviet Union.[4] Before deciding whether to buy an oilfield, the company wants to estimate the number of barrels of oil that the oilfield can supply. For a given well, the company is interested in a purchase if it can determine that the well will produce, on average, at least 1,500 barrels a day. A random sample of 30 days gives a sample mean of 1,482 and the population standard deviation is 430. Construct a 95% confidence interval. What should be the company's decision?

6–11. Recently, three new airlines, MAXjet, L'Avion, and Eos, began operations selling business or first-class-only service.[5] These airlines need to estimate the highest fare a business-class traveler would pay on a New York to Paris route, roundtrip. Suppose that one of these airlines will institute its route only if it can be reasonably certain (90%) that passengers would pay $1,800. Suppose also that a random sample of 50 passengers reveals a sample average maximum fare of $1,700 and the population standard deviation is $800.

    a. Construct a 90% confidence interval.

    b. Should the airline offer to fly this route based on your answer to part (*a*)?

---

[4]Jason Bush, "The Kremlin's Big Squeeze," *BusinessWeek,* April 30, 2007, p. 42.

[5]Susan Stellin, "Friendlier Skies to a Home Abroad," *The New York Times,* May 4, 2007, p. D1.

6–12.   According to *Money*, the average price of a home in Albuquerque is $165,000.[6] Suppose that the reported figure is a sample estimate based on 80 randomly chosen homes in this city, and that the population standard deviation was known to be $55,000. Give an 80% confidence interval for the population mean home price.

6–13.   A mining company needs to estimate the average amount of copper ore per ton mined. A random sample of 50 tons gives a sample mean of 146.75 pounds. The population standard deviation is assumed to be 35.2 pounds. Give a 95% confidence interval for the average amount of copper in the "population" of tons mined. Also give a 90% confidence interval and a 99% confidence interval for the average amount of copper per ton.

6–14.   A new low-calorie pizza introduced by Pizza Hut has an average of 150 calories per slice. If this number is based on a random sample of 100 slices, and the population standard deviation is 30 calories, give a 90% confidence interval for the population mean.

6–15.   "Small-fry" funds trade at an average of 20% discount to net asset value. If $\sigma = 8\%$ and $n = 36$, give the 95% confidence interval for average population percentage.

6–16.   Suppose you have a confidence interval based on a sample of size n. Using the same level of confidence, how large a sample is required to produce an interval of one-half the width?

6–17.   The width of a 95% confidence interval for μ is 10 units. If everything else stays the same, how wide would a 90% confidence interval be for μ?

6–3   Confidence Intervals for μ When σ Is Unknown—The *t* Distribution

In constructing confidence intervals for μ, we assume a normal population distribution or a large sample size (for normality via the central limit theorem). Until now, we have also assumed a known population standard deviation. This assumption was necessary for theoretical reasons so that we could use standard normal probabilities in constructing our intervals.

In real sampling situations, however, the population standard deviation σ is rarely known. The reason for this is that both μ and σ are population parameters. When we sample from a population with the aim of estimating its unknown mean, the other parameter of the same population, the standard deviation, is highly unlikely to be known.

The t Distribution

As we mentioned in Chapter 5, when the population standard deviation is not known, we may use the sample standard deviation S in its place. *If the population is normally distributed,* the standardized statistic

$$t = \frac{\overline{X} - \mu}{S/\sqrt{n}} \tag{6–4}$$

has a **t distribution** with $n - 1$ degrees of freedom. The degrees of freedom of the distribution are the degrees of freedom associated with the sample standard deviation S (as explained in the last chapter). The t distribution is also called *Student's distribution,* or *Student's t distribution.* What is the origin of the name *Student*?

---

[6]"The 100 Biggest U.S. Markets," *Money*, May 2007, p. 81.

W. S. Gossett was a scientist at the Guinness brewery in Dublin, Ireland. In 1908, Gossett discovered the distribution of the quantity in equation 6–4. He called the new distribution the *t* distribution. The Guinness brewery, however, did not allow its workers to publish findings under their own names. Therefore, Gossett published his findings under the pen name *Student*. As a result, the distribution became known also as Student's distribution.

The *t* distribution is characterized by its degrees-of-freedom parameter df. For any integer value df = 1, 2, 3, . . . , there is a corresponding *t* distribution. The *t* distribution resembles the standard normal distribution *Z*: it is symmetric and bell-shaped. The *t* distribution, however, has wider tails than the *Z* distribution.

> The mean of a *t* distribution is zero. For df > 2, the variance of the *t* distribution is equal to df/(df − 2).

We see that the mean of *t* is the same as the mean of *Z*, but the variance of *t* is larger than the variance of *Z*. As df increases, the variance of *t* approaches 1.00, which is the variance of *Z*. Having wider tails and a larger variance than *Z* is a reflection of the fact that the *t* distribution applies to situations with a greater inherent *uncertainty*. The uncertainty comes from the fact that σ is unknown and is estimated by the *random variable S*. The *t* distribution thus reflects the uncertainty in *two* random variables, $\bar{X}$ and *S*, while *Z* reflects only an uncertainty due to $\bar{X}$. The greater uncertainty in *t* (which makes confidence intervals based on *t* wider than those based on *Z*) is the price we pay for not knowing σ and having to estimate it from our data. As df increases, the *t* distribution approaches the *Z* distribution.

Figure 6–7 shows the *t*-distribution template. We can enter any desired degrees of freedom in cell B4 and see how the distribution approaches the *Z* distribution, which is superimposed on the chart. In the range K3:O5 the template shows the critical values for all standard α values. The area to the right of the chart in this template can be used for calculating *p*-values, which we will learn in the next chapter.

FIGURE 6–7 **The *t*-Distribution Template**
         [t.xls]

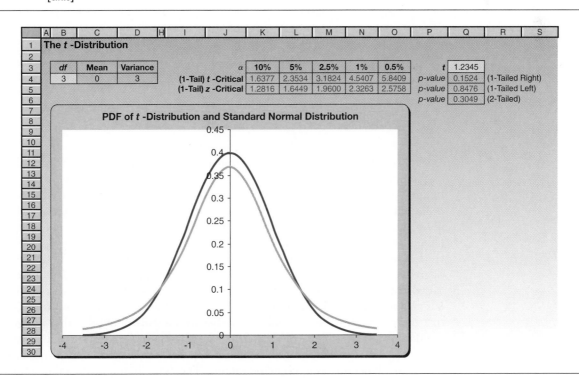

TABLE 6–1   Values and Probabilities of *t* Distributions

Degrees of Freedom	$t_{0.100}$	$t_{0.050}$	$t_{0.025}$	$t_{0.010}$	$t_{0.005}$
1	3.078	6.314	12.706	31.821	63.657
2	1.886	2.920	4.303	6.965	9.925
3	1.638	2.353	3.182	4.541	5.841
4	1.533	2.132	2.776	3.747	4.604
5	1.476	2.015	2.571	3.365	4.032
6	1.440	1.943	2.447	3.143	3.707
7	1.415	1.895	2.365	2.998	3.499
8	1.397	1.860	2.306	2.896	3.355
9	1.383	1.833	2.262	2.821	3.250
10	1.372	1.812	2.228	2.764	3.169
11	1.363	1.796	2.201	2.718	3.106
12	1.356	1.782	2.179	2.681	3.055
13	1.350	1.771	2.160	2.650	3.012
14	1.345	1.761	2.145	2.624	2.977
15	1.341	1.753	2.131	2.602	2.947
16	1.337	1.746	2.120	2.583	2.921
17	1.333	1.740	2.110	2.567	2.898
18	1.330	1.734	2.101	2.552	2.878
19	1.328	1.729	2.093	2.539	2.861
20	1.325	1.725	2.086	2.528	2.845
21	1.323	1.721	2.080	2.518	2.831
22	1.321	1.717	2.074	2.508	2.819
23	1.319	1.714	2.069	2.500	2.807
24	1.318	1.711	2.064	2.492	2.797
25	1.316	1.708	2.060	2.485	2.787
26	1.315	1.706	2.056	2.479	2.779
27	1.314	1.703	2.052	2.473	2.771
28	1.313	1.701	2.048	2.467	2.763
29	1.311	1.699	2.045	2.462	2.756
30	1.310	1.697	2.042	2.457	2.750
40	1.303	1.684	2.021	2.423	2.704
60	1.296	1.671	2.000	2.390	2.660
120	1.289	1.658	1.980	2.358	2.617
∞	1.282	1.645	1.960	2.326	2.576

Values of *t* distributions for selected tail probabilities are given in Table 3 in Appendix C (reproduced here as Table 6–1). Since there are infinitely many *t* distributions—one for every value of the degrees-of-freedom parameter—the table contains probabilities for only some of these distributions. For each distribution, the table gives values that cut off given areas under the curve to the *right*. The *t* table is thus a table of values corresponding to right-tail probabilities.

Let us consider an example. A random variable with a *t* distribution with 10 degrees of freedom has a 0.10 probability of exceeding the value 1.372. It has a 0.025 probability of exceeding the value 2.228, and so on for the other values listed in the table. Since the *t* distributions are symmetric about zero, we also know, for example, that the probability that a random variable with a *t* distribution with 10 degrees of freedom will be less than −1.372 is 0.10. These facts are demonstrated in Figure 6–8.

As we noted earlier, the *t* distribution approaches the standard normal distribution as the df parameter approaches infinity. The *t* distribution with "infinite" degrees

FIGURE 6–8   Table Probabilities for a Selected t Distribution (df = 10)

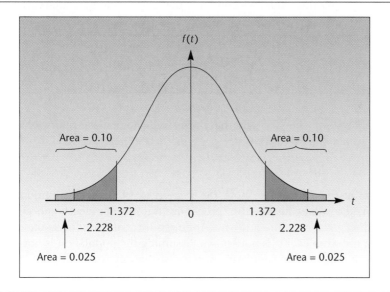

of freedom is defined as the standard normal distribution. The last row in Appendix C, Table 3 (Table 6–1) corresponds to df = ∞, the standard normal distribution. Note that the value corresponding to a right-tail area of 0.025 in that row is 1.96, which we recognize as the appropriate z value. Similarly, the value corresponding to a right-tail area of 0.005 is 2.576, and the value corresponding to a right-tail area of 0.05 is 1.645. These, too, are values we recognize for the standard normal distribution. Look upward from the last row of the table to find cutoff values of the same right-tail probabilities for t distributions with different degrees of freedom. Suppose, for example, that we want to construct a 95% confidence interval for μ using the t distribution with 20 degrees of freedom. We may identify the value 1.96 in the last row (the appropriate z value for 95%) and then move up in the same column until we reach the row corresponding to df = 20. Here we find the required value $t_{\alpha/2} = t_{0.025} = 2.086$.

A $(1 - \alpha)$ 100% confidence interval for μ when σ is not known (assuming a normally distributed population) is

$$\bar{x} \pm t_{\alpha/2}\frac{s}{\sqrt{n}} \qquad\qquad (6\text{–}5)$$

where $t_{\alpha/2}$ is the value of the t distribution with $n - 1$ degrees of freedom that cuts off a tail area of $\alpha/2$ to its right.

EXAMPLE 6–2

A stock market analyst wants to estimate the average return on a certain stock. A random sample of 15 days yields an average (annualized) return of $\bar{x} = 10.37\%$ and a standard deviation of $s = 3.5\%$. Assuming a normal population of returns, give a 95% confidence interval for the average return on this stock.

Solution

Since the sample size is $n = 15$, we need to use the t distribution with $n - 1 = 14$ degrees of freedom. In Table 3, in the row corresponding to 14 degrees of freedom and the column corresponding to a right-tail area of 0.025 (this is $\alpha/2$), we find

$t_{0.025} = 2.145$. (We could also have found this value by moving upward from 1.96 in the last row.) Using this value, we construct the 95% confidence interval as follows:

$$\bar{x} \pm t_{\alpha/2} \frac{s}{\sqrt{n}} = 10.37 \pm 2.145 \frac{3.5}{\sqrt{15}} = [8.43, 12.31]$$

Thus, the analyst may be 95% sure that the average annualized return on the stock is anywhere from 8.43% to 12.31%.

Looking at the *t* table, we note the *convergence* of the *t* distributions to the *Z* distribution—the values in the rows preceding the last get closer and closer to the corresponding *z* values in the last row. Although the *t* distribution is the correct distribution to use whenever σ is not known (assuming the population is normal), when df is *large*, we may use the standard normal distribution as an adequate approximation to the *t* distribution. Thus, instead of using 1.98 in a confidence interval based on a sample of size 121 (df = 120), we will just use the *z* value 1.96.

We divide estimation problems into two kinds: small-sample problems and large-sample problems. Example 6–2 demonstrated the solution of a small-sample problem. In general, *large sample* will mean a sample of 30 items or more, and *small sample* will mean a sample of size less than 30. For small samples, we will use the *t* distribution as demonstrated above. For large samples, we will use the *Z* distribution as an adequate approximation. We note that the larger the sample size, the better the normal approximation. Remember, however, that this division of large and small samples is arbitrary.

> Whenever σ is not known (and the population is assumed normal), the correct distribution to use is the *t* distribution with $n - 1$ degrees of freedom. Note, however, that for large degrees of freedom, the *t* distribution is approximated well by the *Z* distribution.

If you wish, you may always use the more accurate values obtained from the *t* table (when such values can be found in the table) rather than the standard normal approximation. In this chapter and elsewhere (with the exception of some examples in Chapter 14), we will assume that the population satisfies, at least approximately, a normal distribution assumption. For large samples, this assumption is less crucial.

> A large-sample $(1 - \alpha)$ 100% confidence interval for μ is
>
> $$\bar{x} \pm z_{\alpha/2}\frac{s}{\sqrt{n}} \tag{6–6}$$

We demonstrate the use of equation 6–6 in Example 6–3.

EXAMPLE 6–3   An economist wants to estimate the average amount in checking accounts at banks in a given region. A random sample of 100 accounts gives $\bar{x} = \$357.60$ and $s = \$140.00$. Give a 95% confidence interval for μ, the average amount in any checking account at a bank in the given region.

We find the 95% confidence interval for μ as follows:

$$\bar{x} \pm z_{\alpha/2} \frac{s}{\sqrt{n}} = 357.60 \pm 1.96 \frac{140}{\sqrt{100}} = [330.16, 385.04]$$

Thus, based on the data and the assumption of random sampling, the economist may be 95% confident that the average amount in checking accounts in the area is anywhere from $330.16 to $385.04.

PROBLEMS

6–18. A telephone company wants to estimate the average length of long-distance calls during weekends. A random sample of 50 calls gives a mean $\bar{x} = 14.5$ minutes and standard deviation $s = 5.6$ minutes. Give a 95% confidence interval and a 90% confidence interval for the average length of a long-distance phone call during weekends.

6–19. An insurance company handling malpractice cases is interested in estimating the average amount of claims against physicians of a certain specialty. The company obtains a random sample of 165 claims and finds $\bar{x} = \$16,530$ and $s = \$5,542$. Give a 95% confidence interval and a 99% confidence interval for the average amount of a claim.

6–20. The manufacturer of batteries used in small electric appliances wants to estimate the average life of a battery. A random sample of 12 batteries yields $\bar{x} = 34.2$ hours and $s = 5.9$ hours. Give a 95% confidence interval for the average life of a battery.

6–21. A tire manufacturer wants to estimate the average number of miles that may be driven on a tire of a certain type before the tire wears out. A random sample of 32 tires is chosen; the tires are driven on until they wear out, and the number of miles driven on each tire is recorded. The data, in thousands of miles, are as follows:

32, 33, 28, 37, 29, 30, 25, 27, 39, 40, 26, 26, 27, 30, 25, 30, 31, 29, 24, 36, 25, 37, 37, 20, 22, 35, 23, 28, 30, 36, 40, 41

Give a 99% confidence interval for the average number of miles that may be driven on a tire of this kind.

6–22. Digital media have recently begun to take over from print outlets.[7] A newspaper owners' association wants to estimate the average number of times a week people buy a newspaper on the street. A random sample of 100 people reveals that the sample average is 3.2 and the sample standard deviation is 2.1. Construct a 95% confidence interval for the population average.

6–23. Pier 1 Imports is a nationwide retail outlet selling imported furniture and other home items. From time to time, the company surveys its regular customers by obtaining random samples based on customer zip codes. In one mailing, customers were asked to rate a new table from Thailand on a scale of 0 to 100. The ratings of 25 randomly selected customers are as follows: 78, 85, 80, 89, 77, 50, 75, 90, 88, 100, 70, 99, 98, 55, 80, 45, 80, 76, 96, 100, 95, 90, 60, 85, 90. Give a 99% confidence interval for the rating of the table that would be given by an average member of the population of regular customers. Assume normality.

---

[7]"Flat Prospects: Digital Media and Globalization Shake Up an Old Industry," *The Economist*, March 17, 2007, p. 72.

6–24. An executive placement service needs to estimate the average salary of executives placed in a given industry. A random sample of 40 executives gives $\bar{x} =$ \$42,539 and $s =$ \$11,690. Give a 90% confidence interval for the average salary of an executive placed in this industry.

6–25. The following is a random sample of the wealth, in billions of U.S. dollars, of individuals listed on the *Forbes* "Billionaires" list for 2007.[8]

2.1, 5.8, 7.3, 33.0, 2.0, 8.4, 11.0, 18.4, 4.3, 4.5, 6.0, 13.3, 12.8, 3.6, 2.4, 1.0

Construct a 90% confidence interval for the average wealth in \$ billions for the people on the *Forbes* list.

6–26. For advertising purposes, the Beef Industry Council needs to estimate the average caloric content of 3-ounce top loin steak cuts. A random sample of 400 pieces gives a sample mean of 212 calories and a sample standard deviation of 38 calories. Give a 95% confidence interval for the average caloric content of a 3-ounce cut of top loin steak. Also give a 98% confidence interval for the average caloric content of a cut.

6–27. A transportation company wants to estimate the average length of time goods are in transit across the country. A random sample of 20 shipments gives $\bar{x} = 2.6$ days and $s = 0.4$ day. Give a 99% confidence interval for the average transit time.

6–28. To aid in planning the development of a tourist shopping area, a state agency wants to estimate the average dollar amount spent by a tourist in an existing shopping area. A random sample of 56 tourists gives $\bar{x} =$ \$258 and $s =$ \$85. Give a 95% confidence interval for the average amount spent by a tourist at the shopping area.

6–29. According to *Money,* the average home in Ventura County, California, sells for \$647,000.[9] Assume that this sample mean was obtained from a random sample of 200 homes in this county, and that the sample standard deviation was \$140,000. Give a 95% confidence interval for the average value of a home in Ventura County.

6–30. Citibank Visa gives its cardholders "bonus dollars," which may be spent in partial payment for gifts purchased with the Visa card. The company wants to estimate the average amount of bonus dollars that will be spent by a cardholder enrolled in the program during a year. A trial run of the program with a random sample of 225 cardholders is carried out. The results are $\bar{x} =$ \$259.60 and $s =$ \$52.00. Give a 95% confidence interval for the average amount of bonus dollars that will be spent by a cardholder during the year.

6–31. An accountant wants to estimate the average amount of an account of a service company. A random sample of 46 accounts yields $\bar{x} =$ \$16.50 and $s =$ \$2.20. Give a 95% confidence interval for the average amount of an account.

6–32. An art dealer wants to estimate the average value of works of art of a certain period and type. A random sample of 20 works of art is appraised. The sample mean is found to be \$5,139 and the sample standard deviation \$640. Give a 95% confidence interval for the average value of all works of art of this kind.

6–33. A management consulting agency needs to estimate the average number of years of experience of executives in a given branch of management. A random sample of 28 executives gives $\bar{x} = 6.7$ years and $s = 2.4$ years. Give a 99% confidence interval for the average number of years of experience for all executives in this branch.

---

[8]Luisa Krull and Allison Fass, eds., "Billionaires," *Forbes,* March 26, 2007, pp. 104–184.

[9]"The 100 Biggest U.S. Markets," *Money,* May 2007, p. 81.

6–34. The Food and Drug Administration (FDA) needs to estimate the average content of an additive in a given food product. A random sample of 75 portions of the product gives $\bar{x} = 8.9$ units and $s = 0.5$ unit. Give a 95% confidence interval for the average number of units of additive in any portion of this food product.

6–35. The management of a supermarket needs to make estimates of the average daily demand for milk. The following data are available (number of half-gallon containers sold per day): 48, 59, 45, 62, 50, 68, 57, 80, 65, 58, 79, 69. Assuming that this is a random sample of daily demand, give a 90% confidence interval for average daily demand for milk.

6–36. According to an article in *Travel & Leisure,* an average plot of land in Spain's San Martin wine-producing region yields 600 bottles of wine each year.[10] Assume this average is based on a random sample of 25 plots and that the sample standard deviation is 100 bottles. Give a 95% confidence interval for the population average number of bottles per plot.

6–37. The data on the daily consumption of fuel by a delivery truck, in gallons, recorded during 25 randomly selected working days, are as follows:

9.7, 8.9, 9.7, 10.9, 10.3, 10.1, 10.7, 10.6, 10.4, 10.6, 11.6, 11.7, 9.7, 9.7, 9.7, 9.8, 12, 10.4, 8.8, 8.9, 8.4, 9.7, 10.3, 10, 9.2

Compute a 90% confidence interval for the daily fuel consumption.

6–38. According to the Darvas Box stock trading system, a trader looks at a chart of stock prices over time and identifies box-shaped patterns. Then one buys the stock if it appears to be in the lower left corner of a box, and sells if in the upper right corner. In simulations with real data, using a sample of 376 trials, the average hold time for a stock was 41.12 days.[11] If the sample standard deviation was 12 days, give a 90% confidence interval for the average hold time in days.

6–39. Refer to the Darvas Box trading model of problem 6–38. The average profit was 11.46%.[12] If the sample standard deviation was 8.2%, give a 90% confidence interval for average profit using this trading system.

6–4 Large-Sample Confidence Intervals for the Population Proportion p

Sometimes interest centers on a qualitative, rather than a quantitative, variable. We may be interested in the relative frequency of occurrence of some characteristic in a population. For example, we may be interested in the proportion of people in a population who are users of some product or the proportion of defective items produced by a machine. In such cases, we want to estimate the population proportion p.

The estimator of the population proportion p is the sample proportion $\hat{P}$. In Chapter 5, we saw that when the sample size is large, $\hat{P}$ has an approximately normal sampling distribution. The mean of the sampling distribution of $\hat{P}$ is the population proportion p, and the standard deviation of the distribution of $\hat{P}$ is $\sqrt{pq/n}$, where $q = 1 - p$. Since the standard deviation of the estimator depends on the unknown population parameter, its value is also unknown to us. It turns out, however, that for large samples we may use our actual estimate $\hat{P}$ instead of the unknown parameter p in the formula for the standard deviation. We will, therefore, use $\sqrt{\hat{p}\hat{q}/n}$ as our estimate of the standard deviation of $\hat{P}$. Recall our large-sample rule of thumb: For estimating p, a sample is considered large enough when both $n \cdot p$ and $n \cdot q$ are greater

[10]Bruce Schoenfeld, "Wine: Bierzo's Bounty," *Travel & Leisure,* April 2007, p. 119.

[11]Volker Knapp, "The Darvas Box System," *Active Trader,* April 2007, p. 44.

[12]Ibid.

than 5. (We guess the value of p when determining whether the sample is large enough. As a check, we may also compute $n\hat{p}$ and $n\hat{q}$ once the sample is obtained.)

A large-sample $(1 - \alpha)$ 100% confidence interval for the population proportion p is

$$\hat{p} \pm Z_{\alpha/2}\sqrt{\frac{\hat{p}\hat{q}}{n}} \qquad (6\text{--}7)$$

where the sample proportion $\hat{p}$ is equal to the number of successes in the sample x, divided by the number of trials (the sample size) n, and $\hat{q} = 1 - \hat{p}$.

We demonstrate the use of equation 6–7 in Example 6–4.

EXAMPLE 6–4　　A market research firm wants to estimate the share that foreign companies have in the U.S. market for certain products. A random sample of 100 consumers is obtained, and 34 people in the sample are found to be users of foreign-made products; the rest are users of domestic products. Give a 95% confidence interval for the share of foreign products in this market.

Solution　　We have $x = 34$ and $n = 100$, so our sample estimate of the proportion is $\hat{p} = x/n = 34/100 = 0.34$. We now use equation 6–7 to obtain the confidence interval for the population proportion p. A 95% confidence interval for p is

$$\hat{p} \pm z_{\alpha/2}\sqrt{\frac{\hat{p}\hat{q}}{n}} = 0.34 \pm 1.96\sqrt{\frac{(0.34)(0.66)}{100}}$$
$$= 0.34 \pm 1.96(0.04737) = 0.34 \pm 0.0928$$
$$= [0.2472, 0.4328]$$

Thus, the firm may be 95% confident that foreign manufacturers control anywhere from 24.72% to 43.28% of the market.

Suppose the firm is not happy with such a wide confidence interval. What can be done about it? This is a problem of *value of information,* and it applies to all estimation situations. As we stated earlier, for a fixed sample size, the higher the confidence you require, the wider will be the confidence interval. The sample size is in the denominator of the standard error term, as we saw in the case of estimating μ. If we should increase n, the standard error of $\hat{P}$ will decrease, and the uncertainty about the parameter being estimated will be narrowed. If the sample size cannot be increased but you still want a narrower confidence interval, you must reduce your confidence level. Thus, for example, if the firm agrees to reduce the confidence level to 90%, z will be reduced from 1.96 to 1.645, and the confidence interval will shrink to

$$0.34 \pm 1.645(0.04737) = 0.34 \pm 0.07792 = [0.2621, 0.4179]$$

The firm may be 90% confident that the market share of foreign products is anywhere from 26.21% to 41.79%. If the firm wanted a high confidence (say 95%) *and a* narrow

FIGURE 6–9   The Template for Estimating Population Proportions
[Estimating Proportion.xls]

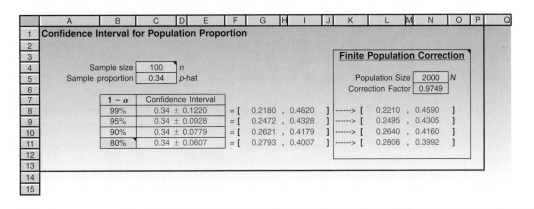

confidence interval, it would have to take a larger sample. Suppose that a random sample of $n = 200$ customers gave us the same result; that is, $x = 68$, $n = 200$, and $\hat{p} = x/n = 0.34$. What would be a 95% confidence interval in this case? Using equation 6–7, we get

$$\hat{p} \pm z_{\alpha/2} \sqrt{\frac{\hat{p}\hat{q}}{n}} = 0.34 \pm 1.96 \sqrt{\frac{(0.34)(0.66)}{200}} = [0.2743, 0.4057]$$

This interval is considerably narrower than our first 95% confidence interval, which was based on a sample of 100.

When proportions using small samples are estimated, the binomial distribution may be used in forming confidence intervals. Since the distribution is discrete, it may not be possible to construct an interval with an exact, prespecified confidence level such as 95% or 99%. We will not demonstrate the method here.

The Template

Figure 6–9 shows the template that can be used for computing confidence intervals for population proportions. The template also has provision for finite population correction. To make this correction, the population size N must be entered in cell N5. If the correction is not needed, it is a good idea to leave this cell blank to avoid creating a distraction.

PROBLEMS

6–40.   A maker of portable exercise equipment, designed for health-conscious people who travel too frequently to use a regular athletic club, wants to estimate the proportion of traveling business people who may be interested in the product. A random sample of 120 traveling business people indicates that 28 may be interested in purchasing the portable fitness equipment. Give a 95% confidence interval for the proportion of all traveling business people who may be interested in the product.

6–41.   The makers of a medicated facial skin cream are interested in determining the percentage of people in a given age group who may benefit from the ointment. A random sample of 68 people results in 42 successful treatments. Give a 99%

confidence interval for the proportion of people in the given age group who may be successfully treated with the facial cream.

6–42. According to *The Economist,* 55% of all French people of voting age are opposed to the proposed European constitution.[13] Assume that this percentage is based on a random sample of 800 French people. Give a 95% confidence interval for the population proportion in France that was against the European constitution.

6–43. According to *BusinessWeek,* many Japanese consider their cell phones toys rather than tools.[14] If a random sample of 200 Japanese cell phone owners reveals that 80 of them consider their device a toy, calculate a 90% confidence interval for the population proportion of Japanese cell phone users who feel this way.

6–44. A recent article describes the success of business schools in Europe and the demand on that continent for the MBA degree. The article reports that a survey of 280 European business positions resulted in the conclusion that only one-seventh of the positions for MBAs at European businesses are currently filled. Assuming that these numbers are exact and that the sample was randomly chosen from the entire population of interest, give a 90% confidence interval for the proportion of filled MBA positions in Europe.

6–45. According to *Fortune,* solar power now accounts for only 1% of total energy produced.[15] If this number was obtained based on a random sample of 8,000 electricity users, give a 95% confidence interval for the proportion of users of solar energy.

6–46. *Money* magazine is on a search for the indestructible suitcase.[16] If in a test of the Helium Fusion Expandable Suiter, 85 suitcases out of a sample of 100 randomly tested survived rough handling at the airport, give a 90% confidence interval for the population proportion of suitcases of this kind that would survive rough handling.

6-47. A machine produces safety devices for use in helicopters. A quality-control engineer regularly checks samples of the devices produced by the machine, and if too many of the devices are defective, the production process is stopped and the machine is readjusted. If a random sample of 52 devices yields 8 defectives, give a 98% confidence interval for the proportion of defective devices made by this machine.

6–48. Before launching its Buyers' Assurance Program, American Express wanted to estimate the proportion of cardholders who would be interested in this automatic insurance coverage plan. A random sample of 250 American Express cardholders was selected and sent questionnaires. The results were that 121 people in the sample expressed interest in the plan. Give a 99% confidence interval for the proportion of all interested American Express cardholders.

6–49. An airline wants to estimate the proportion of business passengers on a new route from New York to San Francisco. A random sample of 347 passengers on this route is selected, and 201 are found to be business travelers. Give a 90% confidence interval for the proportion of business travelers on the airline's new route.

6–50. According to the *Wall Street Journal,* the rising popularity of hedge funds and similar investment instruments has made splitting assets in cases of divorce much more difficult.[17] If a random sample of 250 divorcing couples reveals that 53 of them have great difficulties in splitting their family assets, construct a 90% confidence interval for the proportion of all couples getting divorced who encounter such problems.

---

[13]"Constitutional Conundrum," *The Economist,* March 17, 2007, p. 10.

[14]Moon Ihlwan and Kenji Hall, "New Tech, Old Habits," *BusinessWeek,* March 26, 2007 p. 49.

[15]Jigar Shah, "Question Authority," *Fortune,* March 5, 2007, p. 26.

[16]"Five Bags, Checked," *Money,* May 2007, p. 126.

[17]Rachel Emma Silverman, "Divorce: Counting Money Gets Tougher," *The Wall Street Journal,* May 5–6, 2007, p. B1.

6–51. According to *BusinessWeek,* environmental groups are making headway on American campuses. In a survey of 570 schools, 130 were found to incorporate chapters of environmental organizations.[18] Assume this is a random sample of universities and use the reported information to construct a 95% confidence interval for the proportion of all U.S. schools with environmental chapters.

6–5 Confidence Intervals for the Population Variance

In some situations, our interest centers on the population variance (or, equivalently, the population standard deviation). This happens in production processes, queuing (waiting line) processes, and other situations. As we know, the sample variance S^2 is the (unbiased) estimator of the population variance σ^2.

To compute confidence intervals for the population variance, we must learn to use a new probability distribution: the *chi-square distribution.* Chi (pronounced *ki*) is one of two *X* letters in the Greek alphabet and is denoted by χ. Hence, we denote the chi-square distribution by χ^2.

The chi-square distribution, like the *t* distribution, has associated with it a degrees-of-freedom parameter df. In the application of the chi-square distribution to estimation of the population variance, df $= n - 1$ (as with the *t* distribution in its application to sampling for the population mean). Unlike the *t* and the normal distributions, however, the chi-square distribution is not symmetric.

> The **chi-square distribution** is the probability distribution of the sum of several independent, squared standard normal random variables.

As a sum of squares, the chi-square random variable cannot be negative and is therefore bounded on the left by zero. The resulting distribution is skewed to the right. Figure 6–10 shows several chi-square distributions with different numbers of degrees of freedom.

> The mean of a chi-square distribution is equal to the degrees-of-freedom parameter df. The variance of a chi-square distribution is equal to twice the number of degrees of freedom.

Note in Figure 6–10 that as df increases, the chi-square distribution looks more and more like a normal distribution. In fact, as df increases, the chi-square distribution approaches a normal distribution with mean df and variance 2(df).

FIGURE 6–10   Several Chi-Square Distributions with Different Values of the df Parameter

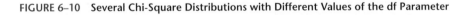

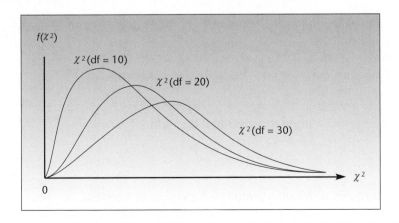

[18]Heather Green, "The Greening of America's Campuses," *BusinessWeek,* April 9, 2007, p. 64.

TABLE 6–2   Values and Probabilities of Chi-Square Distributions

df	0.995	0.990	0.975	0.950	0.900	0.100	0.050	0.025	0.010	0.005
					Area in Right Tail					
1	0.0^4393	0.0^3157	0.0^3982	0.0^2393	0.0158	2.71	3.84	5.02	6.63	7.88
2	0.0100	0.0201	0.0506	0.103	0.211	4.61	5.99	7.38	9.21	10.6
3	0.0717	0.115	0.216	0.352	0.584	6.25	7.81	9.35	11.3	12.8
4	0.207	0.297	0.484	0.711	1.06	7.78	9.49	11.1	13.3	14.9
5	0.412	0.554	0.831	1.15	1.61	9.24	11.1	12.8	15.1	16.7
6	0.676	0.872	1.24	1.64	2.20	10.6	12.6	14.4	16.8	18.5
7	0.989	1.24	1.69	2.17	2.83	12.0	14.1	16.0	18.5	20.3
8	1.34	1.65	2.18	2.73	3.49	13.4	15.5	17.5	20.1	22.0
9	1.73	2.09	2.70	3.33	4.17	14.7	16.9	19.0	21.7	23.6
10	2.16	2.56	3.25	3.94	4.87	16.0	18.3	20.5	23.2	25.2
11	2.60	3.05	3.82	4.57	5.58	17.3	19.7	21.9	24.7	26.8
12	3.07	3.57	4.40	5.23	6.30	18.5	21.0	23.3	26.2	28.3
13	3.57	4.11	5.01	5.89	7.04	19.8	22.4	24.7	27.7	29.8
14	4.07	4.66	5.63	6.57	7.79	21.1	23.7	26.1	29.1	31.3
15	4.60	5.23	6.26	7.26	8.55	22.3	25.0	27.5	30.6	32.8
16	5.14	5.81	6.91	7.96	9.31	23.5	26.3	28.8	32.0	34.3
17	5.70	6.41	7.56	8.67	10.1	24.8	27.6	30.2	33.4	35.7
18	6.26	7.01	8.23	9.39	10.9	26.0	28.9	31.5	34.8	37.2
19	6.84	7.63	8.91	10.1	11.7	27.2	30.1	32.9	36.2	38.6
20	7.43	8.26	9.59	10.9	12.4	28.4	31.4	34.2	37.6	40.0
21	8.03	8.90	10.3	11.6	13.2	29.6	32.7	35.5	38.9	41.4
22	8.64	9.54	11.0	12.3	14.0	30.8	33.9	36.8	40.3	42.8
23	9.26	10.2	11.7	13.1	14.8	32.0	35.2	38.1	41.6	44.2
24	9.89	10.9	12.4	13.8	15.7	33.2	36.4	39.4	43.0	45.6
25	10.5	11.5	13.1	14.6	16.5	34.4	37.7	40.6	44.3	46.9
26	11.2	12.2	13.8	15.4	17.3	35.6	38.9	41.9	45.6	48.3
27	11.8	12.9	14.6	16.2	18.1	36.7	40.1	43.2	47.0	49.6
28	12.5	13.6	15.3	16.9	18.9	37.9	41.3	44.5	48.3	51.0
29	13.1	14.3	16.0	17.7	19.8	39.1	42.6	45.7	49.6	52.3
30	13.8	15.0	16.8	18.5	20.6	40.3	43.8	47.0	50.9	53.7

Table 4 in Appendix C gives values of the chi-square distribution with different degrees of freedom, for given tail probabilities. An abbreviated version of part of the table is given as Table 6–2. We apply the chi-square distribution to problems of estimation of the population variance, using the following property.

In sampling from a normal population, the random variable

$$\chi^2 = \frac{(n-1)s^2}{s^2} \qquad (6\text{–}8)$$

has a chi-square distribution with $n - 1$ degrees of freedom.

The distribution of the quantity in equation 6–8 leads to a confidence interval for σ^2. Since the χ^2 distribution is not symmetric, we cannot use equal values with opposite signs (such as ± 1.96 as we did with Z) and must construct the confidence interval using the two distinct tails of the distribution.

A $(1 - \alpha)$ 100% confidence interval for the population variance σ^2 (where the population is assumed normal) is

$$\left[\frac{(n - 1)s^2}{\chi^2_{\alpha/2}}, \frac{(n - 1)s^2}{\chi^2_{1-\alpha/2}} \right] \qquad (6\text{-}9)$$

where $\chi^2_{\alpha/2}$ is the value of the chi-square distribution with $n - 1$ degrees of freedom that cuts off an area of $\alpha/2$ to its right and $\chi^2_{1-\alpha/2}$ is the value of the distribution that cuts off an area of $\alpha/2$ to its left (equivalently, an area of $1 - \alpha/2$ to its right).

We now demonstrate the use of equation 6–9 with an example.

In an automated process, a machine fills cans of coffee. If the average amount filled is different from what it should be, the machine may be adjusted to correct the mean. If the *variance* of the filling process is too high, however, the machine is out of control and needs to be repaired. Therefore, from time to time regular checks of the variance of the filling process are made. This is done by randomly sampling filled cans, measuring their amounts, and computing the sample variance. A random sample of 30 cans gives an estimate $s^2 = 18,540$. Give a 95% confidence interval for the population variance σ^2.

EXAMPLE 6–5

Figure 6–11 shows the appropriate chi-square distribution with $n - 1 = 29$ degrees of freedom. From Table 6–2 we get, for df = 29, $\chi^2_{0.025} = 45.7$ and $\chi^2_{0.975} = 16.0$. Using these values, we compute the confidence interval as follows:

Solution

$$\left[\frac{29(18,540)}{45.7}, \frac{29(18,540)}{16.0} \right] = [11,765, 33,604]$$

We can be 95% sure that the population variance is between 11,765 and 33,604.

FIGURE 6–11   Values and Tail Areas of a Chi-Square Distribution with 29 Degrees of Freedom

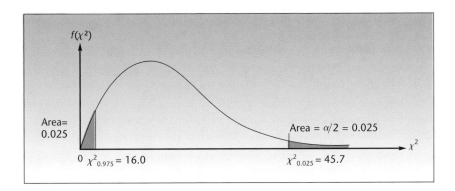

FIGURE 6–12   The Template for Estimating Population Variances
[Estimating Variance.xls; Sheet: Sample Stats]

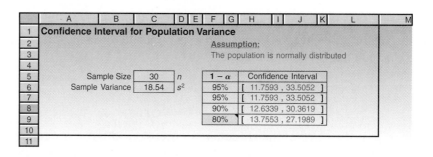

FIGURE 6–13   The Template for Estimating Population Variances
[Estimating Variance.xls; Sheet: Sample Data]

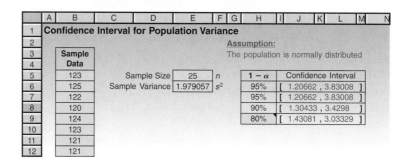

The Template

The workbook named Estimating Variance.xls provides sheets for computing confidence intervals for population variances when

1. The sample statistics are known.
2. The sample data are known.

Figure 6–12 shows the first sheet and Figure 6–13 shows the second. An assumption in both cases is that the population is normally distributed.

PROBLEMS

In the following problems, assume normal populations.

6–52.   The service time in queues should not have a large variance; otherwise, the queue tends to build up. A bank regularly checks service time by its tellers to determine its variance. A random sample of 22 service times (in minutes) gives $s^2 = 8$. Give a 95% confidence interval for the variance of service time at the bank.

6–53.   A sensitive measuring device should not have a large variance in the errors of measurements it makes. A random sample of 41 measurement errors gives $s^2 = 102$. Give a 99% confidence interval for the variance of measurement errors.

6–54.   A random sample of 60 accounts gives a sample variance of 1,228. Give a 95% confidence interval for the variance of all accounts.

6–55.   In problem 6–21, give a 99% confidence interval for the variance of the number of miles that may be driven on a tire.

6–56. In problem 6–25, give a 95% confidence interval for the population of billionaires' worth in dollars.

6–57. In problem 6–26, give a 95% confidence interval for the variance of the caloric content of all 3-ounce cuts of top loin steak.

6–58. In problem 6–27, give a 95% confidence interval for the variance of the transit time for all goods.

6–6 Sample-Size Determination

One of the questions a statistician is most frequently asked before any actual sampling takes place is: "How large should my sample be?" From a *statistical* point of view, the best answer to this question is: "Get as large a sample as you can afford. If possible, 'sample' the entire population." If you need to know the mean or proportion of a population, and you can sample the entire population (i.e., carry out a census), you will have all the information and will know the parameter exactly. Clearly, this is better than any estimate. This, however, is unrealistic in most situations due to economic constraints, time constraints, and other limitations. "Get as large a sample as you can afford" is the best answer if we ignore all costs, because the larger the sample, the smaller the standard error of our statistic. The smaller the standard error, the less uncertainty with which we have to contend. This is demonstrated in Figure 6–14.

When the sampling budget is limited, the question often is how to find the *minimum* sample size that will satisfy some precision requirements. In such cases, you should explain to the designer of the study that he or she must first give you answers to the following three questions:

1. How close do you want your sample estimate to be to the unknown parameter? The answer to this question is denoted by B (for "bound").
2. What do you want the confidence level to be so that the distance between the estimate and the parameter is less than or equal to B?
3. The last, and often misunderstood, question that must be answered is: What is your estimate of the variance (or standard deviation) of the population in question?

Only after you have answers to all three questions can you specify the minimum required sample size. Often the statistician is told: "How can I give you an estimate of the variance? I don't know. You are the statistician." In such cases, try to get from your client some idea about the variation in the population. If the population is approximately normal and you can get 95% bounds on the values in the *population, divide the difference between the upper and lower bounds by* 4; this will give you a rough guess of σ. Or you may take a small, inexpensive *pilot* survey and estimate σ by the sample standard deviation. Once you have obtained the three required pieces of information, all you need to do is to substitute the answers into the appropriate formula that follows:

FIGURE 6–14
Standard Error of a Statistic as a Function of Sample Size

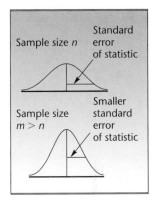

Minimum required sample size in estimating the population mean μ is

$$n = \frac{Z_{\alpha/2}^2 \sigma^2}{B^2} \qquad (6\text{–}10)$$

Minimum required sample size in estimating the population proportion p is

$$n = \frac{Z_{\alpha/2}^2 pq}{B^2} \qquad (6\text{–}11)$$

Equations 6–10 and 6–11 are derived from the formulas for the corresponding confidence intervals for these population parameters based on the normal distribution. In the case of the population mean, B is the half-width of a $(1 - \alpha)$ 100% confidence interval for μ, and therefore

$$B = z_{\alpha/2}\frac{\sigma}{\sqrt{n}} \tag{6-12}$$

Equation 6–10 is the solution of equation 6–12 for the value of n. Note that B is the margin of error. We are solving for the minimum sample size for a given margin of error.

Equation 6–11, for the minimum required sample size in estimating the population proportion, is derived in a similar way. Note that the term pq in equation 6–11 acts as the population variance in equation 6–10. To use equation 6–11, we need a guess of p, the unknown population proportion. Any prior estimate of the parameter will do. When none is available, we may take a pilot sample, or—in the absence of any information—we use the value $p = 0.5$. This value maximizes pq and thus ensures us a minimum required sample size that will work for any value of p.

EXAMPLE 6–6

A market research firm wants to conduct a survey to estimate the average amount spent on entertainment by each person visiting a popular resort. The people who plan the survey would like to be able to determine the average amount spent by all people visiting the resort to within $120, with 95% confidence. From past operation of the resort, an estimate of the population standard deviation is $\sigma = \$400$. What is the minimum required sample size?

Solution   Using equation 6–10, the minimum required sample size is

$$n = \frac{z_{\alpha/2}^2\sigma^2}{B^2}$$

We know that $B = 120$, and σ^2 is estimated at $400^2 = 160,000$. Since we want 95% confidence, $z_{\alpha/2} = 1.96$. Using the equation, we get

$$n = \frac{(1.96)^2 160,000}{120^2} = 42.684$$

Therefore, the minimum required sample size is 43 people (we cannot sample 42.684 people, so we go to the next higher integer).

EXAMPLE 6–7

The manufacturer of a sports car wants to estimate the proportion of people in a given income bracket who are interested in the model. The company wants to know the population proportion p to within 0.10 with 99% confidence. Current company records indicate that the proportion p may be around 0.25. What is the minimum required sample size for this survey?

Using equation 6–11, we get

$$n = \frac{z_{\alpha/2}^2 pq}{B^2} = \frac{(2.576)^2(0.25)(0.75)}{0.10^2} = 124.42$$

The company should, therefore, obtain a random sample of at least 125 people. Note that a different guess of p would have resulted in a different sample size.

PROBLEMS

6–59. What is the required sample size for determining the proportion of defective items in a production process if the proportion is to be known to within 0.05 with 90% confidence? No guess as to the value of the population proportion is available.

6–60. How many test runs of the new Volvo S40 model are required for determining its average miles-per-gallon rating on the highway to within 2 miles per gallon with 95% confidence, if a guess is that the variance of the population of miles per gallon is about 100?

6–61. A company that conducts surveys of current jobs for executives wants to estimate the average salary of an executive at a given level to within $2,000 with 95% confidence. From previous surveys it is known that the variance of executive salaries is about 40,000,000. What is the minimum required sample size?

6–62. Find the minimum required sample size for estimating the average return on real estate investments to within 0.5% per year with 95% confidence. The standard deviation of returns is believed to be 2% per year.

6–63. A company believes its market share is about 14%. Find the minimum required sample size for estimating the actual market share to within 5% with 90% confidence.

6–64. Find the minimum required sample size for estimating the average number of designer shirts sold per day to within 10 units with 90% confidence if the standard deviation of the number of shirts sold per day is about 50.

6–65. Find the minimum required sample size of accounts of the Bechtel Corporation if the proportion of accounts in error is to be estimated to within 0.02 with 95% confidence. A rough guess of the proportion of accounts in error is 0.10.

6–7 The Templates

Optimizing Population Mean Estimates

Figure 6–15 shows the template that can be used for determining minimum sample size for estimating a population mean. Upon entering the three input data—confidence level desired, half-width (B) desired, and the population standard deviation—in the cells C5, C6, and C7, respectively, the minimum required sample size appears in cell C9.

Determining the Optimal Half-Width

Usually, the population standard deviation σ is not known for certain, and we would like to know how sensitive the minimum sample size is to changes in σ. In addition, there is no hard rule for deciding what the half-width B should be. Therefore, a tabulation of the minimum sample size for various values of σ and B will help us to

FIGURE 6–15   The Template for Determining Minimum Sample Size
[Sample Size.xls; Sheet: Population Mean]

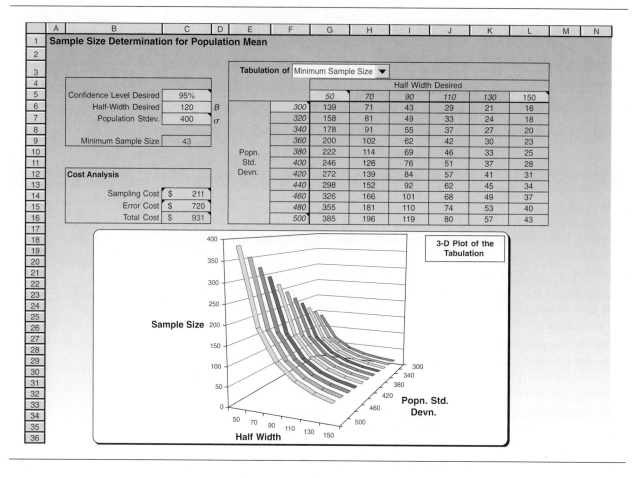

choose a suitable *B*. To create the table, enter the desired starting and ending values of σ in cells F6 and F16, respectively. Similarly, enter the desired starting and ending values for *B* in cells G5 and L5, respectively. The complete tabulation appears immediately. Note that the tabulation pertains to the confidence level entered in cell C5. If this confidence level is changed, the tabulation will be immediately updated.

To visualize the tabulated values a 3-D plot is created below the table. As can be seen from the plot, *the minimum sample size is more sensitive to the half-width* B *than the population standard deviation* σ. That is, when *B* decreases, the minimum sample size increases sharply. This sensitivity emphasizes the issue of how to choose *B*. The natural decision criterion is cost. When *B* is small, the possible error in the estimate is small and therefore the error cost is small. But a small *B* means large sample size, increasing the sampling cost. When *B* is large, the reverse is true. Thus *B* is a compromise between sampling cost and error cost. If cost data are available, an optimal *B* can be found. The template contains features that can be used to find optimal *B*.

The sampling cost formula is to be entered in cell C14. Usually, sampling cost involves a fixed cost that is independent of the sample size and a variable cost that increases linearly with the sample size. The fixed cost would include the cost of planning and organizing the sampling experiment. The variable cost would include the costs of selection, measurement, and recording of each sampled item. For example, if the fixed cost is $125 and the variable cost is $2 per sampled item, then the cost of sampling a total of 43 items will be $125 + $2*43 = $211. In the template, we enter the formula "=125+2*C9" in cell C14, so that the sampling cost appears in cell C14. The instruction for entering the formula appears also in the comment attached to cell C14.

The error cost formula is entered in cell C15. In practice, error costs are more difficult to estimate than sampling costs. Usually, the error cost increases more rapidly than linearly with the amount of error. Often a quadratic formula is suitable for modeling the error cost. In the current case seen in the template, the formula "=0.05*C6^2" has been entered in cell C15. This means the error cost equals $0.05B^2$. Instructions for entering this formula appear in the comment attached to cell C15.

When proper cost formulas are entered in cells C14 and C15, cell C16 shows the total cost. It is possible to tabulate, in place of minimum sample size, the sampling cost, the error cost, or the total cost. You can select what you wish to tabulate using the drop-down box in cell G3.

Using the Solver

By manually adjusting B, we can try to minimize the total cost. Another way to find the optimal B that minimizes the total cost is to use the Solver. Unprotect the sheet and select the Solver command in the Analysis group on the Data tab and click on the Solve button. If the formulas entered in cells C14 and C15 are realistic, the Solver will find a realistic optimal B, and a message saying that an optimal B has been found will appear in a dialog box. Select Keep Solver Solution and press the OK button. In the present case, the optimal B turns out to be 70.4.

For some combinations of sampling and error cost formulas, the Solver may not yield meaningful answers. For example, it may get stuck at a value of zero for B. In such cases, the manual method must be used. At times, it may be necessary to start the Solver with different initial values for B and then take the B value that yields the least total cost.

Note that the total cost also depends on the confidence level (in cell C5) and the population standard deviation (in cell C7). If these values are changed, then the total cost will change and so will the optimal B. The new optimum must be found once again, manually or using the Solver.

Optimizing Population Proportion Estimates

Figure 6–16 shows the template that can be used to determine the minimum sample size required for estimating a population proportion. This template is almost identical to the one in Figure 6–15, which is meant for estimating the population mean. The only difference is that instead of population standard deviation, we have population proportion in cell C7.

The tabulation shows that the minimum sample size increases with population proportion p until p reaches a value of 0.5 and then starts decreasing. Thus, the worst case occurs when p is 0.5.

The formula for error cost currently in cell C15 is "=40000*C6^2." This means the cost equals $40,000B^2$. Notice how different this formula looks compared to the formula $0.05B^2$ we saw in the case of estimating population mean. The coefficient 40,000 is much larger than 0.05. This difference arises because B is a much smaller number in the case of proportions. The formula for sampling cost currently entered in cell C14 is "=125+2*C9" (same as the previous case).

The optimal B that minimizes the total cost in cell C16 can be found using the Solver just as in the case of estimating population mean. Select the Solver command in the Analysis group on the Data tab and press the Solve button. In the current case, the Solver finds the optimal B to be 0.07472.

FIGURE 6–16 The Template for Determining Minimum Sample Size
[Sample Size.xls; Sheet: Population Proportion]

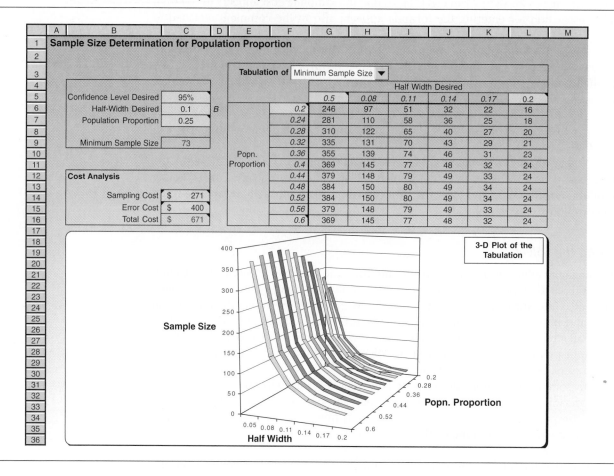

6–8   Using the Computer

Using Excel Built-In Functions for Confidence Interval Estimation

In addition to the Excel templates that were described in this chapter, you can use various statistical functions of Excel to directly build the required confidence intervals. In this section we review these functions.

The function **CONFIDENCE** returns a value that you can use to construct a confidence interval for a population mean. The confidence interval is a range of values. Your sample mean x is at the center of this range and the range is $x \pm$ CONFIDENCE. In the formula CONFIDENCE(alpha, Stdev, Size), *alpha* is the significance level used to compute the confidence level. Thus, the confidence level equals 100*(1 − alpha)%, or, in other words, an alpha of 0.1 indicates a 90% confidence level. *Stdev* is the population standard deviation for the data and is assumed to be known. *Size* is the sample size. The value of alpha should be between zero and one. If Size is not an integer number, it is truncated. As an example, suppose we observe that, in a sample of 40 employees, the average length of travel to work is 20 minutes with a population standard deviation of 3.5. With alpha = .05, CONFIDENCE(.05, 3.5, 40) returns the value 1.084641, so the corresponding confidence interval is 20 ± 1.084641, or [18.915, 21.084].

No function is available for constructing confidence intervals for population proportion or variance per se. But you can use the following useful built-in functions to build the corresponding confidence intervals.

The function **NORMSINV**, which was discussed in Chapter 4, returns the inverse of the standard normal cumulative distribution. For example, NORMSINV(0.975) returns the value 1.95996, or approximately the value of 1.96, which is extensively used for constructing the 95% confidence intervals on the mean. You can use this function to construct confidence intervals on the population mean or population proportion.

The function **TINV** returns the t value of the Student's t distribution as a function of the probability and the degrees of freedom. In the formula TINV(p,df) p is the probability associated with the two-tailed Student's t distribution, and df is the number of degrees of freedom that characterizes the distribution. Note that if df is not an integer, it is truncated. Given a value for probability p, TINV seeks that value t such that P(|T|>t)=P(T>t or T<-t)=p, where T is a random variable that follows the t distribution. You can use TINV for constructing a confidence interval for a population mean when the population standard deviation is not known. For example, for building a 95% confidence interval for the mean of the population assuming a sample of size 15, you need to multiply TINV(0.05, 14) by the sample standard deviation and divide it by the square root of sample size to construct the half width of your confidence interval.

The function **CHIINV** returns the inverse of the one-tailed probability of the chi-squared distribution. You can use this function to construct a confidence interval for the population variance. In the formula CHIINV(p,df), p is a probability associated with the chi-squared distribution, and df is the number of degrees of freedom. Given a value for probability p, CHIINV seeks that value x such that $P(X > x) = p$, where X is a random variable with the chi-square distribution. As an example, CHIINV(0.025, 10) returns the value 20.483.

Using MINITAB for Confidence Interval Estimation

MINITAB can be used for obtaining confidence interval estimates for various population parameters. Let's start by obtaining the confidence interval for the population mean when the population standard deviation is known. In this case start by choosing Stat ▶ Basic Statistics ▶ 1-Sample Z from the menu bar. Then the 1-Sample Z dialog box will appear as shown in Figure 6–17. Enter the name of the column that contains the values of your sample. If you have summarized data of your sample, you

FIGURE 6–17 Confidence Interval on a Population Mean Using MINITAB

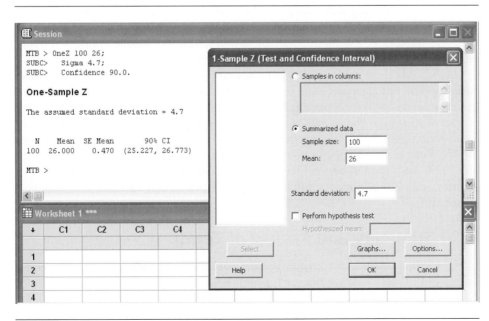

FIGURE 6–18   Confidence Interval on Population Variance Using MINITAB

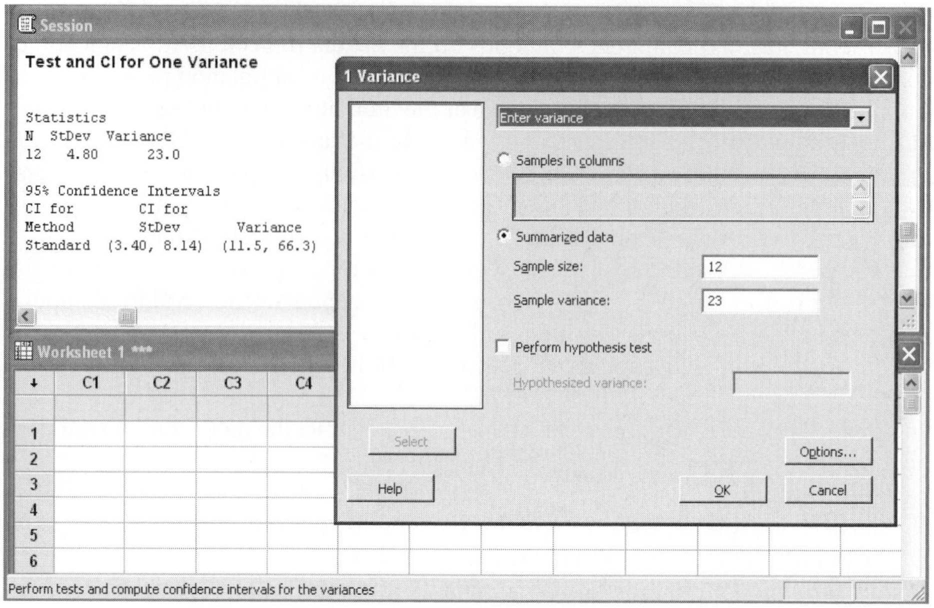

can also enter it in the corresponding section. Enter the value of the population standard deviation in the next box. You can define the desired confidence level of your interval by clicking on the Options button. Then press the OK button. The resulting confidence interval and corresponding Session commands will appear in the Session window as seen in Figure 6–17.

For obtaining the confidence interval for the population mean when the population standard deviation is not known you need to choose Stat ▶ Basic Statistics ▶ 1-Sample t from the menu bar. The setting is the same as the previous dialog box except that you need to determine the sample standard deviation if you choose to enter summarized data of your sample.

MINITAB can also be used for obtaining a confidence interval for a population proportion by selecting Stat ▶ Basic Statistics ▶ 1Proportion from the menu bar. As before, we can define the summarized data of our sample as number of trials (sample size) and number of events (number of samples with the desired condition). After defining the required confidence level press the OK button.

MINITAB also enables you to obtain a confidence interval for the population variance. For this purpose, start by choosing Stat ▶ Basic Statistics ▶ 1 Variance from the menu bar. In the corresponding dialog box, as seen in Figure 6–18, use the drop-down menu to choose whether input values refer to standard deviation or variance. After entering the summarized data or the name of the column that contains the raw data, you can set the desired confidence level by clicking on the Options button. Then press the OK button. The final result, which will be shown in the Session window, contains confidence intervals for both population variance and standard deviation.

6–9   Summary and Review of Terms

In this chapter, we learned how to construct **confidence intervals** for population parameters. We saw how confidence intervals depend on the sampling distributions of the statistics used as estimators. We also encountered two new sampling distributions: the *t* **distribution,** used in estimating the population mean when the population standard deviation is unknown, and the **chi-square distribution,** used in estimating the population variance. The use of either distribution assumes a normal population. We saw how the new distributions, as well as the normal distribution, allow us to construct confidence intervals for population parameters. We saw how to determine the minimum required sample size for estimation.

6-66. Tradepoint, the electronic market set up to compete with the London Stock Exchange, is losing on average $32,000 per day. A potential long-term financial partner for Tradepoint needs a confidence interval for the actual (population) average daily loss, in order to decide whether future prospects for this venture may be profitable. In particular, this potential partner wants to be confident that the true average loss at this period is not over $35,000 per day, which it would consider hopeless. Assume the $32,000 figure given above is based on a random sample of 10 trading days, assume a normal distribution for daily loss, and assume a standard deviation of $s = $6,000$. Construct a 95% confidence interval for the average daily loss in this period. What decision should the potential partner make?

6-67. Landings and takeoffs at Schiphol, Holland, per month are (in 1,000s) as follows:

26, 19, 27, 30, 18, 17, 21, 28, 18, 26, 19, 20, 23, 18, 25, 29, 30, 26, 24, 22, 31, 18, 30, 19

Assume a random sample of months. Give a 95% confidence interval for the average monthly number of takeoffs and landings.

6-68. Thomas Stanley, who surveyed 200 millionaires in the United States for his book *The Millionaire Mind,* found that those in that bracket had an average net worth of $9.2 million. The sample variance was 1.3 million ^{2}. Assuming that the surveyed subjects are a random sample of U.S. millionaires, give a 99% confidence interval for the average net worth of U.S. millionaires.

6-69. The Java computer language, developed by Sun Microsystems, has the advantage that its programs can run on types of hardware ranging from mainframe computers all the way down to handheld computing devices or even smart phones. A test of 100 randomly selected programmers revealed that 71 preferred Java to their other most used computer languages. Construct a 95% confidence interval for the proportion of all programmers in the population from which the sample was selected who prefer Java.

6-70. According to an advertisement in *Worth,* in a survey of 68 multifamily office companies, the average client company had assets of $55.3 million.[19] If this is a result of a random sample and the sample standard deviation was $21.6 million, give a 95% confidence interval for the population average asset value.

6-71. According to the *Wall Street Journal,* an average of 44 tons of carbon dioxide will be saved per year if new, more efficient lamps are used.[20] Assume that this average is based on a random sample of 15 test runs of the new lamps and that the sample standard deviation was 18 tons. Give a 90% confidence interval for average annual savings.

6-72. Finjan is a company that makes a new security product designed to protect software written in the Java programming language against hostile interference. The market for this program materialized recently when Princeton University experts

---

[19] Ad: "The FMO Industry," *Worth,* April 2007, p. 55.

[20] John J. Fialka and Kathryn Kranhold, "Households Would Need New Bulbs to Meet Lighting Efficiency Rules," *The Wall Street Journal,* May 5–6, 2007, p. A1.

showed that a hacker could write misleading applets that fool Java's built-in security rules. If, in 430 trials, the system was fooled 47 times, give a 95% confidence interval for p = probability of successfully fooling the machine.

6–73. Sony's new optical disk system prototype tested and claimed to be able to record an average of 1.2 hours of high-definition TV. Assume $n = 10$ trials and $\sigma = 0.2$ hour. Give a 90% confidence interval.

6–74. The average customer of the Halifax bank in Britain (of whom there are 7.6 million) received $3,600 when the institution changed from a building society to a bank. If this is based on a random sample of 500 customers with standard deviation = $800, give a 95% confidence interval for the average amount paid to any of the 7.6 million bank customers.

6–75. FinAid is a new, free Web site that helps people obtain information on 180,000 college tuition aid awards. A random sample of 500 such awards revealed that 368 were granted for reasons other than financial need. They were based on the applicant's qualifications, interests, and other variables. Construct a 95% confidence interval for the proportion of all awards on this service made for reasons other than financial need.

6–76. In May 2007, a banker was arrested and charged with insider trading after government investigators had secretly looked at a sample of nine of his many trades and found that on these trades he had made a total of $7.5 million.[21] Compute the average earning per trade. Assume also that the sample standard deviation was $0.5 million and compute a 95% confidence interval for the average earning per trade for all trades made by this banker. Use the assumption that the nine trades were randomly selected.

6–77. In problem 6–76, suppose the confidence interval contained the value 0.00. How could the banker's attorney use this information to defend his client?

6–78. A small British computer-game firm, Eidos Interactive PLC, stunned the U.S.- and Japan-dominated market for computer games when it introduced Lara Croft, an Indiana Jones-like adventuress. The successful product took two years to develop. One problem was whether Lara should have a swinging ponytail, which was decided after taking a poll. If in a random sample of 200 computer-game enthusiasts, 161 thought she should have a swinging ponytail (a computer programmer's nightmare to design), construct a 95% confidence interval for the proportion in this market. If the decision to incur the high additional programming cost was to be made if $p > 0.90$, was the right decision made (when Eidos went ahead with the ponytail)?

6–79. In a survey, *Fortune* rated companies on a 0 to 10 scale. A random sample of 10 firms and their scores is as follows.[22]

   FedEx 8.94, Walt Disney 8.76, CHS 8.67, McDonald's 7.82, CVS 6.80, Safeway 6.57, Starbucks 8.09, Sysco 7.42, Staples 6.45, HNI 7.29.

Construct a 95% confidence interval for the average rating of a company on *Fortune*'s entire list.

6–80. According to a survey published in the *Financial Times,* 56% of executives at Britain's top 500 companies are less willing than they had been five years ago to sacrifice their family lifestyle for their career. If the survey consisted of a random sample of 40 executives, give a 95% confidence interval for the proportion of executives less willing to sacrifice their family lifestyle.

6–81. Fifty years after the birth of duty-free shopping at international airports and border-crossing facilities, the European commission announced plans to end this form of business. A study by Cranfield University was carried out to estimate the average

[21]Eric Dash, "Banker Jailed in Trading on 9 Deals," *The New York Times,* May 4, 2007, p. C1.

[22]Anne Fisher, "America's Most Admired Companies," *Fortune,* March 19, 2007, pp. 88–115.

percentage rise in airline landing charges that would result as airlines try to make up for the loss of on-board duty-free shopping revenues. The study found the average increase to be 60%. If this was based on a random sample of 22 international flights and the standard deviation of increase was 25%, give a 90% confidence interval for the average increase.

6–82. When NYSE, NASDAQ, and the British government bonds market were planning to change prices of shares and bonds from powers of 2, such as 1/2, 1/4, 1/8, 1/16, 1/32, to decimals (hence $1/32 = 0.03125$), they decided to run a test. If the test run of trading rooms using the new system revealed that 80% of the traders preferred the decimal system and the sample size was 200, give a 95% confidence interval for the percentage of all traders who will prefer the new system.

6–83. A survey of 5,250 business travelers worldwide conducted by OAG Business Travel Lifestyle indicated that 91% of business travelers consider legroom the most important in-flight feature. (Angle of seat recline and food service were second and third, respectively.) Give a 95% confidence interval for the proportion of all business travelers who consider legroom the most important feature.

6–84. Use the following random sample of suitcase prices to construct a 90% confidence interval for the average suitcase price.[23]

$285, 110, 495, 119, 450, 125, 250, 320

6–85. According to *Money*, 60% of men have significant balding by age 50.[24] If this finding is based on a random sample of 1,000 men of age 50, give a 95% confidence interval for the population of men of 50 who show some balding.

6–86. An estimate of the average length of pins produced by an automatic lathe is wanted to within 0.002 inch with a 95% confidence level. σ is guessed to be 0.015 inch.

  a. What is the minimum sample size?

  b. If the value of σ may be anywhere between 0.010 and 0.020 inch, tabulate the minimum sample size required for σ values from 0.010 to 0.020 inch.

  c. If the cost of sampling and testing n pins is $(25 + 6n)$ dollars, tabulate the costs for σ values from 0.010 to 0.020 inch.

6–87. Wells Fargo Bank, based in San Francisco, offered the option of applying for a loan over the Internet. If a random sample of 200 test runs of the service reveal an average of 8 minutes to fill in the electronic application and standard deviation = 3 minutes, construct a 75% confidence interval for μ.

6–88. An estimate of the percentage defective in a lot of pins supplied by a vendor is desired to within 1% with a 90% confidence level. The actual percentage defective is guessed to be 4%.

  a. What is the minimum sample size?

  b. If the actual percentage defective may be anywhere between 3% and 6%, tabulate the minimum sample size required for actual percentage defective from 3% to 6%.

  c. If the cost of sampling and testing n pins is $(25 + 6n)$ dollars, tabulate the costs for the same percentage defective range as in part (*b*).

6–89. The lengths of pins produced by an automatic lathe are normally distributed. A random sample of 20 pins gives a sample mean of 0.992 inch and a sample standard deviation of 0.013 inch.

  a. Give a 95% confidence interval for the average lengths of all pins produced.

  b. Give a 99% confidence interval for the average lengths of all pins produced.

---

[23]Charles Passy, "Field Test," *Money,* May 2007, p. 127.

[24]Patricia B. Gray, "Forever Young," *Money,* March 2007, p. 94.

6–90.   You take a random sample of 100 pins from the lot supplied by the vendor and test them. You find 8 of them defective. What is the 95% confidence interval for percentage defective in the lot?

6–91.   A statistician estimates the 90% confidence interval for the mean of a normally distributed population as 172.58 ± 3.74 at the end of a sampling experiment, assuming a known population standard deviation. What is the 95% confidence interval?

6–92.   A confidence interval for a population mean is to be estimated. The population standard deviation σ is guessed to be anywhere from 14 to 24. The half-width B desired could be anywhere from 2 to 7.

    a. Tabulate the minimum sample size needed for the given ranges of σ and B.

    b. If the fixed cost of sampling is $350 and the variable cost is $4 per sample, tabulate the sampling cost for the given ranges of σ and B.

    c. If the cost of estimation error is given by the formula $10B^2$, tabulate the total cost for the given ranges of σ and B. What is the value of B that minimizes the total cost when $\sigma = 14$? What is the value of B that minimizes the total cost when $\sigma = 24$?

6–93.   A marketing manager wishes to estimate the proportion of customers who prefer a new packaging of a product to the old. He guesses that 60% of the customers would prefer the new packaging. The manager wishes to estimate the proportion to within 2% with 90% confidence. What is the minimum required sample size?

6–94.   According to *Money,* a survey of 1,700 executives revealed that 51% of them would likely choose a different field if they could start over.[25] Construct a 95% confidence interval for the proportion of all executives who would like to start over, assuming the sample used was random and representative of all executives.

6–95.   According to *Shape,* on the average, 1/2 cup of edamame beans contains 6 grams of protein.[26] If this conclusion is based on a random sample of 50 half-cups of edamames and the sample standard deviation is 3 grams, construct a 95% confidence interval for the average amount of protein in 1/2 cup of edamames.

---

[25]Jean Chatzky, "To Invent the New You, Don't Bankrupt Old You," *Money,* May 2007, p. 30.

[26]Susan Learner Barr, "Smart Eating," *Shape,* June 2007, p. 202.

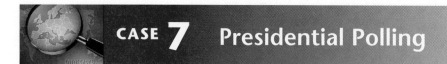

CASE 7   Presidential Polling

A company wants to conduct a telephone survey of randomly selected voters to estimate the proportion of voters who favor a particular candidate in a presidential election, to within 2% error with 95% confidence. It is guessed that the proportion is 53%.

1. What is the required minimum sample size?
2. The project manager assigned to the survey is not sure about the actual proportion or about the 2%

error limit. The proportion may be anywhere from 40% to 60%. Construct a table for the minimum sample size required with half-width ranging from 1% to 3% and actual proportion ranging from 40% to 60%.

3. Inspect the table produced in question 2 above. Comment on the relative sensitivity of the minimum sample size to the actual proportion and to the desired half-width.

4. At what value of the actual proportion is the required sample size the maximum?

5. The cost of polling includes a fixed cost of $425 and a variable cost of $1.20 per person sampled, thus the cost of sampling n voters is $(425 + 1.20n)$. Tabulate the cost for range of values as in question 2 above.

6. A competitor of the company that had announced results to within $\pm 3\%$ with 95% confidence has started to announce results to within $\pm 2\%$ with 95% confidence. The project manager wants to go one better by improving the company's estimate to be within $\pm 1\%$ with 95% confidence. What would you tell the manager?

CASE 8   Privacy Problem

A business office has private information about its customers. A manager finds it necessary to check whether the workers inadvertently give away any private information over the phone. To estimate the percentage of times that a worker does give away such information, an experiment is proposed. At a randomly selected time, a call will be placed to the office and the caller will ask several routine questions. The caller will intersperse the routine questions with three questions (attempts) that ask for private information that should not be given out. The caller will note how many attempts were made and how many times private information was given away.

The true proportion of the times that private information is given away during an attempt is guessed to be 7%. The cost of making a phone call, including the caller's wages, is $2.25. This cost is per call, or per three attempts. Thus the cost per attempt is $0.75. In addition, the fixed cost to design the experiment is $380.

1. What is the minimum sample size (of attempts) if the proportion is to be estimated within $\pm 2\%$ with 95% confidence? What is the associated total cost?

2. What is the minimum sample size if the proportion is to be estimated within $\pm 1\%$ with 95% confidence? What is the associated total cost?

3. Prepare a tabulation and a plot of the total cost as the desired accuracy varies from $\pm 1\%$ to $\pm 3\%$ and the population proportion varies from 5% to 10%.

4. If the caller can make as many as five attempts in one call, what is the total cost for $\pm 2\%$ accuracy with 95% confidence? Assume that cost per call and the fixed cost do not change.

5. If the caller can make as many as five attempts in one call, what is the total cost for $\pm 1\%$ accuracy with 95% confidence? Assume that the cost per call and the fixed cost do not change.

6. What are the problems with increasing the number of attempts in one call?

HYPOTHESIS TESTING

7–1   Using Statistics   257
7–2   The Concepts of Hypothesis Testing   260
7–3   Computing the *p*-Value   265
7–4   The Hypothesis Test   272
7–5   Pretest Decisions   289
7–6   Using the Computer   298
7–7   Summary and Review of Terms   300
Case 9   Tiresome Tires I   301

LEARNING OBJECTIVES

After studying this chapter, you should be able to:

- Explain why hypothesis testing is important.
- Describe the role of sampling in hypothesis testing.
- Identify type I and type II errors and discuss how they conflict with each other.
- Interpret the confidence level, the significance level, and the power of a test.
- Compute and interpret *p*-values.
- Determine the sample size and significance level for a given hypothesis test.
- Use templates for *p*-value computations.
- Plot power curves and operating characteristic curves using templates.

On June 18, 1964, a woman was robbed while walking home along an alley in San Pedro, California. Some time later, police arrested Janet Collins and charged her with the robbery. The interesting thing about this case of petty crime is that the prosecution had *no* direct evidence against the defendant. Janet Collins was convicted of robbery on purely statistical grounds.

The case, *People v. Collins,* drew much attention because of its use of probability—or, rather, what was perceived as a probability—in determining guilt. An instructor of mathematics at a local college was brought in by the prosecution and testified as an expert witness in the trial. The instructor "calculated the probability" that the defendant was a person *other* than the one who committed the crime as 1 in 12,000,000. This led the jury to convict the defendant.

The Supreme Court of California later reversed the guilty verdict against Janet Collins when it was shown that the method of calculating the probability was incorrect. The mathematics instructor had made some very serious errors.[1]

Despite the erroneous procedure used in deriving the probability, and the justified reversal of the conviction by the Supreme Court of California, the *Collins* case serves as an excellent analogy for statistical hypothesis testing. Under the U.S. legal system, the accused is assumed innocent until proved guilty "beyond a reasonable doubt." We will call this the *null hypothesis*—the hypothesis that the accused is *innocent.* We will hold the null hypothesis as true until a time when we can prove, beyond a reasonable doubt, that it is false and that the *alternative hypothesis*—the hypothesis that the accused is guilty—is true. We want to have a small probability (preferably *zero*) of convicting an innocent person, that is, of rejecting a null hypothesis when the null hypothesis is actually true.

In the *Collins* case, the prosecution claimed that the accused was guilty since, otherwise, an event with a very small probability had just been observed. The argument was that if Collins were *not* guilty, then another woman fitting her exact characteristics had committed the crime. According to the prosecution, the probability of this event was 1/12,000,000, and since the probability was so small, Collins was very likely the person who committed the robbery.

The *Collins* case illustrates **hypothesis testing,** an important application of statistics. A *thesis* is something that has been proven to be true. A *hypothesis* is something that has not yet been proven to be true. Hypothesis testing is the process of determining whether or not a given hypothesis is true. Most of the time, a hypothesis is tested through statistical means that use the concepts we learned in previous chapters.

The Null Hypothesis

The first step in a hypothesis test is to formalize it by specifying the *null hypothesis*.

A **null hypothesis** is an assertion about the value of a population parameter. It is an assertion that we hold as true unless we have sufficient statistical evidence to conclude otherwise.

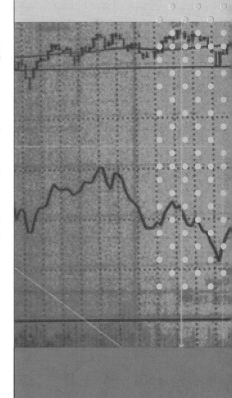

---

[1]The instructor *multiplied* the probabilities of the separate events comprising the reported description of the robber: the event that a woman has blond hair, the event that she drives a yellow car, the event that she is seen with an African-American man, the event that the man has a beard. Recall that the probability of the intersection of several events is equal to the product of the probabilities of the separate events *only* if the events are independent. In this case, there was no reason to believe that the events were independent. There were also some questions about how the separate "probabilities" were actually derived since they were presented by the instructor with no apparent justification. See W. Fairley and F. Mosteller, "A Conversation about Collins," *University of Chicago Law Review* 41, no. 2 (Winter 1974), pp. 242–53.

For example, a null hypothesis might assert that the population mean is equal to 100. Unless we obtain sufficient evidence that it is not 100, we will accept it as 100. We write the null hypothesis compactly as

$$H_0: \mu = 100$$

where the symbol H_0 denotes the null hypothesis.

The **alternative hypothesis** is the *negation* of the null hypothesis.

For the null hypothesis $\mu = 100$, the alternative hypothesis is $\mu \neq 100$. We will write it as

$$H_1: \mu \neq 100$$

using the symbol H_1 to denote the alternative hypothesis.[2] Because the null and alternative hypotheses assert exactly opposite statements, only one of them can be true. Rejecting one is equivalent to accepting the other.

Hypotheses about other parameters such as population proportion or population variance are also possible. In addition, a hypothesis may assert that the parameter in question is at least or at most some value. For example, the null hypothesis may assert that the population proportion p is *at least* 40%. In this case, the null and alternative hypotheses are

$$H_0: p \geq 40\%$$
$$H_1: p < 40\%$$

Yet another example is where the null hypothesis asserts that the population variance is *at most* 50. In this case

$$H_0: \sigma^2 \leq 50$$
$$H_1: \sigma^2 > 50$$

Note that in all cases the equal to sign appears in the null hypothesis.

Although the idea of a null hypothesis is simple, determining what the null hypothesis should be in a given situation may be difficult. Generally what the statistician aims to prove is the alternative hypothesis, the null hypothesis standing for the status quo, do-nothing situation.

---

[2]In some books, the symbol H_a is used for alternative hypothesis.

A vendor claims that his company fills any accepted order, on the average, in at most six working days. You suspect that the average is greater than six working days and want to test the claim. How will you set up the null and alternative hypotheses?

EXAMPLE 7–1

The claim is the null hypothesis and the suspicion is the alternative hypothesis. Thus, with μ denoting the average time to fill an order,

Solution

$$H_0: \mu \leq 6 \text{ days}$$
$$H_1: \mu > 6 \text{ days}$$

A manufacturer of golf balls claims that the variance of the weights of the company's golf balls is controlled to within 0.0028 oz^2. If you wish to test this claim, how will you set up the null and alternative hypotheses?

EXAMPLE 7–2

The claim is the null hypothesis. Thus, with σ^2 denoting the variance,

Solution

$$H_0: \sigma^2 \leq 0.0028 \text{ oz}^2$$
$$H_1: \sigma^2 > 0.0028 \text{ oz}^2$$

At least 20% of the visitors to a particular commercial Web site where an electronic product is sold are said to end up ordering the product. If you wish to test this claim, how will you set up the null and alternative hypotheses?

EXAMPLE 7–3

With p denoting the proportion of visitors ordering the product,

Solution

$$H_0: p \geq 0.20$$
$$H_1: p < 0.20$$

PROBLEMS

7–1. A pharmaceutical company claims that four out of five doctors prescribe the pain medicine it produces. If you wish to test this claim, how would you set up the null and alternative hypotheses?

7–2. A medicine is effective only if the concentration of a certain chemical in it is at least 200 parts per million (ppm). At the same time, the medicine would produce an undesirable side effect if the concentration of the same chemical exceeds 200 ppm. How would you set up the null and alternative hypotheses to test the concentration of the chemical in the medicine?

7–3. It is found that Web surfers will lose interest in a Web page if downloading takes more than 12 seconds at 28K baud rate. If you wish to test the effectiveness of a newly designed Web page in regard to its download time, how will you set up the null and alternative hypotheses?

7–4.   The average cost of a traditional open-heart surgery is claimed to be, $49,160. If you suspect that the claim exaggerates the cost, how would you set up the null and alternative hypotheses?

7–5.   During the sharp increase in gasoline prices in the summer of the year 2006, oil companies claimed that the average price of unleaded gasoline with minimum octane rating of 89 in the Midwest was not more than $3.75. If you want to test this claim, how would you set up the null and alternative hypotheses?

7–2   The Concepts of Hypothesis Testing

We said that a null hypothesis is held as true unless there is sufficient evidence against it. When can we say that we have sufficient evidence against it and thus reject it? This is an important and difficult question. Before we can answer it we have to understand several preliminary concepts.

Evidence Gathering

After the null and alternative hypotheses are spelled out, the next step is to gather evidence. The best evidence is, of course, data that leave no uncertainty at all. If we could measure the whole population and calculate the exact value of the population parameter in question, we would have perfect evidence. Such evidence is perfect in that we can check the null hypothesis against it and be 100% confident in our conclusion that the null hypothesis is or is not true. But in all real-world cases, the evidence is gathered from a random sample of the population. In the rest of this chapter, unless otherwise specified, the evidence is from a random sample.

An important limitation of making inferences from sample data is that we cannot be 100% confident about it. How confident we can be depends on the sample size and parameters such as the population variance. In view of this fact, the sampling experiment for evidence gathering must be carefully designed. Among other considerations, the sample size needs to be large enough to yield a desired confidence level and small enough to contain the cost. We will see more details of sample size determination later in this chapter.

Type I and Type II Errors

CHAPTER 11

In our professional and personal lives we often have to make an accept–reject type of decision based on incomplete data. An inspector has to accept or reject a batch of parts supplied by a vendor, usually based on test results of a random sample. A recruiter has to accept or reject a job applicant, usually based on evidence gathered from a résumé and interview. A bank manager has to accept or reject a loan application, usually based on financial data on the application. A person who is single has to accept or reject a suitor's proposal of marriage, perhaps based on the experiences with the suitor. A car buyer has to buy or not buy a car, usually based on a test drive. As long as such decisions are made based on evidence that does not provide 100% confidence, there will be chances for error. No error is committed when a good prospect is accepted or a bad one is rejected. But there is a small chance that a bad prospect is accepted or a good one is rejected. Of course, we would like to minimize the chances of such errors.

In the context of statistical hypothesis testing, rejecting a true null hypothesis is known as a **type I error** and accepting[3] a false null hypothesis is known as a **type II error.** (Unfortunately, these names are unimaginative and nondescriptive. Because they are nondescriptive, you have to memorize which is which.) Table 7–1 shows the instances of type I and type II errors.

---

[3]Later we will see that "not rejecting" is a more accurate term than "accepting."

TABLE 7–1   Instances of Type I and Type II Errors

	H_0 True	H_0 False
Accept H_0	No error	Type II error
Reject H_0	Type I error	No error

Let us see how we can minimize the chances of type I and type II errors. Is it possible, even with imperfect sample evidence, to reduce the probability of type I error all the way down to zero? The answer is yes. Just accept the null hypothesis, no matter what the evidence is. Since you will never reject any null hypothesis, you will never reject a true null hypothesis and thus you will never commit a type I error! We immediately see that this would be foolish. Why? If we always accept a null hypothesis, then given a false null hypothesis, no matter how wrong it is, we are sure to accept it. In other words, our probability of committing a type II error will be 1. Similarly, it would be foolish to reduce the probability of type II error all the way to zero by always rejecting a null hypothesis, for we would then reject every true null hypothesis, no matter how right it is. Our probability of type I error will be 1.

The lesson is that we should not try to completely avoid either type of error. We should plan, organize, and settle for some small, optimal probability of each type of error. Before we can address this issue, we need to learn a few more concepts.

The p-Value

Suppose the null and alternative hypotheses are

$$H_0: \mu \geq 1{,}000$$
$$H_1: \mu < 1{,}000$$

A random sample of size 30 yields a sample mean of only 999. Because the sample mean is less than 1,000, the evidence goes against the null hypothesis (H_0). Can we reject H_0 based on this evidence? Immediately we realize the dilemma. If we reject it, there is some chance that we might be committing a type I error, and if we accept it, there is some chance that we might be committing a type II error. A natural question to ask at this situation is, What is the probability that H_0 can still be true despite the evidence? The question asks for the "credibility" of H_0 in light of unfavorable evidence. Unfortunately, due to mathematical complexities, computing the probability that H_0 is true is impossible. We therefore settle for a question that comes very close. Recall that $H_0: \mu \geq 1{,}000$. We ask,

> When the actual $\mu = 1{,}000$, and with sample size 30, what is the probability of getting a sample mean that is less than or equal to 999?

The answer to this question is then taken as the "credibility rating" of H_0. Study the question carefully. There are two aspects to note:

1. The question asks for the probability of the evidence being as unfavorable or more unfavorable to H_0. The reason is that in the case of continuous distributions, probabilities can be calculated only for a range of values. Here we pick a range for the sample mean that disfavors H_0, namely, less than or equal to 999.

2. The condition assumed is $\mu = 1,000$, although H_0 states $\mu \geq 1,000$. The reason for assuming $\mu = 1,000$ is that *it gives the most benefit of doubt to H_0.* If we assume $\mu = 1,001$, for instance, the probability of the sample mean being less than or equal to 999 will only be smaller, and H_0 will only have less credibility. Thus the assumption $\mu = 1,000$ gives the maximum credibility to H_0.

Suppose the answer to the question is 26%. That is, there is a 26% chance for a sample of size 30 to yield a sample mean less than or equal to 999 when the actual $\mu = 1,000$. Statisticians call this 26% the **p-value.** As mentioned before, the p-value is a kind of "credibility rating" of H_0 in light of the evidence. The formal definition of the p-value follows:

> Given a null hypothesis and sample evidence with sample size n, the **p-value** is the probability of getting a sample evidence that is equally or more unfavorable to the null hypothesis while the null hypothesis is actually true. The p-value is calculated giving the null hypothesis the maximum benefit of doubt.

Most people in most circumstances would consider a 26% chance of committing a type I error to be too high and would not reject H_0. That is understandable. Now consider another scenario where the sample mean was 998 rather than 999. Here the evidence is more unfavorable to the null hypothesis. Hence there will be less credibility to H_0 and the p-value will be smaller. Suppose the new p-value is 2%, meaning that H_0 has only 2% credibility. Can we reject H_0 now? We clearly see a need for a *policy* for rejecting H_0 based on p-value. Let us see the most common policy.

The Significance Level

The most common policy in statistical hypothesis testing is to establish a **significance level,** denoted by α, and to reject H_0 when the p-value falls below it. When this policy is followed, one can be sure that the maximum probability of type I error is α.

Rule: When the p-value is less than α, reject H_0.

The standard values for α are 10%, 5%, and 1%. Suppose α is set at 5%. This means that whenever the p-value is less than 5%, H_0 will be rejected. In the preceding example, for a sample mean of 999 the p-value was 26%, and H_0 will not be rejected. For a sample mean of 998 the p-value was 2%, which has fallen below $\alpha = 5\%$. Hence H_0 will be rejected.

Let us see in more detail the implications of using a significance level α for rejecting a null hypothesis. The first thing to note is that *if we do not reject H_0, this does not prove that H_0 is true.* For example, if $\alpha = 5\%$ and the p-value $= 6\%$, we will not reject H_0. But the credibility of H_0 is only 6%, which is hardly proof that H_0 is true. It may very well be that H_0 is false and by not rejecting it, we are committing a type II error. For this reason, under these circumstances we should say "We cannot reject H_0 at an α of 5%" rather than "We accept H_0."

The second thing to note is that α is the maximum probability of type I error we set for ourselves. Since α is the maximum p-value at which we reject H_0, it is the maximum probability of committing a type I error. In other words, setting $\alpha = 5\%$ means that we are willing to put up with up to 5% chance of committing a type I error.

The third thing to note is that the selected value of α indirectly determines the probability of type II error as well. Consider the case of setting $\alpha = 0$. Although this may appear good because it reduces the probability of type I error to zero, this corresponds to the foolish case we already discussed: never rejecting H_0. Every H_0, no matter how

FIGURE 7–1   Probability of Type II Error versus α for the Case H_0: $\mu \geq 1,000$, $\sigma = 10$, $n = 30$, Assumed μ for Type II Error = 994

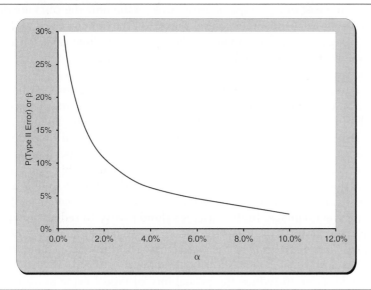

wrong it is, is accepted and thus the probability of type II error becomes 1. To decrease the probability of type II error we have to increase α. In general, *other things remaining the same, increasing the value of α will decrease the probability of type II error.* This should be intuitively obvious. For example, increasing α from 5% to 10% means that in those instances with a *p*-value in the range 5% to 10% the H_0 that would not have been rejected before would now be rejected. Thus, some cases of false H_0 that escaped rejection before may not escape now. As a result, the probability of type II error will decrease.

Figure 7–1 is a graph of the probability of type II error versus α, for a case where H_0: $\mu \geq 1,000$, the evidence is from a sample of size 30, and the probability of type II error is calculated for the case $\mu = 994$. Notice how the probability of type II error decreases as α increases. That the probability of type II error decreases is good news. But as α increases, the probability of type I error increases. That is bad news. This brings out the important compromise between type I and type II errors. If we set a low value for α, we enjoy a low probability of type I error but suffer a high probability of type II error; if we set a high value for α, we will suffer a high probability of type I error but enjoy a low probability of type II error. Finding an optimal α is a difficult task. We will address the difficulties in the next subsection.

Our final note about α is the meaning of $(1 - \alpha)$. If we set $\alpha = 5\%$, then $(1 - \alpha) = 95\%$ is the minimum **confidence level** that we set in order to reject H_0. In other words, we want to be *at least* 95% confident that H_0 is false before we reject it. This concept of confidence level is the same that we saw in the previous chapter. It should explain why we use the symbol α for the significance level.

Optimal α and the Compromise between Type I and Type II Errors

Setting the value of α affects both type I and type II error probabilities as seen in Figure 7–1. But this figure is only one snapshot of a much bigger picture. In the figure, the type II error probability corresponds to the case where the actual $\mu = 994$. But the actual μ can be any one of an infinite number of possible values. For each one of those values, the graph will be different. In addition, the graph is only for a sample size of 30. When the sample size changes, so will the curve. This is the first difficulty in trying to find an optimal α.

Moreover, we note that selecting a value for α is a question of compromise between type I and type II error probabilities. To arrive at a fair compromise we should know the cost of each type of error. Most of the time the costs are difficult to estimate since they depend, among other things, on the unknown actual value of the parameter being tested. Thus, arriving at a "calculated" optimal value for α is impractical. Instead, we follow an intuitive approach of assigning one of the three standard values, 1%, 5%, and 10%, to α.

In the intuitive approach, we try to estimate the relative costs of the two types of errors. For example, suppose we are testing the average tensile strength of a large batch of bolts produced by a machine to see if it is above the minimum specified. Here type I error will result in rejecting a good batch of bolts and the cost of the error is roughly equal to the cost of the batch of bolts. Type II error will result in accepting a bad batch of bolts and its cost can be high or low depending on how the bolts are used. If the bolts are used to hold together a structure, then the cost is high because defective bolts can result in the collapse of the structure, causing great damage. In this case, we should strive to reduce the probability of type II error more than that of type I error. *In such cases where type II error is more costly, we keep a large value for α, namely, 10%.* On the other hand, if the bolts are used to secure the lids on trash cans, then the cost of type II error is not high and we should strive to reduce the probability of type I error more than that of type II error. *In such cases where type I error is more costly, we keep a small value for α, namely, 1%.*

Then there are cases where we are not able to determine which type of error is more costly. *If the costs are roughly equal, or if we have not much knowledge about the relative costs of the two types of errors, then we keep $\alpha = 5\%$.*

β *and Power*

The symbol used for the probability of type II error is β. Note that β depends on the actual value of the parameter being tested, the sample size, and α. Let us see exactly how it depends. In the example plotted in Figure 7–1, if the actual μ is 993 rather than 994, H_0 would be "even more wrong." This should make it easier to detect that it is wrong. Therefore, the probability of type II error, or β, will decrease. If the sample size increases, then the evidence becomes more reliable and the probability of any error, including β, will decrease. As Figure 7–1 depicts, as α increases, β decreases. Thus, β is affected by several factors.

The complement of β $(1 - \beta)$ is known as the *power* of the test.

> The **power** of a test is the probability that a false null hypothesis will be detected by the test.

You can see how α and β as well as $(1 - \alpha)$ and $(1 - \beta)$ are counterparts of each other and how they apply respectively to type I and type II errors. In a later section, we will see more about β and power.

Sample Size

Figure 7–1 depicts how α and β are related. In the discussion above we said that we can keep a low α or a low β depending on which type of error is more costly. What if both types of error are costly and we want to have low α as well as low β? The only way to do this is to make our evidence more reliable, which can be done only by increasing the sample size. Figure 7–2 shows the relationship between α and β for various values of the sample size n. As n increases, the curve shifts downward, reducing both α and β. Thus, when the costs of both types of error are high, the best policy is to have a large sample and a low α, such as 1%.

FIGURE 7–2   β versus α for Various Values of n
[*Taken from* Testing Population Mean.xls; Sheet: Beta vs. Alpha]

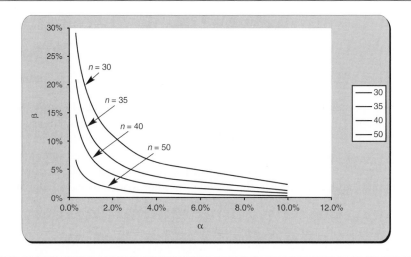

In this section, we have seen a number of important concepts about hypothesis testing. The mechanical details of computations, templates, and formulas remain. You must have a clear understanding of all the concepts discussed before proceeding. If necessary, reread this entire section.

PROBLEMS

7–6.   What is the power of a hypothesis test? Why is it important?

7–7.   How is the power of a hypothesis test related to the significance level α?

7–8.   How can the power of a hypothesis test be increased without increasing the sample size?

7–9.   Consider the use of metal detectors in airports to test people for concealed weapons. In essence, this is a form of hypothesis testing.

   a. What are the null and alternative hypotheses?

   b. What are type I and type II errors in this case?

   c. Which type of error is more costly?

   d. Based on your answer to part (*c*), what value of α would you recommend for this test?

   e. If the sensitivity of the metal detector is increased, how would the probabilities of type I and type II errors be affected?

   f. If α is to be increased, should the sensitivity of the metal detector be increased or decreased?

7–10.   When planning a hypothesis test, what should be done if the probabilities of both type I and type II errors are to be small?

7–3   Computing the *p*-Value

We will now examine the details of calculating the *p*-value. Recall that given a null hypothesis and sample evidence, the *p*-value is the probability of getting evidence that is equally or more unfavorable to H_0. Using what we have already learned in the previous two chapters, this probability can be calculated for hypotheses regarding population mean, proportion, and variance.

The Test Statistic

Consider the case

$$H_0: \mu \geq 1,000$$
$$H_1: \mu < 1,000$$

Suppose the population standard deviation σ is known and a random sample of size $n \geq 30$ is taken and the sample mean $\overline{X}$ is calculated. From sampling theory we know that when $\mu = 1,000$, $\overline{X}$ will be normally distributed with mean 1,000 and standard deviation $\sigma/\sqrt{n}$. This implies that $(\overline{X} - 1,000)/(\sigma/\sqrt{n})$ will follow a standard normal distribution, or Z distribution. Since we know the Z distribution well, we can calculate any probability and, in particular, the p-value. In other words, by calculating first

$$Z = \frac{\overline{X} - 1,000}{\sigma/\sqrt{n}}$$

we can then calculate the p-value and decide whether or not to reject H_0. Since the test result boils down to checking just one value, the value of Z, we call Z the *test statistic* in this case.

> A **test statistic** is a random variable calculated from the sample evidence, which follows a well-known distribution and thus can be used to calculate the p-value.

Most of the time, the test statistic we see in this book will be Z, t, χ^2, or F. The distributions of these random variables are well known and spreadsheet templates can be used to calculate the p-value.

p-Value Calculations

Once again consider the case

$$H_0: \mu \geq 1,000$$
$$H_1: \mu < 1,000$$

Suppose the population standard deviation σ is known and a random sample of size $n \geq 30$ is taken. This means $Z = (\overline{X} - 1,000)/(\sigma/\sqrt{n})$ is the test statistic. If the sample mean $\overline{X}$ is 1,000 or more, we have nothing against H_0 and we will not reject it. But if $\overline{X}$ is less than 1,000, say 999, then the evidence disfavors H_0 and we have reason to suspect that H_0 is false. If $\overline{X}$ decreases below 999, it becomes even more unfavorable to H_0. Thus the p-value when $\overline{X} = 999$ is the probability that $\overline{X} \leq 999$. This probability is the shaded area shown in Figure 7–3. But the usual practice is to calculate the probability using the distribution of the test statistic Z. So let us switch to the Z statistic.

Suppose the population standard deviation σ is 5 and the sample size n is 100. Then

$$Z = \frac{\overline{X} - 1,000}{\sigma/\sqrt{n}} = \frac{999 - 1,000}{5/\sqrt{100}} = -2.00$$

FIGURE 7–3 The *p*-Value Shaded in the Distribution of $\overline{X}$

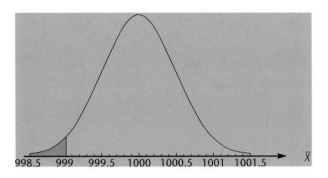

FIGURE 7–4 The *p*-Value Shaded in the Distribution of the Test Statistic *Z* where H_0: $\mu \geq 1,000$

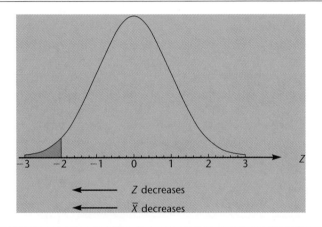

Thus the *p*-value $= P(Z < -2.00)$. See Figure 7–4, in which the probability is shaded. The figure also shows the direction in which $\overline{X}$ and *Z* decrease. The probability $P(Z < -2.00)$ can be calculated from the tables or using a spreadsheet template. We will see full details of the templates later. For now, let us use the tables. From the standard normal distribution table, the *p*-value is $0.5 - 0.4772 = 0.0228$, or 2.28%. This means H_0 will be rejected when α is 5% or 10% but will not be rejected when α is 1%.

One-Tailed and Two-Tailed Tests

Let us repeat the null and alternative hypotheses for easy reference:

$$H_0: \mu \geq 1,000$$
$$H_1: \mu < 1,000$$

In this case, only when $\overline{X}$ is significantly less than 1,000 will we reject H_0, or only when *Z* falls significantly below zero will we reject H_0. Thus the rejection occurs only when *Z* takes a significantly low value in the *left tail* of its distribution. Such a case where rejection occurs in the left tail of the distribution of the test statistic is called a **left-tailed test,** as seen in Figure 7–5. At the bottom of the figure the direction in which *Z*, $\overline{X}$, and the *p*-value decrease is shown.

FIGURE 7–5   A Left-Tailed Test: The Rejection Region for H_0: $\mu \geq 1,000$; $\alpha = 5\%$

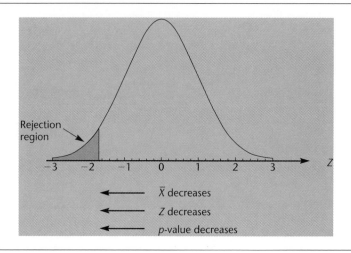

FIGURE 7–6   A Right-Tailed Test: The Rejection Region for H_0: $\mu \leq 1,000$; $\alpha = 5\%$

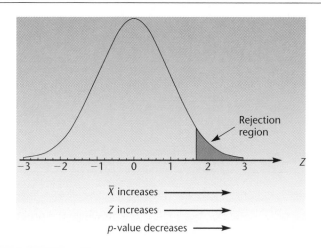

In the case of a left-tailed test, the p*-value is the area to the left of the calculated value of the test statistic.* The case we saw above is a good example. Suppose the calculated value of Z is -2.00. Then the area to the left of it, using tables, is $0.5 - 0.4772 = 0.0228$, or the p-value is 2.28%.

Now consider the case where H_0: $\mu \leq 1,000$. Here rejection occurs when $\overline{X}$ is significantly greater than 1,000 or Z is significantly greater than zero. In other words, rejection occurs on the right tail of the Z distribution. This case is therefore called a **right-tailed test,** as seen in Figure 7–6. At the bottom of the figure the direction in which the p-value decreases is shown.

In the case of a right-tailed test, the p*-value is the area to the right of the calculated value of the test statistic.* Suppose the calculated $z = +1.75$. Then the area to the right of it, using tables, is $0.5 - 0.4599 = 0.0401$, or the p-value is 4.01%.

In left-tailed and right-tailed tests, rejection occurs only on one tail. Hence each of them is called a **one-tailed test.**

Finally, consider the case H_0: $\mu = 1,000$. In this case, we have to reject H_0 in both cases, that is, whether $\overline{X}$ is significantly less than or greater than 1,000. Thus, rejection occurs when Z is significantly less than or greater than zero, which is to say that

FIGURE 7-7   A Two-Tailed Test: Rejection Region for H$_0$: μ = 1,000, α = 5%

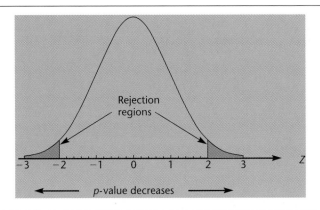

rejection occurs on both tails. Therefore, this case is called a **two-tailed test.** See Figure 7–7, where the shaded areas are the rejection regions. As shown at the bottom of the figure, the p-value decreases as the calculated value of test statistic moves away from the center in either direction.

In the case of a two-tailed test, the p*-value is twice the tail area. If the calculated value of the test statistic falls on the left tail, then we take the area to the left of the calculated value and multiply it by 2. If the calculated value of the test statistic falls on the right tail, then we take the area to the right of the calculated value and multiply it by 2.* For example, if the calculated $z = +1.75$, the area to the right of it is 0.0401. Multiplying that by 2, we get the p-value as 0.0802.

In a hypothesis test, the test statistic $Z = -1.86$.

EXAMPLE 7–4

1. Find the p-value if the test is (a) left-tailed, (b) right-tailed, and (c) two-tailed.
2. In which of these three cases will H$_0$ be rejected at an α of 5%?

1. (a) The area to the left of -1.86, from the tables, is $0.5 - 0.4686 = 0.0314$, or the p-value is 3.14%. (b) The area to the right of -1.86, from the tables, is $0.5 + 0.4686 = 0.9686$, or the p-value is 96.86%. (Such a large p-value means that the evidence greatly favors H$_0$, and there is no basis for rejecting H$_0$.) (c) The value -1.86 falls on the left tail. The area to the left of -1.86 is 3.14%. Multiplying that by 2, we get 6.28%, which is the p-value.
2. Only in the case of a left-tailed test does the p-value fall below the α of 5%. Hence that is the only case where H$_0$ will be rejected.

Solution

Computing β

In this section we shall see how to compute β, the probability of type II error. We consider the null and alternative hypotheses:

$$H_0: \mu \geq 1,000$$
$$H_1: \mu < 1,000$$

Let $\sigma = 5$, $\alpha = 5\%$, and $n = 100$. We wish to compute β when $\mu = \mu_1 = 998$.

FIGURE 7–8   Computing β for a Left-Tailed Test

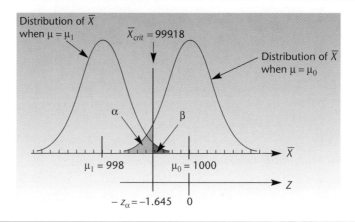

We will use Figure 7–8, which shows the distribution of $\overline{X}$ when $\mu = \mu_0 = 1,000$ and when $\mu = \mu_1 = 998$. First we note that H_0 will be rejected whenever $\overline{X}$ is less than the critical value given by

$$\overline{X}_{\text{crit}} = \mu_0 - z_\alpha \sigma/\sqrt{n} = 1,000 - 1.645 * 5/\sqrt{100} = 999.18$$

CHAPTER 11

Conversely, H_0 will not be rejected whenever $\overline{X}$ is greater than $\overline{X}_{\text{crit}}$. When $\mu = \mu_1 = 998$, β will be the probability of not rejecting H_0, which therefore equals $P(\overline{X} > \overline{X}_{\text{crit}})$. Also, when $\mu = \mu_1$, $\overline{X}$ will follow a normal distribution with mean μ_1 and standard deviation $= \sigma/\sqrt{n}$. Thus

$$\beta = P\left[Z > \frac{\overline{X}_{\text{crit}} - \mu_1}{\sigma/\sqrt{n}}\right] = P(Z > 1.18/0.5) = P(Z > 2.36) = 0.0091$$

The power is the complement of β. For this example, power $= 1 - 0.0091 = 0.9909$. The power and β can also be calculated using the template shown in Figure 7–22.

Note that β is 0.0091 only when $\mu = 998$. If μ is greater than 998, say, 999, what will happen to β? Referring to Figure 7–8, you can see that the distribution of $\overline{X}$ when $\mu = 999$ will be to the right of the one shown for 998. $\overline{X}_{\text{crit}}$ will remain where it is. As a result, β will increase.

Figure 7–9 shows a similar figure for a right-tailed test with

$$H_0: \mu \leq 1,000$$
$$H_1: \mu > 1,000$$

and with $\sigma = 5$, $\alpha = 5\%$, $n = 100$. The figure shows β when $\mu = 1,002$.

Figure 7–10 shows β for a two-tailed test with

$$H_0: \mu = 1,000$$
$$H_1: \mu \neq 1,000$$

and with $\sigma = 5$, $\alpha = 5\%$, $n = 100$. The figure shows β when $\mu = \mu_1 = 1,000.2$.

FIGURE 7–9   β for a Right-Tailed Test

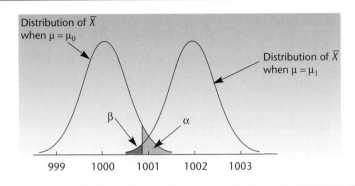

FIGURE 7–10   β for a Two-Tailed Test

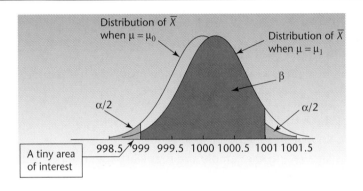

A tiny area of interest is seen in Figure 7–10 on the left tail of the distribution of $\overline{X}$ when $\mu = \mu_1$. It is the area where H_0 is rejected because $\overline{X}$ is significantly smaller than 1,000. The true μ, though, is more than 1,000, namely, 1,000.2. That is to say, H_0 is false because μ is more than 1,000 and thus it deserves to be rejected. It is indeed rejected but the reason for rejection is that the evidence suggests μ is smaller than 1,000. The tiny area thus marks the chances of rejecting a false H_0 through faulty evidence.

PROBLEMS

7–11.   For each one of the following null hypotheses, determine if it is a left-tailed, a right-tailed, or a two-tailed test.

    a. $\mu \geq 10$.

    b. $p \leq 0.5$.

    c. μ is at least 100.

    d. $\mu \leq -20$.

    e. p is exactly 0.22.

    f. μ is at most 50.

    g. $\sigma^2 = 140$.

7–12.   The calculated z for a hypothesis test is -1.75. What is the p-value if the test is (*a*) left-tailed, (*b*) right-tailed, and (*c*) two-tailed?

7–13. In which direction of $\overline{X}$ will the *p*-value decrease for the null hypotheses (*a*) $\mu \geq 10$, (*b*) $\mu \leq 10$, and (*c*) $\mu = 10$?

7–14. What is a test statistic? Why do we have to know the distribution of the test statistic?

7–15. The null hypothesis is $\mu \leq 12$. The test statistic is Z. Assuming that other things remain the same, will the *p*-value increase or decrease when (*a*) $\overline{X}$ increases, (*b*) σ increases, and (*c*) n increases?

7–4 The Hypothesis Test

We now consider the three common types of hypothesis tests:

1. Tests of hypotheses about population means.
2. Tests of hypotheses about population proportions.
3. Tests of hypotheses about population variances.

Let us see the details of each type of test and the templates that can be used.

Testing Population Means

CHAPTER 9

When the null hypothesis is about a population mean, the test statistic can be either Z or t. There are two cases in which it will be Z.

Cases in Which the Test Statistic Is Z
 1. σ is known and the population is normal.
 2. σ is known and the sample size is at least 30. (The population need not be normal.)

The normality of the population may be established by direct tests or the normality may be assumed based on the nature of the population. Recall that if a random variable is affected by many independent causes, then it can be assumed to be normally distributed.

The formula for calculating Z is

$$Z = \frac{\overline{X} - \mu}{\sigma / \sqrt{n}}$$

The value of μ in this equation is the claimed value that gives the maximum benefit of doubt to the null hypothesis. For example, if H_0: $\mu \geq 1,000$, we use the value of 1,000 in the equation. Once the Z value is known, the *p*-value is calculated using tables or the template described below.

Cases in Which the Test Statistic Is t
The population is normal and σ is unknown but the sample standard deviation S is known.

In this case, as we saw in the previous chapter, the quantity $(\overline{X} - \mu)/(S/\sqrt{n})$ will follow a t distribution with $(n - 1)$ degrees of freedom. Thus

$$t = \frac{\overline{X} - \mu}{S / \sqrt{n}}$$

becomes the test statistic. The value of μ used in this equation is the claimed value that gives the maximum benefit of doubt to the null hypothesis. For example, if H_0: $\mu \geq 1,000$, then we use the value of 1,000 for μ in the equation for calculating t.

A Note on t Tables and p-Values

Since the t table provides only the critical values, it cannot be used to find exact p-values. We have to use the templates described below or use other means of calculation. If we do not have access to the templates or other means, then the critical values found in the tables can be used to infer the *range* within which the p-value will fall. For example, if the calculated value of t is 2.000 and the degrees of freedom are 24, we see from the tables that $t_{0.05}$ is 1.711 and $t_{0.025}$ is 2.064. Thus, the one-tailed p-value corresponding to $t = 2.000$ must be somewhere between 0.025 and 0.05, but we don't know its exact value. Since the exact p-value for a hypothesis test is generally desired, it is advisable to use the templates.

A careful examination of the cases covered above, in which Z or t is the test statistic, reveals that a few cases do not fall under either category.

V S

CHAPTER 5

Cases Not Covered by the Z or t Test Statistic

1. The population is not normal and σ is unknown. (Many statisticians will be willing to accept a t test here, as long as the sample size is "large enough." The size is large enough if it is at least 30 in the case of populations believed to be not very skewed. If the population is known to be very skewed, then the size will have to be correspondingly larger.)

2. The population is not normal and the sample size is less than 30.

3. The population is normal and σ is unknown. Whoever did the sampling provided only the sample mean $\overline{X}$ but not the sample standard deviation S. The sample data are also not provided and thus S cannot be calculated. (Obviously, this case is rare.)

Using templates to solve hypothesis testing problems is always a better alternative. But to understand the computation process, we shall do one example manually with Z as the test statistic.

EXAMPLE 7–5

An automatic bottling machine fills cola into 2-liter (2,000-cm^3) bottles. A consumer advocate wants to test the null hypothesis that the average amount filled by the machine into a bottle is at least 2,000 cm^3. A random sample of 40 bottles coming out of the machine was selected and the exact contents of the selected bottles are recorded. The sample mean was 1,999.6 cm^3. The population standard deviation is known from past experience to be 1.30 cm^3.

1. Test the null hypothesis at an α of 5%.
2. Assume that the population is normally distributed with the same σ of 1.30 cm^3. Assume that the sample size is only 20 but the sample mean is the same 1,999.6 cm^3. Conduct the test once again at an α of 5%.
3. If there is a difference in the two test results, explain the reason for the difference.

Solution

1.	
	H_0: $\mu \geq 2,000$
	H_1: $\mu < 2,000$

Since σ is known and the sample size is more than 30, the test statistic is Z. Then

$$z = \frac{\bar{x} - \mu}{\sigma/\sqrt{n}} = \frac{1{,}999.6 - 2{,}000}{1.30/\sqrt{40}} = -1.95$$

Using the table for areas of Z distribution, the p-value $= 0.5000 - 0.4744 = 0.0256$, or 2.56%. Since this is less than the α of 5%, we reject the null hypothesis.

2. Since the population is normally distributed, the test statistic is once again Z:

$$z = \frac{\bar{x} - \mu}{\sigma/\sqrt{n}} = \frac{1{,}999.6 - 2{,}000}{1.30/\sqrt{20}} = -1.38$$

Using the table for areas of Z distribution, the p-value $= 0.5000 - 0.4162 = 0.0838$, or 8.38%. Since this is greater than the α of 5%, we do not reject the null hypothesis.

3. In the first case we could reject the null hypothesis but in the second we could not, although in both cases the sample mean was the same. The reason is that in the first case the sample size was larger and therefore the evidence against the null hypothesis was more reliable. This produced a smaller p-value in the first case.

The Templates

Figure 7–11 shows the template that can be used to test hypotheses about population means when sample statistics are known (rather than the raw sample data). The top portion of the template is used when σ is known and the bottom portion when σ is unknown. On the top part, entries have been made to solve Example 7–5, part 1. The p-value of 0.0258 in cell G13 is read off as the answer to the problem. This answer is more accurate than the value of 0.0256 manually calculated using tables.

Correction for finite population is possible in the panel on the right. It is applied when $n/N > 1\%$. If no correction is needed, it is better to leave the cell K8, meant for the population size N, blank to avoid causing distraction.

Note that the hypothesized value entered in cell F12 is copied into cells F13 and F14. Only cell F12 is unlocked and therefore that is the only place where the hypothesized value of μ can be entered regardless of which null hypothesis we are interested in.

Once a value for α is entered in cell H11, the "Reject" message appears wherever the p-value is less than the α. All the templates on hypothesis testing work in this manner. In the case shown in Figure 7–11, the appearance of "Reject" in cell H13 means that the null hypothesis $\mu \geq 2{,}000$ is to be rejected at an α of 5%.

Figure 7–12 shows the template that can be used to test hypotheses about population means, when the sample data are known. Sample data are entered in column B. Correction for finite population is possible in the panel on the right.

EXAMPLE 7–6

A bottling machine is to be tested for accuracy of the amount it fills in 2-liter bottles. The null hypothesis is $\mu = 2{,}000$ cm³. A random sample of 37 bottles is taken and the contents are measured. The data are shown below. Conduct the test at an α of 5%.

1. Assume $\sigma = 1.8$ cm³. What is the test statistic and what is its value? What is the p-value?

FIGURE 7–11   Testing Hypotheses about Population Means Using Sample Statistics
               [Testing Population Mean.xls; Sheet: Sample Stats]

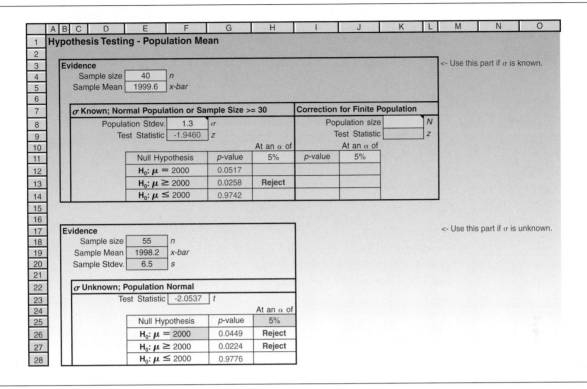

FIGURE 7–12   Testing Hypotheses about Population Means Using Sample Data
               [Testing Population Mean.xls; Sheet: Sample Data]

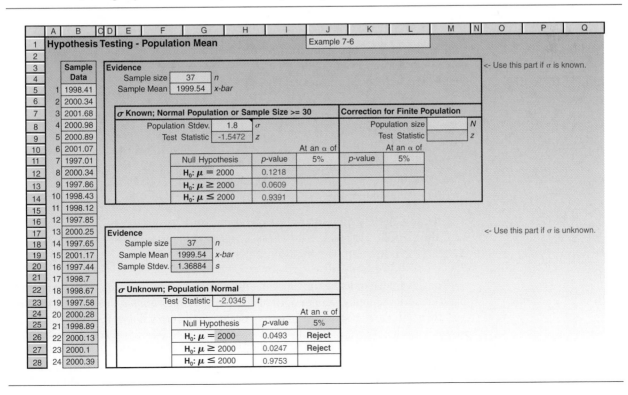

2. Assume σ is not known and the population is normal. What is the test statistic and what is its value? What is the p-value?

3. Looking at the answers to parts 1 and 2, comment on any difference in the two results.

Sample Data

1998.41	1998.12	1998.89	2001.68
2000.34	1997.85	2000.13	2000.76
2001.68	2000.25	2000.1	1998.53
2000.98	1997.65	2000.39	1998.24
2000.89	2001.17	2001.27	1998.18
2001.07	1997.44	1998.98	2000.67
1997.01	1998.7	2000.21	2001.11
2000.34	1998.67	2000.36	
1997.86	1997.58	2000.17	
1998.43	2000.28	1998.67	

Solution　Open the template shown in Figure 7–12. Enter the data in column B. To answer part 1, use the top panel. Enter 1.8 for σ in cell H8, 2000 in cell H12, and 5% in cell J11. Since cell J12 is blank, the null hypothesis cannot be rejected. The test statistic is Z, and its value of -1.5472 appears in cell H9. The p-value is 0.1218, as seen in cell I12.

To answer part 2, use the bottom panel. Enter 2000 in cell H26 and 5% in cell J25. Since cell J26 says "Reject," we reject the null hypothesis. The test statistic is t, and its value of -2.0345 appears in cell H23. The p-value is 0.0493, as seen in cell I26.

The null hypothesis is not rejected in part 1, but is rejected in part 2. The main difference is that the sample standard deviation of 1.36884 (in cell G20) is less than the 1.8 used in part 1. This makes the value of the test statistic $t = -2.0345$ in part 2, significantly different from $Z = -1.5472$ in part 1. As a result, the p-value falls below 5% in part 2 and the null hypothesis is rejected.

Testing Population Proportions

Hypotheses about population proportions can be tested using the binomial distribution or normal approximation to calculate the p-value. The cases in which each approach is to be used are detailed below.

Cases in Which the Binomial Distribution Can Be Used

The binomial distribution can be used whenever we are able to calculate the necessary binomial probabilities. This means for calculations using tables, the sample size n and the population proportion p should have been tabulated. For calculations using spreadsheet templates, sample sizes up to 500 are feasible.

Cases in Which the Normal Approximation Is to Be Used

If the sample size n is too large (> 500) to calculate binomial probabilities, then the normal approximation method is to be used.

The advantage of using the binomial distribution, and therefore of this template, is that it is more accurate than the normal approximation. *When the binomial distribution is used, the number of successes X serves as the test statistic.* The p-value is the appropriate tail area, determined by X, of the binomial distribution defined by n and the hypothesized value of population proportion p. Note that X follows a *discrete* distribution, and recall that the p-value is the probability of the test statistic being *equally or more unfavorable to H_0 than* the value obtained from the evidence. As an example, consider a right-tailed test with $H_0: p \leq 0.5$. For this case, the p-value $= P(X \geq$ observed number of successes).

A coin is to be tested for fairness. It is tossed 25 times and only 8 heads are observed. Test if the coin is fair at $\alpha = 5\%$.

EXAMPLE 7-7

Let p denote the probability of getting a head, which must be 0.5 for a fair coin. Hence the null and alternative hypotheses are

Solution

$$H_0: p = 0.5$$
$$H_1: p \neq 0.5$$

Because this is a two-tailed test, the p-value $= 2*P(X \leq 8)$. From the binomial distribution table (Appendix C, Table 1), this value is $2*0.054 = 0.108$. Since this value is more than the α of 5%, we cannot reject the null hypothesis. (For the use of the template to solve this problem, see Figure 7–13.)

Figure 7–13 shows the template that can be used to test hypotheses regarding population proportions using the binomial distribution. *This template will work only for sample sizes up to approximately 500.* Beyond that, the template that uses normal approximation (shown in Figure 7–14) should be used. The data entered in Figure 7–13 correspond to Example 7–7.

FIGURE 7–13 Testing Population Proportion Using the Binomial Distribution
[Testing Population Proportion.xls; Sheet: Binomial]

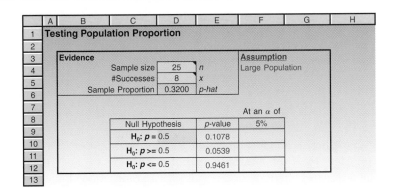

FIGURE 7–14 A Normal Distribution Template for Testing Population Proportion
[Testing Population Proportion.xls; Sheet: Normal]

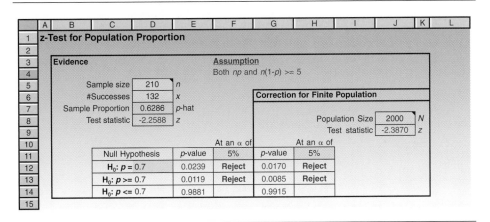

FIGURE 7–15   The Template for Testing Population Variances
[Testing Population Variance.xls; Sheet: Sample Stats]

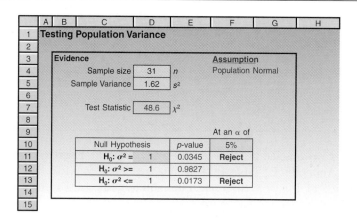

Figure 7–14 shows the template that can be used to test hypotheses regarding population means using normal distribution. The test statistic is Z defined by

$$Z = \frac{\hat{p} - p_0}{\sqrt{p_0(1 - p_0)/n}}$$

where p_0 is the hypothesized value for the proportion, $\hat{p}$ is the sample proportion, and n is the sample size. A correction for finite population can also be applied in this case. The correction is based on the hypergeometric distribution, and is applied if the sample size is more than 1% of the population size. If a correction is not needed, it is better to leave the cell J8, meant for population size N, blank to avoid any distraction.

Testing Population Variances

For testing hypotheses about population variances, the test statistic is $\chi^2 = (n - 1)S^2/\sigma_0^2$. Here σ_0 is the claimed value of population variance in the null hypothesis. The degrees of freedom for this χ^2 is $(n - 1)$. Since the χ^2 table provides only the critical values, it cannot be used to calculate exact p-values. As in the case of t tables, only a range of possible values can be inferred. Use of a spreadsheet template is therefore better for this test. Figure 7–15 shows the template that can be used for testing hypotheses regarding population variances when sample statistics are known.

CHAPTER 5
CHAPTER 9

EXAMPLE 7–8

A manufacturer of golf balls claims that the company controls the weights of the golf balls accurately so that the variance of the weights is not more than 1 mg². A random sample of 31 golf balls yields a sample variance of 1.62 mg². Is that sufficient evidence to reject the claim at an α of 5%?

Solution   The null and alternative hypotheses are

$$H_0: \sigma^2 \leq 1$$
$$H_1: \sigma^2 > 1$$

FIGURE 7–16   The Template for Testing Population Variances with Raw Sample Data
[Testing Population Variance.xls; Sheet: Sample Data]

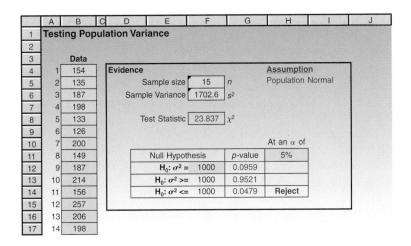

In the template (see Figure 7–15), enter 31 for sample size and 1.62 for sample variance. Enter the hypothesized value of 1 in cell D11. The p-value of 0.0173 appears in cell E13. Since this value is less than the α of 5%, we reject the null hypothesis. This conclusion is also confirmed by the "Reject" message appearing in cell F13 with 5% entered in cell F10.

Figure 7–16 shows the template that can be used to test hypotheses regarding population variances when the sample data are known. The sample data are entered in column B.

7–16.   An automobile manufacturer substitutes a different engine in cars that were known to have an average miles-per-gallon rating of 31.5 on the highway. The manufacturer wants to test whether the new engine changes the miles-per-gallon rating of the automobile model. A random sample of 100 trial runs gives $\bar{x} = 29.8$ miles per gallon and $s = 6.6$ miles per gallon. Using the 0.05 level of significance, is the average miles-per-gallon rating on the highway for cars using the new engine different from the rating for cars using the old engine?

7–17.   In controlling the quality of a new drug, a dose of medicine is supposed to contain an average of 247 parts per million (ppm) of a certain chemical. If the concentration is higher than 247 ppm, the drug may cause some side effects; and if the concentration is below 247 ppm, the drug may be ineffective. The manufacturer wants to check whether the average concentration in a large shipment is the required 247 ppm or not. A random sample of 60 portions is tested, and the sample mean is found to be 250 ppm and the sample standard deviation 12 ppm. Test the null hypothesis that the average concentration in the entire large shipment is 247 ppm versus the alternative hypothesis that it is not 247 ppm using a level of significance $\alpha = 0.05$. Do the same using $\alpha = 0.01$. What is your conclusion? What is your decision about the shipment? If the shipment were guaranteed to contain an average concentration of 247 ppm, what would your decision be, based on the statistical hypothesis test? Explain.

7–18.   The Boston Transit Authority wants to determine whether there is any need for changes in the frequency of service over certain bus routes. The transit authority needs to know whether the frequency of service should increase, decrease, or remain the same. The transit authority determined that if the average number of miles traveled by bus over the routes in question by all residents of a given area is about 5 per day, then no change will be necessary. If the average number of miles traveled per person per day is either more than 5 or less than 5, then changes in service may be necessary. The authority wants, therefore, to test the null hypothesis that the average number of miles traveled per person per day is 5.0 versus the alternative hypothesis that the average is not 5.0 miles. The required level of significance for this test is $\alpha = 0.05$. A random sample of 120 residents of the area is taken, and the sample mean is found to be 2.3 miles per resident per day and the sample standard deviation 1.5 miles. Advise the authority on what should be done. Explain your recommendation. Could you state the same result at different levels of significance? Explain.

7–19.   Many recent changes have affected the real estate market.[4] A study was undertaken to determine customer satisfaction from real estate deals. Suppose that before the changes, the average customer satisfaction rating, on a scale of 0 to 100, was 77. A survey questionnaire was sent to a random sample of 50 residents who bought new plots after the changes in the market were instituted, and the average satisfaction rating for this sample was found to be $\bar{x} = 84$; the sample standard deviation was found to be $s = 28$. Use an α of your choice, and determine whether statistical evidence indicates a change in customer satisfaction. If you determine that a change did occur, state whether you believe customer satisfaction has improved or deteriorated.

7–20.   According to *Money*, the average appreciation, in percent, for stocks has been 4.3% for the five-year period ending in May 2007.[5] An analyst tests this claim by looking at a random sample of 50 stocks and finds a sample mean of 3.8% and a sample standard deviation of 1.1%. Using $\alpha = 0.05$, does the analyst have statistical evidence to reject the claim made by the magazine?

7–21.   A certain commodity is known to have a price that is stable through time and does not change according to any known trend. Price, however, does change from day to day in a random fashion. If the price is at a certain level one day, it is as likely to be at any level the next day within some probability bounds approximately given by a normal distribution. The mean daily price is believed to be $14.25. To test the hypothesis that the average price is $14.25 versus the alternative hypothesis that it is not $14.25, a random sample of 16 daily prices is collected. The results are $\bar{x} = \$16.50$ and $s = \$5.8$. Using $\alpha = 0.05$, can you reject the null hypothesis?

7–22.   Average total daily sales at a small food store are known to be $452.80. The store's management recently implemented some changes in displays of goods, order within aisles, and other changes, and it now wants to know whether average sales volume has changed. A random sample of 12 days shows $\bar{x} = \$501.90$ and $s = \$65.00$. Using $\alpha = 0.05$, is the sampling result significant? Explain.

7–23.   New software companies that create programs for World Wide Web applications believe that average staff age at these companies is 27. To test this two-tailed hypothesis, a random sample is collected:

> 41, 18, 25, 36, 26, 35, 24, 30, 28, 19, 22, 22, 26, 23, 24, 31, 22, 22, 23, 26, 27, 26, 29, 28, 23, 19, 18, 18, 24, 24, 24, 25, 24, 23, 20, 21, 21, 21, 21, 32, 23, 21, 20

Test, using $\alpha = 0.05$.

7–24.   A study was undertaken to evaluate how stocks are affected by being listed in the Standard & Poor's 500 Index. The aim of the study was to assess average excess returns

---

[4]Elizabeth Harris, "Luxury Real Estate Investment," *Worth,* April 2007, p. 73.

[5]Marlys Harris, "Real Estate vs. Stocks," *Money,* May 2007, p. 94.

for these stocks, above returns on the market as a whole. The average excess return on *any* stock is zero because the "average" stock moves with the market as a whole. As part of the study, a random sample of 13 stocks newly included in the S&P 500 Index was selected. Before the sampling takes place, we allow that average "excess return" for stocks newly listed in the Standard & Poor's 500 Index may be either positive or negative; therefore, we want to test the null hypothesis that average excess return is equal to zero versus the alternative that it is not zero. If the excess return on the sample of 13 stocks averaged 3.1% and had a standard deviation of 1%, do you believe that inclusion in the Standard & Poor's 500 Index changes a stock's excess return on investment, and if so, in which direction? Explain. Use $\alpha = 0.05$.

7-25.   A new chemical process is introduced by Duracell in the production of lithium-ion batteries. For batteries produced by the old process, the average life of a battery is 102.5 hours. To determine whether the new process affects the average life of the batteries, the manufacturer collects a random sample of 25 batteries produced by the new process and uses them until they run out. The sample mean life is found to be 107 hours, and the sample standard deviation is found to be 10 hours. Are these results significant at the $\alpha = 0.05$ level? Are they significant at the $\alpha = 0.01$ level? Explain. Draw your conclusion.

7-26.   Average soap consumption in a certain country is believed to be 2.5 bars per person per month. *The standard deviation of the population is known to be* $\sigma = 0.8$. While the standard deviation is not believed to have changed (and this may be substantiated by several studies), the mean consumption may have changed either upward or downward. A survey is therefore undertaken to test the null hypothesis that average soap consumption is still 2.5 bars per person per month versus the alternative that it is not. A sample of size $n = 20$ is collected and gives $\bar{x} = 2.3$. The population is assumed to be normally distributed. What is the appropriate test statistic in this case? Conduct the test and state your conclusion. Use $\alpha = 0.05$. Does the choice of level of significance change your conclusion? Explain.

7-27.   According to *Money,* which not only looked at stocks (as in problem 7-20) but also compared them with real estate, the average appreciation for all real estate sold in the five years ending May 2007 was 12.4% per year. To test this claim, an analyst looks at a random sample of 100 real estate deals in the period in question and finds a sample mean of 14.1% and a sample standard deviation of 2.6%. Conduct a two-tailed test using the 0.05 level of significance.

7-28.   Suppose that the Goodyear Tire Company has historically held 42% of the market for automobile tires in the United States. Recent changes in company operations, especially its diversification to other areas of business, as well as changes in competing firms' operations, prompt the firm to test the validity of the assumption that it still controls 42% of the market. A random sample of 550 automobiles on the road shows that 219 of them have Goodyear tires. Conduct the test at $\alpha = 0.01$.

7-29.   The manufacturer of electronic components needs to inform its buyers of the proportion of defective components in its shipments. The company has been stating that the percentage of defectives is 12%. The company wants to test whether the proportion of all components that are defective is as claimed. A random sample of 100 items indicates 17 defectives. Use $\alpha = 0.05$ to test the hypothesis that the percentage of defective components is 12%.

7-30.   According to *BusinessWeek,* the average market value of a biotech company is less than $250 million.[6] Suppose that this indeed is the alternative hypothesis you want to prove. A sample of 30 firms reveals an average of $235 million and a standard deviation of $85 million. Conduct the test at $\alpha = 0.05$ and $\alpha = 0.01$. State your conclusions.

---

[6]Arlene Weintraub, "Biotech's Unlikely New Pal," *BusinessWeek,* March 26, 2007, p. 116.

7–31. A company's market share is very sensitive to both its level of advertising and the levels of its competitors' advertising. A firm known to have a 56% market share wants to test whether this value is still valid in view of recent advertising campaigns of its competitors and its own increased level of advertising. A random sample of 500 consumers reveals that 298 use the company's product. Is there evidence to conclude that the company's market share is no longer 56%, at the 0.01 level of significance?

7–32. According to a financial planner, individuals should in theory save 7% to 10% of their income over their working life, if they desire a reasonably comfortable retirement. An agency wants to test whether this actually happens with people in the United States, suspecting the overall savings rate may be lower than this range. A random sample of 41 individuals revealed the following savings rates per year:

4, 0, 1.5, 6, 3.1, 10, 7.2, 1.2, 0, 1.9, 0, 1.0, 0.5, 1.7, 8.5, 0, 0, 0.4, 0, 1.6, 0.9, 10.5, 0, 1.2, 2.8, 0, 2.3, 3.9, 5.6, 3.2, 0, 1, 2.6, 2.2, 0.1, 0.6, 6.1, 0, 0.2, 0, 6.8

Conduct the test and state your conclusions. Use the lower value, 7%, in the null hypothesis. Use $\alpha = 0.01$. Interpret.

7–33. The theory of finance allows for the computation of "excess" returns, either above or below the current stock market average. An analyst wants to determine whether stocks in a certain industry group earn either above or below the market average at a certain time period. The null hypothesis is that there are no excess returns, on the average, in the industry in question. "No average excess returns" means that the population excess return for the industry is zero. A random sample of 24 stocks in the industry reveals a sample average excess return of 0.12 and sample standard deviation of 0.2. State the null and alternative hypotheses, and carry out the test at the $\alpha = 0.05$ level of significance.

7–34. According to *Fortune,* on February 27, 2007, the average stock in all U.S. exchanges fell by 3.3%.[7] If a random sample of 120 stocks reveals a drop of 2.8% on that day and a standard deviation of 1.7%, are there grounds to reject the magazine's claim?

7–35. According to *Money,* the average amount of money that a typical person in the United States would need to make him or her feel rich is $1.5 million. A researcher wants to test this claim. A random sample of 100 people in the United States reveals that their mean "amount to feel rich" is $2.3 million and the standard deviation is $0.5 million. Conduct the test.

7–36. The U.S. Department of Commerce estimates that 17% of all automobiles on the road in the United States at a certain time are made in Japan. An organization that wants to limit imports believes that the proportion of Japanese cars on the road during the period in question is higher than 17% and wants to prove this. A random sample of 2,000 cars is observed, 381 of which are made in Japan. Conduct the hypothesis test at $\alpha = 0.01$, and state whether you believe the reported figure.

7–37. Airplane tires are sensitive to the heat produced when the plane taxis along runways. A certain type of airplane tire used by Boeing is guaranteed to perform well at temperatures as high as 125°F. From time to time, Boeing performs quality control checks to determine whether the average maximum temperature for adequate performance is as stated, or whether the average maximum temperature is lower than 125°F, in which case the company must replace all tires. Suppose that a random sample of 100 tires is checked. The average maximum temperature for adequate performance in the sample is found to be 121°F and the sample standard deviation 2°F. Conduct the hypothesis test, and conclude whether the company should take action to replace its tires.

7–38. An advertisement for Qualcomm appearing in various business publications in fall 2003 said: "The average lunch meeting starts seven minutes late." A research

---

[7]Nelson D. Schwartz, "Volatility? No Big Deal," *Fortune,* April 2, 2007, p. 113.

firm tested this claim to see whether it is true. Using a random sample of 100 business meetings, the researchers found that the average meeting in this sample started 4 minutes late and the standard deviation was 3 minutes. Conduct the test using the 0.05 level of significance.

7–39. A study of top executives' midlife crises indicates that 45% of all top executives suffer from some form of mental crisis in the years following corporate success. An executive who had undergone a midlife crisis opened a clinic providing counseling for top executives in the hope of reducing the number of executives who might suffer from this problem. A random sample of 125 executives who went through the program indicated that only 49 eventually showed signs of a midlife crisis. Do you believe that the program is beneficial and indeed reduces the proportion of executives who show signs of the crisis?

7–40. The unemployment rate in Britain during a certain period was believed to have been 11%. At the end of the period in question, the government embarked on a series of projects to reduce unemployment. The government was interested in determining whether the average unemployment rate in the country had decreased as a result of these projects, or whether previously employed people were the ones hired for the project jobs, while the unemployed remained unemployed. A random sample of 3,500 people was chosen, and 421 were found to be unemployed. Do you believe that the government projects reduced the unemployment rate?

7–41. Certain eggs are stated to have reduced cholesterol content, with an average of only 2.5% cholesterol. A concerned health group wants to test whether the claim is true. The group believes that more cholesterol may be found, on the average, in the eggs. A random sample of 100 eggs reveals a sample average content of 5.2% cholesterol, and a sample standard deviation of 2.8%. Does the health group have cause for action?

7–42. An ad for flights to Palm Springs, California, claims that "the average temperature (in Fahrenheit) on Christmas Day in Palm Springs is 56°."[8] Suppose you think this ad exaggerates the temperature upwards, and you look at a random sample of 30 Christmas days and find an average of 50° and standard deviation of 8°. Conduct the test and give the p-value.

7–43. An article in *Active Trader* claims that using the Adaptive Renko trading system seems to give a 75% chance of beating the market.[9] Suppose that in a random simulation of 100 trades using this system, the trading rule beat the market only 61 times. Conduct the test at the 0.05 level of significance.

7–44. Several U.S. airlines carry passengers from the United States to countries in the Pacific region, and the competition in these flight routes is keen. One of the leverage factors for United Airlines in Pacific routes is that, whereas most other airlines fly to Pacific destinations two or three times weekly, United offers daily flights to Tokyo, Hong Kong, and Osaka. Before instituting daily flights, the airline needed to get an idea as to the proportion of frequent fliers in these routes who consider daily service an important aspect of business flights to the Pacific. From previous information, the management of United estimated that 60% of the frequent business travelers to the three destinations believed that daily service was an important aspect of airline service. Following changes in the airline industry, marked by reduced fares and other factors, the airline management wanted to check whether the proportion of frequent business travelers who believe that daily service is an important feature was still about 60%. A random sample of 250 frequent business fliers revealed that 130 thought daily service was important. Compute the p-value for this test (is this a one-tailed or a two-tailed test?), and state your conclusion.

---

[8] Ad for flights to Palm Springs, California, in *U.S. Airways Magazine,* December 2006, p. 30.

[9] Volker Knapp, "Adaptive Renko System," *Active Trader,* April 2007, p. 49.

7–45.   An advertisement for the Audi TT model lists the following performance specifications: standing start, 0–50 miles per hour in an average of 5.28 seconds; braking, 60 miles per hour to 0 in 3.10 seconds on the average. An independent testing service hired by a competing manufacturer of high-performance automobiles wants to prove that Audi's claims are exaggerated. A random sample of 100 trial runs gives the following results: standing start, 0–50 miles per hour in an average of $\bar{x} = 5.8$ seconds and $s = 1.9$ seconds; braking, 60 miles per hour to 0 in an average of $\bar{x} = 3.21$ seconds and $s = 0.6$ second. Carry out the two hypothesis tests, state the p-value of each test, and state your conclusions.

7–46.   Borg-Warner manufactures hydroelectric miniturbines that generate low-cost, clean electric power from the energy in small rivers and streams. One of the models was known to produce an average of 25.2 kilowatts of electricity. Recently the model's design was improved, and the company wanted to test whether the model's average electric output had changed. The company had no reason to suspect, a priori, a change in either direction. A random sample of 115 trial runs produced an average of 26.1 kilowatts and a standard deviation of 3.2 kilowatts. Carry out a statistical hypothesis test, give the p-value, and state your conclusion. Do you believe that the improved model has a different average output?

7–47.   Recent near misses in the air, as well as several fatal accidents, have brought air traffic controllers under close scrutiny. As a result of a high-level inquiry into the accuracy of speed and distance determinations through radar sightings of airplanes, a statistical test was proposed to check the air traffic controllers' claim that a commercial jet's position can be determined, on the average, to within 110 feet in the usual range around airports in the United States. The proposed test was given as H_0: $\mu \leq 110$ versus the alternative H_1: $\mu > 110$. The test was to be carried out at the 0.05 level of significance using a random sample of 80 airplane sightings. The statistician designing the test wants to determine the power of this test if the actual average distance at detection is 120 feet. An estimate of the standard deviation is 30 feet. Compute the power at $\mu_1 = 120$ feet.

7–48.   According to the *New York Times,* the Martha Stewart Living Omnimedia Company concentrates mostly on food.[10] An analyst wants to disprove a claim that 60% of the company's public statements have been related to food products in favor of a left-tailed alternative. A random sample of 60 public statements revealed that only 21 related to food. Conduct the test and provide a p-value.

7–49.   According to the *Wall Street Journal,* the average American jockey makes only $25,000 a year.[11] Suppose you try to disprove this claim against a right-tailed alternative and your random sample of 100 U.S. jockeys gives you a sample mean of $45,600 and sample standard deviation of $20,000. What is your p-value?

7–50.   A large manufacturing firm believes that its market share is 45%. From time to time, a statistical hypothesis test is carried out to check whether the assertion is true. The test consists of gathering a random sample of 500 products sold nationally and finding what percentage of the sample constitutes brands made by the firm. Whenever the test is carried out, there is no suspicion as to the direction of a possible change in market share, that is, increase or decrease; the company wants to detect any change at all. The tests are carried out at the $\alpha = 0.01$ level of significance. What is the probability of being able to statistically determine a true change in the market share of magnitude 5% in either direction? (That is, find the power at $p = 0.50$ or $p = 0.40$. *Hint:* Use the methods of this section in the case of sampling for proportions. You will have to derive the formulas needed for computing the power.)

[10]Michael Barbaro, "Next Venture from Stewart: Costco Food," *The New York Times,* May 4, 2007, p. C1.

[11]Rick Brooks, "Getting a Leg Up on the Competition at the U.S. Only Jockey College," *The Wall Street Journal,* May 5–6, 2007, p. A1.

7–51.   The engine of the Volvo model S70 T-5 is stated to provide 246 horsepower. To test this claim, believing it is too high, a competitor runs the engine $n = 60$ times, randomly chosen, and gets a sample mean of 239 horsepower and standard deviation of 20 horsepower. Conduct the test, using $\alpha = 0.01$.

7–52.   How can we increase the power of a test without increasing the sample size?

7–53.   According to *BusinessWeek*, the Standard & Poor's 500 Index posted an average gain of 13% for 2006.[12] If a random sample of 50 stocks from this index reveals an average gain of 11% and standard deviation of 6%, can you reject the magazine's claim in a two-tailed test? What is your p-value?

7–54.   A recent marketing and promotion campaign by Charles of the Ritz more than doubled the sales of the suntan lotion Bain de Soleil, which has become the nation's number 2 suntan product. At the end of the promotional campaign, the company wanted to test the hypothesis that the market share of its product was 0.35 versus the alternative hypothesis that the market share was higher than 0.35. The company polled a random sample of bathers on beaches from Maine to California and Hawaii, and found that out of the sample of 3,850 users of suntan lotions, 1,367 were users of Bain de Soleil. Do you reject the null hypothesis? What is the p-value? Explain your conclusion.

7–55.   Efforts are under way to make the U.S. automobile industry more efficient and competitive so that it will be able to survive intense competition from foreign automakers. An industry analyst is quoted as saying, "GM is sized for 60% of the market, and they only have 43%." General Motors needs to know its actual market share because such knowledge would help the company make better decisions about trimming down or expanding so that it could become more efficient. A company executive, pushing for expansion rather than for cutting down, is interested in proving that the analyst's claim that GM's share of the market is 43% is false and that, in fact, GM's true market share is higher. The executive hires a market research firm to study the problem and carry out the hypothesis test she proposed. The market research agency looks at a random sample of 5,500 cars throughout the country and finds that 2,521 are GM cars. What should be the executive's conclusion? How should she present her results to GM's vice president for operations?

7–56.   According to *Money*, the average house owner stays with the property for 6 years.[13] Suppose that a random sample of 120 house owners reveals that the average ownership period until the property is sold was 7.2 years and the standard deviation was 3.5 years. Conduct a two-tailed hypothesis test using $\alpha = 0.05$ and state your conclusion. What is your p-value?

7–57.   Before a beach is declared safe for swimming, a test of the bacteria count in the water is conducted with the null and alternative hypotheses formulated as

H_0: Bacteria count is less than or equal to the specified upper limit for safety

H_1: Bacteria count is more than the specified upper limit for safety

    a. What are type I and type II errors in this case?

    b. Which error is more costly?

    c. In the absence of any further information, which standard value will you recommend for α?

7–58.   Other things remaining the same, which of the following will result in an increase in the power of a hypothesis test?

    a. Increase in the sample size.

    b. Increase in α.

    c. Increase in the population standard deviation.

---

[12]Emily Thornton, "Lehman," *BusinessWeek*, March 26, 2007, p. 68.

[13]Marlys Harris, "How Profitable Is That House?" *Money*, May 2007, p. 97.

7–59. The null and alternative hypotheses of a t test for the mean are

$$H_0: \mu \geq 1{,}000$$
$$H_1: \mu < 1{,}000$$

Other things remaining the same, which of the following will result in an increase in the p-value?

   a. Increase in the sample size.

   b. Increase in the sample mean.

   c. Increase in the sample standard deviation.

   d. Increase in α.

7–60. The null and alternative hypotheses of a test for population proportion are

$$H_0: p \leq 0.25$$
$$H_1: p > 0.25$$

Other things remaining the same, which of the following will result in an increase in the p-value?

   a. Increase in sample size.

   b. Increase in sample proportion.

   c. Increase in α.

7–61. While designing a hypothesis test for population proportion, the cost of a type I error is found to be substantially greater than originally thought. It is possible, as a response, to change the sample size and/or α. Should they be increased or decreased? Explain.

7–62. The p-value obtained in a hypothesis test for population mean is 8%. Select the most precise statement about what it implies. Explain why the other statements are not precise, or are false.

   a. If H_0 is rejected based on the evidence that has been obtained, the probability of type I error would be 8%.

   b. We can be 92% confident that H_0 is false.

   c. There is at most an 8% chance of obtaining evidence that is even more unfavorable to H_0 when H_0 is actually true.

   d. If $\alpha = 1\%$, H_0 will not be rejected and there will be an 8% chance of type II error.

   e. If $\alpha = 5\%$, H_0 will not be rejected and no error will be committed.

   f. If $\alpha = 10\%$, H_0 will be rejected and there will be an 8% chance of type I error.

7–63. Why is it useful to know the power of a test?

7–64. Explain the difference between the p-value and the significance level α.

7–65. Corporate women are still struggling to break into senior management ranks, according to a study of senior corporate executives by Korn/Ferry International, New York recruiter. Of 1,362 top executives surveyed by the firm, only 2%, or 29, were women. Assuming that the sample reported is a random sample, use the results to test the null hypothesis that the percentage of women in top management is 5% or more, versus the alternative hypothesis that the true percentage is less than 5%. If the test is to be carried out at $\alpha = 0.05$, what will be the power of the test if the true percentage of female top executives is 4%?

7–66. According to *The Economist,* the current office vacancy rate in San Jose, California, is 21%.[14] An economist knows that this British publication likes to disparage America and suspects that *The Economist* is overestimating the office vacancy rate in San Jose. Suppose that this economist looks at a random sample of 250 office-building properties in San Jose and finds that 12 are vacant. Using $\alpha = 0.05$, conduct the appropriate hypothesis test and state your conclusion. What is the p-value?

7–67. At Armco's steel plant in Middletown, Ohio, statistical quality-control methods have been used very successfully in controlling slab width on continuous casting units. The company claims that a large reduction in the steel slab width variance resulted from the use of these methods. Suppose that the variance of steel slab widths is expected to be 156 (squared units). A test is carried out to determine whether the variance is above the required level, with the intention to take corrective action if it is concluded that the variance is greater than 156. A random sample of 25 slabs gives a sample variance of 175. Using $\alpha = 0.05$, should corrective action be taken?

7–68. According to the mortgage banking firm Lomas & Nettleton, 95% of all households in the second half of last year lived in rental accommodations. The company believes that lower interest rates for mortgages during the following period reduced the percentage of households living in rental units. The company therefore wants to test H_0: $p \geq 0.95$ versus the alternative H_1: $p < 0.95$ for the proportion during the new period. A random sample of 1,500 households shows that 1,380 are rental units. Carry out the test, and state your conclusion. Use an α of your choice.

7–69. A recent study was aimed at determining whether people with increased workers' compensation stayed off the job longer than people without the increased benefits. Suppose that the average time off per employee per year is known to be 3.1 days. A random sample of 21 employees with increased benefits yielded the following number of days spent off the job in one year: 5, 17, 1, 0, 2, 3, 1, 1, 5, 2, 7, 5, 0, 3, 3, 4, 22, 2, 8, 0, 1. Conduct the appropriate test, and state your conclusions.

7–70. Environmental changes have recently been shown to improve firms' competitive advantages. The approach is called the multiple-scenario approach. A study was designed to find the percentage of the *Fortune* top 1,000 firms that use the multiple-scenario approach. The null hypothesis was that 30% or fewer of the firms use the approach. A random sample of 166 firms in the *Fortune* top 1,000 was chosen, and 59 of the firms replied that they used the multiple-scenario approach. Conduct the hypothesis test at $\alpha = 0.05$. What is the p-value? (Do you need to use the finite-population correction factor?)

7–71. According to an article in the *New York Times,* new Internet dating Web sites use sex to advertise their services. One such site, True.com, reportedly received an average of 3.8 million visitors per month.[15] Suppose that you want to disprove this claim, believing the actual average is lower, and your random sample of 15 months revealed a sample mean of 2.1 million visits and a standard deviation of 1.2 million. Conduct the test using $\alpha = 0.05$. What is the approximate p-value?

7–72. Executives at Gammon & Ninowski Media Investments, a top television station brokerage, believe that the current average price for an independent television station in the United States is $125 million. An analyst at the firm wants to check whether the executives' claim is true. The analyst has no prior suspicion that the claim is incorrect in any particular direction and collects a random sample of 25 independent TV stations around the country. The results are (in millions of dollars) 233, 128, 305, 57, 89, 45, 33, 190, 21, 322, 97, 103, 132, 200, 50, 48, 312, 252, 82, 212, 165, 134, 178, 212, 199. Test the hypothesis that the average station price nationwide

---

[14]"Where the Lights Aren't Bright," *The Economist,* March 3–9, 2007, p. 39.

[15]Brad Stone, "Hot but Virtuous Is an Unlikely Match for an Online Dating Service," *The New York Times,* March 19, 2007, p. C1.

is $125 million versus the alternative that it is not $125 million. Use a significance level of your choice.

7–73. Microsoft Corporation makes software packages for use in microcomputers. The company believes that if at least 25% of present owners of microcomputers of certain types would be interested in a particular new software package, then the company will make a profit if it markets the new package. A company analyst therefore wants to test the null hypothesis that the proportion of owners of microcomputers of the given kinds who will be interested in the new package is at most 0.25, versus the alternative that the proportion is greater than 0.25. A random sample of 300 microcomputer owners shows that 94 are interested in the new Microsoft package. Should the company market its new product? Report the *p*-value.

7–74. A recent National Science Foundation (NSF) survey indicates that more than 20% of the staff in U.S. research and development laboratories are foreign-born. Results of the study have been used for pushing legislation aimed at limiting the number of foreign workers in the United States. An organization of foreign-born scientists wants to prove that the NSF survey results do not reflect the true proportion of foreign workers in U.S. laboratories. The organization collects a random sample of 5,000 laboratory workers in all major laboratories in the country and finds that 876 are foreign. Can these results be used to prove that the NSF study overestimated the proportion of foreigners in U.S. laboratories?

7–75. The average number of weeks that banner ads run at a Web site is estimated to be 5.5. You want to check the accuracy of this estimate. A sample of 50 ads reveals a sample average of 5.1 weeks with a sample standard deviation of 2.3 weeks. State the null and alternative hypotheses and carry out the test at the 5% level of significance.

7–76. According to *The New York Times,* 3-D printers are now becoming a reality.[16] If a manufacturer of the new high-tech printers claims that the new device can print a page in 3 seconds on average, and a random sample of 20 pages shows a sample mean of 4.6 seconds and sample standard deviation of 2.1 seconds, can the manufacturer's claim be rejected? Explain and provide numerical support for your answer.

7–77. Out of all the air-travel bookings in major airlines, at least 58% are said to be done online. A sample of 70 airlines revealed that 52% of bookings for last year were done online. State the null and alternative hypotheses and carry out the test at the 5% level of significance.

7–78. According to *The Economist,* investors in Porsche are the dominant group within the larger VW company that now owns the sportscar maker.[17] Let's take dominance to mean 50% ownership, and suppose that a random sample of 700 VW shareholders reveals that 220 of them own Porsche shares. Conduct the left-tailed test aimed at proving that Porsche shareholders are not dominant. What is the *p*-value?

7–79. Suppose that a claim is made that the average billionaire is 60 years old or younger. The following is a random sample of billionaires' ages, drawn from the *Forbes* list.[18]

80, 70, 76, 54, 59, 52, 74, 64, 76, 67, 39, 67, 43, 62, 57, 91, 55

Conduct the test using the 0.05 level of significance.

7–80. An article in *BusinessWeek* says: "Today companies use a mere 40% of their space."[19] Suppose you want to disprove this claim, suspecting that it is an upward exaggeration. A random sample of the percentage used space for companies is 38, 18,

---

[16]Saul Hansell, "3-D Printers Could Be in Homes Much Sooner Than You Think," *The New York Times,* May 7, 2007, p. C1.

[17]"Our Company Right or Wrong," *The Economist,* March 17, 2007, p. 75.

[18]Louisa Kroll and Allison Fass, eds., "Billionaires," *Forbes,* March 26, 2007, pp. 104–184.

[19]Michelle Conlin, "Rolling Out the Instant Office," *BusinessWeek,* May 7, 2007, p. 71.

91, 37, 55, 80, 71, 92, 68, 78, 40, 36, 50, 45, 22, 19, 62, 70, 82, 25. Conduct the test using $\alpha = 0.05$.

7–81. Redo problem 7–80 using a two-tailed test. Did your results change? Compare the p-values of the two tests. Explain.

7–82. The best places in the United States to be a job seeker are state capitals and university towns, which are claimed to have jobless rates below the national average of 4.2%. A sample of 50 towns and state capitals showed average jobless rate of 1.4% with a standard deviation of 0.8%. State the null and alternative hypotheses and carry out the test at the 1% level of significance.

7–5 Pretest Decisions

Sampling costs money, and so do errors. In the previous chapter we saw how to minimize the total cost of sampling and estimation errors. In this chapter, we do the same for hypothesis testing. Unfortunately, however, finding the cost of errors in hypothesis testing is not as straightforward as in estimation. The reason is that the probabilities of type I and type II errors depend on the actual value of the parameter being tested. Not only do we not know the actual value, but we also do not usually know its distribution. It is therefore difficult, or even impossible, to estimate the expected cost of errors. As a result, people follow a simplified policy of fixing a standard value for α (1%, 5%, or 10%) and a certain minimum sample size for evidence gathering. With the advent of spreadsheets, we can look at the situation more closely and, if needed, change policies.

To look at the situation more closely, we can use the following templates that compute various parameters of the problem and plot helpful charts:

1. Sample size template.
2. β versus α for various sample sizes.
3. The power curve.
4. The operating characteristic curve.

We will see these four templates in the context of testing population means. Similar templates are also available for testing population proportions.

Testing Population Means

Figure 7–17 shows the template that can be used for determining sample sizes when α has been fixed and a limit on the probability of type II error at a predetermined actual value of the population mean has also been fixed. Let us see the use of the template through an example.

The tensile strength of parts made of an alloy is claimed to be at least 1,000 kg/cm². The population standard deviation is known from past experience to be 10 kg/cm². It is desired to test the claim at an α of 5% with the probability of type II error, β, restricted to 8% when the actual strength is only 995 kg/cm². The engineers are not sure about their decision to limit β as described and want to do a sensitivity analysis of the sample size on actual μ ranging from 994 to 997 kg/cm² and limits on β ranging from 5% to 10%. Prepare a plot of the sensitivity.

EXAMPLE 7–9

We use the template shown in Figure 7–17. The null and alternative hypotheses in this case are

Solution

$$H_0: \mu \geq 1,000 \text{ kg/cm}^2$$
$$H_1: \mu < 1,000 \text{ kg/cm}^2$$

FIGURE 7–17   The Template for Computing and Plotting Required Sample Size
[Testing Population Mean.xls; Sheet: Sample Size]

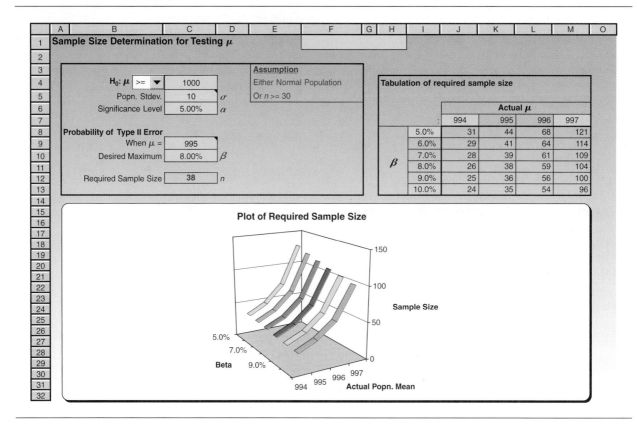

To enter the null hypothesis, choose ">=" in the drop-down box, and enter 1000 in cell C4. Enter σ of 10 in cell C5 and α of 5% in cell C6. Enter 995 in cell C9 and the limit of 8% in cell C10. The result 38 appears in cell C12. Since this is greater than 30, the assumption of $n \geq 30$ is satisfied and all calculations are valid.

To do the sensitivity analysis, enter 5% in cell I8, 10% in cell I13, 994 in cell J7, and 997 in cell M7. The required tabulation and the chart appear, and they may be printed and reported to the engineers.

Manual Calculation of Required Sample Size

The equation for calculating the required sample size is

$$n = \left\lceil \left(\frac{(|z_0| + |z_1|)\sigma}{\mu_0 - \mu_1} \right)^2 \right\rceil$$

where μ_0 = hypothesized value of μ in H_0
μ_1 = the value of μ at which type II error is to be monitored
$z_0 = z_\alpha$ or $z_{\alpha/2}$ depending on whether the test is one-tailed or two-tailed
$z_1 = z_\beta$ where β is the limit on type II error probability when $\mu = \mu_1$

The symbol $\lceil \ \rceil$ stands for rounding up to the next integer. For example, $\lceil 35.2 \rceil = 36$. Note that the formula calls for the absolute values of z_0 and z_1, so enter positive values regardless of right-tailed or left-tailed test. If the template is not available, this equation can be used to calculate the required n manually.

FIGURE 7–18 The Template for Plotting β versus α for Various *n*
[Testing Population Mean.xls; Sheet: Beta vs. Alpha]

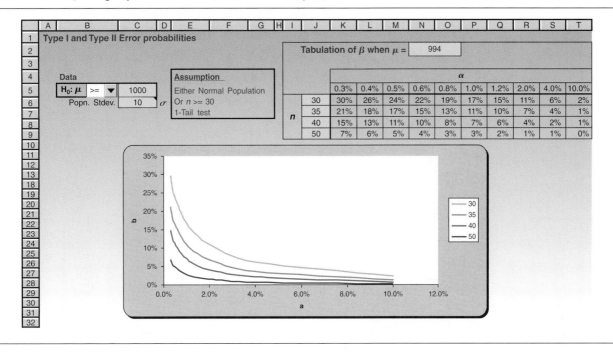

The manual calculation of required sample size for Example 7–9 is

$$n = \left\lceil \left(\frac{(1.645 + 1.4)10}{1{,}000 - 995} \right)^2 \right\rceil = \lceil 37.1 \rceil = 38$$

Figure 7–18 shows the template that can be used to plot β versus α for four different values of *n*. We shall see the use of this template through an example.

EXAMPLE 7–10

The tensile strength of parts made of an alloy is claimed to be at least 1,000 kg/cm². The population standard deviation is known from past experience to be 10 kg/cm². The engineers at a company want to test this claim. To decide *n*, α, and the limit on β, they would like to look at a plot of β when actual μ = 994 kg/cm² versus α for *n* = 30, 35, 40, and 50. Further, they believe that type II errors are more costly and therefore would like β to be not more than half the value of α. Can you make a suggestion for the selection of α and *n*?

Solution

Use the template shown in Figure 7–18. Enter the null hypothesis H_0: μ ≥ 1000 in the range B5:C5. Enter the σ value of 10 in cell C6. Enter the actual μ = 994 in the range N2:O2. Enter the *n* values 30, 35, 40, and 50 in the range J6:J9. The desired plot of β versus α is created.

Looking at the plot, for the standard α value of 5%, a sample size of 40 yields a β of approximately 2.5%. Thus the combination α = 5% and *n* = 40 is a good choice.

Figure 7–19 shows the template that can be used to plot the **power curve** of a hypothesis test once α and *n* have been determined. This curve is useful in determining the power of the test for various actual μ values. Since α and *n* are usually selected

FIGURE 7–19   The Template for Plotting the Power Curve
[Testing Population Mean; Sheet: Power]

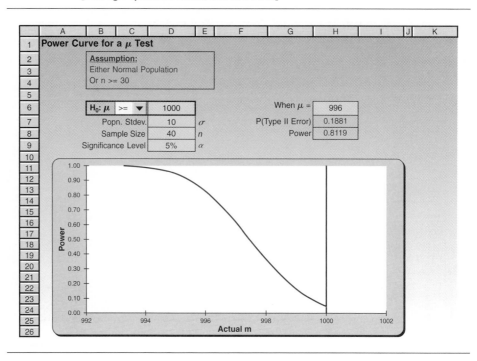

CHAPTER 11

without knowing the actual μ, this plot can be used to check if they have been select-ed well with respect to power. In Example 7–10, if the engineers wanted a power curve of the test, the template shown in Figure 7–19 can be used to produce it. The data and the chart in the figure correspond to Example 7–10. A vertical line appears at the hypothesized value of the population mean, which in this case is 1,000.

The **operating characteristic curve** (OC curve) of a hypothesis test shows how the probability of not rejecting (accepting) the null hypothesis varies with the actual μ. The advantage of an OC curve is that it shows both type I and type II error instances. See Figure 7–20, which shows an OC curve for the case H_0: $\mu \geq 75$; $\sigma = 10$; $n = 40$; $\alpha = 10\%$. A vertical line appears at 75, which corresponds to the hypothe-sized value of the population mean. Areas corresponding to errors in the test deci-sions are shaded. The dark area at the top right represents type I error instances, because in that area $\mu > 75$, which makes H_0 true, but H_0 is rejected. The shaded area below represents instances of type II error, because $\mu < 75$, which makes H_0 false, but H_0 is accepted. By looking at both type I and type II error instances on a single chart, we can design a test more effectively.

Figure 7–21 shows the template that can be used to plot OC curves. The tem-plate will not shade the areas corresponding to the errors. But that is all right, because we would like to superpose two OC curves on a single chart corresponding to two sample sizes, n_1 and n_2 entered in cells H7 and H8. We shall see the use of the template through an example.

EXAMPLE 7–11   Consider the problem in Example 7–10. The engineers want to see the complete picture of type I and type II error instances. In particular, when $\alpha = 10\%$, they want to know the effect of increasing the sample size from 40 to 100 on type I and type II error possibilities. Construct the OC curves for $n_1 = 40$ and $n_2 = 100$ and comment on the effects.

FIGURE 7–20   An Operating Characteristic Curve for the Case H_0: $\mu \geq 75$; $\sigma = 10$; $n = 40$; $\alpha = 10\%$

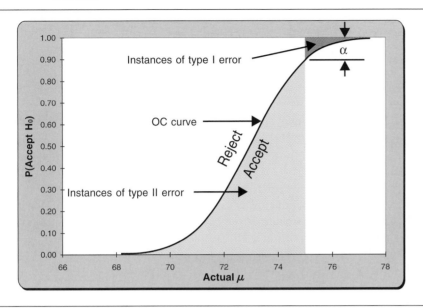

FIGURE 7–21   The Template for Plotting the Operating Characteristic Curve
[Testing Population Mean.xls; Sheet: OC Curve]

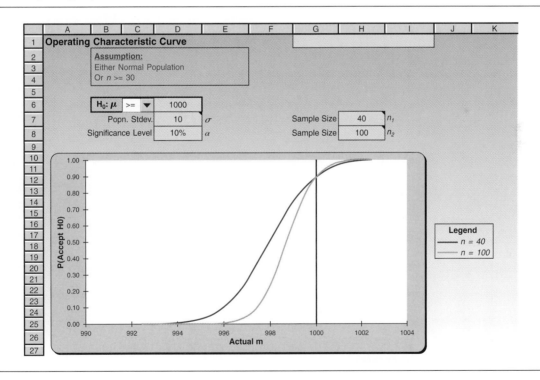

Solution

Open the template shown in Figure 7–21. Enter the null hypothesis in the range B6:D6, and the σ value of 10 in cell D7. Enter the α value of 10% in cell D8. Enter 40 and 100 in cells H7 and H8. The needed OC curves appear in the chart.

Looking at the OC curves, we see that increasing the sample size from 40 to 100 does not affect the instances of type I error much but substantially reduces type II error instances. For example, the chart reveals that when actual $\mu = 998$ the probability of type II error, β, is reduced by more than 50% and when actual $\mu = 995$ β is almost zero. If these gains outweigh the cost of additional sampling, then it is better to go for a sample size of 100.

Testing Population Proportions

Figure 7–22 shows the template that can be used to calculate the required sample size while testing population means.

EXAMPLE 7–12

At least 52% of a city's population is said to oppose the construction of a highway near the city. A test of the claim at $\alpha = 10\%$ is desired. The probability of type II error when the actual proportion is 49% is to be limited to 6%.

1. How many randomly selected residents of the city should be polled to test the claim?
2. Tabulate the required sample size for limits on β varying from 2% to 10% and actual proportion varying from 46% to 50%.
3. If the budget allows only a sample size of 2,000 and therefore that is the number polled, what is the probability of type II error when the actual proportion is 49%?

FIGURE 7–22   The Template for Finding the Required Sample Size
[Testing Population Proportion.xls; Sheet: Sample Size]

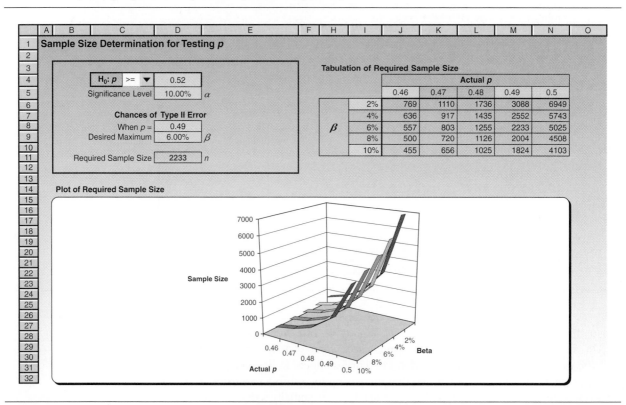

Open the template shown in Figure 7–22. Enter the null hypothesis, H_0: $p \geq 52\%$ *Solution*
in the range C4:D4. Enter α in cell D5, and type II error information in cells D8
and D9.

1. The required sample size of 2233 appears in cell D11.
2. Enter the β values 2% in cell I6 and 10% in cell I10. Enter 0.46 in J5 and 0.50
   in cell N5. The needed tabulation appears in the range I5:N10.
3. In the tabulation of required sample size, in the column corresponding to $p =$
   0.49, the value 2004 appears in cell M9, which corresponds to a β value of 8%.
   Thus the probability of type II error is about 8%.

Manual Calculation of Sample Size

If the template is not available, the required sample size for testing population
proportions can be calculated using the equation

$$n = \left\lceil \left(\frac{(|z_0|\sqrt{p_0(1-p_0)} + |z_1|\sqrt{p_1(1-p_1)})}{p_0 - p_1} \right)^2 \right\rceil$$

where p_0 = hypothesized value of μ in H_0
p_1 = the value of p at which type II error is to be monitored
$z_0 = z_\alpha$ or $z_{\alpha/2}$ depending on whether the test is one-tailed or two-tailed
$z_1 = z_\beta$ where β is the limit on type II error probability when $p = p_1$

For the case in Example 7–12, the calculation will be

$$n = \left\lceil \left(\frac{(1.28\sqrt{0.52(1-0.52)} + 1.555\sqrt{0.49(1-0.49)})}{0.52 - 0.49} \right)^2 \right\rceil = \lceil 2{,}230.5 \rceil = 2{,}231$$

The difference of 2 in the manual and template results is due to the approximation
of z_0 and z_1 in manual calculation.

The power curve and the OC curves can be produced for hypothesis tests regarding population proportions using the templates shown in Figures 7–23 and 7–24. Let
us see the use of the charts through an example.

The hypothesis test in Example 7–12 is conducted with sample size 2,000 and $\alpha = 10\%$.   **EXAMPLE 7–13**
Draw the power curve and the OC curve of the test.

For the power curve, open the template shown in Figure 7–23. Enter the null hypoth-   *Solution*
esis, sample size, and α in their respective places. The power curve appears below the
data. For the power at a specific point use the cell F7. Entering 0.49 in cell F7 shows
that the power when $p = 0.49$ is 0.9893.

For the OC curve open the template shown in Figure 7–24. Enter the null
hypothesis and α in their respective places. Enter the sample size 2000 in cell C7 and
leave cell D7 blank. The OC curve appears below the data.

FIGURE 7–23   The Template for Drawing a Power Curve
[Testing Population Proportion.xls; Sheet: Power]

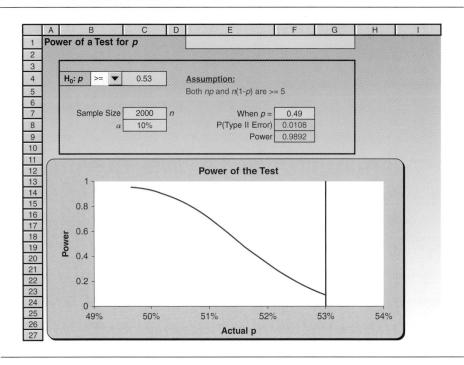

FIGURE 7–24   The Template for Drawing OC Curves
[Testing Population Proportion.xls; Sheet: OC Curve]

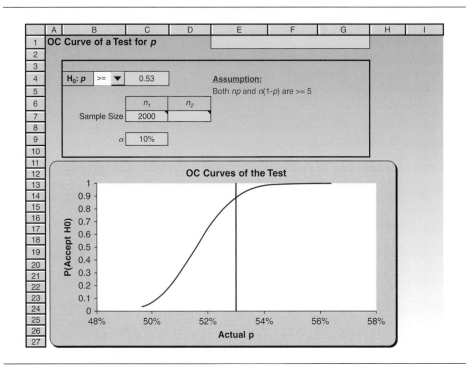

7–83. Consider the null hypothesis $\mu \geq 56$. The population standard deviation is guessed to be 2.16. Type II error probabilities are to be calculated at $\mu = 55$.

    a. Draw a β versus α chart with sample sizes 30, 40, 50, and 60.

    b. The test is conducted with a random sample of size 50 with $\alpha = 5\%$. Draw the power curve. What is the power when $\mu = 55.5$?

    c. Draw an OC curve with $n = 50$ and 60; $\alpha = 5\%$. Is there a lot to gain by going from $n = 50$ to $n = 60$?

7–84. The null hypothesis $p = 0.25$ is tested with $n = 1,000$ and $\alpha = 5\%$.

    a. Draw the power curve. What is the power when $p = 0.22$?

    b. Draw the OC curve for $n = 1,000$ and 1,200. Is there a lot to gain by going from $n = 1,000$ to $n = 1,200$?

7–85. The null hypothesis $\mu \leq 30$ is to be tested. The population standard deviation is guessed to be 0.52. Type II error probabilities are to be calculated at $\mu = 30.3$.

    a. Draw a β versus α chart with sample sizes 30, 40, 50, and 60.

    b. The test is conducted with a random sample of size 30 with an α of 5%. Draw the power curve. What is the power when $\mu = 30.2$?

    c. Draw an OC curve with $n = 30$ and 60; $\alpha = 5\%$. If type II error is to be almost zero when $\mu = 30.3$, is it better to go for $n = 60$?

7–86. If you look at the power curve or the OC curve of a two-tailed test, you see that there is no *region* that represents instances of type I error, whereas there are large regions that represent instances of type II error. Does this mean that there is no chance of type I error? Think carefully, and explain the chances of type I error and the role of α in a two-tailed test.

7–87. The average weight of airline food packaging material is to be controlled so that the total weight of catering supplies does not exceed desired limits. An inspector who uses random sampling to accept or reject a batch of packaging materials uses the null hypothesis H_0: $\mu \leq 248$ grams and an α of 10%. He also wants to make sure that when the average weight in a batch is 250 grams, β must be 5%. The population standard deviation is guessed to be 5 grams.

    a. What is the minimum required sample size?

    b. For the sample size found in the previous question, plot the OC curve.

    c. For actual μ varying from 249 to 252 and β varying from 3% to 8%, tabulate the minimum required sample size.

7–88. A company orders bolts in bulk from a vendor. The contract specifies that a shipment of bolts will be accepted by testing the null hypothesis that the percentage defective in the shipment is not more than 3% at an α of 5% using random sampling from the shipment. The company further wishes that any shipment containing 8% defectives should have no more than 10% chance of acceptance.

    a. Find the minimum sample size required.

    b. For the sample size found in the previous question, plot the OC curve.

    c. For the actual percentage defective varying from 6% to 10% and β varying from 8% to 12%, tabulate the minimum sample size required.

7–89. According to *Money,* "3 in 5 executives said they anticipate making a major career change."[20] Suppose a random sample of 1,000 executives shows that 55% said they anticipate making a major career change. Can you reject the claim made by the magazine? What is the p-value?

---

[20]Jean Chatzky, "To Invent the New You, Don't Bankrupt Old You," *Money,* May 2007, p. 30.

7–6   Using the Computer

Using Excel for One-Sample Hypothesis Testing

In addition to the templates discussed in this chapter, you can use Microsoft Excel functions to directly run hypothesis tests using Excel.

To perform a Z test of a hypothesis for the mean when the population standard deviation is known, use the function **ZTEST**. This function returns the one-tailed probability value of a z test. For a given hypothesized population mean μ_0, ZTEST returns the p-value corresponding to the alternative hypothesis $\mu > \mu_0$, where μ represents the population mean. In the syntax ZTEST(array, μ_0, sigma), *array* represents the range of data against which to test μ_0, μ_0 is the value to test, and *sigma* is the population (known) standard deviation. If omitted, the sample standard deviation is used. In terms of Excel formulas we can say ZTEST is calculated as follows when sigma is not omitted:

$$\text{ZTEST(array, } \mu_0, \text{ sigma)} = 1 - \text{NORMSDIST}((\bar{x} - \mu_0)/(\text{sigma}/\sqrt{n}))$$

When sigma is omitted ZTEST is calculated as follows:

$$\text{ZTEST(array, } \mu_0\text{)} = 1 - \text{NORMSDIST}((\bar{x} - \mu_0)/(s/\sqrt{n}))$$

In the preceding formulas $\bar{x}$=AVERAGE(array) is the sample mean, s=STDEV(array) is the sample standard deviation, and n=COUNT(array) is the number of observations in the sample. It is obvious that when the population standard deviation sigma is not known, ZTEST returns an approximately valid result if the size of the sample is greater than 30. Since ZTEST returns the p-value, it actually represents the probability that the sample mean would be greater than the observed value AVERAGE(array) when the hypothesized population mean is μ_0. From the symmetry of the normal distribution, if AVERAGE(array) $< \mu_0$, ZTEST will return a value greater than 0.5. In this case you have to use 1-ZTEST as your desired and valid p-value. If you need to run a two-tailed ZTEST on the alternative hypothesis $\mu \neq \mu_0$, the following Excel formula can be used for obtaining the corresponding p-value:

$$= 2*\text{MIN(ZTEST(array, } \mu_0, \text{ sigma)}, 1 - \text{ZTEST(array, } \mu_0, \text{ sigma))}$$

Excel does not have a specific test entitled one-sample t test. So when the population standard deviation is not known and sample size is less than 30, we need to use the other Excel formulas to do the mathematical calculations required for this test. At first we need to describe the **TDIST** function of Excel. In the syntax TDIST(t,df,tails), t is the numeric value at which to evaluate the distribution, *df* is an integer indicating the number of degrees of freedom, and *tails* specifies the number of distribution tails to return. If tails = 1, TDIST returns the one-tailed distribution, which means TDIST is calculated as $P(T > t)$ in which T is a random variable that follows a t distribution. If tails = 2, TDIST returns the two-tailed distribution. In this case TDIST is calculated as $P(|T| > t) = P(T < -t \text{ or } T > t)$. Note that the value of t has to be positive. So, if you need to use TDIST when $t < 0$, you can consider the symmetrical behavior of the t distribution and use the relation TDIST($-t$,df,1) = 1 $-$ TDIST(t,df,1) as well as TDIST($-t$,df,2) = TDIST(t,df,2). As an example, TDIST(2.33,10,1) returns the value 0.021025, while TDIST(2.33,10,2) returns the value 0.04205, which is twice 0.021025.

To use this function for conducting a hypothesis test for a population mean, we need to first calculate the value of the test statistics. Let *array* represent the array or range of values against which you test μ_0. Calculate the sample mean, sample standard deviation, and number of observations in the sample by the functions AVERAGE(array), STDEV(array), and COUNT(array), respectively. Then the value of the test statistic t is calculated as

$$t = \text{(AVERAGE(array)} - \mu_0)/(\text{STDEV(array)}/\text{SQRT(COUNT(array))})$$

while SQRT(n) returns the square root of n.

If your null hypothesis is in the form of $\mu > \mu_0$, you need to use the TDIST function as `TDIST(t, COUNT(array)-1, 1)`. The obtained result is the *p*-value corresponding to the obtained test statistics. By comparing the obtained *p*-value with the desired significance level, you can decide to reject or accept the null hypothesis. Note that if you wish to run a test of the hypothesis that $\mu \neq \mu_0$, you need to set the tails parameter of the TDIST function to the value of 2. The obtained result is the *p*-value corresponding to a two-tailed *t* test.

To run a one-sample *z* test for a population proportion, again you need to first find the test statistic *z* based on the formula described in the chapter. Then the function `NORMSDIST(z)` or `1- NORMSDIST(z)` is used to return the *p*-value corresponding to the alternative hypotheses $p < p_0$ or $p > p_0$, respectively. For a two-tailed test $p \neq p_0$, the *p*-value is obtained by the following formula:

```
p-value = 2*MIN(NORMSDIST(z), 1-NORMSDIST(z))
```

To run a test for a population variance, the required function that will return the *p*-value corresponding to the test statistic is `CHIDIST(x, degrees_freedom)`. In this function *x* represents the value for which you want to find the cumulative distribution, and *degrees_freedom* is the number of degrees of freedom for the chi-square distribution.

Using MINITAB for One-Sample Hypothesis Testing

MINITAB can be used to carry out different one-sample hypothesis tests. Suppose we need to run a test on the population mean when the population standard deviation is known. Start by choosing Stat ▶ Basic Statistics ▶ 1-Sample z from the menu bar. In the corresponding dialog box you can define the name of the column that contains your sample data or you can directly enter the summarized data of your sample. Enter the value of the population standard deviation in the next box. You need to check the box to perform the hypothesis test. Enter the hypothesized mean μ_0 in the corresponding edit box. To define the desired significance level of the test as well as the form of your null hypothesis, click on the Options button. In the alternative drop-down list box, select less than or greater than for one-tailed tests, or not equal for a two-tailed test. Click the OK button. The results and corresponding Session commands will appear in the Session window. Figure 7–25 shows the result of an example in which we run a test of the population mean based on a sample of size 15. The population standard deviation is known and equal to 11.5. The hypothesized mean is 62 and the corresponding alternative hypothesis is in the form of $\mu > 62$. The desired significance level is 0.05. As can be seen, based on the obtained *p*-value 0.203, we cannot reject the null hypothesis at the stated significance level.

In cases where the population standard deviation is not known, start by choosing Stat ▶ Basic Statistics ▶ 1-Sample t. The required setting is the same as the previous dialog box except that you need to specify the sample standard deviation instead of the population standard deviation.

To run a test of the population proportion start by selecting Stat ▶ Basic Statistics ▶ 1 Proportion from the menu bar. In the corresponding dialog box you need to define your sample in the form of a column of data or in the form of summarized data by number of trials (sample size) and number of events (number of samples with desired condition). Check the box to perform the hypothesis test. Enter the hypothesized proportion p_0 in the corresponding box. Click the Options button to define the desired significance level of the test as well as the form of the alternative hypothesis. Then click the OK button. The results and corresponding Session commands will appear in the Session window.

For a test of the population variance or standard deviation start by choosing Stat ▶ Basic Statistics ▶ 1 Variance from the menu bar. The required setting follows the same structure that we described for previous dialog boxes. As an example, suppose we have a sample of size 31. Our sample variance is 1.62. We wish to test the null

FIGURE 7–25   Using MINITAB for a Hypothesis Test of the Mean (σ known)

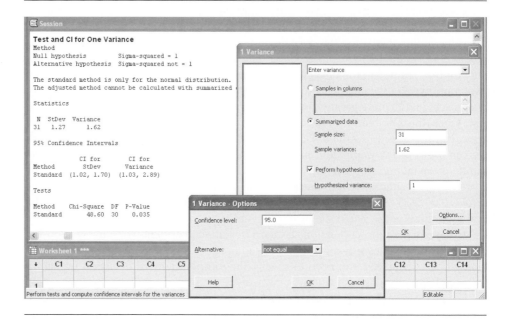

FIGURE 7–26   Using MINITAB for a Hypothesis Test on Population Variance

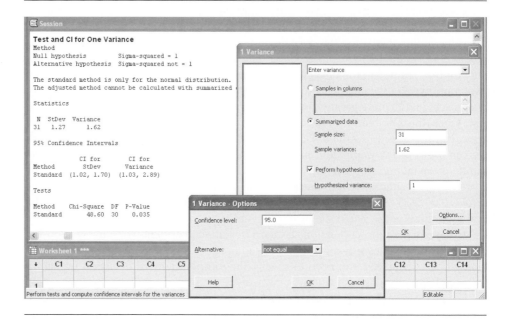

hypothesis that the population variance is equal to 1 at significance level 0.05. Figure 7–26 shows the corresponding dialog box and Session commands for this test. Based on the obtained p-value 0.035, we reject the null hypothesis at significance level 0.05.

7–7   Summary and Review of Terms

In this chapter, we introduced the important ideas of statistical hypothesis testing. We discussed the philosophy behind hypothesis tests, starting with the concepts of **null hypothesis** and **alternative hypothesis.** Depending on the type of null hypothesis, the rejection occurred either on one or both tails of the **test statistic.** Correspondingly, the test became either a **one-tailed test** or a **two-tailed test.** In any test, we saw that there will be chances for **type I** and **type II errors.** We saw how the *p*-value is used in an effort to systematically contain the chances of both types of error. When the *p*-value is less than the **level of significance** α, the null hypothesis is rejected. The probability of not committing a type I error is known as the **confidence level,** and the probability of not committing a type II error is known as the **power** of the test. We also saw how increasing the sample size decreases the chances of both types of errors.

In connection with pretest decisions we saw the compromise between the costs of type I and type II errors. These cost considerations help us in deciding the **optimal sample size** and a suitable level of significance α. In the next chapter we extend these ideas of hypothesis testing to *differences* between two population parameters.

CASE 9 Tiresome Tires I

When a tire is constructed of more than one ply, the interply shear strength is an important property to check. The specification for a particular type of tire calls for a strength of 2,800 pounds per square inch (psi). The tire manufacturer tests the tires using the null hypothesis

$$H_0\colon \mu \geq 2{,}800 \text{ psi}$$

where μ is the mean strength of a large batch of tires. From past experience, it is known that the population standard deviation is 20 psi.

Testing the shear strength requires a costly destructive test and therefore the sample size needs to be kept at a minimum. A type I error will result in the rejection of a large number of good tires and is therefore costly. A type II error of passing a faulty batch of tires can result in fatal accidents on the roads, and therefore is extremely costly. (For purposes of this case, the probability of type II error, β, is always calculated at $\mu = 2{,}790$ psi.) It is believed that β should be at most 1%. Currently, the company conducts the test with a sample size of 40 and an α of 5%.

1. To help the manufacturer get a clear picture of type I and type II error probabilities, draw a β versus α chart for sample sizes of 30, 40, 60, and 80. If β is to be at most 1% with $\alpha = 5\%$, which sample size among these four values is suitable?

2. Calculate the exact sample size required for $\alpha = 5\%$ and $\beta = 1\%$. Construct a sensitivity analysis table for the required sample size for μ ranging from 2,788 to 2,794 psi and β ranging from 1% to 5%.

3. For the current practice of $n = 40$ and $\alpha = 5\%$ plot the power curve of the test. Can this chart be used to convince the manufacturer about the high probability of passing batches that have a strength of less than 2,800 psi?

4. To present the manufacturer with a comparison of a sample size of 80 versus 40, plot the OC curve for those two sample sizes. Keep an α of 5%.

5. The manufacturer is hesitant to increase the sample size beyond 40 due to the concomitant increase in testing costs and, more important, due to the increased time required for the tests. The production process needs to wait until the tests are completed, and that means loss of production time. A suggestion is made by the production manager to increase α to 10% as a means of reducing β. Give an account of the benefits and the drawbacks of that move. Provide supporting numerical results wherever possible.

THE COMPARISON OF TWO POPULATIONS

8–1   Using Statistics   303

8–2   Paired-Observation Comparisons   304

8–3   A Test for the Difference between Two Population Means Using Independent Random Samples   310

8–4   A Large-Sample Test for the Difference between Two Population Proportions   324

8–5   The *F* Distribution and a Test for Equality of Two Population Variances   330

8–6   Using the Computer   338

8–7   Summary and Review of Terms   341

Case 10   Tiresome Tires II   346

LEARNING OBJECTIVES

After studying this chapter, you should be able to:

- Explain the need to compare two population parameters.
- Conduct a paired-difference test for difference in population means.
- Conduct an independent-samples test for difference in population means.
- Describe why a paired-difference test is better than an independent-samples test.
- Conduct a test for difference in population proportions.
- Test whether two population variances are equal.
- Use templates to carry out all tests.

Study Offers Proof of an Obesity–Soda Link

School programs discouraging carbonated drinks appear to be effective in reducing obesity among children, a new study suggests.

A high intake of sweetened carbonated drinks probably contributes to childhood obesity, and there is a growing movement against soft drinks in schools. But until now there have been no studies showing that efforts to lower children's consumption of soft drinks would do any good.

The study outlined this week on the Web site of *The British Medical Journal,* found that a one-year campaign discouraging both sweetened and diet soft drinks led to a decrease in the percentage of elementary school children who were overweight or obese. The improvement occurred after a reduction in consumption of less than a can a day.

Representatives of the soft drink industry contested the implications of the results.

The investigators studied 644 children, ages 7 to 11, in the 2001–2002 school year.

The percentage of overweight and obese children increased by 7.5 percent in the group that did not participate and dipped by 0.2 percent among those who did.

Excerpt from "Study offers proof of an obesity-soda link" Associated Press, © 2004. Used with permission.

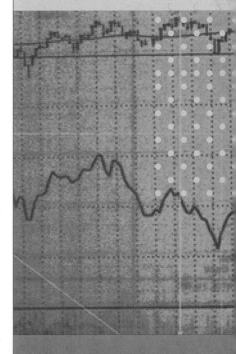

The comparison of two populations with respect to some population parameter—the population mean, the population proportion, or the population variance—is the topic of this chapter. Testing hypotheses about population parameters in the single-population case, as was done in Chapter 7, is an important statistical undertaking. However, the true usefulness of statistics manifests itself in allowing us to make *comparisons,* as in the article above, where the weight of children who drink soda was compared to that of those who do not. Almost daily we compare products, services, investment opportunities, management styles, and so on. In this chapter, we will learn how to conduct such comparisons in an objective and meaningful way.

We will learn first how to find statistically significant differences between two populations. If you understood the methodology of hypothesis testing presented in the last chapter and the idea of a confidence interval from Chapter 6, you will find the extension to two populations straightforward and easy to understand. We will learn how to conduct a test for the existence of a difference between the means of two populations. In the next section, we will see how such a comparison may be made in the special case where the observations may be paired in some way. Later we will learn how to conduct a test for the equality of the means of two populations, using independent random samples. Then we will see how to compare two population proportions. Finally, we will encounter a test for the equality of the variances of two populations. In addition to statistical hypothesis tests, we will learn how to construct confidence intervals for the difference between two population parameters.

8–2 Paired-Observation Comparisons

In this section, we describe a method for conducting a hypothesis test and constructing a confidence interval when our observations come from two populations and are *paired* in some way. What is the advantage of pairing observations? Suppose that a taste test of two flavors is carried out. It seems intuitively plausible that if we let every person in our sample rate each one of the two flavors (with random choice of which flavor is tasted first), the resulting *paired* responses will convey more information about the taste difference than if we had used two different sets of people, each group rating only one flavor. Statistically, when we use the same people for rating the two products, we tend to remove much of the *extraneous variation* in taste ratings—the variation in people, experimental conditions, and other extraneous factors—and concentrate on the difference between the two flavors. When possible, pairing the observations is often advisable, as this makes the experiment more precise. We will demonstrate the paired-observation test with an example.

EXAMPLE 8–1

Home Shopping Network, Inc., pioneered the idea of merchandising directly to customers through cable television. By watching what amounts to 24 hours of commercials, viewers can call a number to buy products. Before expanding their services, network managers wanted to test whether this method of direct marketing increased sales on the average. A random sample of 16 viewers was selected for an experiment. All viewers in the sample had recorded the amount of money they spent shopping during the holiday season of the previous year. The next year, these people were given access to the cable network and were asked to keep a record of their total purchases during the holiday season. The paired observations for each shopper are given in Table 8–1. Faced with these data, Home Shopping Network managers want to test the null hypothesis that their service does not increase shopping volume, versus the alternative hypothesis that it does. The following solution of this problem introduces the *paired-observation t test*.

Solution

The test involves two populations: the population of shoppers who have access to the Home Shopping Network and the population of shoppers who do not. We want to test the null hypothesis that the mean shopping expenditure in both populations is

TABLE 8–1 Total Purchases of 16 Viewers with and without Home Shopping

Shopper	Current Year's Shopping ($)	Previous Year's Shopping ($)	Difference ($)
1	405	334	71
2	125	150	−25
3	540	520	20
4	100	95	5
5	200	212	−12
6	30	30	0
7	1,200	1,055	145
8	265	300	−35
9	90	85	5
10	206	129	77
11	18	40	−22
12	489	440	49
13	590	610	−20
14	310	208	102
15	995	880	115
16	75	25	50

equal versus the alternative hypothesis that the mean for the home shoppers is greater. Using the same people for the test and pairing their observations in a before-and-after way makes the test more precise than it would be without pairing. The pairing removes the influence of factors other than home shopping. The shoppers are the same people; thus, we can concentrate on the effect of the new shopping opportunity, leaving out of the analysis other factors that may affect shopping volume. Of course, we must consider the fact that the first observations were taken a year before. Let us assume, however, that relative inflation between the two years has been accounted for and that people in the sample have not had significant changes in income or other variables since the previous year that might affect their buying behavior.

Under these circumstances, it is easy to see that the variable in which we are interested is the difference between the present year's per-person shopping expenditure and that of the previous year. The population parameter about which we want to draw an inference is the mean difference between the two populations. We denote this parameter by μ_D, the mean difference. This parameter is defined as $\mu_D = \mu_1 - \mu_2$, where μ_1 is the average holiday season shopping expenditure of people who use home shopping and μ_2 is the average holiday season shopping expenditure of people who do not. Our null and alternative hypotheses are, then,

$$H_0\colon \mu_D \leq 0$$
$$H_1\colon \mu_D > 0 \tag{8-1}$$

Looking at the null and alternative hypotheses and the data in the last column of Table 8–1, we note that the test is a simple t test with $n - 1$ degrees of freedom, where our variable is the *difference* between the two observations for each shopper. In a sense, our two-population comparison test has been reduced to a hypothesis test about one parameter—the difference between the means of two populations. The test, as given by equation 8–1, is a right-tailed test, but it need not be. In general, the paired-observation t test can be done as one-tailed or two-tailed. In addition, the hypothesized difference need not be zero. We can state any other value as the difference in the null hypothesis (although zero is most commonly used). The only assumption we make when we use this test is that *the population of differences is normally distributed.* Recall that this assumption was used whenever we carried out a test or constructed a confidence interval using the t distribution. Also note that, for large samples, the standard normal distribution may be used instead. This is also true for a normal population if you happen to know the population standard deviation of the differences σ_D. The test statistic (assuming σ_D is not known and is estimated by s_D, the sample standard deviation of the differences) is given in equation 8–2.

The test statistic for the paired-observation t test is

$$t = \frac{\overline{D} - \mu_{D_0}}{s_D/\sqrt{n}} \tag{8-2}$$

where $\overline{D}$ is the sample average difference between each pair of observations, s_D is the sample standard deviation of these differences, and the sample size n is the number of pairs of observations (here, the number of people in the experiment). The symbol μ_{D_0} is the population mean difference under the null hypothesis. When the null hypothesis is true and the population mean difference is μ_{D_0}, the statistic has a t distribution with $n - 1$ degrees of freedom.

Let us now conduct the hypothesis test. From the differences reported in Table 8–1, we find that their mean is $\bar{D} = \$32.81$ and their standard deviation is $s_D = \$55.75$. Since the sample size is small, $n = 16$, we use the t distribution with $n - 1 = 15$ degrees of freedom. The null hypothesis value of the population mean is $\mu_{D_0} = 0$. The value of our test statistic is obtained as

$$t = \frac{32.81 - 0}{55.75/\sqrt{16}} = 2.354$$

This computed value of the test statistic is greater than 1.753, which is the critical point for a right-tailed test at $\alpha = 0.05$ using a t distribution with 15 degrees of freedom (see Appendix C, Table 3). The test statistic value is less than 2.602, which is the critical point for a one-tailed test using $\alpha = 0.01$, but greater than 2.131, which is the critical point for a right-tailed area of 0.025. We may conclude that the p-value is between 0.025 and 0.01. This is shown in Figure 8–1. Home Shopping Network managers may conclude that the test gave significant evidence for increased shopping volume by network viewers.

The Template

Figure 8–2 shows the template that can be used to test paired differences in population means when the sample data are known. The data are entered in columns B and C. The data and the results seen in the figure correspond to Example 8–1. The hypothesized value of the difference is entered in cell F12, and this value is automatically copied into cells F13 and F14 below. The desired α is entered in cell H11. For the present case, the null hypothesis is $\mu_1 - \mu_2 \leq 0$. The corresponding p-value of 0.0163 appears in cell G14. As seen in cell H14, the null hypothesis is to be rejected at an α of 5%.

If a confidence interval is desired, then the confidence level must be entered in cell J12. The α corresponding to the confidence level in cell J12 need not be the same as the α for the hypothesis test entered in cell H11. If a confidence interval is not desired, then cell J12 may be left blank to avoid creating a distraction.

FIGURE 8–1　Carrying Out the Test of Example 8–1

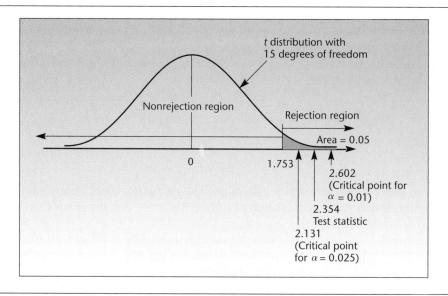

FIGURE 8–2 **The Template for Testing Paired Differences**
[Testing Paired Difference.xls; Sheet: Sample Data]

	A	B	C	D	E	F	G	H	I	J	K	L	M	N	O	P	Q	R	S
1		**Paired Difference Test**																	
2			Data																
3		Current	Previous		Evidence														
4		Sample1	Sample2		Size	16		n		Assumption									
5	1	405	334		Average Difference	32.8125		μ_D		Populations Normal									
6	2	125	150		Stdev. of Difference	55.7533		s_D											
7	3	540	520							Note: Difference has been defined as									
8	4	100	95		Test Statistic	2.3541		t		Sample1 - Sample2									
9	5	200	212		df	15													
10	6	30	30		Hypothesis Testing						At an α of		Confidence Intervals for the Difference in Means						
11	7	1200	1055		Null Hypothesis		p-value			5%			$(1 - \alpha)$		Confidence Interval				
12	8	265	300		$H_0: \mu_1 - \mu_2 = 0$		0.0326		Reject				95%		32.8125	$\pm$	29.7088	=[3.10367 , 62.5213]	
13	9	90	85		$H_0: \mu_1 - \mu_2 >= 0$		0.9837												
14	10	206	129		$H_0: \mu_1 - \mu_2 <= 0$		0.0163		Reject										
15	11	18	40																
16	12	489	440																

EXAMPLE 8–2

Recently, returns on stocks have been said to change once a story about a company appears in the *Wall Street Journal* column "Heard on the Street." An investment portfolio analyst wants to check the statistical significance of this claim. The analyst collects a random sample of 50 stocks that were recommended as winners by the editor of "Heard on the Street." The analyst proceeds to conduct a two-tailed test of whether the annualized return on stocks recommended in the column differs between the month before the recommendation and the month after the recommendation. The analyst decides to conduct a two-tailed rather than a one-tailed test because she wants to allow for the possibility that stocks may be recommended in the column after their price has appreciated (and thus returns may actually decrease in the following month), as well as allowing for an increased return. For each stock in the sample of 50, the analyst computes the return before and after the *event* (the appearance of the story in the column) and the difference between the two return figures. Then the sample average difference of returns is computed, as well as the sample standard deviation of return differences. The results are $\overline{D} = 0.1\%$ and $s_D = 0.05\%$. What should the analyst conclude?

Solution

The null and alternative hypotheses are $H_0: \mu_D = 0$ *and* $H_1: \mu_D \neq 0$. We now use the test statistic given in equation 8–2, noting that the distribution may be well approximated by the normal distribution because the sample size $n = 50$ is large. We have

$$t = \frac{\overline{D} - \mu_{D_0}}{s_D \sqrt{n}} = \frac{0.1 - 0}{0.05/7.07} = 14.14$$

The value of the test statistic falls very far in the right-hand rejection region, and the *p*-value, therefore, is very small. The analyst should conclude that the test offers strong evidence that the average returns on stocks increase (because the rejection occurred in the right-hand rejection region and D = current price − previous price) for stocks recommended in "Heard on the Street," as asserted by financial experts.

Confidence Intervals

In addition to tests of hypotheses, confidence intervals can be constructed for the average population difference μ_D. Analogous to the case of a single-population parameter, we define a $(1 - \alpha)$ 100% confidence interval for the parameter μ_D as follows.

A $(1 - \alpha)$ 100% confidence interval for the mean difference μ_D is

$$\overline{D} \pm t_{\alpha/2}\frac{s_D}{\sqrt{n}} \qquad (8\text{--}3)$$

where $t_{\alpha/2}$ is the value of the t distribution with $n - 1$ degrees of freedom that cuts off an area of $\alpha/2$ to its right. When the sample size n is large, we may approximate $t_{\alpha/2}$ as $z_{\alpha/2}$.

In Example 8–2, we may construct a 95% confidence interval for the average difference in annualized return on a stock before and after its being recommended in "Heard on the Street." The confidence interval is

$$\overline{D} \pm t_{\alpha/2} \frac{s_D}{\sqrt{n}} = 0.1 \pm 1.96 \frac{0.05}{7.07} = [0.086\%, 0.114\%]$$

Based on the data, the analyst may be 95% confident that the average difference in annualized return rate on a stock, measured the month before and the month following a positive recommendation in the column, is anywhere from 0.086% to 0.114%.

The Template

Figure 8–3 shows the template that can be used to test paired differences, when sample statistics rather than sample data are known. The data and results in this figure correspond to Example 8–2.

In this section, we compared population means for paired data. The following sections compare means of two populations where samples are drawn randomly and *independently* of each other from the two populations. When pairing can be done, our results tend to be more precise because the *experimental units* (e.g., the people, each trying two different products) are different from each other, but each acts as an independent measuring device for the two products. This pairing of similar items is called *blocking,* and we will discuss it in detail in Chapter 9.

FIGURE 8–3   **The Template for Testing Paired Differences**
      [Testing Paired Difference.xls; Sheet: Sample Stats]

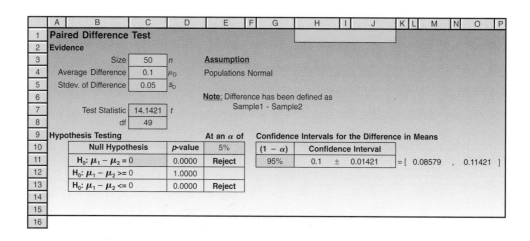

8–1. A market research study is undertaken to test which of two popular electric shavers, a model made by Norelco or a model made by Remington, is preferred by consumers. A random sample of 25 men who regularly use an electric shaver, but not one of the two models to be tested, is chosen. Each man is then asked to shave one morning with the Norelco and the next morning with the Remington, or vice versa. The order, which model is used on which day, is randomly chosen for each man. After every shave, each man is asked to complete a questionnaire rating his satisfaction with the shaver. From the questionnaire, a total satisfaction score on a scale of 0 to 100 is computed. Then, for each man, the difference between the satisfaction score for Norelco and that for Remington is computed. The score differences (Norelco score − Remington score) are 15, −8, 32, 57, 20, 10, −18, −12, 60, 72, 38, −5, 16, 22, 34, 41, 12, −38, 16, −40, 75, 11, 2, 55, 10. Which model, if either, is statistically preferred over the other? How confident are you of your finding? Explain.

8–2. The performance ratings of two sports cars, the Mazda RX7 and the Nissan 300ZX, are to be compared. A random sample of 40 drivers is selected to drive the two models. Each driver tries one car of each model, and the 40 cars of each model are chosen randomly. The time of each test drive is recorded for each driver and model. The difference in time (Mazda time − Nissan time) is computed, and from these differences a sample mean and a sample standard deviation are obtained. The results are $\overline{D} = 5.0$ seconds and $s_D = 2.3$ seconds. Based on these data, which model has higher performance? Explain. Also give a 95% confidence interval for the average time difference, in seconds, for the two models over the course driven.

8–3. Recent advances in cell phone screen quality have enabled the showing of movies and commercials on cell phone screens. But according to the *New York Times,* advertising is not as successful as movie viewing.[1] Suppose the following data are numbers of viewers for a movie (M) and for a commercial aired with the movie (C). Test for equality of movie and commercial viewing, on average, using a two-tailed test at $\alpha = 0.05$ (data in thousands):

M:	15	17	25	17	14	18	17	16	14
C:	10	9	21	16	11	12	13	15	13

8–4. A study is undertaken to determine how consumers react to energy conservation efforts. A random group of 60 families is chosen. Their consumption of electricity is monitored in a period before and a period after the families are offered certain discounts to reduce their energy consumption. Both periods are the same length. The difference in electric consumption between the period before and the period after the offer is recorded for each family. Then the average difference in consumption and the standard deviation of the difference are computed. The results are $\overline{D} = 0.2$ kilowatt and $s_D = 1.0$ kilowatt. At $\alpha = 0.01$, is there evidence to conclude that conservation efforts reduce consumption?

8–5. A nationwide retailer wants to test whether new product shelf facings are effective in increasing sales volume. New shelf facings for the soft drink Country Time are tested at a random sample of 15 stores throughout the country. Data on total sales of Country Time for each store, for the week before and the week after the new facings are installed, are given below:

Store :	1	2	3	4	5	6	7	8	9	10	11	12	13	14	15
Before:	57	61	12	38	12	69	5	39	88	9	92	26	14	70	22
After :	60	54	20	35	21	70	1	65	79	10	90	32	19	77	29

Using the 0.05 level of significance, do you believe that the new shelf facings increase sales of Country Time?

8–6. *Travel & Leisure* conducted a survey of affordable hotels in various European countries.[2] The following list shows the prices (in U.S. dollars) for one night of a double hotel room at comparable paired hotels in France and Spain.

France:	258	289	228	200	190	350	310	212	195	175	200	190
Spain:	214	250	190	185	114	285	378	230	160	120	220	105

Conduct a test for equality of average hotel room prices in these two countries against a two-tailed alternative. Which country has less expensive hotels? Back your answer using statistical inference, including the *p*-value. What are the limitations of your analysis?

8–7. In problem 8–4, suppose that the *population* standard deviation is 1.0 and that the true average reduction in consumption for the entire population in the area is $\mu_D = 0.1$. For a sample size of 60 and $\alpha = 0.01$, what is the power of the test?

8–8. Consider the information in the following table.

	Program Rating (Scale: 0 to 100)	
Program	**Men**	**Women**
60 Minutes	99	96
ABC Monday Night Football	93	25
American Idol	88	97
Entertainment Tonight	90	35
Survivor	81	33
Jeopardy	61	10
Dancing with the Stars	54	50
Murder, She Wrote	60	48
The Sopranos	73	73
The Heat of the Night	44	33
The Simpsons	30	11
Murphy Brown	25	58
Little People, Big World	38	18
L. A. Law	52	12
ABC Sunday Night Movies	32	61
King of Queens	16	96
Designing Women	8	94
The Cosby Show	18	80
Wheel of Fortune	9	20
NBC Sunday Night Movies	10	6

Assume that the television programs were randomly selected from the population of all prime-time TV programs. Also assume that ratings are normally distributed. Conduct a statistical test to determine whether there is a significant difference between average men's and women's ratings of prime-time television programs.

8–3   A Test for the Difference between Two Population Means Using Independent Random Samples

CHAPTER 10

The paired-difference test we saw in the last section is more powerful than the tests we are going to see in this section. It is more powerful because with the same data and the same α, the chances of type II error will be less in a paired-difference test than in other tests. The reason is that pairing gets at the difference between two populations more

---

[2]"Affordable European Hotels," *Travel & Leisure*, May 2007, pp. 158–165.

directly. Therefore, if it is possible to pair the samples and conduct a paired-difference test, then that is what we must do. But in many situations the samples cannot be paired, so we cannot take a paired difference. For example, suppose two different machines are producing the same type of parts and we are interested in the difference between the average time taken by each machine to produce one part. To pair two observations we have to make the same part using each of the two machines. But producing the same part once by one machine and once again by the other machine is impossible. What we can do is time the machines as randomly and independently selected parts are produced on each machine. We can then compare the average time taken by each machine and test hypotheses about the difference between them.

When independent random samples are taken, the sample sizes need not be the same for both populations. We shall denote the sample sizes by n_1 and n_2. The two population means are denoted by μ_1 and μ_2 and the two population standard deviations are denoted by σ_1 and σ_2. The sample means are denoted by $\overline{X}_1$ and $\overline{X}_2$. We shall use $(\mu_1 - \mu_2)_0$ to denote the claimed difference between the two population means.

The null hypothesis can be any one of the three usual forms:

$H_0: \mu_1 - \mu_2 = (\mu_1 - \mu_2)_0$ leading to a two-tailed test

$H_0: \mu_1 - \mu_2 \geq (\mu_1 - \mu_2)_0$ leading to a left-tailed test

$H_0: \mu_1 - \mu_2 \leq (\mu_1 - \mu_2)_0$ leading to a right-tailed test

The test statistic can be either Z or t.

Which statistic is applicable to specific cases? This section enumerates the criteria used in selecting the correct statistic and gives the equations for the test statistics. Explanations about why the test statistic is applicable follow the listed cases.

Cases in Which the Test Statistic Is Z

1. The sample sizes n_1 and n_2 are both at least 30 and the population standard deviations σ_1 and σ_2 are known.
2. Both populations are normally distributed and the population standard deviations σ_1 and σ_2 are known.

The formula for the test statistic Z is

$$Z = \frac{(\overline{X}_1 - \overline{X}_2) - (\mu_1 - \mu_2)_0}{\sqrt{\sigma_1^2/n_1 + \sigma_2^2/n_2}} \qquad (8\text{--}4)$$

where $(\mu_1 - \mu_2)_0$ is the hypothesized value for the difference in the two population means.

In the preceding cases, $\overline{X}_1$ and $\overline{X}_2$ each follows a normal distribution and therefore $(\overline{X}_1 - \overline{X}_2)$ also follows a normal distribution. Because the two samples are independent, we have

$$\text{Var}(\overline{X}_1 - \overline{X}_2) = \text{Var}(\overline{X}_1) + \text{Var}(\overline{X}_2) = \sigma_1^2/n_1 + \sigma_2^2/n_2.$$

Therefore, if the null hypothesis is true, then the quantity

$$\frac{(\overline{X}_1 - \overline{X}_2) - (\mu_1 - \mu_2)_0}{\sqrt{\sigma_1^2/n_1 + \sigma_2^2/n_2}}$$

must follow a Z distribution.

The templates to use for cases where Z is the test statistic are shown in Figures 8–4 and 8–5.

FIGURE 8–4   **The Template for Testing the Difference in Population Means**
[Testing Difference in Means.xls; Sheet: *Z*-Test from Data]

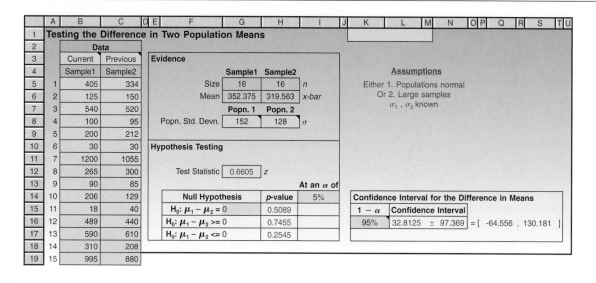

FIGURE 8–5   **The Template for Testing Difference in Means**
[Testing Difference in Means.xls; Sheet: *Z*-Test from Stats]

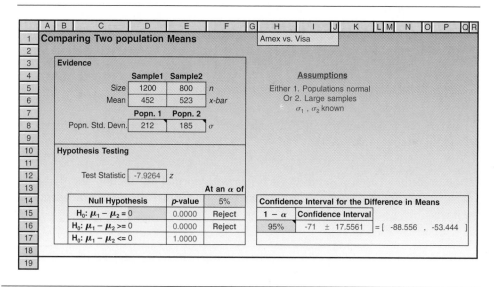

Cases in Which the Test Statistic Is *t*

Both populations are normally distributed; population standard deviations σ_1 and σ_2 are unknown, but the sample standard deviations S_1 and S_2 are known. The equations for the test statistic *t* depends on two subcases:

Subcase 1: σ_1 and σ_2 are believed to be equal (although unknown). In this subcase, we calculate *t* using the formula

$$t = \frac{(\bar{X}_1 - \bar{X}_2) - (\mu_1 - \mu_2)_0}{\sqrt{S_p^2(1/n_1 + 1/n_2)}} \qquad (8\text{--}5)$$

where S_p^2 is the pooled variance of the two samples, which serves as the estimate of the common population variance given by the formula

$$S_p^2 = \frac{(n_1 - 1)S_1^2 + (n_2 - 1)S_2^2}{n_1 + n_2 - 2} \qquad (8\text{--}6)$$

The degrees of freedom for *t* are $(n_1 + n_2 - 2)$.

  Subcase 2: σ_1 and σ_2 are believed to be unequal (although unknown). In this subcase, we calculate *t* using the formula

$$t = \frac{(\bar{X}_1 - \bar{X}_2) - (\mu_1 - \mu_2)_0}{\sqrt{S_1^2/n_1 + S_2^2/n_2}} \qquad (8\text{--}7)$$

The degrees of freedom for this *t* are given by

$$df = \left\lfloor \frac{(S_1^2/n_1 + S_2^2/n_2)^2}{(S_1^2/n_1)^2/(n_1 - 1) + (S_2^2/n_2)^2/(n_2 - 1)} \right\rfloor \qquad (8\text{--}8)$$

Subcase 1 is the easier of the two. In this case, let $\sigma_1 = \sigma_2 = \sigma$. Because the two populations are normally distributed, $\bar{X}_1$ and $\bar{X}_2$ each follows a normal distribution and thus $(\bar{X}_1 - \bar{X}_2)$ also follows a normal distribution. Because the two samples are independent, we have

$$\mathrm{Var}(\bar{X}_1 - \bar{X}_2) = \mathrm{Var}(\bar{X}_1) + \mathrm{Var}(\bar{X}_2) = \sigma^2/n_1 + \sigma^2/n_2 = \sigma^2(1/n_1 + 1/n_2)$$

We estimate σ^2 by

$$S_p^2 = \frac{(n_1 - 1)S_1^2 + (n_2 - 1)S_2^2}{(n_1 + n_2 - 2)}$$

which is a weighted average of the two sample variances. As a result, if the null hypothesis is true, then the quantity

$$\frac{(\bar{X}_1 - \bar{X}_2) - (\mu_1 - \mu_2)_0}{S_p\sqrt{1/n_1 + 1/n_2}}$$

must follow a *t* distribution with $(n_1 + n_1 - 2)$ degrees of freedom.

Subcase 2 does not neatly fall into a t distribution as it combines two sample means from two populations with two different unknown variances. When the null hypothesis is true, the quantity

$$\frac{(\overline{X}_1 - \overline{X}_2) - (\mu_1 - \mu_2)_0}{\sqrt{S_1^2/n_1 + S_2^2/n_2}}$$

can be shown to *approximately* follow a t distribution with degrees of freedom given by the complex equation 8–8. The symbol $\lfloor \; \rfloor$ used in this equation means rounding down to the nearest integer. For example, $\lfloor 15.8 \rfloor = 15$. We round the value down to comply with the principle of giving the benefit of doubt to the null hypothesis.

Because approximation is involved in this case, it is better to use subcase 1 whenever possible, to avoid approximation. But, then, subcase 1 requires the strong assumption that the two population variances are equal. To guard against overuse of subcase 1 we check the assumption using an F test that will be described later in this chapter. In any case, if we use subcase 1, we should understand fully why we believe that the two variances are equal. In general, if the sources or the causes of variance in the two populations are the same, then it is reasonable to expect the two variances to be equal.

The templates that can be used for cases where t is the test statistic are shown in Figures 8–7 and 8–8 on pages 319 and 320.

Cases Not Covered by Z or t

1. At least one population is not normally distributed and the sample size from that population is less than 30.
2. At least one population is not normally distributed and the standard deviation of that population is unknown.
3. For at least one population, neither the population standard deviation nor the sample standard deviation is known. (This case is rare.)

In the preceding cases, we are unable to find a test statistic that would follow a known distribution. It may be possible to apply the nonparametric method, the Mann-Whitney U test, described in Chapter 14.

The Templates

Figure 8–4 shows the template that can be used to test differences in population means when sample data are known. The data are entered in columns B and C. If a confidence interval is desired, enter the confidence level in cell K16.

Figure 8–5 shows the template that can be used to test differences in population means when sample statistics rather than sample data are known. The data in the figure correspond to Example 8–3.

EXAMPLE 8–3   Until a few years ago, the market for consumer credit was considered to be segmented. Higher-income, higher-spending people tended to be American Express cardholders, and lower-income, lower-spending people were usually Visa cardholders. In the last few years, Visa has intensified its efforts to break into the higher-income segments of the market by using magazine and television advertising to create a high-class image. Recently, a consulting firm was hired by Visa to determine whether average monthly charges on the American Express Gold Card are approximately equal to the average monthly charges on Preferred Visa. A random sample of 1,200 Preferred Visa cardholders was selected, and the sample average monthly charge was found to be $x_1 = \$452$. An independent random sample of 800 Gold Card members revealed a sample mean $\overline{x}_2 = \$523$. Assume $\sigma_1 = \$212$ and $\sigma_2 = \$185$. (Holders of both the Gold Card and Preferred Visa were excluded from the study.) Is there evidence to conclude that the average monthly charge in the entire population of

FIGURE 8–6   Carrying Out the Test of Example 8–3

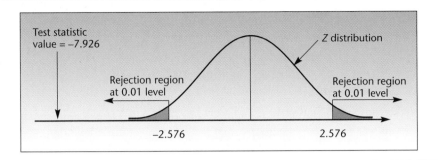

American Express Gold Card members is different from the average monthly charge in the entire population of Preferred Visa cardholders?

Solution

Since we have no prior suspicion that either of the two populations may have a higher mean, the test is two-tailed. The null and alternative hypotheses are

$$H_0: \mu_1 - \mu_2 = 0$$
$$H_1: \mu_1 - \mu_2 \neq 0$$

The value of our test statistic (equation 8–4) is

$$z = \frac{452 - 523 - 0}{\sqrt{212^2/1{,}200 + 185^2/800}} = -7.926$$

The computed value of the Z statistic falls in the left-hand rejection region for any commonly used α, and the p-value is very small. We conclude that there is a statistically significant difference in average monthly charges between Gold Card and Preferred Visa cardholders. Note that this does not imply any *practical significance*. That is, while a difference in average spending in the two populations may exist, we cannot necessarily conclude that this difference is large. The test is shown in Figure 8–6.

EXAMPLE 8–4

Suppose that the makers of Duracell batteries want to demonstrate that their size AA battery lasts an average of at least 45 minutes longer than Duracell's main competitor, the Energizer. Two independent random samples of 100 batteries of each kind are selected, and the batteries are run continuously until they are no longer operational. The sample average life for Duracell is found to be $\bar{x}_1 = 308$ minutes. The result for the Energizer batteries is $\bar{x}_2 = 254$ minutes. Assume $\sigma_1 = 84$ minutes and $\sigma_2 = 67$ minutes. Is there evidence to substantiate Duracell's claim that its batteries last, on average, at least 45 minutes longer than Energizer batteries of the same size?

Solution

Our null and alternative hypotheses are

$$H_0: \mu_1 - \mu_2 \leq 45$$
$$H_1: \mu_1 - \mu_2 > 45$$

The makers of Duracell hope to demonstrate their claim by rejecting the null hypothesis. Recall that failing to reject a null hypothesis is not a strong conclusion. This is why—in order to demonstrate that Duracell batteries last an average of at least 45 minutes longer—the claim to be demonstrated is stated as the *alternative* hypothesis.

The value of the test statistic in this case is computed as follows:

$$z = \frac{308 - 254 - 45}{\sqrt{84^2/100 + 67^2/100}} = 0.838$$

This value falls in the nonrejection region of our right-tailed test at any conventional level of significance α. The *p*-value is equal to 0.2011. We must conclude that there is insufficient evidence to support Duracell's claim.

Confidence Intervals

Recall from Chapter 7 that there is a strong connection between hypothesis tests and confidence intervals. In the case of the difference between two population means, we have the following:

A large-sample $(1 - \alpha)$ 100% confidence interval for the difference between two population means $\mu_1 - \mu_2$, using independent random samples, is

$$\bar{x}_1 - \bar{x}_2 \pm z_{\alpha/2}\sqrt{\frac{\sigma_1^2}{n_1} + \frac{\sigma_2^2}{n_2}} \qquad (8\text{–}9)$$

Equation 8–9 should be intuitively clear. The bounds on the difference between the two population means are equal to the difference between the two sample means, plus or minus the *z* coefficient for $(1 - \alpha)$ 100% confidence times the standard deviation of the difference between the two sample means (which is the expression with the square root sign).

In the context of Example 8–3, a 95% confidence interval for the difference between the average monthly charge on the American Express Gold Card and the average monthly charge on the Preferred Visa Card is, by equation 8–9,

$$523 - 452 \pm 1.96 \sqrt{\frac{212^2}{1,200} + \frac{185^2}{800}} = [53.44, 88.56]$$

The consulting firm may report to Visa that it is 95% confident that the average American Express Gold Card monthly bill is anywhere from $53.44 to $88.56 higher than the average Preferred Visa bill.

With one-tailed tests, the analogous interval is a one-sided confidence interval. We will not give examples of such intervals in this chapter. In general, we construct confidence intervals for population parameters when we have no *particular* values of the parameters we want to test and are interested in estimation only.

PROBLEMS

8–9. Ethanol is getting wider use as car fuel when mixed with gasoline.[3] A car manufacturer wants to evaluate the performance of engines using ethanol mix with that of pure gasoline. The sample average for 100 runs using ethanol is 76.5 on a 0 to

---

[3]John Carey, "Ethanol Is Not the Only Green in Town," *BusinessWeek*, April 30, 2007, p. 74.

100 scale and the sample standard deviation is 38. For a sample of 100 runs of pure gasoline, the sample average is 88.1 and the standard deviation is 40. Conduct a two-tailed test using $\alpha = 0.05$, and also provide a 95% confidence interval for the difference between means.

8–10. The photography department of a fashion magazine needs to choose a camera. Of the two models the department is considering, one is made by Nikon and one by Minolta. The department contracts with an agency to determine if one of the two models gets a higher average performance rating by professional photographers, or whether the average performance ratings of these two cameras are not statistically different. The agency asks 60 different professional photographers to rate one of the cameras (30 photographers rate each model). The ratings are on a scale of 1 to 10. The average sample rating for Nikon is 8.5, and the sample standard deviation is 2.1. For the Minolta sample, the average sample rating is 7.8, and the standard deviation is 1.8. Is there a difference between the average population ratings of the two cameras? If so, which one is rated higher?

8–11. Marcus Robert Real Estate Company wants to test whether the average sale price of residential properties in a certain size range in Bel Air, California, is approximately equal to the average sale price of residential properties of the same size range in Marin County, California. The company gathers data on a random sample of 32 properties in Bel Air and finds $\bar{x} = \$2.5$ million and $s = \$0.41$ million. A random sample of 35 properties in Marin County gives $\bar{x} = \$4.32$ million and $s = \$0.87$ million. Is the average sale price of all properties in both locations approximately equal or not? Explain.

8–12. *Fortune* compared global equities versus investments in the U.S. market. For the global market, the magazine found an average of 15% return over five years, while for U.S. markets it found an average of 6.2%.[4] Suppose that both numbers are based on random samples of 40 investments in each market, with a standard deviation of 3% in the global market and 3.5% in U.S. markets. Conduct a test for equality of average return using $\alpha = 0.05$, and construct a 95% confidence interval for the difference in average return in the global versus U.S. markets.

8–13. Many companies that cater to teenagers have learned that young people respond to commercials that provide dance-beat music, adventure, and a fast pace rather than words. In one test, a group of 128 teenagers were shown commercials featuring rock music, and their purchasing frequency of the advertised products over the following month was recorded as a single score for each person in the group. Then a group of 212 teenagers was shown commercials for the same products, but with the music replaced by verbal persuasion. The purchase frequency scores of this group were computed as well. The results for the music group were $\bar{x} = 23.5$ and $s = 12.2$; and the results for the verbal group were $\bar{x} = 18.0$ and $s = 10.5$. Assume that the two groups were randomly selected from the entire teenage consumer population. Using the $\alpha = 0.01$ level of significance, test the null hypothesis that both methods of advertising are equally effective versus the alternative hypothesis that they are not equally effective. If you conclude that one method is better, state which one it is, and explain how you reached your conclusion.

8–14. New corporate strategies take years to develop. Two methods for facilitating the development of new strategies by executive strategy meetings are to be compared. One method is to hold a two-day retreat in a posh hotel; the other is to hold a series of informal luncheon meetings on company premises. The following are the results of two independent random samples of firms following one of these two methods. The data are the number of months, for each company, that elapsed from the time an idea was first suggested until the time it was implemented.

---

[4]Katie Banner, "Global Strategies: Finding Pearls in Choppy Waters," *Fortune*, March 19, 2007, p. 191.

Hotel	On-Site
17	6
11	12
14	13
25	16
9	4
18	8
36	14
19	18
22	10
24	5
16	7
31	12
23	10

Test for a difference between means, using $\alpha = 0.05$.

8–15. A fashion industry analyst wants to prove that models featuring Liz Claiborne clothing earn on average more than models featuring clothes designed by Calvin Klein. For a given period of time, a random sample of 32 Liz Claiborne models reveals average earnings of $4,238.00 and a standard deviation of $1,002.50. For the same period, an independent random sample of 37 Calvin Klein models has mean earnings of $3,888.72 and a sample standard deviation of $876.05.

    a. Is this a one-tailed or a two-tailed test? Explain.

    b. Carry out the hypothesis test at the 0.05 level of significance.

    c. State your conclusion.

    d. What is the *p*-value? Explain its relevance.

    e. Redo the problem, assuming the results are based on a random sample of 10 Liz Claiborne models and 11 Calvin Klein models.

8–16. *Active Trader* compared earnings on stock investments when companies made strong pre-earnings announcements versus cases where pre-earnings announcements were weak. Both sample sizes were 28. The average performance for the strong pre-earnings announcement group was 0.19%, and the average performance for the weak pre-earnings group was 0.72%. The standard deviations were 5.72% and 5.10%, respectively.[5] Conduct a test for equality of means using $\alpha = 0.01$ and construct a 99% confidence interval for difference in means.

8–17. A brokerage firm is said to provide both brokerage services and "research" if, in addition to buying and selling securities for its clients, the firm furnishes clients with advice about the value of securities, information on economic factors and trends, and portfolio strategy. The Securities and Exchange Commission (SEC) has been studying brokerage commissions charged by both "research" and "nonresearch" brokerage houses. A random sample of 255 transactions at nonresearch firms is collected as well as a random sample of 300 transactions at research firms. These samples reveal that the difference between the average sample percentage of commission at research firms and the average percentage of commission in the nonresearch sample is 2.54%. The standard deviation of the research firms' sample is 0.85%, and that of the nonresearch firms is 0.64%. Give a 95% confidence interval for the difference in the average percentage of commissions in research versus nonresearch brokerage houses.

The Templates

Figure 8–7 shows the template that can be used to conduct *t* tests for difference in population means when sample data are known. The top panel can be used if there is

---

[5]David Bukey, "The Earnings Guidance Game," *Active Trader*, April 2007, p. 16.

FIGURE 8–7 The Template for the *t* Test for Difference in Means
[Testing Difference in Means.xls; Sheet: *t*-Test from Data]

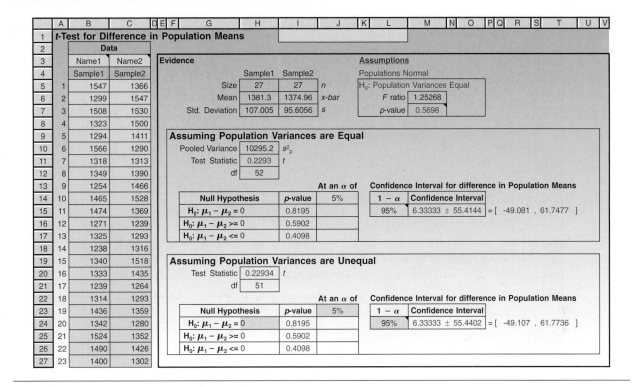

reason to believe that the two population variances are equal; the bottom panel should be used in all other cases. As an additional aid to deciding which panel to use, the null hypothesis H_0: $\sigma_1^2 - \sigma_2^2 = 0$ is tested at top right. The *p*-value of the test appears in cell M7. If this value is at least, say, 20%, then there is no problem in using the top panel. If the *p*-value is less than 10%, then it is not wise to use the top panel. In such circumstances, a warning message—"Warning: Equal variance assumption is questionable"—will appear in cell K10.

If a confidence interval for the difference in the means is desired, enter the confidence level in cell L15 or L24.

Figure 8–8 shows the template that can be used to conduct *t* tests for difference in population means when sample statistics rather than sample data are known. The top panel can be used if there is reason to believe that the two population variances are equal; the bottom panel should be used otherwise. As an additional aid to deciding which panel to use, the null hypothesis that the population variances are equal is tested at top right. The *p*-value of the test appears in cell J7. If this value is at least, say, 20%, then there is no problem in using the top panel. If it is less than 10%, then it is not wise to use the top panel. In such circumstances, a warning message—"Warning: Equal variance assumption is questionable"—will appear in cell H10.

If a confidence interval for the difference in the means is desired, enter the confidence level in cell I15 or I24.

Changes in the price of oil have long been known to affect the economy of the United States. An economist wants to check whether the price of a barrel of crude oil affects the consumer price index (CPI), a measure of price levels and inflation. The economist collects two sets of data: one set comprises 14 monthly observations on increases in the CPI, in percentage per month, when the price of crude oil is $66.00 per barrel;

EXAMPLE 8–5

FIGURE 8–8   The Template for the *t* Test for Difference in Means
[Testing Difference in Means.xls; Sheet: *t*-Test from Stats]

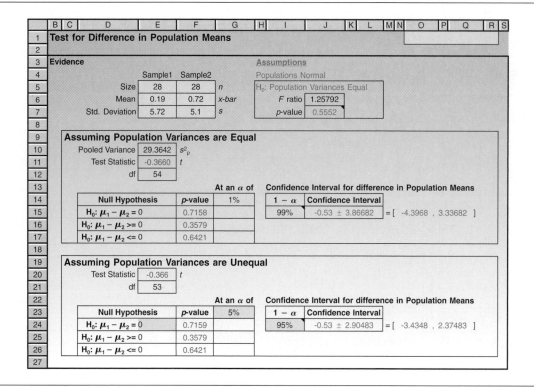

the other set consists of 9 monthly observations on percentage increase in the CPI when the price of crude oil is \$58.00 per barrel. The economist assumes that her data are a random set of observations from a population of monthly CPI percentage increases when oil sells for \$66.00 per barrel, and an independent set of random observations from a population of monthly CPI percentage increases when oil sells for \$58.00 per barrel. She also assumes that the two populations of CPI percentage increases are normally distributed and that the variances of the two populations are equal. Considering the nature of the economic variables in question, these are reasonable assumptions. If we call the population of monthly CPI percentage increases when oil sells for \$66.00 population 1, and that of oil at \$58.00 per barrel population 2, then the economist's data are as follows: $\bar{x}_1 = 0.317\%$, $s_1 = 0.12\%$, $n_1 = 14$; $\bar{x}_2 = 0.210\%$, $s_2 = 0.11\%$, $n_2 = 9$. Our economist is faced with the question: Do these data provide evidence to conclude that average percentage increase in the CPI differs when oil sells at these two different prices?

Solution   Although the economist may have a suspicion about the possible direction of change in the CPI as oil prices decrease, she decides to approach the situation with an open mind and let the data speak for themselves. That is, she wants to carry out the two-tailed test. Her test is H_0: $\mu_1 - \mu_2 = 0$ versus H_1: $\mu_1 - \mu_2 \neq 0$. Using equation 8–5, the economist computes the value of the test statistic, which has a *t* distribution with $n_1 + n_2 - 2 = 21$ degrees of freedom:

$$t = \frac{0.317 - 0.210 - 0}{\sqrt{\dfrac{(13)(0.12)^2 + (8)(0.11)^2}{21}\left(\dfrac{1}{14} + \dfrac{1}{9}\right)}} = 2.15$$

The computed value of the test statistic $t = 2.15$ falls in the right-hand rejection region at $\alpha = 0.05$, but not very far from the critical point 2.080. The p-value is therefore just less than 0.05. The economist may thus conclude that, based on her data and the validity of the assumptions made, evidence suggests that the average monthly increase in the CPI is greater when oil sells for \$66.00 per barrel than it is when oil sells for \$58.00 per barrel.

EXAMPLE 8-6

The manufacturers of compact disk players want to test whether a small price reduction is enough to increase sales of their product. Randomly chosen data on 15 weekly sales totals at outlets in a given area before the price reduction show a sample mean of \$6,598 and a sample standard deviation of \$844. A random sample of 12 weekly sales totals after the small price reduction gives a sample mean of \$6,870 and a sample standard deviation of \$669. Is there evidence that the small price reduction is enough to increase sales of compact disk players?

Solution

This is a one-tailed test, except that we will reverse the notation 1 and 2 so we can conduct a right-tailed test to determine whether reducing the price increases sales (if sales increase, then μ_2 will be greater than μ_1, which is what we want the alternative hypothesis to be). We have $H_0: \mu_1 - \mu_2 \geq 0$ and $H_1: \mu_1 - \mu_2 < 0$. We assume an equal variance of the populations of sales at the two price levels. Our test statistic has a t distribution with $n_1 + n_2 - 2 = 15 + 12 - 2 = 25$ degrees of freedom. The computed value of the statistic, by equation 8–7, is

$$t = \frac{(6{,}870 - 6{,}598) - 0}{\sqrt{\dfrac{(14)(844)^2 + (11)(669)^2}{25}\left(\dfrac{1}{15} + \dfrac{1}{12}\right)}} = 0.91$$

This value of the statistic falls inside the nonrejection region for any usual level of significance.

Confidence Intervals

As usual, we can construct confidence intervals for the parameter in question—here, the difference between the two population means. The confidence interval for this parameter is based on the t distribution with $n_1 + n_2 - 2$ degrees of freedom (or z when df is large).

CHAPTER 10

A $(1 - \alpha)$ 100% confidence interval for $(\mu_1 - \mu_2)$, assuming equal population variance, is

$$\bar{x}_1 - \bar{x}_2 \pm t_{\alpha/2}\sqrt{s_p^2\left(\frac{1}{n_1} + \frac{1}{n_2}\right)} \qquad (8\text{–}10)$$

The confidence interval in equation 8–10 has the usual form: Estimate ± Distribution coefficient × Standard deviation of estimator.

In Example 8–6, forgetting that the test was carried out as a one-tailed test, we compute a 95% confidence interval for the difference between the two means. Since the test resulted in nonrejection of the null hypothesis (and would have also resulted so had it been carried out as two-tailed), our confidence interval should contain the null hypothesis difference between the two population means: zero. This is due to the connection between hypothesis tests and confidence intervals. Let us see if this really happens. The 95% confidence interval for $\mu_1 - \mu_2$ is

$$\overline{x}_1 - \overline{x}_2 \pm t_{0.025}\sqrt{s_p^2\left(\frac{1}{n_1} + \frac{1}{n_2}\right)} = (6{,}870 - 6{,}598) \pm 2.06\sqrt{(595{,}835)(0.15)}$$

$$= [-343.85,\ 887.85]$$

We see that the confidence interval indeed contains the null-hypothesized difference of zero, as expected from the fact that a two-tailed test would have resulted in nonrejection of the null hypothesis.

PROBLEMS

In each of the following problems assume that the two populations of interest are normally distributed with equal variance. Assume independent random sampling from the two populations.

8–18. The recent boom in sales of travel books has led to the marketing of other travel-related guides, such as video travel guides and audio walking-tour tapes. Waldenbooks has been studying the market for these travel guides. In one market test, a random sample of 25 potential travelers was asked to rate audiotapes of a certain destination, and another random sample of 20 potential travelers was asked to rate videotapes of the same destination. Both ratings were on a scale of 0 to 100 and measured the potential travelers' satisfaction with the travel guide they tested and the degree of possible purchase intent (with 100 the highest). The mean score for the audio group was 87, and their standard deviation was 12. The mean score for the video group was 64, and their standard deviation was 23. Do these data present evidence that one form of travel guide is better than the other? Advise Waldenbooks on a possible marketing decision to be made.

8–19. Business schools at certain prestigious universities offer nondegree management training programs for high-level executives. These programs supposedly develop executives' leadership abilities and help them advance to higher management positions within 2 years after program completion. A management consulting firm wants to test the effectiveness of these programs and sets out to conduct a one-tailed test, where the alternative hypothesis is that graduates of the programs under study do receive, on average, salaries more than \$4,000 per year higher than salaries of comparable executives without the special university training. To test the hypotheses, the firm traces a random sample of 28 top executives who earn, at the time the sample is selected, about the same salaries. Out of this group, 13 executives—randomly selected from the group of 28 executives—are enrolled in one of the university programs under study. Two years later, average salaries for the two groups and standard deviations of salaries are computed. The results are $\overline{x} = 48$ and $s = 6$ for the nonprogram executives and $\overline{x} = 55$ and $s = 8$ for the program executives. All numbers are in thousands of dollars per year. Conduct the test at $\alpha = 0.05$, and evaluate the effectiveness of the programs in terms of increased average salary levels.

8–20. Recent low-fare flights between Britain and eastern European destinations have brought large groups of English partygoers to cities such as Prague and Budapest. According to the *New York Times*, cheap beer is a big draw, with an average price of \$1 as compared with \$6 in Britain.[6] Assume these two reported averages were obtained from two random samples of 20 establishments in London and in Prague, and that the sample standard deviation in London was \$2.5 and in Prague \$1.1. Conduct a test for

[6]Craig S. Smith, "British Bachelor Partiers Are Taking Their Revels East," *The New York Times*, May 8, 2007, p. A10.

equality of means using $\alpha = 0.05$ and provide a 95% confidence interval for the average savings per beer for a visitor versus the amount paid at home in London.

8-21. As the U.S. economy cools down, investors look to emerging markets to offer growth opportunities. In China, investments have continued to grow.[7] Suppose that a random sample of 15 investments in U.S. corporations had an average annual return of 3.8% and standard deviation of 2.2%. For a random sample of 18 investments in China, the average return was 6.1% and the standard deviation was 5.3%. Conduct a test for equality of population means using $\alpha = 0.01$.

8-22. Ikarus, the Hungarian bus maker, lost its important Commonwealth of Independent States market and is reported on the verge of collapse. The company is now trying a new engine in its buses and has gathered the following random samples of miles-per-gallon figures for the old engine versus the new:

Old engine: 8, 9, 7.5, 8.5, 6, 9, 9, 10, 7, 8.5, 6, 10, 9, 8, 9, 5, 9.5, 10, 8

New engine: 10, 9, 9, 6, 9, 11, 11, 8, 9, 6.5, 7, 9, 10, 8, 9, 10, 9, 12, 11.5, 10, 7, 10, 8.5

Is there evidence that the new engine is more economical than the old one?

8-23. *Air Transport World* recently named the Dutch airline KLM "Airline of the Year." One measure of the airline's excellent management is its research effort in developing new routes and improving service on existing routes. The airline wanted to test the profitability of a certain transatlantic flight route and offered daily flights from Europe to the United States over a period of 6 weeks on the new proposed route. Then, over a period of 9 weeks, daily flights were offered from Europe to an alternative airport in the United States. Weekly profitability data for the two samples were collected, under the assumption that these may be viewed as independent random samples of weekly profits from the two populations (one population is flights to the proposed airport, and the other population is flights to an alternative airport). Data are as follows. For the proposed route, $\bar{x} = \$96,540$ per week and $s = \$12,522$. For the alternative route, $\bar{x} = \$85,991$ and $s = \$19,548$. Test the hypothesis that the proposed route is more profitable than the alternative route. Use a significance level of your choice.

8-24. According to *Money*, the average yield of a 6-month bank certificate of deposit (CD) is 3.56%, and the average yield for money market funds (MMFs) is 4.84%.[8] Assume that these two averages come from two random samples of 20 each from these two kinds of investments, and that the sample standard deviation for the CDs is 2.8% and for the MMFs it is 3.2%. Use statistical inference to determine whether, on average, one mode of investment is better than the other.

8-25. Mark Pollard, financial consultant for Merrill Lynch, Pierce, Fenner & Smith, Inc., is quoted in national advertisements for Merrill Lynch as saying: "I've made more money for clients by saying no than by saying yes." Suppose that Pollard allowed you access to his files so that you could conduct a statistical test of the correctness of his statement. Suppose further that you gathered a random sample of 25 clients to whom Pollard said yes when presented with their investment proposals, and you found that the clients' average gain on investments was 12% and the standard deviation was 2.5%. Suppose you gathered another sample of 25 clients to whom Pollard said no when asked about possible investments; the clients were then offered other investments, which they consequently made. For this sample, you found that the average return was 13.5% and the standard deviation was 1%. Test Pollard's claim at $\alpha = 0.05$. What assumptions are you making in this problem?

---

[7]James Mehring, "As Trade Deficit Shrinks, a Plus for Growth," *BusinessWeek*, April 30, 2007, p. 27.

[8]Walter Updegrave, "Plan Savings and Credit: Wave and You've Paid," *Money*, March 2007, p. 40.

8–26. An article reports the results of an analysis of stock market returns before and after antitrust trials that resulted in the breakup of AT&T. The study concentrated on two periods: the pre-antitrust period of 1966 to 1973, denoted period 1, and the antitrust trial period of 1974 to 1981, called period 2. An equation similar to equation 8–7 was used to test for the existence of a difference in mean stock return during the two periods. Conduct a two-tailed test of equality of mean stock return in the population of all stocks before and during the antitrust trials using the following data: $n_1 = 21$, $\bar{x}_1 = 0.105$, $s_1 = 0.09$; $n_2 = 28$, $\bar{x}_2 = 0.1331$, $s_2 = 0.122$. Use $\alpha = 0.05$.

8–27. The cosmetics giant Avon Products recently hired a new advertising firm to promote its products.[9] Suppose that following the airing of a random set of 8 commercials made by the new firm, company sales rose an average of 3% and the standard deviation was 2%. For a random set of 10 airings of commercials by the old advertising firm, average sales rise was 2.3% and the standard deviation was 2.1%. Is there evidence that the new advertising firm hired by Avon is more effective than the old one? Explain.

8–28. In problem 8–25, construct a 95% confidence interval for the difference between the average return to investors following a no recommendation and the average return to investors following a yes recommendation. Interpret your results.

8–4 A Large-Sample Test for the Difference between Two Population Proportions

When sample sizes are large enough that the distributions of the sample proportions $\hat{P}_1$ and $\hat{P}_2$ are both approximated well by a normal distribution, the difference between the two sample proportions is also approximately normally distributed, and this gives rise to a test for equality of two population proportions based on the standard normal distribution. It is also possible to construct confidence intervals for the difference between the two population proportions. Assuming the sample sizes are large and assuming independent random sampling from the two populations, the following are possible hypotheses (we consider situations similar to the ones discussed in the previous two sections; other tests are also possible).

Situation I:	$H_0: p_1 - p_2 = 0$
	$H_1: p_1 - p_2 \neq 0$
Situation II:	$H_0: p_1 - p_2 \leq 0$
	$H_1: p_1 - p_2 > 0$
Situation III:	$H_0: p_1 - p_2 \leq D$
	$H_1: p_1 - p_2 > D$

Here D is some number other than 0.

In the case of tests about the difference between two population proportions, there are two test statistics. One statistic is appropriate when the null hypothesis is that the difference between the two population proportions is equal to (or greater than or equal to, or less than or equal to) zero. This is the case, for example, in situations I and II. The other test statistic is appropriate when the null hypothesis difference is some number D different from zero. This is the case, for example, in situation III (or in a two-tailed test, situation I, with D replacing 0).

---

[9] Stuart Elliott, "Avon Comes Calling with a New Campaign," *The New York Times,* March 15, 2007, p. C4.

The test statistic for the difference between two population proportions where the null hypothesis difference is zero is

$$z = \frac{\hat{p}_1 - \hat{p}_2 - 0}{\sqrt{\hat{p}(1 - \hat{p})(1/n_1 + 1/n_2)}} \qquad (8\text{--}11)$$

where $\hat{p}_1 = x_1/n_1$ is the sample proportion in sample 1 and $\hat{p}_2 = x_2/n_2$ is the sample proportion in sample 2. The symbol $\hat{p}$ stands for the *combined sample proportion in both samples,* considered as a single sample. That is,

$$\hat{p} = \frac{x_1 + x_2}{n_1 + n_2} \qquad (8\text{--}12)$$

Note that 0 in the numerator of equation 8–11 is the null hypothesis difference between the two population proportions; we retain it only for conceptual reasons—to maintain the form of our test statistic: (Estimate − Hypothesized value of the parameter)/(Standard deviation of the estimator). When we carry out computations using equation 8–11, we will, of course, ignore the subtraction of zero. Under the null hypothesis that the difference between the two population proportions is zero, both sample proportions $\hat{p}_1$ and $\hat{p}_2$ are estimates of the same quantity, and therefore—assuming, as always, that the null hypothesis is true—we pool the two estimates when computing the estimated standard deviation of the difference between the two sample proportions: the denominator of equation 8–11.

When the null hypothesis is that the difference between the two population proportions is a number other than zero, we cannot assume that $\hat{p}_1$ and $\hat{p}_2$ are estimates of the same population proportion (because the null hypothesis difference between the two population proportions is $D \neq 0$); in such cases we cannot pool the two estimates when computing the estimated standard deviation of the difference between the two sample proportions. In such cases, we use the following test statistic.

The test statistic for the difference between two population proportions when the null hypothesis difference between the two proportions is some number *D*, other than zero, is

$$z = \frac{\hat{p}_1 - \hat{p}_2 - D}{\sqrt{\hat{p}_1(1 - \hat{p}_1)/n_1 + \hat{p}_2(1 - \hat{p}_2)/n_2}} \qquad (8\text{--}13)$$

We will now demonstrate the use of the test statistics presented in this section with the following examples.

Finance incentives by the major automakers are reducing banks' share of the market for automobile loans. Suppose that in 2000, banks wrote about 53% of all car loans, and in 2007, the banks' share was only 43%. Suppose that these data are based on a random sample of 100 car loans in 2000, where 53 of the loans were found to be bank loans; and the 2007 data are also based on a random sample of 100 loans, 43 of which were found to be bank loans. Carry out a two-tailed test of the equality of banks' share of the car loan market in 2000 and in 2007.

EXAMPLE 8–7

Our hypotheses are those described as situation I, a two-tailed test of the equality of two population proportions. We have $H_0: p_1 - p_2 = 0$ and $H_1: p_1 - p_2 \neq 0$. Since the null hypothesis difference between the two population proportions is zero, we can

Solution

FIGURE 8–9   Carrying Out the Test of Example 8–7

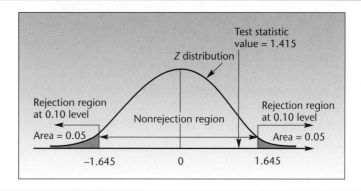

use the test statistic of equation 8–11. First we calculate $\hat{p}$, the combined sample proportion, using equation 8–12:

$$\hat{p} = \frac{x_1 + x_2}{n_1 + n_2} = \frac{53 + 43}{100 + 100} = 0.48$$

We also have $1 - \hat{p} = 0.52$.
    We now compute the value of the test statistic, equation 8–11:

$$z = \frac{\hat{p}_1 - \hat{p}_2}{\sqrt{\hat{p}(1 - \hat{p})(1/n_1 + 1/n_2)}} = \frac{0.53 - 0.43}{\sqrt{(0.48)(0.52)(0.01 + 0.01)}} = 1.415$$

This value of the test statistic falls in the nonrejection region even if we use $\alpha = 0.10$.
In fact, the p-value, found using the standard normal table, is equal to 0.157. We conclude that the data present insufficient evidence that the share of banks in the car
loan market has changed from 2000 to 2007. The test is shown in Figure 8–9.

EXAMPLE 8–8

From time to time, BankAmerica Corporation comes out with its Free and Easy Travelers
Cheques Sweepstakes, designed to increase the amounts of BankAmerica traveler's
checks sold. Since the amount bought per customer determines the customer's chances of
winning a prize, a manager hypothesizes that, during sweepstakes time, the proportion of
BankAmerica traveler's check buyers who buy more than $2,500 worth of checks will
be at least 10% higher than the proportion of traveler's check buyers who buy more
than $2,500 worth of checks when there are no sweepstakes. A random sample of
300 traveler's check buyers, taken when the sweepstakes are on, reveals that 120 of
these people bought checks for more than $2,500. A random sample of 700 traveler's
check buyers, taken when no sweepstakes prizes are offered, reveals that 140 of these
people bought checks for more than $2,500. Conduct the hypothesis test.

Solution   The manager wants to prove that the population proportion of traveler's check buyers
who buy at least $2,500 in checks when sweepstakes prizes are offered is at least 10%
higher than the proportion of such buyers when no sweepstakes are on. Therefore, this

FIGURE 8–10   Carrying Out the Test of Example 8–8

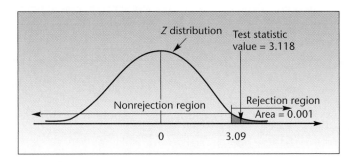

should be the manager's alternative hypothesis. We have H_0: $p_1 - p_2 \leq 0.10$ and H_1: $p_1 - p_2 > 0.10$. The appropriate test statistic is the statistic given in equation 8–13:

$$z = \frac{\hat{p}_1 - \hat{p}_2 - D}{\sqrt{\hat{p}_1(1 - \hat{p}_1)/n_1 + \hat{p}_2(1 - \hat{p}_2)/n_2}}$$

$$= \frac{120/300 - 140/700 - 0.10}{\sqrt{[(120/300)(180/300)]/300 + [(140/700)(560/700)]/700}}$$

$$= \frac{(0.4 - 0.2) - 0.1}{\sqrt{(0.4)(0.6)/300 + (0.2)(0.8)/700}} = 3.118$$

This value of the test statistic falls in the rejection region for $\alpha = 0.001$ (corresponding to the critical point 3.09 from the normal table). The p-value is therefore less than 0.001, and the null hypothesis is rejected. The manager is probably right. Figure 8–10 shows the result of the test.

Confidence Intervals

When constructing confidence intervals for the difference between two population proportions, we do not use the pooled estimate because we do not assume that the two proportions are equal. The estimated standard deviation of the difference between the two sample proportions, to be used in the confidence interval, is the denominator in equation 8–13.

A large-sample $(1 - \alpha)$ 100% confidence interval for the difference between two population proportions is

$$\hat{p}_1 - \hat{p}_2 \pm z_{\alpha/2} \sqrt{\frac{\hat{p}_1(1 - \hat{p}_1)}{n_1} + \frac{\hat{p}_2(1 - \hat{p}_2)}{n_2}} \qquad (8\text{–}14)$$

In the context of Example 8–8, let us now construct a 95% confidence interval for the difference between the proportion of BankAmerica traveler's check buyers who buy more than $2,500 worth of checks during sweepstakes and the proportion of

FIGURE 8–11   The Template for Testing Differences in Proportions
[Testing Difference in Proportions.xls]

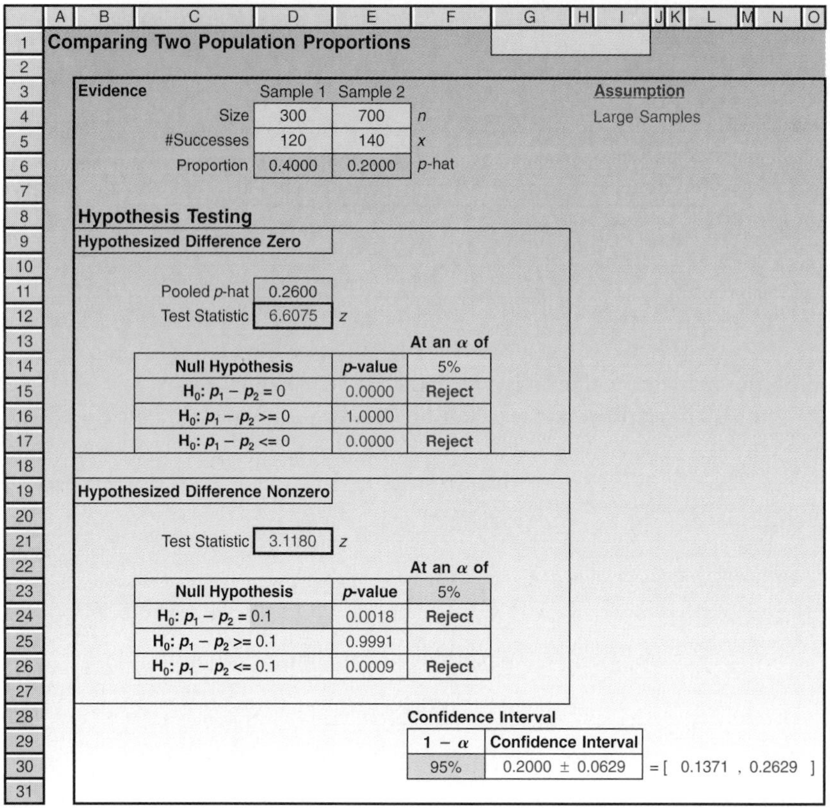

buyers of checks greater than this amount when no sweepstakes prizes are offered. Using equation 8–14, we get

$$0.4 - 0.2 \pm 1.96 \sqrt{\frac{(0.4)(0.6)}{300} + \frac{(0.2)(0.8)}{700}} = 0.2 \pm 1.96(0.032)$$
$$= [0.137, 0.263]$$

The manager may be 95% confident that the difference between the two proportions of interest is anywhere from 0.137 to 0.263.

The Template

Figure 8–11 shows the template that can be used to test differences in population proportions. The middle panel is used when the hypothesized difference is zero. The bottom panel is used when the hypothesized difference is nonzero. The data in the figure correspond to Example 8–8, where $H_0: p_1 - p_2 \le 0.10$. The bottom panel shows that the p-value is 0.009, and H_0 is to be rejected.

PROBLEMS

8–29.   Airline mergers cause many problems for the airline industry. One variable often quoted as a measure of an airline's efficiency is the percentage of on-time departures. Following the merger of Republic Airlines with Northwest Airlines, the percentage of on-time departures for Northwest planes declined from approximately

85% to about 68%. Suppose that the percentages reported above are based on two random samples of flights: a sample of 100 flights over a period of two months before the merger, of which 85 are found to have departed on time; and a sample of 100 flights over a period of two months after the merger, 68 of which are found to have departed on time. Based on these data, do you believe that Northwest's on-time percentage declined during the period following its merger with Republic?

8–30. A physicians' group is interested in testing to determine whether more people in small towns choose a physician by word of mouth in comparison with people in large metropolitan areas. A random sample of 1,000 people in small towns reveals that 850 chose their physicians by word of mouth; a random sample of 2,500 people living in large metropolitan areas reveals that 1,950 chose a physician by word of mouth. Conduct a one-tailed test aimed at proving that the percentage of popular recommendation of physicians is larger in small towns than in large metropolitan areas. Use $\alpha = 0.01$.

8–31. A corporate raider has been successful in 11 of 31 takeover attempts. Another corporate raider has been successful in 19 of 50 takeover bids. Assuming that the success rate of each raider at each trial is independent of all other attempts, and that the information presented can be regarded as based on two independent random samples of the two raiders' overall performance, can you say whether one of the raiders is more successful than the other? Explain.

8–32. A random sample of 2,060 consumers shows that 13% prefer California wines. Over the next three months, an advertising campaign is undertaken to show that California wines receive awards and win taste tests. The organizers of the campaign want to prove that the three-month campaign raised the proportion of people who prefer California wines by at least 5%. At the end of the campaign, a random sample of 5,000 consumers shows that 19% of them now prefer California wines. Conduct the test at $\alpha = 0.05$.

8–33. In problem 8–32, give a 95% confidence interval for the increase in the population proportion of consumers preferring California wines following the campaign.

8–34. Federal Reserve Board regulations permit banks to offer their clients commercial paper. A random sample of 650 customers of Bank of America reveals that 48 own commercial paper as part of their investment portfolios with the bank. A random sample of customers of Chemical Bank reveals that out of 480 customers, only 20 own commercial paper as part of their investments with the bank. Can you conclude that Bank of America has a greater share of the new market for commercial paper? Explain.

8–35. Airbus Industrie, the European maker of the A380 long-range jet, is currently trying to expand its market worldwide. At one point, Airbus managers wanted to test whether their potential market in the United States, measured by the proportion of airline industry executives who would prefer the A380, is greater than the company's potential market for the A380 in Europe (measured by the same indicator). A random sample of 120 top executives of U.S. airlines looking for new aircraft were given a demonstration of the plane, and 34 indicated that they would prefer the model to other new planes on the market. A random sample of 200 European airline executives were also given a demonstration of the plane, and 41 indicated that they would be interested in the A380. Test the hypothesis that more U.S. airline executives prefer the A380 than their European counterparts.

8–36. Data from the Bureau of Labor Statistics indicate that in one recent year the unemployment rate in Cleveland was 7.5% and the unemployment rate in Chicago was 7.2%. Suppose that both figures are based on random samples of 1,000 people in each city. Test the null hypothesis that the unemployment rates in both cities are equal versus the alternative hypothesis that they are not equal. What is the p-value? State your conclusion.

8–37. Recently, Venezuela instituted a new accounting method for its oil revenues.[10] Suppose that a random sample of 100 accounting transactions using the old method

---

[10] José de Córdoba, "Chávez Moves Suggest Inflation Worry," *The Wall Street Journal*, May 5–6, 2007, p. A4.

reveals 18 in error, and a random sample of 100 accounts using the new method reveals 6 errors. Is there evidence of difference in method effectiveness? Explain.

8–38. According to *USA Today*, 32% of the public think that credit cards are safer than debit cards, while 19% believe that debit cards are safer than credit cards.[11] If these results are based on two independent random samples, one of people who use primarily credit cards, and the other of people who use mostly debit cards, and the two samples are of size 100 each, test for equality of proportions using the 0.01 level of significance.

8–39. Several companies have been developing electronic guidance systems for cars. Motorola and Germany's Blaupunkt are two firms in the forefront of such research. Out of 120 trials of the Motorola model, 101 were successful; and out of 200 tests of the Blaupunkt model, 110 were successful. Is there evidence to conclude that the Motorola electronic guidance system is superior to that of the German competitor?

8–5   The *F* Distribution and a Test for Equality of Two Population Variances

CHAPTER 10

In this section, we encounter the last of the major probability distributions useful in statistics, the *F distribution*. The *F* distribution is named after the English statistician Sir Ronald A. Fisher.

> The **F distribution** is the distribution of the ratio of two chi-square random variables that are independent of each other, each of which is divided by its own degrees of freedom.

If we let χ_1^2 be a chi-square random variable with k_1 degrees of freedom, and χ_2^2 another chi-square random variable independent of χ_1^2 and having k_2 degrees of freedom, the ratio in equation 8–15 has the *F* distribution with k_1 and k_2 degrees of freedom.

An *F* random variable with k_1 and k_2 degrees of freedom is

$$F_{(k1,\ k2)} = \frac{\chi_1^2/k_1}{\chi_2^2/k_2} \tag{8–15}$$

The *F* distribution thus has two kinds of degrees of freedom: k_1 is called the *degrees of freedom of the numerator* and is always listed as the first item in the parentheses; k_2 is called the *degrees of freedom of the denominator* and is always listed second inside the parentheses. The degrees of freedom of the numerator, k_1, are "inherited" from the chi-square random variable in the numerator; similarly, k_2 is "inherited" from the other, independent chi-square random variable in the denominator of equation 8–15.

Since there are so many possible degrees of freedom for the *F* random variable, tables of values of this variable for given probabilities are even more concise than the chi-square tables. Table 5 in Appendix C gives the critical points for *F* distributions with different degrees of freedom of the numerator and the denominator corresponding to right-tailed areas of 0.10, 0.05, 0.025, and 0.01. The second part of Table 5 gives critical points for $\alpha = 0.05$ and $\alpha = 0.01$ for a wider ranger of *F* random variables. For example, use Table 5 to verify that the point 3.01 cuts off an area of 0.05 to its right for an *F* random variable with 7 degrees of freedom for the numerator and 11 degrees of freedom

---

[11]"Credit Card vs. Debit Card," *USA Today*, March 14, 2007, p. 1B.

FIGURE 8–12 An *F* Distribution with 7 and 11 Degrees of Freedom

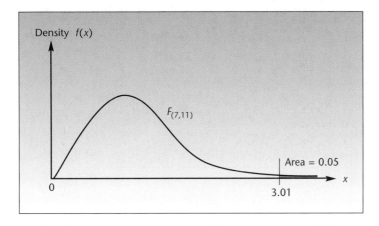

FIGURE 8–13 Several *F* Distributions

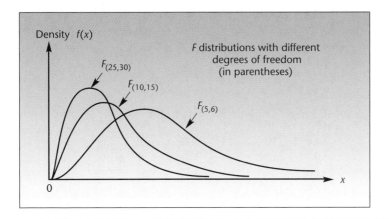

for the denominator. This is demonstrated in Figure 8–12. Figure 8–13 shows various *F* distributions with different degrees of freedom. The *F* distributions are asymmetric (a quality inherited from their chi-square parents), and their shape resembles that of the chi-square distributions. Note that $F_{(7, 11)} \neq F_{(11, 7)}$. It is important to keep track of which degrees of freedom are for the numerator and which are for the denominator.

Table 8–2 is a reproduction of a part of Table 5, showing values of *F* distributions with different degrees of freedom cutting off a right-tailed area of 0.05.

The *F* distribution is useful in testing the equality of two population variances. Recall that in Chapter 7 we defined a chi-square random variable as

$$\chi^2 = \frac{(n-1)S^2}{\sigma^2} \qquad (8\text{--}16)$$

where S^2 is the sample variance from a *normally distributed population*. This was the definition in the single-sample case, where $n-1$ was the appropriate number of degrees of freedom. Now suppose that we have two *independent* random samples from two *normally distributed populations*. The two samples will give rise to two sample

TABLE 8–2   Critical Points Cutting Off a Right-Tailed Area of 0.05 for Selected F Distributions

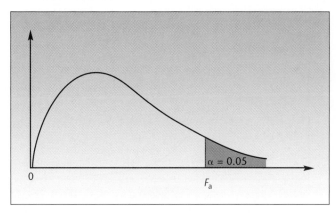

Degrees of Freedom of the Denominator (k_2)	Degrees of Freedom of the Numerator (k_1)								
	1	2	3	4	5	6	7	8	9
1	161.4	199.5	215.7	224.6	230.2	234.0	236.8	238.9	240.5
2	18.51	19.00	19.16	19.25	19.30	19.33	19.35	19.37	19.38
3	10.13	9.55	9.28	9.12	9.01	8.94	8.89	8.85	8.81
4	7.71	6.94	6.59	6.39	6.26	6.16	6.09	6.04	6.00
5	6.61	5.79	5.41	5.19	5.05	4.95	4.88	4.82	4.77
6	5.99	5.14	4.76	4.53	4.39	4.28	4.21	4.15	4.10
7	5.59	4.74	4.35	4.12	3.97	3.87	3.79	3.73	3.68
8	5.32	4.46	4.07	3.84	3.69	3.58	3.50	3.44	3.39
9	5.12	4.26	3.86	3.63	3.48	3.37	3.29	3.23	3.18
10	4.96	4.10	3.71	3.48	3.33	3.22	3.14	3.07	3.02
11	4.84	3.98	3.59	3.36	3.20	3.09	3.01	2.95	2.90
12	4.75	3.89	3.49	3.26	3.11	3.00	2.91	2.85	2.80
13	4.67	3.81	3.41	3.18	3.03	2.92	2.83	2.77	2.71
14	4.60	3.74	3.34	3.11	2.96	2.85	2.76	2.70	2.65
15	4.54	3.68	3.29	3.06	2.90	2.79	2.71	2.64	2.59

variances, S_1^2 and S_2^2, with $n_1 - 1$ and $n_2 - 1$ degrees of freedom, respectively. The ratio of these two random variables is the random variable

$$\frac{S_1^2}{S_2^2} = \frac{\chi_1^2 \sigma_1^2 / (n_1 - 1)}{\chi_2^2 \sigma_2^2 / (n_2 - 1)} \qquad (8-17)$$

When the two population variances σ_1^2 and σ_2^2 are *equal,* the two terms σ_1^2 and σ_2^2 cancel, and equation 8–17 is equal to equation 8–15, which is the ratio of two independent chi-square random variables, each divided by its own degrees of freedom (k_1 is $n_1 - 1$, and k_2 is $n_2 - 1$). This, therefore, is an F random variable with $n_1 - 1$ and $n_2 - 1$ degrees of freedom.

The test statistic for the equality of the variances of two normally distributed populations is

$$F_{(n_1-1,\, n_2-1)} = \frac{S_1^2}{S_2^2} \qquad (8-18)$$

Now that we have encountered the important F distribution, we are ready to define the test for the equality of two population variances. Incidentally, the F distribution has many more uses than just testing for equality of two population variances. In chapters that follow, we will find this distribution extremely useful in a variety of involved statistical contexts.

A Statistical Test for Equality of Two Population Variances

We assume independent random sampling from the two populations in question. We also assume that the two populations are normally distributed. Let the two populations be labeled 1 and 2. The possible hypotheses to be tested are the following:

$$A \text{ two-tailed test:} \quad H_0: \sigma_1^2 = \sigma_2^2$$
$$H_1: \sigma_1^2 \neq \sigma_2^2$$
$$A \text{ one-tailed test:} \quad H_0: \sigma_1^2 \leq \sigma_2^2$$
$$H_1: \sigma_1^2 > \sigma_2^2$$

We will consider the one-tailed test first, because it is easier to handle. Suppose that we want to test whether σ_1^2 is greater than σ_2^2. We collect the two independent random samples from populations 1 and 2, and we compute the statistic in equation 8–18. We must be sure to put s_1^2 in the numerator, because in a one-tailed test, rejection may occur only on the right. If s_1^2 is actually less than s_2^2, we can immediately not reject the null hypothesis because the statistic value will be less than 1.00 and, hence, certainly within the nonrejection region for any level α.

In a two-tailed test, we may do one of two things:

1. We may use the convention of always placing the *larger* sample variance in the *numerator*. That is, we label the population with the larger sample variance population 1. Then, if the test statistic value is greater than a critical point cutting off an area of, say, 0.05 to its right, we reject the null hypothesis that the two variances are equal at $\alpha = 0.10$ (that is, at *double* the level of significance from the table). This is so because, under the null hypothesis, either of the two sample variances could have been greater than the other, and we are carrying out a two-tailed test on one tail of the distribution. Similarly, if we can get a p-value on the one tail of rejection, we need to *double* it to get the actual p-value. Alternatively, we can conduct a two-tailed test as described next.

2. We may choose not to relabel the populations such that the greater sample variance is on top. Instead, we find the right-hand critical point for $\alpha = 0.01$ or 0.05 (or another level) from Appendix C, Table 5. We compute the left-hand critical point for the test (not given in the table) as follows:

The left-hand critical point to go along with $F_{(k_1, k_2)}$ is given by

$$\frac{1}{F_{(k_2, k_1)}} \tag{8–19}$$

where $F_{(k_2, k_1)}$ is the right-hand critical point from the table for an F random variable with the *reverse order of degrees of freedom*.

Thus, the left-hand critical point is the reciprocal of the right-hand critical point obtained from the table and using the reverse order of degrees of freedom for numerator and denominator. Again, the level of significance α must be doubled. For example, from Table 8–2, we find that the right-hand critical point for $\alpha = 0.05$ with degrees of freedom for the numerator equal to 6 and degrees of freedom for the

FIGURE 8–14   The Critical Points for a Two-Tailed Test Using $F_{(6, 9)}$ and $\alpha = 0.10$

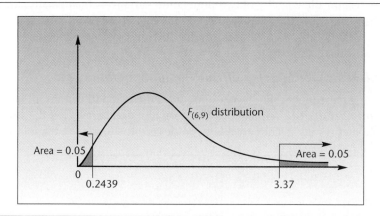

denominator equal to 9 is $C = 3.37$. So, for a two-tailed test at $\alpha = 0.10$ (double the significance level from the table), the critical points are 3.37 and the point obtained using equation 8–19, $1/F_{(9, 6)}$, which, using the table, is found to be $1/4.10 = 0.2439$. This is shown in Figure 8–14.

We will now demonstrate the use of the test for equality of two population variances with examples.

EXAMPLE 8–9

One of the problems that insider trading supposedly causes is unnaturally high stock price volatility. When insiders rush to buy a stock they believe will increase in price, the buying pressure causes the stock price to rise faster than under usual conditions. Then, when insiders dump their holdings to realize quick gains, the stock price dips fast. Price volatility can be measured as the variance of prices.

An economist wants to study the effect of the insider trading scandal and ensuing legislation on the volatility of the price of a certain stock. The economist collects price data for the stock during the period before the event (interception and prosecution of insider traders) and after the event. The economist makes the assumptions that prices are approximately normally distributed and that the two price data sets may be considered independent random samples from the populations of prices before and after the event. As we mentioned earlier, the theory of finance supports the normality assumption. (The assumption of random sampling may be somewhat problematic in this case, but later we will deal with time-dependent observations more effectively.) Suppose that the economist wants to test whether the event has decreased the variance of prices of the stock. The 25 daily stock prices before the event give $s_1^2 = 9.3$ (dollars squared), and the 24 stock prices after the event give $s_1^2 = 3.0$ (dollars squared). Conduct the test at $\alpha = 0.05$.

Solution

Our test is a right-tailed test. We have $H_0: \sigma_1^2 \leq \sigma_2^2$ and $H_1: \sigma_1^2 > \sigma_2^2$. We compute the test statistic of equation 8–18:

$$F_{(n_1-1,\, n_2-1)} = F_{(24,\, 23)} = \frac{s_1^2}{s_2^2} = \frac{9.3}{3.0} = 3.1$$

As can be seen from Figure 8–15, this value of the test statistic falls in the rejection region for $\alpha = 0.05$ and for $\alpha = 0.01$. The critical point for $\alpha = 0.05$, from Table 5,

FIGURE 8–15   Carrying Out the Test of Example 8–9

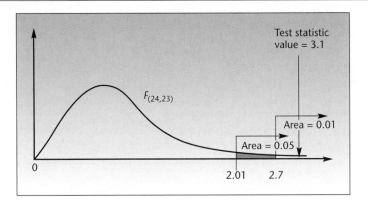

is equal to 2.01 (see 24 degrees of freedom for the numerator and 23 degrees of freedom for the denominator). Referring to the F table for $\alpha = 0.01$ with 24 degrees of freedom for the numerator and 23 degrees of freedom for the denominator gives a critical point of 2.70. The computed value of the test statistic, 3.1, is greater than both of these values. The p-value is less than 0.01, and the economist may conclude that (subject to the validity of the assumptions) the data present significant evidence that the event in question has reduced the variance of the stock's price.

EXAMPLE 8–10

Use the data of Example 8–5—$n_1 = 14$, $s_1 = 0.12$; $n_2 = 9$, $s_2 = 0.11$—to test the assumption of equal population variances.

Solution

The test statistic is the same as in the previous example, given by equation 8–18:

$$F_{(13, 8)} = \frac{s_1^2}{s_2^2} = \frac{0.12^2}{0.11^2} = 1.19$$

Here we placed the larger variance in the numerator because it was already labeled 1 (we did not purposely label the larger variance as 1). We can carry this out as a one-tailed test, even though it is really two-tailed, remembering that we must double the level of significance. Choosing $\alpha = 0.05$ from the table makes this a test at true level of significance equal to $2(0.05) = 0.10$. The critical point, using 12 and 8 degrees of freedom for numerator and denominator, respectively, is 3.28. (This is the closest value, since our table does not list critical points for 13 and 8 degrees of freedom.) As can be seen, our test statistic falls inside the nonrejection region, and we may conclude that at the 0.10 level of significance, there is no evidence that the two population variances are different from each other.

Let us now see how this test may be carried out using the alternative method of solution: finding a left-hand critical point to go with the right-hand one. The right-hand critical point remains 3.28 (let us assume that this is the exact value for 13 and 8 degrees of freedom). The left-hand critical point is found by equation 8–19 as $1/F_{(8, 13)} = 1/2.77 = 0.36$ (recall that the left-hand critical point is the inverse of the critical point corresponding to reversed-order degrees of freedom). The two tails are shown

FIGURE 8–16   Carrying Out the Two-Tailed Test of Example 8–10

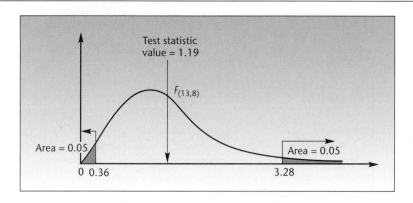

FIGURE 8–17   The *F*-Distribution Template [F.xls]

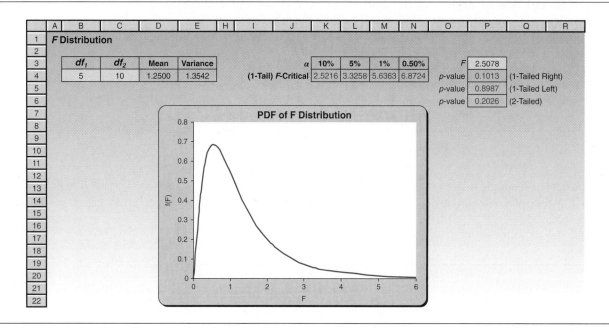

in Figure 8–16. Again, the value of the test statistic falls inside the nonrejection region for this test at $\alpha = 2(0.05) = 0.10$.

The Templates

Figure 8–17 shows the *F*-distribution template. The numerator and denominator degrees of freedom are entered in cells B4 and C4. For any combination of degrees of freedom, the template can be used to visualize the distribution, get critical *F* values, or compute *p*-values corresponding to a calculated *F* value.

Figure 8–18 shows the template that can be used to test the *equality* of two population variances from sample data. In other words, the hypothesized difference between the variances can only be zero.

Figure 8–19 shows the template that can be used to test the equality of two population variances when sample statistics, rather than sample data, are known. The data in the figure correspond to Example 8–9.

FIGURE 8–18 The Template for Testing Equality of Variances [Testing Equality of Variances.xls; Sheet: Sample Data]

F-Test for Equality of Variances

	Data	
	Name 1	Name 2
	Sample1	Sample2
1	334	405
2	150	125
3	520	540
4	95	100
5	212	200
6	30	30
7	1055	1200
8	300	265
9	85	90
10	129	206
11	40	18
12	440	489
13	610	590
14	208	310

	Sample 1	Sample 2	
Size	16	16	n
Variance	95858.8	118367.7	s^2

Test Statistic	0.809839	F
df1	15	
df2	15	

Null Hypothesis	p-value	At an α of 5%
H_0: $\sigma^2_1 - \sigma^2_2 = 0$	0.6882	
H_0: $\sigma^2_1 - \sigma^2_2 >= 0$	0.3441	
H_0: $\sigma^2_1 - \sigma^2_2 <= 0$	0.6559	

FIGURE 8–19 The Template for Testing Equality of Variances [Testing Equality of Variances.xls; Sheet: Sample Stats]

F-Test for Equality of Variances — Stock Price Volatility

	Sample 1	Sample 2	
Size	25	24	n
Variance	9.3	3	s^2

Test Statistic	3.1	F
df1	24	
df2	23	

Null Hypothesis	p-value	At an α of 5%
H_0: $\sigma^2_1 - \sigma^2_2 = 0$	0.0085	Reject
H_0: $\sigma^2_1 - \sigma^2_2 >= 0$	0.9958	
H_0: $\sigma^2_1 - \sigma^2_2 <= 0$	0.0042	Reject

PROBLEMS

In the following problems, assume that all populations are normally distributed.

8–40. Compaq Computer Corporation has an assembly plant in Houston, where the company's Deskpro computer is built. Engineers at the plant are considering a new production facility and are interested in going online with the new facility if and only if they can be fairly sure that the variance of the number of computers assembled per day using the new facility is lower than the production variance of the old system. A random sample of 40 production days using the old production method gives a sample variance of 1,288; and a random sample of 15 production days using the proposed new method gives a sample variance of 1,112. Conduct the appropriate test at $\alpha = 0.05$.

8–41. Test the validity of the equal-variance assumption in problem 8–27.

8–42. Test the validity of the equal-variance assumption for the data presented in problem 8–25.

8–43. Test the validity of the equal-variance assumption for the data presented in problem 8–26.

8–44. The following data are independent random samples of sales of the Nissan Pulsar model made in a joint venture of Nissan and Alfa Romeo. The data represent sales at dealerships before and after the announcement that the Pulsar model will no longer be made in Italy. Sales numbers are monthly.

Before: 329, 234, 423, 328, 400, 399, 326, 452, 541, 680, 456, 220
After: 212, 630, 276, 112, 872, 788, 345, 544, 110, 129, 776

Do you believe that the variance of the number of cars sold per month before the announcement is equal to the variance of the number of cars sold per month after the announcement?

8–45. A large department store wants to test whether the variance of waiting time in two checkout counters is approximately equal. Two independent random samples of 25 waiting times in each of the counters gives $s_1 = 2.5$ minutes and $s_2 = 3.1$ minutes. Carry out the test of equality of variances, using $\alpha = 0.02$.

8–46. An important measure of the risk associated with a stock is the standard deviation, or variance, of the stock's price movements. A financial analyst wants to test the one-tailed hypothesis that stock A has a greater risk (larger variance of price) than stock B. A random sample of 25 daily prices of stock A gives $s_A^2 = 6.52$, and a random sample of 22 daily prices of stock B gives a sample variance of $s_B^2 = 3.47$. Carry out the test at $\alpha = 0.01$.

8–47. Discuss the assumptions made in the solution of the problems in this section.

8–6   Using the Computer

Using Excel for Comparison of Two Populations

A built-in facility is available in Excel to test differences in population means. It is described below. We shall first see the paired-difference test.

- Enter the data from the two samples in columns B and C. See Figure 8–20, where the data are in the range B4:C12. The columns are labeled Before and After.
- Select Data Analysis in the Analysis group on the Data tab.
- In the dialog box that appears, select t-Test: Paired Two Sample for Means.

FIGURE 8–20   Paired-Difference Test Using Excel

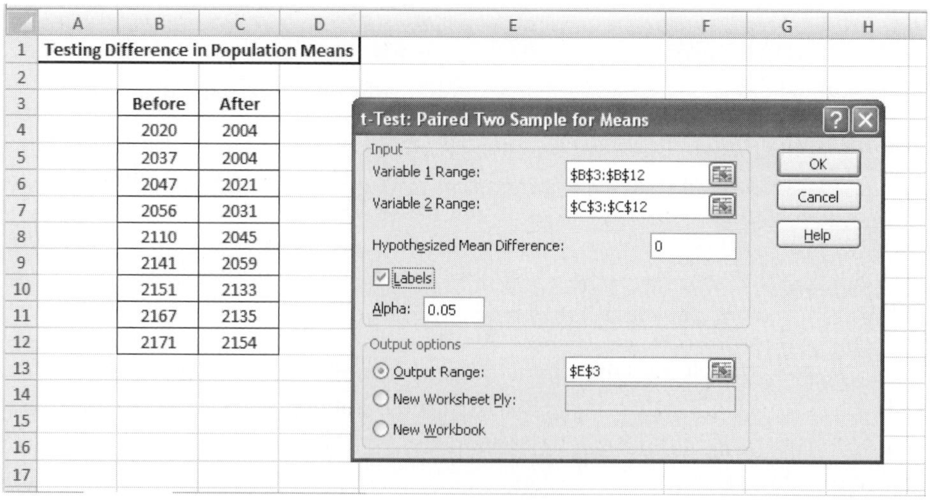

FIGURE 8–21 Paired-Difference Test Output

	A	B	C	D	E	F	G	H
1	Testing Difference in Population Means							
2								
3		Before	After		t-Test: Paired Two Sample for Means			
4		2020	2004					
5		2037	2004			Before	After	
6		2047	2021		Mean	2100	2065.111	
7		2056	2031		Variance	3628.25	3551.861	
8		2110	2045		Observations	9	9	
9		2141	2059		Pearson Correlation	0.925595		
10		2151	2133		Hypothesized Mean Difference	0		
11		2167	2135		df	8		
12		2171	2154		t Stat	4.52678		
13					P(T<=t) one-tail	0.000966		
14					t Critical one-tail	1.859548		
15					P(T<=t) two-tail	0.001933		
16					t Critical two-tail	2.306004		
17								

- In the next dialog box that appears, enter the Variable 1 range. For the case in the figure this range is B3:B12. Note that the range includes the label "Before."
- Enter Variable 2 range. In the figure it is C3:C12.
- In the next box, enter the hypothesized difference between the two populations. Often it is zero.
- If the range you entered for Variables 1 and 2 includes labels, click the Labels box. Otherwise, leave it blank.
- Enter the desired alpha.
- Select Output range and enter E3.
- Click the OK button. You should see an output similar to the one shown in Figure 8–21.

The output shows that the *p*-value for the example is 0.000966 for the one-tailed test and 0.001933 for the two-tailed test. While the null hypothesis for the two-tailed test is obvious, Excel output does not make explicit what the null hypothesis for the one-tailed test is. By looking at the means in the first line of the output we see that the mean is larger for Before than for After. Thus we infer that the null hypothesis is $\mu_{Before} \leq \mu_{After}$.

Since the *p*-values are so small the null hypotheses will be rejected even at an α of 1%.

To conduct an independent random sample test,

- Select Data Analysis in the Analysis group on the Data tab.
- In the dialog box that appears, select t-Test: Two Sample Assuming Equal Variances.
- Fill in the dialog box as before. (See Figure 8–20.)
- Click the OK button and you should see an output similar to the one in Figure 8–22.

This time, the *p*-value for the one-tailed test is 0.117291 and for the two-tailed test, 0.234582. Since these values are larger than 10%, the null hypotheses cannot be rejected even at an α of 10%.

You can see, from the Data Analysis dialog box, that a *t*-test is available for the unequal variance case and a *Z*-test is available for known σ's case. The procedure is similar for these two cases. In the case of the *Z*-test you will have to enter the two σ's as well.

FIGURE 8–22   Output of *t*-Test Assuming Equal Variances

	A	B	C	D	E	F	G	H
1	**Testing Difference in Population Means**							
2								
3		**Before**	**After**		t-Test: Two-Sample Assuming Equal Variances			
4		2020	2004					
5		2037	2004			*Before*	*After*	
6		2047	2021		Mean	2100	2065.111	
7		2056	2031		Variance	3628.25	3551.861	
8		2110	2045		Observations	9	9	
9		2141	2059		Pooled Variance	3590.056		
10		2151	2133		Hypothesized Mean Difference	0		
11		2167	2135		df	16		
12		2171	2154		t Stat	1.235216		
13					P(T<=t) one-tail	0.117291		
14					t Critical one-tail	1.745884		
15					P(T<=t) two-tail	0.234582		
16					t Critical two-tail	2.119905		
17								

FIGURE 8–23   Output of *F*-Test for Equality of Population Variances

	A	B	C	D	E	F	G	H
1	**Testing Difference in Population Means**							
2								
3		**Before**	**After**		F-Test: Two-Sample for Variances			
4		2020	2004					
5		2037	2004			*Before*	*After*	
6		2047	2021		Mean	2100	2065.111	
7		2056	2031		Variance	3628.25	3551.861	
8		2110	2045		Observations	9	9	
9		2141	2059		df	8	8	
10		2151	2133		F	1.021507		
11		2167	2135		P(F<=f) one-tail	0.488365		
12		2171	2154		F Critical one-tail	3.438101		
13								

A built-in *F*-test in Excel can be used to test if two population variances are equal:

- Enter the sample data from the two populations in columns B and C. For our example, we will use the same data we used above.
- Select Data Analysis in the Analysis group on the Data tab.
- In the dialog box that appears, select F-Test Two Sample for Variances.
- Fill in the F-Test dialog box as in the previous examples.
- Click the OK button. You should see an output similar to Figure 8–23.

Using MINITAB for Comparison of Two Samples

In this section we illustrate the use of MINITAB for hypothesis testing to compare two populations.

To run a *t* test of the difference between two population means, start by choosing Stat ▶ Basic Statistics ▶ 2-Sample t. This option performs an independent two-sample *t* test and generates a confidence interval. When the corresponding dialog box appears as shown in Figure 8–24, select Samples in one column if the sample data are in a single column, differentiated by subscript values (group codes) in a second column. Enter the column containing the data in Samples and the column containing the sample subscripts in Subscripts. If the data of the two samples are in separate columns, select Samples in different columns and enter the column containing each

FIGURE 8–24 Using MINITAB for the *t* Test of the Difference between Two Means

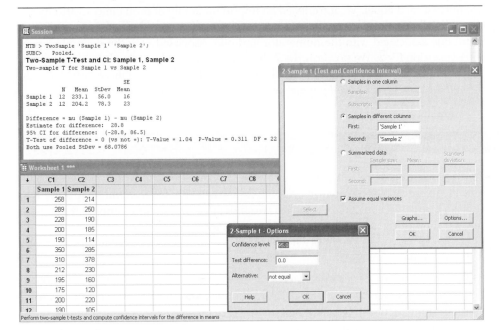

sample in the corresponding box. You can also choose Summarized data if you have summary values for the sample size, mean, and standard deviation for each sample. Check Assume equal variances to assume that the populations have equal variances. The default is to assume unequal variances. If you check Assume equal variances, the sample standard deviations are pooled to obtain a single estimate of σ. Then click on the Options button. Enter the level of confidence desired. You can also define the null hypothesis value in the Test difference box. The default is zero, or that the two population means are equal. Choose less than (left-tailed), not equal (two-tailed), or greater than (right-tailed) from Alternative, depending on the kind of test that you want. Then click the OK button. The corresponding Session commands and dialog box are shown in Figure 8–24.

MINITAB can also run a paired *t* test. Choose Stat ▶ Basic Statistics ▶ Paired t to compute a confidence interval and perform a hypothesis test of the mean difference between paired observations in the population. Paired *t* evaluates the first sample minus the second sample. The settings are similar to the previous dialog box.

You can also use MINITAB to perform a test for comparing two population proportions. Choose Stat ▶ Basic Statistics ▶ 2 Proportions from the menu bar to compute a confidence interval and perform a hypothesis test of the difference between two proportions.

Many statistical procedures, including the two-sample *t*-test procedures, assume that the two samples are from populations with equal variance. The two-variances test procedure will test the validity of this assumption. To perform a hypothesis test for equality, or homogeneity, of variance in two populations, choose Stat ▶ Basic Statistics ▶ 2 Variances from the menu bar.

8–7 Summary and Review of Terms

In this chapter, we extended the ideas of hypothesis tests and confidence intervals to the case of two populations. We discussed the comparisons of two population means, two population proportions, and two population variances. We developed a hypothesis test and confidence interval for the difference between two population means when the population variances were believed to be equal, and in the general case when they are not assumed equal. We introduced an important family of probability distributions: the **F distributions**. We saw that each *F* distribution has two kinds of degrees of freedom: one associated with the numerator and one associated with the denominator of the expression for *F*. We saw how the *F* distribution is used in testing hypotheses about two population variances. In the next chapter, we will make use of the *F* distribution in tests of the equality of *several* population means: the analysis of variance.

ADDITIONAL PROBLEMS

8-48. According to *Money,* the average cost of repairing a broken leg is $10,402, and the average cost of repairing a knee injury is $11,359.[12] Assume that these two statistics are sample averages based on two independent random samples of 200 people each and that the sample standard deviation for the cost of repairing a broken leg was $8,500 and for a knee injury it was $9,100. Conduct a test for equality of means using $\alpha = 0.05$.

8-49. In problem 8–48, construct a 99% confidence interval for the difference between the average cost of repairing a broken leg and the average cost of repairing an injured knee. Interpret your results.

8-50. "Strategizing for the future" is management lingo for sessions that help managers make better decisions. Managers who deliver the best stock performance get results by bold, rule-breaking strategies. To test the effectiveness of "strategizing for the future," companies' 5-year average stock performance was considered before, and after, consultant-led "strategizing for the future" sessions were held.

Before (%)	After (%)
10	12
12	16
8	−2
−5	10
−1	11
5	18
−3	−8
16	20
−2	−1
13	21
17	24

Test the effectiveness of the program, using $\alpha = 0.05$.

8-51. For problem 8–50, construct a 95% confidence interval for the difference in stock performance.

8-52. According to a study reported in the *New York Times,* 48% of the viewers who watched NFL Football on TiVo viewed 1 to 6 commercials, while 26% of the viewers who watched *Survivor: Cook Islands* on TiVo viewed 1 to 6 commercials.[13] If this information is based on two independent random samples of 200 viewers each, test for equality of proportions using $\alpha = 0.05$.

8-53. For problem 8-52, give a 99% confidence interval for the difference between the proportions for viewers of the two shows who watched 1 to 6 commercials. Interpret the results.

---

[12]"Why Buy Your New Grad Some Health Coverage," *Money,* May 2007, p. 20.

[13]Louise Story, "Viewers Fast-Forwarding Past Ads? Not Always," *The New York Times,* February 16, 2007, p. A1.

8–54. According to the *New York Times,* the average number of roses imported to the United States from Costa Rica is 1,242 per month, while the average number imported from Guatemala each month is 1,240.[14] Assume that these two numbers are the averages of samples of 15 months each, and that both sample standard deviations are 50. Conduct a test for equality of means using the 0.05 level of significance.

8–55. Two movies were screen-tested at two different samples of theaters. *Mystic River* was viewed at 80 theaters and was considered a success in terms of box office sales in 60 of these theaters. *Swimming Pool* was viewed at a random sample of 100 theaters and was considered a success in 65. Based on these data, do you believe that one of these movies was a greater success than the other? Explain.

8–56. For problem 8–55, give a 95% confidence interval for the difference in proportion of theaters nationwide where one movie will be preferred over the other. Is the point 0 contained in the interval? Discuss.

8–57. Two 12-meter boats, the K boat and the L boat, are tested as possible contenders in the America's Cup races. The following data represent the time, in minutes, to complete a particular track in independent random trials of the two boats:

K boat: 12.0, 13.1, 11.8, 12.6, 14.0, 11.8, 12.7, 13.5, 12.4, 12.2, 11.6, 12.9
L boat: 11.8, 12.1, 12.0, 11.6, 11.8, 12.0, 11.9, 12.6, 11.4, 12.0, 12.2, 11.7

Test the null hypothesis that the two boats perform equally well. Is one boat faster, on average, than the other? Assume equal population variances.

8–58. In problem 8–57, assume that the data points are paired as listed and that each pair represents performance of the two boats at a single trial. Conduct the test, using this assumption. What is the advantage of testing using the paired data versus independent samples?

8–59. Home loan delinquencies have recently been causing problems throughout the American economy. According to *USA Today,* the percentage of homeowners falling behind on their mortgage payments in some sections of the West has been 4.95%, while in some areas of the South that rate was 6.79%.[15] Assume that these numbers are derived from two independent samples of 1,000 homeowners in each region. Test for equality of proportions of loan default in the two regions using $\alpha = 0.05$.

8–60. The IIT Technical Institute claims "94% of our graduates get jobs." Assume that the result is based on a random sample of 100 graduates of the program. Suppose that an independent random sample of 125 graduates of a competing technical institute reveals that 92% of these graduates got jobs. Is there evidence to conclude that one institute is more successful than the other in placing its graduates?

8–61. The power of supercomputers derives from the idea of parallel processing. Engineers at Cray Research are interested in determining whether one of two parallel processing designs produces faster average computing time, or whether the two designs are equally fast. The following are the results, in seconds, of independent random computation times using the two designs.

Design 1	Design 2
2.1, 2.2, 1.9, 2.0, 1.8, 2.4,	2.6, 2.5, 2.0, 2.1, 2.6, 3.0,
2.0, 1.7, 2.3, 2.8, 1.9, 3.0,	2.3, 2.0, 2.4, 2.8, 3.1, 2.7,
2.5, 1.8, 2.2	2.6

Assume that the two populations of computing time are normally distributed and that the two population variances are equal. Is there evidence that one parallel processing design allows for faster average computation than the other?

---

[14]"Faraway Flowers," *The New York Times,* February 11, 2007, p. B2.

[15]Noelle Knox, "Record Foreclosures Reel Lenders," *USA Today,* March 14, 2007, p. 1B.

8–62. Test the validity of the equal-variance assumption in problem 8–61. If you reject the null hypothesis of equal-population variance, redo the test of problem 8–61 using another method.

8–63. The senior vice president for marketing at Westin Hotels believes that the company's recent advertising of the Westin Plaza in New York has increased the average occupancy rate at that hotel by at least 5%. To test the hypothesis, a random sample of daily occupancy rates (in percentages) before the advertising is collected. A similar random sample of daily occupancy rates is collected after the advertising took place. The data are as follows.

Before Advertising (%)	After Advertising (%)
86, 92, 83, 88, 79, 81, 90,	88, 94, 97, 99, 89, 93, 92,
76, 80, 91, 85, 89, 77, 91,	98, 89, 90, 97, 91, 87, 80,
83	88, 96

Assume normally distributed populations of occupancy rates with equal population variances. Test the vice president's hypothesis.

8–64. For problem 8–63, test the validity of the equal-variance assumption.

8–65. Refer to problem 8–48. Test the null hypothesis that the variance of the cost of repairing a broken leg is equal to the variance of the cost of repairing an injured knee.

8–66. Refer to problem 8–57. Do you believe that the variance of performance times for the K boat is about the same as the variance of performance times for the L boat? Explain. What are the implications of your result on the analysis of problem 8–57? If needed, redo the analysis in problem 8–57.

8–67. A company is interested in offering its employees one of two employee benefit packages. A random sample of the company's employees is collected, and each person in the sample is asked to rate each of the two packages on an overall preference scale of 0 to 100. The order of presentation of each of the two plans is randomly selected for each person in the sample. The paired data are:

Program *A:*   45, 67, 63, 59, 77, 69, 45, 39, 52, 58, 70, 46, 60, 65, 59, 80
Program *B:*   56, 70, 60, 45, 85, 79, 50, 46, 50, 60, 82, 40, 65, 55, 81, 68

Do you believe that the employees of this company prefer, on the average, one package over the other? Explain.

8–68. A company that makes electronic devices for use in hospitals needs to decide on one of two possible suppliers for a certain component to be used in the devices. The company gathers a random sample of 200 items made by supplier *A* and finds that 12 items are defective. An independent random sample of 250 items made by supplier *B* reveals that 38 are defective. Is one supplier more reliable than the other? Explain.

8–69. Refer to problem 8–68. Give a 95% confidence interval for the difference in the proportions of defective items made by suppliers *A* and *B*.

8–70. Refer to problem 8–63. Give a 90% confidence interval for the difference in average occupancy rates at the Westin Plaza hotel before and after the advertising.

8–71. Toys are entering the virtual world, and Mattel recently developed a digital version of its famous Barbie. The average price of the virtual doll is reported to be $60.[16] A competing product sells for an average of $65. Suppose both averages are sample estimates based on independent random samples of 25 outlets selling Barbie

---

[16]Christopher Palmeri, "Barbie Goes from Vinyl to Virtual," *BusinessWeek,* May 7, 2007, p. 68.

software and 20 outlets selling the competing virtual doll, and suppose the sample standard deviation for Barbie is $14 and for the competing doll it is $8. Test for equality of average price using the 0.05 level of significance.

8–72. Microlenders are institutions that lend relatively small amounts of money to businesses. An article on microlenders compared the average return on equity for lenders of two categories based on their credit ratings: Alpha versus Beta. For the Alpha group, a random sample of 74 firms, the average return on equity was 28%. For the Beta group, a random sample of 65 firms, the average return on equity was 22%.[17] Assume both sample standard deviations were 6%, and test for equality of mean return on investment using $\alpha = 0.05$.

8–73. Refer to the situation of problem 8–72. The study also compared average portfolios of microloans. For the Alpha group it was $50 million, and for the Beta group it was $14 million. Assume the Alpha group had a standard deviation of $20 million and the Beta group had a standard deviation of $8 million. Construct a 95% confidence interval for the difference in mean portfolio size for firms in the two groups of credit ratings.

8–74. According to Labor Department statistics, the average U.S. work week shortened from 39 hours in the 1950s and early 1960s to 35 hours in the 1990s. Assume the two statistics are based on independent t samples of 2,500 workers each, and the standard deviations are both 2 hours.

    a. Test for significance of change.

    b. Give a 95% confidence interval for the difference.

8–75. According to *Fortune,* there has been an average decrease of 86% in the Atlantic cod catch over the last two decades.[18] Suppose that two areas are monitored for catch sizes and one of them has a daily average of 1.7 tons and a standard deviation of 0.4 ton, while the other has an average daily catch of 1.5 tons and a standard deviation of 0.7 ton. Both estimates are obtained from independent random samples of 25 days. Conduct a test for equality of mean catch and report your p-value.

8–76. A survey finds that 62% of lower-income households have Internet access at home as compared to 70% of upper-income households. Assume that the data are based on random samples of size 500 each. Does this demonstrate that lower-income households are less likely to have Internet access than the upper-income households? Use $\alpha = 0.05$.

8–77. For problem 8–75, construct a 95% confidence interval for the difference between average catch in the two locations.

8–78. Two statisticians independently estimate the variance of the same normally distributed population, each using a random sample of size 10. One of their estimates is 3.18 times as large as the other. In such situations, how likely is the larger estimate to be at least 3.18 times the smaller one?

8–79. A manufacturer uses two different trucking companies to ship its merchandise. The manufacturer suspects that one company is charging more than the other and wants to test it. A random sample of the amounts charged for one truckload shipment from Chicago to Detroit on various days is collected for each trucking company. The data (in dollars) is given below.

Company 1:   2,570, 2,480, 2,870, 2,975, 2,660, 2,380, 2,590, 2,550, 2,485, 2,585, 2,710

Company 2:   2,055, 2,940, 2,850, 2,475, 1,940, 2,100, 2,655, 1,950, 2,115

---

[17]"Small Loans and Big Ambitions," *The Economist,* March 17, 2007, p. 84.

[18] Susan Casey, "Eminence Green," *Fortune,* April 2, 2007, p. 67.

a. Assuming that the two populations are normally distributed with equal variance, test the null hypothesis that the two companies' average charges are equal.

b. Test the assumption of equal variance.

c. Assuming unequal variance, test the null hypothesis that the two companies' average charges are equal.

CASE 10 Tiresome Tires II

A tire manufacturing company invents a new, cheaper method for carrying out one of the steps in the manufacturing process. The company wants to test the new method before adopting it, because the method could alter the interply shear strength of the tires produced.

To test the acceptability of the new method, the company formulates the null and alternative hypotheses as

$$H_0: \mu_1 - \mu_2 \leq 0$$
$$H_1: \mu_1 - \mu_2 > 0$$

where μ_1 is the population mean of the interply shear strength of the tires produced by the old method and μ_2 that of the tires produced by the new method. The evidence is gathered through a destructive test of 40 randomly selected tires from each method. Following are the data gathered:

No.	Sample 1	Sample 2	No.	Sample 1	Sample 2
1	2792	2713	13	2718	2680
2	2755	2741	14	2719	2786
3	2745	2701	15	2751	2737
4	2731	2731	16	2755	2740
5	2799	2747	17	2685	2760
6	2793	2679	18	2700	2748
7	2705	2773	19	2712	2660
8	2729	2676	20	2778	2789
9	2747	2677	21	2693	2683
10	2725	2721	22	2740	2664
11	2715	2742	23	2731	2757
12	2782	2775	24	2707	2736
25	2754	2741	33	2741	2757
26	2690	2767	34	2789	2788
27	2797	2751	35	2723	2676
28	2761	2723	36	2713	2779
29	2760	2763	37	2781	2676
30	2777	2750	38	2706	2690
31	2774	2686	39	2776	2764
32	2713	2727	40	2738	2720

1. Test the null hypothesis at $\alpha = 0.05$.

2. Later it was found that quite a few tires failed on the road. As a part of the investigation, the above hypothesis test is reviewed. Considering the high cost of type II error, the value of 5% for α is questioned. The response was that the cost of type I error is also high because the new method could save millions of dollars. What value for α would you say is appropriate? Will the null hypothesis be rejected at that α?

3. A review of the tests conducted on the samples reveals that 40 otherwise identical pairs of tires were randomly selected and used. The two tires in each pair underwent the two different methods, and all other steps in the manufacturing process were identically carried out on the two tires. By virtue of this fact, it is argued that a paired difference test is more appropriate. Conduct a paired difference test at $\alpha = 0.05$.

4. The manufacturer moves to reduce the variance of the strength by improving the process. Will the reduction in the variance of the process increase or decrease the chances of type I and type II errors?

ANALYSIS OF VARIANCE

9–1   Using Statistics   349
9–2   The Hypothesis Test of Analysis of Variance   350
9–3   The Theory and the Computations of ANOVA   355
9–4   The ANOVA Table and Examples   364
9–5   Further Analysis   371
9–6   Models, Factors, and Designs   378
9–7   Two-Way Analysis of Variance   380
9–8   Blocking Designs   393
9–9   Using the Computer   398
9–10   Summary and Review of Terms   403
Case 11   Rating Wines   406
Case 12   Checking Out Checkout   406

LEARNING OBJECTIVES

After studying this chapter, you should be able to:

- Explain the purpose of ANOVA.
- Describe the model and computations behind ANOVA.
- Explain the test statistic F.
- Conduct a one-way ANOVA.
- Report ANOVA results in an ANOVA table.
- Apply a Tukey test for pairwise analysis.
- Conduct a two-way ANOVA.
- Explain blocking designs.
- Apply templates to conduct one-way and two-way ANOVA.

Recently, interest has been growing around the world in good wine. But navigating the enchanting world of wines is not easy. There are hundreds of kinds of grapes, thousands of wineries, some very small and some huge, and then there are the vintage years—some excellent in some regions, some not remarkable. The wine-making industry has therefore been researched heavily. Several agencies as well as newspapers, magazines, and Web sites rate wines, either on a five-star system or on a 0-to-100 scale, giving a rating for a particular wine made from a given grape at a given winery, located at a given wine-making region in a particular year. Often wines are compared to see which one the public and wine experts like best. Often grapes themselves are rated in wine tests. For example, wine experts will rate many wines broken into the four important types of grapes used in making the wine: chardonnay, merlot, chenin blanc, and cabernet sauvignon. A wine industry researcher will want to know whether, on average, these four wine categories based on grape used are equally rated by experts. Since more than two populations are to be compared (there are four kinds of grape in this example), the methods of the previous chapter no longer apply. A set of pairwise tests cannot be conducted because the power of the test will decrease. To carry out a comparison of the means of several populations calls for a new statistical method, analysis of variance. The method is often referred to by its acronym: ANOVA. Analysis of variance is the first of several advanced statistical techniques to be discussed in this book. Along with regression analysis, described in the next two chapters, ANOVA is the most commonly quoted advanced research method in the professional business and economic literature. What is analysis of variance? The name of the technique may seem misleading.

> ANOVA is a statistical method for determining the existence of differences among several population means.

While the aim of ANOVA is to detect differences among several population *means,* the technique requires the analysis of different forms of *variance* associated with the random samples under study—hence the name *analysis of variance.*

The original ideas of analysis of variance were developed by the English statistician Sir Ronald A. Fisher during the first part of the 20th century. (Recall our mention of Fisher in Chapter 8 in reference to the *F* distribution.) Much of the early work in this area dealt with agricultural experiments where crops were given different "treatments," such as being grown using different kinds of fertilizers. The researchers wanted to determine whether all treatments under study were equally effective or whether some treatments were better than others. *Better* referred to those treatments that would produce crops of greater average weight. This question is answerable by the analysis of variance. Since the original work involved different *treatments,* the term remained, and we use it interchangeably with *populations* even when no actual treatment is administered. Thus, for example, if we compare the mean income in four different communities, we may refer to the four populations as four different *treatments.*

In the next section, we will develop the simplest form of analysis of variance—the one-factor, fixed-effects, completely randomized design model. We may ignore this long name for now.

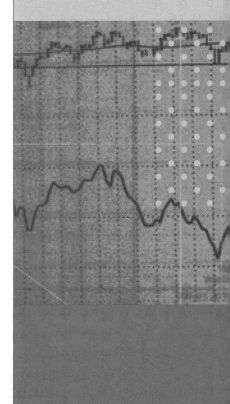

9–2   The Hypothesis Test of Analysis of Variance

The hypothesis test of analysis of variance is as follows:

$$H_0: \mu_1 = \mu_2 = \mu_3 = \cdots = \mu_r$$
$$H_1: \text{Not all } \mu_i \ (i = 1, \ldots, r) \text{ are equal} \qquad (9\text{--}1)$$

CHAPTER 12

There are r populations, or treatments, under study. We draw an independent random sample from each of the r populations. The size of the sample from population $i\ (i = 1, \ldots, r)$ is n_i, and the total sample size is

$$n = n_1 + n_2 + \cdots + n_r$$

From the r samples we compute several different quantities, and these lead to a computed value of a test statistic that follows a known F distribution when the null hypothesis is true and some assumptions hold. From the value of the statistic and the critical point for a given level of significance, we are able to make a determination of whether we believe that the r population means are equal.

Usually, the number of compared means r is greater than 2. Why greater than 2? If r is equal to 2, then the test in equation 9–1 is just a test for equality of two population means; although we could use ANOVA to conduct such a test, we have seen relatively simple tests of such hypotheses: the two-sample t tests discussed in Chapter 8. In this chapter, we are interested in investigating whether *several* population means may be considered equal. This is a test of a *joint hypothesis* about the equality of several population parameters. But why can we not use the two-sample t tests repeatedly? Suppose we are comparing $r = 5$ treatments. Why can we not conduct all possible pairwise comparisons of means using the two-sample t test? There are 10 such possible comparisons (10 choices of five items taken two at a time, found by using a combinatorial formula presented in Chapter 2). It should be possible to make all 10 comparisons. However, if we use, say, $\alpha = 0.05$ for each test, then this means that the probability of committing a type I error in any particular test (deciding that the two population means are not equal when indeed they are equal) is 0.05. If each of the 10 tests has a 0.05 probability of a type I error, what is the probability of a type I error if we state, "Not all the means are equal" (i.e., rejecting H_0 in equation 9–1)? The answer to this question is not known![1]

If we need to compare more than two population means and we want to remain in control of the probability of committing a type I error, we need to conduct a *joint test*. Analysis of variance provides such a joint test of the hypotheses in equation 9–1. The reason for ANOVA's widespread applicability is that in many situations we need to compare more than two populations simultaneously. Even in cases in which we need to compare only two treatments, say, test the relative effectiveness of two different prescription drugs, our actual test may require the use of a third treatment: a control treatment, or a placebo.

We now present the assumptions that must be satisfied so that we can use the analysis-of-variance procedure in testing our hypotheses of equation 9–1.

---

[1]The problem is complicated because we cannot assume independence of the 10 tests, and therefore we cannot use a probability computation for independent events. The sample statistics used in the 10 tests are not independent since two such possible statistics are $\bar{X}_1 - \bar{X}_2$ and $\bar{X}_2 - \bar{X}_3$. Both statistics contain a common term $\bar{X}_3$ and thus are not independent of each other.

FIGURE 9–1   Three Normally Distributed Populations with Different Means
              but with Equal Variance

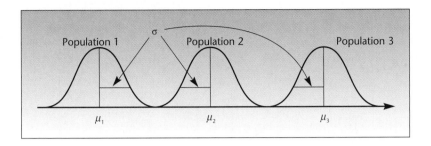

The required assumptions of ANOVA:

1. We assume *independent random sampling* from each of the *r* populations.
2. We assume that the *r* populations under study are *normally distributed,* with means μ_i that may or may not be equal, but with *equal variances* σ^2.

Suppose, for example, that we are comparing three populations and want to determine whether the three population means μ_1, μ_2, and μ_3 are equal. We draw separate random samples from each of the three populations under study, and we assume that the three populations are distributed as shown in Figure 9–1.

These model assumptions are necessary for the test statistic used in analysis of variance to possess an *F* distribution when the null hypothesis is true. If the populations are not exactly normally distributed, but have distributions that are close to a normal distribution, the method still yields good results. If, however, the distributions are highly skewed or otherwise different from normality, or if the population variances are not approximately equal, then ANOVA should not be used, and instead we must use a nonparametric technique called the Kruskal-Wallis test. This alternative technique is described in Chapter 14.

The Test Statistic

As mentioned earlier, when the null hypothesis is true, the test statistic of analysis of variance follows an *F* distribution. As you recall from Chapter 8, the *F* distribution has two kinds of degrees of freedom: degrees of freedom for the numerator and degrees of freedom for the denominator.

In the analysis of variance, the numerator degrees of freedom are $r - 1$, and the denominator degrees of freedom are $n - r$. In this section, we will not present the calculations leading to the computed value of the test statistic. Instead, we will assume that the value of the statistic is given. The computations are a topic in themselves and will be presented in the next section. Analysis of variance is an involved technique, and it is difficult and time-consuming to carry out the required computations by hand. Consequently, computers are indispensable in most situations involving analysis of variance, and we will make extensive use of the computer in this chapter. For now, let us assume that a computer is available to us and that it provides us with the value of the test statistic.

CHAPTER 12

$$\text{ANOVA test statistic} = F_{(r-1,\, n-r)} \qquad (9\text{–}2)$$

FIGURE 9–2   Distribution of the ANOVA Test Statistic for $r = 4$ Populations and a Total Sample Size $n = 54$

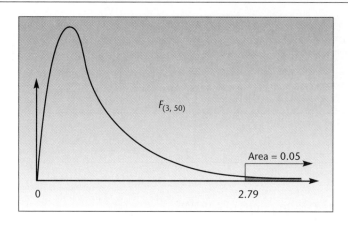

Figure 9–2 shows the F distribution with 3 and 50 degrees of freedom, which would be appropriate for a test of the equality of four population means using a total sample size of 54. Also shown is the critical point for $\alpha = 0.05$, found in Appendix C, Table 5. The critical point is 2.79. For reasons explained in the next section, the test is carried out as a right-tailed test.

We now have the basic elements of a statistical hypothesis test within the context of ANOVA: the null and alternative hypotheses, the required assumptions, and a distribution of the test statistic when the null hypothesis is true. Let us look at an example.

EXAMPLE 9–1

Major roasters and distributors of coffee in the United States have long felt great uncertainty in the price of coffee beans. Over the course of one year, for example, coffee futures prices went from a low of $1.40 per pound up to $2.50 and then down to $2.03. The main reason for such wild fluctuations in price, which strongly affect the performance of coffee distributors, is the constant danger of drought in Brazil. Since Brazil produces 30% of the world's coffee, the market for coffee beans is very sensitive to the annual rumors of impending drought.

Recently a domestic coffee distributor decided to avert the problem altogether by eliminating Brazilian coffee from all blends the company distributes. Before taking such action, the distributor wanted to minimize the chances of suffering losses in sales volume. Therefore, the distributor hired a market research firm to conduct a statistical test of consumers' taste preferences. The research firm made arrangements with several large restaurants to serve randomly chosen groups of their customers different kinds of after-dinner coffee. Three kinds of coffee were served: a group of 21 randomly chosen customers were served pure Brazilian coffee; another group of 20 randomly chosen customers were served pure Colombian coffee; and a third group of 22 randomly chosen customers were served pure African-grown coffee.

This is the *completely randomized design* part of the name of the ANOVA technique we mentioned at the end of the last section. In completely randomized design, the experimental units (in this case, the people involved in the experiment) are randomly assigned to the three treatments, the treatment being the kind of coffee they are served. Later in this chapter, we will encounter other designs useful in many situations. To prevent a response bias, the people in this experiment were not told the kind of coffee they were being served. The coffee was listed as a "house blend."

Suppose that data for the three groups were consumers' ratings of the coffee on a scale of 0 to 100 and that certain computations were carried out with these data (computations will be discussed in the next section), leading to the following value of the ANOVA test statistic: $F = 2.02$. Is there evidence to conclude that any of the three kinds of coffee leads to an average consumer rating different from that of the other two kinds?

The null and alternative hypotheses here are, by equation 9–1,

$$H_0: \mu_1 = \mu_2 = \mu_3$$
$$H_1: \text{Not all three } \mu_i \text{ are equal}$$

Let us examine the meaning of the null and alternative hypotheses in this example. The null hypothesis states that average consumer responses to each of the three kinds of coffee are equal. The alternative hypothesis says that not all three population means are equal. What are the possibilities covered under the alternative hypothesis? The possible relationships among the relative magnitudes of any three real numbers μ_1, μ_2, and μ_3 are shown in Figure 9–3.

As you can see from Figure 9–3, the alternative hypothesis is composed of several different possibilities—it includes all the cases where *not all* three means are equal. Thus, if we reject the null hypothesis, all we know is that statistical evidence allows us to conclude that not all three population means are equal. However, we do not know in what way the means are different. Therefore, once we reject the null hypothesis, we need to conduct further analysis to determine which population means are different from one another. The further analysis following ANOVA will be discussed in a later section.

We have a null hypothesis and an alternative hypothesis. We also assume that the conditions required for ANOVA are met; that is, we assume that the three populations of consumer responses are (approximately) normally distributed with equal population variance. Now we need to conduct the test.

Since we are studying three populations, or treatments, the degrees of freedom for the numerator are $r - 1 = 3 - 1 = 2$. Since the total sample size is $n = n_1 + n_2 + n_3 = 21 + 20 + 22 = 63$, we find that the degrees of freedom for the denominator are

FIGURE 9–3   Some of the Possible Relationships among the Relative Magnitudes of the Three Population Means μ_1, μ_2, and μ_3

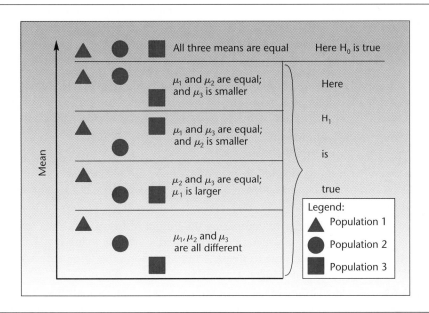

FIGURE 9–4   Carrying Out the Test of Example 9–1

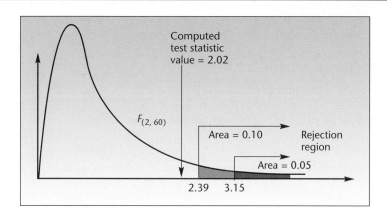

$n - r = 63 - 3 = 60$. Thus, when the null hypothesis is true, our test statistic has an F distribution with 2 and 60 degrees of freedom: $F_{(2, 60)}$. From Appendix C, Table 5, we find that the right-tailed critical point at $\alpha = 0.05$ for an F distribution with 2 and 60 degrees of freedom is 3.15. Since the computed value of the test statistic is equal to 2.02, we may conclude that at the 0.05 level of significance there is insufficient evidence to conclude that the three means are different. The null hypothesis that all three population means are equal cannot be rejected. Since the critical point for $\alpha = 0.10$ is 2.39, we find that the p-value is greater than 0.10.

Our data provide no evidence that consumers tend to prefer the Brazilian coffee to the other two brands. The distributor may substitute one of the other brands for the price-unstable Brazilian coffee. Note that we usually prefer to make conclusions based on the *rejection* of a null hypothesis because nonrejection is often considered a weak conclusion. The results of our test are shown in Figure 9–4.

In this section, we have seen the basic elements of the hypothesis test underlying analysis of variance: the null and alternative hypotheses, the required assumptions, the test statistic, and the decision rule. We have not, however, seen how the test statistic is computed from the data or the reasoning behind its computation. The theory and the computations of ANOVA are explained in the following sections.

PROBLEMS

9–1.   Four populations are compared by analysis of variance. What are the possible relations among the four population means covered under the null and alternative hypotheses?

9–2.   What are the assumptions of ANOVA?

9–3.   Three methods of training managers are to be tested for relative effectiveness. The management training institution proposes to test the effectiveness of the three methods by comparing two methods at a time, using a paired-t test. Explain why this is a poor procedure.

9–4.   In an analysis of variance comparing the output of five plants, data sets of 21 observations per plant are analyzed. The computed F statistic value is 3.6. Do you believe that there are differences in average output among the five plants? What is the approximate p-value? Explain.

9–5.   A real estate development firm wants to test whether there are differences in the average price of a lot of a given size in the center of each of four cities: Philadelphia,

New York, Washington, and Baltimore. Random samples of 52 lots in Philadelphia, 38 lots in New York, 43 lots in Washington, and 47 lots in Baltimore lead to a computed test statistic value of 12.53. Do you believe that average lot prices in the four cities are equal? How confident are you of your conclusion? Explain.

9–3   The Theory and the Computations of ANOVA

Recall that the purpose of analysis of variance is to detect differences among several population means based on evidence provided by random samples from these populations. How can this be done? We want to compare r population means. We use r random samples, one from each population. Each random sample has its own mean. The mean of the sample from population i will be denoted by x_i. We may also compute the mean of all data points in the study, regardless of which population they come from. The mean of all the data points (when all data points are considered a single set) is called the *grand mean* and is denoted by $\bar{\bar{x}}$. These means are given by the following equations.

The mean of sample i ($i = 1, \ldots, r$) is

$$\bar{x}_i = \frac{\sum_{j=1}^{n_i} x_{ij}}{n_i} \qquad (9\text{–}3)$$

The **grand mean,** the mean of all the data points, is

$$\bar{\bar{x}} = \frac{\sum_{j=1}^{r} \sum_{j=1}^{n_i} x_{ij}}{n} \qquad (9\text{–}4)$$

where x_{ij} is the particular data point in position j within the sample from population i. The subscript i denotes the population, or treatment, and runs from 1 to r. The subscript j denotes the data point within the sample from population i; thus, j runs from 1 to n_i.

In Example 9–1, $r = 3$, $n_1 = 21$, $n_2 = 20$, $n_3 = 22$, and $n = n_1 + n_2 + n_3 = 63$. The third data point (person) in the group of 21 people who consumed Brazilian coffee is denoted by x_{13} (that is, $i = 1$ denotes treatment 1 and $j = 3$ denotes the third point in that sample).

We will now define the main principle behind the analysis of variance.

> If the r population means are different (i.e., at least two of the population means are *not* equal), then the variation of the data points about their respective sample means $\bar{x}_i$ is likely to be *small* when compared with the variation of the r sample means about the grand mean $\bar{\bar{x}}$.

We will demonstrate the ANOVA principle, using three hypothetical populations, which we will call the triangles, the squares, and the circles. Table 9–1 gives the values of the sample points from the three populations. For demonstration purposes, we use very small samples. In real situations, the sample sizes should be much larger. The data given in Table 9–1 are shown in Figure 9–5. The figure also shows the deviations of the data points from their sample means and the deviations of the sample means from the grand mean.

Look carefully at Figure 9–5. Note that the *average* distance (in absolute value) of data points from their respective group means (i.e., the average distance, in absolute value, of a triangle from the mean of the triangles x_1 and similarly for the squares and

CHAPTER 12

TABLE 9–1   Data and the Various Sample Means for Triangles, Squares, and Circles

Treatment i	Sample Point j	Value x_{ij}
$i = 1$ Triangle	1	4
Triangle	2	5
Triangle	3	7
Triangle	4	8
Mean of triangles		6
$i = 2$ Square	1	10
Square	2	11
Square	3	12
Square	4	13
Mean of squares		11.5
$i = 3$ Circle	1	1
Circle	2	2
Circle	3	3
Mean of circles		2
Grand mean of all data points		6.909

FIGURE 9–5   Deviations of the Triangles, Squares, and Circles from Their Sample Means and the Deviations of the Sample Means from the Grand Mean

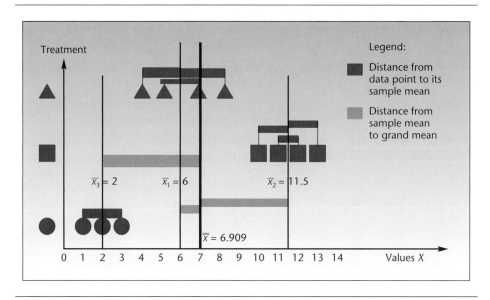

the circles) is *relatively small* compared with the average distance (in absolute value) of the three sample means from the grand mean. If you are not convinced of this, note that there are only three distances of sample means to the grand mean (in the computation, each distance is weighted by the actual number of points in the group), and that only one of them, the smallest distance—that of $\bar{x}_1$ to $\bar{\bar{x}}$—is of the relative magnitude of the distances between the data points and their respective sample means. The two other distances are much greater; hence, the average distance of the sample means from the grand mean is greater than the average distance of all data points from their respective sample means.

The *average* deviation from a mean is zero. We talk about the average absolute deviation—actually, we will use the average *squared* deviation—to prevent the deviations from canceling. This should remind you of the definition of the sample variance in Chapter 1. Now let us define some terms that will make our discussion simpler.

We define an **error deviation** as the difference between a data point and its sample mean. Errors are denoted by e, and we have

$$e_{ij} = x_{ij} - \bar{x}_i \qquad (9\text{–}5)$$

Thus, all the distances from the data points to their sample means in Figure 9–5 are errors (some are positive, and others are negative). The reason these distances are called errors is that they are unexplained by the fact that the corresponding data points belong to population i. The errors are assumed to be due to natural variation, or pure randomness, within the sample from treatment i.

On the other hand,

We define a **treatment deviation** as the deviation of a sample mean from the grand mean. Treatment deviations t_i are given by

$$t_i = \bar{x}_i - \bar{\bar{x}} \qquad (9\text{–}6)$$

The ANOVA principle thus says:

When the population means are not equal, the "average" error is relatively small compared with the "average" treatment deviation.

Again, if we actually averaged all the deviations, we would get zero. Therefore, when we apply the principle computationally, we will square the error and treatment deviations before averaging them. This way, we will maintain the relative (squared) magnitudes of these quantities. The averaging process is further complicated because we have to average based on degrees of freedom (recall that degrees of freedom were used in the definition of a sample variance). For now, let the term *average* be used in a simplified, intuitive sense.

Since we noted that the average error deviation in our triangle-square-circle example looks small relative to the average treatment deviation, let us see what the populations that brought about our three samples look like. Figure 9–6 shows the three

FIGURE 9–6 **Samples of Triangles, Squares, and Circles and Their Respective Populations (the three populations are normal with equal variance but with different means)**

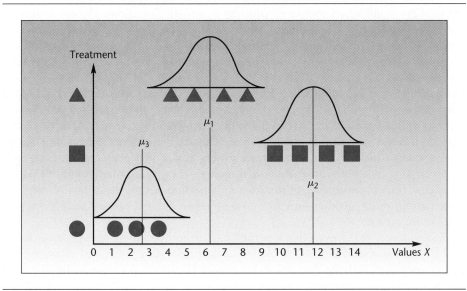

FIGURE 9–7   Samples of Triangles, Squares, and Circles Where the Average Error Deviation Is Not Smaller than the Average Treatment Deviation

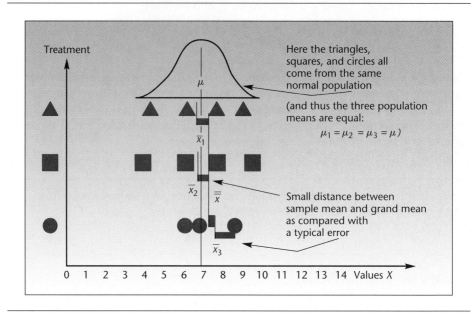

populations, assumed normally distributed with equal variance. (This can be seen from the equal width of the three normal curves. Note also that the three samples seem to have equal dispersion about their sample means.) The figure also shows that the three population means are not equal.

Figure 9–7, in contrast, shows three samples of triangles, squares, and circles in which the average error deviation is of about the same magnitude as (*not* smaller than) the average treatment deviation. As can be seen from the superimposed normal populations from which the samples have arisen in this case, the three population means μ_1, μ_2, and μ_3 are all equal. Compare the two figures to convince yourself of the ANOVA principle.

The Sum-of-Squares Principle

We have seen how, when the population means are different, the error deviations in the data are small when compared with the treatment deviations. We made general statements about the average error being small when compared with the average treatment deviation. The error deviations measure how close the data *within* each group are to their respective group means. The treatment deviations measure the distances *between* the various groups. It therefore seems intuitively plausible (as seen in Figures 9–5 to 9–7) that when these two kinds of deviations are of about equal magnitude, the population means are about equal. Why? Because when the average error is about equal to the average treatment deviation, the treatment deviation may itself be viewed as just another error. That is, the treatment deviation in this case is due to pure chance rather than to any real differences among the population means. In other words, when the average t is of the same magnitude as the average e, both are estimates of the internal variation within the data and carry no information about a difference between any two groups—about a difference in population means.

We will now make everything quantifiable, using the *sum-of-squares principle*. We start by returning to Figure 9–5, looking at a particular data point, and analyzing distances associated with the data point. We choose the fourth data point from the sample of squares (population 2). This data point is $x_{24} = 13$ (verify this from Table 9–1).

FIGURE 9–8 Total Deviation as the Sum of the Treatment Deviation and the Error Deviation for a Particular Data Point

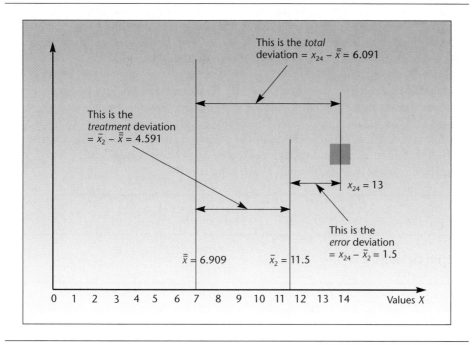

We now magnify a section of Figure 9–5, the section surrounding this particular data point. This is shown in Figure 9–8.

We define the **total deviation** of a data point x_{ij} (denoted by Tot_{ij}) as the deviation of the data point from the grand mean:

$$\text{Tot}_{ij} = x_{ij} - \bar{\bar{x}} \tag{9–7}$$

Figure 9–8 shows that the total deviation is equal to the treatment deviation plus the error deviation. This is true for *any* point in our data set (even when some of the numbers are negative).

For any data point x_{ij},

$$\text{Tot} = t + e \tag{9–8}$$

In words:

Total deviation = Treatment deviation + Error deviation

In the case of our chosen data point x_{24}, we have

$$t_2 + e_{24} = 4.591 + 1.5 = 6.091 = \text{Tot}_{24}$$

Equation 9–8 works for every data point in our data set. Here is how it is derived algebraically:

$$t_i + e_{ij} = (\bar{x}_i - \bar{\bar{x}}) + (x_{ij} - \bar{x}_i) = x_{ij} - \bar{\bar{x}} = \text{Tot}_{ij} \tag{9–9}$$

As seen in equation 9–9, the term $\bar{x}_i$ cancels out when the two terms in parentheses are added. This shows that for every data point, the total deviation is equal to the treatment part of the deviation plus the error part. This is also seen in Figure 9–8. The *total* deviation of a data point from the grand mean is thus partitioned into a deviation due to *treatment* and a deviation due to *error*. The deviation due to treatment differences is the *between-treatments* deviation, while the deviation due to error is the *within-treatment* deviation.

We have considered only one point, x_{24}. To determine whether the error deviations are small when compared with the treatment deviations, we need to aggregate the partition over all data points. This is done, as we noted earlier, by averaging the deviations. We take the partition of the deviations in equation 9–9 and we square each of the three terms (otherwise our averaging process would lead to zero).[2] The squaring of the terms in equation 9–9 gives, on one side,

$$t_i^2 + e_{ij}^2 = (\bar{x}_i - \bar{\bar{x}})^2 + (x_{ij} - \bar{x}_i)^2 \qquad (9\text{–}10)$$

and, on the other side,

$$\text{Tot}_{ij}^2 = (x_{ij} - \bar{\bar{x}})^2 \qquad (9\text{–}11)$$

Note an interesting thing: The two sides of equation 9–9 are equal, but when all three terms are squared, the two sides (now equations 9–10 and 9–11) are *not* equal. Try this with any of the data points. The surprising thing happens next.

We take the squared deviations of equations 9–10 and 9–11, and we *sum them over all our data points.* Interestingly, the sum of the squared error deviations and the sum of the squared treatment deviations do add up to the sum of the squared total deviations. Mathematically, cross-terms in the equation drop out, allowing this to happen. The result is the sum-of-squares principle.

We have the following:

$$\sum_{i=1}^{r} \sum_{j=1}^{n_i} \text{Tot}_{ij}^2 = \sum_{i=1}^{r} n_i t_i^2 + \sum_{i=1}^{r} \sum_{j=1}^{n_i} e_{ij}^2$$

This can be written in longer form as

$$\sum_{i=1}^{r} \sum_{j=1}^{n_i} (x_{ij} - \bar{\bar{x}})^2 = \sum_{i=1}^{r} n_i (\bar{x}_i - \bar{\bar{x}})^2 + \sum_{i=1}^{r} \sum_{j=1}^{n_i} (x_{ij} - \bar{x}_i)^2$$

The Sum-of-Squares Principle
The sum-of-squares total (SST) is the sum of the two terms: the sum of squares for treatment (SSTR) and the sum of squares for error (SSE).

$$\text{SST} = \text{SSTR} + \text{SSE} \qquad (9\text{–}12)$$

[2]This can be seen from the data in Table 9–1. Note that the sum of the deviations of the triangles from their mean of 6 is $(4 - 6) + (5 - 6) + (7 - 6) + (8 - 6) = 0$; hence, an average of these deviations, or those of the squares or circles, leads to zero.

The sum-of-squares principle partitions the sum-of-squares total within the data SST into a part due to treatment effect SSTR and a part due to errors SSE. The squared deviations of the treatment means from the grand mean are *counted for every data point*—hence the term n_i in the first summation on the right side (SSTR) of equation 9–12. The second term on the right-hand side is the sum of the squared errors, that is, the sum of the squared deviations of the data points from their respective sample means.

See Figure 9–8 for the different deviations associated with a single point. Imagine a similar relation among the three kinds of deviations for every one of the data points, as shown in Figure 9–5. Then imagine all these deviations squared and added together—errors to errors, treatments to treatments, and totals to totals. The result is equation 9–12, the sum-of-squares principle.

Sums of squares measure variation within the data. SST is the total amount of variation within the data set. SSTR is that part of the variation within the data that is due to differences among the groups, and SSE is that part of the variation within the data that is due to error—the part that cannot be explained by differences among the groups. Therefore, SSTR is sometimes called the sum of squares *between* (variation among the groups), and SSE is called the sum of squares *within* (within-group variation). SSTR is also called the *explained variation* (because it is the part of the total variation that can be explained by the fact that the data points belong to several different groups). SSE is then called the *unexplained variation*. The partition of the sum of squares in analysis of variance is shown in Figure 9–9.

Breaking down the sum of squares is not enough, however. If we want to determine whether the errors are small compared with the treatment part, we need to find the *average* (squared) error and the *average* (squared) treatment deviation. Averaging, in the context of variances, is achieved by dividing by the appropriate number of degrees of freedom associated with each sum of squares.

The Degrees of Freedom

Recall our definition of degrees of freedom in Chapter 5. The degrees of freedom are the number of data points that are "free to move," that is, the number of elements in the data set minus the number of restrictions. A restriction on a data set is a quantity already computed from the entire data set under consideration; thus, knowledge of this quantity makes one data point fixed and reduces by 1 the effective number of data points that are free to move. This is why, as was shown in Chapter 5, knowledge of the sample mean reduces the degrees of freedom of the sample variance to $n - 1$. What are the degrees of freedom in the context of analysis of variance?

FIGURE 9–9 Partition of the Sum-of-Squares Total into Treatment and Error Parts

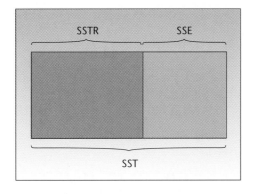

Consider the total sum of squares, SST. In computing this sum of squares, we use the entire data set and information about *one* quantity computed from the data: the grand mean (because, by definition, SST is the sum of the squared deviations of all data points from the grand mean). Since we have a total of n data points and one restriction,

The number of degrees of freedom associated with SST is $n - 1$.

The sum of squares for treatment SSTR is computed from the deviations of r sample means from the grand mean. The r sample means are considered r independent data points, and the grand mean (which can be considered as having been computed from the r sample means) thus reduces the degrees of freedom by 1.

The number of degrees of freedom associated with SSTR is $r - 1$.

The sum of squares for error SSE is computed from the deviations of a total of n data points $(n = n_1 + n_2 + \cdots + n_r)$ from r different sample means. Since each of the sample means acts as a restriction on the data set, the degrees of freedom for error are $n - r$. This can be seen another way: There are r groups with n_i data points in group i. Thus, each group, with its own sample mean acting as a restriction, has degrees of freedom equal to $n_i - 1$. The total number of degrees of freedom for error is the sum of the degrees of freedom in the r groups: $\text{df} = (n_1 - 1) + (n_2 - 1) + \cdots + (n_r - 1) = n - r$.

The number of degrees of freedom associated with SSE is $n - r$.

An important principle in analysis of variance is that the degrees of freedom of the three components are *additive* in the same way that the sums of squares are additive.

$$\text{df(total)} = \text{df(treatment)} + \text{df(error)} \qquad (9\text{--}13)$$

This can easily be verified by noting the following: $n - 1 = (r - 1) + (n - r)$—the r drops out. We are now ready to compute the average squared deviation due to treatment and the average squared deviation due to error.

The Mean Squares

In finding the average squared deviations due to treatment and to error, we divide each sum of squares by its degrees of freedom. We call the two resulting averages **mean square treatment (MSTR)** and **mean square error (MSE),** respectively.

$$\text{MSTR} = \frac{\text{SSTR}}{r - 1} \qquad (9\text{--}14)$$

$$\text{MSE} = \frac{\text{SSE}}{n - r} \qquad (9\text{--}15)$$

The Expected Values of the Statistics MSTR and MSE under the Null Hypothesis

When the null hypothesis of ANOVA is true, all r population means are equal, and in this case there are *no treatment effects.* In such a case, the average squared deviation due to "treatment" is just another realization of an average squared error. In terms of the expected values of the two mean squares, we have

$$E(\text{MSE}) = \sigma^2 \qquad (9\text{–}16)$$

and

$$E(\text{MSTR}) = \sigma^2 + \frac{\sum n_i(\mu_i - \mu)^2}{r - 1} \qquad (9\text{–}17)$$

where μ_i is the mean of population i and μ is the combined mean of all r populations.

Equation 9–16 says that *MSE is an unbiased estimator of* σ^2, *the assumed common variance of the* r *populations*. The mean square error in ANOVA is therefore just like the sample variance in the one-population case of earlier chapters.

The mean square treatment, however, comprises two components, as seen from equation 9–17. The first component is σ^2, as in the case of MSE. The second component is a measure of the differences among the r population means μ_i. If the null hypothesis is true, all r population means are equal—they are all equal to μ. In such a case, the second term in equation 9–17 is equal to *zero*. When this happens, the expected value of MSTR and the expected value of MSE are both equal to σ^2.

When the null hypothesis of ANOVA is true and all r population means are equal, MSTR and MSE are two independent, unbiased estimators of the common population variance σ^2.

If, on the other hand, the null hypothesis is not true and differences do exist among the r population means, then *MSTR will tend to be larger than MSE*. This happens because, when not all population means are equal, the second term in equation 9–17 is a positive number.

The F *Statistic*

The preceding discussion suggests that the ratio of MSTR to MSE is a good indicator of whether the r population means are equal. If the r population means are equal, then MSTR/MSE would tend to be close to 1.00. Remember that both MSTR and MSE are sample statistics derived from our data. As such, MSTR and MSE will have some randomness associated with them, and they are not likely to exactly equal their expected values. Thus, when the null hypothesis is true, MSTR/MSE will vary around the value 1.00. When not all the r population means are equal, the ratio MSTR/MSE will tend to be greater than 1.00 because the expected value of MSTR, from equation 9–17, will be larger than the expected value of MSE. How large is "large enough" for us to reject the null hypothesis?

This is where statistical inference comes in. We want to determine whether the difference between our observed value of MSTR/MSE and the number 1.00 is due just to chance variation, or whether MSTR/MSE is *significantly* greater than 1.00— implying that not all the population means are equal. We will make the determination with the aid of the F distribution.

Under the assumptions of ANOVA, the ratio MSTR/MSE possesses an F distribution with $r - 1$ degrees of freedom for the numerator and $n - r$ degrees of freedom for the denominator when the null hypothesis is true.

In Chapter 8, we saw how the F distribution is used in determining differences between two population variances—noting that if the two variances are equal, then the ratio of the two independent, unbiased estimators of the assumed common variance follows an F distribution. There, too, the appropriate degrees of freedom for the numerator and the denominator of F came from the degrees of freedom of the sample variance in the numerator and the sample variance in the denominator of the ratio. In ANOVA, the numerator is MSTR and has $r - 1$ degrees of freedom; the denominator is MSE and has $n - r$ degrees of freedom. We thus have the following:

> The test statistic in analysis of variance is
> $$F_{(r-1,\ n-r)} = \frac{\text{MSTR}}{\text{MSE}} \qquad (9\text{--}18)$$

In this section, we have seen the theoretical rationale for the F statistic we used in Section 9–2. We also saw the computations required for arriving at the value of the test statistic. In the next section, we will encounter a convenient tool for keeping track of computations and reporting our results: the ANOVA table.

PROBLEMS

9–6. Define *treatment* and *error*.

9–7. Explain why trying to compute a simple average of all error deviations and of all treatment deviations will not lead to any results.

9–8. Explain how the total deviation is partitioned into the treatment deviation and the error deviation.

9–9. Explain the sum-of-squares principle.

9–10. Where do errors come from, and what do you think are their sources?

9–11. If, in an analysis of variance, you find that MSTR is greater than MSE, why can you not immediately reject the null hypothesis without determining the F ratio and its distribution? Explain.

9–12. What is the main principle behind analysis of variance?

9–13. Explain how information about the variance components in a data set can lead to conclusions about population means.

9–14. An article in *Advertising Age* discusses the need for corporate transparency of all transactions and hails the imperative "Get naked," which, it said, appeared on the cover of a recent issue of *Wired.* The article tried to compare the transparency policies of Microsoft, Google, Apple, and Wal-Mart.[3] Suppose that four independent random samples of 20 accountants each rate the transparency of these four corporations on a scale of 0 to 100.

> *a.* What are the degrees of freedom for Factor?
>
> *b.* What are the degrees of freedom for Error?
>
> *c.* What are the degrees of freedom for Total?

9–15. By the sum-of-squares principle, SSE and SSTR are additive, and their sum is SST. Does such a relation exist between MSE and MSTR? Explain.

9–16. Does the quantity MSTR/MSE follow an F distribution when the null hypothesis of ANOVA is false? Explain.

9–17. (A mathematically demanding problem) Prove the sum-of-squares principle, equation 9–12.

9–4   The ANOVA Table and Examples

Table 9–2 shows the data for our triangles, squares, and circles. In addition, the table shows the deviations from the group means, and their squares. From these quantities, we find the sum of squares and mean squares.

---

[3]Matthew Creamer, "You Call This Transparency? They Can See Right Through You," *Advertising Age,* April 30, 2007, p. 7.

TABLE 9-2 Computations for Triangles, Squares, and Circles

Treatment i	j	Value x_{ij}	$x_{ij} - \bar{x}_i$	$(x_{ij} - \bar{x}_i)^2$
Triangle	1	4	$4 - 6 = -2$	$(-2)^2 = 4$
Triangle	2	5	$5 - 6 = -1$	$(-1)^2 = 1$
Triangle	3	7	$7 - 6 = 1$	$(1)^2 = 1$
Triangle	4	8	$8 - 6 = 2$	$(2)^2 = 4$
Square	1	10	$10 - 11.5 = -1.5$	$(-1.5)^2 = 2.25$
Square	2	11	$11 - 11.5 = -0.5$	$(-0.5)^2 = 0.25$
Square	3	12	$12 - 11.5 = 0.5$	$(0.5)^2 = 0.25$
Square	4	13	$13 - 11.5 = 1.5$	$(1.5)^2 = 2.25$
Circle	1	1	$1 - 2 = -1$	$(-1)^2 = 1$
Circle	2	2	$2 - 2 = 0$	$(0)^2 = 0$
Circle	3	3	$3 - 2 = 1$	$(1)^2 = 1$
			Sum = 0	Sum = 17

As we see in the last row of the table, the sum of all the deviations of the data points from their group means is zero, as expected. The sum of the *squared* deviations from the sample means (which, from equation 9-12, is SSE) is equal to 17.00:

$$\text{SSE} = \sum_{i=1}^{r} \sum_{j=1}^{n_i} (x_{ij} - \bar{x}_i)^2 = 17.00$$

Now we want to compute the sum of squares for treatment. Recall from Table 9-1 that $\bar{\bar{x}} = 6.909$. Again using the definitions in equation 9-12, we have

$$\text{SSTR} = \sum_{i=1}^{r} n_i (\bar{x}_i - \bar{\bar{x}})^2 = 4(6 - 6.909)^2 + 4(11.5 - 6.909)^2 + 3(2 - 6.909)^2$$
$$= 159.9$$

We now compute the mean squares. From equations 9-14 and 9-15, respectively, we get

$$\text{MSTR} = \frac{\text{SSTR}}{r - 1} = \frac{159.9}{2} = 79.95$$
$$\text{MSE} = \frac{\text{SSE}}{n - r} = \frac{17}{8} = 2.125$$

Using equation 9-18, we get the computed value of the F statistic:

$$F_{(2, 8)} = \frac{\text{MSTR}}{\text{MSE}} = \frac{79.95}{2.125} = 37.62$$

We are finally in a position to conduct the ANOVA hypothesis test to determine whether the means of the three populations are equal. From Appendix C, Table 5, we find that the critical point at $\alpha = 0.01$ (for a right-tailed test) for the F distribution with 2 degrees of freedom for the numerator and 8 degrees of freedom for the denominator

FIGURE 9–10   Rejecting the Null Hypothesis in the Triangles, Squares, and Circles Example

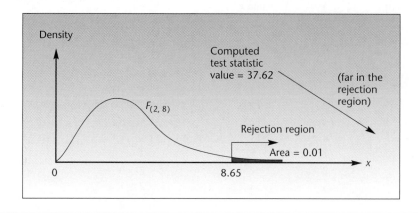

is 8.65. We can therefore reject the null hypothesis. Since 37.62 is much greater than 8.65, the p-value is much smaller than 0.01. This is shown in Figure 9–10.

As usual, we must exercise caution in the interpretation of results based on such small samples. As we noted earlier, in real situations we use large data sets, and the computations are usually done by computer. In the rest of our examples, we will assume that sums of squares and other quantities are produced by a computer.[4]

An essential tool for reporting the results of an analysis of variance is the ANOVA table. An ANOVA table lists the sources of variation: treatment, error, and total. (In the two-factor ANOVA, which we will see in later sections, there will be more sources of variation.) The ANOVA table lists the sums of squares, the degrees of freedom, the mean squares, and the F ratio. The table format simplifies the analysis and the interpretation of the results. The structure of the ANOVA table is based on the fact that both the sums of squares and the degrees of freedom are additive. We will now present an ANOVA table for the triangles, squares, and circles example. Table 9–3 shows the results computed above.

Note that the entries in the second and third columns, sum of squares and degrees of freedom, are both additive. The entries in the fourth column, mean square, are obtained by dividing the appropriate sums of squares by their degrees of freedom. We do not define a mean square total, which is why no entry appears in that particular

TABLE 9–3   ANOVA Table

Source of Variation	Sum of Squares	Degrees of Freedom	Mean Square	F Ratio
Treatment	SSTR = 159.9	$r - 1 = 2$	$\text{MSTR} = \dfrac{\text{SSTR}}{r - 1}$	$F = \dfrac{\text{MSTR}}{\text{MSE}}$
			$= 79.95$	$= 37.62$
Error	SSE = 17.0	$n - r = 8$	$\text{MSE} = \dfrac{\text{SSE}}{n - r}$	
			$= 2.125$	
Total	SST = 176.9	$n - 1 = 10$		

---

[4]If you must carry out ANOVA computations by hand, there are equivalent computational formulas for the sums of squares that may be easier to apply than equation 9–12. These are

$$\text{SST} = \Sigma_i \Sigma_j (x_{ij})^2 - (\Sigma_i \Sigma_j x_{ij})^2 / n$$
$$\text{SSTR} = \Sigma_i [(\Sigma_j x_{ij})^2 / n_i] - (\Sigma_i \Sigma_j x_{ij})^2 / n$$

and we obtain SSE by subtraction: SSE = SST − SSTR.

position in the table. The last entry in the table is the main objective of our analysis: the F ratio, which is computed as the ratio of the two entries in the previous column. No other entries appear in the last column. Example 9–2 demonstrates the use of the ANOVA table.

EXAMPLE 9–2

Club Med has more than 30 major resorts worldwide, from Tahiti to Switzerland. Many of the beach resorts are in the Caribbean, and at one point the club wanted to test whether the resorts on Guadeloupe, Martinique, Eleuthera, Paradise Island, and St. Lucia were all equally well liked by vacationing club members. The analysis was to be based on a survey questionnaire filled out by a random sample of 40 respondents in each of the resorts. From every returned questionnaire, a general satisfaction score, on a scale of 0 to 100, was computed. Analysis of the survey results yielded the statistics given in Table 9–4.

The results were computed from the responses by using a computer program that calculated the sums of squared deviations from the sample means and from the grand mean. Given the values of SST and SSE, construct an ANOVA table and conduct the hypothesis test. (*Note:* The reported sample means in Table 9–4 will be used in the next section.)

Solution

Let us first construct an ANOVA table and fill in the information we have: SST = 112,564, SSE = 98,356, $n = 200$, and $r = 5$. This has been done in Table 9–5. We now compute SSTR as the difference between SST and SSE and enter it in the appropriate place in the table. We then divide SSTR and SSE by their respective degrees of freedom to give us MSTR and MSE. Finally, we divide MSTR by MSE to give us the F ratio. All these quantities are entered in the ANOVA table. The result is the complete ANOVA table for the study, Table 9–6.

TABLE 9–4 Club Med Survey Results

Resort i	Mean Response $\bar{X}_i$
1. Guadeloupe	89
2. Martinique	75
3. Eleuthera	73
4. Paradise Island	91
5. St. Lucia	85
SST = 112,564	SSE = 98,356

TABLE 9–5 Preliminary ANOVA Table for Club Med Example

Source of Variation	Sum of Squares	Degrees of Freedom	Mean Square	F Ratio
Treatment	SSTR =	$r - 1 = 4$	MSTR =	F =
Error	SSE = 98,356	$n - r = 195$	MSE =	
Total	SST = 112,564	$n - 1 = 199$		

TABLE 9–6 ANOVA Table for Club Med Example

Source of Variation	Sum of Squares	Degrees of Freedom	Mean Square	F Ratio
Treatment	SSTR = 14,208	$r - 1 = 4$	MSTR = 3,552	F = 7.04
Error	SSE = 98,356	$n - r = 195$	MSE = 504.4	
Total	SST = 112,564	$n - 1 = 199$		

FIGURE 9–11   Club Med Test

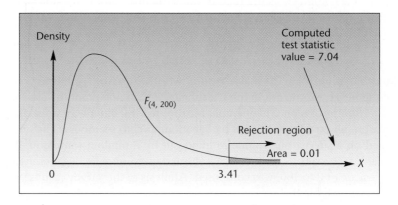

Table 9–6 contains all the pertinent information for this study. We are now ready to conduct the hypothesis test.

$H_0: \mu_1 = \mu_2 = \mu_3 = \mu_4 = \mu_5$ (average vacationer satisfaction for each of the five resorts is equal)

H_1: Not all μ_i $(i = 1, \ldots, 5)$ are equal   (on average, vacationer satisfaction is not equal among the five resorts)

As shown in Table 9–6, the test statistic value is $F_{(4, 195)} = 7.04$. As often happens, the exact number of degrees of freedom we need does not appear in Appendix C, Table 5. We use the nearest entry, which is the critical point for F with 4 degrees of freedom for the numerator and 200 degrees of freedom for the denominator. The critical point for $\alpha = 0.01$ is $C = 3.41$. The test is illustrated in Figure 9–11.

Since the computed test statistic value falls in the rejection region for $\alpha = 0.01$, we reject the null hypothesis and note that the p-value is smaller than 0.01. We may conclude that, based on the survey results and our assumptions, it is likely that the five resorts studied are not equal in terms of average vacationer satisfaction. Which resorts are more satisfying than others? This question will be answered when we return to this example in the next section.

EXAMPLE 9–3

Recent research studied job involvement of salespeople in the four major career stages: exploration, establishment, maintenance, and disengagement. Results of the study included an analysis of variance aimed at determining whether salespeople in each of the four career stages are, on average, equally involved with their jobs. Involvement is measured on a special scale developed by psychologists. The analysis is based on questionnaires returned by a total of 543 respondents, and the reported F value is 8.52. The authors note the result is "significant at $p < .01$." Assuming that MSE $= 34.4$, construct an ANOVA table for this example. Also verify the authors' claim about the significance of their results.

Solution

In this problem, another exercise in the construction of ANOVA tables, we are doing the opposite of what is usually done: We are going from the final result of an F ratio to the earlier stages of an analysis of variance. First, multiplying the F ratio by MSE gives us MSTR. Then, from the sample size $n = 543$ and from $r = 4$, we get the number of degrees of freedom for treatment, error, and total. Using our information, we construct the ANOVA table (Table 9–7).

TABLE 9–7 ANOVA Table for Job Involvement

Source of Variation	Sum of Squares	Degrees of Freedom	Mean Square	F Ratio
Treatment	SSTR = 879.3	$r - 1 = 3$	MSTR = 293.1	$F = 8.52$
Error	SSE = 18,541.6	$n - r = 539$	MSE = 34.4	
Total	SST = 19,420.9	$n - 1 = 542$		

From Appendix C, Table 5, we find that the critical point for a right-tailed test at $\alpha = 0.01$ for an F distribution with 3 and 400 degrees of freedom (the entry for degrees of freedom closest to the needed 3 and 539) is 3.83. Thus, we may conclude that differences do exist among the four career stages with respect to average job involvement. The authors' statement about the p-value is also true: the p-value is much smaller than 0.01.

PROBLEMS

9–18. Gulfstream Aerospace Company produced three different prototypes as candidates for mass production as the company's newest large-cabin business jet, the *Gulfstream IV*. Each of the three prototypes has slightly different features, which may bring about differences in performance. Therefore, as part of the decision-making process concerning which model to produce, company engineers are interested in determining whether the three proposed models have about the same average flight range. Each of the models is assigned a random choice of 10 flight routes and departure times, and the flight range on a full standard fuel tank is measured (the planes carry additional fuel on the test flights, to allow them to land safely at certain destination points). Range data for the three prototypes, in nautical miles (measured to the nearest 10 miles), are as follows.[5]

Prototype A	Prototype B	Prototype C
4,420	4,230	4,110
4,540	4,220	4,090
4,380	4,100	4,070
4,550	4,300	4,160
4,210	4,420	4,230
4,330	4,110	4,120
4,400	4,230	4,000
4,340	4,280	4,200
4,390	4,090	4,150
4,510	4,320	4,220

Do all three prototypes have the same average range? Construct an ANOVA table, and carry out the test. Explain your results.

9–19. In the theory of finance, a market for any asset or commodity is said to be *efficient* if items of identical quality and other attributes (such as risk, in the case of stocks) are sold at the same price. A Geneva-based oil industry analyst wants to test the hypothesis that the spot market for crude oil is efficient. The analyst chooses the Rotterdam oil market, and he selects Arabian Light as the type of oil to be studied. (Differences in location may cause price differences because of transportation costs, and differences in the type of oil—hence, in the quality of oil—also affect the price.

---

[5]General information about the capabilities of the *Gulfstream IV* is provided courtesy of Gulfstream Aerospace Company.

Therefore, both the type and the location must be fixed.) A random sample of eight observations from each of four sources of the spot price of a barrel of oil during February 2007 is collected. Data, in U.S. dollars per barrel, are as follows.

U.K.	Mexico	U.A.E.	Oman
$62.10	$56.30	$55.60	$53.11
63.20	59.45	54.22	52.90
55.80	60.02	53.18	53.75
56.90	60.00	56.12	54.10
61.20	58.75	60.01	59.03
60.18	59.13	53.20	52.35
60.90	53.30	54.00	52.80
61.12	60.17	55.19	54.95

Based on these data, what should the analyst conclude about whether the market for crude oil is efficient? Are conclusions valid only for the Rotterdam market? Are conclusions valid for all types of crude oil? What assumptions are necessary for the analysis? Do you believe that all the assumptions are met in this case? What are the limitations, if any, of this study? Discuss.

9–20.   A study was undertaken to assess how both majority and minority groups perceive the degree of participation of African-American models in television commercials. The authors designated the three groups in this study as European Americans, African Americans, and Other. The purpose of this research was to determine if there were any statistically significant differences in the average perceptions within these three groups of the extent of the role played by African-American models in commercials the subjects viewed. The results of the ANOVA carried out were summarized as $F(2, 101) = 3.61$.[6] Analyze this result and state a conclusion about this study.

9–21.   Research has shown that in the fast-paced world of electronics, the key factor that separates the winners from the losers is actually how *slow* a firm is in making decisions: The most successful firms take longer to arrive at strategic decisions on product development, adopting new technologies, or developing new products. The following values are the number of months to arrive at a decision for firms ranked high, medium, and low in terms of performance:

High	Medium	Low
3.5	3	1
4.8	5.5	2.5
3.0	6	2
6.5	4	1.5
7.5	4	1.5
8	4.5	6
2	6	3.8
6	2	4.5
5.5	9	0.5
6.5	4.5	2
7	5	3.5
9	2.5	1.0
5	7	2
10		
6		

Do an ANOVA. Use $\alpha = 0.05$.

---

[6] Donnel A. Briley, J.L. Shrum, and Robert S. Wyer Jr., "Subjective Impressions of Minority Group Representation in the Media: A Comparison of Majority and Minority Viewers' Judgments and Underlying Processes," *Journal of Consumer Psychology* 17, no. 1 (2007), pp. 36–48.

9–22. In assessing South Korean monetary policy, researchers at the Bank of Korea studied the effects of three inflation-fighting policies the bank had instituted, to determine whether there were any statistically significant differences in the average monetary-economic reaction to these three policies. The results of an ANOVA the bank carried out were reported as df $= (2, 55)$, F-distribution statistic $= 52.787$.[7] Interpret these ANOVA results. Are all three policies equally effective?

9–23. A study was undertaken to assess the effect of sheer size of a portfolio (leaving out all other effects, such as degree of diversification) on abnormal performance, that is, performance of a stock portfolio that is above what one can expect based on the stock market as a whole. In a four-factor design based on portfolio size for well-diversified portfolios, with 240 data points, the F statistic was significant at the 1% level of significance.[8] Explain.

9–5 Further Analysis

You have rejected the ANOVA null hypothesis. What next? This is an important question often overlooked in elementary introductions to analysis of variance. After all, what is the meaning of the statement "not all r population means are equal" if we cannot tell *in what way* the population means are not equal? We need to know which of our population means are large, which are small, and the magnitudes of the differences among them. These issues are addressed in this section.

ANOVA can be viewed as a machine or a box: In go the data, and out comes a conclusion—"all r population means are equal" or "not all r population means are equal." If the ANOVA null hypothesis H_0: $\mu_1 = \mu_2 = \cdots = \mu_r$ is not rejected and we therefore state that there is no strong evidence to conclude that differences exist among the r population means, then there is nothing more to say or do (unless, of course, you believe that differences do exist and you are able to gather more information to prove so). If the ANOVA null hypothesis is rejected, then we have evidence that not all r population means are equal. This calls for *further analysis*—other hypothesis tests and/or the construction of confidence intervals to determine where the differences exist, their directions, and their magnitudes. The schematic diagram of the "ANOVA box" is shown in Figure 9–12.

FIGURE 9–12 The ANOVA Diagram

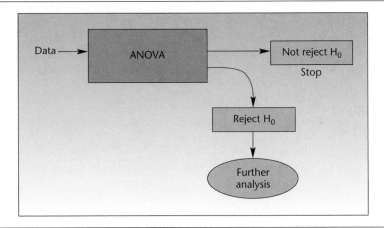

---

[7]Young Sun Kwon, "Estimation of the Asymmetric Monetary Policy Reaction Functions in Korea," *Bank of Korea Economic Papers* 9, no. 2 (2006), pp. 20–37.

[8]Marcin Kacperczyk, Clemens Sialm, and Lu Zheng, "Industry Concentration and Mutual Fund Performance," *Journal of Investment Management* 5, no. 1 (first quarter 2007), pp. 50–64.

Several methods have been developed for further analysis following the rejection of the null hypothesis in ANOVA. All the methods make use of the following two properties:

1. The sample means $\bar{X}_i$ are unbiased estimators of the corresponding population means μ_i.
2. The mean square error, MSE, is an unbiased estimator of the common population variance σ^2.

Since MSE can be read directly from the ANOVA table, we have another advantage of using an ANOVA table. This extends the usefulness of the table beyond the primary stages of analysis. The first and simplest post-ANOVA analysis is the estimation of separate population means μ_i. Under the assumptions of analysis of variance, we can show that each sample mean $\bar{X}_i$ *has a normal distribution with mean* μ_i *and standard deviation* $\sigma/\sqrt{n_i}$, where σ is the common standard deviation of the r populations. Since σ is not known, we estimate it by $\sqrt{\text{MSE}}$. We get the following relation:

$$\frac{\bar{X}_i - \mu_i}{\sqrt{\text{MSE}}/\sqrt{n_i}} \text{ has a } t \text{ distribution with } n - r \text{ degrees of freedom} \qquad (9\text{--}19)$$

This property leads us to the possibility of constructing confidence intervals for individual population means.

A $(1 - \alpha)$ 100% confidence interval for μ_i, the mean of population i, is

$$\bar{x} \pm t_{\alpha/2}\frac{\sqrt{\text{MSE}}}{\sqrt{n_i}} \qquad (9\text{--}20)$$

where $t_{\alpha/2}$ is the value of the t distribution with $n - r$ degrees of freedom that cuts off a right-tailed area equal to $\alpha/2$.

Confidence intervals given by equation 9–20 are included in the template.

We now demonstrate the use of equation 9–20 with the continuation of Example 9–2, the Club Med example. From Table 9–4, we get the sample means $\bar{x}_i$:

Guadeloupe:	$\bar{x}_1 = 89$
Martinique:	$\bar{x}_2 = 75$
Eleuthera:	$\bar{x}_3 = 73$
Paradise Island:	$\bar{x}_4 = 91$
St. Lucia:	$\bar{x}_5 = 85$

From Table 9–6, the ANOVA table for this example, we get MSE $= 504.4$ and degrees of freedom for error $= n - r = 195$. We also know that the sample size in each group is $n_i = 40$ for all $i = 1, \ldots, 5$. Since a t distribution with 195 degrees of freedom is, for all practical purposes, a standard normal distribution, we use $z = 1.96$ in constructing 95% confidence intervals for the population mean responses of vacationers on the five islands. We will construct a 95% confidence interval for the mean response on Guadeloupe and will leave the construction of the other four confidence intervals as an exercise. For Guadeloupe, we have the following 95% confidence interval for the population mean μ_1:

$$\bar{x}_1 \pm t_{\alpha/2} \frac{\sqrt{\text{MSE}}}{\sqrt{n_1}} = 89 \pm 1.96 \frac{\sqrt{504.4}}{\sqrt{40}} = [82.04, 95.96]$$

The real usefulness of ANOVA, however, does not lie in the construction of individual confidence intervals for population means (these are of limited use because the confidence coefficient does not apply to a *series* of estimates). The power of ANOVA lies in providing us with the ability to make *joint* conclusions about population parameters.

As mentioned earlier, several procedures have been developed for further analysis. The method we will discuss here is the *Tukey method* of pairwise comparisons of the population means. The method is also called the *HSD* (honestly significant differences) *test*. This method allows us to compare every possible pair of means by using a *single level of significance*, say $\alpha = 0.05$ (or a single confidence coefficient, say, $1 - \alpha = 0.95$). The single level of significance applies to the *entire set* of pairwise comparisons.

The Tukey Pairwise-Comparisons Test

We will use the *studentized range distribution*.

> The **studentized range distribution** q has a probability distribution with degrees of freedom r and $n - r$.

Note that the degrees of freedom of q are similar, but not identical, to the degrees of freedom of the F distribution in ANOVA. The F distribution has $r - 1$ and $n - r$ degrees of freedom. The q distribution has degrees of freedom r and $n - r$. Critical points for q with different numbers of degrees of freedom for $\alpha = 0.05$ and for $\alpha = 0.01$ are given in Appendix C, Table 6. Check, for example, that for $\alpha = 0.05$, $r = 3$, and $n - r = 20$, we have the critical point $q_\alpha = 3.58$. The table gives right-hand critical points, which is what we need since our test will be a right-tailed test. We now define the Tukey criterion T.

The Tukey Criterion

$$T = q_\alpha \frac{\sqrt{\text{MSE}}}{\sqrt{n_i}} \tag{9–21}$$

Equation 9–21 gives us a critical point, at a given level α, with which we will compare the computed values of test statistics defined later. Now let us define the hypothesis tests. As mentioned, the usefulness of the Tukey test is that it allows us to perform *jointly* all possible pairwise comparisons of the population means using a single, "family" level of significance. What are all the possible pairwise comparisons associated with an ANOVA?

Suppose that we had $r = 3$. We compared the means of three populations, using ANOVA, and concluded that not all the means were equal. Now we would like to be able to compare every *pair* of means to determine where the differences among population means exist. How many pairwise comparisons are there? With three populations, there are

$$\binom{3}{2} = \frac{3!}{2!\,1!} = 3 \text{ comparisons}$$

These comparisons are

$$
\begin{array}{c}
1 \text{ with } 2 \\
2 \text{ with } 3 \\
1 \text{ with } 3
\end{array}
$$

As a general rule, the number of possible pairwise comparisons of r means is

$$
\binom{r}{2} = \frac{r!}{2!(r-2)!} \tag{9-22}
$$

You do not really need equation 9–22 for cases where listing all the possible pairs is relatively easy. In the case of Example 9–2, equation 9–22 gives us $5!/(2!3!) = (5)(4)(3)(2)/(2)(3)(2) = 10$ possible pairwise comparisons. Let us list all the comparisons:

Guadeloupe (1)–Martinique (2)
Guadeloupe (1)–Eleuthera (3)
Guadeloupe (1)–Paradise Island (4)
Guadeloupe (1)–St. Lucia (5)
Martinique (2)–Eleuthera (3)
Martinique (2)–Paradise Island (4)
Martinique (2)–St. Lucia (5)
Eleuthera (3)–Paradise Island (4)
Eleuthera (3)–St. Lucia (5)
Paradise Island (4)–St. Lucia (5)

These pairings are apparent if you look at Table 9–4 and see that we need to compare the first island, Guadeloupe, with all four islands below it. Then we need to compare the second island, Martinique, with all three islands below it (we already have the comparison of Martinique with Guadeloupe). We do the same with Eleuthera and finally with Paradise Island, which has only St. Lucia listed below it; therefore, this is the last comparison. (In the preceding list, we wrote the number of each population in parentheses after the population name.)

The parameter μ_1 denotes the population mean of all vacationer responses for Guadeloupe. The parameters μ_2 to μ_5 have similar meanings. To compare the population mean vacationer responses for every pair of island resorts, we use the following *set of hypothesis tests:*

I. $H_0: \mu_1 = \mu_2$ $H_1: \mu_1 \neq \mu_2$	VI. $H_0: \mu_2 = \mu_4$ $H_1: \mu_2 \neq \mu_4$
II. $H_0: \mu_1 = \mu_3$ $H_1: \mu_1 \neq \mu_3$	VII. $H_0: \mu_2 = \mu_5$ $H_1: \mu_2 \neq \mu_5$
III. $H_0: \mu_1 = \mu_4$ $H_1: \mu_1 \neq \mu_4$	VIII. $H_0: \mu_3 = \mu_4$ $H_1: \mu_3 \neq \mu_4$
IV. $H_0: \mu_1 = \mu_5$ $H_1: \mu_1 \neq \mu_5$	IX. $H_0: \mu_3 = \mu_5$ $H_1: \mu_3 \neq \mu_5$
V. $H_0: \mu_2 = \mu_3$ $H_1: \mu_2 \neq \mu_3$	X. $H_0: \mu_4 = \mu_5$ $H_1: \mu_4 \neq \mu_5$

The Tukey method allows us to carry out simultaneously all 10 hypothesis tests at a single given level of significance, say, $\alpha = 0.05$. Thus, if we use the Tukey procedure for reaching conclusions as to which population means are equal and which are not, we know that the probability of reaching at least one erroneous conclusion, stating that two means are not equal when indeed they are equal, is at most 0.05.

The **test statistic** for each test is the *absolute difference of the appropriate sample means.*

Thus, the test statistic for the first test (I) is

$$|\bar{x}_1 - \bar{x}_2| = |89 - 75| = 14$$

Conducting the Tests

We conduct the tests as follows. We compute each of the test statistics and compare them with the value of T that corresponds to the desired level of significance α. *We reject a particular null hypothesis if the absolute difference between the corresponding pair of sample means exceeds the value of T.*

Using $\alpha = 0.05$, we now conduct the Tukey test for Example 9–2. All absolute differences of sample means corresponding to the pairwise tests I through X are computed and compared with the value of T. For $\alpha = 0.05$, $r = 5$, and $n - r = 195$ (we use ∞, the last row in the table), we get, from Appendix C, Table 6, $q = 3.86$. We also know that MSE $= 504.4$ and $n_i = 40$ for all i. (Later we will see what to do when not all r samples are of equal size.) Therefore, from equation 9–21,

$$T = q_\alpha \sqrt{\frac{MSE}{n_i}} = 3.86 \sqrt{\frac{504.4}{40}} = 13.7$$

We now compute all 10 pairwise absolute differences of sample means and compare them with $T = 13.7$ to determine which differences are statistically significant at $\alpha = 0.05$ (these are marked with an asterisk).

$$
\begin{aligned}
|\bar{x}_1 - \bar{x}_2| &= |89 - 75| = 14 > 13.7^* \\
|\bar{x}_1 - \bar{x}_3| &= |89 - 73| = 16 > 13.7^* \\
|\bar{x}_1 - \bar{x}_4| &= |89 - 91| = 2 < 13.7 \\
|\bar{x}_1 - \bar{x}_5| &= |89 - 85| = 4 < 13.7 \\
|\bar{x}_2 - \bar{x}_3| &= |75 - 73| = 2 < 13.7 \\
|\bar{x}_2 - \bar{x}_4| &= |75 - 91| = 16 > 13.7^* \\
|\bar{x}_2 - \bar{x}_5| &= |75 - 85| = 10 < 13.7^* \\
|\bar{x}_3 - \bar{x}_4| &= |73 - 91| = 18 > 13.7^* \\
|\bar{x}_3 - \bar{x}_5| &= |73 - 85| = 12 < 13.7 \\
|\bar{x}_4 - \bar{x}_5| &= |91 - 85| = 6 < 13.7
\end{aligned}
$$

From these comparisons we determine that our data provide statistical evidence to conclude that μ_1 is different from μ_2; μ_1 is different from μ_3; μ_2 is different from μ_4; and μ_3 is different from μ_4. *There are no other statistically significant differences at $\alpha = 0.05$.*

Drawing a diagram of the significant differences that we found will aid in interpretation. This has been done in Figure 9–13. Looking at the figure, you may be puzzled by the fact that we believe, for example, that μ_1 is different from μ_2, yet we believe that μ_1 is no different from μ_5 and that μ_5 is no different from μ_2. You may

FIGURE 9–13   **Differences among the Population Means in Example 9–2 Suggested by the Tukey Procedure**

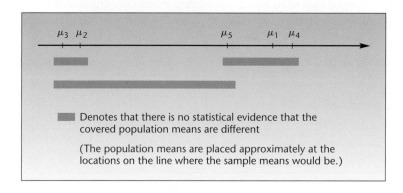

say: If A is equal to B, and B is equal to C, then mathematically we must have A equal to C (the transitivity of equality). But remember that we are doing statistics, not discussing mathematical equality. In statistics, not rejecting the null hypothesis that two parameters are equal does not mean that they are necessarily equal. The nonrejection just means that we have no statistical evidence to conclude that they are different. Thus, in our present example, we conclude that there is statistical evidence to support the claim that, on average, vacationers give higher ratings to Guadeloupe (1) than they give to Martinique (2) or Eleuthera (3), as well as the claim that Paradise Island (4) is, on average, rated higher than Martinique or Eleuthera. No statistical evidence supports any other claim of differences in average ratings among the five island resorts. Note also that we do not have to hypothesize any of the assertions of tests I through X *before* doing the analysis. The Tukey method allows us to make all the above conclusions at a single level of significance, $\alpha = 0.05$.

The Case of Unequal Sample Sizes, and Alternative Procedures

What can we do if the sample sizes are not equal in all groups? We use the *smallest sample size* of all the n_i in computing the criterion T of equation 9–21. The Tukey procedure is the best follow-up to ANOVA when the sample sizes are all equal. The case of equal sample sizes is called the *balanced design*. For very unbalanced designs (i.e., when sample sizes are very different), other methods of further analysis can be used following ANOVA. Two of the better-known methods are the Bonferroni method and the Scheffé method. We will not discuss these methods.

The Template

Figure 9–14 shows the template that can be used to carry out single-factor ANOVA computations. The ANOVA table appears at the top right. Below it appears a table of confidence intervals for each group mean. The α used for confidence intervals need not be the same as the one used in cell S3 for the F test in the ANOVA table. Below the confidence intervals appears a Tukey comparison table. Enter the q_0 corresponding to r, $n - r$, and desired α in cell O21 before reading off the results from this table. The message "Sig" appears in a cell if the difference between the two corresponding groups is significant at the α used for q_0 in cell O21.

PROBLEMS

9–24. Give 95% confidence intervals for the remaining four population mean responses to the Club Med resorts (the one for Guadeloupe having been given in the text).

FIGURE 9–14   The Template for Single-Factor ANOVA
[Anova.xls; Sheet: 1-Way]

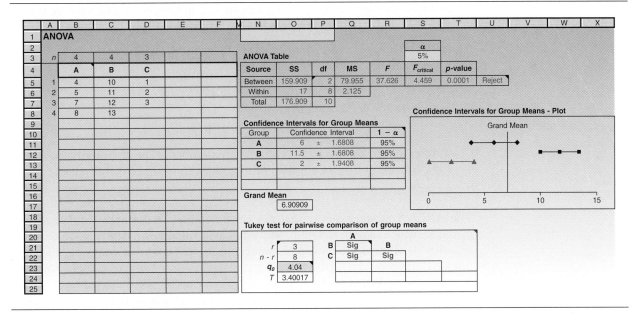

9–25. Use the data of Table 9–1 and the Tukey procedure to determine where differences exist among the triangle, circle, and square population means. Use $\alpha = 0.01$.

9–26. For problem 9–18, find which, if any, of the three prototype planes has an average range different from the others. Use $\alpha = 0.05$.

9–27. For problem 9–19, use the Tukey method to determine which oil types, if any, have an average price different from the others. Use $\alpha = 0.05$.

9–28. For problem 9–20, suppose that the appropriate sample means are 6.4, 2.5, and 4.9 (as scores for participation by European American, African-American, and Other models in commercials). Find where differences, if any, exist among the three population means. Use $\alpha = 0.05$.

9–29. Researchers in retail studies wanted to find out how children and adults react to companies' pricing tactics. They looked at a random sample of 44 10th-grade students, a random sample of pretested adults consisting of 42 people, and a third sample of 71 adults. For each person, they evaluated the response to a pricing tactic. The reported overall level of significance was $p < 0.01$. A further analysis of differences between every pair of groups was reported as all $p < 0.01$.[9] Interpret these reported findings. What were the degrees of freedom for Factor, Error, and Total?

9–30. A study was carried out to find out whether prices differed, on average, within three possible market conditions: monopoly, limited competition, and strong competition. The results were reported as $F(2, 272) = 44.8$. Further analysis reported that for the difference between monopoly and limited competition, $F(1, 272) = 67.9$ and for the difference between monopoly and strong competition, $F(1, 272) = 71.3$.[10]

    a. What was the total sample size used?

    b. Is the overall ANOVA statistically significant?

    c. Interpret the results of the further analysis. Explain.

[9]David M. Hardesty, William O. Bearden, and Jay P. Carlson, "Persuasion Knowledge and Consumer Reactions to Pricing Tactics," *Journal of Retailing* 83, no. 2 (2007), pp. 199–210.

[10]Marcus Christen and Miklos Sarvary, "Competitive Pricing of Information: A Longitudinal Experiment," *Journal of Marketing Research*, February 2007, pp. 42–56.

9–6   Models, Factors, and Designs

A **statistical model** is a set of equations and assumptions that capture the essential characteristics of a real-world situation.

The model discussed in this chapter is the one-factor ANOVA model. In this model, the populations are assumed to be represented by the following equation.

The one-factor ANOVA model is

$$x_{ij} = \mu_i + \epsilon_{ij} = \mu + \alpha_i + \epsilon_{ij} \qquad (9\text{–}23)$$

where ϵ_{ij} is the error associated with the jth member of the ith population. The errors are assumed to be normally distributed with mean zero and variance σ^2.

The ANOVA model assumes that the r populations are normally distributed with means μ_i, which may be different, and with equal variance σ^2. The right-hand side of equation 9–23 breaks the mean of population i into a common component μ and a unique component due to the particular population (or treatment) i. This component is written as α_i. When we sample, the sample means $\overline{X}_i$ are unbiased estimators of the respective population means μ_i. The grand mean $\overline{\overline{x}}$ is an unbiased estimator of the common component of the means μ. The treatment deviations a_i are estimators of the differences among population means α_i. The data errors e_{ij} are estimates of the population errors ϵ_{ij}.

Much more will be said about statistical models in the next chapter, dealing with regression analysis. The one-factor ANOVA null hypothesis $H_0: \mu_1 = \mu_2 = \cdots = \mu_r$ may be written in an equivalent form, using equation 9–23, as $H_0: \alpha_i = 0$ for all i. (This is so because if $\mu_i = \mu$ for all i, then the "extra" components α_i are all zero.) This form of the hypothesis will be extended in the two-factor ANOVA model, also called the two-way ANOVA model, discussed in the following section.

We may want to check that the assumptions of the ANOVA model are indeed met. To check that the errors are approximately normally distributed, we may draw a histogram of the observed errors e_{ij}, which are called *residuals*. If serious deviations from the normal-distribution assumption exist, the histogram will not resemble a normal curve. Plotting the residuals for each of the r samples under study will reveal whether the population variances are indeed (at least approximately) equal. If the *spread* of the data sets around their group means is not approximately equal for all r groups, then the population variances may not be equal. When model assumptions are violated, a nonparametric alternative to ANOVA must be used. An alternative method of analysis uses the Kruskal-Wallis test, discussed in Chapter 14. Residual analysis will be discussed in detail in the next chapter.

One-Factor versus Multifactor Models

In each of the examples and problems you have seen so far, we were interested in determining whether differences existed among several populations, or treatments. These treatments may be considered as *levels* of a single *factor*.

A **factor** is a set of populations or treatments of a single kind.

Examples of factors are vacationer ratings of a *set of resorts*, the range of different *types of airplanes*, and the durability of different *kinds of sweaters*.

Sometimes, however, we may be interested in studying more than one factor. For example, an accounting researcher may be interested in testing whether there are differences in average error percentage rate among the Big Eight accounting firms, *and* among different geographical locations, such as the Eastern Seaboard, the South, the

Midwest, and the West. Such an analysis involves *two factors:* the different firms (factor A, with eight levels) and the geographical location (factor B, with four levels).

Another example is that of an advertising firm interested in studying how the public is influenced by color, shape, and size in an advertisement. The firm could carry out an ANOVA to test whether there are differences in average responses to three different colors, as well as to four different shapes of an ad, and to three different ad sizes. This would be a three-factor ANOVA. Important statistical reasons for jointly studying the effects of several factors in a multifactor ANOVA will be explained in the next section, on two-factor ANOVA.

Fixed-Effects versus Random-Effects Models

Recall Example 9–2, where we wanted to determine whether differences existed among the five particular island resorts of Guadeloupe, Martinique, Eleuthera, Paradise Island, and St. Lucia. Once we reject or do not reject the null hypothesis, *the inference is valid only for the five islands studied.* This is a *fixed-effects model.*

> A **fixed-effects model** is a model in which the levels of the factor under study (the treatments) are *fixed* in advance. Inference is valid only for the levels under study.

Consider another possible context for the analysis. Suppose that Club Med had no particular interest in the five resorts listed, but instead wanted to determine whether differences existed among *any* of its more than 30 resorts. In such a case, we may consider all Club Med resorts as a *population of resorts,* and we may draw a random sample of five (or any other number) of the resorts and carry out an ANOVA to determine differences among population means. The ANOVA would be carried out in exactly the same way. However, since the resorts themselves were randomly selected for analysis from the population of all Club Med resorts, the inference would be valid for *all* Club Med resorts. This is called the *random-effects model.*

> The **random-effects model** is an ANOVA model in which the levels of the factor under study are *randomly chosen* from an entire population of levels (treatments). Inference is valid for the entire population of levels.

The idea should make sense to you if you recall the principle of inference using random sampling, discussed in Chapter 5, and the story of the *Literary Digest.* To make inferences that are valid for an entire population, we must randomly sample from the entire population. Here this principle is applied to a population of treatments.

Experimental Design

Analysis of variance often involves the ideas of **experimental design.** If we want to study the effects of different treatments, we are sometimes in a position to design the experiment by which we plan to study these effects. Designing the experiment involves the choice of elements from a population or populations and the assignment of elements to different treatments. The model we have been using involves a *completely randomized design.*

> A **completely randomized design** is a design in which elements are assigned to treatments *completely at random.* Thus, every element chosen for the study has an equal chance of being assigned to any treatment.

Among the other types of design are **blocking designs,** which are very useful in reducing experimental errors, that is, reducing variation due to factors other than the ones under study. In the *randomized complete block design,* for example, experimental units are assigned to treatments in blocks of similar elements, with randomized treatment order within each block. In the Club Med situation of Example 9–2, a randomized complete block design could involve sending each vacationer in the sample to all five resorts, the order of the resorts chosen randomly; each vacationer is then asked to rate all the resorts. A design such as this one, with *experimental units* (here, people) given all the treatments, is called a *repeated-measures design*. More will be said about blocking designs later.

9–31. For problem 9–18, suppose that four more prototype planes are built after the study is completed. Could the inference from the ANOVA involving the first three prototypes be extended to the new planes? Explain.

9–32. What is a blocking design?

9–33. For problem 9–18, can you think of a blocking design that would reduce experimental errors?

9–34. How can we determine whether there are violations of the ANOVA model assumptions? What should we do if such violations exist?

9–35. Explain why the factor levels must be randomly chosen in the random-effects model to allow inference about an entire collection of treatments.

9–36. For problem 9–19, based on the given data, can you tell whether the world oil market is efficient?

9–7   Two-Way Analysis of Variance

In addition to being interested in possible differences in the general appeal of its five Caribbean resorts (Example 9–2), suppose that Club Med is also interested in the respective appeal of four vacation attributes: friendship, sports, culture, and excitement.[11] Club Med would like to have answers to the following two questions:

1. Are there differences in average vacationer satisfaction with the five Caribbean resorts?
2. Are there differences in average vacationer satisfaction in terms of the four vacation attributes?

In cases such as this one, where interest is focused on *two* factors—resort and vacation attribute—we can answer the two questions *jointly*. In addition, we can answer a *third,* very important question, which may not be apparent to us:

3. Are there any *interactions* between some resorts and some attributes?

The three questions are statistically answerable by conducting a two-factor, or two-way, ANOVA. Why a two-way ANOVA? Why not conduct each of the two ANOVAs separately?

Several reasons justify conducting a two-way ANOVA. One reason is *efficiency*. When we conduct a two-way ANOVA, we may use a smaller total sample size for the analysis than would be required if we were to conduct each of the two tests separately. Basically, we use the same data resources to answer the two main questions. In the case of Club Med, the club may run a friendship program at each of the five resorts for one week; then the next week (with different vacationers) it may run a sports program in each of the five resorts; and so on. All vacationer responses could then be used for evaluating *both* the satisfaction from the resorts and the satisfaction from the attributes, rather than conducting two separate surveys, requiring twice the effort and number of respondents. A more important reason for conducting a two-way ANOVA is that *three* questions must be answered.

---

[11]Information on the attributes and the resorts was provided through the courtesy of Club Med.

Let us call the first factor of interest (here, resorts) factor A and the second factor (here, attributes) factor B. The effects of each factor alone are the factor's *main effects*. The combined effects of the two factors, beyond what we may expect from the consideration of each factor separately, are the *interaction* between the two factors.

Two factors are said to **interact** if the difference between levels (treatments) of one factor depends on the level of the other factor. Factors that do not interact are called *additive*.

An interaction is thus an *extra effect* that appears as a result of a particular combination of a treatment from one factor with a treatment from another factor. An interaction between two factors exists when, for at least one combination of treatments—say Eleuthera and sports—the effect of the combination is not additive: some special "chemistry" appears between the two treatments. Suppose that Eleuthera is rated lowest of all resorts and that sports is rated lowest of all attributes. We then expect the Eleuthera–sports combination to be rated, on average, lowest of all combinations. If this does not happen, the two levels are said to interact.

The three questions answerable by two-way ANOVA:

1. Are there any factor A main effects?
2. Are there any factor B main effects?
3. Are there any interaction effects of factors A and B?

Let n_{ij} be the sample size in the "cell" corresponding to level i of factor A and level j of factor B. Assume there is a uniform sample size for each factor A–factor B combination, say, $n_{ij} = 4$. The layout of the data of a two-way ANOVA, using the Club Med example, is shown in Figure 9–15. Figure 9–16 shows the effects of an interaction. We arrange the levels of each factor in increasing order of sample mean responses. The general two-variable trend of increasing average response is the response plane shown in Figure 9–16. An exception to the plane is the Eleuthera–sports interaction, which leads to a higher-than-expected average response for this combination of levels.

The Two-Way ANOVA Model

There are a levels of factor A ($a = 5$ resorts in the Club Med example) and b levels of factor B ($b = 4$ attributes in the same example). Thus, there are $a \times b$ combinations of levels, or cells, as shown in Figure 9–15. Each one is considered a treatment. We must

FIGURE 9–15   Two-Way ANOVA Data Layout

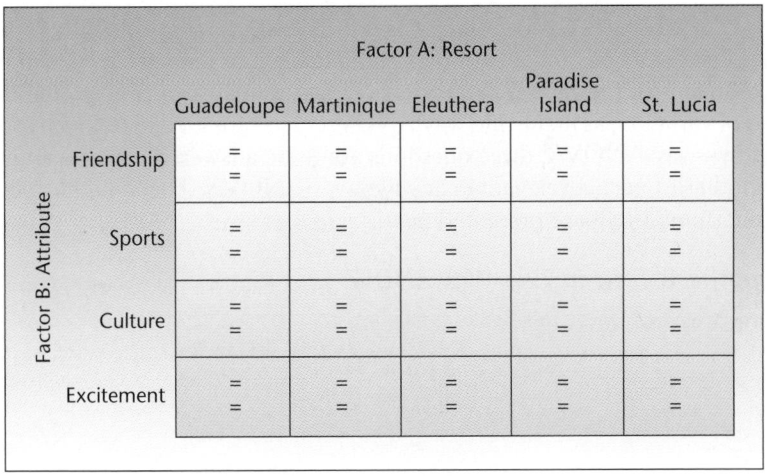

FIGURE 9–16   Graphical Display of Interaction Effects

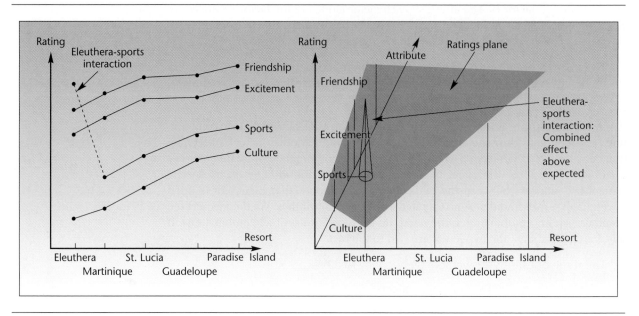

assume equal sample sizes in all the cells. If we do not have equal sample sizes, we must use an alternative to the method of this chapter and solve the ANOVA problem by using multiple regression analysis (Chapter 11). Since we assume an equal sample size in each cell, we will simplify our notation and will call the sample size in each cell n, omitting the subscripts i, j. We will denote the total sample size (formerly called n) by the symbol N. In the two-way ANOVA model, the assumptions of normal populations and equal variance for each two-factor combination treatment are still maintained.

> The **two-way ANOVA model** is
>
> $$x_{ijk} = \mu + \alpha_i + \beta_j + (\alpha\beta)_{ij} + \epsilon_{ijk} \qquad (9\text{–}24)$$
>
> where μ is the overall mean; α_i is the effect of level i ($i = 1, \ldots , a$) of factor A; β_j is the effect of level j ($j = 1, \ldots , b$) of factor B; $(\alpha\beta)_{ij}$ is the interaction effect of levels i and j; and ϵ_{ijk} is the error associated with the kth data point from level i of factor A and level j of factor B. As before, we assume that the error ϵ_{ijk} is normally distributed[12] with mean zero and variance σ^2 for all $i, j,$ and k.

Our data, assumed to be random samples from populations modeled by equation 9–24, give us estimates of the model parameters. These estimates—as well as the different measures of variation, as in the one-way ANOVA case—are used in testing hypotheses. Since, in two-way ANOVA, three questions are to be answered rather than just one, three hypothesis tests are relevant to any two-way ANOVA. The hypothesis tests that answer questions 1 to 3 are presented next.

The Hypothesis Tests in Two-Way ANOVA

Factor A main-effects test:

$$H_0: \alpha_i = 0 \text{ for all } i = 1, \ldots , a$$
$$H_1: \text{Not all } \alpha_i \text{ are } 0$$

---

[12]Since the terms α_i, β_j, and $(\alpha\beta)_{ij}$ are deviations from the overall mean μ, in the fixed-effects model the sums of all these deviations are all zero: $\Sigma\alpha_i = 0$, $\Sigma\beta_j = 0$, and $\Sigma(\alpha\beta)_{ij} = 0$.

This hypothesis test is designed to determine whether there are any factor A main effects. That is, the null hypothesis is true if and only if there are no differences in means due to the different treatments (populations) of factor A.

Factor B main-effects test:

$$H_0: \beta_j = 0 \text{ for all } j = 1, \ldots, b$$
$$H_1: \text{Not all } \beta_j \text{ are } 0$$

This test will detect evidence of any factor B main effects. The null hypothesis is true if and only if there are no differences in means due to the different treatments (populations) of factor B.

Test for AB interactions:

$$H_0: (\alpha\beta)_{ij} = 0 \text{ for all } i = 1, \ldots, a \text{ and } j = 1, \ldots, b$$
$$H_1: \text{Not all } (\alpha\beta)_{ij} \text{ are } 0$$

This is a test for the existence of interactions between levels of the two factors. The null hypothesis is true if and only if there are no two-way interactions between levels of factor A and levels of factor B, that is, if the factor effects are additive.

In carrying out a two-way ANOVA, we should test the third hypothesis first. We do so because it is important to first determine whether interactions exist. If interactions do exist, our interpretation of the ANOVA results will be different from the case where no interactions exist (i.e., in the case where the effects of the two factors are additive).

Sums of Squares, Degrees of Freedom, and Mean Squares

We define the data, the various means, and the deviations from the means as follows.

x_{ijk} is the kth data point from level i of factor A and level j of factor B.
$\bar{\bar{x}}$ is the grand mean.
$\bar{x}_{ij}$ is the mean of cell ij.
$\bar{x}_i$ is the mean of all data points in level i of factor A.
$\bar{x}_j$ is the mean of all data points in level j of factor B.

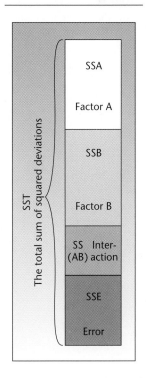

FIGURE 9–17
Partition of the Sum of Squares in Two-Way ANOVA

Using these definitions, we have

$$\sum_1^{a_i} \sum_1^b \sum_1^n (x_{ijk} - \bar{\bar{x}})^2 = \sum\sum\sum (\bar{x}_{ij} - \bar{\bar{x}})^2 + \sum\sum\sum (x_{ijk} - \bar{x}_{ij})^2$$

$$\text{SST} = \text{SSTR} + \text{SSE} \qquad\qquad (9\text{–}25)$$

(This can be further partitioned.)

Equation 9–25 is the usual decomposition of the sum of squares, where each cell (a combination of a level of factor A and a level of factor B) is considered a separate treatment. Deviations of the data points from the cell means are squared and summed. Equation 9–25 is the same as equation 9–12 for the partition of the total sum of squares into sum-of-squares treatment and sum-of-squares error in one-way ANOVA. The only difference between the two equations is that here the summations extend over three subscripts: one subscript for levels of each of the two factors and one subscript for the data point number. The interesting thing is that SSTR can be further partitioned into a component due to factor A, a component due to factor B, and a component due to interactions of the two factors. The partition of the total sum of squares into its components is given in equation 9–26.

Do not worry about the mathematics of the summations. Two-way ANOVA is prohibitively tedious for hand computation, and we will always use a computer. The important thing to understand is that the total sum of squares is partitioned into a part due to factor A, a part due to factor B, a part due to interactions of the two factors, and a part due to error. This is shown in Figure 9–17.

What are the degrees of freedom? Since there are a levels of factor A, the degrees of freedom for factor A are $a - 1$. Similarly, there are $b - 1$ degrees of freedom for factor B, and there are $(a - 1)(b - 1)$ degrees of freedom for AB interactions. The degrees of freedom for error are $ab(n - 1)$. The total degrees of freedom are $abn - 1$. But we knew that [because $(a - 1) + (b - 1) + (a - 1)(b - 1) + ab(n - 1) = a + b - 2 + ab - a - b + 1 + abn - ab = abn - 1$]! Note that since we assume an equal sample size n in each cell and since there are ab cells, we have $N = abn$, and the total number of degrees of freedom is $N - 1 = abn - 1$.

$$\text{SST} \quad = \quad \text{SSTR} \quad + \quad \text{SSE}$$

$$\underbrace{\sum\sum\sum(x - \bar{\bar{x}})^2 = \sum\sum\sum(\bar{x} - \bar{\bar{x}})^2 + \sum\sum\sum(x - \bar{x})^2}$$

$$\underbrace{\sum\sum\sum(\bar{x}_i - \bar{\bar{x}})^2}_{\text{SSA}} + \underbrace{\sum\sum\sum(\bar{x}_j - \bar{\bar{x}})^2}_{\text{SSB}} + \underbrace{\sum(\bar{x}_{ij} - \bar{x}_i - \bar{x}_j + \bar{\bar{x}})^2}_{\text{SS(AB)}}$$

Thus,

$$\text{SST} = \text{SSA} + \text{SSB} + \text{SS(AB)} + \text{SSE} \qquad (9\text{–}26)$$

where SSA = sum of squares due to factor A, SSB = sum of squares due to factor B, and SS(AB) = sum of squares due to the interactions of factors A and B.

Let us now construct an ANOVA table. The table includes the sums of squares, the degrees of freedom, and the mean squares. The mean squares are obtained by dividing each sum of squares by its degrees of freedom. The final products of the table are three F ratios. We define the F ratios as follows.

The F Ratios and the Two-Way ANOVA Table

The F ratio for each one of the hypothesis tests is the ratio of the appropriate mean square to the MSE. That is, for the test of factor A main effects, we use $F = \text{MSA/MSE}$; for the test of factor B main effects, we use $F = \text{MSB/MSE}$; and for the test of interactions of the two factors, we use $F = \text{MS(AB)/MSE}$. We now construct the ANOVA table for two-way analysis, Table 9–8.

The degrees of freedom associated with each F ratio are the degrees of freedom of the respective numerator and denominator (the denominator is the same for all three tests). For the testing of factor A main effects, our test statistic is the first F ratio

TABLE 9–8 ANOVA Table for Two-Way Analysis

Source of Variation	Sum of Squares	Degrees of Freedom	Mean Square	F Ratio
Factor A	SSA	$a - 1$	$\text{MSA} = \dfrac{\text{SSA}}{a - 1}$	$F = \dfrac{\text{MSA}}{\text{MSE}}$
Factor B	SSB	$b - 1$	$\text{MSB} = \dfrac{\text{SSB}}{b - 1}$	$F = \dfrac{\text{MSB}}{\text{MSE}}$
Interaction	SS(AB)	$(a - 1)(b - 1)$	$\text{MS(AB)} = \dfrac{\text{SS(AB)}}{(a - 1)(b - 1)}$	$F = \dfrac{\text{MS(AB)}}{\text{MSE}}$
Error	SSE	$ab(n - 1)$	$\text{MSE} = \dfrac{\text{SSE}}{ab(n - 1)}$	
Total	SST	$abn - 1$		

in the ANOVA table. When the null hypothesis is true (there are no factor A main effects), the ratio $F = \text{MSA}/\text{MSE}$ follows an F distribution with $a - 1$ degrees of freedom for the numerator and $ab(n - 1)$ degrees of freedom for the denominator. We denote this distribution by $F_{[a-1, ab(n-1)]}$. Similarly, for the test of factor B main effects, when the null hypothesis is true, the distribution of the test statistic is $F_{[b-1, ab(n-1)]}$. The test for the existence of AB interactions uses the distribution $F_{[(a-1)(b-1), ab(n-1)]}$.

We will demonstrate the use of the ANOVA table in two-way analysis, and the three tests, with a new example.

EXAMPLE 9–4

There are claims that the Japanese have now joined the English and people in the United States in paying top dollar for paintings at art auctions. Suppose that an art dealer is interested in testing two hypotheses. The first is that paintings sell for the same price, on average, in London, New York, and Tokyo. The second hypothesis is that works of Picasso, Chagall, and Dali sell for the same average price. The dealer is also aware of a third question. This is the question of a possible interaction between the location (and thus the buyers: people from the United States, English, Japanese) and the artist. Data on auction prices of 10 works of art by each of the three painters at each of the three cities are collected, and a two-way ANOVA is run on a computer. The results include the following: The sums of squares associated with the location (factor A) is 1,824. The sum of squares associated with the artist (factor B) is 2,230. The sum of squares for interactions is 804. The sum of squares for error is 8,262. Construct the ANOVA table, carry out the hypothesis tests, and state your conclusions.

Solution

We enter the sums of squares into the table. Since there are three levels in each of the two factors, and the sample size in each cell is 10, the degrees of freedom are $a - 1 = 2$, $b - 1 = 2$, $(a - 1)(b - 1) = 4$, and $ab(n - 1) = 81$. Also, $abn - 1 = 89$, which checks as the sum of all other degrees of freedom. These values are entered in the table as well. The mean squares are computed, and so are the appropriate F ratios. Check to see how each result in the ANOVA table, Table 9–9, is obtained.

Let us now conduct the three hypothesis tests relevant to this problem. We will state the hypothesis tests in words. The factor A test is

H_0: There is no difference in the average price of paintings of the kind studied across the three locations
H_1: There are differences in average price across locations

The test statistic is an F random variable with 2 and 81 degrees of freedom (see Table 9–9). The computed value of the test statistic is 8.94. From Appendix C, Table 5, we find that the critical point for $\alpha = 0.01$ is close to 4.88. Thus, the null hypothesis is rejected, and we know that the p-value is much smaller than 0.01. Computer printouts of ANOVA results often list p-values in the ANOVA table, in a column after the F

TABLE 9–9 ANOVA Table for Example 9–4

Source of Variation	Sum of Squares	Degrees of Freedom	Mean Square	F Ratio
Location	1,824	2	912	8.94
Artist	2,230	2	1,115	10.93
Interaction	804	4	201	1.97
Error	8,262	81	102	
Total	13,120	89		

FIGURE 9–18   Example 9–4: Location Hypothesis Test

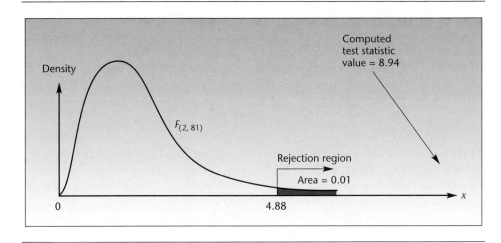

ratios. Often, the computer output will show $p = 0.0000$. This means that the p-value is smaller than 0.0001. The results of the hypothesis test are shown in Figure 9–18.

Now we perform the hypothesis test for factor B:

> H_0: There are no differences in the average price of paintings by the three artists studied
> H_1: There are differences in the average price of paintings by the three artists

Here again, the test statistic is an F random variable with 2 and 81 degrees of freedom, and the computed value of the statistic is 10.93. The null hypothesis is rejected, and the p-value is much smaller than 0.01. The test is shown in Figure 9–19.

The hypothesis test for interactions is

> H_0: There are no interactions of the locations and the artists under study
> H_1: There is at least one interaction of a location and an artist

FIGURE 9–19   Example 9–4: Artist Hypothesis Test

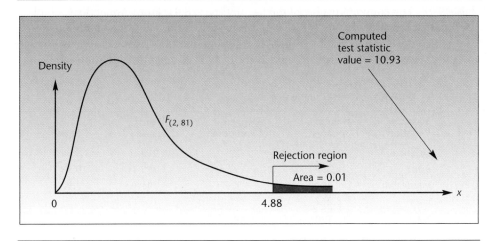

FIGURE 9–20   Example 9–4: Test for Interaction

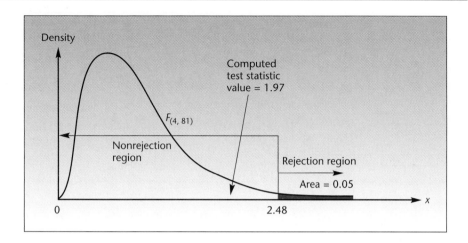

The test statistic is an F random variable with 4 and 81 degrees of freedom. At a level of significance $\alpha = 0.05$, the critical point (see Appendix C, Table 5) is approximately equal to 2.48, and our computed value of the statistic is 1.97, leading us not to reject the null hypothesis of no interaction at levels of significance greater than 0.05. This is shown in Figure 9–20.

As mentioned earlier, we look at the test for interactions first. Since the null hypothesis of no interactions was not rejected, we have no statistical evidence of interactions of the two factors. This means, for example, that if a work by Picasso sells at a higher average price than works by the other two artists, then his paintings will fetch—on average—higher prices in all three cities. It also means that if paintings sell for a higher average price in London than in the other two cities, then this holds true—again, on average—for all three artists. Now we may interpret the results of the two main-effects tests.

We may conclude that there is statistical evidence that paintings (by these artists) do not fetch the same average price across the three cities. We may similarly conclude that paintings by the three artists under study do not sell, on average, for the same price. Where do the differences exist? This can be determined by a method for further analysis, such as the Tukey method.

In cases where we *do* find evidence of an interaction effect, our results have a different interpretation. In such cases, we must qualify any statement about differences among levels of one factor (say, factor A) as follows: *There exist differences among levels of factor A, averaged over all levels of factor B.*

We demonstrate this with a brief example. An article in *Accounting Review* reports the results of a two-way ANOVA on the factors "accounting" and "materiality." The exact nature of the study need not concern us here, as it is very technical. The results of the study include the following:

Source	df	Mean Square	F	Probability
Materiality	2	1.3499	4.5	0.0155
Accounting–materiality interaction	4	0.8581	2.9	0.0298

From these partial results, we see that the p-values ("probability") are each less than 0.05. Therefore, at the 0.05 level of significance for each of the two tests (separately), we find that there is an interaction effect, and we find a main effect for materiality. We may now conclude that, at the 0.05 level of significance, there are differences among the levels of materiality, *averaged over all levels* of accounting.

FIGURE 9–21 The Template for Two-Way ANOVA [Anova.xls; Sheet: 2-Way]

2-Way ANOVA

^ Press the + button to see row means. Scroll down for column and cell means.

This template can be used only if there are an equal number of replications in each cell.

	C1	C2	C3	C4
R1	158	147	139	144
	154	143	135	145
	146	140	142	139
	150	144	139	136

ANOVA Table

Source	SS	df	MS	F	$F_{critical}$ (α = 5%)	p-value	
Row	128.625	2	64.3125	3.5868	3.2594	0.0380	Reject
Column	1295.42	3	431.806	24.082	2.8663	0.0000	Reject
Interaction	159.708	6	26.6181	1.4845	2.3638	0.2112	
Error	645.5	36	17.9306				
Total	2229.25	47					

The Template

Figure 9–21 shows the template that can be used for computing two-way ANOVA. *This template can be used only if the number of replications in each cell is equal.* Up to 5 levels of row factor, 5 levels of column factor, and 10 replications in each cell can be entered in this template. Be sure that the data are entered properly in the cells.

To see the row means, unprotect the sheet and click on the "+" button above column M. Scroll down to see the column means and the cell means.

The Overall Significance Level

Remember our discussion of the Tukey analysis and its importance in allowing us to conduct a family of tests at a single level of significance. In two-way ANOVA, as we have seen, there is a family of *three tests,* each carried out at a given level of significance. Here the question arises: What is the level of significance of the *set* of three tests? A bound on the probability of making at least one type I error in the three tests is given by *Kimball's inequality.* If the hypothesis test for factor A main effects is carried out at α_1, the hypothesis test for factor B main effects is carried out at α_2, and the hypothesis test for interactions is carried out at α_3, then the level of significance α of the three tests together is bounded from above as follows.

Kimball's Inequality

$$\alpha \leq 1 - (1 - \alpha_1)(1 - \alpha_2)(1 - \alpha_3) \qquad (9\text{–}27)$$

In Example 9–4 we conducted the first two tests—the tests for main effects—at the 0.01 level of significance. We conducted the test for interactions at the 0.05 level. Using equation 9–27, we find that the level of significance of the family of three tests is *at most* $1 - (1 - 0.01)(1 - 0.01)(1 - 0.05) = 0.0689$.

The Tukey Method for Two-Way Analysis

Equation 9–21, the Tukey statistic for pairwise comparisons, is easily extended to two-way ANOVA. We are interested in comparing the levels of a factor once the ANOVA has led us to believe that differences do exist for that factor. The only difference in the Tukey formula is the number of degrees of freedom. In making pairwise comparisons of the levels of factor A, the test statistics are the pairwise differences between the sample means for all levels of factor A, regardless of factor B. For example, the pairwise comparisons of all the mean prices at the three locations in Example 9–4 will be done as follows. We compute the absolute differences of all the pairs of sample means:

$$|\bar{x}_{\text{London}} - \bar{x}_{\text{NY}}|$$
$$|\bar{x}_{\text{Tokyo}} - \bar{x}_{\text{London}}|$$
$$|\bar{x}_{\text{NY}} - \bar{x}_{\text{Tokyo}}|$$

Now we compare these differences with the Tukey criterion:

Tukey criterion for factor A is

$$T = q_\alpha \sqrt{\frac{\text{MSE}}{bn}} \tag{9-28}$$

where the degrees of freedom of the q distribution are now a and $ab(n-1)$. Note also that MSE is divided by bn.

In Example 9-4 both a and b are 3. The sample size in each cell is $n = 10$. At $\alpha = 0.05$, the Tukey criterion is equal to $(3.4)(\sqrt{102}/\sqrt{30}) = 6.27$.[13] Suppose that the sample mean in New York is 19.6 (hundred thousand dollars), in Tokyo it is 21.4, and in London it is 15.1. Comparing all absolute differences of the sample means leads us to the conclusion that the average prices in London and Tokyo are significantly different; but the average prices in Tokyo and New York are not different, and neither are the average prices in New York and London. The overall significance level of these joint conclusions is $\alpha = 0.05$.

Extension of ANOVA to Three Factors

To carry out a three-way ANOVA, we assume that in addition to a levels of factor A and b levels of factor B, there are c levels of factor C. Three pairwise interactions of factors and one triple interaction of factors are possible. These are denoted AB, BC, AC, and ABC. Table 9-10 is the ANOVA table for three-way analysis.

Examples of three-way ANOVA are beyond the scope of this book. However, the extension of two-way analysis to this method is straightforward, and if you should need to carry out such an analysis, Table 9-10 will provide you with all the information you need. Three-factor interactions ABC imply that at least some of the two-factor interactions AB, BC, and AC are dependent on the level of the third factor.

Two-Way ANOVA with One Observation per Cell

The case of one data point in every cell presents a problem in two-way ANOVA. Can you guess why? (*Hint:* Degrees of freedom for error are the answer.) Look at Figure 9-22, which shows the layout of the data in a two-way ANOVA with five levels of factor A and four levels of factor B. Note that the sample size in each of the 20 cells is $n = 1$.

As you may have guessed, there are no degrees of freedom for error! With one observation per cell, $n = 1$; the degrees of freedom for error are $ab(n-1) = ab(1-1) = 0$. This can be seen from Table 9-11. What can we do? If we *believe* that there are no interactions (this assumption cannot be statistically tested when $n = 1$), then our sum of squares SS(AB) is due to error and contains no other information. In such a case, we can use SS(AB) and its associated degrees of freedom $(a-1)(b-1)$ in place of SSE and its degrees of freedom. We can thus conduct the tests for the main effects by dividing MSA by MS(AB) when testing for factor A main effects. The

---

[13]If the interaction effect is ignored because it was not significant, then MSE $= (8{,}262 + 804)/(81 + 4) = 107$; $T = 6.41$ with df $= 2, 85$.

TABLE 9–10   Three-Way ANOVA Table

Source of Variation	Sum of Squares	Degrees of Freedom	Mean Square	F Ratio
Factor A	SSA	$a - 1$	$MSA = \dfrac{SSA}{a - 1}$	$F = \dfrac{MSA}{MSE}$
Factor B	SSB	$b - 1$	$MSB = \dfrac{SSB}{b - 1}$	$F = \dfrac{MSB}{MSE}$
Factor C	SSC	$c - 1$	$MSC = \dfrac{SSC}{c - 1}$	$F = \dfrac{MSC}{MSE}$
AB	SS(AB)	$(a - 1)(b - 1)$	$MS(AB) = \dfrac{SS(AB)}{(a - 1)(b - 1)}$	$F = \dfrac{MS(AB)}{MSE}$
BC	SS(BC)	$(b - 1)(c - 1)$	$MS(BC) = \dfrac{SS(BC)}{(b - 1)(c - 1)}$	$F = \dfrac{MS(BC)}{MSE}$
AC	SS(AC)	$(a - 1)(c - 1)$	$MS(AC) = \dfrac{SS(AC)}{(a - 1)(c - 1)}$	$F = \dfrac{MS(AC)}{MSE}$
ABC	SS(ABC)	$(a - 1)(b - 1)(c - 1)$	MS(ABC)	$F = \dfrac{MS(ABC)}{MSE}$
Error	SSE	$abc(n - 1)$	MSE	
Total	SST	$abcn - 1$		

FIGURE 9–22   Data Layout in a Two-Way ANOVA with $n = 1$

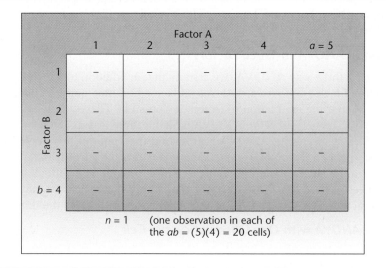

TABLE 9–11   ANOVA Table for Two-Way Analysis with One Observation per Cell, Assuming No Interactions

Source of Variation	Sum of Squares	Degrees of Freedom	Mean Square	F Ratio
Factor A	SSA	$a - 1$	$MSA = \dfrac{SSA}{a - 1}$	$F = \dfrac{MSA}{MS(AB)}$
Factor B	SSB	$b - 1$	$MSB = \dfrac{SSB}{b - 1}$	$F = \dfrac{MSB}{MS(AB)}$
"Error"	SS(AB)	$(a - 1)(b - 1)$	$MS(AB) = \dfrac{SS(AB)}{(a - 1)(b - 1)}$	
Total	SST	$ab - 1$		

resulting F statistic has $a - 1$ and $(a - 1)(b - 1)$ degrees of freedom. Similarly, when testing for factor B main effects, we divide MSB by MS(AB) and obtain an F statistic with $b - 1$ and $(a - 1)(b - 1)$ degrees of freedom.

Remember that this analysis assumes no interactions between the two factors. Remember also that in statistics, having as many data as possible is always desirable. Therefore, the two-way ANOVA with one observation per cell is, in itself, of limited use. The idea of two factors and one observation per cell is useful, however, as it brings us closer to the idea of blocking, presented in the next section.

> The two-way ANOVA model with one observation per cell is
>
> $$x_{ij} = \mu + \alpha_i + \beta_j + \epsilon_{ij} \qquad (9\text{–}29)$$
>
> where μ is the overall mean, α_i is the effect of level i of factor A, β_j is the effect of level j of factor B, and ϵ_{ij} is the error associated with x_{ij}. We assume the errors are normally distributed with zero mean and variance σ^2.

PROBLEMS

9–37. Discuss the context in which Example 9–4 can be analyzed by using a random-effects model.

9–38. What are the reasons for conducting a two-way analysis rather than two separate one-way ANOVAs? Explain.

9–39. What are the limitations of two-way ANOVA? What problems may be encountered?

9–40. (This is a hard problem.) Suppose that a limited data set is available. Explain why it is not desirable to increase the number of factors under study (say, four-way ANOVA, five-way ANOVA, and so on). Give two reasons for this—one of the reasons should be a statistical one.

9–41. Market researchers carried out an analysis of the emotions that arise in customers who buy or do not buy a product at an unintended purchase opportunity and how these emotions later affect the subjects' responses to advertisements by the makers of the product they bought or declined to buy. The results were analyzed using a mixed design and blocking, and the reported results were as follows.[14]

$$
\begin{aligned}
\text{Main effects:} &\quad F(1, 233) = 26.04 \\
\text{Interactions:} &\quad F(1, 233) = 14.05
\end{aligned}
$$

Interpret these findings.

9–42. The following table reports salaries, in thousands of dollars per year, for executives in three job types and three locations. Conduct a two-way ANOVA on these data.

Location	Job		
	Type I	Type II	Type III
East	54, 61, 59, 56, 70, 62, 63, 57, 68	48, 50, 49, 60, 54, 52, 49, 55, 53	71, 76, 65, 70, 68, 62, 73, 60, 79
Central	52, 50, 58, 59, 62, 57, 58, 64, 61	44, 49, 54, 53, 51, 60, 55, 47, 50	61, 64, 69, 58, 57, 63, 65, 63, 50
West	63, 67, 68, 72, 68, 75, 62, 65, 70	65, 58, 62, 70, 57, 61, 68, 65, 73	82, 75, 79, 77, 80, 69, 84, 83, 76

---

[14]Anirban Mukhopadhyay and Gita Venkataramani Johar, "Tempted or Not? The Effect of Recent Purchase History on Responses to Affective Advertising," *Journal of Consumer Research* 33 (March 2007), pp. 445–453.

9–43.   The Neilsen Company, which issues television popularity rating reports, is interested in testing for differences in average viewer satisfaction with morning news, evening news, and late news. The company is also interested in determining whether differences exist in average viewer satisfaction with the three main networks: CBS, ABC, and NBC. Nine groups of 50 randomly chosen viewers are assigned to each combination cell CBS–morning, CBS–evening, . . . , NBC–late. The viewers' satisfaction ratings are recorded. The results are analyzed via two-factor ANOVA, one factor being network and the other factor being news time. Complete the following ANOVA table for this study, and give a full interpretation of the results.

Source of Variation	Sum of Squares	Degrees of Freedom	Mean Square	F Ratio
Network	145			
News time	160			
Interaction	240			
Error	6,200			
Total				

9–44.   An article reports the results of an analysis of salespersons' performance level as a function of two factors: task difficulty and effort. Included in the article is the following ANOVA table:

Variable	df	F Value	p
Task difficulty	1	0.39	0.5357
Effort	1	53.27	<0.0001
Interaction	1	1.95	0.1649

   a. How many levels of task difficulty were studied?

   b. How many levels of effort were studied?

   c. Are there any significant task difficulty main effects?

   d. Are there any significant effort main effects?

   e. Are there any significant interactions of the two factors? Explain.

9–45.   A study evaluated the results of a two-way ANOVA on the effects of the two factors—exercise price of an option and the time of expiration of an option—on implied interest rates (the measured variable). Included in the article is the following ANOVA table.

Source of Variation	Degrees of Freedom	Sum of Squares	Mean Square	F Ratio
Exercise prices	2	2.866	1.433	0.420
Time of expiration	1	16.518	16.518	4.845
Interaction	2	1.315	0.658	0.193
Explained	5	20.699	4.140	1.214
Residuals (error)	144	490.964	3.409	

   a. What is meant by *Explained* in the table, and what is the origin of the information listed under that source?

   b. How many levels of exercise price were used?

   c. How many levels of time of expiration were used?

   d. How large was the total sample size?

   e. Assuming an equal number of data points in each cell, how large was the sample in each cell?

   f. Are there any exercise price main effects?

   g. Are there any time-of-expiration main effects?

   h. Are there any interactions of the two factors?

    i. Interpret the findings of this study.

    j. Give approximate *p*-values for the tests.

    k. In this particular study, what other equivalent distribution may be used for testing for time-of-expiration main effects? (*Hint:* df.) Why?

9–46. An analysis was recently carried out to assess the effects of competency similarity and new service performance on the reputation durability of service companies. The results of a two-factor analysis of variance, with interaction of factors, is given below.[15] Completely interpret and explain these findings.

Source	df	F Statistic
Competence similarity (CS)	1	0.01
New service performance (P)	1	0.65
CS × P	1	5.71
Error	313	

9–8 Blocking Designs

In this section, we discuss alternatives to the completely randomized design. We seek special designs for data analysis that will help us reduce the effects of extraneous factors (factors not under study) on the measured variable. That is, we seek to reduce the errors. These designs allow for *restricted randomization* by grouping the experimental units (people, items in our data) into homogeneous groups called **blocks** and then randomizing the treatments within each block.

The first, and most important, blocking design we will discuss is the *randomized complete block design.*

Randomized Complete Block Design

Recall the first part of the Club Med example, Example 9–2, where we were interested only in determining possible differences in average ratings among the five resorts (no attributes factor). Suppose that Club Med can get information about its vacationers' age, sex, marital status, socioeconomic level, etc., and then can randomly assign vacationers to the different resorts. The club could form groups of five vacationers each such that the vacationers within each group are similar to one another in age, sex, and marital status, etc. Each group of five vacationers is a *block*. Once the blocks are formed, one member from each block is *randomly assigned* to one of the five resorts (Guadeloupe, Martinique, Eleuthera, Paradise Island, or St. Lucia). Thus, the vacationers sent to each resort will comprise a mixture of ages, of males and females, of married and single people, of different socioeconomic levels, etc. The vacationers within each block, however, will be more or less homogeneous.

The vacationers' ratings of the resorts are then analyzed using an ANOVA that utilizes the blocking structure. Since the members of each block are similar to one another (and different from members of other blocks), we expect them to react to similar conditions in similar ways. This brings about a *reduction in the experimental errors.* Why? If we cannot block, it is possible, for example, that the sample of people we get for Eleuthera will happen to be wealthier (or predominantly married, predominantly male, or whatever) and will tend to react less favorably to a resort of this kind than a more balanced sample would react. In such a case, we will have greater experimental error. If, on the other hand, we can *block* and send one member of each homogeneous group of people to each of the resorts and then compare the responses of the block as a whole, we will be more likely to find real differences among the resorts than differences among the people. Thus, the errors (differences among people and

---

[15]Ananda R. Ganguly, Joshua Herbold, and Mark E. Peecher, "Assurer Reputation for Competence in a Multiservice Context," *Contemporary Accounting Research* 24, no. 1 (2007), pp. 133–170.

FIGURE 9–23   Blocking in the Club Med Example

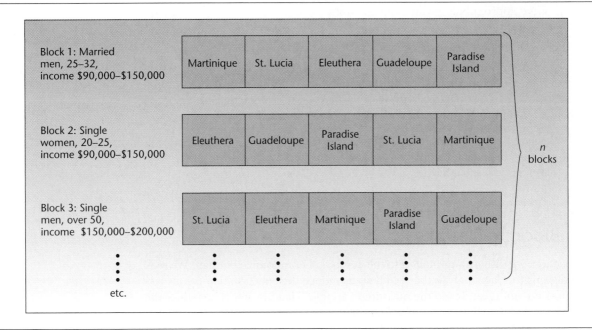

not among the resorts) are reduced by the blocking design. When all members of every block are randomly assigned to all treatments, such as in this example, our design is called the **randomized complete block design.**

> The model for randomized complete block design is
>
> $$x_{ij} = \mu + \alpha_i + \beta_j + \epsilon_{ij} \qquad (9\text{–}30)$$
>
> where μ is the overall mean, α_i is the effect of level i of factor A, β_j is the effect of block j on factor B, and ϵ_{ij} is the error associated with x_{ij}. We assume the errors are normally distributed with zero mean and variance σ^2.

Figure 9–23 shows the formation of blocks in the case of Club Med. We assume that the club is able—for the purpose of a specific study—to randomly assign vacationers to resorts.

The analysis of the results in a randomized complete block design, with a single factor, is very similar to the analysis of two-factor ANOVA with one observation per cell (see Table 9–11). Here, one "factor" is the blocks, and the other is the factor of interest (in our example, resorts). The ANOVA table for a randomized complete block design is illustrated in Table 9–12. Compare this table with Table 9–11. There are n blocks of r elements each. We assume that there are no interactions between blocks and treatments; thus, the degrees of freedom for error are $(n - 1)(r - 1)$. The F ratio reported in the table is for use in testing for treatment effects. It is possible to test for block effects with a similar F ratio, although usually such a test is of no interest.

As an example, suppose that Club Med did indeed use a blocking design with $n = 10$ blocks. Suppose the results are SSTR = 3,200, SSBL = 2,800, and SSE = 1,250. Let us conduct the following test:

> H_0: The average ratings of the five resorts are equal
> H_1: Not all the average ratings of the five resorts are equal

TABLE 9–12 ANOVA Table for Randomized Complete Block Design

Source of Variation	Sum of Squares	Degrees of Freedom	Mean Square	F Ratio
Blocks	SSBL	$n - 1$	MSBL	
Treatments	SSTR	$r - 1$	MSTR	$F = \dfrac{\text{MSTR}}{\text{MSE}}$
Error	SSE	$(n - 1)(r - 1)$	MSE	
Total		$nr - 1$		

TABLE 9–13 Club Med Blocking Design ANOVA Table

Source of Variation	Sum of Squares	Degrees of Freedom	Mean Square	F Ratio
Blocks	2,800	9	311.11	
Resorts	3,200	4	800.00	23.04
Error	1,250	36	34.72	
Total	7,250			

We enter the information into the ANOVA table and compute the remaining entries we need and the F statistic value, which has an F distribution with $r - 1$ and $(n - 1)(r - 1)$ degrees of freedom when H_0 is true. We have as a result Table 9–13.

We see that the value of the F statistic with 4 and 36 degrees of freedom is 23.04. This value exceeds, by far, the critical point of the F distribution with 4 and 36 degrees of freedom at $\alpha = 0.01$, which is 3.89. The p-value is, therefore, much smaller than 0.01. We thus reject the null hypothesis and conclude that there is evidence that not all resorts are rated equally, on average. By blocking the respondents into homogeneous groups, Club Med was able to reduce the experimental errors.

You can probably find many examples where blocking can be useful. For example, recall the situation of problem 9–18. Three prototype airplanes were tested on different flight routes to determine whether differences existed in the average range of the planes. A design that would clearly reduce the experimental errors is a blocking design where all planes are flown over the same routes, at the same time, under the same weather conditions, etc. That is, fly all three planes using each of the sample route conditions. A block in this case is a route condition, and the three treatments are the three planes.

A special case of the randomized complete block design is the **repeated-measures design.** In this design, each experimental unit (person or item) is assigned to *all* treatments in a randomly selected order. Suppose that a taste test is to be conducted, where four different flavors are to be rated by consumers. In a repeated-measures design, each person in the random sample of consumers is assigned to taste all four flavors, in a randomly determined order, independent of all other consumers. A block in this design is one consumer. We demonstrate the repeated-measures design with the following example.

EXAMPLE 9–5

Weintraub Entertainment is a new movie company backed by financial support from Coca-Cola Company. For one of the company's first movies, the director wanted to find the best actress for the leading role. "Best" naturally means the actress who would get the highest average viewer rating. The director was considering three candidates for the role and had each candidate act in a particular test scene. A random group of 40 viewers was selected, and each member of the group watched the same scene enacted by each of the three actresses. The order of actresses was randomly

TABLE 9–14 The ANOVA Table for Example 9–5

Source of Variation	Sum of Squares	Degrees of Freedom	Mean Square	F Ratio
Blocks	2,750	39	70.51	
Treatments	2,640	2	1,320.00	12.93
Error	7,960	78	102.05	
Total	13,350	119		

FIGURE 9–24 Data Layout for Example 9–5

	Randomized Viewing Order		
First sampled person	Actress B	Actress C	Actress A
Second sampled person	Actress C	Actress B	Actress A
Third sampled person	Actress A	Actress C	Actress B
Fourth sampled person etc.	Actress B	Actress A	Actress C

and independently chosen for each viewer. Ratings were on a scale of 0 to 100. The results were analyzed using a block design ANOVA, where each viewer constituted a block of treatments. The results of the analysis are given in Table 9–14. Figure 9–24 shows the layout of the data in this example. Analyze the results. Are all three actresses equally rated, on average?

Solution The test statistic has an *F* distribution with 2 and 78 degrees of freedom when the following null hypothesis is true.

> H_0: There are no differences among average population ratings of the three actresses

Check the appropriate critical point for $\alpha = 0.01$ in Appendix C, Table 5, to see that this null hypothesis is rejected in favor of the alternative that differences do exist and that not all three actresses are equally highly rated, on average. Since the null hypothesis is rejected, there is place for further analysis to determine which actress rates best. Such analysis can be done using the Tukey method or another method of further analysis.

Another method of analysis can be used in cases where a repeated-measures design is used on *rankings* of several treatments—here, if we had asked each viewer to rank the three actresses as 1, 2, or 3, rather than rate them on a 0-to-100 scale. This method is the *Friedman test,* discussed in Chapter 14.

The Template

Figure 9–25 shows the template that can be used for computing ANOVA in the case of a randomized block design. The group means appear at the top of each column and the block means appear in each row to the right of the data.

FIGURE 9–25   The Template for Randomized Block Design ANOVA
[Anova.xls; Sheet: RBD]

	A	B	C	D	E	F	G	N	S	T	U	V	W	X	Y	Z	AA
1	Randomized Complete Block Design																
2															α		
3	Mean	10.7143	13	15.4286						ANOVA Table					5%		
4		A	B	C				Mean		Source	SS	df	MS	F	$F_{critical}$	p-value	
5	1	12	16	15				14.3333		Treatment	40.952	6	6.8254	3.1273	2.9961	0.0439	Reject
6	2	11	10	14				11.6667		Block	77.81	2	38.9048	17.825	3.8853	0.0003	Reject
7	3	10	11	17				12.6667		Error	26.19	12	2.18254				
8	4	12	15	19				15.3333		Total	144.95	20					
9	5	11	14	17				14									
10	6	10	12	13				11.6667									

PROBLEMS

9–47. Explain the advantages of blocking designs.

9–48. A study of emerging markets was conducted on returns on equity, bonds, and preferred stock. Data are available on a random sample of firms that issue all three types of instruments. How would you use blocking in this study, aimed at finding which instrument gives the highest average return?

9–49. Suggest a blocking design for the situation in problem 9–19. Explain.

9–50. Suggest a blocking design for the situation in problem 9–21. Explain.

9–51. Is it feasible to design a study utilizing blocks for the situation in problem 9–20? Explain.

9–52. Is it possible to design a blocking design for the situation in problem 9–23?

9–53. How would you design a block ANOVA for the two-way analysis of the situation described in problem 9–42? Which ANOVA method is appropriate for the analysis?

9–54. What important assumption about the relation between blocks and treatments is necessary for carrying out a block design ANOVA?

9–55. Public concern has recently focused on the fact that although people in the United States often try to lose weight, statistics show that the general population has gained weight, on average, during the last 10 years. A researcher hired by a weight-loss organization is interested in determining whether three kinds of artificial sweetener currently on the market are approximately equally effective in reducing weight. As part of a study, a random sample of 300 people is chosen. Each person is given one of the three sweeteners to use for a week, and the number of pounds lost is recorded. To reduce experimental errors, the people in the sample are divided into 100 groups of three persons each. The three people in every group all weigh about the same at the beginning of the test week and are of the same sex and approximately the same age. The results are SSBL = 2,312, SSTR = 3,233, and SSE = 12,386. Are all three sweeteners equally effective in reducing weight? How confident are you of your conclusion? Discuss the merits of blocking in this case as compared with the completely randomized design.

9–56. IBM Corporation has been retraining many of its employees to assume marketing positions. As part of this effort, the company wanted to test four possible methods of training marketing personnel to determine if at least one of the methods was better than the others. Four groups of 70 employees each were assigned to the four training methods. The employees were pretested for marketing ability and put into groups of four, each group constituting a block with approximately equal prior ability. Then the four employees in each group were randomly assigned to the four training methods and retested after completion of the three-week training session.

The differences between their initial scores and final scores were computed. The results were analyzed using a block design ANOVA. The results of the analysis include: SSTR = 9,875, SSBL = 1,445, and SST = 22,364. Are all four training methods equally effective? Explain.

9–9   Using the Computer

Using Excel for Analysis of Variance

An ANOVA can be conducted using built-in Excel commands. In this section, we shall solve the sample problems in this chapter using the built-in commands.

ONE-WAY ANOVA

- Enter the sample data in the range B3:D7 as shown in Figure 9–26.
- Select Data Analysis in the Analysis group on the Data tab.
- In the dialog box that appears select ANOVA: Single Factor, and click OK.
- In the ANOVA dialog box, fill in the Input Range as B3:D7. Note that the input range includes a blank cell D7. But the blank cell cannot be avoided since the range has to be of rectangular shape. You must select a rectangular input range such that it includes all the data. Blanks do not matter.
- Select Columns for Grouped By entry, because the three groups appear as columns in the input range.
- Click the Labels in First Row box, because the input range includes group labels.
- Enter the desired alpha of 0.05.
- Select Output Range and enter F3. This tells Excel to start the output report at F3.
- Click OK. You should see the results shown in Figure 9–27.

Note that the p-value in cell K14 appears as 8.53E-05, which is the scientific notation for 0.0000853. Since the p-value is so small, the null hypothesis that all group means are equal is rejected.

TWO-WAY ANOVA

Another built-in command is available for a two-way ANOVA. We shall see the details by solving a problem. For our sample problem the data are entered in the range A3:E15 as shown in Figure 9–28. (There should be no gaps in the data. The data entered in the template in Figure 9–21 has gaps because each cell in the template has 10 rows.)

FIGURE 9–26   One-Way ANOVA Setup

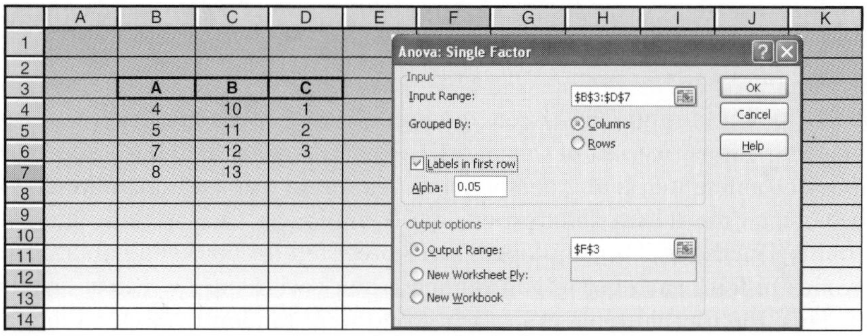

FIGURE 9–27   One-Way ANOVA Results

	A	B	C	D	E	F	G	H	I	J	K	L
1												
2												
3		A	B	C	Anova: Single Factor							
4		4	10	1								
5		5	11	2	SUMMARY							
6		7	12	3	Groups	Count	Sum	Average	Variance			
7		8	13		A	4	24	6	3.333333			
8					B	4	46	11.5	1.666667			
9					C	3	6	2	1			
10												
11												
12					ANOVA							
13					Source of Variation	SS	df	MS	F	P-value	F crit	
14					Between Groups	159.9091	2	79.95455	37.62567	8.53E-05	4.45897	
15					Within Groups	17	8	2.125				
16												
17					Total	176.9091	10					

FIGURE 9–28   Two-Way ANOVA Setup

	A	B	C	D	E	F	G	H	I	J	K
1	2-Way ANOVA										
2											
3			C1	C2	C3	C4	Anova: Two-Factor With Replication				
4		R1	158	147	139	144					
5			154	143	135	145	Input				
6			146	140	142	139	Input Range:	$A$3:$E$15			
7			150	144	139	136					
8		R2	155	158	147	150	Rows per sample:	4			
9			154	154	136	141	Alpha:	0.05			
10			150	149	134	149					
11			154	150	143	134	Output options				
12		R3	152	150	144	142	Output Range:	$G$3			
13			150	151	136	148	New Worksheet Ply:				
14			150	157	140	144	New Workbook				
15			154	155	135	147					
16											

- Select Data Analysis in the Analysis group on the Data tab.
- In the dialog box that appears, select ANOVA: Two-Factor With Replication.
- In the ANOVA dialog box that appears enter the Input Range. For the sample problem it is A3:E15. *The input range must include the first row and the first column that contain the labels.*
- For the Rows per sample box, enter the number of replications per cell, which in this case is 4.
- Enter the desired alpha as 0.05.
- Select Output Range and enter G3.
- Click OK. You should see results similar to those seen in Figure 9–29.

In the results you can see the ANOVA table at the bottom. Above the ANOVA table, you see the count, sum, average, and variance for each cell. In the Total columns and rows you see the count, sum, average, and variance for row factors and column factors.

You can also use Microsoft Excel for the randomized block design by choosing ANOVA: Two Factors Without Replication from Data Analysis in the Analysis group on the Data tab. In this case, the data are classified on two different dimensions as in Two-Factor With Replication. However, for this tool, it is assumed that there is only a single observation for each pair.

FIGURE 9–29   Two-Way ANOVA Results

	A	B	C	D	E	F	G	H	I	J	K	L	M	N
1	2-Way ANOVA													
3		C1	C2	C3	C4		Anova: Two-Factor with Replication							
4	R1	158	147	139	144									
5		154	143	135	145		SUMMARY	C1	C2	C3	C4	Total		
6		146	140	142	139		R1							
7		150	144	139	136		Count	4	4	4	4	16		
8	R2	155	158	147	150		Sum	608	574	555	564	2301		
9		154	154	136	141		Average	152	143.5	138.75	141	143.8125		
10		150	149	134	149		Variance	26.66667	8.333333	8.25	18	39.09583		
11		154	150	143	134									
12	R3	152	150	144	142		R2							
13		150	151	136	148		Count	4	4	4	4	16		
14		150	157	140	144		Sum	613	611	560	574	2358		
15		154	155	135	147		Average	153.25	152.75	140	143.5	147.375		
16							Variance	4.916667	16.91667	36.66667	56.33333	58.38333		
18							R3							
19							Count	4	4	4	4	16		
20							Sum	606	613	555	581	2355		
21							Average	151.5	153.25	138.75	145.25	147.1875		
22							Variance	3.666667	10.91667	16.91667	7.583333	42.5625		
24							Total							
25							Count	12	12	12	12			
26							Sum	1827	1798	1670	1719			
27							Average	152.25	149.8333	139.1667	143.25			
28							Variance	10.20455	31.78788	17.24242	25.65909			
30							ANOVA							
31							Source of Variation	SS	df	MS	F	P-value	F crit	
32							Sample	128.625	2	64.3125	3.586754	0.037978	3.259446	
33							Columns	1295.417	3	431.8056	24.08211	1E-08	2.866266	
34							Interaction	159.7083	6	26.61806	1.484508	0.211233	2.363751	
35							Within	645.5	36	17.93056				
37							Total	2229.25	47					

Using MINITAB for Analysis of Variance

To perform a one-way analysis of variance, with the response variable in one column and factor levels in another, choose Stat ▸ ANOVA ▸ One-way from the menu bar. If each group is entered in its own column, use Stat ▸ ANOVA ▸ One-Way (Unstacked). After choosing Stat ▸ ANOVA ▸ One-way, the One-way Analysis of Variance dialog box appears. Then enter the column containing the response variable in the Response edit box and the column containing the factor levels in the Factor edit box. Check Residuals to store residuals in the next available column. Check Store fits to store the fitted values (level means) in the next available column. You can also enter the desired confidence level. The button Comparison provides you with confidence intervals for all pairwise differences between level means, using four different methods. Click on the Graphs button if you want to display an individual value plot, a box plot, or a residual plot. MINITAB built-in graphs help you check the validity of your assumptions.

As an example, suppose the following data represent the result of running an experiment under four different levels, A, B, C, and D, of a single factor.

A	B	C	D
18	17.75	17.92	18.01
17.98	18	18.01	17.94
18.2	17.77	17.88	18.23
18	18.01	18.3	18.2
17.99	18.01	18.22	18
18.1	18.12	18.56	17.84
17.9	18.2	18.1	18.11

We wish to run a one-way ANOVA to test for equality of means among these four groups. After choosing Stat ▸ ANOVA ▸ One-way from the menu, the corresponding dialog box appears as shown in Figure 9–30. Note that we have to enter data corresponding to the

FIGURE 9–30   One-Way ANOVA Using MINITAB

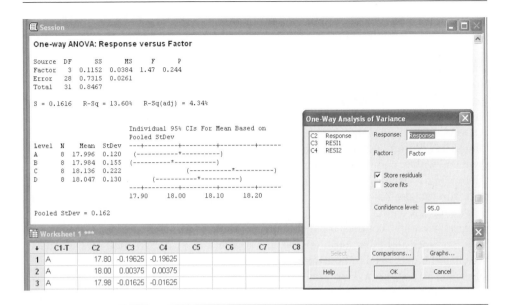

response variable in one column and the factor variable in another column in the MINITAB worksheet (stacked format). As we can see in Figure 9–30, MINITAB generates an ANOVA table as well as the confidence intervals on the means of all groups. Based on the obtained p-value, 0.244, we don't reject the null hypothesis. So there is no significant difference among the means of these four groups.

If you choose the Comparisons button to find confidence intervals for all pairwise differences between level means, MINITAB will generate the confidence intervals on the differences between every two means as well. In our example, Tukey's method was chosen in the One-Way Multiple Comparison window that appears after you click on the Comparison button. The obtained confidence intervals are seen in Figure 9–31.

FIGURE 9–31   Pairwise Comparison between Level Means Using Tukey's Method

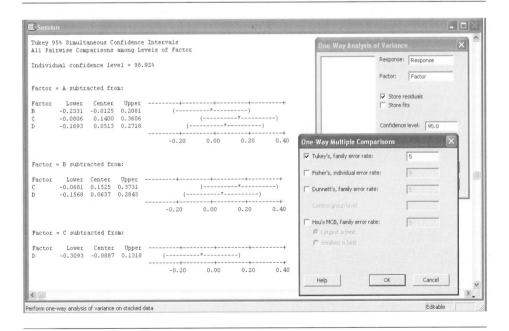

As we can see, all confidence intervals on pairwise comparisons of the means contain the value zero, which shows that the means of every two groups are equal. This result confirms the validity of our earlier conclusion regarding not rejecting the null hypothesis based on the obtained p-value from the ANOVA table.

MINITAB also enables you to run a two-way analysis of variance for testing the equality of populations' means when classification of treatments is by two factors. For this procedure, the data must be balanced (all cells must have the same number of observations) and factors must be fixed. Start by choosing Stat ▶ ANOVA ▶ Two-Way. When the corresponding dialog box appears, enter the column containing the response variable in Response. Enter one of the factor level columns in Row Factor and the other factor level column in Column Factor. You can check Display means for both row and column factors if you wish to compute marginal means and confidence intervals for each level of the column or row factor. Check Fit additive model to fit a model without an interaction term. You can also have access to various built-in graphs using the Graphs button. Then click on the OK button.

As an example, consider the data set of problem 9–42, the salaries for executives in three job types and three locations. We aim to run a two-way ANOVA on these data. Note that the data need to be entered in a stacked format in the MINITAB worksheet. Select Stat ▶ ANOVA ▶ Two-Way from the menu bar. The corresponding dialog box, Session commands, and obtained ANOVA table are shown in Figure 9–32.

As you can see, the p-values corresponding to the location and job main effects are zero. So we reject the null hypothesis and state that the main effects exist for both factors, location and job. But the p-value of the interaction effect is not significant at significance level 0.05. So we do not reject the null hypothesis and conclude that there is no interaction between these two factors. If we check Box plots of data by clicking on the Graphs button, we will observe the corresponding box plot.

Finally, if you wish to run a test at which certain factors are random, you need to choose Stat ▶ ANOVA ▶ Balanced ANOVA from the menu bar when your data are balanced. If your data are unbalanced, you have to choose Stat ▶ ANOVA ▶ General Linear Model from the menu bar. The settings are similar to the previous dialog boxes.

FIGURE 9–32   Two-Way ANOVA Using MINITAB

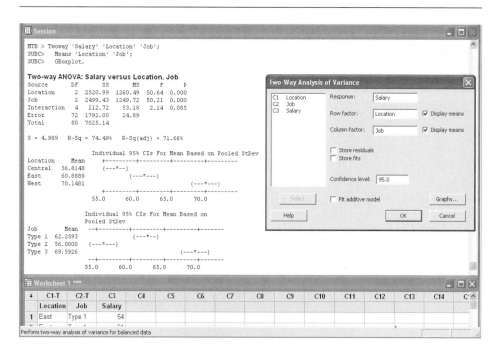

9–10   Summary and Review of Terms

In this chapter, we discussed a method of making statistical comparisons of more than two population means. The method is **analysis of variance,** often referred to as **ANOVA.** We defined **treatments** as the populations under study. A set of treatments is a **factor.** We defined **one-factor ANOVA,** also called one-way ANOVA, as the test for equality of means of treatments belonging to one factor. We defined a **two-factor ANOVA,** also called two-way ANOVA, as a set of three hypothesis tests: (1) a test for main effects for one of the two factors, (2) a test for main effects for the second factor, and (3) a test for the **interaction** of the two factors. We defined the **fixed-effects** model and the **random-effects** model. We discussed one method of further analysis to follow an ANOVA once the ANOVA leads to rejection of the null hypothesis of equal treatment means. The method is the **Tukey HSD procedure.** We also mentioned two other alternative methods of further analysis. We discussed experimental design in the ANOVA context. Among these designs, we mentioned **blocking** as a method of reducing experimental errors in ANOVA by grouping similar items. We also discussed the **repeated-measures design.**

ADDITIONAL PROBLEMS

9–57. An enterprising art historian recently started a new business: the production of walking-tour audiotapes for use by those visiting major cities. She originally produced tapes for eight cities: Paris, Rome, London, Florence, Jerusalem, Washington, New York, and New Haven. A test was carried out to determine whether all eight tapes (featuring different aspects of different cities) were equally appealing to potential users. A random sample of 160 prospective tourists was selected, 20 per city. Each person evaluated the tape he or she was given on a scale of 0 to 100. The results were analyzed using one-way ANOVA and included SSTR = 7,102 and SSE = 10,511. Are all eight tapes equally appealing, on average? What can you say about the p-value?

9–58. NAMELAB is a San Francisco–based company that uses linguistic analysis and computers to invent catchy names for new products. The company is credited with the invention of Acura, Compaq, Sentra, and other names of successful products. Naturally, statistical analysis plays an important role in choosing the final name for a product. In choosing a name for a compact disk player, NAMELAB is considering four names and uses analysis of variance for determining whether all four names are equally liked, on average, by the public. The results include $n_1 = 32$, $n_2 = 30$, $n_3 = 28$, $n_4 = 41$, SSTR = 4,537, and MSE = 412. Are all four names approximately equally liked, on average? What is the approximate p-value?

9–59. As software for microcomputers becomes more and more sophisticated, the element of time becomes more crucial. Consequently, manufacturers of software packages need to work on reducing the time required for running application programs. Speed of execution also depends on the computer used. A two-way ANOVA is suggested for testing whether differences exist among three software packages, and among four microcomputers made by NEC, Toshiba, Kaypro, and Apple, with respect to the average time for performing a certain analysis. The results include SS(software) = 77,645, SS(computer) = 54,521, SS(interaction) = 88,699, and SSE = 434,557. The analysis used a sample of 60 runs of each software package–computer combination. Complete an ANOVA table for this analysis, carry out the tests, and state your conclusions.

9–60. An ANOVA assessing the effects of three blocks of respect and three levels of altruism was carried out.[16] The F-statistic value was 13.65 and the degrees of freedom

[16]May Chiun Lo, T. Ramayah, and Jerome Kueh Swee Hui, "An Investigation of Leader Member Exchange Effects on Organizational Citizenship Behavior," *Journal of Business and Management* 12, no. 1 (2006), pp. 5–24.

were 74 for blocks, 2 for treatment, and 224 for total. What was the total sample size? Are the results of the ANOVA significant? Explain.

9–61. Young affluent U.S. professionals are creating a growing demand for exotic pets. The most popular pets are the Shiba Inu dog breed, Rottweilers, Persian cats, and Maine coons. Prices for these pets vary and depend on supply and demand. A breeder of exotic pets wants to know whether these four pets fetch the same average prices, whether prices for these exotic pets are higher in some geographic areas than in others, and whether there are any interactions—one or more of the four pets being more favored in one location than in others. Prices for 10 of each of these pets at four randomly chosen locations around the country are recorded and analyzed. The results are SS(pet) = 22,245, SS(location) = 34,551, SS(interaction) = 31,778, and SSE = 554,398. Are there any pet main effects? Are there any location main effects? Are there any pet–location interactions? Explain your findings.

9–62. Analysis of variance has long been used in providing evidence of the effectiveness of pharmaceutical drugs. Such evidence is required before the Food and Drug Administration (FDA) will allow a drug to be marketed. In a recent test of the effectiveness of a new sleeping pill, three groups of 25 patients each were given the following treatments. The first group was given the drug, the second group was given a placebo, and the third group was given no treatment at all. The number of minutes it took each person to fall asleep was recorded. The results are as follows.

Drug group:	12, 17, 34, 11, 5, 42, 18, 27, 2, 37, 50, 32, 12, 27, 21, 10, 4, 33, 63, 22, 41,19, 28, 29, 8
Placebo group:	44, 32, 28, 30, 22, 12, 3, 12, 42, 13, 27, 54, 56, 32, 37, 28, 22, 22, 24, 9, 20, 4, 13, 42, 67
No-treatment group:	32, 33, 21, 12, 15, 14, 55, 67, 72, 1, 44, 60, 36, 38, 49, 66, 89, 63, 23, 6, 9, 56, 28, 39, 59

Use a computer (or hand calculations) to determine whether the drug is effective. What about the placebo? Give differences in average effectiveness, if any exist.

9–63. A more efficient experiment than the one described in problem 9–62 was carried out to determine whether a sleeping pill was effective. Each person in a random sample of 30 people was given the three treatments: drug, placebo, nothing. The order in which these treatments were administered was randomly chosen for each person in the sample.

    a. Explain why this experiment is more efficient than the one described for the same investigation in problem 9–62. What is the name of the experimental design used here? Are there any limitations to the present method of analysis?

    b. The results of the analysis include SSTR = 44,572, SSBL = 38,890, and SSE = 112,672. Carry out the analysis, and state your conclusions. Use $\alpha = 0.05$.

9–64. Three new high-definition television models are compared. The distances (in miles) over which a clear signal is received in random trials for each of the models are given below.

General Instrument:	111, 121, 134, 119, 125, 120, 122, 138, 115, 123, 130, 124, 132, 127, 130
Philips:	120, 121, 122, 123, 120, 132, 119, 116, 125, 123, 116, 118, 120, 131, 115
Zenith:	109, 100, 110, 102, 118, 117, 105, 104, 100, 108, 128, 117, 101, 102, 110

Carry out a complete analysis of variance, and report your results in the form of a memorandum. State your hypotheses and your conclusions. Do you believe there are differences among the three models? If so, where do they lie?

9-65. A professor of food chemistry at the University of Wisconsin recently developed a new system for keeping frozen foods crisp and fresh: coating them with watertight, edible film. The Pillsbury Company wants to test whether the new product is tasty. The company collects a random sample of consumers who are given the following three treatments, in a randomly chosen order for each consumer: regular frozen pizza, frozen pizza packaged in a plastic bag, and the new edible-coating frozen pizza (all reheated, of course). Fifty people take part in the study, and the results include SSTR = 128,899, SSBL = 538,217, and SSE = 42,223,987. (These are ANOVA results for taste scores on a 0–1000 scale.) Based on these results, are all three frozen pizzas perceived as equally tasty?

9-66. Give the statistical reason for the fact that a one-way ANOVA with only two treatments is equivalent to a two-sample t test discussed in Chapter 8.

9-67. Following is a computer output of an analysis of variance based on randomly chosen rents in four cities. Do you believe that the average rent is equal in the four cities studied? Explain.

```
ANALYSIS OF VARIANCE

SOURCE      DF        SS         MS          F

FACTOR       3      37402      12467       1.76

ERROR       44     311303       7075

TOTAL       47     348706
```

9-68. One of the oldest and most respected survey research firms is the Gallup Organization. This organization makes a number of special reports available at its corporate Web site www.gallup.com. Select and read one of the special reports available at this site. Based on the information in this report, design a 3×3 ANOVA on a response of interest to you, such as buying behavior. The design should include two factors that you think influence the response, such as location, age, income, or education. Each factor should have three levels for testing in the model.

www.exercise

9-69. Interpret the following computer output.

```
ANALYSIS OF VARIANCE ON SALES

SOURCE     DF      SS       MS       F        p

STORE       2   1017.33   508.67   156.78   0.000

ERROR      15     48.67     3.24

TOTAL      17   1066.00

                          INDIVIDUAL 95 PCT CI'S FOR MEAN BASED
                          ON POOLED STDEV

LEVEL   N    MEAN   STDEV   -+---------+---------+---------+----

    1   6  53.667   1.862              (-*--)

    2   6  67.000   1.673                              (-*-)

    3   6  49.333   1.862        (-*-)

                          -+---------+---------+---------+----

POOLED STDEV = 1.801      48.0      54.0      60.0      66.0
```

CASE 11 Rating Wines

Let us continue discussing the ideas about studying wines using analysis of variance begun in the introduction to this chapter. The four important wine grapes in the introduction are to be compared using ANOVA to see whether experts rate random samples of wines in these groups similarly, on average, or whether differences in average ratings exist that are due to the kind of grape used. The following data are scores on a 0-to-100 scale for these wines.

Chardonnay	Merlot	Chenin Blanc	Cabernet Sauvignon
89	91	81	92
88	88	81	89
89	99	81	89
78	90	82	91
80	91	81	92

86	88	78	90
87	88	79	91
88	89	80	93
88	90	83	91
89	87	81	97
88		88	88
		85	
		86	

The above data are independent random samples of wine ratings in the four groups. Carry out an analysis of variance to determine whether average population ratings are equal for all groups, or whether there is statistical evidence for differences due to the kind of grape used. If you find such evidence, carry out further analysis to find out where these differences are.

CASE 12 Checking Out Checkout

Three checkout lines at a supermarket use three different scanner systems that read the UPC symbols on products and find the prices. The store manager suspects that the three scanner systems have different efficiencies and wants to check their speeds. He measures at randomly selected times the speed of each system in number of items scanned per minute. The measurements are given in the table below. Assume normal distribution with equal variance for the three systems.

Scan 1	Scan 2	Scan 3
16	13	18
15	18	19
12	13	15
15	15	14
16	18	19
15	14	16
15	15	17
14	15	14
12	14	15
14	16	17

1. Conduct a one-way ANOVA to test the null hypothesis that all three scanner systems have the same average number scanned per minute. Use an α of 0.05.

After studying the test results, a representative of the manufacturer of one of the three scanner systems remarks that the ANOVA results may be affected by the differing skills of the checkout clerks. The clerks were not the same for all measurements.

Wanting to know the difference in the efficiencies of the clerks as well as the systems, the manager redesigns the experiment to yield measurements for all combinations of five clerks and three systems. The measurements from this experiment are tabulated below. Assume normal distribution with equal variance for all cells.

	Scan 1	Scan 2	Scan 3
Clerk 1	15	16	18
	15	17	17
	14	14	15
	15	12	15
Clerk 2	14	15	14
	15	17	18
	13	16	19
	12	13	20
Clerk 3	15	16	17
	14	14	18
	16	13	17
	13	14	16
Clerk 4	14	15	20
	15	17	19
	16	18	17
	15	14	16
Clerk 5	15	16	20
	17	16	18
	14	17	18
	13	19	17

2. Conduct a two-way ANOVA with the above data. Interpret your findings.

10

SIMPLE LINEAR REGRESSION AND CORRELATION

10–1	Using Statistics	409
10–2	The Simple Linear Regression Model	411
10–3	Estimation: The Method of Least Squares	414
10–4	Error Variance and the Standard Errors of Regression Estimators	424
10–5	Correlation	429
10–6	Hypothesis Tests about the Regression Relationship	434
10–7	How Good Is the Regression?	438
10–8	Analysis-of-Variance Table and an F Test of the Regression Model	443
10–9	Residual Analysis and Checking for Model Inadequacies	445
10–10	Use of the Regression Model for Prediction	454
10–11	Using the Computer	458
10–12	Summary and Review of Terms	464
Case 13	Firm Leverage and Shareholder Rights	466
Case 14	Risk and Return	467

LEARNING OBJECTIVES

After studying this chapter, you should be able to:

- Determine whether a regression experiment would be useful in a given instance.
- Formulate a regression model.
- Compute a regression equation.
- Compute the covariance and the correlation coefficient of two random variables.
- Compute confidence intervals for regression coefficients.
- Compute a prediction interval for a dependent variable.
- Test hypotheses about regression coefficients.
- Conduct an ANOVA experiment using regression results.
- Analyze residuals to check the validity of assumptions about the regression model.
- Solve regression problems using spreadsheet templates.
- Use the LINEST function to carry out a regression.

10–1 Using Statistics

In 1855, a 33-year-old Englishman settled down to a life of leisure in London after several years of travel throughout Europe and Africa. The boredom brought about by a comfortable life induced him to write, and his first book was, naturally, *The Art of Travel*. As his intellectual curiosity grew, he shifted his interests to science and many years later published a paper on heredity, "Natural Inheritance" (1889). He reported his discovery that sizes of seeds of sweet pea plants appeared to "revert," or "regress," to the mean size in successive generations. He also reported results of a study of the relationship between heights of fathers and the heights of their sons. A straight line was fit to the data pairs: height of son versus height of father. Here, too, he found a "regression to mediocrity": The heights of the sons represented a movement away from their fathers, toward the average height. The man was Sir Francis Galton, a cousin of Charles Darwin. We credit him with the idea of statistical regression.

While most applications of regression analysis may have little to do with the "regression to the mean" discovered by Galton, the term **regression** remains. It now refers to the statistical technique of modeling the relationship between variables. In this chapter on **simple linear regression,** we model the relationship between two variables: a **dependent variable,** denoted by Y, and an **independent variable,** denoted by X. The model we use is a *straight-line relationship* between X and Y. When we model the relationship between the dependent variable Y and a set of several independent variables, or when the assumed relationship between Y and X is curved and requires the use of more terms in the model, we use a technique called *multiple regression.* This technique will be discussed in the next chapter.

Figure 10–1 is a general example of simple linear regression: fitting a straight line to describe the relationship between two variables X and Y. The points on the graph are randomly chosen observations of the two variables X and Y, and the straight line describes the general *movement* in the data—an increase in Y corresponding to an increase in X. An inverse straight-line relationship is also possible, consisting of a general decrease in Y as X increases (in such cases, the slope of the line is negative).

Regression analysis is one of the most important and widely used statistical techniques and has many applications in business and economics. A firm may be interested in estimating the relationship between advertising and sales (one of the most important topics of research in the field of marketing). Over a short range of values—when advertising is not yet overdone, giving diminishing returns—the relationship between advertising and sales may be well approximated by a straight line. The X variable in Figure 10–1 could denote advertising expenditure, and the Y variable could stand for the resulting sales for the same period. The data points in this case would be pairs of observations of the form $x_1 = \$75,570$, $y_1 = 134,679$ units; $x_2 = \$83,090$, $y_2 = 151,664$ units; etc. That is, the first month the firm spent \$75,570 on advertising, and sales for the month were 134,679 units; the second month the company spent \$83,090 on advertising, with resulting sales of 151,664 units for that month; and so on for the entire set of available data.

The data pairs, values of X paired with corresponding values of Y, are the points shown in a sketch of the data (such as Figure 10–1). A sketch of data on two variables is called a **scatter plot.** In addition to the scatter plot, Figure 10–1 shows the straight line believed to best show how the general trend of increasing sales corresponds, in this example, to increasing advertising expenditures. This chapter will teach you how to find the best line to fit a data set and how to use the line once you have found it.

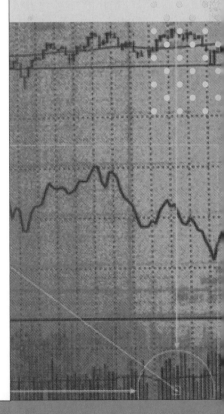

FIGURE 10–1   Simple Linear Regression

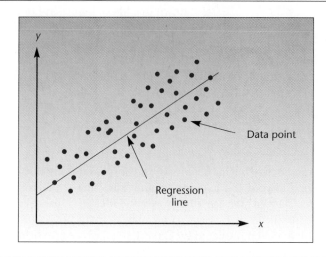

Although, in reality, our sample may consist of all available information on the two variables under study, we always assume that our data set constitutes a random sample of observations from a population of possible pairs of values of X and Y. Incidentally, in our hypothetical advertising sales example, we assume no carryover effect of advertising from month to month; every month's sales depend only on that month's level of advertising. Other common examples of the use of simple linear regression in business and economics are the modeling of the relationship between job performance (the dependent variable Y) and extent of training (the independent variable X); the relationship between returns on a stock (Y) and the riskiness of the stock (X); and the relationship between company profits (Y) and the state of the economy (X).

Model Building

Like the analysis of variance, both simple linear regression and multiple regression are *statistical models*. Recall that a statistical model is a set of mathematical formulas and assumptions that describe a real-world situation. We would like our model to explain as much as possible about the process underlying our data. However, due to the uncertainty inherent in all real-world situations, our model will probably not explain everything, and we will always have some remaining errors. The errors are due to unknown outside factors that affect the process generating our data.

A good statistical model is *parsimonious,* which means that it uses as few mathematical terms as possible to describe the real situation. The model captures the systematic behavior of the data, leaving out the factors that are nonsystematic and cannot be foreseen or predicted–the errors. The idea of a good statistical model is illustrated in Figure 10–2. The errors, denoted by ϵ, constitute the random component in the model. In a sense, the statistical model breaks down the data into a nonrandom, systematic component, which can be described by a formula, and a purely random component.

How do we deal with the errors? This is where probability theory comes in. Since our model, we hope, captures everything systematic in the data, the remaining random errors are probably due to a large number of minor factors that we cannot trace. We assume that the random errors ϵ are *normally distributed*. If we have a properly constructed model, the resulting observed errors will have an average of zero (although few, if any, will actually equal zero), and they should also be *independent* of one another. We note that the assumption of a normal distribution of the errors is not absolutely necessary in the regression model. The assumption is made so that we can carry out statistical hypothesis tests using the F and t distributions. The only necessary assumption is that the errors ϵ have mean zero and a constant variance σ^2 and that they be uncorrelated with one another. In the

**FIGURE 10–2
A Statistical Model**

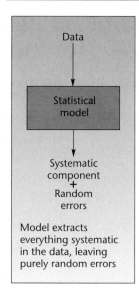

FIGURE 10–3 Steps in Building a Statistical Model

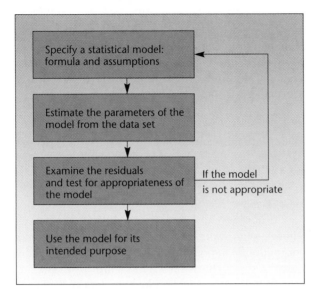

next section, we describe the simple linear regression model. We now present a general model-building methodology.

First, we propose a particular model to describe a given situation. For example, we may propose a simple linear regression model for describing the relationship between two variables. Then we estimate the model parameters from the random sample of data we have. The next step is to consider the observed errors resulting from the fit of the model to the data. These observed errors, called **residuals,** represent the information in the data not explained by the model. For example, in the ANOVA model discussed in Chapter 9, the within-group variation (leading to SSE and MSE) is due to the residuals. If the residuals are found to contain some nonrandom, *systematic* component, we reevaluate our proposed model and, if possible, adjust it to incorporate the systematic component found in the residuals; or we may have to discard the model and try another. When we believe that model residuals contain nothing more than pure randomness, we use the model for its intended purpose: *prediction* of a variable, *control* of a variable, or the *explanation* of the relationships among variables.

In the advertising sales example, once the regression model has been estimated and found to be appropriate, the firm may be able to use the model for predicting sales for a given level of advertising within the range of values studied. Using the model, the firm may be able to control its sales by setting the level of advertising expenditure. The model may help explain the effect of advertising on sales within the range of values studied. Figure 10–3 shows the usual steps of building a statistical model.

10–2 The Simple Linear Regression Model

Recall from algebra that the equation of a straight line is $Y = A + BX$, where A is the Y intercept and B is the slope of the line. In simple linear regression, we model the relationship between two variables X and Y as a straight line. Therefore, our model must contain two parameters: an intercept parameter and a slope parameter. The usual notation for the **population intercept** is β_0, and the notation for the **population slope** is β_1. If we include the error term ϵ, the population regression model is given in equation 10–1.

CHAPTER 15

> The population simple linear regression model is
>
> $$Y = \beta_0 + \beta_1 X + \epsilon \qquad (10\text{--}1)$$
>
> where Y is the dependent variable, the variable we wish to explain or predict; X is the independent variable, also called the *predictor* variable; and ϵ is the error term, the only random component in the model and thus the only source of randomness in Y.

The model parameters are as follows:

> β_0 is the Y intercept of the straight line given by $Y = \beta_0 + \beta_1 X$ (the line does not contain the error term).
>
> β_1 is the slope of the line $Y = \beta_0 + \beta_1 X$.

FIGURE 10–4
Simple Linear Regression Model

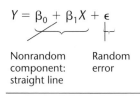

$Y = \beta_0 + \beta_1 X + \epsilon$

Nonrandom component: straight line   Random error

The simple linear regression model of equation 10–1 is composed of two components: a nonrandom component, which is the line itself, and a purely random component—the error term ϵ. This is shown in Figure 10–4. The nonrandom part of the model, the straight line, is the equation for the *mean of Y, given X*. We denote the conditional mean of Y, given X, by $E(Y|X)$. Thus, if the model is correct, the *average* value of Y for a given value of X falls right *on* the regression line. The equation for the mean of Y, given X, is given as equation 10–2.

> The conditional mean of Y is
>
> $$E(Y \mid X) = \beta_0 + \beta_1 X \qquad (10\text{--}2)$$

Comparing equations 10–1 and 10–2, we see that our model says that each value of Y comprises the average Y for the given value of X (this is the straight line), plus a random error. We will sometimes use the simplified notation $E(Y)$ for the line, remembering that this is the *conditional* mean of Y for a given value of X. As X increases, the average population value of Y also increases, assuming a positive slope of the line (or decreases, if the slope is negative). The *actual* population value of Y is equal to the average Y conditional on X, plus a random error ϵ. We thus have, for a given value of X,

> $$Y = \text{Average } Y \text{ for given } X + \text{Error}$$

Figure 10–5 shows the population regression model.

We now state the assumptions of the simple linear regression model.

> Model assumptions:
>
> 1. The relationship between X and Y is a straight-line relationship.
> 2. The values of the independent variable X are assumed fixed (not random); the only randomness in the values of Y comes from the error term ϵ.

FIGURE 10–5   Population Regression Line

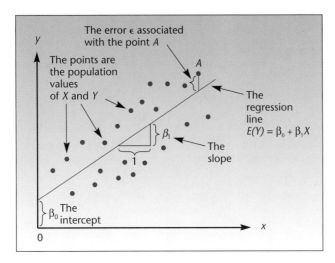

3. The errors ε are normally distributed with mean 0 and a constant variance σ^2. The errors are uncorrelated (not related) with one another in successive observations.[1] In symbols:

$$\epsilon \sim N(0, \sigma^2) \qquad (10\text{–}3)$$

FIGURE 10–6
Distributional Assumptions of the Linear Regression Model

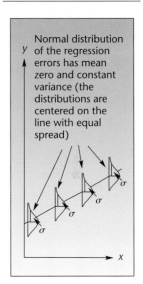

Figure 10–6 shows the distributional assumptions of the errors of the simple linear regression model. The population regression errors are normally distributed about the population regression line, with mean zero and equal variance. (The errors are equally spread about the regression line; the error variance does not increase or decrease as X increases.)

The simple linear regression model applies only if the true relationship between the two variables X and Y is a straight-line relationship. If the relationship is curved (*curvilinear*), then we need to use the more involved methods of the next chapter. In Figure 10–7, we show various relationships between two variables. Some are straight-line relationships that can be modeled by simple linear regression, and others are not.

So far, we have described the population model, that is, the assumed true relationship between the two variables X and Y. Our interest is focused on this unknown population relationship, and we want to *estimate* it, using sample information. We obtain a random sample of observations on the two variables, and we estimate the regression model parameters β_0 and β_1 from this sample. This is done by the *method of least squares*, which is discussed in the next section.

PROBLEMS

10–1. What is a statistical model?

10–2. What are the steps of statistical model building?

10–3. What are the assumptions of the simple linear regression model?

10–4. Define the parameters of the simple linear regression model.

---

[1]The idea of statistical *correlation* will be discussed in detail in Section 10–5. In the case of the regression errors, we assume that successive errors $\epsilon_1, \epsilon_2, \epsilon_3, \ldots$ are uncorrelated: they are not related with one another; there is no trend, no joint movement in successive errors. Incidentally, the assumption of zero correlation together with the assumption of a normal distribution of the errors implies the assumption that the errors are independent of one another. Independence implies noncorrelation, but noncorrelation does not imply independence, except in the case of a normal distribution (this is a technical point).

FIGURE 10–7   **Some Possible Relationships between** *X* **and** *Y*

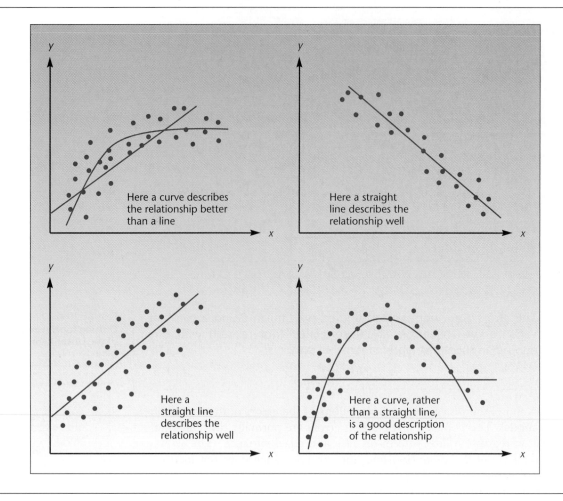

10–5. What is the conditional mean of *Y*, given *X*?

10–6. What are the uses of a regression model?

10–7. What are the purpose and meaning of the error term in regression?

10–8. A simple linear regression model was used for predicting the success of private-label products, which, according to the authors of the study, now account for 20% of global grocery sales, and the per capita gross domestic product for the country at which the private-label product is sold.[2] The regression equation is given as

$$PLS = \beta\ GDPC + \epsilon$$

where PLS = private label success, GDPC = per capita gross domestic product, β = regression slope, and ϵ = error term. What kind of regression model is this?

CHAPTER 15

10–3   Estimation: The Method of Least Squares

We want to find good estimates of the regression parameters β_0 and β_1. Remember the properties of good estimators, discussed in Chapter 5. Unbiasedness and efficiency are among these properties. A method that will give us good estimates of the regression

[2]Lien Lamey et al., "How Business Cycles Contribute to Private-Label Success: Evidence from the United States and Europe," *Journal of Marketing* 71 (January 2007), pp. 1–15.

coefficients is the **method of least squares.** The method of least squares gives us the *best linear unbiased estimators* (BLUE) of the regression parameters β_0 and β_1. These estimators both are unbiased and have the lowest variance of all possible unbiased estimators of the regression parameters. These properties of the least-squares estimators are specified by a well-known theorem, the *Gauss-Markov theorem.* We denote the least-squares estimators by b_0 and b_1.

The least-squares estimators are

$$b_0 \xrightarrow{\text{estimates}} \beta_0$$

$$b_1 \xrightarrow{\text{estimates}} \beta_1$$

The estimated regression equation is

$$Y = b_0 + b_1 X + e \qquad (10\text{--}4)$$

where b_0 estimates β_0, b_1 estimates β_1, and e stands for the observed errors—the residuals from fitting the line $b_0 + b_1 X$ to the data set of n points.

In terms of the data, equation 10–4 can be written with the subscript i to signify each particular data point:

$$y_i = b_0 + b_1 x_i + e_i \qquad (10\text{--}5)$$

where $i = 1, 2, \ldots, n$. Then e_1 is the first residual, the distance from the first data point to the fitted regression line; e_2 is the distance from the second data point to the line; and so on to e_n, the nth error. The errors e_i are viewed as estimates of the true population errors ϵ_i. The equation of the regression line itself is as follows:

The regression line is

$$\hat{Y} = b_0 + b_1 X \qquad (10\text{--}6)$$

where $\hat{Y}$ (pronounced "Y hat") is the Y value *lying on the fitted regression line* for a given X.

Thus, $\hat{y}_1$ is the fitted value corresponding to x_1, that is, the value of y_1 without the error e_1, and so on for all $i = 1, 2, \ldots, n$. The fitted value Y is also called the *predicted value of $\hat{Y}$* because if we do not know the actual value of Y, it is the value we would predict for a given value of X, using the estimated regression line.

Having defined the estimated regression equation, the errors, and the fitted values of Y, we will now demonstrate the principle of least squares, which gives us the BLUE regression parameters. Consider the data set shown in Figure 10–8(a). In parts (b), (c), and (d) of the figure, we show different lines passing through the data set and the resulting errors e_i.

As can be seen from Figure 10–8, the regression line proposed in part (b) results in very large errors. The errors corresponding to the line of part (c) are smaller than the ones of part (b), but the errors resulting from using the line proposed in part (d) are by far the smallest. The line in part (d) seems to move with the data and *minimize* the resulting errors. This should convince you that the line that best describes the trend in the data is the line that lies "inside" the set of

FIGURE 10–8   A Data Set of *X* and *Y* Pairs, and Different Proposed Straight Lines to Describe the Data

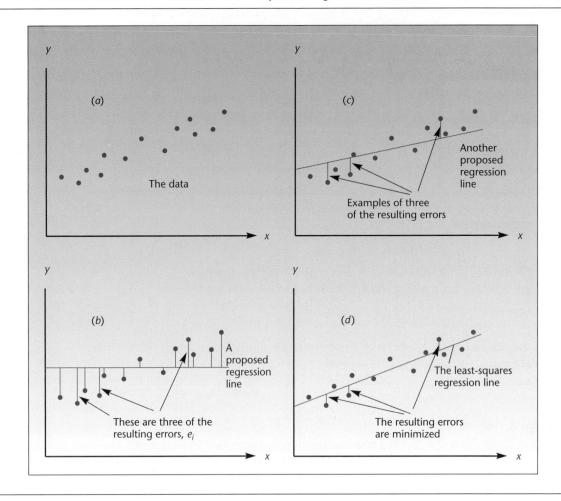

points; since some of the points lie above the fitted line and others below the line, some errors will be positive and others will be negative. If we want to minimize all the errors (both positive and negative ones), we should minimize the *sum of the squared errors* (SSE, as in ANOVA). Thus, we want to find the *least-squares* line–the line that minimizes SSE. We note that least squares is not the only method of fitting lines to data; other methods include minimizing the sum of the absolute errors. The method of least squares, however, is the most commonly used method to estimate a regression relationship. Figure 10–9 shows how the errors lead to the calculation of SSE.

We define the sum of squares for error in regression as

$$\text{SSE} = \sum_{i=1}^{n} e_i^2 = \sum_{i=1}^{n} (y_i - \hat{y}_i)^2 \qquad (10\text{–}7)$$

Figure 10–10 shows different values of SSE corresponding to values of b_0 and b_1. The least-squares line is the particular line specified by values of b_0 and b_1 that minimize SSE, as shown in the figure.

FIGURE 10–9   Regression Errors Leading to SSE

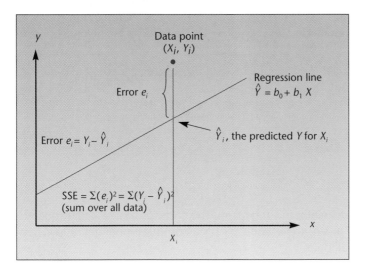

FIGURE 10–10   The Particular Values b_0 and b_1 That Minimize SSE

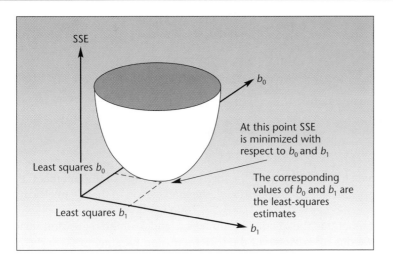

Calculus is used in finding the expressions for b_0 and b_1 that minimize SSE. These expressions are called the *normal equations* and are given as equations 10–8.[3] This system of two equations with two unknowns is solved to give us the values of b_0 and b_1 that minimize SSE. The results are the least-squares estimators b_0 and b_1 of the simple linear regression parameters β_0 and β_1.

The **normal equations** are

$$\sum_{i=1}^{n} y_i = nb_0 + b_1 \sum_{i=1}^{n} x_i$$

$$\sum_{i=1}^{n} x_i y_i = b_0 \sum_{i=1}^{n} x_i + b_1 \sum_{i=1}^{n} x_i^2 \qquad (10\text{--}8)$$

---

[3]We leave it as an exercise to the reader with background in calculus to derive the normal equations by taking the partial derivatives of SSE with respect to b_0 and b_1 and setting them to zero.

Before we present the solutions to the normal equations, we define the sums of squares SS_X and SS_Y and the sum of the cross-products SS_{XY}. These will be very useful in defining the least-squares estimates of the regression parameters, as well as in other regression formulas we will see later. The definitions are given in equations 10–9.

Definitions of sums of squares and cross-products useful in regression analysis:

$$SS_x = \sum (x - \bar{x})^2 = \sum x^2 - \frac{(\sum x)^2}{n}$$

$$SS_y = \sum (y - \bar{y})^2 = \sum y^2 - \frac{(\sum y)^2}{n}$$

$$SS_{xy} = \sum (x - \bar{x})(y - \bar{y}) = \sum xy - \frac{(\sum x)(\sum y)}{n} \qquad (10\text{–}9)$$

The first definition in each case is the conceptual one using squared distances from the mean; the second part is a computational definition. Summations are over all data.

We now give the solutions of the normal equations, the least-squares estimators b_0 and b_1.

Least-squares regression estimators include the slope

$$b_1 = \frac{SS_{xy}}{SS_x}$$

and the intercept

$$b_0 = \bar{y} - b_1 \bar{x} \qquad (10\text{–}10)$$

The formula for the estimate of the intercept makes use of the fact that the *least-squares line always passes through the point* $(\bar{x}, \bar{y})$, the intersection of the mean of X and the mean of Y.

Remember that the obtained estimates b_0 and b_1 of the regression relationship are just realizations of *estimators* of the true regression parameters β_0 and β_1. As always, our estimators have standard deviations (and variances, which, by the Gauss-Markov theorem, are as small as possible). The estimates can be used, along with the assumption of normality, in the construction of confidence intervals for, and the conducting of hypothesis tests about, the true regression parameters β_0 and β_1. This will be done in the next section.

We demonstrate the process of estimating the parameters of a simple linear regression model in Example 10–1.

EXAMPLE 10–1   American Express Company has long believed that its cardholders tend to travel more extensively than others—both on business and for pleasure. As part of a comprehensive research effort undertaken by a New York market research firm on behalf of American Express, a study was conducted to determine the relationship between travel and charges on the American Express card. The research firm selected a random sample of 25 cardholders from the American Express computer file and recorded their total charges over a specified period. For the selected cardholders, information was also obtained, through a mailed questionnaire, on the total number of miles traveled by each cardholder during the same period. The data for this study are given in Table 10–1. Figure 10–11 is a scatter plot of the data.

As can be seen from the figure, it seems likely that a straight line will describe the trend of increase in dollar amount charged with increase in number of miles traveled. The least-squares line that fits these data is shown in Figure 10–12.

We will now show how the least-squares regression line in Figure 10–12 is obtained. Table 10–2 shows the necessary computations. From equations 10–9, using sums at the bottom of Table 10–2, we get

$$SS_X = \sum x^2 - \frac{(\sum x)^2}{n} = 293{,}426{,}946 - \frac{79{,}448^2}{25} = 40{,}947{,}557.84$$

and

$$SS_{XY} = \sum xy - \frac{(\sum x)(\sum y)}{n} = 390{,}185{,}014 - \frac{(79{,}448)(106{,}605)}{25} = 51{,}402{,}852.4$$

FIGURE 10–11   Data for the American Express Study

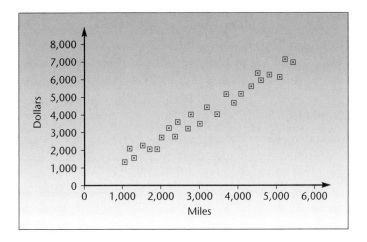

FIGURE 10–12   Least-Squares Line for the American Express Study

The least-squares line:
$\hat{Y} = 274.8497 + 1.2553X$

Solution

TABLE 10–1
American Express Study Data

Miles	Dollars
1,211	1,802
1,345	2,405
1,422	2,005
1,687	2,511
1,849	2,332
2,026	2,305
2,133	3,016
2,253	3,385
2,400	3,090
2,468	3,694
2,699	3,371
2,806	3,998
3,082	3,555
3,209	4,692
3,466	4,244
3,643	5,298
3,852	4,801
4,033	5,147
4,267	5,738
4,498	6,420
4,533	6,059
4,804	6,426
5,090	6,321
5,233	7,026
5,439	6,964

TABLE 10–2   The Computations Required for the American Express Study

Miles X	Dollars Y	X^2	Y^2	XY
1,211	1,802	1,466,521	3,247,204	2,182,222
1,345	2,405	1,809,025	5,784,025	3,234,725
1,422	2,005	2,022,084	4,020,025	2,851,110
1,687	2,511	2,845,969	6,305,121	4,236,057
1,849	2,332	3,418,801	5,438,224	4,311,868
2,026	2,305	4,104,676	5,313,025	4,669,930
2,133	3,016	4,549,689	9,096,256	6,433,128
2,253	3,385	5,076,009	11,458,225	7,626,405
2,400	3,090	5,760,000	9,548,100	7,416,000
2,468	3,694	6,091,024	13,645,636	9,116,792
2,699	3,371	7,284,601	11,363,641	9,098,329
2,806	3,998	7,873,636	15,984,004	11,218,388
3,082	3,555	9,498,724	12,638,025	10,956,510
3,209	4,692	10,297,681	22,014,864	15,056,628
3,466	4,244	12,013,156	18,011,536	14,709,704
3,643	5,298	13,271,449	28,068,804	19,300,614
3,852	4,801	14,837,904	23,049,601	18,493,452
4,033	5,147	16,265,089	26,491,609	20,757,851
4,267	5,738	18,207,289	32,924,644	24,484,046
4,498	6,420	20,232,004	41,216,400	28,877,160
4,533	6,059	20,548,089	36,711,481	27,465,447
4,804	6,426	23,078,416	41,293,476	30,870,504
5,090	6,321	25,908,100	39,955,041	32,173,890
5,233	7,026	27,384,289	49,364,676	36,767,058
5,439	6,964	29,582,721	48,497,296	37,877,196
79,448	106,605	293,426,946	521,440,939	390,185,014

Using equations 10–10 for the least-squares estimates of the slope and intercept parameters, we get

$$b_1 = \frac{\text{SS}_{XY}}{\text{SS}_X} = \frac{51,402,852.40}{40,947,557.84} = 1.255333776$$

and

$$b_0 = \bar{y} - b_1\bar{x} = \frac{106,605}{25} - 1.2553337776\left(\frac{79,448}{25}\right) = 274.8496866$$

Always carry out as many significant digits as you can in these computations. Here we carried out the computations by hand, for demonstration purposes. Usually, all computations are done by computer or by calculator. There are many hand calculators with a built-in routine for simple linear regression. From now on, we will present only the computed results, the least-squares estimates. The estimated least-squares relationship for Example 10–1 is reporting estimates to the second significant decimal:

$$Y = 274.85 + 1.26X + e \qquad (10\text{--}11)$$

The equation of the line itself, that is, the predicted value of Y for a given X, is

$$\hat{Y} = 274.85 + 1.26X \qquad (10\text{--}12)$$

The Template

Figure 10–13 shows the template that can be used to carry out a simple regression. The X and Y data are entered in columns B and C. The scatter plot at the bottom shows the regression equation and the regression line. Several additional statistics regarding the regression appear in the remaining parts of the template; these are explained in later sections. The error values appear in column D.

Below the scatter plot is a panel for residual analysis. Here you will find the Durbin-Watson statistic, the residual plot, and the normal probability plot. The Durbin-Watson statistic will be explained in the next chapter, and the normal probability plot will be explained later in this chapter. The residual plot shows that there is no relationship between X and the residuals. Figure 10–14 shows the panel.

FIGURE 10–13 The Simple Regression Template
[Simple Regression.xls; Sheet: Regression]

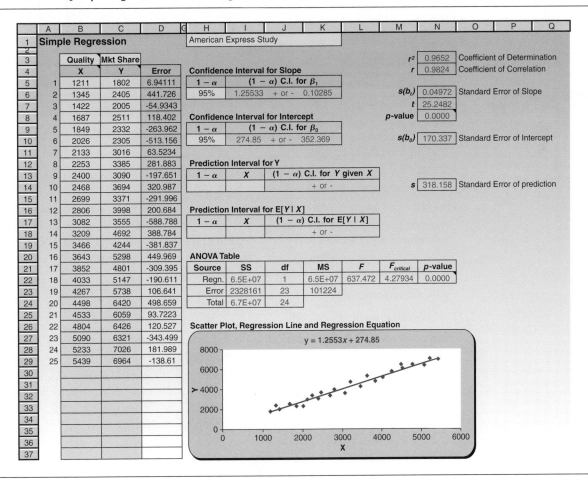

FIGURE 10–14   Residual Analysis in the Template
[Simple Regression.xls; Sheet: Regression]

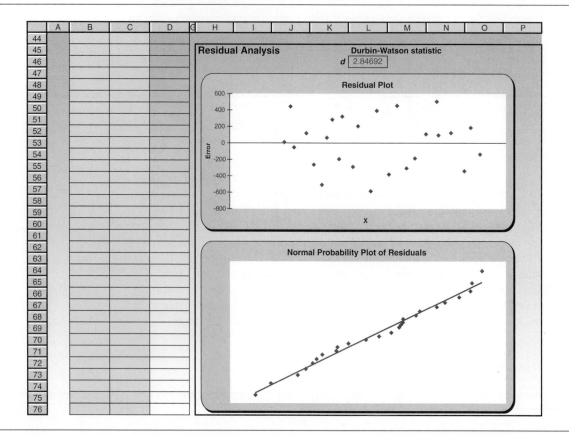

PROBLEMS

10–9. Explain the advantages of the least-squares procedure for fitting lines to data. Explain how the procedure works.

10–10. (A conceptually advanced problem) Can you think of a possible limitation of the least-squares procedure?

10–11. An article in the *Journal of Monetary Economics* assesses the relationship between percentage growth in wealth over a decade and a half of savings for baby boomers of age 40 to 55 with these people's income quartiles. The article presents a table showing five income quartiles, and for each quartile there is a reported percentage growth in wealth. The data are as follows.[4]

Income quartile:	1	2	3	4	5
Wealth growth (%):	17.3	23.6	40.2	45.8	56.8

Run a simple linear regression of these five pairs of numbers and estimate a linear relationship between income and percentage growth in wealth.

10–12. A financial analyst at Goldman Sachs ran a regression analysis of monthly returns on a certain investment (Y) versus returns for the same month on the Standard & Poor's index (X). The regression results included $SS_X = 765.98$ and $SS_{XY} = 934.49$. Give the least-squares estimate of the regression slope parameter.

[4]Edward N. Wolff, "The Retirement Wealth of the Baby Boom Generation," *Journal of Monetary Economics* 54 (January 2007), pp. 1–40.

10–13. Recently, research efforts have focused on the problem of predicting a manufacturer's market share by using information on the quality of its product. Suppose that the following data are available on market share, in percentage (Y), and product quality, on a scale of 0 to 100, determined by an objective evaluation procedure (X):

X:	27	39	73	66	33	43	47	55	60	68	70	75	82
Y:	2	3	10	9	4	6	5	8	7	9	10	13	12

Estimate the simple linear regression relationship between market share and product quality rating.

10–14. A pharmaceutical manufacturer wants to determine the concentration of a key component of cough medicine that may be used without the drug's causing adverse side effects. As part of the analysis, a random sample of 45 patients is administered doses of varying concentration (X), and the severity of side effects (Y) is measured. The results include $\bar{x} = 88.9$, $\bar{y} = 165.3$, $SS_X = 2,133.9$, $SS_{XY} = 4,502.53$, $SS_Y = 12,500$. Find the least-squares estimates of the regression parameters.

10–15. The following are data on annual inflation and stock returns. Run a regression analysis of the data and determine whether there is a linear relationship between inflation and total return on stocks for the periods under study.

Inflation (%)	Total Return on Stocks (%)
1	−3
2	36
12.6	12
−10.3	−8
0.51	53
2.03	−2
−1.8	18
5.79	32
5.87	24

10–16. An article in *Worth* discusses the immense success of one of the world's most prestigious cars, the Aston Martin Vanquish. This car is expected to keep its value as it ages. Although this model is new, the article reports resale values of earlier Aston Martin models over various decades.

Decade:	1960s	1970s	1980s	1990s	2000s
Present value of Aston Martin model (average):	$180,000	$40,000	$60,000	$160,000	$200,000

Based on these limited data, is there a relationship between age and average price of an Aston Martin? What are the limitations of this analysis? Can you think of some hidden variables that could affect what you are seeing in the data?

10–17. For the data given below, regress one variable on the other. Is there an implication of causality, or are both variables affected by a third?

Sample of Annual Transactions ($ millions)

Year	Credit Card	Online Debit Card
2002	156	211
2003	204	280
2004	279	386
2005	472	551
2006	822	684
2007	1,213	905

10–18. (A problem requiring knowledge of calculus) Derive the normal equations (10–8) by taking the partial derivatives of SSE with respect to b_0 and b_1 and setting them to zero. [*Hint:* Set SSE $= \Sigma e^2 = \Sigma(y - \hat{y})^2 = \Sigma(y - b_0 - b_1 x)^2$, and take the derivatives of the last expression on the right.]

10–4   Error Variance and the Standard Errors of Regression Estimators

CHAPTER 15

Recall that σ^2 is the variance of the population regression errors ϵ and that this variance is assumed to be constant for all values of X in the range under study. The error variance is an important parameter in the context of regression analysis because it is a measure of the spread of the population elements about the regression line. Generally, the smaller the error variance, the more closely the population elements follow the regression line. The error variance is the variance of the dependent variable Y as "seen" by an eye looking in the direction of the regression line (the error variance is not the variance of Y). These properties are demonstrated in Figure 10–15.

The figure shows two regression lines. The top regression line in the figure has a larger error variance than the bottom regression line. The error variance for each regression is the variation in the data points as seen by the eye located at the base of the line, looking *in the direction of the regression line*. The variance of Y, on the other hand, is the variation in the Y values regardless of the regression line. That is, the variance of Y for each of the two data sets in the figure is the variation in the data as seen by an eye looking in a direction parallel to the X axis. Note also that the spread of the data is constant along the regression lines. This is in accordance with our assumption of equal error variance for all X.

Since σ^2 is usually unknown, we need to estimate it from our data. An unbiased estimator of σ^2, denoted by S^2, is the *mean square error (MSE)* of the regression. As you will soon see, sums of squares and mean squares in the context of regression analysis are very similar to those of ANOVA, presented in the preceding chapter. The degrees of freedom for error in the context of simple linear regression are $n - 2$ because we have n data points, from which two parameters, β_0 and β_1, are estimated (thus, two restrictions are imposed on the n points, leaving df $= n - 2$). The sum of squares for error (SSE) in regression analysis is defined as the sum of squared deviations of the data values Y from the fitted values $\hat{Y}$. The sum of squares for error may also be defined in terms of a computational formula using SS_X, SS_Y, and SS_{XY} as defined in equations 10–9. We state these relationships in equations 10–13.

FIGURE 10-15   Two Examples of Regression Lines Showing the Error Variance

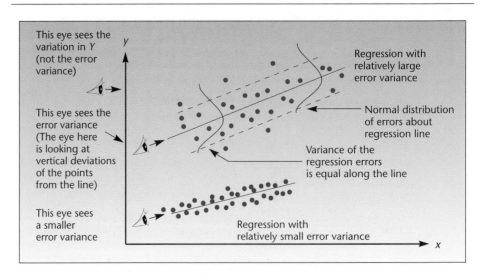

$$df(error) = n - 2$$

$$SSE = \sum (Y - \hat{Y})^2$$

$$= SS_Y - \frac{(SS_{XY})^2}{SS_X}$$

$$= SS_Y - b_1 SS_{XY} \qquad (10\text{--}13)$$

An unbiased estimator of σ^2, denoted by S^2, is

$$MSE = \frac{SSE}{n - 2}$$

In Example 10–1, the sum of squares for error is

$$SSE = SS_Y - b_1 SS_{XY} = 66{,}855{,}898 - (1.255333776)(51{,}402{,}852.4)$$
$$= 2{,}328{,}161.2$$

and

$$MSE = \frac{SSE}{n - 2} = \frac{2{,}328{,}161.2}{23} = 101{,}224.4$$

An estimate of the standard deviation of the regression errors σ is s, which is the square root of MSE. (The estimator S is not unbiased because the square root of an unbiased estimator, such as S^2, is not itself unbiased. The bias, however, is small, and the point is a technical one.) The estimate $s = \sqrt{MSE}$ of the standard deviation of the regression errors is sometimes referred to as *standard error of estimate*. In Example 10–1 we have

$$s = \sqrt{MSE} = \sqrt{101{,}224.4} = 318.1578225$$

The computation of SSE and MSE for Example 10–1 is demonstrated in Figure 10–16.

The standard deviation of the regression errors σ and its estimate s play an important role in the process of estimation of the values of the regression parameters β_0 and β_1.

FIGURE 10–16   Computing SSE and MSE in the American Express Study

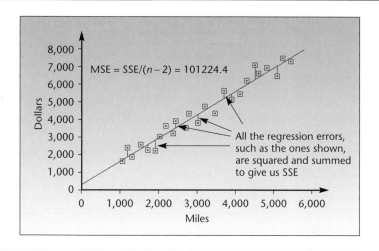

This is so because σ is part of the expressions for the standard errors of both parameter estimators. The standard errors are defined next; they give us an idea of the accuracy of the least-squares estimates b_0 and b_1. *The standard error of* b_1 *is especially important because it is used in a test for the existence of a linear relationship between* X *and* Y. This will be seen in Section 10–6.

The standard error of b_0 is

$$s(b_0) = \frac{s\sqrt{\sum x^2}}{\sqrt{n\,SS_x}} \qquad (10\text{--}14)$$

where $s = \sqrt{MSE}$.

The standard error of b_1 is very important, for the reason just mentioned. The true standard deviation of b_1 is $\sigma/\sqrt{SS_x}$, but since σ is not known, we use the estimated standard deviation of the errors, s.

The standard error of b_1 is

$$s(b_1) = \frac{s}{\sqrt{SS_X}} \qquad (10\text{--}15)$$

Formulas such as equation 10–15 are nice to know, but you should not worry too much about having to use them. Regression analysis is usually done by computer, and the computer output will include the standard errors of the regression estimates. We will now show how the regression parameter estimates and their standard errors can be used in the construction of confidence intervals for the true regression parameters β_0 and β_1. In Section 10–6, as mentioned, we will use the standard error of b_1 for conducting the very important hypothesis test about the existence of a linear relationship between X and Y.

Confidence Intervals for the Regression Parameters

Confidence intervals for the true regression parameters β_0 and β_1 are easy to compute.

A $(1 - \alpha)$ 100% confidence interval for β_0 is

$$b_0 \pm t_{(\alpha/2,\, n-2)} s(b_0) \qquad (10\text{--}16)$$

where $s(b_0)$ is as given in equation 10–14.

A $(1 - \alpha)$ 100% confidence interval for β_1 is

$$b_1 \pm t_{(\alpha/2,\, n-2)} s(b_1) \qquad (10\text{--}17)$$

where $s(b_1)$ is as given in equation 10–15.

Let us construct 95% confidence intervals for β_0 and β_1 in the American Express example. Using equations 10–14 to 10–17, we get

$$s(b_0) = \frac{s\sqrt{\sum x^2}}{\sqrt{n\,SS_X}} = 318.16\,\frac{\sqrt{293,426,946}}{\sqrt{(25)(40,947,557.84)}} = 170.338 \qquad (10\text{--}18a)$$

where the various quantities were computed earlier, including $\sum x^2$, which is found at the bottom of Table 10–2.

A 95% confidence interval for β_0 is

$$b_0 \pm t_{(\alpha/2, \, n-2)}s(b_0) = 274.85 \pm 2.069(170.338) = [-77.58, 627.28] \qquad (10\text{-}18b)$$

where the value 2.069 is obtained from Appendix C, Table 3, for $1 - \alpha = 0.95$ and 23 degrees of freedom. We may be 95% confident that the true regression intercept is anywhere from -77.58 to 627.28. Again using equations 10–14 to 10–17, we get

$$s(b_1) = \frac{s}{\sqrt{SS_X}} = \frac{318.16}{\sqrt{40{,}947{,}557.84}} = 0.04972 \qquad (10\text{-}19a)$$

A 95% confidence interval for β_1 is

$$b_1 \pm t_{(\alpha/2, \, n-2)}s(b_1) = 1.25533 \pm 2.069(0.04972)$$
$$= [1.15246, \, 1.35820] \qquad (10\text{-}19b)$$

From the confidence interval given in equation 10–19b, we may be 95% confident that the *true* slope of the (*population*) regression line is anywhere from 1.15246 to 1.3582. This range of values is far from zero, and so we may be quite confident that the true regression slope is not zero. This conclusion is very important, as we will see in the following sections. Figure 10–17 demonstrates the meaning of the confidence interval given in equation 10–19b.

In the next chapter, we will discuss *joint* confidence intervals for both regression parameters β_0 and β_1, an advanced topic of secondary importance. (Since the two estimates are related, a joint interval will give us greater accuracy and a more meaningful, single confidence coefficient $1 - \alpha$. This topic is somewhat similar to the Tukey analysis of Chapter 9.) Again, we want to deemphasize the importance of inference about β_0, even though information about the standard error of the estimator of this parameter is reported in computer regression output. It is the inference about β_1 that is of interest to us. Inference about β_1 has implications for the existence of a linear relationship between X and Y; inference about β_0 has no such implications. In addition, you may be tempted to use the results of the inference about β_0 to "force" this parameter to equal

FIGURE 10–17 Interpretation of the Slope Estimation for Example 10–1

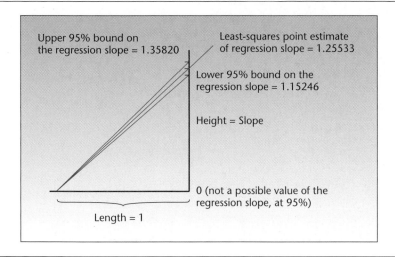

Upper 95% bound on
the regression slope = 1.35820

Least-squares point estimate
of regression slope = 1.25533

Lower 95% bound on the
regression slope = 1.15246

Height = Slope

0 (not a possible value of the
regression slope, at 95%)

Length = 1

zero or another number. Such temptation should be resisted for reasons that will be explained in a later section; therefore, we deemphasize inference about β_0.

EXAMPLE 10–2   The data below are international sales versus U.S. sales for the McDonald's chain for 10 years.

Sales for McDonald's at Year End (in billions)

U.S. Sales	International Sales
7.6	2.3
7.9	2.6
8.3	2.9
8.6	3.2
8.8	3.7
9.0	4.1
9.4	4.8
10.2	5.7
11.4	7.0
12.1	8.9

Use the template to regress McDonald's international sales, then answer the following questions:

1. What is the regression equation?
2. What is the 95% confidence interval for the slope?
3. What is the standard error of estimate?

Solution

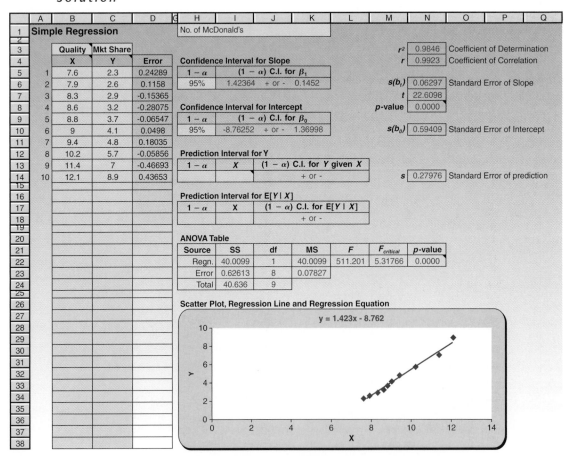

1. From the template, the regression equation is $\hat{Y} = 1.4326X - 8.7625$.
2. The 95% confidence interval for the slope is 1.4236 ± 0.1452.
3. The standard error of estimate is 0.2798.

10–19. Give a 99% confidence interval for the slope parameter in Example 10–1. Is zero a credible value for the true regression slope?

10–20. Give an unbiased estimate for the error variance in the situation of problem 10–11. In this problem and others, you may either use a computer or do the computations by hand.

10–21. Find the standard errors of the regression parameter estimates for problem 10–11.

10–22. Give 95% confidence intervals for the regression slope and the regression intercept parameters for the situation of problem 10–11.

10–23. For the situation of problem 10–13, find the standard errors of the estimates of the regression parameters; give an estimate of the variance of the regression errors. Also give a 95% confidence interval for the true regression slope. Is zero a plausible value for the true regression slope at the 95% level of confidence?

10–24. Repeat problem 10–23 for the situation in problem 10–17. Comment on your results.

10–25. In addition to its role in the formulas of the standard errors of the regression estimates, what is the significance of s^2?

10–5 Correlation

We now digress from regression analysis to discuss an important related concept: statistical *correlation*. Recall that one of the assumptions of the regression model is that the independent variable X is fixed rather than random and that the only randomness in the values of Y comes from the error term ϵ. Let us now relax this assumption and *assume that both* X *and* Y *are random variables*. In this new context, the study of the relationship between two variables is called *correlation analysis*.

CHAPTER 14

In correlation analysis, we adopt a symmetric approach: We make no distinction between an independent variable and a dependent one. The correlation between two variables is a measure of the linear relationship between them. The correlation gives an indication of how well the two variables move together in a straight-line fashion. The correlation between X and Y is the same as the correlation between Y and X. We now define correlation more formally.

> The **correlation** between two random variables X and Y is a measure of the *degree of linear association* between the two variables.

Two variables are highly correlated if they move well together. Correlation is indicated by the **correlation coefficient.**

> The population correlation coefficient is denoted by ρ. The coefficient ρ can take on any value from -1, through 0, to 1.

The possible values of ρ and their interpretations are given below.

1. When ρ is equal to zero, there is no correlation. That is, there is no linear relationship between the two random variables.

2. When $\rho = 1$, there is a perfect, positive, linear relationship between the two variables. That is, whenever one of the variables, X or Y, increases, the other variable also increases; and whenever one of the variables decreases, the other one must also decrease.

3. When $\rho = -1$, there is a perfect negative linear relationship between X and Y. When X or Y increases, the other variable decreases; and when one decreases, the other one must increase.

4. When the value of ρ is between 0 and 1 in absolute value, it reflects the relative strength of the linear relationship between the two variables. For example, a correlation of 0.90 implies a relatively strong positive relationship between the two variables. A correlation of -0.70 implies a weaker, negative (as indicated by the minus sign), linear relationship. A correlation $\rho = 0.30$ implies a relatively weak (positive) linear relationship between X and Y.

A few sets of data on two variables, and their corresponding population correlation coefficients, are shown in Figure 10–18.

How do we arrive at the concept of correlation? Consider the pair of random variables X and Y. In correlation analysis, *we will assume that both* X *and* Y *are normally distributed random variables with means* μ_X *and* μ_Y *and standard deviations* σ_X *and* σ_Y, *respectively.* We define the *covariance* of X and Y as follows:

The **covariance** of two random variables X and Y is

$$Cov(X, Y) = E[(X - \mu_X)(Y - \mu_Y)] \qquad (10\text{–}20)$$

where μ_X is the (population) mean of X and μ_Y is the (population) mean of Y.

The covariance of X and Y is thus the expected value of the product of the deviation of X from its mean and the deviation of Y from its mean. The covariance is positive when the two random variables move together in the same direction, it is negative when the two random variables move in opposite directions, and it is zero when the two variables are not linearly related. Other than this, the covariance does not convey much. Its magnitude cannot be interpreted as an indication of the *degree* of linear association between the two variables, because the covariance's magnitude depends on the magnitudes of the standard deviations of X and Y. But if we divide the covariance by these standard deviations, we get a measure that is constrained to the range of values -1 to 1 and conveys information about the relative strength of the linear relationship between the two variables. This measure is the population correlation coefficient ρ.

The **population correlation coefficient** is

$$\rho = \frac{Cov(X,Y)}{\sigma_X \sigma_Y} \qquad (10\text{–}21)$$

Figure 10–18 gives an idea of what data from populations with different values of ρ may look like.

Like all population parameters, the value of ρ is not known to us, and we need to estimate it from our random sample of (X, Y) observation pairs. It turns out that a sample estimator of $Cov(X, Y)$ is $SS_{XY}/(n - 1)$; an estimator of σ_X is $\sqrt{SS_X/(n - 1)}$; and an estimator of σ_Y is $\sqrt{SS_Y/(n - 1)}$. Substituting these estimators for their population counterparts in equation 10–21, and noting that the term $n - 1$ cancels, we get the *sample correlation coefficient,* denoted by r. This estimate of ρ, also referred to as the *Pearson product-moment correlation coefficient,* is given in equation 10–22.

FIGURE 10–18   Several Possible Correlations between Two Variables

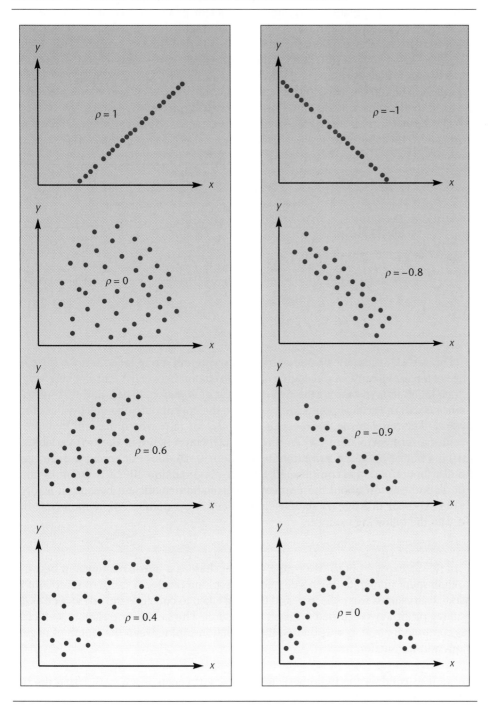

The **sample correlation coefficient** is

$$r = \frac{SS_{XY}}{\sqrt{SS_x SS_Y}}$$

(10–22)

In regression analysis, the square of the sample correlation coefficient, or r^2, has a special meaning and importance. This will be seen in Section 10–7.

We often use the sample correlation coefficient for descriptive purposes as a point estimator of the population correlation coefficient ρ. When r is large and positive (closer to $+1$), we say that the two variables are highly correlated in a positive way; when r is large and negative (toward -1), we say that the two variables are highly correlated in an inverse direction, and so on. That is, we view r as if it were the parameter ρ, which r estimates. However, r can be used as an estimator in testing hypotheses about the true correlation coefficient ρ. When such hypotheses are tested, the assumption of normal distributions of the two variables is required.

The most common test is a test of whether two random variables X and Y are correlated. The hypothesis test is

$$H_0: \rho = 0 \qquad\qquad\qquad (10\text{--}23)$$
$$H_1: \rho \neq 0$$

The test statistic for this particular test is

$$t_{(n-2)} = \frac{r}{\sqrt{(1 - r^2)/(n - 2)}} \qquad\qquad (10\text{--}24)$$

This test statistic may also be used for carrying out a one-tailed test for the existence of a positive only, or a negative only, correlation between X and Y. These would be one-tailed tests instead of the two-tailed test of equation 10–23, and the only difference is that the critical points for t would be the appropriate one-tailed values for a given α. The test statistic, however, is good *only* for tests where the null hypothesis assumes a zero correlation. When the true correlation between the two variables is anything but zero, the t distribution in equation 10–24 does not apply; in such cases the distribution is more complicated.[5] The test in equation 10–23 is the most common hypothesis test about the population correlation coefficient because it is a test for the existence of a linear relationship between two variables. We demonstrate this test with the following example.

EXAMPLE 10–3

A study was carried out to determine whether there is a linear relationship between the time spent in negotiating a sale and the resulting profits. A random sample of 27 market transactions was collected, and the time taken to conclude the sale as well as the resulting profit were recorded for each transaction. The sample correlation coefficient was computed: $r = 0.424$. Is there a linear relationship between the length of negotiations and transaction profits?

Solution

We want to conduct the hypothesis test $H_0: \rho = 0$ versus $H_1: \rho \neq 0$. Using the test statistic in equation 10–24, we get

$$t_{(25)} = \frac{r}{\sqrt{(1 - r^2)/(n - 2)}} = \frac{0.424}{\sqrt{(1 - 0.424^2)/25}} = 2.34$$

---

[5]In cases where we want to test $H_0: \rho = a$ versus $H_1: \rho \neq a$, where a is some number other than zero, we may do so by using the Fisher transformation: $z' = (1/2) \log [(1 + r)/(1 - r)]$, where z' is approximately normally distributed with mean $\mu' = (1/2) \log [(1 + \rho)/(1 - \rho)]$ and standard deviation $\sigma' = 1/\sqrt{n - 3}$. (Here *log* is taken to mean *natural logarithm*.) Such tests are less common, and a more complete description may be found in advanced texts. As an exercise, the interested reader may try this test on some data. [You need to transform z' to an approximate standard normal $z = (z' - \mu')/\sigma'$; use the null-hypothesis value of ρ in the formula for μ'.]

From Appendix C, Table 3, we find that the critical points for a t distribution with 25 degrees of freedom and $\alpha = 0.05$ are ± 2.060. Therefore, we reject the null hypothesis of no correlation in favor of the alternative that the two variables are linearly related. Since the critical points for $\alpha = 0.01$ are ± 2.787, and $2.787 > 2.34$, we are unable to reject the null hypothesis of no correlation between the two variables if we want to use the 0.01 level of significance. If we wanted to test (before looking at our data) only for the existence of a positive correlation between the two variables, our test would have been H_0: $\rho \leq 0$ versus H_1: $\rho > 0$ and we would have used only the right tail of the t distribution. At $\alpha = 0.05$, the critical point of t with 25 degrees of freedom is 1.708, and at $\alpha = 0.01$ it is 2.485. The null hypothesis would, again, be rejected at the 0.05 level but not at the 0.01 level of significance.

In regression analysis, the test for the existence of a linear relationship between X and Y is a test of whether the regression slope β_1 is equal to zero. The regression slope parameter is related to the correlation coefficient (as an exercise, compare the equations of the estimates r and b_1); when two random variables are uncorrelated, the population regression slope is zero.

We end this section with a word of caution. First, the existence of a correlation between two variables does not necessarily mean that one of the variables *causes* the other one. The determination of **causality** is a difficult question that cannot be directly answered in the context of correlation analysis or regression analysis. Also, the statistical determination that two variables are correlated may not always mean that they are correlated in any direct, meaningful way. For example, if we study any two population-related variables and find that both variables increase "together," this may merely be a reflection of the general increase in population rather than any direct correlation between the two variables. We should look for outside variables that may affect both variables under study.

PROBLEMS

10-26. What is the main difference between correlation analysis and regression analysis?

10-27. Compute the sample correlation coefficient for the data of problem 10–11.

10-28. Compute the sample correlation coefficient for the data of problem 10–13.

10-29. Using the data in problem 10–16, conduct the hypothesis test for the existence of a linear correlation between the two variables. Use $\alpha = 0.01$.

10-30. Is it possible that a sample correlation of 0.51 between two variables will not indicate that the two variables are really correlated, while a sample correlation of 0.04 between another pair of variables will be statistically significant? Explain.

10-31. The following data are indexed prices of gold and copper over a 10-year period. Assume that the indexed values constitute a random sample from the population of possible values. Test for the existence of a linear correlation between the indexed prices of the two metals.

Gold: 76, 62, 70, 59, 52, 53, 53, 56, 57, 56
Copper: 80, 68, 73, 63, 65, 68, 65, 63, 65, 66

Also, state one limitation of the data set.

10-32. Follow daily stock price quotations in the *Wall Street Journal* for a pair of stocks of your choice, and compute the sample correlation coefficient. Also, test for the existence of a nonzero linear correlation in the "population" of prices of the two stocks. For your sample, use as many daily prices as you can.

10-33. Again using the *Wall Street Journal* as a source of data, determine whether there is a linear correlation between morning and afternoon price quotations in London for an ounce of gold (for the same day). Any ideas?

10-34. A study was conducted to determine whether a correlation exists between consumers' perceptions of a television commercial (measured on a special scale) and their interest in purchasing the product (measured on a scale). The results are $n = 65$ and $r = 0.37$. Is there statistical evidence of a linear correlation between the two variables?

10-35. (Optional, advanced problem) Using the Fisher transformation (described in footnote 5), carry out a two-tailed test of the hypothesis that the population correlation coefficient for the situation of problem 10–34 is $\rho = 0.22$. Use $\alpha = 0.05$.

10-6   Hypothesis Tests about the Regression Relationship

When X and Y have no linear relationship, the population regression slope β_1 is equal to zero. Why? The population regression slope is equal to zero in either of two situations:

1. When Y is *constant* for all values of X. For example, $Y = 457.33$ for all X. This is shown in Figure 10–19(*a*). If Y is constant for all values of X, the slope of Y with respect to X, parameter β_1, is identically zero; there is no linear relationship between the two variables.

FIGURE 10–19   Two Possibilities Where the Population Regression Slope Is Zero

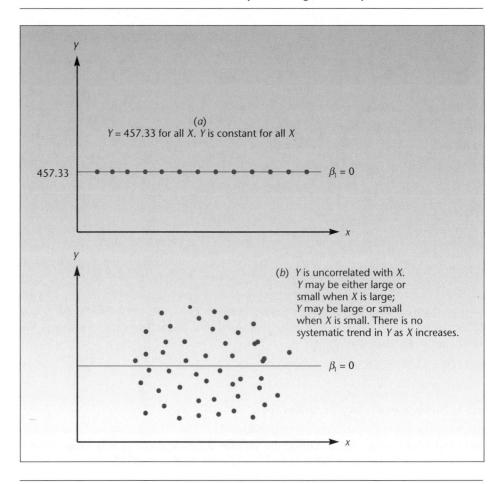

2. When the two variables are *uncorrelated*. When the correlation between X and Y is zero, as X increases Y may increase, or it may decrease, or it may remain constant. There is no *systematic* increase or decrease in the values of Y as X increases. This case is shown in Figure 10–19(b). As can be seen in the figure, data from this process are not "moving" in any pattern; thus, the line has no direction to follow. With no direction, the slope of the line is, again, zero.

Also, remember that the relationship may be curved, with no linear correlation, as was seen in the last part of Figure 10–18. In such cases, the slope may also be zero.

In all cases other than these, at least *some* linear relationship exists between the two variables X and Y; the slope of the line in all such cases would be either positive or negative, but not zero. Therefore, *the most important statistical test in simple linear regression is the test of whether the slope parameter* β_1 *is equal to zero*. If we conclude in any particular case that the true regression slope is equal to zero, this means that there is no linear relationship between the two variables: Either the dependent variable is constant, or—more commonly—the two variables are not linearly related. We thus have the following test for determining the existence of a linear relationship between two variables X and Y:

A hypothesis test for the existence of a linear relationship between X and Y is

$$H_0: \beta_1 = 0$$
$$H_1: \beta_1 \neq 0 \tag{10–25}$$

This test is, of course, a two-tailed test. Either the true regression slope is equal to zero, or it is not. If it is equal to zero, the two variables have no linear relationship; if the slope is not equal to zero, then it is either positive or negative (the two tails of rejection), in which case there is a linear relationship between the two variables. The test statistic for determining the rejection or nonrejection of the null hypothesis is given in equation 10–26. Given the assumption of normality of the regression errors, the test statistic possesses the t distribution with $n - 2$ degrees of freedom.

CHAPTER 15

The test statistic for the existence of a linear relationship between X and Y is

$$t_{(n-2)} = \frac{b_1}{s(b_1)} \tag{10–26}$$

where b_1 is the least-squares estimate of the regression slope and $s(b_1)$ is the standard error of b_1. When the null hypothesis is true, the statistic has a t distribution with $n - 2$ degrees of freedom.

This test statistic is a special version of a general test statistic

$$t_{(n-2)} = \frac{b_1 - (\beta_1)_0}{s(b_1)} \tag{10–27}$$

where $(\beta_1)_0$ is the value of β_1 under the null hypothesis. This statistic follows the format (Estimate − Hypothesized parameter value)/(Standard error of estimator). Since, in the test of equation 10–25, the hypothesized value of β_1 is zero, we have the simplified version of the test statistic, equation 10–26. One advantage of the simple form of our test statistic is that it allows us to conduct the test very quickly. Computer output for regression analysis usually contains a table similar to Table 10–3.

TABLE 10–3   An Example of a Part of the Computer Output for Regression

Variable	Estimate	Standard Error	t Ratio
Constant	5.22	0.5	10.44
X	4.88	0.1	48.80

The estimate associated with X (or whatever name the user may have given to the independent variable in the computer program) is b_1. The standard error associated with X is $s(b_1)$. To conduct the test, all you need to do is to divide b_1 by $s(b_1)$. In the example of Table 10–3, $4.88/0.1 = 48.8$. The answer is reported in the table as the t ratio. The t ratio can now be compared with critical points of the t distribution with $n - 2$ degrees of freedom. Suppose that the sample size used was 100. Then the critical points for $\alpha = 0.05$, from the spreadsheet, are ± 1.98, and since $48.8 > 1.98$, we conclude that there is evidence of a linear relationship between X and Y in this hypothetical example. (Actually, the p-value is very small. Some computer programs will also report the p-value in an extra column on the right.) What about the first row in the table? The test suggested here is a test of whether the intercept β_0 (this is the constant) is equal to zero. The test statistic is the same as equation 10–26, but with subscripts 0 instead of 1. As we mentioned earlier, this test, although suggested by the output of computer routines, is usually not meaningful and should generally be avoided.

We now conduct the hypothesis test for the existence of a linear relationship between miles traveled and amount charged on the American Express card in Example 10–1. Our hypotheses are H_0: $\beta_1 = 0$ and H_1: $\beta_1 \neq 0$. Recall that for the American Express study, $b_1 = 1.25533$ and $s(b_1) = 0.04972$ (from equations 10–11 and 10–19a). We now compute the test statistic, using equation 10–26:

$$t = \frac{b_1}{s(b_1)} = \frac{1.25533}{0.04972} = 25.25$$

From the magnitude of the computed value of the statistic, we know that there is statistical evidence of a linear relationship between the variables, because 25.25 is certainly greater than any critical point of a t distribution with 23 degrees of freedom. We show the test in Figure 10–20. The critical points of t with 23 degrees of freedom and $\alpha = 0.01$ are obtained from Appendix C, Table 3. We conclude that there is evidence of a linear relationship between the two variables "miles traveled" and "dollars charged" in Example 10–1.

FIGURE 10–20   Test for a Linear Relationship for Example 10–1

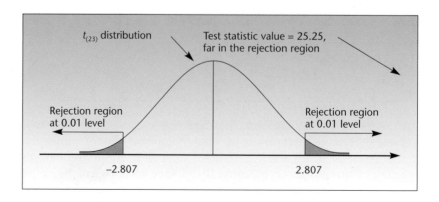

Other Tests[6]

Although the test of whether the slope parameter is equal to zero is a very important test, because it is a test for the existence of a linear relationship between the two variables, other tests are possible in the context of regression. These tests serve secondary purposes. In financial analysis, for example, it is often important to determine from past performance data of a particular stock whether the stock generally moves with the market as a whole. If the stock does move with the stock market as a whole, the slope parameter of the regression of the stock's returns (Y) versus returns on the market as a whole (X) would be equal to 1.00. That is, $\beta_1 = 1$. We demonstrate this test with Example 10–4.

EXAMPLE 10–4

The *Market Sensitivity Report,* issued by Merrill Lynch, Inc., lists estimated beta coefficients of common stocks as well as their standard errors. *Beta* is the term used in the finance literature for the estimate b_1 of the regression of returns on a stock versus returns on the stock market as a whole. Returns on the stock market as a whole are taken by Merrill Lynch as returns on the Standard & Poor's 500 index. The report lists the following findings for common stock of Time, Inc.: beta = 1.24, standard error of beta = 0.21, $n = 60$. Is there statistical evidence to reject the claim that the Time stock moves, in general, with the market as a whole?

Solution

We want to carry out the special-purpose test $H_0: \beta_1 = 1$ versus $H_1: \beta_1 \neq 1$. We use the general test statistic of equation 10–27:

$$t_{(n-2)} = \frac{b_1 - (\beta_1)_0}{s(b_1)} = \frac{1.24 - 1}{0.21} = 1.14$$

Since $n - 2 = 58$, we use the standard normal distribution. The test statistic value is in the nonrejection region for any usual level α, and we conclude that there is no statistical evidence against the claim that Time moves with the market as a whole.

PROBLEMS

10–36. An interesting marketing research effort has recently been reported, which incorporates within the variables that predict consumer satisfaction from a product not only attributes of the product itself but also characteristics of the consumer who buys the product. In particular, a regression model was developed, and found successful, regressing consumer satisfaction S on a consumer's materialism M measured on a psychologically devised scale. For satisfaction with the purchase of sunglasses, the estimate of beta, the slope of S with respect to M, was $b = -2.20$. The reported t statistic was -2.53. The sample size was $n = 54$.[7] Is this regression statistically significant? Explain the findings.

10–37. A regression analysis was carried out of returns on stocks (Y) versus the ratio of book to market value (X). The resulting prediction equation is

$$Y = 1.21 + 3.1X \, (2.89)$$

where the number in parentheses is the standard error of the slope estimate. The sample size used is $n = 18$. Is there evidence of a linear relationship between returns and book to market value?

---

[6]This subsection may be skipped without loss of continuity.

[7]Jeff Wang and Melanie Wallendorf, "Materialism, Status Signaling, and Product Satisfaction," *Journal of the Academy of Marketing Science* 34, no. 4 (2006), pp. 494–505.

10–38. In the situation of problem 10–11, test for the existence of a linear relationship between the two variables.

10–39. In the situation of problem 10–13, test for the existence of a linear relationship between the two variables.

10–40. In the situation of problem 10–16, test for the existence of a linear relationship between the two variables.

10–41. For Example 10–4, test for the existence of a linear relationship between returns on the stock and returns on the market as a whole.

10–42. A regression analysis was carried out to determine whether wages increase for blue-collar workers depending on the extent to which firms that employ them engage in product exportation. The sample consisted of 585,692 German blue-collar workers. For each of these workers, the income was known as well as the percentage of the work that was related to exportation. The regression slope estimate was 0.009, and the t-statistic value was 1.51.[8] Carefully interpret and explain these findings.

10–43. An article in *Financial Analysts Journal* discusses results of a regression analysis of average price per share P on the independent variable X/k, where X/k is the contemporaneous earnings per share divided by firm-specific discount rate. The regression was run using a random sample of 213 firms listed in the *Value Line Investment Survey*. The reported results are

$$P = 16.67 + 0.68X/k(12.03)$$

where the number in parentheses is the standard error. Is there a linear relationship between the two variables?

10–44. A management recruiter wants to estimate a linear regression relationship between an executive's experience and the salary the executive may expect to earn after placement with an employer. From data on 28 executives, which are assumed to be a random sample from the population of executives that the recruiter places, the following regression results are obtained: $b_1 = 5.49$ and $s(b_1) = 1.21$. Is there a linear relationship between the experience and the salary of executives placed by the recruiter?

10–7 How Good Is the Regression?

Once we have determined that a linear relationship exists between the two variables, the question is: How strong is the relationship? If the relationship is a strong one, prediction of the dependent variable can be relatively accurate, and other conclusions drawn from the analysis may be given a high degree of confidence.

We have already seen one measure of the regression fit: the mean square error. The MSE is an estimate of the variance of the true regression errors and is a measure of the variation of the data about the regression line. The MSE, however, depends on the nature of the data, and what may be a large error variation in one situation may not be considered large in another. What we need, therefore, is a *relative* measure of the degree of variation of the data about the regression line. Such a measure allows us to compare the fits of different models.

The relative measure we are looking for is a measure that compares the variation of Y about the regression line with the variation of Y without a regression line. This should remind you of analysis of variance, and we will soon see the relation of ANOVA to regression analysis. It turns out that the relative measure of regression fit

---

[8]Thorsten Schank, Claus Schnabel, and Joachim Wagner, "Do Exporters Really Pay Higher Wages? First Evidence from German Linked Employer–Employee Data," *Journal of International Economics* 72 (May 2007), pp. 52–74.

FIGURE 10–21   The Three Deviations Associated with a Data Point

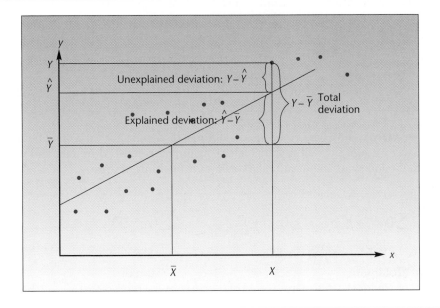

we are looking for is the square of the estimated correlation coefficient r. It is called the *coefficient of determination*.

> The **coefficient of determination r^2** is a descriptive measure of the strength of the regression relationship, a measure of how well the regression line fits the data.

The coefficient of determination r^2 is an estimator of the corresponding population parameter ρ^2, which is the square of the population coefficient of correlation between two variables X and Y. Usually, however, we use r^2 as a descriptive statistic—a relative measure of how well the regression line fits the data. Ordinarily, we do not use r^2 for inference about ρ^2.

We will now see how the coefficient of determination is obtained directly from a decomposition of the variation in Y into a component due to error and a component due to the regression. Figure 10–21 shows the least-squares line that was fit to a data set. One of the data points (x, y) is highlighted. For this data point, the figure shows three kinds of deviations: the deviation of y from its mean $y - \bar{y}$, the deviation of y from its predicted value using the regression $y - \hat{y}$, and the deviation of the regression-predicted value of y from the mean of y, which is $\hat{y} - \bar{y}$. Note that the least-squares line passes through the point $(\bar{x}, \bar{y})$.

We will now follow exactly the same mathematical derivation we used in Chapter 9 when we derived the ANOVA relationships. There we looked at the deviation of a data point from its respective group mean—the error; here the error is the deviation of a data point from its regression-predicted value. In ANOVA, we also looked at the total deviation, the deviation of a data point from the grand mean; here we have the deviation of the data point from the mean of Y. Finally, in ANOVA we also considered the treatment deviation, the deviation of the group mean from the grand mean; here we have the *regression deviation*—the deviation of the predicted value from the mean of Y.

The error is also called the *unexplained deviation* because it is a deviation that cannot be explained by the regression relationship; the regression deviation is also called the *explained deviation* because it is that part of the deviation of a data point from the mean that can be explained by the regression relationship between X and Y. We *explain* why the Y value of a particular data point is above the mean of Y by the fact that its X component

CHAPTER 15

happens to be above the mean of X and by the fact that X and Y are linearly (and positively) related. As can be seen from Figure 10–21, and by simple arithmetic, we have

$$
\begin{array}{ccccc}
y - \overline{y} & = & y - \hat{y} & + & \hat{y} - \overline{y} \\
\text{Total} & = & \text{Unexplained} & + & \text{Explained} \\
\text{deviation} & & \text{deviation (error)} & & \text{deviation (regression)}
\end{array} \quad (10\text{--}28)
$$

As in the analysis of variance, we square all three deviations for each one of our data points, and we sum over all n points. Here, again, cross-terms drop out, and we are left with the following important relationship for the sums of squares:[9]

$$
\begin{array}{ccccc}
\displaystyle\sum_{i=1}^{n}(y_i - \overline{y})^2 & = & \displaystyle\sum_{i=1}^{n}(y_i - \hat{y}_i)^2 & + & \displaystyle\sum_{i=1}^{n}(\hat{y}_i - \overline{y})^2 \\
\text{SST} & = & \text{SSE} & + & \text{SSR} \\
\text{(Total sum} & & \text{(Sum of} & & \text{(Sum of} \\
\text{of squares)} & = & \text{squares for error)} & + & \text{squares for regression)}
\end{array} \quad (10\text{--}29)
$$

The term SSR is also called the *explained variation;* it is the part of the variation in Y that is explained by the relationship of Y with the explanatory variable X. Similarly, SSE is the *unexplained variation,* due to error; the sum of the two is the *total variation* in Y.

We define the coefficient of determination as the sum of squares due to the regression divided by the total sum of squares. Since by equation 10–29 SSE and SSR add to SST, the coefficient of determination is equal to 1 minus SSE/SST. We have

$$
r^2 = \frac{\text{SSR}}{\text{SST}} = 1 - \frac{\text{SSE}}{\text{SST}} \quad (10\text{--}30)
$$

The coefficient of determination can be interpreted as *the proportion of the variation in Y that is explained by the regression relationship of* Y *with* X.

Recall that the correlation coefficient r can be between -1 and 1. Its square, r^2, can therefore be anywhere from 0 to 1. This is in accordance with the interpretation of r^2 as the *percentage of the variation in* Y *explained by the regression.* The coefficient is a measure of how closely the regression line fits the data; it is a measure of how much the variation in the values of Y is reduced once we regress Y on variable X. When $r^2 = 1$, we know that 100% of the variation in Y is explained by X. This means that the data all lie right on the regression line, and no errors result (because, from equation 10–30, SSE must be equal to zero). Since r^2 cannot be negative, we do not know whether the line slopes upward or downward (the direction can be found from b_1 or r), but we know that the line gives a *perfect fit* to the data. Such cases do not occur in business or economics. In fact, when there are no errors, no natural variation, there is no need for statistics.

At the other extreme is the case where the regression line explains nothing. Here the errors account for everything, and SSR is zero. In this case, we see from equation 10–30 that $r^2 = 0$. In such cases, X and Y have no linear relationship, and the true regression slope is probably zero (we say *probably* because r^2 is only an estimator, given to chance variation; it could possibly be estimating a nonzero ρ^2). Between the two cases $r^2 = 0$ and $r^2 = 1$ are values of r^2 that give an indication of the *relative fit* of the regression model to the data. *The higher* r^2 *is, the better the fit and the higher our confidence*

---

[9]The proof of the relation is left as an exercise for the mathematically interested reader.

in the regression. Be wary, however, of situations where the reported r^2 is exceptionally high, such as 0.99 or 0.999. In such cases, something may be wrong. We will see an example of this in the next chapter. Incidentally, in the context of multiple regression, discussed in the next chapter, we will use the notation R^2 for the coefficient of determination to indicate that the relationship is based on several explanatory X variables.

How high should the coefficient of determination be before we can conclude that a regression model fits the data well enough to use the regression with confidence? This question has no clear-cut answer. The answer depends on the intended use of the regression model. If we intend to use the regression for *prediction,* the higher the r^2, the more accurate will be our predictions.

An r^2 value of 0.9 or more is very good, a value greater than 0.8 is good, and a value of 0.6 or more may be satisfactory in some applications, although we must be aware of the fact that, in such cases, errors in prediction may be relatively high. When the r^2 value is 0.5 or less, the regression explains only 50% or less of the variation in the data; therefore, predictions may be poor. If we are interested only in understanding the relationship between the variables, lower values of r^2 may be acceptable, as long as we realize that the model does not explain much.

Figure 10–22 shows several regressions and their corresponding r^2 values. If you think of the total sum of squared deviations as being in a box, then r^2 is the proportion of the box that is filled with the explained sum of squares, the remaining part being the squared errors. This is shown for each regression in the figure.

Computing r^2 is easy if we express SSR, SSE, and SST in terms of the computational sums of squares and cross-products (equations 10–9):

$$\text{SST} = \text{SS}_Y \qquad \text{SSR} = b_1\text{SS}_{XY} \qquad \text{SSE} = \text{SS}_Y - b_1\text{SS}_{XY} \qquad (10\text{–}31)$$

We will now use equation 10–31 in computing the coefficient of determination for Example 10–1. For this example, we have

$$\text{SST} = \text{SS}_Y = 66{,}855{,}898$$
$$\text{SSR} = b_1\text{SS}_{XY} = (1.255333776)(51{,}402{,}852.4) = 64{,}527{,}736.8$$

and

$$\text{SSE} = \text{SST} - \text{SSR} = 2{,}328{,}161.2$$

(These were computed when we found the MSE for this example.) We now compute r^2 as

$$r^2 = \frac{\text{SSR}}{\text{SST}} = \frac{64{,}527{,}736.8}{66{,}855{,}898} = 0.96518$$

The r^2 in this example is very high. The interpretation is that over 96.5% of the variation in charges on the American Express card can be explained by the relationship between charges on the card and extent of travel (miles). Again we note that while the computational formulas are easy to use, r^2 is always reported in a prominent place in regression computer output.

FIGURE 10–22   Value of the Coefficient of Determination in Different Regressions

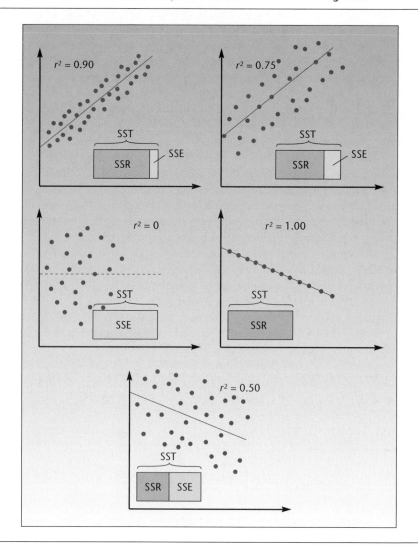

In the next section, we will see how the sums of squares, along with the corresponding degrees of freedom, lead to mean squares—and to an analysis of variance in the context of regression. In closing this section, we note that in Chapter 11, we will introduce an adjusted coefficient of determination that accounts for degrees of freedom.

PROBLEMS

10–45.   In problem 10–36, the coefficient of determination was found to be $r^2 = 0.09$.[10] What can you say about this regression, as far as its power to predict customer satisfaction with sunglasses using information on a customer's materialism score?

---

[10]Jeff Wang and Melanie Wallendorf, "Materialism, Status Signaling, and Product Satisfaction," *Journal of the Academy of Marketing* 34, no. 4 (2006), pp. 494–505.

10–46. Results of a study reported in *Financial Analysts Journal* include a simple linear regression analysis of firms' pension funding (Y) versus profitability (X). The regression coefficient of determination is reported to be $r^2 = 0.02$. (The sample size used is 515.)

   a. Would you use the regression model to predict a firm's pension funding?

   b. Does the model explain much of the variation in firms' pension funding on the basis of profitability?

   c. Do you believe these regression results are worth reporting? Explain.

10–47. What percentage of the variation in percent growth in wealth is explained by the regression in problem 10–11?

10–48. What is r^2 in the regression of problem 10–13? Interpret its meaning.

10–49. What is r^2 in the regression of problem 10–16?

10–50. What is r^2 for the regression in problem 10–17? Explain its meaning.

10–51. A financial regression analysis was carried out to estimate the linear relationship between long-term bond yields and the yield spread, a problem of significance in finance. The sample sizes were 242 monthly observations in each of five countries, and the results were the obtained regression r^2 values for these countries. The results were as follows.[11]

Canada	Germany	Japan	U.K.	U.S.
5.9%	13.3%	3.5%	31.7%	3.3%

Assuming that all five linear regressions were statistically significant, comment on and interpret the reported r^2 values.

10–52. Analysts assessed the effects of bond ratings on bond yields. They reported a regression with $r^2 = 61.56\%$, which, they said, confirmed the economic intuition that predicted higher yields for bonds with lower ratings (by economic theory, an investor would require a higher expected yield for investing in a riskier bond). The conclusion was that, on average, each notch down in rating added an approximate 14.6 basis points to the bond's yield.[12] How accurate is this prediction?

10–53. Find r^2 for the regression in problem 10–15.

10–54. (A mathematically demanding problem) Starting with equation 10–28, derive equation 10–29.

10–55. Using equation 10–31 for SSR, show that $\text{SSR} = (\text{SS}_{XY})^2/\text{SS}_X$.

10–8 Analysis-of-Variance Table and an *F* Test of the Regression Model

We know from our discussion of the *t* test for the existence of a linear relationship that the degrees of freedom for *error* in simple linear regression are $n - 2$. For the *regression,* we have 1 degree of freedom because there is one independent *X* variable in the regression. The *total* degrees of freedom are $n - 1$ because here we only consider the mean of *Y*, to which 1 degree of freedom is lost. These are similar to the degrees of freedom for ANOVA in the last chapter. Mean squares are obtained, as usual, by dividing the sums of squares by their corresponding degrees of freedom. This gives us the mean square regression (MSR) and mean square error (MSE), which we encountered earlier. Further dividing MSR by MSE gives us an *F* ratio

CHAPTER 15

[11]Huarong Tang and Yihong Xia, "An International Examination of Affine Term Structure Models and the Expectations Hypothesis," *Journal of Financial and Quantitative Analysis* 42, no. 1 (2007), pp. 111–180.

[12]William H. Beaver, Catherine Shakespeare, and Mark T. Soliman, "Differential Properties in the Ratings of Certified versus Non-Certified Bond-Rating Agencies," *Journal of Accounting sind Economics* 42 (December 2006), pp. 303–334.

TABLE 10–4 ANOVA Table for Regression

Source of Variation	Sum of Squares	Degrees of Freedom	Mean Square	F Ratio
Regression	SSR	1	$MSR = \dfrac{SSR}{1}$	$F_{(1,\,n-2)} = \dfrac{MSR}{MSE}$
Error	SSE	$n-2$	$MSE = \dfrac{SSE}{n-2}$	
Total	SST	$n-1$		

TABLE 10–5 ANOVA Table for American Express Example

Source of Variation	Sum of Squares	Degrees of Freedom	Mean Square	F Ratio	p
Regression	64,527,736.8	1	64,527,736.8	637.47	0.000
Error	2,328,161.2	23	101,224.4		
Total	66,855,898.0	24			

with degrees of freedom 1 and $n-2$. All these can be put in an ANOVA table for regression. This has been done in Table 10–4.

In regression, three sources of variation are possible (see Figure 10–21): *regression*—the explained variation; *error*—the unexplained variation; and their sum, the *total* variation. We know how to obtain the sums of squares and the degrees of freedom, and from them the mean squares. Dividing the mean square regression by the mean square error should give us another measure of the accuracy of our regression because MSR is the average squared explained deviation and MSE is the average squared error (where averaging is done using the appropriate degrees of freedom). The ratio of the two has an F distribution with 1 and $n-2$ degrees of freedom *when there is no regression relationship between* X *and* Y. This suggests an F test for the existence of a linear relationship between X and Y. *In simple linear regression, this test is equivalent to the* t *test.* In multiple regression, as we will see in the next chapter, the F test serves a general role, and separate t tests are used to evaluate the significance of different variables. In simple linear regression, we may conduct either an F test or a t test; the results of the two tests will be the same. The hypothesis test is as given in equation 10–25; the test is carried on the right tail of the F distribution with 1 and $n-2$ degrees of freedom. We illustrate the analysis with data from Example 10–1. The ANOVA results are given in Table 10–5.

To carry out the test for the existence of a linear relationship between miles traveled and dollars charged on the card, we compare the computed F ratio of 637.47 with a critical point of the F distribution with 1 degree of freedom for the numerator and 23 degrees of freedom for the denominator. Using $\alpha = 0.01$, the critical point from Appendix C, Table 5, is found to be 7.88. Clearly, the computed value is far in the rejection region, and the p-value is very small. We conclude, again, that there is evidence of a linear relationship between the two variables.

Recall from Chapter 8 that an F distribution with 1 degree of freedom for the numerator and k degrees of freedom for the denominator is the *square* of a t distribution with k degrees of freedom. In Example 10–1 our computed F statistic value is 637.47, which is the square of our obtained t statistic 25.25 (to within rounding error). The same relationship holds for the critical points: for $\alpha = 0.01$, we have a critical point for $F_{(1,\,23)}$ equal to 7.88, and the (right-hand) critical point of a two-tailed test at $\alpha = 0.01$ for t with 23 degrees of freedom is $2.807 = \sqrt{7.88}$.

10–56. Conduct the F test for the existence of a linear relationship between the two variables in problem 10–11.

10–57. Carry out an F test for a linear relationship in problem 10–13. Compare your results with those of the t test.

10–58. Repeat problem 10–57 for the data of problem 10–17.

10–59. Conduct an F test for the existence of a linear relationship in the case of problem 10–15.

10–60. In a regression, the F statistic value is 6.3. Assume the sample size used was $n = 104$, and conduct an F test for the existence of a linear relationship between the two variables.

10–61. In a simple linear regression analysis, it is found that $b_1 = 2.556$ and $s(b_1) = 4.122$. The sample size is $n = 22$. Conduct an F test for the existence of a linear relationship between the two variables.

10–62. (A mathematically demanding problem) Using the definition of the t statistic in terms of sums of squares, prove (in the context of simple linear regression) that $t^2 = F$.

10–9 Residual Analysis and Checking for Model Inadequacies

Recall our discussion of statistical models in Section 10–1. We said that a good statistical model accounts for the systematic movement in the process, leaving out a series of uncorrelated, purely random errors ϵ, which are assumed to be normally distributed with mean zero and a constant variance σ^2. In Figure 10–3, we saw a general methodology for statistical model building, consisting of model identification, estimation, tests of validity, and, finally, use of the model. We are now at the third stage of the analysis of a simple linear regression model: examining the residuals and testing the validity of the model.

Analysis of the residuals could reveal whether the assumption of normally distributed errors holds. In addition, the analysis could reveal whether the variance of the errors is indeed constant, that is, whether the spread of the data around the regression line is uniform. The analysis could also indicate whether there are any missing variables that should have been included in our model (leading to a multiple regression equation). The analysis may reveal whether the order of data collection (e.g., time of observation) has any effect on the data and whether the order should have been incorporated as a variable in the model. Finally, analysis of the residuals may determine whether the assumption that the errors are uncorrelated is satisfied. A test of this assumption, the Durbin-Watson test, entails more than a mere examination of the model residuals, and discussion of this test is postponed until the next chapter. We now describe some graphical methods for the examination of the model residuals that may lead to discovery of model inadequacies.

A Check for the Equality of Variance of the Errors

A graph of the regression errors, the residuals, versus the independent variable X, or versus the predicted values $\hat{Y}$, will reveal whether the variance of the errors is constant. The variance of the residuals is indicated by the width of the scatter plot of the residuals as X increases. If the width of the scatter plot of the residuals either increases or decreases as X increases, then the assumption of constant variance is not met. This problem is called

FIGURE 10–23   A Residual Plot Indicating Heteroscedasticity

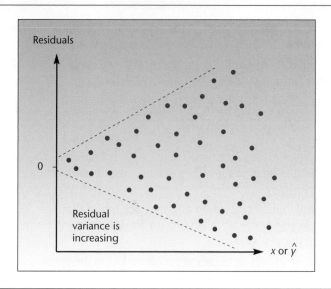

FIGURE 10–24   A Residual Plot Indicating No Heteroscedasticity

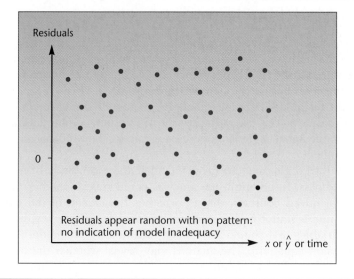

heteroscedasticity. When heteroscedasticity exists, we cannot use the ordinary least-squares method for estimating the regression and should use a more complex method, called *generalized least squares*. Figure 10–23 shows how a plot of the residuals versus X or $\hat{Y}$ looks in the case of heteroscedasticity. Figure 10–24 shows a residual plot in a good regression, with no heteroscedasticity.

Testing for Missing Variables

Figure 10–24 also shows how the residuals should look when plotted against time (or the order in which data are collected). No trend should be seen in the residuals when plotted versus time. A linear trend in the residuals plotted versus time is shown in Figure 10–25.

FIGURE 10–25   A Residual Plot Indicating a Trend with Time

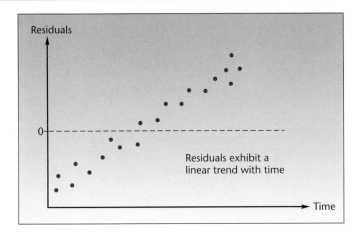

If the residuals exhibit a pattern when plotted versus time, then time should be incorporated as an explanatory variable in the model in addition to X. The same is true for any other variable against which we may plot the residuals: If any trend appears in the plot, the variable should be included in our model along with X. Incorporating additional variables leads to a multiple regression model.

Detecting a Curvilinear Relationship between Y and X

If the relationship between X and Y is curved, "forcing" a straight line to fit the data will result in a poor fit. This is shown in Figure 10–26. In this case, the residuals are at first large and negative, then decrease, become positive, and again become negative. The residuals are not random and independent; they show curvature. This pattern appears in a plot of the residuals versus X, shown in Figure 10–27.

The situation can be corrected by adding the variable X^2 to the model. This also entails the techniques of multiple regression analysis. We note that, in cases where we have repeated Y observations at some levels of X, there is a statistical test for model lack of fit such as that shown in Figure 10–26. The test entails

VS

CHAPTER 18

FIGURE 10–26   Results of Forcing a Straight Line to Fit a Curved Data Set

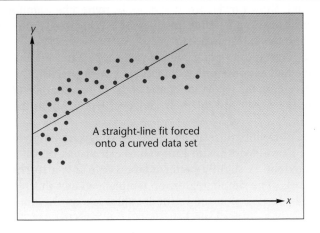

FIGURE 10–27   Resulting Pattern of the Residuals When a Straight Line Is Forced to Fit a Curved Data Set

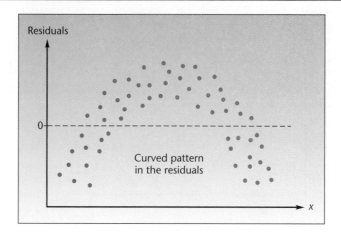

decomposing the sum of squares for error into a component due to lack of fit and a component due to pure error. This gives rise to an F test for lack of fit. This test is described in advanced texts. We point out, however, that examination of the residuals is an excellent tool for detecting such model deficiencies, and this simple technique does not require the special data format needed for the formal test.

The Normal Probability Plot

One of the assumptions in the regression model is that the errors are normally distributed. This assumption is necessary for calculating prediction intervals and for hypothesis tests about the regression. One of several ways to test for the normality of the residuals is to plot a histogram of the residuals and visually observe whether the shape of the histogram is close to the shape of a normal distribution. To do this we can use the histogram template, Histogram.xls, from Chapter 1, shown in Figure 10–28.

Let us plot the histogram for the residuals in the American Express study (Example 10–1) seen in Figure 10–13. First we copy the residuals from column D and paste them (using the Paste Special command and choosing "values" only to be pasted) into the data area (column Y) of the histogram template. We then enter suitable Start, Interval Width, and End values, which in this case could be −600, 100, and 600. The resulting histogram, shown in Figure 10–28, looks more like a uniform distribution than like a normal distribution. But this is only a visual test rather than a formal hypothesis test, and therefore we do not get a p-value for this test. In Chapter 14, we will see a formal χ^2 test for normality, which yields a p-value and thus can be used to possibly reject the null hypothesis that the residuals are normally distributed. Coming back to the histogram, to the extent the shape of the histogram deviates from the normal distribution, the prediction intervals and t or F tests about the regression are questionable.

Checking the normality of residuals using a histogram may work, but a wrong choice of Start, Interval Width, and End values can distort the shape of the distribution to some extent. A slightly better method to use is a **normal probability plot** of the residuals. The simple regression template creates this plot automatically (see Figure 10–14). In this plot, the residual values are on the horizontal axis and

FIGURE 10–28   A Histogram of the Residuals

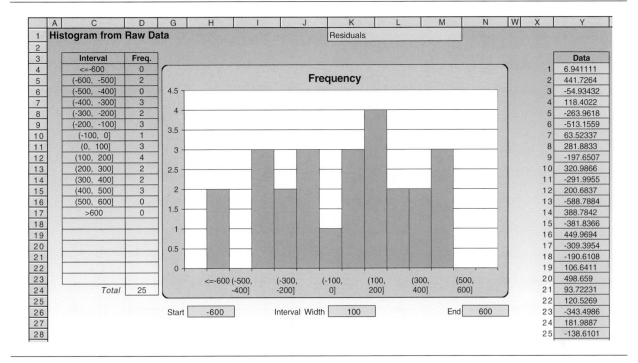

the corresponding z values from the normal distribution are on the vertical axis. If the residuals are normal, then they should align themselves along the straight line that appears on the plot. To the extent the points deviate from this straight line, the residuals deviate from a normal distribution. Note that this also is only a visual test and does not provide a p-value. In Figure 10–14, the points do deviate from the straight line, causing some concern and confirming what we saw in the histogram.

The normal probability plot is constructed as follows. For each value e of the residual, its quartile (cumulative probability) is calculated using the equation

$$q = \frac{l + 1 + m/2}{n + 1}$$

where l is the number of residuals less than e, m is the number of residuals equal to e, and n is the total number of observations. Then the z value corresponding to the quartile q, denoted by z_q, is calculated. A point with this z_q on the vertical axis and e on the horizontal axis is plotted. This process is repeated, with one point plotted for each observation. The diagonal straight line is drawn by connecting 3 standard deviations on either side of zero both on vertical and horizontal axes.

It is useful to recognize different nonnormal cases on a normal probability plot. Figure 10–29 shows four different patterns of lines along which the points will align. Figure 10–30 shows a case where the residuals are clearly nonnormal. From the pattern of the points we can infer that the distribution of the residuals is flatter than the normal distribution.

FIGURE 10–29   Patterns of Nonnormal Distributions on the Normal Probability Plot

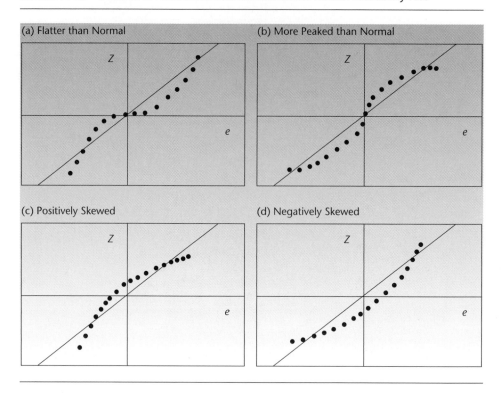

FIGURE 10–30   Distribution of the Residuals Is Flatter Than Normal

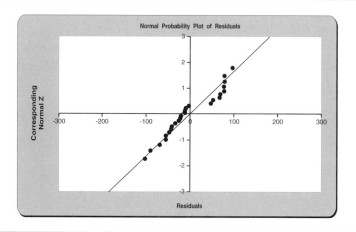

PROBLEMS

10–63. For each of the following plots of regression residuals versus X, state whether there is any indication of model inadequacy; if so, identify the inadequacy.

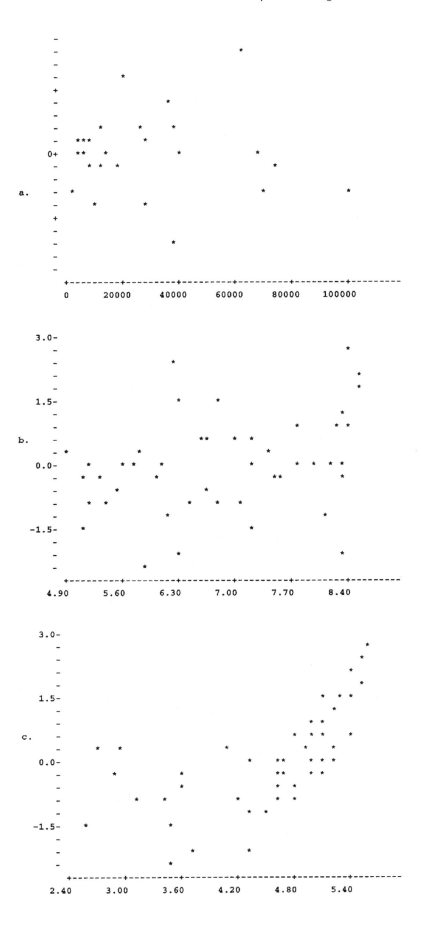

10–64. In the following plots of the residuals versus time of observation, state whether there is evidence of model inadequacy. How would you correct any inadequacy?

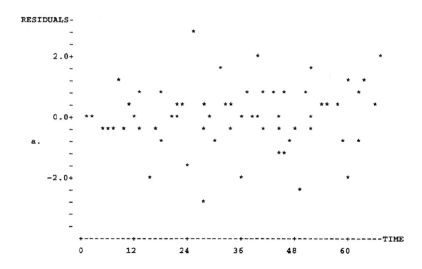

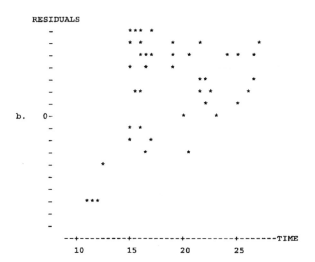

10-65. Is there any indication of model inadequacy in the following plots of residuals on a normal probability scale?

a.

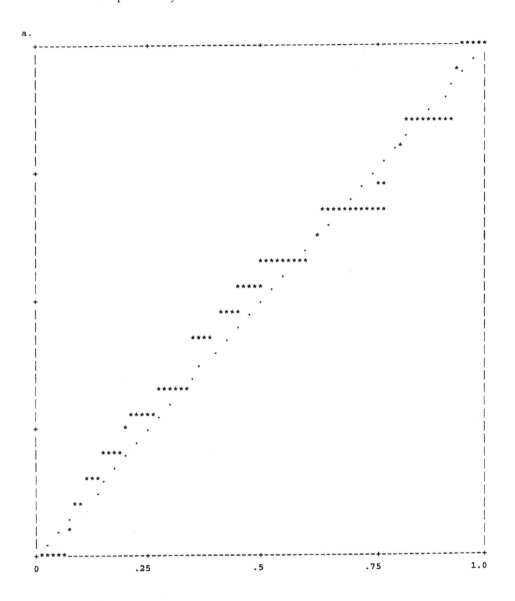

b.

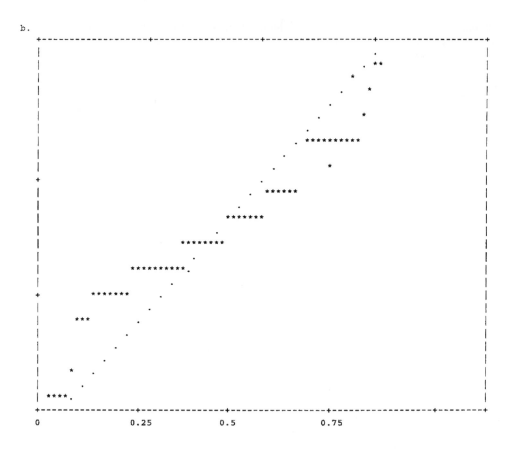

10–66. Produce residual plots for the regression of problem 10–11. Is there any apparent model inadequacy?

10–67. Repeat problem 10–66 for the regression of problem 10–13.

10–68. Repeat problem 10–66 for the regression of problem 10–16.

10–10   Use of the Regression Model for Prediction

CHAPTER 15

As mentioned in the first section of this chapter, a regression model has several possible uses. One is to understand the relationship between the two variables. As with correlation analysis, understanding a relationship between two variables in regression does not imply that one variable causes the other. Causality is a much more complicated issue and cannot be determined by a simple regression analysis.

A more frequent use of a regression analysis is *prediction*: providing estimates of values of the dependent variable by using the prediction equation $\hat{Y} = b_0 + b_1X$. It is important that prediction be done in the region of the data used in the estimation process. *You should be aware that using a regression for extrapolating outside the estimation range is risky, as the estimated relationship may not be appropriate outside this range.* This is demonstrated in Figure 10–31.

Point Predictions

Producing point predictions using the estimated regression equation is very easy. All we need to do is to substitute the value of X for which we want to predict Y into the prediction equation. In Example 10–1 suppose that American Express wants to

FIGURE 10–31   The Danger of Extrapolation

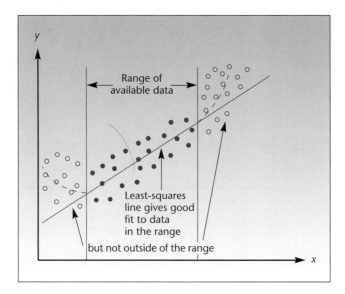

predict charges on the card for a member who traveled 4,000 miles during a period equal to the one studied (note that $x = 4,000$ is in the range of X values used in the estimation). We use the prediction equation, equation 10–12, but with greater accuracy for b_1:

$$\hat{y} = 274.85 + 1.2553x = 274.85 + 1.2553(4,000) = 5,296.05 \text{ (dollars)}$$

The process of prediction in this example is demonstrated in Figure 10–32.

Prediction Intervals

Point predictions are not perfect and are subject to error. The error is due to the uncertainty in estimation as well as the natural variation of points about the regression line. A $(1 - \alpha)$ 100% prediction interval for Y is given in equation 10–32.

A $(1 - \alpha)$ 100% prediction interval for Y is

$$\hat{y} \pm t_{\alpha/2}\, s \sqrt{1 + \frac{1}{n} + \frac{(x - \bar{x})^2}{SS_X}} \qquad (10\text{–}32)$$

As can be seen from the formula, the width of the interval depends on the distance of our value x (for which we wish to predict Y) from the mean $\bar{x}$. This is shown in Figure 10–33.

We will now use equation 10–32 to compute a 95% prediction interval for the amount charged on the American Express card by a member who traveled 4,000 miles. We know that in this example $\bar{x} = \Sigma x/n = 79,448/25 = 3,177.92$. We also know

FIGURE 10–32   Prediction in American Express Study

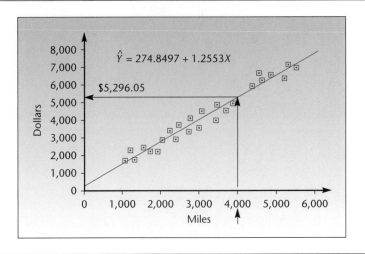

FIGURE 10–33   Prediction Band and Its Width

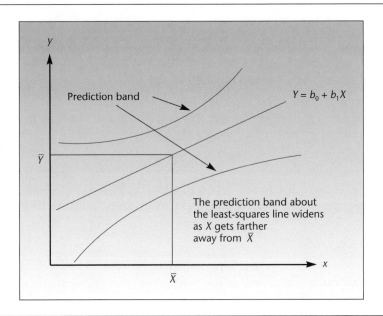

that $SS_X = 40{,}947{,}557.84$ and $s = 318.16$. From Appendix C, Table 3, we get the critical point for t with 23 degrees of freedom: 2.069. Applying equation 10–32, we get

$$5{,}296.05 \pm (2.069)(318.16)\sqrt{1 + 1/25 + (4{,}000 - 3{,}177.92)^2/40{,}947{,}577.84}$$
$$= 5{,}296.05 \pm 676.62 = [4{,}619.43, 5{,}972.67]$$

Based on the validity of the study, we are 95% confident that a cardholder who traveled 4,000 miles during a period of the given length will have charges on her or his card totaling anywhere from $4,619.43 to $5,972.67.

What about the *average* total charge of all cardholders who traveled 4,000 miles? This is $E(Y\,|\,x = 4{,}000)$. The point estimate of $E(Y\,|\,x = 4{,}000)$ is also equal to $\hat{Y}$, but the confidence interval for this quantity is different.

A Confidence Interval for the Average Y, Given a Particular Value of X

We may compute a confidence interval for $E(Y\,|\,X)$, the expected value of Y for a given X. Here the variation is smaller because we are dealing with the average Y for a given X, rather than a particular Y. Thus, the confidence interval is narrower than a prediction interval of the same confidence level. The confidence interval for $E(Y\,|\,X)$ is given in equation 10–33:

A $(1 - \alpha)$ 100% confidence interval for $E(Y\,|\,X)$ is

$$\hat{y} \pm t_{\alpha/2}\, s \sqrt{\frac{1}{n} + \frac{(x - \bar{x})^2}{SS_X}} \qquad (10\text{--}33)$$

The confidence band for $E(Y\,|\,X)$ around the regression line looks like Figure 10–33 except that the band is narrower. The standard error of the estimator of the conditional mean $E(Y\,|\,X)$ is smaller than the standard error of the predicted Y. Therefore, the 1 is missing from the square root quantity in equation 10–33 as compared with equation 10–32.

For the American Express example, let us now compute a 95% confidence interval for $E(Y\,|\,x = 4{,}000)$. Applying equation 10–33, we have

$$5{,}296.05 \pm (2.069)(318.16)\sqrt{1/25 + (4{,}000 - 3{,}177.92)^2/40{,}947{,}557.84}$$
$$= 5{,}296.05 \pm 156.48 = [5{,}139.57,\ 5{,}452.53]$$

Being a confidence interval for a conditional mean, the interval is much narrower than the prediction interval, which has the same confidence level for covering *any given* observation at the level of X.

PROBLEMS

10–69. For the American Express example, give a 95% prediction interval for the amount charged by a member who traveled 5,000 miles. Compare the result with the one for $x = 4{,}000$ miles.

10–70. In problem 10–52, if the rating for a bond falls by three levels, how much higher must be its yield?

10–71. For problem 10–69, give a 99% prediction interval.

10–72. For problem 10–11, give a point prediction and a 99% prediction interval for wealth growth when the income quartile is 5.

10–73. For problem 10–72, give a 99% prediction interval for wealth growth when the income quartile is 5.

10–74. For problem 10–16, give a 95% prediction interval for the present value when the model is from the 1990s.

10–75. For problem 10–16, give a 95% prediction interval for the present value when the model is from the 2000s.

10–76. For problem 10–15 predict the total return on stocks when the inflation rate is 5%.

10–11   Using the Computer

The Excel Solver Method for Regression

The Solver macro available in Excel can also be used to conduct a simple linear regression. The advantage of using this method is that additional constraints can be imposed on the slope and the intercept. For instance, if we want the intercept to be a particular value, or if we want to force the regression line to go through a desired point, we can do that by imposing appropriate constraints. As an example, suppose we are regressing the weight of a certain amount of a chemical against its volume (in order to find the average density). We know that when the volume is zero, the weight should be zero. This means the intercept for the regression line must be zero. We can impose this as a constraint, if we use the Solver method, and be assured that the intercept will be zero. The slope obtained with the constraint can be quite different from the slope obtained without the constraint.

As another example, consider a common type of regression carried out in the area of finance. The risk of a stock (or any capital asset) is measured by regressing its returns against the market return (which is the average return from all the assets in the market) during the same period. The Capital Asset Pricing Model (CAPM) stipulates that when the market return equals the risk-free interest rate (such as the interest rate of short-term Treasury bills), the stock will also return the same amount. In other words, if the market return = risk-free interest rate = 7%, then the stock's return, according to the CAPM, will also be 7%. This means that according to the CAPM, the regression line must pass through the point (7, 7). This can be imposed as a constraint in the Solver method of regression.

Note that forcing a regression line through the origin, (0, 0), is the same as forcing the intercept to equal zero, and forcing the line through the point (0, 5) is the same as forcing the intercept to equal 5.

The criterion for the line of best fit by the Solver method is still the same as before—minimize the sum of squared errors (SSE).

A limitation of this method is that we cannot find confidence intervals for the regression coefficients or prediction intervals for Y. All we get is the constrained line of best fit and point predictions based on that line. Also, we cannot conduct hypothesis tests about the regression, because we are deviating from the model assumptions given in equation 10–3. In particular, the errors may not be normally distributed.

We shall see the use of this method through an example.

EXAMPLE 10–5

A certain fuel produced by a chemical company varies in its composition and therefore in its density. The average density of the fuel is to be determined for engineering purposes. Rather than take the average of all the densities observed, it was decided to estimate the density through regression, thus minimizing SSE. Different amounts of the fuel were sampled at different times and the weights (in grams) and volumes (in cubic centimeters) were accurately measured. The results are in Figure 10–34.

1. Regress the weight against the volume and find the regression equation. Predict the weight when the volume is 7 cm³.

2. Force the regression line through the origin and find the regression line that minimizes SSE. What is the new regression equation? What is the density implied by this regression equation? Predict the weight when the volume is 7 cm³.

FIGURE 10–34 **The Template for Using the Solver for Regression [Simple Regression.xls; Sheet: Solver]**

	Volume X	Weight Y	Error
1	6.23	7.75	0.1513
2	6.87	6.5	0.1207
3	5.54	6.85	0.0929
4	5.9	6.78	-0.4162
5	6.45	8	0.1330
6	6.55	7.8	-0.1890
7	5.75	7.05	0.0368
8	6	7.35	0.0318
9	6.2	7.3	-0.2621
10	6.7	8	-0.1719
11	7	8.59	0.1521
12	7.23	8.86	0.0416
13	5.3	6.25	-0.2144
14	6.35	7.9	0.1549
15	7.15	8.96	0.2392

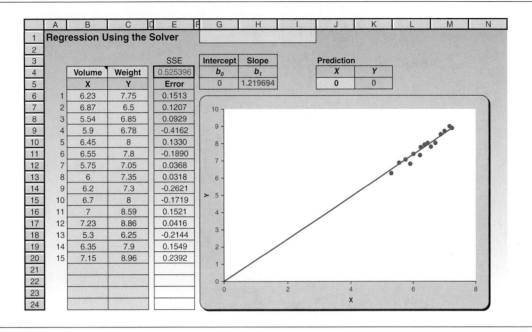

FIGURE 10–35 **The Add Constraint Dialog Box**

Solution

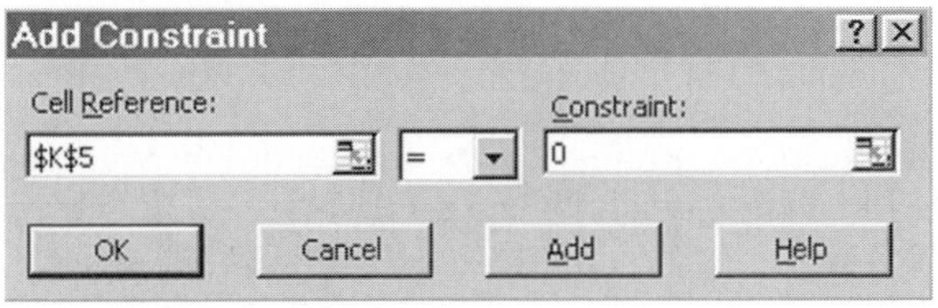

1. Without any constraint, the regression equation is $\hat{Y} = 1.352X - 0.847$ (obtained from the template for regular regression). For a volume of 7 cm^3, the predicted weight is 8.62 grams.
2. Use the template shown in Figure 10–34. Enter the data in columns B and C. Enter zero in cell J5. Choose the Solver command in the Analysis group on the Data tab. In the dialog box that appears, press the Add button. The dialog box shown in Figure 10–35 appears. In this Add Constraint dialog box, enter the constraint K5 = 0. Note the use of the drop-down box in the middle to choose the relationship. Press the OK button. The Solver dialog box appears again, as seen in Figure 10–36. Click the Solve button. When the problem is solved the dialog box shown in Figure 10–37 appears. Make sure Keep Solver Solution is selected. Click the OK button.

The result is seen in Figure 10–34. The intercept is zero, as expected, and the slope is 1.21969. Thus the new regression equation is $\hat{Y} = 1.21969X$. The average density implied by the equation is 1.21969 g/cm^3.

To get the predicted value for $X = 7$, enter 7 in cell J5. The predicted value of 8.53785 g appears in cell K5.

FIGURE 10–36　The Solver Dialog Box

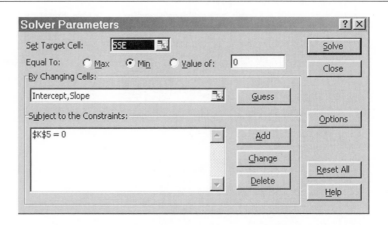

FIGURE 10–37　The Solver Results Dialog Box

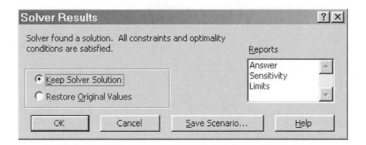

Several other types of constraints can be imposed. For example, we can impose the condition that the slope must be less than or equal to 10. We can even impose a condition that the slope must be numerically less than the intercept, although why we would want such a constraint is not clear. In any case, all constraints are entered using the dialog box seen in Figure 10–35. Some syntax rules must be followed when entering constraints in this dialog box. For example, the entry in the right-hand-side box of Figure 10–35 (0 in the figure) cannot be a formula, whereas the entry in the left-hand-side box ($K$5 in the figure) can be a formula such as 3*$K$5 + 6. Such details can be obtained from the help screens.

PROBLEMS

10–77.　Consider the following sample data of X and Y:

X	Y
8	22.30
6	16.71
9	25.21
6	15.84
1	2.75
8	21.22
2	5.27
1	2.32
10	27.39
7	19.35

    a. Regress *Y* against *X* without any constraints. What is the regression equation? Predict *Y* when *X* = 10.

    b. Force the regression line through the origin. What is the new regression equation? Predict *Y* when *X* = 10 with this equation.

    c. Force the regression line to go through the point (5, 13). What is the new regression line? What is the new regression equation? Predict *Y* when *X* = 10 with this equation.

    d. Regress *Y* against *X* with the constraint that the slope must be less than or equal to 2. What is the new regression equation? Predict *Y* when *X* = 10 with this equation.

10–78. Why would it be silly to force a regression line through two distinct points at the same time?

The Excel LINEST Function

The LINEST function available in Excel can be used to carry out a quick regression if you do not have access to the template for any reason. The following discussion explains the use of the function.

- Enter the data in columns B and C as shown in Figure 10–38.
- Select the range E5:F9. The area you select is going to contain the results. You need five rows and two columns for the results.
- Click the Insert Function in the Formulas tab.
- Select Statistical under Function Category. In the list of functions that appear at right, select LINEST.
- In the LINEST dialog box make the entries as follows (see Figure 10–38):
    - In the box for Known_y's, enter the range that contains the Y values.
    - In the box for Known_x's, enter the range that contains the X values.
    - Leave the Const box blank. Entering TRUE in that box will force the intercept to be zero. We don't need that.

FIGURE 10–38 Using the LINEST Function for Simple Regression

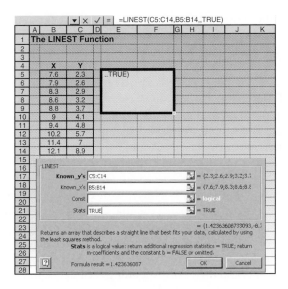

FIGURE 10–39   LINEST Output and Legend

	A	B	C	D	E	F	G	H	I
1	**The LINEST Function**								
2									
3									
4		**X**	**Y**		LINEST Output			Legend	
5		7.6	2.3		1.423636	-8.76252		b_1	b_0
6		7.9	2.6		0.062966	0.594093		$s(b_1)$	$s(b_0)$
7		8.3	2.9		0.984592	0.279761		r^2	s
8		8.6	3.2		511.2009	8		F	$df(SSE)$
9		8.8	3.7		40.00987	0.626131		SSR	SSE
10		9	4.1						
11		9.4	4.8						
12		10.2	5.7						
13		11.4	7						
14		12.1	8.9						

- *Keeping the CTRL and SHIFT keys pressed,* click the OK button. The reason for keeping the CTRL and SHIFT keys pressed is that the formula we are entering is an *array formula.* An array formula is simultaneously entered in a range of cells at once, and that range behaves as one cell. When an array formula is entered, Excel will add the { } braces around the formula.
- You should see the results seen in Figure 10–39.

Unfortunately, Excel does not label the results and therefore it is not immediately clear which result is where. A legend has been provided in Figure 10–39 for reference. If you do not have the legend, you may consult Excel help screens to see which result is where.

Looking at the results and the legend, you can see that the estimated slope $b_1 = 1.423636$, and the estimated intercept $b_0 = -8.76252$. Thus the regression equation is

$$\hat{Y} = -8.76252 + 1.423636X$$

In addition to the tools and functions mentioned above, Excel also provides a very useful and easy-to-use regression analysis tool that performs linear regression analysis by using the least-squares method to fit a line through a set of observations. This tool enables you to analyze how a single dependent variable is affected by the values of one or more independent variables. The Regression tool uses the worksheet function LINEST described earlier. To access these tools click **Data Analysis** in the Analysis group on the Data tab. In the Data Analysis window select **Regression**. The corresponding Regression window will appear as shown in Figure 10–40. Assuming you have your raw data of X and Y in a worksheet, you can define the range of Y and X in the input section. If the ranges contain the label of the X and Y columns, check **Label**. Define the desired confidence level that will be used to construct a confidence interval for all coefficients of the estimated model. Check the **Constant is Zero** check box if you wish to impose the constraint that the intercept is zero. Define the range of output in the next section. You can also get other statistics and graphs such as residual plot or probability plot by checking corresponding check boxes. Then click the OK button. The result will contain a summary output, ANOVA table, model coefficients and their corresponding confidence intervals, residuals, and related graphs as shown in Figure 10–41.

FIGURE 10-40 Using the Excel Regression Tool for a Simple Linear Regression

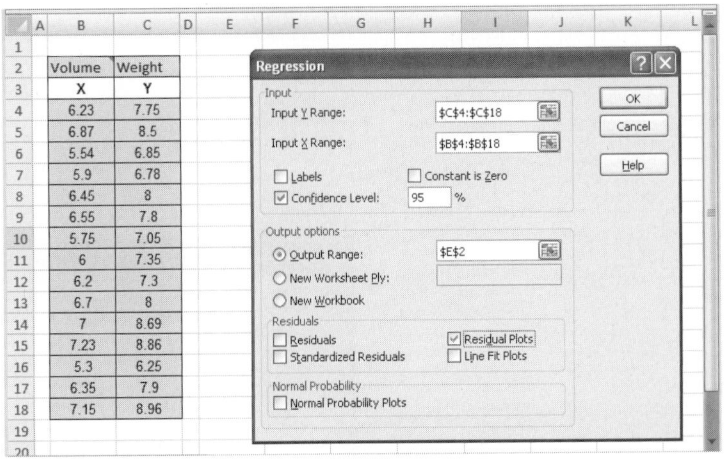

FIGURE 10-41 Excel Results for Simple Linear Regression

	B	C	D	E	F	G	H	I	J	K	L	M
2	Volume	Weight		SUMMARY OUTPUT								
3	X	Y										
4	6.23	7.75		*Regression Statistics*								
5	6.87	8.5		Multiple R	0.975561951							
6	5.54	6.85		R Square	0.95172112							
7	5.9	6.78		Adjusted R Square	0.94800736							
8	6.45	8		Standard Error	0.184266157							
9	6.55	7.8		Observations	15							
10	5.75	7.05										
11	6	7.35		ANOVA								
12	6.2	7.3			df	SS	MS	F	Significance F			
13	6.7	8		Regression	1	8.701357783	8.701358	256.2689	6.17069E-10			
14	7	8.69		Residual	13	0.441402217	0.033954					
15	7.23	8.86		Total	14	9.14276						
16	5.3	6.25										
17	6.35	7.9			Coefficients	Standard Error	t Stat	p-value	Lower 95%	Upper 95%	Lower 95.0%	Upper 95.0%
18	7.15	8.96		Intercept	-0.846543368	0.538234411	-1.57282	0.139775	-2.009328117	0.316241381	-2.009328117	0.316241381
19				X Variable 1	1.352007462	0.084456126	16.0084	6.17E-10	1.169551096	1.534463828	1.169551096	1.534463828
20												
21				RESIDUAL OUTPUT								
22				Observation	Predicted Y	Residuals						
23				1	7.57646312	0.17353688						
24				2	8.441747895	0.058252105						
25				3	6.643577971	0.206422029						
26				4	7.130300657	-0.350300657						
27				5	7.873904761	0.126095239						
28				6	8.009105507	-0.209105507						
29				7	6.927499538	0.122500462						
30				8	7.265501403	0.084498597						
31				9	7.535902896	-0.235902896						
32				10	8.211906627	-0.211906627						

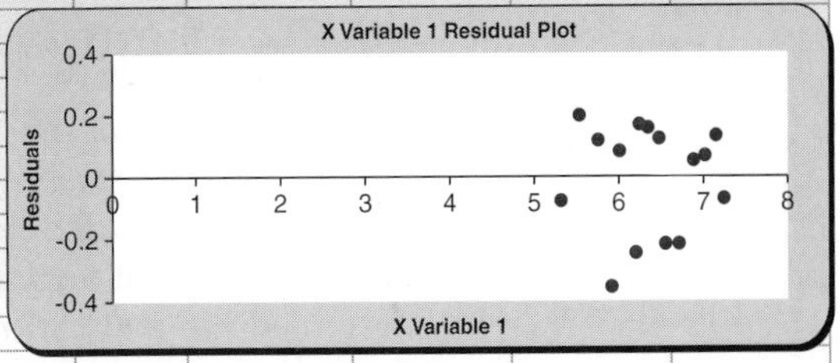

Using MINITAB for Simple Linear Regression Analysis

MINITAB enables you to perform simple linear regression using least squares. Choose Stat ▶ Regression ▶ Regression for fitting general least-squares models, storing regression statistics, examining residual diagnostics, generating point estimates, generating prediction and confidence intervals, and performing lack-of-fit tests. When the Regression dialog box appears, select the column containing the Y, or enter the response variable in the **Response** edit box. The column(s) containing the X,

FIGURE 10-42   Using MINITAB for Simple Regression Analysis

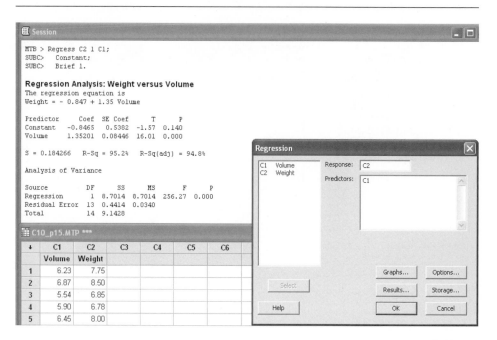

or predictor variable(s), are entered in the Predictors edit box. The Graphs button provides you with different plots such as residual plot or normal plot of residuals, which can be used for validating the assumptions of your analysis. The Options button enables you to define the desired confidence level for confidence intervals as well as prediction intervals of new observations. The Results button controls the level of detail in the display of output to the Session window. By clicking the Storage button you can set to store diagnostic measures and characteristics of the estimated regression equation such as residuals, coefficients, and fits. The result of using the MINITAB regression tool for the data set that was used in the previous example (Excel Regression Tool) appears in Figure 10-42.

10–12   Summary and Review of Terms

In this chapter, we introduced simple linear regression, a technique for estimating the straight-line relationship between two variables. We defined the **dependent variable** as the variable we wish to predict by, or understand the relation with, the **independent variable** (also called the **explanatory** or **predictor** variable). We described the **least-squares** estimation procedure as the procedure that produces the **best linear unbiased estimators (BLUE)** of the regression coefficients, the **slope** and **intercept** parameters. We learned how to conduct two statistical tests for the existence of a linear relationship between the two variables: the t test and the F test. We noted that in the case of simple linear regression, the two tests are equivalent. We saw how to evaluate the fit of the regression model by considering the **coefficient of determination r^2**. We learned how to check the validity of the assumptions of the simple linear regression model by examining the **residuals.** We saw how the regression model can be used for prediction. In addition, we discussed a linear **correlation** model. We saw that the correlation model is appropriate when the two variables are viewed in a symmetric role: both being normally distributed random variables, rather than one of them (X) being considered nonrandom, as in regression analysis.

10–79. A regression was carried out aimed at assessing the effect of the offer price of an initial public offering (IPO) on the chances of failure of the firm issuing the IPO over various time periods from the time of the offering (the maximum length of time being 5 years). The sample was of 2,058 firms, and the regression slope estimate was -0.051. The reported p-value was 0.034.[13] What was the standard error of the slope estimate? Interpret the findings.

10–80. A study was undertaken to find out whether neuroticism affected job performance. The slope estimate of the regression line was 0.16 and the r^2 was 0.19. The sample size was 151. The reported value of the statistical significance of the slope estimate was $p < 0.001$, two-tailed.[14] Interpret and discuss these findings. Does the degree of "neurosis" affect a worker's performance for the particular jobs studied in this research?

10–81. A regression analysis was performed to assess the impact of the perception of risk (credit card information theft, identity theft, etc.) on the frequency of online shopping. The estimated slope of the regression line of frequency of shopping versus level of perceived risk was found to be -0.233 and the standard error was 0.055. The sample size was 72.[15] Is there statistical evidence of a linear relationship between frequency of online shopping and the level of perceived risk?

10–82. The following data are operating income X and monthly stock close Y for Clorox, Inc. Graph the data. Then regress log Y on X.

X ($ millions): 240, 250, 260, 270, 280, 300, 310, 320, 330, 340, 350, 360, 370, 400, 410, 420, 430, 450

Y ($s): 45, 42, 44, 46, 47, 50, 48, 60, 61, 59, 67, 75, 74, 85, 95, 110, 125, 130

Predict Y for $X = 305$.

10–83. One of several simple linear regressions run to assess firms' stock performance based on the Capital Asset Pricing Model (CAPM) for firms with high ratios of cash flow to stock price was the following.[16]

Firm excess return = 0.95 + 0.92 Market excess return + Error

The standard error of the slope estimate was 0.01 and the sample size was 600 (50 years of monthly observations).

    a. Is this regression relationship statistically significant?

    b. If the market excess return is 1%, predict the excess return for a firm's stock.

10–84. A simple regression produces the regression equation $\hat{Y} = 5X + 7$.

    a. If we add 2 to all the X values in the data (and keep the Y values the same as the original), what will the new regression equation be?

    b. If we add 2 to all the Y values in the data (and keep the X values the same as the original), what will the new regression equation be?

    c. If we multiply all the X values in the data by 2 (and keep the Y values the same as the original), what will the new regression equation be?

    d. If we multiply all the Y values in the data by 2 (and keep the X values the same as the original), what will the new regression equation be?

---

[13]Elizabeth Demers and Philip Joos, "IPO Failure Risk," *Journal of Accounting Research* 45, no. 2 (2007), pp. 333–384.

[14]Eric A. Fong and Henry L. Tosi Jr., "Effort, Performance, and Conscientiousness: An Agency Theory Perspective," *Journal of Management* 33, no. 2 (2007), pp. 161–179.

[15]Hyun-Joo Lee and Patricia Huddleston, "Effects of E-Tailer and Product Type on Risk Handling in Online Shopping," *Journal of Marketing Channels* 13, no. 3 (2006), pp. 5–28.

[16]Martin Lettau and Jessica A. Wachter, "Why Is Long-Horizon Equity Less Risky? A Duration-Based Explanation of the Value Premium," *Journal of Finance* 62, no. 1 (2007), pp. 55–92.

10–85.   In a simple regression the regression equation is $\hat{Y} = 5X + 7$. Now if we interchange the X and Y data (that is, what was originally X is now Y and vice versa) and repeat the regression, we would expect the slope of the new regression line to be exactly equal to $1/5 = 0.2$. But the slope will only be approximately equal to 0.2 and almost never exactly equal to 0.2. Why?

10–86.   Regress Y against X with the following data from a random sample of 15 observations:

X	Y
12	100
4	60
10	96
15	102
6	68
4	70
13	102
11	92
10	95
18	125
20	134
22	133
8	87
20	122
11	101

a. What is the regression equation?

b. What is the 90% confidence interval for the slope?

c. Test the null hypothesis "X does not affect Y" at an α of 1%.

d. Test the null hypothesis "the slope is zero" at an α of 1%.

e. Make a point prediction of Y when $X = 10$.

f. Assume that the value of X is controllable. What should be the value of X if the desired value for Y is 100?

g. Construct a residual plot. Are the residuals random?

h. Construct a normal probability plot. Are the residuals normally distributed?

 **CASE 13**   Firm Leverage and Shareholder Rights

A study was undertaken to assess the relationship between a firm's level of leverage and the strength of its shareholders' rights. The authors found that firms with more restricted shareholder rights tended to use higher leverage: they assumed more debt. This empirical result is consistent with the theory of finance. The regression resulted in an intercept estimate of -0.118 and a slope estimate of -0.040. The t-statistic value was -2.62, and the sample size was 1,309.

1. Write the estimated regression equation predicting leverage (L) based on shareholder rights (R).

2. Carry out a statistical test for the existence of a linear relationship between the two variables.

3. The reported r^2 value was 16.50%. Comment on the predictive power of the regression equation linking a firm's leverage with the strength of the rights of its shareholders.

Source: Pornsit Jiraporn and Kimberly C. Gleason, "Capital Structure, Shareholder Rights, and Corporate Governance," *Journal of Financial Research* 30, no. 1 (2007), pp. 21–33.

CASE 14 Risk and Return

According to the Capital Asset Pricing Model (CAPM), the risk associated with a capital asset is proportional to the slope β_1 (or simply β) obtained by regressing the asset's past returns with the corresponding returns of the average portfolio called the *market portfolio*. (The return of the market portfolio represents the return earned by the average investor. It is a weighted average of the returns from all the assets in the market.) The larger the slope β of an asset, the larger is the risk associated with that asset. A β of 1.00 represents average risk.

The returns from an electronics firm's stock and the corresponding returns for the market portfolio for the past 15 years are given below.

Market Return (%)	Stock's Return (%)
16.02	21.05
12.17	17.25
11.48	13.1
17.62	18.23
20.01	21.52
14	13.26
13.22	15.84
17.79	22.18
15.46	16.26
8.09	5.64
11	10.55
18.52	17.86
14.05	12.75
8.79	9.13
11.6	13.87

1. Carry out the regression and find the β for the stock. What is the regression equation?

2. Does the value of the slope indicate that the stock has above-average risk? (For the purposes of this case assume that the risk is average if the slope is in the range 1 ± 0.1, below average if it is less than 0.9, and above average if it is more than 1.1.)

3. Give a 95% confidence interval for this β. Can we say the risk is above average with 95% confidence?

4. If the market portfolio return for the current year is 10%, what is the stock's return predicted by the regression equation? Give a 95% confidence interval for this prediction.

5. Construct a residual plot. Do the residuals appear random?

6. Construct a normal probability plot. Do the residuals appear to be normally distributed?

7. (Optional) The *risk-free rate of return* is the rate associated with an investment that has no risk at all, such as lending money to the government. Assume that for the current year the risk-free rate is 6%. According to the CAPM, when the return from the market portfolio is equal to the risk-free rate, the return from every asset must also be equal to the risk-free rate. In other words, if the market portfolio return is 6%, then the stock's return should also be 6%. It implies that the regression line must pass through the point $(6, 6)$. Repeat the regression forcing this constraint. Comment on the risk based on the new regression equation.

11 MULTIPLE REGRESSION

11–1 Using Statistics 469

11–2 The *k*-Variable Multiple Regression Model 469

11–3 The *F* Test of a Multiple Regression Model 473

11–4 How Good Is the Regression? 477

11–5 Tests of the Significance of Individual Regression Parameters 482

11–6 Testing the Validity of the Regression Model 494

11–7 Using the Multiple Regression Model for Prediction 500

11–8 Qualitative Independent Variables 503

11–9 Polynomial Regression 513

11–10 Nonlinear Models and Transformations 521

11–11 Multicollinearity 531

11–12 Residual Autocorrelation and the Durbin-Watson Test 539

11–13 Partial *F* Tests and Variable Selection Methods 542

11–14 Using the Computer 548

11–15 Summary and Review of Terms 554

Case 15 Return on Capital for Four Different Sectors 556

LEARNING OBJECTIVES

After studying this chapter, you should be able to:

- Determine whether multiple regression would be applicable to a given instance.
- Formulate a multiple regression model.
- Carry out a multiple regression using the spreadsheet template.
- Test the validity of a multiple regression by analyzing residuals.
- Carry out hypothesis tests about the regression coefficients.
- Compute a prediction interval for the dependent variable.
- Use indicator variables in a multiple regression.
- Carry out a polynomial regression.
- Conduct a Durbin-Watson test for autocorrelation in residuals.
- Conduct a partial *F* test.
- Determine which independent variables are to be included in a multiple regression model.
- Solve multiple regression problems using the Solver macro.

People often think that if something is good, then more of it is even better. In the case of the simple linear regression, explained in Chapter 10, this turns out to be true—as long as some rules are followed. Thus, if one X variable can help predict the value of Y, then several X variables may do an even better job—as long as they contain more information about Y.

A survey of the research literature in all areas of business reveals an overwhelmingly wide use of an extension of the method of Chapter 10, a model called **multiple regression**, which uses several independent variables in predicting a variable of interest.

11–2 The *k*-Variable Multiple Regression Model

> The population regression model of a dependent variable Y on a set of k independent variables $X_1, X_2, \ldots, X_k$ is given by
>
> $$Y = \beta_0 + \beta_1 X_1 + \beta_2 X_2 + \cdots + \beta_k X_k + \epsilon \qquad (11\text{–}1)$$
>
> where β_0 is the Y intercept of the regression surface and each β_i, $i = 1, \ldots, k$, is the slope of the regression surface—sometimes called the **response surface**—with respect to variable X_i.

As with the simple linear regression model, we have some assumptions.

> Model assumptions:
>
> 1. For each observation, the error term ϵ is normally distributed with mean zero and standard deviation σ and is independent of the error terms associated with all other observations. That is,
>
> $$\epsilon_j \sim N(0, \sigma^2) \qquad \text{for all } j = 1, 2, \ldots, n \qquad (11\text{–}2)$$
>
> independent of other errors.[1]
>
> 2. In the context of regression analysis, the variables X_j are considered *fixed quantities,* although in the context of correlational analysis, they are random variables. In any case, X_j *are independent of the error term* ϵ. When we assume that X_j are fixed quantities, we are assuming that we have realizations of k variables X_j and that the only randomness in Y comes from the error term ϵ.

For a case with $k = 2$ variables, the response surface is a plane in three dimensions (the dimensions are Y, X_1, and X_2). The plane is the surface of average response $E(Y)$ for any combination of the two variables X_1 and X_2. The response surface is given by the equation for $E(Y)$, which is the expected value of equation 11–1 with two independent variables. Taking the expected value of Y gives the value 0 to the

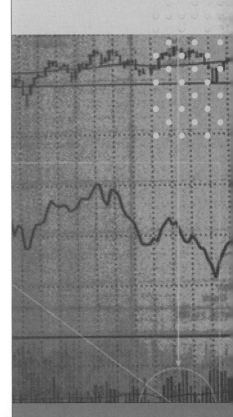

---

[1]The multiple regression model is valid under less restrictive assumptions than these. The assumptions of normality of the errors allows us to perform t tests and F tests of model validity. Also, all we need is that the errors be *uncorrelated* with one another. However, normal distribution + noncorrelation = independence.

error term ϵ. The equations for Y and $E(Y)$ in the case of regression with two independent variables are

$$Y = \beta_0 + \beta_1 X_1 + \beta_2 X_2 + \epsilon \qquad (11\text{–}3)$$

$$E(Y) = \beta_0 + \beta_1 X_1 + \beta_2 X_2 \qquad (11\text{–}4)$$

FIGURE 11–1

A Two-Dimensional Response Surface $E(Y) = \beta_0 + \beta_1 X_1 + \beta_2 X_2$ **and Some Points**

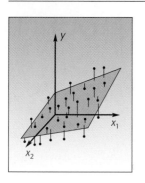

These are equations analogous to the case of simple linear regression. Here, instead of a regression line, we have a regression plane. Some values of Y (i.e., combinations of the X_i variables times their coefficients β_i, and the errors ϵ) are shown in Figure 11–1. The figure shows the response surface, the plane corresponding to equation 11–4.

We estimate the regression parameters of equation 11–3 by the method of least squares. This is an extension of the procedure used in simple linear regression. In the case of two independent variables where the population model is equation 11–3, we need to estimate an equation of a plane that will minimize the sum of the squared errors $(Y - \hat{Y})^2$ over the entire data set of n points. The method is extendable to any k independent variables. In the case of $k = 2$, there are three equations, and their solutions are the least-squares estimates b_0, b_1, and b_2. These are estimates of the Y intercept, the slope of the plane with respect to X_1, and the slope of the plane with respect to X_2. The normal equations for $k = 2$ follow.

When the various sums Σy, Σx_1, and the other sums and products are entered into these equations, it is possible to solve the three equations for the three unknowns b_0, b_1, and b_2. These computations are always done by computer. We will, however, demonstrate the solution of equations 11–5 with a simple example.

The normal equations for the case of two independent variables:

$$\Sigma y = nb_0 + b_1 \Sigma x_1 + b_2 \Sigma x_2$$

$$\Sigma x_1 y = b_0 \Sigma x_1 + b_1 \Sigma x_1^2 + b_2 \Sigma x_1 x_2$$

$$\Sigma x_2 y = b_0 \Sigma x_2 + b_1 \Sigma x_1 x_2 + b_2 \Sigma x_2^2 \qquad (11\text{–}5)$$

EXAMPLE 11–1

Alka-Seltzer recently embarked on an in-store promotional campaign, with displays of its antacid featured prominently in supermarkets. The company also ran its usual radio and television commercials. Over a period of 10 weeks, the company kept track of its expenditure on radio and television advertising, variable X_1, as well as its spending on in-store displays, variable X_2. The resulting sales for each week in the area studied were recorded as the dependent variable Y. The company analyst conducting the study hypothesized a linear regression model of the form

$$Y = \beta_0 + \beta_1 X_1 + \beta_2 X_2 + \epsilon$$

linking sales volume with the two independent variables, advertising and in-store promotions. The analyst wanted to use the available data, considered a random sample of 10 weekly observations, to estimate the parameters of the regression relationship.

Solution   Table 11–1 gives the data for this study in terms of Y, X_1, and X_2, all in thousands of dollars. The table also gives additional columns of products and squares of data

TABLE 11–1   Various Quantities Needed for the Solution of the Normal Equations for
Example 11–1 (numbers are in thousands of dollars)

Y	X_1	X_2	X_1X_2	x_1^2	x_2^2	X_1Y	X_2Y
72	12	5	60	144	25	864	360
76	11	8	88	121	64	836	608
78	15	6	90	225	36	1,170	468
70	10	5	50	100	25	700	350
68	11	3	33	121	9	748	204
80	16	9	144	256	81	1,280	720
82	14	12	168	196	144	1,148	984
65	8	4	32	64	16	520	260
62	8	3	24	64	9	496	186
90	18	10	180	324	100	1,620	900
743	123	65	869	1,615	509	9,382	5,040

values needed for the solution of the normal equations. These columns are X_1X_2, X_1^2, X_2^2, X_1Y, and X_2Y. The sums of these columns are then substituted into equations 11–5, which are solved for the estimates b_0, b_1, and b_2 of the regression parameters.

From Table 11–1, the sums needed for the solution of the normal equations are $\Sigma y = 743$, $\Sigma x_1 = 123$, $\Sigma x_2 = 65$, $\Sigma x_1 y = 9{,}382$, $\Sigma x_2 y = 5{,}040$, $\Sigma x_1 x_2 = 869$, $\Sigma x_1^2 = 1{,}615$, and $\Sigma x_2^2 = 509$. When these sums are substituted into equations 11–5, we get the resulting normal equations:

$$743 = 10b_0 + 123b_1 + 65b_2$$
$$9{,}382 = 123b_0 + 1{,}615b_1 + 869b_2$$
$$5{,}040 = 65b_0 + 869b_1 + 509b_2$$

Solution of this system of equations by substitution, or by any other method of solution, gives

$$b_0 = 47.164942 \qquad b_1 = 1.5990404 \qquad b_2 = 1.1487479$$

These are the *least-squares estimates* of the true regression parameters β_0, β_1, and β_2. Recall that the normal equations (equations 11–5) are originally obtained by calculus methods. (They are the results of differentiating the sum of squared errors with respect to the regression coefficients and setting the results to zero.)

Figure 11–2 shows the results page of the template on which the same problem has been solved. The template is described later.

The meaning of the estimates b_0, b_1, and b_2 as the Y intercept, the slope with respect to X_1, and the slope with respect to X_2, respectively, of the estimated regression surface is illustrated in Figure 11–3.

The general multiple regression model, equation 11–1, has one Y intercept parameter and k slope parameters. Each slope parameter β_i, $i = 1, \ldots, k$, represents the amount of increase (or decrease, in case it is negative) in $E(Y)$ for an increase of 1 unit in variable X_i when all other variables are kept constant. The regression coefficients β_i are therefore sometimes referred to as *net regression coefficients* because they represent the net change in $E(Y)$ for a change of 1 unit in the variable they represent, all else

FIGURE 11–2   The Results from the Template
[Multiple Regression.xls; Sheet: Results]

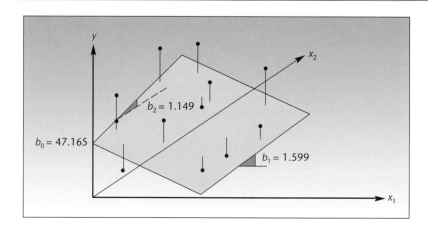

	A	B	C	D	E	F	G	H	I	J	K	L	M
1	**Multiple Regression Results**					Example 11-1							
2													
3		0	1	2	3	4	5	6	7	8	9	10	
4		Intercept	**X1**	**X2**									
5	**b**	47.1649	1.59904	1.1487									
6	**s(b)**	2.47041	0.28096	0.3052									
7	**t**	19.0919	5.69128	3.7633									
8	**p-value**	0.0000	0.0007	0.0070									
9													
10		**VIF**	2.2071	2.2071									
11													
12	**ANOVA Table**												
13		**Source**	**SS**	**df**	**MS**	**F**	**F**_Critical_	**p-value**					
14		Regn.	630.538	2	315.27	86.335	4.7374	0.0000		**s**	1.9109		
15		Error	25.5619	7	3.6517								
16		Total	656.1	9			R^2	0.9610		Adjusted R^2	0.9499		
17													
18													

FIGURE 11–3   The Least-Squares Regression Surface for Example 11–1

remaining constant.[2] This is often difficult to achieve in multiple regression analysis since the explanatory variables are often interrelated in some way.

The Estimated Regression Relationship

The **estimated regression relationship** is

$$\hat{Y} = b_0 + b_1 X_1 + b_2 X_2 + \cdots + b_k X_k \qquad (11\text{–}6)$$

where $\hat{Y}$ is the predicted value of Y, the value lying *on* the estimated regression surface. The terms b_i, $i = 0, \ldots, k$, are the least-squares estimates of the population regression parameters β_i.

The least-squares estimators giving us the b_i are BLUEs (best linear unbiased estimators).

---

[2]For the reader with knowledge of calculus, we note that the coefficient β_i is the partial derivative of $E(Y)$ with respect to X_i: $\beta_i = \partial E(Y)/\partial X_i$.

The estimated regression relationship can also be written in a way that shows how each value of Y is expressed as a linear combination of the values of X_i plus an error term. This is given in equation 11–7.

$$y_j = b_0 + b_1 x_{1j} + b_2 x_{2j} + \cdots + b_k x_{kj} + e_j \qquad j = 1, \ldots, n \qquad (11\text{–}7)$$

In Example 11–1 the estimated regression relationship of sales volume Y on advertising X_1 and in-store promotions X_2 is given by

$$\hat{Y} = 47.164942 + 1.5990404 X_1 + 1.1487479 X_2$$

PROBLEMS

11–1. What are the assumptions underlying the multiple regression model? What is the purpose of the assumption of normality of the errors?

11–2. In a regression analysis of sales volume Y versus the explanatory variables advertising expenditure X_1 and promotional expenditures X_2, the estimated coefficient b_2 is equal to 1.34. Explain the meaning of this estimate in terms of the impact of promotional expenditure on sales volume.

11–3. In terms of model assumptions, what is the difference between a multiple regression model with k independent variables and a correlation analysis involving these variables?

11–4. What is a response surface? For a regression model with seven independent variables, what is the dimensionality of the response surface?

11–5. Again, for a multiple regression model with $k = 7$ independent variables, how many normal equations are there leading to the values of the estimates of the regression parameters?

11–6. What are the BLUEs of the regression parameters?

11–7. For a multiple regression model with two independent variables, results of the analysis include $\Sigma y = 852$, $\Sigma x_1 = 155$, $\Sigma x_2 = 88$, $\Sigma x_1 y = 11{,}423$, $\Sigma x_2 y = 8{,}320$, $\Sigma x_1 x_2 = 1{,}055$, $\Sigma x_1^2 = 2{,}125$, and $\Sigma x_2^2 = 768$, $n = 100$. Solve the normal equations for this regression model, and give the estimates of the parameters.

11–8. A realtor is interested in assessing the impact of size (in square feet) and distance from the center of town (in miles) on the value of homes (in thousands of dollars) in a certain area. Nine randomly chosen houses are selected; data are as follows.

Y (value): 345, 238, 452, 422, 328, 375, 660, 466, 290
X_1 (size): 1,650, 1,870, 2,230, 1,740, 1,900, 2,000, 3,200, 1,860, 1,230
X_2 (distance): 3.5, 0.5, 1.5, 4.5, 1.8, 0.1, 3.4, 3.0, 1.0

Compute the estimated regression coefficients, and explain their meaning.

11–9. The estimated regression coefficients in Example 11–1 are $b_0 = 47.165$, $b_1 = 1.599$, and $b_2 = 1.149$ (rounded to three decimal places). Explain the meaning of each of the three numbers in terms of the situation presented in the example.

11–3 The *F* Test of a Multiple Regression Model

The first statistical test we need to conduct in our evaluation of a multiple regression model is a test that will answer the basic question: Is there a linear regression relationship between the dependent variable Y and *any* of the explanatory, independent variables X_i suggested by the regression equation under consideration? If the proposed regression relationship is given in equation 11–1, a statistical test that can answer this important question is as follows.

A statistical hypothesis test for the existence of a linear relationship between Y and any of the X_i is

$$H_0: \beta_1 = \beta_2 = \beta_3 = \cdots = \beta_k = 0$$
$$H_1: \text{Not all the } \beta_i \ (i = 1, \ldots, k) \text{ are zero} \tag{11–8}$$

If the null hypothesis is true, no linear relationship exists between Y and any of the independent variables in the proposed regression equation. In such a case, there is nothing more to do. There is no regression. If, on the other hand, we reject the null hypothesis, there is statistical evidence to conclude that a regression relationship exists between Y and at least one of the independent variables proposed in the regression model.

To carry out the important test in equation 11–8, we will perform an analysis of variance. The ANOVA is the same as the one given in Chapter 10 for simple linear regression, except that here we have k independent variables instead of just 1. Therefore, the F test of the analysis of variance is not equivalent to the t test for the significance of the slope parameter, as was the case in Chapter 10. Since in multiple regression there are k slope parameters, we have k different t tests to follow the ANOVA.

Figure 11–4 is an extension of Figure 10–21 to the case of $k = 2$ independent variables–to a regression plane instead of a regression line. The figure shows a particular data point y, the predicted point $\hat{y}$ which lies on the estimated regression surface, and the mean of the dependent variable $\bar{y}$. The figure shows the three deviations associated with the data point: the error deviation $y - \hat{y}$, the regression deviation $\hat{y} - \bar{y}$, and the total deviation $y - \bar{y}$. As seen from the figure, the three deviations satisfy the relation: Total deviation = Regression deviation + Error deviation. As in the case of simple linear regression, when we square the deviations and sum them over all n data points, we get the following relation for the sums of squares. The sums of

FIGURE 11–4   Decomposition of the Total Deviation in Multiple Regression Analysis

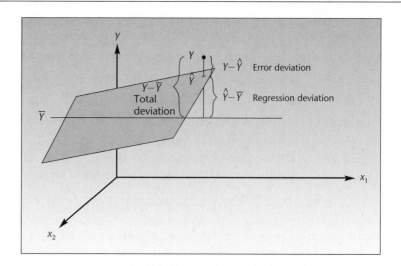

squares are denoted by SST for the total sum of squares, SSR for the regression sum of squares, and SSE for the error sum of squares.

$$SST = SSR + SSE \qquad (11\text{–}9)$$

This is the same as equation 10–29. The difference lies in the degrees of freedom. In simple linear regression, the degrees of freedom for error were $n - 2$ because two parameters, an intercept and a slope, were estimated from a data set of n points. In multiple regression, we estimate k slope parameters and an intercept from a data set of n points. Therefore, the degrees of freedom for error are $n - (k + 1)$. The degrees of freedom for the regression are k, and the total degrees of freedom are $n - 1$. Again, the degrees of freedom are additive. Table 11–2 is the ANOVA table for a multiple regression model with k independent variables.

For Example 11–1, we present the ANOVA table computed by using the template. The results are shown in Table 11–3. Since the p-value is small, we reject the null hypothesis that both slope parameters β_1 and β_2 are zero (equation 11–8), in favor of the alternative that the slope parameters are not both zero. We conclude that there is evidence of a linear regression relationship between sales and at least one of the two variables, advertising or in-store promotions (or both). The F test is shown in Figure 11–5.

Note that since Example 11–1 has two independent variables, we do not yet know whether there is a regression relationship between sales and both advertising and in-store promotions, or whether the relationship exists between sales and one of the two variables only—and if so, which one. All we know is that our data present statistical evidence to conclude that a relationship exists between sales and at least one of the two independent variables. This is, of course, true for all cases with two or more independent variables. The F test only tells us that there is evidence of a relationship between the dependent variable and at least one of the independent variables in the full regression equation under consideration. Once we conclude that a relationship exists, we need to conduct separate tests to determine which of the slope parameters β_i, where $i = 1, \ldots, k$, are different from zero. Therefore, k further tests are needed.

TABLE 11–2   ANOVA Table for Multiple Regression

Source of Variation	Sum of Squares	Degrees of Freedom	Mean Square	F Ratio
Regression	SSR	k	$MSR = \dfrac{SSR}{k}$	$F = \dfrac{MSR}{MSE}$
Error	SSE	$n - (k + 1)$	$MSE = \dfrac{SSE}{n - (k + 1)}$	
Total	SST	$n - 1$		

TABLE 11–3   ANOVA Table Produced by the Template
[Multiple Regression.xls; Sheet: Results]

	ANOVA Table									
11	**ANOVA Table**									
12		Source	SS	df	MS	F	$F_{Critical}$	p-value		
13		Regn.	630.538	2	315.27	86.335	4.7374	0.0000	s	1.9109
14		Error	25.5619	7	3.6517					
15		Total	656.1	9		R^2	0.9610		Adjusted R^2	0.9499
16										

FIGURE 11–5   Regression *F* Test for Example 11–1

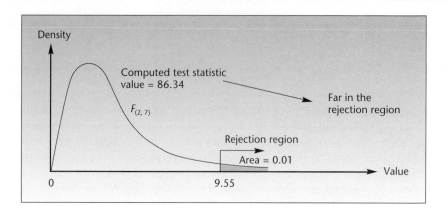

Compare the use of ANOVA tables in multiple regression with the analysis of variance discussed in Chapter 9. Once we rejected the null hypothesis that all *r* population means are equal, we required further analysis (the Tukey procedure or an alternative technique) to determine where the differences existed. In multiple regression, the further tests necessary for determining which variables are important are *t* tests. These tests tell us which variables help explain the variation in the values of the dependent variable and which variables have no explanatory power and should be eliminated from the regression model. Before we get to the separate tests of multiple regression parameters, we want to be able to evaluate how good the regression relationship is as a whole.

PROBLEMS

11–10.   Explain what is tested by the hypothesis test in equation 11–8. What conclusion should be reached if the null hypothesis is not rejected? What conclusion should be reached if the null hypothesis is rejected?

11–11.   In a multiple regression model with 12 independent variables, what are the degrees of freedom for error? Explain.

11–12.   A study was reported about the effects of the number of hours worked, on average, and the average hourly income on unemployment in different countries.[3] Suppose that the regression analysis resulted in SSE = 8,650, SSR = 988, and the sample size was 82 observations. Is there a regression relationship between the unemployment rate and at least one of the explanatory variables?

11–13.   Avis is interested in estimating weekly costs of maintenance of its rental cars of a certain size based on these variables: number of miles driven during the week, number of renters during the week, the car's total mileage, and the car's age. A regression analysis is carried out, and the results include *n* = 45 cars (each car selected randomly, during a randomly selected week of operation), SSR = 7,768, and SST = 15,673. Construct a complete ANOVA table for this problem, and test for the existence of a linear regression relationship between weekly maintenance costs and any of the four independent variables considered.

[3]Christopher A. Pissarides, "Unemployment and Hours of Work," *International Economic Review,* February 2007, pp. 1–36.

11–14. Nissan Motor Company wanted to find leverage factors for marketing the Maxima model in the United States. The company hired a market research firm in New York City to carry out an analysis of the factors that make people favor the model in question. As part of the analysis, the market research firm selected a random sample of 17 people and asked them to fill out a questionnaire about the importance of three automobile characteristics: prestige, comfort, and economy. Each respondent reported the importance he or she gave to each of the three attributes on a 0–100 scale. Each respondent then spent some time becoming acquainted with the car's features and drove it on a test run. Finally, each of the respondents gave an overall appeal score for the model on a 0–100 scale. The appeal score was considered the dependent variable, and the three attribute scores were considered independent variables. A multiple regression analysis was carried out, and the results included the following ANOVA table. Complete the table. Based on the results, is there a regression relationship between the appeal score and at least one of the attribute variables? Explain.

```
Analysis of Variance
   SOURCE      DF      SS       MS
Regression          7474.0
Error
Total               8146.5
```

11–4 How Good Is the Regression?

The mean square error MSE is an unbiased estimator of the variance of the population errors ϵ, which we denote by σ^2. The mean square error is defined in equation 11–10.

The **mean square error** is

$$\text{MSE} = \frac{\text{SSE}}{n - (k + 1)} = \frac{\sum_{j=1}^{n}(y_j - \hat{y}_j)^2}{n - (k + 1)} \qquad (11\text{–}10)$$

The errors resulting from the fit of a regression surface to our set of n data points are shown in Figure 11–6. The smaller the errors, the better the fit of the regression

FIGURE 11–6   Errors in a Multiple Regression Model (shown for $k = 2$)

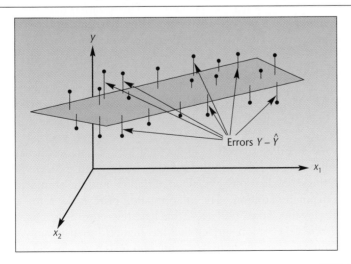

model. Since the mean square error is the average squared error, where averaging is done by dividing by the degrees of freedom, MSE is a measure of how well the regression fits the data. The square root of MSE is an estimator of the standard deviation of the population regression errors σ. (Note that a square root of an unbiased estimator is not unbiased; therefore, $\sqrt{\text{MSE}}$ is not an unbiased estimator of σ, but is still a good estimator.) The square root of MSE is usually denoted by s and is referred to as the *standard error of estimate.*

The **standard error of estimate** is

$$s = \sqrt{\text{MSE}} \qquad (11\text{–}11)$$

This statistic is usually reported in computer output of multiple regression analysis. The mean square error and its square root are measures of the size of the errors in regression and give no indication about the *explained* component of the regression fit (see Figure 11–4, showing the breakdown of the total deviation of any data point to the error and regression components). A measure of regression fit that does incorporate the explained as well as the unexplained components is the *multiple coefficient of determination,* denoted by R^2. This measure is an extension to multiple regression of the coefficient of determination in simple linear regression, denoted by r^2.

The **multiple coefficient of determination** R^2 measures the proportion of the variation in the dependent variable that is explained by the combination of the independent variables in the multiple regression model:

$$R^2 = \frac{\text{SSR}}{\text{SST}} = 1 - \frac{\text{SSE}}{\text{SST}} \qquad (11\text{–}12)$$

Note that R^2 is also equal to SSR/SST because SST = SSR + SSE. We prefer the definition in equation 11–12 for consistency with another measure of how well the regression model fits our data, the *adjusted* multiple coefficient of determination, which will be introduced shortly.

The measures SSE, SSR, and SST are reported in the ANOVA table for multiple regression. Because of the importance of R^2, however, it is reported separately in computer output of multiple regression analysis. The square root of the multiple coefficient of determination, $R = \sqrt{R^2}$, is the **multiple correlation coefficient.** In the context of multiple regression analysis (rather than correlation analysis), the multiple coefficient of determination R^2 is the important measure, not R. The coefficient of determination measures the percentage of variation in Y explained by the X variables; thus, it is an important measure of how well the regression model fits the data. In correlation analysis, where the X_i variables as well as Y are assumed to be random variables, the multiple correlation coefficient R measures the strength of the linear relationship between Y and the k variables X_i.

Figure 11–7 shows the breakdown of the total sum of squares (the sum of squared deviations of all n data points from the mean of Y; see Figure 11–6) into the sum of squares due to the regression (the explained variation) and the sum of squares due to error (the unexplained variation). The interpretation of R^2 is the same as that of r^2 in simple linear regression. The difference is that here the regression errors are measured as deviations from a regression surface that has higher dimensionality than a regression line. The multiple coefficient of determination R^2 is a very useful measure of performance of a multiple regression model. It does, however, have some limitations.

FIGURE 11–7   Decomposition of the Sum of Squares in Multiple Regression, and the Definition of R^2

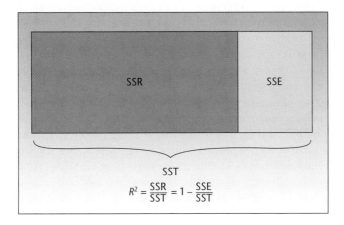

$$R^2 = \frac{SSR}{SST} = 1 - \frac{SSE}{SST}$$

Recall the story at the beginning of this chapter about the student who wanted to predict the nation's economic future with a multiple regression model that had many variables. It turns out that, for any given data set of n points, as the number of variables in the regression model increases, so does R^2. You have already seen how this happens: The greater the number of variables in the regression equation, the more the regression surface "chases" the data until it overfits them. Since the fit of the regression model increases as we increase the number of variables, R^2 cannot decrease and approaches 1.00, or 100% explained variation in Y. This can be very deceptive, as the model–while appearing to fit the data very well–would produce poor predictions.

Therefore, a new measure of fit of a multiple regression model must be introduced: the *adjusted* (or corrected) *multiple coefficient of determination*. The adjusted multiple coefficient of determination, denoted $\overline{R}^2$, is the multiple coefficient of determination corrected for degrees of freedom. It accounts, therefore, not only for SSE and SST, but also for their appropriate degrees of freedom. This measure does not always increase as new variables are entered into our regression equation. When $\overline{R}^2$ does increase as a new variable is entered into the regression equation, including the variable in the equation may be worthwhile. The adjusted measure is defined as follows:

The **adjusted multiple coefficient of determination** is

$$\overline{R}^2 = 1 - \frac{SSE/[n - (k + 1)]}{SST/(n - 1)} \qquad (11\text{–}13)$$

The adjusted R^2 is the R^2 (defined in equation 11–12) where both SSE and SST are divided by their respective degrees of freedom. Since $SSE/[n - (k + 1)]$ is the MSE, we can say that, in a sense, $\overline{R}^2$ is a mixture of the two measures of the performance of a regression model: MSE and R^2. The denominator on the right-hand side of equation 11–13 would be *mean square total,* were we to define such a measure.

Computer output for multiple regression analysis usually includes the adjusted R^2. If it is not reported, we can get $\overline{R}^2$ from R^2 by a simple formula:

$$\overline{R}^2 = 1 - (1 - R^2)\frac{n - 1}{n - (k + 1)} \qquad (11\text{–}14)$$

The proof of the relation between R^2 and $\overline{R}^2$ has instructional value and is left as an exercise. *Note:* Unless the number of variables is relatively large compared to the number of data points (as in the economics student's problem), R^2 and $\overline{R}^2$ are close to each other in value. Thus, in many situations, consideration of only the uncorrected measures R^2 is sufficient. We evaluate the fit of a multiple regression model based on this measure. When we are considering whether to include an independent variable in a regression model that already contains other independent variables, the increase in R^2 when the new variable is added must be weighed against the loss of 1 degree of freedom for error resulting from the addition of the variable (a new parameter would be added to the equation). With a relatively small data set and several independent variables in the model, adding a new variable if R^2 increases, say, from 0.85 to 0.86, may not be worthwhile. As mentioned earlier, in such cases, the adjusted measure $\overline{R}^2$ may be a good indicator of whether to include the new variable. We may decide to include the variable if $\overline{R}^2$ increases when the variable is added.

Of several possible multiple regression models with different independent variables, the model that minimizes MSE will also maximize $\overline{R}^2$. This should not surprise you, since MSE is related to the adjusted measure $\overline{R}^2$. The use of the two criteria MSE and $\overline{R}^2$ in selecting variables to be included in a regression model will be discussed in a later section.

We now return to the analysis of Example 11–1. Note that in Table 11–3 $R^2 = 0.961$, which means that 96.1% of the variation in sales volume is explained by the combination of the two independent variables, advertising and in-store promotions. Note also that the adjusted R^2 is 0.95, which is very close to the unadjusted measure. We conclude that the regression model fits the data very well since a high percentage of the variation in Y is explained by X_1, and/or X_2 (we do not yet know which of the two variables, if not both, is important). The standard error of estimate s is an estimate of σ, the standard deviation of the population regression errors. Note that R^2 is also a *statistic,* like s or MSE. It is a sample estimate of the population multiple coefficient of determination ρ^2, a measure of the proportion of the explained variation in Y in the entire population of Y and X_i values.

All three measures of the performance of a regression model—MSE (and its square root s), the coefficient of determination R^2, and the adjusted measure $\overline{R}^2$—are obtainable from quantities reported in the ANOVA table. This is shown in Figure 11–8, which demonstrates the relations among the different measures.

FIGURE 11–8   Measures of Performance of a Regression Model and the ANOVA Table

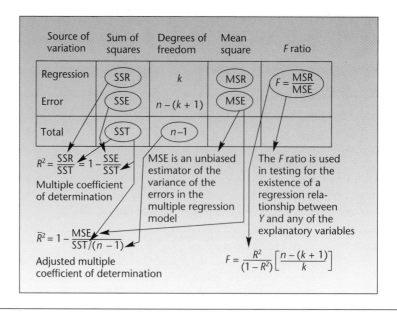

11–15. Under what conditions is it important to consider the adjusted multiple coefficient of determination?

11–16. Explain why the multiple coefficient of determination never decreases as variables are added to the multiple regression model.

11–17. Would it be useful to consider an adjusted coefficient of determination in a simple linear regression situation? Explain.

11–18. Prove equation 11–14.

11–19. Can you judge how well a regression model fits the data by considering the mean square error only? Explain.

11–20. A regression analysis was carried out of the stock return on the first day of an IPO (initial public offering) based on four variables: assessed benefit of the IPO, assessed improved market perception, assessed perception of market strength at the time of the IPO, and assessed growth potential due to patent or copyright ownership. The adjusted R^2 was 2.1%, and the F value was 2.27. The sample consisted of 438 responses from the chief financial officers of firms who issued IPOs from January 1, 1996, through June 15, 2002.[4] Analyze these results.

11–21. A portion of the regression output for the Nissan Motor Company study of problem 11–14 follows. Interpret the findings, and show how these results are obtainable from the ANOVA table results presented in problem 11–14. How good is the regression relationship between the overall appeal score for the automobile and the attribute-importance scores? Also, obtain the adjusted R^2 from the multiple coefficient of determination.

```
s = 7.192        R² = 91.7%       R² (ADJ) = 89.8%
```

11–22. A study of the market for mortgage-backed securities included a regression analysis of security effects and time effects on market prices as dependent variable. The sample size was 383 and the R^2 was 94%.[5] How good is this regression? Would you confidently predict market price based on security and time effects? Explain.

11–23. In the Nissan Motor Company situation in problem 11–21, suppose that a new variable is considered for inclusion in the equation and a new regression relationship is analyzed with the new variable included. Suppose that the resulting multiple coefficient of determination is $R^2 = 91.8\%$. Find the adjusted multiple coefficient of determination. Should the new variable be included in the final regression equation? Give your reasons for including or excluding the variable.

11–24. An article on pricing and competition in marketing reports the results of a regression analysis.[6] Information price was the dependent variable, and the independent variables were six marketing measures. The R^2 was 76.9%. Interpret the strength of this regression relationship. The number of data points was 242, and the F-test value was 44.8. Conduct the test and state your conclusions.

11–25. The following excerpt reports the results of a regression of excess stock returns on firm size and stock price, both variables being ranked on some scale. Explain, critique, and evaluate the reported results.

[4]James C. Brau, Patricia A. Ryan, and Irv DeGraw, "Initial Public Offerings: CFO Perceptions," *Financial Review* 41 (2006), pp. 483–511.

[5]Xavier Garbaix, Arvind Krishnamurthy, and Olivier Vigneron, "Limits of Arbitrage: Theory and Evidence from the Mortgage-Backed Securities Market," *Journal of Finance* 42, no. 2 (2007), pp. 557–595.

[6]Markus Christen and Miklos Sarvary, "Competitive Pricing of Information: A Longitudinal Experiment," *Journal of Marketing Research* 44 (February 2007), pp. 42–56.

Estimated Coefficient Value (*t* Statistic)

INTCPT	X1	X2	ADJUSTED-R²

Ordinary Least-Squares Regression Results

0.484	−0.030	−0.017	0.093
(5.71)***	(−2.91)***	(−1.66)*	

*Denotes significance at the 10% level.

**Denotes significance at the 5% level.

***Denotes significance at the 1% level.

11-26.   A study of Dutch tourism behavior included a regression analysis using a sample of 713 respondents. The dependent variable, number of miles traveled on vacation, was regressed on the independent variables, family size and family income; and the multiple coefficient of determination was $R^2 = 0.72$. Find the adjusted multiple coefficient of determination $\overline{R}^2$. Is this a good regression model? Explain.

11-27.   A regression analysis was carried out to assess sale prices of land in Uganda based on many variables that describe the owner of the land: age, educational level, number of males in the household, and more.[7] Suppose that there are eight independent variables, 500 data points, SSE = 6,179, and SST = 23,108. Construct an ANOVA table, conduct the F test, find R^2 and $\overline{R}^2$, and find the MSE.

11-5   Tests of the Significance of Individual Regression Parameters

Until now, we have discussed the multiple regression model in general. We saw how to test for the existence of a regression relationship between Y and at least one of a set of independent X_i variables by using an F test. We also saw how to evaluate the fit of the general regression model by using the multiple coefficient of determination and the adjusted multiple coefficient of determination. We have not yet seen, however, how to evaluate the significance of individual regression parameters β_i. A test for the significance of an individual parameter is important because it tells us whether the variable in question, X_h, has explanatory power with respect to the dependent variable. Such a test tells us whether the variable in question should be included in the regression equation.

In the last section, we saw that some indication about the benefit from inclusion of a particular variable in the regression equation is gained by comparing the adjusted coefficient of determination of a regression that includes the variable of interest with the value of this measure when the variable is not included. In this section, we will perform individual t tests for the significance of each slope parameter β_i. As we will see, however, we must use caution in interpreting the results of the individual t tests.

In Chapter 10 we saw that the hypothesis test

$$H_0: \beta_1 = 0$$
$$H_1: \beta_1 \neq 0$$

can be carried out using either a t statistic $t = b_1/s(b_1)$ or an F statistic. Both tests were shown to be equivalent because F with 1 degree of freedom for the numerator is a squared t random variable with the same number of degrees of freedom as the denominator of F. A simple linear regression has only one slope, β_1, and if that slope is zero, there is no linear regression relationship. In multiple regression, where $k > 1$, the two

---

[7]J.M. Baland et al., "The Distributive Impact of Land Markets in Uganda," *Economic Development and Cultural Change* 55, no. 2 (2007), pp. 283–311.

tests are not equivalent. The *F* test tells us whether a relationship exists between *Y* and at least one of the X_i, and the *k* ensuing *t* tests tell us which of the X_i variables are important and should be included in the regression equation. From the similarity of this situation with the situation of analysis of variance discussed in Chapter 9, you probably have guessed at least one of the potential problems: The individual *t* tests are each carried out at a single level of significance α, and we cannot determine the level of significance of the family of all *k* tests of the regression slopes jointly. The problem is further complicated by the fact that the tests are not independent of each other because the regression estimates come from the same data set.

Recall that hypothesis tests and confidence intervals are related. We may test hypotheses about regression slope parameters (in particular, the hypothesis that a slope parameter is equal to zero), or we may construct confidence intervals for the values of the slope parameters. If a 95% confidence interval for a slope parameter β_h contains the point zero, then the hypothesis test $H_0: \beta_h = 0$ carried out using $\alpha = 0.05$ would lead to nonrejection of the null hypothesis and thus to the conclusion that there is no evidence that the variable X_h has a linear relationship with *Y*.

We will demonstrate the interdependence of the separate tests of significance of the slope parameters with the use of confidence intervals for these parameters. When $k = 2$, there are two regression slope parameters: β_1 and β_2. (As in simple linear regression, usually there is no interest in testing hypotheses about the intercept parameter.) The sample estimators of the two regression parameters are b_1 and b_2. These estimators (and their standard errors) are correlated with each other (and assumed to be normally distributed). Therefore, the joint confidence region for the pair of parameters (β_1, β_2) is an *ellipse*. If we consider the estimators b_1 and b_2 separately, the joint confidence region will be a rectangle, with each side a separate confidence interval for a single parameter. This is demonstrated in Figure 11–9. A point inside the rectangle formed by the two separate confidence intervals for the parameters, such as point *A* in the figure, seems like a plausible value for the pair of regression slopes (β_1, β_2) but is not *jointly* plausible for the parameters. Only points inside the ellipse in the figure are jointly plausible for the pair of parameters.

Another problem that may arise in making inferences about individual regression slope coefficients is due to **multicollinearity**—the problem of correlations among the independent variables themselves. In multiple regression, we hope to have a strong correlation between each independent variable and the dependent

FIGURE 11–9 Joint Confidence Region and Individual Confidence Intervals for the Slope Parameters β_1 and β_2

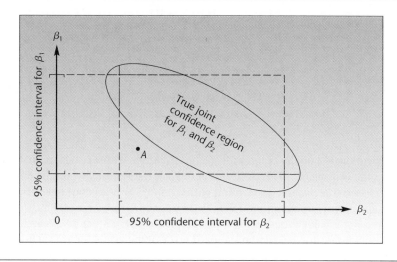

variable Y. Such correlations give the independent X_i variables predictive power with respect to Y. However, we do not want the independent variables to be correlated with one another. When the independent variables are correlated with one another, we have multicollinearity. When this happens, the independent variables rob one another of explanatory power. Many problems may then arise. One problem is that the standard errors of the individual slope estimators become unusually high, making the slope coefficients seem statistically not significant (not different from zero). For example, if we run a regression of job performance Y versus the variables age X_1 and experience X_2, we may encounter multicollinearity. Since, in general, as age increases so does experience, the two independent variables are not independent of each other; the two variables rob each other of explanatory power with respect to Y. If we run this regression, it is likely that—even though experience affects job performance—the individual test for significance of the slope parameter β_2 would lead to nonrejection of the null hypothesis that this slope parameter is equal to zero. Much will be said later about the problem of multicollinearity. Remember that in the presence of multicollinearity, the significance of any regression parameter depends on the other variables included in the regression equation. Multicollinearity may also cause the signs of some estimated regression parameters to be the opposite of what we expect.

Another problem that may affect the individual tests of significance of model parameters occurs when one of the model assumptions is violated. Recall from Section 11–2 that one of the assumptions of the regression model is that the error terms ϵ_j are uncorrelated with one another. When this condition does not hold, as may happen when our data are time series observations (observations ordered by time: yearly data, monthly data, etc.), we encounter the problem of autocorrelation of the errors. This causes the standard errors of the slope estimators to be unusually small, making some parameters seem more significant than they really are. This problem, too, should be considered, and we will discuss it in detail later.

Forewarned of problems that may arise, we now consider the tests of the individual regression parameters. In a regression model of Y versus k independent variables X_1, $X_2, \ldots, X_k$, we have k tests of significance of the slope parameters $\beta_1, \beta_2, \ldots, \beta_k$:

Hypothesis tests about individual regression slope parameters:

$$
\begin{aligned}
&(1) & &H_0\colon \beta_1 = 0 \\
& & &H_1\colon \beta_1 \neq 0 \\
&(2) & &H_0\colon \beta_2 = 0 \\
& & &H_1\colon \beta_2 \neq 0 \\
& & &\quad\vdots \\
&(k) & &H_0\colon \beta_k = 0 \\
& & &H_1\colon \beta_k \neq 0
\end{aligned}
\qquad (11\text{–}15)
$$

These tests are carried out by comparing each test statistic with a critical point of the distribution of the test statistic. The distribution of each test statistic, when the appropriate null hypothesis is true, is the t distribution with $n - (k + 1)$ degrees of freedom. The distribution depends on our assumption that the regression errors are normally distributed. The test statistic for each hypothesis test (i) in equations 11–15 (where $i = 1, 2, \ldots, k$) is the slope estimate b_i, divided by the standard error of the estimator $s(b_i)$. The estimates and the standard errors are reported in the computer output. Each $s(b_i)$ is an estimate of the population standard deviation of the estimator $\sigma(b_i)$, which is unknown to us.[8] The test statistics for the hypothesis tests (1) through (k) in equations 11–15 are as follows:

Test statistics for tests about individual regression slope parameters:

For test i ($i = 1, \ldots, k$):

$$t_{[n-(k+1)]} = \frac{b_i - 0}{s(b_i)}$$

(11–16)

We write each test statistic as the estimate minus zero (the null-hypothesis value of β_i) to stress the fact that we may test the null hypothesis that β_i is equal to any number, not necessarily zero. Testing for equality to zero is most important because it tells us whether there is evidence that variable X_i has a linear relationship with Y. It tells us whether there is statistical evidence that variable X_i has explanatory power with respect to the dependent variable.

Let us look at a quick example. Suppose that a multiple regression analysis is carried out relating the dependent variable Y to five independent variables X_1, X_2, X_3, X_4, and X_5. In addition, suppose that the F test resulted in rejection of the null hypothesis that none of the predictor variables has any explanatory power with respect to Y; suppose also that R^2 of the regression is respectably high. As a result, we believe that the regression equation gives a good fit to the data and potentially may be used for prediction purposes. Our task now is to test the importance of each of the X_i variables separately. Suppose that the sample size used in this regression analysis is $n = 150$. The results of the regression estimation procedure are given in Table 11–4.

From the information in Table 11–4, which variables are important, and which are not? Note that the first variable listed is "Constant." This is the Y intercept. As we noted earlier, testing whether the intercept is zero is less important than testing whether the coefficient parameter of any of the k variables is zero. Still, we may do so by dividing the reported coefficient estimate, 53.12, by its standard error, 5.43. The result is the value of the test statistic that has a t distribution with $n - (k + 1) = 150 - 6 = 144$ degrees of freedom when the null hypothesis that the intercept is zero is true. For manual calculation purposes, we shall approximate this t random variable as a standard normal variable Z. The test statistic value is $z = 53.12/5.43 = 9.78$. This value is greater than 1.96, and we may reject the null hypothesis that β_0 is equal to zero at the $\alpha = 0.05$ level of significance. Actually, the p-value is very small. The regression hyperplane, therefore, most probably does not pass through the origin.

TABLE 11–4 Regression Results for Individual Parameters

Variable	Coefficient Estimate	Standard Error
Constant	53.12	5.43
X_1	2.03	0.22
X_2	5.60	1.30
X_3	10.35	6.88
X_4	3.45	2.70
X_5	−4.25	0.38

---

[8]Each $s(b_i)$ is the product of $s = \sqrt{\text{MSE}}$ and a term denoted by c_i, which is a diagonal element in a matrix obtained in the regression computations. You need not worry about matrices. However, the matrix approach to multiple regression is discussed in a section at the end of this chapter for the benefit of students familiar with matrix theory.

Let us now turn to the tests of significance of the slope parameters of the variables in the regression equation. We start with the test for the significance of variable X_1 as a predictor variable. The hypothesis test is H_0: $\beta_1 = 0$ versus H_1: $\beta_1 \neq 0$. We now compute our test statistic (again, we will use Z for $t_{(144)}$):

$$z = \frac{b_1 - 0}{s(b_1)} = \frac{2.03}{0.22} = 9.227$$

The value of the test statistic, 9.227, lies far in the right-hand rejection region of Z for any conventional level of significance; the p-value is very small. We therefore conclude that there is statistical evidence that the slope of Y with respect to X_1, the population parameter β_1, is not zero. Variable X_1 is shown to have some explanatory power with respect to the dependent variable.

If it is not zero, what is the value of β_1? The parameter, as in the case of all population parameters, is not known to us. An unbiased estimate of the parameter's value is $b_1 = 2.03$. We can also compute a confidence interval for β_1. A 95% confidence interval for β_1 is $b_1 \pm 1.96 s(b_1) = 2.03 \pm 1.96(0.22) = [1.599, 2.461]$. Based on our data and the validity of our assumptions, we can be 95% confident that the true slope of Y with respect to X_1 is anywhere from 1.599 to 2.461. Figure 11–10 shows the hypothesis test for the significance of variable X_1.

For the other variables X_2 through X_5, we show the hypothesis tests without figures. The tests are carried out in the same way, with the same distribution. We also do not show the computation of confidence intervals for the slope parameters. These are done exactly as shown for β_1. Note that when the hypothesis test for the significance of a slope parameter leads to nonrejection of the null hypothesis that the slope parameter is zero, the point zero will be included in a confidence interval with the same confidence level as the level of significance of the test.

The hypothesis test for β_2 is H_0: $\beta_2 = 0$ versus H_1: $\beta_2 \neq 0$. The test statistic value is $z = 5.60/1.30 = 4.308$. This value, too, is in the right-hand rejection region for usual levels of significance; the p-value is small. We conclude that X_2 is also an important variable in the regression equation.

The hypothesis test for β_3 is H_0: $\beta_3 = 0$ versus H_1: $\beta_3 \neq 0$. Here the test statistic value is $z = 10.35/6.88 = 1.504$. This value lies in the nonrejection region for levels of α even larger than 0.10. The p-value is greater than 0.133, as you can verify from a normal table. We conclude that variable X_3 is probably not important. Remember our cautionary comments that preceded this discussion—there is a possibility that X_3 is actually an important variable. The variable may *appear* to have a

FIGURE 11–10 Testing Whether $\beta_1 = 0$

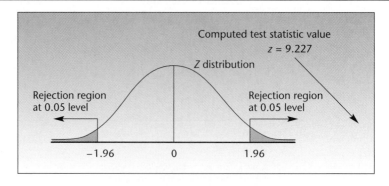

TABLE 11–5 Multiple Regression Results from the Template
[Multiple Regression.xls; Sheet: Results]

	A	B	C	D	E	F	G	H	I	J	K	L	M
1	Multiple Regression Results					Example 11-1							
2													
3		0	1	2	3	4	5	6	7	8	9	1 0	
4		Intercept	Advt.	Promo									
5	b	47.165	1.599	1.1487									
6	s(b)	2.4704	0.281	0.3052									
7	t	19.092	5.6913	3.7633									
8	p-value	0.0000	0.0007	0.0070									

slope that is not different from zero because its standard error, $s(b_3) = 6.88$, may be unduly inflated; the variable may be correlated with another explanatory variable (the problem of multicollinearity). A way out of this problem is to drop another variable, one that we suspect to be correlated with X_3, and see if X_3 becomes significant in the new regression model. We will come back to this problem in the section on multicollinearity and in the section on selection of variables to be included in a regression model.

The hypothesis test about β_4 is $H_0: \beta_4 = 0$ versus $H_1: \beta_4 \neq 0$. The value of the test statistic for this test is $z = 3.45/2.70 = 1.278$. Again, we cannot reject the null hypothesis that the slope parameter of X_4 is zero and that the variable has no explanatory power. Note, however, the caution in our discussion of the test of β_3. It is possible, for example, that X_3 and X_4 are collinear and that this is the reason for their respective tests resulting in nonsignificance. It would be wise to drop one of these two variables and check whether the other variable then becomes significant. If it does, the reason for our test result is multicollinearity, and not the absence of explanatory power of the variable in question. Another point worth mentioning is the idea of joint inference, discussed earlier. Although the separate tests of β_3 and β_4 both may lead to the nonrejection of the hypothesis that the parameters are zero, it may be that the two parameters are not jointly equal to zero. This would be the situation if, in Figure 11–9, the rectangle contained the point zero while the ellipse—the true joint confidence region for both parameters—did not contain that point. Note that the *t* tests are *conditional*. The significance or nonsignificance of a variable in the equation is conditional on the fact that the regression equation contains the other variables.

Finally, the test for parameter β_5 is $H_0: \beta_5 = 0$ versus $H_1: \beta_5 \neq 0$. The computed value of the test statistic is $z = -4.25/0.38 = -11.184$. This value falls far in the left-hand rejection region, and we conclude that variable X_5 has explanatory power with respect to the dependent variable and therefore should be included in the regression equation. The slope parameter is negative, which means that, everything else staying constant, the dependent variable Y decreases on average as X_5 increases. We note that these tests can be carried out very quickly by just considering the *p*-values.

We now return to Example 11–1 and look at the rest of the results from the template. For easy reference the results from Table 11–4 are repeated here in Table 11–5. As seen in the table, the test statistic *t* is very significant for both advertisement and promotion variables, because the *p*-value is less than 1% in both cases. We therefore declare that both of these variables affect the sales.

EXAMPLE 11–2

In recent years, many U.S. firms have intensified their efforts to market their products in the Pacific Rim. Among the major economic powers in that area are Japan, Hong Kong, and Singapore. A consortium of U.S. firms that produce raw materials used in Singapore is interested in predicting the level of exports from the United

States to Singapore, as well as understanding the relationship between U.S. exports to Singapore and certain variables affecting the economy of that country. Understanding this relationship would allow the consortium members to time their marketing efforts to coincide with favorable conditions in the Singapore economy. Understanding the relationship would also allow the exporters to determine whether expansion of exports to Singapore is feasible. The economist hired to do the analysis obtained from the Monetary Authority of Singapore (MAS) monthly data on five economic variables for the period of January 1989 to August 1995. The variables were U.S. exports to Singapore in billions of Singapore dollars (the dependent variable, Exports), money supply figures in billions of Singapore dollars (variable M1), minimum Singapore bank lending rate in percentages (variable Lend), an index of local prices where the base year is 1974 (variable Price), and the exchange rate of Singapore dollars per U.S. dollar (variable Exchange). The monthly data are given in Table 11–6.

TABLE 11–6   Example 11–2 Data

Row	Exports	M1	Lend	Price	Exchange
1	2.6	5.1	7.8	114	2.16
2	2.6	4.9	8.0	116	2.17
3	2.7	5.1	8.1	117	2.18
4	3.0	5.1	8.1	122	2.20
5	2.9	5.1	8.1	124	2.21
6	3.1	5.2	8.1	128	2.17
7	3.2	5.1	8.3	132	2.14
8	3.7	5.2	8.8	133	2.16
9	3.6	5.3	8.9	133	2.15
10	3.4	5.4	9.1	134	2.16
11	3.7	5.7	9.2	135	2.18
12	3.6	5.7	9.5	136	2.17
13	4.1	5.9	10.3	140	2.15
14	3.5	5.8	10.6	147	2.16
15	4.2	5.7	11.3	150	2.21
16	4.3	5.8	12.1	151	2.24
17	4.2	6.0	12.0	151	2.16
18	4.1	6.0	11.4	151	2.12
19	4.6	6.0	11.1	153	2.11
20	4.4	6.0	11.0	154	2.13
21	4.5	6.1	11.3	154	2.11
22	4.6	6.0	12.6	154	2.09
23	4.6	6.1	13.6	155	2.09
24	4.2	6.7	13.6	155	2.10
25	5.5	6.2	14.3	156	2.08
26	3.7	6.3	14.3	156	2.09
27	4.9	7.0	13.7	159	2.10
28	5.2	7.0	12.7	161	2.11
29	4.9	6.6	12.6	161	2.15
30	4.6	6.4	13.4	161	2.14
31	5.4	6.3	14.3	162	2.16
32	5.0	6.5	13.9	160	2.17
33	4.8	6.6	14.5	159	2.15
34	5.1	6.8	15.0	159	2.10
35	4.4	7.2	13.2	158	2.06
36	5.0	7.6	11.8	155	2.05

(*Continued*)

Row	Exports	M1	Lend	Price	Exchange
37	5.1	7.2	11.2	155	2.06
38	4.8	7.1	10.1	154	2.11
39	5.4	7.0	10.0	154	2.12
40	5.0	7.5	10.2	154	2.13
41	5.2	7.4	11.0	153	2.04
42	4.7	7.4	11.0	152	2.14
43	5.1	7.3	10.7	152	2.15
44	4.9	7.6	10.2	152	2.16
45	4.9	7.8	10.0	151	2.17
46	5.3	7.8	9.8	152	2.20
47	4.8	8.2	9.3	152	2.21
48	4.9	8.2	9.3	152	2.15
49	5.1	8.3	9.5	152	2.08
50	4.3	8.3	9.2	150	2.08
51	4.9	8.0	9.1	147	2.09
52	5.3	8.2	9.0	147	2.10
53	4.8	8.2	9.0	146	2.09
54	5.3	8.0	8.9	145	2.12
55	5.0	8.1	9.0	145	2.13
56	5.1	8.1	9.0	146	2.14
57	4.8	8.1	9.0	147	2.14
58	4.8	8.1	8.9	147	2.13
59	5.2	8.6	8.9	147	2.13
60	4.9	8.8	9.0	146	2.13
61	5.5	8.4	9.1	147	2.13
62	4.3	8.2	9.0	146	2.13
63	5.2	8.3	9.2	146	2.09
64	4.7	8.3	9.6	146	2.09
65	5.4	8.4	10.0	146	2.10
66	5.2	8.3	10.0	147	2.11
67	5.6	8.2	10.1	146	2.15

Solution

Use the template to perform a multiple regression analysis with Exports as the dependent variable and the four economic variables M1, Lend, Price, and Exchange as the predictor variables. Table 11–7 shows the results.

Let us analyze the regression results. We start with the ANOVA table and the F test for the existence of linear relationships between the independent variables and exports from the United States to Singapore. We have $F_{(4, 62)} = 73.059$ with a p-value of "0.000." We conclude that there is strong evidence of a linear regression relationship here. This is further confirmed by noting that the coefficient of determination is high: $R^2 = 0.825$. Thus, the combination of the four economic variables explains 82.5% of the variation in exports to Singapore. The adjusted coefficient of determination $\overline{R}^2$ is a little smaller: 0.8137. Now the question is, Which of the four variables are important as predictors of export volume to Singapore and which are not? Looking at the reported p-values, we see that the Singapore money supply M1 is an important variable; the level of prices in Singapore is also an important variable. The remaining two variables, minimum lending rate and exchange rate, have very large p-values. Surprisingly, the lending rate and the exchange rate of Singapore dollars to U.S. dollars seem to have no effect on the volume of Singapore's imports from the United States. Remember, however, that we may have a problem of multicollinearity.

CHAPTER 17

TABLE 11–7   Regression Results from the Template for Exports to Singapore [Multiple Regression.xls]

Multiple Regression Results				Exports						
	0	1	2	3	4	5	6	7	8	9	10
	Intercept	M1	Lend	Price	Exch.						
b	-4.0155	0.3685	0.0047	0.0365	0.2679						
s(b)	2.7664	0.0638	0.0492	0.0093	1.1754						
t	-1.4515	5.7708	0.0955	3.9149	0.2279						
p-value	0.1517	0.0000	0.9242	0.0002	0.8205						

ANOVA Table

Source	SS	df	MS	F	$F_{Critical}$	p-value		
Regn.	32.946	4	8.2366	73.059	2.5201	0.0000	s	0.3358
Error	6.9898	62	0.1127					
Total	39.936	66		R^2 0.8250		Adjusted R^2 0.8137		

This is especially true when we are dealing with economic variables, which tend to be correlated with one another.[9]

When M1 is dropped from the equation and the new regression analysis considers the independent variables Lend, Price, and Exchange, we see that the lending rate, which was not significant in the full regression equation, now becomes significant! This is seen in Table 11–8. Note that R^2 has dropped greatly with the removal of M1. The fact that the lending rate is significant in the new equation is an indication of *multicollinearity;* variables M1 and Lend are correlated with each other. Therefore, Lend is not significant when M1 is in the equation, but in the absence of M1, Lend does have explanatory power.

Note that the exchange rate is still not significant. Since R^2 and the adjusted R^2 both decrease significantly when the money supply M1 is dropped, let us put that variable back into the equation and run U.S. exports to Singapore versus the independent variables M1 and Price only. The results are shown in Table 11–9. In this regression equation, both independent variables are significant. Note that R^2 in this regression is virtually the same as R^2 with all four variables in the equation (see

TABLE 11–8   Regression Results for Singapore Exports without M1

Multiple Regression Results				Exports						
	0	1	2	3	4	5	6	7	8	9	10
	Intercept	Lend	Price	Exch.							
b	-0.2891	-0.2114	0.0781	-2.095							
s(b)	3.3085	0.0393	0.0073	1.3551							
t	-0.0874	-5.3804	10.753	-1.546							
p-value	0.9306	0.0000	0.0000	0.1271							

ANOVA Table

Source	SS	df	MS	F	$F_{Critical}$	p-value		
Regn.	29.192	3	9.7306	57.057	2.7505	0.0000	s	0.413
Error	10.744	63	0.1705					
Total	39.936	66		R^2 0.7310		Adjusted R^2 0.7182		

---

[9]The analysis of economic variables presents special problems. Economists have developed methods that account for the intricate interrelations among economic variables. These methods, based on multiple regression and time series analysis, are usually referred to as *econometric methods.*

TABLE 11–9 Regressing Exports against M1 and Price

Multiple Regression Results							Exports			
	0	1	2	3	4	5	6	7	8	9	10
	Intercept	M1	Price								
b	-3.423	0.3614	0.0037								
s(b)	0.5409	0.0392	0.0041								
t	-6.3288	9.209	9.0461								
p-value	0.0000	0.0000	0.0000								

ANOVA Table

Source	SS	df	MS	F	$F_{Critical}$	p-value		
Regn.	32.94	2	16.47	150.67	3.1404	0.0000	s	0.3306
Error	6.9959	64	0.1093					
Total	39.936	66		R^2 0.8248		Adjusted R^2 0.8193		

Table 11–7). However, the adjusted coefficient of determination $\overline{R}^2$ is different. The adjusted R^2 actually *increases* as we drop the variables Lend and Exchange. In the full model with the four variables (Table 11–7), $\overline{R}^2 = 0.8137$, while in the reduced model, with variables M1 and Price only (Table 11–9), $\overline{R}^2 = 0.8193$. This demonstrates the usefulness of the adjusted R^2. When unimportant variables are added to the equation (unimportant in the presence of other variables), $\overline{R}^2$ decreases even if R^2 increases. The best model, in terms of explanatory power gauged against the loss of degrees of freedom, is the reduced model in Table 11–9, which relates exports to Singapore with only the money supply and price level. This is also seen by the fact that the other two variables are not significant once M1 and Price are in the equation. Later, when we discuss stepwise regression–a method of letting the computer choose the best variables to be included in the model–we will see that this automatic procedure also chooses the variables M1 and Price as the best combination for predicting U.S. exports to Singapore.

PROBLEMS

11–28. A regression analysis is carried out, and a confidence interval for β_1 is computed to be [1.25, 1.55]; a confidence interval for β_2 is [2.01, 2.12]. Both are 95% confidence intervals. Explain the possibility that the point (1.26, 2.02) may not lie inside a joint confidence region for (β_1, β_2) at a confidence level of 95%.

11–29. A multiple regression model was developed for predicting firms' governance level, measured on a scale, based on firm size, firm profitability, fixed-asset ratio, growth opportunities, and nondebt tax shield size. For firm size, the coefficient estimate was 0.06 and the standard error was 0.005. For firm profitability, the estimate was −0.166 and the standard error was 0.03. For fixed-asset ratio the estimate was −0.004 and standard error 0.05. For growth opportunities the estimate was –0.018 and standard error 0.025. And for nondebt tax shield the estimate was 0.649 and standard error 0.151. The F statistic was 44.11 and the adjusted R^2 was 16.5%.[10] Explain these results completely and offer a next step in this analysis. Assume a very large sample size.

---

[10]Pornsit Jiraporn and Kimberly C. Gleason, "Capital Structure, Shareholder Rights, and Corporate Governance," *Journal of Financial Research* 30, no. 1 (2007), pp. 21–33.

11–30. Give three reasons why caution must be exercised in interpreting the significance of single regression slope parameters.

11–31. Give 95% confidence intervals for the slope parameters β_2 through β_5, using the information in Table 11–4. Which confidence intervals contain the point $(0, 0)$? Explain the interpretation of such outcomes.

11–32. A regression analysis was carried out to predict a firm's reputation (defined on a scale called the Carter-Manaster reputation ranking) on the basis of unexpected accruals, auditor quality, return on investment, and expenditure on research and development. The parameter estimates (and standard errors, in parentheses), in the order these predictor variables are listed, are $-2.0775(0.4111)$, $-0.1116(0.2156)$, $0.4192(0.2357)$, and $0.0328(0.0155)$. The number of observations was 487, and the R^2 was 36.51%.[11] Interpret these findings.

11–33. A computer program for regression analysis produces a joint confidence region for the two slope parameters considered in the regression equation, β_1 and β_2. The elliptical region of confidence level 95% does not contain the point $(0, 0)$. Not knowing the value of the F statistic, or R^2, do you believe there is a linear regression relationship between Y and at least one of the two explanatory variables? Explain.

11–34. In the Nissan Motor Company situation of problems 11–14 and 11–21, the regression results, using MINITAB, are as follows. Give a complete interpretation of these results.

```
The regression equation is
RATING = 24.1 − 0.166 PRESTIGE + 0.324 COMFORT + 0.514 ECONOMY

Predictor       Coef        Stdev
Constant        24.14       18.22
PRESTIGE       −0.1658      0.1215
COMFORT         0.3236      0.1228
ECONOMY         0.5139      0.1143
```

11–35. Refer to Example 11–2, where exports to Singapore were regressed on several economic variables. Interpret the results of the following MINITAB regression analysis, and compare them with the results reported in the text. How does the present model fit with the rest of the analysis? Explain.

```
The regression equation is
EXPORTS = − 3.40 + 0.363 M1 + 0.0021 LEND + 0.0367 PRICE

Predictor       Coef        Stdev       t-ratio      P
CONSTANT       −3.4047      0.6821       −4.99      0.000
M1              0.36339     0.05940       6.12      0.000
LEND            0.00211     0.04753       0.04      0.965
PRICE           0.036666    0.009231      3.97      0.000

s = 0.3332     R-sq = 82.5%     R-sq (adj) = 81.6%
```

11–36. After the model of problem 11–35, the next model was run:

```
The regression equation is
EXPORTS = − 1.09 + 0.552 M1 + 0.171 LEND
```

---

[11]Hoje Jo, Yongtae Kim, and Myung Seok Park, "Underwriter Choice and Earnings Management: Evidence from Seasoned Equity Offerings," *Review of Accounting Studies* 12, no. 1 (2007), pp. 23–59.

```
Predictor       Coef       Stdev      t-ratio       P

Constant      -1.0859      0.3914      -2.77       0.007

M1             0.55222     0.03950     13.98       0.000

LEND           0.17100     0.02357      7.25       0.000

s = 0.3697      R-sq = 78.1%     R-sq (adj) = 77.4%

Analysis of Variance

  SOURCE      DF       SS         MS          F          P

Regression    2      31.189     15.594     114.09     0.000

Error        64       8.748      0.137

Total        66      39.936
```

a. What happened when Price was dropped from the regression equation? Why?

b. Compare this model with all previous models of exports versus the economic variables, and draw conclusions.

c. Which model is best overall? Why?

d. Conduct the F test for this particular model.

e. Compare the reported value of s in this model with the reported s value in the model of problem 11–35. Why is s higher in this model?

f. For the model in problem 11–35, what is the mean square error?

11–37. A regression analysis of monthly sales versus four independent variables is carried out. One of the variables is known not to have any effect on sales, yet its slope parameter in the regression is significant. In your opinion, what may have caused this to happen?

11–38. A study of 14,537 French firms was carried out to assess employment growth based on levels of new technological process, organizational innovation, commercial innovation, and research and development. The R^2 was 74.3%. The coefficient estimates for these variables (and standard errors) were reported, in order, as follows: $-0.014(0.004)$, $0.001(0.004)$, $0.016(0.005)$, and $0.027(0.006)$.[12] Which of these variables have explanatory power over a firm's employment growth? Explain.

11–39. Run a regression of profits against revenues and number of employees for the airline industry using the data in the following table. Interpret all your findings.

Profit ($ billion)	Revenue ($ billion)	Employees (thousands)
−1.2	17	96
−2.8	13	68
−0.2	13	70
0.2	9.5	39
0.03	8.8	38
1.4	6.8	32
0.4	5.9	33
0.01	2.4	13
0.06	2.3	11
0.1	1.3	6

---

[12]Pierre Biscourp and Francis Kramarz, "Employment, Skill Structure and Internal Trade: Firm-Level Evidence for France," *Journal of International Economics* 72 (May 2007), pp. 22–51.

11–6   Testing the Validity of the Regression Model

In Chapter 10, we stressed the importance of the three stages of statistical model building: model specification, estimation of parameters, and testing the validity of the model assumptions. We will now discuss the third and very important stage of checking the validity of the model assumptions in multiple regression analysis.

Residual Plots

CHAPTER 17

As with simple linear regression, the analysis of regression residuals is an important tool for determining whether the assumptions of the multiple regression model are met. Residual plots are easy to use, and they convey much information quickly. The saying "A picture is worth a thousand words" is a good description of the technique of examining plots of regression residuals. As with simple linear regression, we may plot the residuals against the predicted values of the dependent variable, against each independent variable, against time (or the order of selection of the data points), and on a probability scale, to check the normality assumption. Since we have already discussed the use of residual plots in Chapter 10, we will demonstrate only some of the residual plots, using Example 11–2. Figure 11–11 is a plot of the residuals produced from the model with the two independent variables M1 and Price (Table 11–9) against variable M1. It appears that the residuals are randomly distributed with no pattern and with equal variance as M1 increases.

Figure 11–12 is a plot of the regression residuals against the variable Price. Here the picture is quite different. As we examine this figure carefully, we see that the spread of the residuals increases as Price increases. Thus, the variance of the residuals is not constant. We have the situation called *heteroscedasticity*—a violation of the assumption of equal error variance. In such cases, the ordinary least-squares (OLS) estimation method is not efficient, and an alternative method, called *weighted least squares* (*WLS*), should be used instead. The WLS procedure is discussed in advanced texts on regression analysis.

Figure 11–13 is a plot of the regression residuals against the variable Time, that is, the order of the observations. (The observations are a time sequence of monthly data.) This variable was not included in the model, and the plot could reveal whether time should have been included as a variable in our regression model. The plot of the residuals against time reveals no pattern in the residuals as time increases. The residuals seem to be more or less randomly distributed about their mean of zero.

Figure 11–14 is a plot of the regression residuals against the predicted export values $\hat{Y}$. We leave it as an exercise to the reader to interpret the information in this plot.

Standardized Residuals

Remember that under the assumptions of the regression model, the population errors ϵ_j are normally distributed with mean zero and standard deviation σ. As a result,

FIGURE 11–11   Residuals versus M1

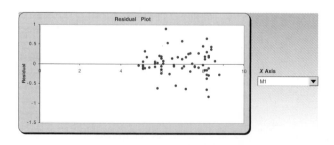

FIGURE 11–12   Residuals versus Price

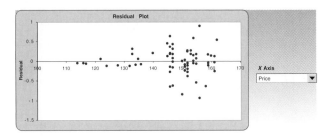

FIGURE 11–13   Residuals versus Time

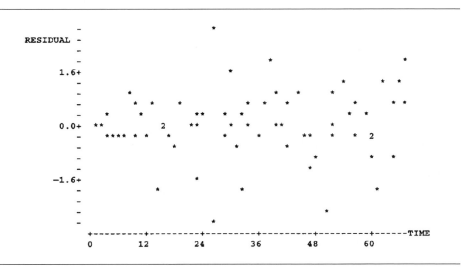

FIGURE 11–14   Residuals versus Predicted *Y* Values

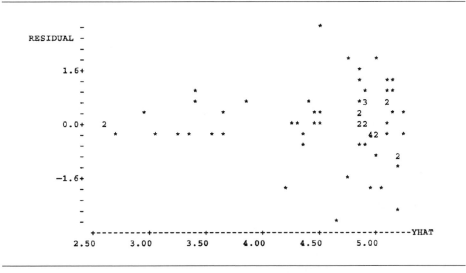

FIGURE 11–15   The Normal Probability Plot of the Residuals
[Multiple Regression.xls; Sheet: Residuals]

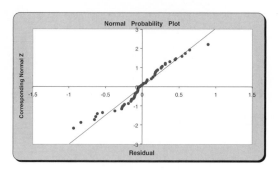

CHAPTER 17

the errors divided by their standard deviation should follow the standard normal distribution:

$$\frac{\epsilon_j}{\sigma} \sim N(0, 1) \quad \text{for all } j$$

Therefore, dividing the observed regression errors e_j by their estimated standard deviation s will give us standardized residuals. Examination of a histogram of these residuals may give us an idea as to whether the normal assumption is valid.[13]

The Normal Probability Plot

Just as we saw in the simple regression template, the multiple regression template also produces a normal probability plot of the residuals. If the residuals are perfectly normally distributed, they will lie along the diagonal straight line in the plot. The more they deviate from the diagonal line, the more they deviate from the normal distribution. In Figure 11–15, the deviations do not appear to be significant. Consequently, we assume that the residuals are normally distributed.

CHAPTER 17

Outliers and Influential Observations

An **outlier** is an extreme observation. It is a point that lies away from the rest of the data set. Because of this, outliers may exert greater influence on the least-squares estimates of the regression parameters than do other observations. To see why, consider the data in Figure 11–16. The graph shows the estimated least-squares regression line without the outlier and the line obtained when the outlier is considered.

As can be seen from Figure 11–16, the outlier has a strong effect on the estimation of model parameters. (We used a line showing Y versus variable X_1. The same is true for a regression plane or hyperplane: The outlier "tilts" the regression surface away from the other points.) The reason for this effect is the nature of least squares: The procedure minimizes the squared deviations of the data points from the regression surface. A point with an unusually large deviation "attracts" the surface toward itself so as to make its squared deviation smaller.

We must, therefore, pay special attention to outliers. If an outlier can be traced to an error in recording the data or to another type of error, it should, of course, be removed. On the other hand, if an outlier is not due to error, it may have been caused by special circumstances, and the information it provides may be important. For example, an outlier may be an indication of a missing variable in the regression equation.

---

[13]Actually, the residuals are not independent and do not have equal variance; therefore, we really should divide the residuals e_j by something a little more complicated than s. However, the simpler procedure outlined here and implemented in some computer packages is usually sufficiently accurate.

FIGURE 11–16   A Least-Squares Regression Line Estimated with and without the Outlier

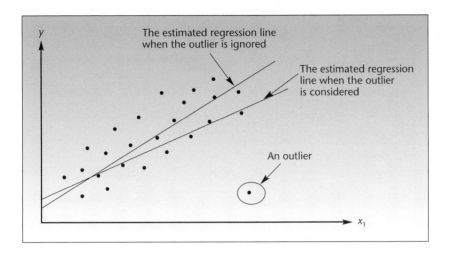

The data shown in Figure 11–16 may be maximum speed for an automobile as a function of engine displacement. The outlier may be an automobile with four cylinders, while all others are six-cylinder cars. Thus, the fact that the point lies away from the rest may be explained. Because of the possible information content in outliers, they should be carefully scrutinized before being discarded. Some alternative regression methods do not use a squared-distance approach and are therefore more robust—less sensitive to the influence of outliers.

Sometimes an outlier is actually a point that is distant from the rest because the value of one of its independent variables is larger than the rest of the data. For example, suppose we measure chemical yield Y as a function of temperature X_1. There may be other variables, but we will consider only these two. Suppose that most of our data are obtained at low temperatures within a certain range, but one observation is taken at a high temperature. This outlying point, far in the X_1 direction, exerts strong influence on the estimation of the model parameters. This is shown in Figure 11–17. Without the point at high temperature, the regression line may have slope zero, and no relationship may be detected, as can be seen from the figure. We must also be

FIGURE 11–17   Influence of an Observation Far in the X_1 Direction

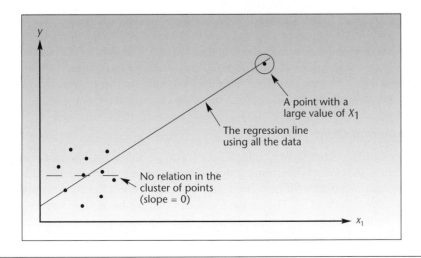

FIGURE 11–18   **Possible Relation in the Region between the Available Cluster of Data and the Far Point**

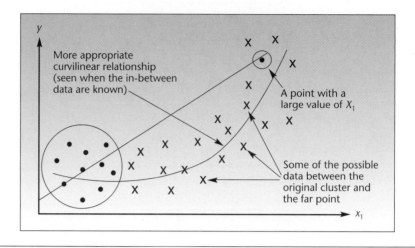

careful in such cases to guard against estimating a straight-line relation where a curvilinear one may be more appropriate. This could become evident if we had more data points in the region between the far point and the rest of the data. This is shown in Figure 11–18.

Figure 11–18 serves as a good reminder that regression analysis should not be used for extrapolation. We do not know what happens in the region in which we have no data. This region may be between two regions where we have data, or it may lie beyond the last observation in a given direction. The relationship may be quite different from what we estimate from the data. This is also a reason why forcing the regression surface to go through the origin (that is, carrying out a regression with no constant term $\beta_0 = 0$), as is done in some applications, is not a good idea. The reasoning in such cases follows the idea expressed in the statement "In this particular case, when there is zero input, there must be zero output," which may very well be true. Forcing the regression to go through the origin, however, may make the estimation procedure biased. This is because in the region where the data points are located—assuming they are not near the origin—the best straight line to describe the data may not have an intercept of zero. This happens when the relationship is not a straight-line relationship. We mentioned this problem in Chapter 10.

A data point far from the other point in some X_i direction is called an *influential observation* if it strongly affects the regression fit. Statistical techniques can be used to test whether the regression fit is strongly affected by a given observation. Computer routines such as MINITAB automatically search for outliers and influential observations, reporting them in the regression output so that the user is alerted to the possible effects of these observations. Table 11–10 shows part of the MINITAB output for the analysis of Example 11–2. The table reports "unusual observations": large residuals and influential observations that affect the estimation of the regression relationship.

Lack of Fit and Other Problems

Model lack of fit occurs if, for example, we try to fit a straight line to curved data. The statistical method of determining the existence of lack of fit consists of breaking down the sum of squares for error to a sum of squares due to pure error and a sum of squares due to lack of fit. The method requires that we have observations at equal values of the independent variables or near-neighbor points. This method is described in advanced texts on regression.

TABLE 11–10 Part of the MINITAB Output for Example 11–2

Unusual Observations

Obs.	M1	EXPORTS	Fit	Stdev.Fit	Residual	St.Resid
1	5.10	2.6000	2.6420	0.1288	−0.0420	−0.14 X
2	4.90	2.6000	2.6438	0.1234	−0.0438	−0.14 X
25	6.20	5.5000	4.5949	0.0676	0.9051	2.80R
26	6.30	3.7000	4.6311	0.0651	−0.9311	−2.87R
50	8.30	4.3000	5.1317	0.0648	−0.8317	−2.57R
67	8.20	5.6000	4.9474	0.0668	0.6526	2.02R

R denotes an obs. with a large st.resid.

X denotes an obs. whose X value gives it large influence.

A statistical method for determining whether the errors in a regression model are correlated through time (thus violating the regression model assumptions) is the Durbin-Watson test. This test is discussed in a later section of this chapter. Once we determine that our regression model is valid and that there are no serious violations of assumptions, we can use the model for its intended purpose.

PROBLEMS

11–40. Analyze the following plot of the residuals versus $\hat{Y}$.

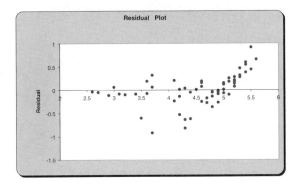

11–41. The normal probability plots of two regression experiments are given below. For each case, give your comments.

a.

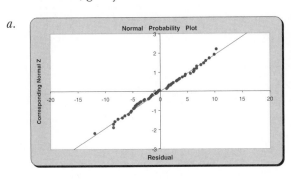

b.

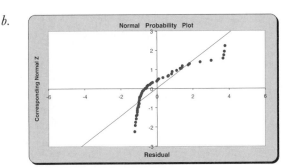

11–42. Explain what an outlier is.

11–43. How can you detect outliers? Discuss two ways of doing so.

11–44. Why should outliers not be discarded and the regression run without them?

11–45. Discuss the possible effects of an outlier on the regression analysis.

11–46.   What is an influential observation? Give a few examples.

11–47.   What are the limitations of forcing the regression surface to go through the origin?

11–48.   Analyze the residual plot of Figure 11–14.

11–7   Using the Multiple Regression Model for Prediction

The use of the multiple regression model for prediction follows the same lines as in the case of simple linear regression, discussed in Chapter 10. We obtain a regression model prediction of a value of the dependent variable Y, based on given values of the independent variables, by substituting the values of the independent variables into the prediction equation. That is, we substitute the values of X_i variables into the equation for $\hat{Y}$. We demonstrate this in Example 11–1.

The predicted value of Y is given by substituting the given values of advertising X_1 and in-store promotions X_2 for which we want to predict sales Y into equation 11–6, using the parameter estimates obtained in Section 11–2. Let us predict sales when advertising is at a level of \$10,000 and in-store promotions are at a level of \$5,000.

$$\hat{Y} = 47.165 + 1.599X_1 + 1.149X_2$$
$$= 47.165 + (1.599)(10) + (1.149)(5) = 68.9 \text{ (thousand dollars)}$$

This prediction is not bad, since the value of Y actually occurring for these values of X_1 and X_2 is known from Table 11–1 to be $Y = 70$ (thousand dollars). Our point estimate of the expected value of Y, denoted $E(Y)$, given these values of X_1 and X_2, is also 68.9 (thousand dollars). Note that our predictions lie *on* the estimated regression surface. The estimated regression surface for Example 11–1 is the plane shown in Figure 11–19.

FIGURE 11–19   Estimated Regression Plane for Example 11–1

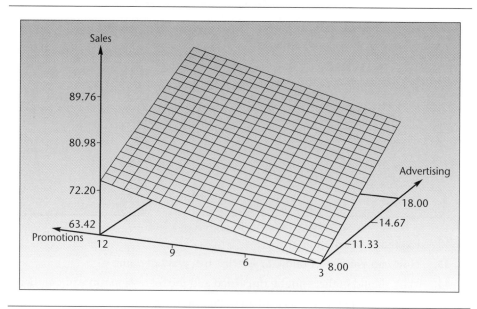

We may also compute prediction intervals as well as confidence intervals for $E(Y)$, given values of the independent variables. As you recall, while the predicted value and the estimate of the mean value of Y are equal, the prediction interval is wider than a confidence interval for $E(Y)$ using the same confidence level. There is more uncertainty about the predicted value than there is about the average value of Y given the values X_i. The equation for a $(1 - \alpha)$ 100% prediction interval is an extension of equation 10–32 for simple linear regression. The only difference is that the degrees of freedom of the t distribution are $n - (k + 1)$ rather than just $n - 2$, as is the case for $k = 1$. The standard error, when there are several explanatory variables, is a complicated expression, and we will not give it here; we will denote it by $s(\hat{Y})$. The prediction interval is given in equation 11–17.

A $(1 - \alpha)$ 100% prediction interval for a value of Y given values of X_i is

$$\hat{y} \pm t_{[\alpha/2,\, n-(k+1)]} \sqrt{s^2(\hat{Y}) + \text{MSE}} \qquad (11\text{–}17)$$

While the expression in the square root is complex, it is computed by most computer packages for regression. The prediction intervals for any values of the independent variables and a given level of confidence are produced as output.

Similarly, the equation for a $(1 - \alpha)$ 100% confidence interval for the conditional mean of Y is an extension of equation 10–33 for the simple linear regression. It is given as equation 11–18. Again, the degrees of freedom are $n - (k + 1)$. The formula for the standard error is complex and will not be given here. We will call the standard error $s[E(\hat{Y})]$. The confidence interval for the conditional mean of Y is computable and may be reported, upon request, in the output of most computer packages that include regression analysis.

A $(1 - \alpha)$ 100% confidence interval for the conditional mean of Y is

$$\hat{y} \pm t_{[\alpha/2,\, n-(k+1)]} s\,[E(\hat{y})] \qquad (11\text{–}18)$$

Equations 11–17 and 11–18 are implemented in the template on the Results sheet. These equations are also produced by other computer packages for regression, and are presented here—as many other formulas—for information only.[14] To make a prediction, we enter the values of the independent variables in row 22 and the confidence level desired in row 25. Table 11–11 shows the case of Example 11–2 with

TABLE 11–11   Prediction Using Multiple Regression
[Multiple Regression.xls; Sheet: Results]

19	Prediction Interval									
20										
21	Given X		M1	Price						
22			5	150						
23										
24		$1-\alpha$	$(1-\alpha)$ P.I. for Y for given X			$1-\alpha$	$(1-\alpha)$ P.I. for E[Y	X]		
25		95%	3.939	+ or -	0.6846		95%	3.939	+ or -	0.1799
26										

---

[14]Note also that equations 11–17 and 11–18 are extensions to multiple regression of the analogous equations, 10–32 and 10–33, of simple linear regression–which is a special case of multiple regression with one explanatory variable.

independent variables M1 and Price. The 95% prediction interval has been computed for the exports when M1 = 5 and Price = 150. A similar interval for the expected value of the exports for the given M1 and Price values has also been computed. The two prediction intervals appear in row 24.

The predictions are not very reliable because of the heteroscedasticity we discovered in the last section, but they are useful as a demonstration of the procedure. Remember that it is never a good idea to try to predict values outside the region of the data used in the estimation of the regression parameters, because the regression relationship may be different outside that range. In this example, all predictions use values of the independent variables within the range of the estimation data.

When using regression models, remember that a regression relationship between the dependent variable and some independent variables does not imply causality. Thus, if we find a linear relationship between Y and X, it does not necessarily mean that X causes Y. Causality is very different to determine and to prove. There is also the issue of spurious correlations between variables—correlations that are not real. Montgomery and Peck give an example of a regression analysis of the number of mentally disturbed people in the United Kingdom versus the number of radio receiver licenses issued in that country.[15] The regression relationship is close to a perfect straight line, with $r^2 = 0.9842$. Can the conclusion be drawn that there is a relationship between the number of radio receiver licenses and the incidence of mental illness? Probably not. Both variables—the number of licenses and the incidence of mental illness—are related to a third variable: population size. The increase in both of these variables reflects the growth of the population in general, and there is probably no *direct* connection between the two variables. We must be very careful in our interpretation of regression results.

The Template

The multiple regression template [Multiple Regression.xls] consists of a total of five sheets. The sheet titled "Data" is used to enter the data (see Figure 11–28 for an example). The sheet titled "Results" contains the regression coefficients, their standard errors, the corresponding t tests, the ANOVA table, and a panel for prediction intervals. The sheet titled "Residuals" contains a plot of the residuals, the Durbin-Watson statistic (described later), and a normal probability plot for testing the normality assumption of the error term. The sheet titled "Correl" displays the correlation coefficient between every pair of variables. The use of the correlation matrix is described later in this chapter. The sheet titled "Partial F" can be used to find partial F, which is also described later in this chapter.

Setting Recalculation to "Manual" on the Template

Since the calculations performed in the multiple regression template are voluminous, a recalculation can take a little longer than in other templates. Therefore, entering data in the Data sheet may be difficult, especially on slower PCs (Pentium II or earlier), because the computer will recalculate every result before taking in the next data entry. If this problem occurs, set the Recalculation feature to manual. This can be done by clicking the Microsoft Office button and then Formulas. Choose Manual under the Calculation options. When this is done, a change made in the data or in any cell *will not cause the spreadsheet to automatically update itself.* Only when recalculation is manually initiated will the spreadsheet update itself. To initiate recalculation, *press the F9 key* on the keyboard. A warning message about pressing the F9 key is displayed at a few places in the template. If the recalculation has not been set to manual, this message can be ignored.

---

[15]D. Montgomery, E. Peck, and G. G. Vining, *Introduction to Linear Regression Analysis,* 4th ed. (New York: Wiley, 2006).

Note also that when the recalculation is set to manual, *none of the open spreadsheets* will update itself. That is, if other spreadsheets were open, they will not update themselves either. The F9 key needs to be pressed on every open spreadsheet to initiate recalculation. This state of manual recalculation will continue until the Excel program is closed and reopened. For this reason, set the recalculation to manual only after careful consideration.

11–49. Explain why it is not a good idea to use the regression equation for predicting values outside the range of the estimation data set.

11–50. Use equation 11–6 to predict sales in Example 11–1 when the level of advertising is $8,000 and in-store promotions are at a level of $12,000.

11–51. Using the regression relationship you estimated in problem 11–8, predict the value of a home 1,800 square feet located 2.0 miles from the center of the town.

11–52. Using the regression equation from problem 11–25, predict excess stock return when SIZRNK = 5 and PRCRNK = 6.

11–53. Using the information in Table 11–11, what is the standard error of $\hat{Y}$? What is the standard error of $E(\hat{Y})$?

11–54. Use a computer to produce a prediction interval and a confidence interval for the conditional mean of Y for the prediction in problem 11–50. Use the data in Table 11–1.

11–55. What is the difference between a predicted value of the dependent variable and the conditional mean of the dependent variable?

11–56. Why is the prediction interval of 95% wider than the 95% confidence interval for the conditional mean, using the same values of the independent variables?

11–8 Qualitative Independent Variables

The variables we have encountered so far in this chapter have all been *quantitative* variables: variables that can take on values on a scale. Sales volume, advertising expenditure, exports, the money supply, and people's ratings of an automobile are all examples of quantitative variables. In this section, we will discuss the use of *qualitative* variables as explanatory variables in a regression model. Qualitative variables are variables that describe a quality rather than a quantity. This should remind you of analysis of variance in Chapter 9. There we had qualitative variables: the kind of resort in the Club Med example, type of airplane, type of coffee, and so on.

CHAPTER 19

In some cases, including information on one or more qualitative variables in our multiple regression model is very useful. For example, a hotel chain may be interested in predicting the number of occupied rooms as a function of the economy of the area in which the hotel is located, as well as advertising level and some other quantitative variables. The hotel may also want to know whether the peak season is in progress—a qualitative variable that may have a lot to do with the level of occupancy at the hotel. A property appraiser may be interested in predicting the value of different residential units on the basis of several quantitative variables, such as age of the unit and area in square feet, as well as the qualitative variable of whether the unit is owned or rented.

Each of these qualitative variables has only two *levels:* peak season versus nonpeak season, rental unit versus nonrental unit. An easy way to quantify such a qualitative variable is by way of a single **indicator variable**, also called a **dummy variable**. An indicator variable is a variable that indicates whether some condition holds. It has the value 1 when the condition holds and the value 0 when the condition does not hold. If you are familiar with computer science, you probably know the indicator variable by another name: *binary variable*, because it takes on only two possible values, 0 and 1.

When included in the model of hotel occupancy, the indicator variable will equal 0 if it is not peak season and 1 if it is (or vice versa; it makes no difference). Similarly, in the property value analysis, the dummy variable will have the value 0 when the unit is rented and the value 1 when the unit is owned, or vice versa. We define the general form of an indicator variable in equation 11–19.

An indicator variable of qualitative level A is

$$X_h = \begin{cases} 1 & \text{if level A is obtained} \\ 0 & \text{if level A is not obtained} \end{cases} \qquad (11\text{–}19)$$

The use of indicator variables in regression analysis is very simple. No special computational routines are required. All we do is code the indicator variable as 1 whenever the quality of interest is obtained for a particular data point and as 0 when it is not obtained. The rest of the variables in the regression equation are left the same. We demonstrate the use of an indicator variable in modeling a qualitative variable with two levels in the following example.

EXAMPLE 11–3   A motion picture industry analyst wants to estimate the gross earnings generated by a movie. The estimate will be based on different variables involved in the film's production. The independent variables considered are X_1 = production cost of the movie and X_2 = total cost of all promotional activities. A third variable that the analyst wants to consider is the qualitative variable of whether the movie is based on a book published before the release of the movie. This third, qualitative variable is handled by the use of an indicator variable: $X_3 = 0$ if the movie is not based on a book, and $X_3 = 1$ if it is. The analyst obtains information on a random sample of 20 Hollywood movies made within the last 5 years (the inference is to be made only about the population of movies in this particular category). The data are given in Table 11–12. The variable Y is gross earnings, in millions of dollars. The two quantitative independent variables are also in millions of dollars.

Solution   The data are entered into the template. The resulting output is presented in Figure 11–20. The coefficient of determination of this regression is very high; the F statistic value is very significant, and we have a good regression relationship. From the individual t ratios and their p-values, we find that all three independent variables are important in the equation.

From the intercept of 7.84, we could (erroneously, of course) deduce that a movie costing nothing to produce or promote, and that is not based on a book, would still gross $7.84 million! The point 0 ($X_1 = 0$, $X_2 = 0$, $X_3 = 0$) is outside the estimation region, and the regression relationship may not hold for that region. In our case, it evidently does not. The intercept is merely a reference point used to move the regression surface upward to where it should be in the estimation region.

The estimated slope for the cost variable, 2.85, means that—within the estimation region—an increase of $1 million in a movie's production cost (the other variables held constant) increases the movie's gross earnings by an average of $2.85 million. Similarly, the estimated slope coefficient for the promotion variable means that, in the estimation region of the variables, an increase of $1 million in promotional

TABLE 11–12   Data for Example 11–3

Movie	Gross Earnings Y, Million $	Production Cost X₁, Million $	Promotion Cost X₂, Million $	Book X₃
1	28	4.2	1	0
2	35	6.0	3	1
3	50	5.5	6	1
4	20	3.3	1	0
5	75	12.5	11	1
6	60	9.6	8	1
7	15	2.5	0.5	0
8	45	10.8	5	0
9	50	8.4	3	1
10	34	6.6	2	0
11	48	10.7	1	1
12	82	11.0	15	1
13	24	3.5	4	0
14	50	6.9	10	0
15	58	7.8	9	1
16	63	10.1	10	0
17	30	5.0	1	1
18	37	7.5	5	0
19	45	6.4	8	1
20	72	10.0	12	1

activities (with the other variables constant) increases the movie's gross earnings by an average of $2.28 million.

How do we interpret the estimated coefficient of variable X_3? The estimated coefficient of 7.17 means that having the movie based on a published book $(X_3 = 1)$ increases the movie's gross earnings by an average of $7.17 million. Again, the inference is valid only for the region of the data used in the estimation. When $X_3 = 0$, that is, when the movie is not based on a book, the last term in the estimated equation for $\hat{Y}$ drops out—there is no added $7.17 million.

What do we learn from this example about the function of the indicator variable? Note that the predicted value of Y, given the values of the quantitative independent

FIGURE 11–20   Multiple Regression Results for Example 11–3.
[Multiple Regression.xls; Sheet: Results]

	A	B	C	D	E	F	G	H	I	J	K	L
1	**Multiple Regression Results**					Movies						
2												
3			0	1	2	3	4	5	6	7	8	9	10
4			Intercept	rod.Cos	Promo	Book						
5		*b*	7.8362	2.8477	2.2782	7.1661						
6		*s(b)*	2.3334	0.3923	0.2534	1.818						
7		*t*	3.3583	7.2582	8.9894	3.9418						
8		*p-value*	0.0040	0.0000	0.0000	0.0012						
9												
10												
11	**ANOVA Table**											
12		**Source**	**SS**	**df**	**MS**	**F**	**F**Critical	**p-value**				
13		Regn.	6325.2	3	2108.4	154.89	3.2389	0.0000	*s*	3.6895		
14		Error	217.8	16	13.612							
15		Total	6543	19		R²	0.9667		Adjusted R²	0.9605		
16												

FIGURE 11–21   Two Regression Planes of Example 11–3

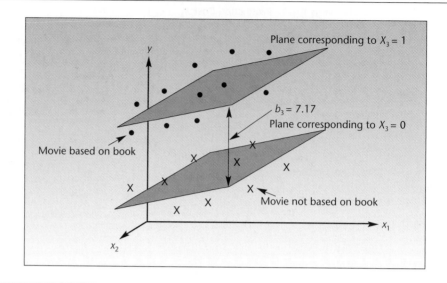

variables, shifts upward (or downward, depending on the sign of the estimated coefficient) by an amount equal to the coefficient of the indicator variable whenever the variable is equal to 1. In this particular case, the surface of the regression—the plane formed by the variables Y, X_1, and X_2—is split into two surfaces: one corresponding to movies based on books and the other corresponding to movies not based on books. The appropriate surface depends on whether $X_3 = 0$ or $X_3 = 1$; the two estimated surfaces are separated by a distance equal to $b_3 = 7.17$. This is demonstrated in Figure 11–21. The regression surface in this example is a plane, so we can draw its image (for a higher-dimensional surface, the same idea holds).

We will now look at the simpler case, with one independent quantitative variable and one indicator variable. Here we assume an estimated regression relationship of the form $\hat{Y} = b_0 + b_1X_1 + b_2X_2$, where X_1 is a quantitative variable and X_2 is an indicator variable. The regression relationship is a straight line, and the indicator variable splits the line into two parallel straight lines, one for each level (0 or 1) of the qualitative variable. The points belonging to one level (a level could be Book, as in Example 11–3) are shown as triangles, and the points belonging to the other level are shown as squares. The distance between the two parallel lines (measured as the difference between the two intercepts) is equal to the estimated coefficient of the dummy variable X_2. The situation is demonstrated in Figure 11–22.

We have been dealing with qualitative variables that have only two levels. Therefore, it has sufficed to use an indicator variable with two possible values, 0 and 1. What about situations where we have a qualitative variable with more than two levels? Should we use an "indicator" variable with more than two values? The answer is no. Were we to do this and give our variable values such as 0, 1, 2, 3, . . . , to indicate qualitative levels, we would be using a quantitative variable that has several discrete values but no values in between. Also, the assignment of the qualities to the values would be arbitrary. Since there may be no justification for using the values 1, 2, 3, etc., we would be imposing a very special measuring scale on the regression problem—a scale that may not be appropriate. Instead, we will use several indicator variables.

We account for a qualitative variable with r levels by the use of $r - 1$ indicator (0/1) variables.

FIGURE 11–22   A Regression with One Quantitative Variable and One Dummy Variable

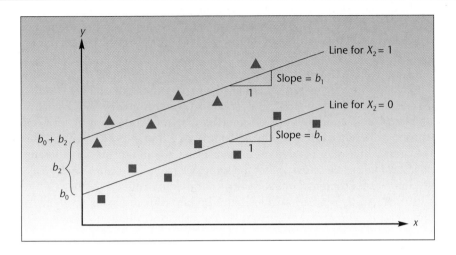

We will now demonstrate the use of this rule by changing Example 11–3 somewhat. Suppose that the analyst is interested not in whether a movie is based on a book, but rather in using an explanatory variable that represents the category to which each movie belongs: adventure, drama, or romance. Since this qualitative variable has $r = 3$ levels, the rule tells us that we need to model this variable by using $r - 1 = 2$ indicator variables. Each of the two indicator variables will have one of two possible values, as before: 0 or 1. The setup of the two dummy variables indicating the level of the qualitative variable, movie category, is shown in the following table. For simplicity, let us also assume that the only quantitative variable in the equation is production cost (we leave out the promotion variable). This will allow us to have lines rather than planes. We let $X_1 = $ production cost, as before. We now define the two dummy variables X_2 and X_3.

Category	X_2	X_3
Adventure	0	0
Drama	0	1
Romance	1	0

The definition of the values of X_2 and X_3 for representing the different categories is arbitrary; we could just as well have assigned the values $X_2 = 0$, $X_3 = 0$ to drama or to romance as to adventure. The important thing to remember is that the number of dummy variables is 1 less than the number of categories they represent. Otherwise our model will be overspecified, and problems will occur. In this example, variable X_2 is the indicator variable for romance; when a movie is in the romance category, this variable has the value 1. Similarly, X_3 is the indicator for drama and has the value 1 in cases where a movie is in the drama category. Only three categories are under consideration, so when both X_2 and X_3 are zero, the movie is neither a drama nor a romance; therefore, it must be an adventure movie.

If we use the model

$$Y = \beta_0 + \beta_1 X_1 + \beta_2 X_2 + \beta_3 X_3 + \epsilon \qquad (11\text{–}20)$$

with X_2 and X_3 as defined, we will be estimating three regression lines, one line per category. The line for adventure movies will be $\hat{Y} = b_0 + b_1 X_1$ because here both X_2

and X_3 are zero. The drama line will be $\hat{Y} = b_0 + b_3 + b_1X_1$ because here $X_3 = 1$ and $X_2 = 0$. In the case of romance movies, our line will be $\hat{Y} = b_0 + b_2 + b_1X_1$ because in this case $X_2 = 1$ and $X_3 = 0$. Since the estimated coefficients b_i may be negative as well as positive, the different parallel lines may position themselves above or below one another, as determined by the data. Of course, the b_i may be estimates of zero. If we did not reject the null hypothesis H_0: $\beta_3 = 0$, using the usual t test, it would mean that there was no evidence that the adventure and the drama lines were different. That is, it would mean that, on average, adventure movies and drama movies have the same gross earnings as determined by the production costs. If we determine that β_2 is not different from zero, the adventure and romance lines will be the same and the drama line may be different. In case the adventure line is different from drama and romance, these two being the same, we would determine statistically that both β_2 and β_3 are different from zero, but not different from each other.

If we have three regression lines, why bother with indicator variables at all? Why not just run three separate regressions, each for a different movie category? One answer to this question has already been given: The use of indicator variables and their estimated regression coefficients with their standard errors allows us to *test statistically* whether the qualitative variable of interest has any effect on the dependent variable. We are able to test whether we have one distinct line, two lines, three lines, or as many lines as there are levels of the qualitative variable. Another reason is that even if we know that there are, say, three distinct lines, estimating them together via a regression analysis with dummy variables allows us to pool the degrees of freedom for the three regressions, leading to better estimation and a more efficient analysis.

Figure 11–23 shows the three regression lines of our new version of Example 11–3; each line shows the regression relationship between a movie's production cost and the resulting movie's gross earnings in its category. In case there are two independent quantitative variables, say, if we add promotions as a second quantitative variable, we will have three regression *planes* like the two planes shown in Figure 11–21. In Figure 11–23, we show adventure movies as triangles, romance movies as squares, and drama movies as circles. Assuming that adventure movies have the highest average

FIGURE 11–23   The Three Possible Regression Lines, Depending on Movie Category (modified Example 11–3)

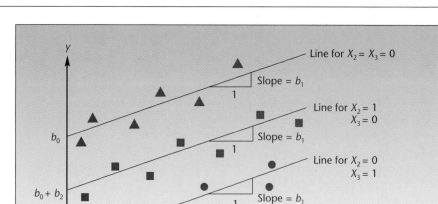

gross earnings, followed by romance and drama, the estimated coefficients b_2 and b_3 have to be negative, as can be seen from the figure.

Can we run a regression on a qualitative variable (by use of dummy variables) only? Yes. You have already seen this model, essentially. Running a regression on a qualitative variable only means modeling some quantitative response by levels of a qualitative factor: it is the *analysis of variance,* discussed in Chapter 9. Doing the analysis by regression means using a different computational procedure than was done in Chapter 9, but it is still the analysis of variance. Two qualitative variables make the analysis a two-way ANOVA, and interaction terms are cross-products of the appropriate dummy variables, such as $X_2 X_3$. We will say more about cross-products a little later. For now, we note that the regression approach to ANOVA allows us more freedom. Remember that a two-way ANOVA, using the method in Chapter 9, required a balanced design (equal sample size in each cell). If we use the regression approach, we are no longer restricted to the balanced design and may use any sample size.

Let us go back to regressions using quantitative independent variables with some qualitative variables. In some situations, we are not interested in using a regression equation for prediction or for any of the other common uses of regression analysis. Instead, we are intrinsically interested in a qualitative variable used in the regression. Let us be more specific. Recall our original Example 11–3. Suppose we are not interested in predicting a movie's gross earnings based on the production cost, promotions, and whether the movie is based on a book. Suppose instead that we are interested in answering the question: Is there a difference in average gross earnings between movies based on books and movies not based on books?

To answer this question, we use the estimated regression relationship. We use the estimate b_3 and its standard error in testing the null hypothesis H_0: $\beta_3 = 0$ versus the alternative H_1: $\beta_3 \neq 0$. The question is really an ANOVA question. We want to know whether a difference exists in the population means of the two groups of movies based on books and movies not based on books. However, we have some quantitative variables that affect the variable we are measuring (gross earnings). We therefore incorporate information on these variables (production cost and promotions) in a regression model aimed at answering our ANOVA question. When we do this, that is, when we attempt to answer the question of whether differences in population means exist, using a regression equation to account for other sources of variation in our data (the quantitative independent variables), we are conducting an **analysis of covariance.** The independent variables used in the analysis of covariance are called **concomitant variables,** and their purpose in the analysis is not to explain or predict the independent variable, but rather to reduce the errors in the test of significance of the indicator variable or variables.

One of the interesting applications of analysis of covariance is in providing statistical evidence in cases of sex or race discrimination. We demonstrate this particular use in the following example.

A large service company was sued by its female employees in a class action suit alleging sex discrimination in salary levels. The claim was that, on average, a man and a woman of the same education and experience received different salaries: the man's salary was believed to be higher than the woman's salary. The attorney representing the women employees hired a statistician to provide statistical evidence supporting the women's side of the case. The statistician was allowed access to the company's payroll files and obtained a random sample of 100 employees, 40 of whom were women. In addition to salary, the files contained information on education and experience. The statistician then ran a regression analysis of salary Y versus three variables: education level X_1 (on a scale based on the total number of years in school, with an additional value added to the score for each college degree earned, by type),

EXAMPLE 11–4

TABLE 11–13   Regression Results for Example 11–4

Variable	Coefficient Estimate	Standard Error
Constant	8,547	32.6
Education	949	45.1
Experience	1,258	78.5
Sex	−3,256	212.4

years of experience X_2 (on a scale that combined the number of years of experience directly related to the job assignment with the number of years of similar job experience), and gender X_3 (0 if the employee was a man and 1 if the employee was a woman). The computer output for the regression included the results F ratio = 1,237.56 and $R^2 = 0.67$, as well as the coefficient estimates and standard errors given in Table 11–13. Based on this information, does the attorney for the women employees have a case against the company?

Solution   Let us analyze the regression results. Remember that we are using a regression with a dummy variable to perform an analysis of covariance. There is certainly a regression relationship between salary and at least some of the variables, as evidenced by the very large F value, which is beyond any critical point we can find in a table. The p-value is very small. The coefficient of determination is not extremely high, but then we are using very few variables to explain variation in salary levels. This being the case, 67% explained variation, based on these variables only, is quite respectable. Now we consider the information in Table 11–13.

Dividing the four coefficient estimates by their standard errors, we find that all three variables are important, and the intercept is different from zero. However, we are particularly interested in the hypothesis test:

$$H_0: \beta_3 = 0$$
$$H_1: \beta_3 \neq 0$$

Our test statistic is $t_{(96)} = b_3/s(b_3) = -3,256/212.4 = -15.33$. Since t with 96 degrees of freedom [df $= n - (k + 1) = 100 - 4 = 96$] is virtually a standard normal random variable, we conduct this as a Z test. The computed test statistic value of -15.33 lies very far in the left-hand rejection region. This means that there are two regressions: one for men and one for women. Since we coded X_3 as 0 for a man and 1 for a woman, the women's estimated regression plane lies \$3,256 below the regression plane for men. Since the parameter of the sex variable is significantly different from zero (with an extremely small p-value) and is negative, there is statistical evidence of sex discrimination in this case. The situation here is as seen in Figure 11–21 for the previous example: We have two regression planes, one below the other. The only difference is that in this example, we were not interested in using the regression for prediction, but rather for an ANOVA-type statistical test.

Interactions between Qualitative and Quantitative Variables

Do the different regression lines or higher-dimensional surfaces have to be parallel? The answer is no. Sometimes, there are *interactions* between a qualitative variable and one or more quantitative variables. The idea of an interaction in regression analysis is the same as the idea of interaction between factors in a two-way ANOVA model (as well as higher-order ANOVAs). In regression analysis with qualitative variables,

CHAPTER 19

FIGURE 11–24   **Effects of an Interaction between a Qualitative Variable and a Quantitative Variable**

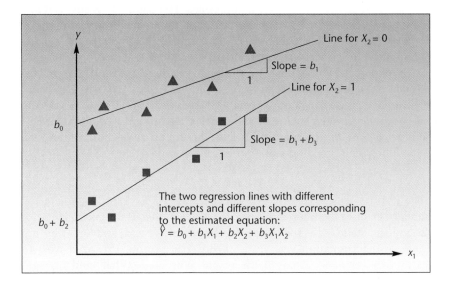

the interaction between a qualitative variable and a quantitative variable makes the regression lines or planes at different levels of the dummy variables have *different slopes.* Let us look at the simple case where we have one independent quantitative variable X_1 and one qualitative variable with two levels, modeled by the dummy variable X_2. When an interaction exists between the qualitative and the quantitative variables, the slope of the regression line for $X_2 = 0$ is different from the slope of the regression line for $X_2 = 1$. This is shown in Figure 11–24.

We model the interactions between variables by the cross-product of the variables. The interaction of X_1 with X_2 in this case is modeled by adding the term X_1X_2 to the regression equation. We are thus interested in the model

$$Y = \beta_0 + \beta_1X_1 + \beta_2X_2 + \beta_3X_1X_2 + \epsilon \qquad (11\text{--}21)$$

We can use the results of the estimation procedure to test for the existence of an interaction. We do so by testing the significance of parameter β_3.

When regression parameters β_1, β_2, and β_3 are all nonzero, we have two distinct lines with different intercepts and different slopes. When β_2 is zero, we have two lines with the same intercept and different slopes (this is unlikely to happen, except when both intercepts are zero). When β_3 is zero, we have two parallel lines, as in the case of equation 11–20. If β_1 is zero, of course, we have no regression—just an ANOVA model; we then assume that β_3 is also zero. Assuming the full model of equation 11–21, representing two distinct lines with different slopes and different intercepts, the intercept and the slope of each line will be as shown in Figure 11–24. By substituting $X_2 = 0$ or $X_2 = 1$ into equation 11–21, verify the definition of each slope and each intercept.

Again, estimating a single model for the different levels of the indicator variable offers two advantages. These are the pooling of degrees of freedom (we assume that the spread of the data about the two or more lines is equal) and an understanding of the joint process generating the data. More important, we may use the model to statistically test for the equality of intercepts and slopes. Note that when several indicator variables are used in modeling one or more qualitative variables, the model has several possible interaction terms. We will learn more about interactions in general in the next section.

PROBLEMS

11-57. Echlin, Inc., makes parts for automobiles. The company is engaged in strong competition with Japanese, Taiwanese, and Korean manufacturers of the same automobile parts. Recently, the company hired a statistician to study the relationship between monthly sales and the independent variable, number of cars on the road. Data on the explanatory variable are published in national statistical reports. Because of the keen competition with Asian firms, an indicator variable was also used. This variable was given the value 1 during months when restrictions on imports from Asia were in effect and 0 when such restrictions were not in effect. Denoting sales by Y, total number of cars on the road by X_1, and the import restriction dummy variable by X_2, the following regression equation was estimated:

$$\hat{Y} = -567.3 + 0.006X_1 + 26,540X_2$$

The standard error of the intercept estimate was 38.5, that of the coefficient of X_1 was 0.0002, and the standard error of the coefficient of X_2 was 1,534.67. The multiple coefficient of determination was $R^2 = 0.783$. The sample size used was $n = 60$ months (5 years of data). Analyze the results presented. What kind of regression model was used? Comment on the significance of the model parameters and the value of R^2. How many distinct regression lines are there? What likely happens during times of restricted trade with Asia?

11-58. A regression analysis was carried out based on 7,016 observations of firms, aimed at assessing the factors that determine the level of a firm's leverage. The independent variables included amount of fixed assets, profitability, firm size, volatility, and abnormal earnings level, as well as a dummy variable that indicated whether the firm was regulated (1) or unregulated (0). The coefficient estimate for this dummy variable was -0.003 and its standard error was -0.29.[16] Does a firm's being regulated affect its leverage level? Explain.

11-59. If we have a regression model with no quantitative variables and only two qualitative variables, represented by some indicator variables and cross-products, what kind of analysis is carried out?

11-60. Recall our Club Med example of Chapter 9. Suppose that not all vacationers at Club Med resorts stay an equal length of time at the resort—different people stay different numbers of days. The club's research director knows that people's ratings of the resorts tend to differ depending on the number of days spent at the resort. Design a new method for studying whether there are differences among the average population ratings of the five Caribbean resorts. What is the name of your method of analysis, and how is the analysis carried out? Explain.

11-61. A financial institution specializing in venture capital is interested in predicting the success of business operations that the institution helps to finance. Success is defined by the institution as return on its investment, as a percentage, after 3 years of operation. The explanatory variables used are Investment (in thousands of dollars), Early investment (in thousands of dollars), and two dummy variables denoting the category of business. The values of these variables are (0, 0) for high-technology industry, (0, 1) for biotechnology companies, and (1, 0) for aerospace firms. Following is part of the computer output for this analysis. Interpret the output, and give a complete analysis of the results of this study based on the provided information.

---

[16]Matthew T. Billett, Tao-Hsien Dolly King, and David Mauer, "Growth Opportunities and the Choice of Leverage, Debt Maturity, and Covenants," *Journal of Finance* 42, no. 2 (2007), pp. 697–730.

```
The regression equation is
Return = 6.16 + 0.617 INVEST + 0.151 EARLY + 11.1 DUM1 + 4.15 DUM2
  Predictor     Coef       Stdev
  Constant      6.162      1.642
  INVEST        0.6168     0.1581
  EARLY         0.1509     0.1465
  DUM1         11.051      1.355
  DUM2          4.150      1.315
  s = 2.148     R-sq = 91.6%     R-sq (adj) = 89.4%


Analysis of Variance

   SOURCE       DF       SS
Regression      4      755.99
Error          15       69.21
Total          19      825.20
```

11–9 Polynomial Regression

Often, the relationship between the dependent variable Y and one or more of the independent X variables is not a straight-line relationship but, rather, has some curvature to it. Several such situations are shown in Figure 11–25 (we show the curved relationship between Y and a *single* explanatory variable X). In each of the situations shown, a straight line provides a poor fit to the data. Instead, polynomials of order higher than 1, that is, functions of higher powers of X, such as X^2 and X^3, provide much better fit to our data. Such polynomials in the X variable or in several X_i variables are still considered linear regression models. Only models where the parameters β_i are not all of the first power are called *nonlinear models*. The multiple linear regression model thus covers situations of fitting data to polynomial functions. The general form of a polynomial regression model in one variable X is given in equation 11–22.

CHAPTER 18

FIGURE 11–25   Situations Where the Relationship between *X* and *Y* Is Curved

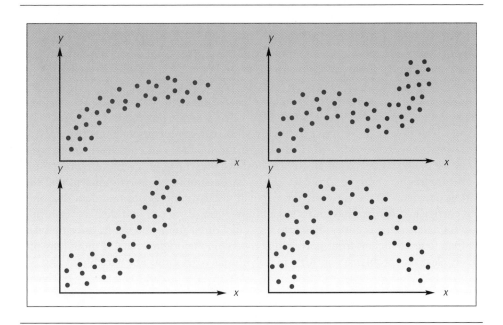

FIGURE 11–26   The Fits Provided for the Data Sets in Figure 11–25 by Polynomial Models

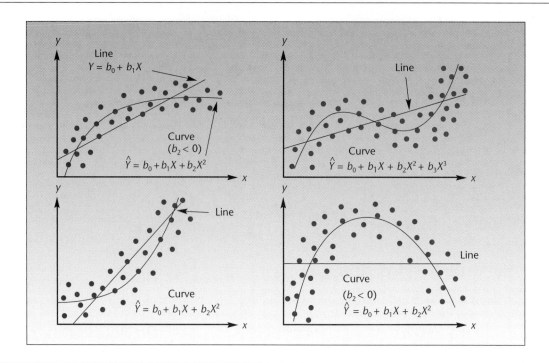

A one-variable polynomial regression model is

$$Y = \beta_0 + \beta_1 X + \beta_2 X^2 + \beta_3 X^3 + \cdots + \beta_m X^m + \epsilon \qquad (11\text{–}22)$$

where m is the *degree* of the polynomial—the highest power of X appearing in the equation. The degree of the polynomial is the *order* of the model.

Figure 11–26 shows how second- and third-degree polynomial models provide good fits for the data sets in Figure 11–25. A straight line is also shown in each case, for comparison. Compare the fit provided in each case by a polynomial with the poor fit provided by a straight line. Some authors, for example, Cook and Weisberg, recommend using polynomials of order no greater than 2 (the third-order example in Figure 11–26 would be an exception) because of the overfitting problem.[17] At any rate, models should never be of order 6 or higher (unless the powers of X have been transformed in a special way). Seber shows that when a polynomial of degree 6 or greater is fit to a data set, a matrix involved in regression computations becomes *ill-conditioned,* which means that very small errors in the data cause relatively large errors in the estimated model parameters.[18] In short, we must be very careful with polynomial regression models and try to obtain the most parsimonious polynomial model that will fit our data. In the next section, we will discuss *transformations* of data that often can change curved data sets into a straight-line form. If we can find such a transformation for a data set, it is always better to use a first-order model on the transformed data set than to use a higher-order polynomial model on the original data. It should be intuitively clear that problems may arise in polynomial regression. The variables X and X^2,

---

[17]R. Dennis Cook and Sanford Weisberg, *Applied Regression Including Computing and Graphics* (New York: Wiley, 1999).

[18]George A. F. Seber and Alan J. Lee, *Linear Regression Analysis,* 2nd ed. (New York: Wiley, 2003).

for example, are clearly not independent of each other. This may cause the problem of multicollinearity in cases where the data are confined to a narrow range of values.

Having seen what to beware of in using polynomial regression, now we see how these models are used. Since powers of X can be obtained directly from the value of variable X, it is relatively easy to run polynomial models. We enter the data into the computer and add a command that uses X to form a new variable. In a second-order model, we create an X^2 column using spreadsheet commands. Then we run a multiple regression model with two "independent" variables: X and X^2. We demonstrate this with a new example.

EXAMPLE 11–5

Sales response to advertising usually follows a curve reflecting the diminishing returns to advertising expenditure. As a firm increases its advertising expenditure, sales increase, but the rate of increase drops continually after a certain point. If we consider company sales profits as a function of advertising expenditure, we find that the response function can be very well approximated by a second-order (quadratic) model of the form

$$Y = \beta_0 + \beta_1 X + \beta_2 X^2 + \epsilon$$

A quadratic response function such as this one is shown in Figure 11–27.

It is very important for a firm to identify its own point X_m, shown in the figure. At this point, a maximum benefit is achieved from advertising in terms of the resulting sales profits. Figure 11–27 shows a general form of the sales response to advertising. To find its own maximum point X_m, a firm needs to estimate its response-to-advertising function from its own operation data, obtained by using different levels of advertising at different time periods and observing the resulting sales profits. For a particular firm, the data on monthly sales Y and monthly advertising expenditure X, both in hundred thousand dollars, are given in Table 11–14. The table also shows the values of X^2 used in the regression analysis.

FIGURE 11–27   A Quadratic Response Function of Sales Profits to Advertising Expenditure

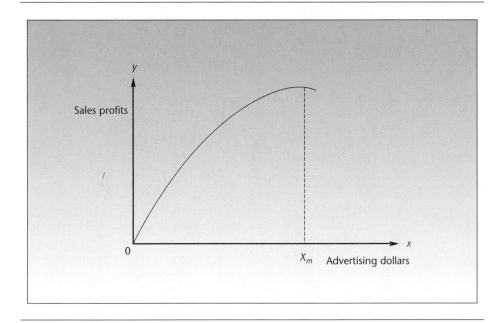

TABLE 11–14 Data for Example 11–5

Row	Sales	Advert	Advsqr
1	5.0	1.0	1.00
2	6.0	1.8	3.24
3	6.5	1.6	2.56
4	7.0	1.7	2.89
5	7.5	2.0	4.00
6	8.0	2.0	4.00
7	10.0	2.3	5.29
8	10.8	2.8	7.84
9	12.0	3.5	12.25
10	13.0	3.3	10.89
11	15.5	4.8	23.04
12	15.0	5.0	25.00
13	16.0	7.0	49.00
14	17.0	8.1	65.61
15	18.0	8.0	64.00
16	18.0	10.0	100.00
17	18.5	8.0	64.00
18	21.0	12.7	161.29
19	20.0	12.0	144.00
20	22.0	15.0	225.00
21	23.0	14.4	207.36

Solution Figure 11–28 shows the data entered in the template. In cell E5, the formula "`=D5^2`" has been entered. This calculates X^2. The formula has been copied down through cell E25. The regression results from the Results sheet of the template are shown in

FIGURE 11–28 Data for the Regression [Multiple Regression.xls; Sheet: Data]

E5 = =D5^2

	A	B	C	D	E	F	G
1	**Multiple Regression**					Example 11-5	
2							
3		Y	1	X1	X2	X3	X4
4	Sl.No.	**Sales**		**Advert**	**Advsqr**		
5	1	5	1	1	1		
6	2	6	1	1.8	3.24		
7	3	6.5	1	1.6	2.56		
8	4	7	1	1.7	2.89		
9	5	7.5	1	2	4		
10	6	8	1	2	4		
11	7	10	1	2.3	5.29		
12	8	10.8	1	2.8	7.84		
13	9	12	1	3.5	12.25		
14	10	13	1	3.3	10.89		
15	11	15.5	1	4.8	23.04		
16	12	15	1	5	25		
17	13	16	1	7	49		
18	14	17	1	8.1	65.61		
19	15	18	1	8	64		
20	16	18	1	10	100		
21	17	18.5	1	8	64		
22	18	21	1	12.7	161.29		
23	19	20	1	12	144		
24	20	22	1	15	225		
25	21	23	1	14.4	207.36		

TABLE 11–15   **Results of the Regression**
[Multiple Regression; Sheet: Results]

	0	1	2	3	4	5	6	7	8	9	10
	Intercept	Advert	Advsqr								
b	3.51505	2.51478	-0.0875								
s(b)	0.73840	0.25796	0.0166								
t	4.7599	9.7487	-5.2751								
p-value	0.0002	0.0000	0.0001								

ANOVA Table

Source	SS	df	MS	F	$F_{Critical}$	p-value		
Regn.	630.258	2	315.13	208.99	3.5546	0.0000	s	1.228
Error	27.142	18	1.5079					
Total	657.4	20		R^2	0.9587		Adjusted R^2	0.9541

Table 11–15. The coefficient of determination is $R^2 = 0.9587$, the F ratio is significant, and both Advert and Advsqr are very significant. The minus sign of the squared variable, Advsqr, is logical because a quadratic function with a maximum point has a negative leading coefficient (the coefficient of X^2). We may write the estimated quadratic regression model of Y in terms of X and X^2 as follows:

$$Y = 3.52 + 2.51X - 0.0875X^2 + e \qquad (11\text{–}23)$$

The equation of the estimated regression curve itself is given by dropping the error term e, giving an equation for the predicted values $\hat{Y}$ that lie on the quadratic curve

$$\hat{Y} = 3.52 + 2.51X - 0.0875X^2 \qquad (11\text{–}24)$$

In our particular example, the equation of the curve (equation 11–24) is of importance, as it can be differentiated with respect to X, with the derivative then set to zero and the result solved for the maximizing value X_m shown in Figure 11–27. (If you have not studied calculus, you may ignore the preceding statement.) The result here is $x_m = 14.34$ (hundred thousand dollars). This value maximizes sales profits with respect to advertising (within estimation error of the regression). Thus, the firm should set its advertising level at $1.434 million. The fact that polynomials can always be differentiated gives these models an advantage over alternative models. Remember, however, to keep the order of the model low.

Other Variables and Cross-Product Terms

The polynomial regression model in one variable X, given in equation 11–22, can easily be extended to include more than one independent explanatory variable. The new model, which includes several variables at different powers, is a mixture of the usual multiple regression model in k variables (equation 11–1) and the polynomial regression model (equation 11–22). When several variables are in a regression equation, we may also consider interactions among variables. We have already encountered interactions in the previous section, where we discussed interactions between an indicator variable and a quantitative variable. We saw that an interaction term is just the cross-product of the two variables involved. In this section, we discuss the general concept of interactions between variables, quantitative or not.

The interaction term $X_i X_j$ is a second-order term (the product of two variables is classified the same way as an X^2 term). Similarly, $X_i X_j^2$, for example, is a third-order term. Thus, models that incorporate interaction terms find their natural place within the class of polynomial models. Equation 11–25 is a second-order regression model in two variables X_1 and X_2. This model includes both first and second powers of both variables and an interaction term.

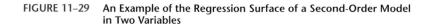

$$Y = \beta_0 + \beta_1 X_1 + \beta_2 X_2 + \beta_3 X_1^2 + \beta_4 X_2^2 + \beta_5 X_1 X_2 + \epsilon \qquad (11\text{–}25)$$

A regression surface of a model like that of equation 11–25 is shown in Figure 11–29. Of course, many surfaces are possible, depending on the values of the coefficients of all terms in the equation. Equation 11–25 may be generalized to more than two explanatory variables, to higher powers of each variable, and to more interaction terms.

When we are considering polynomial regression models in several variables, it is very important not to get carried away by the number of possible terms we can include in the model. The number of variables, as well as the powers of these variables and the number of interaction terms, should be kept to a minimum.

How do we choose the terms to include in a model? This question will be answered in Section 11–13, where we discuss methods of variable selection. You already know several criteria for the inclusion of variables, powers of variables, and interaction terms in a model. One thing to consider is the adjusted coefficient of determination. If this measure decreases when a term is included in the model, then the term should be dropped. Also, the significance of any particular term in a model depends on which other variables, powers, or interaction terms are in the model. We must consider the significance of each term by its t statistic, and we must consider what happens to the significance of regression terms once other terms are added to the model or removed from it. For example, let us consider the regression output in Table 11–16.

The results in the table clearly show that only X_1, X_2, and X_1^2 are significant. The apparent nonsignificance of X_2^2 and $X_1 X_2$ may be due to multicollinearity. At any

FIGURE 11–29   An Example of the Regression Surface of a Second-Order Model in Two Variables

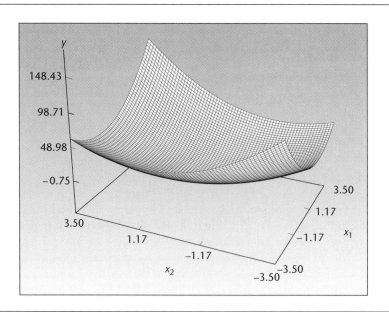

TABLE 11–16   Example of Regression Output for a Second-Order Model in Two Variables

Variable	Estimate	Standard Error	t Ratio
X_1	2.34	0.92	2.54
X_2	3.11	1.05	2.96
X_1^2	4.22	1.00	4.22
X_2^2	3.57	2.12	1.68
$X_1 X_2$	2.77	2.30	1.20

rate, a regression without these last two variables should be carried out. We must also look at R^2 and the adjusted R^2 of the different regressions, and find the most parsimonious model with statistically significant parameters that explain as much as possible of the variation in the values of the dependent variable. Incidentally, the surface in Figure 11–29 was generated by computer, using all the coefficient estimates given in Table 11–16 (regardless of their significance) and an intercept of zero.

PROBLEMS

11–62. The following results pertain to a regression analysis of the difference between the mortgage rate and the Treasury bill rate (SPREAD) on the shape of the yield curve (S) and the corporate bond yields spread (R). What kind of regression model is used? Explain.

$$\text{SPREAD} = b_0 + b_1 S + b_2 R + b_3 S^2 + b_4 S * R$$

11–63. Use the data in Table 11–6 to run a polynomial regression model of exports to Singapore versus M1 and M1 squared, as well as Price and Price squared, and an interaction term. Also try to add a squared exchange rate variable into the model. Find the best, most parsimonious regression model for the data.

11–64. Use the data of Example 11–3, presented in Table 11–12, to try to fit a polynomial regression model of movie gross earnings on production cost and production cost squared. Also try promotion and promotion squared. What is the best, most parsimonious model?

11–65. An ingenious regression analysis was reported in which the effects of the 1985 French banking deregulation were assessed. Bank equity was the dependent variable, and each data point was a tax return for a particular quarter and bank in France from 1978 to the time the research was done. This resulted in 325,928 data points, assumed a random sample. The independent variables were Bankdep—average debt in the industry during this period; ROA—the given firm's average return on assets for the entire period, and After—0 before 1985, and 1 after 1985. The variables used in this regression were all cross-products. These variables and their coefficient estimates (with their standard errors) are given below.

After * Bankdep	−0.398 (0.035)
After * Bankdep * ROA	0.155 (0.057)
After * ROA	−0.072 (0.024)
Bankdep * ROA	−0.286 (0.073)

The adjusted R^2 was 53%.[19] Carefully analyze these results and try to draw a conclusion about the effects of the 1985 French Banking Deregulation Act.

[19]Marianne Bertrand, Antoinette Schoar, and David Thesmar, "Banking Deregulation and Industry Structure: Evidence from the French Banking Reforms of 1985," *Journal of Finance* 42, no. 2 (2007), pp. 597–628.

11–66.   A regression model of sales Y versus advertising X_1, advertising squared X_1^2, competitors' advertising X_2, competitors' advertising squared X_2^2, and the interaction of X_1 and X_2 is run. The results are as follows.

Variable	Parameter Estimate	Standard Error
X_1	5.324	2.478
X_2	3.229	1.006
X_1^2	4.544	3.080
X_2^2	1.347	0.188
$X_1 X_2$	2.692	1.517
$R^2 = 0.657$	Adjusted $R^2 = 0.611$	$n = 197$

Interpret the regression results. Which regression equation should be tried next? Explain.

11–67.   What regression model would you try for the following data? Give your reasons why.

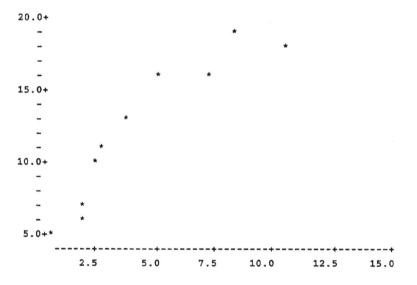

11–68.   The regression model $Y = \beta_0 + \beta_1 X + \beta_2 X^2 + \beta_3 X^3 + \beta_4 X^4 + \epsilon$ was fit to the following data set. Can you suggest a better model? If so, which?

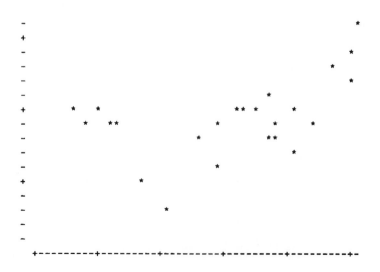

11–10   Nonlinear Models and Transformations

Sometimes the relationship between Y and one or more of the independent X_i variables is nonlinear. Remember that powers of the X_i variables in the regression model still keep the model linear, but that powers of the coefficients β_i make the model nonlinear. We may have prior knowledge about the process generating the data that indicates that a nonlinear model is appropriate; or we may observe that the data follow one of the general nonlinear curves shown in the figures in this section.

CHAPTER 18

In many cases, a nonlinear model may be changed to a linear model by use of an appropriate **transformation.** Models that can be transformed to linear models are called **intrinsically linear** models. These models are the subject of this section. The "hard-core" nonlinear models, those that cannot be transformed into linear models, are difficult to analyze and therefore are outside the scope of this book.

The first model we will encounter is the *multiplicative model,* given by equation 11–26.

The multiplicative model is

$$Y = \beta_0 X_1^{\beta_1} X_2^{\beta_2} X_3^{\beta_3} \epsilon \qquad\qquad (11\text{–}26)$$

This is a multiplicative model in the three variables X_1, X_2, and X_3. The generalization to k variables is clear. The β_i are unknown parameters, and ϵ is a multiplicative random error.

The multiplicative model of equation 11–26 can be transformed to a linear regression model by the use of a **logarithmic transformation.** A logarithmic transformation is the most common transformation of data in statistical analysis. We will use natural logarithms–logs to base e–although any log transformation would do (we may use logs to any base, as long as we are consistent throughout the equation). Taking natural logs (sometimes denoted by ln) of both sides of equation 11–26 gives us the following linear model:

$$\log Y = \log \beta_0 + \beta_1 \log X_1 + \beta_2 \log X_2 + \beta_3 \log X_3 + \log \epsilon \qquad (11\text{–}27)$$

Equation 11–27 is now in the form of equation 11–1: It is a linear regression equation of log Y in terms of log X_1, log X_2, and log X_3 as independent variables. The error term in the linearized model is log ϵ. To conform with the assumptions of the multiple regression model and to allow us to perform tests of significance of model parameters, we must assume that the linearized errors log ϵ are normally distributed with mean 0 and equal variance σ^2 for successive observations and that these errors are independent of each other.

When we consider only one independent variable, the model of equation 11–26 is a power curve in X, of the form

$$Y = \beta_0 X^{\beta_1} \epsilon \qquad\qquad (11\text{–}28)$$

Depending on the values of parameters β_0 and β_1, equation 11–28 gives rise to a wide-range family of power curves. Several members of this family of curves, showing the relationship between X and Y, leaving out the errors ϵ, are shown in Figure 11–30. When more than one independent variable is used, as in equation 11–26, the graph

FIGURE 11–30   A Family of Power Curves of the Form $Y = \beta_0 X^{\beta_1}$

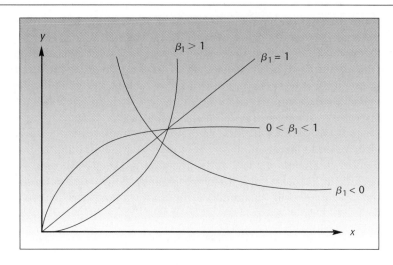

of the relationship between the X_i variables and Y is a multidimensional extension of Figure 11–30.

As you can see from the figure, many possible data relationships may be well modeled by a power curve in one variable or its extension to several independent variables. The resemblance of the curves in Figure 11–30 to at least two curves shown in Figure 11–26 is also evident. As you look at Figure 11–30, we repeat our suggestion from the last section that, when possible, a transformed model with few parameters is better than a polynomial model with more parameters.

When dealing with a multiplicative, or power, model, we take logs of both sides of the equation and run a linear regression model on the logs of the variables. Again, understanding that the errors must be multiplicative is important. This makes sense in situations where the magnitude of an error is proportional to the magnitude of the response variable. We assume that the logs of the errors are normally distributed and satisfy all the assumptions of the linear regression model. Models where the error term is additive rather than multiplicative, such as $Y = \beta_0 X_1^{\beta_1} X_2^{\beta_2} X_3^{\beta_3} + \epsilon$, are *not* intrinsically linear because they include no expression for logs of *sums*.

When using a model such as equation 11–26 or equation 11–28, we enter the data into the computer, form new variables by having the computer take logs of the Y and X_i variables, and run a regression on the transformed variables. In addition to making sure that the model assumptions seem to hold, we must remember that computer-generated predictions and confidence intervals will be in terms of the transformed variables unless the computer algorithm is designed to convert information back to the original variables. The conversion back to the original variables is done by taking antilogs.

In many situations, we can determine the need for a log transformation by inspecting a scatter plot of the data. We demonstrate the analysis, using the data of Example 11–5. We will assume that a model of the form of equation 11–28 fits the relationship between sales profits Y and advertising dollars X. We assume a power curve with multiplicative errors. Thus, we assume that the relationship between X and Y is given by

$$Y = \beta_0 X^{\beta_1} \epsilon$$

Taking logs of both sides of the equation, we get the linearized model

$$\log Y = \log \beta_0 + \beta_1 \log X + \log \epsilon \qquad (11\text{-}29)$$

Our choice of a power curve and a transformation using logarithms is prompted by the fact that our data in this example exhibit curvature that may resemble a member of the family of curves in Figure 11–30, and by the fact that a quadratic regression model, which is similar to a power curve, was found to fit the data well. (Data for this example are shown in Figure 11–28.)

To solve this problem using the template we use the "=LN()" function available in Excel. This function calculates the natural logarithm of the number in parentheses. Unprotect the Data sheet and enter the Sales and Advert data in some unused columns, say, columns N and O, as in Figure 11–31. Then enter the formula "=LN(N5)" in cell B5. Copy that formula down to cell B25. Next, in cell D5, enter the formula "=LN(O5)" and copy it down to cell D25. Press the F9 key and the regression is complete. Protect the Data sheet. Table 11–17 shows the regression results.

Comparing the results in Table 11–17 with those of the quadratic regression, given in Table 11–15, we find that, in terms of R^2 and the adjusted R^2, the quadratic regression is slightly better than the log Y versus log X regression.

Do we have to take logs of both X and Y, or can we take the log of one of the variables only? That depends on the kind of nonlinear model we wish to linearize. It turns out that there is indeed a nonlinear model that may be linearized by taking the log of one of the variables. Equation 11–30 is a nonlinear regression model of Y versus the independent variable X that may be linearized by taking logs of both sides of

FIGURE 11–31   Data Entry for the Exponential Model
[Multiple Regression.xls; Sheet: Data]

	A	B	C	D	E	F	G	N	O
1	Multiple Regression					Exponential Model			
2									
3		Y	1	X1	X2	X3	X4		
4	Sl.No.	Log Sales		Log Advt				Sales	Advert
5	1	1.60944	1	0				5	1
6	2	1.79176	1	0.5878				6	1.8
7	3	1.8718	1	0.47				6.5	1.6
8	4	1.94591	1	0.5306				7	1.7
9	5	2.0149	1	0.6931				7.5	2
10	6	2.07944	1	0.6931				8	2
11	7	2.30259	1	0.8329				10	2.3
12	8	2.37955	1	1.0296				10.8	2.8
13	9	2.48491	1	1.2528				12	3.5
14	10	2.56495	1	1.1939				13	3.3
15	11	2.74084	1	1.5686				15.5	4.8
16	12	2.70805	1	1.6094				15	5
17	13	2.77259	1	1.9459				16	7
18	14	2.83321	1	2.0919				17	8.1
19	15	2.89037	1	2.0794				18	8
20	16	2.89037	1	2.3026				18	10
21	17	2.91777	1	2.0794				18.5	8
22	18	3.04452	1	2.5416				21	12.7
23	19	2.99573	1	2.4849				20	12
24	20	3.09104	1	2.7081				22	15
25	21	3.13549	1	2.6672				23	14.4
26									

TABLE 11–17   **Regression Results**
[Multiple Regression.xls; Sheet: Results]

	0	1	2	3	4	5	6	7	8	9	10
	Intercept	**Log Advt**									
b	1.70082	0.55314									
s(b)	0.05123	0.03011									
t	33.2006	18.3727									
p-value	0.0000	0.0000									

ANOVA Table

Source	SS	df	MS	F	$F_{Critical}$	p-value
Regn.	4.27217	1	4.2722	337.56	4.3808	0.0000
Error	0.24047	19	0.0127			
Total	4.51263	20				

s = 0.1125

R^2 0.9467   Adjusted R^2 0.9439

the equation. To use the resulting linear model, given in equation 11–31, we run a regression of $\log Y$ versus X (not $\log X$).

> The **exponential model** is
> $$Y = \beta_0 e^{\beta_1 x} \,\epsilon \qquad (11\text{–}30)$$

The linearized model of the exponential relationship, obtained by taking logs of both sides of equation 11–30, is given by

$$\log Y = \log \beta_0 + \beta_1 X + \log \epsilon \qquad (11\text{–}31)$$

When the relationship between Y and X is of the exponential form, the relationship is mildly curved upward or downward. Thus, taking log of Y only and running a regression of $\log Y$ versus X may be useful when our data display mild curvature.

The exponential model of equation 11–30 is extendable to several independent X_i variables. The model is given in equation 11–32.

> An exponential model in two independent variables is
> $$Y = e^{\beta_0 + \beta_1 x_1 + \beta_2 x_2} \epsilon \qquad (11\text{–}32)$$

The letter e in equation 11–32, as in equation 11–30, denotes the natural number $e = 2.7182\ldots$, the base of the natural logarithm. Taking the natural logs of both sides of equation 11–32 gives us the following linear regression model:

$$\log Y = \beta_0 + \beta_1 X_1 + \beta_2 X_2 + \log \epsilon \qquad (11\text{–}33)$$

This relationship is extendable to any number of independent variables. The transformation of log Y, leaving the X_i variables in their natural form, allows us to perform linear regression analysis. The data of Example 11–5, shown in Figure 11–28, do not display a mild curvature. The next model we discuss, however, may be more promising.

Figure 11–32 shows curves corresponding to the logarithmic model given in equation 11–34.

FIGURE 11–32
Curves Corresponding
to a Logarithmic Model

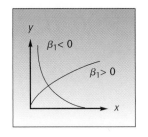

The **logarithmic model** is

$$Y = \beta_0 + \beta_1 \log X + \epsilon \qquad (11\text{–}34)$$

This nonlinear model can be linearized by substituting the variable $X' = \log X$ into the equation. This gives us the linear model in X':

$$Y = \beta_0 + \beta_1 X' + \epsilon \qquad (11\text{–}35)$$

From Figure 11–30, the logarithmic model with $\beta_1 > 0$ seems to fit the data of Example 11–5. We will therefore try to fit this model. The required transformation to obtain the linearized model in equation 11–35 is to take the log of X only, leaving Y as is. We will tell the computer program to run Y versus log X. By doing so, we assume that our data follow the logarithmic model of equation 11–34. The results of the regression analysis of sales profits versus the natural logarithm of advertising expenditure are given in Table 11–18.

As seen from the regression results, the model of equation 11–35 is probably the best model to describe the data of Example 11–5. The coefficient of determination is $R^2 = 0.978$, which is higher than those of both the quadratic model and the power curve model we tried earlier. Figure 11–33 is a plot of the sales variable versus the log of advertising (the regression model of equation 11–35). As can be seen from the figure, we have a straight-line relationship between log advertising and sales. Compare this figure with Figure 11–34, which is the relationship of log sales versus log advertising, the model of equation 11–31 we tried earlier. In the latter graph, some extra curvature appears, and a straight line does not quite fit the transformed variable. We conclude that the model given by equation 11–34 fits the sales

TABLE 11–18   Results of the Logarithmic Model
[Multiple Regression.xls; Sheet: Results]

	0	1	2	3	4	5	6	7	8	9	10
	Intercept	Log Advt									
b	3.66825	6.784									
s(b)	0.40159	0.23601									
t	9.13423	28.7443									
p-value	0.0000	0.0000									

ANOVA Table

Source	SS	df	MS	F	$F_{Critical}$	p-value		
Regn.	642.622	1	642.62	826.24	4.3808	0.0000	s	0.8819
Error	14.7777	19	0.7778					
Total	657.4	20		R^2 0.9775		Adjusted R^2 0.9763		

FIGURE 11–33   Plot of Sales versus the Natural Log of Advertising Expenditure (Example 11–5)

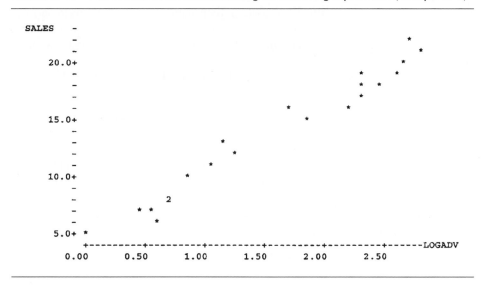

FIGURE 11–34   Plot of Log Sales versus Log Advertising Expenditure (Example 11–5)

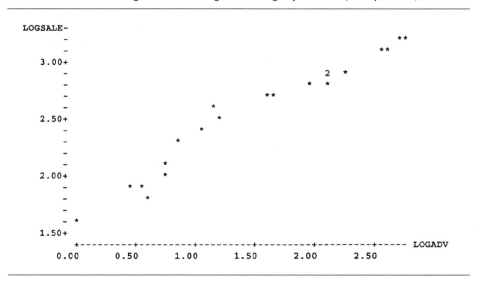

profits–advertising expenditure relationship best. The estimated regression relationship is as given in Table 11–18: Sales = 3.67 + 6.78 Log Advt.

Remember that when we transform our data, the least-squares method minimizes the sum of the squared errors for the *transformed* variables. It is, therefore, very important for us to check for any violations of model assumptions that may occur as a result of the transformations. We must be especially careful with the assumptions about the regression errors and their distribution. This is why residual plots are very important when transformations of variables are used. In our present model for the data of Example 11–5, a plot of the residuals versus the predicted sales values $\hat{Y}$ is given in Figure 11–35. The plot of the residuals does not indicate any violation of assumptions, and we therefore conclude that the model is adequate. We note also that confidence intervals for transformed models do not always correspond to correct intervals for the original model.

**FIGURE 11–35   Residual Plot of the Logarithmic Model; X Axis Is Sales
[Multiple Regression.xls; Sheet: Residuals]**

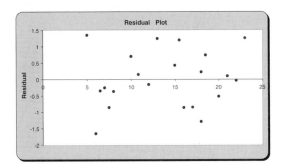

Another nonlinear model that may be linearized by an appropriate transformation is the *reciprocal model*. A reciprocal model in several variables is given in equation 11–36.

The **reciprocal model** is

$$Y = \frac{1}{\beta_0 + \beta_1 X_1 + \beta_2 X_2 + \beta_3 X_3 + \epsilon} \qquad (11\text{–}36)$$

This model becomes a linear model upon taking the reciprocals of both sides of the equation. In practical terms, we run a regression of $1/Y$ versus the X_i variables unchanged. A particular reciprocal model with one independent variable has a complicated form, which will not be explicitly stated here. This model calls for linearization by taking the reciprocals of both X and Y. Two curves corresponding to this particular reciprocal model are shown in Figure 11–36. When our data display the acute curvature of one of the curves in the figure, running a regression of $1/Y$ versus $1/X$ may be fruitful.

Next we will discuss transformations of the dependent variable Y only. These are transformations designed to stabilize the variance of the regression errors.

**FIGURE 11–36
Two Examples of a
Relationship Where
a Regression of $1/Y$ versus
$1/X$ Is Appropriate**

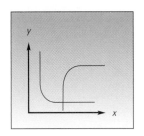

Variance-Stabilizing Transformations

Remember that one of the assumptions of the regression model is that the regression errors ϵ have equal variance. If the variance of the errors increases or decreases as one or more of the independent variables change, we have the problem of heteroscedasticity. When heteroscedasticity is present, our regression coefficient estimators are not efficient. This violation of the regression assumptions may sometimes be corrected by the use of a transformation. We will consider three major transformations of the dependent variable Y to correct for heteroscedasticity.

Transformations of Y that may help correct the problem of heteroscedasticity:

1. The square root transformation: $Y' = \sqrt{Y}$
   This is the least "severe" transformation. It is useful when the variance of the regression errors is approximately proportional to the mean of Y, conditional on the values of the independent variables X_i.

2. The logarithmic transformation: $Y' = \log Y$ (to any base)
   This is a transformation of a stronger nature and is useful when the variance of the errors is approximately proportional to the square of the conditional mean of Y.

3. The reciprocal transformation: $Y' = 1/Y$
   This is the most severe of the three transformations and is required when the violation of equal variance is serious. This transformation is useful when the variance of the errors is approximately proportional to the conditional mean of Y to the fourth power.

Other transformations are possible, although the preceding transformations are most commonly used. In a given situation, we want to find the transformation that makes the errors have approximately equal variance as evidenced by the residual plots. An alternative to using transformations to stabilize the variance is the use of the weighted least-squares procedure mentioned in our earlier discussion of the heteroscedasticity problem. We note that a test for heteroscedasticity exists. The test is the Goldfeld-Quandt test, discussed in econometrics books.

It is important to note that transformations may also correct problems of nonnormality of the errors. A variance-stabilizing transformation may thus make the distribution of the new errors closer to a normal distribution. In using transformations—whether to stabilize the variance, to make the errors approximate a normal distribution, or to make a nonlinear model linear—remember that all results should be converted back to the original variables. As a final example of a nonlinear model that can be linearized by using a transformation, we present the *logistic regression model*.

Regression with Dependent Indicator Variable

In Section 11–8, we discussed models with indicator variables as independent X_i variables. In this subsection, we discuss regression analysis where the dependent variable Y is an indicator variable and may obtain only the value 0 or the value 1. This is the case when the response to a set of independent variables is in binary form: success or failure. An example of such a situation is the following.

A bank is interested in predicting whether a given loan applicant would be a good risk, i.e., pay back his or her loan. The bank may have data on past loan applicants, such as applicant's income, years of employment with the same employer, and value of the home. All these independent variables may be used in a regression analysis where the dependent variable is binary: $Y = 0$ if the applicant did not repay the loan, and $Y = 1$ if she or he did pay back the loan. When only one explanatory variable X is used, the model is the *logistic function*, given in equation 11–37.

The **logistic function** is

$$E(Y \mid X) = \frac{e^{\beta_0 + \beta_1 X}}{1 + e^{\beta_0 + \beta_1 X}} \qquad (11\text{–}37)$$

The expected value of Y given X, that is, $E(Y|X)$, has a special meaning: It is the probability that Y will equal 1 (the probability of success), given the value of X. Thus, we write $E(Y|X) = p$. The transformation given below linearizes equation 11–37.

Transformation to linearize the logistic function:

$$p' = \log\left(\frac{p}{1 - p}\right) \tag{11–38}$$

FIGURE 11–37
The Logistic Function

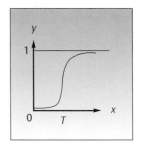

We leave it to the reader to show that the resulting regression equation is linear. In practical terms, the transformed model is difficult to employ because resulting errors are intrinsically heteroscedastic. A better approach is to use the more involved methods of nonlinear regression analysis. We present the example to show that, in many cases, the dependent variable may be an indicator variable as well. Much research is being done today on the logistic regression model, which reflects the model's growing importance. Fitting data to the curve of the logistic function is called *logit analysis*. A graph of the logistic function of equation 11–37 is shown in Figure 11–37. Note the typical elongated S shape of the graph. This function is useful as a "threshold model," where the probability that the dependent variable Y will be equal to 1 (a success in the experiment) increases as X increases. This increase becomes very dramatic as X reaches a certain threshold value (the point T in the figure).

PROBLEMS

11–69. What are the two main reasons for using transformations?

11–70. Explain why a transformed model may be better than a polynomial model. Under what conditions is this true?

11–71. Refer to the residual plot in Figure 11–12. What transformation would you recommend be tried to correct the situation?

11–72. For the Singapore data of Example 11–2, presented in Table 11–6, use several different data transformations of the variables Exports, M1, and Price, and find a better model to describe the data. Comment on the properties of your new model.

11–73. Which transformation would you try for modeling the following data set?

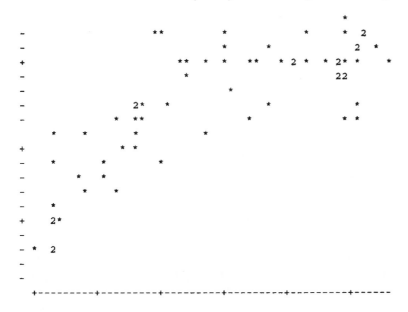

11-74. Which transformation would you recommend for the following data set?

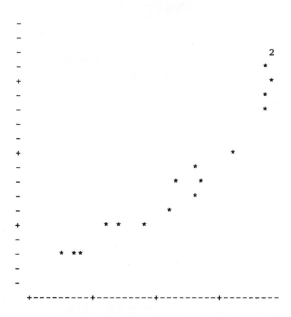

11-75. An analysis of the effect of advertising on consumer price sensitivity is carried out. The log of the quantity purchased (ln q), the dependent variable, is run against the log of an advertising-related variable called RP (the log is variable ln RP). An additive error term ϵ is included in the transformed regression. What assumptions about the model relating q and RP are implied by the transformation?

11-76. The following regression model is run.

$$\log Y = 3.79 + 1.66X_1 + 2.91X_2 + \log e$$

Give the equation of the original, nonlinear model linking the explanatory variables with Y.

11-77. Consider the following nonlinear model.

$$Y = e^{\beta_1 X_1} + e^{\beta_2 X_2} + \epsilon$$

Is this model intrinsically linear? Explain.

11-78. The model used in economics to describe production is

$$Q = \beta_0 C^{\beta_1} K^{\beta_2} L^{\beta_3} \epsilon$$

where the dependent variable Q is the quantity produced, C is the capacity of a production unit, K is the capital invested in the project, and L is labor input, in days. Transform the model to linear regression form.

11–79. Consider the nonlinear model

$$Y = \frac{1}{\beta_0 + \beta_1 X_1 + \beta_2 X_2 + \epsilon}$$

What transformation linearizes this model?

11–80. If the residuals from fitting a linear regression model display mild heteroscedasticity, what data transformation may correct the problem?

11–81. The model in problem 11–78 is transformed to a linear regression model and analyzed with a computer. Do the estimated regression coefficients minimize the sum of the squared deviations of the data from the original curve? Explain.

11–82. In the French banking deregulation analysis of problem 11–65, part of the analysis included adding to the equation a variable that was the logarithm of the firm's total assets. In your opinion, what might be the reason for including such a variable? (The estimate and standard error for the effect of this variable were not reported in this study.)

11–11 Multicollinearity

The idea of multicollinearity permeates every aspect of multiple regression, and we have encountered this idea in earlier sections of this chapter. The reason multicollinearity (or simply *collinearity*) has such a pervasive effect on multiple regression is that whenever we study the relationship between Y and several X_i variables, we are bound to encounter some relationships among the X_i variables themselves. Ideally, the X_i variables in a regression equation are uncorrelated with one another; each variable contains a unique piece of information about Y—information that is not contained in any of the other X_i. When the ideal occurs in practice, we have no multicollinearity. On the other extreme, we encounter the case of perfect collinearity. Suppose that we run a regression of Y on two explanatory variables X_1 and X_2. Perfect collinearity occurs when one X variable can be expressed precisely in terms of the other X variable for all elements in our data set.

Variables X_1 and X_2 are perfectly collinear if

$$X_1 = a + bX_2 \tag{11–39}$$

for some real numbers a and b.

In the case of equation 11–39, the two variables are on a straight line, and one of them perfectly determines the other. No new information about Y is gained by adding X_2 to a regression equation that already contains X_1 (or vice versa).

In practice, most situations fall between the two extremes. Often, several of the independent variables in a regression equation show some degree of collinearity. A measure of the collinearity between two X_i variables is the *correlation* between the two. Recall that in regression analysis we assume that the X_i are constants and not random variables. Here we relax this assumption and measure the correlation between the independent variables (this assumes they are random variables in their own right). When two independent X_i variables are found to be highly correlated with each other, we may expect the adverse effects of multicollinearity on the regression estimation procedure.

FIGURE 11–38   Collinearity Viewed as the Relationship between Two Directions in Space

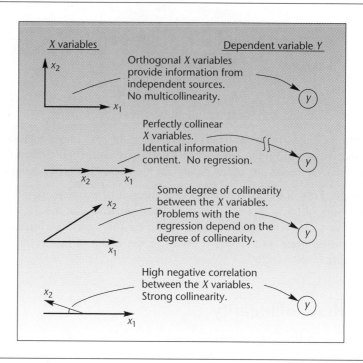

In the case of perfect collinearity, the regression algorithm breaks down completely. Even if we were able to get regression coefficient estimates in such a case, their variance would be infinite. When the degree of collinearity is less severe, we may expect the variance of the regression estimators (and the standard errors) to be large. Other problems may occur, and we will discuss them shortly. Multicollinearity is a problem of degree. When the correlations among the independent regression variables are minor, the effects of multicollinearity may not be serious. In cases of strong correlations, the problem may affect the regression more adversely, and we may need to take some corrective action. Note that in a multiple regression analysis with several independent variables, *several* of the X_i may be correlated. A set of independent variables that are correlated with one another is called a *multicollinearity set*.

Let us imagine a variable and its information content as a direction in space. Two uncorrelated variables can be viewed as *orthogonal* directions in space—directions that are at 90° to each other. Perfectly correlated variables represent directions that have an angle of 0° or 180° between them, depending on whether the correlation is +1 or −1. Variables that are partly correlated are directions that form an angle greater than 0° but less than 90° (or between 90° and 180° if the correlation is negative). The closer the angle between the directions is to 0° or 180°, the greater the collinearity. This is illustrated in Figure 11–38.

Causes of Multicollinearity

Several different factors cause multicollinearity. A data collection method may produce multicollinearity if, without intention, we tend to gather data with related values on several variables. For example, we may be interested in running a regression of size of home Y versus family income X_1 and family size X_2. If, unwittingly, we always sample families with high income and large size (rather than also obtaining sample families with low income and large size or high income and small size), then we have multicollinearity. In such cases, improving the sampling method would solve the problem. In other cases, the variables may by nature be related to one another, and sampling adjustments may not work. In such cases, one of the correlated variables should probably be excluded from the model to avoid the collinearity problem.

In industrial processes, sometimes there are physical constraints on the data. For example, if we run a regression of chemical yield Y versus the concentration of two elements X_1 and X_2, and the total amount of material in the process is constant, then as one chemical increases in concentration, we must reduce the concentration of the other. In this case, X_1 and X_2 are (negatively) correlated, and multicollinearity is present.

Yet another source of collinearity is the inclusion of higher powers of the X_i. Including X^2 in a model that contains the variable X may cause collinearity if our data are restricted to a narrow range of values. This was seen in one of the problems in an earlier section.

Whatever the source of the multicollinearity, we must remain aware of its existence so that we may guard against its adverse effects on the estimation procedure and the ensuing use of the regression equation in prediction, control, or understanding the underlying process. In particular, it is hard to separate out the effects of each collinear variable; and it is hard to know which model is correct, because removing one collinear variable may cause large changes in the coefficient estimates of other variables. We now present several methods of detecting multicollinearity and a description of its major symptoms.

Detecting the Existence of Multicollinearity

Many statistical computer packages have built-in warnings about severe cases of multicollinearity. When multicollinearity is extreme (i.e., when we have near-perfect correlation between some of the explanatory variables), the program may automatically drop collinear variables so that computations may be possible. In such cases, the MINITAB program, for example, will print the following message:

```
[variable name] is highly correlated with other X variables.
[variable name] has been omitted from the equation.
```

CHAPTER 17

In less serious cases, the program prints the first line of the warning above but does not drop the variable.

In cases where multicollinearity is not serious enough to cause computational problems, it may still disturb the statistical estimation procedure and make our estimators have large variances. In such cases, the computer may not print a message telling us about multicollinearity, but we will still want to know about it. Two methods are available in most statistical packages to help us determine the extent of multicollinearity present in our regression.

The first method is the computation of a **correlation matrix** of the independent regression variables. The correlation matrix is an array of all estimated pairwise correlations between the independent variables X_i. The format of the correlation matrix is shown in Figure 11–39. The correlation matrix allows us to identify those explanatory variables that are highly correlated with one another and thus cause the problem of multicollinearity when they are included together in the regression equation. For example, in the correlation matrix shown in Figure 11–39, we see that the correlation between variable X_1 and variable X_2 is very high (0.92). This means that the two variables represent very much the same direction in space, as was shown in Figure 11–38. Being highly correlated with each other, the two variables contain much of the same information about Y and therefore cause multicollinearity when both are in the regression equation. A similar statement can be made about X_3 and X_6, which have a 0.89 correlation. Remember that multicollinearity is a matter of extent or degree. It is hard to give a rule of thumb as to how high a correlation may be

FIGURE 11–39   A Correlation Matrix

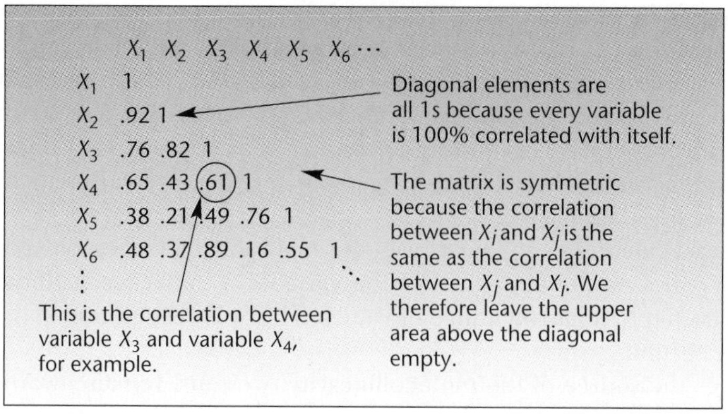

$$X_1 \; X_2 \; X_3 \; X_4 \; X_5 \; X_6 \cdots$$

X_1	1					
X_2	.92	1				
X_3	.76	.82	1			
X_4	.65	.43	(.61)	1		
X_5	.38	.21	.49	.76	1	
X_6	.48	.37	.89	.16	.55	1

Diagonal elements are all 1s because every variable is 100% correlated with itself.

The matrix is symmetric because the correlation between X_i and X_j is the same as the correlation between X_j and X_i. We therefore leave the upper area above the diagonal empty.

This is the correlation between variable X_3 and variable X_4, for example.

before multicollinearity has adverse effects on the regression analysis. Correlations as high as the ones just mentioned are certainly large enough to cause multicollinearity problems.

The template has a sheet titled "Correl" in which the correlation matrix is computed and displayed. Table 11–19 shows the correlation matrix among all the variables in Example 11–2.

The highest pairwise correlation exists between Lend and Price. This correlation of 0.745 is the source of the multicollinearity detected in problem 11–36. Recall that the model we chose as best in our solution of Example 11–2 did not include the lending rate. In our solution of Example 11–2, we discussed other collinear variables as well. The multicollinearity may have been caused by the smaller pairwise correlations in Table 11–19, or it may have been caused by more complex correlations in the data than just the pairwise correlations. This brings us to the second statistical method of detecting multicollinearity: variance inflation factors.

The degree of multicollinearity introduced to the regression by variable X_h, once variables $X_1, \ldots, X_k$ are in the regression equation, is a function of the multiple correlation between X_h and the other variables $X_1, \ldots, X_k$. Thus, suppose we run a multiple regression—not of Y, but of X_h—on all the other X variables. From this multiple regression, we get an R^2 value. This R^2 is a measure of the multicollinearity

TABLE 11–19   The Correlation Matrix for Example 11–2
[Multiple Regression.xls; Sheet: Correl]

		0 M1	1 Lend	2 Price	3 Exch.	4	5	6	7	8	9	10
1	M1	1										
2	Lend	-0.112	1									
3	Price	0.4471	0.7451	1								
4	Exch.	-0.4097	-0.2786	-0.4196	1							
5												
6												
7												
8												
9												
10												
Y	Exports	0.7751	0.335	0.7699	-0.4329							

FIGURE 11–40   Relationship between R_h^2 and VIF

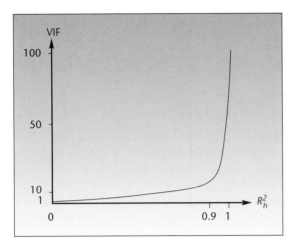

"exerted" by variable X_h. Recall that a major problem caused by multicollinearity is the inflation of the variance of the regression coefficient estimators. To measure this ill effect of multicollinearity, we use the *variance inflation factor (VIF)* associated with variable X_h.

> The **variance inflation factor** associated with X_h is
>
> $$\text{VIF}(X_h) = \frac{1}{1 - R_h^2} \qquad (11\text{–}40)$$
>
> where R_h^2 is the R^2 value obtained for the regression of X_h, as dependent variable, on the other X variables in the original equation aimed at predicting Y.

The VIF of variable X_h can be shown to be equal to the ratio of the variance of the coefficient estimator b_h in the original regression (with Y as dependent variable) and the variance of the estimator b_h in a regression where X_h is orthogonal to the other X variables.[20] The VIF is the inflation factor of the variance of the estimator as compared with what that variance would have been if X_h were not collinear with any of the other X variables in the regression. A graph of the relationship between R_h^2 and the VIF is shown in Figure 11–40.

As can be seen from the figure, when the R^2 value of X_h versus the other X variables increases from 0.9 to 1, the VIF rises very dramatically. In fact, for $R_h^2 = 1.00$, the VIF is infinite. The graph, however, should not deceive you. Even for values of R_h^2 less than 0.9, the VIF is still large. A VIF of 6, for example, means that the variance of the regression coefficient estimator b_h is 6 times what it should be (when no collinearity exists). Most computer packages will report, on request, the VIFs for all the independent variables in a regression model.

Table 11–20 shows the template output for the regression from Example 11–2, which contains the VIF values in row 10. We note that the VIF for variables Lend

---

[20]J. Johnston, *Econometric Methods,* 4th ed. (New York: McGraw-Hill, 2001).

TABLE 11–20   VIF Values for the Regression from Example 11–2

	A	B	C	D	E	F
1	Multiple Regression Results					Exports
2						
3		0	1	2	3	4
4		Intercept	M1	Lend	Price	Exch.
5	b	-4.0155	0.36846	0.0047	0.0365	0.2679
6	s(b)	2.7664	0.06385	0.04922	0.00933	1.17544
7	t	-1.45151	5.7708	0.09553	3.91491	0.22791
8	p-value	0.1517	0.0000	0.9242	0.0002	0.8205
9						
10	VIF		3.2072	5.3539	6.2887	1.3857

and Price are greater than 5 and thus indicate that some degree of multicollinearity exists with respect to these two variables. Some action, as described in the next subsection, is required to take care of this multicollinearity.

What symptoms and effects of multicollinearity would we find without looking at a variable correlation matrix or the VIFs? Multicollinearity has several noticeable effects. The major ones are presented in the following list.

The effects of multicollinearity:

1. The variances (and standard errors) of regression coefficient estimators are inflated.
2. The magnitudes of the regression coefficient estimates may be different from what we expect.
3. The signs of the regression coefficient estimates may be the opposite of what we expect.
4. Adding or removing variables produces large changes in the coefficient estimates or their signs.
5. Removing a data point causes large changes in the coefficient estimates or their signs.
6. In some cases, the F ratio is significant, but none of the t ratios is.

When any of or all these effects are present, multicollinearity is likely to be present. How bad is the problem? What are the adverse consequences of multicollinearity? The problem is not always as bad as it may seem. Actually, if we wish to use the regression model for prediction purposes, multicollinearity may not be a serious problem.

From the effects of multicollinearity just listed (some of them were mentioned in earlier sections), we know that the regression coefficient estimates are not reliable when multicollinearity is present. The most serious effect is the variance inflation, which makes some variables seem not significant. Then there is the problem of the magnitudes of the estimates, which may not be accurate, and the problem of the signs of the estimates. We see that in the presence of multicollinearity, we may be unable to assess the impact of a particular variable on the dependent variable Y because we do not have a reliable estimate of the variable's coefficient. If we are interested in prediction only and do not care about understanding the net effect of each independent variable on Y, the regression model may be adequate even in the presence of multicollinearity. Even though individual regression parameters may be poorly estimated when collinearity exists, the combination of all regression coefficients in the regression may, in some cases, be estimated with sufficient accuracy that satisfactory predictions are possible. In such cases, however, we must be very careful to predict values of Y only within the range of the X variables where the multicollinearity is the same as in the region of estimation. If we try to predict in regions of the X variables where the multicollinearity is not present or is different from that present in the estimation region, large errors may result. We will now explore some of the solutions commonly used to remedy the problem of multicollinearity.

Solutions to the Multicollinearity Problem

1. One of the best solutions to the problem of multicollinearity is to *drop collinear variables from the regression equation.* Suppose that we have a regression of Y on X_1, X_2, X_3, and X_4 and we find that X_1 is highly correlated with X_4. In this case, much of the information about Y in X_1 is also contained in X_4. If we dropped one of the two variables from the regression model, we would solve the multicollinearity problem and lose little information about Y. By comparing the R^2 and the adjusted R^2 of different regressions with and without one of the variables, we can decide which of the two independent variables to drop from the regression. We want to maintain a high R^2 and therefore should drop a variable if R^2 is not reduced much when the variable is removed from the equation. When the adjusted R^2 increases when a variable is deleted, we certainly want to drop the variable. For example, suppose that the R^2 of the regression with all four independent variables is 0.94, the R^2 when X_1 is removed is 0.87, and the R^2 of the regression of X_1, X_2, and X_3 on Y (X_4 removed) is 0.92. In this case, we clearly want to drop X_4 and not X_1. The variable selection methods to be discussed in Section 11–13 will help us determine which variables to include in a regression model.

We note a limitation of this remedy to multicollinearity. In some areas, such as economics, theoretical considerations may require that certain variables be in the equation. In such cases, the bias resulting from deletion of a collinear variable must be weighed against the increase in the variance of the coefficient estimators when the variable is included in the model. The method of weighing the consequences and choosing the best model is presented in advanced books.

2. When the multicollinearity is caused by sampling schemes that, by their nature, tend to favor elements with similar values of some of the independent variables, a change in the sampling plan to include elements outside the multicollinearity range may reduce the extent of this problem.

3. Another method that sometimes helps to reduce the extent of the multicollinearity, or even eliminate it, is to change the form of some of the variables. This can be done in several ways. The best way is to form new combinations of the X variables that are uncorrelated with one another and then run the regression on the new combinations instead of on the original variables. Thus the information content in the original variables is maintained, but the multicollinearity is removed. Other ways of changing the form of the variables include centering the data—a technique of subtracting the means from the variables and running a regression on the resulting new variables.

4. The problem of multicollinearity may be remedied by using an alternative to the least-squares procedure called *ridge regression.* The coefficient estimators produced by ridge regression are biased, but in some cases, some bias in the regression estimators can be tolerated in exchange for a reduction in the high variance of the estimators that results from multicollinearity.

In summary, the problem of multicollinearity is an important one. We need to be aware of the problem when it exists and to try to solve it when we can. Removing collinear variables from the equation, when possible, is the simplest method of solving the multicollinearity problem.

PROBLEMS

11–83. For the data of Example 11–3 presented in Table 11–12, find the sample correlations between every pair of variables (the correlation matrix), and determine whether you believe that multicollinearity exists in the regression.

11–84. For the data of Example 11–3, find the variance inflation factors, and comment on their relative magnitudes.

11–85. Find the correlation between X_1 and X_2 for the data of Example 11–1 presented in Table 11–1. Is multicollinearity a problem here? Also find the variance inflation factors, and comment on their magnitudes.

11–86. Regress Y against X_1, X_2, and X_3 with the following sample data:

Y	X_1	X_2	X_3
13.79	76.45	44.47	8.00
21.23	24.37	37.45	7.56
66.49	98.46	95.04	19.00
35.97	49.21	2.17	0.44
37.88	76.12	36.75	7.50
72.70	82.93	42.83	8.74
81.73	23.04	82.17	16.51
58.91	80.98	7.84	1.59
30.47	47.45	88.58	17.86
8.51	65.09	25.59	5.12
39.96	44.82	74.93	15.05
67.85	85.17	55.70	11.16
10.77	27.71	30.60	6.23
72.30	62.32	12.97	2.58

a. What is the regression equation?

b. Change the first observation of X_3 from 8.00 to 9.00. Repeat the regression. What is the new regression equation?

c. Compare the old and the new regression equations. Does the comparison prove multicollinearity in the data? What is your suggestion for getting rid of the multicollinearity?

d. Looking at the results of the original regression only, could you have figured out that there is a multicollinearity problem? How?

11–87. How does multicollinearity manifest itself in a regression situation?

11–88. Explain what is meant by perfect collinearity. What happens when perfect collinearity is present?

11–89. Is it true that the regression equation can never be used adequately for prediction purposes if multicollinearity exists? Explain.

11–90. In a regression of Y on the two explanatory variables X_1 and X_2, the F ratio was found not to be significant. Neither t ratio was found to be significant, and R^2 was found to be 0.12. Do you believe that multicollinearity is a problem here? Explain.

11–91. In a regression of Y on X_1, X_2, and X_3, the F ratio is very significant, and R^2 is 0.88, but none of the t ratios are significant. Then X_1 is dropped from the equation, and a new regression is run of Y on X_2 and X_3 only. The R^2 remains approximately the same, and F is still very significant, but the two t ratios are still not significant. What do you think is happening here?

11–92. A regression is run of Y versus X_1, X_2, X_3, and X_4. The R^2 is high, and F is significant, but only the t ratio corresponding to X_1 is significant. What do you propose to do next? Why?

11–93. In a regression analysis with several X variables, the sign of the coefficient estimate of one of the variables is the opposite of what you believe it should be. How would you test to determine whether multicollinearity is the cause?

11–12 Residual Autocorrelation and the Durbin-Watson Test

Remember that one of the assumptions of the regression model is that the errors ϵ are independent from observation to observation. This means that successive errors are not correlated with one another at any lag; that is, the error at position i is not correlated with the error at position $i - 1$, $i - 2$, $i - 3$, etc. The idea of correlation of the values of a variable (in this case we consider the errors as a variable) with values of the same variable lagged one, two, three, or more time periods back is called *autocorrelation.*

CHAPTER 16

> An **autocorrelation** is a correlation of the values of a variable with values of the same variable lagged one or more time periods back.

Here we demonstrate autocorrelation in the case of regression errors. Suppose that we have 10 observed regression errors $e_{10} = 1$, $e_9 = 0$, $e_8 = -1$, $e_7 = 2$, $e_6 = 3$, $e_5 = -2$, $e_4 = 1$, $e_3 = 1.5$, $e_2 = 1$, and $e_1 = -2.5$. We arrange the errors in descending order of occurrence i. Then we form the lag 1 errors, the regression errors lagged one period back in time. The first error is now $e_{10-1} = e_9 = 0$, the second error is now $e_{9-1} = e_8 = -1$, and so on. We demonstrate the formation of variable e_{i-1} from variable e_i (that is, the formation of the lag 1 errors from the original errors), as well as the variables e_{i-2}, e_{i-3}, etc., in Table 11–21.

We now define the autocorrelations. The error autocorrelation of lag 1 is the correlation between the *population* errors ϵ_i and ϵ_{i-1}. We denote this correlation by ρ_1. This autocorrelation is estimated by the *sample* error autocorrelation of lag 1, denoted r_1, which is the computed correlation between variables e_i and e_{i-1}. Similarly ρ_2 is the lag 2 error autocorrelation. This autocorrelation is estimated by r_2, computed from the data for e_i and e_{i-2} in the table. Note that lagging the data makes us lose data points; one data point is lost for each lag. When computing the estimated error autocorrelations r_j, we use as many points as we have for e_{i-j} and shorten e_i appropriately. We will not do any of these computations.

The assumption that the regression errors are uncorrelated means that they are uncorrelated at *any* lag. That is, we assume $\rho_1 = \rho_2 = \rho_3 = \rho_4 = \cdots = 0$. A statistical test was developed in 1951 by Durbin and Watson for the purpose of detecting when the assumption is violated. The test, called the *Durbin-Watson test,* checks for evidence of the existence of a first-order autocorrelation.

TABLE 11–21   Formation of the Lagged Errors

i	e_i	e_{i-1}	e_{i-2}	e_{i-3}	e_{i-4}	$\cdots$
10	1	0	−1	2	3	
9	0	−1	2	3	−2	
8	−1	2	3	−2	1	
7	2	3	−2	1	1.5	
6	3	−2	1	1.5	1	
5	−2	1	1.5	1	−2.5	
4	1	1.5	1	−2.5	—	
3	1.5	1	−2.5	—	—	
2	1	−2.5	—	—	—	
1	−2.5	—	—	—	—	

TABLE 11–22   Critical Points of the Durbin-Watson Statistic d at $\alpha = 0.05$ (n = sample size, k = number of independent variables in the regression) (partial table)

	$k = 1$		$k = 2$		$k = 3$		$k = 4$		$k = 5$	
n	d_L	d_U	d_L	d_U	d_L	d_U	d_L	d_U	d_L	d_U
15	1.08	1.36	0.95	1.54	0.82	1.75	0.69	1.97	0.56	2.21
16	1.10	1.37	0.98	1.54	0.86	1.73	0.74	1.93	0.62	2.15
17	1.13	1.38	1.02	1.54	0.90	1.71	0.78	1.90	0.67	2.10
18	1.16	1.39	1.05	1.53	0.93	1.69	0.82	1.87	0.71	2.06
.	.	.	.	.	.	.	.	.	.	.
.	.	.	.	.	.	.	.	.	.	.
65	1.57	1.63	1.54	1.66	1.50	1.70	1.47	1.73	1.44	1.77
70	1.58	1.64	1.55	1.67	1.52	1.70	1.49	1.74	1.46	1.77
75	1.60	1.65	1.57	1.68	1.54	1.71	1.51	1.74	1.49	1.77
80	1.61	1.66	1.59	1.69	1.56	1.72	1.53	1.74	1.51	1.77
85	1.62	1.67	1.60	1.70	1.57	1.72	1.55	1.75	1.52	1.77
90	1.63	1.68	1.61	1.70	1.59	1.73	1.57	1.75	1.54	1.78
95	1.64	1.69	1.62	1.71	1.60	1.73	1.58	1.75	1.56	1.78
100	1.65	1.69	1.63	1.72	1.61	1.74	1.59	1.76	1.57	1.78

The **Durbin-Watson test** is

$$H_0: \rho_1 = 0$$

$$H_1: \rho_1 \neq 0 \qquad\qquad (11\text{–}41)$$

In testing for the existence of a first-order error autocorrelation, we use the Durbin-Watson test statistic. Critical points for this test statistic are given in Appendix C, Table 7. Part of the table is reproduced here as Table 11–22. The formula of the Durbin-Watson test statistic is equation 11–42.

The **Durbin-Watson test** is

$$d = \frac{\sum_{i=2}^{n}(e_i - e_{i-1})^2}{\sum_{i=1}^{n}e_1^2} \qquad\qquad (11\text{–}42)$$

Note that the test statistic[21] d is not the sample autocorrelation r_1. The statistic d has a known, tabulated distribution. Also note that the summation in the numerator extends from 2 to n rather than from 1 to n, as in the denominator. An inspection of the first two columns in Table 11–21, corresponding to e_i and e_{i-1}, and our comment on the "lost" data points (here, one point) reveal the reason for this.

Using a given level α from the table (0.05 or 0.01), we may conduct either a test for $\rho_1 < 0$ or a test for $\rho_1 > 0$. The test has two critical points for testing for a positive autocorrelation (the one-tailed half of H_1 in equation 11–41). When the test statistic d falls to the left of the lower critical point d_L, we conclude that there is evidence of a

---

[21]Actually, d is approximately equal to $2(1 - r_1)$.

FIGURE 11–41   **Critical Regions of the Durbin-Watson Test**

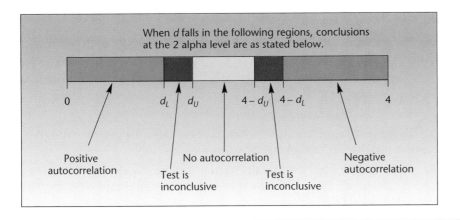

positive error autocorrelation of order 1. When d falls between d_L and the upper critical point d_U, the test is inconclusive. When d falls above d_U, we conclude that there is no evidence of a positive first-order autocorrelation (conclusions are at the appropriate level α). Similarly, when testing for negative autocorrelation, if d is greater than $4 - d_L$, we conclude that there is evidence of negative first-order error autocorrelation. When d is between $4 - d_U$ and $4 - d_L$, the test is inconclusive; and when d is below $4 - d_U$, there is no evidence of negative first-order autocorrelation of the errors. When we test the two-tailed hypothesis in equation 11–41, the actual level of significance α is double what is shown in the table. In cases where we have no prior suspicion of one type of autocorrelation (positive or negative), we carry out the two-tailed test and double the α. The critical points for the two-tailed test are shown in Figure 11–41.

For example, suppose we run a regression using $n = 18$ data points and $k = 3$ independent variables, and the computed value of the Durbin-Watson statistic is $d = 3.1$. Suppose that we want to conduct the two-tailed test. From Table 11–22 (or Appendix C, Table 7), we find that at $\alpha = 0.10$ (twice the level of the table) we have $d_L = 0.93$ and $d_U = 1.69$. We compute $4 - d_L = 3.07$ and $4 - d_U = 2.31$. Since the computed value $d = 3.1$ is greater than $4 - d_L$, we conclude that there is evidence of a negative first-order autocorrelation in the errors. As another example, suppose $n = 80$, $k = 2$, and $d = 1.6$. In this case, the statistic value falls between d_L and d_U, and the test is inconclusive.

The Durbin-Watson statistic helps us test for first-order autocorrelation in the errors. In most cases, when autocorrelation exists, there is a first-order autocorrelation. In some cases, however, second- or higher-order autocorrelation exists without there being a first-order autocorrelation. In such cases, the test does not help us. Fortunately, such cases are not common.

In the template, the Durbin-Watson statistic appears in cell H4 of the Residuals sheet. For the Exports problem of Example 11–2, the template computes the statistic to be 2.58. Recall that for this example, $n = 67$ and $k = 4$ (in this version of the equation). At $\alpha = 0.10$, for a two-tailed test, we have $d_U = 1.73$, $d_L = 1.47$, $4 - d_L = 2.53$, and $4 - d_U = 2.27$. We conclude that there is evidence that our regression errors are negatively correlated at lag 1. This, of course, sheds doubt on the regression results; an alternative to least-squares estimation should be used. One alternative procedure that is useful in cases where the ordinary least-squares routine produces autocorrelated errors is a procedure called *generalized least squares* (*GLS*). This method is described in advanced books.

PROBLEMS

11-94. What is the purpose of the Durbin-Watson test?

11-95. Discuss the meaning of autocorrelation. What is a third-order autocorrelation?

11-96. What is a first-order autocorrelation? If a fifth-order autocorrelation exists, is it necessarily true that a first-order autocorrelation exists as well? Explain.

11-97. State three limitations of the Durbin-Watson test.

11-98. Find the value of the Durbin-Watson statistic for the data of Example 11–5, and conduct the Durbin-Watson test. State your conclusion.

11-99. Find the value of the Durbin-Watson statistic for the model of Example 11–3, and conduct the Durbin-Watson test. Is the assumption of no first-order error autocorrelation satisfied? Explain.

11-100. Do problem 11–99 for the data of Example 11–1.

11-101. State the conditions under which a one-sided Durbin-Watson test is appropriate (i.e., a test for positive autocorrelation only, or a test for a negative autocorrelation only).

11-102. For the regression you performed in problem 11–39, produce and interpret the Durbin-Watson statistic.

11–13 Partial *F* Tests and Variable Selection Methods

Our method of deciding which variables to include in a given multiple regression model has been trial and error. We started by asserting that several variables may have an effect on our variable of interest *Y*, and we tried to run a multiple linear regression model of *Y* versus these variables. The "independent" variables have included dummy variables, powers of a variable, transformed variables, and a combination of all the above. Then we scrutinized the regression model and tested the significance of any individual variable (while being cautious about multicollinearity). We also tested the predictive power of the regression equation as a whole. If we found that an independent variable seemed insignificant due to a low *t* ratio, we dropped the variable and reran the regression without it, observing what happened to the remaining independent variables. By a process of adding and deleting variables, powers, or transformations, we hoped to end up with the best model: the most parsimonious model with the highest relative predictive power.

Partial F Tests

In this section, we present a statistical test, based on the *F* distribution and, in simple cases, the *t* distribution, for evaluating the relative significance of parts of a regression model. The test is sometimes called a *partial* F *test* because it is an *F* test (or a *t* test, in simple cases) of a part of our regression model.

Suppose that a regression model of *Y* versus *k* independent variables is postulated, and the analysis is carried out (the *k* variables may include dummy variables, powers, etc.). Suppose that the equation of the regression model is as given in equation 11–1:

$$Y = \beta_0 + \beta_1 X_1 + \beta_2 X_2 + \beta_3 X_3 + \cdots + \beta_k X_k + \epsilon$$

We will call this model the *full model*. It is the full model in the sense that it includes the maximal set of independent variables X_i that we consider as predictors of *Y*. Now suppose that we want to test the relative significance of a subset of *r* of the *k* independent variables in the full model. (By relative significance we mean the significance of the r variables given that the remaining $k - r$ variables are in the model.) We will do this by comparing the *reduced model*, consisting of Y and the $k - r$ independent variables that remain once the r variables have been removed, with the full model, equation 11–1. The statistical comparison of the reduced model with the full model is done by the **partial F test.**

We will present the partial F test, using a more specific example. Suppose that we are considering the following two models.

Full model:

$$Y = \beta_0 + \beta_1 X_1 + \beta_2 X_2 + \beta_3 X_3 + \beta_4 X_4 + \epsilon \qquad (11\text{–}43)$$

Reduced model:

$$Y = \beta_0 + \beta_1 X_1 + \beta_2 X_2 + \epsilon \qquad (11\text{–}44)$$

By comparing the two models, we are asking the question: Given that variables X_1 and X_2 are already in the regression model, would we be gaining anything by adding X_3 and X_4 to the model? Will the reduced model be improved in terms of its predictive power by the addition of the two variables X_3 and X_4?

The statistical way of posing and answering this question is, of course, by way of a test of a hypothesis. The null hypothesis that the two variables X_3 and X_4 have no additional value once X_1 and X_2 are in the regression model is the hypothesis that both β_3 and β_4 are zero (given that X_1 and X_2 are in the model). The alternative hypothesis is that the two slope coefficients are not both zero. The hypothesis test is stated in equation 11–45.

Partial F test:

H_0: $\beta_3 = \beta_4 = 0$ (given that X_1 and X_2 are in the model)

H_1: β_3 and β_4 are not both zero $\qquad (11\text{–}45)$

The test statistic for this hypothesis test is the partial F statistic.

The **partial F statistic** is

$$F_{[r,\, n-(k+1)]} = \frac{(SSE_R - SSE_F)/r}{MSE_F} \qquad (11\text{–}46)$$

where SSE_R is the sum of squares for error of the reduced model; SSE_F is the sum of squares for error of the full model; MSE_F is the mean square error of the full model: $MSE_F = SSE_F/[n - (K + 1)]$; k is the number of independent variables in the full model ($k = 4$ in the present example); and r is the number of variables dropped from the full model in creating the reduced model (in the present example, $r = 2$).

The difference $SSE_R - SSE_F$ is called the *extra sum of squares* associated with the reduced model. Since this additional sum of squares for error is due to r variables, it has r degrees of freedom. (Like the sums of squares, degrees of freedom are additive. Thus, the extra sum of squares for error has degrees of freedom $[n - (k + 1)] - [n - (k - r + 1)] = r$.)

Suppose that the sum of squares for error of the full model, equation 11–43, is 37,653 and that the sum of squares for error of the reduced model, equation 11–44, is 42,900. Suppose also that the regression analysis is based on a data set of $n = 45$ points. Is there a statistical justification for including X_3 and X_4 in a model already containing X_1 and X_2?

To answer this question, we conduct the hypothesis test, equation 11–45. To do so, we compute the F statistic of equation 11–46:

$$F_{(2, 40)} = \frac{(\text{SSE}_R - \text{SSE}_F)/2}{\text{SSE}_F/40} = \frac{(42{,}900 - 37{,}653)/2}{37{,}653/40} = 2.79$$

This value of the statistic falls in the nonrejection region for $\alpha = 0.05$, and so we do not reject the null hypothesis and conclude that the decrease in the sum of squares for error when we go from the reduced model to the full model, adding X_3 and X_4 to the model that already has X_1 and X_2, is not statistically significant. It is not worthwhile to add the two variables.

Figure 11–42 shows the Partial F sheet of the Multiple Regression template. When we enter the value of r in cell D4, the partial F value appears in cell C9 and the corresponding p-value appears in cell C10. We can also see the SSE values for the full and reduced models in cells C6 and C7.

Figure 11–42 shows the partial F calculation for the exports problem of Example 11–2. Recall that the four independent variables in the problem are M1, Price, Lend, and Exchange. The p-value of 0.0010 for the partial F indicates that we should reject the null hypothesis H_0: the slopes for Lend and Exchange are zero (when M1 and Price are in the model).

In this example, we conducted a partial F test for the conditional significance of a set of $r = 2$ independent variables. This test can be carried out for the significance of any number of independent variables, powers of variables, or transformed variables, considered *jointly* as a set of variables to be added to a model. Frequently, however, we are interested in considering the relative merit of a single variable at a time. We may be interested in sequentially testing the conditional significance of a single independent variable, once other variables are already in the model (when no other variables are in the model, the F test is just a test of the significance of a single-variable regression). The F statistic for this test is still given by equation 11–46, but since the degrees of freedom are 1 and $n - (k + 1)$, this statistic is equal to the square of a t statistic with $n - (k + 1)$ degrees of freedom. Thus, the partial F test for the significance of a *single* variable may be carried out as a t test.

It may have occurred to you that a computer may be programmed to sequentially test the significance of each variable as it is added to a potential regression model,

FIGURE 11–42   Partial F from the Template
[Multiple Regression.xls; Sheet: Partial F]

	A	B	C	D	E	F
1	**Partial *F* Calculations**		Exports			
2						
3		#Independent variables in full model	4	*k*		
4		#Independent variables **dropped** from the model	2	*r*		
5						
6		SSE_F	6.989784			
7		SSE_R	8.747573			
8						
9		**Partial *F***	7.79587			
10		*p*-value	0.0010			

starting with one variable and building up until a whole set of variables has been tested and the best subset of variables chosen for the final regression model. We may also start with a full model, consisting of the entire set of potential variables, and delete variables from the model, one by one, whenever these variables are found not to be significant. Indeed, computers have been programmed to carry out both kinds of sequential single-variable tests and even a combination of the two methods. We will now discuss these three methods of variable selection called, respectively, *forward selection, backward elimination,* and their combination, *stepwise regression.* We will also discuss a fourth method, called *all possible regressions.*

Variable Selection Methods

1. **All possible regressions:** This method consists of running all possible regressions when k independent variables are considered and choosing the best model. If we assume that every one of the models we consider has an intercept term, then there are 2^k possible models. This is so because each of the k variables may be either included in the model or not included, which means that there are two possibilities for each variable—2^k possibilities for a model consisting of k potential variables. When four potential variables are considered, such as in Example 11–2, there are $2^4 = 16$ possible models: four models with a single variable, six models with a pair of variables, four models with three variables, one model with all four variables, and one model with no variables (an intercept term only). As you can see, the number of possible regression models increases very quickly as the number of variables considered increases.

    The different models are evaluated according to some criterion of model performance. There are several possible criteria: We may choose to select the model with the highest adjusted R^2 or the model with the lowest MSE (an equivalent condition). We may also choose to find the model with the highest R^2 for a given number of variables and then assess the increase in R^2 as we go to the best model with one more variable, to see if the increase in R^2 is worth the addition of a parameter to the model. Other criteria, such as Mallows' C_p statistic, are described in advanced books. The SAS System software has a routine called RSQUARE that runs all possible regressions and identifies the model with the highest R^2 for each number of variables included in the model. The all-possible-regressions procedure is thorough but tedious to carry out. The next three methods we describe are all stepwise procedures for building the best model. While the procedure called stepwise regression is indeed stepwise, the other two methods, forward selection and backward elimination, are also stepwise methods. These procedures are usually listed in computer manuals as variations of the stepwise method.

2. **Forward selection:** Forward selection starts with a model with no variables. The method then considers all k models with one independent variable and chooses the model with the highest significant F statistic, assuming that at least one such model has an F statistic with a p-value smaller than some predetermined value (this may be set by the user; otherwise a default value is used). Then the procedure looks at the variables remaining outside the model, considers all partial F statistics (i.e., keeping the added variables in the model, the statistic is equation 11–46), and adds the variable with the highest F value to the equation, again assuming that at least one variable is found to meet the required level of significance. The procedure is then continued until no variable left outside the model has a partial F statistic that satisfies the level of significance required to enter the model.

3. **Backward elimination:** This procedure works in a manner opposite to forward selection. We start with a model containing all k variables. Then the partial F statistic, equation 11–46, is computed for each variable, treated as if it were the last variable to enter the regression (i.e., we evaluate each variable in terms of its

contribution to a model that already contains all other variables). When the significance level of a variable's partial F statistic is found not to meet a preset standard (i.e., when the p-value is above the preset p-value), the variable is removed from the equation. All statistics are then computed for the new, reduced model, and the remaining variables are screened to see if they meet the significance standard. When a variable is found to have a higher p-value than required, the variable is dropped from the equation. The process continues until all variables left in the equation are significant in terms of their partial F statistic.

4. **Stepwise regression:** This is probably the most commonly used, wholly computerized method of variable selection. The procedure is an interesting mixture of the backward elimination and the forward selection methods. In forward selection, once a variable enters the equation, it remains there. This method does not allow for a reevaluation of a variable's significance once it is in the model. Recall that multicollinearity may cause a variable to become redundant in a model once other variables with much of the same information are included. This is a weakness of the forward selection technique. Similarly, in the backward elimination method, once a variable is out of the model, it stays out. Since a variable that was not significant due to multicollinearity and was dropped may have predictive power once other variables are removed from the model, backward elimination has limitations as well.

   Stepwise regression is a combination of forward selection and backward elimination that reevaluates the significance of every variable at every stage. This minimizes the chance of leaving out important variables or keeping unimportant ones. The procedure works as follows. The algorithm starts, as with the forward selection method, by finding the most significant single-variable regression model. Then the variables left out of the model are checked via a partial F test, and the most significant variable, assuming it meets the entry significance requirement, is added to the model. At this point, the procedure diverges from the forward selection scheme, and the logic of backward elimination is applied. The original variable in the model is reevaluated to see if it meets preset significance standards for staying in the model once the new variable has been added. If not, the variable is dropped. Then variables still outside the model are screened for the entry requirement, and the most significant one, if found, is added. All variables in the model are then checked again for staying significance once the new variable has been added. The procedure continues until there are no variables outside that should be added to the model and no variables inside the model that should be out.

The minimum significance requirements to enter the model and to stay in the model are often called P_{IN} and P_{OUT}, respectively. These are significance levels of the partial F statistic. For example, suppose that P_{IN} is 0.05 and P_{OUT} is also 0.05. This means that a variable will enter the equation if the p-value associated with its partial F statistic is less than 0.05, and it will stay in the model as long as the p-value of its partial F statistic is less than 0.05 after the addition of other variables. The two significance levels P_{IN} and P_{OUT} do not have to be equal, but we must be careful when setting them (or leave their values as programmed) because if P_{IN} is less strict than P_{OUT} (that is, $P_{IN} > P_{OUT}$), then we may end up with a circular routine where a variable enters the model, then leaves it, then reenters, etc., in an infinite loop. We demonstrate the stepwise regression procedure as a flowchart in Figure 11–43. Note that since we test the significance of one variable at a time, our partial F test may be carried out as a t test. This is done in some computer packages.

It is important to note that computerized variable selection algorithms may not find the best model. When a model is found, it may not be a unique best model; there may be several possibilities. The best model based on one evaluation criterion may not be best based on other criteria. Also, since there is order dependence in the selection process, we may not always arrive at the same "best" model. We must remember

FIGURE 11–43   The Stepwise Regression Algorithm

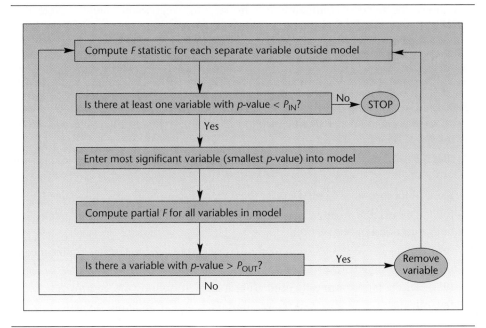

that computers do only what we tell them to do; and so if we have not considered some good variables to include in the model, including cross-products of variables, powers, and transformations, our model may not be as good as it could be. We must always use judgment in model selection and not rely blindly on the computer to find the best model. The computer should be used as an aid.

Table 11–23 shows output from a MINITAB stepwise regression for the Singapore exports example, Example 11–2. Note that the procedure chose the same "best"

TABLE 11–23   Stepwise Regression Using MINITAB for Example 11–2

```
MTB >  Stepwise 'Exports' 'M1' 'Lend' 'Price' 'Exch.';
SUBC>  AEnter 0.15;
SUBC>  ARemove 0.15;
SUBC>  Best 0;
SUBC>  Constant.
```

Stepwise Regression: Exports versus M1, Lend, Price, Exch.

```
  Alpha-to-Enter: 0.15 Alpha-to-Remove: 0.15

Response is Exports on 4 predictors, with N = 67
```

Step	1	2
Constant	0.9348	-3.4230
M1	0.520	0.361
T-Value	9.89	9.21
P-Value	0.000	0.000
Price		0.0370
T-Value		9.05
P-Value		0.000
S	0.495	0.331
R-Sq	60.08	82.48
R-Sq(adj)	59.47	81.93
Mallows Cp	78.4	1.1

model (out of the 16 possible regression models) as we did in our analysis. The table also shows the needed commands for the stepwise regression analysis. Note that MINITAB uses t tests rather than the equivalent F tests.

11–103.   Use equation 11–46 and the information in Tables 11–7 and 11–9 to conduct a partial F test for the significance of the lending rate and the exchange rate in the model of Example 11–2.

11–104.   Use a stepwise regression program to find the best set of variables for Example 11–1.

11–105.   Redo problem 11–104, using the data of Example 11–3.

11–106.   Discuss the relative merits and limitations of the four variable selection methods described in this section.

11–107.   In the stepwise regression method, why do we need to test the significance of a variable that is already determined to be included in the model, assuming $P_{IN} = P_{OUT}$?

11–108.   Discuss the commonly used criteria for determining the best model.

11–109.   Is there always a single "best" model in a given situation? Explain.

11–14   Using the Computer

Multiple Regression Using the Solver

Just as we did in simple regression, we can conduct a multiple regression using the Solver command in Excel. The advantage of the method is that we can impose all kinds of constraints on the regression coefficients. The disadvantage is that our assumptions about the errors being normally distributed will not be valid. Hence, hypothesis tests about the regression coefficients and calculation of prediction intervals are not possible. We can make point predictions, though.

Figure 11–44 shows the template that can be used to carry out a multiple regression using the Solver. After entering the data, we may start with zeroes for all the regression coefficients in row 6. Enter zeroes even in unused columns. (Strictly, this row of cells should have been shaded in green. For the sake of clarity, they have not been shaded.) Then the Solver is invoked by selecting the Solver command under the Data tab. If a constraint needs to be entered, the Add button in the Solver dialog box should be used to enter the constraint. Click the Solve button to start the Solver. When the problem is solved, select Keep Solver Solution and press the OK button.

The results seen in Figure 11–44 are for the exports to Singapore problem (Example 11–2) using all four independent variables. One way to drop an independent variable from the model is to force the regression coefficient (slope) of that variable to equal zero. Figure 11–45 presents the Solver dialog box showing the constraints needed to drop the variables Lend and Exchange from the model. Figure 11–46 shows the results of this constrained regression. Note that the regression coefficients for Lend and Exchange show up as zeroes.

As we saw in simple regression, many different types of constraint can be imposed. The possibilities are more extensive in the case of multiple regression since there are more regression coefficients. For instance, we can enter a constraint such as

$$2b_1 + 5b_2 - 6b_3 \leq 10$$

Such constraints may be needed in econometric regression problems.

FIGURE 11–44   The Template for Multiple Regression by Solver
[Mult Regn by Solver.xls]

	A	B	C	D	E	F	G	H	I	J	K	L	M	N	O
1	**Using the Solver**					Exports									
2	Unprotect the sheet before using the Solver.														
3															
4			Regression Coefficients												
5			b_0	b_1	b_2	b_3	b_4	b_5	b_6	b_7	b_8	b_9	b_{10}		
6			-4.024	0.3686	0.0048	0.0365	0.2714	0	0	0	0	0	0		
7															**SSE**
8		Y	1	X1	X2	X3	X4	X5	X6	X7	X8	X9	X10		6.98979
9	Sl.No.	Exports	Ones	M1	Lend	Price	Exch.								Error
10	1	2.6	1	5.1	7.8	114	2.16								-0.04107
11	2	2.6	1	4.9	8	116	2.17								-0.04404
12	3	2.7	1	5.1	8.1	117	2.18								-0.05744
13	4	3	1	5.1	8.1	122	2.2								0.05459
14	5	2.9	1	5.1	8.1	124	2.21								-0.12114

FIGURE 11–45   Solver Dialog Box Containing Two Constraints

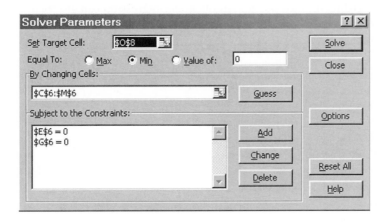

FIGURE 11–46   Results of Constrained Regression

	A	B	C	D	E	F	G	H	I	J	K	L	M	N	O
1	**Using the Solver**					Exports									
2	Unprotect the sheet before using the Solver.														
3															
4			Regression Coefficients												
5			b_0	b_1	b_2	b_3	b_4	b_5	b_6	b_7	b_8	b_9	b_{10}		
6			-3.423	0.361	0	0.037	0	0	0	0	0	0	0		
7															**SSE**
8		Y	1	X1	X2	X3	X4	X5	X6	X7	X8	X9	X10		6.9959
9	Sl.No.	Exports	Ones	M1	Lend	Price	Exch.								Error
10	1	2.6	1	5.1	7.8	114	2.16								-0.042
11	2	2.6	1	4.9	8	116	2.17								-0.0438
12	3	2.7	1	5.1	8.1	117	2.18								-0.0531
13	4	3	1	5.1	8.1	122	2.2								0.0617

A COMMENT ON R²

The idea of constrained regression makes it easy to understand an important concept in multiple regression. Note that the SSE in the unconstrained regression (Figure 11–44) is 6.9898, whereas it has increased to 6.9959 in the constrained regression (Figure 11–46). When a constraint is imposed, it cannot decrease SSE. Why? Whatever values we have for the regression coefficients in the constrained version are certainly feasible in the unconstrained version. Thus, whatever SSE is achieved in the constrained version can be achieved in the unconstrained version just as well. Thus the SSE in the constrained version will be more than, or at best equal to, the SSE in the unconstrained version. Therefore, *a constraint cannot decrease SSE*. Dropping an independent variable from the model is the same as constraining its slope to zero. Thus dropping a variable cannot decrease SSE. Note that $R^2 = 1 - SSE/SST$. We can therefore say that dropping a variable cannot increase R^2. Conversely, introducing a new variable cannot increase SSE, which is to say, *introducing a new variable cannot decrease R^2*.

In an effort to increase R^2, an experimenter may be tempted to include more and more independent variables in the model, reasoning that this cannot decrease R^2 but will very likely increase R^2. This is an important reason why we have to look carefully at the included variables in any model. In addition, we should also look at adjusted R^2 and the difference between R^2 and adjusted R^2. A large difference means that some questionable variables have been included.

LINEST Function for Multiple Regression

The LINEST function we saw for simple linear regression can also be used for multiple regression. We will solve the problem introduced in Example 11–2 using the LINEST function.

- Enter the Y values in the range B5:B71 as shown in Figure 11–47.
- Enter the X1, X2, X3, X4 values in the range D5:G71.
- Select the 5 rows × 5 columns range I5:M9. The selected range should have 5 rows and $k + 1$ columns where k is the number of X variables in the data. In our problem $k = 4$.
- Click the Insert Function in the Formulas tab.
- Select Statistical under Function category. In the list of functions that appear at right, select LINEST.
- Fill in the LINEST dialog box as follows (see Figure 11–47):
    - –In the box for Known_y's, enter the range that contains the Y values.
    - –In the box for Known_x's, enter the range that contains the X values.
    - –Leave the Const box blank. Entering TRUE in that box will force the intercept to be zero. We don't need that.

FIGURE 11–47   Using the LINEST Function for Multiple Regression

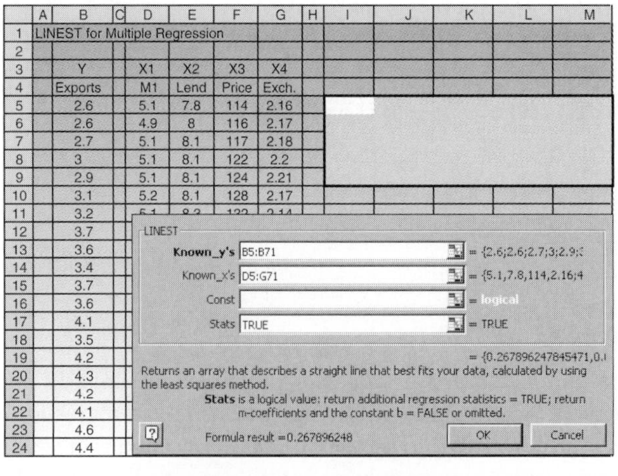

FIGURE 11–48   LINEST Output for Multiple Regression

	A	B	C	D	E	F	G	H	I	J	K	L	M
1		LINEST for Multiple Regression											
2													
3		Y		X1	X2	X3	X4						
4		Exports		M1	Lend	Price	Exch.		LINEST Output				
5		2.6		5.1	7.8	114	2.16		0.267896	0.036511	0.004702	0.368456	-4.015461
6		2.6		4.9	8	116	2.17		1.17544	0.009326	0.049222	0.063848	2.766401
7		2.7		5.1	8.1	117	2.18		0.824976	0.335765	#N/A	#N/A	#N/A
8		3		5.1	8.1	122	2.2		73.05922	62	#N/A	#N/A	#N/A
9		2.9		5.1	8.1	124	2.21		32.94634	6.989784	#N/A	#N/A	#N/A
10		3.1		5.2	8.1	128	2.17						
11		3.2		5.1	8.3	132	2.14		Legend				
12		3.7		5.2	8.8	133	2.16		b_4	b_3	b_2	b_1	b_0
13		3.6		5.3	8.9	133	2.15		$s(b_4)$	$s(b_3)$	$s(b_2)$	$s(b_1)$	$s(b_0)$
14		3.4		5.4	9.1	134	2.16		R^2	s			
15		3.7		5.7	9.2	135	2.18		F	df(SSE)			
16		3.6		5.7	9.5	136	2.17		SSR	SSE			

- *Keeping the CTRL and SHIFT keys pressed,* click the OK button. The reason for keeping the CTRL and SHIFT keys pressed is that the formula we are entering is an *array formula.* An array formula is simultaneously entered in a range of cells at once, and that range behaves as one cell. When an array formula is entered, Excel will add the { } braces around the formula.
- You should see the results seen in Figure 11–48.

LINEST does not label any of its outputs. You need a legend to see which result is where. The legend is shown is Figure 11–48. Note that there are some unused cell in the output range, and LINEST fills them with #N/A, which stands for "Not Applicable."

Using the legend, you can see that the regression equation is

$$\hat{Y} = -4.01546 + 0.368456 X_1 + 0.004702 X_2 + 0.036511 X_3 + 0.267896 X_4$$

As in the previous chapter, we can use the Excel Regression tool to perform a multiple regression analysis. The Regression tool uses the worksheet function LINEST that was described before. Start by clicking the Data Analysis in the Analysis group on the Data tab. In the Data Analysis window select Regression. The corresponding Regression window will appear as shown in Figure 11–49. The setting is very similar to what we described in Chapter 10 for a single regression analysis using the Excel Regression tool.

Using the data of Example 11–2, the obtained result will contain a summary output, ANOVA table, model coefficients and their corresponding confidence intervals, residuals, and related graphs if they have been selected. Figure 11–50 shows the result.

Using MINITAB for Multiple Regression

In Chapter 10, we provided instructions for using MINITAB for simple linear regression analysis choosing Stat ► Regression ► Regression from the menu bar. The same set of instructions can be applied to using MINITAB in a multiple as well as polynomial

FIGURE 11–49   Using the Excel Regression Tool for a Multiple Regression

	A	B	C	D	E	F	G	H	I	J	K	L	M	N
1														
2		Exports	M1	Lend	Price	Exch.		Regression					?⏷ ✕	
3		2.6	5.1	7.8	114	2.16		Input					OK	
4		2.6	4.9	8	116	2.17		Input Y Range:		$B$2:$B$69			Cancel	
5		2.7	5.1	8.1	117	2.18								
6		3	5.1	8.1	122	2.2		Input X Range:		$C$2:$F$69			Help	
7		2.9	5.1	8.1	124	2.21		☑ Labels		☐ Constant is Zero				
8		3.1	5.2	8.1	128	2.17		☑ Confidence Level:		95 %				
9		3.2	5.1	8.3	132	2.14								
10		3.7	5.2	8.8	133	2.16		Output options						
11		3.6	5.3	8.9	133	2.15		⦿ Output Range:		$H$2				
12		3.4	5.4	9.1	134	2.16		○ New Worksheet Ply:						
13		3.7	5.7	9.2	135	2.18		○ New Workbook						
14		3.6	5.7	9.5	136	2.17		Residuals						
15		4.1	5.9	10.3	140	2.15		☐ Residuals		☐ Residual Plots				
16		3.5	5.8	10.6	147	2.16		☐ Standardized Residuals		☐ Line Fit Plots				
17		4.2	5.7	11.3	150	2.21		Normal Probability						
18		4.3	5.8	12.1	151	2.24		☐ Normal Probability Plots						
19		4.2	6	12	151	2.16								
20		4.1	6	11.4	151	2.12								

FIGURE 11–50   Excel Results for Multiple Regression

	A	B	C	D	E	F	G	H	I	J	K	L	M	N	O	P
1																
2		Exports	M1	Lend	Price	Exch.		SUMMARY OUTPUT				Excel Regression Tool for Multiple Regression Analysis				
3		2.6	5.1	7.8	114	2.16										
4		2.6	4.9	8	116	2.17		Regression Statistics								
5		2.7	5.1	8.1	117	2.18		Multiple R	0.908281831							
6		3	5.1	8.1	122	2.2		R Square	0.824975884							
7		2.9	5.1	8.1	124	2.21		Adjusted R Square	0.813684006							
8		3.1	5.2	8.1	128	2.17		Standard Error	0.335765471							
9		3.2	5.1	8.3	132	2.14		Observations	67							
10		3.7	5.2	8.8	133	2.16										
11		3.6	5.3	8.9	133	2.15		ANOVA								
12		3.4	5.4	9.1	134	2.16			df	SS	MS	F	Significance F			
13		3.7	5.7	9.2	135	2.18		Regression	4	32.94633542	8.236584	73.05922	9.13052E-23			
14		3.6	5.7	9.5	136	2.17		Residual	62	6.989783981	0.112738					
15		4.1	5.9	10.3	140	2.15		Total	66	39.9361194						
16		3.5	5.8	10.6	147	2.16										
17		4.2	5.7	11.3	150	2.21			Coefficients	Standard Error	t Stat	p-value	Lower 95%	Upper 95%	Lower 95.0%	Upper 95.0%
18		4.3	5.8	12.1	151	2.24		Intercept	-4.015461451	2.766400566	-1.45151	0.151679	-9.545417333	1.514494431	-9.545417333	1.514494431
19		4.2	6	12	151	2.16		M1	0.368456401	0.063848409	5.7708	2.71E-07	0.24082525	0.496087551	0.24082525	0.496087551
20		4.1	6	11.4	151	2.12		Lend	0.004702202	0.049221863	0.095531	0.924201	-0.0936909	0.103095304	-0.0936909	0.103095304
21		4.6	6	11.1	153	2.11		Price	0.036510524	0.009326009	3.914914	0.000228	0.017868098	0.05515295	0.017868098	0.05515295
22		4.4	6	11	154	2.13		Exch.	0.267896248	1.175440162	0.227911	0.820465	-2.081775134	2.617567629	-2.081775134	2.617567629
23		4.5	6.1	11.3	154	2.11										

regression analysis. Figure 11–51 shows the Regression window as well as corresponding Session commands for running a multiple regression analysis on the data of Example 11–2. Note that by clicking the Options button in the main dialog box, you can choose to display variance inflation factors (VIF) to check for multicollinearity effects associated with each predictor. In addition, you can display the Durbin-Watson statistic to detect autocorrelation in the residuals by selecting the Durbin-Watson statistic check box.

Based on the obtained p-value of the ANOVA table, which is approximately zero, we conclude that a linear relation exists between the dependent and independent variables. On the other hand, the p-value corresponding to the coefficients of the independent variables Lend and Exch are considerably large. So the estimated coefficients of these two variables are not statistically significant. This conclusion can also be confirmed by considering the 95% confidence intervals on the model coefficients obtained in Figure 11–50. As we can see, the only two intervals that contain the value zero belong to the variables Lend and Exch.

FIGURE 11–51   Using MINITAB for Multiple Regression Analysis

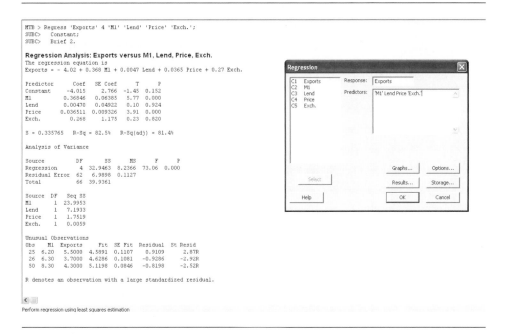

```
MTB > Regress 'Exports' 4 'M1' 'Lend' 'Price' 'Exch.';
SUBC>   Constant;
SUBC>   Brief 2.

Regression Analysis: Exports versus M1, Lend, Price, Exch.
The regression equation is
Exports = - 4.02 + 0.368 M1 + 0.0047 Lend + 0.0365 Price + 0.27 Exch.

Predictor      Coef    SE Coef      T      P
Constant     -4.015      2.766  -1.45  0.152
M1          0.36846    0.06385   5.77  0.000
Lend        0.00470    0.04922   0.10  0.924
Price      0.036511   0.009326   3.91  0.000
Exch.         0.268      1.175   0.23  0.820

S = 0.335765   R-Sq = 82.5%   R-Sq(adj) = 81.4%

Analysis of Variance

Source          DF       SS      MS      F      P
Regression       4  32.9463  8.2366  73.06  0.000
Residual Error  62   6.9898  0.1127
Total           66  39.9361

Source  DF   Seq SS
M1       1  23.9953
Lend     1   7.1933
Price    1   1.7519
Exch.    1   0.0059

Unusual Observations
Obs    M1  Exports     Fit  SE Fit  Residual  St Resid
 25  6.20   5.5000  4.5891  0.1107    0.9109      2.87R
 26  6.30   3.7000  4.6286  0.1081   -0.9286     -2.92R
 50  8.30   4.3000  5.1198  0.0846   -0.8198     -2.52R

R denotes an observation with a large standardized residual.
```

Perform regression using least squares estimation

If you need to use MINITAB for a polynomial regression or adding cross-product terms to the model, you have to transform variables before starting the regression analysis. Select Calc ▶ Calculator to enter the column number or name of the new variable in the Store result in the variable edit box. Choose the function, such as power, square root, or natural log, that should be used in the transformation from the Functions drop-down box. The names of the independent variables that should be transformed are entered in the Expression edit box. Click the OK button and continue with your regression analysis.

MINITAB can also be used to build a model based on the stepwise regression method. As described earlier in this chapter, this method enables you to identify a useful subset of the predictors by removing and adding variables to the regression model. MINITAB provides three frequently used procedures: standard stepwise regression (adds and removes variables), forward selection (adds variables), and backward elimination (removes variables). Start by choosing Stat ▶ Regression ▶ Stepwise. When the Stepwise Regression dialog box appears, enter the response variable in the Response edit box. The columns containing the predictor variables to include in the model are entered in the Predictors edit box. Indicate which predictors should never be removed from the model in Predictors to include in every model. Click on the Methods button. Check Use alpha value if you wish to use the alpha value as the criterion for adding or removing a variable to or from the model. When you choose the stepwise or forward selection method, you can set the value of α for entering a new variable in the model in Alpha to enter. If you wish to run a stepwise or backward elimination method, you can set the value of α for removing a variable from the model in Alpha to remove. If you check Use F values, then the F value will be used as the criterion for adding or removing a variable to or from the model. The value of F for entering or removing a new variable in the model can be defined in the F to enter and F to remove edit boxes, respectively. You can also enter a starting set of predictor variables in Predictors in initial model. Figure 11–52 shows the corresponding dialog box as well as corresponding Session commands for the data set of Example 11–2.

As we can see, as the result of the stepwise regression method, M1 and Price compose the best subset of independent variables that have been chosen to build the

FIGURE 11–52   Using MINITAB for a Stepwise Regression

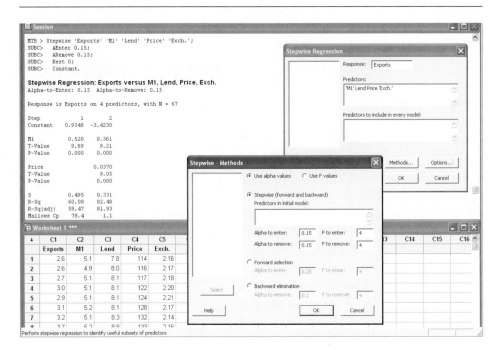

model. Note that MINITAB has used the t test to add or eliminate the independent variables. The obtained coefficients and adjusted R^2 are the same as the result we obtained by applying the regular regression method.

MINITAB has many other options and tools that enable you to run different types of regression analysis. All these options are available via Stat ▶ Regression from the menu bar.

11–15   Summary and Review of Terms

In this chapter, we extended the simple linear regression method of Chapter 10 to include several independent variables. We saw how the F test and the t test are adapted to the extension: The F test is aimed at determining the existence of a linear relationship between Y and any of the explanatory variables, and the separate t tests are each aimed at checking the significance of a single variable. We saw how the geometry of least-squares estimation is extended to planes and to higher-dimensional surfaces as more independent variables are included in a model. We extended the coefficient of determination to multiple regression situations, as well as the correlation coefficient. We discussed the problem of **multicollinearity** and its effects on estimation and prediction. We extended our discussion of the use of residual plots and mentioned the problem of **outliers** and the problem of **autocorrelation** of the errors and its detection. We discussed **qualitative variables** and their modeling using **indicator (dummy) variables.** We also talked about higher-order models: **polynomials** and **cross-product terms.** We emphasized the need for parsimony. We showed the relationship between regression and ANOVA and between regression and **analysis of covariance.** We also talked about **nonlinear** models and about **transformations.** Finally, we discussed methods for selecting variables to find the "best" multiple regression model: **forward selection, backward elimination, stepwise regression,** and **all possible regressions.**

www.exercise

11–110. Go to the Web site http://www.lib.umich.edu/govdocs/stforeig.html, which lists economic variables in foreign countries. Choose a number of economic variables for various years, and run a multiple regression aimed at predicting one variable based on a set of independent variables.

11–111. A multiple regression analysis of mutual fund performance includes a number of variables as they are, but the variable *size of fund* is used only as the logarithm of the actual value.[22] Why?

11–112. A multiple regression of price versus the independent variables quality, industry, category, and quality $\times$ industry and quality $\times$ category was carried out. The R^2 was 67.5%. The t statistic for each variable alone was significant, but the cross-products were not.[23] Explain.

11–113. An article in *Psychology and Marketing* describes four variables that have been found to impact the effectiveness of commercials for high-performance automobiles: sincerity, excitement, ruggedness, and sophistication.[24] Suppose that the following data are available on commercials' effectiveness and these variables, all on appropriate scales.

Commercial Effectiveness	Assessed Sincerity	Assessed Excitement	Assessed Ruggedness	Assessed Sophistication
75	12	50	32	17
80	10	55	32	18
71	20	48	33	16
90	15	57	32	15
92	21	56	34	19
60	17	42	33	14
58	18	41	30	16
65	22	49	31	18
81	20	54	30	19
90	14	58	33	11
95	10	59	31	12
76	17	51	30	20
61	21	42	29	11

Is there a regression relation here between commercial effectiveness and any of the independent variables? Explain.

11–114. The following data are the asking price and other variables for condominiums in a small town. Try to construct a prediction equation for the asking price based on any of or all the other reported variables.

Price ($)	Number of Rooms	Number of Bedrooms	Number of Baths	Age	Assessed Value ($)	Area (square feet)
145,000	4	1	1	69	116,500	790
144,900	4	2	1	70	127,200	915
145,900	3	1	1	78	127,600	721
146,500	4	1	1	75	121,700	800
146,900	4	2	1	40	94,800	718
147,900	4	1	1	12	169,700	915
148,000	3	1	1	20	151,800	870

(continued)

[22]Josh Lerner, Antoinette Schoar, and Wan Wongsunwai, "Smart Institutions, Foolish Choices: The Limited Partner Performance Puzzle," *Journal of Finance* 62, no. 2 (2007), pp. 731–764.

[23]Markus Christen and Miklos Sarvary, "Competitive Pricing of Information: A Longitudinal Experiment," *Journal of Marketing Research* 44 (February 2007), pp. 42–56.

[24]Kong Cheen Lau and Ian Phav, "Extending Symbolic Brands Using Their Personality," *Psychology and Marketing* 24, no. 5 (2007), pp. 421–443.

Price ($)	Number of Rooms	Number of Bedrooms	Number of Baths	Age	Assessed Value ($)	Area (square feet)
148,900	3	1	1	20	147,800	875
149,000	4	2	1	70	140,500	1,078
149,000	4	2	1	60	120,400	705
149,900	4	2	1	65	160,800	834
149,900	3	1	1	20	135,900	725
149,900	4	2	1	65	125,400	900
152,900	5	2	1	37	134,500	792
153,000	3	1	1	100	132,100	820
154,000	3	1	1	18	140,800	782
158,000	5	2	1	89	158,000	955
158,000	4	2	1	69	127,600	920
159,000	4	2	1	60	152,800	1,050
159,000	5	2	2	49	157,000	1,092
179,900	5	2	2	90	165,800	1,180
179,900	6	3	1	89	158,300	1,328
179,500	5	2	1	60	148,100	1,175
179,000	6	3	1	87	158,500	1,253
175,000	4	2	1	80	156,900	650

11–115. By definition, the U.S. trade deficit is the sum of the trade deficits it has with all its trading partners. Consider a model of the trade deficit based on regions such as Asia, Africa, and Europe. Whether there is collinearity, meaning the deficits move in the same direction, among these trading regions depends on the similarities of the goods that the United States trades in each region. You can investigate the collinearity of these regional deficits from data available from the U.S. Census Bureau, www.census.gov/. At this site, locate the trade data in the International Trade Reports. (*Hint:* Start at the A–Z area; locate foreign trade by clicking on "F.")

Read the highlights of the current report, and examine current-year country-by-commodity detailed data for a selection of countries in each of the regions of Asia, Africa, and Europe. Based on the country-by-commodity detailed information, would you expect the deficits in these regions to be correlated? How would you design a statistical test for collinearity among these regions?

www.exercise

CASE 15 Return on Capital for Four Different Sectors

The table that follows presents financial data of some companies drawn from four different industry sectors. The data include return on capital, sales, operating margin, and debt-to-capital ratio all pertaining to the same latest 12 months for which data were available for that company. The period may be different for different companies, but we shall ignore that fact.

Using suitable indicator variables to represent the sector of each company, regress the return on capital against all other variables, including the indicator variables.

1. The sectors are to be ranked in descending order of return on capital. Based on the regression results, what will that ranking be?

2. It is claimed that the sector that a company belongs to does not affect its return on capital. Conduct a partial *F* test to see if all the indicator variables can be dropped from the regression model.

3. For each of the four sectors, give a 95% prediction interval for the *expected* return on capital for a company with the following annual data: sales of $2 billion, operating margin of 35%, and a debt-to-capital ratio of 50%.

	Return on Capital (%)	Sales ($ millions)	Operating Margin (%)	Debt/ Capital (%)
Banking				
Bank of New York	17.2	7,178	38.1	28.5
Bank United	11.9	1,437	26.7	24.3
Comerica	17.1	3,948	38.9	65.6
Compass Bancshares	15.4	1,672	27	26.4
Fifth Third Bancorp	16.6	4,123	34.8	46.4
First Tennessee National	15.1	2,317	21.3	20.1
Firstar	13.7	6,804	36.6	17.7
Golden State Bancorp	15.9	4,418	21.5	65.8
Golden West Financial	14.6	3,592	23.8	17
GreenPoint Financial	11.3	1,570	36	14.1
Hibernia	14.7	1,414	26	0
M&T Bank	13.4	1,910	30.2	21.4
Marshall & Ilsley	14.7	2,594	24.4	19.2
Northern Trust	15.3	3,379	28.4	35.7
Old Kent Financial	16.6	1,991	26	21.9
PNC Financial Services	15	7,548	32	29.5
SouthTrust	12.9	3,802	24	26.1
Synovus Financial	19.7	1,858	27.3	5.1
UnionBanCal	16.5	3,085	31.4	14.6
Washington Mutual	13.8	15,197	24.7	39.6
Wells Fargo	11.9	24,532	38.9	50.7
Zions Bancorp	7.7	1,845	23.5	19.3
Computers				
Agilent Technologies	22.4	10,773	14	0
Altera	32.4	1,246	41.7	0
American Power Conversion	21.2	1,459	22.2	0
Analog Devices	36.8	2,578	35.3	34
Applied Materials	42.2	9,564	32.5	7.4
Atmel	16.4	1,827	30.8	28.1
Cisco Systems	15.5	21,529	27.3	0
Dell Computer	38.8	30,016	9.6	7.8
EMC	24.9	8,127	31	0.2
Gateway	26.6	9,461	9.8	0.1
Intel	28.5	33,236	46.3	1.5
Jabil Circuit	25	3,558	8.4	1.9
KLA-Tencor	21.8	1,760	26.7	0
Micron Technology	26.5	7,336	44.8	11.8
Palm	10.1	1,282	7.8	0
Sanmina	14.1	3,912	13.9	39
SCI Systems	12.5	8,707	5.8	35.9
Solectron	14.6	14,138	7	46.6
Sun Microsystems	30.5	17,621	19.6	14.7
Tech Data	13	19,890	2	22.6
Tektronix	41.3	1,118	12.3	13.2
Teradyne	40.4	2,804	27	0.54
Texas Instruments	25.5	11,406	29.9	8.4
Xilinx	35.8	1,373	36.8	0

(continued)

	Return on Capital (%)	Sales ($ millions)	Operating Margin (%)	Debt/ Capital (%)
Construction				
Carlisle Companies	15.7	1,752	13.9	34.3
Granite Construction	14.1	1,368	9.8	13.7
DR Horton	12.3	3,654	9.3	58
Kaufman & Broad Home	12.1	3,910	9.2	58.4
Lennar	14.7	3,955	10.7	59.7
Martin Marietta Materials	10.3	1,354	26.4	39.3
Masco	14.3	7,155	18.4	38.3
MDC Holdings	21.4	1,674	12.3	28.4
Mueller Industries	15	1,227	15.9	14.2
NVR	40.8	2,195	11.9	31.5
Pulte Homes	11.5	4,052	8.9	37.6
Standard Pacific	13.7	1,198	10.7	52.9
Stanley Works	16.9	2,773	14	18.9
Toll Brothers	11	1,642	14.7	53.5
URS	8.7	2,176	9.8	62.9
Vulcan Materials	11.8	2,467	23.5	27.1
Del Webb	8.2	2,048	10.3	64.8
Energy				
Allegheny Energy	7.8	3,524	26.4	47.9
Apache	12.5	2,006	79.8	32.3
BJ Services	9.8	1,555	19.1	10.6
BP Amoco	19.4	131,450	15.4	17.9
Chevron	16.6	43,957	23	16
Cinergy	7.7	7,130	16.7	42.3
Conoco	17.5	30	14	36.7
Consol Energy	20.4	2,036	17.1	55.9
Duke Energy	7.8	40,104	10.4	37.7
Dynegy	18.4	24,074	3.7	39.4
Enron	8.1	71,011	3.2	40.6
Exelon	8.6	5,620	33.9	56.8
ExxonMobil	14.9	196,956	14.7	7.9
FPL Group	8.6	6,744	33.1	32.8
Halliburton	11.9	12,424	8	18.2
Kerr-McGee	17.2	3,760	54.7	45
KeySpan	8.9	4,123	23.1	39.9
MDU Resources	8.7	1,621	17.7	40.5
Montana Power	10.5	1,055	23.5	24
Murphy Oil	17.5	3,172	20.5	22.1
Noble Affiliates	13.5	1,197	42.4	36
OGE Energy	7.9	2,894	18.7	48.6
Phillips Petroleum	14.9	19,414	21.6	47
PPL	10.1	5,301	26.4	54
Progress Energy	8.3	3,661	40.8	38.7
Reliant Energy	8.3	23,576	11.9	37.8
Royal Dutch Petroleum	17.9	129,147	19.8	5.7
Scana	7.2	2,839	42.5	47.4
Smith International	7	2,539	9.3	22.8
Sunoco	13.4	11,791	6.4	34.3
TECO Energy	9	2,189	31.2	40.4
Tosco	16.7	21,287	5.9	41.5
Valero Energy	14.5	13,188	4.7	35.8

Source: *Forbes*, January 8, 2001.

12

TIME SERIES, FORECASTING, AND INDEX NUMBERS

12–1 Using Statistics 561

12–2 Trend Analysis 561

12–3 Seasonality and Cyclical Behavior 566

12–4 The Ratio-to-Moving-Average Method 569

12–5 Exponential Smoothing Methods 577

12–6 Index Numbers 582

12–7 Using the Computer 588

12–8 Summary and Review of Terms 591

Case 16 Auto Parts Sales Forecast 592

LEARNING OBJECTIVES

After studying this chapter, you should be able to:

- Differentiate between qualitative and quantitative methods of forecasting.
- Carry out a trend analysis in time series data.
- Identify seasonal and cyclical patterns in time series data.
- Forecast using simple and weighted moving-average methods.
- Forecast using the exponential smoothing method.
- Forecast when the time series contains both trend and seasonality.
- Assess the efficiency of forecasting methods using measures of error.
- Make forecasts using templates.
- Compute index numbers.

12–1 Using Statistics

Everything in life changes through time. Even the value of money is not constant in this world: A dollar today is not the same as a dollar a year ago, or a dollar a year from now. While most people know this, they think that the cause is inflation. In fact, the value of one dollar a year from now should be lower than the value of a dollar today for a basic economic reason. A dollar today can be invested or put in the bank or loaned to someone. Since the investor (or bank depositor or lender) must be paid for giving someone else his dollar for a year, that one dollar now must be equal to a dollar plus some amount a year from now—the amount it earns the investor in one year. Thus, one dollar today is worth more than a dollar a year hence.

So how can we evaluate the worth of money across years? One way to do this is to use the most famous time series data in America, called the **consumer price index** (CPI), which is computed and published by the U.S. Bureau of Labor Statistics (and can be found at http://www.bls.gov). This index defines a base year (1967, or the years 1982–84; the user can choose which one to use), for which the value is defined as 100. Using base year 1967, the series value for 2006 was 603.9. This means that one dollar in 1967 was worth 6.039 dollars in 2006.

This chapter will teach you about the CPI and its uses. The chapter also presents methods for forecasting time series—data sets that are ordered through time.

12–2 Trend Analysis

Sometimes a time series displays a steady tendency of increase or decrease through time. Such a tendency is called a **trend.** When we plot the observations against time, we may notice that a straight line can describe the increase or decrease in the series as time goes on. This should remind us of simple linear regression, and, indeed, in such cases we will use the method of least squares to estimate the parameters of a straight-line model.

At this point, we make an important remark. *When one is dealing with time series data, the errors of the regression model may not be independent of one another: Time series observations tend to be sequentially correlated.* Therefore, we cannot give much credence to regression results. Our estimation and hypothesis tests may not be accurate. We must be aware of such possible problems and must realize that fitting lines to time series data is less an accurate statistical method than a simple *descriptive* method that may work in some cases. We will now demonstrate the procedure of trend analysis with an example.

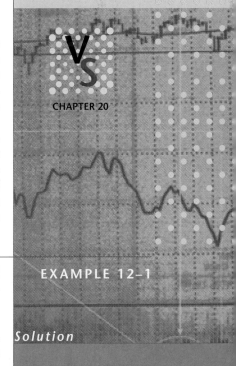

CHAPTER 20

EXAMPLE 12–1

An economist is researching banking activity and wants to find a model that would help her forecast total net loans by commercial banks. The economist gets the hypothetical data presented in Table 12–1. A plot of the data is shown in Figure 12–1.

Solution

As can be seen from the figure, the observations may be described by a straight line. A simple linear regression equation is fit to the data by least squares. A straight-line model to account for a trend is of the form

$$Z_t = \beta_0 + \beta_1 t + a_t \qquad (12\text{–}1)$$

where t is time and a_t is the error term. The coefficients β_0 and β_1 are the regression intercept and slope, respectively. The regression can be carried out as we saw in Chapter 10. To simplify the calculation, the first year in the data (2000) is coded $t = 1$, and next $t = 2$, and so on. We shall see the regression results in a template.

TABLE 12–1
Annual Total Net Loans
by Commercial Banks

Year	Loans ($ billions)
2000	833
2001	936
2002	1,006
2003	1,120
2004	1,212
2005	1,301
2006	1,490
2007	1,608

FIGURE 12–1   Hypothetical Annual Total Net Loans by Commercial Banks

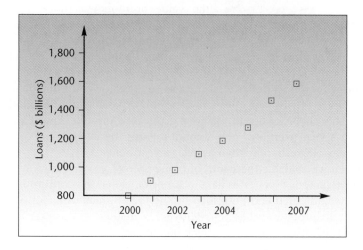

Figure 12–2 shows the template that can be used for trend forecast. The data are entered in columns B and D. The coded t values appear in column C. As seen in the range M7:M8, the slope and the intercept of the regression line are, respectively, 109.19 and 696.89. In other words, the regression equation is

$$Z_t = 696.89 + 109.19t$$

By substituting 9 for t, we get the forecast for year 2008 as 1,679.61. In the template, this appears in cell G5. Indeed, the template contains forecasts for $t = 9$ through 20, which correspond to the years 2008 to 2019. In the range I5:I16, we can enter any desired values for t and get the corresponding forecast in the range J5:J16.

Remember that forecasting is an extrapolation outside the region of the estimation data. This, in addition to the fact that the regression assumptions are not met in trend analysis, causes our forecast to have an unknown accuracy. We will, therefore, not construct any prediction interval.

Trend analysis includes cases where the trend is not necessarily a straight line. *Curved* trends can be modeled as well, and here we may use either polynomials or transformations, as we saw in Chapter 11. In fact, a careful examination of the data in Figure 12–1 and of the fitted line in Figure 12–2 reveals that the data are actually curved upward somewhat. We will, therefore, fit an exponential model $Z = \beta_0 e^{\beta_1 t} a_t$, where β_0 and β_1 are constants and e is the number 2.71828 . . . , the base of the natural logarithm. We assume a multiplicative error a_t. We run a regression of the natural log of Z on variable t. The transformed regression, in terms of the original exponential equation, is shown in Figure 12–3. The coefficient of determination of this model is very close to 1.00. The figure also shows the forecast for 2002, obtained from the equation by substituting $t = 9$, as we did when we tried fitting the straight line.

A polynomial regression with t and t^2 leads to a fit very similar to the one shown in Figure 12–3, and the forecast is very close to the one obtained by the exponential equation. We do not elaborate on the details of the analysis here because much was explained about regression models in Chapters 10 and 11. Remember that trend analysis does not enjoy the theoretical strengths that regression analysis does in

FIGURE 12–2   The Template for Trend Analysis
[Trend Forecast.xls]

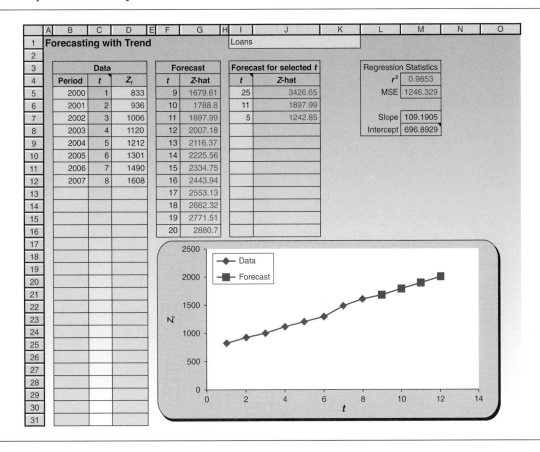

FIGURE 12–3   Fitting an Exponential Model to the Data of Example 12–1

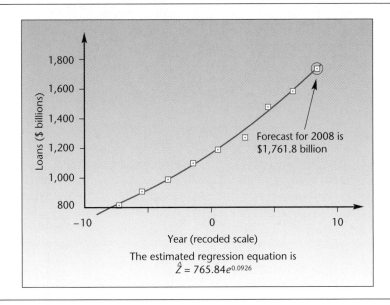

non-time-series contexts; therefore, your forecasts are of questionable accuracy. In the case of Example 12–1, we conclude that an exponential or quadratic fit is probably better than a straight line, but there is no way to objectively evaluate our forecast. The main advantage of trend analysis is that when the model is appropriate and the data exhibit a clear trend, we may carry out a simple analysis.

EXAMPLE 12–2   The following data are a price index for industrial metals for the years 1999 to 2007. A company that uses the metals in this index wants to construct a time series model to forecast future values of the index.

	A	B
1	**Time Series**	
2	**A Price Index**	
3		
4	Year	Price
5	1999	122.55
6	2000	140.64
7	2001	164.93
8	2002	167.24
9	2003	211.28
10	2004	242.17
11	2005	247.08
12	2006	277.72
13	2007	353.40

Solution   Figure 12–4 shows the results on the template. As seen in the template, the regression equation is $Z_t = 82.96 + 26.23t$. The forecast for $t = 10$, or year 2008, is 345.27.

FIGURE 12–4   Price Index Forecast
[Trend Forecast.xls]

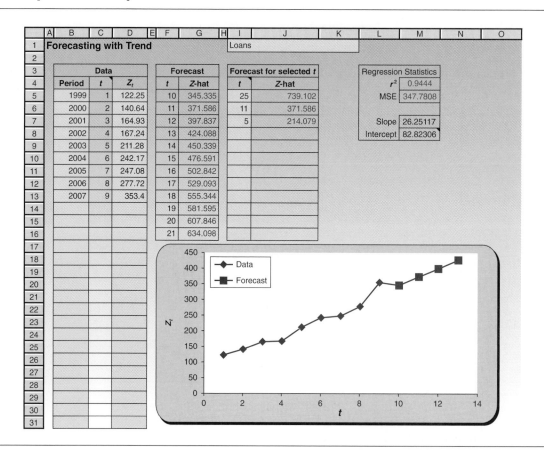

12–1. What are the advantages and disadvantages of trend analysis? When would you use this method of forecasting?

12–2. An article in *Real Estate Finance* displays the following data for Brazil's short-term interest rates (in percent).[1]

January	1996	43%
July	1996	31
January	1997	23
July	1997	20
January	1998	21
July	1998	25
January	1999	26
July	1999	25
January	2000	21
July	2000	17
January	2001	15
July	2001	15
January	2002	16
July	2002	17
January	2003	18
July	2003	22
January	2004	20
July	2004	16
January	2005	15
July	2005	17
January	2006	17
July	2006	15
January	2007	14

Develop a good forecasting model, and use it to forecast Brazil's short-term rate for July 2007.

12–3. The following data are a local newspaper's readership figures, in thousands:

Year:	1996	1997	1998	1999	2000	2001	2002	2003	2004	2005	2006	2007
Readers:	53	65	74	85	92	105	120	128	144	158	179	195

Do a trend regression on the data, and forecast the total number of readers for 2008 and for 2009.

12–4. The following data are the share of foreign shareholding as a percentage of total market capitalization in Korea for the past 12 years: 5, 10, 10, 12, 13, 14, 18, 21, 30, 37, 37, 40.[2] Develop a forecasting model for these data and forecast foreign share-holding percentage for Korea in the following year.

12–5. Would trend analysis, by itself, be a useful forecasting tool for monthly sales of swimming suits? Explain.

12–6. A firm's profits are known to vary with a business cycle of several years. Would trend analysis, by itself, be a good forecasting tool for the firm's profits? Why?

---

[1]Paulo Gomez and Gretchen Skedsvold, "Brazil: Trying to Realize Potential," *Real Estate Finance* 23, no. 5 (2007), pp. 8–20.

[2]Joshua Aizenman, Yeonho Lee, and Youngseop Rhee, "International Reserves Management and Capital Mobility in a Volatile World: Policy Considerations and a Case Study of Korea," *Journal of the Japanese and International Economies* 21, no. 1 (2007), pp. 1–15.

$\overset{V}{S}$

CHAPTER 20

12–3   Seasonality and Cyclical Behavior

Monthly time series observations very often display seasonal variation. The seasonal variation follows a complete cycle throughout a whole year, with the same general pattern repeating itself year after year. The obvious examples of such variation are sales of seasonal items, for example, suntan oil. We expect that sales of suntan oil will be very high during the summer months. We expect sales to taper off during the onset of fall and to decline drastically in winter—with another peak during the winter holiday season, when many people travel to sunny places on vacation—and then increase again as spring progresses into summer. The pattern repeats itself the following year.

Seasonal variation, which is very obvious in a case such as suntan oil, actually exists in many time series, even those that may not appear at first to have a seasonal characteristic. Electricity consumption, gasoline consumption, credit card spending, corporate profits, and sales of most discretionary items display distinct seasonal variation. Seasonality is not confined to monthly observations. Monthly time series observations display a 12-month period: a 1-year cycle. If our observations of a seasonal variable are quarterly, these observations will have a four-quarter period. Weekly observations of a seasonal time series will display a 52-week period. The term *seasonality*, or *seasonal variation*, frequently refers to a 12-month cycle.

In addition to a linear or curvilinear trend and seasonality, a time series may exhibit cyclical variation (where the period is not 1 year). In the context of business and economics, cyclical behavior is often referred to as the *business cycle*. The business cycle is marked by troughs and peaks of business activity in a cycle that lasts several years. The cycle is often of irregular, unpredictable pattern, and the period may be anything from 2 to 15 years and may change within the same time series. We repeat the distinction between the terms *seasonal variation* and *cyclical variation:*

> When a cyclical pattern in our data has a period of 1 year, we usually call the pattern **seasonal variation.** When a cyclical pattern has a period other than 1 year, we refer to it as **cyclical variation.**

We now give an example of a time series with a linear trend and with seasonal variation and no cyclical variation. Figure 12–5 shows sales data for suntan oil. Note

FIGURE 12–5   Monthly Sales of Suntan Oil

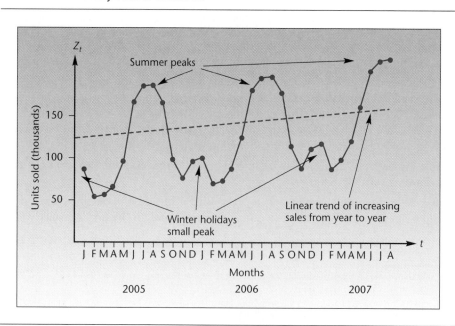

FIGURE 12–6 Annual Corporate Gross Earnings

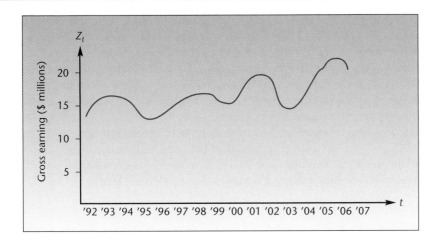

FIGURE 12–7 Monthly Total Numbers of Airline Passengers Traveling between Two Cities

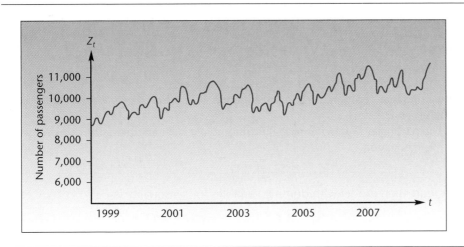

that the data display both a trend (increasing sales as one compares succeeding years) and a seasonal variation.

Figure 12–6 shows a time series of annual corporate gross earnings for a given company. Since the data are annual, there is no seasonal variation. As seen in the figure, the data exhibit both a trend and a cyclical pattern. The business cycle here has a period of approximately 4 years (the period does change during the time span under study). Figure 12–7 shows monthly total numbers of airline passengers traveling between two cities. See what components you can visually detect in the plot of the time series.

How do we incorporate seasonal behavior in a time series model? Several different approaches can be applied to the problem. Having studied regression analysis, and having used it (somewhat informally) in trend analysis, we now extend regression analysis to account for seasonal behavior. If you think about it for a while and recall the methods described in Chapter 11, you probably realize that one of the tools of multiple regression—the dummy variable—is applicable here. We can formulate a regression model for the trend, whether linear or curvilinear, and add 11 dummy variables to the model to account for seasonality if our data are monthly. (Why 11? Reread the appropriate section of Chapter 11 if you do not know.) If data are quarterly, we use three dummy variables to denote the particular quarter. You have probably spotted a limitation to this analysis, in addition to the fact that the assumptions of the regression model are not met in the context of time series. The new limitation is lack of parsimony. If you have 2 years' worth of monthly data and you use the dummy variable technique along with linear trend, then you have a regression analysis of 24 observations using a model with 12 variables. If, on the other hand, your data are quarterly and you have many years of data, then the problem of the proliferation of variables does not arise. Since the regression assumptions are not met anyway, we will not worry about this problem.

Using the dummy variable regression approach to seasonal time series assumes that the effect of the seasonal component of the series is additive. The seasonality is added to the trend and random error, as well as to the cycle (nonseasonal periodicity)—if one exists. We are thus assuming a model of the following form.

An additive model is

$$Z_t = T_t + S_t + C_t + I_t \tag{12–2}$$

where T is the trend component of the series, S is the seasonal component, C is the cyclical component, and I is the irregular component

---

(The irregular component is the error a_t; we use I_t because it is the usual notation in decomposition models.) Equation 12–2 states the philosophy inherent in the use of dummy variable regression to account for seasonality: The time series is viewed as comprising four components that are added to each other to give the observed values of the series.

The particular regression model, assuming our data are quarterly, is given by the following equation.

A regression model with dummy variables for seasonality is

$$Z_t = \beta_0 + \beta_1 t + \beta_2 Q_1 + \beta_3 Q_2 + \beta_4 Q_3 + a_t \tag{12–3}$$

where $Q_1 = 1$ if the observation is in the first quarter of the year and 0 otherwise; $Q_2 = 1$ if the observation is in the second quarter of the year and 0 otherwise; $Q_3 = 1$ if the observation is in the third quarter of the year and 0 otherwise; and all three Q_i are 0 if the observation is in the fourth quarter of the year.

Since the procedure is a straightforward application of the dummy variable regression technique of Chapter 11, we will not give an example.

A second way of modeling seasonality assumes a *multiplicative* model for the components of the time series. This is more commonly used than the additive model, equation 12–2, and is found to describe appropriately time series in a wide range of applications. The overall model is of the following form.

A multiplicative model is

$$Z_t = (T_t)(S_t)(C_t)(I_t) \tag{12–4}$$

Here the observed time series values are viewed as the *product* of the four components, when all exist. If there is no cyclicity, for example, then $C_t = 1$. When equation 12–4 is the assumed overall model for the time series, we deal with the seasonality by using a method called *ratio to moving average*. Once we account for the seasonality, we may also model the cyclical variation and the trend. We describe the procedure in the next section.

12–7. Explain the difference between the terms *seasonal variation* and *cyclical variation*.

12–8. What particular problem would you encounter in fitting a dummy variable regression to 70 weekly observations of a seasonal time series?

12–9. In your opinion, what could be the reasons why the seasonal component is not constant? Give examples where you believe the seasonality may change.

12–10. The following data are the monthly profit margins, in dollars per gallon, for an ethanol marketer from January 2005 through December 2006.[3]

0.5, 0.7, 0.8, 1.0, 1.0, 0.9, 1.1, 1.4, 1.5, 1.4, 0.7, 0.8, 0.8, 0.7, 1.1, 1.5, 1.7, 1.5, 1.6, 1.9, 2.1, 2.4, 2.6, 1.4

Construct a forecasting model for these data and forecast the profit margin for January 2007.

12–4 The Ratio-to-Moving-Average Method

A **moving average** of a time series is an average of a fixed number of observations (say, five observations) that moves as we progress down the series.[4]

A moving average based on five observations is demonstrated in Table 12–2. Figure 12–8 shows how the moving average in Table 12–2 is obtained and how this average *moves* as the series progresses. Note that the first moving average is obtained from the first five observations, so we must wait until $t = 5$ to produce the first moving average. Therefore, there are fewer observations in the moving-average series than there are in the original series, Z_t. A moving average smoothes the data of their variations. The original data of Table 12–2 along with the smoothed moving-average series are displayed in Figure 12–9.

The idea may have already occurred to you that if we have a seasonal time series and we compute a moving-average series for the data, then we will smooth out the seasonality. This is indeed the case. Assume a multiplicative time series model of the form given in equation 12–4:

$$Z = TSCI$$

TABLE 12–2 Demonstration of a Five-Observation Moving Average

Time t:	1	2	3	4	5	6	7	8	9	10	11	12	13	14
Series values, Z_t:	15	12	11	18	21	16	14	17	20	18	21	16	14	19
Corresponding series of five-observation moving average:			15.4	15.6	16	17.2	17.6	17	18	18.4	17.8	17.6		

---

[3]William K. Caesar, Jens Riese, and Thomas Seitz, "Betting on Biofuels," *McKinsey Quarterly,* no. 3 (2007), pp. 53–64.

[4]The term *moving average* has another meaning within the Box-Jenkins methodology (an advanced forecasting technique not discussed in this book).

FIGURE 12–8   Computing the Five-Observation Moving Averages for the Data in Table 12–2

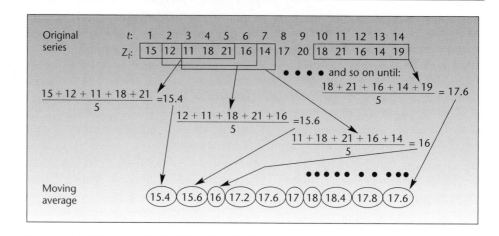

FIGURE 12–9   Original Series and Smoothed Moving-Average Series

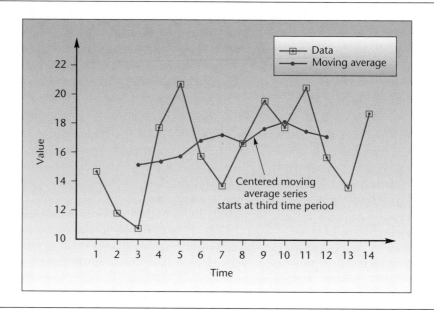

(here we drop the subscript t). If we smooth out the series by using a 12-month moving average when data are monthly, or four-quarter moving average when data are quarterly, then the resulting smoothed series will contain trend and cycle but not seasonality or the irregular component; the last two will have been smoothed out by the moving average. If we then divide each observation by the corresponding value of the moving-average (MA) series, we will have isolated the seasonal and irregular components. Notationally,

$$\frac{Z_t}{\text{MA}} = \frac{TSCI}{TC} = SI \qquad (12\text{–}5)$$

This is the **ratio to moving average.** If we average each seasonal value with all values of Z_t/MA for the same season (i.e., for quarterly data, we average all values corresponding to the first quarter, all values of the second quarter, and so on), then we cancel out *most* of the irregular component I_t and isolate the seasonal component of the series. Two more steps must be followed in the general procedure just described: (1) we compute the seasonal components as percentages by multiplying Z_t/MA by 100; and (2) we *center* the dates of the moving averages by averaging them. In the case of quarterly data, we average every two consecutive moving averages and center them midway between quarters. Centering is required because the number of terms in the moving average is even (4 quarters or 12 months).

Summary of the ratio-to-moving-average procedure for quarterly data (a similar procedure is carried out when data are monthly):

1. Compute a four-quarter moving-average series.
2. Center the moving averages by averaging every consecutive pair.
3. For each data point, divide the original series value by the corresponding moving average. Then multiply by 100.
4. For each quarter, average all data points corresponding to the quarter. The averaging can be done in one of several ways: find the simple average; find a modified average, which is the average after dropping the highest and lowest points; or find the median. Once we average the ratio-to-moving-average figures for each quarter, we will have four *quarterly indexes*. Finally, we adjust the indexes so that their mean will be 100. This is done by multiplying each by 400 and dividing by their sum.

We demonstrate the procedure with Example 12–3.

EXAMPLE 12–3

The distribution manager of Northern Natural Gas Company needs to analyze the time series of quarterly sales of natural gas in a Midwestern region served by the company. Quarterly data for 2004 through 2007 are given in Table 12–3. The table also shows the four-quarter moving averages, the centered moving averages, and the ratio to moving average (multiplied by 100 to give percentages). Figure 12–10 shows both the original series and the centered four-quarter moving-average series. Note how the seasonal variation is smoothed out.

Solution

The ratio-to-moving-average column in Table 12–3 gives us the contribution of the seasonal component and the irregular component within the multiplicative model,

TABLE 12–3   Data and Four-Quarter Moving Averages for Example 12–3

Quarter		Sales (billions Btu)	Four-Quarter Moving Average	Centered Moving Average	Ratio to Moving Average (%)
2004	W	170			
	Sp	148		(141/151.125)100	
	Su	141	152.25	151.125	93.3
	F	150	150	148.625	100.9
2005	W	161	147.25	146.125	110.2
	Sp	137	145	146	93.8
	Su	132	147	146.5	90.1
	F	158	146	147	107.5
2006	W	157	148	147.5	106.4
	Sp	145	147	144	100.7
	Su	128	141	141.375	90.5
	F	134	141.75	141	95.0
2007	W	160	140.25	140.5	113.9
	Sp	139	140.75	142	97.9
	Su	130	143.25	(139/142)100	
	F	144			

FIGURE 12–10   Northern Natural Gas Sales: Original Series and Moving Average

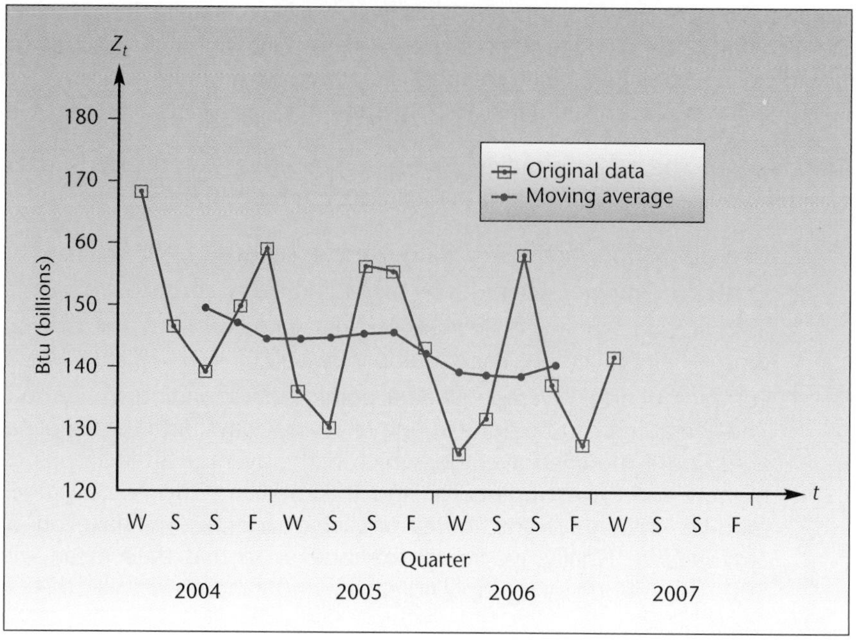

as seen from equation 12–5. We now come to step 4 of the procedure—averaging each seasonal term so as to average out the irregular effects and isolate the purely seasonal component as much as possible. We will use the simple average in obtaining the four seasonal indexes. This is done in Table 12–4, with the ratio-to-moving-average figures from Table 12–3.

Due to rounding, the indexes do not add to exactly 400, but their sum is very close to 400. The seasonal indexes quantify the seasonal effects in the time series of natural gas sales. We will see shortly how these indexes and other quantities are used in forecasting future values of the time series.

The ratio-to-moving-average procedure, which gives us the seasonal indexes, may also be used for **deseasonalizing** the data. Deseasonalizing a time series is a procedure that is often used to display the general movement of a series without regard to the seasonal effects. Many government economic statistics are reported in the form of deseasonalized time series. To deseasonalize the data, we divide every data point by its appropriate seasonal index. If we assume a multiplicative time series

TABLE 12–4   Obtaining the Seasonal Indexes for Example 12–3

	Quarter			
	Winter	Spring	Summer	Fall
2004			93.3	100.9
2005	110.2	93.8	90.1	107.5
2006	106.4	100.7	90.5	95.0
2007	113.9	97.9		
Sum	330.5	292.4	273.9	303.4
Average	110.17	97.47	91.3	101.13
Sum of averages = 400.07				
Seasonal index = (Average)(400)/(400.07):				
	110.15	97.45	91.28	101.11

TABLE 12–5 Deseasonalizing the Series for Example 12–3

Quarter		Sales Z (billions Btu)	Seasonal Indexes S	Deseasonalized Series (Z/S)(100)
2004	Winter	170	110.15	154.33
	Spring	148	97.45	151.87
	Summer	141	91.28	154.47
	Fall	150	101.11	148.35
2005	Winter	161	110.15	146.16
	Spring	137	97.45	140.58
	Summer	132	91.28	144.61
	Fall	158	101.11	156.27
2006	Winter	157	110.15	142.53
	Spring	145	97.45	148.79
	Summer	128	91.28	140.23
	Fall	134	101.11	132.53
2007	Winter	160	110.15	145.26
	Spring	139	97.45	142.64
	Summer	130	91.28	142.42
	Fall	144	101.11	142.42

model (equation 12–4), then dividing by the seasonal index gives us a series containing the other components only:

$$\frac{Z}{S} = \frac{TSCI}{S} = CTI \tag{12-6}$$

Table 12–5 shows how the series of Example 12–3 is deseasonalized. The deseasonalized natural gas time series, along with the original time series, is shown in Figure 12–11. Note that we have to multiply our results Z/S by 100 to cancel out the fact that our seasonal indexes were originally multiplied by 100 by convention.

FIGURE 12–11 Original and Deseasonalized Series for the Northern Natural Gas Example

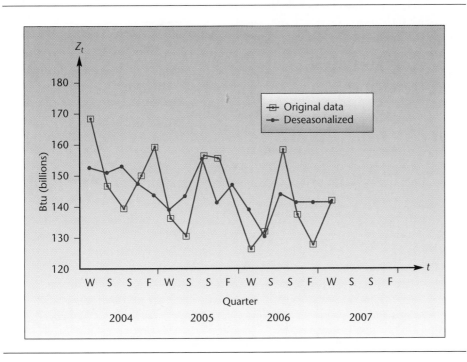

The deseasonalized series in Figure 12–11 does have some variation in it. Comparing this series with the moving-average series in Figure 12–10, containing only the trend and cyclical components *TC*, we conclude that the relatively high residual variation in the deseasonalized series is due to the irregular component *I* (because the deseasonalized series is *TCI* and the moving-average series is *TC*). The large irregular component is likely due to variation in the weather throughout the period under study.

The Template

The template that can be used for Trend + Season Forecasting using the ratio-to-moving-average method is shown in Figure 12–12. In this figure, the sheet meant for quarterly data is shown. The same workbook, Trend+Season Forecasting.xls, includes a sheet meant for monthly data, which is shown in Figure 12–13.

The Cyclical Component of the Series

Since the moving-average series is *TC*, we could isolate the cyclical component of the series by dividing the moving-average series by the trend *T*. We must, therefore, first estimate the trend. By visually inspecting the moving-average series in Figure 12–10, we notice a slightly decreasing linear trend and what looks like two cycles. We should therefore try to fit a straight line to the data. The line, fit by simple linear regression of centered moving average against *t*, is shown in Figure 12–14. The estimated trend line is

$$\hat{Z} = 152.26 - 0.837t \tag{12-7}$$

FIGURE 12–12 The Template for the Ratio-to-Moving-Average Method of Trend+Season Forecasting [Trend+Season Forecast.xls; Sheet: Quarterly]

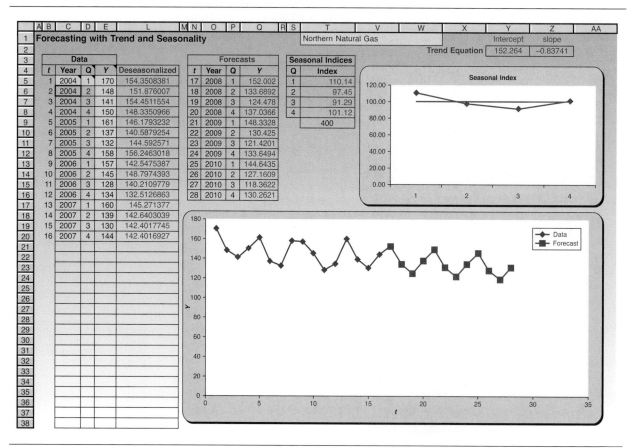

FIGURE 12–13   The Template for Trend+Season Forecasting with Monthly Data
[Trend+Season Forecast.xls; Sheet: Monthly]

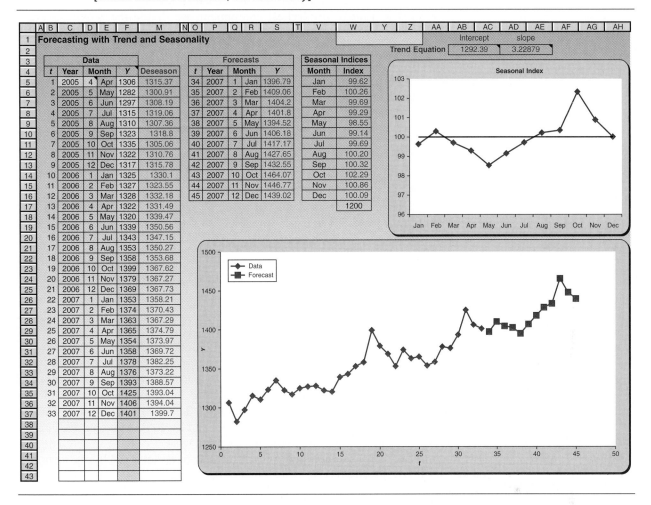

FIGURE 12–14   Trend Line and Moving Average for the Northern Natural Gas Example

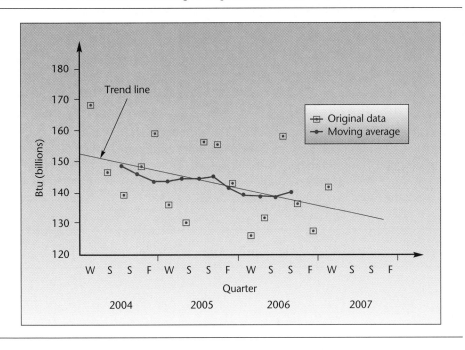

From Figure 12–14, it seems that the cyclical component is relatively small in comparison with the other components of this particular series.

If we want to isolate the cyclical component, we divide the moving-average series (the product TC) by the corresponding trend value for the period. Multiplying the answer by 100 gives us a kind of cyclical index for each data point. There are problems, however, in dealing with the cycle. Unlike the seasonal component, which is fairly regular (with a 1-year cycle), the cyclical component of the time series may not have a dependable cycle at all. Both the amplitude and the cycle (peak-to-peak distance) of the cyclical component may be erratic, and it may be very difficult, if not impossible, to predict. Thus forecasting future series observations is difficult.

Forecasting a Multiplicative Series

Forecasting a series of the form $Z = TSCI$ entails trying to forecast the three "regular" components C, T, and S. We try to forecast each component separately and then multiply them to get a series forecast:

> The forecast of a multiplicative series is
> $$\hat{Z} = TSC \qquad\qquad (12\text{–}8)$$

As we noted, obtaining reliable forecasts of the cyclical component is very difficult. The trend is forecast simply by substituting the appropriate value of t in the least-squares line, as was done in Section 12–2. Then we multiply the value by the seasonal index (expressed as a decimal—divided by 100) to give us TS. Finally, we follow the cyclical component and try to guess what it may be at the point we need to forecast; then we multiply by this component to get TSC. In our example, since the cyclical component seems small, we may avoid the nebulous task of guessing the future value of the cyclical component. We will therefore forecast using only S and T.

Let us forecast natural gas sales for winter 2008. Equation 12–7 for the trend was estimated with each quarter sequentially numbered from 1 to 16. Winter 2008 is $t = 17$. Substituting this value into equation 12–7, we get

$$\hat{z} = 152.26 - 0.837(17) = 138.03 \text{ (billion Btu)}$$

The next stage is to multiply this result by the seasonal index (divided by 100). Since the point is a winter quarter, we use the winter index. From the bottom of Table 12–4 (or the second column of Table 12–5), we get the seasonal index for winter: 110.15. Ignoring the (virtually unforecastable) cyclical component by letting it equal 1, we find, using the forecast equation, equation 12–8:

$$\hat{z} = TSC = (1)(138.03)(1.1015) = 152.02 \text{ (billion Btu)}$$

This is our forecast of sales for winter 2008. See Figure 12–12 for further forecasts.

12–11. The following data, from the U.S. Department of the Treasury's *Treasury Bulletin,* are monthly total federal debt, in millions of dollars, for December 2005 through December 2006.[5]

Dec 2005	Jan 2006	Feb 2006	Mar 2006	Apr 2006	May 2006	Jun 2006
8,194,251	8,219,745	8,293,333	8,394,740	8,379,083	8,380,354	8,443,683

Jul 2006	Aug 2006	Sep 2006	Oct 2006	Nov 2006	Dec 2006
8,467,856	8,538,350	8,530,366	8,607,540	8,656,590	8,703,738

Forecast total federal debt for January 2007. How confident are you in your forecast?

12–12. The following data are monthly figures of factory production, in millions of units, from July 2004 through April 2007:

7.4, 6.8, 6.4, 6.6, 6.5, 6.0, 7.0, 6.7, 8.2, 7.8, 7.7, 7.3, 7.0, 7.1, 6.9, 7.3, 7.0, 6.7, 7.6, 7.2, 7.9, 7.7, 7.6, 6.7, 6.3, 5.7, 5.6, 6.1, 5.8, 5.9, 6.2, 6.0, 7.3, 7.4

Decompose the series into its components, using the methods of this section, and forecast steel production for May 2007.

12–13. The following data are monthly price discovery contributions for gold prices from the COMEX open outcry contract for November 2004 through August 2006.[6]

0.38, 0.38, 0.44, 0.42, 0.44, 0.46, 0.48, 0.49, 0.51, 0.52, 0.45, 0.40, 0.39, 0.37, 0.38, 0.37, 0.33, 0.33, 0.32, 0.32, 0.32, 0.31

Construct a forecasting model and forecast the next period's value.

12–14. An article in *Harvard Business Review* looked at the percentage of negative media stories about British Petroleum (BP) in 2005 and 2006. The monthly data, in percent, from January 2005 through September 2006, are as follows.[7]

14, 10, 50, 24, 16, 15, 20, 42, 18, 26, 21, 20, 18, 10, 22, 24, 26, 24, 18, 58, 40

Can you predict the percentage of negative media stories about BP for October 2006? Comment on the value of such an analysis.

12–15. The following are quarterly data, in millions of dollars, of corporate revenues for a firm in the apparel industry from first quarter 2005 through first quarter 2007:

3.4, 4.5, 4.0, 5.0, 4.2, 5.4, 4.9, 5.7, 4.6

Predict corporate revenue for the second quarter of 2004.

12–5 Exponential Smoothing Methods

One method that is often useful in forecasting time series is *exponential smoothing*. There are exponential smoothing methods of varying complexity, but we will discuss only the simplest model, called *simple exponential smoothing*. Simple exponential smoothing is a useful method for forecasting time series that have no pronounced trend or seasonality. The concept is an extension of the idea of a moving average, introduced in the last section. Look at Figures 12–9 and 12–10, and notice how the moving average *smoothes* the original series of its sharp variations. The idea of exponential smoothing is to smooth

---

[5]Summary of Federal Debt, *Treasury Bulletin,* March 2007, p. 24.

[6]Valeria Martinez and Yiuman Tse, "Multi-Market Trading of Gold Futures," *Review of Futures Markets* 15, no. 3 (2006/2007), pp. 239–263.

[7]Robert G. Eccles, Scott C. Newquist, and Ronald Schatz, "Reputation and Its Risks," *Harvard Business Review,* February 2007, pp. 104–114.

the original series the way the moving average does and to use the smoothed series in forecasting future values of the variable of interest. In exponential smoothing, however, we want to allow the more recent values of the series to have greater influence on the forecasts of future values than the more distant observations.

> **Exponential smoothing** is a forecasting method in which the forecast is based on a *weighted average* of current and past series values. The largest weight is given to the present observation, less weight to the immediately preceding observation, even less weight to the observation before that, and so on. *The weights decline geometrically as we go back in time.*

We define a **weighting factor *w*** as a selected number between 0 and 1

$$0 < w < 1 \qquad\qquad (12\text{--}9)$$

Once we select *w*—for example, $w = 0.4$—we define the forecast equation. The forecast equation is

$$\hat{Z}_{t+1} = w(Z_t) + w(1 - w)(Z_{t-1}) + w(1 - w)^2(Z_{t-2})$$
$$+\ w(1 - w)^3(Z_{t-3}) + \cdots \qquad\qquad (12\text{--}10)$$

where $\hat{Z}_{t+1}$ is the *forecast* value of the variable Z at time $t + 1$ from knowledge of the *actual* series values Z_t, Z_{t-1}, Z_{t-2}, and so on back in time to the first known value of the time series Z_1.

The series of weights used in producing the forecast $\hat{Z}_{t+1}$ is w, $w(1 - w)$, $w(1 - w)^2$, ... These weights decline toward 0 in an *exponential* fashion; thus, as we go back in the series, each value has a smaller weight in terms of its effect on the forecast. If $w = 0.4$, then the rest of the weights are $w(1 - w) = 0.24$, $w(1 - w)^2 = 0.144$, $w(1 - w)^3 = 0.0864$, $w(1 - w)^4 = 0.0518$, $w(1 - w)^5 = 0.0311$, $w(1 - w)^6 = 0.0187$, and so on. The exponential decline of the weights toward 0 is evident. This is shown in Figure 12–15.

FIGURE 12–15   Exponentially Declining Weights

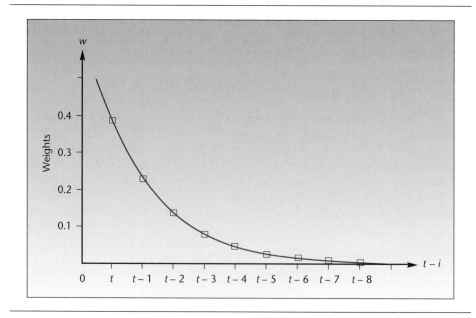

Before we show how the exponential smoothing model is used, we will rewrite the model in a recursive form that uses both previous observations and previous forecasts. Let us look at the forecast of the series value at time $t + 1$, denoted $\hat{Z}_{t+1}$. The exponential smoothing model of equation 12–10 can be shown to be equivalent to the following model.

The exponential smoothing model is

$$\hat{Z}_{t+1} = w(Z_t) + (1 - w)(\hat{Z}_t) \qquad (12\text{–}11)$$

where Z_t is the actual, known series value at time t and $\hat{Z}_t$ is the forecast value for time t.

The recursive equation, equation 12–11, can be restated in words as

---

Next forecast $= w$(Present actual value) $+ (1 - w)$(Present forecast)

The forecast value for time period $t + 1$ is thus seen as a weighted average of the actual value of the series at time t and the forecast value of the series at time t (the forecast having been made at time $t - 1$). Yet a third way of writing the formula for the simple exponential smoothing model follows.

An equivalent form of the exponential smoothing model is

$$\hat{Z}_{t+1} = Z_t + (1 - w)(\hat{Z}_t - Z_t) \qquad (12\text{–}12)$$

The proofs of the equivalence of equations 12–10, 12–11, and 12–12 are left as exercises at the end of this section. The importance of equation 12–12 is that it describes the forecast of the value of the variable at time $t + 1$ as the actual value of the variable at the previous time period t plus a fraction of the previous *forecast error*. The forecast error is the difference between the forecast $\hat{Z}_t$ and the actual series value Z_t. We will formally define the forecast error soon.

The recursive equation (equation 12–11) allows us to compute the forecast value of the series for each time period in a sequential manner. This is done by substituting values for t ($t = 1, 2, 3, 4, \ldots$) and using equation 12–11 for each t to produce the forecast at the next period $t + 1$. Then the forecast and actual values at the last known time period, $\hat{Z}_t$ and Z_t, are used in producing a forecast of the series into the future. The recursive computation is done by applying equation 12–11 as follows:

$$\hat{Z}_2 = w(Z_1) + (1 - w)(\hat{Z}_1)$$
$$\hat{Z}_3 = w(Z_2) + (1 - w)(\hat{Z}_2)$$
$$\hat{Z}_4 = w(Z_3) + (1 - w)(\hat{Z}_3)$$
$$\hat{Z}_5 = w(Z_4) + (1 - w)(\hat{Z}_4)$$
$$\cdot$$
$$\cdot$$
$$\cdot \qquad\qquad\qquad\qquad\qquad (12\text{–}13)$$

The problem is how to determine the first forecast $\hat{Z}_1$. Customarily, we use $\hat{Z}_1 = Z_1$. Since the effect of the first forecast in a series of values diminishes as the series progresses toward the future, the choice of the first forecast is of little importance (it is an *initial value* of the series of forecasts, and its influence diminishes exponentially).

The choice of w, which is up to the person carrying out the analysis, is very important, however. *The larger the value of w, the faster the forecast series responds to change in the original series.* Conversely, the smaller the value of w, the less sensitive is the forecast to changes in the variable Z_t. If we want our forecasts not to respond quickly to changes in the variable, we set w to be a relatively small number. Conversely, if we want the forecast to quickly follow abrupt changes in variable Z_t, we set w to be relatively large (closer to 1.00 than to 0). We demonstrate this, as well as the computation of the exponentially smoothed series and the forecasts, in Example 12–4.

EXAMPLE 12–4   A sales analyst is interested in forecasting weekly firm sales in thousands of units. The analyst collects 15 weekly observations in 2007 and recursively computes the exponentially smoothed series of forecasts, using $w = 0.4$ and the exponentially smoothed forecast series for $w = 0.8$. The original data and both exponentially smoothed series are given in Table 12–6.

Solution   The original series and the two exponentially smoothed forecast series, corresponding to $w = 0.4$ and $w = 0.8$, are shown in Figure 12–16. The figure also shows the forecasts of the unknown value of the series at the 16th week produced by the two exponential smoothing procedures ($w = 0.4$ and $w = 0.8$). As was noted earlier, the smoothing coefficient w is set at the discretion of the person carrying out the analysis. Since w has a strong effect on the magnitude of the forecast values, the forecast accuracy depends on guessing a "correct" value for the smoothing coefficient. We have presented a simple exponential smoothing method. When the data exhibit a trend or a seasonal variation, or both, more complicated exponential smoothing methods apply.

TABLE 12–6   Exponential Smoothing Sales Forecasts Using $w = 0.4$ and $w = 0.8$

Day	Z_t Original Series	$\hat{Z}_t$ Forecast Using $w = 0.4$	$\hat{Z}_t$ Forecast Using $w = 0.8$
1	925	925	925
2	940	$0.4(925) + 0.6(925) = 925$	925
3	924	$0.4(940) + 0.6(925) = 931$	937
4	925	928.2	926.6
5	912	926.9	925.3
6	908	920.9	914.7
7	910	915.7	909.3
8	912	913.4	909.9
9	915	912.8	911.6
10	924	913.7	914.3
11	943	917.8	922.1
12	962	927.9	938.8
13	960	941.5	957.4
14	958	948.9	959.5
15	955	952.5	958.3
16 (Forecasts)		953.5	955.7

FIGURE 12–16   The Sales Data: Original Series and Two Exponentially Smoothed Series

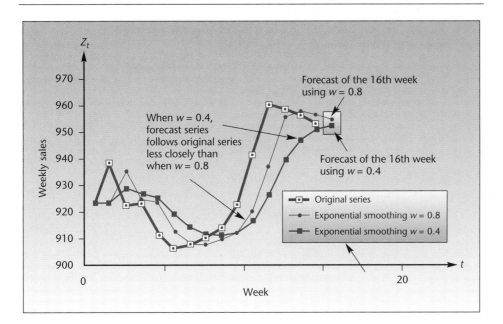

The Template

The template that can be used for exponential smoothing is shown in Figure 12–17. An additional feature available on the template is the use of the Solver to find the optimal w. We saw the results of using $w = 0.4$ and $w = 0.8$ in Example 12–4. Suppose we want to find the optimal w that minimizes MSE. To do this, unprotect the sheet and invoke the Solver. Click the Solve button, and when the Solver is done, choose Keep Solver Solution. The value of w found in the template is the optimal w that minimizes MSE. These instructions are also available in the comment at cell C4.

**FIGURE 12–17   The Template for Exponential Smoothing
[Exponential Smoothing.xls]**

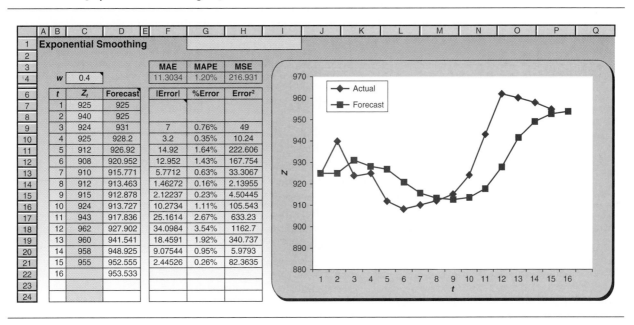

The Solver works better with MSE than MAPE (mean absolute percent error), because MSE is a "smooth" function of w whereas MAPE is not. With MAPE, the Solver may be stuck at a local minimum and miss the global minimum.

PROBLEMS

12–16. The following data are Vodafone's quarterly market share of revenue (in percent) for 1992 through 2003 in Portugal.[8]

28, 39, 41, 43, 46, 48, 53, 55, 59, 60, 61, 60, 58, 59, 60, 60, 57, 55, 56, 52, 49, 52, 52, 53, 46, 45, 42, 40, 39, 40, 39, 38, 35, 37, 36, 33, 30, 32, 33, 32, 27, 28, 28, 26, 27, 26, 27, 28

Forecast Vodafone's revenue market share in Portugal for the following quarter, using an exponential smoothing model.

12–17. The following are weekly sales data, in thousands of units, for microcomputer disks:

57, 58, 60, 54, 56, 53, 55, 59, 62, 57, 50, 48, 52, 55, 58, 61

Use $w = 0.3$ and $w = 0.8$ to produce an exponential smoothing model for these data. Which value of w produces better forecasts? Explain.

12–18. Construct an exponential smoothing forecasting model, using $w = 0.7$, for new orders reported by a manufacturer. Monthly data (in thousands of dollars) to April 2007 are

195, 193, 190, 185, 180, 190, 185, 186, 184, 185, 198, 199, 200, 201, 199, 187, 186, 191, 195, 200, 200, 190, 186, 196, 198, 200, 200

12–19. The following data are from the *Treasury Bulletin,* published by the U.S. Department of the Treasury. They represent total U.S. liabilities to foreigners for the years 2000 to 2006 in millions of dollars[9]:

2000	2001	2002	2003	2004	2005	2006
2,565,942	2,724,292	3,235,231	3,863,508	4,819,747	5,371,689	6,119,114

Can you forecast total U.S. liabilities to foreigners for 2007?

12–20. Use the *Wall Street Journal* or another source to gather information on the daily price of gold. Collect a series of prices, and construct an exponential smoothing model. Choose the weighting factor w that seems to fit the data best. Forecast the next day's price of gold, and compare the forecast with the actual price once it is known.

12–21. Prove that equation 12–10 is equivalent to equation 12–11.

12–22. Prove the equivalence of equations 12–11 and 12–12.

12–6 Index Numbers

It was dubbed the "Crash of '87." Measured as a percentage, the decline was worse than the one that occurred during the same month in 1929 and ushered in the Great Depression. Within a few hours on Monday, October 19, 1987, the Dow Jones Industrial Average plunged 508.32 points, a drop of 22.6%—the greatest percentage drop ever recorded in one day.

What is the Dow Jones Industrial Average, and why is it useful? The Dow Jones average is an example of an **index.** It is one of several quantitative measures of price movements of stocks through time. Another commonly used index is the New York

---

[8]Philippe Gagnepain and Pedro Pereira, "Entry, Costs Reduction, and Competition in the Portuguese Mobile Telephony Industry," *International Journal of Industrial Organization* 25, no. 3 (2007), pp. 461–481.

[9]Selected U.S. Liability to Foreigners, *Treasury Bulletin,* March 2007, p. 56.

Stock Exchange (NYSE) Index, and there are others. The Dow Jones captures in one number (e.g., the 508.32 points just mentioned) the movements of 30 industrial stocks considered by some to be representative of the entire market. Other indexes are based on a wider proportion of the market than just 30 big firms.

Indexes are useful in many other areas of business and economics. Another commonly quoted index is the **consumer price index (CPI),** which measures price fluctuations. The CPI is a single number representing the general level of prices that affect consumers.

> An **index number** is a number that measures the relative change in a set of measurements over time.

When the measurements are of a *single variable,* for example, the price of a certain commodity, the index is called a *simple index number.* A simple index number is the ratio of two values of a variable, expressed as a percentage. First, a *base period* is chosen. The value of the index at any time period is equal to the ratio of the current value of the variable divided by the base-period value, times 100.

EXAMPLE 12–5

The following data are annual cost figures for residential natural gas for the years 1984 to 1997 (in dollars per thousand cubic feet):

121, 121, 133, 146, 162, 164, 172, 187, 197, 224, 255, 247, 238, 222

Solution

If we want to describe the relative change in price of residential natural gas, we construct a simple index of these prices. Suppose that we are interested in comparing prices of residential natural gas of any time period to the price in 1984 (the first year in our series). In this case, 1984 is our base year, and the index for that year is defined as 100. The index for any year is defined by equation 12–14.

$$\text{Index number for period } i = 100\left(\frac{\text{Value in period } i}{\text{Value in base period}}\right) \qquad (12\text{–}14)$$

Thus, the index number for 1986 (using the third data point in the series) is computed as

$$\text{Index number for 1986} = 100\left(\frac{\text{Price in 1986}}{\text{Price in 1984}}\right)$$
$$= 100\left(\frac{133}{121}\right) = 109.9$$

This means that the price of residential natural gas increased by 9.9% from 1984 to 1986. Incidentally, the index for 1985 is also 100 since the price did not change from 1984 to 1985. Let us now compute the index for 1987:

$$\text{Index number for 1987} = 100\left(\frac{146}{121}\right) = 120.66$$

Thus, compared with the price in 1984, the price in 1987 was 20.66% higher. It is very important to understand that changes in the index from year to year *may not be interpreted as percentages* except when one of the two years is the base year. The fact that the index for 1987 is 120.66 and for 1986 is 109.9 does not imply that the price in 1987 was $20.66 - 9.9 = 10.76\%$ higher than in 1986. Comparisons in terms of

FIGURE 12–18   Price and Index (Base Year 1984) of Residential Natural Gas

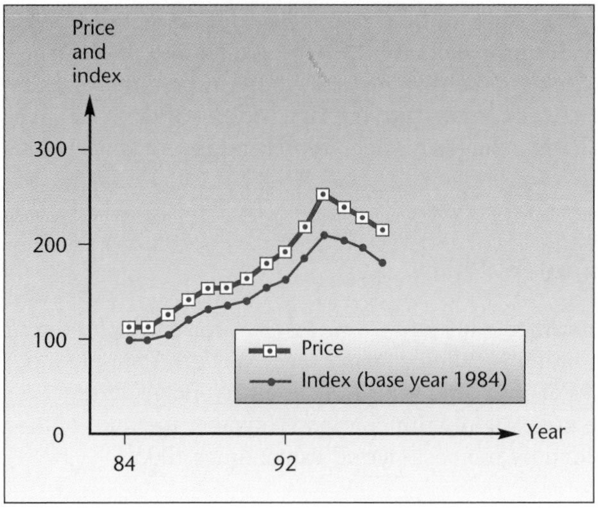

TABLE 12–7
Price Index for Residential Natural Gas, Base Year 1984

Year	Price	Index
1984	121	100
1985	121	100
1986	133	109.9
1987	146	120.7
1988	162	133.9
1989	164	135.5
1990	172	142.1
1991	187	154.5
1992	197	162.8
1993	224	185.1
1994	255	210.7
1995	247	204.1
1996	238	196.7
1997	222	183.5

percentages may be made only with the base year. We can only say that the price in 1986 was 9.9% higher than 1984, and the price in 1987 was 20.66% higher than in 1984. Table 12–7 shows the year, the price, and the price index for residential natural gas from 1984 to 1997, inclusive.

From the table, we see, for example, that the price in 1994 was more than 210% of what it was in 1984 and that by 1997 the price declined to only 183.5% of what it was in 1984. Figure 12–18 shows both the raw price and the index with base year 1984. (The units of the two plots are different, and no comparison between them is suggested.)

As time goes on, the relevance of any base period in the past decreases in terms of comparison with values in the present. Therefore, changing the base period and moving it closer to the present is sometimes useful. Many indexed economic variables, for example, use the base year 1967. As we move into more recent years, the base year for these variables is changed to 1980 or later. To easily change the base period of an index, all we need to do is to change the index number of the new base period so that it will equal 100 and to change all other numbers using the *same operation*. Thus, we divide all numbers in the index by the index value of the proposed new base period and multiply them by 100. This is shown in equation 12–15.

Changing the base period of an index:

$$\text{New index value} = \frac{\text{Old index value}}{\text{Index value of new base}} \times 100 \qquad (12\text{–}15)$$

Suppose that we want to change the base period of the residential natural gas index (Table 12–7) from 1984 to 1991. We want the index for 1991 to equal 100, so we divide all index values in the table by the current value for 1991, which is 154.5, and we multiply these values by 100. For 1992, the new index value is $(162.8/154.5)100 = 105.4$. The new index, using 1991 as base, is shown in Table 12–8.

Figure 12–19 shows the two indexes of the price of residential natural gas using the two different base years. Note that the changes in the index numbers that use 1984 as the base year are more pronounced. This is so because 1991, when used as the base year, is close to the middle of the series, and percentage changes with respect to that year are smaller.

TABLE 12–8   Residential Natural Gas Price Index

Year	Index Using 1984 Base	Index Using 1991 Base
1984	100	64.7
1985	100	64.7
1986	109.9	71.1
1987	120.7	78.1
1988	133.9	86.7
1989	135.5	87.7
1990	142.1	92.0
1991	154.5	100
1992	162.8	105.4
1993	185.1	119.8
1994	210.7	136.4
1995	204.1	132.1
1996	196.7	127.3
1997	183.5	118.7

Note: All entries in the rightmost column are obtained from the entries in the middle column by multiplication by 100/154.5.

FIGURE 12–19   Comparison of the Two Price Indexes for Residential Natural Gas

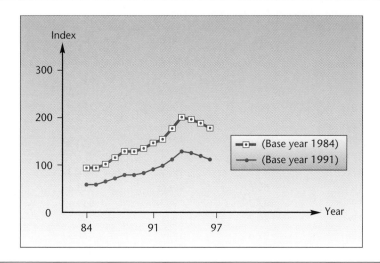

An important use of index numbers is as *deflators*. This allows us to compare prices or quantities through time in a meaningful way. Using information on the relative price of natural gas at different years, as measured by the price index for this commodity, we can better assess the effect of changes in consumption by consumers. The most important use of index numbers as deflators, however, is in the case of *composite index numbers*. In particular, the consumer price index is an overall measure of relative changes in prices of many goods and thus reflects changes in the value of the dollar. We all know that a dollar today is not worth the same as a dollar 20 years ago. Using the consumer price index, or another composite index, allows us to compare prices through time in "constant" dollars.

The Consumer Price Index

The CPI is probably the best-known price index. It is published by the U.S. Bureau of Labor Statistics and is based on the prices of several hundred items. The base year is 1967. For obtaining the base-year quantities used as weights, the Bureau of Labor

Statistics interviewed thousands of families to determine their consumption patterns. Since the CPI reflects the general price level in the country, it is used, among other purposes, in converting nominal amounts of money to what are called *real* amounts of money: amounts that can be compared through time without requiring us to consider changes in the value of money due to inflation. This use of the CPI is what we referred to earlier as using an index as a *deflator*. By simply dividing *X* dollars in year *i* by the CPI value for year *i* and multiplying by 100, we convert our *X nominal* (year *i*) dollars to *constant* (base-year) dollars. This allows us to compare amounts of money across time periods. Let us look at an example.

EXAMPLE 12–6   Table 12–9 gives the CPI values for the years 1950 to 2007. The base year is 1967. This is commonly denoted by [1967 = 100]. The data in Table 12–9 are from the U.S. Bureau of Labor Statistics Web site, http://data.bls.gov.

We see, for example, that the general level of prices in the United States in 1994 was almost 4½ times what it was in 1967 (the base year). Thus, a dollar in 1994 could buy, on average, only what $1/4.44 = \$0.225$, or 22.5 cents, could buy in 1967. By dividing any amount of money in a given year by the CPI value for that year and multiplying by 100, we convert the amount to constant (1967) dollars. The term *constant* means dollars of a constant point in time—the base year.

TABLE 12–9   The Consumer Price Index [1967 = 100]

Year	CPI	Year	CPI
1950	72.1	1978	195.4
1951	77.8	1979	217.4
1952	79.5	1980	246.8
1953	80.1	1981	272.4
1954	80.5	1982	289.1
1955	80.2	1983	298.4
1956	81.4	1984	311.1
1957	84.3	1985	322.2
1958	86.6	1986	328.4
1959	87.3	1987	340.4
1960	88.7	1988	354.3
1961	89.6	1989	371.3
1962	90.6	1990	391.4
1963	91.7	1991	408.0
1964	92.9	1992	420.3
1965	94.5	1993	432.7
1966	97.2	1994	444.0
1967	100.0	1995	456.0
1968	104.2	1996	469.9
1969	109.8	1997	480.8
1970	116.3	1998	488.3
1971	121.3	1999	499.0
1972	125.3	2000	515.8
1973	133.1	2001	530.4
1974	147.7	2002	538.8
1975	161.2	2003	551.1
1976	170.5	2004	565.8
1977	181.5	2005	585.0
		2006	603.9
		2007	619.1 (estimate)

Let us illustrate the use of the CPI as a price deflator. Suppose that during the years 1980 to 1985, an analyst was making the following annual salaries:

1980	$29,500	1983	$35,000
1981	31,000	1984	36,700
1982	33,600	1985	38,000

Looking at the raw numbers, we may get the impression that this analyst has done rather well. His or her salary has increased from $29,500 to $38,000 in just 5 years. Actually the analyst's salary has not even kept up with inflation! That is, in *real* terms of *actual buying power,* this analyst's 1985 salary is smaller than what it was in 1980. To see why this is true, we use the CPI.

Solution

If we divide the 1980 salary of $29,500 by the CPI value for that year and multiply by 100, we will get the equivalent salary in 1967 dollars: $(29,500/246.8)(100) = \$11,953$. We now take the 1985 salary of $38,000 and divide it by the CPI value for 1985 and multiply by 100. This gives us $(38,000/322.2)(100) = \$11,794$—a *decrease* of $159 (1967)!

If you perform a similar calculation for the salaries of all other years, you will find that none of them have kept up with inflation. If we transform all salaries to 1967 dollars (or for that matter, to dollars of any single year), the figures can be compared with one another. Often, time series data such as these are converted to constant dollars of a single time period and then are analyzed by using methods of time series analysis such as the ones presented earlier in this chapter. To convert to dollars of another year (not the base year), you need to divide the salary by the CPI for the current year and multiply by the CPI value for the constant year in which you are interested. For example, let us convert the 1985 salary to 1980 (rather than 1967) dollars. We do this as follows: $(38,000/322.2)(246.8) = \$29,107$. Thus, in terms of 1980 dollars, the analyst was making only $29,107 in 1985, whereas in 1980 he or she was making $29,500 (1980)!

The Template

The template that can be used for index calculations is shown in Figure 12–20. The data entered in the template are from Table 12–7.

**FIGURE 12–20 The Template for Index Calculations
[Index.xls]**

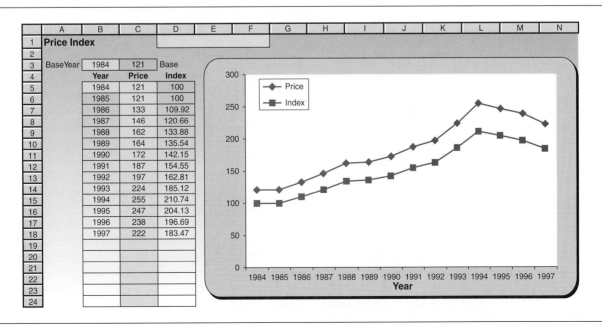

PROBLEMS

12–23. In 1987, the base year was changed to [1982 = 100]. Change the base for all the figures in Table 12–9.

12–24. The percentage change in the price index of food and beverages in the United States from July 2000 to July 2001 was +3.1%. The change in the same index from June 2001 to July 2001 was +0.3%. The index was 174.0 in July 2001, with base year 1982. Calculate what the index was in July 2000 and June 2001, with base year 1982.

12–25. What is a simple price index?

12–26. What are the uses of index numbers?

12–27. The following is Nigeria's Industrial Output Index for the years 1984 to 1997:

Year	Index of Output
1984	175
1985	190
1986	132
1987	96
1988	100
1989	78
1990	131
1991	135
1992	154
1993	163
1994	178
1995	170
1996	145
1997	133

   a. What is the base year used here?

   b. Change the base year to 1993.

   c. What happened to Nigeria's industrial output from 1996 to 1997?

   d. Describe the trends in industrial output throughout the years 1984 to 1997.

12–28. The following data are June 2003 to June 2004 commodity price index for a category of goods: 142, 137, 143, 142, 145, 151, 147, 144, 149, 154, 148, 153, 154. Form a new index, using January 2004 as the base month.

12–7   Using the Computer

Using Microsoft Excel in Forecasting and Time Series

Microsoft Excel Analysis Toolpack provides you with several tools that are used widely in forecasting. The Moving Average analysis tool is one of them, and it enables you to forecast the trend in your data based on the average value of the variable over a specific number of preceding periods. To start, choose Data Analysis in the Analysis group on the Data tab. Click Moving Average in the Data Analysis dialog box and then press OK. Then the Moving Average dialog box appears. In the Input Range box, enter a single row or column of your original data. Based on the example shown in Figure 12–21, enter $B$4:$B$15 in the corresponding edit box. In the Interval box, enter the number of values that you want to include in the moving average. Enter 4 in our example.

FIGURE 12–21 **Moving Average Generated by Excel Moving Average Tool**

Original Data	Forecast
96	#N/A
10	#N/A
10	#N/A
72	47
72	41
60	53.5
60	66
14	51.5
2	34
93	42.25
94	50.75
26	53.75

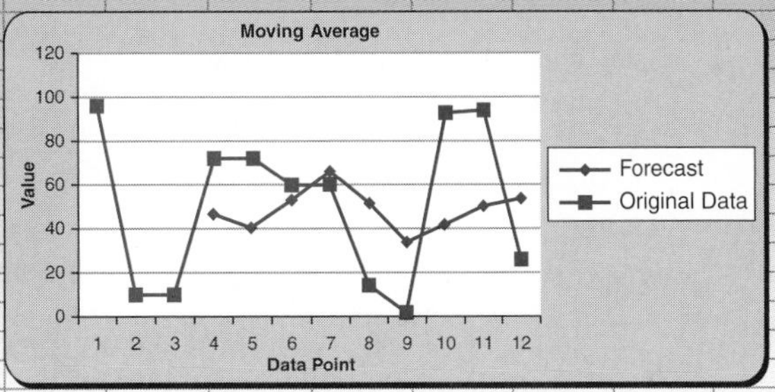

Note that larger intervals provide you with smoother moving average lines. For smaller intervals, the moving average is more strongly affected by individual data point fluctuations. In the Output Range box, enter the cell address where you want the results to start. Enter $C$4 in our example. Select the Chart Output check box to see a graph comparing the actual and forecasted inventory levels. Then click the OK button. Figure 12–21 shows the result. The generated moving average is stored in a column starting from cell C4. We have labeled this column Forecast.

The next Excel forecasting tool is Exponential Smoothing. As before, you need to select the Exponential Smoothing tool from the Data Analysis dialog box. When the corresponding dialog box appears, enter the cell reference for the range of data you want to analyze in the Input Range. The range must contain a single column or row with four or more cells of data. In the Damping factor edit box enter the damping factor you want to use as the exponential smoothing constant. The damping factor is obtained by deducting the weighting factor w from 1. The default damping factor is 0.3. Enter the reference for the output table as the next step. If you select the Standard Errors check box, Microsoft Excel generates a two-column output table with standard error values in the right column. If you have insufficient historical values to project a forecast or calculate a standard error, Microsoft Excel returns the #N/A error value. Figure 12–22 shows the Exponential Smoothing dialog box as well as the obtained result stored in a column labeled Forecast. The original data set we used belongs to Example 12–4.

Using MINITAB in Forecasting and Time Series

MINITAB provides you with a set of statistical tools that can be used in time series and forecasting. You can access these tools by choosing Stat ▶ Time Series from the menu bar. The first option is a time series plot. You can select this tool either from Stat ▶ Time Series ▶ Time Series Plot or from Graph ▶ Time Series Plot. This tool is used for evaluating patterns in data over time. MINITAB plots the data in worksheet order, in equally spaced time intervals. For cases in which your data were not collected at regular intervals or are not entered in chronological order, you may want to use Graph ▶ Scatterplot. The next feature is the MINITAB trend analysis tool, which fits a trend line using a linear, quadratic, growth, or *S*-curve model. Trend analysis fits a general trend model to time series data and provides forecasts. This tool is accessible via Stat ▶ Time Series ▶ Trend Analysis from the menu bar.

MINITAB also enables you to run a moving average analysis. This procedure calculates moving averages, which can be used either to smooth a time series or to

FIGURE 12–22   Exponential Smoothing for w = 0.4 Performed by the Excel Exponential
                Smoothing Tool

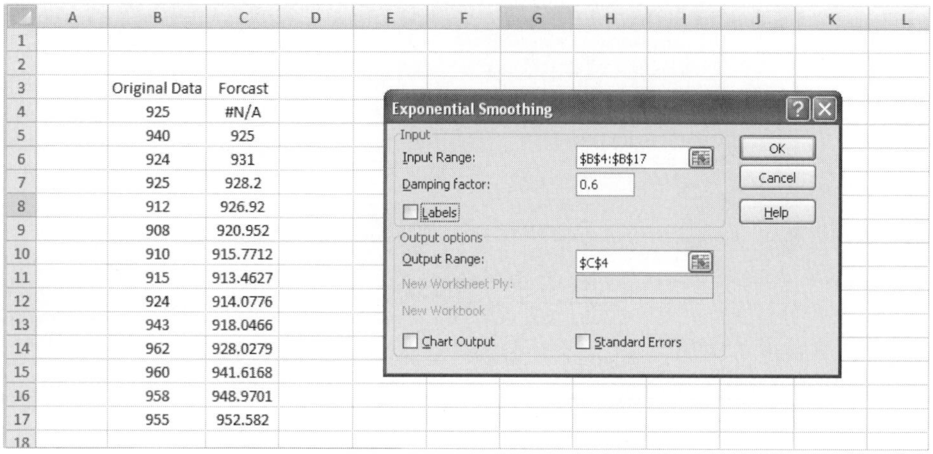

	A	B	C	D	E	F	G	H	I	J	K	L
1												
2												
3		Original Data	Forcast									
4		925	#N/A									
5		940	925									
6		924	931									
7		925	928.2									
8		912	926.92									
9		908	920.952									
10		910	915.7712									
11		915	913.4627									
12		924	914.0776									
13		943	918.0466									
14		962	928.0279									
15		960	941.6168									
16		958	948.9701									
17		955	952.582									
18												

Exponential Smoothing

Input
Input Range: $B$4:$B$17
Damping factor: 0.6
☐ Labels

Output options
Output Range: $C$4
New Worksheet Ply:
New Workbook
☐ Chart Output   ☐ Standard Errors

OK   Cancel   Help

generate forecasts. Start by choosing Stat ▶ Time Series ▶ Moving Average from the menu bar. When the dialog box appears enter the column containing the time series in the Variable edit box. Enter a positive integer to indicate the desired length for the moving average in the MA Length edit box. If you check Center the moving averages, MINITAB places the moving average values at the period which is in the center of the range rather than at the end of the range. This is called centering the moving average. You can also generate forecasts by checking the option Generate forecasts. Enter an integer in the Number of forecasts edit box to indicate how many forecasts you want. The forecasts will appear in green on the time series plot with 95% prediction interval bands. You can set a starting point for your forecast by entering a positive integer in Starting from origin edit box. If you leave this space blank, MINITAB generates forecasts from the end of the data. You can specify your data time scale by clicking on the Time button. By clicking on the Storage button, you can store various statistics generated during the process. If you check the Moving averages in the Storage dialog box, MINITAB will store the averages of consecutive groups of data in a time series. If you choose to center the moving average in previous steps, MINITAB will store the centered moving average instead. As an example, we use this tool to run a moving average analysis of the data of Example 12–3. Don't forget to click the Time button and choose Quarter in the Calendar drop-down box. In addition, choose Moving Average from the Storage dialog box. Figure 12–23 shows the generated Session commands, the predicted value for the following quarter, the centered moving averages stored in the second column of the worksheet, as well as the plot of smoothed versus actual values.

MINITAB can also be used for running an exponential smoothing procedure. This procedure works best for data without a trend or seasonal component. To start choose Stat ▶ Time Series ▶ Single Exp Smoothing from the menu bar. Single exponential smoothing smoothes your data by computing exponentially weighted averages and provides short-term forecasts. In the corresponding dialog box you need to define the column that contains the time series, weight to use in smoothing, how many forecasts you want, and other required settings. The Graphs, Storage, and Time buttons work the same as before. Other time series tools and procedures of MINITAB are also available via Stat ▶ Time Series from the menu bar.

FIGURE 12–23   Result of Using the MINITAB Moving Average Procedure on the
Data of Example 12–3

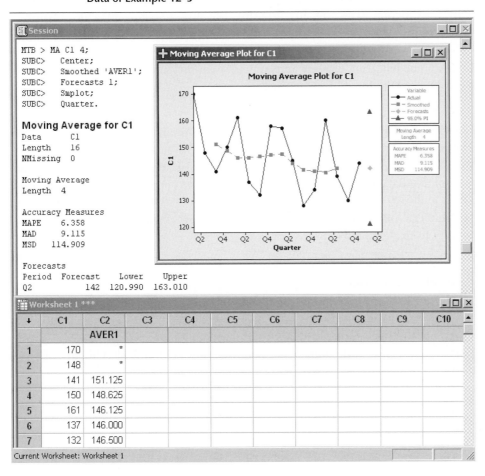

12–8   Summary and Review of Terms

In this chapter, we discussed forecasting methods. We saw how simple **Cycle** × **Trend** × **Seasonality** × **Irregular components models** are created and used. We then talked about **exponential smoothing models.** We also discussed **index numbers.**

ADDITIONAL PROBLEMS

12–29.   The following data are monthly existing-home sales, in millions of dwelling units, for January 2006 through June 2007. Construct a forecasting model for these data, and use it in forecasting sales for July 2007.

4.4, 4.2, 3.8, 4.1, 4.1, 4.0, 4.0, 3.9, 3.9, 3.8, 3.7, 3.7, 3.8, 3.9, 3.8, 3.7, 3.5, 3.4

12–30.   Discuss and compare all the forecasting methods presented in this chapter. What are the relative strengths and weaknesses of each method? Under what conditions would you use any of the methods?

12–31.   Discuss the main principle of the exponential smoothing method of forecasting. What effect does the smoothing constant w have on the forecasts?

12–32.   The following data represent the performance of a constant-proportion debt obligation (CPDO), executed on October 10, 2006, from that day until March 10, 2007, recorded biweekly: 99, 102, 102, 101, 103, 103, 104, 103, 104, 106, 101, 102.[10] Construct a forecasting model for these data and predict the CPDO's performance for the following period.

12–33.   The following data are annual time series measurements of market segmentation in Thailand for 1991 and onward.[11]

> 18, 17, 15, 14, 15, 11, 8, 5, 4, 3, 5, 4, 6, 5, 7, 8

Construct a forecasting model for these data and predict market segmentation in Thailand for the following year, 2007.

12–34.   Open the Trend+Season Forecasting template shown in Figure 12–13, used for monthly data and do a sensitivity analysis on this template. Change some of the values in the table and see how the forecasts change. Are there large relative changes?

12–35.   The following data are annual percentage changes in GDP for a small country from 2001 to 2007:

> 6.3, 6.6, 7.3, 7.4, 7.8, 6.9, 7.8

Do trend-line forecasting.

12–36.   Use your library to research the Standard & Poor's 500 index. Write a short report explaining this index, its construction, and its use.

12–37.   The CPI is the most pervasively used index number in existence. You can keep current with it at the Bureau of Labor Statistics site http://stats.bls.gov/. Locate the CPI index-All urban consumers.

If the majority of new college graduates in 1978 could expect to land a job earning $20,000 per year, what must the starting salary be for the majority of new college graduates in 2007 in order for them to be at the same standard of living as their counterparts in 1978? Is today's typical college graduate better or worse off than her or his 1978 counterpart?

www.exercise

---

[10]Navroz Patel, "Credit Market Ricochet," *Risk,* April 2007, pp. 23–26.

[11]George P. Nishiotis, "Further Evidence on Closed-End Country Fund Prices and International Capital Flows," *Journal of Business* 79, no. 4 (2006), pp. 1727–1743.

CASE 16 Auto Parts Sales Forecast

The quarterly sales of a large manufacturer of spare parts for automobiles are tabulated below. Since the sales are in millions of dollars, forecast errors can be costly. The company wants to forecast the sales as accurately as possible.

Quarter	Sales	M2 Index	Non-Farm-Activity Index	Oil Price
04 Q1	$35,452,300	2.356464	34.2	19.15
04 Q2	$41,469,361	2.357643	34.27	16.46
04 Q3	$40,981,634	2.364126	34.3	18.83
04 Q4	$42,777,164	2.379493	34.33	19.75
05 Q1	$43,491,652	2.373544	34.4	18.53
05 Q2	$57,669,446	2.387192	34.33	17.61
05 Q3	$59,476,149	2.403903	34.37	17.95
05 Q4	$76,908,559	2.42073	34.43	15.84
06 Q1	$63,103,070	2.431623	34.37	14.28
06 Q2	$84,457,560	2.441958	34.5	13.02
06 Q3	$67,990,330	2.447452	34.5	15.89
06 Q4	$68,542,620	2.445616	34.53	16.91
07 Q1	$73,457,391	2.45601	34.6	16.29
07 Q2	$89,124,339	2.48364	34.7	17
07 Q3	$85,891,854	2.532692	34.67	18.2
07 Q4	$69,574,971	2.564984	34.73	17

1. Carry out a Trend+Season forecast with the sales data, and forecast the sales for the four quarters of 2008.

The director of marketing research of the company believes that the sales can be predicted better using a multiple regression of sales against three selected econometric variables that the director believes have significant impact on the sales. These variables are M2 Index, Non-Farm-Activity Index, and Oil Price. The values of these variables for the corresponding periods are available in the data tabulated to the left.

2. Conduct a multiple regression of sales against the three econometric variables, following the procedure learned in Chapter 11. What is the regression equation?

3. Make a prediction for the four quarters of 2008 based on the regression equation using projected values of the following econometric variables:

Quarter	M2 Index	Non-Farm-Activity Index	Oil Price
08 Q1	2.597688	34.7	17.1
08 Q2	2.630159	34.4	17.3
08 Q3	2.663036	34.5	18
08 Q4	2.696324	34.5	18.2

After seeing large errors and wide prediction intervals in the multiple regression approach to forecasting, the director of marketing research decides to include indicator variables to take into account the seasonal effects that may not be captured in the three independent variables. He adds the following three indicator variables:

	Indicator		
	Q2	Q3	Q4
Q1	0	0	0
Q2	1	0	0
Q3	0	1	0
Q4	0	0	1

He wants to run the multiple regression with a total of six independent variables–the original three plus the three indicator variables.

4. Carry out the multiple regression with the six independent variables and report the regression equation.

5. Make a forecast for the next four quarters with this new regression model.

6. Conduct a partial F test to test the claim that the three indicator variables can be dropped from the model.

7. Compare the forecasts from the three methods employed and rank order them according to their forecast accuracy.

13

QUALITY CONTROL AND IMPROVEMENT

13–1   Using Statistics 595

13–2   W. Edwards Deming Instructs 596

13–3   Statistics and Quality 596

13–4   The $\bar{x}$ Chart 604

13–5   The R Chart and the s Chart 608

13–6   The p Chart 611

13–7   The c Chart 614

13–8   The x Chart 615

13–9   Using the Computer 616

13–10 Summary and Review of Terms 617

Case 17   Quality Control and Improvement at Nashua Corporation 618

LEARNING OBJECTIVES

After studying this chapter, you should be able to:

- Determine when to use control charts.
- Create control charts for sample means, ranges, and standard deviations.
- Create control charts for sample proportions.
- Create control charts for a number of defectives.
- Draw Pareto charts using spreadsheet templates.
- Draw control charts using spreadsheet templates.

594

13–1 Using Statistics

Not long after the Norman Conquest of England, the Royal Mint was established in London. The Mint has been in constant operation from its founding to this very day, producing gold and silver coins for the Crown (and in later periods, coins from cheaper metals). Sometime during the reign of Henry II (1154–1189), a mysterious ceremony called the "Trial of the Pyx" was initiated.

The word *pyx* is Old English for "box," and the ceremony was an actual trial by jury of the contents of a box. The ancient trial had religious overtones, and the jurors were all members of the Worshipful Company of Goldsmiths. The box was thrice locked and held under guard in a special room, the Chapel of the Pyx, in Westminster Abbey. It was ceremoniously opened at the trial, which was held once every three or four years.

What did the Pyx box contain, and what was the trial? Every day, a single coin of gold (or silver, depending on what was being minted) was randomly selected by the minters and sent to Westminster Abbey to be put in the Pyx. In three or four years, the Pyx contained a large number of coins. For a given type of coin, say a gold sovereign, the box also contained a royal standard, which was the exact desired weight of a sovereign. At the trial, the contents of the box were carefully inspected and counted, and later some coins were assayed. The total weight of all gold sovereigns was recorded. Then the weight of the royal standard was multiplied by the number of sovereigns in the box and compared with the actual total weight of the sovereigns. A given tolerance was allowed in the total weight, and the trial was declared a success if the total weight was within the tolerance levels established above and below the computed standard.

The trial was designed so that the King or Queen could maintain control of the use of the gold and silver ingots furnished to the Mint for coinage. If, for example, coins were too heavy, then the monarch's gold was being wasted. A shrewd merchant could then melt down such coins and sell them back to the Mint at a profit. This actually happened often enough that such coins were given the name *come again guineas* as they would return to the Mint in melted-down form, much to the minters' embarrassment. On the other hand, if coins contained too little gold, then the currency was being debased and would lose its value. In addition, somebody at the Mint could then be illegally profiting from the leftover gold.

When the trial was successful, a large banquet would be held in celebration. We may surmise that when the trial was not successful . . . the Tower of London was not too far away. The Trial of the Pyx is practiced (with modifications) to this very day. Interestingly, the famous scientist and mathematician Isaac Newton was at one time (1699 to 1727) Master of the Mint. In fact, one of the trials during Newton's tenure was not successful, but he survived.[1]

The Trial of the Pyx is a classic example, and probably the earliest on record, of a two-tailed statistical test for the population mean. The Crown wants to test the null hypothesis that, on average, the weight of the coins is as specified. The Crown wants to test this hypothesis against the two-tailed alternative that the average coin is either too heavy or too light—both having negative consequences for the Crown. The test statistic used is the sum of the weights of n coins, and the critical points are obtained as n times the standard weight, plus or minus the allowed tolerance.[2] The Trial of the Pyx is also a wonderful example of *quality control*. We have a production process, the minting of coins, and we want to ensure that high quality is maintained throughout

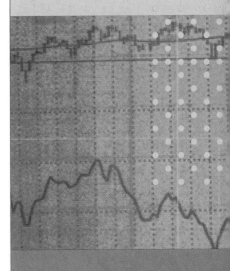

---

[1]Adapted from the article "Eight Centuries of Sampling Inspection: The Trial of the Pyx," by S. Stigler, originally published in the *Journal of the American Statistical Association,* copyright 1977 by the American Statistical Association. All rights reserved.

[2]According to Professor Stigler, the tolerance was computed in a manner incongruent with statistical theory, but he feels we may forgive this error as the trial seems to have served its purpose well through the centuries.

the operation. We sample from the production process, and we take corrective action whenever we believe that the process is *out of control*—producing items that, on average, lie outside our specified target limits.

13–2   W. Edwards Deming Instructs

We now jump 800 years, to the middle of the 20th century and to the birth of modern quality control theory. In 1950 Japan was trying to recover from the devastation of World War II. Japanese industry was all but destroyed, and its leaders knew that industry must be rebuilt well if the nation was to survive. But how? By an ironic twist of fate, Japanese industrialists decided to hire a U.S. statistician as their consultant. The man they chose was the late W. Edwards Deming, at the time a virtually unknown government statistician. No one in the United States paid much attention to Deming's theories on how statistics could be used to improve industrial quality. The Japanese wanted to listen. They brought Deming to Japan in 1950, and in July of that year he met with the top management of Japan's leading companies. He then gave the first of many series of lectures to Japanese management. The title of the course was "Elementary Principles of the Statistical Control of Quality," and it was attended by 230 Japanese managers of industrial firms, engineers, and scientists.

The Japanese listened closely to Deming's message. In fact, they listened so well that in a few short decades, Japan became one of the most successful industrial nations on earth. Whereas "Made in Japan" once meant low quality, the phrase has now come to denote the highest quality. In 1960, Emperor Hirohito awarded Dr. Deming the Medal of the Sacred Treasure. The citation with the medal stated that the Japanese people attribute the rebirth of Japanese industry to W. Edwards Deming. In addition, the Deming Award was instituted in Japan to recognize outstanding developments and innovations in the field of quality improvement. On the walls of the main lobby of Toyota's headquarters in Tokyo hang three portraits. One portrait is of the company's founder, another is of the current chairman, and the largest portrait is of Dr. Deming.

Ironically, Dr. Deming's ideas did get recognized in the United States—alas, when he was 80 years old. For years, U.S. manufacturing firms had been feeling the pressure to improve quality, but not much was actually being done while the Japanese were conquering the world markets. In June 1980, Dr. Deming appeared in a network television documentary entitled "If Japan Can, Why Can't We?" Starting the next morning, Dr. Deming's mail quadrupled, and the phone was constantly ringing. Offers came from Ford, General Motors, Xerox, and many others.

While well into his 90s, Dr. Ed Deming was one of the most sought-after consultants to U.S. industry. His appointment book was filled years in advance, and companies were willing to pay very high fees for an hour of his time. He traveled around the country, lecturing on quality and how to achieve it. The first U.S. company to adopt the Deming philosophy and to institute a program of quality improvement at all levels of production was Nashua Corporation. The company kindly agreed to provide us with actual data of a production process and its quality improvement. This is presented as Case 17 at the end of this chapter. How did Deming do it? How did he apply statistical quality control schemes so powerful that they could catapult a nation to the forefront of the industrialized world and are now helping U.S. firms improve as well? This chapter should give you an idea.

13–3   Statistics and Quality

In all fairness, Dr. Deming did not invent the idea of using statistics to control and improve quality; that honor goes to a colleague of his. What Deming did was to expand the theory and demonstrate how it could be used very successfully in industry. Since then, Deming's theories have gone beyond statistics and quality control, and they now encompass the entire firm. His tenets to management are the well-known "14 points" he advocated, which deal with the desired corporate approach to costs, prices, profits, labor, and other factors. Deming even liked to expound about antitrust laws and capitalism and to have fun with his audience. At a lecture attended by one author (A.D.A.) around Deming's 90th birthday, Dr. Deming opened by writing on a transparency: "Deming's Second Theorem: 'Nobody gives a hoot about profits.'" He then stopped and addressed the audience, "Ask me what is Deming's First Theorem." He looked expectantly at his listeners and answered, "I haven't thought of it yet!" The philosophical approach to quality and the whole firm, and how it relates to profits and costs, is described in the ever-growing literature on this subject. It is sometimes referred to as *total quality management* (TQM). Dr. Deming's vision of what a firm can do by using the total quality management approach to continual improvement is summarized in his famous 14 points. The Deming approach centers on creating an environment in which the 14 points can be implemented toward the achievement of quality.

Deming's 14 Points

1. Create constancy of purpose for continual improvement of products and service to society, allocating resources to provide for long-range needs rather than only short-term profitability, with a plan to become competitive, to stay in business, and to provide jobs.

2. Adopt the new philosophy. We are in a new economic age, created in Japan. We can no longer live with commonly accepted levels of delays, mistakes, defective materials, and defective workmanship. Transformation of Western management style is necessary to halt the continued decline of industry.

3. Eliminate the need for mass inspection as the way of life to achieve quality by building quality into the product in the first place. Require statistical evidence of built-in quality in both manufacturing and purchasing functions.

4. End the practice of awarding business solely on the basis of price tag. Instead, require meaningful measures of quality along with the price. Reduce the number of suppliers for the same item by eliminating those that do not qualify with statistical and other evidence of quality. The aim is to minimize *total* cost, not merely initial cost, by minimizing variation. This may be achievable by moving toward a single supplier for any one item, on a long-term relationship of loyalty and trust. Purchasing managers have a new job and must learn it.

5. Improve constantly and forever every process for planning, production, and service. Search continually for problems in order to improve every activity in the company, to improve quality and productivity, and thus to constantly decrease costs. Institute innovation and constant improvement of product, service, and process. It is the management's job to work continually on the system (design, incoming materials, maintenance, improvement of machines, supervision, training, and retraining).

6. Institute modern methods of training on the job for all, including management, to make better use of every employee. New skills are required to keep up with changes in materials, methods, product design, machinery, techniques, and service.

7. Adopt and institute leadership aimed at helping people to do a better job. The responsibility of managers and supervisors must be changed from sheer numbers to quality. Improvement of quality will automatically improve productivity. Management must ensure that immediate action is taken on reports of inherited defects, maintenance requirements, poor tools, fuzzy operational definitions, and all conditions detrimental to quality.

8. Encourage effective two-way communication and other means to drive out fear throughout the organization so that everybody may work effectively and more productively for the company.

9. Break down barriers between departments and staff areas. People in different areas, such as research, design, sales, administration, and production, must work in teams to tackle problems that may be encountered with products or service.

10. Eliminate the use of slogans, posters, and exhortations for the workforce, demanding zero defects and new levels of productivity, without providing methods. Such exhortations only create adversarial relationships; the bulk of the causes of low quality and low productivity belong to the system, and thus lie beyond the power of the workforce.

11. Eliminate work standards that prescribe quotas for the workforce and numerical goals for people in management. Substitute aids and helpful leadership in order to achieve continual improvement of quality and productivity.

12. Remove the barriers that rob hourly workers, and people in management, of their right to pride of workmanship. This implies, *inter alia,* abolition of the annual merit rating (appraisal of performance) and of management by objective. Again, the responsibility of managers, supervisors, and foremen must be changed from sheer numbers to quality.

13. Institute a vigorous program of education, and encourage self-improvement for everyone. What an organization needs is not just good people; it needs people who are improving with education. Advances in competitive position will have their roots in knowledge.

14. Clearly define top management's permanent commitment to ever-improving quality and productivity, and their obligation to implement all these principles. Indeed, it is not enough that top managers commit themselves for life to quality and productivity. They must know what it is that they are committed to—that is, what they must do. Create a structure in top management that will push every day on the preceding 13 points, and take action in order to accomplish the transformation. Support is not enough: Action is required.

Process Capability

Process capability is the best in-control performance that an existing process can achieve without major expenditures. The *capability* of any process is the natural behavior of the particular process after disturbances are eliminated. In an effort to improve quality and productivity in the firm, it is important to first try to establish the capability of the process. An investigation is undertaken to actually achieve a state of statistical control in a process based on current data. This gives a live image of the process. For example, in trying to improve the quality of car production, we first try to find how the process operates in the best way, then make improvements. Control charts are a useful tool in this analysis.

Control Charts

The first modern ideas on how statistics could be used in quality control came in the mid-1920s from a colleague of Deming's, Walter Shewhart of Bell Laboratories. Shewhart invented the **control chart** for industrial processes. A control chart is a graphical display of measurements (usually aggregated in the form of means or other statistics) of an industrial process through time. By carefully scrutinizing the chart, a quality control engineer can identify any potential problems with the production process. The idea is that when a process is in control, the variable being measured—the mean of every four observations, for example—should remain stable through

FIGURE 13–1   A Control Chart

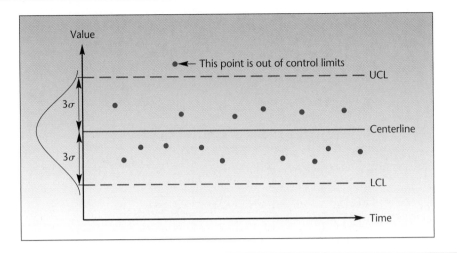

time. The mean should stay somewhere around the middle line (the grand mean for the process) and not wander off "too much." By now you understand what "too much" means in statistics: more than several standard deviations of the process. The required number of standard deviations is chosen so that there will be a small probability of exceeding them when the process is in control. Addition and subtraction of the required number of standard deviations (generally three) give us the **upper control limit** (UCL) and the **lower control limit** (LCL) of the control chart. The UCL and LCL are similar to the "tolerance" limits in the story of the Pyx. When the bounds are breached, the process is deemed **out of control** and must be corrected. A control chart is illustrated in Figure 13–1. We assume throughout that the variable being charted is at least approximately normally distributed.

In addition to looking for the process exceeding the bounds, quality control workers look for patterns and trends in the charted variable. For example, if the mean of four observations at a time keeps increasing or decreasing, or it stays too long above or below the centerline (even if the UCL and LCL are not breached), the process may be out of control.

> A **control chart** is a time plot of a statistic, such as a sample mean, range, standard deviation, or proportion, with a centerline and *upper and lower control limits*. The limits give the desired range of values for the statistic. When the statistic is outside the bounds, or when its time plot reveals certain patterns, the process may be out of control.

Central to the idea of a control chart—and, in general, to the use of statistics in quality control—is the concept of **variance.** If we were to summarize the entire field of statistical quality control (also called *statistical process control,* or SPC) in one word, that word would have to be *variance.* Shewhart, Deming, and others wanted to bring the statistical concept of variance down to the shop floor. If supervisors and production line workers could understand the existence of variance in the production process, then this awareness by itself could be used to help minimize the variance. Furthermore, the variance in the production process could be partitioned into two kinds: the natural, random variation of the process and variation due to assignable causes. Examples of assignable causes are fatigue of workers and breakdown of components. Variation due to assignable causes is especially undesirable because it is due to something's being wrong with the production process, and may result in low quality

FIGURE 13–2   A Production Process in, and out of, Statistical Control

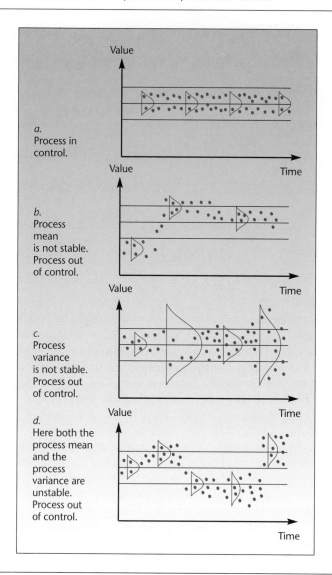

of the produced items. Looking at the chart helps us detect an assignable cause, by asking what has happened at a particular time on the chart where the process looks unusual.

A process is considered in **statistical control** when it has no assignable causes, only natural variation.

Figure 13–2 shows how a process could be in control or out of control. Recall the assumption of a normal distribution—this is what is meant by the normal curves shown on the graphs. These curves stand for the hypothetical populations from which our data are assumed to have been randomly drawn.

Actually, any kind of variance is undesirable in a production process. Even the natural variance of a process due to purely random causes rather than to assignable causes can be detrimental. The control chart, however, will detect only assignable causes. As the following story shows, one could do very well by removing all variance.

FIGURE 13–3   Pareto Diagram for Ceramics Example

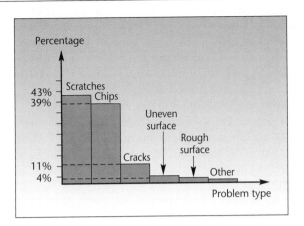

An American car manufacturer was having problems with transmissions made at one of its domestic plants, and warranty costs were enormous. The identical type of transmission made in Japan was not causing any problems at all. Engineers carefully examined 12 transmissions made at the company's American plant. They found that variations existed among the 12 transmissions, but there were no assignable causes and a control chart revealed nothing unusual. All transmissions were well within specifications. Then they looked at 12 transmissions made at the Japanese plant. The engineer who made the measurements reported that the measuring equipment was broken: in testing one transmission after the other, the needle did not move at all. A closer investigation revealed that the measuring equipment was perfectly fine: the transmissions simply had *no variation*. They did not just satisfy specifications; for all practical purposes, the 12 transmissions were identical![3]

Such perfection may be difficult to achieve, but the use of control charts can go a long way toward improving quality. Control charts are the main topic of this chapter, and we will discuss them in later sections. We devote the remainder of this section to brief descriptions of other quality control tools.

Pareto Diagrams

In instituting a quality control and improvement program, one important question to answer is: What are the exact causes of lowered quality in the production process? A ceramics manufacturer may be plagued by several problems: scratches, chips, cracks, surface roughness, uneven surfaces, and so on. It would be very desirable to find out which of these problems were serious and which not. A good and simple tool for such analysis is the **Pareto diagram**. Although the diagram is named after an Italian economist, its use in quality control is due to J. M. Juran.

A **Pareto diagram** is a bar chart of the various problems in production and their percentages, which must add to 100%.

A Pareto diagram for the ceramics example above is given in Figure 13–3. As can be seen from the figure, scratches and chips are serious problems, accounting for most of the nonconforming items produced. Cracks occur less frequently, and the other problems are relatively rare. A Pareto diagram thus helps management to identify the most significant problems and concentrate on their solution rather than waste time and resources on unimportant causes.

---

[3]From "Ed Deming wants big changes and he wants them fast," by Lloyd Dobyns, *Smithsonian Magazine*, August 1990, pp. 74–83. Copyright © 1990 Lloyd Dobyns. Used with permission.

Six Sigma

Six Sigma is a further innovation, beyond Deming's work, in the field of quality assurance and control. This system of quality control practices was developed by Bill Smith at Motorola Inc. in 1986.

The purpose of Six Sigma was to push the defect levels at Motorola to below the threshold defined as 3.4 defects per million opportunities (3.4 DPMO), meaning that with this new methodology, the company was hoping that only 3.4 or fewer items out of 1 million produced would be found defective.

The key to Six Sigma is a precise definition of the production process, followed by accurate measurements and valid collection of data. A detailed analysis then measures the relationships and causality of factors in production. Experimental design (as described in Chapter 9) is used in an effort to identify key factors. Finally, strict control of the production process is exercised. Any variations are corrected, and the process is further monitored as it goes on line.

Six Sigma has been a very successful undertaking at Motorola, and has since been adopted by Caterpillar, Raytheon, General Electric, and even service companies such as Bank of America and Merrill Lynch. The essence of Six Sigma is the statistical methods described in this chapter.

Acceptance Sampling

Finished products are grouped in lots before being shipped to customers. The lots are numbered, and random samples from these lots are inspected for quality. Such checks are made both before lots are shipped out and when lots arrive at their destination. The random samples are measured to find out which and how many items do not meet specifications.

A lot is rejected whenever the sample mean exceeds or falls below some prespecified limit. For attribute data, the lot is rejected when the number of defective or nonconforming items in the sample exceeds a prespecified limit. Acceptance sampling does not, by itself, improve quality; it simply removes bad lots. To improve quality, it is necessary to control the production process itself, removing any assignable causes and striving to reduce the variation in the process.

Analysis of Variance and Experimental Design

As statistics in general is an important collection of tools to improve quality, so in particular is experimental design. Industrial experiments are performed to find production methods that can bring about high quality. Experiments are designed to identify the factors that affect the variable of interest, for example, the diameter of a rod. We may find that method B produces rods with diameters that conform to specifications more often than those produced by method A or C. Analysis of variance (as well as regression and other techniques) is used in making such a determination. These tools are more "active" in the quest for improved quality than the control charts, which are merely diagnostic and look at a process already in place. However, both types of tool should be used in a comprehensive quality improvement plan.

Taguchi Methods

The Japanese engineer Genichi Taguchi developed new notions about quality engineering. Taguchi's ideas transcend the customary wisdom of tolerance limits, where we implicitly assume that any value for a parameter within the specified range is as good as any other value. Taguchi aims at the ideal *optimal* value for a parameter in question. For example, if we look at a complete manufactured product, such as a car, the car's quality may not be good even if all its components are within desired levels when considered alone. The idea is that the quality of a large system deteriorates as we add the small variations in quality for all its separate components.

To try to solve this problem, Taguchi developed the idea of a total loss to society due to the lowered quality of any given item. That loss to society is to be minimized.

FIGURE 13–4 **The Template for Pareto Diagrams**
[Pareto.xls]

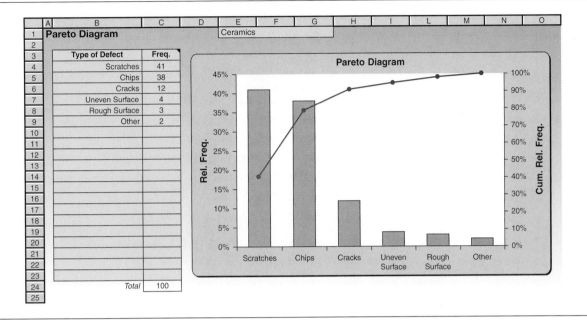

That is, we want to *minimize* the variations in product quality, not simply keep them within limits. This is done by introducing a *loss function* associated with the parameter in question (e.g., rod diameter) and by trying to create production systems that minimize this loss both for components and for finished products.

The Template

Figure 13–4 shows the template that can be used to draw Pareto diagrams. After entering the data in columns B and C, make sure that the frequencies are in descending order. To sort them in descending order, select the whole range of data, B4:C23, choose the Sort command under the Data menu and click the OK button.

The chart has a cumulative relative frequency line plotted on top of the histogram. This line helps to calculate the cumulative percentage of cases that are covered by a set of defects. For example, we see from the cumulative percentage line that approximately 90% of the cases are covered by the first three types: scratches, chips, and cracks. Thus, a quality control manager can hope to remedy 90% of the problems by concentrating on and eliminating the first three types.

In the following sections, we describe Shewhart's control charts in detail, since they are the main tool currently used for maintaining and improving quality. Information on the other methods we mentioned in this section can be found in the ever-increasing literature on quality improvement. (For example, see the appropriate references in Appendix A at the end of this book.) Our discussion of control charts will roughly follow the order of their frequency of use in industry today. The charts we will discuss are the $\bar{x}$ chart, the R chart, the s chart, the p chart, the c chart, and the x chart.

PROBLEMS

13–1. Discuss what is meant by *quality control* and *quality improvement*.

13–2. What is the main statistical idea behind current methods of quality control?

13–3. Describe the two forms of variation in production systems and how they affect quality.

13–4. What is a quality control chart, and how is it used?

13–5.   What are the components of a quality control chart?

13–6.   What are the limitations of quality control charts?

13–7.   What is acceptance sampling?

13–8.   Describe how one would use experimental design in an effort to improve industrial quality.

13–9.   The errors in the inventory records of a company were analyzed for their causes. The findings were 164 cases of omissions, 103 cases of wrong quantity entered, 45 cases of wrong part numbers entered, 24 cases of wrong dates entered, and 8 cases of withdrawal versus deposit mixup. Draw a Pareto diagram for the different causes.

   a. What percentage of the cases is covered by the top two causes?

   b. If at least 90% of the cases are to be covered, which causes must be addressed?

13–10.   Out of 1,000 automobile engines tested for quality, 62 had cracked blocks, 17 had leaky radiators, 106 had oil leaks, 29 had faulty cylinders, and 10 had ignition problems. Draw a Pareto diagram for these data, and identify the key problems in this particular production process.

13–11.   In an effort to improve quality, AT&T has been trying to control pollution problems. Problem causes and their relative seriousness, as a percentage of the total, are as follows: chlorofluorocarbons, 61%; air toxins, 30%; manufacturing wastes, 8%; other, 1%. Draw a Pareto diagram of these causes.

13–12.   The journal *People Management* reports on new ways to use directive training to improve the performance of managers. The percentages of managers who benefited from the training from 2003 to 2007 are: 34%, 36%, 38%, 39%, and 41% for 2007.[4] Comment on these results from a quality-management viewpoint.

13–4   The $\bar{x}$ Chart

CHAPTER 21

We want to compute the centerline and the upper and lower control limits for a process believed to be in control. Then future observations can be checked against these bounds to make sure the process remains in control. To do this, we first conduct an *initial run*. We determine trial control limits to test for control of past data, and then we remove out-of-control observations and recompute the control limits. We apply these improved control limits to future data. This is the philosophy behind all control charts discussed in this chapter. Although we present the $\bar{x}$ chart first, in an actual quality control program we would first want to test that the process variation is under control. This is done by using the R (range) or the s (standard deviation) chart. Unless the process variability is under statistical control, there is no stable distribution of values with a fixed mean.

An $\bar{x}$ **chart** can help us to detect shifts in the process mean. One reason for a control chart for the process mean (rather than for a single observation) has to do with the central limit theorem. We want to be able to use the known properties of the normal curve in designing the control limits. By the central limit theorem, the distribution of the sample mean tends toward a normal distribution as the sample size increases. Thus, when we aggregate data from a process, the aggregated statistic, or sample mean, becomes closer to a normal random variable than the original, unaggregated quantity. Typically, a set number of observations will be aggregated and averaged. For example, a set of four measurements of rod diameter will be made every hour of production. The four rods will be chosen randomly from all rods made during that hour.

[4]Daniel Wain, "Learning Center," *People Management,* April 19, 2007, p. 34.

If the distribution of rod diameters is roughly mound-shaped, then the sample means of the groups of four diameters will have a distribution closer to normal.

The mean of the random variable $\overline{X}$ is the population mean μ, and the standard deviation of $\overline{X}$ is $\sigma/\sqrt{4}$, where σ is the population standard deviation. We know all this from the theory in Chapter 5. We also know from the theory that the probability that a normal random variable will exceed 3 of its standard deviations on either side of the mean is 0.0026 (check this by using the normal table). Thus, the interval

$$\mu \pm 3\sigma/\sqrt{n} \qquad (13\text{-}1)$$

should contain about 99.74% of the sample means. This is, in fact, the logic of the control chart for the process mean. The idea is the same as that of a hypothesis test (conducted in a form similar to a confidence interval). We try to select the bounds so that they will be as close as possible to equation 13-1. We then chart the bounds, with an estimate of μ in the center (the centerline) and the upper and lower bounds (UCL and LCL) as close as possible to the bounds of the interval specified by equation 13-1. Out of 1,000 $\overline{x}$'s, fewer than 3 are expected to be out of bounds. Therefore, with a limited number of $\overline{x}$'s on the control chart, observing even one of them out of bounds is cause to reject the null hypothesis that the process is in control, in favor of the alternative that it is out of control. (One could also compute a p-value here, although it is more complicated since we have several $\overline{x}$'s on the chart, and in general this is not done.)

We note that the assumption of random sampling is important here as well. If somehow the process is such that successively produced items have values that are correlated—thus violating the independence assumption of random sampling—the interpretation of the chart may be misleading. Various new techniques have been devised to solve this problem.

To construct the control chart for the sample mean, we need estimates of the parameters in equation 13-1. The grand mean of the process, that is, the mean of all the sample means (the mean of all the observations of the process), is our estimate of μ. This is our centerline. To estimate σ, we use s, the standard deviation of all the process observations. However, this estimate is good only for large samples, $n > 10$. For smaller sample sizes we use an alternative procedure. When sample sizes are small, we use the *range* of the values in each sample used to compute an $\overline{x}$. Then we average these ranges, giving us a mean range $\overline{R}$. When the mean range $\overline{R}$ is multiplied by a constant, which we call A_2, the result is a good estimate for 3σ. Values of A_2 for all sample sizes up to 25 are found in Appendix C, Table 13, at the end of the book. The table also contains the values for all other constants required for the quality control charts discussed in this chapter.

The box on page 606 shows how we compute the centerline and the upper and lower control limits when constructing a control chart for the process mean.

In addition to a sample mean being outside the bounds given by the UCL and LCL, other occurrences on the chart may lead us to conclude that there is evidence that the process is out of control. Several such sets of rules have been developed, and the idea behind them is that they represent occurrences that have a very low probability when the process is indeed in control. The set of rules we use is given in Table 13-1.[5]

---

[5]This particular set of rules was provided courtesy of Dr. Lloyd S. Nelson of Nashua Corporation, one of the pioneers in the area of quality control. See L. S. Nelson, "The Shewhart Control Chart—Tests for Special Causes," *Journal of Quality Technology* Issue 16 (1984), pp. 237–239. The MINITAB package tests for special causes using Nelson's criteria. © 1984 American Society for Quality. Reprinted by permission.

TABLE 13–1 Tests for Assignable Causes

Test 1: One point beyond 3σ ($3s$)
Test 2: Nine points in a row on one side of the centerline
Test 3: Six points in a row steadily increasing or decreasing
Test 4: Fourteen points in a row alternating up and down
Test 5: Two out of three points in a row beyond 2σ ($2s$)
Test 6: Four out of five points in a row beyond 1σ ($1s$)
Test 7: Fifteen points in a row within 1σ ($1s$) of the centerline
Test 8: Eight points in a row on both sides of the centerline, all beyond 1σ ($1s$)

Elements of a control chart for the process mean:

Centerline:
$$\bar{\bar{x}} = \frac{\sum_{i=1}^{k} \bar{x}_i}{k}$$

UCL:
$$\bar{\bar{x}} + A_2\bar{R} \qquad \bar{R} = \frac{\sum_{i=1}^{k} R_i}{k}$$

LCL:
$$\bar{\bar{x}} - A_2\bar{R}$$

where k = number of samples, each of size n
$\bar{x}$ = sample mean for ith sample
R_i = range of the ith sample

If the sample size in each group is over 10, then

$$UCL = \bar{\bar{x}} + 3\frac{\bar{s}/c_4}{\sqrt{n}} \qquad LCL = \bar{\bar{x}} - 3\frac{\bar{s}/c_4}{\sqrt{n}}$$

where $\bar{s}$ is the average of the standard deviations of all groups and c_4 is a constant found in Appendix C, Table 13.

The Template

The template for drawing X-bar charts is shown in Figure 13–5. Its use is illustrated through Example 13–1.

EXAMPLE 13–1

A pharmaceutical manufacturer needs to control the concentration of the active ingredient in a formula used to restore hair to bald people. The concentration should be around 10%, and a control chart is desired to check the sample means of 30 observations, aggregated in groups of 3. The template containing the data, as well as the control chart it produced, are given in Figure 13–5. As can be seen from the control chart, there is no evidence here that the process is out of control.

The grand mean is $\bar{\bar{x}} = 10.253$. The ranges of the groups of three observations each are 0.15, 0.53, 0.69, 0.45, 0.55, 0.71, 0.90, 0.68, 0.11, and 0.24. Thus, $\bar{R} = 0.501$. From Table 13 we find for $n = 3$, $A_2 = 1.023$. Thus, UCL $= 10.253 + 1.023(0.501) = 10.766$, and LCL $= 10.253 - 1.023(0.501) = 9.74$. Note that the $\bar{x}$ chart cannot be interpreted unless the R or s chart has been examined and is in control. These two charts are presented in the next section.

FIGURE 13–5 The Template for *X*-bar Chart
[Control Charts.xls; Sheet: X-bar R s Charts]

	1	2	3	4	5	6	7	8	9	10	11	12	13	14	15
1	10.22	10.46	10.82	9.88	9.92	10.15	10.69	10.12	10.31	10.07					
2	10.25	10.06	10.52	10.31	9.94	10.85	10.32	10.8	10.23	10.15					
3	10.37	10.59	10.13	10.33	9.39	10.14	9.79	10.26	10.2	10.31					
4															
5															
6															
7															
8															
9															
10															
x-bar	10.28	10.37	10.49	10.17	9.75	10.38	10.27	10.39	10.25	10.18					
R	0.15	0.53	0.69	0.45	0.55	0.71	0.9	0.68	0.11	0.24					
s	0.079	0.276	0.346	0.254	0.312	0.407	0.452	0.359	0.057	0.122					

n = 3   x-bar-bar = 10.25   R-bar = 0.501   s-bar = 0.267
          UCL = 10.77   UCL = 1.29   UCL = 0.684
          LCL = 9.74   LCL = 0   LCL = 0

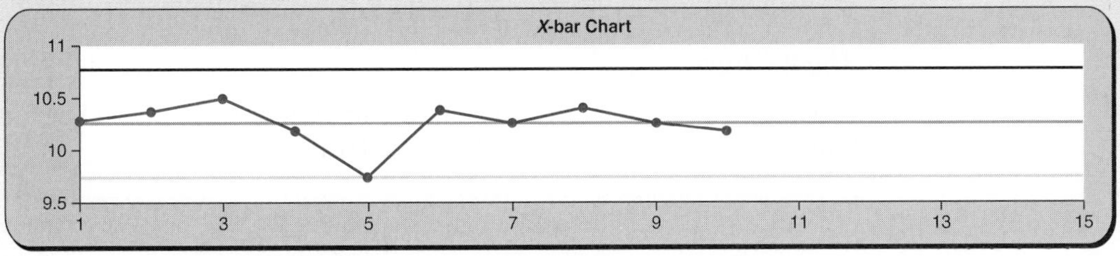

PROBLEMS

13–13. What is the logic behind the control chart for the sample mean, and how is the chart constructed?

13–14. Boston-based Legal Seafoods prides itself on having instituted an advanced quality control system that includes the control of both food quality and service quality. The following are successive service times at one of the chain's restaurants on a Saturday night in May 2007 (time is stated in minutes from customer entry to appearance of waitperson):

5, 6, 5, 5.5, 7, 4, 12, 4.5, 2, 5, 5.5, 6, 6, 13, 2, 5, 4, 4.5, 6.5, 4, 1,
2, 3, 5.5, 4, 4, 8, 12, 3, 4.5, 6.5, 6, 7, 10, 6, 6.5, 5, 3, 6.5, 7

Aggregate the data into groups of four, and construct a control chart for the process mean. Is the waiting time at the restaurant under control?

13–15. What assumptions are necessary for constructing an $\bar{x}$ chart?

13–16. Rolls Royce makes the Trent 900 jet engines used in the new Airbus A380 planes, and needs to control the maximum thrust delivered by the engines. The following are readings related to power for successive engines produced:

121, 122, 121, 125, 123, 121, 129, 123, 122, 122, 120, 121, 119, 118, 121,
125, 139, 150, 121, 122, 120, 123, 127, 123, 128, 129, 122, 120, 128, 120

Aggregate the data in groups of 3, and create a control chart for the process mean. Use the chart to test the assumption that the production process is under control.

13–17. The following data are tensile strengths, in pounds, for a sample of string for industrial use made at a plant. Construct a control chart for the mean, using groups of 5 observations each. Test for statistical control of the process mean.

5, 6, 4, 6, 5, 7, 7, 7, 6, 5, 3, 5, 5, 5, 6, 5, 5, 6, 7, 7, 7, 7, 6, 7, 5,
5, 5, 6, 7, 7, 7, 7, 7, 5, 5, 6, 4, 6, 6, 6, 7, 6, 6, 6, 6, 6, 7, 5, 7, 6

13–5   The *R* Chart and the *s* Chart

In addition to the process mean, we want to control the process variance. When the variation in the production process is high, produced items will have a wider range of values, and this jeopardizes the product's quality. Recall also that in general we want as small a variance as possible. As noted earlier, it is advisable first to check the process variance and then to check its mean. Two charts are commonly used to achieve this aim. The more frequently used of the two is a control chart for the process range, called the **R chart.** The other is a control chart for the process standard deviation, the **s chart.** A third chart is a chart for the actual variance, called the s^2 chart, but we will not discuss it since it is the least frequently used of the three.

The R *Chart*

Like the $\bar{x}$ chart, the R chart contains a centerline and upper and lower control limits. One would expect the limits to be of the form

$$\bar{R} \pm 3\sigma_{\bar{R}} \qquad (13\text{--}2)$$

CHAPTER 21

But the distribution of R is not normal and hence the limits need not be symmetric. Additionally, the lower limit cannot go below zero and is therefore bounded by zero. With these considerations in mind, the limits are calculated using the formulas in the box below, where the constants D_3 and D_4 are obtained from Table 13 of Appendix C. Notice that the constant D_3 is bounded below at zero for small samples.

> The elements of an *R* chart:
>
> Centerline: $\bar{R}$
>
> LCL: $D_3\bar{R}$
>
> UCL: $D_4\bar{R}$
>
> where $\bar{R}$ is the sum of group ranges, divided by the number of groups.

Returning to Example 13–1, we find that $\bar{R} = 0.501$, and from Table 13, $D_3 = 0$ and $D_4 = 2.574$. Thus, the centerline is 0.501, the lower control limit is 0, and the upper control limit is $(0.501)(2.574) = 1.29$. Figure 13–6 gives the control chart for the process range for this example.

The test for control in the case of the process range is just to look for at least one observation outside the bounds. Based on the R chart for Example 13–1, we conclude that the process range seems to be in control.

The s *Chart*

The R chart is in common use because it is easier (by hand) to compute ranges than to compute standard deviations. Today (as compared with the 1920s, when these

FIGURE 13–6 The *R* Chart for Example 13–1
[Control Charts.xls; Sheet: X-bar R s charts]

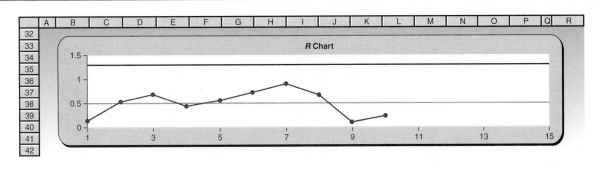

FIGURE 13–7 The *s* Chart for Example 13–1
[Control Charts.xls; Sheet: X-bar R s charts]

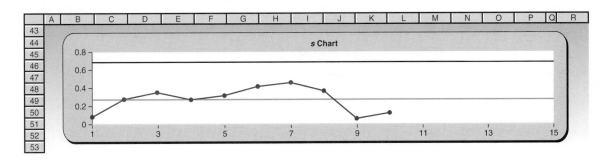

charts were invented), computers are usually used to create control charts, and an *s* chart should be at least as good as an *R* chart. We note, however, that the standard deviation suffers from the same nonnormality (skewness) as does the range. Again, symmetric bounds as suggested by equation 13–2, with *s* replacing *R*, are still used. The control chart for the process standard deviation is similar to that for the range. Here we use constants B_3 and B_4, also found in Appendix C, Table 13. The bounds and the centerline are given in the following box.

Elements of the *s* chart:

Centerline: $\bar{s}$

LCL: $B_3\bar{s}$

UCL: $B_4\bar{s}$

where $\bar{s}$ is the sum of group standard deviations, divided by the number of groups.

The *s* chart for Example 13–1 is given in Figure 13–7.

Again, we note that the process standard deviation seems to be in control. Since *s* charts are done by computer, we will not carry out the computations of the standard deviations of all the groups.

FIGURE 13–8   The Charts for Example 13–2
[Control Charts.xls; Sheet: X-bar R s charts]

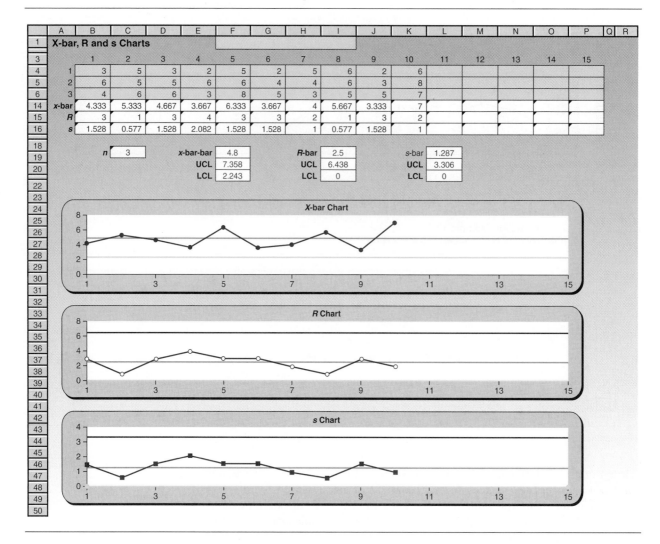

EXAMPLE 13–2

The nation's largest retailer wants to make sure that supplier delivery times are under control. Consistent supply times are critical factors in forecasting. The actual number of days it took each of the 30 suppliers to deliver goods last month is grouped into 10 sets in Figure 13–8.

PROBLEMS

13–18.   Why do we need a control chart for the process range?

13–19.   Compare and contrast the control charts for the process range and the process standard deviation.

13–20.   What are the limitations of symmetric LCL and UCL? Under what conditions are symmetric bounds impossible in practice?

13–21.   Create R and s charts for problem 13–14. Is the process in control?

13–22.   Create R and s charts for problem 13–16. Is the process in control?

13–23.   Create R and s charts for problem 13–17. Is the process in control?

13-24. Create X-bar, R, and s charts for the following data on the diameter of pins produced by an automatic lathe. The data summarize 12 samples of size 5 each, obtained at random on 12 different days. Is the process in control? If it is not, remove the sample that is out of control and redraw the charts.

1	2	3	4	5	6	7	8	9	10	11	12
1.300	1.223	1.310	1.221	1.244	1.253	1.269	1.325	1.306	1.255	1.221	1.268
1.207	1.232	1.290	1.218	1.206	1.289	1.318	1.285	1.288	1.260	1.256	1.208
1.287	1.289	1.255	1.200	1.294	1.279	1.270	1.301	1.243	1.296	1.245	1.207
1.237	1.310	1.317	1.273	1.302	1.303	1.224	1.315	1.288	1.270	1.239	1.218
1.258	1.228	1.260	1.219	1.269	1.229	1.224	1.224	1.238	1.307	1.265	1.238

13-25. The capacity of the fuel tank of the 2007 Volvo S40 is designed to be 12.625 gallons. The actual capacity of tanks produced is controlled using a control chart. The data of 9 random samples of size 5 each collected on 9 different days are tabulated below. Draw X-bar, R, and s charts. Is the process in control? If it is not, remove the sample that is out of control, and redraw the charts.

1	2	3	4	5	6	7	8	9
12.667	12.600	12.599	12.607	12.738	12.557	12.646	12.710	12.529
12.598	12.711	12.583	12.524	12.605	12.745	12.647	12.627	12.725
12.685	12.653	12.515	12.718	12.640	12.626	12.651	12.605	12.306
12.700	12.703	12.653	12.615	12.653	12.694	12.607	12.648	12.551
12.722	12.579	12.599	12.554	12.507	12.574	12.589	12.545	12.600

13-26. The amount of mineral water filled in 2-liter bottles by an automatic bottling machine is monitored using a control chart. The actual contents of random samples of 4 bottles collected on 8 different days are tabulated below. Draw X-bar, R, and s charts. Is the process in control? If it is not, remove the sample that is out of control, and redraw the charts.

1	2	3	4	5	6	7	8
2.015	2.006	1.999	1.983	2.000	1.999	2.011	1.983
2.012	1.983	1.988	2.008	2.016	1.982	1.983	1.991
2.001	1.996	2.012	1.999	2.016	1.997	1.983	1.989
2.019	2.003	2.015	1.999	1.988	2.005	2.000	1.998
2.018	1.981	2.004	2.005	1.986	2.017	2.006	1.990

13-6 The p Chart

The example of a quality control problem used most frequently throughout the book has been that of controlling the proportion of defective items in a production process. This, indeed, is the topic of this section. Here we approach the problem by using a control chart.

The number of defective items in a random sample chosen from a population has a binomial distribution: the number of successes x out of a number of trials n with a constant probability of success p in each trial. The parameter p is the proportion of defective items in the population. If the sample size n is fixed in repeated samplings, then the sample proportion $\hat{P}$ derives its distribution from a binomial distribution. Recall that the binomial distribution is symmetric when $p = 0.5$, and it is skewed for other values of p. By the central limit theorem, as n increases, the distribution of $\hat{P}$ approaches a normal distribution. Thus, a normal approximation to the binomial should work well with large sample sizes; a relatively small sample size would suffice if $p = 0.5$ because of the symmetry of the binomial in this case.

The chart for p is called the **p chart**. Using the normal approximation, we want bounds of the form

$$\hat{p} \pm 3\sigma_{\hat{p}} \qquad (13\text{–}3)$$

The idea is, again, that the probability of a sample proportion falling outside the bounds is small when the process is under control. When the process is not under control, the proportion of defective or nonconforming items will tend to exceed the upper bound of the control chart. The lower bound is sometimes zero, which happens when $\hat{p}$ is sufficiently small. Being at the lower bound of zero defectives is, of course, a very good occurrence.

Recall that the sample proportion $\hat{p}$ is given by the number of defectives x, divided by the sample size n. We estimate the population proportion p by the total number of defectives in all the samples of size n we have obtained, divided by the entire sample size (all the items in all our samples). This is denoted by $\bar{p}$, and it serves as the centerline of the chart. Also recall that the standard deviation of this statistic is given by

$$\sqrt{\frac{\bar{p}(1-\bar{p})}{n}}$$

Thus, the control chart for the proportion of defective items is given in the following box. The process is believed to be out of control when at least one sample proportion falls outside the bounds.

> The elements of a control chart for the process proportion:
>
> Centerline: $\bar{p}$
>
> LCL: $\bar{p} - 3\sqrt{\dfrac{\bar{p}(1-\bar{p})}{n}}$
>
> UCL: $\bar{p} + 3\sqrt{\dfrac{\bar{p}(1-\bar{p})}{n}}$
>
> where n is the number of items in each sample and $\bar{p}$ is the proportion of defectives in the combined, overall sample.

The Template

The template for drawing p charts can be seen in Figure 13–9. Example 13–3 demonstrates use of the template.

EXAMPLE 13–3

The French tire manufacturer Michelin randomly samples 40 tires at the end of each shift to test for tires that are defective. The number of defectives in 12 shifts is as follows: 4, 2, 0, 5, 2, 3, 14, 2, 3, 4, 12, 3. Construct a control chart for this process. Is the production process under control?

FIGURE 13–9   **The Template for *p* Charts**
[Control Charts.xls; Sheet: p Chart]

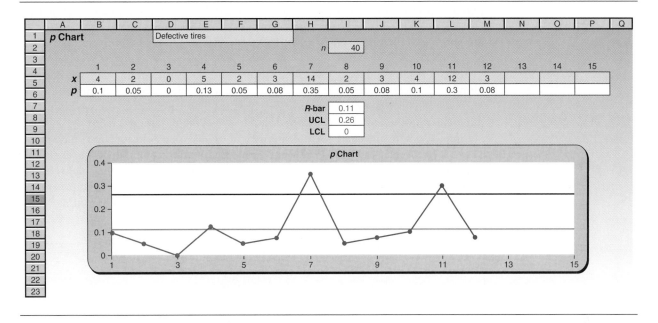

The results are shown in Figure 13–9. Our estimate of p, the centerline, is the sum of all the defective tires, divided by 40×12. It is $\bar{p} = 0.1125$. Our standard error of $\bar{p}$ is $\sqrt{\bar{p}(1 - \bar{p})/n} = 0.05$; thus, LCL $= 0.1125 - 3(0.05) = -0.0375$, which means that the LCL should be 0. Similarly, UCL $= 0.1125 + 3(0.05) = 0.2625$.

Solution

As we can see from the figure, two sample proportions are outside the UCL. These correspond to the samples with 14 and 12 defective tires, respectively. There is ample evidence that the production process is out of control.

PROBLEMS

13–27. The manufacturer of steel rods used in the construction of a new nuclear reactor in Shansi Province in China in Spring 2007 looks at random samples of 20 items from each production shift and notes the number of nonconforming rods in these samples. The results of 10 shifts are 8, 7, 8, 9, 6, 7, 8, 6, 6, 8. Is there evidence that the process is out of control? Explain.

13–28. A battery manufacturer looks at samples of 30 batteries at the end of every day of production and notes the number of defective batteries. Results are 1, 1, 0, 0, 1, 2, 0, 1, 0, 0, 2, 5, 0, 1. Is the production process under control?

13–29. BASF Inc. makes CDs for use in computers. A quality control engineer at the plant tests batches of 50 disks at a time and plots the proportions of defective disks on a control chart. The first 10 batches used to create the chart had the following numbers of defective disks: 8, 7, 6, 7, 8, 4, 3, 5, 5, 8. Construct the chart and interpret the results.

13–30. If the proportion of defective items in a production process of specially designed carburetors used in a limited-edition model Maserati introduced in 2007 is very small, and few items are tested in each batch, what problems do you foresee? Explain.

13–7   The c Chart

Often in production activities we want to control the *number of defects or imperfections per item*. When fabric is woven, for example, the manufacturer may keep a record of the number of blemishes per yard and take corrective action when this number is out of control.

Recall from Chapter 3 that the random variable representing the count of the number of errors occurring in a fixed time or space is often modeled using the *Poisson distribution*. This is the model we use here. For the Poisson distribution, we know that the mean and the variance are both equal to the same parameter. Here we call that parameter c, and our chart for the number of defects per item (or yard, etc.) is the **c chart**. In this chart we plot a random variable, the number of defects per item. We estimate c by $\bar{c}$, which is the average number of defects per item, the total number averaged over all the items we have. The standard deviation of the random variable is thus the square root of c. Now, the Poisson distribution can be approximated by the normal distribution for large c, and this again suggests the form

$$\bar{c} \pm 3\sqrt{\bar{c}} \qquad\qquad (13\text{–}4)$$

Equation 13–4 leads to the control bounds and centerline given in the box that follows.

Elements of the c chart:

Centerline: $\bar{c}$

LCL: $\bar{c} - 3\sqrt{\bar{c}}$

UCL: $\bar{c} + 3\sqrt{\bar{c}}$

where $\bar{c}$ is the average number of defects or imperfections per item (or area, volume, etc.).

The Template

The template that produces c charts can be seen in Figure 13–10. We shall see the use of the template through Example 13–4.

EXAMPLE 13–4

The following data are the numbers of nonconformities in bolts for use in cars made by the Ford Motor Company:[6] 9, 15, 11, 8, 17, 11, 5, 11, 13, 7, 10, 12, 4, 3, 7, 2, 3, 3, 6, 2, 7, 9, 1, 5, 8. Is there evidence that the process is out of control?

Solution

We need to find the mean number of nonconformities per item. This is the sum of the numbers, divided by 25, or 7.56. The standard deviation of the statistic is the square root of this number, or 2.75, and the control limits are obtained as shown in the box. Figure 13–10 gives the template solution.

---

[6]From T. P. Ryan, *Statistical Methods for Quality Improvement* (New York: Wiley, 1989), p. 198.

FIGURE 13–10   **The Template for *c* Charts**
                [Control Charts.xls; Sheet: c Chart]

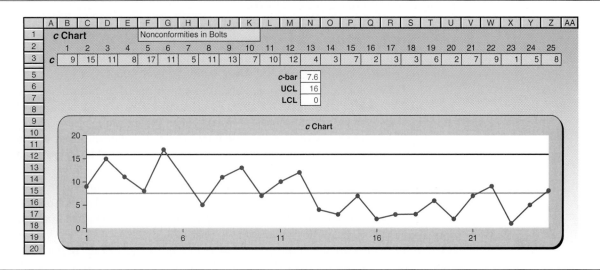

From the figure we see that one observation is outside the upper control limit, indicating that the production process may be out of control. We also note a general downward trend, which should be investigated (maybe the process is improving).

PROBLEMS

13–31.   The following are the numbers of imperfections per yard of yarn produced in a mill in Pennsylvania in May 2007: 5, 3, 4, 8, 2, 3, 1, 2, 5, 9, 2, 2, 2, 3, 4, 2, 1. Is there evidence that the process is out of control?

13–32.   The following are the numbers of blemishes in the coat of paint of new automobiles made by Ford in June 2007: 12, 25, 13, 20, 5, 22, 8, 17, 31, 40, 9, 62, 14, 16, 9, 28. Is there evidence that the painting process is out of control?

13–33.   The following are the numbers of imperfections in rolls of wallpaper made by Laura Ashley: 5, 6, 3, 4, 5, 2, 7, 4, 5, 3, 5, 5, 3, 2, 0, 5, 5, 6, 7, 6, 9, 3, 3, 4, 2, 6. Construct a *c* chart for the process, and determine whether there is evidence that the process is out of control.

13–34.   What are the assumptions underlying the use of the *c* chart?

13–8   The *x* Chart

Sometimes we are interested in controlling the process mean, but our observations come so slowly from the production process that we cannot aggregate them into groups. In such a case, and in other situations as well, we may consider an **x chart**. An *x* chart is a chart for the raw values of the variable in question.

As you may guess, the chart is effective if the variable in question has a distribution that is close to normal. We want to have the bounds as mean of the process ± 3 standard deviations of the process. The mean is estimated by $\bar{x}$, and the standard deviation is estimated by s/c_4.

The tests for special causes in Table 13–1 can be used in conjunction with an *x* chart as well. Case 17 at the end of this chapter will give you an opportunity to study an actual *x* chart using all these tests.

13–9   Using the Computer

Using MINITAB for Quality Control

MINITAB offers many tools to help you detect and eliminate quality problems. MINITAB's quality tools can assist with a wide variety of tasks, for example, control charts, Pareto charts, and capability analysis. To look for any evidence of patterns in your process data you can choose Stat ▶ Quality Tools ▶ Run Chart from the menu bar. Run Chart plots all of the individual observations versus their number. You can also choose Stat ▶ Quality Tools ▶ Pareto Chart to plot a Pareto chart. Pareto charts can help focus improvement efforts on areas where the largest gains can be made.

MINITAB draws a wide variety of control charts by choosing Stat ▶ Control Charts from the menu bar. One of the available options is Variables control charts, which creates control charts for measurement data in subgroups. Let's start by selecting Stat ▶ Control Charts ▶ Variables Charts for Subgroups ▶ Xbar-R from the menu bar to display a control chart for subgroup means (an X chart) and a control chart for subgroup ranges (an R chart) in the same graph window. The X chart is drawn in the upper half of the screen; the R chart in the lower half. By default, MINITAB's X and R Chart bases the estimate of the process variation, σ, on the average of the subgroup ranges. You can also use a pooled standard deviation or enter a historical value for σ, as we will describe later. When the Xbar-R Chart dialog box appears choose whether the data are in one or more columns and then enter the columns. Enter a number or a column of subscripts in the Subgroup sizes edit box. If subgroups are arranged in rows across several columns, choose Observations for a subgroup are in one row of columns and enter the columns. The Multiple Graphs button controls the placement and scales of multiple control charts. Click on the Data Options button to include or exclude rows when creating a graph. Click on the Xbar-R button. When the corresponding dialog box appears, you can enter the historical data for estimating σ and μ in the Parameters tab. If you do not specify a value for σ or μ, MINITAB estimates it from the data. In the Estimate tab you can omit or include certain subgroups to estimate σ and μ. You can also select one of two methods to estimate σ. In the Test tab select a subset of the tests to detect a specific pattern in the data plotted on the chart. MINITAB marks the point that fails a test with the test number on the plot. In cases at which a point fails more than one test, MINITAB marks it by the lowest numbered test. As an example, we have used MINITAB Xbar-R tool to plot the control charts for the data of Example 13–1. Figure 13–11 shows the corresponding dialog box, Session commands, and the obtained control charts. As you can see in this example, subgroups have been arranged in rows across several columns.

You can also choose Stat ▶ Control Charts ▶ Variables Charts for Subgroups ▶ Xbar-S to display a control chart for subgroup means (an X chart) and a control chart for subgroup standard deviations (an S chart) in the same graph window. The X chart is drawn in the upper half of the screen; the S chart in the lower half. By default, MINITAB's X and S Chart command bases the estimate of the process variation, s, on the average of the subgroup standard deviations. You can also use a pooled standard deviation or enter a historical value for s. Required settings for the corresponding dialog box are the same as those we discussed for an Xbar-R control chart. Choosing Stat ▶ Control Charts ▶ Variables Charts for Subgroups also provides you with three other options for constructing Xbar, R, and S control charts separately.

To construct a P chart or a C chart using MINITAB you need to choose Stat ▶ Control Charts ▶ Attributes Charts from menu bar. Attributes control charts plot statistics from count data rather than measurement data. MINITAB control charts for defectives are the P Chart and NP Chart. P Chart shows the proportion of defectives in each subgroup, while NP Chart shows the number of defectives in each subgroup. In addition, MINITAB provides you with two other charts that can be used for classifying a product by its number of defects. The control charts for defects are the C Chart and U Chart. The former charts the number of defects in each subgroup, while the latter

FIGURE 13–11 Xbar-R Control Chart Using MINITAB

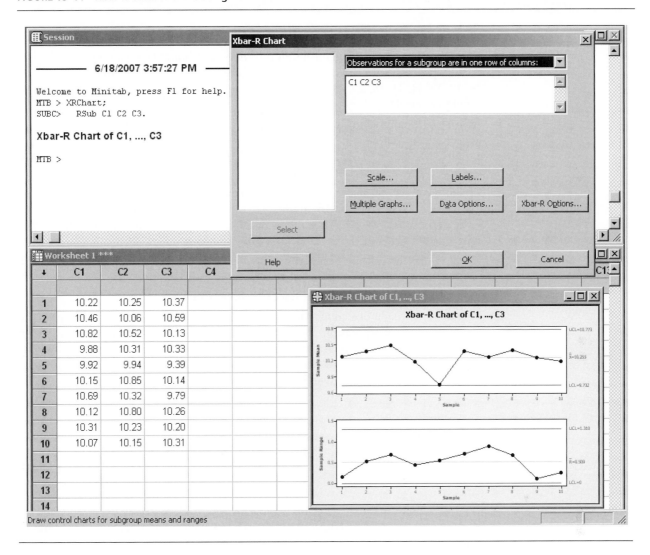

charts the number of defects per unit sampled in each subgroup. U Chart is used when the subgroup size varies. The corresponding dialog boxes and required settings are very similar to what we have discussed for the Xbar-R control chart.

13–10 Summary and Review of Terms

Quality control and improvement is a fast-growing, important area of application of statistics in both production and services. We discussed **Pareto diagrams,** which are relatively simple graphical ways of looking at problems in production. We discussed quality control in general and how it relates to statistical theory and hypothesis testing. We mentioned **process capability** and **Deming's 14 points.** Then we described **control charts,** graphical methods of determining when there is evidence that a process is out of statistical control. The control chart has a **centerline,** an **upper control limit,** and a **lower control limit.** The process is believed to be out of control when one of the limits is breached at least once. The control charts we discussed were the $\bar{x}$ **chart,** for the mean; the **R chart,** for the range; the **s chart,** for the standard deviation; the **p chart,** for the proportion; the **c chart,** for the number of defects per item; and the **x chart,** a chart of individual observations for controlling the process mean.

13–35. Discuss and compare the various control charts discussed in this chapter.

13–36. The number of blemishes in rolls of Scotch brand tape coming out of a production process at a plant of the 3M Company in Minnesota is as follows: 17, 12, 13, 18, 12, 13, 14, 11, 18, 29, 13, 13, 15, 16. Is there evidence that the production process is out of control?

13–37. The number of defective items out of random samples of 100 windshield wipers selected at the end of each production shift at a factory is as follows: 4, 4, 5, 4, 4, 6, 6, 3, 3, 3, 3, 2, 2, 4, 5, 3, 4, 6, 4, 12, 2, 2, 0, 1, 1, 1, 2, 3, 1. Is there evidence that the production process is out of control?

13–38. Weights of pieces of tile made in Arizona in April 2007 (in ounces) are as follows: 2.5, 2.66, 2.8, 2.3, 2.5, 2.33, 2.41, 2.88, 2.54, 2.11, 2.26, 2.3, 2.41, 2.44, 2.17, 2.52, 2.55, 2.38, 2.89, 2.9, 2.11, 2.12, 2.13, 2.16. Create an R chart for these data, using subgroups of size 4. Is the process variation under control?

13–39. Use the data in problem 13–38 to create an $\bar{x}$ chart to test whether the process mean is under control.

13–40. Create an s chart for the data in problem 13–38.

13–41. The weight of a connecting rod used in a diesel engine made at a plant of the General Motors Corporation needs to be strictly uniform to minimize vibrations in the engine. The connecting rod is produced by a forging process. Every day, five rods coming out of the process are selected at random and weighed. The data for 10 days' samples in early 2007 are given below.

	1	2	3	4	5	6	7	8	9	10
1	577	579	576	579	577	579	579	577	577	584
2	577	580	580	580	580	576	578	579	579	580
3	579	578	580	580	578	578	580	578	579	582
4	580	580	579	578	580	577	578	579	577	579
5	578	580	576	577	578	578	577	580	576	580

On the 10th day, the supervisor stopped the process, declaring it out of control. Prepare one or more appropriate control charts and test whether the process is indeed out of control.

CASE 17 Quality Control and Improvement at Nashua Corporation

In 1979, Nashua Corporation, with an increasing awareness of the importance of always maintaining and improving quality, invited Dr. W. Edwards Deming for a visit and a consultation. Dr. Deming, then almost 80 years old, was the most sought-after quality guru in the United States.

Following many suggestions by Deming, Nashua hired Dr. Lloyd S. Nelson the following year as director of statistical methods. The idea was to teach everyone at the company about quality and how it can be maintained and improved by using statistics.

Dr. Nelson instituted various courses and workshops lasting 4 to 10 weeks for all the employees. Workers on the shop floor became familiar with statistical process control (SPC) charts and their use in maintaining and improving quality. Nashua uses individual x charts as well as $\bar{x}$, R, and p charts. These are among the most commonly used SPC charts today. Here we will consider the x chart. This chart is used when values come slowly, as in the following example, and taking the time to form the subgroups necessary for an $\bar{x}$ or R chart is not practical.

Among the many products Nashua makes is thermally responsive paper, which is used in printers and recording instruments. The paper is coated with a chemical mixture that is sensitive to heat, thus producing marks in a printer or instrument when heat is applied by a print head or stylus. The variable of interest is the amount of material coated on the paper (the *weight coat*). Large rolls, some as long as 35,000 feet, are coated, and samples are taken from the ends of the rolls. A template 12 × 18 inches is used in cutting through four layers of the paper—first from an area that was coated and second from an uncoated area. A gravimetric comparison of the coated and uncoated samples gives four measurements of the weight coat. The average of these is the individual *x* value for that roll.

Assume that 12 rolls are coated per shift and that each roll is tested as described above. For two shifts, the 24 values of weight coat, in pounds per 3,000 square feet, were

3.46, 3.56, 3.58, 3.49, 3.45, 3.51, 3.54, 3.48, 3.54, 3.49, 3.55, 3.60, 3.62, 3.60, 3.53, 3.60, 3.51, 3.54, 3.60, 3.61, 3.49, 3.60, 3.60, 3.49.

Exhibit 1 shows the individual control chart for this process, using all 24 values to calculate the limits. Is the production process in statistical control? Explain. Discuss any possible actions or solutions.

We are indebted to Dr. Lloyd S. Nelson of Nashua Corporation for providing us with this interesting and instructive case.

EXHIBIT 1   Standardized *x* Chart

SAMPLE NO.	WEIGHT COAT
1.	3.46
2.	3.56
3.	3.58
4.	3.49
5.	3.45
6.	3.51
7.	3.54
8.	3.48
9.	3.54
10.	3.49
11.	3.55
12.	3.60
13.	3.62
14.	3.60
15.	3.53
16.	3.60
17.	3.51
18.	3.54
19.	3.60
20.	3.61
21.	3.49
22.	3.60
23.	3.60
24.	3.49

x - bar equals 3.54333

s (est sigma) = 5.12725e - 2

14

NONPARAMETRIC METHODS AND CHI-SQUARE TESTS

14–1 Using Statistics 621

14–2 The Sign Test 621

14–3 The Runs Test—A Test for Randomness 626

14–4 The Mann-Whitney *U* Test 633

14–5 The Wilcoxon Signed-Rank Test 639

14–6 The Kruskal-Wallis Test—A Nonparametric Alternative to One-Way ANOVA 645

14–7 The Friedman Test for a Randomized Block Design 653

14–8 The Spearman Rank Correlation Coefficient 657

14–9 A Chi-Square Test for Goodness of Fit 661

14–10 Contingency Table Analysis—A Chi-Square Test for Independence 669

14–11 A Chi-Square Test for Equality of Proportions 675

14–12 Using the Computer 680

14–13 Summary and Review of Terms 682

Case 18 The Nine Nations of North America 684

LEARNING OBJECTIVES

After studying this chapter, you should be able to:

- Differentiate between parametric and nonparametric tests.
- Conduct a sign test to compare population means.
- Conduct a runs test to detect abnormal sequences.
- Conduct a Mann-Whitney test for comparing population distributions.
- Conduct a Wilcoxon test for paired differences.
- Conduct a Friedman test for randomized block designs.
- Compute Spearman's rank correlation coefficient for ordinal data.
- Conduct a chi-square test for goodness of fit.
- Conduct a chi-square test for independence.
- Conduct a chi-square test for equality of proportions.

14–1 Using Statistics

An article in *Technical Analysis of Stocks and Commodities* discussed the many definitions of the business cycle. According to the Kondratieff definition, the U.S. business cycle is 54 years long.[1] Research on aspects of the economy and the stock and commodity markets that employ this definition–rather than definitions of a business cycle lasting only four or five years–face a serious statistical problem. Since most models of the economy consider its behavior after World War II, a 54-year cycle would imply at most two postwar peaks. Thus a researcher would be left with only two data points in studying postwar peak-cycle behavior. This is a real example of the fact that a statistical analyst is sometimes constrained by having few data points.

Although two observations is not enough for any meaningful analysis, this chapter will teach you how to perform a statistical analysis when at least some of the requirements of the standard statistical methods are not met. Nonparametric methods are alternative statistical methods of analysis in such cases.

Many hypothesis-testing situations have nonparametric alternatives to be used when the usual assumptions we make are not met. In other situations, nonparametric methods offer *unique* solutions to problems at hand. Because a nonparametric test usually requires fewer assumptions and uses less information in the data, it is often said that *a parametric procedure is an exact solution to an approximate problem,* whereas *a nonparametric procedure is an approximate solution to an exact problem.*

In short, we define a **nonparametric method** as one that satisfies at least one of the following criteria.

1. The method deals with *enumerative data* (data that are frequency counts).
2. The method *does not deal with specific population parameters* such as μ or σ.
3. The method *does not require assumptions about specific population distributions* (in particular, the assumption of normality).

Since nonparametric methods require fewer assumptions than do parametric ones, the methods are useful when the scale of measurement is weaker than required for parametric methods. As we will refer to different measurement scales, you may want to review Section 1–7 at this point.

14–2 The Sign Test

In Chapter 8, we discussed statistical methods of comparing the means of two populations. There we used the *t* test, which required the assumption that the populations were normally distributed with equal variance. In many situations, one or both of these assumptions are not satisfied. In some situations, it may not even be possible to make exact measurements except for determining the relative magnitudes of the observations. In such cases, the **sign test** is a good alternative. The sign test is also useful in testing for a trend in a series of ordinal values and in testing for a correlation, as we will see soon.

[1]Martha Stokes, "The Missing Cycle," *Technical Analysis of Stocks and Commodities,* April 2007, p. 19.

As a test for comparing two populations, the sign test is stated in terms of the probability that values of one population are greater than values of a second population that are paired with the first in some way. For example, we may be interested in testing whether consumer responses to one advertisement are about the same as responses to a second advertisement. We would take a random sample of consumers, show them both ads, and ask them to rank the ads on some scale. For each person in our sample, we would then have two responses: one response for each advertisement. The null hypothesis is that the probability that a consumer's response to one ad will be greater than his or her response to the other ad is equal to 0.50. The alternative hypothesis is that the probability is not 0.50. Note that these null and alternative hypotheses are more general than those of the analogous parametric test—the paired-t test—which is stated in terms of the means of the two populations. When the two populations under study are symmetric, the test is equivalent to a test of the equality of two means, like the parametric t test. As stated, however, the sign test is more general and requires fewer assumptions.

We define p as the probability that X will be greater than Y, where X is the value from population 1 and Y is the value from population 2. Thus,

$$p = P(X > Y) \tag{14–1}$$

The test could be a two-tailed test, or a one-tailed test in either direction. Under the null hypothesis, X is as likely to exceed Y as Y is to exceed X: The probability of either occurrence is 0.50. We leave out the possibility of a tie, that is, the possibility that $X = Y$. When we gather our random sample of observations, we denote every pair (X, Y) where X is greater than Y by a plus sign $(+)$, and we denote every pair where Y is greater than X by a minus sign $(-)$ (hence the name *sign test*). In terms of signs, the null hypothesis is that the probability of a plus sign [that is, $P(X > Y)$] is equal to the probability of a minus sign [that is, $P(X < Y)$], and both are equal to 0.50. These are the possible hypothesis tests:

Possible hypotheses for the sign test:

Two-tailed test

$$H_0: p = 0.50$$
$$H_1: p \neq 0.50 \tag{14–2}$$

Right-tailed test

$$H_0: p \leq 0.50$$
$$H_1: p > 0.50 \tag{14–3}$$

Left-tailed test

$$H_0: p \geq 0.50$$
$$H_1: p < 0.50 \tag{14–4}$$

The test assumes that the pairs of (X, Y) values are independent and that the measurement scale within each pair is at least *ordinal*. After discarding any ties, we are left

FIGURE 14–1 The Template for the Sign Test
[Nonparametric.xls; Sheet: Sign]

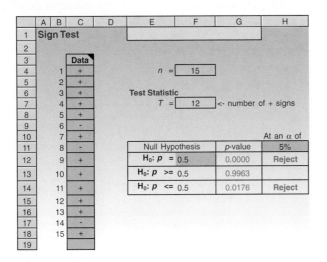

with the number of plus signs and the number of minus signs. These are used in defining the test statistic.

> The test statistic is
> $$T = \text{number of plus signs} \qquad (14\text{–}5)$$

Suppose the null hypothesis is $p \leq 0.5$, which makes it a right-tailed test. Then the larger the T, the more unfavorable it would be to the null hypothesis. The p-value[2] is therefore the binomial probability of observing a value greater than or equal to the observed T. The calculation of a binomial probability requires two parameters, n and p. The value of n used is the sample size minus the tied cases, and the value of p used is 0.5 (which gives the maximum benefit of doubt to the null hypothesis).

If the null hypothesis is $p \geq 0.5$, which makes it a left-tailed test, the p-value is the probability of observing a value less than or equal to the observed T. If the null hypothesis is $p = 0.5$, which makes it a two-tailed test, the p-value is twice the tail area.

Figure 14–1 shows the template that can be used for conducting a sign test. Its use will be illustrated in Example 14–1.

EXAMPLE 14–1

According to a recent survey of 220 chief executive officers (CEOs) of *Fortune 1000* companies, 18.3% of the CEOs in these firms hold MBA degrees. A management consultant wants to test whether there are differences in attitude toward CEOs who hold MBA degrees. In order to control for extraneous factors affecting attitudes toward different CEOs, the consultant designed a study that recorded the attitudes toward the same group of 19 CEOs before and after these people completed an MBA program. The consultant had no prior intention of proving one kind of

[2]Unfortunately, we cannot avoid using the p symbol in two different senses. Take care not to confuse the two senses.

attitudinal change; she believed it was possible that the attitude toward a CEO could change for the better, change for the worse, or not change at all following the completion of an MBA program. Therefore, the consultant decided to use the following two-tailed test.

> H_0: There is no change in attitude toward a CEO following his or her being awarded an MBA degree

versus

> H_1: There is a change in attitude toward a CEO following the award of an MBA degree

The consultant defined variable X_i as the attitude toward CEO i before receipt of the MBA degree, as rated by his or her professional associates on a scale of 1 to 5 (5 being highest). Similarly, she defined Y_i as the attitude toward CEO i following receipt of the MBA degree, as rated by his or her professional associates on the same scale.

Solution In this framework, the null and alternative hypotheses may be stated in terms of the probability that the attitude score *after* (Y) is greater than the attitude *before* (X). The null hypothesis is that the probability that the attitude after receipt of the degree is higher than the attitude before is 0.50 (i.e., the attitude is as likely to improve as it is to become worse, where *worse* means a lower numerical score). The alternative hypothesis is that the probability is not 0.50 (i.e., the attitude is likely to change in one or the other direction). The null and alternative hypotheses can now be stated in the form of equation 14–2:

> H_1: $p \neq 0.50$

versus

> H_0: $p = 0.50$

The consultant looked at her data of general attitude scores toward the 17 randomly chosen CEOs both before and after these CEOs received their MBAs. Data are given in Table 14–1. The first thing to note is that there are two ties: for CEOs 2 and 5. We thus remove these two from our data set and reduce the sample size to $n = 15$. We now (arbitrarily) define a plus sign to be any data point where the after-attitude score is greater than the before score. In terms of plus and minus symbols, the data in Table 14–1 are as follows:

> $+ \ + \ + \ + \ - \ + \ - \ + \ + \ + \ + \ + \ - \ +$

TABLE 14–1 Data for Example 14–1

CEO:	1	2	3	4	5	6	7	8	9	10	11	12	13	14	15	16	17
Attitude before:	3	5	2	2	4	2	1	5	4	5	3	2	2	2	1	3	4
Attitude after:	4	5	3	4	4	3	2	4	5	4	4	5	5	3	2	2	5

According to our definition of the test statistic (equation 14–5), we have

$$T = \text{number of pluses} = 12$$

We now carry out the statistical hypothesis test. From Appendix C, Table 1 (pages 755–757), the binomial table, we find for $p = 0.5$, $n = 15$ that the point $C_1 = 3$ corresponds to a "tail" probability of 0.018. That is, $F(3) = 0.018$. The p-value is 0.036. Since the rejection happened in the right-hand rejection region, the consultant may conclude that there is evidence that attitudes toward CEOs who recently received their MBA degrees have become more positive (as defined by the attitude test).

Figure 14–1 shows the same results obtained through the template. The data, entered in column C, should consist of only + and − symbols. All ties should be removed from the data before entry. The p-value for the null hypothesis $p = 0.5$ appears in cell G12; it is 0.0352. It is more accurate than the manually calculated 0.036. As seen in cell H12, the null hypothesis is rejected at an α of 5%.

The sign test can be viewed as a test of the hypothesis that the *median* difference between two populations is zero. As such, the test may be adapted for testing whether the median of a single population is equal to any prespecified number. The null and alternative hypotheses here are

$$H_0: \text{Population median} = a$$
$$H_1: \text{Population median} \neq a$$

where a is some number. One-tailed tests of this hypothesis are also possible, and the extension is straightforward.

To conduct the test, we pair our data observations with the null-hypothesis value of the median and perform the sign test. If the null hypothesis is true, then we expect that about one-half of the signs will be pluses and one-half minuses because, by the definition of the median, one-half of the population values are above it and one-half are below it.

Suppose that we wish to test the null hypothesis that median income in a certain region is $24,000 per family per year. The following random sample of family incomes is available (in thousands of dollars): 22, 30, 28, 22, 34, 19, 42, 18, 16, 26, 30, 25, 29, 20, 17, 33, 32, 24, 15, 31. In terms of + signs, − signs, and ties (t), the data are as follows when paired with the hypothesized median of 24: − + + − + − + − − + + + + − − + + t − +. (The choice of how to define a + versus a − is, again, arbitrary.) Discarding the single tie, we see that the number of plus signs is 11, and the sample size is $n = 19$.

Since 11 is more than the average of 9.5 ($= np = 19 * 0.5$), the tail area is to the right of 11. The tail area is the binomial probability $P(T \geq 11)$ with $n = 19$, $p = 0.5$. From the binomial template, this probability is 0.3238. The p-value is twice the tail area and therefore equal to $2 * 0.3238 = 0.6476$. Since this p-value is so large, we cannot reject the null hypothesis that the median equals 24.

14–1. An article in *Bloomberg Markets* compares returns for the Hermitage Fund with those of the Russian Trading System Index.[3] Paired data of rates of return for the two funds during 12 randomly chosen years are as follows:

Year	Hermitage	Russian Trading
1	12	15
2	15	10
3	12	7
4	17	12
5	8	8
6	7	11
7	21	16
8	13	7
9	15	17
10	22	12
11	17	15
12	25	19

Conduct the sign test for determining whether returns on the Hermitage Fund and the Russian Trading System Index are equal.

14–2. Breakstone Company makes whipped butter and whipped margarine. A company market analyst wanted to test whether people prefer the taste of one of these products over the other. A random sample of consumers was selected, and each one was asked to taste both the butter and the margarine and then to state a preference. The data follow. Is there evidence that one of the two products is preferred over the other? (M denotes margarine and B is for butter.) M B B B M B B M B B B B M M B M M M B B M B B M B B B B (no pref.) M B B B B (no pref.) M M M B M B B B B B M B

14–3. The median amount of accounts payable to a CVS retail outlet in May 2007 is believed to be $78.50. Conduct a test to assess whether this assumption is still true after several changes in company operations have taken place. A random sample of 30 accounts is collected. The data follow (in dollars):

34.12, 58.90, 73.25, 33.70, 69.00, 70.53, 12.68, 100.00, 82.55, 23.12, 57.55, 124.20, 89.60, 79.00, 150.13, 30.35, 42.45, 50.00, 90.25, 65.20, 22.28, 165.00, 120.00, 97.25, 78.45, 24.57, 12.11, 5.30, 234.00, 76.65

14–4. Biometrics is a technology that helps identify people by facial and body features and is used by banks to reduce fraud. If in 15 trials the machine correctly identified 10 people, test the hypothesis that the machine's identification rate is 50%.

14–5. The median age of a tourist to Aruba in the summer of 2007 was believed to be 41 years. A random sample of 18 tourists gives the following ages:

25, 19, 38, 52, 57, 39, 46, 46, 30, 49, 40, 27, 39, 44, 63, 31, 67, 42

Test the hypothesis against a two-tailed alternative using $\alpha = 0.05$.

14–3   The Runs Test—A Test for Randomness

In his well-known book *Introduction to Probability Theory and Its Applications* (New York: John Wiley & Sons, 1973), William Feller tells of noticing how people occupy bar stools. Let S denote an occupied seat and E an empty seat. Suppose that, entering a bar, you find the following sequence:

S E S E S E S E S E S E S E S E S E S E   (case 1)

---

[3]Stephanie Baker-Said, "Russia's Hedge Fund Outcast," *Bloomberg Markets,* July 2006, pp. 58–66.

Do you believe that this sequence was formed at random? Is it likely that the 10 seated persons took their seats by a random choice, or did they purposely make sure they sat at a distance of one seat away from their neighbors? Just looking at the perfect regularity of this sequence makes us doubt its randomness.

Let us now look at another way the people at the bar might have been occupying 10 out of 20 seats:

$$SSSSSSSSSSEEEEEEEEEE \qquad \text{(case 2)}$$

Is it likely that this sequence was formed at random? In this case, rather than perfect separation between people, there is a perfect clustering together. This, too, is a form of regularity not likely to have arisen by chance.

Let us now look at yet a third case:

$$SEESSEEESESSESEESSSE \qquad \text{(case 3)}$$

This last sequence seems more random. It is much more likely that this sequence was formed by chance than the sequences in cases 1 and 2. There does not seem to be any consistent regularity in the series in case 3.

What we feel intuitively about order versus randomness in these cases can indeed be quantified. There is a statistical test that can help us determine whether we believe that a sequence of symbols, items, or numbers resulted from a random process. The statistical test for randomness depends on the concept of a *run*.

A **run** is a sequence of like elements that are preceded and followed by different elements or no element at all.

Using the symbols S and E, Figure 14–2 demonstrates the definition of a run by showing all runs in a particular sequence of symbols. There are seven runs in the sequence of elements in Figure 14–2.

Applying the definition of runs to cases 1, 2, and 3, we see that case 1 has 20 runs in a sequence of 20 elements! This is clearly the largest possible number of runs. The sequence in case 2 has only two runs (the smallest possible number). In the first case, there are too many runs, and in the second case, there are too few runs for randomness to be a probable generator of the process. Case 3 has 12 runs—neither too few nor too many. This sequence could very well have been generated by a random process. To quantify how many runs are acceptable before we begin to doubt the randomness of the process, we use a probability distribution. This distribution leads to a *statistical test for randomness.*

Let us call the number of elements of one kind (S) n_1 and the number of elements of the second kind (E) n_2. The total sample size is $n = n_1 + n_2$. In all three cases, both n_1 and n_2 are equal to 10. For a given pair (n_1, n_2) and a given number of runs, Appendix C, Table 8 (pages 778–779), gives the probability that the number of runs will be less than or equal to the given number (i.e., left-hand "tail" probabilities).

FIGURE 14–2 **Examples of Runs**

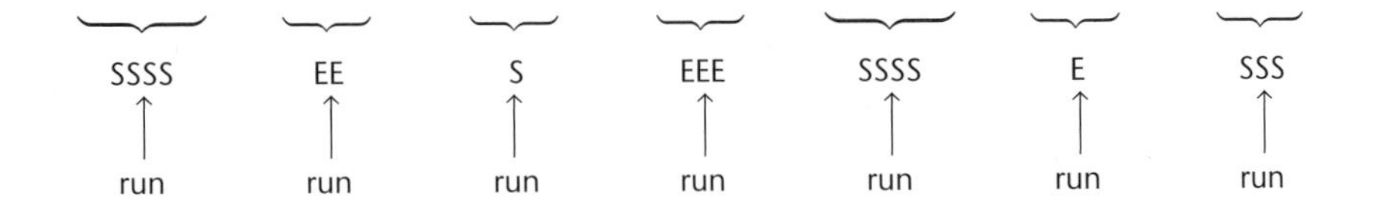

SSSS	EE	S	EEE	SSSS	E	SSS
↑	↑	↑	↑	↑	↑	↑
run	run	run	run	run	run	run

Based on our example, look at the row in Table 8 corresponding to $(n_1, n_2) =$ (10, 10). We find that the probability that four or fewer runs will occur is 0.001; the probability that five or fewer will occur is 0.004; the probability that six or fewer runs will occur is 0.019; and so on.

The logic of the test for randomness is as follows. We know the probabilities of obtaining any number of runs, and if we obtain an extreme number of runs—too many or too few—we will decide that the elements in our sequence were not generated in a random fashion.

A two-tailed hypothesis test for randomness:

H_0: Observations are generated randomly

H_1: Observations are not randomly generated   (14–6)

The test statistic is

$$R = \text{number of runs} \qquad (14\text{–}7)$$

The decision rule is to reject H_0 at level α if $R \leq C_1$ or $R \geq C_2$, where C_1 and C_2 are critical values obtained from Appendix C, Table 8, with total tail probability $P(R \leq C_1) + P(R \geq C_2) = \alpha$.

Let us conduct the hypothesis test for randomness (equation 14–6) for the sequences in cases 1, 2, and 3. Note that the tail probability for 6 or fewer runs is 0.019, and the probability for 16 or more runs is $P(R \geq 16) = 1 - F(15) = 1 - 0.981 = 0.019$. Thus, if we choose $\alpha = 2(0.019) = 0.038$, which is as close to 0.05 as we can get with this discrete distribution, our decision rule will be to reject H_0 for $R \geq 16$ or $R \leq 6$.

In case 1, we have $R = 20$. We reject the null hypothesis. In fact, the p-value obtained by looking in the table is less than 0.001. The same is true in case 2, where $R = 2$. In case 3, we have $R = 12$. We find the p-value as follows: $2[P(R \geq 12)] = 2[(1 - F(11)] = 2(1 - 0.586) = 2(0.414) = 0.828$. The null hypothesis cannot be rejected.

Large-Sample Properties

As you may have guessed, as the sample sizes n_1 and n_2 increase, the distribution of the number of runs approaches a normal distribution.

The mean of the normal distribution of the number of runs is

$$E(R) = \frac{2n_1 n_2}{n_1 + n_2} + 1 \qquad (14\text{–}8)$$

The standard deviation is

$$\sigma_R = \sqrt{\frac{2n_1 n_2 (2n_1 n_2 - n_1 - n_2)}{(n_1 + n_2)^2 (n_1 + n_2 - 1)}} \qquad (14\text{–}9)$$

Therefore, when the sample size is large, we may use a *standard normal test statistic* given by

$$z = \frac{R - E(R)}{\sigma_R} \qquad (14\text{–}10)$$

We demonstrate the large-sample test for randomness with Example 14–2.

One of the most important uses of the test for randomness is its application in residual analysis. Recall that a regression model, or a time series model, is adequate if the errors are random (no regular pattern). A time series model was fitted to sales data of multiple-vitamin pills. After the model was fitted to the data, the following residual series was obtained from the computer. Is there any statistical evidence to conclude that the time series errors are not random and, hence, that the model should be corrected?

EXAMPLE 14-2

$$-23, 30, 12, -10, -5, -17, -22, 57, 43, -23, 31, 42, 50, 61, -28, -52, 10, 34, 28, 55, 60,$$
$$32, 88, -75, -22, -56, -89, -34, -20, -2, -5, 29, 12, 45, 77, 78, 91, 25, 60, -25, 45, 42,$$
$$30, -59, -60, -40, -75, -25, -34, -66, -90, 10, -20$$

(The sequence of residuals continues, and their sum is zero.) Using this part of the sequence, we reason that since the mean residual is zero, we may look at the sign of the residuals and write them as plus or minus signs. Then we may count the number of runs of positive and negative residuals and perform the runs test for randomness.

We have the following signs:

Solution

```
− + + − − − + + − + + + + − − + + + + + + + − − − − − − − −
+ + + + + + + + − + + + − − − − − − − − − + − 
```

Letting n_1 be the number of positive residuals and n_2 the number of negative ones, we have $n_1 = 27$ and $n_2 = 26$. We count the number of runs and find that $R = 15$.

We now compute the value of the Z statistic from equation 14–10. We have, for the mean and standard deviation given in equations 14–8 and 14–9, respectively,

$$E(R) = \frac{2(27)(26)}{27 + 26} + 1 = 27.49$$

and

$$\sigma_R = \sqrt{\frac{2(27)(26)[2(27)(26) - 27 - 26]}{(27 + 26)^2(27 + 26 - 1)}} = 3.6$$

The computed value of the Z test statistic is

$$z = \frac{R - E(R)}{\sigma_R} = \frac{15 - 27.49}{3.6} = -3.47$$

From the Z table we know that the p-value is 0.0006 (this is a two-tailed test). We reject the null hypothesis that the residuals are random and conclude that the time series model needs to be corrected.

The Template

The same results for Example 14–2 could have been obtained using the template shown in Figure 14–3. The data, which should be + or − only, are entered in column B. The p-value appears in cell F18. For the current example the p-value of 0.0005 is more accurate than the manually calculated value of 0.0006.

FIGURE 14–3   The Template for the Runs Test
[Nonparametric Tests.xls; Sheet: Runs]

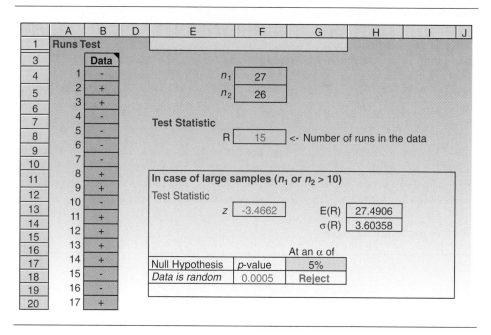

The Wald-Wolfowitz Test

An extension of the runs test for determining whether two populations have the same distribution is the **Wald-Wolfowitz test.**

The null and alternative hypotheses for the Wald-Wolfowitz test are

H_0: The two populations have the same distribution

H_1: The two populations have different distributions   (14–11)

This is one nonparametric analog to the t test for equality of two population means. Since the test is nonparametric, it is stated in terms of the distributions of the two populations rather than their means; however, the test is aimed at determining the difference between the two means. The test is two-tailed, but it is carried out on one tail of the distribution of the number of runs.

The only assumptions required for this test are that the two samples are independently and randomly chosen from the two populations of interest, and that values are on a continuous scale. The test statistic is, as before, $R =$ number of runs.

We arrange the values of the two samples in increasing order in one sequence, regardless of the population from which each is taken. We denote each value by the symbol representing its population, and this gives us a sequence of symbols of two types. We then count the number of runs in the sequence. This gives us the value of R.

Logically, if the two populations have the same distribution, we may expect a higher degree of overlapping of the symbols of the two populations (i.e., a large number of runs). If, on the other hand, the two populations are different, we may expect a clustering of the sample items from each of the groups. If, for example, the values in population 1 tend to be larger than the values in population 2, then we may expect the items from sample 1 to be clustered to the right of the items from sample 2. This produces a small number of runs. We would like to reject the null

FIGURE 14–4   Overlap versus Clustering of Two Samples

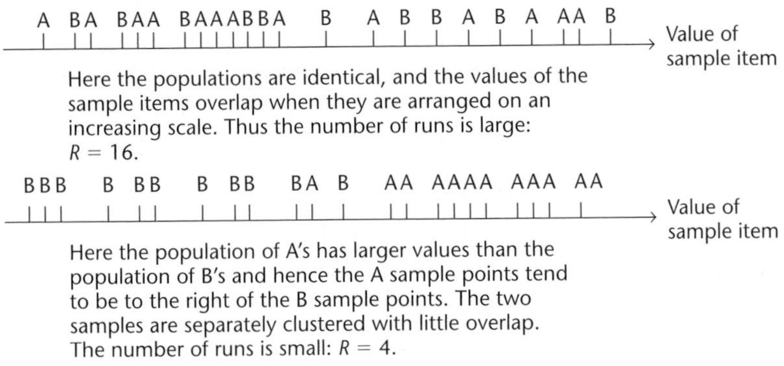

Here the populations are identical, and the values of the sample items overlap when they are arranged on an increasing scale. Thus the number of runs is large: $R = 16$.

Here the population of A's has larger values than the population of B's and hence the A sample points tend to be to the right of the B sample points. The two samples are separately clustered with little overlap. The number of runs is small: $R = 4$.

hypothesis when the number of runs is too small. We illustrate the idea of overlapping versus clustering in Figure 14–4.

We demonstrate the Wald-Wolfowitz test with Example 14–3.

EXAMPLE 14–3

The manager of a record store wants to test whether her two salespeople are equally effective. That is, she wants to test whether the number of sales made by each salesperson is about the same or whether one salesperson is better than the other. The manager gets the following random samples of daily sales made by each salesperson.

Salesperson A: 35, 44, 39, 50, 48, 29, 60, 75, 49, 66
Salesperson B: 17, 23, 13, 24, 33, 21, 18, 16, 32

Solution

We have $n_1 = 10$ and $n_2 = 9$. We arrange the items from the two samples in increasing order and denote them by A or B based on which population they came from. We get

BBBBBBBABBBAAAAAAAAA

The total number of runs is $R = 4$.

From Appendix C, Table 8, we find that the probability of four or fewer runs for sample sizes of 9 and 10 is 0.002. As the p-value is 0.002, we reject the null hypothesis that the two salespeople are equally effective. Since salesperson A had the larger values, we conclude that he or she tends to sell more than salesperson B.

We have assumed here that the sales of the two salespersons cannot be paired as taking place on the same days. Otherwise, a paired test would be more efficient, as it would reduce day-to-day variations.

The Wald-Wolfowitz test is a *weak test*. There are other nonparametric tests, as we will see, that are more powerful than this test in determining differences between two populations. The advantage of the present test is that it is easy to carry out. There is no need to compute any quantity from the data values—all we need to do is to order the data on an increasing scale and to count the number of runs of elements from the two samples.

PROBLEMS

14–6. According to *Strategic Finance,* Medtronic, Inc., recently applied two quality improvement methods to its global finance operations. The two methods were aimed at reducing the cycle time of an operation.[4] The following data are time, in seconds, for the operation, using Method A and Method B.

Method A: 477 482 471 419 470 410
Method B: 453 469 450 423 472 425

Is there statistical evidence that one method is better than the other?

14–7. A computer is used for generating random numbers. It is necessary to test whether the numbers produced are indeed random. A common method of doing this is to look at runs of odd versus even digits. Conduct the test using the following sequence of numbers produced by the computer.

2765898376445449986752138797563745876453426789876334821910934736 40898763

14–8. In a regression analysis, 12 out of 30 residuals are greater than 1.00 in value, and the rest are not. With A denoting a residual greater than 1 and B a residual less than 1, the residuals are as follows:

B B B B B B B B B A A A A A A A A A A B B B B B B B B B A A

Do you believe that the regression errors are random? Explain.

14–9. A messenger service employs eight men and nine women. Every day, the assignments of errands are supposed to be done at random. On a certain day, all the best jobs, in order of desirability, were given to the eight men. Is there evidence of sex discrimination? Discuss this also in the context of a continuing, daily operation. What would happen if you tested the randomness hypothesis every day?

14–10. Bids for a government contract are supposed to be opened in a random order. For a given contract, there were 42 bids, 30 of them from domestic firms and 12 from foreign firms. The order in which the sealed bids were opened was as follows (D denotes a domestic firm and F a foreign one):

D D D D D D D D F D D D D D D D F F D D D D D D D D D F D D F
D D D D D D F F F F F F F

Could the foreign firms claim that they had been discriminated against? Explain.

14–11. Two advertisements for tourism and vacation on Turks and Caicos Islands, which ran in business publications in May 2007, were compared for their appeal. A random sample of eight people was selected, and their responses to ad 1 were recorded. Another random sample, of nine people, was shown ad 2, and their responses were also recorded. The response data are as follows (10 is highest appeal).

Ad 1:   7, 8, 6, 7, 8, 9, 9, 10
Ad 2:   3, 4, 3, 5, 5, 4, 2, 5, 4

Is there a quick statistical proof that one ad is better than the other?

---

[4]Renee Cveykus and Erin Carter, "Fix the Process, Not the People," *Strategic Finance,* July 2006, pp. 27–33.

14–12. The following data are salaries of seven randomly chosen managers of furniture-making firms and eight randomly chosen managers of paper product firms. The data are in thousands of dollars per year.

Furniture: 175, 170, 166, 168, 204, 96, 147

Paper products: 89, 120, 136, 160, 111, 101, 98, 80

Use the Wald-Wolfowitz test to determine whether there is evidence that average owner salaries in the two business lines are not equal.

14–4   The Mann-Whitney *U* Test

In this section, we present the first of several statistical procedures that are based on *ranks*. In these procedures, we rank the observations from smallest to largest and then use the ranks instead of the actual sample values in our computations. Sometimes, our data are themselves ranks. Methods based on ranks are useful when the data are at least on an ordinal scale of measurement. Surprisingly, when we substitute ranks for actual observations, the loss of information does not weaken the tests very much. In fact, when the assumptions of the corresponding parametric tests are met, the nonparametric tests based on ranks are often about 95% as efficient as the parametric tests. When the assumptions needed for the parametric tests (usually, a normal distribution) are not met, the tests based on ranks are excellent, powerful alternatives.

We demonstrate the ranking procedure with a simple set of numbers: 17, 32, 99, 12, 14, 44, 50. We rank the observations from smallest to largest. This gives us 3, 4, 7, 1, 2, 5, 6. (The reason is that the smallest observation is 12, the next one up is 14, and so on. The largest observation—the seventh—is 99.) This simple ranking procedure is the basis of the test presented in this section, as well as of the tests presented in the next few sections. Tests based on ranks are probably the most widely used nonparametric procedures.

In this section, we present the **Mann-Whitney *U* test**, also called the *Wilcoxon rank sum test,* or just the *rank sum test*. This test is different from the test we discuss in the next section, called the Wilcoxon *signed-rank* test. Try not to get confused by these names. The Mann-Whitney test is an adaptation of a procedure due to Wilcoxon, who also developed the signed-rank test. The most commonly used name for the rank sum test, however, is the Mann-Whitney *U* test.

The Mann-Whitney *U* test is a test of equality of two population distributions. The test is most useful, however, in testing for equality of two population means. As such, the test is an alternative to the two-sample *t* test and is used when the assumption of normal population distributions is not met. The test is only slightly weaker than the *t* test and is more powerful than the Wald-Wolfowitz runs test described in the previous section.

The null and alternative hypotheses for the Mann-Whitney *U* test are

H_0: The distributions of the two populations are identical

H_1: The two population distributions are not identical   (14–12)

Often, the hypothesis test in equation 14–12 is written in terms of equality versus nonequality of two population means or equality versus nonequality of two population medians. As such, we may also have one-tailed versions of the test. We may test whether one population mean is greater than the other. We may state these hypotheses in terms of population medians.

The only assumptions required by the test are that the samples be random samples from the two populations of interest and that they be drawn independently of each other. If we want to state the hypotheses in terms of population means or medians, however, we need to add an assumption, namely, that if a difference exists between the two populations, the difference is in *location* (mean, median).

The Computational Procedure

We combine the two random samples and rank all our observations from smallest to largest. To any ties we assign the *average* rank of the tied observations. Then we sum all the ranks of the observations from one of the populations and denote that population as population 1. The sum of the sample ranks is R_1.

The Mann-Whitney U statistic is

$$U = n_1 n_2 + \frac{n_1(n_1 + 1)}{2} - R_1 \qquad (14\text{--}13)$$

where n_1 is the sample size from population 1 and n_2 is the sample size from population 2

The U statistic is a measure of the difference between the ranks of the two samples. Large values of the statistic, or small ones, provide evidence of a difference between the two populations. If we assume that differences between the two populations are only in location, then large or small values of the statistic provide evidence of a difference in the location (mean, median) of the two populations.

The distribution of the U statistic for small samples is given in Appendix C, Table 9 (pages 780–784). The table assumes that n_1 is the smaller sample size. For large samples, we may, again, use a normal approximation. The convergence to the normal distribution is relatively fast, and when both n_1 and n_2 are greater than 10 or so, the normal approximation is good.

The mean of the distribution of U is

$$E(U) = \frac{n_1 n_2}{2} \qquad (14\text{--}14)$$

The standard deviation of U is

$$\sigma_U = \sqrt{\frac{n_1 n_2 (n_1 + n_2 + 1)}{12}} \qquad (14\text{--}15)$$

The large-sample test statistic is

$$z = \frac{U - E(U)}{\sigma_U} \qquad (14\text{--}16)$$

For large samples, the test is straightforward. In a two-tailed test, we reject the null hypothesis if z is greater than or less than the values that correspond to our chosen level of α (for example, ± 1.96 for $\alpha = 0.05$). Similarly, in a one-tailed test, we reject H_0 if z is greater than (or less than) the appropriate critical point. Note that U is large when R_1 is small, and vice versa. Thus, if we want to prove the alternative hypothesis that the location parameter of population 1 is greater than the location parameter of population 2, we reject on the left tail of the normal distribution.

With small samples, we have a problem because the U table lists only left-hand-side probabilities of the statistic [the table gives $F(U)$ values]. Here we will use the following procedure. For a two-tailed test, we define R_1 as the larger of the two sums of ranks. This will make U small so it can be tested against a left-hand critical point with tail probability $\alpha/2$. For a one-tailed test, if we want to prove that the location parameter of population 1 is greater than that of population 2, we look at the sum of the ranks of sample 1 and do not reject H_0 if this sum is smaller than that for sample 2. Otherwise, we compute the statistic and test on the left side of the distribution. We choose the left-hand critical point corresponding to α. Relabel populations 1 and 2 if you want to prove the other one-tailed possibility.

We demonstrate the Mann-Whitney test with two examples.

FIGURE 14–5 Ordering and Ranking the Data for Example 14–4

Model A:					35	36		38		40	41	42
Model B:	27	29	30	33			37		39			
Rank:	1	2	3	4	(5)	(6)	7	(8)	9	(10)	(11)	(12)

EXAMPLE 14–4

Federal aviation officials tested two proposed versions of the Copter-plane, a twin-engine plane with tilting propellers that make takeoffs and landings easy and save time during short flights. The two models, made by Bell Helicopter Textron, Inc., were tested on the New York–Washington route. The officials wanted to know whether the two models were equally fast or whether one was faster than the other. Each model was flown six times, at randomly chosen departure times. The data, in minutes of total flight time for models A and B, are as follows.

Model A: 35, 38, 40, 42, 41, 36
Model B: 29, 27, 30, 33, 39, 37

Solution

First we order the data so that they can be ranked. This has been done in Figure 14–5. We note that the sum of the ranks of the sample points from the population of model A should be higher since the ranks for this model are higher. We will thus define R_1 as the sum of the ranks from this sample because we need a small value of U (which happens when R_1 is large) for comparison with table values. We find the value of R_1 as $R_1 = 5 + 6 + 8 + 10 + 11 + 12 = 52$. This is the sum of the circled ranks in Figure 14–5, the ranks belonging to the sample for model A.

We now compute the test statistic U. From equation 14–13, we find

$$U = n_1 n_2 + \frac{n_1(n_1 + 1)}{2} - R_1 = (6)(6) + \frac{(6)(7)}{2} - 52 = 5$$

Looking at Appendix C, Table 9, we find that the probability that U will attain a value of 5 or less is 0.0206. Since this is a two-tailed test, we want to reject the null hypothesis if the value of the statistic is less than or equal to the (left-hand) critical point corresponding to $\alpha/2$; if we choose $\alpha = 0.05$, then $\alpha/2 = 0.025$. Since 0.0206 is less than 0.025, we reject the null hypothesis at the 0.05 level. The p-value for this test is $2(0.0206) = 0.0412$. (Why?)

Suppose that we had chosen to conduct this as a one-tailed test. If we had originally wanted to test whether model B was slower than model A, then we would not be able to reject the null hypothesis that model B was *not* slower because the sum of the ranks of model B is smaller than the sum of the ranks of model A, and, hence, U would be large and not in the (left-side) rejection region. If, on the other hand, we wanted to test whether model A was slower, the test statistic would have been the same as the one we used, except that we could have rejected with a value of U as high as 7 (from Table 9, the tail probability for $U = 7$ is 0.0465, which is less than $\alpha = 0.05$). Remember that in a one-tailed test, we use the (left-hand) critical point corresponding to α and not to $\alpha/2$. In any case, we reject the null hypothesis and state that there is evidence to conclude that model B is generally faster. Note that Table 9 values are approximate and will differ slightly from the values obtained by the computer.

When the sample sizes are large and we use the normal approximation, conducting the test is much easier since we do not have to redefine U so that it is always on the left-hand side of the distribution. We just compute the standardized Z statistic, using equations 14–14 through 14–16, and consult the standard normal table. This is demonstrated in Example 14–5.

EXAMPLE 14–5   A multinational corporation is about to open a subsidiary in Greece. Since the operation will involve a large number of executives who will have to move to that country, the company plans to offer an extensive program of teaching the language to the executives who will operate in Greece. For its previous operation starts in France and Italy, the company used cassettes and books provided by Educational Services Teaching Cassettes, Inc. Recently one of the company directors suggested that the book-and-cassette program offered by Metacom, Inc., sold under the name *The Learning Curve,* might provide a better introduction to the language. The company therefore decided to test the null hypothesis that the two programs were equally effective versus the one-tailed alternative that students who go through The Learning Curve program achieve better proficiency scores in a comprehensive examination following the course. Two groups of 15 executives were randomly selected, and each group studied the language under a different program. The final scores for the two groups, Educational Services (ES) and Learning Curve (LC), are as follows. Is there evidence that The Learning Curve method is more effective?

ES: 65, 57, 74, 43, 39, 88, 62, 69, 70, 72, 59, 60, 80, 83, 50
LC: 85, 87, 92, 98, 90, 88, 75, 72, 60, 93, 88, 89, 96, 73, 62

Solution   We order the scores and rank them. When ties occur, we assign to each tied observation the average rank of the ties.

ES: 39 43 50 57 59 60 62 65 69 70 72   74   80 83   88
LC: 60 62   72 73   75   85 87 88 89 90 92 93 96 98
                                                         88

The tied observations are 60 (two—one from each group), 62 (two—one from each group), 72 (two—one from each group), and 88 (three—one from ES and two from LC). If we disregarded ties, the two observations of 60 would have received ranks 6 and 7. Since either one of them could have been rank 6 or rank 7, each gets the *average* rank of 6.5 (and the next rank up is 8). The next two observations are also tied (both are 62). They would have received ranks 8 and 9, so each gets the average rank of 8.5, and we continue with rank 10, which goes to the observation 65. The two 72 observations each get the average rank of 13.5 [(13 + 14)/2]. There are three 88 observations; they occupy ranks 22, 23, and 24. Therefore, each of them gets the average rank of 23.
We now list the ranks of all the observations in each of the two groups:

ES: 1   2   3   4   5   6.5   8.5   10   11   12 13.5   16   18   19   23
LC: 6.5 8.5 13.5   15   17   20   21   23   23   25   26   27   28   29   30

Note that 2 of the 23 ranks belong to LC and 1 belongs to ES. We may now compute the test statistic U. To be consistent with the small-sample procedure, let us define LC as population 1. We have

$$R_1 = 6.5 + 8.5 + 13.5 + 15 + 17 + 20 + 21 + 23 + 23 + 25 + 26 + 27$$
$$+ 28 + 29 + 30$$
$$= 312.5$$

Thus, the value of the statistic is

$$U = (15)(15) + \frac{(15)(16)}{2} - 312.5 = 32.5$$

We now compute the value of the standardized Z statistic, equation 14–16. From equation 14–14,

$$E(U) = \frac{(15)(15)}{2} = 112.5$$

and from equation 14–15,

$$\sigma_U = \sqrt{\frac{(15)(15)(31)}{12}} = 24.1$$

We get

$$z = \frac{U - E(U)}{\sigma_U} = \frac{32.5 - 112.5}{24.1} = -3.32$$

We want to reject the null hypothesis if we believe that LC gives higher scores. Our test statistic is defined to give a negative value in such a case. Since the computed value of the statistic is in the rejection region for any usual α value, we reject the null hypothesis and conclude that there is evidence that the LC program is more effective. Our p-value is 0.0005. Figure 14–6 shows the same result was obtained by the Mann-Whitney analysis tool of MINITAB.

FIGURE 14–6   Mann-Whitney Test Using MINITAB

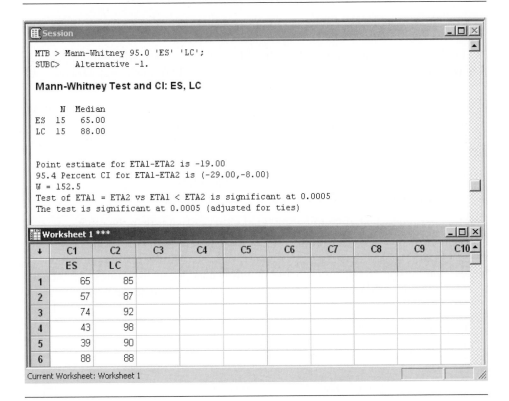

In Example 14–5 we used the Mann-Whitney test instead of the parametric t test because some people have a facility with language and tend to score high on language tests, whereas others do not and tend to score low. This can create a bimodal distribution (one with two modes) rather than a normal curve, which is required for the t test.

In Example 14–4, we had small samples. When small samples are used, the parametric tests are sensitive to deviations from the normal assumption required for the t distribution. In such cases, use of a nonparametric method such as the Mann-Whitney test is more suitable, unless there is a good indication that the populations in question are approximately normally distributed.

PROBLEMS

14–13. Gotex is considering two possible bathing suit designs for the 2008 summer season. One is called Nautical Design, and the other is Geometric Prints. Since the fashion industry is very competitive, Gotex needs to test before marketing the bathing suits. Ten randomly chosen top models are selected for modeling Nautical Design, and 10 other randomly chosen top models are selected to model Geometric Prints bathing suits. The results of the judges' ratings of the 20 bathing suits follow.

ND: 86, 90, 77, 81, 86, 95, 99, 92, 93, 85

GP: 67, 72, 60, 59, 78, 69, 70, 85, 65, 62

Is there evidence to conclude that one design is better than the other? If so, which one is it, and why?

14–14. The May 1, 2007, College Retirement Equity Fund (CREF) prospectus lists the following sample returns on $1 invested in two of the fund's accounts, per year.[5]

Equity Index Account ($):   1.636, 1.441, 0.973, 1.055, 1.400
Money Market Account ($):   1.169, 1.273, 0.976, 0.998, 0.953

Assuming these data are random samples, is there statistical evidence that one account is better than the other?

14–15. Explain when you would use the Mann-Whitney test, when you would use the two-sample t test, and when you would use the Wald-Wolfowitz test. Discuss your reasons for choosing each test in the appropriate situation.

14–16. An article in *Money* compares investment in an income annuity, offered by insurance companies, and a mix of low-cost mutual funds.[6] Suppose the following data are annualized returns (in percent) randomly sampled from these two kinds of investments.

Income Annuity: 9, 7.5, 8.3, 6.2, 9.1, 6.8, 7.9, 8.8
Mutual Funds Mix: 10, 10.5, 11.0, 8.9, 12.1, 10.3, 9.1, 9.7

Test to determine which investment mode, if either, is better than the other.

14–17. Shearson Lehman Brothers, Inc., now encourages its investors to consider real estate limited partnerships. The company offers two limited partnerships—one in a condominium project in Chicago and one in Dallas. Annualized rates of return for the two investments during separate eight-month periods are as follows. Is one type of investment better than the other? Explain.

Chicago (%):   12, 13, 10, 14, 15, 9, 11, 10
Dallas (%):   10, 9, 8, 7, 9, 11, 6, 13

---

[5]Prospectus of College Retirement Equity Fund (CREF), May 1, 2007, pp. 8–10.

[6]Walter Updegrave, "Those Annuity Ads on TV? Monkey Feathers!" *Money*, March 2007, p. 42.

14–18. An article in *BusinessWeek* discusses the salvage value of bankrupt hedge funds compared with the salvage value of bankrupt consumer lenders.[7] Suppose the following data are the value a shareholder can salvage, in cents per invested dollar, for random samples of the two kinds of institutions.

Hedge funds: 10, 15, 10, 17, 10, 11, 9, 9, 12
Consumer lenders: 25, 15, 15, 28, 33, 10, 29, 25, 18

Which kind of institution, if either, falls harder and leaves its unfortunate investors in more trouble?

14–5   The Wilcoxon Signed-Rank Test

The **Wilcoxon signed-rank test** is useful in comparing two populations for which we have paired observations. This happens when our data can be paired off in a natural way, for example, husband's score and wife's score in a consumer rating study. As such, the test is a good alternative to the paired-observations *t* test in cases where the differences between paired observations are not believed to be normally distributed. We have already seen a nonparametric test for such a situation—the sign test. Unlike the sign test, the Wilcoxon test accounts for the magnitude of differences between paired values, not only their signs. The test does so by considering the *ranks* of these differences. The test is therefore more efficient than the sign test when the differences may be quantified rather than just given a positive or negative sign. The sign test, on the other hand, is easier to carry out.

The Wilcoxon procedure may also be adapted for testing whether the location parameter of a single population (its median or its mean) is equal to any given value. Each test has one-tailed and two-tailed versions. We start with the paired-observations test for the equality of two population distributions (or the equality of the location parameters of the two populations).

The Paired-Observations Two-Sample Test

The null hypothesis is that the median difference between the two populations is zero. The alternative hypothesis is that it is not zero.

The hypothesis test is

H_0: The median difference between populations 1 and 2 is zero
H_1: The median difference between populations 1 and 2
    is not zero   (14–17)

We assume that the distribution of differences between the two populations is symmetric, that the differences are mutually independent, and that the measurement scale is at least interval. By the assumption of symmetry, hypotheses may be stated in terms of means. The alternative hypothesis may also be a directed one: that the mean (or median) of one population is greater than the mean (or median) of the other population.

First, we list the pairs of observations we have on the two variables (the two populations). The data are assumed to be a random sample of paired observations. For each pair, we compute the difference

$$D = x_1 - x_2 \qquad (14\text{–}18)$$

Then we rank the absolute values of the differences D.

[7] Matthew Goldstein, "Vultures to the Rescue: A New Market Gives Holders of Distressed Hedge Funds a Quick Escape," *BusinessWeek,* April 9, 2007, p. 78.

In the next step, we form sums of the ranks of the positive and of the negative differences.

The Wilcoxon T statistic is defined as the smaller of the two sums of ranks—the sum of the negative or the positive ones

$$T = \min\left[\Sigma(+), \Sigma(-)\right] \qquad (14\text{–}19)$$

where $\Sigma(+)$ is the sum of the ranks of the positive differences and $\Sigma(-)$ is the sum of the ranks of the negative differences

---

The **decision rule:** Critical points of the distribution of the test statistic T (when the null hypothesis is true) are given in Appendix C, Table 10 (page 785). We carry out the test on the left tail; that is, we reject the null hypothesis if the computed value of the statistic is less than a critical point from the table, for a given level of significance.

For a one-tailed test, suppose that the alternative hypothesis is that the mean (median) of population 1 is greater than that of population 2; that is,

$$H_0: \mu_1 \leq \mu_2$$
$$H_1: \mu_1 > \mu_2 \qquad (14\text{–}20)$$

Here we use the sum of the ranks of negative differences. If the alternative hypothesis is reversed (populations 1 and 2 are switched), then we use the sum of the ranks of the positive differences as the statistic. In either case, the test is carried out on the left "tail" of the distribution. Appendix C, Table 10, gives critical points for both one-tailed and two-tailed tests.

Large-Sample Version of the Test

As in other situations, when the sample size increases, the distribution of the Wilcoxon statistic T approaches the normal probability distribution. In the Wilcoxon test, n is defined as the number of *pairs* of observations from populations 1 and 2. As the number of pairs n gets large (as a rule of thumb, $n > 25$ or so), T may be approximated by a normal random variable as follows.

The mean of T is

$$E(T) = \frac{n(n+1)}{4} \qquad (14\text{–}21)$$

The standard deviation of T is

$$\sigma_T = \sqrt{\frac{n(n+1)(2n+1)}{24}} \qquad (14\text{–}22)$$

The standardized z statistic is

$$z = \frac{T - E(T)}{\sigma_T} \qquad (14\text{–}23)$$

We now demonstrate the Wilcoxon signed-rank test with Example 14–6.

EXAMPLE 14–6

The Sunglass Hut of America, Inc., operates kiosks occupying previously unused space in the well-traveled aisles of shopping malls. Sunglass Hut owner Sanford Ziff hopes to expand within a few years to every major shopping mall in the United States. He is using the present $4.5 million business as a test of the marketability of different types of sunglasses. Two types of sunglasses are sold: violet and pink. Ziff wants to know whether there is a difference in the quantities sold of each type. The numbers of sunglasses sold of each kind are paired by store; these data for each of 16 stores during the first month of operation are given in Table 14–2. The table also shows how the differences and their absolute values are computed and ranked, and how the signed ranks are summed, leading to the computed value of T.

Solution

Note that a difference of zero is discarded, and the sample size is reduced by 1. The effective sample size for this experiment is now $n = 15$. Note also that ties are handled as before: We assign the average rank to tied differences. Since the smaller sum is the one associated with the negative ranks, we define T as that sum. We therefore have the following value of the Wilcoxon test statistic:

$$T = \Sigma(-) = 34$$

We now conduct the test of the hypotheses in equation 14–17. We compare the computed value of the statistic $T = 34$ with critical points of T from Appendix C, Table 10. For a two-tailed test, we find that for $\alpha = 0.05$ ($P = 0.05$ in the table) and $n = 15$, the critical point is 25. Since the test is carried out on the "left tail"— that is, we do not reject the null hypothesis if the computed value of T is *greater than or equal to* the table value—we do not reject the null hypothesis that the distribution of sales of the violet sunglasses is identical to the distribution of sales of the pink sunglasses.

TABLE 14–2 Data and Computations for Example 14–6

Store	Number of Violet Sold X_1	Number of Pink Sold X_2	Difference $D = X_1 - X_2$	Rank of Absolute Difference $|D|$	Rank of Positive D	Rank of Negative D
1	56	40	16	9	9	
2	48	70	−22	12		12
3	100	60	40	15	15	
4	85	70	15	8	8	
5	22	8	14	7	7	
6	44	40	4	2	2	
7	35	45	−10	6		6
8	28	7	21	11	11	
9	52	60	−8	5		5
10	77	70	7	3.5	3.5	
11	89	90	−1	1		1
12	10	10	0			
13	65	85	−20	10		10
14	90	61	29	13	13	
15	70	40	30	14	14	
16	33	26	7	3.5	3.5	
					$\Sigma(+) = 86$	$\Sigma(-) = 34$

A Test for the Mean or Median of a Single Population

As stated earlier, the Wilcoxon signed-rank test may be adapted for testing whether the mean (or median) of a single population is equal to any given number. There are three possible tests. The first is a left-tailed test where the alternative hypothesis is that the mean (or median—both are equal if we assume a *symmetric* population distribution) is smaller than some value specified in the null hypothesis. The second is a right-tailed test where the alternative hypothesis is that the mean (or median) is greater than some value. The third is a two-tailed test where the alternative hypothesis is that the mean (or median) is not equal to the value specified in the null hypothesis.

The computational procedure is as follows. Using our n data points $x_1, x_2, \ldots, x_n$, we form pairs: $(x_1, m), (x_2, m), \ldots, (x_n, m)$, where m is the value of the mean (or median) specified in the null hypothesis. Then we perform the usual Wilcoxon signed-rank test on these pairs.

In a right-tailed test, if the negative ranks have a larger sum than the positive ranks, we do not reject the null hypothesis. If the negative ranks have a smaller sum than the positive ones, we conduct the test (on the left tail of the distribution, as usual) and use the critical points in the table corresponding to the one-tailed test. We use the same procedure in the left-tailed test. For a two-tailed test, we use the two-tailed critical points. In any case, we always reject the null hypothesis if the computed value of T is less than or equal to the appropriate critical point from Appendix C, Table 10.

We will now demonstrate the single-sample Wilcoxon test for a mean using the large-sample normal approximation.

EXAMPLE 14–7

The average hourly number of messages transmitted by a private communications satellite is believed to be 149. The satellite's owners have recently been worried about the possibility that demand for this service may be declining. They therefore want to test the null hypothesis that the average number of messages is 149 (or more) versus the alternative hypothesis that the average hourly number of relayed messages is less than 149. A random sample of 25 operation hours is selected. The data (numbers of messages relayed per hour) are

151, 144, 123, 178, 105, 112, 140, 167, 177, 185, 129, 160, 110, 170, 198, 165, 109, 118, 155, 102, 164, 180, 139, 166, 182

Is there evidence of declining use of the satellite?

Solution

We form 25 pairs, each pair consisting of a data point and the null-hypothesis mean of 149. Then we subtract the second number from the first number in each pair (i.e., we subtract 149 from every data point). This gives us the differences D.

2, −5, −26, 29, −44, −37, −9, 18, 28, 36, −20, 11, −39, 21, 49, 16, −40, −31, 6, −47, 15, 31, −10, 17, 33

The next step is to rank the absolute value of the differences from smallest to largest. We have the following ranks, in the order of the data:

1, 2, 13, 15, 23, 20, 4, 10, 14, 19, 11, 6, 21, 12, 25, 8, 22, 16.5, 3, 24, 7, 16.5, 5, 9, 18

Note that the differences 31 and −31 are tied, and since they would occupy positions 16 and 17, each is assigned the average of these two ranks, or 16.5.

The next step is to compute the sum of the ranks of the positive differences and the sum of the ranks of the negative differences. The ranks associated with the positive differences are 1, 15, 10, 14, 19, 6, 12, 25, 8, 3, 7, 16.5, 9, and 18. (Check this.) The sum of these ranks is $\Sigma(+) = 163.5$. When using the normal approximation, we may use either sum of ranks. Since this is a left-tailed test, we want to reject the null hypothesis that the mean is 149 only if there is evidence that the mean is less than 149, that is, when the sum of the positive ranks is too small. We will therefore carry out the test on the left tail of the normal distribution.

Using equations 14–21 to 14–23, we compute the value of the test statistic Z as

$$z = \frac{T - E(T)}{\sigma_T} = \frac{T - n(n+1)/4}{\sqrt{n(n+1)(2n+1)/24}} = \frac{163.5 - (25)(26)/4}{\sqrt{(25)(26)(51)/24}} = 0.027$$

This value of the statistic lies inside the nonrejection region, far from the critical point for any conventional level of significance. (If we had decided to carry out the test at $\alpha = 0.05$, our critical point would have been -1.645.) We do not reject the null hypothesis and conclude that there is no evidence that use of the satellite is declining.

In closing this section, we note that the Wilcoxon signed-rank test assumes that the distribution of the population is symmetric in the case of the single-sample test, and that the distribution of differences between the two populations in the paired, two-sample case is symmetric. This assumption allows us to make inferences about population means or medians. Another assumption inherent in our analysis is that the random variables in question are continuous. The measurement scale of the data is at least ordinal.

The Template

Figure 14–7 shows the use of the template for testing the mean (or median). The data entered correspond to Example 14–7. Note that we enter the claimed value of the mean (median) in every used row of the second column of data. In the problem, the null hypothesis is $\mu_1 \geq \mu_2$. Since the sample size is large, the p-values appear in the range J17:J19. The p-value we need is 0.5107. Since this is too large, we cannot reject the null hypothesis.

Note that the template always uses the sum of the negative ranks to calculate the test statistic Z. Hence its sign differs from the manual calculation. The final results—the p-value and whether or not we reject the null hypothesis—will be the same in both cases.

FIGURE 14–7 Wilcoxon Test for the Mean or Median [Nonparametric Tests.xls; Sheet: Wilcoxon]

Wilcoxon's Signed Rank Test — # Message Transmitted

	# Message X_1	Mean X_2
1	151	149
2	144	149
3	123	149
4	178	149
5	105	149
6	112	149
7	140	149
8	167	149
9	177	149
10	185	149
11	129	149
12	160	149
13	110	149
14	170	149
15	198	149
16	165	149

$\Sigma(+)$ 163.5
$\Sigma(-)$ 161.5
n 25

Null Hypothesis	Test Statistic T
H_0: $\mu_1 = \mu_2$	161.5
H_0: $\mu_1 >= \mu_2$	163.5
H_0: $\mu_1 <= \mu_2$	161.5

For Large Samples (n >= 25)
Test Statistic

z −0.026907 $E[T]$ 162.5 $\sigma(T)$ 37.1652

Null Hypothesis	p-value	At an α of 5%
H_0: $\mu_1 = \mu_2$	0.9785	
H_0: $\mu_1 >= \mu_2$	0.5107	
H_0: $\mu_1 <= \mu_2$	0.4893	

PROBLEMS

14–19. Explain the purpose of the Wilcoxon signed-rank test. When is this test useful? Why?

14–20. For problem 14–17, suppose that the returns for the Chicago and Dallas investments are paired by month: the first observation for each investment is for the first month (say, January), the second is for the next month, and so on. Conduct the analysis again, using the Wilcoxon signed-rank test. Is there a difference in your conclusion? Explain.

14–21. According to an article in the *New York Times,* a new trend has been introduced by some of America's finest restaurants: refusing to offer diners bottled water, and pushing instead the restaurant's filtered tap water.[8] A restaurant owner is considering following this new trend but wants to research the option. The owner collects a random sample of paired observations on the numbers of bottled water orders per night and the number of customers who agreed to drink filtered tap water that night. The data are (15, 8), (17, 12), (25, 10), (19, 3), (28, 5), (17, 18), (12, 13), (20, 11), (16, 18). Is there evidence that tap water can be as popular as bottled water?

14–22. The average life of a 100-watt lightbulb is stated on the package to be 750 hours. The quality control director at the plant making the lightbulbs needs to check whether the statement is correct. The director is only concerned about a possible reduction in quality and will stop the production process only if statistical evidence exists to conclude that the average life of a lightbulb is under 750 hours. A random sample of 20 bulbs is collected and left on until they burn out. The lifetime of each bulb is recorded. The data are (in hours of continuous use) 738, 752, 710, 701, 689, 779, 650, 541, 902, 700, 488, 555, 870, 609, 745, 712, 881, 599, 659, 793. Should the process be stopped and corrected? Explain why or why not.

14–23. A retailer of tapes and compact disks wants to test whether people can differentiate the two products by the quality of sound only. A random sample of consumers who agreed to participate in the test and who have no particular experience with high-quality audio equipment is selected. The same musical performance is played for each person, once on a disk and once on a tape. The listeners do not know which is playing, and the order has been determined randomly. Each person is asked to state which of the two performances he or she prefers. What statistical test is most appropriate here? Why?

14–24. From experience, a manager knows that the commissions earned by her salespeople are very well approximated by a normal distribution. The manager wants to test whether the average commission is $439 per month. A random sample of 100 observations is available. What statistical test is best in this situation? Why?

14–25. Returns on stock of small firms have been shown to be symmetrically distributed, but the distributions are believed to be "long-tailed"—not well approximated by the normal distribution. To test whether the average return on a stock of a small firm is equal to 12% per year, what test would you recommend? Why?

14–26. According to *Money,* a water filter (which costs about $26) will save a consumer more than $1 per gallon of water over one year compared with buying bottled water.[9] Suppose that a random sample of 15 consumers agrees to participate in a study aimed at proving this claim, and that their results, extrapolated to savings per gallon per year are ($): 0.95, 1.07, 1.09, 1.12, 0.85, 1.17, 1.25, 0.82, 0.99, 1.02, 1.15, 0.90, 1.32, 1.01, 0.88. Conduct the test and state your conclusion.

---

[8]Marian Burros, "Fighting the Tide, a Few Restaurants Tilt to Tap Water," *The New York Times*, May 30, 2007, p. D1.

[9]Jean Chatzky, "Save a Buck, Save the World," *Money*, June 2007, p. 32.

14–27. Fidelity Investments' February 2007 prospectus compares the value of $10,000 invested in the S&P 500 versus its value invested in Fidelity's Select Natural Resources Portfolio over the life of this fund. The paired data below are the values, in dollars, of the $10,000 invested in the S&P 500, and in the Fidelity Select Natural Resources (FSNR) fund for a random sample of years:[10] (9,200, 14,500), (16,300, 21,000), (18,700, 33,100) (28,500, 36,700), (19,600, 29,200), (35,300, 37,200), (8,900, 21,700), (20,700, 36,100), (14,800, 7,800). Within the limitations of this analysis, is FSNR a better investment, over the range of years reported, than the S&P 500?

14–28. A stock market analyst wants to test whether there are higher-than-usual returns on stocks following a two-for-one split. A random sample of 10 stocks that recently split is available. For each stock, the analyst records the percentage return during the month preceding the split and the percentage return for the month following the split. The data are

Before split (%):   0.5, 20.2, 0.9, 1.1, 20.7, 1.5, 2.0, 1.3, 1.6, 2.1
After split (%):   1.1, 0.3, 1.2, 1.9, −0.2, 1.4, 1.8, 1.8, 2.4, 2.2

Is there evidence that a stock split causes excess returns for the month following the split? Redo the problem, using the sign test. Compare the results of the sign test with those of the Wilcoxon test.

14–29. Much has been said about airline deregulation and the effects it has had on the airline industry and its performance. Following a deluge of complaints from passengers, the public relations officer of one of the major airlines asked the company's operations manager to look into the problem. The operations manager obtained average takeoff delay figures for a random sample of the company's routes over time periods of equal length before and after the deregulation. The data, in minutes of average delay per route, are as follows.

Before: 3, 2, 4, 5, 1, 0, 1, 5, 6, 3, 10, 4, 11, 7
After: 6, 8, 2, 9, 8, 2, 6, 12, 5, 9, 8, 12, 11, 10

Is there evidence in these data that the airline's delays have increased after deregulation?

14–30. The following data are the one-year return to investors in world stock investment funds, as published in *Pensions & Investments*.[11] The data are in percent return (%): 35.9, 34.5, 33.7, 31.7, 27.5, 27.3, 27.3, 27.2, 27.1 25.5. Assume these data constitute a random sample of such funds, and use them to test the claim that the average world stock fund made more than 25% for its investors during this period.

14–6 The Kruskal-Wallis Test—A Nonparametric Alternative to One-Way ANOVA

Remember that the ANOVA procedure discussed in Chapter 9 requires the assumption that the populations being compared are all normally distributed with equal variance. When we have reason to believe that the populations under study are not normally distributed, we cannot use the ANOVA procedure. However, a nonparametric test that was designed to detect differences among populations requires no assumptions about the shape of the population distributions. This test is the **Kruskal-Wallis test.** The test is the nonparametric alternative to the (completely randomized design) one-way analysis of variance. In the next section, we will see a nonparametric alternative to the randomized block design analysis of variance, the *Friedman test.* Both of these tests use ranks.

---

[10]*Fidelity Select Portfolios,* Fidelity Investments, February 28, 2007, p. 27.

[11]Mark Bruno, "Value Comeback," *Pensions & Investments,* May 14, 2007, p. 14.

The Kruskal-Wallis test is an analysis of variance that uses the ranks of the observations rather than the data themselves. This assumes, of course, that the observations are on an interval scale. If our data are in the form of ranks, we use them as they are. The Kruskal-Wallis test is identical to the Mann-Whitney test when only two populations are involved. We thus use the Kruskal-Wallis test for comparing k populations, where k is greater than 2. The null hypothesis is that the k populations under study have the same distribution, and the alternative hypothesis is that at least two of the population distributions are different from each other.

The Kruskal-Wallis hypothesis test is

> H$_0$: All k populations have the same distribution
> H$_1$: Not all k populations have the same distribution   (14–24)

Although the hypothesis test is stated in terms of the distributions of the populations of interest, the test is most sensitive to differences in the locations of the populations. Therefore, the procedure is actually used to test the ANOVA hypothesis of equality of k population means. The only assumptions required for the Kruskal-Wallis test are that the k samples are random and are independently drawn from the respective populations. The random variables under study are continuous, and the measurement scale used is at least ordinal.

We rank all data points in the entire set from smallest to largest, without regard to which sample they come from. Then we sum all the ranks from each separate sample. Let n_1 be the sample size from population 1, n_2 the sample size from population 2, and so on up to n_k, which is the sample size from population k. Define n as the total sample size: $n = n_1 + n_2 + \cdots + n_k$. We define R_1 as the sum of the ranks from sample 1, R_2 as the sum of the ranks from sample 2, and so on to R_k, the sum of the ranks from sample k. We now define the Kruskal-Wallis test statistic H.

The Kruskal-Wallis test statistic is

$$H = \frac{12}{n(n+1)} \left(\sum_{j=1}^{k} \frac{R_j^2}{n_j} \right) - 3(n+1) \qquad (14\text{–}25)$$

For very small samples ($n_j < 5$), tables for the exact distribution of H under the null hypothesis are found in books devoted to nonparametric statistics. Usually, however, we have samples that are greater than 5 for each group (remember the serious limitations of inference based on very small samples). For larger samples, as long as each n_j is at least 5, the distribution of the test statistic H under the null hypothesis is well approximated by the chi-square distribution with $k - 1$ degrees of freedom.

We reject the null hypothesis on the right-hand tail of the chi-square distribution. That is, we reject the null hypothesis if the computed value of H is too large, exceeding a critical point of $\chi^2_{(k-1)}$ for a given level of significance α. We demonstrate the Kruskal-Wallis test with an example.

EXAMPLE 14–8   A company is planning to buy a word processing software package to be used by its office staff. Three available packages, made by different companies, are considered: Multimate, WordPerfect, and Microsoft Word. Demonstration packages of the three alternatives are available, and the company selects a random sample of 18 staff members, 6 members assigned to each package. Every person in the sample learns how to

TABLE 14–3 The Data (in minutes) and Ranks for Example 14–8

Multimate		WordPerfect		Microsoft Word	
Time	Rank	Time	Rank	Time	Rank
45	14	30	8	22	4
38	10	40	11	19	3
56	16	28	7	15	1
60	17	44	13	31	9
47	15	25	5	27	6
65	18	42	12	17	2
	$R_1 = 90$		$R_2 = 56$		$R_3 = 25$

use the particular package to which she or he is assigned. The time required for every member to learn how to use the word processing package is recorded. The question is: Is approximately the same amount of time needed to learn how to use each package proficiently?

None of the office staff has used any of these packages before, and because of similarity in use, each person is assigned to learn only one package. The staff, however, have varying degrees of experience. In particular, some are very experienced typists, and others are beginners. Therefore, it is believed that the three populations of time it takes to learn how to use a package are not normally distributed. If a conclusion is reached that one package takes longer to learn than the others, then learning time will be a consideration in the purchase decision. Otherwise, the decision will be based only on package capabilities and price. Table 14–3 gives the data, in minutes, for every person in the three samples. It also shows the ranks and the sum of the ranks for each group.

Solution

Using the obtained sums of ranks for the three groups, we compute the Kruskal-Wallis statistic H. From equation 14–25 we get

$$H = \frac{12}{n(n+1)}\left(\sum \frac{R_j^2}{n_j}\right) - 3(n+1) = \frac{12}{(18)(19)}\left(\frac{90^2}{6} + \frac{56^2}{6} + \frac{25^2}{6}\right) - 3(19)$$
$$= 12.3625$$

We now perform the test of the hypothesis that the populations of the learning times of the three software packages are identical. We compare the computed value of H with critical points of the chi-square distribution with $k - 1 = 3 - 1 = 2$ degrees of freedom. Using Appendix C, Table 4 (pages 760–761), we find that $H = 12.36$ exceeds the critical point for $\alpha = 0.01$, which is given as 9.21. We therefore reject the null hypothesis and conclude that there is evidence that the time required to learn how to use the word processing packages is not the same for all three; at least one package takes longer to learn. Our p-value is smaller than 0.01. The test is demonstrated in Figure 14–8.

We note that even though our example had a balanced design (equal sample sizes in all groups), the Kruskal-Wallis test can also be performed if sample sizes are different. We also note that we had no ties in this example. If ties do exist, we assign them the average rank, as we have done in previous tests based on ranks. The effect

FIGURE 14–8 **Carrying Out the Test for Example 14–8**

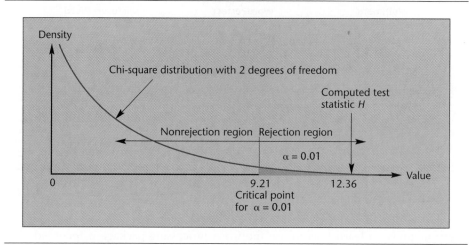

FIGURE 14–9 **The Template for the Kruskal-Wallis Test [Nonparametric Tests.xls; Sheet: Kruskal-Wallis]**

Kruskal-Wallis Test

	Group	Data	Rank
1	1	45	14
2	1	38	10
3	1	56	16
4	1	60	17
5	1	47	15
6	1	65	18
7	2	30	8
8	2	40	11
9	2	28	7
10	2	44	13
11	2	25	5
12	2	42	12
13	3	22	4
14	3	19	3
15	3	15	1
16	3	31	9
17	3	27	6
18	3	17	2

Group	*R*	*n*	Avg. *R*
1	90	6	15
2	56	6	9.3333
3	25	6	4.1667
3	*Total*	18	

Test Statistic

H 12.363

Null Hypothesis

H_0: *All the Groups have the same distribution*

	At an α of
p-value	5%
0.0021	Reject

Further Analysis

	1	2	3
2			
3	Sig		

of ties can be corrected for by using a correction formula, which may be found in advanced books.

The Template

The template for the Kruskal-Wallis test is shown in Figure 14–9. Note that the group numbers are to be entered in the first column of data as 1, 2, 3, ... The group numbers need not be in a particular order.

The data seen in the template correspond to Example 14–8. The advantage in using the template is that we get to know the exact *p*-value. It is 0.0021, seen in cell K10. In addition, the tabulation in the range G18:O26 shows if the difference in the means of every pair of groups is significant. The appearance of "Sig" means the corresponding difference is significant. In the current problem, the difference in the means of groups 1 and 3 is significantly more than zero. This aspect of the problem is discussed a little later, in the subsection "Further Analysis."

EXAMPLE 14–9

Because its delivery times are too slow, a trucking company is on the verge of losing an important customer. A manager wants to explore upgrading the fleet of trucks. There are three new models to choose from, each of which claims significant fuel efficiency improvements. Better gas mileage translates to fewer stops on long trips, cutting delivery times.

The manager is allowed to test-drive the trucks for a few days and randomly picks 15 drivers to do so. Five drivers will test each truck. The mpg results are as follows. Conduct a Kruskal-Wallis rank test for differences in the three population medians.

	A	B
	Truck	**MPG**
1	Truck A	17.00
2	Truck A	18.20
3	Truck A	18.50
4	Truck C	18.70
5	Truck A	19.40
6	Truck C	19.90
7	Truck C	20.30
8	Truck C	21.10
9	Truck B	22.70
10	Truck A	23.50
11	Truck B	23.80
12	Truck C	23.90
13	Truck B	24.20
14	Truck B	25.10
15	Truck B	26.30

Solution

Figure 14–10 shows the template solution to the problem. Since the p-value of 0.014 is less than 5%, we reject the null hypothesis that the medians of the mileage for the three groups are equal at an α of 5%.

FIGURE 14–10 The Template Solution to Example 14–9 [Nonparametric Tests.xls; Sheet: Kruskal-Wallis]

	Group	Data	Rank
1	1	17	1
2	1	18.2	2
3	1	18.5	3
4	3	18.7	4
5	1	19.4	5
6	3	19.9	6
7	3	20.3	7
8	3	21.1	8
9	2	22.7	9
10	1	23.5	10
11	2	23.8	11
12	3	23.9	12
13	2	24.2	13
14	2	25.1	14
15	2	26.3	15

Group	*R*	*n*	Avg. *R*
1	21	5	4.2
2	62	5	12.4
3	37	5	7.4
3	*Total*	15	

Test Statistic

H 8.54

Null Hypothesis

H_0: *All the Groups have the same distribution*

	At an α of
p-value	5%
0.0140	Reject

Further Analysis

	1	2	3
2	Sig		
3			

Further Analysis

As in the case of the usual ANOVA, once we reject the null hypothesis of no difference among populations, the question arises: Where are the differences? That is, which populations are different from which? Here we use a procedure that is similar to the Tukey method of further analysis following ANOVA. For every pair of populations we wish to compare (populations i and j, for example), we compute the average rank of the sample.

$$\bar{R}_i = \frac{R_i}{n_i} \quad \text{and} \quad \bar{R}_j = \frac{R_i}{n_j} \tag{14-26}$$

where R_i and R_j are the sums of the ranks from samples i and j, respectively, computed as part of the original Kruskal-Wallis test. We now define the test statistic D as the absolute difference between $\bar{R}_i$ and $\bar{R}_j$.

The test statistic for determining whether there is evidence to reject the null hypothesis that populations i and j are identical is

$$D = |\bar{R}_i - \bar{R}_j| \tag{14-27}$$

We carry out the test by comparing the test statistic D with a quantity that we compute from the critical point of the chi-square distribution at the same level α at which we carried out the Kruskal-Wallis test. The quantity is computed as follows.

The critical point for the paired comparisons is

$$C_{KW} = \sqrt{\chi^2_{\alpha,k-1} \frac{n(n+1)}{12} \left(\frac{1}{n_i} + \frac{1}{n_j} \right)} \tag{14-28}$$

where $\chi^2_{\alpha,k-1}$ is the critical point of the chi-square distribution used in the original, overall test.

By comparing the value of the statistic D with C_{KW} for every pair of populations, we can perform all pairwise comparisons *jointly* at the level of significance α at which we performed the overall test. We reject the null hypothesis if and only if $D > C_{KW}$. We demonstrate the procedure by performing all three pairwise comparisons of the populations in Example 14–8.

Since we have a balanced design, $n_i = n_j = 6$ for all three samples, the critical point C_{KW} will be the same for all pairwise comparisons. Using equation 14–28 and 9.21 as the value of chi-square for the overall test at $\alpha = 0.01$, we get

$$C_{KW} = \sqrt{9.21 \frac{(18)(19)}{12} \left(\frac{1}{6} + \frac{1}{6} \right)} = 9.35$$

Comparing populations 1 and 2: From the bottom of Table 14–3, we find that $R_1 = 90$ and $R_2 = 56$. Since the sample sizes are each 6, we find that the average rank for sample 1 is $90/6 = 15$, and the average rank for sample 2 is $56/6 = 9.33$. Hence, the test statistic for comparing these two populations is the absolute value of the difference between 15 and 9.33, which is 5.67. This value is less than C_{KW}, and we must conclude that there is no evidence, at $\alpha = 0.01$, of a difference between populations 1 and 2.

Comparing populations 1 and 3: Here the absolute value of the difference between the average ranks is $|(90/6) - (25/6)| = 10.83$. Since 10.83 is greater than $C_{KW} = 9.35$, we conclude that there is evidence, at $\alpha = 0.01$, that population 1 is different from population 3.

Comparing populations 2 and 3: Here we have $D = |(56/6) - (25/6)| = 5.17$, which is less than 9.35. Therefore we conclude that there is no evidence, at $\alpha = 0.01$, that populations 2 and 3 are different.

Our interpretation of the data is that at $\alpha = 0.01$, significant differences are evident only between the time it takes to learn Multimate and the time it takes to learn Microsoft Word. Since the values for Multimate are larger, we conclude that the study provides evidence that Multimate takes longer to learn.

PROBLEMS

14–31. With the continuing surge in the number of mergers and acquisitions in 2007, research effort has been devoted to determining whether the size of an acquisition has an effect on stockholders' abnormal returns (in percent) following the announcement of an impending acquisition.[12] Given the data below about abnormal stockholder returns for three size groups of acquired firms, test for equality of mean abnormal return.

Large: 11.9, 13.2, 8.7, 9.8, 12.1, 8.8, 10.3, 11.0
Medium: 8.6, 8.9, 5.3, 4.1, 6.2, 8.1, 6.0, 7.1
Small: 5.2, 4.1, 8.8, 10.7, 12.6, 13.0, 9.1, 8.0

14–32. An analyst in the publishing industry wants to find out whether the cost of a newspaper advertisement of a given size is about the same in four large newspaper groups. Random samples of seven newspapers from each group are selected, and the cost of an ad is recorded. The data follow (in dollars). Do you believe that there are differences in the price of an ad across the four groups?

Group A: 57, 65, 50, 45, 70, 62, 48
Group B: 72, 81, 64, 55, 90, 38, 75
Group C: 35, 42, 58, 59, 46, 60, 61
Group D: 73, 85, 92, 68, 82, 94, 66

14–33. Lawyers representing the Beatles filed a $15 million suit in New York against Nike, Inc., over Nike's Air Max shoe commercial set to the Beatles' 1968 hit song "Revolution." As part of all such lawsuits, the plaintiff must prove a financial damage—in this case, that Nike improperly gained from the unlicensed use of the Beatles' song. In proving their case, lawyers for the Beatles had to show that "Revolution," or any Beatles' song, is not just a tune played with the commercial and that, in fact, the use of the song made the Nike commercial more appealing than it would have been if it had featured another song or melody. A statistician was hired to aid in proving this point. The statistician designed a study in which the Air Max commercial was recast using two other randomly chosen songs that were in the public domain and did not require permission, and that were not sung by the Beatles. Then three groups of 12 people

[12]Martin Sikora, "Changes in SEC Price Rule Should Spark More Tenders," *Mergers & Acquisitions,* January 2007, p. 22.

each were randomly selected. Each group was shown one of the commercials, and every person's appeal score for the commercial was recorded. Using the following appeal scores, determine whether there is statistical evidence that not all three songs would be equally effective in the commercial. If you do reject the null hypothesis of equal appeal, go the required extra step to prove that the Beatles' "Revolution" does indeed have greater appeal over other songs, and that Nike should pay the Beatles for using it.

"Revolution":	95, 98, 96, 99, 91, 90, 97, 100, 96, 92, 88, 93
Random alternative A:	65, 67, 66, 69, 60, 58, 70, 64, 64, 68, 61, 62
Random alternative B:	59, 57, 55, 63, 59, 44, 49, 48, 46, 60, 47, 45

14–34. According to *Mediaweek,* there are three methods of advertising on the Web. Method 1 is to serve ads to users who clicked on an icon for the ad. Method 2 serves ads through visits to the company's Web site. And Method 3 uses highly targeted content sites.[13] Which method, if any, is most effective? Suppose the following data are the numbers of responders to each method who have eventually made a purchase, taken over a random sample of days for each method.

Method 1:	55, 79, 88, 41, 29, 85, 70, 68, 90
Method 2:	42, 21, 38, 40, 39, 61, 44, 26, 28
Method 3:	108, 111, 81, 65, 89, 100, 92, 97, 80

Conduct the test and state your conclusion.

14–35. According to an article in *Real Estate Finance,* developers and hotel operators have three ways of controlling shared facilities: the square footage allocation (SF) method, the revenue-generating (RG) allocation method, and the purchase price value (PPV) method.[14] An industry analyst wants to know if one of these methods is more successful than the others and collects random samples of return on equity data (in percent) for firms that have used one of these methods. The data are as follows.

SF:	15, 17, 8.5, 19, 22, 16, 15, 11.5, 16.5, 17
RG:	8.6, 9.5, 11, 15, 10.3, 16, 9.5, 12, 10.2
PPV:	3.8, 5.7, 12, 6.8, 10.1, 11.2, 9.9, 10.4, 6.1

Test for equality of means, and state your conclusion.

14–36. According to an article in *Risk,* three Danish financial institutions recently offered new structured investment programs.[15] Suppose that data, in percent return, for a random sample of investments offered by these banks, are as follows.

Bank 1:	8.5, 7.9, 8.3, 8.2, 8.2, 7.7, 8.1, 7.9
Bank 2:	6.8, 7.1, 6.6, 7.3, 7.5, 6.9, 7.7, 8.0
Bank 3:	5.9, 6.0, 6.1, 5.8, 7.3, 5.9, 6.5, 6.3

Conduct a test for equality of means and state your conclusions.

14–37. What assumptions did you use when solving problems 14–31 through 14–36? What assumptions did you not make about the populations in question? Explain.

---

[13]Michael Cassidy, "Remarketing 101: This New Form of Online Behavioral Marketing Takes Three Forms," *Mediaweek,* May 14, 2007, p. 12.

[14]Melissa Turra and Melissa Nelson, "How Developers and Hotel Operators Can Control Shared Facilities and Fairly Allocate Shared Facilities Expenses," *Real Estate Finance,* April 2007, pp. 12–14.

[15]"Structured Products," *Risk,* April 2007, p. 62.

14–7 The Friedman Test for a Randomized Block Design

Recall the randomized block design, which was discussed in Chapter 9. In this design, each block of units is assigned all k treatments, and our aim is to determine possible differences among treatments or treatment means (in the context of ANOVA). A *block* may be one person who is given all k treatments (asked to try k different products, to rate k different items, etc.). The Kruskal-Wallis test discussed in the previous section is a nonparametric version of the one-way ANOVA with completely randomized design. Similarly, the **Friedman test,** the subject of this section, is a nonparametric version of the randomized block design ANOVA. Sometimes this design is referred to as a two-way ANOVA with one item per cell because the blocks may be viewed as one factor and the treatment levels as the other. In the randomized block design, however, we are interested in the treatments as a factor and not in the blocks themselves. Like the methods we discussed in preceding sections, the Friedman test is based on ranks. The test may be viewed as an extension of the Wilcoxon signed-rank test or an extension of the sign test to more than two treatments per block. Recall that in each of these tests, two treatments are assigned to each element in the sample—the observations are paired. In the Friedman test, the observations are more than paired: each block, or person, is assigned to all $k > 2$ treatments.

Since the Friedman test is based on the use of ranks, it is especially useful for testing treatment effects when the observations are in the form of ranks. In fact, in such situations, we cannot use the randomized block design ANOVA because the assumption of a normal distribution cannot hold for very discrete data such as ranks. The Friedman test is a unique test for a situation where data are in the form of ranks within each block. Our example will demonstrate the use of the test in this particular situation. When our data are on an interval scale and not in the form of ranks, but we believe that the assumption of normality may not hold, we use the Friedman test instead of the parametric ANOVA and transform our data to ranks.

> The null and alternative hypotheses of the Friedman test are
>
> H_0: The distributions of the k treatment populations are identical
> H_1: Not all k distributions are identical   (14–29)

The data for the Friedman test are arranged in a table in which the rows are blocks (or units, if each unit is a block). There are n blocks. The columns are treatments, and there are k of them. Let us assume that each block is one person who is assigned to all treatments. The data in this case are arranged as in Table 14–4.

TABLE 14–4   Data Layout for the Friedman Test

	Treatment 1	Treatment 2	Treatment 3	. . .	Treatment k
Person 1					
Person 2					
Person 3					
⋮	⋮	⋮	⋮	. . .	⋮
Person n					
Sum of ranks:	R_1	R_2	R_3	. . .	R_k

If the data are not already in the form of ranks within each block, we rank the observations within each block from 1 to k. That is, the smallest observation in the block is given rank 1, the second smallest gets rank 2, and the largest gets rank k. Then we sum all the ranks for every treatment. The sum of all the ranks for treatment 1 is R_1, the sum of the ranks for treatment 2 is R_2, and so on to R_k, the sum of all the ranks given to treatment k.

If the distributions of the k populations are indeed identical, as stated in the null hypothesis, then we expect that the sum of the ranks for each treatment would not differ much from the sum of the ranks of any other treatment. The differences among the sums of the ranks are measured by the Friedman test statistic, denoted by X^2. When this statistic is too large, we reject the null hypothesis and conclude that at least two treatments do not have the same distribution.

The Friedman test statistic is

$$X^2 = \frac{12}{nk(k+1)} \sum_{j=1}^{k} R_j^2 - 3n(k+1) \qquad (14\text{–}30)$$

When the null hypothesis is true, the distribution of X^2 approaches the chi-square distribution with $k - 1$ degrees of freedom as n increases. For small values of k and n, tables of the exact distribution of X^2 under the null hypothesis may be found in nonparametric statistics books. Here we will use the chi-square distribution as our decision rule. We note that for small n, the chi-square approximation is *conservative;* that is, we may not be able to reject the null hypothesis as easily as we would if we use the exact distribution table. Our decision rule is to reject H_0 at a given level, α, if X^2 exceeds the critical point of the chi-square distribution with $k - 1$ degrees of freedom and right-tail area α. We now demonstrate the use of the Friedman test with an example.

EXAMPLE 14–10   A particular segment of the population, mostly retired people, frequently go on low-budget cruises. Many travel agents specialize in this market and maintain mailing lists of people who take frequent cruises. One such travel agent in Fort Lauderdale wanted to find out whether "frequent cruisers" prefer some of the cruise lines in the low-budget range over others. If so, the agent would concentrate on selling tickets on the preferred line(s) rather than on a wider variety of lines. From a mailing list of people who have taken at least one cruise on each of the three cruise lines Carnival, Costa, and Sitmar, the agent selected a random sample of 15 people and asked them to rank their overall experiences with the three lines. The ranks were 1 (best), 2 (second best), and 3 (worst). The results are given in Table 14–5. Are the three cruise lines equally preferred by people in the target population?

Solution   Using the sums of the ranks of the three treatments (the three cruise lines), we compute the Friedman test statistic. From equation 14–30, we get

$$X^2 = \frac{12}{nk(k+1)} (R_1^2 + R_2^2 + R_3^2) - 3n(k+1)$$

$$= \frac{12}{(15)(3)(4)} (31^2 + 21^2 + 38^2) - 3(15)(4) = 9.73$$

TABLE 14–5 Sample Results of Example 14–10

Respondent	Carnival	Costa	Sitmar
1	1	2	3
2	2	1	3
3	1	3	2
4	2	1	3
5	3	1	2
6	3	1	2
7	1	2	3
8	3	1	2
9	2	1	3
10	1	2	3
11	2	1	3
12	3	1	2
13	1	2	3
14	3	1	2
15	3	1	2
	$R_1 = 31$	$R_2 = 21$	$R_3 = 38$

We now compare the computed value of the statistic with values of the right tail of the chi-square distribution with $k - 1 = 2$ degrees of freedom. The critical point for $\alpha = 0.01$ is found from Appendix C, Table 4, to be 9.21. Since 9.73 is greater than 9.21, we conclude that there is evidence that not all three low-budget cruise lines are equally preferred by the frequent cruiser population.

The Template

Figure 14–11 shows the template that can be used to conduct a Friedman test. The data seen in the figure correspond to Example 14–10. The RowSum column in the template can be used to make a quick check of data entry. All the sums must be equal.

FIGURE 14–11 The Template for the Friedman Test [Nonparametric Tests.xls; Sheet: Friedman]

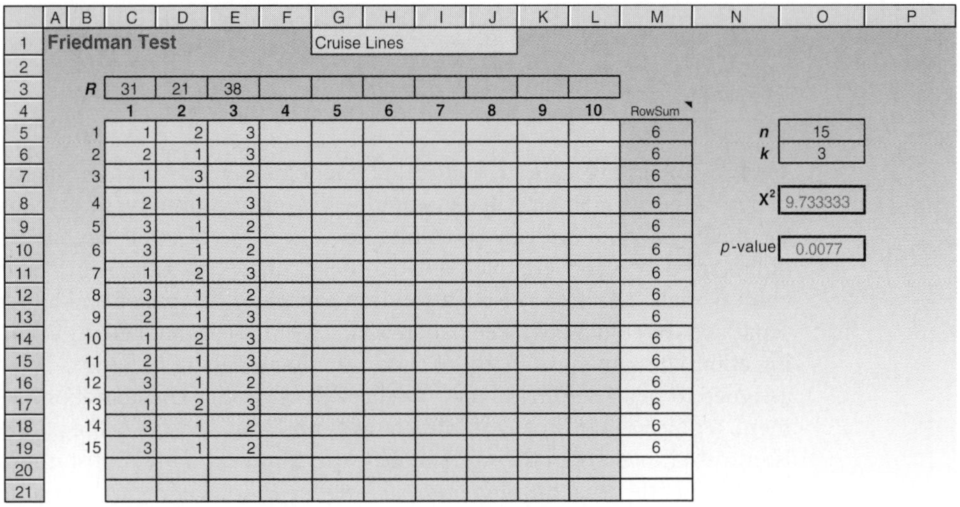

	A	B	C	D	E	F	G	H	I	J	K	L	M	N	O	P
1	Friedman Test						Cruise Lines									
2																
3		R	31	21	38											
4			1	2	3	4	5	6	7	8	9	10	RowSum			
5		1	1	2	3								6	*n*	15	
6		2	2	1	3								6	*k*	3	
7		3	1	3	2								6			
8		4	2	1	3								6	X^2	9.733333	
9		5	3	1	2								6			
10		6	3	1	2								6	*p*-value	0.0077	
11		7	1	2	3								6			
12		8	3	1	2								6			
13		9	2	1	3								6			
14		10	1	2	3								6			
15		11	2	1	3								6			
16		12	3	1	2								6			
17		13	1	2	3								6			
18		14	3	1	2								6			
19		15	3	1	2								6			
20																
21																

The template provides the *p*-value in cell O10. Since it is less than 1%, we can reject the null hypothesis that all cruise lines are equally preferred at an α of 1%.

PROBLEMS

14–38. A random sample of 12 consumers are asked to rank their preferences of four new fragrances that Calvin Klein wants to introduce to the market in the fall of 2008. The data are as follows (best liked denoted by 1 and least liked denoted by 4). Do you believe that all four fragrances are equally liked? Explain.

Respondent	Fragrance 1	Fragrance 2	Fragrance 3	Fragrance 4
1	1	2	4	3
2	2	1	3	4
3	1	3	4	2
4	1	2	3	4
5	1	3	4	2
6	1	4	3	2
7	1	3	4	2
8	2	1	4	3
9	1	3	4	2
10	1	3	2	4
11	1	4	3	2
12	1	3	4	2

14–39. While considering three managers for a possible promotion, the company president decided to solicit information from employees about the managers' relative effectiveness. Each person in a random sample of 10 employees who had worked with all three managers was asked to rank the managers, where best is denoted by 1, second best by 2, and worst by 3. The data follow. Based on the survey, are all three managers perceived as equally effective? Explain.

Respondent	Manager 1	Manager 2	Manager 3
1	3	2	1
2	3	2	1
3	3	1	2
4	3	2	1
5	2	3	1
6	3	1	2
7	3	2	1
8	3	2	1
9	3	1	2
10	3	1	2

14–40. In testing to find a cure for congenital heart disease, the condition of a patient after he or she has been treated with a drug cannot be directly quantified, but the patient's condition can be compared with those of other patients with the same illness severity who were treated with other drugs. A pharmaceutical firm conducting clinical trials therefore selects a random sample of 27 patients. The sample is then separated into blocks of three patients each, with the three patients in each block having about the same pretreatment condition. Each person in a block is then randomly assigned to be treated by one of the three drugs under consideration. After the treatment, a physician evaluates each person's condition and ranks the patient in comparison with the others in the same block (with 1 indicating the most improvement and 3 indicating the least improvement). Using the following data, do you believe that all three drugs are equally effective?

Block	Drug A	Drug B	Drug C
1	2	3	1
2	2	3	1
3	2	3	1
4	2	3	1
5	1	3	2
6	2	3	1
7	2	1	3
8	2	3	1
9	1	2	3

14-41. Four different processes for baking Oreo cookies are considered for the 2008 season. The cookies produced by each process are evaluated in terms of their overall quality. Since the cookies sometimes may not bake correctly, the distribution of quality ratings is different from a normal distribution. When conducting a test of the quality of the four processes, cookies are blocked into groups of four according to the ingredients used. The ratings of the cookies baked by the four processes are as follows. (Ratings are on a scale of 0 to 100.) Are the four processes equally good? Explain.

Block	Process 1	Process 2	Process 3	Process 4
1	87	65	73	20
2	98	60	39	45
3	85	70	50	60
4	90	80	85	50
5	78	40	60	45
6	95	35	70	25
7	70	60	55	40
8	99	70	45	60

14–8   The Spearman Rank Correlation Coefficient

Recall our discussion of correlation in Chapter 10. There we stressed the assumption that the distributions of the two variables in question, X and Y, are normal. In cases where this assumption is not realistic, or in cases where our data are themselves in the form of ranks or are otherwise on an ordinal scale, we have alternative measures of the degree of association between the two variables. The most frequently used nonparametric measure of the correlation between two variables is the *Spearman rank correlation coefficient,* denoted by r_s.

Our data are pairs of n observations on two variables X and Y—pairs of the form (x_i, y_i), where $i = 1, \ldots, n$. To compute the Spearman correlation coefficient, we first rank all the observations of one variable within themselves from smallest to largest. Then we independently rank the values of the second variable from smallest to largest. *The Spearman rank correlation coefficient is the usual (Pearson) correlation coefficient applied to the ranks.* When no ties exist, that is, when there are no two values of X or two values of Y with the same rank, there is an easier computational formula for the Spearman correlation coefficient. The formula follows.

The **Spearman rank correlation coefficient** (assuming no ties) is

$$r_s = 1 - \frac{6\sum_{i=1}^{n}d_i^2}{n(n^2 - 1)} \qquad (14\text{–}31)$$

where d_i, $i = 1, \ldots, n$, are the differences in the ranks of x_i and y_i; $d_i = R(x_i) - R(y_i)$.

If we do have ties within the X values or the Y values, but the number of ties is small compared with n, equation 14–31 is still useful.

The Spearman correlation coefficient satisfies the usual requirements of correlation measures. It is equal to 1 when the variables X and Y are perfectly positively related, that is, when Y increases whenever X does, and vice versa. It is equal to -1 in the opposite situation, where X increases whenever Y decreases. It is equal to 0 when there is no relation between X and Y. Values between these extremes give a relative indication of the degree of association between X and Y.

As with the parametric Pearson correlation coefficient, the Spearman statistic has two possible uses. It may be used as a descriptive statistic giving us an indication of the association between X and Y. We may also use it for *statistical inference*. In the context of inference, we assume a certain correlation in the ranks of the values of the bivariate population of X and Y. This population rank correlation is denoted by ρ_s. We want to test whether $\rho_s = 0$, that is, whether there is an association between the two variables X and Y.

The hypothesis test for association between two variables is
$$H_0: \rho_s = 0$$
$$H_1: \rho_s \neq 0 \tag{14–32}$$

This is a two-tailed test for the existence of a relation between X and Y. One-tailed versions of the test are also possible. If we want to test for a positive association between the variables, then the alternative hypothesis is that the parameter ρ_s is strictly greater than zero. If we want to test for a negative association only, then the alternative hypothesis is that ρ_s is strictly less than zero. The test statistic is simply r_s, as defined in equation 14–31.

When the sample size is less than or equal to 30, we use Appendix C, Table 11 (page 786). The table gives critical points for various levels of significance α. For a two-tailed test, we double the α level given in the table and reject the null hypothesis if r_s is either greater than or equal to the table value C or less than or equal to $-C$. In a right-tailed test, we reject only if r_s is greater than or equal to C; and in a left-tailed test, we reject only if r_s is less than or equal to $-C$. In either one-tailed case, we use the α given in one of the columns in the table (we do not double it).

For larger sample sizes, we use the normal approximation to the distribution of r_s under the null hypothesis. The Z statistic for such a case is as follows.

A large-sample test statistic for association is
$$z = r_s \sqrt{n - 1} \tag{14–33}$$

We demonstrate the computation of Spearman's statistic, and a test of whether the population rank correlation is zero, with Example 14–11.

EXAMPLE 14–11   The S&P 100 Index is an index of 100 stock options traded on the Chicago Board Options Exchange. The MMI is an index of 20 stocks with options traded on the American Stock Exchange. Since options are volatile, the assumption of a normal distribution may not be appropriate, and the Spearman rank correlation coefficient may provide us with information about the association between the two indexes.[16] Using the reported data on the two indexes, given in Table 14–6, compute the r_s

---

[16] *Volatility* means that there are jumps to very small and very large values. This gives the distribution long tails and makes it different from the normal distribution. For *stock returns,* however, the normal assumption is a good one, as mentioned in previous chapters.

statistic, and test the null hypothesis that the MMI and the S&P 100 are not related against the alternative that they are positively correlated.

We rank the MMI values and the S&P 100 values and compute the 10 differences: $d_i = \text{rank}(MMI_i) - \text{rank}(S\&P100_i)$. This is shown in Table 14–7. The order of the values in the table corresponds to their order in Table 14–6.

We now use equation 14–31 and compute r_s:

TABLE 14–6
Data on the MMI and S&P 100 Indexes for Example 14–11

$$r_s = 1 - \frac{6(d_1^2 + d_2^2 + \cdots + d_{10}^2)}{10(10^2 - 1)} = 1 - \frac{24}{990} = 0.9758$$

The sample correlation is very high.

We now use the r_s statistic in testing the hypotheses:

$$H_0: \rho_s \le 0$$
$$H_1: \rho_s > 0 \qquad (14\text{–}34)$$

MMI	S&P 100
220	151
218	150
216	148
217	149
215	147
213	146
219	152
236	165
237	162
235	161

We want to test for the existence of a positive rank correlation between MMI and S&P 100 in the *population* of values of the two indexes. We want to test whether the high sample rank correlation we found is statistically significant. Since this is a right-tailed test, we reject the null hypothesis if r_s is greater than or equal to a point C found in Appendix C, Table 11, at a level of α given in the table. We find from the table that for $\alpha = 0.005$ and $n = 10$, the critical point is 0.794. Since $r_s = 0.9758 > 0.794$, we reject the null hypothesis and conclude that the MMI and the S&P 100 are positively correlated. The p-value is less than 0.005.

In closing this section, we note that Spearman's rank correlation coefficient is sometimes referred to as *Spearman's rho* (the Greek letter ρ). There is another commonly used nonparametric measure of correlation. This one was developed by Kendall and is called *Kendall's tau* (the Greek letter τ). Since Kendall's measure is not as simple to compute as the Spearman coefficient of rank correlation, we leave it to texts on nonparametric statistics.

The Template

Figure 14–12 shows the template that can be used for calculating and testing Spearman's rank correlation coefficients. The data entered in columns B and C can be raw data or ranks themselves. The p-values in the range J15:J17 appear only if the sample is large ($n > 30$). Otherwise, the message "Look up the tables for p-value" appears in cell J6.

TABLE 14–7   Ranks and Rank Differences for Example 14–11

Rank(MMI)	Rank(S&P 100)	Difference
7	6	1
5	5	0
3	3	0
4	4	0
2	2	0
1	1	0
6	7	−1
9	10	−1
10	9	1
8	8	0

FIGURE 14–12 The Template for Calculating Spearman's Rank Correlation [Nonparametric Tests.xls; Sheet: Spearman]

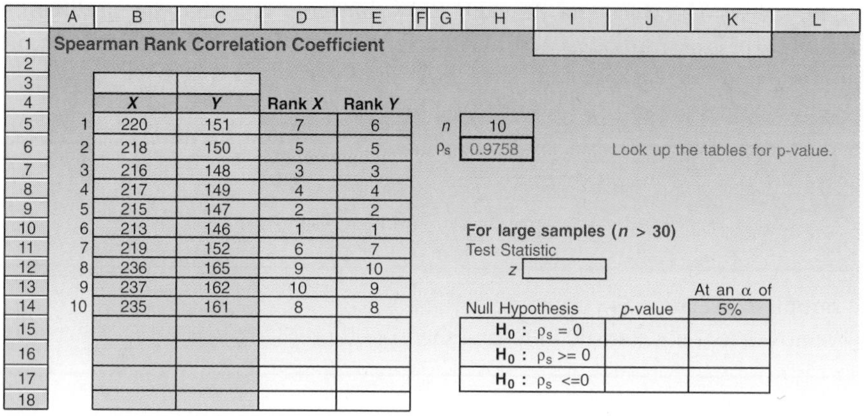
Spearman Rank Correlation Coefficient

	X	Y	Rank X	Rank Y
1	220	151	7	6
2	218	150	5	5
3	216	148	3	3
4	217	149	4	4
5	215	147	2	2
6	213	146	1	1
7	219	152	6	7
8	236	165	9	10
9	237	162	10	9
10	235	161	8	8

n 10

ρ_s 0.9758

Look up the tables for p-value.

For large samples ($n > 30$)

Test Statistic

z

Null Hypothesis	p-value	At an α of 5%
$H_0: \rho_s = 0$		
$H_0: \rho_s >= 0$		
$H_0: \rho_s <= 0$		

PROBLEMS

14–42. The director of a management training program wants to test whether there is a positive association between an applicant's score on a test prior to her or his being admitted to the program and the same person's success in the program. The director ranks 15 participants according to their performance on the pretest and separately ranks them according to their performance in the program:

Participant:	1	2	3	4	5	6	7	8	9	10	11	12	13	14	15
Pretest rank:	8	9	4	2	3	10	1	5	6	15	13	14	12	7	11
Performance rank:	7	5	9	6	1	8	2	10	15	14	4	3	11	12	13

Using these data, carry out the test for a positive rank correlation between pretest scores and success in the program.

14–43. An article in *Money* looks at the relationship between people's investments in large-cap stocks and international stocks.[17] Suppose that the following data are available for a random sample of families, the percentage of the portfolio invested in large-cap stocks, and the percentage invested in international stocks:

Large-cap (%):	25	28	15	17	30	22	12	13	20
International (%):	30	32	23	25	40	29	17	21	32

Compute the Spearman rank correlation coefficient and test for the existence of a population correlation.

14–44. Recently the European Community (EC) decided to lower its subsidies to makers of pasta. In deciding by what amount to reduce total subsidies, experiments were carried out for determining the possible reduction in exports, mainly to the United States, that would result from the subsidy reduction. Over a small range of values, economists wanted to test whether there is a positive correlation between level of subsidy and level of exports. A computer simulation of the economic variables involved in the pasta exports market was carried out. The results follow. Assuming that the simulation is an accurate description of reality and that the values obtained may be viewed as a random sample of the populations of possible outcomes, state

[17] "The Portfolio," *Money*, June 2007, p. 69.

whether you believe that a positive rank correlation exists between subsidy level and exports level over the short range of values studied.

Subsidy (millions of dollars/year):	5.1	5.3	5.2	4.9	4.8	4.7	4.5	5.0	4.6	4.4	5.4
Exports (millions of dollars/year):	22	30	35	29	27	36	40	39	42	45	21

14–45. An advertising research analyst wanted to test whether there is any relationship between a magazine advertisement's color intensity using a new digital photography technique introduced in 2007 and the ad's appeal. Ten ads of varying degrees of color intensity, but identical in other ways, were shown to randomly selected groups of respondents. The respondents rated each ad for its general appeal. The respondents were segmented in such a way that each group viewed a different ad, and every group's responses were aggregated. The results were ranked as follows.

Color intensity:	8	7	2	1	3	4	10	6	5	9
Appeal score:	1	3	4	2	5	8	7	6	9	10

Is there a rank correlation between color intensity and appeal?

14–9 A Chi-Square Test for Goodness of Fit

CHAPTER 13

In this section and the next two, we describe tests that make use of the chi-square distribution. The data used in these tests are *enumerative:* The data are counts, or frequencies. Our actual observations may be on a nominal (or higher) scale of measurement. Because many real-world situations in business and other areas allow for the collection of count data (e.g., the number of people in a sample who fall into different categories of age, sex, income, and job classification), chi-square analysis is very common and very useful. The tests are easy to carry out and are versatile: we can employ them in a wide variety of situations. The tests presented in this and the next two sections are among the most useful statistical techniques of analyzing data. Quite often, in fact, a computer program designed merely to count the number of items falling in some categories automatically prints out a chi-square value. The user then has to consider the question: What statistical test is implied by the chi-square statistic in this particular situation? Among their other purposes, these sections should help you answer this question.

We will discuss a common principle of all the chi-square tests. The principle is summarized in the following steps:

Steps in a chi-square analysis:

1. We hypothesize about a population by stating the null and alternative hypotheses.
2. We compute frequencies of occurrence of certain events that we expect under the null hypothesis. These give us the *expected* counts of data points in different cells.
3. We note the *observed* counts of data points falling in the different cells.
4. We consider the difference between the observed and the expected. This difference leads us to a computed value of the chi-square statistic. The formula of the statistic is given as equation 14–35.
5. We compare the value of the statistic with critical points of the chi-square distribution and make a decision.

The analysis in this section and the next two involves tables of data counts. The chi-square statistic has the same form in the applications in all three sections. The statistic is equal to the *squared difference between the observed count and the expected count in each cell, divided by the expected count, summed over all cells.* If our data table has k cells, let the observed count in cell i be O_i and the expected count (expected under H_0) be E_i. The definition is for all cells $i = 1, 2, \ldots, k$.

The chi-square statistic is

$$X^2 = \sum_{i=1}^{k} \frac{(O_i - E_i)^2}{E_i} \qquad (14\text{--}35)$$

As the total sample size increases, for a given number of cells k, the distribution of the statistic X^2 in equation 14–35 approaches the chi-square distribution. The degrees of freedom of the chi-square distribution are determined separately in each situation.

Remember the binomial experiment, where the number of *successes* (items falling in a particular category) is a random variable. The probability of a success is a fixed number p. Recall from the beginning of Chapter 4 that as the number of trials n increases, the distribution of the number of binomial successes approaches a normal distribution. In the situations in this and the next two sections, the number of items falling in any of *several* categories is a random variable, and as the number of trials increases, the observed number in any cell O_i approaches a normal random variable. Remember also that the sum of several squared standard normal random variables has a chi-square distribution. The terms summed in equation 14–35 are standardized random variables that are squared. Each one of these variables approaches a normal random variable. The sum, therefore, approaches a chi-square distribution as the sample size n gets large.

> A **goodness-of-fit test** is a statistical test of how well our data support an assumption about the distribution of a population or random variable of interest. The test determines how well an assumed distribution fits the data.

For example, we often make an assumption of a normal population. A test of how well a normal distribution fits a given data set may be of interest. Shortly we will see how to carry out a test of the normal distribution assumption.

We start our discussion of goodness-of-fit tests with a simpler test, and a very useful one—a test of goodness of fit in the case of a **multinomial distribution.** The multinomial distribution is a generalization of the binomial distribution to more than two possibilities (success versus failure). In the multinomial situation, we have $k > 2$ possible categories for the data. A data point can fall into only one of the k categories, and the probability that the point will fall in category i (where $i = 1, 2, \ldots, k$) is constant and equal to p_i. The sum of all k probabilities p_i is 1.

Given five categories, for example, such as five age groups, a respondent can fall into only one of the (nonoverlapping) groups. If the probabilities that the respondent will fall into any of the k groups are given by the five parameters p_1, p_2, p_3, p_4, and p_5, then the multinomial distribution with these parameters and n, the number of people in a random sample, specifies the probability of any combination of cell counts. For example, if $n = 100$ people, the multinomial distribution gives us the probability that 10 people will fall in category 1; 15 in category 2; 12 in category 3; 50 in category 4; and the remaining 13 in category 5. The distribution gives us the probabilities of *all possible counts* of 100 people (or items) distributed into five cells.

When we have a situation such as this, we may use the multinomial distribution to test how well our data fit the assumption of k fixed probabilities $p_1, \ldots, p_k$ of falling into k cells. However, working with the multinomial distribution is difficult, and the chi-square distribution is a very good alternative when sample size considerations allow its use.

A Goodness-of-Fit Test for the Multinomial Distribution

> The null and the alternative hypotheses for the multinomial distribution are
>
> H_0: The probabilities of occurrence of events $E_1, E_2, \ldots, E_k$ are given by the specified probabilities $p_1, p_2, \ldots, p_k$
>
> H_1: The probabilities of the k events are not the p_i stated in the null hypothesis   (14–36)

The test statistic is as given in equation 14–35. For large enough n (a rule for how large is "enough" will be given shortly), the distribution of the statistic may be approximated by a chi-square distribution with $k - 1$ degrees of freedom. We demonstrate the test with Example 14–12.

EXAMPLE 14–12

Raymond Weil is about to come out with a new watch and wants to find out whether people have special preferences for the color of the watchband, or whether all four colors under consideration are equally preferred. A random sample of 80 prospective watch buyers is selected. Each person is shown the watch with four different band colors and asked to state his or her preference. The results—the *observed counts*—are given in Table 14–8.

Solution

The null and alternative hypotheses, equation 14–36, take the following specific form:

> H_0: The four band colors are equally preferred; that is, the probabilities of choosing any of the four colors are equal: $p_1 = p_2 = p_3 = p_4 = 0.25$
>
> H_1: Not all four colors are equally preferred (the probabilities of choosing the four colors are not all equal)

To compute the value of our test statistic (equation 14–35), we need to find the *expected* counts in all four cells (in this example, each cell corresponds to a color).

Recall that for a binomial random variable, the mean—the *expected value*—is equal to the number of trials n times the probability of success in a single trial p. Here, in the multinomial experiment, we have k cells, each with probability p_i, where $i = 1, 2, \ldots, k$. For each cell, we have a binomial experiment with probability p_i and number of trials n. The expected number in each cell is therefore equal to n times p_i.

> The expected count in cell i is
> $$E_i = np_i \qquad (14–37)$$

In this example, the number of trials is the number of people in the random sample: $n = 80$. Under the null hypothesis, the expected number of people who will choose

TABLE 14–8   Watchband Color Preferences

	Tan	Brown	Maroon	Black	Total
	12	40	8	20	80

color i is equal to $E_i = np_i$. Furthermore, since all the probabilities in this case are equal to 0.25, we have the following:

$$E_1 = E_2 = E_3 = E_4 = (80)(0.25) = 20$$

When the null hypothesis is true, and the probability that any person will choose any one of the four colors is equal to 0.25, we may not observe 20 people in every cell. In fact, observing *exactly* 20 people in each of the four cells is an event with a small probability. However, the number of people we observe in each cell should not be too far from the expected number, 20. Just how far is "too far" is determined by the chi-square distribution. We use the expected counts and the observed counts in computing the value of the chi-square test statistic. From equation 14–35, we get the following:

$$X^2 = \sum_{i=1}^{k} \frac{(O_i - E_i)^2}{E_i} = \frac{(12 - 20)^2}{20} + \frac{(40 - 20)^2}{20} + \frac{(8 - 20)^2}{20} + \frac{(20 - 20)^2}{20}$$

$$= \frac{64}{20} + \frac{400}{20} + \frac{144}{20} + 0 = 3.2 + 20 + 7.2 + 0 = 30.4$$

We now conduct the test by comparing the computed value of our statistic, $X^2 = 30.4$, with critical points of the chi-square distribution with $k - 1 = 4 - 1 = 3$ degrees of freedom. From Appendix C, Table 4, we find that the critical point for a chi-square random variable with 3 degrees of freedom and right-hand-tail area $\alpha = 0.01$ is 11.3. (*Note that all the chi-square tests in this chapter are carried out only on the right-hand tail of the distribution.*) Since the computed value is much greater than the critical point at $\alpha = 0.01$, we conclude that there is evidence to reject the null hypothesis that all four colors are equally likely to be chosen. Some colors are probably preferable to others. Our p-value is very small.

The Template

The template for conducting chi-square tests for goodness of fit is shown in Figure 14–13. The data in the template correspond to Example 14–12. The results agree with the hand calculations. In addition, the template reveals that the p-value is almost zero.

Unequal Probabilities

The test for multinomial probabilities does not always entail equal probabilities, as was the case in our example. The probabilities may very well be different. All we need to

FIGURE 14–13   The Template for Goodness of Fit
[Chi-Square Tests.xls; Sheet: Goodness-of-Fit]

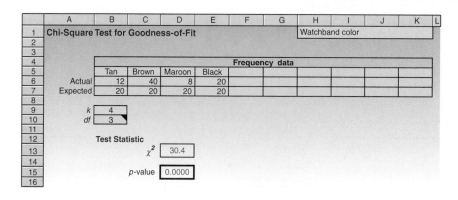

do is to specify the probabilities in the null hypothesis and then use the hypothesized probabilities in computing the expected cell counts (using equation 14–37). Then we use the expected counts along with the observed counts in computing the value of the chi-square statistic.

Under what conditions can we assume that, under the null hypothesis, the distribution of the test statistic in equation 14–37 is well-approximated by a chi-square distribution? This important question has no exact answer. As the sample size n increases, the approximation gets better and better. On the other hand, there is also a dependence on the cell k. If the expected number of counts in some cells is too small, the approximation may not be valid. We will give a good rule of thumb that specifies the minimum expected count in each cell needed for the chi-square approximation to be valid. The rule is conservative in the sense that other rules have been given that allow smaller expected counts under certain conditions. If we follow the rule given here, we will usually be safe using the chi-square distribution.

> The chi-square distribution may be used as long as the expected count in every cell is at least 5.0.

Suppose that while conducting an analysis, we find that for one or more cells, the expected number of items is less than 5. We may still continue our analysis if we can *combine cells* so that the expected number has a total of at least 5. For example, suppose that our null hypothesis is that the distribution of ages in a certain population is as follows: 20% are between the ages of 0 to 15, 10% are in the age group of 16 to 25, 10% are in the age group of 26 to 35, 20% are in the age group of 36 to 45, 30% are in the age group of 45 to 60, and 10% are age 61 or over. If we number the age group cells consecutively from 1 to 6, then the null hypothesis is H_0: $p_1 = 0.20$, $p_2 = 0.10$, $p_3 = 0.10$, $p_4 = 0.20$, $p_5 = 0.30$, $p_6 = 0.10$.

Now suppose that we gather a random sample of $n = 40$ people from this population and use this group to test for goodness of fit of the multinomial assumption in the null hypothesis. What are our expected cell counts? In the 0–15 cell, the expected number of people is $np_1 = (40)(0.20) = 8$, which is fine. But for the next age group, 16 to 25, we find that the expected number is $np_2 = (40)(0.10) = 4$, which is less than 5. If we want to continue the analysis, we may combine age groups that have small expected counts with other age groups. We may combine the 16–25 age group with the 26–35 age group, which also has a low expected count. Or we may combine the 16–25 group with the 0–15 group, and the 26–35 group with the 36–45 group—whichever makes more sense in terms of the interpretation of the analysis. We also need to combine the 61-and-over group with the 45–60 age group. Once we make sure that all expected counts are at least 5, we may use the chi-square distribution. Instead of combining groups, we may choose to increase the sample size.

We will now discuss the determination of the number of degrees of freedom, denoted by df. The total sample size is $n = 80$ in Table 14–8 of Example 14–12. The total count acts similarly to the way $\bar{x}$ does when we use it in computing the sample standard deviation. *The total count reduces the number of degrees of freedom by 1.* Why? Because knowing the total allows us not to know directly *any one* of the cell counts. If we knew, for example, the counts in the cells corresponding to tan, black, and maroon but did not know the count in the brown cell, we could still figure out the count for this cell by subtracting the sum of the three cell counts we do know from the total of 80. Thus, when we know the total, 1 degree of freedom is lost from the category cells. Out of four cells in this example, any three are free to move. Out of k cells, since we know their total, only $k − 1$ are free to move: df $= k − 1$.

Next we note another fact that will be important in our next example.

> If we have to use the data for estimating the parameters of the probability distribution stated in the null hypothesis, then for every parameter we estimate from the data, we lose an additional degree of freedom.

The chi-square goodness-of-fit test may be applied to testing any hypothesis about the distribution of a population or a random variable. As mentioned earlier, the test may be applied in particular to testing how well an assumption of a normal distribution is supported by a given data set. The standard normal distribution table, Appendix C, Table 2, gives us the probability that a standard normal random variable will be between any two given values. Through the transformation $X = \mu + \sigma Z$, we may then find boundaries in terms of the original variable X for any given probabilities of occurrence. These boundaries can be used in forming cells with known probabilities and, hence, known expected counts for a given sample size. This analysis, however, assumes that we know μ and σ, the mean and the standard deviation of the population or variable in question.

When μ and σ are *not* known and when the null and alternative hypotheses are stated as

> H_0: The population (or random variable) has a normal distribution
> H_1: The population (or random variable) is not normally distributed   (14–38)

there is no mention in the statement of the hypotheses of what the mean or standard deviation may be, and we need to estimate them directly from our data. When this happens, we lose a degree of freedom for each parameter estimated from the data (unless we use another data set for the estimation). We estimate μ by $\overline{X}$ and σ by S, as usual. The degrees of freedom of the chi-square statistic are $df = k - 2 - 1 = k - 3$ (instead of $k - 1$, as before). We will now demonstrate the test for a normal distribution with Example 14–13.

EXAMPLE 14–13

An analyst working for a department store chain wants to test the assumption that the amount of money spent by a customer in any store is approximately normally distributed. It is important to test this assumption because the analyst plans to conduct an analysis of variance to determine whether average sales per customer are equal at several stores in the same chain (as we recall, the normal-distribution assumption is required for ANOVA). A random sample of 100 shoppers at one of the department stores reveals that the average spending is $\bar{x} = \$125$ and the standard deviation is $s = \$40$. These are sample estimates of the *population* mean and standard deviation. (The breakdown of the data into cells is included in the solution.)

Solution

We begin by defining boundaries with known probabilities for the standard normal random variable Z. We know that the probability that the value of Z will be between -1 and $+1$ is about 0.68. We also know that the probability that Z will be between -2 and $+2$ is about 0.95, and we know other such probabilities. We may use Appendix C, Table 2, to find more exact probabilities. Let us use the table and define several nonoverlapping intervals for Z with known probabilities. We will form intervals of about the same probability. Figure 14–14 shows one possible partition of the standard normal distribution to intervals and their probabilities, obtained from Table 2. You may use any partition you desire.

The partition was obtained as follows. We know that the area under the curve between 0 and 1 is 0.3413 (from Table 2). Looking for an area of about half that size, 0.1700, we find that the appropriate point is $z = 0.44$. A similar relationship exists on the negative side of the number line. Thus, using just the values 0.44 and 1 and their negatives, we get a complete partition of the Z scale into the six intervals: $-\infty$ to -1, with associated probability of 0.1587; -1 to -0.44, with probability 0.1713; -0.44 to 0, with probability 0.1700; 0 to 0.44, with probability 0.1700; 0.44 to 1, with probability 0.1713; and, finally, 1 to ∞, with probability 0.1587. Breakdowns into other intervals may also be used.

FIGURE 14–14 Intervals and Their Standard Normal Probabilities

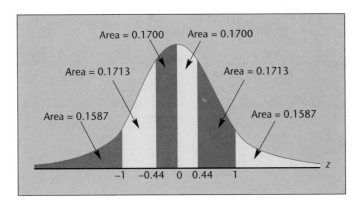

Now we transform the Z scale values to interval boundaries for the original problem. Taking $\bar{x}$ and s as if they were the mean and the standard deviation of the *population*, we use the transformation $X = \mu + \sigma Z$ with $\bar{x} = 125$ and $s = 40$ substituted for the unknown parameters. The Z value boundaries we just obtained are substituted into the transformation, giving us the following cell boundaries:

$$x_1 = 125 + (-1)(40) = 85$$
$$x_2 = 125 + (-0.44)(40) = 107.4$$
$$x_3 = 125 + (0)(40) = 125$$
$$x_4 = 125 + (0.44)(40) = 142.6$$
$$x_5 = 125 + (1)(40) = 165$$

The cells and their expected counts are given in Table 14–9. Cell boundaries are broken at the nearest cent. Recall that the expected count in each cell is equal to the cell probability times the sample size $E_i = np_i$. In this example, the p_i are obtained from the normal table and are, in order, 0.1587, 0.1713, 0.1700, 0.1700, 0.1713, and 0.1587. Multiplying these probabilities by $n = 100$ gives us the expected counts. (Note that the theoretical boundaries of $-\infty$ and $+\infty$ have no practical meaning; therefore, the lowest bound is replaced by 0 and the highest bound by *and above*.) Note that all expected cell counts are above 5, and, therefore, the chi-square distribution is an adequate approximation to the distribution of the test statistic X^2 in equation 14–35 under the null hypothesis.

Table 14–10 gives the observed counts of the sales amounts falling in each of the cells. The table was obtained by the analyst by looking at each data point in the sample and classifying the amount into one of the chosen categories.

To facilitate the computation of the chi-square statistic, we arrange the observed and expected cell counts in a single table and show the computations necessary for obtaining the value of the test statistic. This has been done in Table 14–11. The sum of all the entries in the last column in the table is the value of the chi-square statistic. The appropriate distribution has $k - 3 = 6 - 3 = 3$ degrees of freedom. We now consult

TABLE 14–9 Cells and Their Expected Counts

0–$84.99	$85.00–$107.39	$107.4–$124.99	$125–$142.59	$142.6–$164.99	$165 and above	
15.87	17.13	17.00	17.00	17.13	15.87	Total = 100

TABLE 14–10   Observed Cell Counts

0–$84.99	$85.00–$107.39	$107.4–$124.99	$125–$142.59	$142.6–$164.99	$165 and above	
14	20	16	19	16	15	Total = 100

TABLE 14–11   Computing the Value of the Chi-Square Statistic for Example 14–13

Cell	i	O_i	E_i	$O_i - E_i$	$(O_i - E_i)^2$	$(O_i - E_i)^2/E_i$
0–$84.99	1	14	15.87	−1.87	3.50	0.22
$85.00–$107.39	2	20	17.13	2.87	8.24	0.48
$107.40–$124.99	3	16	17.00	−1.00	1.00	0.06
$125.00–$142.59	4	19	17.00	2.00	4.00	0.24
$142.60–$164.99	5	16	17.13	−1.13	1.28	0.07
$165.00 and above	6	15	15.87	−0.87	0.76	0.05
						1.12

the chi-square table, Appendix C, Table 4, and we find that the computed statistic value $X^2 = 1.12$ falls in the nonrejection region for any level of α in the table. There is therefore no statistical evidence that the population is not normally distributed.

The Template

The template for testing the normal distribution of a given data set is shown in Figure 14–15. Since the calculated mean and standard deviation of the data set are used to define the class intervals, the degrees of freedom = $k - 3 = 3$.

The chi-square goodness-of-fit test may be applied to testing the fit of any hypothesized distribution. In general, we use an appropriate probability table for obtaining probabilities of intervals of values. The intervals define our data cells. Using the sample size, we then find the expected count in each cell. We compare the expected counts with the observed counts and compute the value of the chi-square test statistic.

The chi-square statistic is useful in other areas as well. In the next section, we will describe the use of the chi-square statistic in the analysis of contingency tables—an analysis of whether two principles of classification are contingent on each other or independent of each other. The following section extends the contingency table analysis to a test of homogeneity of several populations.

FIGURE 14–15   The Template for Testing Normal Distributions
[Chi-Square Tests.xls; Sheet: Normal Fit]

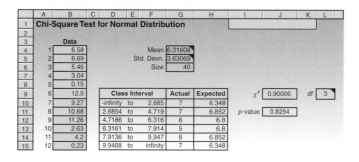

14–46. A company is considering five possible names for its new product. Before choosing a name, the firm decides to test whether all five names are equally appealing. A random sample of 100 people is chosen, and each person is asked to state her or his choice of the best name among the five possibilities. The numbers of people who chose each one of the names are as follows.

Name:	A	B	C	D	E
Number of choices:	4	12	34	40	10

Conduct the test.

14–47. A study reports an analysis of 35 key product categories. At the time of the study, 72.9% of the products sold were of a national brand, 23% were private label, and 4.1% were generic. Suppose that you want to test whether these percentages are still valid for the market today. You collect a random sample of 1,000 products in the 35 product categories studied, and you find the following: 610 products are of a national brand, 290 are private label, and 100 are generic. Conduct the test, and state your conclusions.

14–48. Overbooking of airline seats has now become a major problem for everyone who flies, because in order to stay profitable despite rising fuel costs, airlines now fly at an unprecedented average seat occupancy of 85%.[18] The following are the results, occupancy rates and counts, for some flights. Assume these data represent a random sample, and test the assumption that occupancy rates are normally distributed given that the mean is 85% and the standard deviation is 5%.

Range (%):	65–70	71–75	76–80	81–85	86–90	91–95
Count (number of flights):	21	18	11	9	5	4

14–49. Returns on an investment have been known to be normally distributed with mean 11% (annualized rate) and standard deviation 2%. A brokerage firm wants to test the null hypothesis that this statement is true and collects the following returns data in percent (assume a random sample): 8, 9, 9.5, 9.5, 8.6, 13, 14.5, 12, 12.4, 19, 9, 10, 10, 11.7, 15, 10.1, 12.7, 17, 8, 9.9, 11, 12.5, 12.8, 10.6, 8.8, 9.4, 10, 12.3, 12.9, 7. Conduct the analysis and state your conclusion.

14–50. Using the data provided in problem 14–49, test the null hypothesis that returns on the investment are normally distributed, but with *unknown* mean and standard deviation. That is, test only for the validity of the normal-distribution assumption. How is this test different from the one in problem 14–49?

14–10 Contingency Table Analysis— A Chi-Square Test for Independence

CHAPTER 14

Recall the important concept of *independence* of events, which we discussed in Chapter 2. Two events A and B are independent if the probability of their joint occurrence is equal to the product of their marginal (i.e., separate) probabilities. This was given as:

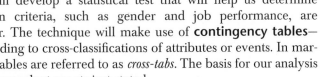

A and B are independent if $P(A \cap B) = P(A)P(B)$

In this section, we will develop a statistical test that will help us determine whether two classification criteria, such as gender and job performance, are independent of each other. The technique will make use of **contingency tables**— tables with cells corresponding to cross-classifications of attributes or events. In market research studies, such tables are referred to as *cross-tabs*. The basis for our analysis will be the property of independent events just stated.

---

[18]Jeff Bailey, "Overbooking: Bumped Fliers and No Plan B," *The New York Times*, May 30, 2007, p. A1.

FIGURE 14–16   Layout of a Contingency Table

Second Classification Category	First Classification Category						Total
	1	2	3	4	5	6	
1	O_{11}	O_{12}	O_{13}	O_{14}	O_{15}	O_{16}	R_1
2	O_{21}	O_{22}	O_{23}	O_{24}	O_{25}	O_{26}	R_2
3	O_{31}	O_{32}	O_{33}	O_{34}	O_{35}	O_{36}	R_3
4	O_{41}	O_{42}	O_{43}	O_{44}	O_{45}	O_{46}	R_4
5	O_{51}	O_{52}	O_{53}	O_{54}	O_{55}	O_{56}	R_5
Total	C_1	C_2	C_3	C_4	C_5	C_6	n

The contingency tables may have several rows and several columns. The rows correspond to levels of one classification category, and the columns correspond to another. We will denote the number of rows by r, and the number of columns by c. The total sample size is n, as before. The count of the elements in cell (i, j), that is, the cell in row i and column j (where $i = 1, 2, \ldots, r$ and $j = 1, 2, \ldots, c$), is denoted by O_{ij}. The total count for row i is R_i, and the total count for column j is C_j. The general form of a contingency table is shown in Figure 14–16. The table is demonstrated for $r = 5$ and $c = 6$. Note that n is also the sum of all r row totals and the sum of all c column totals.

Let us now state the null and alternative hypotheses.

> The hypothesis test for independence is
>
> H_0: The two classification variables are independent of each other
>
> H_1: The two classification variables are not independent   (14–39)

The principle of our analysis is the same as that used in the previous section. The chi-square test statistic for this set of hypotheses is the one we used before, given in equation 14–35. The only difference is that the summation extends over all cells in the table: the c columns and the r rows (in the previous application, goodness-of-fit tests, we only had one row). We will rewrite the statistic to make it clearer:

> The chi-square test statistic for independence is
>
> $$X^2 = \sum_{i=1}^{r} \sum_{j=1}^{c} \frac{(O_{ij} - E_{ij})^2}{E_{ij}}$$ (14–40)

The double summation in equation 14–40 means summation over all rows and all columns.

> The degrees of freedom of the chi-square statistic are
>
> $$df = (r - 1)(c - 1)$$ (14–41)

Now all we need to do is to find the expected cell counts E_{ij}. Here is where we use the assumption that the two classification variables are independent. Remember that the philosophy of hypothesis testing is to assume that H_0 is true and to use this assumption in determining the distribution of the test statistic. Then we try to show that the result is unlikely under H_0 and thus reject the null hypothesis.

Assuming that the two classification variables are independent, let us derive the expected counts in all cells. Look at a particular cell in row i and column j. Recall from equation 14–37 that the expected number of items in a cell is equal to the sample size times the probability of the occurrence of the event signified by the particular cell. In the context of an $r \times c$ contingency table, the probability associated with cell (i, j) is the probability of occurrence of event i and event j. Thus, the expected count in cell (i, j) is $E_{ij} = nP(i \cap j)$. If we assume independence of the two classification variables, then event i and event j are independent events, and by the law of independence of events, $P(i \cap j) = P(i)P(j)$.

From the row totals, we can estimate the probability of event i as R_i/n. Similarly, we estimate the probability of event j by C_j/n. Substituting these estimates of the marginal probabilities, we get the following expression for the expected count in cell (i, j): $E_{ij} = n(R_i/n)(C_j/n) = R_iC_j/n$.

> The expected count in cell (i, j) is
> $$E_{ij} = \frac{R_iC_j}{n} \tag{14–42}$$

Equation 14–42 allows us to compute the expected cell counts. These, along with the observed cell counts, are used in computing the value of the chi-square statistic, which leads us to a decision about the null hypothesis of independence.

We will now illustrate the analysis with two examples. The first example is an illustration of an analysis of the simplest contingency table, a 2×2 table. In such tables, the two rows correspond to the occurrence versus nonoccurrence of one event, and the two columns correspond to the occurrence or nonoccurrence of another event.

EXAMPLE 14–14

In order to study the profits and losses of firms by industry, a random sample of 100 firms is selected, and for each firm in the sample, we record whether the company made money or lost money, and whether the firm is a service company. The data are summarized in the 2×2 contingency table, Table 14–12. Using the information in the table, determine whether you believe that the two events "the company made a profit this year" and "the company is in the service industry" are independent.

Solution

Table 14–12 is the table of observed counts. We now use its marginal totals R_1, R_2, C_1, and C_2 as well as the sample size n, in creating a table of expected counts. Using equation 14–42, we get

> $$E_{11} = R_1C_1/n = (60)(48)/100 = 28.8$$
> $$E_{12} = R_1C_2/n = (60)(52)/100 = 31.2$$
> $$E_{21} = R_2C_1/n = (40)(48)/100 = 19.2$$
> $$E_{22} = R_2C_2/n = (40)(52)/100 = 20.8$$

We now arrange these values in a table of expected counts, Table 14–13. Using the values shown in the table, we now compute the chi-square test statistic of equation 14–40:

> $$X^2 = \frac{(42 - 28.8)^2}{28.8} + \frac{(18 - 31.2)^2}{31.2} + \frac{(6 - 19.2)^2}{19.2} + \frac{(34 - 20.8)^2}{20.8} = 29.09$$

TABLE 14–12 Contingency Table of Profit/Loss versus Industry Type

	Industry Type		
	Service	Nonservice	Total
Profit	42	18	60
Loss	6	34	40
Total	48	52	100

TABLE 14–13 Expected Counts (with the observed counts shown in parentheses) for Example 14–14

	Service	Nonservice
Profit	28.8	31.2
	(42)	(18)
Loss	19.2	20.8
	(6)	(34)

To conduct the test, we compare the computed value of the statistic with critical points of the chi-square distribution with $(r - 1)(c - 1) = (2 - 1)(2 - 1) = 1$ degree of freedom. From Appendix C, Table 4, we find that the critical point for $\alpha = 0.01$ is 6.63, and since our computed value of the X^2 statistic is much greater than the critical point, we reject the null hypothesis and conclude that the two qualities, profit/loss and industry type, are probably not independent.

In the analysis of 2×2 contingency tables, our chi-square statistic has *1 degree of freedom*. In such cases, the value of the statistic frequently is "corrected" so that its discrete distribution will be better approximated by the *continuous* chi-square distribution. The correction is called the **Yates correction** and entails subtracting the number $1/2$ from the absolute value of the difference between the observed and the expected counts before squaring them as required by equation 14–40. The Yates-corrected form of the statistic is as follows.

$$\text{Yates-corrected } X^2 = \sum_{i=1}^{r} \sum_{j=1}^{c} \frac{(|O_{ij} - E_{ij}| - 0.5)^2}{E_{ij}} \qquad (14\text{–}43)$$

For our example, the corrected value of the chi-square statistic is found as

$$\begin{aligned}
\text{Yates-corrected } X^2 \\
= \frac{(13.2 - 0.5)^2}{28.8} + \frac{(13.2 - 0.5)^2}{31.2} + \frac{(13.2 - 0.5)^2}{19.2} + \frac{(13.2 - 0.5)^2}{20.8} \\
= 26.92
\end{aligned}$$

As we see, the correction yields a smaller computed value. This value still leads to a strong rejection of the null hypothesis of independence. In many cases, the correction will not significantly change the results of the analysis. We will not emphasize the correction in the applications in this book.

The Template

The template for testing independence using the chi-square distribution is shown in Figure 14–17. The data correspond to Example 14–14.

EXAMPLE 14–15

To better identify its target market, Alfa Romeo conducted a market research study. A random sample of 669 respondents was chosen, and each was asked to select one of four qualities that best described him or her as a driver. The four possible self-descriptive qualities were *defensive, aggressive, enjoying,* and *prestigious.* Each respondent was then

FIGURE 14–17 The Template for Testing Independence
[Chi-Square Tests.xls; Sheet: Independence]

	A	B	C	D	E	F	G	H	I	J	K	L	N	N	O	P
1	Chi-Square Test for Independence								Alfa Romeo							
2																
3		Frequencies Data												Yates Correction	0.5	
4		1	2	3	4	5	6	7	8	9	10	Total				
5	1	42	18									60		#Rows	2	
6	2	6	34									40		#Cols	2	
7	3											0		df	1	
8	4											0				
9	5											0		Test Statistic		
10	6											0		χ^2	26.925	
11	7											0				
12	8											0		p-value	0.0000	
13	9											0				
14	10											0				
15	Total	48	52	0	0	0	0	0	0	0	0	100				
16																

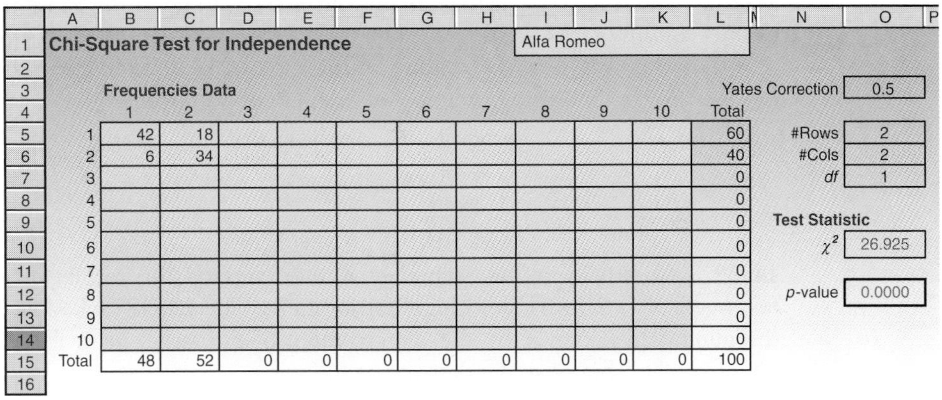

TABLE 14–14 The Observed Counts: Alfa Romeo Study

Alfa Romeo Model	Self-Image				
	Defensive	Aggressive	Enjoying	Prestigious	Total
Alfasud	22	21	34	56	133
Giulia	39	45	42	68	194
Spider	77	89	96	80	342
Total	138	155	172	204	669

FIGURE 14–18 Template Solution to Example 14–15
[Chi-Square Tests.xls; Sheet: Independence]

	A	B	C	D	E	F	G	H	I	J	K	L	N	N	O	P
1	Chi-Square Test for Independence								Alfa Romeo							
2																
3		Frequencies Data												Yates Correction	0	
4		1	2	3	4	5	6	7	8	9	10	Total				
5	1	22	21	34	56							133		#Rows	3	
6	2	39	45	42	68							194		#Cols	4	
7	3	77	89	96	80							342		df	6	
8	4											0				
9	5											0		Test Statistic		
10	6											0		χ^2	20.867	
11	7											0				
12	8											0		p-value	0.0019	
13	9											0				
14	10											0				
15	Total	138	155	172	204	0	0	0	0	0	0	669				
16																

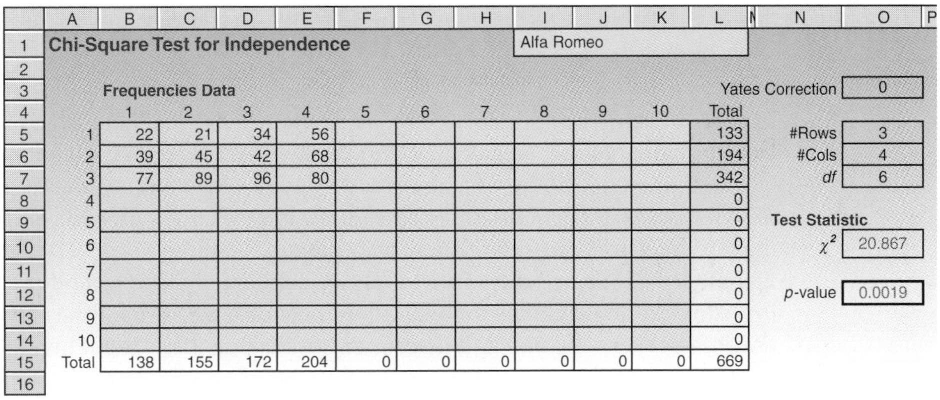

asked to choose one of three Alfa Romeo models as her or his choice of the most suitable car. The three models were Alfasud, Giulia, and Spider. The purpose of the study was to determine whether a relationship existed between a driver's self-image and choice of an Alfa Romeo model. The response data are given in Table 14–14.

Figure 14–18 shows the template solution to Example 14–15. The p-value of 0.0019 is less than 1% and therefore we reject the null hypothesis that the choice of Alfa Romeo model and self-image are independent.

Solution

14–51. An article reports that smaller firms seem to be hiring more than large ones as the economy picks up its pace. The table below gives numbers of employees hired and those laid off, out of a random sample of 1,032, broken down by firm size. Is there evidence that hiring practices are dependent on firm size?

	Small Firm	Medium-Size Firm	Large Firm	Total
Number hired	210	290	325	825
Number laid off	32	95	80	207
Total	242	385	405	1,032

14–52. An article in the *Journal of Business* reports the results of an analysis of takeovers of U.S. firms by foreign corporations. The article looked at the reaction to the attempted takeover by the management of the target firm: friendly, hostile, or white knight.[19] Suppose the data are as follows.

Managerial Reaction	Successful Takeover	Unsuccessful Takeover	Total
Friendly	174	8	182
Hostile	18	12	30
White knight	14	2	16
Total	206	22	228

Does managerial reaction by the target firm affect the success of the takeover?

14–53. The table below gives the number of cars, out of a random sample of 100 rental cars, belonging to each of the listed firms in 2005 and in 2007. Is there evidence of a change in the market shares of the car rental firms?

	Hertz	Avis	National	Budget	Other	Total
2005	39	26	18	14	3	100
2007	29	25	16	19	11	100

14–54. The following table describes recent purchases of U.S. stocks by individual or institution as well as domestic or foreign. Is there evidence of a dependence to institutional buying on whether the buyer is foreign or domestic?

	Domestic	Foreign
Individual	25	32
Institution	30	13

14–55. A study was conducted to determine whether a relationship existed between certain shareholder characteristics and the level of risk associated with the shareholders' investment portfolios. As part of the analysis, portfolio risk (measured by the portfolio beta) was divided into three categories: low-risk, medium-risk, and high-risk; and the portfolios were cross-tabulated according to the three risk levels and seven family-income levels. The results of the analysis, conducted using a random sample of 180 investors, are shown in the following contingency table. Test for the existence of a relationship between income and investment risk taking. [Be careful here! (Why?)]

Income Level ($)	Portfolio Risk Level			
	Low	Medium	High	Total
0 to 60,000	5	4	1	10
61,000 to 100,000	6	3	0	9
101,000 to 150,000	22	30	11	63
151,000 to 200,000	11	20	20	51
201,000 to 250,000	8	10	4	22
251,000 to 300,000	2	0	10	12
301,000 and above	1	1	11	13
Total	55	68	57	180

[19]Jun-Koo Kang et al., "Post Takeover Restructuring and the Sources of Gains in Foreign Takeovers: Evidence from U.S. Targets," *Journal of Business* 79, no. 5 (2006), pp. 2503–2537.

14–56. When new paperback novels are promoted at bookstores, a display is often arranged with copies of the same book with differently colored covers. A publishing house wanted to find out whether there is a dependence between the place where the book is sold and the color of its cover. For one of its latest novels, the publisher sent displays and a supply of copies of the novel to large bookstores in five major cities. The resulting sales of the novel for each city–color combination are as follows. Numbers are in thousands of copies sold over a 3-month period.

City	Red	Blue	Green	Yellow	Total
New York	21	27	40	15	103
Washington	14	18	28	8	68
Boston	11	13	21	7	52
Chicago	3	33	30	9	75
Los Angeles	30	11	34	10	85
Total	79	102	153	49	383

a. Assume that the data are random samples for each particular color–city combination and that the inference may apply to all novels. Conduct the overall test for independence of color and location.

b. Before the analysis, the publisher stated a special interest in the issue of whether there is any dependence between the red versus blue preference and the two cities Chicago versus Los Angeles. Conduct the test. Explain.

14–11   A Chi-Square Test for Equality of Proportions

Contingency tables and the chi-square statistic are also useful in another kind of analysis. Sometimes we are interested in whether the proportion of some characteristic is equal in several populations. An insurance company, for example, may be interested in finding out whether the proportion of people who submit claims for automobile accidents is about the same for the three age groups 25 and under, over 25 and under 50, and 50 and over. In a sense, the question of whether the proportions are equal is a question of whether the three age populations are *homogeneous* with respect to accident claims. Therefore, tests of equality of proportions across several populations are also called *tests of homogeneity.*

The analysis is carried out in exactly the same way as in the previous application. We arrange the data in cells corresponding to population-characteristic combinations, and for each cell, we compute the expected count based on its row and column totals. The chi-square statistic is computed exactly as before. Two things are different in this analysis. First, we identify our populations of interest before the analysis and sample directly from these populations. Contrast this with the previous application, where we sampled from one population and then cross-classified according to two criteria. Second, because we identify populations and sample from them directly, the sizes of the samples from the different populations of interest are fixed. This is called a *chi-square analysis with fixed marginal totals.* This fact, however, does not affect the analysis.

We will demonstrate the analysis with the insurance company example just mentioned. The null and alternative hypotheses are

H_0: The proportion of claims is the same for all three age groups (i.e., the age groups are homogeneous with respect to claim proportions)

H_1: The proportion of claims is not the same across age groups (the age groups are not homogeneous)   (14–44)

TABLE 14–15   Data for the Insurance Company Example

| | Age Group | | | |
	25 and under	Over 25 and under 50	50 and over	Total
Claim	40	35	60	135
No claim	60	65	40	165
Total	100	100	100	300

There are fixed sample sizes for all three populations.

Suppose that random samples, selected from company records for the three age categories, are classified according to *claim* versus *no claim* and are counted. The data are presented in Table 14–15.

To carry out the test, we first calculate the expected counts in all the cells. The expected cell counts are obtained, as before, by using equation 14–42. The expected count in each cell is equal to the row total times the column total, divided by the total sample size (the pooled sample size from all populations). The reason for the formula in this new context is that if the proportion of items in the class of interest (here, the proportion of people who submit a claim) is equal across all populations, as stated in the null hypothesis, then *pooling* this proportion across populations gives us the expected proportion in the cells for the class. Thus, the expected proportion in the claim class is estimated by the total in the claim class divided by the grand total, or $R_1/n = 135/300 = 0.45$. If we multiply this pooled proportion by the total number in the sample from the population of interest (say, the sample of people 25 and under), this should give us the *expected* count in the cell *claim—25 and under*. We get $E_{11} = C_1(R_1/n) = (C_1 R_1)/n$. This is exactly as prescribed by equation 14–42 in the test for independence. Here we get $E_{11} = (100)(0.45) = 45$. This is the expected count under the null hypothesis. We compute the expected counts for all other cells in the table in a similar manner. Table 14–16 is the table of expected counts in this example.

Note that since we used equal sample sizes (100 from each age population), the expected count is equal in all cells corresponding to the same class. The proportions are expected to be equal under the null hypothesis. Since these proportions are multiplied by the same sample size, the counts are also equal.

We are now ready to compute the value of the chi-square test statistic. From equation 14–40, we get

$$X^2 = \sum_{\text{all cells}} \frac{(O-E)^2}{E} = \frac{(40-45)^2}{45} + \frac{(35-45)^2}{45} + \frac{(60-45)^2}{45}$$
$$+ \frac{(60-551)^2}{55} + \frac{(65-55)^2}{55} + \frac{(40-55)^2}{55} = 14.14$$

The degrees of freedom are obtained as usual. We have two rows and three columns, so the degrees of freedom are $(2-1)(3-1) = 2$. Alternatively, cross out

TABLE 14–16   Expected Counts for the Insurance Company Example

	25 and under	Over 25 and under 50	50 and over	Total
Claim	45	45	45	135
No claim	55	55	55	165
Total	100	100	100	300

any one row and any one column in Table 14–15 or 14–16 (ignoring the *Total* row and column). This leaves you with two cells, giving df = 2.

Comparing the computed value of the statistic with critical points of the chi-square distribution with 2 degrees of freedom, we find that the null hypothesis may be rejected and that the p-value is less than 0.01. (Check this, using Appendix C, Table 4.) We conclude that the proportions of people who submit claims to the insurance company are not the same across the age groups studied.

In general, when we compare c populations (or r populations, if they are arranged as the rows of the table rather than the columns), the hypotheses in equation 14–44 may be written as

$$H_0: p_1 = p_2 = \cdots = p_c$$
$$H_1: \text{Not all } p_i, i = 1, \ldots, c, \text{ are equal} \qquad (14\text{--}45)$$

where p_i $(i = 1, \ldots, c)$ is the proportion in population i of the characteristic of interest. The test of equation 14–45 is a generalization to c populations of the test of equality of two population proportions discussed in Chapter 8. In fact, when $c = 2$, the test is identical to the simple test for equality of two population proportions. In our present context, the two-population test for proportion may be carried out using a 2×2 contingency table. The results of such a test would be identical to the results of a test using the method of Chapter 8 (a Z test).

The test presented in this section may also be applied to several proportions within each population. That is, instead of just testing for the proportion of *claim* versus *no claim,* we could be testing a more general hypothesis about the proportions of *several* different types of claims: no claim, claim under $1,000, claim of $1,000 to $5,000, and claim over $5,000. Here the null hypothesis would be that the proportion of each type of claim is equal across all populations. (This does not mean that the proportions of all types of claims are equal within a population.) The alternative hypothesis would be that not all proportions are equal across all populations under study. The analysis is done using an $r \times c$ contingency table (instead of the $2 \times c$ table we used in the preceding example). The test statistic is the same, and the degrees of freedom are as before: $(r - 1) \times (c - 1)$. We now discuss another extension of the test presented in this section.

The Median Test

The hypotheses for the median test are

$$H_0: \text{The } c \text{ populations have the same median}$$
$$H_1: \text{Not all } c \text{ populations have the same median} \qquad (14\text{--}46)$$

Using the c random samples from the populations of interest, we determine the grand median, that is, the median of all our data points regardless of which population they are from. Then we divide each sample into two sets. One set contains all points that are greater than the grand median, and the second set contains all points in the sample that are less than or equal to the grand median. We construct a $2 \times c$ contingency table in which the cells in the top row contain the counts of all points above the median for all c samples. The second row contains cells with the counts of the data points in each sample that are less than or equal to the grand median. Then we conduct the usual chi-square analysis of the contingency table. If we reject H_0, then we may conclude that there is evidence that not all c population medians are equal. We now demonstrate the median test with Example 14–16.

TABLE 14–17   Family Incomes ($1,000s per year)

	Region A	Region B	Region C
	22	31	28
	29	37	42
	36	26	21
	40	25	47
	35	20	18
	50	43	23
	38	27	51
	25	41	16
	62	57	30
	16	32	48

EXAMPLE 14–16   An economist wants to test the null hypothesis that median family incomes in three rural areas are approximately equal. Random samples of family incomes in the three regions (in thousands of dollars per year) are given in Table 14–17.

Solution   For simplicity, we chose an equal sample size of 10 in each population. This is not necessary; the sample sizes may be different. There is a total of 30 observations, and the median is therefore the average of the 15th and the 16th observations. Since the 15th observation (counting from smallest to largest) is 31 and the 16th is 32, the grand median is 31.5. Table 14–18 shows the counts of the sample points in each sample that are above the grand median and those that are less than or equal to the grand median. The table also shows the expected cell counts (in parentheses). Note that all expected counts are 5—the minimum required for the chi-square test. We now compute the value of the chi-square statistic.

$$X^2 = \frac{1}{5}\left[(4-5)^2 + (5-5)^2 + (6-5)^2 + (6-5)^2 + (5-5)^2 + (4-5)^2\right]$$

$$= \frac{4}{5} = 0.8$$

Comparing this value with critical points of the chi-square distribution with 2 degrees of freedom, we conclude that there is no evidence to reject the null hypothesis. The p-value is greater than 0.20.

Note that the median test is a weak test. Other tests could have resulted in the rejection of the null hypothesis (try them). We presented the test as an illustration of the wide variety of possible uses of the chi-square statistic. Other uses may be found in advanced books. We note that if the test had led to rejection, then other tests would probably have done so, too. Sometimes this test is easier to carry out and may lead to a quick answer (when we reject the null hypothesis).

TABLE 14–18   Observed and Expected Counts for Example 14–16

	Region A	Region B	Region C	Total
Less than or equal to	4	5	6	15
	(5)	(5)	(5)	
Above grand median	6	5	4	15
	(5)	(5)	(5)	
Total	10	10	10	30

14–57. An advertiser runs a commercial on national television and wants to determine whether the proportion of people exposed to the commercial is equal throughout the country. A random sample of 100 people is selected at each of five locations, and the number of people in each location who have seen the commercial at least once during the week is recorded. The numbers are as follows: location A, 32 people; location B, 59 people; location C, 78 people; location D, 40 people; and location E, 10 people. Do you believe that the proportion of people exposed to the commercial is equal across the five locations?

14–58. An accountant wants to test the hypothesis that the proportion of incorrect transactions at four client accounts is about the same. A random sample of 80 transactions of one client reveals that 21 are incorrect; for the second client, the sample proportion is 25 out of 100; for the third client, the proportion is 30 out of 90 sampled; and for the fourth, 40 are incorrect out of a sample of 110. Conduct the test at $\alpha = 0.05$.

14–59. An article in *BusinessWeek* describes how three online news services now supply Web surfers quick information on developing stories.[20] Suppose that a random sample of users is available from various parts of the country. Data are shown in the table below. Is there evidence that the three Web news services have different success rates at different regions of the country?

	Northeast	South	West	Midwest
Google News	78	15	109	65
PBS Online	115	10	88	50
New York Times	208	3	52	40

14–60. Data mining for use in marketing products to consumers has recently undergone much growth.[21] HP, NCR, and IBM have been involved in this business, and suppose the following data are available about successful marketing efforts by these three firms within three industry groups. Based on these data, are the three firms equally successful in the three industry groups? Explain.

	Consumer Goods	Luxury Items	Financial Services
HP	2,517	1,112	850
NCR	7,042	8,998	12,420
IBM	15,103	6,014	1,997

14–61. As markets become more and more international, many firms invest in research aimed at determining the maximum possible extent of sales in foreign markets. A U.S. manufacturer of coffeemakers wants to find out whether the company's market share and the market shares of two main competitors are about the same in three European countries to which all three companies export their products. The results of a market survey are summarized in the following table. The data are random samples of 150 consumers in each country. Conduct the test of equality of population proportions across the three countries.

	Country			
	France	England	Spain	Total
Company	55	38	24	117
First competitor	28	30	21	79
Second competitor	20	18	31	69
Other	47	64	74	185
Total	150	150	150	450

---

[20]Burt Helm and Paula Lehman, "Buying Clicks to a Tragedy," *BusinessWeek,* May 7, 2007, p. 42.

[21]Louise Lee, "HP Sees a Gold Mine in Data Mining," *BusinessWeek,* April 30, 2007, p. 71.

14–62.   New production methods stressing teamwork have recently been instituted at car manufacturing plants in Detroit. Three teamwork production methods are to be compared to see if they are equally effective. Since large deviations often occur in the numbers produced daily, it is desired to test for equality of medians (rather than means). Samples of daily production volume for the three methods are as follows. Assume that these are random samples from the populations of daily production volume. Use the median test to help determine whether the three methods are equally effective.

Method A:	5, 7, 19, 8, 10, 16, 14, 9, 22, 4, 7, 8, 15, 18, 7
Method B:	8, 12, 15, 28, 5, 14, 19, 16, 23, 19, 25, 17, 20
Method C:	14, 28, 13, 10, 8, 29, 30, 26, 17, 13, 10, 31, 27, 20

14–12   Using the Computer

Using MINITAB for Nonparametric Tests

MINITAB enables you to carry out a variety of nonparametric tests by the commands that are available via Stat ▶ Nonparametrics in the menu bar.

To perform a one-sample sign test of the median or calculate the corresponding point estimate and confidence interval, choose Stat ▶ Nonparametrics ▶ 1-Sample Sign from the menu bar. This test is used as a nonparametric alternative to one-sample Z tests and to one-sample t tests, which use the mean instead of median. When the corresponding dialog box appears you need to select the column(s) containing the variable(s) you want to test. Enter a confidence level between 0 and 100 for calculating confidence intervals. Check Test Median to perform a sign test, and then specify the null hypothesis value. You also need to choose the kind of test performed by selecting less than (left-tailed), not equal (two-tailed), or greater than (right-tailed) from the drop-down box.

You can also perform a one-sample Wilcoxon signed rank test by choosing Stat ▶ Nonparametrics ▶ 1-Sample Wilcoxon from the menu bar. An assumption for this test is that the data are a random sample from a continuous, symmetric population. The dialog box setting is the same as for the previous test. MINITAB also carries out a two-sample Wilcoxon rank sum test or Mann-Whitney test of the equality of two population medians. Start by choosing Stat ▶ Nonparametrics ▶ Mann-Whitney from the menu bar. The assumption for the Mann-Whitney test is that the data were chosen randomly and independently from two populations that have the same shape and equal variances. The required settings are as before.

A Kruskal-Wallis test of the equality of medians for two or more populations is performed via Stat ▶ Nonparametrics ▶ Kruskal-Wallis. This test offers a nonparametric alternative to the one-way analysis of variance. An assumption for this test is that the samples were chosen randomly and independently from continuous distributions with the same shape. When the corresponding dialog box appears, you need to enter the column that contains the response variable from all the samples as well as the column that contains the factor levels.

MINITAB can also perform the Friedman test for the analysis of a randomized block experiment, and thus provides an alternative to the two-way analysis of variance. Start by choosing Stat ▶ Nonparametrics ▶ Friedman from the menu bar. When the corresponding dialog box appears, enter the column containing the response variable in the Response edit box. Enter the column that contains the treatments in the Treatment edit box, and enter the column that contains the blocks in the Block edit box. You can also check to store the residuals or fitted values in the worksheet. MINITAB prints the test statistic, which has approximately a chi-square distribution, and the associated degrees of freedom. If there are ties within one or more blocks, the average rank is used, and a test statistic corrected for ties is also printed. An estimated median for each treatment level will be displayed as well.

FIGURE 14–19   Chi-Square Goodness-of-Fit Test (One Variable) Using MINITAB

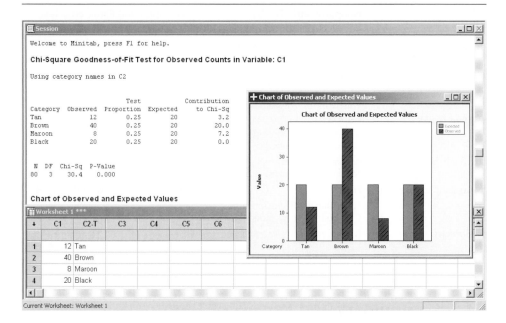

To perform a runs test choose Stat ▶ Nonparametrics ▶ Runs Test. A *run* is defined as a set of consecutive observations that are all either less than or greater than a specified value. This test is used when you want to determine if the order of responses above or below a specified value is random. When the corresponding dialog box appears, select the columns containing the variables you want to test for randomness in the Variables edit box. Check Above and below the mean if you want to use the mean as the baseline to determine the number of runs. If you want to choose a value other than the mean as the baseline, choose Above and below and then enter a value.

MINITAB tools for chi-square tests are available via Stat ▶ Tables from the menu bar. To evaluate whether the data follow a multinomial distribution with certain proportions choose Stat ▶ Tables ▶ Chi-Square Goodness-of-Fit Test (One Variable). Note that the results may not be accurate if the expected frequency of any category is less than 5. In the corresponding dialog box you need to choose if you have summary values of observed counts for each category. Enter the column containing the observed counts or type the observed counts for each category in the Observed counts edit box. Enter the column containing the category names or type each category's name in the Category names. If you have raw categorical data in a column, enter the column name in the Categorical data edit box. Check Equal proportions to assume equal proportions across categories. If you have different proportions for each category, select Specific proportions and then enter the column name that contains the proportions. If you want to type the proportion for each category, choose Input constants. Then you can type the proportions for the corresponding categories. The Graph button enables you to display a bar chart of the observed and the expected values as well as a bar chart of each category's contribution to the chi-square value. Figure 14–19 shows the Session commands and the chart obtained by using the MINITAB chi-square test on the data of Example 14–12.

You can also perform a chi-square test of independence between variables if your data are in table form. Start by choosing Stat ▶ Tables ▶ Chi-Square Test (Two-Way Table in Worksheet) from the menu bar. Enter the columns containing the contingency table data in the Columns containing the table edit box. Rows with missing data should be deleted before using this procedure.

TABLE 14–19   Summary of Nonparametric Tests

Situation	Nonparametric Test(s)	Corresponding Parametric Test
Single-sample test for location	Sign test Wilcoxon test (more powerful)	Single-sample t test
Goodness of fit	Chi-square test	
Randomness	Runs test	
Paired-differences test	Sign test Wilcoxon test (more powerful)	Paired-data t test
Test for difference of two independent samples	Wald-Wolfowitz (weaker) Mann-Whitney (more powerful) Median test (weaker)	Two-sample t test
Test for difference of more than two independent samples	Kruskal-Wallis test Median test (weaker)	ANOVA
Test for difference of more than two samples, blocked	Friedman test	Randomized block-design ANOVA
Correlation	Spearman's statistic and test Chi-square test for independence	
Equality of several population proportions	Chi-square test	

14–13   Summary and Review of Terms

This chapter was devoted to **nonparametric tests** (summarized in Table 14–19). Interpreted loosely, the term refers to statistical tests in situations where stringent assumptions about the populations of interest may not be warranted. Most notably, the very common assumption of a normal distribution—required for the parametric t and F tests—is not necessary for the application of nonparametric methods. The methods often use less of the information in the data and thus tend to be less powerful than parametric methods, when the assumptions of the parametric methods are met. The nonparametric methods include methods for handling categorical data, and here the analysis entails use of a limiting chi-square distribution for our test statistic. **Chi-square analysis** is often discussed separately from nonparametric methods, although the analysis is indeed "nonparametric," as it usually involves no specific reference to population *parameters* such as μ and σ. The other nonparametric methods (ones that require no assumptions about the distribution of the population) are often called *distribution-free* methods.

Besides chi-square analyses of **goodness of fit, independence,** and tests for **equality of proportions,** the methods we discussed included many based on **ranks.** These included a **rank correlation coefficient** due to Spearman; a test analogous to the parametric paired-sample t test—the **Wilcoxon signed-rank test;** a ranks-based ANOVA—the **Kruskal-Wallis test;** and a method for investigating two independent samples analogous to the parametric two-sample t test, called the **Mann-Whitney test.** We also discussed a test for randomness—the **runs test;** a paired-difference test called the **sign test,** which uses less information than the Wilcoxon signed-rank test; and several other methods.

ADDITIONAL PROBLEMS

14–63. The following data are daily price quotations of two stocks:

Stock A: 12.50, 12.75, 12.50, 13.00, 13.25, 13.00, 13.50, 14.25, 14.00
Stock B: 35.25, 36.00, 37.25, 37.25, 36.50, 36.50, 36.00, 36.00, 36.25

Is there a correlation between the two stocks? Explain.

14–64. The Hyatt Gold Passport is a card designed to allow frequent guests at Hyatt hotels to enjoy privileges similar to the ones enjoyed by frequent air travelers. When the program was initiated, a random sample of 15 Hyatt Gold Passport members were asked to rate the program on a scale of 0 to 100 and also to rate (on the same scale) an airline frequent-flier card that all of them had. The results are as follows.

Hyatt card: 98, 99, 87, 56, 79, 89, 86, 90, 95, 99, 76, 88, 90, 95
Airline card: 84, 62, 90, 77, 80, 98, 65, 97, 58, 74, 80, 90, 85, 70

Is the Hyatt Gold Passport better liked than the airline frequent-flier card by holders of both cards? Explain.

14–65. Two telecommunication systems are to be compared. A random sample of 14 users of one system independently rate the system on a scale of 0 to 100. An independent random sample of 12 users of the other system rate their system on the same scale. The data are as follows.

System A: 65, 67, 83, 39, 45, 20, 95, 64, 99, 98, 76, 78, 82, 90
System B: 45, 57, 76, 54, 60, 72, 34, 50, 63, 39, 44, 70

Based on these data, are the two telecommunication systems equally liked? Explain.

14–66. What is the distinction between *distribution-free* methods and *nonparametric* methods?

14–67. The following data are the net wealth, in billions of dollars, of a random sample of U.S. billionaires in the *Forbes* 2007 list:[22] 1.0, 1.0, 1.2, 1.3, 2.5, 2.3, 4.1, 4.8, 2.5, 2.5, 2.7, 5.2, 2.3, 5.5, 2.0, 2.1, 3.5, 4.0, 52.0, 21.5, 5.5, 2.1, 6.0, 1.8, 16.7, 1.8, 18.0, 2.1, 1.9, 3.1, 3.5, 1.4, 1.2, 1.3, 1.1. Do you believe that the wealth of American billionaires is normally distributed?

14–68. In a chi-square analysis, the expected count in one of the cells is 2.1. Can you conduct the analysis? If not, what can be done?

14–69. New credit card machines use two receipts, to be signed by the payer. This has recently caused confusion as many customers forget to sign the copy they leave with the establishment. If 6 out of 17 randomly selected patrons forgot to sign their slips, test the hypothesis that a full one-half of the customers do so, using $\alpha = 0.05$, against a left-tailed alternative.

14–70. An article in *The Economist* compares divorce procedures in New York to those in England, France, and Germany.[23] Suppose the following data are available for these places on numbers of divorces, broken down by whether a prenuptial agreement had been signed.

	New York	England	France	Germany
Prenuptial agreement	8,049	17,139	3,044	1,014
No prenuptial agreement	75,113	25,108	19,800	16,131

In light of these data, are the percentages of divorcing couples with prenuptial agreements equal in these four places?

---

[22]“Billionaires: United States,” *Forbes,* March 26, 2007, pp. 154–168.

[23]“For Richer and Poorer,” *The Economist,* March 3, 2007, pp. 64–65.

CASE 18 The Nine Nations of North America

In a fascinating article in the *Journal of Marketing* (April 1986), "The Nine Nations of North America and the Value Basis of Geographic Segmentation," Professor Lynn Kahle explores the possible marketing implications of Joel Garreau's idea of the nine nations.

Garreau traveled extensively throughout North America, studying people, customs, traditions, and ways of life. This research led Garreau to the conclusion that state boundaries or the Census Bureau's divisions of the United States into regions are not very indicative of the cultural and social boundaries that really exist on the continent. Instead, Garreau suggested in his best-selling book *The Nine Nations of North America* (New York: Avon, 1981) that the real boundaries divide the entire North American continent into nine separate, homogeneous regions, which he called "nations." Each nation, according to Garreau, is inhabited by people who share the same traditions, values, hopes, and world outlook and are different from the people of the other nations. The nine nations cross national boundaries of the United States, Canada, and the Caribbean. Garreau named his nations very descriptively, as follows: New England, Quebec, The Foundry, Dixie, The Islands, Empty Quarter, Breadbasket, MexAmerica, and Ecotopia. Exhibit 1 shows the boundaries of these nations.

Geographic segmentation is a very important concept in marketing. Thus, Garreau's novel idea promised potential gains in marketing. Professor Kahle suggested a statistical test of whether Garreau's division of the country (without the nation of Quebec, which lies entirely outside the United States) could be found valid with respect to marketing-related values. Such a division could then replace currently used geographic segmentation methods.

Two currently used segmentation schemes studied by Kahle were the quadrants and the Census Bureau regions. Kahle used a random sample of 2,235 people across the country and collected responses pertaining to eight self-assessed personal attributes: self-respect, security, warm relationships with others, sense of accomplishment, self-fulfillment, being well respected, sense of belonging, and fun–enjoyment–excitement. Kahle showed that these self-assessment attributes were directly related to marketing variables. The attributes determine, for example, the magazines a person is likely to read and the television programs he or she is likely to watch.

Kahle's results, using the nine-nations division (without Quebec), the quadrants division, and the Census

EXHIBIT 1   The Nine Nations

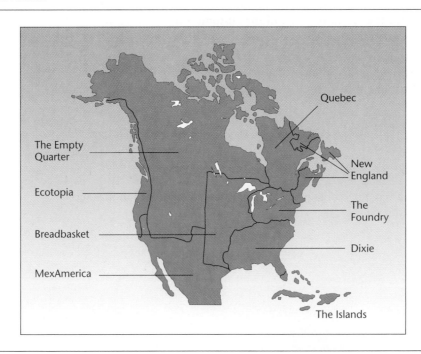

EXHIBIT 2 Distribution of Values across the Nine Nations

Value	New England	The Foundry	Dixie	The Islands	Bread-basket	Mex-America	Empty Quarter	Eco-topia	N
Self-respect	22.5%	20.5%	22.5%	25.0%	17.9%	22.7%	35.3%	18.0%	471
Security	21.7	19.6	23.3	15.6	20.2	17.3	17.6	19.6	461
Warm relationships with others	14.2	16.7	13.8	9.4	20.5	18.0	5.9	18.5	362
Sense of accomplishment	14.2	11.7	10.0	9.4	12.4	11.3	8.8	12.2	254
Self-fulfillment	9.2	9.9	8.4	3.1	7.5	16.0	5.9	12.7	214
Being well respected	8.3	8.7	11.0	15.6	10.1	2.7	2.9	4.2	196
Sense of belonging	5.0	8.4	7.5	12.5	7.8	6.7	17.6	7.9	177
Fun–enjoyment–excitement	5.0	4.5	3.5	9.4	3.6	5.3	5.9	6.9	100
Total	100.0	100.0	100.0	100.0	100.0	100.0	100.0	100.0	2,235
N	120	750	653	32	307	150	34	189	

EXHIBIT 3 Distribution of Values across Quadrants of the United States

Value	East	Midwest	South	West	N
Self-respect	19.7%	19.1%	23.4%	21.6%	471
Security	18.9	21.6	22.0	18.4	461
Warm relationships with others	16.0	17.8	14.5	17.1	362
Sense of accomplishment	13.2	12.5	9.2	11.4	254
Self-fulfillment	9.5	9.0	8.1	13.5	214
Being well respected	8.0	9.1	11.6	3.6	196
Sense of belonging	8.4	7.3	8.0	8.3	117
Fun–enjoyment–excitement	6.3	3.3	3.4	6.2	100
Total	100.0	100.0	100.0	100.0	2,235
N	476	634	740	385	

EXHIBIT 4 Distribution of Values across Census Regions of the United States

Value	New England	Middle Atlantic	South Atlantic	East South Central	East North Central	West North Central	West South Central	Mountain	Pacific	N
Self-respect	22.6%	18.6%	23.1%	23.4%	20.2%	16.7%	23.8%	29.2%	19.8%	471
Security	21.2	18.0	18.3	26.9	22.1	20.6	23.8	18.1	18.5	461
Warm relationships with others	13.9	16.8	15.7	11.4	16.0	21.6	14.9	15.3	17.6	362
Sense of accomplishment	13.9	13.0	10.7	9.6	11.4	14.7	6.8	8.3	12.1	254
Self-fulfillment	8.0	10.0	10.1	7.8	9.3	8.3	5.5	6.9	15.0	214
Being well respected	8.8	7.7	9.8	12.0	10.0	7.4	14.0	4.2	3.5	196
Sense of belonging	7.3	8.8	9.2	7.8	7.4	6.9	6.4	13.9	7.0	177
Fun–enjoyment–excitement	4.4	7.1	3.3	1.2	3.5	3.9	4.7	4.2	6.4	100
Total	100.0	100.0	100.0	100.0	100.0	100.0	100.0	100.0	100.0	2,235
N	137	339	338	167	430	204	235	72	313	

division of the country, are presented in Exhibits 2 through 4. These tables are reprinted by permission from Kahle (1986). (Values reported in the exhibits are percentages.)

Carefully analyze the results presented in the exhibits. Is the nine-nations segmentation a useful alternative to the quadrants or the Census Bureau divisions of the country? Explain.

15

BAYESIAN STATISTICS AND DECISION ANALYSIS

15–1 Using Statistics 687

15–2 Bayes' Theorem and Discrete Probability Models 688

15–3 Bayes' Theorem and Continuous Probability Distributions 695

15–4 The Evaluation of Subjective Probabilities 701

15–5 Decision Analysis: An Overview 702

15–6 Decision Trees 705

15–7 Handling Additional Information Using Bayes' Theorem 714

15–8 Utility 725

15–9 The Value of Information 728

15–10 Using the Computer 731

15–11 Summary and Review of Terms 733

Case 19 Pizzas 'R' Us 735

Case 20 New Drug Development 736

LEARNING OBJECTIVES

After studying this chapter, you should be able to:

- Apply Bayes' theorem to revise population parameters.
- Solve sequential decision problems using the decision tree technique.
- Conduct decision analyses for cases without probability data.
- Conduct decision analyses for cases with probability data.
- Evaluate the expected value of perfect information.
- Evaluate the expected value of sample information.
- Use utility functions to model the risk attitudes of decision makers.
- Solve decision analysis problems using spreadsheet templates.

Anyone who's used the Internet is familiar with *spam*—that ubiquitous, irritating, and sometimes even dangerous, virus-carrying, unwanted e-mail. Many methods have been devised to help people get rid of such unwelcome electronic solicitation for anything from low interest rates to schemes for enlarging of certain body parts. But, as with any statistical method for making a decision—here, the decision to automatically delete a message before you see it on your screen—two errors are possible. One is the error of deleting a good e-mail message, one that may be very important to you. The other is the error of keeping a bad message, one that unnecessarily clogs up your mailbox and may even contain a virus that can destroy your system. These methods, therefore, are never perfect. Most of them have not done well at all.

Recently, a science reporter at the *New York Times,* George Johnson, tried a new method for automatically detecting and deleting spam, and he reported a success rate of over 98%. Johnson used a revolutionary statistical method called **Bayesian analysis.**[1]

The Bayesian approach allows the statistician to use *prior information* about a particular problem, in addition to the information obtained from sampling. This approach is called *Bayesian* because the mathematical link between the probabilities associated with data results and the probabilities associated with the prior information is Bayes' theorem, which was introduced in Chapter 2. The theorem allows us to combine the prior information with the results of our sampling, giving us *posterior* (postsampling) information. A schematic comparison of the classical and the Bayesian approaches is shown in Figure 15–1.

The Bayesian philosophy does not necessarily lead to conclusions that are more accurate than those obtained by using the *frequentist,* or *classical,* approach. If the prior information we have is accurate, then using it in conjunction with sample information leads to more accurate results than would be obtained without prior information. If, on the other hand, the prior information is inaccurate, then using it in conjunction with our sampling results leads to a worse outcome than would be obtained by using frequentist statistical inference. The very use of prior knowledge in a statistical analysis often brings the entire Bayesian methodology under attack.

When prior information is a direct result of previous statistical surveys, or when prior information reflects no knowledge about the problem at hand (in which case the prior probabilities are called *noninformative*), the Bayesian analysis is purely objective, and few people would argue with its validity. Sometimes, however, the prior information reflects the personal opinions of the individual doing the analysis—or possibly those of an expert who has knowledge of the particular problem at hand. In such cases, where the prior information is of a subjective nature, one may criticize the results of the analysis.

One way to classify statisticians is according to whether they are Bayesian or non-Bayesian (i.e., frequentist). The Bayesian group used to be a minority, but in recent years its numbers have grown. Even though differences between the two groups exist, when noninformative prior probabilities are used, the Bayesian results can be shown to parallel the frequentist statistical results. This fact lends credibility to the Bayesian approach. If we are careful with the use of any prior information, we may avoid criticism and produce good results via the Bayesian methodology.

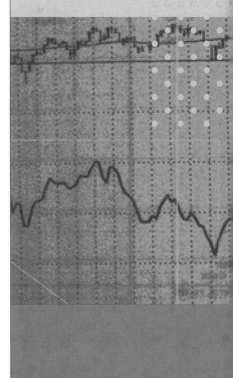

[1]George Johnson, "Cognitive Rascal in the Amorous Swamp: A Robot Battles Spam," *The New York Times,* April 27, 2004, p. D3.

FIGURE 15–1   **A Comparison of Bayesian and Classical Approaches**

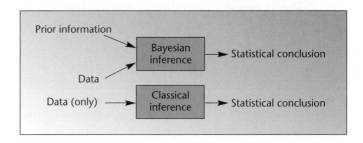

In the next two sections, we give some basic elements of Bayesian statistics. These sections extend the idea of Bayes' theorem, first to discrete random variables and then to continuous ones. Section 15–4 discusses some aspects of subjective probabilities and how they can be elicited from a person who has knowledge of the situation at hand.

There is another important area, not entirely in the realm of statistics, that makes use of Bayes' theorem as well as subjective probabilities. This is the area of **decision analysis.** Decision analysis is a methodology developed in the 1960s, and it quantifies the elements of a decision-making process in an effort to determine the optimal decision.

15–2   Bayes' Theorem and Discrete Probability Models

In Section 2–7, we introduced Bayes' theorem. The theorem was presented in terms of *events.* The theorem was shown to transform *prior probabilities* of the occurrence of certain events into *posterior probabilities* of occurrence of the same events. Recall Example 2–10. In that example, we started with a prior probability that a randomly chosen person has a certain illness, given by $P(I) = 0.001$. Through the information that the person tested positive for the illness, and the reliability of the test, known to be $P(Z \mid I) = 0.92$ and $P(Z \mid \bar{I}) = 0.04$, we obtained through Bayes' theorem (equation 2–21) the posterior probability that the person was sick:

$$P(I \mid Z) = \frac{P(Z \mid I)P(I)}{P(Z \mid I)P(I) + P(Z \mid \bar{I})P(\bar{I})} = 0.0225$$

The fact that the person had a positive reaction to the test may be considered our data. The conditional probabilities $P(Z \mid I)$ and $P(Z \mid \bar{I})$ help incorporate the data in the computation. We will now extend these probabilities to include more than just an event and its complement, as was done in this example, or one of three events, as was the case in Example 2–10. Our extension will cover a whole set of values and their prior probabilities. The *conditional* probabilities, when extended over the entire set of values of a random variable, are called the *likelihood function.*

The **likelihood function** is the set of conditional probabilities $P(x \mid \theta)$ for given data x, considered a function of an unknown population parameter θ.

Using the likelihood function and the prior probabilities $P(\theta)$ of the values of the parameter in question, we define Bayes' theorem for discrete random variables in the following form:

Bayes' theorem for a discrete random variable is

$$P(\theta \mid x) = \frac{P(x \mid \theta)P(\theta)}{\sum_i P(x \mid \theta_i)P(\theta_i)} \qquad (15\text{--}1)$$

where θ is an unknown population parameter to be estimated from the data. The summation in the denominator is over all possible values of the parameter of interest θ_i, and x stands for our particular data set.

In Bayesian statistics, we assume that population parameters such as the mean, the variance, or the population proportion are *random variables* rather than fixed (but unknown) quantities, as in the classical approach.

We assume that the parameter of interest is a random variable; thus, we may specify our prior information about the parameter as a **prior probability distribution** of the parameter. Then we obtain our data, and from them we get the likelihood function, that is, a measure of how likely we are to obtain our particular data, given different values of the parameter specified in the parameter's prior probability distribution. This information is transformed via Bayes' theorem, equation 15–1, to a **posterior probability distribution** of the value of the parameter in question. The posterior distribution includes the prior information as well as the data results. The posterior distribution can then be used in statistical inference. Such inference may include computing confidence intervals. Bayesian confidence intervals are often called **credible sets** of given posterior probability.

The following example illustrates the use of Bayes' theorem when the population parameter of interest is the population proportion p.

A market research analyst is interested in estimating the proportion of people in a certain area who use a product made by her client. That is, the analyst is interested in estimating her client's market share. The analyst denotes the parameter in question—the true (population) market share of her client—by S. From previous studies of a similar nature, and from other sources of information about the industry, the analyst constructs the table of prior probabilities of the possible values of the market share S. This is the analyst's prior probability distribution of S. It contains different values of the parameter in question and the analyst's degree of belief that the parameter is equal to any of the values, given as a probability. The prior probability distribution is presented in Table 15–1.

As seen from the prior probabilities table, the analyst does not believe that her client's market share could be above 0.6 (60% of the market). For example, she may know that a competitor controls 40% of the market, so values above 60% are impossible as her client's share. Similarly, she may know for certain that her client's market share is at least 10%. The assumption that S may equal one of six discrete values is a restrictive approximation. In the next section, we will explore a continuous space of values.

The analyst now gathers a random sample of 20 people and finds out that 4 out of the 20 in the sample do use her client's product. The analyst wishes to use Bayes' theorem to combine her prior distribution of market share with the data results to obtain a posterior distribution of market share. Recall that in the classical approach, all that

EXAMPLE 15–1

TABLE 15–1
Prior Probabilities of Market Share S

S	P(S)
0.1	0.05
0.2	0.15
0.3	0.20
0.4	0.30
0.5	0.20
0.6	0.10
	1.00

TABLE 15–2   Prior Distribution, Likelihood, and Posterior Distribution of Market Share (Example 15–1)

S	$P(S)$	$P(x \mid S)$	$P(S)P(x \mid S)$	$P(S \mid x)$
0.1	0.05	0.0898	0.00449	0.06007
0.2	0.15	0.2182	0.03273	0.43786
0.3	0.20	0.1304	0.02608	0.34890
0.4	0.30	0.0350	0.01050	0.14047
0.5	0.20	0.0046	0.00092	0.01230
0.6	0.10	0.0003	0.00003	0.00040
	1.00		0.07475	1.00000

can be used is the sample estimate of the market share, which is $\hat{p} = x/n = 4/20 = 0.2$ and may be used in the construction of a confidence interval or a hypothesis test.

Solution   Using Bayes' theorem for discrete random variables (equation 15–1), the analyst updates her prior information to incorporate the data results. This is done in a tabular format and is shown in Table 15–2. As required by equation 15–1, the conditional probabilities $P(x \mid S)$ are evaluated. These conditional probabilities are our likelihood function. To evaluate these probabilities, we ask the following questions:

1. How likely are we to obtain the data results we have, that is, 4 successes out of 20 trials, if the probability of success in a single trial (the true *population proportion*) is equal to 0.1?
2. How likely are we to obtain the results we have if the population proportion is 0.2?
3. How likely are we to obtain these results when the population proportion is 0.3?
4. How likely are we to obtain these results when the population proportion is 0.4?
5. How likely are we to obtain these results when the population proportion is 0.5?
6. How likely are we to obtain these results when the population proportion is 0.6?

The answers to these six questions are obtained from a table of the binomial distribution (Appendix C, Table 1) and written in the appropriate places in the third column of Table 15–2. The fourth column is the product, for each value of S, of the prior probability of S and its likelihood. The sum of the entries in the fourth column is equal to the denominator in equation 15–1. When each entry in column 4 is divided by the sum of that column, we get the posterior probabilities, which are written in column 5. This procedure corresponds to an application of equation 15–1 for each one of the possible values of the population proportion S.

By comparing the values in column 2 of Table 15–2 with the values in column 5, we see how the prior probabilities of different possible market share values changed by the incorporation, via Bayes' theorem, of the information in the data (i.e., the fact that 4 people in a sample of 20 were found to be product users). The influence of the prior beliefs about the actual market share is evident in the posterior distribution. This is illustrated in Figure 15–2, which shows the prior probability distribution of S, and Figure 15–3, which shows the posterior probability distribution of S.

As the two figures show, starting with a prior distribution that is spread in a somewhat symmetric fashion over the six possible values of S, we end up, after the incorporation of data results, with a posterior distribution that is concentrated over the three values 0.2, 0.3, and 0.4, with the remaining values having small probabilities.

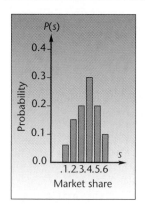

FIGURE 15–2
Prior Distribution of Market Share (Example 15–1)

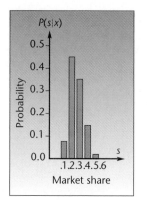

FIGURE 15–3
Posterior Distribution of Market Share (Example 15–1)

The total posterior probability of the three values 0.2, 0.3, and 0.4 is equal to 0.92723 (from summing Table 15–2 entries). The three adjacent values are thus a set of highest posterior probability and can be taken as a credible set of values for S with posterior probability close to the standard 95% confidence level. Recall that with discrete random variables, it is hard to get values corresponding to exact, prespecified levels such as 95%, and we are fortunate in this case to be close to 95%. We may state as our conclusion that we are about 93% confident that the market share is anywhere between 0.2 and 0.4. Our result is a Bayesian conclusion, which may be stated in terms of a probability; it includes both the data results and our prior information. (As a comparison, compute an approximate classical confidence interval based on the sampling result.)

One of the great advantages of the Bayesian approach is the possibility of carrying out the analysis in a sequential fashion. Information obtained from one sampling study can be used as the prior information set when new information becomes available. The second survey results are considered the data set, and the two sources are combined by use of Bayes' theorem. The resulting posterior distribution may then be used as the prior distribution when new data become available, and so on.

We now illustrate the sequential property by continuing Example 15–1. Suppose that the analyst is able to obtain a *second* sample after her analysis of the first sample is completed. She obtains a sample of 16 people and finds 3 users of the product of interest in this sample. The analyst now wants to combine this new sampling information with what she already knows about the market share. To do this, the analyst considers her last posterior distribution, from column 5 of Table 15–2, as her new prior distribution when the new data come in. Note that the last posterior distribution contains *all* the analyst's information about market share before the incorporation of the new data, because it includes both her prior information and the results of the first sampling. Table 15–3 shows how this information is transformed into a new posterior probability distribution by incorporating the new sample results. The likelihood function is again obtained by consulting Appendix C, Table 1. We look for the binomial probabilities of obtaining 3 successes in 16 trials, using the given values of $S(0.1, 0.2, \ldots, 0.6)$, each in turn taken as the binomial parameter p.

The new posterior distribution of S is shown in Figure 15–4. Note that the highest posterior probability after the second sampling is given to the value $S = 0.2$, the posterior probability being 0.6191. With every additional sampling, the posterior distribution will get more peaked at values indicated by the data. The posterior distribution keeps moving toward data-derived results, and the effects of the prior distribution become less and less important. This fact becomes clear as we compare the distributions shown in Figures 15–2, 15–3, and 15–4. This property of Bayesian analysis is reassuring. It allows the data to speak for themselves, thus moving away from prior beliefs if these beliefs are away from reality. In the presence of limited data,

FIGURE 15–4
**Second Posterior
Distribution of Market Share**

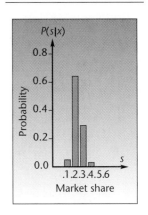

TABLE 15–3   Prior Distribution, Likelihood, and Posterior Distribution of Market Share for Second Sampling

S	$P(S)$	$P(x \mid S)$	$P(S)P(x \mid S)$	$P(S \mid x)$
0.1	0.06007	0.1423	0.0085480	0.049074
0.2	0.43786	0.2463	0.1078449	0.619138
0.3	0.34890	0.1465	0.0511138	0.293444
0.4	0.14047	0.0468	0.0065740	0.037741
0.5	0.01230	0.0085	0.0001046	0.000601
0.6	0.00040	0.0008	0.0000003	0.000002
	1.00000		0.1741856	1.000000

Bayesian analysis allows us to compensate for the small data set by allowing us to use previous information—obtained either by prior sampling or by other means.

Incidentally, what would have happened if our analyst had decided to combine the results of the two surveys before considering them in conjunction with her prior information? That is, what would have happened if the analyst had decided to consider the two samples as one, where the total number of trials is $20 + 16 = 36$ and the total number of successes is $4 + 3 = 7$ users? Surprisingly, the posterior probability distribution for the combined sample incorporated with the prior distribution would have been exactly the same as the posterior distribution presented in Table 15–3. This fact demonstrates how well the Bayesian approach handles successive pieces of information. When or how information is incorporated in the model does not matter—the posterior distribution will contain *all* information available at any given time.

In the next section, we discuss Bayesian statistics in the context of continuous probability distributions. In particular, we develop the normal probability model for Bayesian analysis. As will be seen in the next section, the normal distribution is particularly amenable to Bayesian analysis. If our prior distribution is normal and the likelihood function is normal, then the posterior distribution is also normal. We will develop two simple formulas: one for the posterior mean and one for the posterior variance (and standard deviation) in terms of the prior distribution parameters and the likelihood function.

The Template

Figure 15–5 shows the template for revising binomial probabilities. The data seen in the figure correspond to Example 15–1.

To get the new posterior distribution, copy the posterior probabilities in the range C13:L13 and use the Paste Special (values) command to paste them into the

FIGURE 15–5   The Template for Bayesian Revision—Binomial [Bayesian Revision.xls; Sheet: Binomial]

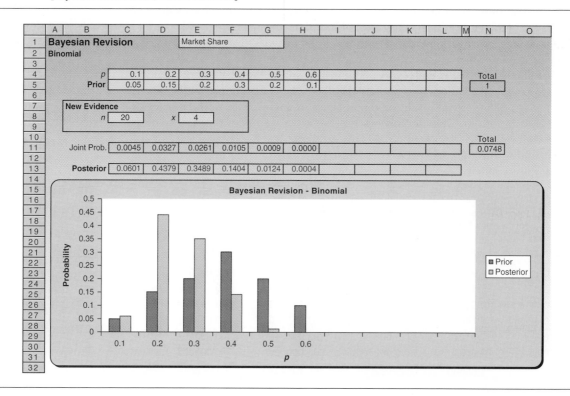

FIGURE 15–6 The New Posterior Probabilities for Example 15–1
[Bayesian Revision.xls; Sheet: Binomial]

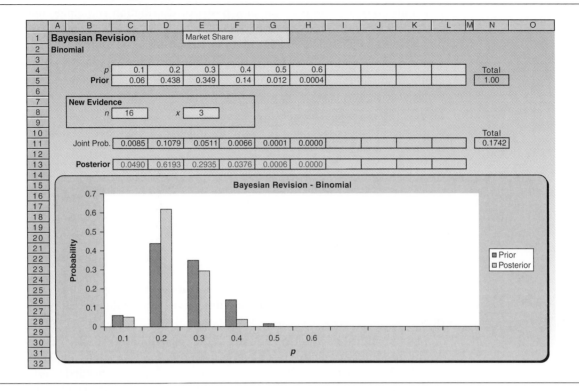

range C5:L5. They thus become the new prior probabilities. Add the new evidence of $n = 16$ and $x = 3$. The new posterior probabilities appear in row 13, as seen in Figure 15–6.

PROBLEMS

15–1. Bank of America recently launched a special credit card designed to reward people who pay their bills on time by allowing them to pay a lower-than-usual interest rate. Some research went into designing the new program. The director of the bank's regular credit card systems was consulted, and she gave her prior probability distribution of the proportion of cardholders who would qualify for the new program. Then a random sample of 20 cardholders was selected and tracked over several months. It was found that 6 of them paid all their credit card bills on time. Using this information and the information in the following table—the director's prior distribution of the proportion of all cardholders who pay their bills on time—construct the posterior probability distribution for this parameter. Also give a credible set of highest posterior probability close to 95% for the parameter in question. Plot both the prior and the posterior distributions of the parameter.

Proportion	Probability
0.1	0.2
0.2	0.3
0.3	0.1
0.4	0.1
0.5	0.1
0.6	0.1
0.7	0.1

15–2.   In the situation of problem 15–1, suppose that a second random sample of cardholders was selected, and 7 out of the 17 people in the sample were found to pay their bills on time. Construct the new posterior distribution containing information from the prior distribution and both samplings. Again, give a credible set of highest posterior probability close to 95%, and plot the posterior distribution.

15–3.   For Example 15–1 suppose that a third sample is obtained. Three out of 10 people in the sample are product users. Update the probabilities of market share after the third sampling, and produce the new posterior distribution.

15–4.   The magazine *Inc.* recently surveyed managers to determine the proportion of managers who participate in planning meetings.[2] Consider the following prior probability distribution for this proportion.

Proportion	Probability
0.80	0.4
0.85	0.5
0.90	0.05
0.95	0.04
1.00	0.01

If a random sample of 10 managers reveals that all of them participate in planning meetings, revise the probabilities to find the posterior probability distribution.

15–5.   Recent years have seen a sharp decline in the Alaska king crab fishery. One problem identified as a potential cause of the decline has been the prevalence of a deadly parasite believed to infect a large proportion of the adult king crab population. A fisheries management agency monitoring crab catches needed to estimate the proportion of the adult crab population infected by the parasite. The agency's biologists constructed the following prior probability distribution for the proportion of infected adult crabs (denoted by R):

R	$P(R)$
0.25	0.1
0.30	0.2
0.35	0.2
0.40	0.3
0.45	0.1
0.50	0.1

A random sample of 10 adult king crabs was collected, and 3 of them were found to be infected with the parasite. Construct the posterior probability distribution of the proportion of infected adult crabs, and plot it.

15–6.   To continue problem 15–5, a second random sample of 12 adult crabs was collected, and it revealed that 4 individual crabs had been infected. Revise your probability distribution, and plot it. Give a credible set of highest posterior probability close to 95%.

15–7.   For problem 15–5, suppose the biologists believed the proportion of infected crabs in the population was equally likely to be anywhere from 10% to 90%. Using the discrete points 0.1, 0.2, etc., construct a uniform prior distribution for the proportion of infected crabs, and compute the posterior distribution after the results of the sampling in problem 15–5.

15–8.   American Airlines is interested in the proportion of flights that are full during the 2008 summer season. The airline uses data from past experience and

---

[2]"How to Vet a Board Member," *Inc.*, May 2007, p. 35.

constructs the following prior distribution of the proportion of flights that are full to capacity:

S	P(S)
0.70	0.1
0.75	0.2
0.80	0.3
0.85	0.2
0.90	0.1
0.95	0.1
	1.0

A sample of 20 flights shows that 17 of these flights are full. Update the probability distribution to obtain a posterior distribution for the proportion of full flights.

15–9. In the situation of problem 15–8, another sample of 20 flights reveals that 18 of them are full. Obtain the second posterior distribution of the proportion of full flights. Graph the prior distribution of problem 15–8, as well as the first posterior and the second posterior distributions. How did the distribution of the proportion in question change as more information became available?

15–10. An article in the *Harvard Business Review* discusses new products and services offered by the famous British department store Marks & Spencer.[3] Suppose that Marks & Spencer plans to offer a new line of women's shoes and estimates the proportion of its customers who will be interested in the new line using the following probability distribution:

Proportion	Probability
0.3	0.1
0.4	0.3
0.5	0.3
0.6	0.2
0.7	0.05
0.8	0.05

A survey of 20 randomly selected customers reveals that 5 of them are interested in the new line. Compute the posterior probability distribution.

15–3 Bayes' Theorem and Continuous Probability Distributions

We will now extend the results of the preceding section to the case of continuous probability models. Recall that a continuous random variable has a probability density function, denoted by $f(x)$. The function $f(x)$ is nonnegative, and the total area under the curve of $f(x)$ must equal 1.00. Recall that the probability of an event is defined as the area under the curve of $f(x)$ over the interval or intervals corresponding to the event.

We define $f(\theta)$ as the **prior probability density** of the parameter θ. We define $f(x \mid \theta)$ as the conditional density of the data x, given the value of θ. This is the likelihood function.

The **joint density** of θ and x is obtained as the product:

$$f(\theta, x) = f(x \mid \theta)f(\theta) \qquad (15\text{–}2)$$

---

[3]Stuart Rose, "Back in Fashion: How We're Reviving a British Icon," *Harvard Business Review*, May 2007, pp. 51–58.

Using these functions, we may now write Bayes' theorem for continuous probability distributions. The theorem gives us the **posterior density** of the parameter θ, *given* the data *x*.

Bayes' theorem for continuous distributions[4] is

$$f(\theta \mid x) = \frac{f(x \mid \theta)\, f(\theta)}{\text{total area under } f(\theta, x)} \tag{15–3}$$

Equation 15–3 is the analog for continuous random variables of equation 15–1. We may use the equation for updating a prior probability density function of a parameter θ once data *x* are available. In general, computing the posterior density is a complicated operation. However, in the case of a normal prior distribution and a normal data-generating process (or large samples, leading to central-limit conditions), the posterior distribution is also a normal distribution. The parameters of the posterior distribution are easy to calculate, as will be shown next.

The Normal Probability Model

Suppose that you want to estimate the population mean μ of a normal population that has a *known* standard deviation σ. Also suppose that you have some prior beliefs about the population in question. Namely, you view the population mean as a random variable with a normal (prior) distribution with mean *M′ and standard deviation σ′.*

If you draw a random sample of size *n* from the normal population in question and obtain a sample mean *M*, then the posterior distribution for the population mean μ is a *normal distribution with mean M″ and standard deviation σ″* obtained, respectively, from equations 15–4 and 15–5.

The posterior mean and variance of the normal distribution of the population mean μ are

$$M'' = \frac{(1/\sigma'^2)M' + (n/\sigma^2)M}{1/\sigma'^2 + n/\sigma^2} \tag{15–4}$$

$$\sigma''^2 = \frac{1}{1/\sigma'^2 + n/\sigma^2} \tag{15–5}$$

The two equations are very useful in many applications. We are fortunate that the normal distribution family is *closed;* that is, when the prior distribution of a parameter is normal and the population (or process) is normal, the posterior distribution of the parameter in question is also normal. Be sure that you understand the distinction among the various quantities involved in the computations—especially the distinction between σ^2 and σ'^2. The quantity σ^2 is the variance of the population, and σ'^2 is the prior variance of the population mean μ. We demonstrate the methodology with Example 15–2.

EXAMPLE 15–2

A stockbroker is interested in the return on investment for a particular stock. Since Bayesian analysis is especially suited for the incorporation of opinion or prior knowledge with data, the stockbroker wishes to use a Bayesian model. The stockbroker

---

[4]For the reader with knowledge of calculus, we note that Bayes' theorem is written as $f(\theta \mid x) = f(x \mid \theta)f(\theta)/[\int_{-\infty}^{\infty} f(x \mid \theta)f(\theta)\, d\theta]$.

quantifies his beliefs about the *average return* on the stock by a normal probability distribution with mean 15 (percentage return per year) and a standard deviation of 8. Since it is relatively large, compared with the mean, the stockbroker's prior standard deviation of μ reflects a state of relatively little prior knowledge about the stock in question. However, the prior distribution allows the broker to incorporate into the analysis some of his limited knowledge about the stock. The broker collects a sample of 10 monthly observations on the stock and computes the annualized average percentage return. He gets a mean $M = 11.54$ (percent) and a standard deviation $s = 6.8$. Assuming that the population standard deviation is equal to 6.8 and that returns are normally distributed, what is the posterior distribution of average stock returns?

Solution

We know that the posterior distribution is normal, with mean and variance given by equations 15–4 and 15–5, respectively. We have

$$M'' = \frac{(1/64)15 + (10/46.24)11.54}{1/64 + 10/46.24} = 11.77$$

$$\sigma'' = \sqrt{\frac{1}{1/64 + 10/46.24}} = 2.077$$

Note how simple it is to update probabilities when you start with a normal prior distribution and a normal population. Incidentally, the assumption of a normal population is very appropriate in our case, as the theory of finance demonstrates that stock returns are well approximated by the normal curve. If the population standard deviation is unknown, the sample standard deviation provides a reasonable estimate.

Figure 15–7 shows the stockbroker's prior distribution, the normal likelihood function (normalized to have a unit area), and the posterior density of the average return on the stock of interest. Note that the prior distribution is relatively flat—this is due to the relatively large standard deviation. The standard deviation is a measure of uncertainty, and here it reflects the fact that the broker does not know much about the stock. Prior distributions such as the one used here are called

FIGURE 15–7 Prior Distribution, Likelihood Function, and Posterior Distribution of Average Return μ (Example 15–2)

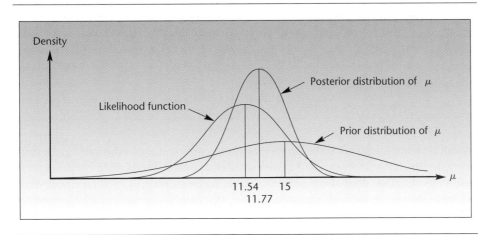

diffuse priors. They convey little a priori knowledge about the process in question. A relatively flat prior normal distribution conveys some information but lets the data tell us more.

Credible Sets

Unlike the discrete case, in the continuous case credible sets for parameters with an exact, prespecified probability level are easy to construct. In Example 15–2, the stockbroker may construct a 95% *highest-posterior-density* (HPD) credible set for the average return on the stock directly from the posterior density. The posterior distribution is normal, with mean 11.77 and standard deviation 2.077. Therefore, the 95% HPD credible set for μ is simply

$$M'' \pm 1.96\sigma'' = 11.77 \pm 1.96(2.077)$$
$$= [7.699, 15.841]$$

Thus, the stockbroker may conclude there is a 0.95 probability that the average return on the stock is anywhere from 7.699% to 15.841% per year.

Recall that in the classical approach, we would have to rely only on the data and would not be able to use prior knowledge. As a conclusion, we would have to say: "Ninety-five percent of the intervals constructed in this manner will contain the parameter of interest." In the Bayesian approach, we are free to make *probability* statements as conclusions. Incidentally, the idea of attaching a probability to a result extends to the Bayesian way of testing hypotheses. A Bayesian statistician can give a posterior probability to the null hypothesis. Contrast this with the classical *p*-value, as defined in Chapter 7.

Suppose the stockbroker believed differently. Suppose that he believed that returns on the stock had a mean of 15 and a standard deviation of 4. In this case, the broker admits less uncertainty in his knowledge about average stock returns. The sampling results are the same, so the likelihood is unchanged. However, the posterior distribution does change as it now incorporates the data (through the likelihood) with a prior distribution that is not diffuse, as in the last case, but more peaked over its mean of 15. In our present case, the broker has a stronger belief that the average return is around 15% per year, as indicated by a normal distribution more peaked around its mean. Using equations 15–4 and 15–5, we obtain the posterior mean and standard deviation:

$$M'' = \frac{(1/16)15 + (10/46.24)11.54}{1/16 + 10/46.24} = 12.32$$

$$\sigma'' = \sqrt{\frac{1}{1/16 + 10/46.24}} = 1.89$$

As can be seen, the fact that the broker felt more confident about the average return's being around 15% (as manifested by the smaller standard deviation of his prior probability distribution) caused the posterior mean to be closer to 15% than it was when the same data were used with a more diffuse prior (the new mean is 12.32, compared with 11.77, obtained earlier). The prior distribution, the likelihood function, and the posterior distribution of the mean return on the stock are shown in Figure 15–8. Compare this figure with Figure 15–7, which corresponds to the earlier case with a more diffuse prior.

The Template

Figure 15–9 shows the template for revising beliefs about the mean of a normal distribution. The data in the figure correspond to Example 15–2.

Changing the 8 in cell E5 to 4 solves the less diffuse case. See Figure 15–10.

FIGURE 15–8 **Prior Distribution, Likelihood Function, and Posterior Distribution of Average Return Using a More Peaked Prior Distribution**

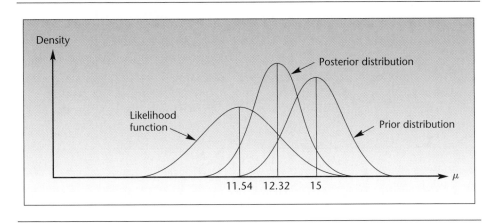

FIGURE 15–9 **The Template for Revising Beliefs about a Normal Mean [Bayesian Revision.xls; Sheet: Normal]**

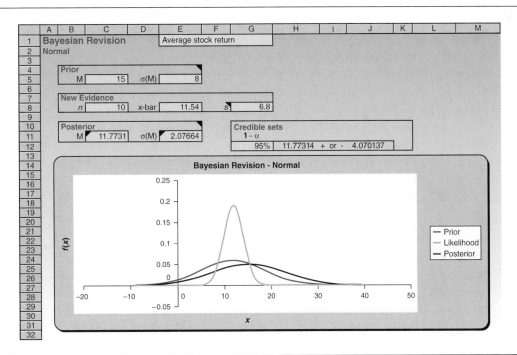

FIGURE 15–10   A Second Case of Revising the Normal Mean
[Bayesian Revision.xls; Sheet: Normal]

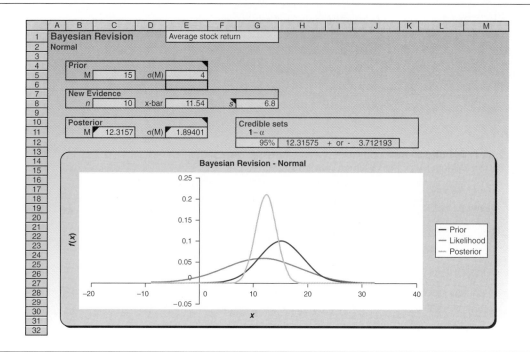

PROBLEMS

15–11.   The partner-manager of a franchise of Au Bon Pain, Inc., the French bakery-restaurant chain, believes that the *average* daily revenue of her business may be viewed as a random variable (she adheres to the Bayesian philosophy) with mean $8,500 and standard deviation $1,000. Her prior probability distribution of average daily revenue is normal. A random sample of 35 days reveals a mean daily revenue of $9,210 and a standard deviation of $365. Construct the posterior distribution of average daily revenue. Assume a normal distribution of daily revenues.

15–12.   *Money* surveyed mutual funds as a good investment instrument.[5] Suppose that the annual average percentage return from mutual funds is a normally distributed random variable with mean 8.7% and standard deviation 5%, and suppose that a random sample of 50 such funds gave a mean return of 10.1% and standard deviation of 4.8%. Compute a 95% highest-posterior-density credible set for the average annual mutual fund return.

15–13.   Claude Vrinat, owner of Taillevent—one of Europe's most highly acclaimed restaurants—is reported to regularly sample the tastes of his patrons. From experience, Vrinat believes that the average rating (on a scale of 0 to 100) that his clients give his *foie gras de canard* may be viewed as normally distributed with mean 94 and standard deviation 2. A random sample of 10 diners gives an average rating of 96 and standard deviation of 1. What should be Vrinat's posterior distribution of average rating of *foie gras de canard,* assuming ratings are normally distributed?

15–14.   In the context of problem 15–13, a second random sample of 15 diners is asked to rate the *foie gras,* giving a mean rating of 95 and standard deviation of 1.

---

[5]"The Best Mutual Funds You Can Buy," *Money,* February 2007, p. 61.

Incorporate the new information to give a posterior distribution that accounts for both samplings and the prior distribution. Give a 95% HPD credible set for mean rating.

15–15.   An article in *Forbes* discusses the problem of oil and gas reserves around the world.[6] Forecasting the amount of oil available is difficult. If the average number of barrels that can be pumped daily from an oil field is a normal random variable with mean 7,200 barrels and standard deviation 505 barrels, and a random sample of 20 days reveals a sample average of 6,100 barrels and standard deviation of 800, give a 95% highest-posterior-density credible set for the average number of barrels that can be pumped daily.

15–16.   Continuing problem 15–15, suppose that a second random sample of 20 days reveals an average of 5,020 barrels and standard deviation of 650. Create a new 95% HPD credible set.

15–17.   In an effort to predict Alaska's oil-related state revenues, a Delphi session is regularly held where experts in the field give their expectations of the average future price of crude oil over the next year. The views of five prominent experts who participated in the last Delphi session may be stated as normal prior distributions with means and standard deviations given in the following table. To protect their identities (the Delphi sessions are closed to the public), we will denote them by the letters A through E. Data are in dollars per barrel.

Expert	Mean	Standard Deviation
A	23	4
B	19	7
C	25	1
D	20	9
E	27	3

Compare the views of the five experts, using this information. What can you say about the different experts' degrees of belief in their own respective knowledge? One of the experts is the governor of Alaska, who, due to the nature of the post, devotes little time to following oil prices. All other experts have varying degrees of experience with price analysis; one of them is the ARCO expert who assesses oil prices on a daily basis. Looking only at the reported prior standard deviations, who is likely to be the governor, and who is likely to be the ARCO expert? Now suppose that at the end of the year the average daily price of crude oil was $18 per barrel. Who should be most surprised (and embarrassed), and why?

15–4   The Evaluation of Subjective Probabilities

Since Bayesian analysis makes extensive use of people's subjective beliefs in the form of prior probabilities, it is only natural that the field should include methods for the elicitation of personal probabilities. We begin by presenting some simple ideas on how to identify a normal prior probability distribution and give a rough estimate of its mean and standard deviation.

Assessing a Normal Prior Distribution

As you well know by now, the normal probability model is useful in a wide variety of applications. Furthermore, since we know probabilities associated with the normal distribution, results can easily be obtained if we do make the assumption of normality. How can we estimate a decision maker's subjective normal probability distribution? For example, how did the stockbroker of Example 15–2 decide that his prior distribution of average returns was normal with mean 15 and standard deviation 8?

---

[6]Steve Forbes, "Will We Rid Ourselves of This Pollution?" *Forbes*, April 16, 2007, pp. 33–34.

The normal distribution appears naturally and as an approximation in many situations due to the central limit theorem. Therefore, in many instances, it makes sense to assume a normal distribution. In other cases, we frequently have a distribution that is not normal but still is *symmetric* with a *single mode*. In such cases, it may still make sense to assume a normal distribution as an approximation because this distribution is easily estimated as a subjective distribution, and the resulting inaccuracies will not be great. In cases where the distribution is *skewed*, however, the normal approximation will not be adequate.

Once we determine that the normal distribution is appropriate for describing our personal beliefs about the situation at hand, we need to estimate the mean and the standard deviation of the distribution. For a symmetric distribution with one mode, the mean is equal to the median and to the mode. Therefore, we may ask the decision maker whose subjective probability we are trying to assess what he or she believes to be the center of the distribution. We may also ask for the most likely value. We may ask for the average, or we may ask for the point that splits the distribution into two equal parts. All these questions would lead us to the central value, which we take to be the mean of the subjective distribution. By asking the person whose probabilities we are trying to elicit several of these questions, we have a few checks on the answer. Any discrepancies in the answers may lead to possible violations of our assumption of the symmetry of the distribution or its unimodality (having only one mode), which would obviate the normal approximation. Presumably, questions such as these lead the stockbroker of Example 15–2 to determine that the mean of his prior distribution for average returns is 15%.

How do we estimate the standard deviation of a subjective distribution? Recall the simple rules of thumb for the normal probability model:

Approximately 68% of the distribution lies within 1 standard deviation of the mean.

Approximately 95% of the distribution lies within 2 standard deviations of the mean.

These rules lead us to the following questions for the decision maker whose probabilities we are trying to assess: "Give me two values of the distribution in question such that you are 95% sure that the variable in question is between the two values," or equivalently, "Give me two values such that 95% of the distribution lies between them." We may also ask for two values such that 68% of the distribution is between these values.

For 95% sureness, assuming symmetry, we know that the two values we obtain as answers are each 2 standard deviations away from the mean. In the case of the stockbroker, he must have felt there was a 0.95 chance that the average return on the stock was anywhere from -1% to 31%. The two points -1 and 31 are 2×8 units on either side of the mean of 15. Hence, the standard deviation is 8. The stockbroker could also have said that he was 68% sure that the average return was anywhere from 7% to 23% (each of these two values is 1 standard deviation away from the mean of 15). Using 95% bounds is more useful than 68% limits because people are more likely to think in terms of 95% sureness. Be sure you understand the difference between this method of obtaining bounds on values of a population (or random variable) and the construction of confidence intervals (or credible sets) for population *parameters*.

15–5   Decision Analysis: An Overview

Some years ago, the state of Massachusetts had to solve a serious problem: an alarming number of road fatalities caused by icy roads in winter. The state department of transportation wanted to solve the problem by salting the roads to reduce ice buildup. The introduction of large amounts of salt into the environment, however, would eventually cause an increase in the sodium content of drinking water, thus increasing the risk of heart problems in the general population.

This is the kind of problem that can be solved by *decision analysis.* There is a decision to be made: to salt or not to salt. With each of the two possible actions, we may associate a final outcome, and each outcome has a probability of occurrence. An additional number of deaths from heart disease would result if roads were salted. The number of deaths is uncertain, but its probability may be assessed. On the other hand, a number of highway deaths would be prevented if salt were used. Here again, the number is uncertain and governed by some probability law. In decision analysis we seek the best decision in a given situation. Although it is unpleasant to think of deaths, the best (optimal) decision here is the decision that would minimize the expected total number of deaths. *Expected* means averaged using the different probabilities as weights.

The area of decision analysis is independent of most of the material in this book. To be able to perform decision analysis, you need to have a rudimentary understanding of probability and of expected values. Some problems make use of additional information, obtained either by sampling or by other means. In such cases, we may have an idea about the *reliability* of our information—which may be stated as a probability—and the information is incorporated in the analysis by use of Bayes' theorem.

When a company is interested in introducing a new product, decision analysis offers an excellent aid in coming to a final decision. When one company considers a merger with another, decision analysis may be used as a way of evaluating all possible outcomes of the move and deciding whether to go ahead based on the best expected outcome. Decision analysis can help you decide which investment or combination of investments to choose. It could help you choose a job or career. It could help you decide whether to pursue an MBA degree.

We emphasize the use of decision analysis as an aid in corporate decision making. Since quantifying the aspects of human decision making is often difficult, it is important to understand that decision analysis should not be the only criterion for making a decision. A stockbroker's hunch, for example, may be a much better indication of the best investment decision than a formal mathematical analysis, which may very well miss some important variables.

Decision analysis, as described in this book, has several elements.

The elements of a decision analysis:

1. Actions
2. Chance occurrences
3. Probabilities
4. Final outcomes
5. Additional information
6. Decision

Actions

By an *action,* we mean anything that the decision maker can do. An action is something you, the decision maker, can control. You may choose to take an action, or you may choose not to take it. Often, there are several choices for action: You may buy one of several different products, travel one of several possible routes, etc. Many decision problems are sequential in nature: You choose one action from among several possibilities; later, you are again in a position to take an action. You may keep taking actions until a final outcome is reached; you keep playing the game until the game is over. Finally, you have reached some final outcome—you have gained a certain amount or lost an amount, achieved a goal or failed.

Chance Occurrences

Even if the decision problem is essentially nonsequential (you take an action, something happens, and that is it), we may gain a better understanding of the problem if we view the problem as sequential. We assume that the decision maker takes an action, and afterward "chance takes an action." The action of chance is the chance occurrence. When you decide to buy ABC stock, you have taken an action. When the stock falls 3 points the next day, chance has taken an action.

Probabilities

All actions of chance are governed by probabilities, or at least we view them that way because we cannot predict chance occurrences. The probabilities are obtained by some method. Often, the probabilities of chance occurrences are the decision maker's (or consulted expert's) subjective probabilities. Thus, the chief executive officer of a firm bidding for another firm will assign certain probabilities to the various outcomes that may result from the attempted merger.

In other cases, the probabilities of chance occurrences are more objective. If we use sampling results as an aid in the analysis (see the section on additional information, which follows), then statistical theory gives us measures of the reliability of results and, hence, probabilities of relevant chance occurrences.

Final Outcomes

We assume that the decision problem is of finite duration. After you, the decision maker, have taken an action or a sequence of actions, and after chance has taken action or a sequence of actions, there is a final outcome. An outcome may be viewed as a *payoff* or *reward,* or it may be viewed as a *loss.* We will look at outcomes as rewards (positive or negative). A payoff is an amount of money (or other measure of benefit, called a *utility*) that you receive at the end of the game—at the end of the decision problem.

Additional Information

Each time chance takes over, a random occurrence takes place. We may have some prior information that allows us to assess the probability of any chance occurrence. Often, however, we may be able to purchase additional information. We may consult an expert, at a cost, or we may sample from the population of interest (assuming such a population exists) for a price. The costs of obtaining additional information are subtracted from our final payoff. Therefore, buying new information is, in itself, an action that we may choose to take or not. Deciding whether to obtain such information is part of the entire decision process. We must weigh the benefit of the additional information against its cost.

Decision

The action, or sequential set of actions, we decide to take is called our *decision.* The decision obtained through a useful analysis is that set of actions that maximizes our expected final-outcome payoff. The decision will often give us a set of *alternative actions* in addition to the optimal set of actions. In a decision to introduce a new product, suppose that the result of the decision analysis indicates that we should proceed with the introduction of the product without any market testing—that is, without any sampling. Suppose, however, that a higher official in the company requires us to test the product even though we may not want to do so. A comprehensive solution to the decision problem would provide us not only with the optimal action (market the product), but also with information on how to proceed in the best possible way when we are forced to take some suboptimal actions along the way. The complete solution to the decision problem would thus include information on how to treat the results of the market test. If the results are unfavorable, the optimal action at this point may be not to go ahead with introducing the product. The solution to the decision problem—the *decision*—gives us all information on how to proceed at any given stage or circumstance.

FIGURE 15–11 An Example of a Decision Tree for New-Product Introduction

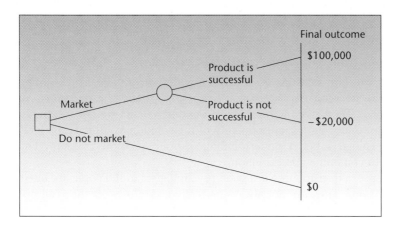

As you see, we have stressed a sequential approach to decision making. At the very least, a decision analysis consists of two stages: The decision maker takes an action out of several possible ones, and then chance takes an action. This sequential approach to decision making is very well modeled and visualized by what is called a **decision tree.**

A decision tree is a set of nodes and branches. At a *decision node,* the decision maker takes an action; the action is the choice of a branch to be followed. The branch leads to a *chance node,* where chance determines the outcome; that is, chance chooses the branch to be followed. Then either the final outcome is reached (the branch ends), or the decision maker gets to take another action, and so on. We mark a decision node by a square and a chance node by a circle. These are connected by the branches of the decision tree. An example of a decision tree is shown in Figure 15–11. The decision tree shown in the figure is a simple one: It consists of only four branches, one decision node, and one chance node. In addition, there is no product-testing option. As we go on, we will see more complicated decision trees, and we will explore related topics.

PROBLEMS

15–18. What are the uses of decision analysis?

15–19. What are the limitations of decision analysis?

15–20. List the elements of a decision problem, and explain how they interrelate.

15–21. What is the role of probabilities in a decision problem, and how do these probabilities arise?

15–22. What is a decision tree?

15–6 Decision Trees

As mentioned in the last section, a decision tree is a useful aid in carrying out a decision analysis because it allows us to visualize the decision problem. If nothing else, the tree gives us a good perspective on our decision problem: It lets us see when we, as decision makers, are in control and when we are not. To handle the instances when we are not in control, we use probabilities. These probabilities—assuming they are assessed in some accurate, logical, and consistent way—are our educated guesses as to what will happen when we are not in control.

The aforementioned use of decision trees in clarifying our perspective on a decision problem may not seem terribly important, say, compared with a quantitatively rigorous solution to a problem involving exact numbers. However, this use of decision trees is actually more important than it seems. After you have seen how to use a decision tree in computing the expected payoff at each chance node and the choice of the optimal action at each decision node, and after you have tried several decision problems, you will find that the trees have an added advantage. You will find that just drawing the decision tree helps you better understand the decision problem you need to solve. Then, even if the probabilities and payoffs are not accurately assessed, making you doubt the exact optimality of the solution you have obtained, you will still have gained a better understanding of your decision problem. This in itself should help you find a good solution.

In a sense, a decision tree is a good psychological tool. People are often confused about decisions. They are not always perfectly aware of what they can do and what they cannot do, and they often lack an understanding of uncertainty and how it affects the outcomes of their decisions. This is especially true of large-scale decision problems, entailing several possible actions at several different points, each followed by chance outcomes, leading to a distant final outcome. In such cases, drawing a decision tree is an indispensable way of gaining familiarity with all aspects of the decision problem. The tree shows which actions affect which, and how the actions interrelate with chance outcomes. The tree shows how combinations of actions and chance outcomes lead to possible final outcomes and payoffs.

Having said all this, let us see how decision problems are transformed to visual decision trees and how these trees are analyzed. Let us see how decision trees can lead us to optimal solutions to decision problems. We will start with the simple new-product introduction example shown in the decision tree in Figure 15–11. Going step by step, we will show how that simple tree was constructed. The same technique is used in constructing more complicated trees, with many branches and nodes.

The Payoff Table

The first step in the solution of any decision problem is to prepare the *payoff table* (also called the *payoff matrix*). The payoff table is a table of the possible payoffs we would receive if we took certain actions and certain chance occurrences followed. Generally, what takes place will be called *state of nature,* and what we do will be called the *decision.* This leads us to a table that is very similar to Table 7–1. There we dealt with hypothesis testing, and the state of nature was whether the null hypothesis was true; our decision was either to reject or not reject the null hypothesis. In that context, we could have associated the result "not reject H_0 when H_0 is true" with some payoff (because a correct decision was made); the outcome "not reject H_0 when H_0 is false" could have been associated with another (negative) payoff, and similarly for the other two possible outcomes. In the context of decision analysis, we might view the hypothesis testing as a sequential process. We make a decision (to reject or not to reject H_0), and then "chance" takes over and makes H_0 either true or false.

Let us now write the payoff table for the new-product introduction problem. Here we assume that if we do not introduce the product, nothing is gained and nothing is lost. This assumes we have not invested anything in developing the product, and it assumes no opportunity loss. If we do not introduce the new product, our payoff is zero.

If our action is to introduce the product, two things may happen: The product may be successful, or it may not. If the product is successful, our payoff will be $100,000; and if it is not successful, we will lose $20,000, so our payoff will be −$20,000. The payoff table for this simple problem is Table 15–4. In real-world situations, we may assess more possible outcomes: finely divided *degrees* of success. For example, the product may be extremely successful—with payoff $150,000; very successful—payoff $120,000; successful—payoff $100,000; somewhat successful—payoff $80,000; barely successful—payoff $40,000; breakeven—payoff $0; unsuccessful—payoff −$20,000;

TABLE 15–4 Payoff Table: New-Product Introduction

Action	Product Is	
	Successful	Not Successful
Market the product	+$100,000	−$20,000
Do not market the product	0	0

FIGURE 15–12 Decision Tree for New-Product Introduction

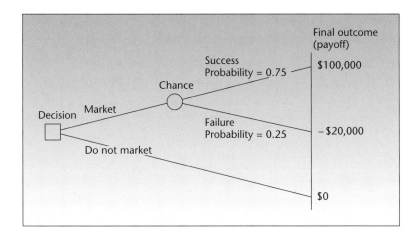

or disastrous—payoff −$50,000. Table 15–4 can be easily extended to cover these expanded states of nature. Instead of two columns, we would have eight, and we would still have two rows corresponding to the two possible actions.

The values in Table 15–4 give rise to the decision tree that was shown in Figure 15–11. We take an action: If we do not market the product, the payoff is zero, as shown by the arc from the decision node to the final outcome of zero. If we choose to market the product, chance either will take us to success and a payoff of $100,000 or will lead us to failure and a loss of $20,000. We now need to deal with chance. We do so by assigning probabilities to the two possible states of nature, that is, to the two possible actions of chance. Here, some elicitation of personal probabilities is done. Suppose that our marketing manager concludes that the probability of success of the new product is 0.75. The probability of failure then must be $1 - 0.75 = 0.25$. Let us write these probabilities on the appropriate branches of our decision tree. The tree, with payoffs and probabilities, is shown in Figure 15–12.

We now have all the elements of the decision tree, and we are ready to solve the decision problem.

> The solution of decision tree problems is achieved by working backward from the final outcomes.

The method we use is called **averaging out and folding back.** Working backward from the final outcomes, we *average out all chance occurrences.* This means that we find the *expected value* at each chance node. At each chance node (each circle in the tree), we write the expected monetary value of all branches leading out of the node; we *fold back* the tree. At each decision node (each square in the tree), we *choose the action that maximizes our (expected) payoff.* That is, we look at all branches emanating from the decision node, and we choose the branch leading to the highest monetary value. Other branches may be *clipped;* they are not optimal. The problem is solved once we reach the beginning: the first decision node.

Let us solve the decision problem of the new-product introduction. We start at the final outcomes. There are three such outcomes, as seen in Figure 15–12. The outcome with payoff $0 emanates directly from the decision node; we leave it for now. The other two payoffs, $100,000 and −$20,000, both emanate from a chance node. We therefore average them out—using their respective probabilities—and fold back to the chance node. To do this, we find the expected monetary value at the chance node (the circle in Figure 15–12). Recall the definition of the expected value of a random variable, given as equation 3–4.

The expected value of X, denoted $E(X)$, is

$$E(X) = \sum_{\text{all } x} xP(x)$$

The outcome as you leave the chance node is a random variable with two possible values: 100,000 and −20,000. The probability of outcome 100,000 is 0.75, and the probability of outcome −20,000 is 0.25. To find the expected value at the chance node, we apply equation 3–4:

$$E(\text{outcome at chance node}) = (100{,}000)(0.75) + (-20{,}000)(0.25)$$
$$= 70{,}000$$

Thus, the expected value associated with the chance node is +$70,000; we write this value next to the circle in our decision tree. We can now look at the decision node (the square), since we have folded back and reached the first node in the tree. We know the (expected) monetary values associated with the two branches emanating from this node. Recall that at decision nodes we do not average. Rather, we choose the best branch to be followed and clip the other branches, as they are not optimal. Thus, at the decision node, we compare the two values +$70,000 and $0. Since 70,000 is greater than 0, the expected monetary outcome of the decision to market the new product is greater than the monetary outcome of the decision not to market the new product. We follow the rule of choosing the decision that maximizes the expected payoff, so we choose to market the product. (We clip the branch corresponding to "not market" and put a little arrow by the branch corresponding to "market.") In Section 15–8, where we discuss *utility,* we will see an alternative to the "maximum expected monetary value" rule, which takes into account our attitudes toward risk rather than simply aims for the highest *average* payoff, as we have done here. The solution of the decision tree is shown in Figure 15–13.

FIGURE 15–13   Solution of the New-Product Introduction Decision Tree

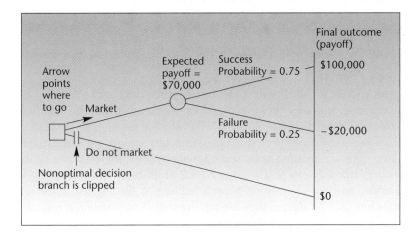

TABLE 15–5   **Possible Outcomes and Their Probabilities**

Outcome	Payoff	Probability
Extremely successful	$150,000	0.1
Very successful	120,000	0.2
Successful	100,000	0.3
Somewhat successful	80,000	0.1
Barely successful	40,000	0.1
Breakeven	0	0.1
Unsuccessful	−20,000	0.05
Disastrous	−50,000	0.05

We follow the arrow and make the decision to market the new product. Then chance takes over, and the product either becomes successful (an event which, a priori, we believe to have a 0.75 probability of occurring) or does not become successful. On average—that is, if we make decisions such as this one very many times—we should expect to make $70,000.

Let us now consider the extended market possibilities mentioned earlier. Suppose that the outcomes and their probabilities in the case of extended possibilities are as given in Table 15–5. In this new example, the payoff is more realistic: It has many possible states. Our payoff is a random variable. The expected value of this random variable is computed, as usual, by multiplying the values by their probabilities and adding (equation 3–4). This can easily be done by adding a column for Payoff $\times$ Probability to Table 15–5 and adding all entries in the column. This gives us $E(\text{payoff}) = \$77,500$ (verify this). The decision tree for this example—with many branches emanating from the chance node—is shown in Figure 15–14. The optimal decision in this case is, again, to market the product.

We have seen how to analyze a decision problem by using a decision tree. Let us now look at an example. In Example 15–3, chance takes over after either action we take, and the problem involves more than one action. We will take an action; then a chance occurrence will take place. Then we will again decide on an action, after which chance will again take over, leading us to a final outcome.

Recently, Digital Equipment Corporation arranged to get the Cunard Lines ship *Queen Elizabeth 2* (QE2) for use as a floating hotel for the company's annual convention. The meeting took place in September and lasted nine days. In agreeing to

EXAMPLE 15–3

FIGURE 15–14   **Extended-Possibilities Decision Tree for New-Product Introduction**

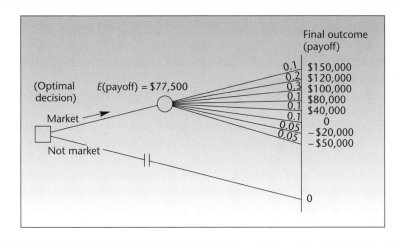

lease the QE2, Cunard had to make a decision. If the cruise ship were leased to Digital, Cunard would get a flat fee and an additional percentage of profits from the gala convention, which could attract as many as 50,000 people. Cunard analysts therefore estimated that if the ship were leased, there would be a 0.50 probability that the company would make $700,000 for the nine days; a 0.30 probability that profits from the venture would be about $800,000; a 0.15 probability that profits would be about $900,000; and a 0.05 probability that profits would be as high as $1 million. If the ship were not leased to Digital, the vessel would be used for its usual Atlantic crossing voyage, also lasting nine days. If this happened, there would be a 0.90 probability that profits would be $750,000 and a 0.10 probability that profits would be about $780,000. The tighter distribution of profits on the voyage was due to the fact that Cunard analysts knew much about the company's usual business of Atlantic crossings but knew relatively little about the proposed venture.

Cunard had one additional option. If the ship were leased to Digital, and it became clear within the first few days of the convention that Cunard's profits from the venture were going to be in the range of only $700,000, the steamship company could choose to promote the convention on its own by offering participants discounts on QE2 cruises. The company's analysts believed that if this action were chosen, there would be a 0.60 probability that profits would increase to about $740,000 and a 0.40 probability that the promotion would fail, lowering profits to $680,000 due to the cost of the promotional campaign and the discounts offered. What should Cunard have done?

Solution   Let us analyze all the components of this decision problem. One of two possible actions must be chosen: to lease or not to lease. We can start constructing our tree by drawing the square denoting this decision node and showing the two appropriate branches leading out of it.

Once we make our choice, chance takes over. If we choose to lease, chance will lead us to one of four possible outcomes. We show these possibilities by attaching a circle node at the end of the lease action branch, with four branches emanating from it. If we choose not to lease, chance again takes over, leading us to two possible outcomes. This is shown by a chance node attached at the end of the not-lease action branch, with two branches leading out of it and into the possible final outcome payoffs of $750,000 and $780,000.

We now go back to the chance occurrences following the lease decision. At the end of the branch corresponding to an outcome of $700,000, we attach another decision node corresponding to the promotion option. This decision node has two branches leaving it: One goes to the final outcome of $700,000, corresponding to nonpromotion of the convention; and the other, the one corresponding to promotion, leads to a chance node, which in turn leads to two possible final outcomes: a profit of $740,000 and a profit of $680,000. All other chance outcomes following the lease decision lead directly to final outcomes. These outcomes are profits of $800,000, $900,000, and $1 million. At each chance branch, we note its probability. The chance outcomes of the lease action have probabilities 0.5, 0.3, 0.15, and 0.05 (in order of increasing monetary outcome). The probabilities of the outcomes following the not-lease action are 0.9 and 0.1, respectively. Finally, the probabilities corresponding to the chance outcomes following the promote action are 0.4 and 0.6, again in order of increasing profit.

Our decision tree for the problem is shown in Figure 15–15. Having read the preceding description of the details of the tree, you will surely agree that "A picture is worth 1,000 words."

We now solve the decision tree. Our method of solution, as you recall, is averaging out and folding back. We start at the end; that is, we look at the final-outcome payoffs and work backward from these values. At every chance node, we average the payoffs, using their respective probabilities. This gives us the expected monetary

FIGURE 15–15   Decision Tree for the Cunard Lease Example

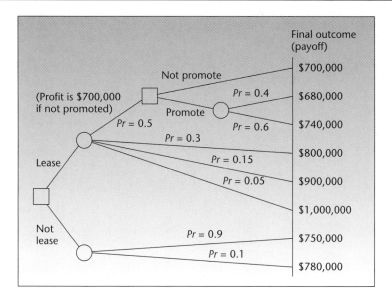

value associated with the chance node. At every decision node, we choose the action with the highest expected payoff and clip the branches corresponding to all other, nonoptimal actions. Once we reach the first decision node in the tree, we are done and will have obtained a complete solution to the decision problem.

Let us start with the closest chance node to the final outcomes—the one corresponding to the possible outcomes of the promote action. The expected payoff at this chance node is obtained as

$$E(\text{payoff}) = (680{,}000)(0.4) + (740{,}000)(0.6) = \$716{,}000$$

We now move back to the promote/not-promote decision node. Here we must choose the action that maximizes the expected payoff. This is done by comparing the two payoffs: the payoff of $700,000 associated with the not-promote action and the expected payoff of $716,000 associated with the promote action. Since the *expected* value of $716,000 is greater, we choose to promote. We show this with an arrow, and we clip the nonoptimal action not to promote. The expected value of $716,000 now becomes associated with the decision node, and we write it next to the node.

We now fold back to the chance node following the lease action. Four branches lead out of that node. One of them leads to the promote decision node, which, as we just decided, is associated with an (expected) outcome of $716,000. The probability of reaching the decision node is 0.5. The next branch leads to an outcome of $800,000 and has a probability of 0.3; and the next two outcomes are $900,000 and $1 million, with probabilities 0.15 and 0.05, respectively. We now average out the payoffs at this chance node as follows:

$$E(\text{payoff}) = (716{,}000)(0.5) + (800{,}000)(0.3) + (900{,}000)(0.15)$$
$$+ (1{,}000{,}000)(0.05) = \$783{,}000$$

This expected monetary value is now written next to the chance node.

FIGURE 15–16   Solution of the Cunard Leasing Problem

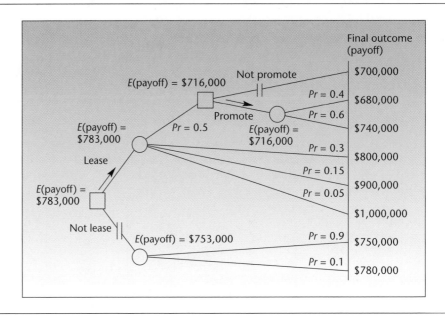

Let us now look at the last chance node, the one corresponding to outcomes associated with the not-lease action. Here, we have two possible outcomes: a payoff of $750,000, with probability 0.9; and a payoff of $780,000, with probability 0.1. We now find the expected monetary value of the chance node:

$$E(\text{payoff}) = (750,000)(0.9) + (780,000)(0.1) = \$753,000$$

We are now finally at the first decision node of the entire tree. Here we must choose the action that maximizes the expected payoff. The choice is done by comparing the expected payoff associated with the lease action, $783,000, and the expected payoff associated with not leasing, $753,000. Since the higher expected payoff is that associated with leasing, the decision is to lease. This is shown by an arrow on the tree and by clipping the not-lease action as nonoptimal. The stages of the solution are shown in Figure 15–16.

We now have a final solution to the decision problem: We choose to *lease* our ship to Digital Equipment Corporation. Then, if we should find out that our profit from the lease were in the range of only $700,000, our action would be to *promote* the convention. Note that in this decision problem, the decision consists of a pair of actions. The decision tells us what to do in any eventuality.

If the tree had more than just two decision nodes, the final solution to the problem would have consisted of a set of optimal actions at all decision nodes. The solution would have told us what to do at any decision node to maximize the expected payoff, given that we arrive at that decision node. Note, again, that our solution is optimal only in an *expected monetary value* sense. If Cunard is very conservative and does not want to take any risk of getting a profit lower than the minimum of $750,000 it is assured of receiving from an Atlantic crossing, then, clearly, the decision to lease would not be optimal because it does admit such a risk. If the steamship company has some risk aversion but would accept some risk of lower profits, then the analysis should be done using utilities rather than pure monetary values. The use of utility in a way that accounts for people's attitudes toward risk is discussed in Section 15–8.

15–23. During the Super Bowl, a 30-second commercial costs \$2.5 million.[7] The maker of Doritos corn chips was considering purchasing such an ad. The marketing director felt that there was a 0.35 probability that the commercial would boost sales volume to \$20 million over the next month; there was a 0.60 probability that excess sales would be \$10 million; and a 0.05 probability that excess sales would be only \$1 million. Carry out an analysis of whether to purchase a 30-second commercial during the Super Bowl using a complete decision tree.

15–24. An article in the *Asia Pacific Journal of Management* discusses the importance for firms to invest in social ties.[8] A company is considering paying \$150,000 for social activities over one year, hoping that productivity for the year will rise. Estimates are that there is a 50% chance that productivity would not change; there is a 20% chance that the company's profits would rise by \$300,000; and there is a 10% chance of a rise of \$500,000. There is also a 20% chance that employees will learn to waste time and that profits would fall by \$50,000. Construct a decision tree and recommend a course of action.

15–25. Drug manufacturing is a risky business requiring much research and development. Recently, several drug manufacturers had to make important decisions.[9] Developing a new drug for Alzheimer's can cost \$250 million. An analyst believes that such a drug would be approved by the FDA with probability 0.70. In this case, the company could make \$850 million over the next few years. If the FDA did not approve the new drug, it could still be sold overseas, and the company could make \$200 million over the same number of years. Construct a decision tree and recommend a decision on whether to develop the new drug.

15–26. Predicting the styles that will prevail in a coming year is one of the most important and difficult problems in the fashion industry. A fashion designer must work on designs for the coming fall long before he or she can find out for certain what styles are going to be "in." A well-known designer believes that there is a 0.20 chance that short dresses and skirts will be popular in the coming fall; a 0.35 chance that popular styles will be of medium length; and a 0.45 chance that long dresses and skirts will dominate fall fashions. The designer must now choose the styles on which to concentrate. If she chooses one style and another turns out to be more popular, profits will be lower than if the new style were guessed correctly. The following table shows what the designer believes she would make, in hundreds of thousands of dollars, for any given combination of her choice of style and the one that prevails in the new season.

Designer's Choice	Prevailing Style		
	Short	Medium	Long
Short	8	3	1
Medium	1	9	2
Long	4	3	10

Construct a decision tree, and determine what style the designer should choose to maximize her expected profits.

---

[7]"Give Consumers Control," *Adweek,* December 11, 2006, p. 14.

[8]Peter Ping Li, "Social Tie, Social Capital, and Social Behavior: Toward an Integrative Model of Informal Exchange," *Asia Pacific Journal of Management* 24, no. 2 (2007), pp. 227–246.

[9]Alex Berenson, "Manufacturer of Risky Drug to Sell Shares," *The New York Times,* May 31, 2007, p. C1.

15-27. For problem 15–26, suppose that if the designer starts working on long designs, she can change them to medium designs after the prevailing style for the season becomes known—although she must then pay a price for this change because of delays in delivery to manufacturers. In particular, if the designer chooses long and the prevailing style is medium, and she then chooses to change to medium, there is a 0.30 chance that her profits will be $200,000 and a 0.70 chance that her profits will be $600,000. No other change from one style to another is possible. Incorporate this information in your decision tree of problem 15–26, and solve the new tree. Give a complete solution in the form of a pair of decisions under given circumstances that maximize the designer's expected profits.

15-28. Commodity futures provide an opportunity for buyers and suppliers of commodities such as wheat to arrange in advance sales of a commodity, with delivery and payment taking place at a specified time in the future. The price is decided at the time the order is placed, and the buyer is asked to deposit an amount less than the value of the order, but enough to protect the seller from loss in case the buyer should decide not to meet the obligation.

An investor is considering investing $15,000 in wheat futures and believes that there is a 0.10 probability that he will lose $5,000 by the expiration of the contract, a 0.20 probability that he will make $2,000, a 0.25 probability that he will make $3,000, a 0.15 probability he will make $4,000, a 0.15 probability he will make $5,000, a 0.10 probability he will make $6,000, and a 0.05 probability that he will make $7,000. If the investor should find out that he is going to lose $5,000, he can pull out of his contract, losing $3,500 for certain and an additional $3,000 with probability 0.20 (the latter amount deposited with a brokerage firm as a guarantee). Draw the decision tree for this problem, and solve it. What should the investor do?

15-29. For problem 15–28, suppose that the investor is considering another investment as an alternative to wheat. He is considering investing his $15,000 in a limited partnership for the same duration of time as the futures contract. This alternative has a 0.50 chance of earning $5,000 and a 0.50 chance of earning nothing. Add this information to your decision tree of problem 15–28, and solve it.

15-7   Handling Additional Information Using Bayes' Theorem

In any kind of decision problem, it is very natural to ask: Can I gain additional information about the situation? Any additional information will help in making a decision under uncertainty. The more we know, the better able we are to make decisions that are likely to maximize our payoffs. If our information is perfect, that is, if we can find out exactly what chance will do, then there really is no randomness, and the situation is perfectly determined. In such cases, decision analysis is unnecessary because we can determine the exact action that will maximize the actual (rather than the expected) payoff. Here we are concerned with making decisions under uncertainty, and we assume that when additional information is available, such information is probabilistic in nature. Our information has a certain degree of reliability. The reliability is stated as a set of conditional probabilities.

If we are considering the introduction of a new product into the market, we would be wise to try to gain information about the prospects for success of the new product by sampling potential consumers and soliciting their views about the product. (Is this not what statistics is all about?) Results obtained from random sampling are always probabilistic; the probabilities originate in the sampling distributions of our statistics. The reliability of survey results may be stated as a set of *conditional probabilities* in the following way. Given that the market is ripe for our product and that it is in fact going to be successful, there is a certain probability that the sampling results will tell us so. Conversely, given that the market will not accept the new product, there is a certain probability that the random sample of people we select will be representative enough of the population in question to tell us so.

To show the use of the conditional probabilities, let S denote the event that the product will be a success and $F = \overline{S}$ (the complement of S) be the event that the product will fail. Let IS be the event that the sample indicates that the product will be a success, and IF the event that the sample indicates that the product will fail. The reliability of the sampling results may be stated by the conditional probabilities $P(\text{IS} \mid \text{S})$, $P(\text{IS} \mid \text{F})$, $P(\text{IF} \mid \text{S})$, and $P(\text{IF} \mid \text{F})$. [Each pair of conditional probabilities with the same condition has a sum of 1.00. Thus, $P(\text{IS} \mid \text{S}) + P(\text{IF} \mid \text{S}) = 1$, and $P(\text{IS} \mid \text{F}) + P(\text{IF} \mid \text{F}) = 1$. So we need to be given only two of the four conditional probabilities.]

Once we have sampled, we know the sample outcome: either the event IS (the sample telling us that the product will be successful) or the event IF (the sample telling us that our product will not be a success). What we need is the probability that the product will be successful given that the sample told us so, or the probability that the product will fail, if that is what the sample told us. In symbols, what we need is $P(\text{S} \mid \text{IS})$ and $P(\text{F} \mid \text{IS})$ (its complement), or the pair of probabilities $P(\text{S} \mid \text{IF})$ and $P(\text{F} \mid \text{IF})$. We have $P(\text{IS} \mid \text{S})$, and we need $P(\text{S} \mid \text{IS})$. The conditions in the two probabilities are reversed. Remember that Bayes' theorem reverses the conditionality of events. This is why decision analysis is usually associated with Bayesian theory. In order to transform information about the reliability of additional information in a decision problem to usable information about the likelihood of states of nature, we need to use Bayes' theorem.

To restate the theorem in this context, suppose that the sample told us that the product will be a success. The (posterior) probability that the product will indeed be a success is given by

$$P(\text{S} \mid \text{IS}) = \frac{P(\text{IS} \mid \text{S}) \, P(\text{S})}{P(\text{IS} \mid \text{S})P(\text{S}) + P(\text{IS} \mid \text{F})P(\text{F})} \qquad (15\text{–}6)$$

The probabilities $P(\text{S})$ and $P(\text{F})$ are our *prior* probabilities of the two possible outcomes: successful product versus unsuccessful product. Knowing these prior probabilities and knowing the reliability of survey results, here in the form of $P(\text{IS} \mid \text{S})$ and $P(\text{IS} \mid \text{F})$, allows us to compute the posterior, updated probability that the product will be successful given that the sample told us that it will be successful.

How is all this used in a decision tree? We extend our decision problem to include two possible actions: to test or not to test, that is, to obtain additional information or not to obtain such information. The decision of whether to test must be made before we make any other decision. In the case of a new-product introduction decision problem, our decision tree must be augmented to include the possibility of testing or not testing before we decide whether to market our new product. We will assume that the test costs $5,000. Our new decision tree is shown in Figure 15–17.

As shown in Figure 15–17, we first decide whether to test. If we test, we get a test result. The result is a *chance outcome*—the test indicates success, or the test indicates failure (event IS or event IF). If the test indicates success, then we may choose to market or not to market. The same happens if the test indicates failure: We may still choose to market, or we may choose not to market. If the test is worthwhile, it is not logical to market once the test tells us the product will fail. But the point of the

FIGURE 15–17 New-Product Decision Tree with Testing

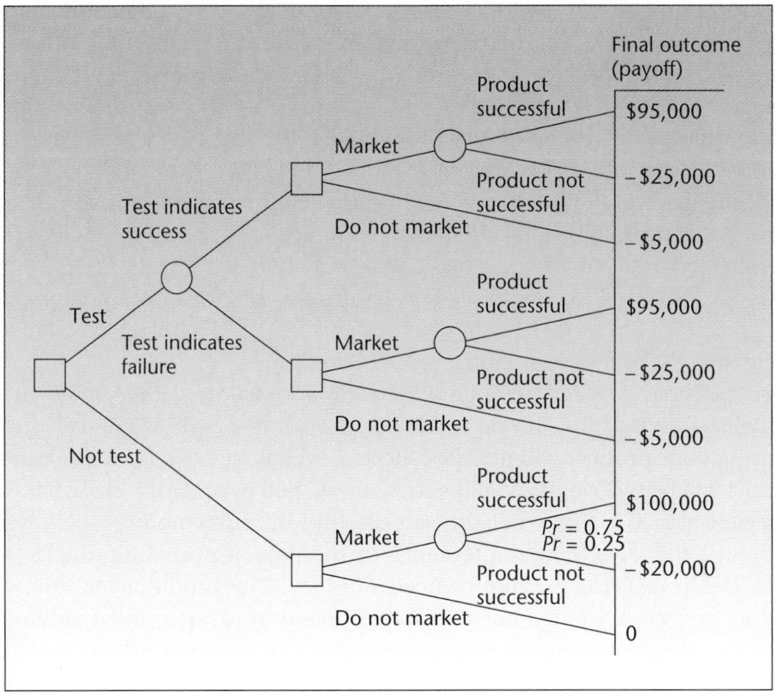

decision analysis is that we do not know whether the test is worthwhile; this is one of the things that we need to decide. Therefore, we allow for the possibility of marketing even if the test tells us not to market, as well as allowing for all other possible combinations of decisions.

Determining the Payoffs

Recall that if the product is successful, we make $100,000, and if it is not successful, we lose $20,000. The test is assumed to cost $5,000. Thus, we must subtract $5,000 from all final-outcome payoffs that are reached via testing. If we test, we spend $5,000. If we then market and the product is successful, we make $100,000, but we must deduct the $5,000 we had to pay for the test, leaving us a net profit of $95,000. Similarly, we must add the $5,000 cost of the market test to the possible loss of $20,000. This brings the payoff that corresponds to product failure to −$25,000.

Determining the Probabilities

We have now reached the crucial step of determining the probabilities associated with the different branches of our decision tree. As shown in Figure 15–17, we know only two probabilities: the probability of a successful product without any testing and the probability of an unsuccessful product without any testing. (These are our old probabilities from the decision tree of Figure 15–12.) These probabilities are $P(S) = 0.75$ and $P(F) = 0.25$. The two probabilities are also our *prior* probabilities—the probabilities before any sampling or testing is undertaken. As such, we will use them in conjunction with Bayes' theorem for determining the posterior probabilities of success and of failure, and the probabilities of the two possible test results $P(IS)$ and $P(IF)$. The latter are the total probabilities of IS and IF, respectively, and are obtained from the *denominator* in equation 15–6 and its analog, using the event IF. These are sometimes called *predictive probabilities* because they predict the test results.

For the decision tree in Figure 15–17, we have *two* probabilities, and we need to fill in the other six. First, let us look at the particular branches and define our probabilities. The probabilities of the two upper branches of the chance node immediately preceding the payoffs correspond to the two sequences

> Test → Test indicates success → Market → Product is successful

and

> Test → Test indicates success → Market → Product is not successful

These are the two sequences of events leading to the payoffs \$95,000 and −\$25,000, respectively. The probabilities we seek for the two final branches are

> P(Product is successful | Test has indicated success)

and

> P(Product is not successful | Test has indicated success)

These are the required probabilities because we have reached the branches success and no-success via the route: Test → Test indicates success. In symbols, the two probabilities we seek are $P(S \mid IS)$ and $P(F \mid IS)$. The first probability will be obtained from Bayes' theorem, equation 15–6, and the second will be obtained as $P(F \mid IS) = 1 - P(S \mid IS)$. What we need for Bayes' theorem—in addition to the prior probabilities—is the conditional probabilities that contain the information about the reliability of the market test. Let us suppose that these probabilities are

> $P(IS \mid S) = 0.9$ $P(IF \mid S) = 0.1$ $P(IF \mid F) = 0.85$ $P(IS \mid F) = 0.15$

Thus, when the product is indeed going to be successful, the test has a 0.90 chance of telling us so. Ten percent of the time, however, when the product is going to be successful, the test erroneously indicates failure. When the product is not going to be successful, the test so indicates with probability 0.85 and fails to do so with probability 0.15. This information is assumed to be known to us at the time we consider whether to test.

Applying Bayes' theorem, equation 15–6, we get

$$P(S \mid IS) = \frac{P(IS \mid S)\,P(S)}{P(IS \mid S)P(S) + P(IS \mid F)P(F)} = \frac{(0.9)(0.75)}{(0.9)(0.75) + (0.15)(0.25)}$$

$$= \frac{0.675}{0.7125} = 0.9474$$

The denominator in the equation, 0.7125, is an important number. Recall from Section 2–7 that this is the *total probability* of the conditioning event; it is the probability of IS. We therefore have

$$P(S \mid IS) \;=\; 0.9474 \qquad \text{and} \qquad P(IS) \;=\; 0.7125$$

These two probabilities give rise to two more probabilities (namely, those of their complements): $P(F \mid IS) = 1 - 0.9474 = 0.0526$ and $P(IF) = 1 - P(IS) = 1 - 0.7125 = 0.2875$.

Using Bayes' theorem and its denominator, we have found that the probability that the test will indicate success is 0.7125, and the probability that it will indicate failure is 0.2875. Once the test indicates success, there is a probability of 0.9474 that the product will indeed be successful and a probability of 0.0526 that it will not be successful. This gives us four more probabilities to attach to branches of the decision tree. Now all we need are the last two probabilities, $P(S \mid IF)$ and $P(F \mid IF)$. These are obtained via an analog of equation 15–6 for when the test indicates failure. It is given as equation 15–7.

$$P(S \mid IF) \;=\; \frac{P(IF \mid S)P(S)}{P(IF \mid S)P(S) \;+\; P(IF \mid F)P(F)} \tag{15–7}$$

The denominator of equation 15–7 is, by the law of total probability, simply the probability of the event IF, and we have just solved for it: $P(IF) = 0.2875$. The numerator is equal to $(0.1)(0.75) = 0.075$. We thus get $P(S \mid IF) = 0.075/0.2875 = 0.2609$. The last probability we need is $P(F \mid IF) = 1 - P(S \mid IF) = 1 - 0.2609 = 0.7391$.

We will now enter all these probabilities into our decision tree. The complete tree with all probabilities and payoffs is shown in Figure 15–18. (To save space in the figure, events are denoted by their symbols: S, F, IS, etc.)

We are finally in a position to solve the decision problem by averaging out and folding back our tree. Let us start by averaging out the three chance nodes closest to the final outcomes:

$$\begin{aligned}
E(\text{payoff}) &= (0.9474)(95{,}000) + (0.0526)(-25{,}000) \\
&= \$88{,}688 \qquad \text{(top chance node)} \\[4pt]
E(\text{payoff}) &= (0.2609)(95{,}000) + (0.7391)(-25{,}000) \\
&= \$6{,}308 \qquad \text{(middle chance node)} \\[4pt]
E(\text{payoff}) &= (0.75)(100{,}000) + (0.25)(-20{,}000) \\
&= \$70{,}000 \qquad \text{(bottom chance node)}
\end{aligned}$$

We can now fold back and look for the optimal actions at each of the three preceding decision nodes. Again, starting from top to bottom, we first compare \$88,688 with −\$5,000 and conclude that—once the test indicates success—we should market the product. Then, comparing \$6,308 with −\$5,000, we conclude that even if the test says that the product will fail, we are still better off if we go ahead and market the product (remember, all our conclusions are based on the expected monetary value and have no allowance for risk aversion). The third comparison again tells us to market the product, because \$70,000 is greater than \$0.

FIGURE 15–18   New-Product Decision Tree with Probabilities

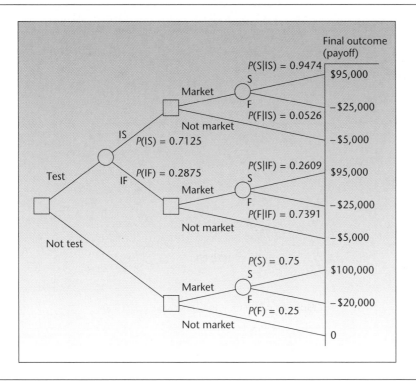

We are now at the chance node corresponding to the outcome of the test. At this point, we need to average out $88,688 and $6,308, with probabilities 0.7125 and 0.2875, respectively. This gives us

$$E(\text{payoff}) = (0.7125)(88,688) + (0.2875)(6,308) = \$65,003.75$$

Finally, we are at the very first decision node, and here we need to compare $65,003.75 with $70,000. Since $70,000 is greater, our optimal decision is not to test and to go right ahead and market the new product. If we must, for some reason, test the product, then we should go ahead and market it regardless of the outcome of the test, if we want to maximize our expected monetary payoff. Note that our solution is, of course, strongly dependent on the numbers we have used. If these numbers were different—for example, if the prior probability of success were not as high as it is—the optimal solution could very well have been to test first and then follow the result of the test. Our solution to this problem is shown in Figure 15–19.

We now demonstrate the entire procedure of decision analysis with additional information by Example 15–4. To simplify the calculations, which were explained earlier on a conceptual level using equations, we will use tables.

Insurance companies need to invest large amounts of money in opportunities that provide high yields and are long-term. One type of investment that has recently attracted some insurance companies is real estate.

EXAMPLE 15–4

FIGURE 15–19   New-Product Introduction: Expected Values and Optimal Decision

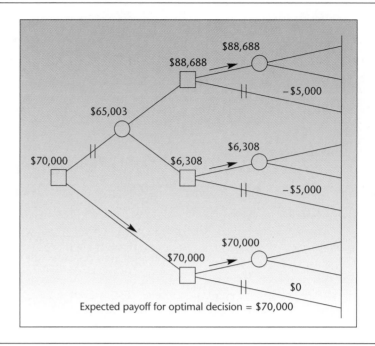

TABLE 15–6   Information for Example 15–4

Profit from Investment	Level of Economic Activity	Probability
$ 3 million	Low	0.20
6 million	Medium	0.50
12 million	High	0.30

Aetna Life and Casualty Company is considering an investment in real estate in central Florida. The investment is for a period of 10 years, and company analysts believe that the investment will lead to returns that depend on future levels of economic activity in the area. In particular, the analysts believe that the invested amount would bring the profits listed in Table 15–6, depending on the listed levels of economic activity and their given (prior) probabilities. The alternative to this investment plan—one that the company has used in the past—is a particular investment that has a 0.5 probability of yielding a profit of $4 million and a 0.5 probability of yielding $7 million over the period in question.

The company may also seek some expert advice on economic conditions in central Florida. For an amount that would be equivalent to $1 million 10 years from now (when invested at a risk-free rate), the company could hire an economic consulting firm to study the future economic prospects in central Florida. From past dealings with the consulting firm, Aetna analysts believe that the reliability of the consulting firm's conclusions is as listed in Table 15–7. The table lists as columns the three conclusions the consultants may reach about the future of the area's economy. The rows of the table correspond to the true level of the economy 10 years in the future, and the table entries are conditional probabilities. For example, if the future level of the economy is going to be high, then the consultants' statement will be "high" with probability 0.85. What should Aetna do?

TABLE 15–7   Reliability of the Consulting Firm

True Future State of Economy	Consultants' Conclusion		
	High	Medium	Low
Low	0.05	0.05	0.90
Medium	0.15	0.80	0.05
High	0.85	0.10	0.05

FIGURE 15–20   Decision Tree for Example 15–4

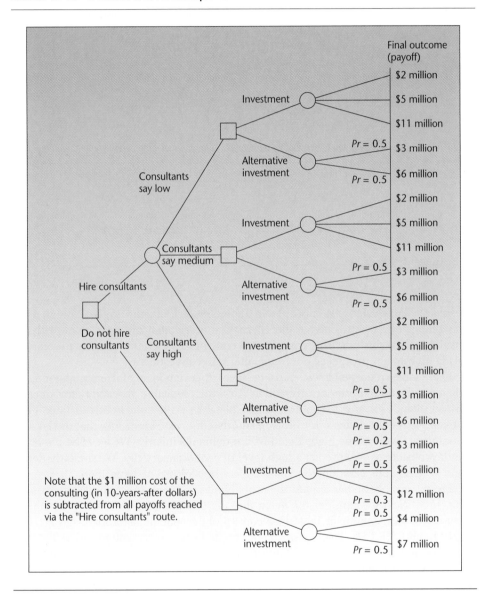

First, we construct the decision tree, including all the known information. The decision tree is shown in Figure 15–20. Now we need to use the prior probabilities in Table 15–6 and the conditional probabilities in Table 15–7 in computing both the posterior probabilities of the different payoffs from the investment given the three possible consultants' conclusions, and the predictive probabilities of the three

Solution

TABLE 15–8 Events and Their Probabilities: Consultants Say "Low"

Event	Prior	Conditional	Joint	Posterior
Low	0.20	0.90	0.180	0.818
Medium	0.50	0.05	0.025	0.114
High	0.30	0.05	0.015	0.068
		P(Consultants say "low") = 0.220		1.000

TABLE 15–9 Events and Their Probabilities: Consultants Say "Medium"

Event	Prior	Conditional	Joint	Posterior
Low	0.20	0.05	0.01	0.023
Medium	0.50	0.80	0.40	0.909
High	0.30	0.10	0.03	0.068
		P(Consultants say medium) = 0.44		1.000

TABLE 15–10 Events and Their Probabilities: Consultants Say "High"

Event	Prior	Conditional	Joint	Posterior
Low	0.20	0.05	0.010	0.029
Medium	0.50	0.15	0.075	0.221
High	0.30	0.85	0.255	0.750
		P(Consultants say high) = 0.340		1.000

consultants' conclusions. This is done in Tables 15–8, 15–9, and 15–10. Note that the probabilities of the outcomes of the alternative investment do not change with the consultants' conclusions (the consultants' conclusions pertain only to the central Florida investment prospects, not to the alternative investment).

These tables represent a way of using Bayes' theorem in an efficient manner. Each table gives the three posterior probabilities and the predictive probability for a particular consultant's statement. The structure of the tables is the same as that of Table 15–2, for example. Let us define our events in shortened form: H indicates that the level of economic activity will be high; L and M are defined similarly. We let *H* be the event that the consultants will predict a high level of economic activity. We similarly define *L* and *M*. Using this notation, the following is a breakdown of Table 15–8.

The prior probabilities are just the probabilities of events H, L, and M, as given in Table 15–6. Next we consider the event that the consultants predict a low economy: event L. The next column in Table 15–8 consists of the conditional probabilities $P(L \mid L)$, $P(L \mid M)$, and $P(L \mid H)$. These probabilities come from the last column of Table 15–7. The joint probabilities column in Table 15–8 consists of the products of the entries in the first two probabilities columns. The sum of the entries in this column is the denominator in Bayes' theorem: It is the total (or predictive) probability of the event L. Finally, dividing each entry in the joint probabilities column by the sum of that column [i.e., by $P(L)$] gives us the posterior probabilities: $P(L \mid L)$, $P(M \mid L)$, and $P(H \mid L)$. Tables 15–9 and 15–10 are interpreted in the same way, for events M and H, respectively.

Now that we have all the required probabilities, we can enter them in the tree. We can then average out at the chance nodes and fold back the tree. At each decision node, we choose the action that maximizes the expected payoff. The tree, with all its probabilities, final-outcome payoffs, expected payoffs at the chance nodes, and

FIGURE 15–21   Solution to Aetna Decision Problem

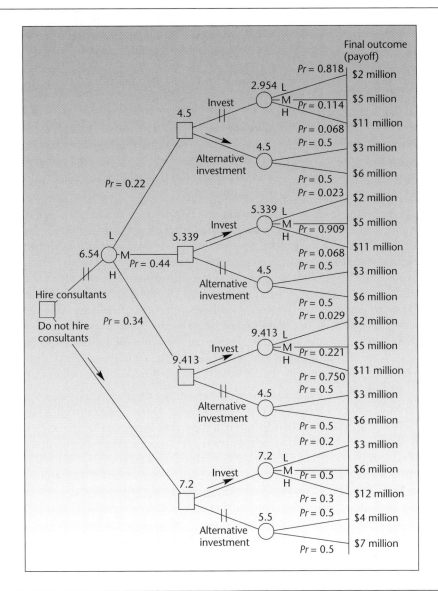

indicators of the optimal action at each decision node, is shown in Figure 15–21. The figure is a complete solution to this problem.

The final solution is not to hire the consultants and to invest in the central Florida project. If we have to consult, then we should choose the alternative investment if the consultants predict a low level of economic activity for the region, and invest in the central Florida project if they predict either a medium or a high level of economic activity. The expected value of the investment project is $7.2 million.

A template solution to this problem is given in Section 15–10.

PROBLEMS

15–30.   Explain why Bayes' theorem is necessary for handling additional information in a decision problem.

15–31.   Explain the meaning of the term *predictive probability*.

15–32.   For Example 15–4, suppose that hiring the economic consultants costs only $100,000 (in 10-years-after dollars). Redo the analysis. What is the optimal decision? Explain.

15–33.   For problem 15–23, suppose that before deciding whether to advertise on television, the company can test the commercial. The test costs $300,000 and has the following reliability. If sales volume would go up by $20 million, the test would indicate this with probability 0.96. It would wrongly indicate that sales would be $10 million more with probability 0.03, and wrongly indicate that sales would be $1 million more with probability 0.01. If sales would increase by $10 million, the test would indicate this with probability 0.90, and the other two (wrong) possibilities with probability 0.05 each. The test would indicate that sales would rise by $1 million with probability 0.80 if that was really to happen, and wrongly indicate the other two possibilities with probability 0.1 each. Redo the decision problem.

15–34.   One of the most powerful people in Hollywood is not an actor, director, or producer. It is Richard Soames, an insurance director for the London-based Film Finances Ltd. Soames is a leading provider of movie completion bond guarantees. The guarantees are like insurance policies that pay the extra costs when films go over budget or are not completed on time. Suppose that Soames is considering insuring the production of a movie and feels there is a 0.65 chance that his company will make $80,000 on the deal (i.e., the production will be on time and not exceed budget). He believes there is a 0.35 chance that the movie will exceed budget and his company will lose $120,000, which would have to be paid to complete production. Soames could pay a movie industry expert $5,000 for an evaluation of the project's success. He believes that the expert's conclusions are true 90% of the time. What should Soames do?

15–35.   Many airlines flying overseas have recently considered changing the kinds of goods they sell at their in-flight duty-free services. Swiss, for example, is considering selling watches instead of the usual liquor and cigarettes. A Swiss executive believes that there is a 0.60 chance that passengers would prefer these goods to the usual items and that revenues from in-flight sales would increase by $500,000 over a period of several years. She believes there is a 0.40 chance that revenues would decrease by $700,000, which would happen should people not buy the watches and instead desire the usual items. Testing the new idea on actual flights would cost $60,000, and the results would have a 0.85 probability of correctly detecting the state of nature. What should Swiss do?

15–36.   For problem 15–26, suppose that the designer can obtain some expert advice for a cost of $30,000. If the fashion is going to be short, there is a 0.90 probability that the expert will predict short, a 0.05 probability that the expert will predict medium, and a 0.05 probability that the expert will predict long. If the fashion is going to be medium, there is a 0.10 probability that the expert will predict short, a 0.75 probability that the expert will predict medium, and a 0.15 probability that the expert will predict long. If the fashion is going to be long, there is a 0.10 probability that the expert will predict short, a 0.10 probability that the expert will predict medium, and a 0.80 probability that the expert will predict long. Construct the decision tree for this problem. What is the optimal decision for the designer?

15–37.   A cable television company is considering extending its services to a rural community. The company's managing director believes that there is a 0.50 chance that profits from the service will be high and amount to $760,000 in the first year, and a 0.50 chance that profits will be low and amount to $400,000 for the year. An alternative operation promises a sure profit of $500,000 for the period in question. The company may test the potential of the rural market for a cost of $25,000. The test has a 90% reliability of correctly detecting the state of nature. Construct the decision tree and determine the optimal decision.

15–38.   An investor is considering two brokerage firms. One is a discount broker offering no investment advice, but charging only $50 for the amount the investor intends to invest. The other is a full-service broker who charges $200 for the amount of the intended investment. If the investor chooses the discount broker, there is a 0.45 chance of a $500 profit (before charges) over the period of the investment, a 0.35 chance of making only $200, and 0.20 chance of losing $100. If the investor chooses the full-service broker, then there is a 0.60 chance that the investment will earn $500, a 0.35 chance that it will earn $200, and a 0.05 chance that it will lose $100. What is the best investment advice in this case?

15–8 Utility

Often we have to make decisions where the rewards are not easily quantifiable. The reputation of a company, for example, is not easily measured in terms of dollars and cents. Such rewards as job satisfaction, pride, and a sense of well-being also fall into this category. Although you may feel that a stroll on the beach is "priceless," sometimes you may order such things on a scale of values by gauging them against the amount of money you would require for giving them up. When such scaling is possible, the value system used is called a **utility.**

If a decision affecting a firm involves rewards or losses that either are nonmonetary or—more commonly—represent a mixture of dollars and other benefits such as reputation, long-term market share, and customer satisfaction, then we need to convert all the benefits to a single scale. The scale, often measured in dollars or other units, is a *utility scale.* Once utilities are assessed, the analysis proceeds as before, with the utility units acting as dollars and cents. If the utility function was correctly evaluated, results of the decision analysis may be meaningful.

The concept of utility is derived not only from seemingly nonquantifiable rewards. Utility is a part of the very way we deal with money. For most people, the value of $1,000 is not constant. For example, suppose you were offered $1,000 to wash someone's dirty dishes. Would you do it? Probably yes. Now suppose that you were given $1 million and then asked if you would do the dishes for $1,000. Most people would refuse because the value of an additional $1,000 seems insignificant once you have $1 million (or more), as compared with the value of $1,000 if you do not have $1 million.

The value you attach to money—the *utility* of money—is not a straight-line function, but a curve. Such a curve is shown in Figure 15–22. Looking at the figure, we see that the utility (the value) of one additional dollar, as measured on the vertical axis,

FIGURE 15–22 A Utility-of-Money Curve

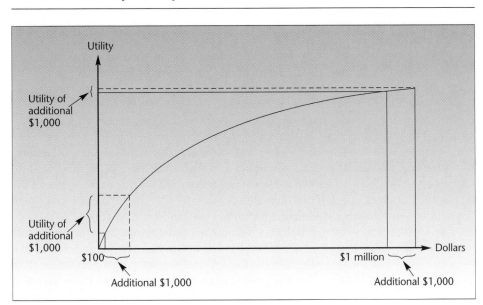

FIGURE 15–23   **Utility of a Risk Avoider**

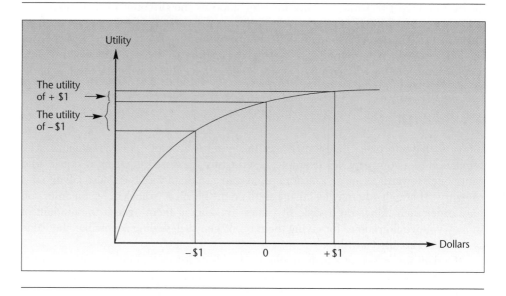

decreases as our wealth (measured on the horizontal axis) increases. The type of function shown in Figure 15–22 is well suited for modeling a situation where an additional amount of money $x has different worth to us depending on our wealth, that is, where the utility of each additional dollar decreases as we acquire more money. This utility function is the utility curve of a *risk-averse* individual. Indeed, utility can be used to model people's attitudes toward risk. Let us see why and how.

Suppose that you are offered the following choice. You can get $5,000 for certain, or you could get a lottery ticket where you have a 0.5 chance of winning $20,000 and a 0.5 chance of losing $2,000. Which would you choose? The expected payoff from the lottery is $E(\text{payoff}) = (0.5)(20,000) + (0.5)(-2,000) = \$9,000$. This is almost twice the amount you could get with probability 1.0, the $5,000. Expected monetary payoff would tell us to choose the lottery. However, few people would really do so; most would choose the $5,000, a sure amount. This shows us that a possible loss of $2,000 is not worth the possible gain of $20,000, even if the expected payoff is large. Such behavior is typical of a risk-averse individual. For such a person, the reward of a possible gain of $1 is not worth the "pain" of a possible loss of the same amount.

Risk aversion is modeled by a utility function (the value-of-money function) such as the one shown in Figure 15–22. Again, let us look at such a function. Figure 15–23 shows how, for a risk-averse individual, the utility of $1 earned ($1 to the right of zero) is less than the value of a dollar lost ($1 to the left of zero).

Not everyone is risk-averse, especially if we consider companies rather than individuals. The utility functions in Figures 15–22 and 15–23 are *concave* functions: They are functions with a decreasing slope, and these are characteristic of a risk-averse person. For a *risk-seeking* person, the utility is a *convex* function: a function with an increasing slope. Such a function is shown in Figure 15–24. Look at the curve in the figure, and convince yourself that an added dollar is worth more to the risk taker than the pain of a lost dollar (use the same technique used in Figure 15–23).

For a *risk-neutral* person, a dollar is a dollar no matter what. Such an individual gives the same value to $1 whether he or she has $10 million or nothing. For such a person, the pain of the loss of a dollar is the same as the reward of gaining a dollar. The utility function for a risk-neutral person is a straight line. Such a utility function is shown in Figure 15–25. Again, convince yourself that the utility of +$1 is equal

FIGURE 15–24
Utility of a Risk Taker

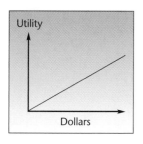

FIGURE 15–25
Utility of a Risk-Neutral Person

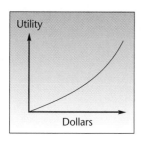

(in absolute value) to the utility of −$1 for such a person. Figure 15–26 shows a mixed utility function. The individual is a risk avoider when his or her wealth is small and a risk taker when his or her wealth is great. We now present a method that may be used for assessing an individual's utility function.

A Method of Assessing Utility

One way of assessing the utility curve of an individual is to do the following:

1. Identify the maximum payoff in a decision problem, and assign it the utility 1: U(maximum value) = 1.
2. Identify the minimum payoff in a decision problem, and assign it the value 0: U(minimum value) = 0.
3. Conduct the following game to determine the utility of any intermediate value in the decision problem (in this chosen scale of numbers). Ask the person whose utility you are trying to assess to determine the probability p such that he or she expresses *indifference* between the two choices: receive the payoff R with certainty or have probability p of receiving the maximum value and probability $1 - p$ of receiving the minimum value. The determined p is the utility of the value R. This is done for all values R whose utility we want to assess.

The assessment of a utility function is demonstrated in Figure 15–27. The utility curve passes through all the points (R_i, p_i) $(i = 1, 2 \ldots)$ for which the utility was assessed. Let us look at an example.

FIGURE 15–26
A Mixed Utility

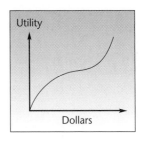

FIGURE 15–27
Assessment of a Utility
Function

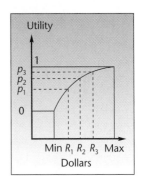

EXAMPLE 15–5

Suppose that an investor is considering decisions that lead to the following possible payoffs: $1,500, $4,300, $22,000, $31,000, and $56,000 (the investments have different levels of risk). We now try to assess the investor's utility function.

Solution

Starting with step 1, we identify the minimum payoff as $1,500. This value is assigned the utility of 0. The maximum payoff is $56,000, and we assign the utility 1 to that figure. We now ask the investor a series of questions that should lead us to the determination of the utilities of the intermediate payoff values. Let us suppose the investor states that he is indifferent between receiving $4,300 for certain and receiving $56,000 with probability 0.2 and $1,500 with probability 0.8. This means that the utility of the payoff $4,300 is 0.2. We now continue to the next payoff, of $22,000. Suppose that the investor is indifferent between receiving $22,000 with certainty and $56,000 with probability 0.7 and $1,500 with probability 0.3. The investor's utility of $22,000 is therefore 0.7. Finally, the investor indicates indifference between a certain payoff of $31,000 and receiving $56,000 with probability 0.8 and $1,500 with probability 0.2. The utility of $31,000 is thus equal to 0.8. We now plot the corresponding pairs (payoff, utility) and run a rough curve through them.

The curve—the utility function of the investor—is shown in Figure 15–28. Whatever the decision problem facing the investor, the *utilities* rather than the actual payoffs are the values to be used in the analysis. The analysis is based on maximizing the investor's *expected utility* rather than the expected monetary outcome.

FIGURE 15–28
Investor's Utility

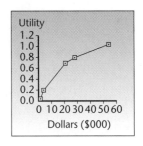

Note that utility is not unique. Many possible scales of values may be used to represent a person's attitude toward risk, as long as the general shape of the curve, for a given individual, remains the same—convex, concave, or linear—and with the same relative curvature. In practice, the assessment of utilities may not always be a feasible procedure, as it requires the decision maker to play the hypothetical game of assessing the indifference probabilities.

15–39.   What is a utility function?

15–40.   What are the advantages of using a utility function?

15–41.   What are the characteristics of the utility function of a risk-averse individual? Of a risk taker?

15–42.   What can you say about the risk attitude of the investor in Example 15–5?

15–43.   Choose a few hypothetical monetary payoffs, and determine your own utility function. From the resulting curve, draw a conclusion about your attitude toward risk.

15–9   The Value of Information

In decision-making problems, the question often arises as to the *value* of information: How much should we be willing to pay for additional information about the situation at hand? The first step in answering this question is to find out how much we should be willing to pay for perfect information, that is, how much we should pay for a crystal ball that would tell us exactly what will happen—what the exact state of nature will be. If we can determine the value of perfect information, this will give us an upper bound on the value of any (imperfect) information. If we are willing to pay D dollars to know exactly what will happen, then we should be willing to pay an amount no greater than D for information that is less reliable. Since sample information is imperfect (in fact, it is probabilistic, as we well know from our discussion of sampling), the value of sample information is less than the value of perfect information. It will equal the value of perfect information only if the entire population is sampled.

Let us see how the upper bound on the value of information is obtained. Since we do not know what the perfect information is, we can only compute the *expected value of perfect information* in a given decision-making situation. The expected value is a *mean* computed using the prior probabilities of the various states of nature. It assumes, however, that at any given point when we actually take an action, we know its exact outcome. Before we (hypothetically) buy the perfect information, we do not know what the state of nature will be, and therefore we must average payoffs using our prior probabilities.

> The **expected value of perfect information (EVPI)** is
>
> EVPI = The expected monetary value of the decision situation when perfect information is available, minus the expected value of the decision situation when no additional information is available

This definition of the expected value of perfect information is logical: It says that the (expected) maximum amount we should be willing to pay for perfect information is equal to the difference between our expected payoff from the decision situation when we have the information and our expected payoff from the decision situation without the information. The expected value of information is equal to what we stand to gain from this information. We will demonstrate the computation of the expected value of perfect information with an example.

An article in the *Journal of Marketing Research* gives an example of decision making in the airline industry. The situation involves a price war that ensues when one airline determines the fare it will set for a particular route. Profits depend on the fare that will be set by a competing airline for the same route. Competitive situations such as this one are modeled using game theory. In this example, however, we will look at the competitor's action as a chance occurrence and consider the problem within the realm of decision analysis.

EXAMPLE 15–6

Table 15–11 shows the payoffs (in millions of dollars) to the airline over a given period of time, for a given fare set by the airline and by its competitor. We assume that there is a certain probability that the competitor will choose the low ($200) price and a certain probability that the competitor will choose the high price. Suppose that the probability of the low price is 0.6 and that the probability of the high price is 0.4.

The decision tree for this situation is given in Figure 15–29. Solving the tree, we find that if we set our price at $200, the expected payoff is equal to $E(\text{payoff}) = (0.6)(8) + (0.4)(9) = \$8.4$ million. If we set our price at $300, then our expected payoff is $E(\text{payoff}) = (0.6)(4) + (0.4)(10) = \$6.4$ million. The optimal action is, therefore, to set our price at $200. This is shown with an arrow in Figure 15–29.

Solution

Now we ask whether it may be worthwhile to obtain more information. Obtaining new information in this case may entail hiring a consultant who is knowledgeable about the operating philosophy of the competing airline. We may seek other ways of obtaining information; we may, for example, make an analysis of the competitor's past pricing behavior. The important question is: What do we stand to gain from the new information? Suppose that we know exactly what our competitor plans to do. If we know that the competitor plans to set the price at $200, then our optimal action is to set ours at $200 as well; this is seen by comparing the two amounts in the first payoff column of Table 15–11, the column corresponding to the competitor's setting

TABLE 15–11 Airline Payoffs (in millions of dollars)

Airline's Fare (Action)	Competitor's Fare (State of Nature)	
	$200	$300
$200	8	9
$300	4	10

FIGURE 15–29 Decision Tree for Example 15–6

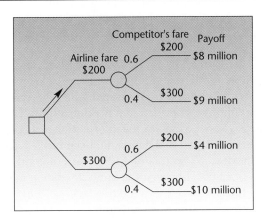

the price at $200. We see that our maximum payoff is then $8 million, obtained by choosing $200 as our own price as well. If the competitor chooses to set its price at $300, then our optimal action is to set our price at $300 as well and obtain a payoff of $10 million.

We know that without any additional information, the optimal decision is to set the price at $200, obtaining an *expected* payoff of $8.4 million (the expected value of the decision situation without any information). What is the expected payoff with *perfect* information? We do not know what the perfect information may be, but we assume that the prior probabilities we have are a true reflection of the long-run proportion of the time our competitor sets either price. Therefore, 60% of the time our competitor sets the low price, and 40% of the time the competitor sets the high price. If we had perfect information, we would know—at the time—how high to set the price. If we knew that the competitor planned to set the price at $200, we would do the same because this would give us the maximum payoff, $8 million. Conversely, when our perfect information tells us that the competitor is setting the price at $300, we again follow suit and gain a maximum payoff, $10 million. Analyzing the situation now, we do not know what the competitor will do (we do not have the perfect information), but we do know the probabilities. We therefore average the maximum payoff in each case, that is, the payoff that would be obtained under perfect information, using our probabilities. This gives us the expected payoff under perfect information. We get E(payoff under perfect information) = (Maximum payoff if the competitor chooses $200) × (Probability that the competitor will choose $200) + (Maximum payoff if the competitor chooses $300) × (Probability that the competitor will choose $300) = (8)(0.6) + (10)(0.4) = $8.8 million. If we could get perfect information, we could expect (on the average) to make a profit of $8.8 million. Without perfect information, we expect to make $8.4 million (the optimal decision without any additional information).

We now use the definition of the expected value of perfect information:

$$\text{EVPI} = E(\text{payoff under perfect information}) - E(\text{payoff without information})$$

Applying the rule in this case, we get EVPI = 8.8 − 8.4 = $0.4 million, or simply $400,000. Therefore, $400,000 is the maximum amount of money we should be willing to pay for additional information about our competitor's price intentions. This is the amount of money we should be willing to pay to know for certain what our competitor plans to do. We should pay less than this amount for all information that is not as reliable.

What about sampling—when sampling is possible? (In the airlines example, it probably is not possible to sample.) The expected value of sample information is equal to the expected value of perfect information, minus the expected cost of sampling errors. The expected cost of sampling errors is obtained from the probabilities of errors—known from sampling theory—and the resulting loss of payoff due to making less-than-optimal decisions. The *expected net gain* from sampling is equal to the expected value of sampling information, minus the cost of sampling. As the sample size increases, the expected net gain from sampling first increases, as our new information is valuable and improves our decision-making ability. Then the expected net gain decreases because we are paying for the information at a constant rate, while the information content in each additional data point becomes less and less important as we get more and more data. (A sample of 1,100 does not contain much more information than a sample of 1,000. However, the same 100 data points may be very valuable if they are all we have.)

At some particular sample size n, we maximize our expected net gain from sampling. Determining the optimal sample size to be used in a decision situation is a

FIGURE 15–30   Expected Net Gain from Sampling (in Dollars) as a Function of the Sample Size

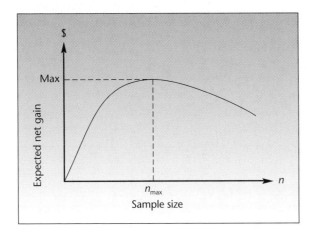

difficult problem, and we will not say more about it here. We will, however, show the relationship between sample size and the expected net gain from sampling in Figure 15–30. The interested reader is referred to advanced works on the subject.[10]

PROBLEMS

15–44. Explain the value of additional information within the context of decision making.

15–45. Explain how we compute the expected value of perfect information, and why it is computed that way.

15–46. Compute the expected value of perfect information for the situation in problem 15–26.

15–47. For the situation in problem 15–26, suppose the designer is offered expert opinion about the new fall styles for a price of $300,000. Should she buy the advice? Explain why or why not.

15–48. What is the expected value of perfect information in the situation of problem 15–23? Explain.

15–10   Using the Computer

Most statistical computer packages do not have extensive Bayesian statistics or decision analysis capabilities. There are, however, several commercial computer programs that do decision analysis. Also, you may be able to write your own computer program for solving a decision tree.

The Template

The decision analysis template can be used only if the problem is representable by a payoff table.[11] In the Aetna decision example, it is possible to represent the problem

---

[10]From C. Barenghi, A. Aczel, and R. Best, "Determining the Optimal Sample Size for Decision Making," *Journal of Statistical Computation and Simulation,* Spring 1986, pp. 135–45. © 1986 Taylor & Francis Ltd. Reprinted with permission.

[11]Theoretically speaking, all the problems can be represented in a payoff table format. But the payoff table can get too large and cumbersome for cases where the set of consequences is different for different decision alternatives.

TABLE 15–12 The Payoff Table for the Aetna Decision Problem (Example 15–4)

	State of the Economy		
	Low	**Medium**	**High**
Real estate investment	$ 3 million	$ 6 million	$ 12 million
Alternative investment	5.5 million	5.5 million	5.5 million

FIGURE 15–31 The Data Sheet for Decision Analysis [Decision Analysis.xls; Sheet: Data]

	A	B	C	D	E	F	G	H	I	J	K	L	M
1	**Data**			Aetna Decision									
2													
3		**Payoff Table**		Low	Medium	High							
4				**s1**	**s2**	**s3**	**s4**	**s5**	**s6**	**s7**	**s8**	**s9**	**s10**
5		Invest	**d1**	3	6	12							
6		Alternative	**d2**	5.5	5.5	5.5							
7			**d3**										
8			**d4**										
9			**d5**										
10			**d6**										
11			**d7**										
12			**d8**										
13			**d9**										
14			**d10**										
16			**Probability**	0.2	0.5	0.3							
17													
18		**Conditional Probabilities of Additional Information**											
19				Low	Medium	High	0	0	0	0	0	0	0
20				**s1**	**s2**	**s3**	**s4**	**s5**	**s6**	**s7**	**s8**	**s9**	**s10**
21		Low	**P(I1I.)**	0.9	0.05	0.05							
22		Med	**P(I2I.)**	0.05	0.8	0.1							
23		High	**P(I3I.)**	0.05	0.15	0.85							
24			**P(I4I.)**										
25			**P(I5I.)**										

by Table 15–12. Note that the returns from the alternative investment have been reduced to a constant *expected value* of $5.5 million to fit the payoff table format. If this manipulation of the payoff were not possible, then we could not use the template.

The template consists of three sheets, Data, Results, and Calculation. The Data sheet is shown in Figure 15–31. On this sheet the payoffs are entered at the top and conditional probabilities of additional information (such as a consultant's information) at the bottom. The probabilities of all the states entered in row 16 must add up to 1, or an error message will appear in row 17. Similarly, every column of the conditional probabilities in the bottom must add up to 1.

Once the data are entered properly, we can read off the results on the Results page shown in Figure 15–32. The optimal decision for each possible information from the consultant appears in row 7. The corresponding expected payoff (EV) appears in row 8. The marginal probability of obtaining each possible information appears in row 9. The maximum expected payoff achieved by correctly following the optimal decision under each information is $7.54 million, which appears in cell H12. It has been labeled as "EV with SI," where SI stands for sample information. The sample information in this example is the consultant's prediction of the state of the economy.

In cell E11, we get the expected value of perfect information (EVPI), and in cell E12, we get the expected value of sample information (EVSI). This EVSI is the expected value of the consultant's information. Recall that the consultant's fee is $1 million. Since EVSI is only $0.34 million, going by expected values, Aetna should not hire the consultant. Note also that the best decision without any information is d1 (seen in cell C7), which stands for real estate investment. Thus Aetna should simply invest in real estate without hiring the consultant. It can then expect a payoff of

FIGURE 15–32   **The Results**
[Decision Analysis.xls; Sheet: Results]

	A	B	C	D	E	F	G	H	I
1		**Results**			Aetna Decision				
10									
11		Decision with probabilities and additional information							
12									
13			Best Decision Under						
14			No Info.	Low	Med	High			
15		*d**	d1	d2	d1	d1			
16		EV	7.2	5.5	6.340909	10.41176			
17		Prob.		0.22	0.44	0.34			
18									
19				EVPI	0.5				
20				EVSI	0.34				
21				Efficiency of SI	68.00%				
22									

$7.2 million (seen in cell C8). All these results agree with what we already saw using manual calculations.

The **efficiency** of the sample information is defined as (EVSI/EVPI) × 100%, and it appears in cell E13.

The third sheet, Calculation, is where all the calculations are carried out. The user need not look at this sheet at all, and it is not shown here.

15–11   Summary and Review of Terms

In this chapter, we presented two related topics: **Bayesian statistics** and **decision analysis.** We saw that the Bayesian statistical methods are extensions of Bayes' theorem to discrete and continuous random variables. We saw how the Bayesian approach allows the statistician to use, along with the data, **prior information** about the situation at hand. The prior information is stated in terms of a **prior probability distribution** of population parameters. We saw that the Bayesian approach is less restrictive in that it allows us to consider an unknown parameter as a random variable. In this context, as more sampling information about a parameter becomes available to us, we can update our prior probability distribution of the parameter, thus creating a **posterior probability distribution.** The posterior distribution may then serve as a prior distribution when more data become available. We also may use the posterior distribution in computing a **credible set** for a population parameter, in the discrete case, and a **highest-posterior-density (HPD) set** in the continuous case. We discussed the possible dangers in using the Bayesian approach and the fact that we must be careful in our choice of prior distributions.

We saw how decision analysis may be used to find the decision that maximizes our **expected payoff** from an uncertain situation. We discussed personal or **subjective probabilities** and saw how these can be assessed and used in a Bayesian statistics problem or in a decision problem. We saw that a **decision tree** is a good method of solving problems of decision making under uncertainty. We learned how to use the method of **averaging out and folding back,** which leads to the determination of the **optimal decision**—the decision that maximizes the expected monetary payoff. We saw how to assess the usefulness of obtaining additional information within the context of the decision problem, using a decision tree and Bayes' theorem. Finally, we saw how to incorporate people's attitudes toward risk into our analysis and how these attitudes lead to a **utility function.** We saw that this leads to solutions to decision problems that maximize the **expected utility** rather than the expected monetary payoff. We also discussed the **expected value of perfect information** and saw how this value serves as an upper bound for the amount of money we are willing to pay for additional information about a decision-making situation.

ADDITIONAL PROBLEMS

15–49.   A quality control engineer believes that the proportion of defective items in a production process is a random variable with a probability distribution that is approximated as follows:

x	P(x)
0.1	0.1
0.2	0.3
0.3	0.2
0.4	0.2
0.5	0.1
0.6	0.1

The engineer collects a random sample of items and finds that 5 out of the 16 items in the sample are defective. Find the engineer's posterior probability distribution of the proportion of defective items.

15–50.   To continue problem 15–49, determine a credible set for the proportion of defective items with probability close to 0.95. Interpret the meaning of the credible set.

15–51.   For problem 15–49, suppose that the engineer collects a second sample of 20 items and finds that 5 items are defective. Update the probability distribution of the population proportion you computed in problem 15–49 to incorporate the new information.

15–52.   What are the main differences between the Bayesian approach to statistics and the classical (frequentist) approach? Discuss these differences.

15–53.   What is the added advantage of the normal probability distribution in the context of Bayesian statistics?

15–54.   GM is designing a new car, the Chevrolet Volt, which is expected to get 100 mpg on the highway.[12] In trying to estimate how much people would be willing to pay for the new car, the company assesses a normal distribution for the average maximum price with mean $29,000 and standard deviation $6,000. A random sample of 30 potential buyers yields an average maximum price of $26,500 and standard deviation $3,800. Give a 95% highest-posterior-density credible set for the average maximum price a consumer would pay.

15–55.   For problem 15–54, give a highest-posterior-density credible set of probability 0.80 for the population mean.

15–56.   For problem 15–54, a second sample of 60 people gives a sample mean of $27,050. Update the distribution of the population mean, and give a new HPD credible set of probability 0.95 for μ.

15–57.   What is a payoff table? What is a decision tree? Can a payoff table be used in decision making without a decision tree?

15–58.   What is a subjective probability, and what are its limitations?

15–59.   Discuss the advantages and the limitations of the assessment of personal probabilities.

15–60.   Why is Bayesian statistics controversial? Try to argue for, and then against, the Bayesian methodology.

15–61.   Suppose that I am indifferent about the following two choices: a sure $3,000 payoff, and a payoff of $5,000 with probability 0.2 and $500 with probability 0.8. Am I a risk taker or a risk-averse individual (within the range $500 to $5,000)? Explain.

15–62.   An investment is believed to earn $2,000 with probability 0.2, $2,500 with probability 0.3, and $3,000 with probability 0.5. An alternative investment may earn $0 with probability 0.1, $3,000 with probability 0.2, $4,000 with probability 0.5, and $7,000 with probability 0.2. Construct a decision tree for this problem, and determine

---

[12]Matt Vella, "In Cars," *BusinessWeek*, March 12, 2007, p. 6.

the investment with the highest expected monetary outcome. What are the limitations of the analysis?

15–63. A company is considering merging with a smaller firm in a related industry. The company's chief executive officer believes that the merger has a 0.55 probability of success. If the merger is successful, the company stands to gain in the next 2 years $5 million with probability 0.2; $6 million with probability 0.3; $7 million with probability 0.3; and $8 million with probability 0.2. If the attempted merger should fail, the company stands to lose $2 million (due to loss of public goodwill) over the next 2 years with probability 0.5 and to lose $3 million over this period with probability 0.5. Should the merger be attempted? Explain.

15–64. For problem 15–63, suppose that the chief executive officer may hire a consulting firm for a fee of $725,000. The consulting firm will advise the CEO about the possibility of success of the merger. This consulting firm is known to have correctly predicted the outcomes of 89% of all successful mergers and the outcomes of 97% of all unsuccessful ones. What is the optimal decision?

15–65. What is the expected value of perfect information about the success or failure of the merger in problem 15–63?

15–66. *Money* suggests an interesting decision problem for family investments.[13] Start with $50,000 to invest over 20 years. There are two possibilities: a low-cost index fund and a fixed-interest investment paying 6.5% per year. The index fund has two possibilities: If equities rise by 6% a year, the $50,000 invested would be worth $160,356. If, on the other hand, equities rise at an average of 10% a year, the $50,000 investment would be worth $336,375. The fixed-interest investment would be worth $176,182. Suppose the probability of equities rising 6% per year is 60% and the probability that they rise 10% per year is 40%. Conduct the decision analysis.

---

[13]Pat Regnier, "The Road Ahead," *Money*, March 2007, pp. 69–74.

CASE 19 Pizzas 'R' Us

Pizzas 'R' Us is a national restaurant chain with close to 100 restaurants across the United States. It is continuously in the process of finding and evaluating possible locations for new restaurants. For any potential site, Pizzas 'R' Us needs to decide the size of the restaurant to build at that site—small, medium, or large—or whether to build none. For a particular prospective site, the accounting department estimates the present value (PV) of possible annual profit, in thousands of dollars, for each size as follows:

Size	Demand		
	Low	Medium	High
Small	48	32	30
Medium	−64	212	78
Large	−100	12	350
No restaurant	0	0	0

The prior probabilities are estimated for low demand at 0.42 and for medium demand at 0.36.

1. What is the best decision if the PV of expected profits is to be maximized?

2. What is the EVPI?

Since the EVPI is large, Pizzas 'R' Us decides to gather additional information. It has two potential market researchers, Alice Miller and Becky Anderson, both of whom it has contracted many times in the past. The company has a database of the demand levels predicted by these researchers in the past and the corresponding actual demand levels realized. The cross-tabulation of these records are as follows:

Alice Miller

	Actual		
Predicted	Low	Medium	High
Low	9	4	2
Medium	8	12	4
High	4	3	13

Becky Anderson

	Actual		
Predicted	Low	Medium	High
Low	12	2	1
Medium	2	15	2
High	0	3	20

3. Alice Miller charges $12,500 for the research and Becky Anderson $48,000. With which one should the company contract for additional information? Why?

FOTOSEARCH

CASE 20 New Drug Development

A pharmaceutical company is planning to develop a new drug. The development will take place in two phases. Phase I will cost $1 million and Phase II will cost $2 million. Any new drug has to be approved by the FDA (U.S. Federal Drug Administration) before it can be marketed. If the drug is approved by the FDA, then a profit contribution of $6,250,000 can be realized by marketing the drug. The only fixed costs to be subtracted from this contribution is the $3 million development cost. In other words, if the drug is approved, the profit would be $3,250,000. If the drug is not approved, then all the development cost has to be written off as a loss.

The managers estimate a 70% chance that the FDA will approve the drug. This still leaves a 30% chance of a $3 million loss. Because of the risk involved, one of the managers proposes a plan to conduct a test at the end of Phase I to determine the chances of FDA approval. The test itself will cost $165,000. If the test result is positive, the company will continue with Phase II; otherwise, the project will be aborted. The motivation

for the test is that in case the chances of FDA approval are slim, at least Phase II costs can be saved by aborting the project.

The manager has drawn the decision tree seen in Exhibit 1 to show possible outcomes. The tree shows the expenses and income along the relevant branches. However, the manager has not been able to arrive at the probabilities for the branches from chance nodes.

The researcher who conducts the test says that the test is not 100% accurate in predicting whether the FDA will approve the drug. He estimates the following probabilities:

$P(\text{Test positive} \mid \text{FDA will approve}) = 0.90$
$P(\text{Test negative} \mid \text{FDA will not approve}) = 0.80$

1. Given the above probabilities, compute the required probabilities for the decision tree. [*Hint:* You need to compute $P(\text{FDA will approve} \mid \text{Test}$

EXHIBIT 1   The Decision Tree

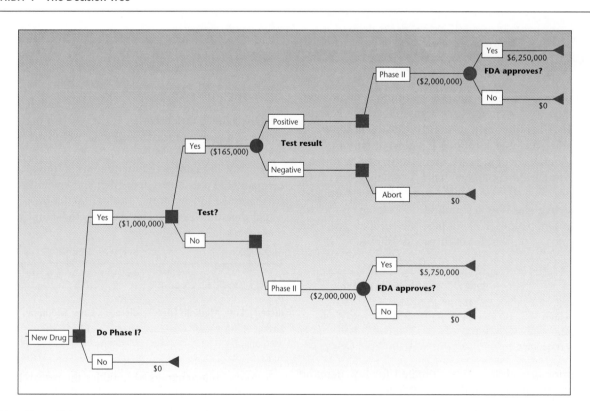

positive) and P(FDA will not approve | Test positive) for the case where the test is conducted. For the case where the test is not conducted, use the given nonconditional P(FDA will approve) and P(FDA will not approve).]

2. Assuming that the company wants to maximize the expected monetary value, what is the best decision strategy?

3. The company assumed that if the test result is negative, the best decision is to abort the project. Prove that it is the best decision.

4. At what cost of the test will the company be indifferent between conducting and not conducting the test?

5. Is your answer to question 4 the same as the EVSI of the test information?

Appendixes

Books on Data Analysis (Chapter 1):

Chambers, J. M.; W. S. Cleveland; B. Kleiner; and P. A. Tukey. *Graphical Methods for Data Analysis*. Boston: Duxbury Press, 1983. An interesting approach to graphical techniques and EDA using computer-intensive methods. The book requires no mathematical training.

Tukey, J. W. *Exploratory Data Analysis*. Reading, Mass.: Addison-Wesley Publishing, 1977. This is the original EDA book. Some material in our Chapter 1 is based on this text.

Books Primarily about Probability and Random Variables (Chapters 2, 3, and 4):

Chung, K. L. *Probability Theory with Stochastic Processes*. New York: Springer-Verlag, 1979. This is a lucidly written book. The approach to the theory of probability is similar to the one used in our text.

Feller, William. *An Introduction to Probability Theory and Its Applications*. Vol. 1, 3rd ed.; vol. 2, 2nd ed. New York: John Wiley & Sons, 1968, 1971. This is a classic textbook in probability theory. Volume 1 should be understandable to a reader of our text. Volume 2, which deals with continuous probability models, is more difficult and requires considerable mathematical ability.

Loève, Michel. *Probability Theory*. New York: Springer-Verlag, 1994. This is a mathematically demanding classic text in probability (an understanding of mathematical analysis is required).

Ross, Sheldon M. *A First Course in Probability*. 3rd ed. New York: Macmillan, 1988. An intuitive introduction to probability that requires a knowledge of calculus.

Ross, Sheldon M. *Introduction to Probability Models*. 4th ed. New York: Academic Press, 1989. A very intuitive introduction to probability theory that is consistent with the development in our text.

Statistical Theory and Sampling (Chapters 5, 6, 7, and 8):

Cochran, William G. *Sampling Techniques*. 3rd ed. New York: John Wiley & Sons, 1977. This is a classic text on sampling methodology.

Cox, D. R., and D. V. Hinkley. *Theoretical Statistics*. London: Chapman and Hall, 1974. A thorough discussion of the theory of statistics.

Fisher, Sir Ronald A. *The Design of Experiments*. 7th ed. Edinburgh: Oliver and Boyd, 1960. A classic treatise on statistical inference.

Fisher, Sir Ronald A. *Statistical Methods for Research Workers*. Edinburgh: Oliver and Boyd, 1941.

Hogg, R. V., and A. T. Craig. *Introduction to Mathematical Statistics*. 4th ed. New York: Macmillan, 1978. A good introduction to mathematical statistics that requires an understanding of calculus.

Kendall, M. G., and A. Stuart. *The Advanced Theory of Statistics*. Vol. 1, 2nd ed.; vols. 2, 3. London: Charles W. Griffin, 1963, 1961, 1966.

Mood, A. M.; F. A. Graybill; and D. C. Boes. *Introduction to the Theory of Statistics*. 3rd ed. New York: McGraw-Hill, 1974.

Rao, C. R. *Linear Statistical Inference and Its Applications*. 2nd ed. New York: John Wiley & Sons, 1973. This is a classic book on statistical inference that provides in-depth coverage of topics ranging from probability to analysis of variance, regression analysis, and multivariate methods. This book contains theoretical results that are the basis of statistical inference. The book requires advanced mathematical ability.

Books Primarily about Experimental Design, Analysis of Variance, Regression Analysis, and Econometrics (Chapters 9, 10, and 11):

Chatterjee, S., and B. Price. *Regression Analysis by Example*. 2nd ed. New York: John Wiley & Sons, 1991.

Cochran, W. G., and G. M. Cox. *Experimental Designs*. 2nd ed. New York: John Wiley & Sons, 1957.

Cook, R. Dennis, and Weisberg, S. *Applied Regression Including Computing and Graphics*. New York: John Wiley & Sons, 1999. A good introduction to regression analysis.

Draper, N. R., and H. Smith. *Applied Regression Analysis*. 3rd ed. New York: John Wiley & Sons, 1998. A thorough text on regression analysis that requires an understanding of matrix algebra.

Johnston, J. *Econometric Methods*. 4th ed. New York: McGraw-Hill, 2001. A good, comprehensive introduction to econometric models and regression analysis at a somewhat higher level than that of our text.

Judge, G. R.; C. Hill; W. Griffiths; H. Lutkepohl; and T. Lee. *Introduction to the Theory and Practice of Econometrics*. 2nd ed. New York: John Wiley & Sons, 1985.

Kutner, M. H., et al. *Applied Linear Regression Models*. 4th ed. New York: McGraw-Hill/Irwin, 2004. A good introduction to regression analysis.

Kutner, M. H., et al. *Applied Linear Statistical Models*. 5th ed. New York: McGraw-Hill/Irwin, 2005. A good introduction to regression and analysis of variance that requires no advanced mathematics.

Montgomery, D. C., and E. A. Peck. *Introduction to Linear Regression Analysis*. 2nd ed. New York: John Wiley & Sons, 1992. A very readable book on regression analysis that is recommended for further reading after our Chapter 11.

Scheffé, H. *The Analysis of Variance*. New York: John Wiley & Sons, 1959. This is a classic text on analysis of variance that requires advanced mathematical ability.

Seber, G. A. F., and Alan J. Lee. *Linear Regression Analysis*. 2nd ed.

New York: John Wiley & Sons, 2003. An advanced book on regression analysis. Some of the results in this book are used in our Chapter 11.

Snedecor, George W., and William G. Cochran. *Statistical Methods*. 7th ed. Ames: Iowa State University Press, 1980. This well-known book is an excellent introduction to analysis of variance and experimental design, as well as regression analysis. The book is very readable and requires no advanced mathematics.

Books on Forecasting (Chapter 12):

Abraham, B., and J. Ledolter. *Statistical Methods for Forecasting*. New York: John Wiley & Sons, 1983. This is an excellent book on forecasting methods.

Armstrong, S. *Long-Range Forecasting*. 2nd ed. New York: John Wiley & Sons, 1985.

Granger, C. W. J., and P. Newbold. *Forecasting Economic Time Series*. 2nd ed. New York: Academic Press, 1986. A good introduction to forecasting models.

Books on Quality Control (Chapter 13):

Duncan, A. J. *Quality Control and Industrial Statistics*. 5th ed. New York: McGraw-Hill/Irwin, 1986.

Gitlow, H.; A. Oppenheim; and R. Oppenheim. *Quality Management*. 3rd ed. New York: McGraw-Hill/Irwin, 2005.

Ott, E. R., and E. G. Schilling. *Process Quality Control*. 2nd ed. New York: McGraw-Hill, 1990.

Ryan, T. P. *Statistical Methods for Quality Improvement*. New York:

John Wiley & Sons, 1989. Much of the material in our Chapter 13 is inspired by the approach in this book.

Books on Nonparametric Methods (Chapter 14):

Conover, W. J. *Practical Nonparametric Statistics*. 2nd ed. New York: John Wiley & Sons, 1980. This is an excellent, readable textbook covering a wide range of nonparametric methods. Much of the material in our Chapter 14 is based on results in this book.

Hollander, M., and D. A. Wolfe. *Nonparametric Statistical Methods*. New York: John Wiley & Sons, 1973.

Siegel, S. *Nonparametric Statistics for the Behavioral Sciences*. 2nd ed. New York: McGraw-Hill, 1988.

Books on Subjective Probability, Bayesian Statistics, and Decision Analysis (Chapter 15 and Chapter 2):

Berger, James O. *Statistical Decision Theory and Bayesian Analysis*. 2nd ed. New York: Springer-Verlag, 1985. A comprehensive book on Bayesian methods at an advanced level.

de Finetti, Bruno. *Probability, Induction, and Statistics*. New York: John Wiley & Sons, 1972. This excellent book on subjective probability and the Bayesian philosophy is the source of the de Finetti game in our Chapter 15. The book is readable at about the level of our text.

de Finetti, Bruno. *Theory of Probability*. Vols. 1 and 2. New York: John Wiley & Sons, 1974, 1975. An excellent introduction to subjective probability and the Bayesian approach by one of its pioneers.

DeGroot, M. H. *Optimal Statistical Decisions.* New York: McGraw-Hill, 1970.

Good, I. J. *Good Thinking: The Foundations of Probability and Its Applications.* Minneapolis: University of Minnesota Press, 1983.

Jeffreys, Sir Harold. *Theory of Probability.* 3rd rev. ed. London: Oxford University Press, 1983. First published in 1939, this book truly came before its time. The book explains the Bayesian philosophy of science and its application in probability and statistics. It is readable and thought-provoking and is highly recommended for anyone with an interest in the ideas underlying Bayesian inference.

Answers to Most Odd-Numbered Problems

Chapter 1

1-1. 1. quantitative/ratio
2. qualitative/nominal
3. quantitative/ratio
4. qualitative/nominal
5. quantitative/ratio
6. quantitative/interval
7. quantitative/ratio
8. quantitative/ratio
9. quantitative/ratio
10. quantitative/ratio
11. quantitative/ordinal

1-3. Weakest to strongest: nominal, ordinal, interval, ratio.

1-5. Ordinal

1-7. Nonrandom sample; frame is random sample

1-11. Ordinal

1-13. LQ = 121
MQ = 128
UQ = 133.5
10th percentile = 114.8
15th percentile = 118.1
65th percentile = 131.1
IQR = 12.5

1-15. Formula (template)
Median = −0.15 (−0.15)
20th percentile = −0.7 (−0.7)
30th percentile = −0.64 (−0.56)
60th percentile = 0.16 (0.14)
90th percentile = 1.52 (0.88)

1-17. Median = 51
LQ = 31.5
UQ = 162.75
IQR = 131.25
45th percentile = 42.2

1-19. mean = 126.64
median = 128
modes = 128, 134, 136

1-21. mean = 66.955
median = 70
mode = 45

1-23. mean = 199.875
median = 51
mode = none

1-25. mean = 21.75
median = 13
mode = 12

1-27. mean = 18.34
median = 19.1

1-29. Variance, standard deviation

1-31. range = 27
var = 57.74
s.d. = 7.5986

1-33. range = 60
var = 321.38
s.d. = 17.927

1-35. range = 1186
var = 110,287.45
s.d. = 332.096

1-37. Chebyshev holds; data not mound-shaped, empirical rule does not apply

1-39. Chebyshev holds; data not mound-shaped, empirical rule does not apply

1-45. mean = 13.33
median = 12.5

1-47. 5 | 5688
6 | 0123677789
7 | 0222333455667889
8 | 224

1-49. Stem-and-leaf is similar to a histogram but it retains the individual data points; box plot is useful in identifying outliers and the shape of the distribution of the data.

1-51. Data are concentrated about the median; 2 outliers

1-53. μ = 127
σ = 11.45
σ² = 131.04
Mode = 127

Suspected outliers: 101, 157

1-55. Can use stem-and-leaf or box plots to identify outliers; outliers need to be evaluated instead of just eliminated.

1-57.

Mine A:	Mine B:
3 | 2457	2 | 3489
4 | 12355689	3 | 24578
5 | 123	4 | 034789
6 | 0	5 | 0129

−out values−
7 | 36
8 | 5

1-59. LW = −0.3
LH = 0.275
median = 0.6
UH = 1.15
UW = 1.6

1-63. mean = 504.688
s.d. = 94.547

1-65. range = 346
90th percentile = 632.7
LQ = 419.25
MQ = 501.5
UQ = 585.75

1-67. 1 | 2456789
2 | 02355
3 | 24
4 | 01

1-69. 1 | 012
−out values−
1 | 9
2 | 1222334556677889
3 | 02457
−out values−
6 | 2

1-71. mean = 8.067
median = 9
mode = 10

1-73. mean = 33.271
s.d. = 16.945
var = 287.15
LQ = 25.41
MQ = 26.71
UQ = 35

1–75. 1. 3.5
2. Right skewed
3. d
4. Nothing will be affected

1–77. mean = 186.7
median = 56.2
s.d. = 355.6
outliers: 1459, 707.1, 481.9

1–79. mean = 1720.2
median = 930
s.d. = 1409.85
var = 1987680.96

1–81. mean = 17.587
var = 0.2172
s.d. = 0.466

1–83. mean = 37.17
median = 34
s.d. = 13.12758
var = 172.33

1–85. *a.* VARP = 3.5 + offset^2
b. VARP = 3.5

1–89. mean = 5.148
median = 5.35
s.d. = 0.6021
var = 0.3625

Chapter 2

2–1. Objective and subjective

2–3. The sample space is the set of all possible outcomes of an experiment.

2–5. $G \cup F$: the baby is either a girl, or is over 5 pounds (of either sex). $G \cap F$: the baby is a girl over 5 pounds.

2–7. 0.417

2–9. $S \cup B$: purchase stock or bonds, or both. $S \cap B$: purchase stock and bonds.

2–11. 0.12

2–13. *a.* 0.1667
b. 0.0556
c. 0.3889

2–15. 0.85 is a typical "very likely" probability.

2–17. The team is very likely to win.

2–19. *a.* Mutually exclusive
b. 0.035
c. 0.985, complements

2–21. 0.49

2–23. 0.7909

2–25. 0.500

2–27. 0.34

2–29. 0.60

2–31. *a.* 0.1002
b. 0.2065
c. 0.59
d. 0.144
e. 0.451
f. 0.571
g. 0.168
h. 0.454
i. 0.569

2–33. *a.* 0.484
b. 0.455
c. 0.138
d. 0.199
e. 0.285
f. 0.634
g. 0.801

2–35. 0.333

2–37. 0.8143

2–39. 0.72675

2–41. 0.99055

2–43. 0.9989

2–45. not independent

2–47. 0.3686

2–49. 0.00048

2–51. 0.0039, 0.684

2–53. 362,880

2–55. 120

2–57. 0.00275

2–59. 0.0000924

2–61. 0.86

2–63. 0.78

2–65. 0.9944

2–67. 0.2857

2–69. 0.8824

2–71. 0.0248

2–73. 0.6

2–75. 0.20

2–77. 0.60

2–79. not independent

2–81. 0.388

2–83. 0.59049, 0.40951

2–85. 0.132, not random

2–87. 0.6667

2–89. *a.* 0.255
b. 0.8235

2–91. 0.5987

2–93. 0.5825

2–95. Practically speaking, the probabilities involved vary only slightly, and their role in the outcome of the game should be more or less unnoticeable when averaged over a span of games.

2–97. 1/2

2–99. 0.767

2–101. *a.* 0.202
b. 1.00
c. 0.0

2–103. P(Pass) = 0.0002; P(Success) = 0.00014

2–105. P(A|def) = 0.3838
P(B|good) = 0.3817

Chapter 3

3–1. *a.* $\Sigma P(x) = 1.0$

b.

x	F(x)
0	0.3
1	0.5
2	0.7
3	0.8
4	0.9
5	1.0

c. 0.3

3–3. *a.* $\Sigma P(x) = 1.0$

b.

x	F(x)
0	0.10
10	0.30
20	0.65
30	0.85
40	0.95
50	1.00

c. 0.35

3–5.

x	P(x)	F(x)
2	1/36	1/36
3	2/36	3/36
4	3/36	6/36
5	4/36	10/36
6	5/36	15/36
7	6/36	21/36
8	5/36	26/36
9	4/36	30/36
10	3/36	33/36
11	2/36	35/36
12	1/36	36/36

Most likely sum is 7

3–7. *a.* 0.30

b.

x	F(x)
400	0.05
600	0.10
800	0.20
1000	0.30
1200	0.60
1500	0.80
1700	1.00

c. 0.30

d. 0.70

3–9. *a.* $\Sigma P(x) = 1.0$

b. 0.50

c.

x	F(x)
9	0.05
10	0.20
11	0.50
12	0.70
13	0.85
14	0.95
15	1.00

3–11. $E(X) = 1.8$

$E(X^2) = 6$

$V(X) = 2.76$

$SD(X) = 1.661$

3–13. $E(X) = 21.5$

$E(X^2) = 625$

$V(X) = 162.75$

3–15. $E(\text{sum of 2 dice}) = 7$

x	P(x)	xP(x)
2	1/36	2/36
3	2/36	6/36
4	3/36	12/36
5	4/36	20/36
6	5/36	30/36
7	6/36	42/36
8	5/36	40/36
9	4/36	36/36
10	3/36	30/36
11	2/36	22/36
12	1/36	12/36
		252/36 = 7

3–17. mean = 1230

var = 137100

s.d. = 370.27

3–19. Three standard deviations

$8/9 = 1 - 1/3^2$ $k = 3$

3–21. *a.* 2000

b. Yes $P(X > 0) = .6$

c. $E(X) = +800$

d. good measure of risk is the standard deviation

$E(X^2) = 2,800,000$

$V(X) = 2,160,000$

$SD(X) = 1,469.69$

3–23. $868.5 million

3–25. Penalty = X^2

$E(X^2) = 12.39$

3–27. Variance is a measure of the spread or uncertainty of the random variable.

3–29. $V(\text{Cost}) = V(aX + b) = a^2 V(X) = 68,687,500$

$SD(\text{Cost}) = 8,287.79$

3–31. 3.11

3–33. X is binomial if sales calls are independent.

3–35. X is not binomial because members of the same family are related and not independent of each other.

3–37. *a.* slightly skewed; becomes more symmetric as n increases.

b. Symmetric if $p = 0.5$. Left-skewed if $p > 0.5$; right-skewed if $p < 0.5$

3–39. *a.* 0.8889

b. 11

c. 0.55

3–41. *a.* 0.9981

b. 0.889, 0.935

c. 4, 5

d. increase the reliability of each engine

3–43. *a.* mean = 6.25, var = 6.77083

b. 61.80%

c. 11

d. $p = 0.7272$

3–45. *a.* mean = 2.857, var = 5.306

b. 82.15%

c. 7

d. $p = 0.5269$

3–47. *a.* 0.5000

b. Add 4 more women or remove 3 men.

3–49. *a.* 0.8430

b. 6

c. $\mu = 1.972$

3–51. *a.* MTBF = 5.74 days

b. $P(x \leq 1) = 0.1599$

c. 0.1599

d. 0.4185

3–55. As s or p increases skewness decreases.

3–57. *a.* 0.7807

b. 0.2858

3–59. *a.* 0.7627

b. 0.2373

3–61. *a.* 0.2119

b. 0.2716

c. 0.1762

3–63. *a.* $P(x = 5) = 0.2061$

b. $P(x = 4) = 0.2252$

c. $P(x = 3) = 0.2501$

d. $P(x = 2) = 0.2903$

e. $P(x = 1) = 0.3006$

3–65. $P(x \geq 2) = 0.5134$

3–67. *a.* $\Sigma P(x) = 1.0$

b.

x	F(x)
0	.05
1	.10
2	.20
3	.35
4	.55
5	.70
6	.85
7	.95
8	1.00

c. $P(3 \leq x \leq 7) = 0.65$

d. $P(X \leq 5) = 0.70$

e. $E(X) = 4.25$

f. $E(X^2) = 22.25$

$V(X) = 4.1875$

$SD(X) = 2.0463$

g. [0.1574, 8.3426] vs $P(1 \leq X \leq 8)$ = 0.95

3–69. *a.* $\Sigma P(x) = 1.0$

b.

x	F(x)
0	.10
1	.30
2	.60
3	.75
4	.90
5	.95
6	1.00

c. 0.35, 0.40, 0.10

d. 0.20

e. 0.0225

f. $E(X) = 2.4$

$SD(X) = 1.562$

3–71. *a.* $E(X) = 17.56875$

profit = $31.875

b. $SD(X) = 0.3149$

a measure of risk

c. the assumption
of stationary and
independence of
the stock prices

3–73. a. Yes.
b. 0.7716

3–75. a. The distribution is
binomial if the cars
are independent of
each other.

b.
x	P(x)
0	.5987
1	.3151
2	.0746
3	.0105
4	.0010
5	.0001

c. 0.0861
d. ½ a car

3–77. $N/n < 10$

3–79. b. 1.00
c. 0.75

3–81. 0.9945

3–83. a. 11.229
b. 20/20 : +1.02
G.B.: −0.33
M.C.: −1.48

3–85. 0.133; 10

3–87. 0.3935

3–89. $P(X \geq 5) = 0.0489$

3–91. 0.9999; 0.0064; 0.6242

3–93. i) MTBF = 103.86 hrs
ii) 49.9 hrs
iii) Because it is right
skewed

Chapter 4

4–1. 0.6826; 0.95; 0.9802

4–3. 0.1805

4–5. 0.0215

4–7. 0.9901

4–9. a very small number,
close to 0

4–11. 0.9544

4–13. Not likely,
$P = 0.00003$

4–15. $z = 0.48$

4–17. $z = 1.175$

4–19. $z = \pm 1.96$

4–21. 0.0164

4–23. 0.927

4–25. 0.003

4–27. 0.8609; 0.2107;
0.6306

4–29. 0.0931

4–31. 0.2525

4–33. 0.8644

4–35. 0.3759; 0.0135; 0.8766

4–37. 0.0344

4–39. 15.67

4–41. 76.35; 99.65

4–43. −46.15

4–45. 832.6; 435.5

4–47. [18,130.2; 35,887.8]

4–49. 74.84

4–51. 1.54

4–53. 0.99998

4–55. 0.3804

4–57. 0.1068

4–59. 0.7642

4–61. 0.1587; 0.9772

4–63. 791,580

4–65. [7.02, 8.98]

4–67. 1555.52, [1372.64,
3223.36]

4–69. 8.856 kW

4–71. more than 0.26%

4–73. $u = 64.31$, s.d.
= 5.49

4–75. 6015.6

4–77. 0.0000

4–79. a. $N(248, 5.3852^2)$
b. 0.6448
c. 0.0687

4–81. a. 0.0873
b. 0.4148
c. 16,764.55
d. 0.0051

4–83. i) Yes
ii) Mean = $7133;
Std. dev = $177.29
iii) 0.7734

Chapter 5

5–1. Parameters are
numerical measures
of populations.
Sample statistics are
numerical measures of
samples. An estimator
is a sample statistic
used for estimating
a population
parameter.

5–3. 5/12 = 0.41667

5–5. mean = 4.368
s.d. = 0.3486

5–11. The probability
distribution of a
sample statistic; useful
in determining the
accuracy of estimation
results.

5–13. $E(\overline{X}) = 125$
$SE(\overline{X}) = 8.944$

5–15. When the population
distribution is
unknown.

5–17. Binomial. Cannot use
normal approximation
since $np = 1.2$

5–19. 0.075

5–21. 1.000

5–23. 0.2308

5–25. 0.000

5–27. 0.0497

5–29. 0.0190

5–31. A consistent estimator
means as $n \to \infty$ the
probability of getting
close to the parameter
increases. A generous
budget affords a large
sample size, making
this probability high.

5–33. Advantage: uses all
information in the
data. Disadvantage:
may be too sensitive
to the influence of
outliers.

5–37. a. mean = 43.667,
SSD = 358,
MSD = 44.75
b. use Means: 40.75,
49.667, 40.5
c. SSD = 195.917,
MSD = 32.6528
d. SSD = 719,
MSD = 89.875

5–39. Yes, we can solve the
equation for the one
unknown amount.

5–41. $E(\overline{X}) = 1065$
$V(\overline{X}) = 2500$

5–43. $E(\overline{X}) = 53$
$SE(\overline{X}) = 0.5$

5–45. $E(\hat{p}) = 0.2$
$SE(\hat{p}) = 0.04216$

5–47. 1.000

5–49. 0.9544

5–51. *a.* 8128.08

 b. 0.012

5–55. The sample median is unbiased. The sample mean is more efficient and is sufficient. Must assume normality for using the sample median to estimate μ; it is more resistant to outliers.

5–57. 0.000

5–59. 1.000

5–61. 0.9503

5–63. No minimum ($n = 1$ is enough for normality).

5–65. This estimator is consistent, and is more efficient than $\overline{X}$, because $\sigma^2/n^2 < \sigma^2/n$

5–67. Relative minimum sample sizes: $n_a < n_b < n_d < n_e < n_c$

5–69. Use a computer simulation, draw repeated samples, determine the empirical distribution.

5–71. $P(Z < -5) = 0.0000003$ Not probable

5–73. 0.923

5–75. 0.1999

5–77. 0.0171

Chapter 6

6–5. [86,978.12, 92,368.12]

6–7. [31.098, 32.902] m.p.g.

6–9. [9.045, 9.555] percent

6–11. *a.* [1513.91, 1886.09]

 b. fly the route

6–13. 95% C.I.: [136.99, 156.51]

 90% C.I.: [138.56, 154.94]

 99% C.I.: [133.93, 159.57]

6–15. [17.4, 22.6] percent

6–17. 8.393

6–19. 95% C.I.: [15,684.37, 17,375.63]

 99% C.I.: [15,418.6, 17,641.4]

6–21. [27.93, 33.19] thousand miles

6–23. [72.599, 89.881]

6–25. [4.92368, 12.06382]

6–27. [2.344, 2.856] days

6–29. [627478.6, 666521.4]

6–31. [15.86, 17.14] dollars

6–33. [5.44, 7.96] years

6–35. [55.85, 67.48] containers

6–37. [9.764, 10.380]

6–39. [10.76, 12.16]

6–41. [0.4658, 0.7695]

6–43. [0.3430, 0.4570]

6–45. [0.0078, 0.0122]

6–47. [0.0375, 0.2702]

6–49. [0.5357, 0.6228]

6–51. [0.1937, 0.2625]

6–53. [61.11, 197.04]

6–55. [19.25, 74.92]

6–57. [1268.03, 1676.68]

6–59. 271

6–61. 39

6–63. 131

6–65. 865

6–67. [21.507, 25.493]

6–69. [0.6211, 0.7989]

6–71. [35.81417, 52.18583]

6–73. [1.0841, 1.3159]

6–75. [0.6974, 0.7746]

6–77. did benefit

6–79. [7.021, 8.341]

6–81. [0.508, 0.692]

6–83. [0.902, 0.918]

6–85. [0.5695, 0.6304]

6–87. 75% C.I.: [7.76, 8.24]

6–89. 95% CI: [0.9859, 0.9981]

 99% CI: [0.9837, 1.0003]

6–95. [5.147, 6.853]

Chapter 7

7–1. H_0: $p = 0.8$

 H_1: $p \neq 0.8$

7–3. H_0: $\mu \leq 12$

 H_1: $\mu > 12$

7–5. H_0: $\mu \leq \$3.75$

 H_1: $\mu > \$3.75$

7–11. *a.* left-tailed H_1: $\mu < 10$

 b. right-tailed H_1: $p > 0.5$

 c. left-tailed H_1: $\mu < 100$

 d. right-tailed H_1: $\mu > 20$

 e. two-tailed H_1: $p \neq 0.22$

 f. right-tailed H_1: $\mu > 50$

 g. two-tailed H_1: $\sigma^2 \neq 140$

7–13. *a.* to the left tail

 b. to the right tail

 c. either to the left or to the right tail

7–15. *a.* p-value will decrease

 b. p-value increases

 c. p-value decreases

7–17. $z = 1.936$, Do not reject H_0 (p-value $= 0.0528$)

7–19. $z = 1.7678$, Reject H_0

7–21. $t_{(15)} = 1.55$, Do not reject H_0 (p-value > 0.10)

7–23. $z = -3.269$, Reject H_0 (p-value $= 0.0011$)

7–25. $t_{(24)} = 2.25$, Do not reject H_0 at $\alpha = 0.01$, reject at $\alpha = 0.05$

7–27. $z = 6.5385$, Reject H_0

7–29. $z = 1.539$, Do not reject H_0 (p-value $= 0.1238$)

7–31. $z = 1.622$, Do not reject H_0 (p-value $= 0.1048$)

7–33. $t_{(23)} = 2.939$, Reject H_0

7–35. $z = 16.0$, Reject H_0

7–37. $z = -20$, Reject H_0

7–39. $z = -1.304$, Do not reject H_0 (p-value $= 0.0962$)

7–41. $z = 9.643$, Reject H_0

7–43. $z = -3.2332$, Reject H_0

7–45. standing start: $z = 2.7368$, Reject H_0 braking: $z = 1.8333$, Reject H_0

7–47. power $= 0.9092$

7–49. $z = 10.30$, Reject H_0

7–51. $z = -2.711$, Reject H_0

7–53. $z = -2.3570$, Reject H_0

7–55. $z = 4.249$, Reject H_0 (p-value $= 0.00001$)

7–65. $z = -4.86$, Reject H_0, power $= 0.5214$

7–67. $\chi^2_{(24)} = 26.923$, Do not reject H_0 (p-value > 0.10)

7–69. $t_{(20)} = 1.06$, Do not reject H_0 at $\alpha = 0.10$ (p-value $= 0.15$)

7–71. $t = -5.4867$, Reject H_0

7–73. $z = 2.53$, Reject H_0 (p-value $= 0.0057$)

7–75. Do not reject H_0 at 0.05 level of significance

7–77. Do not reject H_0 at 0.05 level of significance

7–79. $t = 1.1899$, Do not reject H_0

7–81. Reject H_0, p-value $= 0.0188$

7–83. *b.* power $= 0.4968$
          c. No.

7–85. *b.* power $= 0.6779$
          c. Yes.

7–87. 1. 54

7–89. $z = -3.2275$, Reject H_0

Chapter 8

8–1. $t_{(24)} = 3.11$, Reject H_0 (p-value < 0.01)

8–3. $t = 4.4907$, Reject H_0

8–5. $t_{(14)} = 1.469$, Cannot reject H_0

8–7. Power $= P(Z > 1.55) = 0.0606$

8–9. $t = -2.1025$, Reject H_0

8–11. $t = -11.101$, Reject H_0

8–13. $z = 4.24$, Reject H_0

8–15. *a.* One-tailed: H_0: $\mu_1 - \mu_2 \leq 0$
          b. $z = 1.53$
          c. At $\alpha = .05$, Do not reject H_0
          d. 0.063
          e. $t_{(19)} = 0.846$, Do not reject H_0

8–17. $[2.416, 2.664]$ percent

8–19. $t_{(26)} = -1.132$, Do not reject H_0 (p-value > 0.10)

8–21. $t = -1.676$, Do not reject H_0

8–23. $t_{(13)} = 1.164$, Strongly reject H_0 (p-value > 0.10)

8–25. $z = 2.785$, Reject H_0 (p-value $= 0.0026$)

8–27. $t = 0.7175$, Do not reject H_0

8–29. $z = 2.835$, Reject H_0 (p-value $= 0.0023$)

8–31. $z = -0.228$, Do not reject H_0

8–33. $[0.0419, 0.0781]$

8–35. $z = 1.601$, Do not reject H_0 at $\alpha = .05$ (p-value $= 0.0547$)

8–37. $z = 2.6112$, Reject H_0

8–39. $z = 5.33$, Strongly reject H_0 (p-value is very small)

8–41. $F = 1.1025$, Do not reject H_0

8–43. $F_{(27,20)} = 1.838$, At $\alpha = 0.10$, cannot reject H_0 $[0.652, 4.837]$

8–45. $F_{(24,24)} = 1.538$, Do not reject H_0

8–47. Independent random sampling from the populations and normal population distributions

8–49. $[-3235.97, 1321.97]$

8–51. $[-0.465, 9.737]$

8–53. $[0.0989, 0.3411]$

8–55. $z = 1.447$, Do not reject H_0 (p-value $= 0.1478$)

8–57. $t_{(22)} = 2.719$, Reject H_0 ($0.01 < p$-value < 0.02)

8–59. $z = -1.7503$, Do not reject H_0

8–61. $t_{(26)} = 2.479$, Reject H_0 (p-value $= 0.02$)

8–63. $t_{(29)} = 1.08$, Do not reject H_0

8–65. Since $s_1^2 < s_2^2$, Do not reject H_0

8–67. $t_{(15)} = -0.9751$, Do not reject H_0

8–69. $[0.0366, 0.1474]$

8–71. $t = -1.5048$, Do not reject H_0

8–73. $t = 14.2414$, Reject H_0

8–75. Do not reject H_0

8–77. $[-0.1264, 0.5264]$

8–79. 1. $t = 2.1356$, Reject H_0
          2. $F = 5.11$, Reject H_0

Chapter 9

9–1. H_0: All 4 means are equal
          H_1: All 4 are different; or 2 equal, 2 different; or 3 equal, 1 different; or 2 equal, other 2 equal but different from first 2.

9–3. Series of paired t tests are *dependent* on each other. No control over the probability of a type I error.

9–5. $F_{(3,176)} = 12.53$, Reject H_0

9–7. The sum of all the deviations from a mean is equal to 0.

9–11. Both MSTR and MSE are *sample statistics* given to natural variation about their own means.

9–19.

Source	SS	df
Between	187.696	3
Within	152.413	28
Total	340.108	31

MS	F
62.565	11.494
5.4433	

p-value $= 0.000$, Reject H_0

9–21.

Source	df	SS
Treatment	2	91.043
Error	38	140.529
Total	40	231.571

MS	F
45.521	12.31
3.698	

Critical point $F_{(2,38)}$ for $\alpha = 0.01$ is 3.24, Reject H_0

9–23. Performances of the four different portfolios are significantly different.

9–25. $T = 4.738$. The mean for squares is significantly greater than those for circles and for triangles; circles and triangles show no significant difference.

9–27. UK − UAE, UK-OMAN, MEX-OMAN

9–29. df factor = 2
df error = 154
df total = 156

9–31. No; the 3 prototypes were not randomly chosen from a population.

9–33. Fly all 3 planes on the same route every time.

9–35. Otherwise not a random sample from a population of treatments, and inference is thus not valid for the entire "population."

9–37. If the locations and the artists are chosen randomly, we have a random-effects model.

9–41. Since there are inter-actions, there are differences in emotions averaged over all levels of advertisements.

9–43.

Source	df	SS
Network	145	2
Newstime	160	2
Interaction	240	4
Error	6200	441
Total	6745	449

MS	F
72.5	5.16
80	5.69
60	4.27
14.06	

All are significant at $\alpha = 0.01$. There are

interactions. There are Network main effects averaged over Newstime levels. There are Newstime main effects averaged over Network levels.

9–45.
  a. Explained is treatment = Factor A + Factor B + (AB)
  b. $a = 3$
  c. $b = 2$
  d. $N = 150$
  e. $n = 25$ There are no exercise-price main effects.
  g. There are time-of-expiration main effects at 0.05 but not at 0.01.
  h. There are no interactions.
  i. Some evidence for time-of-expiration main effects; no evidence for exercise-price main effects or interaction effects.
  j. For time-of-expiration main effects, $0.01 < p$-value < 0.05. For the other two tests, the p-values are very high.
  k. Could use a t test for time-of-expiration effects: $t^2_{(144)} = F_{(1,144)}$

9–47. Advantages: reduced experimental errors and great economy of sample size. Disadvantages: restrictive, because it requires that number of treatments = number of rows = number of columns.

9–49. Could use a randomized blocking design.

9–51. Yes; have people of the same occupation/age/demographics use sweaters of the 3 kinds under study. Each group of 3 people is a block.

9–53. Group the executives into blocks according to some choice of common characteristics such as age, sex, or years employed at current firm; these blocks would then form a third variable beyond Location and Type to use in a 3-way ANOVA.

9–55. $F_{(2,198)} = 25.84$, Reject H_0 (p-value very small)

9–57. $F_{(7,152)} = 14.67$, Reject H_0 (p-value very small)

9–59.

Source	SS	df
Software	77,645	2
Computer	54,521	3
Interaction	88,699	6
Error	434,557	708
Total	655,422	719

MS	F
38,822.5	63.25
18,173.667	29.60
14,783.167	24.09
613.78	

Both main effects and the interactions are highly significant.

9–61.

Source	SS	df
Pet	22,245	3
Location	34,551	3
Interaction	31,778	9
Error	554,398	144
Total	642,972	159

MS	F
7,415	1.93
11,517	2.99
3,530.89	0.92
3,849.99	

No interactions; no pet main effects. There are location main effects at $\alpha = 0.05$

9–63. *b.* $F_{(2,58)} = 11.47$,
Reject H_0

9–65. $F_{(2,98)} = 0.14958$,
Do not reject H_0

9–67. Rents are equal on
average; no evidence
of differences among
the four cities.

Chapter 10

10–1. A set of mathematical
formulas and assump-
tions that describe some
real-world situation.

10–3. 1. a straight-line
relationship
between X and Y
2. the values of X are
fixed
3. the regression errors,
ϵ, are identically
normally distributed
random variables,
uncorrelated with
each other through
time.

10–5. It is the population
regression line.

10–7. 1. It captures the
randomness in the
process.
2. It makes the result
(Y) a random
variable.
3. It captures the
effects on Y of
other unknown
components not
accounted by the
regression model.

10–9. The line is the best
unbiased linear
estimator of the true
regression line. Least-
squares line is
obtained by
minimizing the sum of
the squared deviations
of the data points
about the line.

10–11. $b_0 = 6.38$,
$b_1 = 10.12$

10–13. $b_0 = -3.057$,
$b_1 = 0.187$

10–15. $b_0 = 16.096$;
$b_1 = 0.9681$

10–17. $b_0 = 39.6717$,
$b_1 = 0.06129$

10–19. $[1.1158, 1.3949]$

10–21. $s(b_0) = 2.897$,
$s(b_1) = 0.873$

10–23. $s(b_0) = 0.971$
$s(b_1) = 0.016$ Estimate
of error variance is
MSE $= 0.991$

10–25. s^2 gives information
about the variation of
the data points about
the computed
regression line.

10–27. $r = 0.9890$

10–29. $t_{(5)} = 0.601$, Do not
reject H_0

10–31. $t_{(8)} = 5.11$, Reject H_0

10–35. $z = 1.297$, Do not
reject H_0

10–37. $t_{(16)} = 1.0727$, Do not
reject H_0

10–39. $t_{(11)} = 11.69$, Strongly
reject H_0

10–41. $t_{(58)} = 5.90$,   Reject H_0

10–43. $t_{(211)} = 0.0565$, Do not
reject H_0

10–45. 9% of the variation in
customer satisfaction
can be explained by
the changes in a
customer's materialism
measurement.

10–47. $r^2 = 0.9781$

10–49. $r^2 = 0.067$

10–51. U.K. model explains
31.7% of the variation;
next best models:
Germany, Canada,
Japan, then United
States.

10–53. $r^2 = 0.835$

10–57. $F_{(1,11)} = 129.525$
$t_{(11)} = 11.381$ $t^2 = F$
$(11.381)^2 = 129.525$

10–59. $F_{(1,17)} = 85.90$, Very
strongly reject H_0

10–61. $F_{(1,20)} = 0.3845$,
Do not reject H_0

10–63. *a.* Heteroscedasticity
b. No apparent
inadequacy

c. Data display
curvature, not a
linear relationship

10–65. *a.* no serious
inadequacy
b. Yes. A deviation
from the normal-
distribution
assumption is
apparent.

10–69. 6551.35
P.I.: $[5854.4, 7248.3]$

10–71. $[5605.75, 7496.95]$

10–73. $[36.573, 77.387]$

10–75. $[-157990, 477990]$

10–77. *a.* $Y = 2.779337X -$
0.284157. When
$X = 10$, $Y = 27.5092$
b. $Y = 2.741537X$.
When $X = 10$,
$Y = 27.41537$
c. $Y = 2.825566X -$
1.12783. When
$X = 10$,
$Y = 27.12783$
d. $Y = 2X + 4.236$.
When $X = 10$,
$Y = 24.236$

10–79. Reject the null. 19%
of the variation in job
performance can be
explained by
neuroticism.

10–81. Mean $= 13.4\%$;
s.d. $= 5.3563\%$

10–83. $b_0 = 62.292$;
$b_1 = -1.8374$

10–85. $b_0 = -2311$;
$b_1 = 5.2031$

10–87. $b_0 = 713.95$;
$b_1 = -0.0239$

Chapter 11

11–5. 8 equations

11–7. $b_0 = -1.134$
$b_1 = 0.048$
$b_2 = 10.897$

11–11. $n - 13$

11–21. $R^2 = 0.9174$, a good
regression, $\overline{R}^2$
$= 0.8983$

11–23. $\overline{R}^2 = 0.8907$. Do not
include the new
variable.

11–25. *a.* Assume $n = 50$;
Regression is:
Return = 0.484 −
0.030 (Siz rnk) −
0.017 (Prc rnk)
b. $R^2 = 0.130$. 13%
of the variation is
due to the two
independent
variables
c. Adjusted R^2 is quite
low; try regressing
on size alone.

11–27. $F = 168.153$, adj.
$R^2 = 0.7282$,
Reject H_0

11–29. firm size: $z = 12.00$
(significant)
firm profitability: $z = -5.533$ (significant)
fixed-asset ratio:
$z = -0.08$
growth opportunities:
$z = -0.72$
nondebt tax shield:
$z = 4.29$ (significant)

11–31. $\beta_2 = [3.052, 8.148]$
$\beta_3 = [-3.135, 23.835]$
$\beta_4 = [-1.842, 8.742]$
$\beta_5 = [-4.995, -3.505]$

11–33. Yes

11–35. Lend seems
insignificant because
of collinearity with M_1
or price.

11–37. Autocorrelation of the
regression errors.

11–39. $b_0 = 0.578053$
$b_1 = 0.155178$
$b_2 = -0.04974$
$R^2 = 0.355968$
$F = 1.934515$
Regression is not
statistically significant.

11–41. *a.* Residuals appear
to be normally
distributed.
b. Residuals are not
normally distributed.

11–47. Creates a bias. There is
no reason to force the
regression surface to
go through the origin.

11–51. 363.78

11–53. 0.341. 0.085

11–55. The estimators are the
same although their
standard errors are
different.

11–59. Two-way ANOVA

11–61. Early investment is not
statistically significant
(or may be collinear
with another variable).
Rerun the regression
without it. The dummy
variables are both
significant. Investment
is significant.

11–63. The STEPWISE
routine chooses Price
and M_1 *Price as the
best set of explanatory
variables. Exports = $-1.39 + 0.0229$ Price
$+ 0.00248M_1$ *Price.
t statistics: -2.36, 4.57,
9.08, respectively.
$R^2 = 0.822$

11–65. After * Bankdep:
$z = -11.3714$
After * Bankdep *
ROA: $z = 2.7193$
After * ROA:
$z = -3.00$
Bankdep * ROA:
$z = -3.9178$
All interactions
significant.
adj. $R^2 = 0.53$

11–67. Quadratic regression
(should get a negative
estimated x^2 coefficient)

11–69. Linearizing a model;
finding a more
parsimonious model
than is possible without
a transformation;
stabilizing the variance.

11–71. The transformation
$\log Y$

11–73. A logarithmic model

11–77. No

11–79. Taking reciprocals of
both sides of the
equation.

11–81. No. They minimize
the sum of the squared

deviations relevant to
the estimated,
transformed model.

11–83.

	Earn	Prod	Prom
Prod	.867		
Prom	.882	.638	
Book	.547	.402	.319

Multicollinearity does
not seem to be serious.

11–85. Sample correlation is
0.740

11–89. Not true. Predictions
may be good when
carried out within the
same region of the
multicollinearity as
used in the estimation
procedure.

11–91. X_2 and X_3 are
probably collinear.

11–93. Drop some of the other
variables one at a time
and see what happens
to the suspected sign of
the estimate.

11–97. 1. The test checks only
for first-order
autocorrelation.
2. The test may not
be conclusive.
3. The usual
limitations of a
statistical test owing
to the two possible
types of errors.

11–99. DW = 2.13 At the
0.10 level, no evidence
of a first-order
autocorrelation.

11–103. $F_{(r, n-(k+1))} = 0.0275$,
Cannot reject H_0

11–105. The STEPWISE
procedure selects all
three variables.
$R^2 = 0.9667$

11–107. Because a variable
may lose explanatory
power and become
insignificant once
other variables are
added to the model.

11–109. No. There may be
several different "best"
models.

11–111. Transforms a nonlinear model to a linear model.

11–113.

Predictor	Coef
Constant	−36.49
Sincerity	0.0983
Excitement	1.9859
Ruggedness	0.5071
Sophistication	−0.3664

Only Excitement is significant. $R^2 = 0.946$, adj. $R^2 = 0.918$

Chapter 12

12–3. 2005: 198.182
2006: 210.748

12–5. No, because of the seasonality.

12–11. debt = 8728083

12–13. forecast = 0.33587

12–15. 6.2068 using trend + season

12–17. The $w = 0.8$ forecasts follow the raw data much more closely.

12–19. forecast = 6037828

12–23.

Year	Old CPI	New CPI
1950	72.1	24.9
1951	77.8	26.9
1952	79.5	27.5
1953	80.1	27.7

12–25. A simple price index reflects changes in a single price variable of time, relative to a single base time.

12–27. *a.* 1988
b. Divide each index number by 163/100
c. It fell, from 145% of the 1988 output down to 133% of that output.

12–29. Sales = 4.23987 − 0.03870 Month. Forecast for July 1997 (month #19) = 3.5046

12–33. forecast = 6.73

12–35. 7.9

Chapter 13

13–3. 1. Natural, random variation
2. variation due to assignable causes

13–9. *a.* 77.62%
b. Omissions, Quantity Entry, Part Numbers (90.70%)

13–15. Random sampling, so that the observations are independent.

13–17. Process is in control.

13–21. Process is in control.

13–23. Process is in control.

13–25. Process is out of control (9th sample).

13–27. All points are well within the p chart limits; process is in control.

13–29. All points are well within the p chart limits; process is in control.

13–31. The tenth sample barely exceeds the UCL = 8.953; otherwise in control.

13–33. All points within c chart limits; process is in control.

13–37. The 20th observation far exceeds the UCL = 8.92/100; the last nine observations are all on one side of the center line $\overline{P} = 3.45/100$

13–39. Last group's mean is below the LCL = 2.136

13–41. X-bar chart shows the process is out of control.

Chapter 14

14–1. $T = 3$, p-value = 0.2266   Accept H_0.

14–3. $z = 1.46$ Cannot reject H_0.

14–5. $T = 9$ Cannot reject H_0 (p-value = .593).

14–7. $z = 2.145$ Reject H_0.

14–9. $z = -3.756$ Reject H_0.

14–11. $z = -3.756$ Reject H_0.

14–13. $U = 3.5$ Reject H_0.

14–17. $U = 12$ Reject H_0.

14–21. $H_0 : \mu_1 = \mu_2$
$H_1 : \mu_1 \neq \mu_2$
p-value = 0.117

14–23. Sign Test

14–25. Wilcoxon Signed-Rank Test

14–27. $H_0 : \mu_1 = \mu_2$
$H_1 : \mu_1 \neq \mu_2$
p-value = 0.1120

14–29. p-value < 0.001 Reject H_0.

14–31. $H = 8.97$, p-value = 0.0120

14–33. $H = 29.61$ Reject H_0. $C_{KW} = 11.68$

14–35. $H = 12.37$, p-value = 0.002

14–39. The three managers are not equally effective.

14–41. No, the 4 baking processes are not equally good.

14–43. $n = 9$, $r_s = 0.9289$ Reject H_0.

14–45. $\chi^2 = 0.586$ Do not reject H_0.

14–47. $\chi^2 = 12.193$ Reject H_0.

14–49. $\chi^2 = 6.94$ Do not reject H_0 at $\alpha = 0.05$

14–51. $\chi^2 = 50.991$ Reject H_0.

14–53. $\chi^2 = 109.56$ Reject H_0.

14–55. $\chi^2 = 16.15$ Reject H_0.

14–57. $\chi^2 = 24.36$ Reject H_0.

14–59. $\chi^2 = 94.394$ Reject H_0.

14–61. $\Sigma - = 32.5$
$\Sigma + = 72.5$
2-tailed p-value > 0.10

14–63. −0.125. Do not reject H_0

14–67. $\chi^2 = 51.6836$ Reject H_0.

Chapter 15

15–1. 0.02531, 0.46544, 0.27247, 0.17691, 0.05262, 0.00697, 0.00028. Credible set is [0.2, 0.4].

15–3. 0.0126, 0.5829, 0.3658, 0.0384, 0.0003, 0.0000

15–5. 0.1129, 0.2407, 0.2275, 0.2909, 0.0751, 0.0529

15–7. 0.0633, 0.2216, 0.2928, 0.2364, 0.1286, 0.0465, 0.0099, 0.0009, 0.0000

15–9. 0.0071, 0.0638, 0.3001, 0.3962, 0.1929, 0.0399

15–11. Normal with mean 9,207.3 and standard deviation 61.58

15–13. Normal with mean 95.95 and standard deviation 0.312

15–15. [5892.15, 6553.12]

15–17. Governor: D (largest s.d.) ARCO expert: C (smallest s.d.) Most embarrassed: C

15–23. Expected payoff = $10.55 million. Buy the ad.

15–25. Expected payoff = $405 million. Develop the drug.

15–27. Optimal decision is *long*–change if possible. Expected profit is $698,000

15–29. Optimal decision is invest in wheat futures. Expected value is $3,040

15–33. Expected payoff = $11.19 million. Do the test.

15–35. Sell watches, no testing: expected payoff = $20,000 Sell watches, with testing: expected payoff = $127,200 No change in in-flight sales: expected payoff = $700,000 Do not change their in-flight sales.

15–37. Test and follow the test's recommendation. E(payoff) = $587,000

15–39. A utility function is a value-of-money function of an individual.

15–47. EVPI = $290,000. Buy information if it is perfect.

15–49. 0.01142, 0.30043, 0.35004, 0.27066, 0.05561, 0.01184

15–51. 0.0026, 0.3844, 0.4589, 0.1480, 0.0060, 0.0001

15–55. [25649.75, 27416.22]

15–61. 1,400 < 3,000: a risk taker

15–63. Merge; E(payoff) = $2.45 million

15–65. EVPI = $1.125 million

15–67. Hire candidate A

On the CD

Chapter 16

16–1. *a.* $\bar{x}_{st} = 33.48\%$
  b. S.D. = 0.823%
  c. [31.87, 35.09]

16–3. *a.* $\bar{x}_{st} = \$40.01$
  b. S.D. = 0.6854
  c. [38.88, 41.14]
  d. Data has many zero values

16–5. $35,604.5 C.I. = [30,969.19, 40,239.87]

16–9. *a–c.* All no. Clusters need to be randomly chosen.
  d. Consider the companies as strata, ships as clusters. Randomly draw clusters from the strata.

16–11. Arrange elements in a circle, randomly choose a number from 1 to 28, and then add 28 to element number until you have a sample of 30 sales.

16–13. If k is a multiple of 7, we would sample on the same day for different weeks and bias the results due to weekly sales cycles.

16–17. Yes, with each vehicle a cluster.

16–19. OK unless a nonnegligible fraction of the businesses in the community are unlisted in the Yellow Pages.

16–21. [0.055, 0.091]

16–25. Sample about 109 children, 744 young adults, 147 older people.

16–27. Regression and ratio estimators

16–29. No; benefits are not substantial when the number of strata is much greater than 6. Combine some.

Chapter 17

17–1. Statistically classifying elements into one of several groups.

17–3. Classify as default.

17–7. Used the information in a Bayesian formulation of a discriminant function, using $P(G)$, $P(D|G)$, leading to $P(G|D)$

17–9. Group 3

17–11. The discriminant function is not statistically significant and should not be used.

17–13. 5 functions; some may not be significant

17–19. VARIMAX maximizes the sum of the variances of the loadings in the factor matrix. Other rotation methods are QUARTIMAX and EQUIMAX.

17–21. Factor 1 is price items, factor 2 is retailing/selling, factor 3 is advertising, and factor 4 is negative (or opposite) of product ratings.

17–23. Pricing policies: associate with factor 2; communality = 0.501. Record and reporting procedures: associate with factor 2; commonality = 0.077

17–27. 3 functions

17–31. Not a worthwhile result since the dimensionality has not been reduced.

17–33. Communality of a variable

17–37. Wilks' $\lambda = 0.412$ $F(3,21) = 9.987$ (p-value = 0.000) Production cost p-value = 0.009. Number of sponsors p-value = 0.066 (n.s.). Promotions p-value = 0.004. Discriminant function coefficients: production cost = 0.945, promotions = 0.996. 84% correct prediction.

Statistical Tables

TABLE 1 Cumulative Binomial Distribution

$$F(x) = P(X \le x) = \sum_{i=0}^{x} \binom{n}{i} p^i(1-p)^{n-i}$$

Example: if $p = 0.10$, $n = 5$, and $x = 2$, then $F(x) = 0.991$

n	x	.01	.05	.10	.20	.30	.40	.50	.60	.70	.80	.90	.95	.99
5	0	.951	.774	.590	.328	.168	.078	.031	.010	.002	.000	.000	.000	.000
	1	.999	.977	.919	.737	.528	.337	.187	.087	.031	.007	.000	.000	.000
	2	1.000	.999	.991	.942	.837	.683	.500	.317	.163	.058	.009	.001	.000
	3	1.000	1.000	1.000	.993	.969	.913	.813	.663	.472	.263	.081	.023	.001
	4	1.000	1.000	1.000	1.000	.998	.990	.969	.922	.832	.672	.410	.226	.049
6	0	.941	.735	.531	.262	.118	.047	.016	.004	.001	.000	.000	.000	.000
	1	.999	.967	.886	.655	.420	.233	.109	.041	.011	.002	.000	.000	.000
	2	1.000	.998	.984	.901	.744	.544	.344	.179	.070	.017	.001	.000	.000
	3	1.000	1.000	.999	.983	.930	.821	.656	.456	.256	.099	.016	.002	.000
	4	1.000	1.000	1.000	.998	.989	.959	.891	.767	.580	.345	.114	.033	.001
	5	1.000	1.000	1.000	1.000	.999	.996	.984	.953	.882	.738	.469	.265	.059
7	0	.932	.698	.478	.210	.082	.028	.008	.002	.000	.000	.000	.000	.000
	1	.998	.956	.850	.577	.329	.159	.063	.019	.004	.000	.000	.000	.000
	2	1.000	.996	.974	.852	.647	.420	.227	.096	.029	.005	.000	.000	.000
	3	1.000	1.000	.997	.967	.874	.710	.500	.290	.126	.033	.003	.000	.000
	4	1.000	1.000	1.000	.995	.971	.904	.773	.580	.353	.148	.026	.004	.000
	5	1.000	1.000	1.000	1.000	.996	.981	.937	.841	.671	.423	.150	.044	.002
	6	1.000	1.000	1.000	1.000	1.000	.998	.992	.972	.918	.790	.522	.302	.068
8	0	.923	.663	.430	.168	.058	.017	.004	.001	.000	.000	.000	.000	.000
	1	.997	.943	.813	.503	.255	.106	.035	.009	.001	.000	.000	.000	.000
	2	1.000	.994	.962	.797	.552	.315	.145	.050	.011	.001	.000	.000	.000
	3	1.000	1.000	.995	.944	.806	.594	.363	.174	.058	.010	.000	.000	.000
	4	1.000	1.000	1.000	.990	.942	.826	.637	.406	.194	.056	.005	.000	.000
	5	1.000	1.000	1.000	.999	.989	.950	.855	.685	.448	.203	.038	.006	.000
	6	1.000	1.000	1.000	1.000	.999	.991	.965	.894	.745	.497	.187	.057	.003
	7	1.000	1.000	1.000	1.000	1.000	.999	.996	.983	.942	.832	.570	.337	.077
9	0	.914	.630	.387	.134	.040	.010	.002	.000	.000	.000	.000	.000	.000
	1	.997	.929	.775	.436	.196	.071	.020	.004	.000	.000	.000	.000	.000
	2	1.000	.992	.947	.738	.463	.232	.090	.025	.004	.000	.000	.000	.000
	3	1.000	.999	.992	.914	.730	.483	.254	.099	.025	.003	.000	.000	.000
	4	1.000	1.000	.999	.980	.901	.733	.500	.267	.099	.020	.001	.000	.000
	5	1.000	1.000	1.000	.997	.975	.901	.746	.517	.270	.086	.008	.001	.000
	6	1.000	1.000	1.000	1.000	.996	.975	.910	.768	.537	.262	.053	.008	.000
	7	1.000	1.000	1.000	1.000	1.000	.996	.980	.929	.804	.564	.225	.071	.003
	8	1.000	1.000	1.000	1.000	1.000	1.000	.998	.990	.960	.866	.613	.370	.086
10	0	.904	.599	.349	.107	.028	.006	.001	.000	.000	.000	.000	.000	.000
	1	.996	.914	.736	.376	.149	.046	.011	.002	.000	.000	.000	.000	.000
	2	1.000	.988	.930	.678	.383	.167	.055	.012	.002	.000	.000	.000	.000
	3	1.000	.999	.987	.879	.650	.382	.172	.055	.011	.001	.000	.000	.000
	4	1.000	1.000	.998	.967	.850	.633	.377	.166	.047	.006	.000	.000	.000
	5	1.000	1.000	1.000	.994	.953	.834	.623	.367	.150	.033	.002	.000	.000
	6	1.000	1.000	1.000	.999	.989	.945	.828	.618	.350	.121	.013	.001	.000

TABLE 1 *(continued)*   Cumulative Binomial Distribution

n	x	.01	.05	.10	.20	.30	.40	.50	.60	.70	.80	.90	.95	.99
	7	1.000	1.000	1.000	1.000	.998	.988	.945	.833	.617	.322	.070	.012	.000
	8	1.000	1.000	1.000	1.000	1.000	.998	.989	.954	.851	.624	.264	.086	.004
	9	1.000	1.000	1.000	1.000	1.000	1.000	.999	.994	.972	.893	.651	.401	.096
15	0	.860	.463	.206	.035	.005	.000	.000	.000	.000	.000	.000	.000	.000
	1	.990	.829	.549	.167	.035	.005	.000	.000	.000	.000	.000	.000	.000
	2	1.000	.964	.816	.398	.127	.027	.004	.000	.000	.000	.000	.000	.000
	3	1.000	.995	.944	.648	.297	.091	.018	.002	.000	.000	.000	.000	.000
	4	1.000	.999	.987	.836	.515	.217	.059	.009	.001	.000	.000	.000	.000
	5	1.000	1.000	.998	.939	.722	.403	.151	.034	.004	.000	.000	.000	.000
	6	1.000	1.000	1.000	.982	.869	.610	.304	.095	.015	.001	.000	.000	.000
	7	1.000	1.000	1.000	.996	.950	.787	.500	.213	.050	.004	.000	.000	.000
	8	1.000	1.000	1.000	.999	.985	.905	.696	.390	.131	.018	.000	.000	.000
	9	1.000	1.000	1.000	1.000	.996	.966	.849	.597	.278	.061	.002	.000	.000
	10	1.000	1.000	1.000	1.000	.999	.991	.941	.783	.485	.164	.013	.001	.000
	11	1.000	1.000	1.000	1.000	1.000	.998	.982	.909	.703	.352	.056	.005	.000
	12	1.000	1.000	1.000	1.000	1.000	1.000	.996	.973	.873	.602	.184	.036	.000
	13	1.000	1.000	1.000	1.000	1.000	1.000	1.000	.995	.965	.833	.451	.171	.010
	14	1.000	1.000	1.000	1.000	1.000	1.000	1.000	1.000	.995	.965	.794	.537	.140
20	0	.818	.358	.122	.012	.001	.000	.000	.000	.000	.000	.000	.000	.000
	1	.983	.736	.392	.069	.008	.001	.000	.000	.000	.000	.000	.000	.000
	2	.999	.925	.677	.206	.035	.004	.000	.000	.000	.000	.000	.000	.000
	3	1.000	.984	.867	.411	.107	.016	.001	.000	.000	.000	.000	.000	.000
	4	1.000	.997	.957	.630	.238	.051	.006	.000	.000	.000	.000	.000	.000
	5	1.000	1.000	.989	.804	.416	.126	.021	.002	.000	.000	.000	.000	.000
	6	1.000	1.000	.998	.913	.608	.250	.058	.006	.000	.000	.000	.000	.000
	7	1.000	1.000	1.000	.968	.772	.416	.132	.021	.001	.000	.000	.000	.000
	8	1.000	1.000	1.000	.990	.887	.596	.252	.057	.005	.000	.000	.000	.000
	9	1.000	1.000	1.000	.997	.952	.755	.412	.128	.017	.001	.000	.000	.000
	10	1.000	1.000	1.000	.999	.983	.872	.588	.245	.048	.003	.000	.000	.000
	11	1.000	1.000	1.000	1.000	.995	.943	.748	.404	.113	.010	.000	.000	.000
	12	1.000	1.000	1.000	1.000	.999	.979	.868	.584	.228	.032	.000	.000	.000
	13	1.000	1.000	1.000	1.000	1.000	.994	.942	.750	.392	.087	.002	.000	.000
	14	1.000	1.000	1.000	1.000	1.000	.998	.979	.874	.584	.196	.011	.000	.000
	15	1.000	1.000	1.000	1.000	1.000	1.000	.994	.949	.762	.370	.043	.003	.000
	16	1.000	1.000	1.000	1.000	1.000	1.000	.999	.984	.893	.589	.133	.016	.000
	17	1.000	1.000	1.000	1.000	1.000	1.000	1.000	.996	.965	.794	.323	.075	.001
	18	1.000	1.000	1.000	1.000	1.000	1.000	1.000	.999	.992	.931	.608	.264	.017
	19	1.000	1.000	1.000	1.000	1.000	1.000	1.000	1.000	.999	.988	.878	.642	.182
25	0	.778	.277	.072	.004	.000	.000	.000	.000	.000	.000	.000	.000	.000
	1	.974	.642	.271	.027	.002	.000	.000	.000	.000	.000	.000	.000	.000
	2	.998	.873	.537	.098	.009	.000	.000	.000	.000	.000	.000	.000	.000
	3	1.000	.966	.764	.234	.033	.002	.000	.000	.000	.000	.000	.000	.000
	4	1.000	.993	.902	.421	.090	.009	.000	.000	.000	.000	.000	.000	.000
	5	1.000	.999	.967	.617	.193	.029	.002	.000	.000	.000	.000	.000	.000
	6	1.000	1.000	.991	.780	.341	.074	.007	.000	.000	.000	.000	.000	.000
	7	1.000	1.000	.998	.891	.512	.154	.022	.001	.000	.000	.000	.000	.000
	8	1.000	1.000	1.000	.953	.677	.274	.054	.004	.000	.000	.000	.000	.000
	9	1.000	1.000	1.000	.983	.811	.425	.115	.013	.000	.000	.000	.000	.000
	10	1.000	1.000	1.000	.994	.902	.586	.212	.034	.002	.000	.000	.000	.000
	11	1.000	1.000	1.000	.998	.956	.732	.345	.078	.006	.000	.000	.000	.000

TABLE 1 *(concluded)*   Cumulative Binomial Distribution

								p						
n	x	.01	.05	.10	.20	.30	.40	.50	.60	.70	.80	.90	.95	.99
	12	1.000	1.000	1.000	1.000	.983	.846	.500	.154	.017	.000	.000	.000	.000
	13	1.000	1.000	1.000	1.000	.994	.922	.655	.268	.044	.002	.000	.000	.000
	14	1.000	1.000	1.000	1.000	.998	.966	.788	.414	.098	.006	.000	.000	.000
	15	1.000	1.000	1.000	1.000	1.000	.987	.885	.575	.189	.017	.000	.000	.000
	16	1.000	1.000	1.000	1.000	1.000	.996	.946	.726	.323	.047	.000	.000	.000
	17	1.000	1.000	1.000	1.000	1.000	.999	.978	.846	.488	.109	.002	.000	.000
	18	1.000	1.000	1.000	1.000	1.000	1.000	.993	.926	.659	.220	.009	.000	.000
	19	1.000	1.000	1.000	1.000	1.000	1.000	.998	.971	.807	.383	.033	.001	.000
	20	1.000	1.000	1.000	1.000	1.000	1.000	1.000	.991	.910	.579	.098	.007	.000
	21	1.000	1.000	1.000	1.000	1.000	1.000	1.000	.998	.967	.766	.236	.034	.000
	22	1.000	1.000	1.000	1.000	1.000	1.000	1.000	1.000	.991	.902	.463	.127	.002
	23	1.000	1.000	1.000	1.000	1.000	1.000	1.000	1.000	.998	.973	.729	.358	.026
	24	1.000	1.000	1.000	1.000	1.000	1.000	1.000	1.000	1.000	.996	.928	.723	.222

TABLE 2   Areas of the Standard Normal Distribution

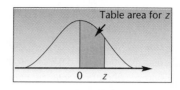

The table areas are probabilities that the standard normal random variable is between 0 and z.

Second Decimal Place in z

z	0.00	0.01	0.02	0.03	0.04	0.05	0.06	0.07	0.08	0.09
0.0	0.0000	0.0040	0.0080	0.0120	0.0160	0.0199	0.0239	0.0279	0.0319	0.0359
0.1	0.0398	0.0438	0.0478	0.0517	0.0557	0.0596	0.0636	0.0675	0.0714	0.0753
0.2	0.0793	0.0832	0.0871	0.0910	0.0948	0.0987	0.1026	0.1064	0.1103	0.1141
0.3	0.1179	0.1217	0.1255	0.1293	0.1331	0.1368	0.1406	0.1443	0.1480	0.1517
0.4	0.1554	0.1591	0.1628	0.1664	0.1700	0.1736	0.1772	0.1808	0.1844	0.1879
0.5	0.1915	0.1950	0.1985	0.2019	0.2054	0.2088	0.2123	0.2157	0.2190	0.2224
0.6	0.2257	0.2291	0.2324	0.2357	0.2389	0.2422	0.2454	0.2486	0.2517	0.2549
0.7	0.2580	0.2611	0.2642	0.2673	0.2704	0.2734	0.2764	0.2794	0.2823	0.2852
0.8	0.2881	0.2910	0.2939	0.2967	0.2995	0.3023	0.3051	0.3078	0.3106	0.3133
0.9	0.3159	0.3186	0.3212	0.3238	0.3264	0.3289	0.3315	0.3340	0.3365	0.3389
1.0	0.3413	0.3438	0.3461	0.3485	0.3508	0.3531	0.3554	0.3577	0.3599	0.3621
1.1	0.3643	0.3665	0.3686	0.3708	0.3729	0.3749	0.3770	0.3790	0.3810	0.3830
1.2	0.3849	0.3869	0.3888	0.3907	0.3925	0.3944	0.3962	0.3980	0.3997	0.4015
1.3	0.4032	0.4049	0.4066	0.4082	0.4099	0.4115	0.4131	0.4147	0.4162	0.4177
1.4	0.4192	0.4207	0.4222	0.4236	0.4251	0.4265	0.4279	0.4292	0.4306	0.4319
1.5	0.4332	0.4345	0.4357	0.4370	0.4382	0.4394	0.4406	0.4418	0.4429	0.4441
1.6	0.4452	0.4463	0.4474	0.4484	0.4495	0.4505	0.4515	0.4525	0.4535	0.4545
1.7	0.4554	0.4564	0.4573	0.4582	0.4591	0.4599	0.4608	0.4616	0.4625	0.4633
1.8	0.4641	0.4649	0.4656	0.4664	0.4671	0.4678	0.4686	0.4693	0.4699	0.4706
1.9	0.4713	0.4719	0.4726	0.4732	0.4738	0.4744	0.4750	0.4756	0.4761	0.4767
2.0	0.4772	0.4778	0.4783	0.4788	0.4793	0.4798	0.4803	0.4808	0.4812	0.4817
2.1	0.4821	0.4826	0.4830	0.4834	0.4838	0.4842	0.4846	0.4850	0.4854	0.4857
2.2	0.4861	0.4864	0.4868	0.4871	0.4875	0.4878	0.4881	0.4884	0.4887	0.4890
2.3	0.4893	0.4896	0.4898	0.4901	0.4904	0.4906	0.4909	0.4911	0.4913	0.4916
2.4	0.4918	0.4920	0.4922	0.4925	0.4927	0.4929	0.4931	0.4932	0.4934	0.4936
2.5	0.4938	0.4940	0.4941	0.4943	0.4945	0.4946	0.4948	0.4949	0.4951	0.4952
2.6	0.4953	0.4955	0.4956	0.4957	0.4959	0.4960	0.4961	0.4962	0.4963	0.4964
2.7	0.4965	0.4966	0.4967	0.4968	0.4969	0.4970	0.4971	0.4972	0.4973	0.4974
2.8	0.4974	0.4975	0.4976	0.4977	0.4977	0.4978	0.4979	0.4979	0.4980	0.4981
2.9	0.4981	0.4982	0.4982	0.4983	0.4984	0.4984	0.4985	0.4985	0.4986	0.4986
3.0	0.4987	0.4987	0.4987	0.4988	0.4988	0.4989	0.4989	0.4989	0.4990	0.4990
3.1	0.4990	0.4991	0.4991	0.4991	0.4992	0.4992	0.4992	0.4992	0.4993	0.4993
3.2	0.4993	0.4993	0.4994	0.4994	0.4994	0.4994	0.4994	0.4995	0.4995	0.4995
3.3	0.4995	0.4995	0.4995	0.4996	0.4996	0.4996	0.4996	0.4996	0.4996	0.4997
3.4	0.4997	0.4997	0.4997	0.4997	0.4997	0.4997	0.4997	0.4997	0.4997	0.4998
3.5	0.4998									
4.0	0.49997									
4.5	0.499997									
5.0	0.4999997									
6.0	0.49999999									

TABLE 3 Critical Values of the _t_ Distribution

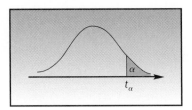

Degrees of Freedom	$t_{.100}$	$t_{.050}$	$t_{.025}$	$t_{.010}$	$t_{.005}$
1	3.078	6.314	12.706	31.821	63.657
2	1.886	2.920	4.303	6.965	9.925
3	1.638	2.353	3.182	4.541	5.841
4	1.533	2.132	2.776	3.747	4.604
5	1.476	2.015	2.571	3.365	4.032
6	1.440	1.943	2.447	3.143	3.707
7	1.415	1.895	2.365	2.998	3.499
8	1.397	1.860	2.306	2.896	3.355
9	1.383	1.833	2.262	2.821	3.250
10	1.372	1.812	2.228	2.764	3.169
11	1.363	1.796	2.201	2.718	3.106
12	1.356	1.782	2.179	2.681	3.055
13	1.350	1.771	2.160	2.650	3.012
14	1.345	1.761	2.145	2.624	2.977
15	1.341	1.753	2.131	2.602	2.947
16	1.337	1.746	2.120	2.583	2.921
17	1.333	1.740	2.110	2.567	2.898
18	1.330	1.734	2.101	2.552	2.878
19	1.328	1.729	2.093	2.539	2.861
20	1.325	1.725	2.086	2.528	2.845
21	1.323	1.721	2.080	2.518	2.831
22	1.321	1.717	2.074	2.508	2.819
23	1.319	1.714	2.069	2.500	2.807
24	1.318	1.711	2.064	2.492	2.797
25	1.316	1.708	2.060	2.485	2.787
26	1.315	1.706	2.056	2.479	2.779
27	1.314	1.703	2.052	2.473	2.771
28	1.313	1.701	2.048	2.467	2.763
29	1.311	1.699	2.045	2.462	2.756
30	1.310	1.697	2.042	2.457	2.750
40	1.303	1.684	2.021	2.423	2.704
60	1.296	1.671	2.000	2.390	2.660
120	1.289	1.658	1.980	2.358	2.617
∞	1.282	1.645	1.960	2.326	2.576

Source: M. Merrington, "Table of Percentage Points of the _t_-Distribution," _Biometrika_ 32 (1941), p. 300.
Reproduced by permission of the _Biometrika_ trustees.

TABLE 4 Critical Values of the Chi-Square Distribution

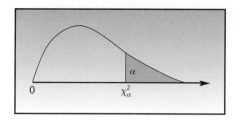

Degrees of Freedom	$\chi^2_{.995}$	$\chi^2_{.990}$	$\chi^2_{.975}$	$\chi^2_{.950}$	$\chi^2_{.900}$
1	0.0000393	0.0001571	0.0009821	0.0039321	0.0157908
2	0.0100251	0.0201007	0.0506356	0.102587	0.210720
3	0.0717212	0.114832	0.215795	0.351846	0.584375
4	0.206990	0.297110	0.484419	0.710721	1.063623
5	0.411740	0.554300	0.831211	1.145476	1.61031
6	0.675727	0.872085	1.237347	1.63539	2.20413
7	0.989265	1.239043	1.68987	2.16735	2.83311
8	1.344419	1.646482	2.17973	2.73264	3.48954
9	1.734926	2.087912	2.70039	3.32511	4.16816
10	2.15585	2.55821	3.24697	3.94030	4.86518
11	2.60321	3.05347	3.81575	4.57481	5.57779
12	3.07382	3.57056	4.40379	5.22603	6.30380
13	3.56503	4.10691	5.00874	5.89186	7.04150
14	4.07468	4.66043	5.62872	6.57063	7.78953
15	4.60094	5.22935	6.26214	7.26094	8.54675
16	5.14224	5.81221	6.90766	7.96164	9.31223
17	5.69724	6.40776	7.56418	8.67176	10.0852
18	6.26481	7.01491	8.23075	9.39046	10.8649
19	6.84398	7.63273	8.90655	10.1170	11.6509
20	7.43386	8.26040	9.59083	10.8508	12.4426
21	8.03366	8.89720	10.28293	11.5913	13.2396
22	8.64272	9.54249	10.9823	12.3380	14.0415
23	9.26042	10.19567	11.6885	13.0905	14.8479
24	9.88623	10.8564	12.4011	13.8484	15.6587
25	10.5197	11.5240	13.1197	14.6114	16.4734
26	11.1603	12.1981	13.8439	15.3791	17.2919
27	11.8076	12.8786	14.5733	16.1513	18.1138
28	12.4613	13.5648	15.3079	16.9279	18.9392
29	13.1211	14.2565	16.0471	17.7083	19.7677
30	13.7867	14.9535	16.7908	18.4926	20.5992
40	20.7065	22.1643	24.4331	26.5093	29.0505
50	27.9907	29.7067	32.3574	34.7642	37.6886
60	35.5346	37.4848	40.4817	43.1879	46.4589
70	43.2752	45.4418	48.7576	51.7393	55.3290
80	51.1720	53.5400	57.1532	60.3915	64.2778
90	59.1963	61.7541	65.6466	69.1260	73.2912
100	67.3276	70.0648	74.2219	77.9295	82.3581

TABLE 4 *(concluded)*   Critical Values of the Chi-Square Distribution

Degrees of Freedom	$\chi^2_{.100}$	$\chi^2_{.050}$	$\chi^2_{.025}$	$\chi^2_{.010}$	$\chi^2_{.005}$
1	2.70554	3.84146	5.02389	6.63490	7.87944
2	4.60517	5.99147	7.37776	9.21034	10.5966
3	6.25139	7.81473	9.34840	11.3449	12.8381
4	7.77944	9.48773	11.1433	13.2767	14.8602
5	9.23635	11.0705	12.8325	15.0863	16.7496
6	10.6446	12.5916	14.4494	16.8119	18.5476
7	12.0170	14.0671	16.0128	18.4753	20.2777
8	13.3616	15.5073	17.5346	20.0902	21.9550
9	14.6837	16.9190	19.0228	21.6660	23.5893
10	15.9871	18.3070	20.4831	23.2093	25.1882
11	17.2750	19.6751	21.9200	24.7250	26.7569
12	18.5494	21.0261	23.3367	26.2170	28.2995
13	19.8119	22.3621	24.7356	27.6883	29.8194
14	21.0642	23.6848	26.1190	29.1413	31.3193
15	22.3072	24.9958	27.4884	30.5779	32.8013
16	23.5418	26.2962	28.8454	31.9999	34.2672
17	24.7690	27.5871	30.1910	33.4087	35.7185
18	25.9894	28.8693	31.5264	34.8053	37.1564
19	27.2036	30.1435	32.8523	36.1908	38.5822
20	28.4120	31.4104	34.1696	37.5662	39.9968
21	29.6151	32.6705	35.4789	38.9321	41.4010
22	30.8133	33.9244	36.7807	40.2894	42.7956
23	32.0069	35.1725	38.0757	41.6384	44.1813
24	33.1963	36.4151	39.3641	42.9798	45.5585
25	34.3816	37.6525	40.6465	44.3141	46.9278
26	35.5631	38.8852	41.9232	45.6417	48.2899
27	36.7412	40.1133	43.1944	46.9630	49.6449
28	37.9159	41.3372	44.4607	48.2782	50.9933
29	39.0875	42.5569	45.7222	49.5879	52.3356
30	40.2560	43.7729	46.9792	50.8922	53.6720
40	51.8050	55.7585	59.3417	63.6907	66.7659
50	63.1671	67.5048	71.4202	76.1539	79.4900
60	74.3970	79.0819	83.2976	88.3794	91.9517
70	85.5271	90.5312	95.0231	100.425	104.215
80	96.5782	101.879	106.629	112.329	116.321
90	107.565	113.145	118.136	124.116	128.299
100	118.498	124.342	129.561	135.807	140.169

Source: C. M. Thompson, "Tables of the Percentage Points of the χ^2-Distribution," *Biometrika* 32 (1941), pp. 188–89. Reproduced by permission of the *Biometrika* Trustees.

TABLE 5   Critical Values of the F Distribution for $\alpha = 0.10$

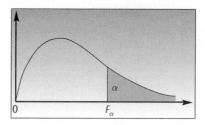

Denominator Degrees of Freedom (k_2)	Numerator Degrees of Freedom (k_1)								
	1	2	3	4	5	6	7	8	9
1	39.86	49.50	53.59	55.83	57.24	58.20	58.91	59.44	59.86
2	8.53	9.00	9.16	9.24	9.29	9.33	9.35	9.37	9.38
3	5.54	5.46	5.39	5.34	5.31	5.28	5.27	5.25	5.24
4	4.54	4.32	4.19	4.11	4.05	4.01	3.98	3.95	3.94
5	4.06	3.78	3.62	3.52	3.45	3.40	3.37	3.34	3.32
6	3.78	3.46	3.29	3.18	3.11	3.05	3.01	2.98	2.96
7	3.59	3.26	3.07	2.96	2.88	2.83	2.78	2.75	2.72
8	3.46	3.11	2.92	2.81	2.73	2.67	2.62	2.59	2.56
9	3.36	3.01	2.81	2.69	2.61	2.55	2.51	2.47	2.44
10	3.29	2.92	2.73	2.61	2.52	2.46	2.41	2.38	2.35
11	3.23	2.86	2.66	2.54	2.45	2.39	2.34	2.30	2.27
12	3.18	2.81	2.61	2.48	2.39	2.33	2.28	2.24	2.21
13	3.14	2.76	2.56	2.43	2.35	2.28	2.23	2.20	2.16
14	3.10	2.73	2.52	2.39	2.31	2.24	2.19	2.15	2.12
15	3.07	2.70	2.49	2.36	2.27	2.21	2.16	2.12	2.09
16	3.05	2.67	2.46	2.33	2.24	2.18	2.13	2.09	2.06
17	3.03	2.64	2.44	2.31	2.22	2.15	2.10	2.06	2.03
18	3.01	2.62	2.42	2.29	2.20	2.13	2.08	2.04	2.00
19	2.99	2.61	2.40	2.27	2.18	2.11	2.06	2.02	1.98
20	2.97	2.59	2.38	2.25	2.16	2.09	2.04	2.00	1.96
21	2.96	2.57	2.36	2.23	2.14	2.08	2.02	1.98	1.95
22	2.95	2.56	2.35	2.22	2.13	2.06	2.01	1.97	1.93
23	2.94	2.55	2.34	2.21	2.11	2.05	1.99	1.95	1.92
24	2.93	2.54	2.33	2.19	2.10	2.04	1.98	1.94	1.91
25	2.92	2.53	2.32	2.18	2.09	2.02	1.97	1.93	1.89
26	2.91	2.52	2.31	2.17	2.08	2.01	1.96	1.92	1.88
27	2.90	2.51	2.30	2.17	2.07	2.00	1.95	1.91	1.87
28	2.89	2.50	2.29	2.16	2.06	2.00	1.94	1.90	1.87
29	2.89	2.50	2.28	2.15	2.06	1.99	1.93	1.89	1.86
30	2.88	2.49	2.28	2.14	2.05	1.98	1.93	1.88	1.85
40	2.84	2.44	2.23	2.09	2.00	1.93	1.87	1.83	1.79
60	2.79	2.39	2.18	2.04	1.95	1.87	1.82	1.77	1.74
120	2.75	2.35	2.13	1.99	1.90	1.82	1.77	1.72	1.68
∞	2.71	2.30	2.08	1.94	1.85	1.77	1.72	1.67	1.63

TABLE 5 *(continued)*   Critical Values of the *F* Distribution for $\alpha = 0.10$

Denominator Degrees of Freedom (k_2)	Numerator Degrees of Freedom (k_1)									
	10	12	15	20	24	30	40	60	120	∞
1	60.19	60.71	61.22	61.74	62.00	62.26	62.53	62.79	63.06	63.33
2	9.39	9.41	9.42	9.44	9.45	9.46	9.47	9.47	9.48	9.49
3	5.23	5.22	5.20	5.18	5.18	5.17	5.16	5.15	5.14	5.13
4	3.92	3.90	3.87	3.84	3.83	3.82	3.80	3.79	3.78	3.76
5	3.30	3.27	3.24	3.21	3.19	3.17	3.16	3.14	3.12	3.10
6	2.94	2.90	2.87	2.84	2.82	2.80	2.78	2.76	2.74	2.72
7	2.70	2.67	2.63	2.59	2.58	2.56	2.54	2.51	2.49	2.47
8	2.54	2.50	2.46	2.42	2.40	2.38	2.36	2.34	2.32	2.29
9	2.42	2.38	2.34	2.30	2.28	2.25	2.23	2.21	2.18	2.16
10	2.32	2.28	2.24	2.20	2.18	2.16	2.13	2.11	2.08	2.06
11	2.25	2.21	2.17	2.12	2.10	2.08	2.05	2.03	2.00	1.97
12	2.19	2.15	2.10	2.06	2.04	2.01	1.99	1.96	1.93	1.90
13	2.14	2.10	2.05	2.01	1.98	1.96	1.93	1.90	1.88	1.85
14	2.10	2.05	2.01	1.96	1.94	1.91	1.89	1.86	1.83	1.80
15	2.06	2.02	1.97	1.92	1.90	1.87	1.85	1.82	1.79	1.76
16	2.03	1.99	1.94	1.89	1.87	1.84	1.81	1.78	1.75	1.72
17	2.00	1.96	1.91	1.86	1.84	1.81	1.78	1.75	1.72	1.69
18	1.98	1.93	1.89	1.84	1.81	1.78	1.75	1.72	1.69	1.66
19	1.96	1.91	1.86	1.81	1.79	1.76	1.73	1.70	1.67	1.63
20	1.94	1.89	1.84	1.79	1.77	1.74	1.71	1.68	1.64	1.61
21	1.92	1.87	1.83	1.78	1.75	1.72	1.69	1.66	1.62	1.59
22	1.90	1.86	1.81	1.76	1.73	1.70	1.67	1.64	1.60	1.57
23	1.89	1.84	1.80	1.74	1.72	1.69	1.66	1.62	1.59	1.55
24	1.88	1.83	1.78	1.73	1.70	1.67	1.64	1.61	1.57	1.53
25	1.87	1.82	1.77	1.72	1.69	1.66	1.63	1.59	1.56	1.52
26	1.86	1.81	1.76	1.71	1.68	1.65	1.61	1.58	1.54	1.50
27	1.85	1.80	1.75	1.70	1.67	1.64	1.60	1.57	1.53	1.49
28	1.84	1.79	1.74	1.69	1.66	1.63	1.59	1.56	1.52	1.48
29	1.83	1.78	1.73	1.68	1.65	1.62	1.58	1.55	1.51	1.47
30	1.82	1.77	1.72	1.67	1.64	1.61	1.57	1.54	1.50	1.46
40	1.76	1.71	1.66	1.61	1.57	1.54	1.51	1.47	1.42	1.38
60	1.71	1.66	1.60	1.54	1.51	1.48	1.44	1.40	1.35	1.29
120	1.65	1.60	1.55	1.48	1.45	1.41	1.37	1.32	1.26	1.19
∞	1.60	1.55	1.49	1.42	1.38	1.34	1.30	1.24	1.17	1.00

TABLE 5 *(continued)*   Critical Values of the *F* Distribution for $\alpha = 0.05$

Denominator Degrees of Freedom (k_2)	Numerator Degrees of Freedom (k_1)								
	1	2	3	4	5	6	7	8	9
1	161.4	199.5	215.7	224.6	230.2	234.0	236.8	238.9	240.5
2	18.51	19.00	19.16	19.25	19.30	19.33	19.35	19.37	19.38
3	10.13	9.55	9.28	9.12	9.01	8.94	8.89	8.85	8.81
4	7.71	6.94	6.59	6.39	6.26	6.16	6.09	6.04	6.00
5	6.61	5.79	5.41	5.19	5.05	4.95	4.88	4.82	4.77
6	5.99	5.14	4.76	4.53	4.39	4.28	4.21	4.15	4.10
7	5.59	4.74	4.35	4.12	3.97	3.87	3.79	3.73	3.68
8	5.32	4.46	4.07	3.84	3.69	3.58	3.50	3.44	3.39
9	5.12	4.26	3.86	3.63	3.48	3.37	3.29	3.23	3.18
10	4.96	4.10	3.71	3.48	3.33	3.22	3.14	3.07	3.02
11	4.84	3.98	3.59	3.36	3.20	3.09	3.01	2.95	2.90
12	4.75	3.89	3.49	3.26	3.11	3.00	2.91	2.85	2.80
13	4.67	3.81	3.41	3.18	3.03	2.92	2.83	2.77	2.71
14	4.60	3.74	3.34	3.11	2.96	2.85	2.76	2.70	2.65
15	4.54	3.68	3.29	3.06	2.90	2.79	2.71	2.64	2.59
16	4.49	3.63	3.24	3.01	2.85	2.74	2.66	2.59	2.54
17	4.45	3.59	3.20	2.96	2.81	2.70	2.61	2.55	2.49
18	4.41	3.55	3.16	2.93	2.77	2.66	2.58	2.51	2.46
19	4.38	3.52	3.13	2.90	2.74	2.63	2.54	2.48	2.42
20	4.35	3.49	3.10	2.87	2.71	2.60	2.51	2.45	2.39
21	4.32	3.47	3.07	2.84	2.68	2.57	2.49	2.42	2.37
22	4.30	3.44	3.05	2.82	2.66	2.55	2.46	2.40	2.34
23	4.28	3.42	3.03	2.80	2.64	2.53	2.44	2.37	2.32
24	4.26	3.40	3.01	2.78	2.62	2.51	2.42	2.36	2.30
25	4.24	3.39	2.99	2.76	2.60	2.49	2.40	2.34	2.28
26	4.23	3.37	2.98	2.74	2.59	2.47	2.39	2.32	2.27
27	4.21	3.35	2.96	2.73	2.57	2.46	2.37	2.31	2.25
28	4.20	3.34	2.95	2.71	2.56	2.45	2.36	2.29	2.24
29	4.18	3.33	2.93	2.70	2.55	2.43	2.35	2.28	2.22
30	4.17	3.32	2.92	2.69	2.53	2.42	2.33	2.27	2.21
40	4.08	3.23	2.84	2.61	2.45	2.34	2.25	2.18	2.12
60	4.00	3.15	2.76	2.53	2.37	2.25	2.17	2.10	2.04
120	3.92	3.07	2.68	2.45	2.29	2.17	2.09	2.02	1.96
∞	3.84	3.00	2.60	2.37	2.21	2.10	2.01	1.94	1.88

TABLE 5 *(continued)*   Critical Values of the *F* Distribution for $\alpha = 0.05$

Denominator Degrees of Freedom (k_2)	Numerator Degrees of Freedom (k_1)									
	10	12	15	20	24	30	40	60	120	∞
1	241.9	243.9	245.9	248.0	249.1	250.1	251.1	252.2	253.3	254.3
2	19.40	19.41	19.43	19.45	19.45	19.46	19.47	19.48	19.49	19.50
3	8.79	8.74	8.70	8.66	8.64	8.62	8.59	8.57	8.55	8.53
4	5.96	5.91	5.86	5.80	5.77	5.75	5.72	5.69	5.66	5.63
5	4.74	4.68	4.62	4.56	4.53	4.50	4.46	4.43	4.40	4.36
6	4.06	4.00	3.94	3.87	3.84	3.81	3.77	3.74	3.70	3.67
7	3.64	3.57	3.51	3.44	3.41	3.38	3.34	3.30	3.27	3.23
8	3.35	3.28	3.22	3.15	3.12	3.08	3.04	3.01	2.97	2.93
9	3.14	3.07	3.01	2.94	2.90	2.86	2.83	2.79	2.75	2.71
10	2.98	2.91	2.85	2.77	2.74	2.70	2.66	2.62	2.58	2.54
11	2.85	2.79	2.72	2.65	2.61	2.57	2.53	2.49	2.45	2.40
12	2.75	2.69	2.62	2.54	2.51	2.47	2.43	2.38	2.34	2.30
13	2.67	2.60	2.53	2.46	2.42	2.38	2.34	2.30	2.25	2.21
14	2.60	2.53	2.46	2.39	2.35	2.31	2.27	2.22	2.18	2.13
15	2.54	2.48	2.40	2.33	2.29	2.25	2.20	2.16	2.11	2.07
16	2.49	2.42	2.35	2.28	2.24	2.19	2.15	2.11	2.06	2.01
17	2.45	2.38	2.31	2.23	2.19	2.15	2.10	2.06	2.01	1.96
18	2.41	2.34	2.27	2.19	2.15	2.11	2.06	2.02	1.97	1.92
19	2.38	2.31	2.23	2.16	2.11	2.07	2.03	1.98	1.93	1.88
20	2.35	2.28	2.20	2.12	2.08	2.04	1.99	1.95	1.90	1.84
21	2.32	2.25	2.18	2.10	2.05	2.01	1.96	1.92	1.87	1.81
22	2.30	2.23	2.15	2.07	2.03	1.98	1.94	1.89	1.84	1.78
23	2.27	2.20	2.13	2.05	2.01	1.96	1.91	1.86	1.81	1.76
24	2.25	2.18	2.11	2.03	1.98	1.94	1.89	1.84	1.79	1.73
25	2.24	2.16	2.09	2.01	1.96	1.92	1.87	1.82	1.77	1.71
26	2.22	2.15	2.07	1.99	1.95	1.90	1.85	1.80	1.75	1.69
27	2.20	2.13	2.06	1.97	1.93	1.88	1.84	1.79	1.73	1.67
28	2.19	2.12	2.04	1.96	1.91	1.87	1.82	1.77	1.71	1.65
29	2.18	2.10	2.03	1.94	1.90	1.85	1.81	1.75	1.70	1.64
30	2.16	2.09	2.01	1.93	1.89	1.84	1.79	1.74	1.68	1.62
40	2.08	2.00	1.92	1.84	1.79	1.74	1.69	1.64	1.58	1.51
60	1.99	1.92	1.84	1.75	1.70	1.65	1.59	1.53	1.47	1.39
120	1.91	1.83	1.75	1.66	1.61	1.55	1.50	1.43	1.35	1.25
∞	1.83	1.75	1.67	1.57	1.52	1.46	1.39	1.32	1.22	1.00

TABLE 5 *(continued)*   Critical Values of the *F* Distribution for $\alpha = 0.025$

Denominator Degrees of Freedom (k_2)	Numerator Degrees of Freedom (k_1)								
	1	2	3	4	5	6	7	8	9
1	647.8	799.5	864.2	899.6	921.8	937.1	948.2	956.7	963.3
2	38.51	39.00	39.17	39.25	39.30	39.33	39.36	39.37	39.39
3	17.44	16.04	15.44	15.10	14.88	14.73	14.62	14.54	14.47
4	12.22	10.65	9.98	9.60	9.36	9.20	9.07	8.98	8.90
5	10.01	8.43	7.76	7.39	7.15	6.98	6.85	6.76	6.68
6	8.81	7.26	6.60	6.23	5.99	5.82	5.70	5.60	5.52
7	8.07	6.54	5.89	5.52	5.29	5.12	4.99	4.90	4.82
8	7.57	6.06	5.42	5.05	4.82	4.65	4.53	4.43	4.36
9	7.21	5.71	5.08	4.72	4.48	4.32	4.20	4.10	4.03
10	6.94	5.46	4.83	4.47	4.24	4.07	3.95	3.85	3.78
11	6.72	5.26	4.63	4.28	4.04	3.88	3.76	3.66	3.59
12	6.55	5.10	4.47	4.12	3.89	3.73	3.61	3.51	3.44
13	6.41	4.97	4.35	4.00	3.77	3.60	3.48	3.39	3.31
14	6.30	4.86	4.24	3.89	3.66	3.50	3.38	3.29	3.21
15	6.20	4.77	4.15	3.80	3.58	3.41	3.29	3.20	3.12
16	6.12	4.69	4.08	3.73	3.50	3.34	3.22	3.12	3.05
17	6.04	4.62	4.01	3.66	3.44	3.28	3.16	3.06	2.98
18	5.98	4.56	3.95	3.61	3.38	3.22	3.10	3.01	2.93
19	5.92	4.51	3.90	3.56	3.33	3.17	3.05	2.96	2.88
20	5.87	4.46	3.86	3.51	3.29	3.13	3.01	2.91	2.84
21	5.83	4.42	3.82	3.48	3.25	3.09	2.97	2.87	2.80
22	5.79	4.38	3.78	3.44	3.22	3.05	2.93	2.84	2.76
23	5.75	4.35	3.75	3.41	3.18	3.02	2.90	2.81	2.73
24	5.72	4.32	3.72	3.38	3.15	2.99	2.87	2.78	2.70
25	5.69	4.29	3.69	3.35	3.13	2.97	2.85	2.75	2.68
26	5.66	4.27	3.67	3.33	3.10	2.94	2.82	2.73	2.65
27	5.63	4.24	3.65	3.31	3.08	2.92	2.80	2.71	2.63
28	5.61	4.22	3.63	3.29	3.06	2.90	2.78	2.69	2.61
29	5.59	4.20	3.61	3.27	3.04	2.88	2.76	2.67	2.59
30	5.57	4.18	3.59	3.25	3.03	2.87	2.75	2.65	2.57
40	5.42	4.05	3.46	3.13	2.90	2.74	2.62	2.53	2.45
60	5.29	3.93	3.34	3.01	2.79	2.63	2.51	2.41	2.33
120	5.15	3.80	3.23	2.89	2.67	2.52	2.39	2.30	2.22
∞	5.02	3.69	3.12	2.79	2.57	2.41	2.29	2.19	2.11

TABLE 5 *(continued)*   Critical Values of the F Distribution for $\alpha = 0.025$

Denominator Degrees of Freedom (k_2)	Numerator Degrees of Freedom (k_1)									
	10	12	15	20	24	30	40	60	120	∞
1	968.6	976.7	984.9	993.1	997.2	1001	1006	1010	1014	1018
2	39.40	39.41	39.43	39.45	39.46	39.46	39.47	39.48	39.49	39.50
3	14.42	14.34	14.25	14.17	14.12	14.08	14.04	13.99	13.95	13.90
4	8.84	8.75	8.66	8.56	8.51	8.46	8.41	8.36	8.31	8.26
5	6.62	6.52	6.43	6.33	6.28	6.23	6.18	6.12	6.07	6.02
6	5.46	5.37	5.27	5.17	5.12	5.07	5.01	4.96	4.90	4.85
7	4.76	4.67	4.57	4.47	4.42	4.36	4.31	4.25	4.20	4.14
8	4.30	4.20	4.10	4.00	3.95	3.89	3.84	3.78	3.73	3.67
9	3.96	3.87	3.77	3.67	3.61	3.56	3.51	3.45	3.39	3.33
10	3.72	3.62	3.52	3.42	3.37	3.31	3.26	3.20	3.14	3.08
11	3.53	3.43	3.33	3.23	3.17	3.12	3.06	3.00	2.94	2.88
12	3.37	3.28	3.18	3.07	3.02	2.96	2.91	2.85	2.79	2.72
13	3.25	3.15	3.05	2.95	2.89	2.84	2.78	2.72	2.66	2.60
14	3.15	3.05	2.95	2.84	2.79	2.73	2.67	2.61	2.55	2.49
15	3.06	2.96	2.86	2.76	2.70	2.64	2.59	2.52	2.46	2.40
16	2.99	2.89	2.79	2.68	2.63	2.57	2.51	2.45	2.38	2.32
17	2.92	2.82	2.72	2.62	2.56	2.50	2.44	2.38	2.32	2.25
18	2.87	2.77	2.67	2.56	2.50	2.44	2.38	2.32	2.26	2.19
19	2.82	2.72	2.62	2.51	2.45	2.39	2.33	2.27	2.20	2.13
20	2.77	2.68	2.57	2.46	2.41	2.35	2.29	2.22	2.16	2.09
21	2.73	2.64	2.53	2.42	2.37	2.31	2.25	2.18	2.11	2.04
22	2.70	2.60	2.50	2.39	2.33	2.27	2.21	2.14	2.08	2.00
23	2.67	2.57	2.47	2.36	2.30	2.24	2.18	2.11	2.04	1.97
24	2.64	2.54	2.44	2.33	2.27	2.21	2.15	2.08	2.01	1.94
25	2.61	2.51	2.41	2.30	2.24	2.18	2.12	2.05	1.98	1.91
26	2.59	2.49	2.39	2.28	2.22	2.16	2.09	2.03	1.95	1.88
27	2.57	2.47	2.36	2.25	2.19	2.13	2.07	2.00	1.93	1.85
28	2.55	2.45	2.34	2.23	2.17	2.11	2.05	1.98	1.91	1.83
29	2.53	2.43	2.32	2.21	2.15	2.09	2.03	1.96	1.89	1.81
30	2.51	2.41	2.31	2.20	2.14	2.07	2.01	1.94	1.87	1.79
40	2.39	2.29	2.18	2.07	2.01	1.94	1.88	1.80	1.72	1.64
60	2.27	2.17	2.06	1.94	1.88	1.82	1.74	1.67	1.58	1.48
120	2.16	2.05	1.94	1.82	1.76	1.69	1.61	1.53	1.43	1.31
∞	2.05	1.94	1.83	1.71	1.64	1.57	1.48	1.39	1.27	1.00

TABLE 5 *(continued)*　　Critical Values of the *F* Distribution for $\alpha = 0.01$

Denominator Degrees of Freedom (k_2)	Numerator Degrees of Freedom (k_1)								
	1	2	3	4	5	6	7	8	9
1	4,052	4,999.5	5,403	5,625	5,764	5,859	5,928	5,982	6,022
2	98.50	99.00	99.17	99.25	99.30	99.33	99.36	99.37	99.39
3	34.12	30.82	29.46	28.71	28.24	27.91	27.67	27.49	27.35
4	21.20	18.00	16.69	15.98	15.52	15.21	14.98	14.80	14.66
5	16.26	13.27	12.06	11.39	10.97	10.67	10.46	10.29	10.16
6	13.75	10.92	9.78	9.15	8.75	8.47	8.26	8.10	7.98
7	12.25	9.55	8.45	7.85	7.46	7.19	6.99	6.84	6.72
8	11.26	8.65	7.59	7.01	6.63	6.37	6.18	6.03	5.91
9	10.56	8.02	6.99	6.42	6.06	5.80	5.61	5.47	5.35
10	10.04	7.56	6.55	5.99	5.64	5.39	5.20	5.06	4.94
11	9.65	7.21	6.22	5.67	5.32	5.07	4.89	4.74	4.63
12	9.33	6.93	5.95	5.41	5.06	4.82	4.64	4.50	4.39
13	9.07	6.70	5.74	5.21	4.86	4.62	4.44	4.30	4.19
14	8.86	6.51	5.56	5.04	4.69	4.46	4.28	4.14	4.03
15	8.68	6.36	5.42	4.89	4.56	4.32	4.14	4.00	3.89
16	8.53	6.23	5.29	4.77	4.44	4.20	4.03	3.89	3.78
17	8.40	6.11	5.18	4.67	4.34	4.10	3.93	3.79	3.68
18	8.29	6.01	5.09	4.58	4.25	4.01	3.84	3.71	3.60
19	8.18	5.93	5.01	4.50	4.17	3.94	3.77	3.63	3.52
20	8.10	5.85	4.94	4.43	4.10	3.87	3.70	3.56	3.46
21	8.02	5.78	4.87	4.37	4.04	3.81	3.64	3.51	3.40
22	7.95	5.72	4.82	4.31	3.99	3.76	3.59	3.45	3.35
23	7.88	5.66	4.76	4.26	3.94	3.71	3.54	3.41	3.30
24	7.82	5.61	4.72	4.22	3.90	3.67	3.50	3.36	3.26
25	7.77	5.57	4.68	4.18	3.85	3.63	3.46	3.32	3.22
26	7.72	5.53	4.64	4.14	3.82	3.59	3.42	3.29	3.18
27	7.68	5.49	4.60	4.11	3.78	3.56	3.39	3.26	3.15
28	7.64	5.45	4.57	4.07	3.75	3.53	3.36	3.23	3.12
29	7.60	5.42	4.54	4.04	3.73	3.50	3.33	3.20	3.09
30	7.56	5.39	4.51	4.02	3.70	3.47	3.30	3.17	3.07
40	7.31	5.18	4.31	3.83	3.51	3.29	3.12	2.99	2.89
60	7.08	4.98	4.13	3.65	3.34	3.12	2.95	2.82	2.72
120	6.85	4.79	3.95	3.48	3.17	2.96	2.79	2.66	2.56
∞	6.63	4.61	3.78	3.32	3.02	2.80	2.64	2.51	2.41

TABLE 5 *(continued)*   Critical Values of the *F* Distribution for $\alpha = 0.01$

Denominator Degrees of Freedom (k_2)	Numerator Degrees of Freedom (k_1)									
	10	12	15	20	24	30	40	60	120	∞
1	6,056	6,106	6,157	6,209	6,235	6,261	6,287	6,313	6,339	6,366
2	99.40	99.42	99.43	99.45	99.46	99.47	99.47	99.48	99.49	99.50
3	27.23	27.05	26.87	26.69	26.60	26.50	26.41	26.32	26.22	26.13
4	14.55	14.37	14.20	14.02	13.93	13.84	13.75	13.65	13.56	13.46
5	10.05	9.89	9.72	9.55	9.47	9.38	9.29	9.20	9.11	9.02
6	7.87	7.72	7.56	7.40	7.31	7.23	7.14	7.06	6.97	6.88
7	6.62	6.47	6.31	6.16	6.07	5.99	5.91	5.82	5.74	5.65
8	5.81	5.67	5.52	5.36	5.28	5.20	5.12	5.03	4.95	4.86
9	5.26	5.11	4.96	4.81	4.73	4.65	4.57	4.48	4.40	4.31
10	4.85	4.71	4.56	4.41	4.33	4.25	4.17	4.08	4.00	3.91
11	4.54	4.40	4.25	4.10	4.02	3.94	3.86	3.78	3.69	3.60
12	4.30	4.16	4.01	3.86	3.78	3.70	3.62	3.54	3.45	3.36
13	4.10	3.96	3.82	3.66	3.59	3.51	3.43	3.34	3.25	3.17
14	3.94	3.80	3.66	3.51	3.43	3.35	3.27	3.18	3.09	3.00
15	3.80	3.67	3.52	3.37	3.29	3.21	3.13	3.05	2.96	2.87
16	3.69	3.55	3.41	3.26	3.18	3.10	3.02	2.93	2.84	2.75
17	3.59	3.46	3.31	3.16	3.08	3.00	2.92	2.83	2.75	2.65
18	3.51	3.37	3.23	3.08	3.00	2.92	2.84	2.75	2.66	2.57
19	3.43	3.30	3.15	3.00	2.92	2.84	2.76	2.67	2.58	2.49
20	3.37	3.23	3.09	2.94	2.86	2.78	2.69	2.61	2.52	2.42
21	3.31	3.17	3.03	2.88	2.80	2.72	2.64	2.55	2.46	2.36
22	3.26	3.12	2.98	2.83	2.75	2.67	2.58	2.50	2.40	2.31
23	3.21	3.07	2.93	2.78	2.70	2.62	2.54	2.45	2.35	2.26
24	3.17	3.03	2.89	2.74	2.66	2.58	2.49	2.40	2.31	2.21
25	3.13	2.99	2.85	2.70	2.62	2.54	2.45	2.36	2.27	2.17
26	3.09	2.96	2.81	2.66	2.58	2.50	2.42	2.33	2.23	2.13
27	3.06	2.93	2.78	2.63	2.55	2.47	2.38	2.29	2.20	2.10
28	3.03	2.90	2.75	2.60	2.52	2.44	2.35	2.26	2.17	2.06
29	3.00	2.87	2.73	2.57	2.49	2.41	2.33	2.23	2.14	2.03
30	2.98	2.84	2.70	2.55	2.47	2.39	2.30	2.21	2.11	2.01
40	2.80	2.66	2.52	2.37	2.29	2.20	2.11	2.02	1.92	1.80
60	2.63	2.50	2.35	2.20	2.12	2.03	1.94	1.84	1.73	1.60
120	2.47	2.34	2.19	2.03	1.95	1.86	1.76	1.66	1.53	1.38
∞	2.32	2.18	2.04	1.88	1.79	1.70	1.59	1.47	1.32	1.00

Source: M. Merrington and C. M. Thompson, "Tables of Percentage Points of the Inverted Beta (*F*)-Distribution," *Biometrika* 33 (1943), pp. 73–88. Reproduced by permission of the *Biometrika* Trustees.

TABLE 5A   The *F* Distribution for $\alpha = 0.05$ and $\alpha = 0.01$ for Many Possible Degrees of Freedom

Denominator Degrees of Freedom (k_2)	Numerator Degrees of Freedom (k_1)																							
	1	2	3	4	5	6	7	8	9	10	11	12	14	16	20	24	30	40	50	75	100	200	500	∞
1	161	200	216	225	230	234	237	239	241	242	243	244	245	246	248	249	250	251	252	253	253	254	254	254
	4,052	4,999	5,403	5,625	5,764	5,859	5,928	5,981	6,022	6,056	6,082	6,106	6,142	6,169	6,208	6,234	6,261	6,286	6,302	6,323	6,334	6,352	6,361	6,366
2	18.51	19.00	19.16	19.25	19.30	19.33	19.36	19.37	19.38	19.39	19.40	19.41	19.42	19.43	19.44	19.45	19.46	19.47	19.47	19.48	19.49	19.49	19.50	19.50
	98.49	99.00	99.17	99.25	99.30	99.33	99.36	99.37	99.39	99.40	99.41	99.42	99.43	99.44	99.45	99.46	99.47	99.48	99.48	99.49	99.49	99.49	99.50	99.50
3	10.13	9.55	9.28	9.12	9.01	8.94	8.88	8.84	8.81	8.78	8.76	8.74	8.71	8.69	8.66	8.64	8.62	8.60	8.58	8.57	8.56	8.54	8.54	8.53
	34.12	30.82	29.46	28.71	28.24	27.91	27.67	27.49	27.34	27.23	27.13	27.05	26.92	26.83	26.69	26.60	26.50	26.41	26.35	26.27	26.23	26.18	26.14	26.12
4	7.71	6.94	6.59	6.39	6.26	6.16	6.09	6.04	6.00	5.96	5.93	5.91	5.87	5.84	5.80	5.77	5.74	5.71	5.70	5.68	5.66	5.65	5.64	5.63
	21.20	18.00	16.69	15.98	15.52	15.21	14.98	14.80	14.66	14.54	14.45	14.37	14.24	14.15	14.02	13.93	13.83	13.74	13.69	13.61	13.57	13.52	13.48	13.46
5	6.61	5.79	5.41	5.19	5.05	4.95	4.88	4.82	4.78	4.74	4.70	4.68	4.64	4.60	4.56	4.53	4.50	4.46	4.44	4.42	4.40	4.38	4.37	4.36
	16.26	13.27	12.06	11.39	10.97	10.67	10.45	10.29	10.15	10.05	9.96	9.89	9.77	9.68	9.55	9.47	9.38	9.29	9.24	9.17	9.13	9.07	9.04	9.02
6	5.99	5.14	4.76	4.53	4.39	4.28	4.21	4.15	4.10	4.06	4.03	4.00	3.96	3.92	3.87	3.84	3.81	3.77	3.75	3.72	3.71	3.69	3.68	3.67
	13.74	10.92	9.78	9.15	8.75	8.47	8.26	8.10	7.98	7.87	7.79	7.72	7.60	7.52	7.39	7.31	7.23	7.14	7.09	7.02	6.99	6.94	6.90	6.88
7	5.59	4.74	4.35	4.12	3.97	3.87	3.79	3.73	3.68	3.63	3.60	3.57	3.52	3.49	3.44	3.41	3.38	3.34	3.32	3.29	3.28	3.25	3.24	3.23
	12.25	9.55	8.45	7.85	7.46	7.19	7.00	6.84	6.71	6.62	6.54	6.47	6.35	6.27	6.15	6.07	5.98	5.90	5.85	5.78	5.75	5.70	5.67	5.65
8	5.32	4.46	4.07	3.84	3.69	3.58	3.50	3.44	3.39	3.34	3.31	3.28	3.23	3.20	3.15	3.12	3.08	3.05	3.03	3.00	2.98	2.96	2.94	2.93
	11.26	8.65	7.59	7.01	6.63	6.37	6.19	6.03	5.91	5.82	5.74	5.67	5.56	5.48	5.36	5.28	5.20	5.11	5.06	5.00	4.96	4.91	4.88	4.86
9	5.12	4.26	3.86	3.63	3.48	3.37	3.29	3.23	3.18	3.13	3.10	3.07	3.02	2.98	2.93	2.90	2.86	2.82	2.80	2.77	2.76	2.73	2.72	2.71
	10.56	8.02	6.99	6.42	6.06	5.80	5.62	5.47	5.35	5.26	5.18	5.11	5.00	4.92	4.80	4.73	4.64	4.56	4.51	4.45	4.41	4.36	4.33	4.31
10	4.96	4.10	3.71	3.48	3.33	3.22	3.14	3.07	3.02	2.97	2.94	2.91	2.86	2.82	2.77	2.74	2.70	2.67	2.64	2.61	2.59	2.56	2.55	2.54
	10.04	7.56	6.55	5.99	5.64	5.39	5.21	5.06	4.95	4.85	4.78	4.71	4.60	4.52	4.41	4.33	4.25	4.17	4.12	4.05	4.01	3.96	3.93	3.91
11	4.84	3.98	3.59	3.36	3.20	3.09	3.01	2.95	2.90	2.86	2.82	2.79	2.74	2.70	2.65	2.61	2.57	2.53	2.50	2.47	2.45	2.42	2.41	2.40
	9.65	7.20	6.22	5.67	5.32	5.07	4.88	4.74	4.63	4.54	4.46	4.40	4.29	4.21	4.10	4.02	3.94	3.86	3.80	3.74	3.70	3.66	3.62	3.60
12	4.75	3.88	3.49	3.26	3.11	3.00	2.92	2.85	2.80	2.76	2.72	2.69	2.64	2.60	2.54	2.50	2.46	2.42	2.40	2.36	2.35	2.32	2.31	2.30
	9.33	6.93	5.95	5.41	5.06	4.82	4.65	4.50	4.39	4.30	4.22	4.16	4.05	3.98	3.86	3.78	3.70	3.61	3.56	3.49	3.46	3.41	3.38	3.36
13	4.67	3.80	3.41	3.18	3.02	2.92	2.84	2.77	2.72	2.67	2.63	2.60	2.55	2.51	2.46	2.42	2.38	2.34	2.32	2.28	2.26	2.24	2.22	2.21
	9.07	6.70	5.74	5.20	4.86	4.62	4.44	4.30	4.19	4.10	4.02	3.96	3.85	3.78	3.67	3.59	3.51	3.42	3.37	3.30	3.27	3.21	3.18	3.16

n																								
14	4.60	3.74	3.34	3.11	2.96	2.85	2.77	2.70	2.65	2.60	2.56	2.53	2.48	2.44	2.39	2.35	2.31	2.27	2.24	2.21	2.19	2.16	2.14	2.13
	8.86	6.51	5.56	5.03	4.69	4.46	4.28	4.14	4.03	3.94	3.86	3.80	3.70	3.62	3.51	3.43	3.34	3.26	3.21	3.14	3.11	3.06	3.02	3.00
15	4.54	3.68	3.29	3.06	2.90	2.79	2.70	2.64	2.59	2.55	2.51	2.48	2.43	2.39	2.33	2.29	2.25	2.21	2.18	2.15	2.12	2.10	2.08	2.07
	8.68	6.36	5.42	4.89	4.56	4.32	4.14	4.00	3.89	3.80	3.73	3.67	3.56	3.48	3.36	3.29	3.20	3.12	3.07	3.00	2.97	2.92	2.89	2.87
16	4.49	3.63	3.24	3.01	2.85	2.74	2.66	2.59	2.54	2.49	2.45	2.42	2.37	2.33	2.28	2.24	2.20	2.16	2.13	2.09	2.07	2.04	2.02	2.01
	8.53	6.23	5.29	4.77	4.44	4.20	4.03	3.89	3.78	3.69	3.61	3.55	3.45	3.37	3.25	3.18	3.10	3.01	2.96	2.90	2.86	2.80	2.77	2.75
17	4.45	3.59	3.20	2.96	2.81	2.70	2.62	2.55	2.50	2.45	2.41	2.38	2.33	2.29	2.23	2.19	2.15	2.11	2.08	2.04	2.02	1.99	1.97	1.96
	8.40	6.11	5.18	4.67	4.34	4.10	3.93	3.79	3.68	3.59	3.52	3.45	3.35	3.27	3.16	3.08	3.00	2.92	2.86	2.79	2.76	2.70	2.67	2.65
18	4.41	3.55	3.16	2.93	2.77	2.66	2.58	2.51	2.46	2.41	2.37	2.34	2.29	2.25	2.19	2.15	2.11	2.07	2.04	2.00	1.98	1.95	1.93	1.92
	8.28	6.01	5.09	4.58	4.25	4.01	3.85	3.71	3.60	3.51	3.44	3.37	3.27	3.19	3.07	3.00	2.91	2.83	2.78	2.71	2.68	2.62	2.59	2.57
19	4.38	3.52	3.13	2.90	2.74	2.63	2.55	2.48	2.43	2.38	2.34	2.31	2.26	2.21	2.15	2.11	2.07	2.02	2.00	1.96	1.94	1.91	1.90	1.88
	8.18	5.93	5.01	4.50	4.17	3.94	3.77	3.63	3.52	3.43	3.36	3.30	3.19	3.12	3.00	2.92	2.84	2.76	2.70	2.63	2.60	2.54	2.51	2.49
20	4.35	3.49	3.10	2.87	2.71	2.60	2.52	2.45	2.40	2.35	2.31	2.28	2.23	2.18	2.12	2.08	2.04	1.99	1.96	1.92	1.90	1.87	1.85	1.84
	8.10	5.85	4.94	4.43	4.10	3.87	3.71	3.56	3.45	3.37	3.30	3.23	3.13	3.05	2.94	2.86	2.77	2.69	2.63	2.56	2.53	2.47	2.44	2.42
21	4.32	3.47	3.07	2.84	2.68	2.57	2.49	2.42	2.37	2.32	2.28	2.25	2.20	2.15	2.09	2.05	2.00	1.96	1.93	1.89	1.87	1.84	1.82	1.81
	8.02	5.78	4.87	4.37	4.04	3.81	3.65	3.51	3.40	3.31	3.24	3.17	3.07	2.99	2.88	2.80	2.72	2.63	2.58	2.51	2.47	2.42	2.38	2.36
22	4.30	3.44	3.05	2.82	2.66	2.55	2.47	2.40	2.35	2.30	2.26	2.23	2.18	2.13	2.07	2.03	1.98	1.93	1.91	1.87	1.84	1.81	1.80	1.78
	7.94	5.72	4.82	4.31	3.99	3.76	3.59	3.45	3.35	3.26	3.18	3.12	3.02	2.94	2.83	2.75	2.67	2.58	2.53	2.46	2.42	2.37	2.33	2.31
23	4.28	3.42	3.03	2.80	2.64	2.53	2.45	2.38	2.32	2.28	2.24	2.20	2.14	2.10	2.04	2.00	1.96	1.91	1.88	1.84	1.82	1.79	1.77	1.76
	7.88	5.66	4.76	4.26	3.94	3.71	3.54	3.41	3.30	3.21	3.14	3.07	2.97	2.89	2.78	2.70	2.62	2.53	2.48	2.41	2.37	2.32	2.28	2.26
24	4.26	3.40	3.01	2.78	2.62	2.51	2.43	2.36	2.30	2.26	2.22	2.18	2.13	2.09	2.02	1.98	1.94	1.89	1.86	1.82	1.80	1.76	1.74	1.73
	7.82	5.61	4.72	4.22	3.90	3.67	3.50	3.36	3.25	3.17	3.09	3.03	2.93	2.85	2.74	2.66	2.58	2.49	2.44	2.36	2.33	2.27	2.23	2.21
25	4.24	3.38	2.99	2.76	2.60	2.49	2.41	2.34	2.28	2.24	2.20	2.16	2.11	2.06	2.00	1.96	1.92	1.87	1.84	1.80	1.77	1.74	1.72	1.71
	7.77	5.57	4.68	4.18	3.86	3.63	3.46	3.32	3.21	3.13	3.05	2.99	2.89	2.81	2.70	2.62	2.54	2.45	2.40	2.32	2.29	2.23	2.19	2.17
26	4.22	3.37	2.98	2.74	2.59	2.47	2.39	2.32	2.27	2.22	2.18	2.15	2.10	2.05	1.99	1.95	1.90	1.85	1.82	1.78	1.76	1.72	1.70	1.69
	7.72	5.53	4.64	4.14	3.82	3.59	3.42	3.29	3.17	3.09	3.02	2.96	2.86	2.77	2.66	2.58	2.50	2.41	2.36	2.28	2.25	2.19	2.15	2.13

TABLE 5A (continued) The F Distribution for $\alpha = 0.05$ and $\alpha = 0.01$ for Many Possible Degrees of Freedom

Denominator Degrees of Freedom (k_2)	Numerator Degrees of Freedom (k_1)																							
	1	2	3	4	5	6	7	8	9	10	11	12	14	16	20	24	30	40	50	75	100	200	500	∞
27	4.21	3.35	2.96	2.73	2.57	2.46	2.37	2.30	2.25	2.20	2.16	2.13	2.08	2.03	1.97	1.93	1.88	1.84	1.80	1.76	1.74	1.71	1.68	1.67
	7.68	**5.49**	**4.60**	**4.11**	**3.79**	**3.56**	**3.39**	**3.26**	**3.14**	**3.06**	**2.98**	**2.93**	**2.83**	**2.74**	**2.63**	**2.55**	**2.47**	**2.38**	**2.33**	**2.25**	**2.21**	**2.16**	**2.12**	**2.10**
28	4.20	3.34	2.95	2.71	2.56	2.44	2.36	2.29	2.24	2.19	2.15	2.12	2.06	2.02	1.96	1.91	1.87	1.81	1.78	1.75	1.72	1.69	1.67	1.65
	7.64	**5.45**	**4.57**	**4.07**	**3.76**	**3.53**	**3.36**	**3.23**	**3.11**	**3.03**	**2.95**	**2.90**	**2.80**	**2.71**	**2.60**	**2.52**	**2.44**	**2.35**	**2.30**	**2.22**	**2.18**	**2.13**	**2.09**	**2.06**
29	4.18	3.33	2.93	2.70	2.54	2.43	2.35	2.28	2.22	2.18	2.14	2.10	2.05	2.00	1.94	1.90	1.85	1.80	1.77	1.73	1.71	1.68	1.65	1.64
	7.60	**5.42**	**4.54**	**4.04**	**3.73**	**3.50**	**3.33**	**3.20**	**3.08**	**3.00**	**2.92**	**2.87**	**2.77**	**2.68**	**2.57**	**2.49**	**2.41**	**2.32**	**2.27**	**2.19**	**2.15**	**2.10**	**2.06**	**2.03**
30	4.17	3.32	2.92	2.69	2.53	2.42	2.34	2.27	2.21	2.16	2.12	2.09	2.04	1.99	1.93	1.89	1.84	1.79	1.76	1.72	1.69	1.66	1.64	1.62
	7.56	**5.39**	**4.51**	**4.02**	**3.70**	**3.47**	**3.30**	**3.17**	**3.06**	**2.98**	**2.90**	**2.84**	**2.74**	**2.66**	**2.55**	**2.47**	**2.38**	**2.29**	**2.24**	**2.16**	**2.13**	**2.07**	**2.03**	**2.01**
32	4.15	3.30	2.90	2.67	2.51	2.40	2.32	2.25	2.19	2.14	2.10	2.07	2.02	1.97	1.91	1.86	1.82	1.76	1.74	1.69	1.67	1.64	1.61	1.59
	7.50	**5.34**	**4.46**	**3.97**	**3.66**	**3.42**	**3.25**	**3.12**	**3.01**	**2.94**	**2.86**	**2.80**	**2.70**	**2.62**	**2.51**	**2.42**	**2.34**	**2.25**	**2.20**	**2.12**	**2.08**	**2.02**	**1.98**	**1.96**
34	4.13	3.28	2.88	2.65	2.49	2.38	2.30	2.23	2.17	2.12	2.08	2.05	2.00	1.95	1.89	1.84	1.80	1.74	1.71	1.67	1.64	1.61	1.59	1.57
	7.44	**5.29**	**4.42**	**3.93**	**3.61**	**3.38**	**3.21**	**3.08**	**2.97**	**2.89**	**2.82**	**2.76**	**2.66**	**2.58**	**2.47**	**2.38**	**2.30**	**2.21**	**2.15**	**2.08**	**2.04**	**1.98**	**1.94**	**1.91**
36	4.11	3.26	2.86	2.63	2.48	2.36	2.28	2.21	2.15	2.10	2.06	2.03	1.98	1.93	1.87	1.82	1.78	1.72	1.69	1.65	1.62	1.59	1.56	1.55
	7.39	**5.25**	**4.38**	**3.89**	**3.58**	**3.35**	**3.18**	**3.04**	**2.94**	**2.86**	**2.78**	**2.72**	**2.62**	**2.54**	**2.43**	**2.35**	**2.26**	**2.17**	**2.12**	**2.04**	**2.00**	**1.94**	**1.90**	**1.87**
38	4.10	3.25	2.85	2.62	2.46	2.35	2.26	2.19	2.14	2.09	2.05	2.02	1.96	1.92	1.85	1.80	1.76	1.71	1.67	1.63	1.60	1.57	1.54	1.53
	7.35	**5.21**	**4.34**	**3.86**	**3.54**	**3.32**	**3.15**	**3.02**	**2.91**	**2.82**	**2.75**	**2.69**	**2.59**	**2.51**	**2.40**	**2.32**	**2.22**	**2.14**	**2.08**	**2.00**	**1.97**	**1.90**	**1.86**	**1.84**
40	4.08	3.23	2.84	2.61	2.45	2.34	2.25	2.18	2.12	2.07	2.04	2.00	1.95	1.90	1.84	1.79	1.74	1.69	1.66	1.61	1.59	1.55	1.53	1.51
	7.31	**5.18**	**4.31**	**3.83**	**3.51**	**3.29**	**3.12**	**2.99**	**2.88**	**2.80**	**2.73**	**2.66**	**2.56**	**2.49**	**2.37**	**2.29**	**2.20**	**2.11**	**2.05**	**1.97**	**1.94**	**1.88**	**1.84**	**1.81**
42	4.07	3.22	2.83	2.59	2.44	2.32	2.24	2.17	2.11	2.06	2.02	1.99	1.94	1.89	1.82	1.78	1.73	1.68	1.64	1.60	1.57	1.54	1.51	1.49
	7.27	**5.15**	**4.29**	**3.80**	**3.49**	**3.26**	**3.10**	**2.96**	**2.86**	**2.77**	**2.70**	**2.64**	**2.54**	**2.46**	**2.35**	**2.26**	**2.17**	**2.08**	**2.02**	**1.94**	**1.91**	**1.85**	**1.80**	**1.78**
44	4.06	3.21	2.82	2.58	2.43	2.31	2.23	2.16	2.10	2.05	2.01	1.98	1.92	1.88	1.81	1.76	1.72	1.66	1.63	1.58	1.56	1.52	1.50	1.48
	7.24	**5.12**	**4.26**	**3.78**	**3.46**	**3.24**	**3.07**	**2.94**	**2.84**	**2.75**	**2.68**	**2.62**	**2.52**	**2.44**	**2.32**	**2.24**	**2.15**	**2.06**	**2.00**	**1.92**	**1.88**	**1.82**	**1.78**	**1.75**
46	4.05	3.20	2.81	2.57	2.42	2.30	2.22	2.14	2.09	2.04	2.00	1.97	1.91	1.87	1.80	1.75	1.71	1.65	1.62	1.57	1.54	1.51	1.48	1.46
	7.21	**5.10**	**4.24**	**3.76**	**3.44**	**3.22**	**3.05**	**2.92**	**2.82**	**2.73**	**2.66**	**2.60**	**2.50**	**2.42**	**2.30**	**2.22**	**2.13**	**2.04**	**1.98**	**1.90**	**1.86**	**1.80**	**1.76**	**1.72**
48	4.04	3.19	2.80	2.56	2.41	2.30	2.21	2.14	2.08	2.03	1.99	1.96	1.90	1.86	1.79	1.74	1.70	1.64	1.61	1.56	1.53	1.50	1.47	1.45
	7.19	**5.08**	**4.22**	**3.74**	**3.42**	**3.20**	**3.04**	**2.90**	**2.80**	**2.71**	**2.64**	**2.58**	**2.48**	**2.40**	**2.28**	**2.20**	**2.11**	**2.02**	**1.96**	**1.88**	**1.84**	**1.78**	**1.73**	**1.70**

50	4.03	3.18	2.79	2.56	2.40	2.29	2.20	2.13	2.07	2.02	1.98	1.95	1.90	1.85	1.78	1.74	1.69	1.63	1.60	1.55	1.52	1.48	1.46	1.44
	7.17	5.06	4.20	3.72	3.41	3.18	3.02	2.88	2.78	2.70	2.62	2.56	2.46	2.39	2.26	2.18	2.10	2.00	1.94	1.86	1.82	1.76	1.71	1.68
55	4.02	3.17	2.78	2.54	2.38	2.27	2.18	2.11	2.05	2.00	1.97	1.93	1.88	1.83	1.76	1.72	1.67	1.61	1.58	1.52	1.50	1.46	1.43	1.41
	7.12	5.01	4.16	3.68	3.37	3.15	2.98	2.85	2.75	2.66	2.59	2.53	2.43	2.35	2.23	2.15	2.06	1.96	1.90	1.82	1.78	1.71	1.66	1.64
60	4.00	3.15	2.76	2.52	2.37	2.25	2.17	2.10	2.04	1.99	1.95	1.92	1.86	1.81	1.75	1.70	1.65	1.59	1.56	1.50	1.48	1.44	1.41	1.39
	7.08	4.98	4.13	3.65	3.34	3.12	2.95	2.82	2.72	2.63	2.56	2.50	2.40	2.32	2.20	2.12	2.03	1.93	1.87	1.79	1.74	1.68	1.63	1.60
65	3.99	3.14	2.75	2.51	2.36	2.24	2.15	2.08	2.02	1.98	1.94	1.90	1.85	1.80	1.73	1.68	1.63	1.57	1.54	1.49	1.46	1.42	1.39	1.37
	7.04	4.95	4.10	3.62	3.31	3.09	2.93	2.79	2.70	2.61	2.54	2.47	2.37	2.30	2.18	2.09	2.00	1.90	1.84	1.76	1.71	1.64	1.60	1.56
70	3.98	3.13	2.74	2.50	2.35	2.23	2.14	2.07	2.01	1.97	1.93	1.89	1.84	1.79	1.72	1.67	1.62	1.56	1.53	1.47	1.45	1.40	1.37	1.35
	7.01	4.92	4.08	3.60	3.29	3.07	2.91	2.77	2.67	2.59	2.51	2.45	2.35	2.28	2.15	2.07	1.98	1.88	1.82	1.74	1.69	1.62	1.56	1.53
80	3.96	3.11	2.72	2.48	2.33	2.21	2.12	2.05	1.99	1.95	1.91	1.88	1.82	1.77	1.70	1.65	1.60	1.54	1.51	1.45	1.42	1.38	1.35	1.32
	6.96	4.88	4.04	3.56	3.25	3.04	2.87	2.74	2.64	2.55	2.48	2.41	2.32	2.24	2.11	2.03	1.94	1.84	1.78	1.70	1.65	1.57	1.52	1.49
100	3.94	3.09	2.70	2.46	2.30	2.19	2.10	2.03	1.97	1.92	1.88	1.85	1.79	1.75	1.68	1.63	1.57	1.51	1.48	1.42	1.39	1.34	1.30	1.28
	6.90	4.82	3.98	3.51	3.20	2.99	2.82	2.69	2.59	2.51	2.43	2.36	2.26	2.19	2.06	1.98	1.89	1.79	1.73	1.64	1.59	1.51	1.46	1.43
125	3.92	3.07	2.68	2.44	2.29	2.17	2.08	2.01	1.95	1.90	1.86	1.83	1.77	1.72	1.65	1.60	1.55	1.49	1.45	1.39	1.36	1.31	1.27	1.25
	6.84	4.78	3.94	3.47	3.17	2.95	2.79	2.65	2.56	2.47	2.40	2.33	2.23	2.15	2.03	1.94	1.85	1.75	1.68	1.59	1.54	1.46	1.40	1.37
150	3.91	3.06	2.67	2.43	2.27	2.16	2.07	2.00	1.94	1.89	1.85	1.82	1.76	1.71	1.64	1.59	1.54	1.47	1.44	1.37	1.34	1.29	1.25	1.22
	6.81	4.75	3.91	3.44	3.14	2.92	2.76	2.62	2.53	2.44	2.37	2.30	2.20	2.12	2.00	1.91	1.83	1.72	1.66	1.56	1.51	1.43	1.37	1.33
200	3.89	3.04	2.65	2.41	2.26	2.14	2.05	1.98	1.92	1.87	1.83	1.80	1.74	1.69	1.62	1.57	1.52	1.45	1.42	1.35	1.32	1.26	1.22	1.19
	6.76	4.71	3.88	3.41	3.11	2.90	2.73	2.60	2.50	2.41	2.34	2.28	2.17	2.09	1.97	1.88	1.79	1.69	1.62	1.53	1.48	1.39	1.33	1.28
400	3.86	3.02	2.62	2.39	2.23	2.12	2.03	1.96	1.90	1.85	1.81	1.78	1.72	1.67	1.60	1.54	1.49	1.42	1.38	1.32	1.28	1.22	1.16	1.13
	6.70	4.66	3.83	3.36	3.06	2.85	2.69	2.55	2.46	2.37	2.29	2.23	2.12	2.04	1.92	1.84	1.74	1.64	1.57	1.47	1.42	1.32	1.24	1.19
1,000	3.85	3.00	2.61	2.38	2.22	2.10	2.02	1.95	1.89	1.84	1.80	1.76	1.70	1.65	1.58	1.53	1.47	1.41	1.36	1.30	1.26	1.19	1.13	1.08
	6.66	4.62	3.80	3.34	3.04	2.82	2.66	2.53	2.43	2.34	2.26	2.20	2.09	2.01	1.89	1.81	1.71	1.61	1.54	1.44	1.38	1.28	1.19	1.11
∞	3.84	2.99	2.60	2.37	2.21	2.09	2.01	1.94	1.88	1.83	1.79	1.75	1.69	1.64	1.57	1.52	1.46	1.40	1.35	1.28	1.24	1.17	1.11	1.00
	6.63	4.60	3.78	3.32	3.02	2.80	2.64	2.51	2.41	2.32	2.24	2.18	2.07	1.99	1.87	1.79	1.69	1.59	1.52	1.41	1.36	1.25	1.15	1.00

Source: Reprinted by permission from *Statistical Methods*, 7th ed., by George W. Snedecor and William G. Cochran, © 1980 by the Iowa State University Press, Ames, Iowa, 50010.

TABLE 6 Critical Values of the Studentized Range Distribution for $\alpha = 0.05$

$n-r$	r																		
	2	3	4	5	6	7	8	9	10	11	12	13	14	15	16	17	18	19	20
1	18.0	27.0	32.8	37.1	40.4	43.1	45.4	47.4	49.1	50.6	52.0	53.2	54.3	55.4	56.3	57.2	58.0	58.8	59.6
2	6.08	8.33	9.80	10.9	11.7	12.4	13.0	13.5	14.0	14.4	14.7	15.1	15.4	15.7	15.9	16.1	16.4	16.6	16.8
3	4.50	5.91	6.82	7.50	8.04	8.48	8.85	9.18	9.46	9.72	9.95	10.2	10.3	10.5	10.7	10.8	11.0	11.1	11.2
4	3.93	5.04	5.76	6.29	6.71	7.05	7.35	7.60	7.83	8.03	8.21	8.37	8.52	8.66	8.79	8.91	9.03	9.13	9.23
5	3.64	4.60	5.22	5.67	6.03	6.33	6.58	6.80	6.99	7.17	7.32	7.47	7.60	7.72	7.83	7.93	8.03	8.12	8.21
6	3.46	4.34	4.90	5.30	5.63	5.90	6.12	6.32	6.49	6.65	6.79	6.92	7.03	7.14	7.24	7.34	7.43	7.51	7.59
7	3.34	4.16	4.68	5.06	5.36	5.61	5.82	6.00	6.16	6.30	6.43	6.55	6.66	6.76	6.85	6.94	7.02	7.10	7.17
8	3.26	4.04	4.53	4.89	5.17	5.40	5.60	5.77	5.92	6.05	6.18	6.29	6.39	6.48	6.57	6.65	6.73	6.80	6.87
9	3.20	3.95	4.41	4.76	5.02	5.24	5.43	5.59	5.74	5.87	5.98	6.09	6.19	6.28	6.36	6.44	6.51	6.58	6.64
10	3.15	3.88	4.33	4.65	4.91	5.12	5.30	5.46	5.60	5.72	5.83	5.93	6.03	6.11	6.19	6.27	6.34	6.40	6.47
11	3.11	3.82	4.26	4.57	4.82	5.03	5.20	5.35	5.49	5.61	5.71	5.81	5.90	5.98	6.06	6.13	6.20	6.27	6.33
12	3.08	3.77	4.20	4.51	4.75	4.95	5.12	5.27	5.39	5.51	5.61	5.71	5.80	5.88	5.95	6.02	6.09	6.15	6.21
13	3.06	3.73	4.15	4.45	4.69	4.88	5.05	5.19	5.32	5.43	5.53	5.63	5.71	5.79	5.86	5.93	5.99	6.05	6.11
14	3.03	3.70	4.11	4.41	4.64	4.83	4.99	5.13	5.25	5.36	5.46	5.55	5.64	5.71	5.79	5.85	5.91	5.97	6.03
15	3.01	3.67	4.08	4.37	4.59	4.78	4.94	5.08	5.20	5.31	5.40	5.49	5.57	5.65	5.72	5.78	5.85	5.90	5.96
16	3.00	3.65	4.05	4.33	4.56	4.74	4.90	5.03	5.15	5.26	5.35	5.44	5.52	5.59	5.66	5.73	5.79	5.84	5.90
17	2.98	3.63	4.02	4.30	4.52	4.70	4.86	4.99	5.11	5.21	5.31	5.39	5.47	5.54	5.61	5.67	5.73	5.79	5.84
18	2.97	3.61	4.00	4.28	4.49	4.67	4.82	4.96	5.07	5.17	5.27	5.35	5.43	5.50	5.57	5.63	5.69	5.74	5.79
19	2.96	3.59	3.98	4.25	4.47	4.65	4.79	4.92	5.04	5.14	5.23	5.31	5.39	5.46	5.53	5.59	5.65	5.70	5.75
20	2.95	3.58	3.96	4.23	4.45	4.62	4.77	4.90	5.01	5.11	5.20	5.28	5.36	5.43	5.49	5.55	5.61	5.66	5.71
24	2.92	3.53	3.90	4.17	4.37	4.54	4.68	4.81	4.92	5.01	5.10	5.18	5.25	5.32	5.38	5.44	5.49	5.55	5.59
30	2.89	3.49	3.85	4.10	4.30	4.46	4.60	4.72	4.82	4.92	5.00	5.08	5.15	5.21	5.27	5.33	5.38	5.43	5.47
40	2.86	3.44	3.79	4.04	4.23	4.39	4.52	4.63	4.73	4.82	4.90	4.98	5.04	5.11	5.16	5.22	5.27	5.31	5.36
60	2.83	3.40	3.74	3.98	4.16	4.31	4.44	4.55	4.65	4.73	4.81	4.88	4.94	5.00	5.06	5.11	5.15	5.20	5.24
120	2.80	3.36	3.68	3.92	4.10	4.24	4.36	4.47	4.56	4.64	4.71	4.78	4.84	4.90	4.95	5.00	5.04	5.09	5.13
∞	2.77	3.31	3.63	3.86	4.03	4.17	4.29	4.39	4.47	4.55	4.62	4.68	4.74	4.80	4.85	4.89	4.93	4.97	5.01

TABLE 6 (concluded) **Critical Values of the Studentized Range Distribution for α = 0.01**

r

$n-r$	2	3	4	5	6	7	8	9	10	11	12	13	14	15	16	17	18	19	20
1	90.0	135	164	186	202	216	227	237	246	253	260	266	272	277	282	286	290	294	298
2	14.0	19.0	22.3	24.7	26.6	28.2	29.5	30.7	31.7	32.6	33.4	34.1	34.8	35.4	36.0	36.5	37.0	37.5	37.9
3	8.26	10.6	12.2	13.3	14.2	15.0	15.6	16.2	16.7	17.1	17.5	17.9	18.2	18.5	18.8	19.1	19.3	19.5	19.8
4	6.51	8.12	9.17	9.96	10.6	11.1	11.5	11.9	12.3	12.6	12.8	13.1	13.3	13.6	13.7	13.9	14.1	14.2	14.4
5	5.70	6.97	7.80	8.42	8.91	9.32	9.67	9.97	10.2	10.5	10.7	10.9	11.1	11.2	11.4	11.6	11.7	11.8	11.9
6	5.24	6.33	7.03	7.56	7.97	8.32	8.61	8.87	9.10	9.30	9.49	9.65	9.81	9.95	10.1	10.2	10.3	10.4	10.5
7	4.95	5.92	6.54	7.01	7.37	7.68	7.94	8.17	8.37	8.55	8.71	8.86	9.00	9.12	9.24	9.35	9.46	9.55	9.65
8	4.74	5.63	6.20	6.63	6.96	7.24	7.47	7.68	7.87	8.03	8.18	8.31	8.44	8.55	8.66	8.76	8.85	8.94	9.03
9	4.60	5.43	5.96	6.35	6.66	6.91	7.13	7.32	7.49	7.65	7.78	7.91	8.03	8.13	8.23	8.32	8.41	8.49	8.57
10	4.48	5.27	5.77	6.14	6.43	6.67	6.87	7.05	7.21	7.36	7.48	7.60	7.71	7.81	7.91	7.99	8.07	8.15	8.22
11	4.39	5.14	5.62	5.97	6.25	6.48	6.67	6.84	6.99	7.13	7.25	7.36	7.46	7.56	7.65	7.73	7.81	7.88	7.95
12	4.32	5.04	5.50	5.84	6.10	6.32	6.51	6.67	6.81	6.94	7.06	7.17	7.26	7.36	7.44	7.52	7.59	7.66	7.73
13	4.26	4.96	5.40	5.73	5.98	6.19	6.37	6.53	6.67	6.79	6.90	7.01	7.10	7.19	7.27	7.34	7.42	7.48	7.55
14	4.21	4.89	5.32	5.63	5.88	6.08	6.26	6.41	6.54	6.66	6.77	6.87	6.96	7.05	7.12	7.20	7.27	7.33	7.39
15	4.17	4.83	5.25	5.56	5.80	5.99	6.16	6.31	6.44	6.55	6.66	6.76	6.84	6.93	7.00	7.07	7.14	7.20	7.26
16	4.13	4.78	5.19	5.49	5.72	5.92	6.08	6.22	6.35	6.46	6.56	6.66	6.74	6.82	6.90	6.97	7.03	7.09	7.15
17	4.10	4.74	5.14	5.43	5.66	5.85	6.01	6.15	6.27	6.38	6.48	6.57	6.66	6.73	6.80	6.87	6.94	7.00	7.05
18	4.07	4.70	5.09	5.38	5.60	5.79	5.94	6.08	6.20	6.31	6.41	6.50	6.58	6.65	6.72	6.79	6.85	6.91	6.96
19	4.05	4.67	5.05	5.33	5.55	5.73	5.89	6.02	6.14	6.25	6.34	6.43	6.51	6.58	6.65	6.72	6.78	6.84	6.89
20	4.02	4.64	5.02	5.29	5.51	5.69	5.84	5.97	6.09	6.19	6.29	6.37	6.45	6.52	6.59	6.65	6.71	6.76	6.82
24	3.96	4.54	4.91	5.17	5.37	5.54	5.69	5.81	5.92	6.02	6.11	6.19	6.26	6.33	6.39	6.45	6.51	6.56	6.61
30	3.89	4.45	4.80	5.05	5.24	5.40	5.54	5.65	5.76	5.85	5.93	6.01	6.08	6.14	6.20	6.26	6.31	6.36	6.41
40	3.82	4.37	4.70	4.93	5.11	5.27	5.39	5.50	5.60	5.69	5.77	5.84	5.90	5.96	6.02	6.07	6.12	6.17	6.21
60	3.76	4.28	4.60	4.82	4.99	5.13	5.25	5.36	5.45	5.53	5.60	5.67	5.73	5.79	5.84	5.89	5.93	5.98	6.02
120	3.70	4.20	4.50	4.71	4.87	5.01	5.12	5.21	5.30	5.38	5.44	5.51	5.56	5.61	5.66	5.71	5.75	5.79	5.83
∞	3.64	4.12	4.40	4.60	4.76	4.88	4.99	5.08	5.16	5.23	5.29	5.35	5.40	5.45	5.49	5.54	5.57	5.61	5.65

Source: E. S. Pearson and H. O. Hartley, eds., *Biometrika Tables for Statisticians*, vol. 1, 3rd ed. (Cambridge University Press, 1966). Reprinted by permission by the *Biometrika* Trustees.

TABLE 7   Critical Values of the Durbin-Watson Test Statistic for $\alpha = 0.05$

n	k = 1		k = 2		k = 3		k = 4		k = 5	
	d_L	d_U	d_L	d_U	d_L	d_U	d_L	d_U	d_L	d_U
15	1.08	1.36	0.95	1.54	0.82	1.75	0.69	1.97	0.56	2.21
16	1.10	1.37	0.98	1.54	0.86	1.73	0.74	1.93	0.62	2.15
17	1.13	1.38	1.02	1.54	0.90	1.71	0.78	1.90	0.67	2.10
18	1.16	1.39	1.05	1.53	0.93	1.69	0.82	1.87	0.71	2.06
19	1.18	1.40	1.08	1.53	0.97	1.68	0.86	1.85	0.75	2.02
20	1.20	1.41	1.10	1.54	1.00	1.68	0.90	1.83	0.79	1.99
21	1.22	1.42	1.13	1.54	1.03	1.67	0.93	1.81	0.83	1.96
22	1.24	1.43	1.15	1.54	1.05	1.66	0.96	1.80	0.86	1.94
23	1.26	1.44	1.17	1.54	1.08	1.66	0.99	1.79	0.90	1.92
24	1.27	1.45	1.19	1.55	1.10	1.66	1.01	1.78	0.93	1.90
25	1.29	1.45	1.21	1.55	1.12	1.66	1.04	1.77	0.95	1.89
26	1.30	1.46	1.22	1.55	1.14	1.65	1.06	1.76	0.98	1.88
27	1.32	1.47	1.24	1.56	1.16	1.65	1.08	1.76	1.01	1.86
28	1.33	1.48	1.26	1.56	1.18	1.65	1.10	1.75	1.03	1.85
29	1.34	1.48	1.27	1.56	1.20	1.65	1.12	1.74	1.05	1.84
30	1.35	1.49	1.28	1.57	1.21	1.65	1.14	1.74	1.07	1.83
31	1.36	1.50	1.30	1.57	1.23	1.65	1.16	1.74	1.09	1.83
32	1.37	1.50	1.31	1.57	1.24	1.65	1.18	1.73	1.11	1.82
33	1.38	1.51	1.32	1.58	1.26	1.65	1.19	1.73	1.13	1.81
34	1.39	1.51	1.33	1.58	1.27	1.65	1.21	1.73	1.15	1.81
35	1.40	1.52	1.34	1.58	1.28	1.65	1.22	1.73	1.16	1.80
36	1.41	1.52	1.35	1.59	1.29	1.65	1.24	1.73	1.18	1.80
37	1.42	1.53	1.36	1.59	1.31	1.66	1.25	1.72	1.19	1.80
38	1.43	1.54	1.37	1.59	1.32	1.66	1.26	1.72	1.21	1.79
39	1.43	1.54	1.38	1.60	1.33	1.66	1.27	1.72	1.22	1.79
40	1.44	1.54	1.39	1.60	1.34	1.66	1.29	1.72	1.23	1.79
45	1.48	1.57	1.43	1.62	1.38	1.67	1.34	1.72	1.29	1.78
50	1.50	1.59	1.46	1.63	1.42	1.67	1.38	1.72	1.34	1.77
55	1.53	1.60	1.49	1.64	1.45	1.68	1.41	1.72	1.38	1.77
60	1.55	1.62	1.51	1.65	1.48	1.69	1.44	1.73	1.41	1.77
65	1.57	1.63	1.54	1.66	1.50	1.70	1.47	1.73	1.44	1.77
70	1.58	1.64	1.55	1.67	1.52	1.70	1.49	1.74	1.46	1.77
75	1.60	1.65	1.57	1.68	1.54	1.71	1.51	1.74	1.49	1.77
80	1.61	1.66	1.59	1.69	1.56	1.72	1.53	1.74	1.51	1.77
85	1.62	1.67	1.60	1.70	1.57	1.72	1.55	1.75	1.52	1.77
90	1.63	1.68	1.61	1.70	1.59	1.73	1.57	1.75	1.54	1.78
95	1.64	1.69	1.62	1.71	1.60	1.73	1.58	1.75	1.56	1.78
100	1.65	1.69	1.63	1.72	1.61	1.74	1.59	1.76	1.57	1.78

TABLE 7 *(concluded)*   Critical Values of the Durbin-Watson Test Statistic for $\alpha = 0.01$

	$k = 1$		$k = 2$		$k = 3$		$k = 4$		$k = 5$	
n	d_L	d_U	d_L	d_U	d_L	d_U	d_L	d_U	d_L	d_U
15	0.81	1.07	0.70	1.25	0.59	1.46	0.49	1.70	0.39	1.96
16	0.84	1.09	0.74	1.25	0.63	1.44	0.53	1.66	0.44	1.90
17	0.87	1.10	0.77	1.25	0.67	1.43	0.57	1.63	0.48	1.85
18	0.90	1.12	0.80	1.26	0.71	1.42	0.61	1.60	0.52	1.80
19	0.93	1.13	0.83	1.26	0.74	1.41	0.65	1.58	0.56	1.77
20	0.95	1.15	0.86	1.27	0.77	1.41	0.68	1.57	0.60	1.74
21	0.97	1.16	0.89	1.27	0.80	1.41	0.72	1.55	0.63	1.71
22	1.00	1.17	0.91	1.28	0.83	1.40	0.75	1.54	0.66	1.69
23	1.02	1.19	0.94	1.29	0.86	1.40	0.77	1.53	0.70	1.67
24	1.05	1.20	0.96	1.30	0.88	1.41	0.80	1.53	0.72	1.66
25	1.05	1.21	0.98	1.30	0.90	1.41	0.83	1.52	0.75	1.65
26	1.07	1.22	1.00	1.31	0.93	1.41	0.85	1.52	0.78	1.64
27	1.09	1.23	1.02	1.32	0.95	1.41	0.88	1.51	0.81	1.63
28	1.10	1.24	1.04	1.32	0.97	1.41	0.90	1.51	0.83	1.62
29	1.12	1.25	1.05	1.33	0.99	1.42	0.92	1.51	0.85	1.61
30	1.13	1.26	1.07	1.34	1.01	1.42	0.94	1.51	0.88	1.61
31	1.15	1.27	1.08	1.34	1.02	1.42	0.96	1.51	0.90	1.60
32	1.16	1.28	1.10	1.35	1.04	1.43	0.98	1.51	0.92	1.60
33	1.17	1.29	1.11	1.36	1.05	1.43	1.00	1.51	0.94	1.59
34	1.18	1.30	1.13	1.36	1.07	1.43	1.01	1.51	0.95	1.59
35	1.19	1.31	1.14	1.37	1.08	1.44	1.03	1.51	0.97	1.59
36	1.21	1.32	1.15	1.38	1.10	1.44	1.04	1.51	0.99	1.59
37	1.22	1.32	1.16	1.38	1.11	1.45	1.06	1.51	1.00	1.59
38	1.23	1.33	1.18	1.39	1.12	1.45	1.07	1.52	1.02	1.58
39	1.24	1.34	1.19	1.39	1.14	1.45	1.09	1.52	1.03	1.58
40	1.25	1.34	1.20	1.40	1.15	1.46	1.10	1.52	1.05	1.58
45	1.29	1.38	1.24	1.42	1.20	1.48	1.16	1.53	1.11	1.58
50	1.32	1.40	1.28	1.45	1.24	1.49	1.20	1.54	1.16	1.59
55	1.36	1.43	1.32	1.47	1.28	1.51	1.25	1.55	1.21	1.59
60	1.38	1.45	1.35	1.48	1.32	1.52	1.28	1.56	1.25	1.60
65	1.41	1.47	1.38	1.50	1.35	1.53	1.31	1.57	1.28	1.61
70	1.43	1.49	1.40	1.52	1.37	1.55	1.34	1.58	1.31	1.61
75	1.45	1.50	1.42	1.53	1.39	1.56	1.37	1.59	1.34	1.62
80	1.47	1.52	1.44	1.54	1.42	1.57	1.39	1.60	1.36	1.62
85	1.48	1.53	1.46	1.55	1.43	1.58	1.41	1.60	1.39	1.63
90	1.50	1.54	1.47	1.56	1.45	1.59	1.43	1.61	1.41	1.64
95	1.51	1.55	1.49	1.57	1.47	1.60	1.45	1.62	1.42	1.64
100	1.52	1.56	1.50	1.58	1.48	1.60	1.46	1.63	1.44	1.65

Source: J. Durbin and G. S. Watson, "Testing for Serial Correlation in Least Squares Regression, II," *Biometrika* 38 (1951), pp. 159–78. Reproduced by permission of the *Biometrika* Trustees.

TABLE 8   Cumulative Distribution Function: $F(r)$ for the Total Number of Runs R in Samples of Sizes n_1 and n_2

(n_1, n_2)	Number of Runs, r								
	2	3	4	5	6	7	8	9	10
(2, 3)	0.200	0.500	0.900	1.000					
(2, 4)	0.133	0.400	0.800	1.000					
(2, 5)	0.095	0.333	0.714	1.000					
(2, 6)	0.071	0.286	0.643	1.000					
(2, 7)	0.056	0.250	0.583	1.000					
(2, 8)	0.044	0.222	0.533	1.000					
(2, 9)	0.036	0.200	0.491	1.000					
(2, 10)	0.030	0.182	0.455	1.000					
(3, 3)	0.100	0.300	0.700	0.900	1.000				
(3, 4)	0.057	0.200	0.543	0.800	0.971	1.000			
(3, 5)	0.036	0.143	0.429	0.714	0.929	1.000			
(3, 6)	0.024	0.107	0.345	0.643	0.881	1.000			
(3, 7)	0.017	0.083	0.283	0.583	0.833	1.000			
(3, 8)	0.012	0.067	0.236	0.533	0.788	1.000			
(3, 9)	0.009	0.055	0.200	0.491	0.745	1.000			
(3, 10)	0.007	0.045	0.171	0.455	0.706	1.000			
(4, 4)	0.029	0.114	0.371	0.629	0.886	0.971	1.000		
(4, 5)	0.016	0.071	0.262	0.500	0.786	0.929	0.992	1.000	
(4, 6)	0.010	0.048	0.190	0.405	0.690	0.881	0.976	1.000	
(4, 7)	0.006	0.033	0.142	0.333	0.606	0.833	0.954	1.000	
(4, 8)	0.004	0.024	0.109	0.279	0.533	0.788	0.929	1.000	
(4, 9)	0.003	0.018	0.085	0.236	0.471	0.745	0.902	1.000	
(4, 10)	0.002	0.014	0.068	0.203	0.419	0.706	0.874	1.000	
(5, 5)	0.008	0.040	0.167	0.357	0.643	0.833	0.960	0.992	1.000
(5, 6)	0.004	0.024	0.110	0.262	0.522	0.738	0.911	0.976	0.998
(5, 7)	0.003	0.015	0.076	0.197	0.424	0.652	0.854	0.955	0.992
(5, 8)	0.002	0.010	0.054	0.152	0.347	0.576	0.793	0.929	0.984
(5, 9)	0.001	0.007	0.039	0.119	0.287	0.510	0.734	0.902	0.972
(5, 10)	0.001	0.005	0.029	0.095	0.239	0.455	0.678	0.874	0.958
(6, 6)	0.002	0.013	0.067	0.175	0.392	0.608	0.825	0.933	0.987
(6, 7)	0.001	0.008	0.043	0.121	0.296	0.500	0.733	0.879	0.966
(6, 8)	0.001	0.005	0.028	0.086	0.226	0.413	0.646	0.821	0.937
(6, 9)	0.000	0.003	0.019	0.063	0.175	0.343	0.566	0.762	0.902
(6, 10)	0.000	0.002	0.013	0.047	0.137	0.288	0.497	0.706	0.864
(7, 7)	0.001	0.004	0.025	0.078	0.209	0.383	0.617	0.791	0.922
(7, 8)	0.000	0.002	0.015	0.051	0.149	0.296	0.514	0.704	0.867
(7, 9)	0.000	0.001	0.010	0.035	0.108	0.231	0.427	0.622	0.806
(7, 10)	0.000	0.001	0.006	0.024	0.080	0.182	0.355	0.549	0.743
(8, 8)	0.000	0.001	0.009	0.032	0.100	0.214	0.405	0.595	0.786
(8, 9)	0.000	0.001	0.005	0.020	0.069	0.157	0.319	0.500	0.702
(8, 10)	0.000	0.000	0.003	0.013	0.048	0.117	0.251	0.419	0.621
(9, 9)	0.000	0.000	0.003	0.012	0.044	0.109	0.238	0.399	0.601
(9, 10)	0.000	0.000	0.002	0.008	0.029	0.077	0.179	0.319	0.510
(10, 10)	0.000	0.000	0.001	0.004	0.019	0.051	0.128	0.242	0.414

TABLE 8 *(concluded)*   Cumulative Distribution Function: $F(r)$ for the Total Number of Runs R in Samples of Sizes n_1 and n_2

(n_1, n_2)	Number of Runs, r									
	11	12	13	14	15	16	17	18	19	20
(2, 3)										
(2, 4)										
(2, 5)										
(2, 6)										
(2, 7)										
(2, 8)										
(2, 9)										
(2, 10)										
(3, 3)										
(3, 4)										
(3, 5)										
(3, 6)										
(3, 7)										
(3, 8)										
(3, 9)										
(3, 10)										
(4, 4)										
(4, 5)										
(4, 6)										
(4, 7)										
(4, 8)										
(4, 9)										
(4, 10)										
(5, 5)										
(5, 6)	1.000									
(5, 7)	1.000									
(5, 8)	1.000									
(5, 9)	1.000									
(5, 10)	1.000									
(6, 6)	0.998	1.000								
(6, 7)	0.992	0.999	1.000							
(6, 8)	0.984	0.998	1.000							
(6, 9)	0.972	0.994	1.000							
(6, 10)	0.958	0.990	1.000							
(7, 7)	0.975	0.996	0.999	1.000						
(7, 8)	0.949	0.988	0.998	1.000	1.000					
(7, 9)	0.916	0.975	0.994	0.999	1.000					
(7, 10)	0.879	0.957	0.990	0.998	1.000					
(8, 8)	0.900	0.968	0.991	0.999	1.000	1.000				
(8, 9)	0.843	0.939	0.980	0.996	0.999	1.000	1.000			
(8, 10)	0.782	0.903	0.964	0.990	0.998	1.000	1.000			
(9, 9)	0.762	0.891	0.956	0.988	0.997	1.000	1.000	1.000		
(9, 10)	0.681	0.834	0.923	0.974	0.992	0.999	1.000	1.000	1.000	
(10, 10)	0.586	0.758	0.872	0.949	0.981	0.996	0.999	1.000	1.000	1.000

Source: Reproduced from F. Swed and C. Eisenhart, "Tables for Testing Randomness of Grouping in a Sequence of Alternatives," *Annals of Mathematical Statistics* 14 (1943) by permission of the authors and of the Editor, *Annals of Mathematical Statistics.*

TABLE 9   Cumulative Distribution Function of the Mann-Whitney U Statistic: $F(u)$ for $n_1 \leq n_2$ and $3 \leq n_2 \leq 10$

| | | $n_2 = 3$ | |
| | | n_1 | |
u	1	2	3
0	0.25	0.10	0.05
1	0.50	0.20	0.10
2		0.40	0.20
3		0.60	0.35
4			0.50

| | | | $n_2 = 4$ | |
| | | | n_1 | |
u	1	2	3	4
0	0.2000	0.0667	0.0286	0.0143
1	0.4000	0.1333	0.0571	0.0286
2	0.6000	0.2667	0.1143	0.0571
3		0.4000	0.2000	0.1000
4		0.6000	0.3143	0.1714
5			0.4286	0.2429
6			0.5714	0.3429
7				0.4429
8				0.5571

| | | | $n_2 = 5$ | | |
| | | | n_1 | | |
u	1	2	3	4	5
0	0.1667	0.0476	0.0179	0.0079	0.0040
1	0.3333	0.0952	0.0357	0.0159	0.0079
2	0.5000	0.1905	0.0714	0.0317	0.0159
3		0.2857	0.1250	0.0556	0.0278
4		0.4286	0.1964	0.0952	0.0476
5		0.5714	0.2857	0.1429	0.0754
6			0.3929	0.2063	0.1111
7			0.5000	0.2778	0.1548
8				0.3651	0.2103
9				0.4524	0.2738
10				0.5476	0.3452
11					0.4206
12					0.5000

TABLE 9 *(continued)*   Cumulative Distribution Function of the Mann-Whitney U Statistic: $F(u)$ for $n_1 \leq n_2$ and $3 \leq n_2 \leq 10$

$n_2 = 6$
n_1

u	1	2	3	4	5	6
0	0.1429	0.0357	0.0119	0.0048	0.0022	0.0011
1	0.2857	0.0714	0.0238	0.0095	0.0043	0.0022
2	0.4286	0.1429	0.0476	0.0190	0.0087	0.0043
3	0.5714	0.2143	0.0833	0.0333	0.0152	0.0076
4		0.3214	0.1310	0.0571	0.0260	0.0130
5		0.4286	0.1905	0.0857	0.0411	0.0206
6		0.5714	0.2738	0.1286	0.0628	0.0325
7			0.3571	0.1762	0.0887	0.0465
8			0.4524	0.2381	0.1234	0.0660
9			0.5476	0.3048	0.1645	0.0898
10				0.3810	0.2143	0.1201
11				0.4571	0.2684	0.1548
12				0.5429	0.3312	0.1970
13					0.3961	0.2424
14					0.4654	0.2944
15					0.5346	0.3496
16						0.4091
17						0.4686
18						0.5314

$n_2 = 7$
n_1

u	1	2	3	4	5	6	7
0	0.1250	0.0278	0.0083	0.0030	0.0013	0.0006	0.0003
1	0.2500	0.0556	0.0167	0.0061	0.0025	0.0012	0.0006
2	0.3750	0.1111	0.0333	0.0121	0.0051	0.0023	0.0012
3	0.5000	0.1667	0.0583	0.0212	0.0088	0.0041	0.0020
4		0.2500	0.0917	0.0364	0.0152	0.0070	0.0035
5		0.3333	0.1333	0.0545	0.0240	0.0111	0.0055
6		0.4444	0.1917	0.0818	0.0366	0.0175	0.0087
7		0.5556	0.2583	0.1152	0.0530	0.0256	0.0131
8			0.3333	0.1576	0.0745	0.0367	0.0189
9			0.4167	0.2061	0.1010	0.0507	0.0265
10			0.5000	0.2636	0.1338	0.0688	0.0364
11				0.3242	0.1717	0.0903	0.0487
12				0.3939	0.2159	0.1171	0.0641
13				0.4636	0.2652	0.1474	0.0825
14				0.5364	0.3194	0.1830	0.1043
15					0.3775	0.2226	0.1297
16					0.4381	0.2669	0.1588
17					0.5000	0.3141	0.1914
18						0.3654	0.2279
19						0.4178	0.2675
20						0.4726	0.3100
21						0.5274	0.3552
22							0.4024
23							0.4508
24							0.5000

TABLE 9 *(continued)*   Cumulative Distribution Function of the Mann-Whitney U Statistic: $F(u)$ for $n_1 \leq n_2$ and $3 \leq n_2 \leq 10$

				$n_2 = 8$ n_1				
u	1	2	3	4	5	6	7	8
0	0.1111	0.0222	0.0061	0.0020	0.0008	0.0003	0.0002	0.0001
1	0.2222	0.0444	0.0121	0.0040	0.0016	0.0007	0.0003	0.0002
2	0.3333	0.0889	0.0242	0.0081	0.0031	0.0013	0.0006	0.0003
3	0.4444	0.1333	0.0424	0.0141	0.0054	0.0023	0.0011	0.0005
4	0.5556	0.2000	0.0667	0.0242	0.0093	0.0040	0.0019	0.0009
5		0.2667	0.0970	0.0364	0.0148	0.0063	0.0030	0.0015
6		0.3556	0.1394	0.0545	0.0225	0.0100	0.0047	0.0023
7		0.4444	0.1879	0.0768	0.0326	0.0147	0.0070	0.0035
8		0.5556	0.2485	0.1071	0.0466	0.0213	0.0103	0.0052
9			0.3152	0.1414	0.0637	0.0296	0.0145	0.0074
10			0.3879	0.1838	0.0855	0.0406	0.0200	0.0103
11			0.4606	0.2303	0.1111	0.0539	0.0270	0.0141
12			0.5394	0.2848	0.1422	0.0709	0.0361	0.0190
13				0.3414	0.1772	0.0906	0.0469	0.0249
14				0.4040	0.2176	0.1142	0.0603	0.0325
15				0.4667	0.2618	0.1412	0.0760	0.0415
16				0.5333	0.3108	0.1725	0.0946	0.0524
17					0.3621	0.2068	0.1159	0.0652
18					0.4165	0.2454	0.1405	0.0803
19					0.4716	0.2864	0.1678	0.0974
20					0.5284	0.3310	0.1984	0.1172
21						0.3773	0.2317	0.1393
22						0.4259	0.2679	0.1641
23						0.4749	0.3063	0.1911
24						0.5251	0.3472	0.2209
25							0.3894	0.2527
26							0.4333	0.2869
27							0.4775	0.3227
28							0.5225	0.3605
29								0.3992
30								0.4392
31								0.4796
32								0.5204

TABLE 9 *(continued)*   Cumulative Distribution Function of the Mann-Whitney *U* Statistic: *F(u)*
for $n_1 \le n_2$ and $3 \le n_2 \le 10$

$n_2 = 9$
n_1

u	1	2	3	4	5	6	7	8	9
0	0.1000	0.0182	0.0045	0.0014	0.0005	0.0002	0.0001	0.0000	0.0000
1	0.2000	0.0364	0.0091	0.0028	0.0010	0.0004	0.0002	0.0001	0.0000
2	0.3000	0.0727	0.0182	0.0056	0.0020	0.0008	0.0003	0.0002	0.0001
3	0.4000	0.1091	0.0318	0.0098	0.0035	0.0014	0.0006	0.0003	0.0001
4	0.5000	0.1636	0.0500	0.0168	0.0060	0.0024	0.0010	0.0005	0.0002
5		0.2182	0.0727	0.0252	0.0095	0.0038	0.0017	0.0008	0.0004
6		0.2909	0.1045	0.0378	0.0145	0.0060	0.0026	0.0012	0.0006
7		0.3636	0.1409	0.0531	0.0210	0.0088	0.0039	0.0019	0.0009
8		0.4545	0.1864	0.0741	0.0300	0.0128	0.0058	0.0028	0.0014
9		0.5455	0.2409	0.0993	0.0415	0.0180	0.0082	0.0039	0.0020
10			0.3000	0.1301	0.0599	0.0248	0.0115	0.0056	0.0028
11			0.3636	0.1650	0.0734	0.0332	0.0156	0.0076	0.0039
12			0.4318	0.2070	0.0949	0.0440	0.0209	0.0103	0.0053
13			0.5000	0.2517	0.1199	0.0567	0.0274	0.0137	0.0071
14				0.3021	0.1489	0.0723	0.0356	0.0180	0.0094
15				0.3552	0.1818	0.0905	0.0454	0.0232	0.0122
16				0.4126	0.2188	0.1119	0.0571	0.0296	0.0157
17				0.4699	0.2592	0.1361	0.0708	0.0372	0.0200
18				0.5301	0.3032	0.1638	0.0869	0.0464	0.0252
19					0.3497	0.1924	0.1052	0.0570	0.0313
20					0.3986	0.2280	0.1261	0.0694	0.0385
21					0.4491	0.2643	0.1496	0.0836	0.0470
22					0.5000	0.3035	0.1755	0.0998	0.0567
23						0.3445	0.2039	0.1179	0.0680
24						0.3878	0.2349	0.1383	0.0807
25						0.4320	0.2680	0.1606	0.0951
26						0.4773	0.3032	0.1852	0.1112
27						0.5227	0.3403	0.2117	0.1290
28							0.3788	0.2404	0.1487
29							0.4185	0.2707	0.1701
30							0.4591	0.3029	0.1933
31							0.5000	0.3365	0.2181
32								0.3715	0.2447
33								0.4074	0.2729
34								0.4442	0.3024
35								0.4813	0.3332
36								0.5187	0.3652
37									0.3981
38									0.4317
39									0.4657
40									0.5000

TABLE 9 *(concluded)*　　Cumulative Distribution Function of the Mann-Whitney U Statistic: $F(u)$ for $n_1 \leq n_2$ and $3 \leq n_2 \leq 10$

| | | | | | $n_2 = 10$ | | | | | |
| | | | | | n_1 | | | | | |
u	1	2	3	4	5	6	7	8	9	10
0	0.0909	0.0152	0.0035	0.0010	0.0003	0.0001	0.0001	0.0000	0.0000	0.0000
1	0.1818	0.0303	0.0070	0.0020	0.0007	0.0002	0.0001	0.0000	0.0000	0.0000
2	0.2727	0.0606	0.0140	0.0040	0.0013	0.0005	0.0002	0.0001	0.0000	0.0000
3	0.3636	0.0909	0.0245	0.0070	0.0023	0.0009	0.0004	0.0002	0.0001	0.0000
4	0.4545	0.1364	0.0385	0.0120	0.0040	0.0015	0.0006	0.0003	0.0001	0.0001
5	0.5455	0.1818	0.0559	0.0180	0.0063	0.0024	0.0010	0.0004	0.0002	0.0001
6		0.2424	0.0804	0.0270	0.0097	0.0037	0.0015	0.0007	0.0003	0.0002
7		0.3030	0.1084	0.0380	0.0140	0.0055	0.0023	0.0010	0.0005	0.0002
8		0.3788	0.1434	0.0529	0.0200	0.0080	0.0034	0.0015	0.0007	0.0004
9		0.4545	0.1853	0.0709	0.0276	0.0112	0.0048	0.0022	0.0011	0.0005
10		0.5455	0.2343	0.0939	0.0376	0.0156	0.0068	0.0031	0.0015	0.0008
11			0.2867	0.1199	0.0496	0.0210	0.0093	0.0043	0.0021	0.0010
12			0.3462	0.1518	0.0646	0.0280	0.0125	0.0058	0.0028	0.0014
13			0.4056	0.1868	0.0823	0.0363	0.0165	0.0078	0.0038	0.0019
14			0.4685	0.2268	0.1032	0.0467	0.0215	0.0103	0.0051	0.0026
15			0.5315	0.2697	0.1272	0.0589	0.0277	0.0133	0.0066	0.0034
16				0.3177	0.1548	0.0736	0.0351	0.0171	0.0086	0.0045
17				0.3666	0.1855	0.0903	0.0439	0.0217	0.0110	0.0057
18				0.4196	0.2198	0.1099	0.0544	0.0273	0.0140	0.0073
19				0.4725	0.2567	0.1317	0.0665	0.0338	0.0175	0.0093
20				0.5275	0.2970	0.1566	0.0806	0.0416	0.0217	0.0116
21					0.3393	0.1838	0.0966	0.0506	0.0267	0.0144
22					0.3839	0.2139	0.1148	0.0610	0.0326	0.0177
23					0.4296	0.2461	0.1349	0.0729	0.0394	0.0216
24					0.4765	0.2811	0.1574	0.0864	0.0474	0.0262
25					0.5235	0.3177	0.1819	0.1015	0.0564	0.0315
26						0.3564	0.2087	0.1185	0.0667	0.0376
27						0.3962	0.2374	0.1371	0.0782	0.0446
28						0.4374	0.2681	0.1577	0.0912	0.0526
29						0.4789	0.3004	0.1800	0.1055	0.0615
30						0.5211	0.3345	0.2041	0.1214	0.0716
31							0.3698	0.2299	0.1388	0.0827
32							0.4063	0.2574	0.1577	0.0952
33							0.4434	0.2863	0.1781	0.1088
34							0.4811	0.3167	0.2001	0.1237
35							0.5189	0.3482	0.2235	0.1399
36								0.3809	0.2483	0.1575
37								0.4143	0.2745	0.1763
38								0.4484	0.3019	0.1965
39								0.4827	0.3304	0.2179
40								0.5173	0.3598	0.2406
41									0.3901	0.2644
42									0.4211	0.2894
43									0.4524	0.3153
44									0.4841	0.3421
45									0.5159	0.3697
46										0.3980
47										0.4267
48										0.4559
49										0.4853
50										0.5147

TABLE 10   Critical Values of the Wilcoxon *T* Statistic

One-Tailed	Two-Tailed	n = 5	n = 6	n = 7	n = 8	n = 9	n = 10
P = 0.05	P = 0.10	1	2	4	6	8	11
P = 0.025	P = 0.05		1	2	4	6	8
P = 0.01	P = 0.02			0	2	3	5
P = 0.005	P = 0.01				0	2	3

One-Tailed	Two-Tailed	n = 11	n = 12	n = 13	n = 14	n = 15	n = 16
P = 0.05	P = 0.10	14	17	21	26	30	36
P = 0.025	P = 0.05	11	14	17	21	25	30
P = 0.01	P = 0.02	7	10	13	16	20	24
P = 0.005	P = 0.01	5	7	10	13	16	19

One-Tailed	Two-Tailed	n = 17	n = 18	n = 19	n = 20	n = 21	n = 22
P = 0.05	P = 0.10	41	47	54	60	68	75
P = 0.025	P = 0.05	35	40	46	52	59	66
P = 0.01	P = 0.02	28	33	38	43	49	56
P = 0.005	P = 0.01	23	28	32	37	43	49

One-Tailed	Two-Tailed	n = 23	n = 24	n = 25	n = 26	n = 27	n = 28
P = 0.05	P = 0.10	83	92	101	110	120	130
P = 0.025	P = 0.05	73	81	90	98	107	117
P = 0.01	P = 0.02	62	69	77	85	93	102
P = 0.005	P = 0.01	55	68	68	76	84	92

One-Tailed	Two-Tailed	n = 29	n = 30	n = 31	n = 32	n = 33	n = 34
P = 0.05	P = 0.10	141	152	163	175	188	201
P = 0.025	P = 0.05	127	137	148	159	171	183
P = 0.01	P = 0.02	111	120	130	141	151	162
P = 0.005	P = 0.01	100	109	118	128	138	149

One-Tailed	Two-Tailed	n = 35	n = 36	n = 37	n = 38	n = 39
P = 0.05	P = 0.10	214	228	242	256	271
P = 0.025	P = 0.05	195	208	222	235	250
P = 0.01	P = 0.02	174	186	198	211	224
P = 0.005	P = 0.01	160	171	183	195	208

One-Tailed	Two-Tailed	n = 40	n = 41	n = 42	n = 43	n = 44	n = 45
P = 0.05	P = 0.10	287	303	319	336	353	371
P = 0.025	P = 0.05	264	279	295	311	327	344
P = 0.01	P = 0.02	238	252	267	281	297	313
P = 0.005	P = 0.01	221	234	248	262	277	292

One-Tailed	Two-Tailed	n = 46	n = 47	n = 48	n = 49	n = 50
P = 0.05	P = 0.10	389	408	427	446	466
P = 0.025	P = 0.05	361	379	397	415	434
P = 0.01	P = 0.02	329	345	362	380	398
P = 0.005	P = 0.01	307	323	339	356	373

Source: Reproduced from F. Wilcoxon and R. A. Wilcox, *Some Rapid Approximate Statistical Procedures* (1964), p. 28, with the permission of American Cyanamid Company.

TABLE 11   Critical Values of Spearman's Rank Correlation Coefficient

n	α = 0.05	α = 0.025	α = 0.01	α = 0.005
5	0.900	—	—	—
6	0.829	0.886	0.943	—
7	0.714	0.786	0.893	—
8	0.643	0.738	0.833	0.881
9	0.600	0.683	0.783	0.833
10	0.564	0.648	0.745	0.794
11	0.523	0.623	0.736	0.818
12	0.497	0.591	0.703	0.780
13	0.475	0.566	0.673	0.745
14	0.457	0.545	0.646	0.716
15	0.441	0.525	0.623	0.689
16	0.425	0.507	0.601	0.666
17	0.412	0.490	0.582	0.645
18	0.399	0.476	0.564	0.625
19	0.388	0.462	0.549	0.608
20	0.377	0.450	0.534	0.591
21	0.368	0.438	0.521	0.576
22	0.359	0.428	0.508	0.562
23	0.351	0.418	0.496	0.549
24	0.343	0.409	0.485	0.537
25	0.336	0.400	0.475	0.526
26	0.329	0.392	0.465	0.515
27	0.323	0.385	0.456	0.505
28	0.317	0.377	0.448	0.496
29	0.311	0.370	0.440	0.487
30	0.305	0.364	0.432	0.478

Source: Reproduced by permission from E. G. Olds, "Distribution of Sums of Squares of Rank Differences for Small Samples," *Annals of Mathematical Statistics* 9 (1938).

TABLE 12 Poisson Probability Distribution

This table gives values of

$$P(x) = \frac{\mu^x e^{-\mu}}{x!}$$

					μ					
x	.005	.01	.02	.03	.04	.05	.06	.07	.08	.09
0	.9950	.9900	.9802	.9704	.9608	.9512	.9418	.9324	.9231	.9139
1	.0050	.0099	.0192	.0291	.0384	.0476	.0565	.0653	.0738	.0823
2	.0000	.0000	.0002	.0004	.0008	.0012	.0017	.0023	.0030	.0037
3	.0000	.0000	.0000	.0000	.0000	.0000	.0000	.0001	.0001	.0001

					μ					
x	0.1	0.2	0.3	0.4	0.5	0.6	0.7	0.8	0.9	1.0
0	.9048	.8187	.7408	.6703	.6065	.5488	.4966	.4493	.4066	.3679
1	.0905	.1637	.2222	.2681	.3033	.3293	.3476	.3595	.3659	.3679
2	.0045	.0164	.0333	.0536	.0758	.0988	.1217	.1438	.1647	.1839
3	.0002	.0011	.0033	.0072	.0126	.0198	.0284	.0383	.0494	.0613
4	.0000	.0001	.0002	.0007	.0016	.0030	.0050	.0077	.0111	.0153
5	.0000	.0000	.0000	.0001	.0002	.0004	.0007	.0012	.0020	.0031
6	.0000	.0000	.0000	.0000	.0000	.0000	.0001	.0002	.0003	.0005
7	.0000	.0000	.0000	.0000	.0000	.0000	.0000	.0000	.0000	.0001

					μ					
x	1.1	1.2	1.3	1.4	1.5	1.6	1.7	1.8	1.9	2.0
0	.3329	.3012	.2725	.2466	.2231	.2019	.1827	.1653	.1496	.1353
1	.3662	.3614	.3543	.3452	.3347	.3230	.3106	.2975	.2842	.2707
2	.2014	.2169	.2303	.2417	.2510	.2584	.2640	.2678	.2700	.2707
3	.0738	.0867	.0998	.1128	.1255	.1378	.1496	.1607	.1710	.1804
4	.0203	.0260	.0324	.0395	.0471	.0551	.0636	.0723	.0812	.0902
5	.0045	.0062	.0084	.0111	.0141	.0176	.0216	.0260	.0309	.0361
6	.0008	.0012	.0018	.0026	.0035	.0047	.0061	.0078	.0098	.0120
7	.0001	.0002	.0003	.0005	.0008	.0011	.0015	.0020	.0027	.0034
8	.0000	.0000	.0001	.0001	.0001	.0002	.0003	.0005	.0006	.0009
9	.0000	.0000	.0000	.0000	.0000	.0000	.0001	.0001	.0001	.0002

					μ					
x	2.1	2.2	2.3	2.4	2.5	2.6	2.7	2.8	2.9	3.0
0	.1225	.1108	.1003	.0907	.0821	.0743	.0672	.0608	.0550	.0498
1	.2572	.2438	.2306	.2177	.2052	.1931	.1815	.1703	.1596	.1494
2	.2700	.2681	.2652	.2613	.2565	.2510	.2450	.2384	.2314	.2240
3	.1890	.1966	.2033	.2090	.2138	.2176	.2205	.2225	.2237	.2240
4	.0992	.1082	.1169	.1254	.1336	.1414	.1488	.1557	.1622	.1680
5	.0417	.0476	.0538	.0602	.0668	.0735	.0804	.0872	.0940	.1008
6	.0146	.0174	.0206	.0241	.0278	.0319	.0362	.0407	.0455	.0504
7	.0044	.0055	.0068	.0083	.0099	.0118	.0139	.0163	.0188	.0216
8	.0011	.0015	.0019	.0025	.0031	.0038	.0047	.0057	.0068	.0081
9	.0003	.0004	.0005	.0007	.0009	.0011	.0014	.0018	.0022	.0027
10	.0001	.0001	.0001	.0002	.0002	.0003	.0004	.0005	.0006	.0008
11	.0000	.0000	.0000	.0000	.0000	.0001	.0001	.0001	.0002	.0002
12	.0000	.0000	.0000	.0000	.0000	.0000	.0000	.0000	.0000	.0001

TABLE 12 *(continued)*   Poisson Probability Distribution

					μ					
x	3.1	3.2	3.3	3.4	3.5	3.6	3.7	3.8	3.9	4.0
0	.0450	.0408	.0369	.0334	.0302	.0273	.0247	.0224	.0202	.0183
1	.1397	.1304	.1217	.1135	.1057	.0984	.0915	.0850	.0789	.0733
2	.2165	.2087	.2008	.1929	.1850	.1771	.1692	.1615	.1539	.1465
3	.2237	.2226	.2209	.2186	.2158	.2125	.2087	.2046	.2001	.1954
4	.1734	.1781	.1823	.1858	.1888	.1912	.1931	.1944	.1951	.1954
5	.1075	.1140	.1203	.1264	.1322	.1377	.1429	.1477	.1522	.1563
6	.0555	.0608	.0662	.0716	.0771	.0826	.0881	.0936	.0989	.1042
7	.0246	.0278	.0312	.0348	.0385	.0425	.0466	.0508	.0551	.0595
8	.0095	.0111	.0129	.0148	.0169	.0191	.0215	.0241	.0269	.0298
9	.0033	.0040	.0047	.0056	.0066	.0076	.0089	.0102	.0116	.0132
10	.0010	.0013	.0016	.0019	.0023	.0028	.0033	.0039	.0045	.0053
11	.0003	.0004	.0005	.0006	.0007	.0009	.0011	.0013	.0016	.0019
12	.0001	.0001	.0001	.0002	.0002	.0003	.0003	.0004	.0005	.0006
13	.0000	.0000	.0000	.0000	.0001	.0001	.0001	.0001	.0002	.0002
14	.0000	.0000	.0000	.0000	.0000	.0000	.0000	.0000	.0000	.0001

					μ					
x	4.1	4.2	4.3	4.4	4.5	4.6	4.7	4.8	4.9	5.0
0	.0166	.0150	.0136	.0123	.0111	.0101	.0091	.0082	.0074	.0067
1	.0679	.0630	.0583	.0540	.0500	.0462	.0427	.0395	.0365	.0337
2	.1393	.1323	.1254	.1188	.1125	.1063	.1005	.0948	.0894	.0842
3	.1904	.1852	.1798	.1743	.1687	.1631	.1574	.1517	.1460	.1404
4	.1951	.1944	.1933	.1917	.1898	.1875	.1849	.1820	.1789	.1755
5	.1600	.1633	.1662	.1687	.1708	.1725	.1738	.1747	.1753	.1755
6	.1093	.1143	.1191	.1237	.1281	.1323	.1362	.1398	.1432	.1462
7	.0640	.0686	.0732	.0778	.0824	.0869	.0914	.0959	.1002	.1044
8	.0328	.0360	.0393	.0428	.0463	.0500	.0537	.0575	.0614	.0653
9	.0150	.0168	.0188	.0209	.0232	.0255	.0280	.0307	.0334	.0363
10	.0061	.0071	.0081	.0092	.0104	.0118	.0132	.0147	.0164	.0181
11	.0023	.0027	.0032	.0037	.0043	.0049	.0056	.0064	.0073	.0082
12	.0008	.0009	.0011	.0014	.0016	.0019	.0022	.0026	.0030	.0034
13	.0002	.0003	.0004	.0005	.0006	.0007	.0008	.0009	.0011	.0013
14	.0001	.0001	.0001	.0001	.0002	.0002	.0003	.0003	.0004	.0005
15	.0000	.0000	.0000	.0000	.0001	.0001	.0001	.0001	.0001	.0002

					μ					
x	5.1	5.2	5.3	5.4	5.5	5.6	5.7	5.8	5.9	6.0
0	.0061	.0055	.0050	.0045	.0041	.0037	.0033	.0030	.0027	.0025
1	.0311	.0287	.0265	.0244	.0225	.0207	.0191	.0176	.0162	.0149
2	.0793	.0746	.0701	.0659	.0618	.0580	.0544	.0509	.0477	.0446
3	.1348	.1293	.1239	.1185	.1133	.1082	.1033	.0985	.0938	.0892
4	.1719	.1681	.1641	.1600	.1558	.1515	.1472	.1428	.1383	.1339
5	.1753	.1748	.1740	.1728	.1714	.1697	.1678	.1656	.1632	.1606
6	.1490	.1515	.1537	.1555	.1571	.1584	.1594	.1601	.1605	.1606
7	.1086	.1125	.1163	.1200	.1234	.1267	.1298	.1326	.1353	.1377
8	.0692	.0731	.0771	.0810	.0849	.0887	.0925	.0962	.0998	.1033
9	.0392	.0423	.0454	.0486	.0519	.0552	.0586	.0620	.0654	.0688
10	.0200	.0220	.0241	.0262	.0285	.0309	.0334	.0359	.0386	.0413
11	.0093	.0104	.0116	.0129	.0143	.0157	.0173	.0190	.0207	.0225
12	.0039	.0045	.0051	.0058	.0065	.0073	.0082	.0092	.0102	.0113
13	.0015	.0018	.0021	.0024	.0028	.0032	.0036	.0041	.0046	.0052
14	.0006	.0007	.0008	.0009	.0011	.0013	.0015	.0017	.0019	.0022
15	.0002	.0002	.0003	.0003	.0004	.0005	.0006	.0007	.0008	.0009
16	.0001	.0001	.0001	.0001	.0001	.0002	.0002	.0002	.0003	.0003
17	.0000	.0000	.0000	.0000	.0000	.0001	.0001	.0001	.0001	.0001

TABLE 12 *(concluded)*   Poisson Probability Distribution

x	6.1	6.2	6.3	6.4	6.5	6.6	6.7	6.8	6.9	7.0
0	.0022	.0020	.0019	.0017	.0015	.0014	.0012	.0011	.0010	.0009
1	.0137	.0126	.0116	.0106	.0098	.0090	.0082	.0076	.0070	.0064
2	.0417	.0390	.0364	.0340	.0318	.0296	.0276	.0258	.0240	.0223
3	.0848	.0806	.0765	.0726	.0688	.0652	.0617	.0584	.0552	.0521
4	.1294	.1249	.1205	.1162	.1118	.1076	.1034	.0992	.0952	.0912
5	.1579	.1549	.1519	.1487	.1454	.1420	.1385	.1349	.1314	.1277
6	.1605	.1601	.1595	.1586	.1575	.1562	.1546	.1529	.1511	.1490
7	.1399	.1418	.1435	.1450	.1462	.1472	.1480	.1486	.1489	.1490
8	.1066	.1099	.1130	.1160	.1188	.1215	.1240	.1263	.1284	.1304
9	.0723	.0757	.0791	.0825	.0858	.0891	.0923	.0954	.0985	.1014
10	.0441	.0469	.0498	.0528	.0558	.0588	.0618	.0649	.0679	.0710
11	.0245	.0265	.0285	.0307	.0330	.0353	.0377	.0401	.0426	.0452
12	.0124	.0137	.0150	.0164	.0179	.0194	.0210	.0227	.0245	.0264
13	.0058	.0065	.0073	.0081	.0089	.0098	.0108	.0119	.0130	.0142
14	.0025	.0029	.0033	.0037	.0041	.0046	.0052	.0058	.0064	.0071
15	.0010	.0012	.0014	.0016	.0018	.0020	.0023	.0026	.0029	.0033
16	.0004	.0005	.0005	.0006	.0007	.0008	.0010	.0011	.0013	.0014
17	.0001	.0002	.0002	.0002	.0003	.0003	.0004	.0004	.0005	.0006
18	.0000	.0001	.0001	.0001	.0001	.0001	.0001	.0002	.0002	.0002
19	.0000	.0000	.0000	.0000	.0000	.0000	.0000	.0001	.0001	.0001

μ

x	7.1	7.2	7.3	7.4	7.5	7.6	7.7	7.8	7.9	8.0
0	.0008	.0007	.0007	.0006	.0006	.0005	.0005	.0004	.0004	.0003
1	.0059	.0054	.0049	.0045	.0041	.0038	.0035	.0032	.0029	.0027
2	.0208	.0194	.0180	.0167	.0156	.0145	.0134	.0125	.0116	.0107
3	.0492	.0464	.0438	.0413	.0389	.0366	.0345	.0324	.0305	.0286
4	.0874	.0836	.0799	.0764	.0729	.0696	.0663	.0632	.0602	.0573
5	.1241	.1204	.1167	.1130	.1094	.1057	.1021	.0986	.0951	.0916
6	.1468	.1445	.1420	.1394	.1367	.1339	.1311	.1282	.1252	.1221
7	.1489	.1486	.1481	.1474	.1465	.1454	.1442	.1428	.1413	.1396
8	.1321	.1337	.1351	.1363	.1373	.1382	.1388	.1392	.1395	.1396
9	.1042	.1070	.1096	.1121	.1144	.1167	.1187	.1207	.1224	.1241
10	.0740	.0770	.0800	.0829	.0858	.0887	.0914	.0941	.0967	.0993
11	.0478	.0504	.0531	.0558	.0585	.0613	.0640	.0667	.0695	.0722
12	.0283	.0303	.0323	.0344	.0366	.0388	.0411	.0434	.0457	.0481
13	.0154	.0168	.0181	.0196	.0211	.0227	.0243	.0260	.0278	.0296
14	.0078	.0086	.0095	.0104	.0113	.0123	.0134	.0145	.0157	.0169
15	.0037	.0041	.0046	.0051	.0057	.0062	.0069	.0075	.0083	.0090
16	.0016	.0019	.0021	.0024	.0026	.0030	.0033	.0037	.0041	.0045
17	.0007	.0008	.0009	.0010	.0012	.0013	.0015	.0017	.0019	.0021
18	.0003	.0003	.0004	.0004	.0005	.0006	.0006	.0007	.0008	.0009
19	.0001	.0001	.0001	.0002	.0002	.0002	.0003	.0003	.0003	.0004
20	.0000	.0000	.0001	.0001	.0001	.0001	.0001	.0001	.0001	.0002
21	.0000	.0000	.0000	.0000	.0000	.0000	.0000	.0000	.0001	.0001

TABLE 13   Control Chart Constants

n	For Estimating Sigma		For $\bar{X}$ Chart		For $\bar{X}$ Chart (Standard Given)	For R Chart		For R Chart (Standard Given)		For s Chart (Standard Given)			
	c_4	d_2	A_2	A_3	A	D_3	D_4	D_1	D_2	B_3	B_4	B_5	B_6
2	0.7979	1.128	1.880	2.659	2.121	0	3.267	0	3.686	0	3.267	0	2.606
3	0.8862	1.693	1.023	1.954	1.732	0	2.575	0	4.358	0	2.568	0	2.276
4	0.9213	2.059	0.729	1.628	1.500	0	2.282	0	4.698	0	2.266	0	2.088
5	0.9400	2.326	0.577	1.427	1.342	0	2.115	0	4.918	0	2.089	0	1.964
6	0.9515	2.534	0.483	1.287	1.225	0	2.004	0	5.078	0.030	1.970	0.029	1.874
7	0.9594	2.704	0.419	1.182	1.134	0.076	1.924	0.205	5.203	0.118	1.882	0.113	1.806
8	0.9650	2.847	0.373	1.099	1.061	0.136	1.864	0.387	5.307	0.185	1.815	0.179	1.751
9	0.9693	2.970	0.337	1.032	1.000	0.184	1.816	0.546	5.394	0.239	1.761	0.232	1.707
10	0.9727	3.078	0.308	0.975	0.949	0.223	1.777	0.687	5.469	0.284	1.716	0.276	1.669
15	0.9823	3.472	0.223	0.789	0.775	0.348	1.652	1.207	5.737	0.428	1.572	0.421	1.544
20	0.9869	3.735	0.180	0.680	0.671	0.414	1.586	1.548	5.922	0.510	1.490	0.504	1.470
25	0.9896	3.931	0.153	0.606	0.600	0.459	1.541	1.804	6.058	0.565	1.435	0.559	1.420

Source: T. P. Ryan, *Statistical Methods for Quality Improvement* © 1989 New York: John Wiley & Sons. This material is used by permission of John Wiley & Sons, Inc.

TABLE 14   Random Numbers

1559	9068	9290	8303	8508	8954	1051	6677	6415	0342
5550	6245	7313	0117	7652	5069	6354	7668	1096	5780
4735	6214	8037	1385	1882	0828	2957	0530	9210	0177
5333	1313	3063	1134	8676	6241	9960	5304	1582	6198
8495	2956	1121	8484	2920	7934	0670	5263	0968	0069
1947	3353	1197	7363	9003	9313	3434	4261	0066	2714
4785	6325	1868	5020	9100	0823	7379	7391	1250	5501
9972	9163	5833	0100	5758	3696	6496	6297	5653	7782
0472	4629	2007	4464	3312	8728	1193	2497	4219	5339
4727	6994	1175	5622	2341	8562	5192	1471	7206	2027
3658	3226	5981	9025	1080	1437	6721	7331	0792	5383
6906	9758	0244	0259	4609	1269	5957	7556	1975	7898
3793	6916	0132	8873	8987	4975	4814	2098	6683	0901
3376	5966	1614	4025	0721	1537	6695	6090	8083	5450
6126	0224	7169	3596	1593	5097	7286	2686	1796	1150
0466	7566	1320	8777	8470	5448	9575	4669	1402	3905
9908	9832	8185	8835	0384	3699	1272	1181	8627	1968
7594	3636	1224	6808	1184	3404	6752	4391	2016	6167
5715	9301	5847	3524	0077	6674	8061	5438	6508	9673
7932	4739	4567	6797	4540	8488	3639	9777	1621	7244
6311	2025	5250	6099	6718	7539	9681	3204	9637	1091
0476	1624	3470	1600	0675	3261	7749	4195	2660	2150
5317	3903	6098	9438	3482	5505	5167	9993	8191	8488
7474	8876	1918	9828	2061	6664	0391	9170	2776	4025
7460	6800	1987	2758	0737	6880	1500	5763	2061	9373
1002	1494	9972	3877	6104	4006	0477	0669	8557	0513
5449	6891	9047	6297	1075	7762	8091	7153	8881	3367
9453	0809	7151	9982	0411	1120	6129	5090	2053	7570
0471	2725	7588	6573	0546	0110	6132	1224	3124	6563
5469	2668	1996	2249	3857	6637	8010	1701	3141	6147
2782	9603	1877	4159	9809	2570	4544	0544	2660	6737
3129	7217	5020	3788	0853	9465	2186	3945	1696	2286
7092	9885	3714	8557	7804	9524	6228	7774	6674	2775
9566	0501	8352	1062	0634	2401	0379	1697	7153	6208
5863	7000	1714	9276	7218	6922	1032	4838	1954	1680
5881	9151	2321	3147	6755	2510	5759	6947	7102	0097
6416	9939	9569	0439	1705	4680	9881	7071	9596	8758
9568	3012	6316	9065	0710	2158	1639	9149	4848	8634
0452	9538	5730	1893	1186	9245	6558	9562	8534	9321
8762	5920	8989	4777	2169	7073	7082	9495	1594	8600
0194	0270	7601	0342	3897	4133	7650	9228	5558	3597
3306	5478	2797	1605	4996	0023	9780	9429	3937	7573
7198	3079	2171	6972	0928	6599	9328	0597	5948	5753
8350	4846	1309	0612	4584	4988	4642	4430	9481	9048
7449	4279	4224	1018	2496	2091	9750	6086	1955	9860
6126	5399	0852	5491	6557	4946	9918	1541	7894	1843
1851	7940	9908	3860	1536	8011	4314	7269	7047	0382
7698	4218	2726	5130	3132	1722	8592	9662	4795	7718
0810	0118	4979	0458	1059	5739	7919	4557	0245	4861
6647	7149	1409	6809	3313	0082	9024	7477	7320	5822
3867	7111	5549	9439	3427	9793	3071	6651	4267	8099
1172	7278	7527	2492	6211	9457	5120	4903	1023	5745
6701	1668	5067	0413	7961	7825	9261	8572	0634	1140
8244	0620	8736	2649	1429	6253	4181	8120	6500	8127
8009	4031	7884	2215	2382	1931	1252	8088	2490	9122
1947	8315	9755	7187	4074	4743	6669	6060	2319	0635
9562	4821	8050	0106	2782	4665	9436	4973	4879	8900
0729	9026	9631	8096	8906	5713	3212	8854	3435	4206
6904	2569	3251	0079	8838	8738	8503	6333	0952	1641

Source: T. P. Ryan, *Statistical Methods for Quality Improvement* © 1989 New York: John Wiley & Sons. This material is used by permission of John Wiley & Sons, Inc.

Page numbers followed by n indicate
material found in notes.

A

Absolute frequencies, 21
Absolute kurtosis, 22
Absolute zero, 4
Acceptable Pins (case), 177–178
Acceptance sampling, 602
Acceptance Sampling of Pins (case), 216
Actions, 703
Aczel, A. D., 88n, 731n
Additive factors, 381, 568
Adjusted multiple coefficient of
    determination, 479
Aizenman, Joshua, 565n
All possible regressions, 545
Alternative actions, 704
Alternative hypothesis, 257–258, 353–354
Analysis of covariance, 509
Analysis of variance (ANOVA), 205,
    349–402, 509
  ANOVA diagram, 371
  ANOVA table and examples, 364–369
  ANOVA table for regression, 443–444
  assumptions of, 351
  blocking designs, 379
  completely randomized design, 379
  computer use and, 398–402
  confidence intervals, 372–373
  defined, 349
  degrees of freedom, 361–362
  error deviation, 357
  Excel for, 398–399
  experimental design, 379
  F statistic, 363–364
  fixed-effects vs. random-effects
      models, 379
  further analysis, 371–373
  grand mean, 355, 359
  hypothesis test of, 350–354
  main principle of, 355
  mean squares, 362–363
  MINITAB for, 400–402
  models, factors, and designs, 378–380
  multiple regression, 475, 480
  one-factor model, 378
  one-factor vs. multifactor models, 378–379
  principle of, 357
  quality control and, 602
  random-effects model, 379
  randomized complete block design, 379,
      393–395

repeated-measures design, 395
sum-of-squares principle, 358–361
template (single-factor ANOVA), 377
test statistic for, 351–354, 364
theory and computations of, 355–358
three factors extension, 389
total deviation of data point, 359
treatment deviation, 357
Tukey pairwise-comparisons test,
    373–376
two-way ANOVA, 380–381
two-way ANOVA with one observation
    per cell, 389–391
unequal sample size, 376
ANOVA; *see* Analysis of variance (ANOVA)
ANOVA table, 364–369
ANOVA test statistic, 351–354, 364
Arithmetic mean, 10
Asimov, Eric, 219
Auto Parts Sales Forecasts (case), 592–593
Autocorrelation, 539
Average, 10; *see also* Mean
Averaging out and folding back, 707

B

Backward elimination, 545–546
Bailey, Jeff, 669n
Baker-Said, Stephanie, 626n
Balanced design, 376
Baland, J. M., 482n
Banner, Katie, 317n
Bar charts, 25, 38
  probability bar chart, 92–93
Barbaro, Michael, 284n
Barenghi, C., 731n
Barr, Susan Learner, 254n
Barrionuevo, Alexei, 185n
Base period, 584
Basic outcome, 54
Bayes, Thomas, 73
Bayes' Theorem, 73–74, 689
  additional information and, 714–716
  continuous probability distributions,
      695–700
  determining the payoff, 716
  determining the probabilities, 716–719
  discrete probability models, 688–693
  extended Bayes' Theorem, 77–79
  normal probability model, 701–702
Bayesian analysis, 687–688
Bayesian statistics, 687–699
  advantages of approach, 691
  classical approaches vs., 688

computer usage for, 731–733
subjective probabilities, evaluation of,
    701–702
template for, 692–693
Bearden, William O., 377n
Beaver, William H., 443n
Bell-shaped normal curve, 147
Berdahl, Robert M., 51
Berenson, Alex, 713n
Bernoulli, Jakob, 112
Bernoulli distribution, 112
Bernoulli process, 113
Bernoulli random variable, 112
Bernoulli trial, 112
Bertrand, Marianne, 519n
Best, R., 731n
Best linear unbiased estimators (BLUE),
    415, 472
B computation of, 269–271
B and power of test, 264, 289
Between-treatments deviation, 360
Bias, 181, 201–203
  nonresponse bias, 5–6, 181
Bigda, Caroline, 25n
Billett, Matthew T., 512n
Binary variable, 504
BINOMDIST function, 133
Binomial distribution, 71, 115
  MINITAB for, 134–135
  negative binomial distribution, 118–120
  normal approximation of, 169–170
  population proportions, 276
  template for, 115–116
Binomial distribution formulas, 114–115
Binomial distribution template, 115–116
Binomial probability formula, 114
Binomial random variable, 93, 113–116
  conditions for, 113–114
Binomial successes, 184
Biscourp, Pierre, 493n
Block, 393, 653
Blocking, 308
Blocking designs, 379, 393–397
  randomized complete block design,
      393–395
  repeated-measures design, 395
BLUE (best linear unbiased estimators),
    415, 472
Bonferroni method, 376
Box-and-whisker plot, 31
Box plots, 31–33, 38
  elements of, 31–32
  uses of, 33
Brav, James C., 481n

Briley, Donnel A., 370n
Brooks, Rick, 284n
Bruno, Mark, 645n
Bukey, David, 318n
Burros, Marian, 644n
Bush, Jason, 227n
Business cycle, 566, 621

C

c chart, 614–615
Caesar, William K., 569n
Callbacks, 189
Capability of any process, 598
Capital Asset Pricing Model (CAPM), 458
Carey, John, 316n
Carlson, Jay P., 377n
Carter, Erin, 632n
Cases
 Acceptable Pins, 177–178
 Acceptance Sampling of Pins, 216
 Auto Parts Sales Forecasts, 592–593
 Checking Out Checkout, 406
 Concepts Testing, 145
 Firm Leverage and Shareholder
  Rights, 466–467
 Job Applications, 89
 Multicurrency Decision, 177–178
 NASDAQ Volatility, 48
 New Drug Development, 736–737
 Nine Nations of North America, 684–685
 Pizzas "R" Us, 735
 Presidential Polling, 254–255
 Privacy Problem, 255
 Quality Control and Improvement at
  Nashua Corporation, 618–619
 Rating Wines, 406
 Return on Capital for Four Different
  Sectors, 556–558
 Risk and Return, 467
 Tiresome Tires I, 301
 Tiresome Tires II, 346
Casey, Susan, 345n
Cassidy, Michael, 652n
Categorical variable, 4
Causality, 433
Center of mass, 103
Centerline, 599, 606, 608–609, 612, 614
Central limit theorem, 194–198, 220
 effects of, 195
 history of, 198
 population standard deviation and, 198
 sample size and, 194
Central tendency; *see* Measures of central
  tendency
Centrality of observations, 10, 102
Chance node, 705
Chance occurrences, 703–704
Chance outcome, 715
Chart Wizard, 37

Charts; *see* Methods of displaying data
Chatzky, Jean, 171, 254n, 297n, 644n
Chebyshev's theorem, 24, 108–109
Checking Out Checkout (case), 406
Chi-square analysis with fixed marginal
  totals, 675
Chi-square distribution, 239, 249, 330
 mean of, 239
 values and probabilities of, 240
Chi-square random variable, 331
Chi-square statistic, 662
Chi-square test for equality of proportions,
  675–678
Chi-square test for goodness of fit, 661–668
 chi-square statistic, 662
 degrees of freedom, 665–666
 multinominal distribution, 662–663
 rule for use of, 665
 steps in analysis, 661
 template for, 664, 668
 unequal probabilities, 664–666
CHIINV function, 249
Christen, Markus, 377n, 481n, 555n
Classes, 20
Classical approach, 687–688
Classical probability, 52
Cluster, 188
Cluster sampling, 188
Coefficient of determination (r^2), 439–442
Collinearity, 531–532; *see also*
  Multicollinearity
Combinations, 71, 81
Combinatorial concepts, 70–72
Comparison of two populations, 303–341
 computer templates for, 338–340
 difference (population-means/independent
  random samples), 310–322
 equality of two population variances,
  333–337
 F distribution, 330–333
 large-sample test (two population
  proportions), 324–328
 paired-observation comparisons, 304–308
Complement, 53–54
 rule of complements, 58
Completely randomized design, 352, 379
Computational formula for the variance
  of a random variable, 105
Computers; *see also* Excel; Templates
 bar charts, 38
 Bayesian statistics/decision analysis,
  731–733
 box plots, 38
 confidence interval estimation, 248–250
 decision analysis, 731–733
 for descriptive statistics and plots, 35–40
 in forecasting and time series, 588–591
 histograms, 36–37
 hypothesis testing, 298–300
 multiple regression using Solver, 548–551

normal distribution, 171–172
one-way ANOVA, 398
paired-difference test, 338–340
percentile/percentile rank computation, 36
pie charts, 37
probability, 80–82
 for quality control, 616–617
 sampling distributions, 209–213
 scatter plots, 38–39
 for standard distributions, 133–134
 time plots, 38
 two-way ANOVA, 398–399
Concepts Testing (case), 145
Concomitant variables, 509
Conditional probability, 61–63, 74,
  688, 715
Confidence, 219
Confidence coefficient, 223
CONFIDENCE function, 248
Confidence intervals, 167, 219–250, 303
 Bayesian approach, 220n
 classical/frequentist interpretation, 220n
 defined, 219
 80% confidence interval, 224
 Excel functions for, 248–250
 expected value of Y for given X, 457
 half-width, determining optimal, 245–246
 important property of, 224
 individual population means, 372
 MININTAB for, 249–250
 95% confidence interval, 221–223
 paired-observation comparisons, 307–308
 population mean (known standard
  deviation), 220–226
 population means, difference between,
  316, 321
 population proportion (large sample),
  235–237
 population proportions, difference
  between, 327
 population variance, 239–242
 regression parameters, 426–428
 sample-size determination, 243–245
 t distribution, 228–233
 templates, 225–226, 242
Confidence level, 223, 263
Conlin, Michelle, 288n
Consistency, 203
Consumer price index (CPI), 561, 583,
  585–587
Contingency table, 62, 669–670
Contingency table analysis, 669–672
 chi-square test for independence, 669–672
 chi-square test statistic for
  independence, 670
 degrees of freedom, chi-square statistic, 670
 expected count in cell, 671
 hypothesis test for independence, 670
 template, 672–673
 Yates correction, 672

Continuity correction, 169–170
Continuous probability distributions, Bayes' theorem and, 695–700
Continuous random variable, 95–96, 126–128
Control chart, 598–601, 606
　centerline, 599, 606, 608–609, 612, 614
　lower control limit (LCL), 599, 606, 608–609, 612, 614
　out of control, 599
　for process mean, 606
　for process proportion, 612
　upper control limit (UCL), 599, 606, 608–609, 612, 614
Control treatment (placebo), 350
Cook, R. Dennis, 514n
Cordoba, Jose de, 329
Correlation, 429–433, 531
Correlation analysis, 429
Correlation coefficient, 429
Correlation matrix, 533–534
Counts of data points, 21
Covariance, 430
CPI (Consumer price index), 561, 583, 585–587
Creamer, Matthew, 364n
Credible sets, 689, 698–699
Creswell, Julie, 100n
Crockett, Roger O., 84n
Cross-product terms, 517–519
Cross-tabs, 669
Cumulative distribution function, 96–98
Cumulative frequency plots (ogives), 25, 27
Cumulative probability function, 97
Curved trends, 562
Curvilinear relationship, 413, 447–448
Cveykus, Renee, 632n
Cycle, 566
Cyclical behavior, 566–569
Cyclical variation, 566

D

Darwin, Charles, 409
Dash, Eric, 252n
Data, 3, 5
　grouped data, 20–22
Data collection, 5
Data set, 5, 102
Data smoothing, 570
de Fermat, Pierre, 52
de Finetti, Bruno, 52n
de Mère, Chevalier, 52
de Moivre, Abraham, 52, 148, 198
Decision, 182, 704, 706
Decision analysis, 688, 702–705
　actions, 703
　additional information, 704
　chance occurrences, 703–704
　decision, 704
　decision tree, 705–712

elements of, 703
final outcomes, 704
overview of, 702–705
payoff table, 706–709
probabilities, 704
utility, 725–728
value of information, 728–731
Decision node, 705
Decision tree, 705–712
Deflators, 585
DeGraw, Irv, 481n
Degree of linear association, 429–431
Degrees of freedom (df), 198, 205–208
　ANOVA and, 361–362, 383–384, 389
　chi-square statistic, 670
　chi-square tests, 665–666
　sum-of-squares for error (SSE), 362
　sum-of-squares total (SST) and, 362
　sum-of-squares for treatment (SSTR), 362
Degrees of freedom of the denominator, 330
Degrees of freedom of the numerator, 330
Demers, Elizabeth, 465n
Deming, W. Edwards, 596–597
Deming Award, 596
Deming's 14 Points, 597–598
Dependent indicator variable, regression with, 528–529
Dependent variable, 409
Descriptive graphs, 25
Descriptive statistics, 3–40, 181n
　computer use for, 35–39
　exploratory data analysis, 29–33
　grouped data and histogram, 20–22
　mean-standard deviation relations, 24–25
　measures of central tendency, 10–14
　measures of variability, 10–14
　methods of displaying data, 25–29
　MINITAB for, 39–40
　percentiles and quartiles, 8–9, 36
　random variable, 91–94
　skewness and kurtosis, 22–23, 33
　templates for random variables, 109–110
Deseasonalizing a time series, 572–573
df; see Degrees of freedom (df)
Diffuse priors, 698
Discrete probability models, 688–689
Discrete random variable, 95–96
　Bayes' theorem for, 689
　cumulative distribution function of, 97
　expected values of, 102–107
　probability distribution of, 96
　variance of, 104–105
Disjoint sets, 54
Dispersion, 14–15, 106; see also Measures of variability
Displaying data; see Methods of displaying data
Distribution of the data, 9
Distribution-free methods, 682; see also Nonparametric tests

Distributions; see also Normal distribution; Probability distribution
　Bernoulli distribution, 112
　cumulative distribution function, 96–98
　exponential distribution, 130–133
　geometric distribution, 120–121
　hypergeometric distribution, 121–124
　kurtosis of, 22–23
　Poisson distribution, 124–126
　sampling distributions, 190–200
　skewness of, 22–23
　uniform distribution, 129–130
Dobyns, L., 601n
Dow Jones Industrial Average, 582–583
Dummy variable, 503, 507, 568
Dummy variable regression technique, 568
Durbin-Watson test, 445, 539–541
Durbin-Watson test statistic, 540

E

Eccles, Robert G., 577n
EDA (Exploratory data analysis), 29–33
Efficiency, 201, 203, 733
80% confidence interval, 224
Elementary event, 54
Elements of a set, 53
Elliot, Stuart, 324n
Empirical rule, 24–25, 163n
Empty set, 53
Enumerative data, 661
Epstein, Edward, 68n
Error deviation, 357, 359
Error probability, 223
Estimated regression relationship, 472
Estimators, 183–184, 201
　consistency of, 201, 203
　efficiency of, 201, 203
　of population parameter, 184–185
　properties of, 201–204, 414
　sufficiency of, 201, 203
　as unbiased, 201–203
Event, 55, 688
EVPI (expected value of perfect information), 728
Excel; see also Solver Macro
　ANOVA and, 398–399
　Bayesian revision of probabilities, 80–81
　descriptive statistics and plots, 25–40
　F-test, 340
　in forecasting and time series, 588–591
　graphs, 27
　histograms, 36–37
　LINEST function, 461–462
　normal distribution, 171–172
　one-sample hypothesis testing, 298–299
　paired-difference test, 338–340
　percentile/percentile rank computation, 36
　probabilities, 80–82
　Random Number Generation analysis, 211

Excel; *see also* Solver Macro—*Cont.*
  regression, 458–459, 462–463
  Sampling analysis tool, 210
  sampling distributions and, 209–213
  standard distributions and, 133–134
  t-test, 340
Excel Analysis Toolpack, 35
Expected net gain from sampling, 730
Expected payoff, 707, 711–712
Expected value of a discrete random
     variable, 102–103
Expected value of a function of a random
     variable, 103–104
Expected value of a linear composite, 107
Expected value of a linear function of a
     random variable, 104
Expected value of perfect information
     (EVPI), 728
Expected value of sample mean, 192
Expected value of the sum of random
     variables, 107
Experiment, 54
Experimental design, 379, 602
Experimental units, 308, 380
Explained deviation, 439–440
Explained variation, 361, 440
Exploratory data analysis (EDA), 29–33
  box plots, 31–33
  stem-and-leaf displays, 30–31
EXPONDIST function, 134
Exponential distribution, 130–133
  common examples of, 130–131
  remarkable property of, 131
  template for, 131–132, 134
Exponential model, 524
Exponential smoothing methods, 577–582
  model for, 579
  template for, 581–582
  weighting factor (*w*), 578–580
Extended Bayes' Theorem, 77
Extra sum of squares, 543
Extrapolation, 498

F

F distribution, 330–333, 351, 444
  degrees of freedom of the denominator,
     330, 351
  degrees of freedom of the numerator,
     330, 351
  equality of two population variances,
     333–334
  templates for, 336–337
F ratio, two-way ANOVA, 384
F statistic, 363–364
F test, 314, 340
  multiple regression model, 473–476
  partial *F* tests, 542–544
  of regression model, 443–444, 448
Factor, 378

Factorial, 70, 81
Fair games, 103
Fairley, W., 257n
Farley, Amy, 99n
Farzad, R., 43n
Fass, Allison, 234n, 288n
Feller, W., 70, 198, 626
Ferry, John, 29n, 69n
Fialka, John J., 251n
50th percentile, 9
Final outcomes, 704
Firm Leverage and Shareholder Rights
     (case), 466–467
First quartile, 9
Fisher, Anne, 252n
Fisher, Sir Ronald A., 330, 349
Fixed-effects vs. random-effects models, 379
Flight simulators, 30
Fong, Eric A., 465n
Forbes, Malcolm, 3
Forbes, Steve, 701n
Forecasting
  Excel/MINITAB in, 588–591
  exponential smoothing methods, 577–582
  index numbers, 582–587
  multiplicative series, 576–577
  ratio-to-moving-average method, 569–576
  seasonality and cyclical behavior, 566–569
  trend analysis, 561–564
Forward selection, 545
Frame, 8, 186
Frequency, 20
Frequency distribution, 183
Frequency polygon, 25–27
Frequentist approach, 687
Friedman test, 396, 645
  data layout for, 653
  null and alternative hypotheses of, 653
  template, 655–656
  test statistic, 654
Fulcrum, 11
Full model (*F* test), 542–543

G

Gagnepain, Philippe, 582n
Galilei, Galileo, 52
Galton, Sir Francis, 409
Gambling models, 52
Ganguly, Ananda, 393n
Garbaix, Xavier, 481n
Gauss, Carl Friedrich, 148
Gauss-Markov theorem, 415
Gaussian distribution, 148
Generalized least squares (GLS), 541
Geometric distribution, 120–121
  formulas for, 120
  template for, 121
Geometric progression, 120
Gleason, Kimberly C., 466n, 491n

GLS (Generalized least squares), 541
Goal seek command, 116, 123, 166
Goldstein, Matthew, 639n
Gomez, Paulo, 565n
Good, I. J., 51
Goodness-of-fit test, 662
  for multinomial distribution, 663–664
Goodstein, Laurie, 6n
Gossett, W. D., 229
Grand mean, 355, 359, 378, 383, 599
Graphs; *see* Methods of displaying data
Gray, Patricia B., 253n
Green, Heather, 239n
Grouped data, 20–22
Grover, Ronald, 225n
Gruley, Bryan, 144n

H

Hall, Kenji, 238n
Hammand, S., 26
Hansell, Saul, 288n
Hardesty, David M., 377n
Harris, Elizabeth, 201n, 280n
Harris, Marlys, 280n, 285n
HDP (highest-posterior-density), 698
Hellmich, Nancy, 69n
Helm, Burt, 87n, 189n, 679n
Herbold, Joshua, 393n
Heteroscedasticity, 446, 494, 502, 527
Highest-posterior-density (HPD), 698
Hinges (of box plot), 31–32
Histogram, 20–22, 25, 36–37, 126–127, 449
Holson, Laura M., 309n
Homogeneity, tests of, 675
Hovanesian, Marader, 44n
HSD (honestly significant differences) test, 373
Huddleston, Patricia, 465n
Hui, Jerome Kueh Swee, 403n
Hypergeometric distribution, 121–124
  formulas for, 122–123
  problem solving with template,
     123–124, 134
  schematic for, 122
HYPGEOMDIST function, 134
Hypothesis, 257
Hypothesis testing, 257–300, 303
  alternative hypothesis, 257–258, 353–354
  ANOVA, 350–354
  association between two variables, 658
  B and power of test, 264
  common types of, 272
  computing *B*, 269
  concepts of, 260–265
  confidence level, 263–264
  evidence gathering, 260
  Excel/MINITAB for, 298–300
  for independence, 670
  individual regression slope parameters, 484
  Kruskal-Wallis test, 646

left-tailed test, 267–270
linear relationship between X and Y, 435
median test, 677
null hypothesis, 257–258, 353–354
one-tailed and two-tailed tests, 267–269
operating characteristic (OC) curve, 292–293
optimal significance level, 263–264
p-value, 261–262, 273
p-value computation, 265–267
paired-observations two-sample test, 639
population means, 272–273, 289–290
population proportions, 276–278, 294–295
population variance, 278–279
power curve, 291–292, 296
power of the test, 264
pretest decisions, 289–296
regression relationship, 434–438, 474
required sample size (manual calculation), 290–291, 295
right-tailed test, 268, 271
sample size, 264–265, 295
significance level, 262–263
t tables, 273
templates, 274–275
test statistic, 272
two-tailed test, 267, 269, 271
two-way ANOVA, 382–383, 386
type I/II errors, 260–261, 263–264

I

Ihlwan, Moon, 238n
Independence of events, 66–68, 669;
        see also Contingency table analysis
    conditions for, 66
    product rules for, 66–68
Independent events, 68
Independent variable, 409
Index, 582
Index numbers, 582–587
    changing base period of index, 584
    Consumer Price Index (CPI), 561, 583, 585–587
    as deflators, 585
    template, 587
Indicator variable, 503–504, 506
Indifference, 727
Inferential statistics, 52, 181
Influential observation, 498
Information, 3
    expected net gain from sampling, 730
    expected value of perfect information (EVPI), 728
    qualitative vs. quantitative, 3
    value of, 728–731
Initial run, 604
Inner fence, 32
Interaction effects, 381–382, 510
Interarrival time, 131

Intercept, 418, 420
Interquartile range (IQR), 9, 14–15, 32
Intersection, 53–54
Intersection rule, 67
Interval estimate, 184
Interval scale, 4
Intrinsically linear models, 521
Introduction to Probability Theory and Its Applications (Feller), 626
Inverse transformation, 157, 162–165
Irregular components models, 591

J

Jiraporn, Pornsit, 466n, 491n
Jo, Hoje, 492n
Job Applications (case), 89
Johar, Gita Venkataramani, 391n
Johnson, George, 687, 687n
Johnston, J., 535n
Joint confidence intervals, 427
Joint density, 695
Joint hypothesis, 350
Joint probability, 59
Joint probability table, 79–80
Joint test, 350
Joos, Philip, 465n
Josephy, N. H., 88n
Juran, J. M., 601

K

k-variable multiple regression model, 469–473
Kacperczyk, Marcin, 371n
Kang, Jun-Koo, 674n
Kendall's tau, 659
Keynes, John Maynard, 3
Kim, Yongtae, 492n
Kimball's inequality, 388
King, Tao-Hsien Dolly, 512n
Kirkland, R., 29n
Knapp, Volker, 235n, 283n
Knox, Noelle, 343n
Kondratieff definition, 621
Kramarz, Francis, 493n
Kranhold, Kathryn, 251n
Krishnamurthy, Arvind, 481n
Kroll, Lovisa, 234n, 288n
Kruskal-Wallis test, 351, 378, 645–651
    further analysis, 650–651
    template for, 648–649
    test statistic, 646
Kurtosis, 22–23
Kwon, Young Sun, 371n

L

Lack of fit, 498–499
Lamey, Lien, 414n

Large sample confidence intervals for population proportion, 324
Large-sample properties, 628
Lav, Kong Cheen, 555n
Law of total probability, 73–75
LCL (lower control limit), 599, 606, 608–609, 612, 614
Least-squares estimates, 471–472, 497
Lee, Alan J., 514n
Lee, Hyun-Joo, 465n
Lee, Louise, 679n
Lee, Yeonho, 565n
Left-skewed distribution, 22
Left-tailed test, 267–270, 622
Lehman, Paula, 679n
Leptokurtic distribution, 23
Lerner, Josh, 555n
Lettav, Martin, 465n
Level of significance, 262–264
Li, Peter Ping, 713n
Likelihood function, 688–689
Linear composite, 107–110
    expected value of, 107
LINEST function, 461–462, 550–551
Literary Digest presidential poll, 181–183
Lo, May Chiun, 403n
Location of observations, 10, 102
Logarithmic model, 525
Logarithmic transformation, 521–523, 528
Logistic function, 528–529
Logistic regression model, 528
Loss, 704
Loss function, 603
Lower control limit (LCL), 599, 606, 608–609, 612, 614
Lower quartile, 9

M

Malkiel, Burton G., 201n
Mann-Whitney *U* test, 314, 633–638
    computational procedure, 634
    MINITAB for, 637–638
    null and alternative hypothesis for, 633
    U statistic, 634
Manual recalculation, 502–503
Marcial, Gene G., 216n
Margin of error, 221
Marginal probabilities, 80
Marketing research, 6
Martin, Mitchell, 161n
Martinez, Valeria, 577n
Mauer, David, 512n
Mean, 10–13, 102
    defined, 10
    extreme observations and, 12
    grand mean, 355
    population mean, 11, 15, 183, 372
    sample mean, 10, 191, 193, 355
    standard deviation and, 24–25

Mean square error (MSE), 362–363
    multiple regression, 477–478
    simple linear regression, 424
Mean square treatment (MSTR),
    362–363
Mean time between failures (MTBF), 130
Measurements, 4
    scales of, 4
Measures of central tendency, 10–14
    mean, 10–13
    median, 9–13
    mode, 10–13
Measures of variability, 14–19, 102
    interquartile range, 9, 14–15
    range, 15
    standard deviation, 15
    variance, 15
Median, 9–12
Median test, 677–678
Mehring, James, 323n
Method of least squares, 415
Methods of displaying data, 25–29
    bar charts, 25
    cautionary note to, 27–28
    exploratory data analysis (EDA),
        29–33
    frequency polygons, 25–27
    histogram, 20–22, 25, 36–37
    ogives, 25–27
    pie charts, 25, 37
    time plots, 28
Middle quartile, 9
MINITAB
    ANOVA and, 400–402
    comparison of two samples, 340–341
    confidence interval estimation,
        249–250
    for descriptive statistics/plots, 39–40
    for factorial, combination, and
        permutation, 81
    in forecasting and time series, 589–591
    Mann-Whitney test, 637
    multicollinearity, 533
    multiple regression, 551–554
    nonparametric tests, 680–681
    normal distribution, 172
    one-sample hypothesis testing,
        299–300
    for quality control, 616–617
    regression analysis, 498
    sampling distributions, 212–213
    simple linear regression analysis,
        463–464
    standard distributions, 134–135
    stepwise regression, 547–548
Missing variables test, 446
Mode, 10–13, 22
Montgomery, D., 502n
Moskin, Julia, 43n
Mosteller, F., 257n

Mound-shaped distribution, 24
Moving average, 569
MSE; see Mean square error (MSE)
MSTR (mean square treatment), 362–363
MTBF (mean time between failures), 130
Mukhopadhyay, Anirban, 391n
Multicollinearity, 483–484, 531–537
    causes of, 515, 532–533
    detecting existence of, 533–536
    effects of, 536
    solutions to problem, 537
Multicollinearity set, 532
Multicurrency Decision (case), 177–178
Multifactor ANOVA models, 378–379
Multinomial distribution, 662
    goodness-of-fit test for, 663
Multiple coefficient of determination (R^2), 478
Multiple correlation coefficient, 478
Multiple regression, 409, 469–554
    adjusted multiple coefficient of
        determination, 479
    ANOVA table for, 475, 480
    assumptions for model, 469
    cross-product terms, 517–519
    decomposition of total deviation, 474
    dependent indicator variable and,
        528–529
    Durbin-Watson test, 539–541
    estimated regression relationship,
        472–473
    F test, 473–476
    how good is the regression, 477–480
    influential observation, 498
    k-variable model, 469–473
    lack of fit and other problems,
        498–499
    least-squares regression surface, 472
    LINEST function for, 550–551
    mean square error (MSE), 477
    measures of performance of, 480
    MINITAB and, 551–552
    multicollinearity, 483–484, 531–537
    multiple coefficient of determination
        R^2, 478–479
    multiple correlation coefficient, 478
    nonlinear models and transformations,
        521–529
    normal equations, two independent
        variables, 470
    normal probability plot, 496
    other variables, 517–519
    outliers and influential observations,
        496–498
    partial F test, 542–544
    polynomial regression, 513–519
    prediction and, 500–503
    qualitative independent variables,
        503–511
    qualitative/quantitative variables
        interactions, 510–511

residual autocorrelation, 539–541
residual plots, 494
significance of individual regression
    parameters, 482–491
Solver, 548–551
standard error of estimate, 478
standardized residuals, 494–497
template for, 472, 487, 490, 496,
    502, 516
validity of model, 494–499
variable selection methods, 545–547
Multiplicative model, 521, 568
Multiplicative series, forecast of, 576–577
Multistage cluster sampling, 188
Murphy, Dean E., 51n
Mutually exclusive events, 59, 68–69
Mutually independent, 107

N

N factorial ($n!$), 70
NASDAQ Volatility (case), 48
Negative binomial distribution, 118–120
    problem solving with template,
        119–120, 134
Negative correlation, 430
Negative skewness, 22
NEGBINOMDIST function, 134
Nelson, Lloyd S., 605n, 619n
Nelson, Melissa, 652n
Net regression coefficients, 471
New Drug Development (case), 736–737
Newquist, Scott C., 577n
Newton, Sir Isaac, 595
Nine Nations of North America (case),
    684–685
95% confidence interval, 221–223
Nominal scale, 4
Noninformative, 687
Nonlinear models, 513, 521–529
Nonparametric tests, 314, 621–682
    chi-square test, 661–662
    chi-square test for equality of proportions,
        675–677
    contingency table analysis, 669–673
    defined, 621
    Friedman test, 653–656
    Kruskal-Wallis test, 351, 645–651
    Mann-Whitney U test, 633–638
    median test, 677–678
    MINITAB for, 680–681
    paired-observations two-sample test,
        639–640
    runs test, 626–629
    sign test, 621–625
    Spearman rank correlation coefficient,
        657–660
    summary of, 682
    Wald-Wolfowitz test, 630–631
    Wilcoxon signed-rank test, 639–643

Nonresponse, 188–189
Nonresponse bias, 5–6, 181
Normal approximation of binomial
        distributions, 169–170
    template, 171–172
Normal distribution, 147–172; *see also*
        Standard normal distribution
    absolute kurtosis of, 23
    Excel functions for, 171–172
    inverse transformation, 162–165
    MINITAB for, 172
    normal approximation of binomial
        distributions, 169–170
    probability density function, 147
    properties of, 148–150
    sampling and, 192, 198
    standard normal distribution,
        151–155
    template for, 166–169
    testing population proportions, 276
    transformation of normal random
        variables, 156–160
Normal equations, 417
Normal prior distribution, 701–702
Normal probability model, 696, 702
Normal probability plot, 448–450, 496
Normal random variables
    inverse transformation, 162–165
    inverse transformation of Z to X, 157
    obtaining values, given
        a probability, 165
    transformation of X to Z, 156, 160
    transformation of, 156–160
    using the normal transformation, 157
Normal sampling distribution,
        192–193
NORMDIST function, 171
NORMSINV function, 249
Null hypothesis, 257, 353–354
    Chi-square test for equality
        of proportions, 675
    of Friedman test, 653
    Mann-Whitney U test, 633
    multinomial distribution, 663

O

Objective probability, 52
OC (Operating characteristic curve), 292
Odds, 58
Ogives, 25–27
1 standard deviation, 24
One-factor ANOVA model, 378
    Excel/MINITAB for, 398, 401
    multifactor models vs., 378–379
One-tailed test, 267–268
One-variable polynomial regression
        model, 514
Operating characteristic curve (OC curve),
        292–293

Optimal decision, 733
Optimal sample size, 301
Optimal value, 602
Ordinal scale, 4
Ordinary least squares (OLS) estimation
        method, 494
Out of control process, 599
Outcomes, 54
Outer fence, 32
Outliers, 12, 33, 496–498

P

p chart, 611–612
    template for, 612–613
p-value, 261–262, 273, 319, 321
    computation of, 265–267
    definition of, 262
    test statistic, 266
Paired-observation comparisons,
        304–308
    advantage of, 304
    confidence intervals, 307–308
    Excel for, 338–340
    template for, 306–308
    test statistic for, 305
Paired-observation t test, 304–306
Paired-observations two-sample
        test, 639
Palmeri, Christopher, 344n
Parameters, 184, 682
Pareto diagrams, 601
    template for, 603
Park, Myung Seok, 492n
Parsimonious model, 410
Partial F statistic, 543
Partial F tests, 542–544
Partition, 73–74
Pascal, Blaise, 52
Passy, Charles, 253n
Payoff, 704, 716
Payoff table/matrix, 706–709
Pearson product-moment correlation
        coefficient, 430, 658
Peck, F., 502n
Peecher, Mark E., 393n
People v. Collins, 257
Percentile, 8–9, 36
Percentile rank computation, 36
Pereira, Pedro, 582n
Permutations, 71, 81
Personal probability, 53
Peters, Ruth, 144n
Phav, Ian, 555n
Pie chart, 25, 37
Pissaeides, Christopher A., 476n
Pizzas "R" Us (case), 735
Platykurtic distribution, 23
Point estimate, 184
Point predictions, 454–455

Poisson distribution, 124–126, 614
    formulas for, 124–125
    problem solving with template,
        125–126, 134
Poisson formula, 124–125
POISSON function, 134
Polynomial regression, 513–519
Pooling, 676
Population, 5, 181, 191, 349
    defined, 5, 183
    sampling from the, 5, 67, 181
Population correlation coefficient,
        429–430
Population intercept, 411
Population mean, 11, 15, 183
    cases not covered by Z or t, 314
    confidence interval, 372
    confidence interval (known standard
        deviation), 220–225
    difference using independent random
        samples, 316
    hypothesis tests of, 272, 289–290
    population mean differences, 316
    templates, 245, 275, 291
    test statistic is t, 272, 313–314
    test statistic is Z, 272, 311–312
Population parameter, 183–184
    comparison of; *see* Comparison of
        two populations
    point estimate of, 184
    sample statistics as estimators of,
        182–186
Population proportion, 184
    binomial distribution/normal
        distribution, 277
    confidence intervals, 327
    hypothesis test of, 276–278, 294
    large-sample confidence intervals,
        235–227
    large-sample test, two population
        proportions, 324
    manual calculation of sample size, 295
    template for, 237, 294, 296, 328
    test statistic for, 325
Population regression line, 413
Population simple linear regression
        model, 412
Population slope, 411
Population standard deviation, 16, 198
Population variance, 15
    confidence intervals for, 239–241
    F distribution and, 330–337
    hypothesis test of, 278
    statistical test for equality of, 333–336
    template for, 242, 278
Positive skewness, 22
Posterior density, 696
Posterior (postsampling) information, 687
Posterior probability, 76, 688
Posterior probability distribution, 689

Power curve, 291–292, 296
Power of the test, 264
Prediction, 457
　multiple regression and, 500–503
　point predictions, 454–455
　prediction intervals, 455–457, 501
　simple linear regression, 454–457
　of a variable, 411
Prediction intervals, 455–457, 501
Predictive probabilities, 717
Presidential Polling (case), 254–255
Pretest decisions, 289–296
Prior information, 687
Prior probabilities, 76, 688, 716
Prior probability density, 695
Prior probability distribution, 689,
　698–699
Privacy Problem (case), 255
Probability, 51–84, 257
　basic definitions for, 55–56
　Bayes' theorem, 75–79
　classical probability, 52
　combinatorial concepts, 70–72
　computer use for, 80–82
　conditional probability, 61–63
　decision analysis, 704, 716–719
　defined, 51, 57
　independence of events, 66–68
　interpretation of, 58
　intersection rule, 67
　joint probability, 59
　joint probability table, 79–80
　law of total probability, 73–75
　marginal probabilities, 80
　mutually exclusive events, 59
　objective, 52
　personal probability, 53
　posterior probability, 76
　prior probabilities, 76
　probability of event A, 55
　range of values, 57–58
　relative-frequency probability, 52
　rule of complements, 58
　rule of unions, 58–59
　rules for, 57–59
　standard normal distribution,
　　151–153
　subjective, 52
　unequal/multinomial probabilities,
　　664–665
　union rule, 67
Probability bar chart, 92–93
Probability density function,
　127–128, 147
Probability distribution, 91, 94–95, 190;
　see also Normal distribution
　cumulative distribution function,
　　96–98
　discrete random variable, 96
　mean as center of mass of, 103

Probability theory, 51–52
Process capability, 598
Process capability index, 176
Product rules, 66
Product rules for independent events,
　67–68
Pth percentile, 8

Q

Qualitative independent variables,
　503–511
Qualitative information, 3
Qualitative variable, 4, 503
　defined, 4
　quantitative variable interactions,
　　510–511
Quality control, 595
Quality control and improvement,
　595–617
　acceptance sampling, 602
　analysis of variance, 602
　c chart, 614–615
　control charts, 598–601
　Deming's 14 points, 597–598
　experimental design, 602
　history of, 596
　p chart, 611–613
　Pareto diagrams, 601, 603
　process capability, 598
　R chart, 608
　s chart, 608–610
　Six Sigma, 602
　statistics and quality, 596–597
　Taguchi methods, 602–603
　x-bar chart, 604–607
　x chart, 615
Quality Control and Improvement
　　at Nashua Corporation (case),
　　618–619
Quantitative information, 3
Quantitative variable, 4, 503, 507
　defined, 4
　qualitative variable interactions,
　　510–511
Quartiles, 8–9

R

R chart, 608–610
Ramayah, T., 403n
Ramsey, Frank, 52n
Random-effects model, 379
Random Number Generation
　　(Excel), 211
Random number table, 186–187
Random sample, 5, 181, 311
　Excel and, 211
　obtaining a, 186–187
　single random sample, 5

Random sampling, 67
Random variables, 91–94, 186
　Bayesian statistics, 689
　Bernoulli random variable, 112
　binomial random variable, 93,
　　113–114
　Chebyshev's theorem, 108–109
　Chi-square random variable, 331
　continuous, 95–96, 126–128
　cumulative distribution function,
　　96–98, 128
　defined, 91–92
　discrete random variable, 95–96
　expected values of, 102–107
　exponential distribution, 130–133
　geometric distribution, 120–121
　hypergeometric distribution,
　　121–124
　linear composites of random
　　variables, 107–108
　negative binomial distribution,
　　118–120
　Poisson distribution, 124–126
　standard deviation of, 106
　sum and linear composites of,
　　107–110
　templates for, 109–110
　uniform distribution, 129–130
　variance of, 104–106
Randomize/randomization, 6
Randomized complete block design, 379,
　　393–395
　repeated-measures design, 393
　template for, 396–397
Range, 15
Range of values, 57–58
Rank sum test, 633
Rating Wines (case), 406
Ratio scale, 4
Ratio to moving average, 570
Ratio-to-moving-average method,
　　569–576
　deseasonalizing data, 572–573
　quarterly/monthly data, 571
　template for, 574
　Trend + Season forecasting,
　　574–576
Reciprocal model, 527–528
Reciprocal transformation, 528
Reduced model (F test), 543
Regnier, Pat, 735n
Regression, 409
Regression analysis; see Multiple
　　regression; Simple linear
　　regression
Regression deviation, 439
Regression line, 415, 424
Relative frequency, 21
Relative-frequency polygon, 26
Relative-frequency probability, 52

Relative kurtosis, 23
Repeated-measures design, 380, 395
Residual analysis, 445–450
Residual autocorrelation, 539–541
Residual plots, 494
Residuals, 378, 411
  histogram of, 449
  standardized residuals, 494–497
Response surface, 469
Restricted randomization, 393
Return on Capital for Four Different
        Sectors (cases), 555–558
Reward, 704
Rhee, Youngseop, 565n
Richtel, Matt, 142n
Ridge regression, 537
Right-skewed distribution, 22–23
Right-tailed test, 268, 271, 622
Rises, Jens, 569n
Risk, 18
Risk-aversion, 726
Risk-neutral, 726
Risk and Return (case), 467
Risk taker, 726
Roberts, Dexter, 166
Rose, Stuart, 695n
Rule of complements, 58
Rule of unions, 58–59
Run, 627
Runs test, 626–631
  large-sample properties, 628–629
  test statistic, 628
  two-tailed hypothesis test, 628
  Wald-Wolfwitz test, 630–631
Ryan, Patricia A., 481n
Ryan, T. P., 614n

S

s chart, 608–610
Sample, 5
  small vs. large samples, 194, 232
Sample correlation coefficient,
        430–431
Sample mean, 10, 191, 193, 355, 378
  expected value of, 192
  standard deviation of, 192
  standardized sampling distribution
        of, 198
Sample proportion, 184–185, 198
Sample-size determination,
        243–245, 248
  hypothesis test, 264–265, 294
  manual calculation of, 290–291, 295
  template for, 290
Sample space, 54–55, 92
Sample standard deviation, 16
Sample statistic, 184
  as estimator of population parameters,
        183–186

Sample variance, 15, 17, 205
Sampling analysis tool (Excel), 210
Sampling distribution, 183, 190–200
  defined, 190
  MINITAB for generating, 212–213
  normal sampling distribution,
        192–193
  sample proportion and, 198
  template for, 209–210
Sampling error, 221
Sampling from the population, 5, 181
Sampling methods, 187–189
  cluster sampling, 188
  multistage cluster sampling, 188
  other methods, 187–188
  single-stage cluster sampling, 188
  stratified sampling, 187
  systematic sampling, 188
  two-stage cluster sampling, 188
Sampling with replacement, 114
Sampling and sampling distributions,
        181–213
  central limit theorem, 194–198
  degrees of freedom, 205–207
  estimators and their properties,
        201–204
  expected net gain from, 730
  Literary Digest sampling error, 181–183
  nonresponse, 188–189
  obtaining a random sample, 186–187
  as population parameters estimators,
        183–186
  small vs. large samples, 194
  standardized sampling distribution of
        sample mean, 198
  template, 209–213
  uses of, 182
  with/without replacement, 114
Sarvary, Miklos, 377n, 481n, 555n
Scales of measurement, 4
  interval scale, 4
  nominal scale, 4
  ordinal scale, 4
  ratio scale, 4
Scatter plots, 38–39, 409
Schank, Thorsten, 438n
Schatz, Ronald, 577n
Scheffé method, 376
Schnabel, Claus, 438n
Schoar, Antoinette, 519n, 555n
Schoenfeld, Bruce, 235n
Schwartz, Nelson D., 282n
Sciolino, Elaine, 70n
Seasonal variation, 566
Seasonality, 566–569
  multiplicative model, 568
  regression model with dummy variables
        for, 568
Seber, George A. F., 514n
Seitz, Thomas, 569n

Semi-infinite intervals, 151
Set, 53
75th percentile, 9
Shah, Jagar, 238n
Shakespeare, Catherine, 443n
Shewhart, Walter, 598
Shrum, J. L., 370n
Sialm, Clemens, 371n
Sigma squared, 15
Sign test, 621–625
  possible hypotheses for, 622
  template for, 623
  test statistic, 623
Significance level, 262–264
Sikora, Martin, 651n
Silverman, Rachel Emma, 238n
Simple exponential smoothing, 577
Simple index number, 583
Simple linear regression, 409, 411–414
  analysis-of-variance table, 443–444
  coefficient of determination, 439
  conditional mean of Y, 412
  confidence intervals for regression
        parameters, 426–428
  correlation, 429–433
  curvilinear relationship between Y and X,
        413, 447–448
  distributional assumptions of errors, 413
  error variance, 424–428
  estimation: method of least squares,
        414–422
  Excel Solver for, 458–460, 463
  F test of, 443–444
  goodness of fit, 438–442
  heteroscedasticity, 446
  how good is the regression, 438–442
  hypothesis tests about, 434–437
  linear relationship between X and Y, 435
  mean square error (MSE), 424–425
  MINITAB for, 463–464
  missing variables test, 446
  model assumptions, 412
  model building, 410–411
  model inadequacies, 445–450
  model parameters, 412
  normal equations, 417
  normal probability plot, 448–450
  population regression line, 413
  population simple linear regression
        model, 412
  residual analysis, 445–450
  slope and intercept, 418, 427
  Solver method for, 458–460
  standard error of estimate, 424–428
  steps in, 411
  sum of squares for error (SSE),
        415–417, 425
  t test, 435, 444
  template for, 421–422
  use for prediction, 454–457

Single mode, 702
Single random sample, 5
Single-stage cluster sampling, 188
Single variable, 583
Six Sigma, 602
Skedevold, Gretchen, 565n
Skewness, 22–23, 33, 702
Slope, 418, 420, 435
Smith, Bill, 602
Smith, Craig S., 322n
Soliman, Mark T., 443n
Solver Macro, 247
   multiple regression and, 548–545
   regression, 458–460
Sorkin, Andrew Ross, 142n
Spearman rank correlation coefficient,
      657–660
   hypothesis test for association, 659
   large-sample test statistic for
         association, 658
   template for, 659–660
Spread, 102
Standard deviation, 15, 102
   defined, 16
   mean and, 24–25
   population standard deviation,
         16, 198
   of random variable, 106
   of sample mean, 192
   sample standard deviation, 16
Standard error, 192, 198
Standard error of estimate,
      425–426
Standard normal distribution,
      151–155
   finding probabilities of, 151–153
   finding values of Z given a probability,
         153–155
   importance of, 156
   table area, 151
Standard normal probabilities
      (table), 152
Standard normal random variable Z, 151
Standard normal test statistic, 628
State of nature, 706
Statista, 3
Statistic, 184
Statistical analysis, information from, 3
Statistical control, 600
Statistical inference, 5–6, 28,
      182–183, 658
   business applications of, 6–7
Statistical model, 378
   checking for inadequacies in, 445
   for control of a variable, 411
   as parsimonious, 410
   for prediction of a variable, 411
   steps in building, 411
   to explain variable relationships, 411

Statistical process control (SPC), 599
Statistical test for randomness, 627
Statistics
   derivation of word, 3
   quality and, 596–603
   as science of inference, 5–6, 28, 181
   use of, 6–7, 147, 181, 219, 257, 303, 349,
         409, 595
Stellin, Susan, 227n
Stem-and-leaf displays, 30–31
Stepwise regression, 546–547
Stigler, S., 595n
Stokes, Martha, 621n
Stone, Brad, 60n, 287n
Story, Louise, 342n
Straight-line relationship, 409
Strata, 187
Stratified sampling, 187
Studentized range distribution, 373
Student's distribution/Student's t
      distribution, 228, 249
Subjective probabilities, 52, 688
   evaluation of, 701–702
   normal prior distribution, 701–702
Subsets, 53
Sufficiency, 203
Sum-of-squares principle, 358–362
Sum-of-squares total (SST), 360–362,
      383–384
Sum of squares for error (SSE),
      360–362, 384
Sum of squares for error (SSE)
      (in regression), 416–417, 425,
      440–441, 475
Sum of squares for regression (SSR),
      440–441, 475
Sum of squares for treatment (SSTR),
      360–362, 384
Surveys, 6
Symmetric data set/population, 13
Symmetric distribution, 22–23, 702
   with two modes, 22–23
Systematic component, 411
Systematic sampling, 188

T

t distribution, 228–233, 305, 314
t table, 273
t test statistic, 272–273, 313–314,
      319–320, 340
Table area, 151–152
Taguchi, Genichi, 602
Taguchi methods, 602
Tahmincioglu, Eva, 189n
Tails of the distribution, 151
Tallying principle, 30
Tang, Huarong, 443n
TDIST function, 298

Templates, 36
   bar charts, 38
   Bayesian revision-binomial probabilities,
         692–693
   Bayesian revision-normal mean, 699
   binomial distribution, 169–170
   binomial probabilities, 115–116
   box plot, 38
   c chart, 615
   chi-square tests, 664, 668, 673
   confidence intervals, 225–226
   control chart, 610, 612–613, 615
   for data (basic statistics), 36
   decision analysis, 731–733
   exponential distribution, 131–132
   exponential smoothing, 581–582
   F-distribution, 336
   Friedman test, 655–656
   geometric distribution, 121
   half-width, determining optimal,
         245–246
   histograms and related charts, 36–37
   hypergeometric distribution, 123–124
   hypothesis testing, population means,
         274–275, 290–293
   hypothesis testing, population proportion,
         277, 294, 296
   index numbers, 587
   Kruskal-Wallis test, 648–649
   manual recalculation, 502–503
   minimum sample size, 248
   multiple regression, 472, 487, 490, 496,
         502, 518, 544
   negative binomial distribution,
         119–120
   normal approximation of binomial
         distribution, 169–170
   normal distribution, 166–169
   operating characteristic (OC) curves,
         292–293
   optimal half-width, 245–247
   paired-observation comparisons,
         306–308
   Pareto diagrams, 603
   partial F test, 544
   percentile/percentile rank
         computation, 36
   pie chart, 37
   Poisson distribution, 125–126
   population mean differences, 312, 314
   population mean estimates,
         optimizing of, 245
   population proportion, 237, 277
   population proportion estimates,
         optimizing of, 247
   population variances, 242, 278–279
   power curve, 292, 296
   problem solving with, 167–169
   random variables, 109–110

randomized block design ANOVA, 396–397
residuals, histogram of, 449
runs test, 629–630
sample size, 290, 294
sampling distribution of sample mean, 209
sampling distribution of sample proportion, 210
scatter plot, 38
sign test, 623
simple regression, 421–422, 459
single-factor ANOVA, 377
Solver, 247, 459
Spearman's rank correlation coefficient, 659–660
t-distribution, 229
t test difference in means, 319–320
testing population mean, 291
time plot, 38
Trend + Season forecasting, 574–576
trend analysis, 563–564
Tukey method, 376
two-way ANOVA, 388
uniform distribution, 130
Wilcoxon signed-rank test, 643
x-bar chart, 606–607
Z-test, 312
Test statistic
  ANOVA, 351–354, 364
  association, large-sample test, 658
  chi-square test for independence, 670
  Durbin-Watson test, 540
  Friedman test, 654
  hypothesis test, 266, 272, 276
  individual regression slope parameters, 485
  Kruskal-Wallis test, 646
  linear relationship between X and Y, 435
  Mann-Whitney U test, 634
  paired-observation t test, 305
  population proportions, 325
  runs test, 628
  sign test, 623
  test statistic is t, 272, 313–314
  test statistic is Z, 272, 311–312
  Tukey pairwise-comparison, 375
  two normally distributed populations/ equality of variances, 332
  two population means/independent random samples, 310–316
Tests of homogeneity, 675
Theory of probability, 51–52
Thesis, 257
Thesmar, David, 519n
Third quartile, 9
"30 rule" (sample size), 194
Thornton, Emily, 285n
3 standard deviations, 24

Three-factor ANOVA, 379, 389–390
Time plots, 29–30, 38
Time series
  Excel/MINITAB in, 588–591
  exponential smoothing methods, 588–582
TINV function, 249
Tiresome Tires I (case), 301
Tiresome Tires II (case), 346
Tolerance limits, 595, 599
Tosi, Henry L., 465n
Total deviation of a data point, 369, 439
Total quality management (TQM), 597
Total sum of squares (SST), 440, 475
Transformation of normal random variables, 156–157
  of X to Z, 156
  inverse transformation of Z to X, 157
  summary of, 160
  use of, 157–160
Transformations of data, 514, 521
  logarithmic transformation, 521–527
  to linearize the logistic function, 529
  variance-stabilizing transformations, 527–528
Treatment deviation, 357, 359
Treatments, 349
Tree diagram, 71, 79
Trend, 561
Trend analysis, 561–564
  curved trends, 562
  template for, 563–564
  trend + Season forecasting, 574–576
Trial of the Pyx, 595
Tse, Yinman, 577n
Tucker, M., 26
Tukey, John W., 29
Tukey pairwise-comparison test, 373–376
  conducting the tests, 375
  studentized range distribution, 373
  template for, 376, 401
  test statistic for, 375
  Tukey criterion, 373
  two-way ANOVA, 388–389
  unequal sample sizes/alternative procedures, 376
Turra, Melissa, 652n
25th percentile, 9
2 standard deviations, 162–163, 702
Two-stage cluster sampling, 188
Two-tailed tests, 267, 269, 271, 435, 622, 628
Two-way ANOVA, 380–391
  extension to three factors, 389–391
  F ratios and, 384–385
  factor B main-effects test, 381
  hypothesis tests in, 382–383
  Kimball's inequality, 388
  model of, 381–382
  one observation per cell, 389–391

overall significance level, 388
sums of squares, degrees of freedom, and mean squares, 383–384
template for, 388, 398–399, 402
test for AB interactions, 383
Tukey method for, 388–389
two-way ANOVA table, 384–385
Type I and Type II errors, 289, 310, 350
  hypothesis testing, 260–261
  instances of, 261
  optimal significance level and, 263–264
  significance level, 262

U
Unbalanced designs, 376
Unbiased estimator, 201
Uncertainty, 196
Uncorrelated variables, 435
Unexplained deviation (error), 439–440
Unexplained variation, 361, 440
Uniform distribution, 129–130
  formulas, 129
  problem solving with template, 130
Union, 53–54
  rule of unions, 67
Union rule, 67
Universal set, 53
Universe, 5
Updegrave, Walter, 323n, 638n
Upper control limit (UCL), 599, 606, 608–609, 612, 614
Upper quartile, 9
Useen, Jerry, 45n
Utility, 725–728
  method of assessing, 727
Utility function, 725–727, 731
Utility scale, 725

V
Value at risk, 132–133
Value of information, 728–731
Variability; see Measures of variability
Variable selection methods, 545–547
  all possible regressions, 545
  backward elimination, 545–546
  forward selection, 545
  stepwise regression, 546
Variance, 15, 102; see also Analysis of variance (ANOVA)
  defined, 15
  of discrete random variable, 104–105
  of linear composite, 108
  of a linear function of a random variable, 106–107
  population variance, 15
  quality control, 599
  sample variance, 15, 17, 205

Variance inflation factor (VIF), 535
Variance-stabilizing transformations,
    527–528
Vella, Matt, 734n
Venn diagram, 53–54
Vigneron, Olivier, 481n
Vining, G. G., 502n
Virtual reality, 30
Volatility, 18, 658n

W

Wachter, Jessica A., 465n
Wagner, Joachim, 438n
Wain, Daniel, 604n
Wald-Wolfowitz test, 630–631
Wallendorf, Melanie, 437n, 442n
Wang, Jeff, 437n, 442n
Weak test, 631, 678

Weighted average, 102
Weighted least squares (WLS), 494
Weighting factor, 578
Weintraub, Arlene, 281n
Weisberg, Sanford, 514n
Whiskers, 32
Wilcoxon rank sum test, 633
Wilcoxon signed-rank test, 639–643
    decision rule, 640
    large-sample version, 640
    paired-observations two-sample test,
        639–640
    template for, 643
    test for mean/median of single
        population, 642
Within-treatment deviation, 360
Wolff, Edward N., 422n
Wongsunwai, Wan, 555n
Wyer, Robrt S., Jr., 370n

X

x-bar chart, 604–607
    template for, 606–607
x chart, 615
Xia, Yihong, 443n

Y

Yates correction, 672

Z

z distribution, 232, 315
z standard deviations, 163
Z test statistic, 272, 311–312
z value, 163
Zero skewness, 22
Zheng, Lu, 371n
ZTEST function, 298